MW00995628

TEACHER'S EDITION

GRADE 9

Program Consultants:

Kylene Beers

Martha Hougen

Elena Izquierdo

Carol Jago

Erik Palmer

Robert E. Probst

Front Cover Photo Credits: (outer ring): ©momente/Shutterstock, (inner ring): ©optimarc/Shutterstock, (c) ©Carrie Garcia/Houghton Murt, (c overlay): ©Eyewire/Getty Images, (bc overlay): ©elenamiv/Shutterstock

Back Cover Photo Credits: (Units 1-6): ©Rigmanyi/Dreamstime; ©John Gomez/Shutterstock; ©Artur Debat/Moment/Getty Images; ©Gerstock; ©Hulton Archive/Getty Images; ©Carlos Amarillo/Shutterstock

Printed in the U.S.A.

ISBN 978-1-328-47487-2

2 3 4 5 6 7 8 9 10 0690 27 26 25 24 23 22 21 20 19

4500752975 B C D E F G

Teacher's Edition Table of Contents

HMH *into* Literature

PROGRAM CONSULTANTS

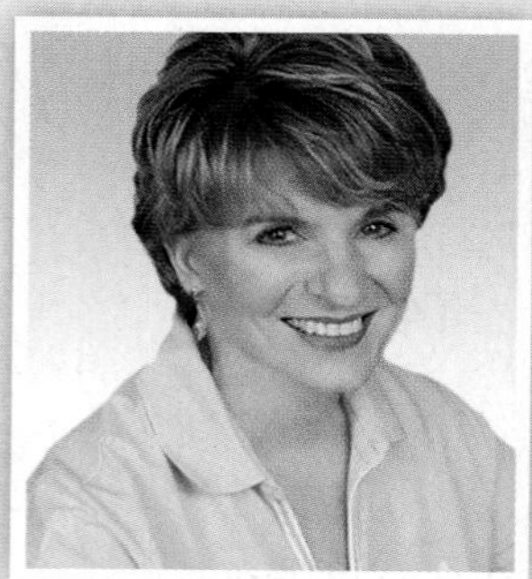

Kylene Beers

Nationally known lecturer and author on reading and literacy; coauthor with Robert Probst of *Disrupting Thinking, Notice & Note: Strategies for Close Reading,* and *Reading Nonfiction*; former president of the National Council of Teachers of English. Dr. Beers is the author of *When Kids Can't Read: What Teachers Can Do* and coeditor of *Adolescent Literacy: Turning Promise into Practice*, as well as articles in the *Journal of Adolescent and Adult Literacy*. Former editor of *Voices from the Middle,* she is the 2001 recipient of NCTE's Richard W. Halle Award, given for outstanding contributions to middle school literacy. She recently served as Senior Reading Researcher at the Comer School Development Program at Yale University as well as Senior Reading Advisor to Secondary Schools for the Reading and Writing Project at Teachers College.

Martha Hougen

National consultant, presenter, researcher, and author. Areas of expertise include differentiating instruction for students with learning difficulties, including those with learning disabilities and dyslexia; and teacher and leader preparation improvement. Dr. Hougen has taught at the middle school through graduate levels. In addition to peer-reviewed articles, curricular documents, and presentations, Dr. Hougen has published two college textbooks: *The Fundamentals of Literacy Instruction and Assessment Pre-K–6* (2012) and *The Fundamentals of Literacy Instruction and Assessment 6–12* (2014). Dr. Hougen has supported Educator Preparation Program reforms while working at the Meadows Center for Preventing Educational Risk at The University of Texas at Austin and at the CEEDAR Center, University of Florida.

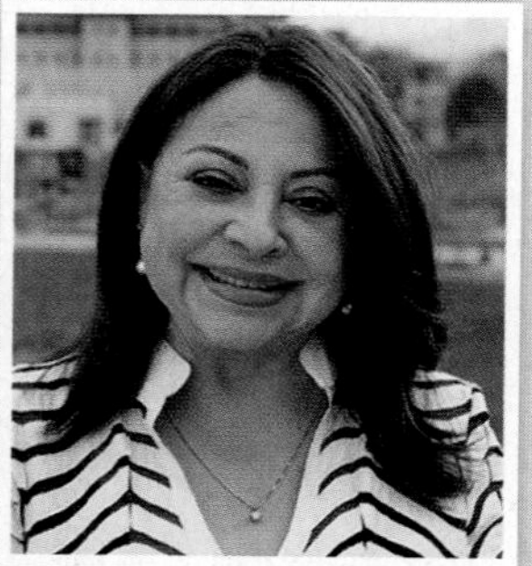

Elena Izquierdo

Nationally recognized teacher educator and advocate for English language learners. Dr. Izquierdo is a linguist by training, with a Ph.D. in Applied Linguistics and Bilingual Education from Georgetown University. She has served on various state and national boards working to close the achievement gaps for bilingual students and English language learners. Dr. Izquierdo is a member of the Hispanic Leadership Council, which supports Hispanic students and educators at both the state and federal levels. She served as Vice President on the Executive Board of the National Association of Bilingual Education and as Publications and Professional Development Chair.

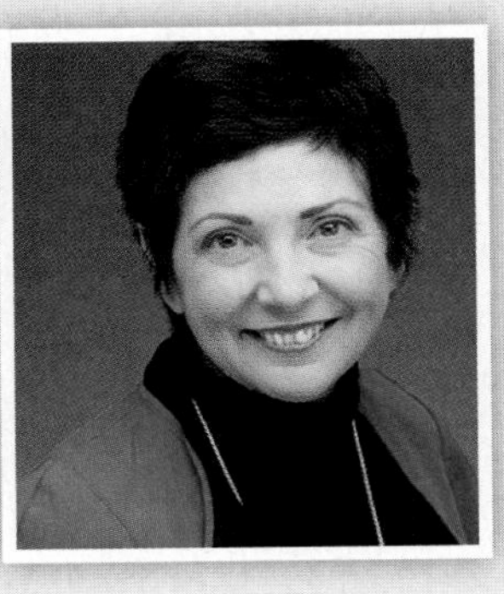

Carol Jago

Teacher of English with 32 years of experience at Santa Monica High School in California; author and nationally known lecturer; former president of the National Council of Teachers of English. Ms. Jago currently serves as Associate Director of the California Reading and Literature Project at UCLA. With expertise in standards assessment and secondary education, Ms. Jago is the author of numerous books on education, including *With Rigor for All* and *Papers, Papers, Papers*, and is active with the California Association of Teachers of English, editing its scholarly journal *California English* since 1996. Ms. Jago also served on the planning committee for the 2009 NAEP Reading Framework and the 2011 NAEP Writing Framework.

Erik Palmer

Veteran teacher and education consultant based in Denver, Colorado. Author of *Well Spoken: Teaching Speaking to All Students* and *Digitally Speaking: How to Improve Student Presentations with Technology*. His areas of focus include improving oral communication, promoting technology in classroom presentations, and updating instruction through the use of digital tools. He holds a bachelor's degree from Oberlin College and a master's degree in curriculum and instruction from the University of Colorado.

Robert E. Probst

Nationally respected authority on the teaching of literature; Professor Emeritus of English Education at Georgia State University. Dr. Probst's publications include numerous articles in *English Journal* and *Voices from the Middle*, as well as professional texts including (as coeditor) *Adolescent Literacy: Turning Promise into Practice* and (as coauthor with Kylene Beers) *Disrupting Thinking, Notice & Note: Strategies for Close Reading*, and *Reading Nonfiction*. He regularly speaks at national and international conventions including those of the International Literacy Association, the National Council of Teachers of English, the Association for Supervision and Curriculum Development, and the National Association of Secondary School Principals. He has served NCTE in various leadership roles, including the Conference on English Leadership Board of Directors, the Commission on Reading, and column editor of the NCTE journal *Voices from the Middle*. He is also the 2004 recipient of the CEL Exemplary Leadership Award.

Lead and Learn

Image Credits: (t): ©Kanetmark/Shutterstock, (b): ©Monkey Business Images/Shutterstock

Students who communicate...

- **Listen** actively
- **Present** effectively
- **Expand** vocabulary
- **Question** appropriately
- **Engage** constructively

SPEAKING AND LISTENING TASK

Create a Podcast

You will now adapt your research report as a podcast that your classmates can listen and respond to. You also will listen to their podcasts, ask questions to better understand their ideas, and help them improve their work.

Go to **Using Media in a Presentation** in the **Listening and Speaking Studio** for help planning and crafting your presentation.

1 Adapt Your Report as a Podcast

Review your research report, and use the chart below to guide you as you adapt your report and follow instructions for creating a script and effects for your podcast. Ensure that the vocabulary, language, and tone of your podcast are appropriate for your audience. Also, make sure to link your ideas clearly using connecting words to transition smoothly from one idea to the next.

Podcast Planning Chart		
Title and Introduction	How will you revise your title and introduction to capture the listener's attention? Is there a catchier way to state your thesis? Consider putting your thesis in the form of a question that you can then answer.	
Audience	Who is your audience? What information will your audience already know? What information can you exclude? What should you add?	
Effective Language and Organization	Which parts of your report should be simplified? What can you change to strike a more informal voice and tone? Make sure you use standard language conventions so your ideas are clear to listeners.	
Sound	Think about whether you want to begin your podcast with music or sound effects. What kind of music is appropriate to the topic? Are there sound effects you c that will help you crea	

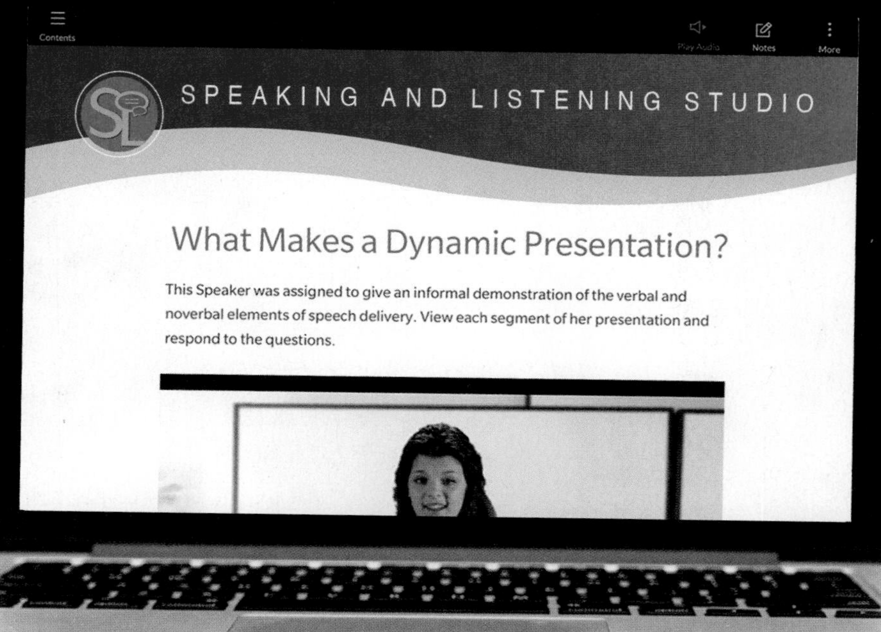

Image Credits: (t): ©kanetmark/Shutterstock, (b): ©Goran Bogicevic/Shutterstock

Question and Respond

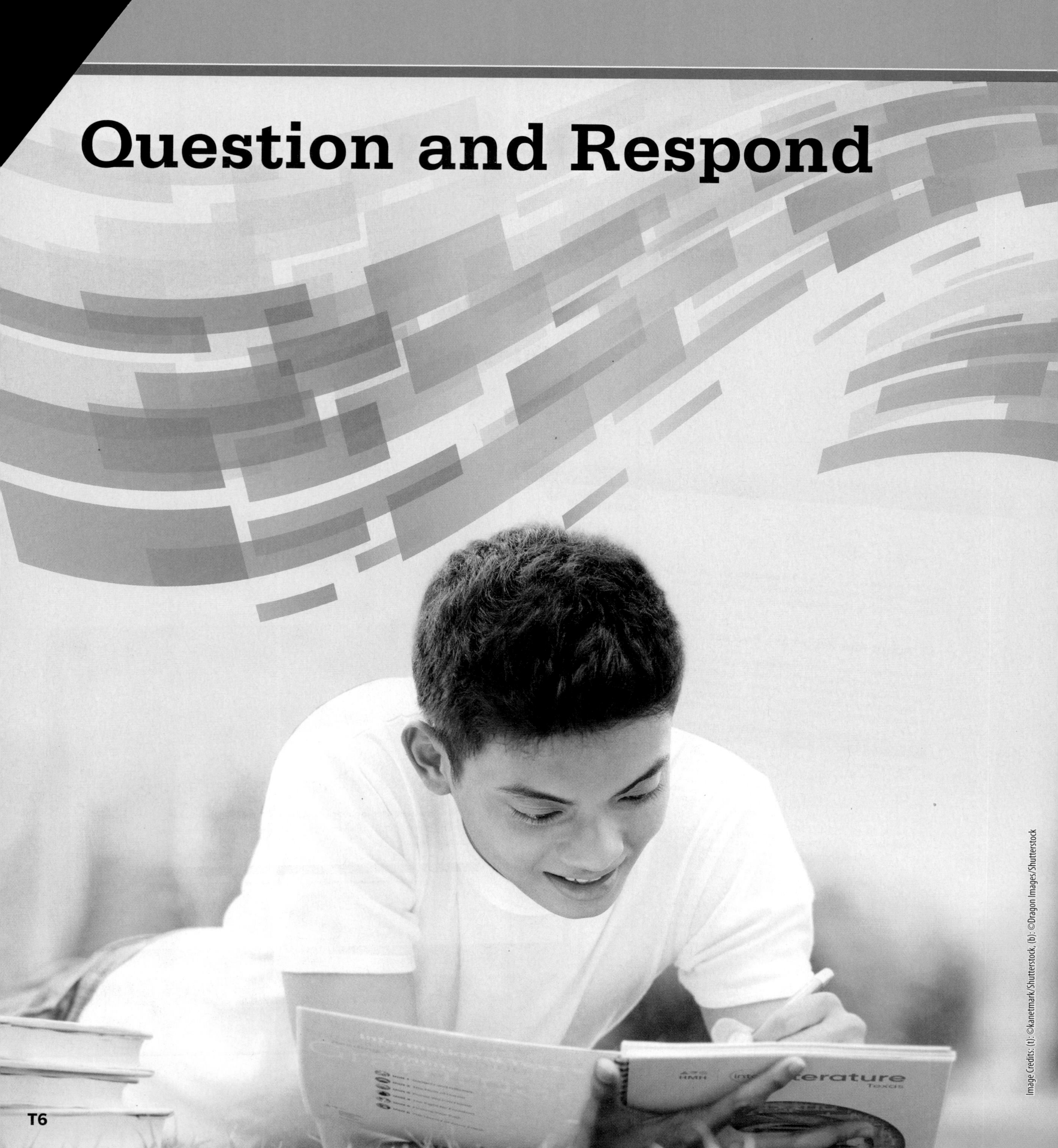

Students who read...

- **Acquire** fluency
- **Choose** independently
- **Monitor** understanding
- **Annotate** and use evidence
- **Write** and discuss within and across texts

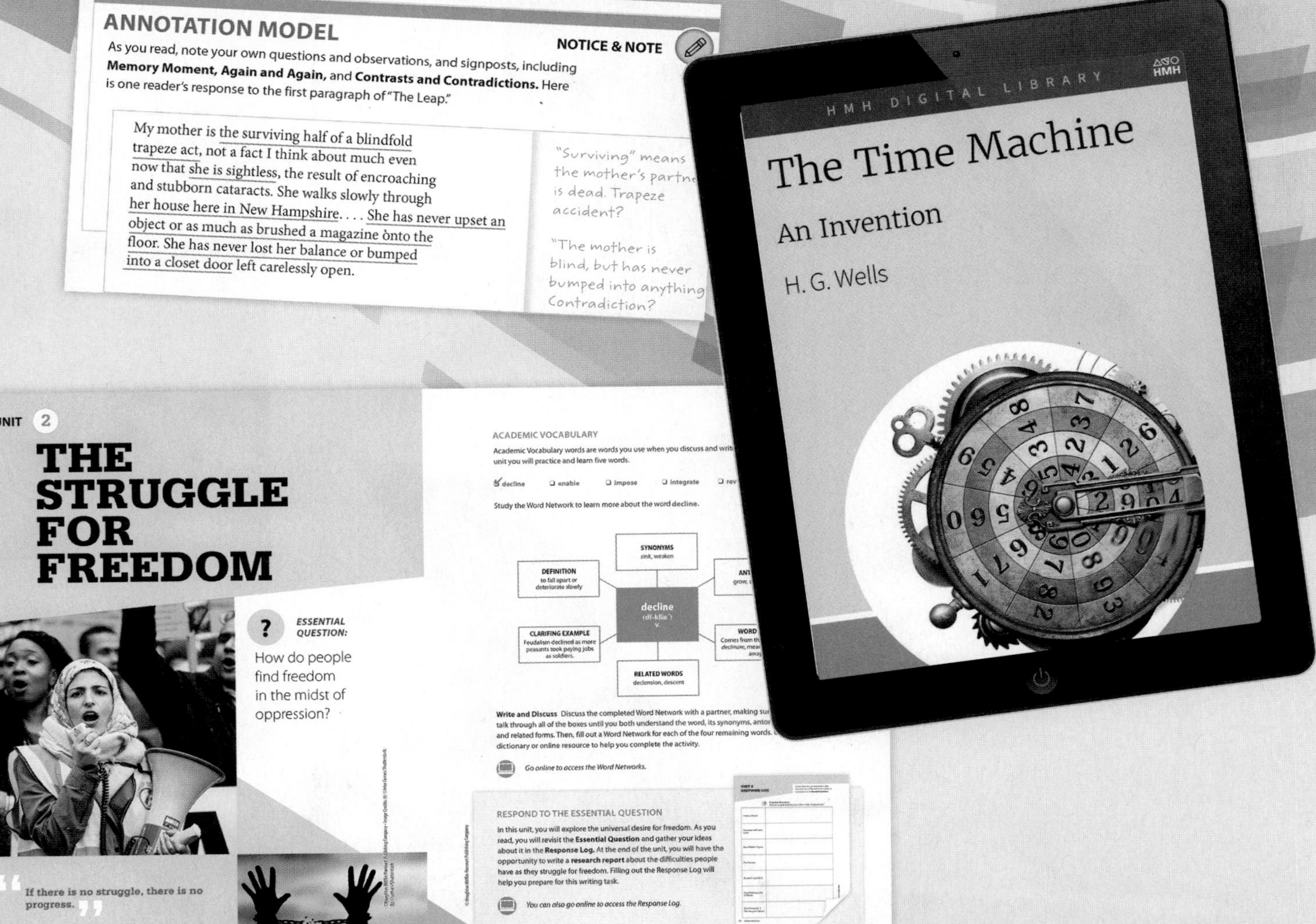

Image Credits: (t): ©kanetmark/Shutterstock, (b): ©MSSA/Shutterstock

Connect Reading and Writing

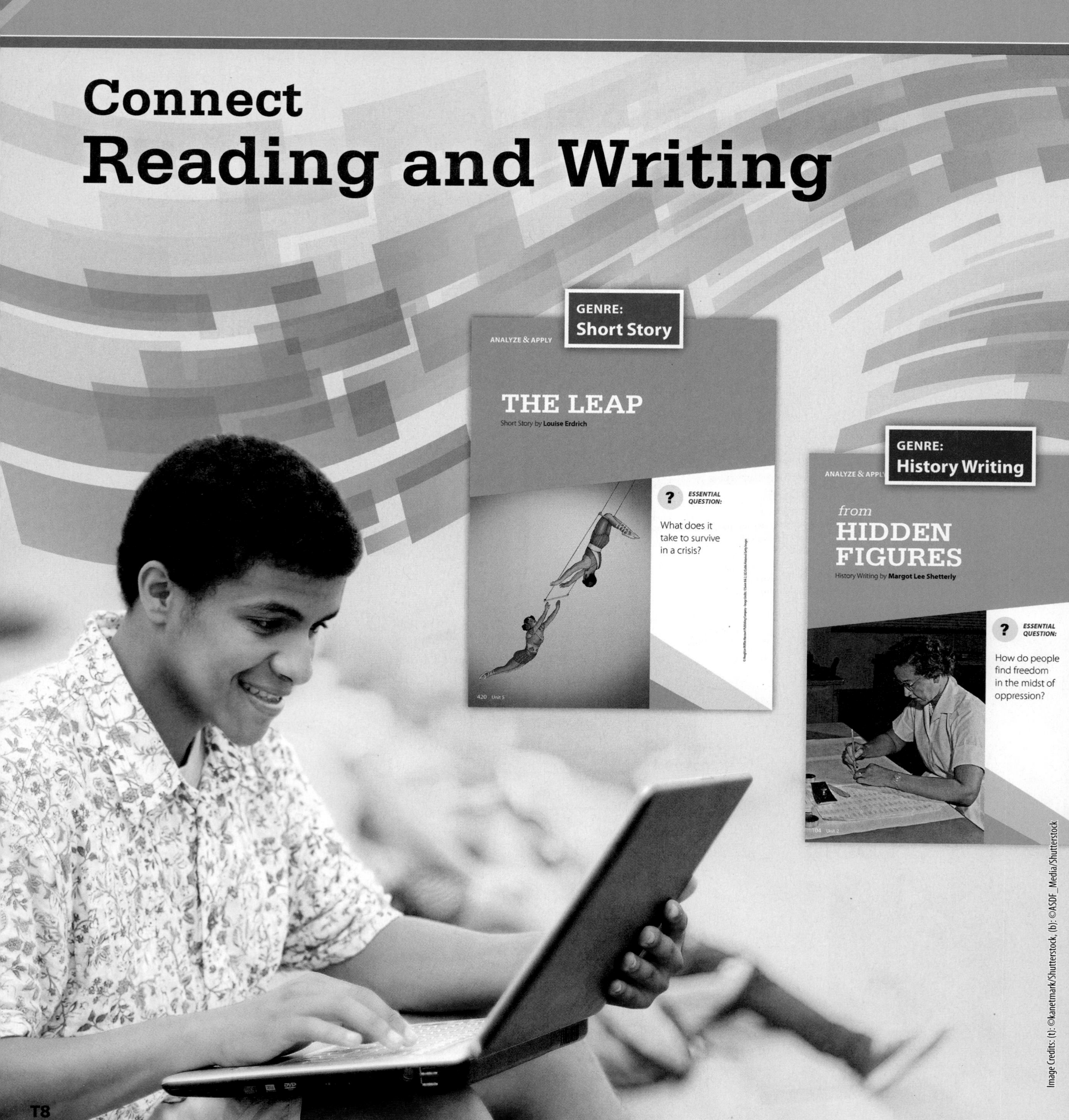

Image Credits: (t): ©kanetmark/Shutterstock, (b): ©ASDF_Media/Shutterstock

Students who explore genre...

- **Analyze** features
- **Understand** effects of authors' choices
- **Emulate** craft
- **Use** mentor texts
- **Synthesize** ideas

GENRE ELEMENTS: HISTORY WRITING
- uses chronological order
- is a form of informational text
- includes evidence to support ideas
- contains text features to help the reader absorb and retain information

GET R

QUICK START

What do you know about opportunities that were once closed to African Americans, women, or other minorities? Name some jobs a woman or an African American might not have been able to apply for in the past.

ANALYZE TEXT STRUCTURE

Authors use a variety of **text structures.** These include thesis or main idea and details; cause and effect; problem and solution; and chronology, or time order. Most historical texts are a combination of chronology, main idea, and cause and effect. Sometimes these organizational designs are intertwined.

As you read, keep track of the important events, the order in which they happen, any causal relationships, and key ideas.

TEXT STRUCTURES	EXAMPLE FROM *HIDDEN FIGURES*
Narration of an Event	By 1943, the American aircraft industry was the largest, most productive, and most sophisticated in the world, making three times more planes than the Germans, who were fighting on the other side of the war.
Cause and Effect	But in the spring of 1943, with World War II in full swing and many men off serving in the military . . . employers were beginning to hire women to do jobs that had once belonged *only* to men.
Thesis/Important Ideas	The NACA's mission was . . . to help the United States develop the most powerful and efficient airplanes in the world. . . . World leaders felt that the country that ruled the skies would win the war.

MAKE PREDICTIONS

To read historical text effectively, it is important to **make predictions** as you read. A prediction is an informed guess about what the author is about to say.
- Before you read, use text features such as the title, headings, and background information to make initial predictions about the text.
- As you read, use text structure as well as genre characteristics to correct your initial predictions and to predict what you will read about next.
- After you read, confirm your predictions. They may not always be correct. If the author surprises you, your predictions will help you evaluate and remember the unexpected information.

Use a chart like this one to help you make and evaluate your predictions:

WHAT I KNOW	MY PREDICTION	WAS IT CORRECT?

GENRE ELEMENTS: HISTORY WRITING
- uses chronological order
- is a form of informational text
- includes evidence to support ideas
- contains text features to help the reader absorb and retain information

Hidden Figures 105

GENRE: Poem

COLLABORATE & COMPARE

POEM
THE JOURNEY
by **Mary Oliver**
pages 555–557

COMPARE THEME AND MAIN IDEA

Now that you've read the excerpt from *The Cruelest Journey: 600 Miles to Timbuktu*, read "The Journey" and consider how this poem explores some of the same ideas. As you read, think about how "The Journey" relates to the idea of a journey or quest as well to your own experiences. After you are finished, you will collaborate with a small group on a final project that involves an analysis of both texts.

? ***ESSENTIAL QUESTION:***

What drives us to take on a challenge?

TRAVEL WRITING
from
THE CRUELEST JOURNEY: 600 MILES TO TIMBUKTU
by **Kira Salak**
pages 539–547

552 Unit 6

Image Credits: (t): ©kanetmark/Shutterstock, (b): ©MSSA/Shutterstock

Craft and Communicate

Image Credits: (t): ©kanetmark/Shutterstock, (b): ©Syda Productions/Shutterstock

Students who compose...

- **Inform,** argue, and connect
- **Create** in a literary genre
- **Imitate** mentor texts
- **Apply** conventions
- **Use** process and partners

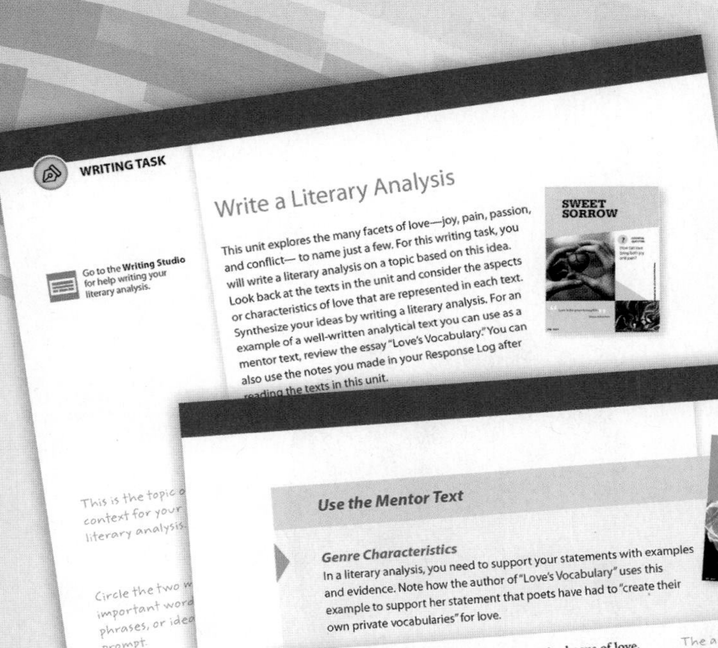
WRITING TASK

Write a Literary Analysis

This unit explores the many facets of love—joy, pain, passion, and conflict— to name just a few. For this writing task, you will write a literary analysis on a topic based on this idea. Look back at the texts in the unit and consider the aspects or characteristics of love that are represented in each text. Synthesize your ideas by writing a literary analysis. For an example of a well-written analytical text you can use as a mentor text, review the essay "Love's Vocabulary." You can also use the notes you made in your Response Log after reading the texts in this unit.

Go to the **Writing Studio** for help writing your literary analysis.

408 Unit 4

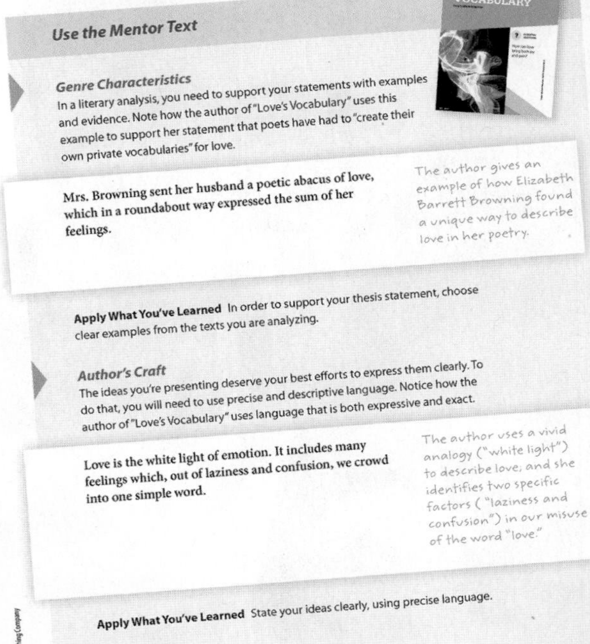
WRITING TASK

Use the Mentor Text

Genre Characteristics
In a literary analysis, you need to support your statements with examples and evidence. Note how the author of "Love's Vocabulary" uses this example to support her statement that poets have had to "create their own private vocabularies" for love.

> Mrs. Browning sent her husband a poetic abacus of love, which in a roundabout way expressed the sum of her feelings.

The author gives an example of how Elizabeth Barrett Browning found a unique way to describe love in her poetry.

Apply What You've Learned In order to support your thesis statement, choose clear examples from the texts you are analyzing.

Author's Craft
The ideas you're presenting deserve your best efforts to express them clearly. To do that, you will need to use precise and descriptive language. Notice how the author of "Love's Vocabulary" uses language that is both expressive and exact.

> Love is the white light of emotion. It includes many feelings which, out of laziness and confusion, we crowd into one simple word.

The author uses a vivid analogy ("white light") to describe love, and she identifies two specific factors ("laziness and confusion") in our misuse of the word "love."

Apply What You've Learned State your ideas clearly, using precise language.

© Houghton Mifflin Harcourt Publishing Company

Write a Literary Analysis 411

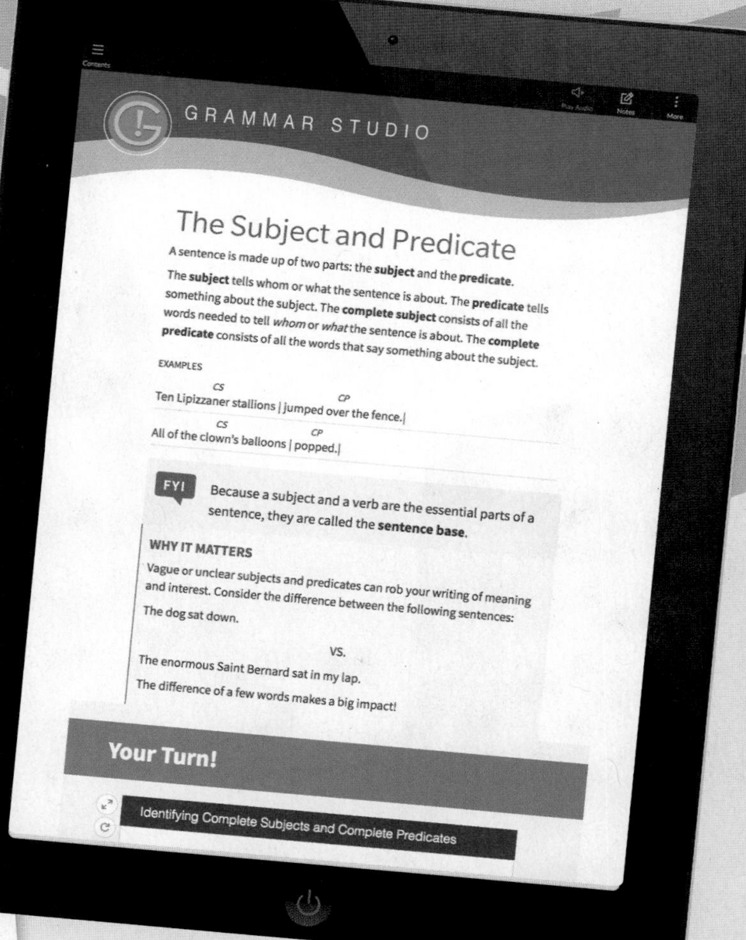
GRAMMAR STUDIO

The Subject and Predicate

A sentence is made up of two parts: the **subject** and the **predicate.**

The **subject** tells whom or what the sentence is about. The **predicate** tells something about the subject. The **complete subject** consists of all the words needed to tell *whom* or *what* the sentence is about. The **complete predicate** consists of all the words that say something about the subject.

EXAMPLES

Ten Lipizzaner stallions (CS) | jumped over the fence. (CP)

All of the clown's balloons (CS) | popped. (CP)

FYI Because a subject and a verb are the essential parts of a sentence, they are called the **sentence base.**

WHY IT MATTERS

Vague or unclear subjects and predicates can rob your writing of meaning and interest. Consider the difference between the following sentences:

The dog sat down.

VS.

The enormous Saint Bernard sat in my lap.

The difference of a few words makes a big impact!

Your Turn!

Identifying Complete Subjects and Complete Predicates

Image Credits: (t): (t): ©kanetmark/Shutterstock, (b): ©MSSA/Shutterstock

Explore and Research

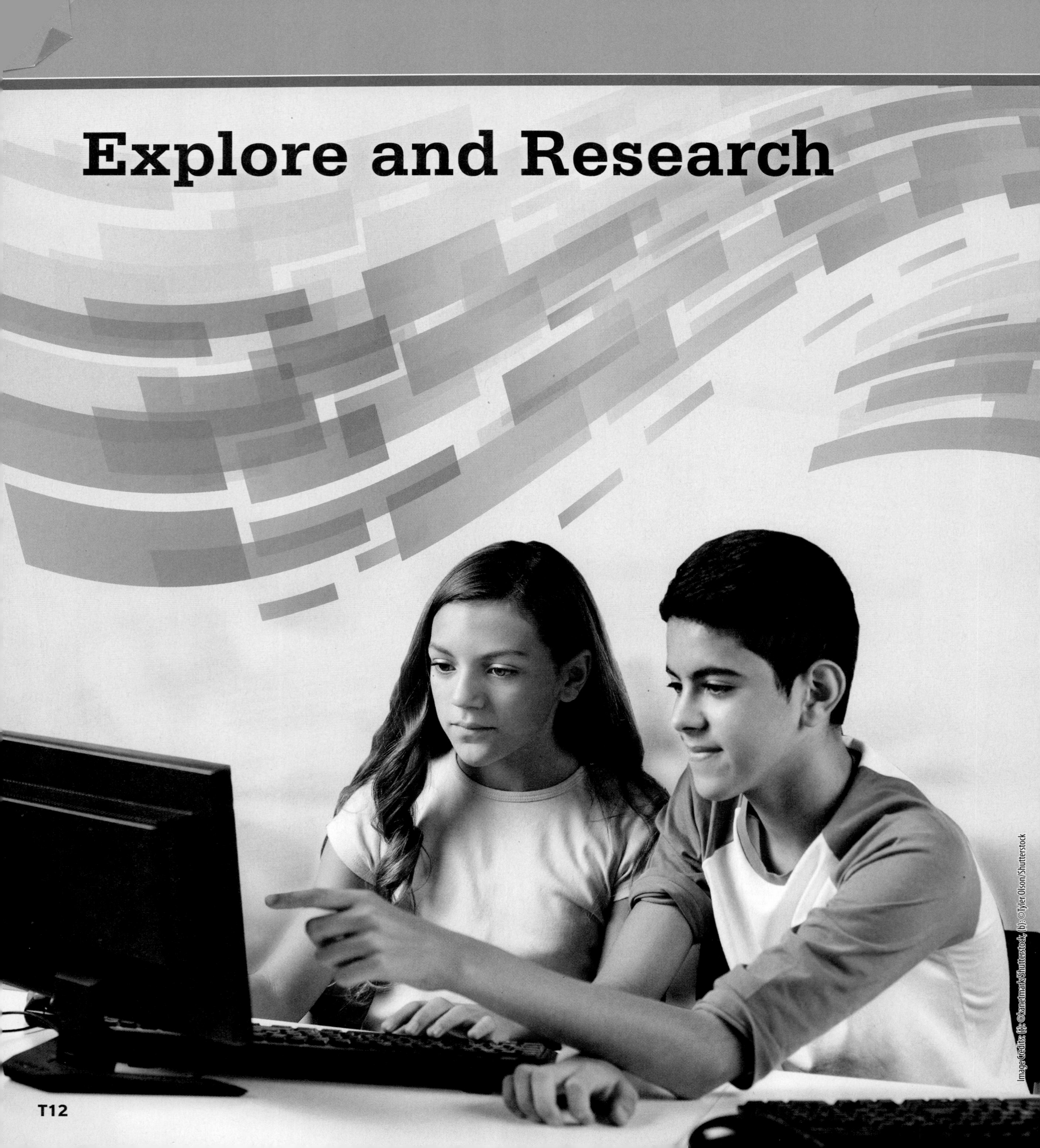

Image Credits: (t): ©kanetmark/Shutterstock; (b): ©Tyler Olson/Shutterstock

Students who inquire...

- **Generate** questions
- **Plan** and revise
- **Synthesize** information
- **Cite** sources
- **Deliver** results

Image Credits: (t): ©kanetmark/Shutterstock, (b): ©MSSA/Shutterstock

Maximize Growth through Data-Driven Differentiation and Assessment

Ongoing assessment and data reporting provide critical feedback loops to teachers and students, so that each experience encourages self-assessment and reflection, and drives positive learning outcomes for all students.

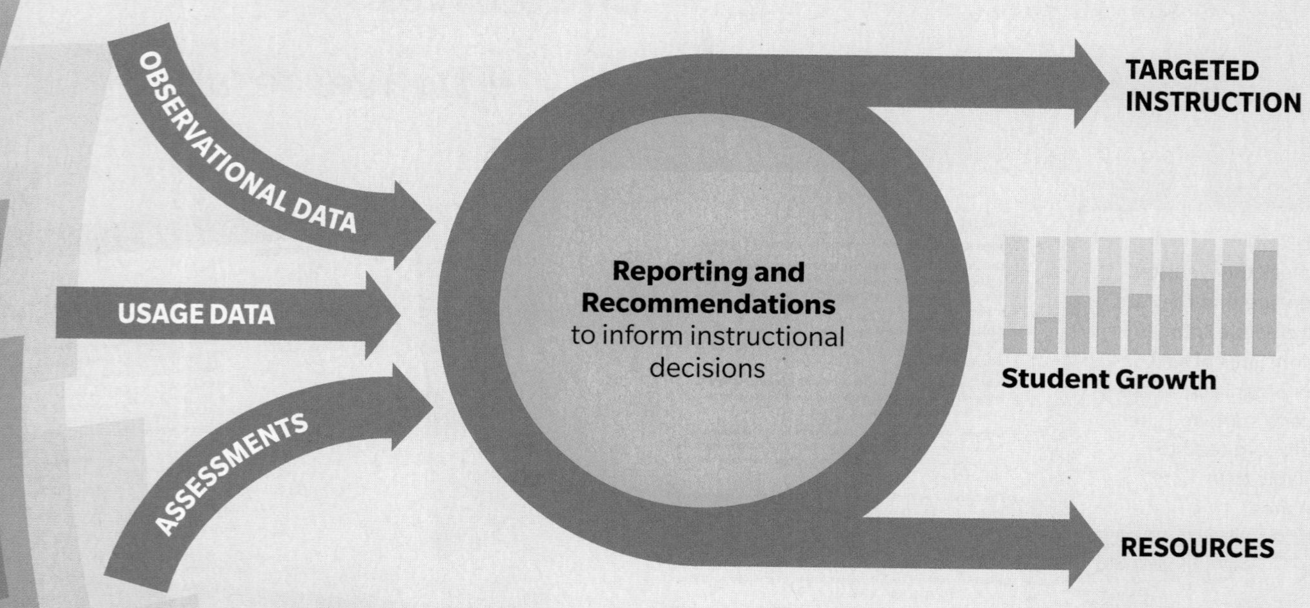

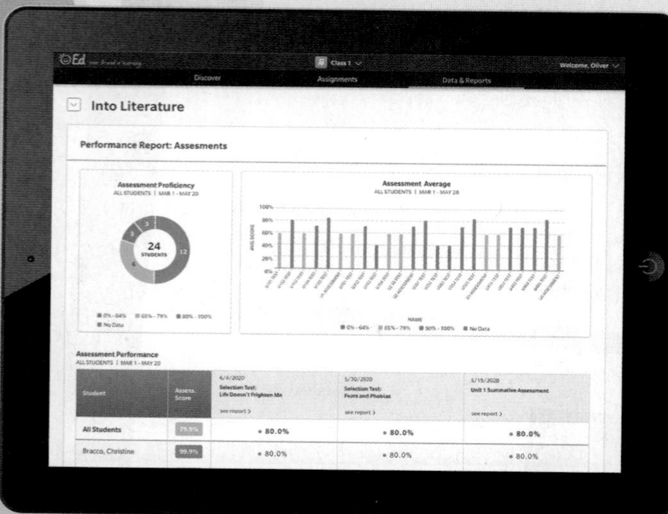

Actionable reports drive grouping and instructional recommendations appropriate for each learner.

Image Credits: (l): ©kanetmark/Shutterstock, (b): ©MSSA

Program Assessments

Adaptive Growth Measure

Adaptive Growth Measure allows teachers to gain an understanding of where students are on the learning continuum and identify students in need of intervention or enrichment.

Unit Assessments

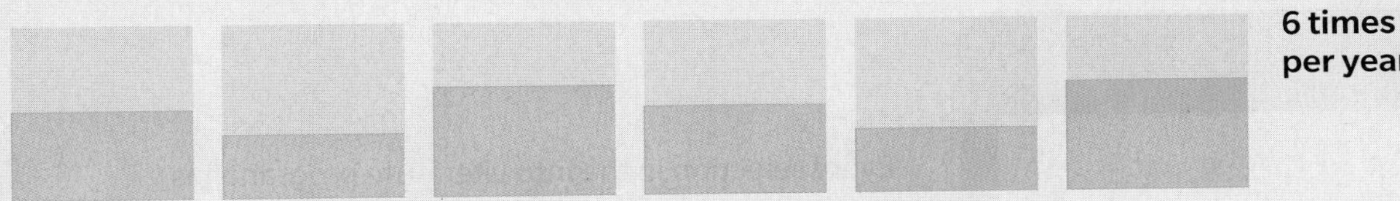

Unit Assessments identify mastery of skills covered during the course of the unit across all literacy strands.

Ongoing Feedback from Daily Classroom Activities

Formative Assessment data is collected across a variety of student activities to help teachers make informed instructional decisions based on data.

- Check Your Understanding
- Selection Tests
- Writing Tasks
- Independent Reading
- Usage Data
- Online Essay Scoring
- Teacher Observations
- Research Projects

Assessments

HMH Into Literature has a comprehensive suite of assessments to help you determine what students already know and how they are progressing through the program lessons.

Diagnostic Assessment for Reading is an informal, criterion-referenced assessment designed to diagnose the specific reading comprehension skills that need attention.

Skills-based Diagnostic Assessments will help you quickly gauge a student's mastery of common, grade-level appropriate skills.

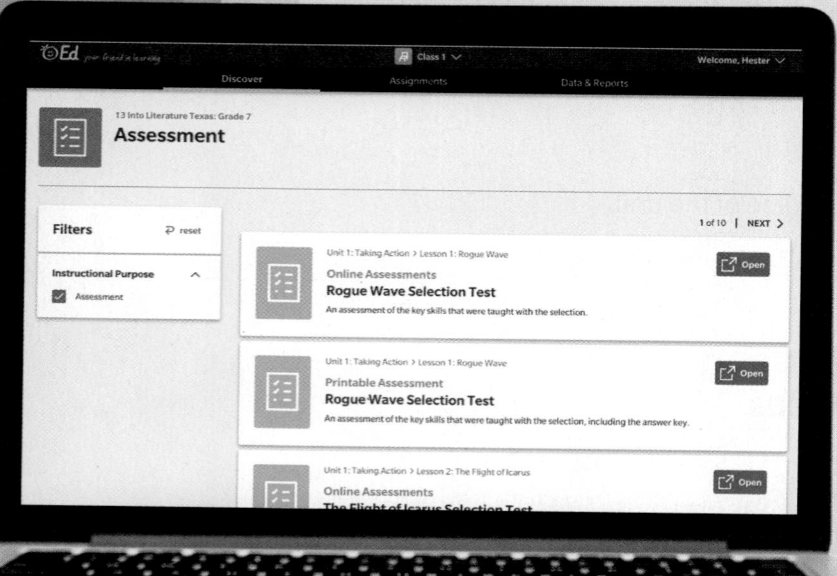

Every selection in the Into Literature program has a corresponding **Selection Test,** focusing on the skills taught in each lesson.

- Analyze & Apply
- Collaborate & Compare, and
- Independent Reading

A **Unit Test** assesses mastery of the skills taught in the entire Unit using new readings aligned with the Unit topic.

The **Diagnostic Screening Test** for Grammar, Usage, and Mechanics provides an assessment of strengths and weaknesses in the conventions of written English.

Each Module in the Grammar Studio has a **Diagnostic Assessment** and a **Summative Assessment,** for before and after instruction.

Foster a Learning Culture

As you encourage a culture of responsibility and collaboration, essential for students' success in the world of work, you will find learning activities that are social, active, and student owned.

Collaborate & Compare Designed to support individual accountability as well as team aptitude, this section requires students to read and annotate texts and compare their responses in small groups.

Peer Review is a critical part of students' creative process. Tools like Checklists for writing and listening and speaking tasks and the Revision Guide with questions, tips, and techniques offer practical support for peer interaction.

Learning Mindset notes and strategies in your Teacher's Edition are designed to help students acquire the attitude of perseverance needed to successfully negotiate learning obstacles. Other resources such as ongoing formative assessments, peer evaluation, and Reflect on the Unit questions encourage students to monitor their progress and develop metacognitive ability.

SETTING GOALS
GRIT
PROBLEM SOLVING
SEEKING CHALLENGES
RESILIENCE
WONDER
CURIOSITY

LEARNING MINDSET

Persistence Remind students that learning requires taking on challenges. Point out that taking on a challenge requires working hard and putting forth real effort. You might use a sports analogy to make your point. Ask students what their favorite football, basketball, or soccer teams do when they are losing early in a game. Discuss how persistence and confidence—a sense that "I can do this"—propel athletes and sports teams to victory. Remind students that academic subjects, like sports, require that same level of confidence and persistence and a commitment to work hard. Just as athletes put in many hours of practice to hone their skills, completing homework and other assignments is, in essence, how students practice and improve upon their academic skills.

Build a Culture of Professional Growth

Embedded and on-going Professional Learning empowers you to develop high-impact learning experiences that provide all students with opportunities for reading and writing success.

Build agency with purposeful, embedded teacher support and high-impact strategies

- Notice & Note Strategies for Close Reading
- Classroom Videos
- On-Demand Professional Learning Modules

A QUILT OF A COUNTRY

You are about to read the argument "A Quilt of a Country." In it, you will encounter notice and note signposts that will give you clues about the essay's claims and evidence. Here are three key signposts to look for as you read this essay and other informative writing.

For more information on these and other signposts to Notice & Note, visit the **Reading Studio**.

When you see phrases like these, pause to see if it's a **Big Questions** signpost:

- "Everyone has heard of..."
- "It goes without saying that."
- "There was a time when..."
- "Most people know that..."

Big Questions Even in a simple conversation between two friends, there are frequent references to information that both speakers already know. Even though they may be exchanging new information, two people communicate better if they understand each other in a variety of ways. Authors count on their readers to understand certain information, such as:

- historical and current events
- shared opinions or ideas
- common words, terms, or concepts

If you're reading a text and feel lost, stop and ask yourself: **What does the author think I already know?** Read this part of "Quilt of a Country" to see one student's annotation of Big Questions.

1 That's because it was built of bits and pieces that seem discordant, like the crazy quilts that have been one of its great folk-art forms, velvet and calico and checks and brocades. Out of many, one. That is the ideal.

2 The reality is often quite different, a great national striving consisting frequently of failure. Many of the oft-told stories of the most pluralistic nation on earth are stories not of tolerance, but of bigotry. Slavery and sweatshops, the burning of crosses and the ostracism of the other. Children learn in social-studies class and in the news of the lynching of blacks, the denial of rights to women, the murders of gay men.

What does the author assume her audience understands about America?	Quindlen has an understanding of America as a melting pot, a mosaic, or a "crazy quilt."
Which historical or social events does the author assume her audience is familiar with?	The author expects that her audience knows about the historical mistreatment of African Americans and other minorities, and the struggle of women for equality.

2 Unit 1

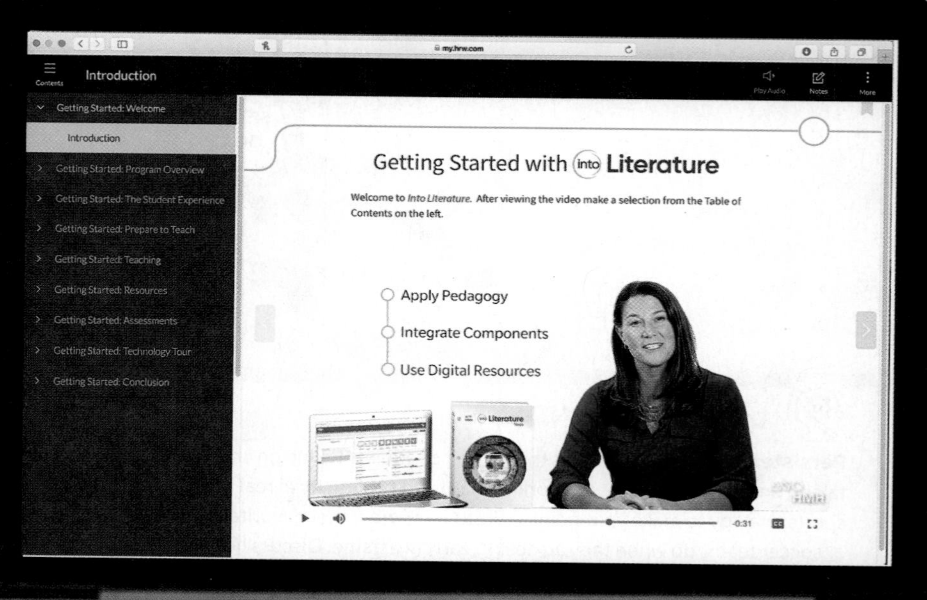

Grow Your Practice with Personalized Blended Professional Learning

- **Getting Started Course and Professional Learning Guide:** Learn the program components, pedagogy, and digital resources to successfully teach with *Into Literature*.
- **Follow-Up:** Choose from relevant instructional topics to create a personalized in-person or online Follow-Up experience to deepen program mastery and enhance teaching practices.
- **Coaching and Modeling:** Experience just-in-time support to ensure continuous professional learning that is student-centered and grounded in data.
- **askHMH:** Get on-demand access to program experts who will answer questions and provide personalized conferencing and digital demonstrations to support implementation.
- **Technical Services:** Plan, prepare, implement, and operate technology with ease.

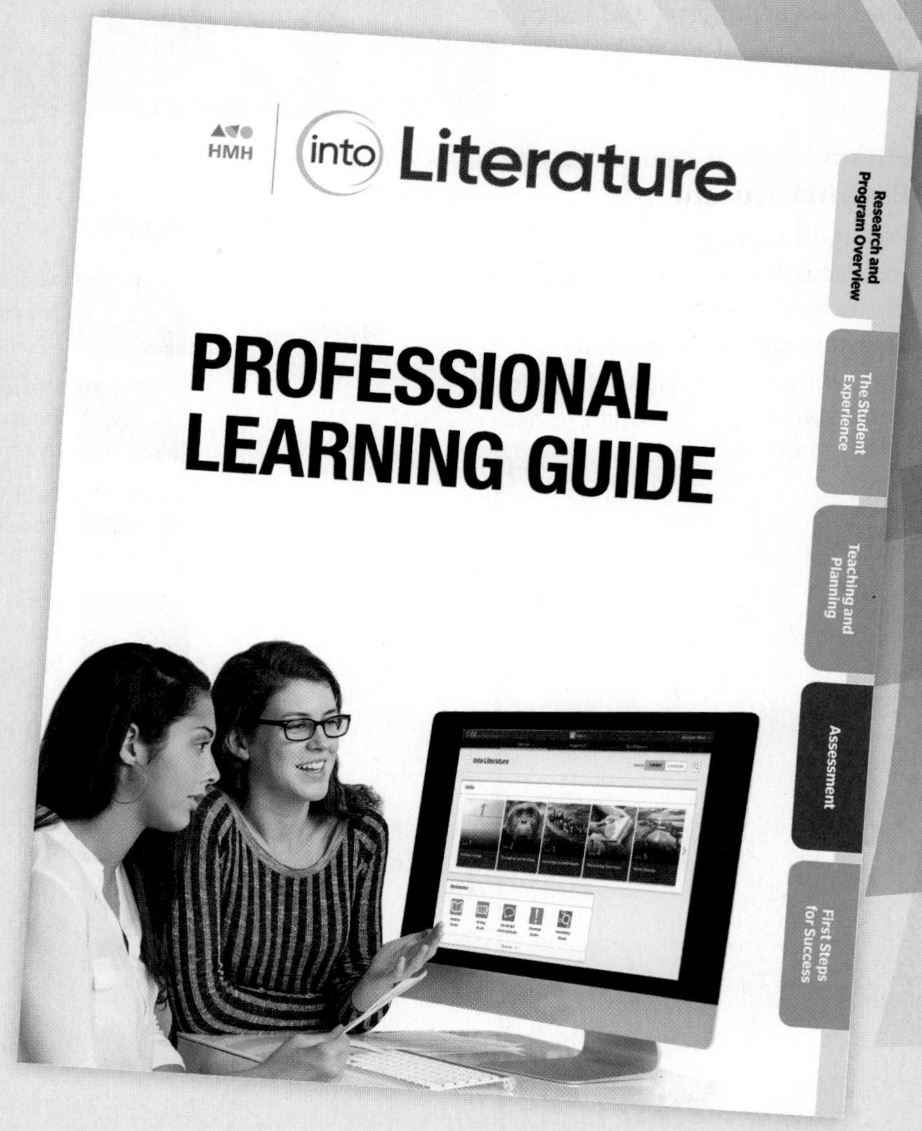

Image Credits: (r): ©kanetmark/Shutterstock, (b): ©Ariel Skelley/Digital Vision/Getty Images

Annotated Student Edition Table of Contents

UNIT 1

Topical Focus
Each unit reflects a topic linking selections, an Essential Question, a quotation, and unit tasks for analysis, discussion, synthesis, and response.

Essential Question
Posing thought-provoking ideas for discussion and reflection as students read, the Essential Question stimulates analysis and synthesis, leading to a richer understanding of the unit's texts.

UNIT 1

FINDING COMMON GROUND

PAGE 1

? ESSENTIAL QUESTION:
How can we come together despite our differences?

ANALYZE & APPLY

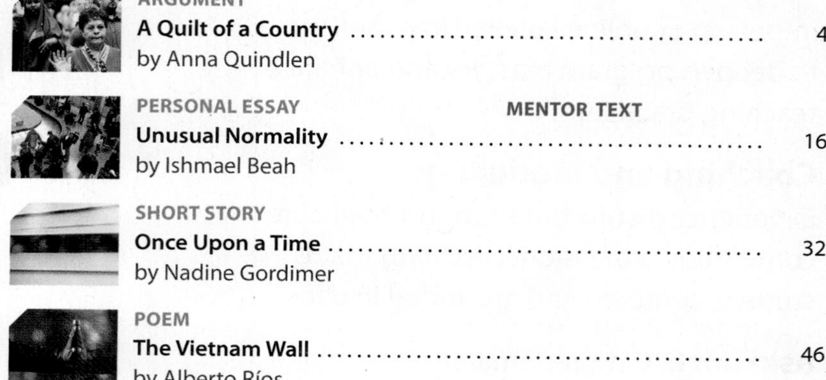

COLLABORATE & COMPARE

UNIT 1

Key Learning Objectives
- Analyze arguments
- Analyze author's purpose and message
- Analyze tone and voice
- Analyze setting and theme
- Analyze graphic elements
- Analyze figurative language
- Analyze digital texts

Visit the Interactive Student Edition for:
- Unit and Selection Videos
- Media Selections
- Selection Audio Recordings
- Enhanced Digital Instruction

Additional Connections
- **The Joy Luck Club**
  by Amy Tan (novel)
- **Freak the Mighty**
  by Rodman Philbrick (novel)

Key Learning Objectives
In abbreviated form, each unit's main instructional goals are listed for planning and quick reference.

Annotated Student Edition Table of Contents

UNIT 2

UNIT 2

THE STRUGGLE FOR FREEDOM

PAGE 82

ESSENTIAL QUESTION:

How do people find freedom in the midst of oppression?

Analyze & Apply

This section of the Table of Contents groups a variety of selections for analysis, annotation, and application of the Notice & Note protocol, as well as standards instruction.

ANALYZE & APPLY

NOTICE & NOTE READING MODEL

Collaborate & Compare

This section of the Table of Contents provides a comparative analysis of two selections linked by topic but different in genre, craft, or focus. Standards instruction and annotation are also applied.

COLLABORATE & COMPARE

COMPARE ACROSS GENRES

UNIT 2

Independent Reading

Interactive digital texts linked to the unit topic and in a wide range of genres and Lexile levels provide additional resources for students' independent reading, expanding student choice and experience.

Additional Connections

- **Goodbye, Vietnam** by Gloria Whelan (novel)
- **Narrative of the Life of Frederick Douglass** by Frederick Douglass (autobiography)

Key Learning Objectives

- Analyze rhetorical devices
- Analyze text structure
- Analyze literary devices
- Analyze setting and theme
- Analyze poetic language
- Analyze setting and purpose
- Analyze multimodal texts

Visit the Interactive Student Edition for:

- Unit and Selection Videos
- Media Selections
- Selection Audio Recordings
- Enhanced Digital Instruction

Annotated Student Edition Table of Contents

UNIT 3

UNIT 3

THE BONDS BETWEEN US

PAGE 168

? ESSENTIAL QUESTION:

How do we form and maintain our connections with others?

Notice & Note Reading Model

Using a gradual release model to teach the signposts referred to as Notice & Note, the Reading Model describes two to three signposts and illustrates them in a selection.

ANALYZE & APPLY

COLLABORATE & COMPARE

Mentor Text

This selection exemplifies genre characteristics and craft choices that will be used in end-of-unit writing tasks as models for students.

UNIT 3

Additional Connections

- **The Miracle Worker** by William Gibson (drama)
- **To Kill a Mockingbird** by Harper Lee (novel)

Key Learning Objectives

- Analyze setting and theme
- Make inferences about theme
- Analyze author's claim
- Summarize and paraphrase texts
- Evaluate details
- Analyze media messages
- Analyze plot and characterization
- Analyze diction and syntax

 **Visit the Interactive Student Edition for:**

- Unit and Selection Videos
- Media Selections
- Selection Audio Recordings
- Enhanced Digital Instruction

UNIT 4

Variety of Genres

Each unit is comprised of different kinds of texts or genres. Essential characteristics of each genre are identified and illustrated. Students then apply those characteristics to their own writing.

UNIT 4

SWEET SORROW

PAGE 246

ESSENTIAL QUESTION:

How can love bring both joy and pain?

ANALYZE & APPLY

COLLABORATE & COMPARE

UNIT 4

Tasks
Each unit concludes with one or two culminating tasks that demonstrate essential understandings, synthesizing ideas and text references in oral and written responses.

Additional Novel Connections
- **Wuthering Heights**
  by Emily Bronte
- **Ethan Frome**
  by Edith Wharton

Key Learning Objectives
- Analyze text meaning and author's purpose
- Analyze informational text
- Generate questions
- Analyze multimodal texts
- Analyze literary devices
- Analyze parallel plots
- Analyze poetry
- Connect ideas

Visit the Interactive Student Edition for:
- Unit and Selection Videos
- Media Selections
- Selection Audio Recordings
- Enhanced Digital Instruction

Annotated Student Edition Table of Contents

UNIT 5

Cultural Diversity
Each unit includes a rich array of selections that represent multicultural authors and experiences.

UNIT 

A MATTER OF LIFE OR DEATH

PAGE 416

ESSENTIAL QUESTION:
What does it take to survive in a crisis?

ANALYZE & APPLY

COLLABORATE & COMPARE

UNIT 5

Suggested Novel Connection

One extended text is recommended for its topical and thematic connection to other texts in the unit.

Additional Novel Connections

- **Call of the Wild**
  by Jack London
- **Monster**
  by Walter Dean Myers

Key Learning Objectives

- Analyze plot
- Make inferences
- Analyze arguments and rhetorical devices
- Analyze poetic language and structure
- Analyze memoirs
- Analyze word choice

Visit the Interactive Student Edition for:

- Unit and Selection Videos
- Media Selections
- Selection Audio Recordings
- Enhanced Digital Instruction

UNIT 6

UNIT 6

HEROES AND QUESTS

PAGE 492

ESSENTIAL QUESTION:

What drives us to take on a challenge?

UNIT 6

Additional Novel Connections

- **The Thief**
  by Megan Whalen Turner
- **The Autobiography of Miss Jane Pittman**
  by Ernest J. Gaines

Reflection

Students may pause and reflect on their process and understanding of the selections and the themes in each unit.

Key Learning Objectives

- Epic heroes and epic poetry
- Analyze technical texts
- Analyze travel writing
- Evaluate graphic features
- Analyze language
- Make connections

Visit the Interactive Student Edition for:

- Unit and Selection Videos
- Media Selections
- Selection Audio Recordings
- Enhanced Digital Instruction

SELECTIONS BY GENRE

FICTION

SHORT STORY

NONFICTION

ARGUMENT

AUTOBIOGRAPHY/MEMOIR

INFORMATIONAL TEXT

NARRATIVE NONFICTION

SPEECH

POETRY

DRAMA

MEDIA STUDY

HMH *Into Literature* Dashboard

Easy to use and personalized for your learning.

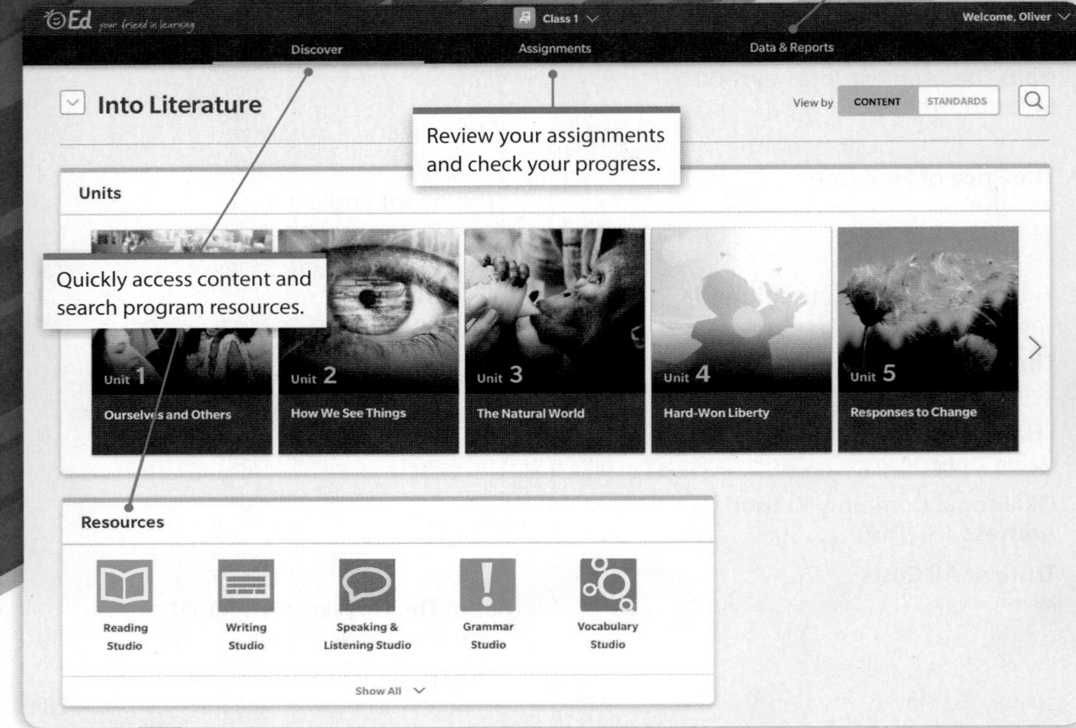

Explore Online to Experience the Power of HMH *Into Literature*

All in One Place

Readings and assignments are supported by a variety of resources to bring literature to life and give you the tools you need to succeed.

Supporting 21st-Century Skills

Whether you're working alone or collaborating with others, it takes effort to analyze the complex texts and competing ideas that bombard us in this fast-paced world. What will help you succeed? Staying engaged and organized. The digital tools in this program will help you take charge of your learning.

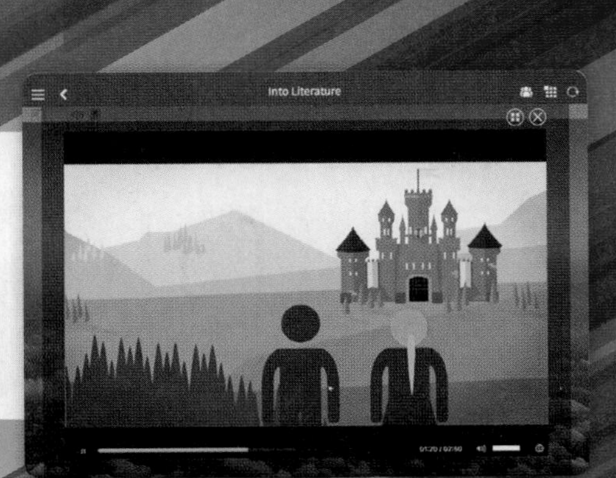

Ignite Your Investigation

You learn best when you're engaged. The **Stream to Start** videos at the beginning of every unit are designed to spark your interest before you read. Get curious and start reading!

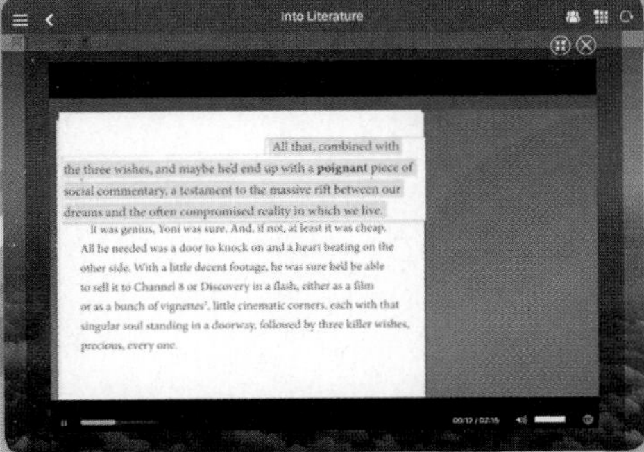

Learn How to Close Read

Close reading effectively is all about examining the details. See how it's done by watching the **Close Read Screencasts** in your eBook. Hear modeled conversations on targeted passages.

Personalized Annotations

My Notes encourages you to take notes as you read and allows you to mark the text in your own customized way. You can easily access annotations to review later as you prepare for exams.

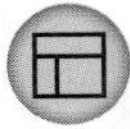

Interactive Graphic Organizers

Graphic organizers help you process, summarize, and keep track of your learning and prepare for end-of-unit writing tasks. **Word Networks** help you learn academic vocabulary, and **Response Logs** help you explore and deepen your understanding of the **Essential Question** in each unit.

No Wi-Fi? No problem!

With HMH *Into Literature,* you always have access: download when you're online and access what you need when you're offline. Work offline and then upload when you're back online.

Communicate "Raise a Hand" to ask or answer questions without having to be in the same room as your teacher.

Collaborate Collaborate with your teacher via chat and work with a classmate to improve your writing.

HMH

Into Literature STUDIOS

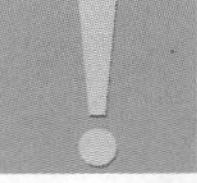

All the help you need to be successful in your literature class is one click away with the Studios. These digital-only lessons are here to tap into the skills that you already use and help you sharpen those skills for the future.

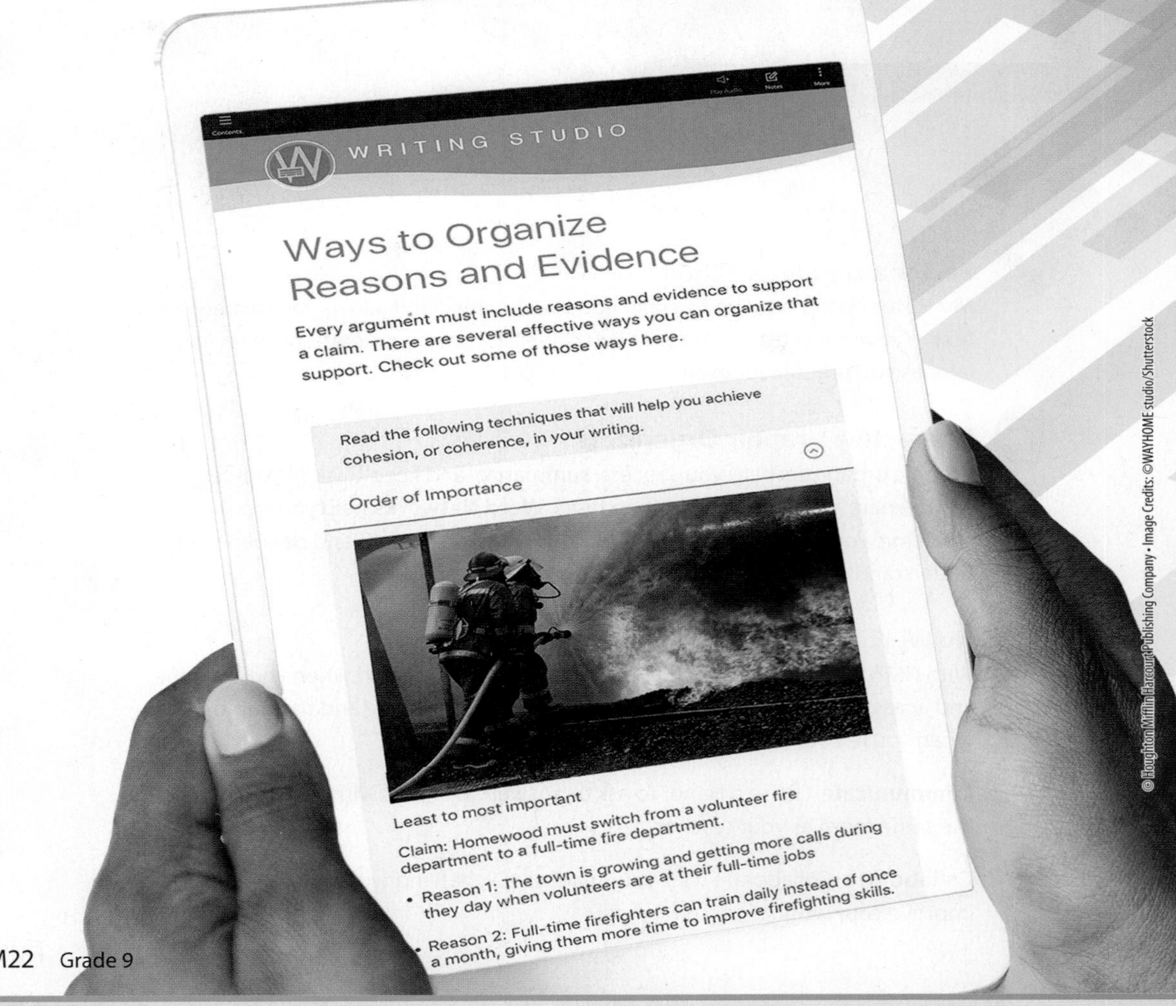

Online Ed

Easy-to-find resources, organized in five separate STUDIOS. On demand and on ED!

Look for links in each lesson to take you to the appropriate Studio.

READING STUDIO

Go beyond the book with the Reading Studio. With over 100 full-length down-loadable titles to choose from, find the right story to continue your journey.

WRITING STUDIO

Being able to write clearly and effectively is a skill that will help you throughout life. The Writing Studio will help you become an expert communicator—in print or online.

SPEAKING & LISTENING STUDIO

Communication is more than just writing. The Speaking & Listening Studio will help you become an effective speaker and a focused listener.

GRAMMAR STUDIO

Go beyond traditional worksheets with the Grammar Studio. These engaging, interactive lessons will sharpen your grammar skills.

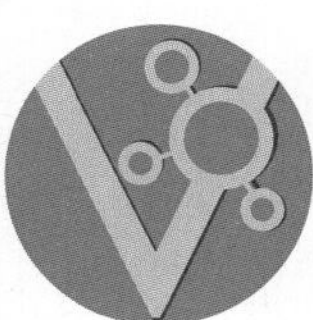

VOCABULARY STUDIO

Learn the skills you need to expand your vocabulary. The interactive lessons in the Vocabulary Studio will grow your vocabulary to improve your reading.

NOTICE & NOTE

This essay is an introduction to the Notice & Note signposts by program consultants Kylene Beers and Robert Probst. It is purposefully informal and designed to motivate students.

Ask students to read the title and first and second paragraphs of the essay. The word "perspicacious" is used repeatedly. Suggest that students use context to define the word.

Discuss the context and how it helped students understand the word.

Definition of "perspicacious": having a ready insight into and understanding of things.

THE PERSPICACIOUS READER (And yes, you want to be one)

Dr. Kylene Beers and Dr. Robert E. Probst

From Dr. Beers:

When Dr. Probst said he wanted to call this essay "The Perspicacious Reader," I had to ask him what that word meant. Did we want kids in high school to be perspicacious? Is that a good thing? Dr. Probst—who knows more words than anyone I know—said, "Of course it is good to be a perspicacious reader," and then he made me look it up. Yes, he's one of those folks who believes looking up words you don't know is good for you. So, off I went, to look it up . . .

I discovered that if you were to be a perspicacious reader, it would be a very good thing. It would mean that you were able to think deeply about what you are reading and make smart inferences. It would mean that you notice a lot as you are reading. And since we wrote a book for teachers titled **Notice and Note**, we like the idea that being a perspicacious reader means you would notice a lot as you read!

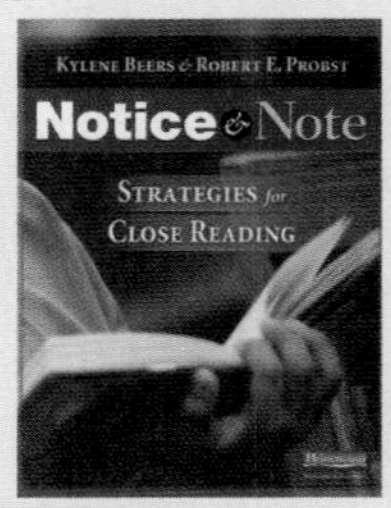

From Both of Us

We both think reading is one of the most important skills you will ever learn. We know that every day you read. Take a moment and think of all you read each day. Here is our combined list.

- Text messages
- Emails
- Tweets
- FB posts
- Newspaper/magazine articles
- How-to info for texting/using our technology
- Novels we choose to read for fun
- Articles for work – some we have to read and some we choose to read
- Bills we get that have to be paid
- Food magazines (Who do you think reads these?)
- Books about teaching
- Articles about technology (And who do you think reads these?)
- Crossword puzzles

And then there are some things we occasionally read:

- Party/wedding invitations
- Birth announcements
- Jokes or cartoons
- Job applications
- Report cards
- School test results
- Income tax information
- Reports from doctors
- Sympathy cards when someone has died
- Information about world events

No matter what you read, we want you to read well. We want you to know what to do when you get confused because we all get confused from time to time as we read. We want you to know what to do when you come to a word you might not know (such as *perspicacious*). We want you to be able to figure out the author's theme if you are reading fiction or the author's purpose and main idea if you are reading nonfiction. We don't want you to have to wait around for someone else to tell you what the text means, which would make you dependent on that person.

We suspect, now that you're in high school, the last thing you want is to depend on others all the time. So, we want you to read smart, read critically, read closely, and always read wondering just what else there is you need to know.

But Sometimes I Hate to Read

We don't doubt that. You've got a lot going on in your life. Friends. Sports. Music. Jobs, maybe. Homework. Worrying about who likes whom and who is invited to what and if your grades are good and how things are going at home and who you'll sit with at lunch, stand with in the hall, go to the party with — even if you'll get invited to the party. First, it will all work out. How do we know? We've been your age. It will all work out.

What's important—along with the many other things that are important in your life right now—is to remember that you want to end up getting smarter about a lot of things each year, and the best way—yes THE BEST WAY—to do that is to make sure you become a better reader each year. So, sometimes this year your teacher may ask you to read a text that makes you say, "Really? Seriously?" We want you to dig in deep and do it because we promise there's a reason, and the reason is about making sure you, the young adult you're becoming, are prepared to deal with all the texts that get thrown your way.

Because here's what most people won't tell you: not all the texts will be honest. Right. That online ad about the used car might not mention everything you need to know. The social media post about your favorite presidential candidate just might be fake news. That Instagram photo showing everyone looking so

Ask students to list at least two examples of what Beers and Probst mean by "reading well." Discuss their examples. Ask students to add additional examples.

Note that Beers and Probst ask students to always read with these three questions in mind:

What surprised me?

What did the author think I already knew?

What changed or confirmed what I already knew?

Ask students to circle these and draw an arrow from them to the margin.

Discuss these three questions.

Beers and Probst introduce the concept of **signposts** which will be used throughout *Into Literature*. Ask students to underline this definition in their book.

perfect, so very happy? Chances are it was posed, shot, reshot, put through several filters, and touched up. The newspaper story about why your school district should or shouldn't build a new school might only offer one perspective. You—not a teacher, not a parent, not your best buddy—you have an obligation to yourself and to the community you live in to always ask yourself if you are reading closely enough to know when you should agree and when you shouldn't. So, we want you to always read with these three questions in mind:

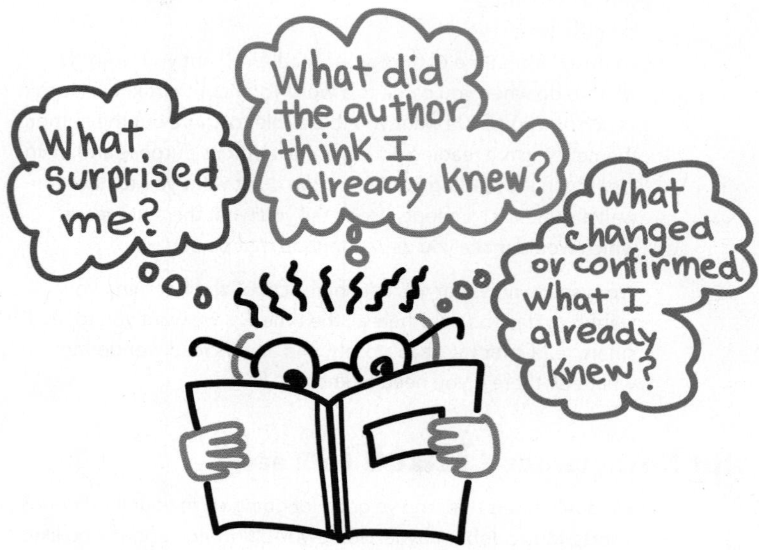

If you'll do that, then we know you'll be on your way to becoming a smarter reader.

AND (Of course there is an AND) . . .

. . . we also want you to learn to read being aware of something we call

signposts.

A signpost is simply a cue an author gives you as you read that can help you figure out the theme (if reading fiction) or author's purpose (if reading nonfiction). In the same way that drivers pay attention (we hope!) to signs as they drive, we want you paying attention to signposts as you read.

So I'm Supposed to Read Just to Look for Signposts?

No, of course not! No one should ever set out to read an article, a chapter in a book, an online essay, a play, or a novel just to hunt for signposts. That would be like taking a drive to your favorite destination just so you can count the stop signs you see on your way there. **No!** You drive to that favorite place to see it and to enjoy the scenery along the way. But if you don't notice the stop signs or one-way signs or curve ahead signs while driving there, you might not ever get there. The signs help you make the journey safely, but noticing the signs isn't the point of the journey.

No!

The same is true of reading. You read to enjoy the journey, to learn some things along the way, and to get to the end of the text with new insights and understandings. Understanding those insights means also noticing the signposts so that you are better able to understand what the author has in mind.

The End!

IN CONCLUSION

This is a signpost showing that we are about to wrap this up!

We are always reading. We may not always be reading books, poems, articles, newspapers, webpages, or texts of any kind, but we are always reading. We read the weather, the teacher's mood, the expression on our friend's face, the demeanor of a group of strangers we encounter on the street, the unusual silence—or noise—in the hallway. We observe and listen, we try to make sense of what we have noticed, and then we act accordingly. We can't get through the day without reading.

And the essence of all of this reading—of both texts and the world around us—is simply paying attention. If we don't see the storm on the horizon, if we don't see the expression on our friend's face, if we don't see the teacher's devious grin, then we won't be able to react intelligently. Noticing is the first step.

So it is with the reading of texts. If you aren't paying attention, if you aren't noticing, then you may as well not be staring at the page at all. If you look out the window and don't notice the storm clouds forming, then you'll be drenched in the afternoon. Looking out the window without seeing what is there—noticing—does you little good.

Ask students why the term *signpost*, which is used in other contexts, is also a good one for reading. ***Possible answer:*** *Writers give us direction, clues, and insight with their words just as drivers are given vital information with stop signs, yield signs, and school zone warnings.*

The authors state that there is much more to the process of reading than just "noticing."

Ask students to answer the following question in writing in the margin of their book:

Explain how reading is more than noticing.

Then ask students to get into groups of three and share their written responses and discuss. Ask for volunteers to share responses. Discuss.

And then you must do more. You must take note of what you have noticed. If you do notice the clouds but fail to ask yourself what they might mean, fail to recognize that they forewarn you of the approaching storm, you'll still get soaked. Noticing alone isn't enough; you have to take note of it and ask what it means.

Again, so it is with reading. If you notice what the character has said, what the author has emphasized or ignored, what the setting is like, and you don't bother asking what all that you have noticed tells you, then you may as well not have noticed it in the first place. Looking out the window and noticing the clouds—without thinking about what they mean—does you little good.

NOW WHAT?

Finally, after noticing and noting, you must do something. You must ask yourself, "So what? Now what do I need to do (or think, or feel, or say)?" If you don't reach that third step, the first two have been little more than an exercise.

Again, so it is with reading texts. If you notice what the text offers, think about it, and simply lay it aside without considering how you might change your own thinking or your own actions, then you will have missed an opportunity to grow and change. The effort of reading will have been wasted. If you notice the clouds forming, take note of that and realize that it warns you of the approaching storm, and still walk out the door without your raincoat or your umbrella, you will ***still*** get drenched. Reading—of the sky or of the book —should enable us to deal with life more effectively.

That's because the pages of a book allow you to explore places you've never been, meet people and characters who are far different from you, and discover through all this that reading— more than anything else— is what gives you the opportunity to reflect and in that reflection perhaps change something about yourself. Reading is a changemaker. We hope this is your year for growing and changing as a reader. We hope this is the year when, as you read, you learn to notice and note.

NOTICE & NOTE SIGNPOSTS

Signpost	Definition	Anchor Question(s)
FICTION		
Contrasts and Contradictions	A sharp contrast between what we would expect and what we observe the character doing; behavior that contradicts previous behavior or well-established patterns	Why would the character act (feel) this way?
Aha Moment	A character's realization of something that shifts his actions or understanding of himself, others, or the world around him	How might this change things?
Tough Questions	Questions a character raises that reveal his or her inner struggles	What does this question make me wonder about?
Words of the Wiser	The advice or insight about life that a wiser character, who is usually older, offers to the main character	What is the life lesson, and how might this affect the character?
Again and Again	Events, images, or particular words that recur over a portion of the story	Why might the author bring this up again and again?
Memory Moment	A recollection by a character that interrupts the forward progress of the story	Why might this memory be important?
NONFICTION		
Contrasts and Contradictions	A sharp contrast between what we would expect and what we observe happening. A difference between two or more elements in the text.	What is the difference, and why does it matter?
Extreme or Absolute Language	Language that leaves no doubt about a situation or an event, allows no compromise, or seems to exaggerate or overstate a case.	Why did the author use this language?
Numbers and Stats	Specific quantities or comparisons to depict the amount, size, or scale. Or, the writer is vague and imprecise about numbers when we would expect more precision.	Why did the author use these numbers or amounts?
Quoted Words	Opinions or conclusions of someone who is an expert on the subject, or someone who might be a participant in or a witness to an event. Or, the author might cite other people to provide support for a point.	Why was this person quoted or cited, and what did this add?
Word Gaps	Vocabulary that is unfamiliar to the reader—for example, a word with multiple meanings, a rare or technical word, a discipline-specific word, or one with a far-removed antecedent.	Do I know this word from someplace else? Does it seem like technical talk for this topic? Can I find clues in the sentence to help me understand the word?

FM29

Ask students to mark this page for future reference.

Read the chart on this page noting that it is divided into **Fiction** and **Nonfiction** signposts and includes a definition and an anchor question for each. An **anchor question** helps students identify the signposts as they read by "questioning" the text.

The essay by program consultant Carol Jago is an accessible explanation of **genre** and its importance. Genre has an elevated role in the new standards—both in reading and writing.

Ask students to read the first and second paragraphs and then to write their own definition of genre in the margin of their book.

If your students need an analogy to better understand **genre**, explain that genre refers to different categories or kinds of texts we read. This is similar to vehicles that we use for transportation. Vehicles transport people and goods but may be trucks, vans, sedans or sports cars—different categories for vehicles—different genres for texts.

Ask students to turn to a partner and provide examples of their favorite genre.

READING AND WRITING ACROSS GENRES

by Carol Jago

Reading is a first-class ticket around the world. Not only can you explore other lands and cultures, but you can also travel to the past and future. That journey is sometimes a wild ride. Other books can feel like comfort food, enveloping you in an imaginative landscape full of friends and good times. Making time for reading is making time for life.

Genre

One of the first things readers do when we pick up something to read is notice its genre. You might not think of it exactly in those terms, but consider how you approach a word problem in math class compared to how you read a science fiction story. Readers go to different kinds of text for different purposes. When you need to know how to do or make something, you want a reliable, trusted source of information. When you're in the mood to spend some time in a world of fantasy, you happily suspend your normal disbelief in dragons.

In every unit of *Into Literature,* you'll find a diverse mix of genres all connected by a common theme, allowing you to explore a topic from many different angles.

GENRE: INFORMATIONAL TEXT

COMING TO OUR SENSES

GENRE: SHORT STORY

WHAT, OF THIS GOLDFISH, WOULD YOU WISH?

GENRE: LITERARY NONFICTION

from TOTAL ECLIPSE

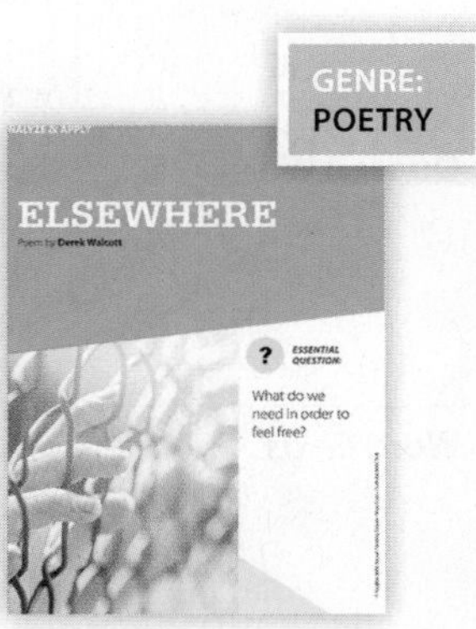

Writer's Craft

Learning how writers use genre to inform, to explain, to entertain, or to surprise readers will help you better understand—as well as enjoy—your reading. Imitating how professional writers employ the tools of their craft—descriptive language, repetition, sensory images, sentence structure, and a variety of other features—will give you many ideas for making your own writing more lively.

Into Literature provides you with the tools you need to understand the elements of all the critical genres and advice on how to learn from professional texts to improve your own writing in those genres.

Reading with Independence

Finding a good book can sometimes be a challenge. Like every other reader, you have probably experienced "book desert" when nothing you pick up seems to have what you are looking for (not that it's easy to explain exactly what you are looking for, but whatever it is, "this" isn't it). If you find yourself in this kind of reading funk, bored by everything you pick up, give yourself permission to range more widely, exploring graphic novels, contemporary biographies, books of poetry, historical fiction. And remember that long doesn't necessarily mean boring. My favorite kind of book is one that I never want to end.

Take control over your own reading with *Into Literature's* Reader's Choice selections and the HMH Digital Library. And don't forget: your teacher, librarian, and friends can offer you many more suggestions.

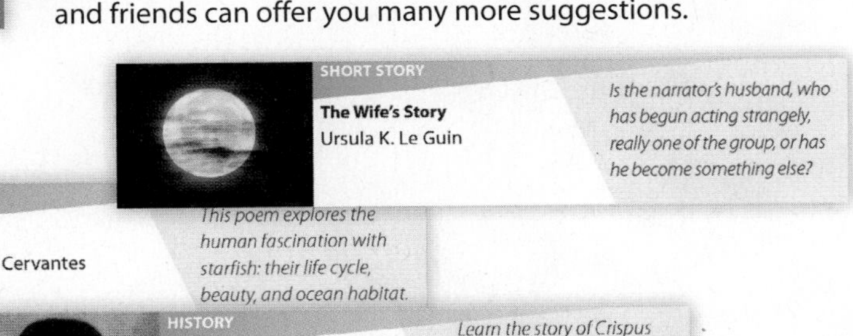

Direct students to read the paragraph under the heading "Writer's Craft." Ask students to write their own definition of *writer's craft* in the margin of *Into Literature*. Discuss, asking students to cite examples.

Encourage students to find the Genre Elements feature with each selection in *Into Literature*.

Call students' attention to the **Reader's Choice** selections listed at the end of each unit and show students how to find the **HMH Digital Library** in the **Reading Studio.**

TEACHER'S EDITION

GRADE 9

Program Consultants:
Kylene Beers
Martha Hougen
Elena Izquierdo
Carol Jago
Erik Palmer
Robert E. Probst

Instructional Overview and Resources

	Instructional Focus	Online Ed Resources
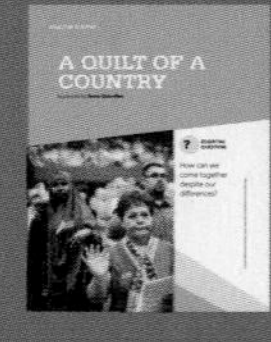 **Unit Introduction** **Finding Common Ground**	**Unit 1 Essential Question** **Unit 1 Academic Vocabulary**	**Stream to Start:** Finding Common Ground **Unit 1 Response Log**
ANALYZE & APPLY		
 **"A Quilt of a Country"** Argument by Anna Quindlen **Lexile 1260L** **NOTICE & NOTE** READING MODEL **Signposts** • Big Questions • Contrasts and Contradictions • Word Gaps	**Reading** • Analyze Arguments • Evaluate Author's Claim **Writing:** Compare Research with a Partner **Speaking and Listening:** Discuss with a Small Group **Vocabulary:** Patterns of Word Changes **Language Conventions:** Noun Clauses	**Audio** **Close Read Screencasts:** Modeled Discussions **Reading Studio:** Notice & Note **Level Up Tutorials:** Analyzing Arguments; Elements of an Argument **Speaking and Listening Studio:** Participating in Collaborative Discussions **Vocabulary Studio:** Words With Multiple Meanings **Grammar Studio:** Module 4: Lesson 4: The Noun Clause
 **Mentor Text** **"Unusual Normality"** Personal Essay by Ishmael Beah **Lexile 820L**	**Reading** • Analyze Purpose and Message • Analyze Voice and Tone **Writing:** Write a Summarizing Report **Speaking and Listening:** Debate with a Small Group **Vocabulary:** Denotative and Connotative Meanings **Language Conventions:** Active and Passive Voice	**Audio** **Reading Studio:** Notice & Note **Level Up Tutorials:** Author's Purpose; Author's Style **Writing Studio:** Introduction: Informative Texts **Speaking and Listening Studio:** Rhetoric and Delivery **Vocabulary Studio:** Denotative and Connotative Meanings **Grammar Studio:** Module 6: Lesson 4: Active and Passive Voice
"Once Upon a Time" Short Story by Nadine Gordimer **Lexile 1390L**	**Reading** • Analyze Setting and Theme • Analyze Plot: Subplots **Writing:** Write a Fairy Tale **Speaking and Listening:** Present to the Class **Vocabulary:** Words from Latin **Language Conventions:** Prepositional Phrases	**Audio** **Close Read Screencasts:** Modeled Discussions **Reading Studio:** Notice & Note **Level Up Tutorial:** Setting: Effect on Plot **Writing Studio:** Writing Narratives **Speaking and Listening Studio:** Giving a Presentation **Vocabulary Studio:** Words from Latin **Grammar Studio:** Module 3: Lesson 1: Prepositional Phrases

SUGGESTED PACING: 30 DAYS

Unit Introduction	A Quilt of a Country	Unusual Normality	Once Upon a Time	The Vietnam Wall
1	2 3 4 5	6 7 8 9	10 11 12 13	14 15 16

English Learner Support		Differentiated Instruction	Online Ed Assessment
• Learn New Expressions • Learning Strategies			
• Text X-Ray • Use Academic Language • Use Cognates • Listen and Derive Meaning • Understand Language Structures • Oral Assessment	• Pronounce Vocabulary Correctly • Language Conventions	**When Students Struggle** • Use Strategies • Analyze Arguments • Reteaching: Analyzing Arguments **To Challenge Students** • Analyze Rhetoric	**Selection Test**
• Text X-Ray • Use Cognates • Practice Phonology • Language Conventions • Use Content-Based Vocabulary • Practice Newly Acquired Vocabulary	• Make Inferences • Expand Reading Skills • Understand Voice • Oral Assessment • Adapt Language • Vocabulary Strategy • Active and Passive Voice	**When Students Struggle** • Analyze Author's Purpose • Analyze Author's Style **To Challenge Students** • Explore Beah's Decision	**Selection Test**
• Text X-Ray • Use Cognates • Make Inferences About Theme • Identify Figurative Language • Describe Setting • Understand Language Structures	• Analyze Descriptive Language • Discuss Environmental Print • Oral Assessment • Analyze Spelling • Confirm Understanding • Use Prepositions and Prepositional Phrases	**When Students Struggle** • Compare and Contrast **To Challenge Students** • Write from Author's Perspective	**Selection Test**

The Gettysburg Address / *from* Saving Lincoln 17 18 19 20 21 22 23 24 25
Independent Reading 26 27
End of Unit 28 29 30

UNIT 1 Continued

	Instructional Focus	 Online Ed Resources
ANALYZE & APPLY		
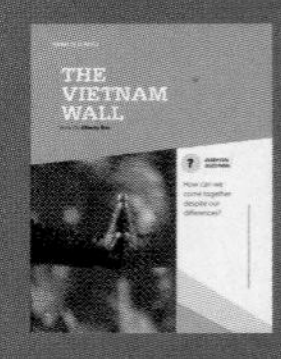 **"The Vietnam Wall"** Poem by Alberto Ríos	**Reading** • Analyze Graphic Elements • Analyze Figurative Language **Writing:** Create an Imagery Board **Speaking and Listening:** Present Your Work	 **Audio** **Reading Studio:** Notice & Note **Level Up Tutorial:** Figurative Language **Writing Studio:** Writing as a Process **Speaking and Listening Studio:** Participating in Collaborative Discussions
COLLABORATE & COMPARE		
 **"The Gettysburg Address"** Speech by Abraham Lincoln **Lexile 1170L**	**Reading** • Analyze Purpose and Audience • Analyze Rhetorical Devices **Writing:** Deliver an Oral Presentation **Speaking and Listening:** Discuss with a Small Group **Vocabulary:** Multiple-Meaning Words **Language Conventions:** Parallel Structure	 **Audio** **Reading Studio:** Notice & Note **Level Up Tutorial:** Elements of an Argument **Speaking and Listening Studio:** Giving a Presentation **Vocabulary Studio:** Multiple-Meaning Words
from *Saving Lincoln* Film Clip	**Reading** • Analyze Digital Texts • Analyze Special Effects **Writing:** Review the Film **Speaking and Listening:** Hold a Panel Discussion	**Reading Studio:** Notice & Note **Level Up Tutorial:** Biographies and Autobiographies **Writing Studio:** Writing Informative Texts **Speaking and Listening Studio:** Giving a Presentation
Collaborate and Compare	**Reading:** Compare Across Genres **Speaking and Listening:** Discuss and Present	**Speaking and Listening Studio:** Participating in Collaborative Discussions

 Online Ed INDEPENDENT READING

The Independent Reading selections are only available in the eBook.

 **Go to the Reading Studio for more information on Notice & Note.**

"Facing It"
Poem by Yusef Komunyakaa

"Making the Future Better, Together"
Blog by Eboo Patel
Lexile 1170L

"Oklahoma Bombing Memorial Address"
Speech by Bill Clinton
Lexile 1060L

END OF UNIT		
Writing Task: Write a Personal Essay **Reflect on the Unit**	**Writing:** Write a Personal Essay **Language Conventions:** Active and Passive Voice	**Unit 1 Response Log** **Mentor Text:** "Unusual Normality" **Writing Studio:** Narrative Context **Reading Studio:** Notice & Note **Grammar Studio:** Module 6: Lesson 4: Active and Passive Voice

English Learner Support	Differentiated Instruction	Online Ed Assessment
• Text X-Ray • Understand Directionality • Oral Assessment	**When Students Struggle** • Analyze Figurative Language • Reteaching: Analyze Figurative Language	**Selection Test**
• Text X-Ray • Apply Directionality • Use Cognates • Oral Assessment • Vocabulary Strategies • Language Conventions	**When Students Struggle** • Analyze Parallel Structure	**Selection Test**
• Text X-Ray • Understand Meanings • Use Cognates • Understand Information	**When Students Struggle** • Analyze Media • Reteaching: Analyze Digital Texts **To Challenge Students** • Write a Sidebar	**Selection Test**
• Express Ideas		
"Night Calls" Short Story by Lisa Fugard **Lexile 1110L**	"Theme for English B" Poem by Langston Hughes	**Selection Tests**
• Language X-Ray • Learning Strategies • Develop a Topic Statement • Use the Mentor Text • Use Transitions Effectively • Check Subject-Verb Agreement	**When Students Struggle** • Use Small Group Brainstorming • Learn Drafting Strategies **To Challenge Students** • Peer Reviews	**Unit Test**

Connect to the
ESSENTIAL QUESTION

Ask a volunteer to read aloud the Essential Question. Discuss the different ways people can "come together" and why it may be important to do so despite possible differences. Prompt students to think of past or current events in their community that resulted in disagreements. Then have them give examples of situations that could be resolved if people with different opinions work together to find a solution.

English Learner Support

Learn New Expressions Make sure students understand the Essential Question. If necessary, explain the following idiomatic expressions:

- *Come together* means "to join or form a group with others."
- *Despite* means "in spite of; even though there is something that may prevent this from happening."

Help students restate the question in simpler language: How can we join with others who are different from us? **SUBSTANTIAL**

DISCUSS THE QUOTATION

Tell students that Kofi Annan (1938) is a diplomat from Ghana who served as the seventh Secretary-General of the United Nations from January 1997 to December 2006. In 2001, Annan was awarded the Nobel Peace Prize for reforming the UN and making human rights a major priority. Ask students to read the quotation thoughtfully and to pause for a moment to reflect on it. Then have students discuss the message Annan is conveying. Have they heard similar sentiments? Can they think of conflicts that resulted from the differences Annan notes? Can they think of times when people came together even when they had long-standing differences?

UNIT  1

FINDING COMMON GROUND

ESSENTIAL QUESTION:

How can we come together despite our differences?

> We may have different religions, different languages, different colored skin, but we all belong to one human race.
>
> Kofi Annan

LEARNING MINDSET

Growth Mindset Explain that people with a "fixed" mindset tend to believe they are simply not good at something or can't learn new things or skills. For example, students who believe they aren't good at math may not try hard to improve because they don't think they can. Emphasize that learning takes effort and time. Tell them to think of mistakes as opportunities to learn and try again; in other words, mistakes are just practice. Provide examples of people who, despite setbacks, continued to work hard in order to improve. Point out that J.K. Rowling—author of the Harry Potter series—didn't stop trying to publish her book, despite originally being rejected by twelve different publishers.

ACADEMIC VOCABULARY

Academic Vocabulary words are words you use when you discuss and write about texts. In this unit you will practice and learn five words.

☑ enforce ☐ entity ☐ internal ☐ presume ☐ resolve

Study the Word Network to learn more about the word **enforce**.

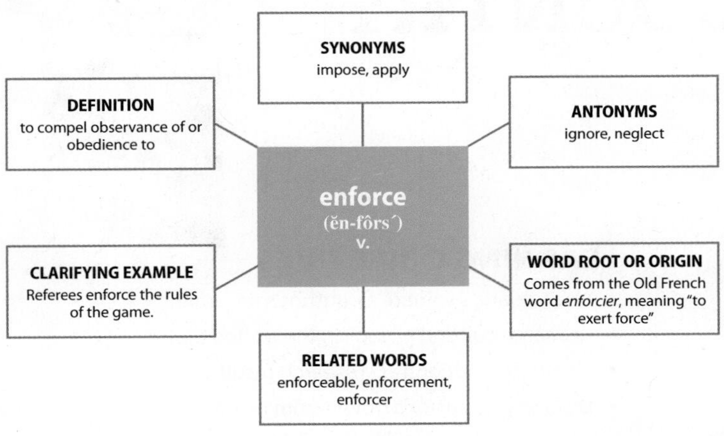

Write and Discuss Discuss the completed Word Network with a partner, making sure to talk through all of the boxes until you both understand the word, its synonyms, antonyms, and related forms. Then, fill out a Word Network for each of the four remaining words. Use a dictionary or online resource to help you complete the activity.

Go online to access the Word Networks.

RESPOND TO THE ESSENTIAL QUESTION

In this unit, you will explore how humanity can unite despite our differences and struggles. As you read, you will revisit the **Essential Question** and gather your ideas about it in the **Response Log** that appears on page R1. At the end of the unit, you will have the opportunity to write a **personal essay** about yourself, sharing an experience, opinion, or response to an event. Filling out the Response Log will help you prepare for this writing task.

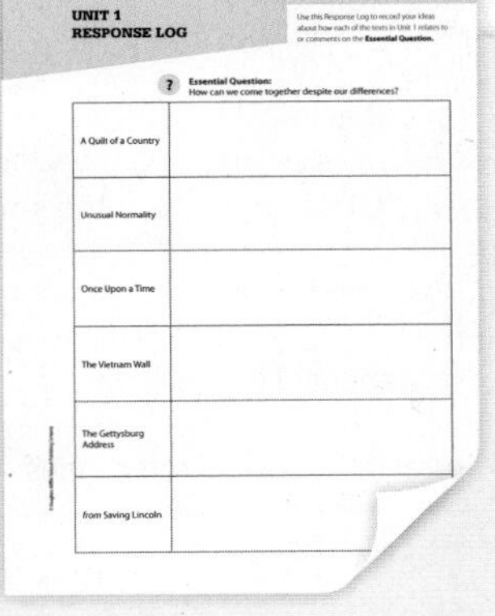

You can also go online to access the Response Log.

TEACH

ACADEMIC VOCABULARY

As students complete Word Networks for the remaining four vocabulary words, encourage them to include all the categories shown in the completed network if possible, but point out that some words do not have clear synonyms or antonyms.

enforce (ĕn-fôrs´) *v.* To compel observance of or obedience to.

entity (ĕn´tĭ-tē) *n.* A thing that exists as a unit. (Spanish cognate: *entidad*)

internal (ĭn-tûr´nəl) *adj.* Inner, located within something or someone. (Spanish cognate: *interno*)

presume (prĭ-zo͞om´) *v.* To take for granted as being true; to assume something is true. (Spanish cognate: *presumir*)

resolve (rĭ-zŏlv´) *v.* To decide or become determined. (Spanish cognate: *resolver*)

RESPOND TO THE ESSENTIAL QUESTION

Direct students to the Unit 1 Response Log. Explain that students will use it to record ideas and details from the selections that help answer the Essential Question. When they work on the writing task at the end of the unit, their Response Logs will help them think about what they have read and make connections between the texts.

ENGLISH LEARNER SUPPORT

Learning Strategies In this unit, students are likely going to come across unfamiliar sayings and expressions. Use this strategy to help students learn how to make sense of ones they do not know:

- Preview each selection. Guide students in looking for phrases they do not know. Model how to look for italics, parentheses, quotation marks, and footnotes and show how to use these as helpful clues to understand unfamiliar sayings and expressions.
- Have students circle or highlight sayings or expressions that are new to them. Model how to figure out meaning by using context clues, writing down their ideas, and then checking their ideas with a partner.
- During and after reading the selection, coach students in using these new sayings and expressions in their discussions and writing.

ALL LEVELS

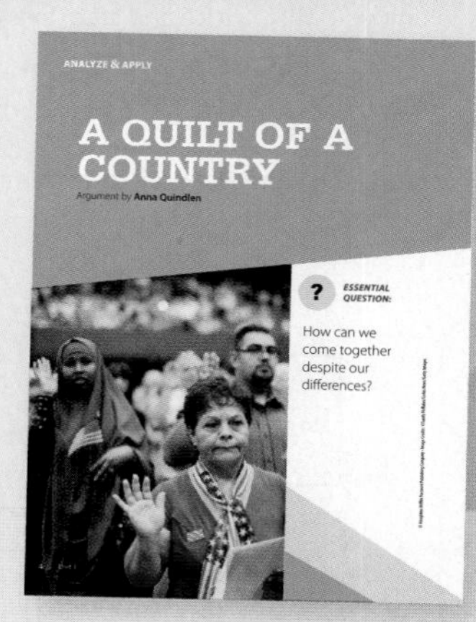

READING MODEL

A QUILT OF A COUNTRY

Argument by Anna Quindlen

GENRE ELEMENTS

ARGUMENT

Remind students that a strong **argument** clearly states the author's **claim,** or position on an issue, and supports it with valid reasons and credible, relevant evidence. It anticipates objections and counterclaims and either reduces their impact by offering concessions or refutes them entirely with rebuttals and counterarguments.

LEARNING OBJECTIVES

- Analyze and evaluate an author's argument.
- Research cultural groups in the United States.
- Compare and contrast research results.
- Discuss conclusions drawn from research.
- Identify and apply knowledge of patterns of word changes.
- Use noun clauses to express meaning and add interest to writing.
- **Language** Compare and contrast information using key expressions such as *both, similarly, unlike,* and *however.*

TEXT COMPLEXITY

Quantitative Measures	**A Quilt of a Country**	Lexile: 1260L
Qualitative Measures	**Ideas Presented** Mostly explicit, but moves to some implied meaning.	
	Structures Used More complex text structures with some deviation from chronology.	
	Language Used Complex sentences; Tier II and III vocabulary not defined at point of use.	
	Knowledge Required Cultural or historical references.	

Online 

RESOURCES

- Unit 1 Response Log
- Selection Audio
-  Close Read Screencasts: Modeled Discussions
-  Reading Studio: Notice & Note
-  Level Up Tutorials: Analyzing Arguments; Elements of an Argument
-  Speaking and Listening Studio: Participating in Collaborative Discussions
-  Vocabulary Studio: Words With Multiple Meanings
-  Grammar Studio: Module 4: Lesson 4: The Noun Clause
- "A Quilt of a Country" Selection Test

SUMMARIES

English

Anna Quindlen argues that patriotism unites Americans despite cultural divisions that have caused conflicts throughout U.S. history. Quindlen develops her claim with an extended metaphor comparing the diversity of the United States to a patchwork quilt that holds together a variety of fabrics. To support her reasoning, Quindlen cites evidence of shared values, work ethics, and ideologies as well as times of crisis when Americans have pulled together to support one another.

Spanish

Anna Quindlen expresa que el patriotismo une a los estadounidenses, a pesar de las divisiones culturales que han causado conflictos a través de la historia de Estados Unidos.

Quindlen desarrolla su afirmación con una metáfora extendida, donde compara la diversidad de Estados Unidos con una colcha de retazos que mantiene unidas una variedad de telas. Para apoyar su razonamiento, Quindlen cita como evidencia la harmonía y la discordia desde la fundación de la nación.

SMALL-GROUP OPTIONS

Have students work in small groups to read and discuss the selection.

Double-Entry Journal

- Instruct students to create a T-chart in their notebooks or journals, labeling the left column *Quotes from the Text* and the right column *My Notes.*
- In the left column, have students record quotes from "A Quilt of a Country" that they view as significant, interesting, or difficult.
- In the right column, instruct students to write their own analyses, interpretations, paraphrases, and questions.
- When students have finished, have them draw a line under their notes and exchange journals with a partner. Then tell students to respond to their partner's notes in the space below the line.

Three-Minute Review

- After students have read and analyzed "A Quilt of a Country," tell them they will conduct a three-minute review in order to identify questions they still have about the text.
- Set a timer for three minutes. Tell students to review the text along with their annotations and notes and write clarifying questions.
- Have students share and discuss their questions in small groups.
- After groups have finished their discussions, invite them to share any questions they still have with the class.

Text X-Ray: English Learner Support
for "A Quilt of a Country"

Use the Text X-Ray and the supports and scaffolds in the Teacher's Edition to help guide students at different proficiency levels through the selection.

INTRODUCE THE SELECTION
DISCUSS UNITY AND DIVISION

In this lesson, students will need to be able to discuss unity and division among Americans. Explain that *unity* and *division* are antonyms, or opposites, referring to the states of being united as a whole or divided into groups. Tell students that "A Quilt of a Country" was written following the terrorist attacks of September 11, 2001. Then display this sentence from paragraph 5: "Terrorism has led to devastation—and unity." Have volunteers share ideas about forces that might bring people together and those that might divide them. Ask: Why might a disaster or tragedy result in unity? What are some situations that might cause division? Why? Supply the following sentence frames:

- *People might feel [united/divided] when they ____ .*
- *[Unity/division] might result from ____ because ____ .*

CULTURAL REFERENCES

The following references to American history may be unfamiliar to students.

- *all men are created equal* (paragraph 1): a belief that is a cornerstone of the Declaration of Independence, the document that formally announced the separation of the American colonies from Great Britain in 1776
- *the burning of crosses* and *the lynching of blacks* (paragraph 2): examples of the kinds of violence and intimidation African Americans faced after slavery ended in 1865

LISTENING

Listen Actively in a Small Group

Support students' participation in the small-group discussion activity on Student Edition page 13.

Use the following supports with students at varying proficiency levels:

- To support students' active listening skills, have them practice asking these questions to seek clarification of key ideas: Would you repeat that please? Would you explain that another way? Alternatively, provide students with an index card with the word *repeat* on it to hold up when they want something repeated. Have them hold up a card with a question mark on it when they want something clarified. **SUBSTANTIAL**
- Provide these frames for students to seek clarification as they listen to the discussion: *Would you please repeat what you said about ____ ? I understand your point about ____ , but what did you mean when you said ____ ? Would you please elaborate on your point about ____ ?* **MODERATE**
- Have students summarize or paraphrase group members' comments to confirm understanding. **LIGHT**

SPEAKING

Compare Research with a Partner

Support students' participation in the partner activity on Student Edition page 13.

Use the following supports with students at varying proficiency levels:

- Have students say *similar* or *different* as they point to details in their and their partner's research charts. **SUBSTANTIAL**
- Provide these frames that students can use to compare and contrast cultural groups: *[Cultural group A] and [cultural group B] are similar because _____. They differ because _____. In other words, [cultural group A] and [cultural group B] both _____, but [cultural group A or B] _____.* **MODERATE**
- Display words and phrases students might use to compare and contrast, such as *both, similarly, unlike, but, however, on the other hand*. Then tell them to utilize as many of these as they can as they compare their research findings. **LIGHT**

READING

Identify Author's Claim

Display an image of a patchwork quilt with varying colors and patterns. Explain that the title "A Quilt of a Country" provides a clue to Quindlen's **claim,** or position, about the United States.

Guide students to underline words and phrases in paragraph 1 that describe America and to circle details Quindlen uses to describe a quilt. Use the following supports with students at varying proficiency levels:

- Have students skim the text for the sole purpose of finding references to the various ethnic groups that make up the United States. Then have them design a "Quilt of the United States," using symbols and pictures or drawings to show how the country is made up of different parts. **SUBSTANTIAL**
- Have students skim the text to find passages that describe the various "parts" and characteristics of the United States' population. Then have them design a quilt that combines images and text passages to represent Quindlen's vision of the United States. **MODERATE**
- Have students identify Quindlen's claim, or position, and write it as a complete sentence. **LIGHT**

WRITING

Explain Ideas

Draw students' attention to the Quick Start activity. Explain that people have different opinions about things that mean America.

Use the following supports with students at varying proficiency levels:

- Have students find or draw pictures of things that mean America to them and then write a simple caption for each image, using this sentence frame: *This means America to me because ______.* **SUBSTANTIAL**
- Have students find or draw pictures of things that mean America to them and then caption each image using a variety of sentence frames. Provide them with these: *This means America to me because ______. This ______ means America to me because ______. This ______ stands for the United States' ______ .* **MODERATE**
- Have students create a chart with three columns and two rows. Tell them to label each column with the name of something that means America to them, and have them label the rows *Description* and *Explanation*. Then have students complete the charts by writing an appropriate sentence or two in each cell. **LIGHT**

EXPLAIN THE SIGNPOSTS

Explain that **NOTICE & NOTE Signposts** are significant moments in the text that help readers understand and analyze works of fiction or nonfiction. Use the instruction on these pages to introduce students to asking **Big Questions** and to using the **Contrasts and Contradictions** and **Word Gaps** signposts. Then use the selection that follows to have students apply the Big Questions and signposts to a text.

For a full list of the fiction and nonfiction signposts, see page 72.

BIG QUESTIONS

Tell students that asking **Big Questions** such as *What does the author think I already know?* can help them realize what they need to clarify in order to understand the author's **main ideas, supporting details,** or **allusions.**

Read aloud the example passage and then say: *The author must think I already know the historical events to which she is alluding, or referring, when she says, "Slavery and sweatshops, the burning of crosses," and so on. But if I didn't know U.S. history well enough to understand her allusions, I would not know what she's referring to and so would not consider her point about bigotry to be adequately supported.*

Tell students that when they encounter a difficult or confusing passage of text, they should pause, mark it in their consumable text, and ask themselves one or more of these Big Questions:

What does the author think I already know?

What surprised me?

What challenged, changed, or confirmed what I thought I already knew?

READING MODEL

A QUILT OF A COUNTRY

For more information on these and other signposts to Notice & Note, visit the **Reading Studio**.

You are about to read the argument "A Quilt of a Country." In it, you will encounter notice and note signposts that will give you clues about the essay's claims and evidence. Here are three key signposts to look for as you read this essay and other informative writing.

When you see phrases like these, pause to see if it's a **Big Questions** signpost:

- "Everyone has heard of…"
- "It goes without saying that.."
- "There was a time when…"
- "Most people know that…"

Big Questions Even in a simple conversation between two friends, there are frequent references to information that both speakers already know. Even though they may be exchanging new information, two people communicate better if they understand each other in a variety of ways. Authors count on their readers to understand certain information, such as:

- historical and current events
- shared opinions or ideas
- common words, terms, or concepts

If you're reading a text and feel lost, stop and ask yourself: **What does the author think I already know?** Read this part of "Quilt of a Country" to see one student's annotation of Big Questions.

1 That's because it was built of bits and pieces that seem discordant, like the crazy quilts that have been one of its great folk-art forms, velvet and calico and checks and brocades. Out of many, one. That is the ideal.

2 The reality is often quite different, a great national striving consisting frequently of failure. Many of the oft-told stories of the most pluralistic nation on earth are stories not of tolerance, but of bigotry. Slavery and sweatshops, the burning of crosses and the ostracism of the other. Children learn in social-studies class and in the news of the lynching of blacks, the denial of rights to women, the murders of gay men.

What does the author assume her audience understands about America?	Quindlen has an understanding of America as a melting pot, a mosaic, or a "crazy quilt."
Which historical or social events does the author assume her audience is familiar with?	The author expects that her audience knows about the historical mistreatment of African Americans and other minorities, and the struggle of women for equality.

Contrasts and Contradictions If someone tells you they are afraid of heights and then wants to try skydiving, you are likely to wonder what they really think. How can two opposites act together to form a true statement?

When an author makes two conflicting—or even contradictory--statements, it can be jarring. You might think the statements would cancel each other out. Yet authors often include **Contrasts and Contradictions** in nonfiction text to bring the reader's attention to something important. Here a student marked a Contrast and Contradiction.

> 2 It is difficult to know how to convince them that this amounts to "crown thy good with brotherhood," that amid all the failures is something spectacularly successful. Perhaps they understand it at this moment, when enormous tragedy, as it so often does, demands a time of reflection on enormous blessings.

When you read and encounter phrases like this, pause to see if they are **Contrasts and Contradictions** signposts:

"It may seem that ____; however ..."

"For every ____, there is ____..."

"Forget what you believe in, I'm here to tell you..."

"You may think that ____ but it's really ..."

Anchor Question
When you notice this signpost, stop and ask: What is the contrast or contradiction, and why does it matter?

What contrasts are expressed here?	Quindlen describes failures and successes. She also mentions "enormous tragedy" that comes with reflecting on "enormous blessings."
How do these opposites work together?	The author's point is that while contradictions exist in America, it still functions as one country.

Word Gaps Authors sometimes use terms that readers will not know. These may include specialized or technical words, or familiar words that are used in an unfamiliar or unusual way. A reader encountering unfamiliar words can ask the following questions:

- Do I know this word from some place else?
- Does this seem like technical talk for experts on this topic?
- Can I find context clues to help me understand the word?

In this example, a student underlined examples of **Word Gaps:**

> 1 America is an improbable idea. A mongrel nation built of ever-changing disparate parts . . . it is held together by a notion, the notion that all men are created equal, though everyone knows that most men consider themselves better than someone.

When you notice one of the following while reading, pause to see if it's a **Word Gaps** signpost:

Descriptive language

Multiple meanings

References to events, art, or ideas

Rare words and technical talk

Anchor Question
When you notice this signpost, stop and ask: Can I find clues in the sentence to help me understand this word?

What strategy can help you understand the words *improbable* and *mongrel*?	I can see the word "probably" and the prefix "im-" in "improbable." Context clues like "ever-changing disparate parts" help me understand the word "mongrel."

WHEN STUDENTS STRUGGLE . . .

Use Strategies If students are struggling to apply the signposts, have them use the Syntax Surgery strategy to help them clarify meaning. Display the Word Gaps example passage and model thinking aloud as you draw lines and arrows to phrases that help define the words *improbable* and *mongrel*. Then circle *it* and explain that the pronoun refers to "America" as you draw a line with an arrow to the word *America*. Finally, circle the word *though* and explain that the word signals a contradiction as you write *contradiction* next to it. Underline the phrases "all men are created equal" and "most men consider themselves better," and draw lines and arrows connecting the phrases to the word *though*. After you model the Syntax Surgery strategy, have students mark up an additional passage on their own and then compare their markings with those of a partner.

CONTRASTS AND CONTRADICTIONS

Explain that authors may use words or phrases such as *however, although*, or *on the other hand* to signal **Contrasts and Contradictions.** Tell students that the presence of **antonyms,** or words with opposite meanings, in close proximity to one another should also alert them to the fact that a **contrast** or **contradiction** is being made. In the example passage, for instance, the author uses antonyms to draw readers' attention to the sad irony that only in times of tragedy might children understand how bonded and unified the American people truly are.

Tell students when they spot a Contrasts and Contradictions signpost, they should pause, mark it in their consumable text, and ask themselves the anchor question: *What is the contrast or contradiction, and why does it matter?*

WORD GAPS

Tell students that the **Word Gaps** signpost can help them **monitor** their comprehension of a text. To apply this signpost as they read, students should note unfamiliar words that are creating gaps in their understanding of key ideas. Monitoring their comprehension and then taking steps to look for **context clues** or to apply other strategies to determine the meaning of unfamiliar words can help them close gaps in understanding.

Read aloud the example passage. Then guide students to use the context clues in the student model to infer that *improbable* means "unlikely" and *mongrel* means "of mixed background."

Tell students when they spot a Word Gap, they should pause, mark it in their consumable text, and ask themselves the anchor question: *Can I find clues in the sentence to help me understand this word?*

APPLY THE SIGNPOSTS

Have students use the selection that follows as a model text to apply the signposts. As students encounter signposts, prompt them to stop, reread, and ask themselves the anchor questions that will help them understand the author's argument.

Tell students to continue to look for these and other signposts as they read the other selections in the unit.

Connect to the
ESSENTIAL QUESTION

"A Quilt of a Country" explores the argument that America's history as both a unified and fractured country gives the nation a unique ability to come together in times of adversity.

A QUILT OF A COUNTRY

Argument by **Anna Quindlen**

ESSENTIAL QUESTION:

How can we come together despite our differences?

QUICK START

People say there is nothing more American than apple pie, baseball, and hot dogs. What things mean America to you? Share and explain your ideas with the class.

ANALYZE ARGUMENTS

In "A Quilt of a Country," Anna Quindlen presents an **argument** about how America works as a country. An argument presents a claim, or position, on an issue and supports it with reasons and evidence. To evaluate the strength of Quindlen's argument, you must describe these elements:

- Identify the **claim**, or Quindlen's position, on the issue.
- Look for the valid, logical **reasons** Quindlen uses to support her claim.
- Evaluate whether the **evidence** Quindlen cites for each reason is credible, or believable, and relevant to the claim. Evidence may include facts, statistics, examples, anecdotes, or quotations.
- Look for **counterarguments**, which are statements that address opposing viewpoints. Does Quindlen anticipate opposing viewpoints and provide counterarguments to disprove them?
- Look for how Quindlen offers a **concession**, or admission that an opposing viewpoint may be correct. Also, notice how she provides a **rebuttal**, or a denial that clarifies and discredits opposing viewpoints.
- Identify the audience Quindlen is addressing.

GENRE ELEMENTS: ARGUMENT

- presents a claim or position on an issue
- includes reasons or evidence that support the claim
- acknowledges and addresses counterclaims through concessions and rebuttals

EVALUATE AUTHOR'S CLAIM

To support a **claim**, authors develop and refine their ideas throughout the text. Authors develop their claims with reasons and **evidence**. Analyzing how a writer like Anna Quindlen cites evidence and develops a claim can help you make your arguments stronger.

Use a chart to help you evaluate how Anna Quindlen develops her claim in "A Quilt of a Country." First, identify her claim. Then, list specific reasons or evidence from the text. Finally, evaluate if the reason or evidence supports the claim. Would you defend her claim, or challenge it?

Read this example from a student newspaper editorial.

CLAIM More time should be given to students to transition between classes.	
REASONS/EVIDENCE FROM TEXT	HOW THE REASONS/EVIDENCE SUPPORT THE CLAIM
"Students have told me how rushed they are to gather materials from their lockers for their next classes."	The evidence is a quotation from the school counselor, an objective observer who hears from many students. Her statement is logical support for the claim because it would be easier to gather materials if students had more time.

TEACH

QUICK START

Have students read the Quick Start question, and invite them to share their ideas about foods, games, traditions, or other things that mean America to them. Ask students to explain the reasons for their choices.

For **writing support** for students at varying proficiency levels, see the **Text X-Ray** on page 2D.

ANALYZE ARGUMENTS

Help students understand the elements of an argument by discussing examples of each of the most basic elements (claim, reasons, evidence). Point out that credible evidence relies on eyewitness accounts or authoritative sources such as encyclopedias, almanacs, or people or organizations with expertise related to the topic. Explain that counterarguments and rebuttals can strengthen an argument by demonstrating that the author has carefully considered the claim from different perspectives and, more obviously, by disproving the opposition's objections and counterclaims. Concessions show a willingness to compromise or to admit to the validity of some aspect of the alternative viewpoint. As such, they show the author of the argument to be reasonable.

EVALUATE AUTHOR'S CLAIM

Explain that students usually can find an author's position, or claim, stated at the beginning of an argument and then repeated at the end. Discuss the differences between reasons and evidence as related to supporting a claim. (A reason describes a general principle that supports a claim; evidence helps prove a claim.) Then briefly review various kinds of evidence (facts, statistics, examples, anecdotes, and quotations).

Suggest that students use these questions to help them evaluate reasons and evidence:

- Does the reason logically and directly support the claim?
- Can the facts or statistics be verified?
- Do the examples or anecdotes present common situations, or do they represent rare or unusual situations?
- Are quotations relevant and from respected sources?

ENGLISH LEARNER SUPPORT

Use Academic Language Display these Spanish cognates: *argument/argumento, position/posición, reason/razón, valid/válido, logical/lógico, evidence/evidencia, relevant/relevante, anecdote/anécdota, statistic/estadística, opposing/opuesto, concession/concesión.* Guide students in using the terms to complete the following sentences: *An ____ presents a claim, or position.* (argument) *____ support a claim.* (Reasons) *____ supports reasons.* (Evidence) *Evidence that is ____ clearly connects to a claim.* (relevant) *____ and ____ are types of evidence.* (Anecdotes, statistics) *Strong arguments address ____ viewpoints.* (opposing) *A ____ agrees with an opposing viewpoint.* (concession) **SUBSTANTIAL/MODERATE**

TEACH

CRITICAL VOCABULARY

Encourage students to read all the sentences before deciding which word best completes each one. Remind them to look for context clues that match the precise meaning of each word.

Answers:

1. *diversity*
2. *pluralistic*
3. *discordant*
4. *interwoven*

English Learner Support

Use Cognates Tell students that three of the Critical Vocabulary words have Spanish cognates: *diversity/diversidad, discordant/discordante, pluralistic/pluralista*. **ALL LEVELS**

LANGUAGE CONVENTIONS

Remind students that a noun names a person, place, thing, or idea. Like a noun, a noun clause can serve as a subject, direct object, object of a preposition, or predicate nominative. Encourage students to use noun clauses in their writing to convey precise meaning and to add variety and interest.

ANNOTATION MODEL

Students can review the Reading Model introduction if they have questions about any of the signposts. Suggest that they underline important phrases or circle key words that help them identify signposts. They may want to color-code their annotations by using a different color highlighter for each signpost. Point out that they may follow this suggestion or use their own system for marking up the selections in their write-in texts.

GET READY

CRITICAL VOCABULARY

discordant **pluralistic** **interwoven** **diversity**

To see how many Critical Vocabulary words you already know, use them to complete the sentences.

1. During the field trip we learned about the __________ of plants and animals in our area.
2. Many people describe the United States as a __________ society.
3. The shouting kindergartners made for a __________ classroom.
4. The teacher's main points were __________ with charts and graphics.

LANGUAGE CONVENTIONS

Noun Clauses A noun clause takes the place of a noun in a sentence. It is a subordinate clause that usually begins with *that, what, whatever, why, whether, how, who, whom, whoever, or whomever.* Like all subordinate clauses it contains a subject and a verb, but it cannot stand alone in a sentence. The noun clauses are boldfaced in these sentences:

> **What Anna Quindlen wrote** was very thoughtful.
>
> Throughout U.S. history, people have noted **that America is made up of many diverse cultures**.

Notice that these noun clauses could not stand alone as a sentence. They could, however, be replaced by the pronoun *it*.

ANNOTATION MODEL

NOTICE & NOTE

As you read, notice and note signposts, including Big Questions, Contrasts and Contradictions, and Word Gaps. Here is an example of how one reader responded to an early paragraph in "A Quilt of a Country."

This is a nation founded on a conundrum, what Mario Cuomo has characterized as "community added to individualism." These two are our defining ideals; they are also in constant conflict. Historians today bemoan the ascendancy of a kind of prideful apartheid in America, saying that the clinging to ethnicity, in background and custom, has undermined the concept of unity.

community and individualism → contrasts and contradictions

Author assumes I know what apartheid is.

BACKGROUND

Anna Quindlen *(b. 1953) was born in Philadelphia. She is a columnist and author who has been described as having a "common touch" because so many people relate to her writings about politics and gender-specific issues. In 1992, she became the third woman to win a Pulitzer Prize for commentary. "A Quilt of a Country" was published after the World Trade Center attacks of September 11, 2001. The piece was written at a time when many people were thinking about what it means to be an American.*

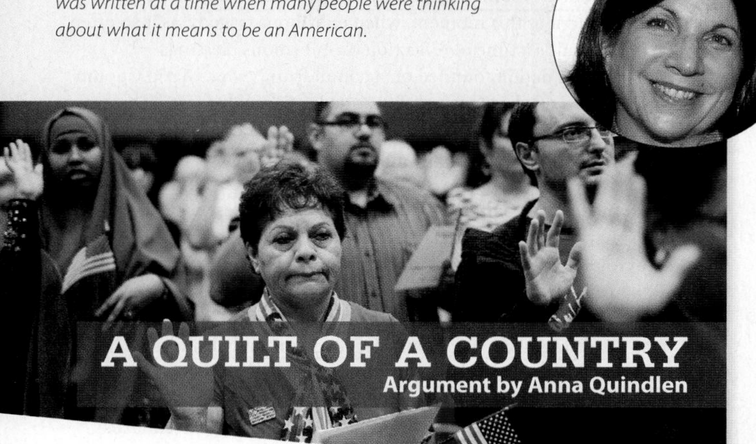

A QUILT OF A COUNTRY

Argument by Anna Quindlen

SETTING A PURPOSE

As you read, look for how the author uses an extended metaphor to convince readers of her claim, or argument. An extended metaphor is a comparison between two unlike things that is explored over and over in a variety of related ways.

1 America is an improbable idea. A mongrel[1] nation built of ever-changing disparate[2] parts, it is held together by a notion, the notion that all men are created equal, though everyone knows that most men consider themselves better than someone. "Of all the nations in the world, the United States was built in nobody's image," the historian Daniel Boorstin wrote. That's because it was built of bits and pieces that seem **discordant,** like the crazy quilts that have been one of its great folk-art forms, velvet and calico and checks and brocades. Out of many, one. That is the ideal.

2 The reality is often quite different, a great national striving consisting frequently of failure. Many of the oft-told stories of the most **pluralistic** nation on earth are stories not of tolerance,

[1] **mongrel:** something produced by mixing different breeds.
[2] **disparate:** distinct or not alike.

Notice & Note

You can use the side margins to notice and note signposts in the text.

discordant (dĭ-skôr´dnt) *adj.* conflicting or not being in accord

pluralistic (plŏŏr´ə-lĭs´tĭc) *adj.* consisting of many ethnic and cultural groups

BACKGROUND

Have students read the Background note. Tell students that the attacks of September 11, 2001, brought expressions of sympathy from around the world. The attacks sparked feelings of patriotism among many Americans, but some became distrustful of Arab immigrants and others of perceived Middle Eastern descent. Many Americans also questioned the nation's immigration and visitation policies.

SETTING A PURPOSE

Direct students to use the Setting a Purpose prompt to focus their reading.

For **reading support** for students at varying proficiency levels, see the **Text X-Ray** on page 2D.

CRITICAL VOCABULARY

discordant Quindlen suggests that the United States has been constructed out of elements that appear to be in conflict with one another.

ASK STUDENTS to describe how a "crazy quilt" might seem discordant. *(The fabrics and colors may clash.)*

pluralistic Quindlen notes that the United States is a combination of many ethnic and cultural groups.

ASK STUDENTS to provide an example of how American society is pluralistic. *(Americans' religious beliefs vary widely.)*

TO CHALLENGE STUDENTS . . .

Analyze Rhetoric Have students identify examples of the following rhetorical devices in "A Quilt of a Country." Then have students share and discuss the impact of each example with a partner.

- rhetorical question: a question that does not require a reply *(paragraph 3: "Do the Cambodians and Mexicans in California coexist less easily today than did the Irish and Italians of Massachusetts a century ago?"; paragraph 7: "Sound familiar?"; emphasizes similarities between immigrants of the past and present)*
- repetition: a technique in which a word or phrase is repeated *(paragraphs 1 and 8: "improbable", "mongrel nation"; emphasizes unique characteristics of the United States)*
- parallelism: the use of similar grammatical constructions to express related ideas *(paragraph 4: questions beginning with "What is the point"; paragraph 7: sentences beginning "There is" and "And there is"; highlights points about unity despite division and American character)* .

ENGLISH LEARNER SUPPORT

Listen and Derive Meaning Point out the phrase "crown thy good with brotherhood" in paragraph 2. Have students repeat it. Then play a recording of the song "America the Beautiful" and tell students to raise their hands when they hear the phrase "crown thy good with brotherhood." Discuss its meaning, noting that *thy* is an archaic form of *your* and *crown* is used as a verb meaning "honor." **MODERATE**

LANGUAGE CONVENTIONS

Remind students that a noun clause contains a subject and a verb and takes the place of a noun in a sentence. A noun clause may function as a direct object, which means that it receives the action of a verb or a verbal. ***(Answer:*** *The noun clauses help to show that the ideal expressed in "America the Beautiful" is sometimes hard to acknowledge because actions of Americans have often fallen short of true brotherhood.)*

ANALYZE ARGUMENTS

Remind students that examples such as **anecdotes** are used to support an author's position, or **claim**. Have students consider what point Quindlen is making by comparing anecdotes about past and present-day ethnic divisions in America. ***(Answer:*** *Ethnic groups have struggled to coexist throughout the country's history.)*

CRITICAL VOCABULARY

interwoven: Quindlen suggests that America could not be split into countries because it is like a piece of cloth with threads woven together.

ASK STUDENTS how ideals and beliefs might be interwoven. *(People's religious beliefs are sometimes closely blended with their political ideals.)*

NOTICE & NOTE

LANGUAGE CONVENTIONS

Annotate: Mark the two noun clauses beginning with *that* in the fifth sentence in paragraph 2.

Respond: How do these noun clauses reveal the contradictions in American society?

ANALYZE ARGUMENTS

Annotate: Mark examples of when ethnicity has divided Americans.

Summarize: What is Quindlen's claim in paragraph 3?

interwoven
(ĭn´tər-wō´vən) *adj.* blended or laced together

but of bigotry. Slavery and sweatshops, the burning of crosses and the ostracism[3] of the other. Children learn in social studies class and in the news of the lynching of blacks, the denial of rights to women, the murders of gay men. It is difficult to know how to convince them that this amounts to "crown thy good with brotherhood," that amid all the failures is something spectacularly successful. Perhaps they understand it at this moment, when enormous tragedy, as it so often does, demands a time of reflection on enormous blessings.

3 This is a nation founded on a conundrum,[4] what Mario Cuomo[5] has characterized as "community added to individualism." These two are our defining ideals; they are also in constant conflict. Historians today bemoan the ascendancy of a kind of prideful apartheid[6] in America, saying that the clinging to ethnicity, in background and custom, has undermined the concept of unity. These historians must have forgotten the past, or have gilded it. The New York of my children is no more Balkanized,[7] probably less so, than the Philadelphia of my father, in which Jewish boys would walk several blocks out of their way to avoid the Irish divide of Chester Avenue. (I was the product of a mixed marriage, across barely bridgeable lines: an Italian girl, an Irish boy. How quaint it seems now, how incendiary then.) The Brooklyn of Francie Nolan's famous tree, the Newark of which Portnoy complained, even the uninflected WASP suburbs of Cheever's characters:[8] they are ghettos, pure and simple. Do the Cambodians and the Mexicans in California coexist less easily today than did the Irish and Italians of Massachusetts a century ago? You know the answer.

4 What is the point of this splintered whole? What is the point of a nation in which Arab cabbies chauffeur Jewish passengers through the streets of New York—and in which Jewish cabbies chauffeur Arab passengers, too, and yet speak in theory of hatred, one for the other? What is the point of a nation in which one part seems to be always on the verge of fisticuffs with another, blacks and whites, gays and straights, left and right, Pole and Chinese and Puerto Rican and Slovenian? Other countries with such divisions have in fact divided into new nations with new names, but not this one, impossibly **interwoven** even in its hostilities.

[3] **ostracism:** exclusion or separation from society.
[4] **conundrum:** a riddle or a puzzle.
[5] **Mario Cuomo:** Governor of New York from 1983 until 1994.
[6] **apartheid:** a political system of racial or ethnic separation and discrimination.
[7] **Balkanized:** divided into small, uncooperative groups like countries in the Balkan Peninsula in the early 20th century.
[8] **Francie Nolan's . . . WASP suburbs of Cheever's characters:** characters in the novels *A Tree Grows in Brooklyn* and *Portnoy's Complaint;* John Cheever's characters were generally White Anglo-Saxon Protestants, or WASPs.

CLOSE READ SCREENCAST

Modeled Discussions In their eBook, have students view the Close Read Screencast, in which readers discuss and annotate the following key passages:

- statement of inherent conflicts within American ideals in paragraph 3, sentences 1–4
- statement of two basic American attitudes in paragraph 7, sentences 1–2

As a class, view and discuss the video. Then have students pair up to do an independent close read of paragraph 8. Students can record their answers on the Close Read Practice PDF.

Close Read Practice PDF

5 Once these disparate parts were held together by a common enemy, by the fault lines of world wars and the electrified fence of communism. With the end of the cold war[9] there was the creeping concern that without a focus for hatred and distrust, a sense of national identity would evaporate, that the left side of the hyphen—African-American, Mexican-American, Irish-American—would overwhelm the right. And slow-growing domestic traumas like economic unrest and increasing crime seemed more likely to emphasize division than community. Today the citizens of the United States have come together once more because of armed conflict and enemy attack. Terrorism has led to devastation—and unity.

6 Yet even in 1994, the overwhelming majority of those surveyed by the National Opinion Research Center agreed with this statement: "The U.S. is a unique country that stands for something special in the world." One of the things that it stands for is this vexing notion that a great nation can consist entirely of refugees from other nations, that people of different, even warring religions and cultures can live, if not side-by-side, then on either side of the country's Chester Avenues. Faced with this **diversity** there is little point in trying to isolate anything remotely resembling a national character, but there are two strains of behavior that, however tenuously, abet the concept of unity.

[9] **cold war:** diplomatic and economic hostility between the United States and the Soviet Union and their respective allies in the decades following World War II.

NOTICE & NOTE

CONTRASTS AND CONTRADICTIONS

Notice & Note: Mark the contrast that Quindlen describes in paragraph 5.

Infer: Why did the author include this contrast? How does it support her claim?

diversity
(dĭ-vûr´sĭ-tē) *n.*
having varied social and/or ethnic backgrounds.

APPLYING ACADEMIC VOCABULARY

❑ **enforce** ☑ **entity** ☑ **internal** ❑ **presume** ❑ **resolve**

Write and Discuss Have students turn to a partner to discuss the following questions. Guide students to include the academic vocabulary words *entity* and *internal* in their responses. Ask volunteers to share their responses with the class.

- Does Quindlen describe America as a single **entity** or more as a collection of disparate cultural groups?
- How are the **internal** forces that separate groups affected by external forces?

TEACH

CONTRASTS AND CONTRADICTIONS

Tell students to review paragraphs 1 and 2 to find the author's **claim** and restate it in their own words. *(Although the population of the United States is made up of many different people, the people are united by their shared belief in the ideal that all people are born as equals.)* Next discuss the similarities between past and present circumstances Quindlen points out in paragraph 5, sentences 1, 4, and 5. *(Americans unite when they have a common enemy.)* Ask students to describe the "creeping concern" Quindlen describes in sentences 2 and 3. *(Without an external focus for hatred and distrust, Americans might start focusing on their differences and lose their sense of unity as a nation.)* Then have students discuss their answers to the guided reading questions. *(**Answer:** The author contrasts the sense of division Americans might feel amidst domestic unrest with the sense of unity they might feel against outside enemies. This supports her claim that although domestic conflicts may at times divide Americans, history has shown that Americans come together in the face of adversity and are still united.)*

English Learner Support

Understand Language Structures Draw students' attention to the time-order signal words and phrases "Once," "With the end of the cold war," and "Today" in paragraph 5. Have students copy these words as headings of a three-column chart. Then have them list phrases the author uses to describe Americans during each period. *(Once: "held together by a common enemy"; With the end of the cold war: "sense of national identity would evaporate"; Today: "come together once more because of armed conflict and enemy attack")* Ask students which period the author contrasts with the other two periods. *(the period following the end of the cold war)* **MODERATE**

CRITICAL VOCABULARY

diversity Quindlen refers to the differences within the United States because it has grown as a country of refugees from opposing countries and religions.

ASK STUDENTS how diversity could both strengthen and weaken a nation. *(Different beliefs could spur innovation but also create conflict.)*

TEACH

EVALUATE AUTHOR'S CLAIM

Remind students of Quindlen's claim, which may be restated as follows: Although the population of the United States is made up of many different people, Americans are united by their shared belief in the ideal that all people are born as equals. Next ask a volunteer to **paraphrase** the quotation. *(While immigrants today may come from different countries than they once did, they still share the same values and work ethic as previous immigrants.)* Ask: Does the observation made by Castillo directly support Quindlen's claim? *(No, pointing out that immigrants today share the same values and work ethic as previous immigrants who are now, presumably, U.S. citizens does not directly support the idea that Americans are united by the belief that all people are born equal.)* Then ask: How might this observation indirectly support Quindlen's claim? *(It might indirectly support it by implying that immigrants today, as always, believe that they are equally capable of success through hard work and perseverance. In other words, the behavior Castillo points out suggests that today's immigrants must share the belief that all people are created equal and therefore equally capable of success.)*

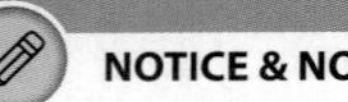

NOTICE & NOTE

7 There is that Calvinist undercurrent[10] in the American psyche that loves the difficult, the demanding, that sees mastering the impossible, whether it be prairie or subway, as a test of character, and so glories in the struggle of this fractured coalescing. And there is a grudging fairness among the citizens of the United States that eventually leads most to admit that, no matter what the English-only advocates try to suggest, the new immigrants are not so different from our own parents or grandparents. Leonel Castillo, former director of the Immigration and Naturalization Service and himself the grandson of Mexican immigrants, once told the writer Studs Terkel proudly, "The old neighborhood Ma-Pa stores are still around. They are not Italian or Jewish or Eastern European any more. Ma and Pa are now Korean, Vietnamese, Iraqi, Jordanian, Latin American. They live in the store. They work seven days a week. Their kids are doing well in school. They're making it. Sound familiar?"

Close Read

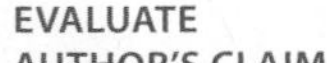

EVALUATE AUTHOR'S CLAIM

Annotate: Mark the quotation Quindlen uses to support her claim about diversity and immigration in America.

Connect: Do you think this quotation adequately supports her claim? Why or why not?

8 Tolerance is the word used most often when this kind of coexistence succeeds, but tolerance is a vanilla-pudding word, standing for little more than the allowance of letting others live unremarked and unmolested. Pride seems excessive, given the American willingness to endlessly complain about them, them being

[10] **Calvinist undercurrent:** the social influence of Calvinism, a Christian religion with a strict moral code and a belief in God as absolutely sovereign.

WHEN STUDENTS STRUGGLE . . .

Analyze Arguments Have individuals or partners use a chart to identify different types of evidence used to support Quindlen's claim.

Evidence	Type
"the United States was built in nobody's image"	*quotation*
The Brooklyn of Francie Nolan's famous tree	*example*

For additional support, go to the **Reading Studio** and assign the following **Level Up Tutorial: Analyzing Arguments.**

whoever is new, different, unknown, or currently under suspicion. But patriotism is partly taking pride in this unlikely ability to throw all of us together in a country that across its length and breadth is as different as a dozen countries, and still be able to call it by one name. When photographs of the faces of all those who died in the World Trade Center destruction are assembled in one place, it will be possible to trace in the skin color, the shape of the eyes and the noses, the texture of the hair, a map of the world. These are the representatives of a mongrel nation that somehow, at times like this, has one spirit. Like many improbable ideas, when it actually works, it's a wonder.

NOTICE & NOTE

WORD GAPS

Notice & Note: Mark three words that Quindlen uses to describe her ideas about diversity in America.

Synthesize: What is the difference between these three words? Which word does Quindlen think is most fitting right now?

CHECK YOUR UNDERSTANDING

Answer these questions before moving on to the **Analyze the Text** questions on the following page.

1 Which of these best describes the purpose of the selection?

A To suggest who is responsible for the 9/11 tragedy
B To show that America consists of different pieces that work together
C To show how immigrants can become legal citizens
D To prove that over time the nation's differences will disappear

2 What can the reader conclude from paragraph 2?

F American history has always favored immigrants.
G The American "story" has included bigotry and intolerance.
H Democracy is an important American system.
J The American republic has changed over time.

3 The author mentions her parents' marriage in order to —

A show how attitudes toward immigrants have evolved over time
B illustrate the difference between the Irish and Italian cultures
C demonstrate how the institution of marriage has changed
D suggest that Philadelphia was more diverse than New York

WORD GAPS

Ask students to share the words they marked. *(tolerance, pride, patriotism)* Then display the words as headings of a three-column chart. Ask students what Quindlen says about each word and write down what they say. *(tolerance: successful coexistence, vanilla-pudding word, allowing others to live unremarked and unmolested; pride: excessive, given that people endlessly complain about whoever is new, different, unknown, or under suspicion; patriotism: taking pride in the ability to throw all of us together in a country that is as different as a dozen countries and still be able to call it by one name)* Then ask: What do you notice about her definition of *patriotism*? *(Possible answers: It means taking pride in our ability to tolerate one another. It is a combination of tolerance and pride.)*

*(**Answer:** Quindlen believes that the word tolerance is too weak because it describes a minimal acceptance of coexistence. The word pride is too strong because it doesn't acknowledge the problems associated with accepting differences. Her choice of patriotism as more fitting supports her claim that Americans come together because they are committed to upholding the ideal upon which the United States was founded: all people are created equal.)*

CHECK YOUR UNDERSTANDING

Have students answer the questions independently.

Answers:

1. *B*
2. *G*
3. *A*

If students answer any questions incorrectly, have them reread the text to confirm their understanding. Then they may proceed to ANALYZE THE TEXT on page 12.

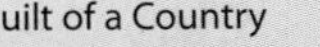

ENGLISH LEARNER SUPPORT

Oral Assessment Use the following questions to assess students' comprehension and speaking skills.

1. What is the author's purpose in this selection? *(The author wants to show that America consists of different pieces that work together.)*
2. Reread paragraph 2. What can you conclude? *(The American "story" includes bigotry and intolerance.)*
3. Why does the author mention her parents' marriage? *(The author mentions her parents' marriage to show how attitudes toward immigrants have evolved over time.)* **ALL LEVELS**

TEACH

ANALYZE THE TEXT

Possible answers:

1. **DOK 2:** *Quindlen's claim is that our country is a united, pluralistic society, no matter how diverse and discordant we may seem. Students who disagree with Quindlen's claim may cite her admission that American history includes acts of bigotry and examples of Americans failing to accept ethnic, racial, and cultural differences. Students who agree with Quindlen's claim may cite evidence of how Americans come together when necessary.*
2. **DOK 2:** *Quindlen is suggesting that all our different heritages and backgrounds are united like the pieces of a quilt, which holds together as one. This extended metaphor supports her claim by showing how many parts can come together to make one crazy but beautiful whole.*
3. **DOK 4:** *Quindlen revisits the terms "mongrel nation" and "tolerance," noting that in times of trouble the nation "has one spirit." This helps support her argument that our nation comes together when it is tested.*
4. **DOK 4:** *Quindlen refers to specific events in American history like slavery, sweatshops, and acts of hate to show that the country has fallen short of its pluralistic ideals. She quotes Mario Cuomo to point out the contradictions in our society. She also cites a public opinion survey to show that people feel that America is a special place.*
5. **DOK 4:** *Quindlen points out the contradiction that the United States is "held together" by the idea that "all men are created equal," yet "most men consider themselves better than someone." Quindlen also contrasts bigotry and tolerance in the United States. However, by conceding the fact that there are these contrasts and contradictions in the United States and nevertheless reasserting that Americans ultimately stand united as one, she discounts and thereby absorbs the criticisms of those who see the United States as more fractured than united.*

RESEARCH

Remind students to confirm the information they find by checking multiple websites and assessing the credibility of each one.

Extend Have pairs or small groups create a list of qualities that help immigrants to succeed. Remind them to provide evidence in the form of facts, statistics, examples, anecdotes, or quotations for each item on their list.

RESPOND

ANALYZE THE TEXT

Support your responses with evidence from the text. NOTEBOOK

1. **Summarize** What is Anna Quindlen's claim in "A Quilt of a Country"? Summarize her claim in your own words. Would you defend her claim, or challenge it?
2. **Interpret** In paragraph 1, what does Quindlen mean when she describes America as being "like the crazy quilts that have been one of its great folk-art forms"? Quindlen uses this image throughout her argument. How does this extended metaphor support her claim?
3. **Analyze** Reread Quindlen's conclusion. What specific words and phrases does she use to link the conclusion to her introduction? How do these words and phrases support her argument?
4. **Evaluate** Quindlen uses many different types of **evidence** throughout the argument to support her claim, such as examples, facts, statistics, and quotations. Identify at least three examples of evidence. Evaluate how she uses each type of evidence to support her claim.
5. **Notice & Note** Quindlen cites many instances of contrasts and contradictions to support her claim. Identify one contrast and one contradiction, and explain how each helps strengthen her argument.

RESEARCH TIP
The best way to find specific information about a topic is to limit your focus. You can start with a general topic, but as you learn more about it, narrow your scope and select a topic that gives you plenty of materials to consult.

RESEARCH

Every city or state in America has a mix of cultural groups. Research one of these groups. Record what you learn in the chart.

CULTURAL GROUP	
Percentage of overall population	
Settlement history	
Customs and traditions (for example, foods)	
Prominent members	

Extend Anna Quindlen discusses how throughout American history different cultural groups have been accepted as part of America's social fabric. What qualities of American society help immigrants to succeed?

CREATE AND DISCUSS

Compare Research with a Partner Meet with a partner to compare the results of your research into the cultural group you have chosen. Write a breakdown of the data each of you found and recorded in your charts. Then share your research.

- ❑ Introduce the cultural group you have chosen and where they are located.
- ❑ Discuss any similarities and differences between your cultural group and the one your partner chose.
- ❑ State a conclusion about these two cultural groups and how Quindlen's claim relates to your conclusion.

Discuss with a Small Group Have a discussion about the information partners have compiled in their research.

- ❑ As a group, review what each partnership has learned about their cultural groups. Make a connection with the claims and evidence Quindlen wrote about immigrants in "A Quilt of a Country."
- ❑ Have group members describe how their cultural group relates to Quindlen's claim. You may include personal connections or experiences as evidence. Remember to be understanding and respectful of all cultural groups.
- ❑ Review the conclusions that the group draws. Work together to suggest ways that cultural groups become another panel of our quilt of a country. Listen closely and respectfully to all ideas. Request assistance from peers or seek clarification as necessary.

Go to the **Speaking and Listening Studio** for help with having a group discussion.

RESPOND TO THE ESSENTIAL QUESTION

? How can we come together despite our differences?

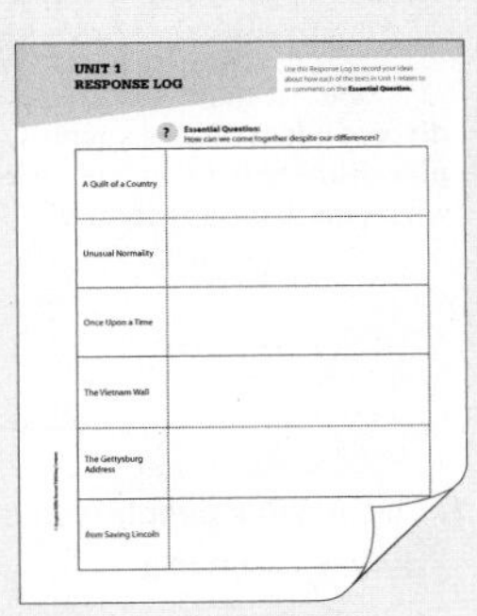

Gather Information Review your annotations and notes on "A Quilt of a Country." Then, add relevant information to your Response Log. As you determine which information to include, think about:

- ways to describe our country as a mixed group of people
- how different cultural groups come together as a nation
- how we as a nation can come together in hard times

At the end of the unit, use your notes to help you write a personal essay.

ACADEMIC VOCABULARY

As you write and discuss what you learned from the argument, be sure to use the Academic Vocabulary words. Check off each of the words that you use.

- ❑ **enforce**
- ❑ **entity**
- ❑ **internal**
- ❑ **presume**
- ❑ **resolve**

TEACH

CREATE AND DISCUSS

Compare Research with a Partner Suggest that partners use a Venn diagram to show similarities and differences between the cultural groups they have researched.

For **listening support** for students at varying proficiency levels, see the **Text X-Ray** on page 2C.

Discuss with a Small Group Remind students that when they do not understand a comment made by another group member, they should ask questions to clarify meaning. The process of asking and answering questions can help everyone understand the issue more clearly and can lead to new ideas.

For **speaking support** for students at varying proficiency levels, see the **Text X-Ray** on page 2D.

RESPOND TO THE ESSENTIAL QUESTION

Allow time for students to add details from "A Quilt of a Country" to their Unit 1 Response Logs.

WHEN STUDENTS STRUGGLE . . .

Reteaching: Analyzing Arguments If students have difficulty identifying the elements of Quindlen's argument, have them reread the essay to answer the following questions:

- What does the author want me to believe or do? *(claim)*
- According to her, why should I believe or do this? *(reasons)*
- What examples, facts, statistics, and quotations does she offer to convince me her reasons are sound? *(evidence)*
- What other viewpoints does she bring up? *(opposing positions)*
- What reasons and evidence does she offer to prove those other viewpoints are flawed, weak, or wrong? *(counterarguments)*

For additional support, go to the **Reading Studio** and assign the following **Level Up Tutorials: Analyzing Arguments** and **Elements of an Argument.**

CRITICAL VOCABULARY

Answers:

1. *an unskilled orchestra; because a discordant orchestra is producing notes that don't sound pleasant together*
2. *at an international conference; because pluralistic is an adjective that describes a gathering made up of many groups*
3. *a musical motif heard several times throughout a movie; because a motif that is repeated throughout a work helps to weave it together*
4. *an all-star team from twenty states; because it would include people from different locations and different social and ethnic backgrounds*

VOCABULARY STRATEGY: Patterns of Word Changes

Answers:

1. *discord*
2. *pluralistic*
3. *discordant*

English Learner Support

Employ Spelling Patterns and Rules Write the base words *discord* and *plural* on the board and point out that each one ends in a consonant. Guide students to see that these words do not change spelling when suffixes such as *-ism, -ize, -ant,* and *-istic* are added. Then discuss the spelling rule that base words ending in silent *e* usually drop the final *e* when a suffix is added. Use these words from the selection as examples: *strive/striving, diverse/diversity, devastate/devastation*. (An exception to the rule is *bridgeable*, with a soft *g* sound.)

Also point out the spelling pattern in which verbs ending in *-ize* replace that ending with *-ism* to create the noun form. Examples include *pluralize/pluralism, ostracize/ostracism, individualize/individualism,* and *terrorize/terrorism*. (An exception is *emphasize/emphasis*.) **MODERATE**

RESPOND

WORD BANK
discordant
pluralistic
interwoven
diversity

CRITICAL VOCABULARY

Practice and Apply Circle the letter of the best answer. Explain your response.

1. Which of the following would be described as **discordant**?
   a. an unskilled orchestra **b.** birds flying in formation
2. Where would a **pluralistic** gathering most likely to be found?
   a. at a family picnic **b.** at an international conference
3. Which of the following would be **interwoven**?
   a. a layer of frosting on a birthday cake **b.** a musical motif heard several times throughout a movie
4. Which of the following is an example of **diversity**?
   a. an all-star team from 20 states **b.** a set of twins

VOCABULARY STRATEGY: Patterns of Word Changes

Go to the **Vocabulary Studio** for more on words with multiple meanings.

Words can have different meanings or be different parts of speech. Many words have several meanings listed in the dictionary. The word *equal* can mean "having the same privileges or rights." It also means "being the same or identical." Knowing different meanings can help you be an effective reader.

Words also change depending on the part of speech. The words *discordant* and *pluralistic* change spelling and meaning when the part of speech changes. Knowing how a word functions in a sentence will help you gain a complete understanding of the word's meaning.

Practice and Apply Complete the sentences with the correct word.

NOUN	VERB	ADJECTIVE
discord—lack of agreement **pluralism**—a condition of society where many groups coexist	**pluralize**—to engage in pluralism	**discordant**—conflicting **pluralistic**—consisting of many ethnic and cultural groups

1. The fact that people were shouting indicated the level of ____________ during the meeting.
2. Some governmental entities claim to be ____________ because people of different ethnic backgrounds work together.
3. Because the groups discussing the plan had ____________ ideas, they made little progress.

ENGLISH LEARNER SUPPORT

Pronounce Vocabulary Correctly Students whose primary language is Spanish, Vietnamese, Hmong, Cantonese, Haitian Creole, or Korean may have difficulty perceiving and pronouncing the short *i* sound, as in *sit*. Help them learn to pronounce this sound by instructing them to listen to you pronounce the vocabulary words correctly and then to say them back to you with the appropriately short *i* sound. Each of the vocabulary words in this lesson contains at least one short *i* sound: *discordant, pluralistic, interwoven,* and *diversity*. Correct pronunciations and repeat as needed. **ALL LEVELS**

LANGUAGE CONVENTIONS: Noun Clauses

Writers use noun clauses to present complicated ideas that can replace a single word or phrase. This allows for a complete expression of ideas and a greater complexity of related concepts.

- Subject

  What Anna Quindlen wrote is still relevant today.

- Predicate Nominative

  "Pride seems excessive, given the American willingness to endlessly complain about them, them being whoever is new, different, unknown, or currently under suspicion."

- Object of a Preposition

  "This is a nation founded on a conundrum, what Mario Cuomo has characterized as 'community added to individualism.'"

- Direct Object

  Many people don't appreciate that America is made up of many diverse cultures

Practice and Apply Write your own sentences with noun phrases. You may write about the cultural group you researched earlier. When you have finished, share your sentences with a partner and compare your use of noun phrases and revise if necessary. Remember that noun phrases can start with the following words: *that, what, whatever, why, whether, how, who, whom, whoever,* or *whomever*.

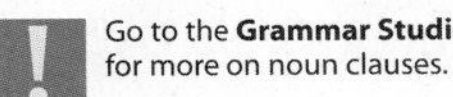

Go to the **Grammar Studio** for more on noun clauses.

LANGUAGE CONVENTIONS: Noun Clauses

Remind students that there is no single correct way to use a noun clause and that the varied use of noun clauses is a way for students to experiment with their writing and refine it to make it lively and interesting. Tell students this can be true in both fiction and nonfiction and may be a way for them to construct a unique and interesting style of writing.

Practice and Apply Have students check their partner's sentences to make sure each noun clause contains a subject and a verb and takes the place of a noun. *(Students' sentences will vary.)*

ENGLISH LEARNER SUPPORT

Language Conventions Use the following supports with students at varying proficiency levels:

- Have students work with partners to find other sentences in "A Quilt of a Country" that use noun clauses and copy them into their notebooks. **SUBSTANTIAL**
- Have students work with partners to write their original sentences with noun clauses. Then have them meet with another pair to compare their sentences and identify the word that starts the noun clause in each sentence. **MODERATE**
- Ask students to write sentences that use noun clauses in each of the following ways—as the subject, direct object, predicate nominative, and object of a preposition. Then have them exchange sentences with partners and identify the function of noun clauses in their partner's sentences. **LIGHT**

MENTOR TEXT

UNUSUAL NORMALITY

Personal Essay by Ishmael Beah

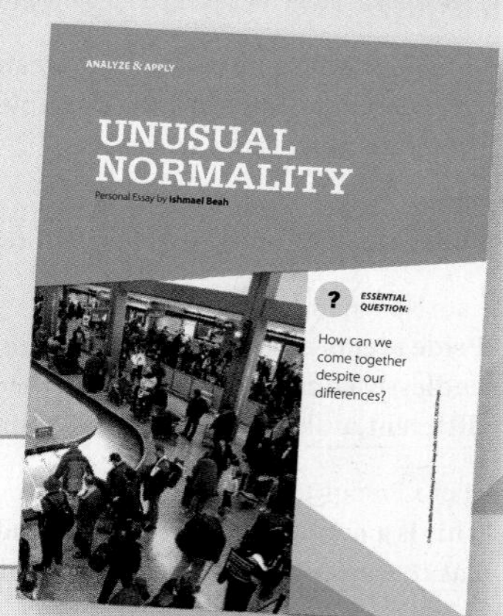

This essay serves as a **mentor text**, a model for students to follow when they come to the Unit 1 Writing Task: Writing a Personal Essay.

GENRE ELEMENTS
PERSONAL ESSAY

Explain to students that a **personal essay** explores the writer's life experiences in ways that are similar to a **memoir.** Unlike a memoir, which typically covers a person's entire life, a personal essay is much shorter and more tightly focused. A personal essay includes the author's feelings and reactions, so understanding the author's purpose and message is key to understanding the essay. In this lesson, students will analyze voice and tone to help them explore the author's experiences as a child soldier trying to adapt to American teen culture in the personal essay "Unusual Normality."

LEARNING OBJECTIVES

- Analyze an author's purpose and message.
- Analyze the voice and tone of a personal essay.
- Conduct research on children forced to serve as soldiers.
- Write a summarizing report about research on child soldiers.
- Debate solutions to the problem of child soldiers.
- Examine denotative and connotative meanings to learn thoughts and feelings associated with words.
- Identify and practice use of active and passive voices.
- **Language** Write, and with a partner review, sentences in the passive and the active voice.

TEXT COMPLEXITY

Quantitative Measures	**Unusual Normality** Lexile: 820L
Qualitative Measures	**Ideas Presented** Mostly explicit, but moves to some implied meanings.
	Structures Used Chronological text structure; events are generally sequenced in time order.
	Language Used Mostly Tier II words; explicit, familiar language; some ironic language.
	Knowledge Required Mostly situations and experiences that can be envisioned; some may be emotionally challenging for students.

Online 

RESOURCES

- Unit 1 Response Log
-  Selection Audio
-  Reading Studio: Notice & Note
-  Level Up Tutorials: Author's Purpose; Author's Style
-  Writing Studio: Introduction: Informative Texts
-  Speaking and Listening Studio: Rhetoric and Delivery
-  Vocabulary Studio: Denotative and Connotative Meanings
- Grammar Studio: Module 6: Lesson 4: Active and Passive Voice
-  "Unusual Normality" Selection Test

SUMMARIES

English

After serving as a child soldier in Sierra Leone, author Ishmael Beah was relocated to New York City and entered high school there. In his personal essay, Beah describes the challenges he faces to fit in with his classmates and the adjustments he makes to adapt to American teen culture. With great insight and understated wit, Beah describes his new life in and out of school, including a memorable weekend playing paintball. His experiences as a child soldier serve him well in paintball, but also keep him distant from his friends as he realizes he will never share their naïve innocence about the world.

Spanish

Después de servir como niño soldado en Sierra Leona, el autor Ishmael Beah fue trasladado a la ciudad de Nueva York y ahí entró en la escuela secundaria. En su ensayo personal, Beah describe los retos que enfrenta para encajar con sus compañeros de clase y los ajustes que hace para adaptarse a la cultura adolescente de Estados Unidos. Con gran perspicacia y sencillo ingenio, Beah describe su nueva vida dentro y fuera de la escuela, incluyendo un memorable fin de semana jugando "paintball". Sus experiencias como niño soldado le ayudan en el "paintball", pero también lo mantienen distante de sus amigos mientras se da cuenta de que él nunca compartirá su ingenua inocencia acerca del mundo.

SMALL-GROUP OPTIONS

Have students work in small groups to read and discuss the selection.

Four Corners

- Write on the board: *No matter where people grow up, they have similar childhood experiences*.
- Display possible responses to the statement, one each in four different classroom corners: *Strongly Agree, Agree, Disagree, Strongly Disagree*.
- Read aloud the statement. Have students choose a response by moving to one of the corners.
- In each corner, have students form a group to discuss their reasons for choosing that response.
- Then, invite volunteers from each group to summarize the group's ideas.

Think-Write-Pair-Share

- Before students read "Unusual Normality," ask: If you had to go to school in another country where you did not know anyone, what are some things you would do to adjust to your new way of life?
- Give students time to reflect and jot down responses individually.
- Have students pair up with partners to discuss their responses and elaborate on one of them. For example, if students respond, *We would try to make new friends*, encourage them to explain how they would do that.
- Call on volunteers to share those responses.
- As students read and discuss the essay, encourage them to make connections to Beah's experiences and add to, or modify, their responses.

Text X-Ray: English Learner Support

for "Unusual Normality"

Use the Text X-Ray and the supports and scaffolds in the Teacher's Edition to help guide students at different proficiency levels through the selection.

INTRODUCE THE SELECTION

DISCUSS EXPRESSIONS

In this lesson, students will need to be able to discuss the ideas of fitting in to adjust to a new culture, and also blending into physical surroundings to avoid being seen. Read the summary with students and offer these explanations:

- Beah wants to *fit in* with his classmates. He wants to belong with them and be like them.
- When people play paintball, they may hide, or *blend into*, their surroundings so no one can see them.

Encourage volunteers to share how a new student might try to fit in with other students. (*Possibilities include dressing, speaking, and acting like them, playing games.*) Mention that Beah has not played paintball before. Ask: What are some questions he might have about the game? Why do you think some players might hide, or try to blend into, their surroundings?

CULTURAL REFERENCES

The following words or phrases may be unfamiliar to students:

- *Manhattan* (paragraph 5), *East Village* (32), *the Bronx* (34), *Bed-Stuy* (34): boroughs or neighborhoods of New York City
- *a great omen* (paragraph 6): a sign of good times ahead
- *weirded out* (paragraph 18): feeling bewildered or disquieted by something that seems very odd
- *ill at ease* (paragraph 28): feeling uncomfortable or uneasy
- *pumped up* (paragraph 57): very excited

LISTENING

Listen for Important Events

Explain that you are going to read aloud paragraphs 1–5. Students can practice listening to ensure their understanding of important events.

Have students listen as you read aloud paragraphs 1–5 of the essay. Then, use the following supports with students at varying proficiency levels:

- Help students understand what happens to the author's baggage. As students listen, use body language to help convey meaning, such as letting your shoulders sag when the bag doesn't come. Give students time to sketch what they visualize. **SUBSTANTIAL**
- Confirm students' understanding by asking them to provide an oral summary of events. Ask students to identify a detail that shows why the author included these events. **MODERATE**
- Have students listen for what happens to the author's baggage. Ask students to tell or show how Beah reacts. **LIGHT**

SPEAKING

Discuss Voice and Tone

Students will analyze the author's voice and tone. Teach and model how to identify and describe specific examples orally.

Use the following supports with students at varying proficiency levels:

- Display, and expressively read aloud, a paragraph. Help students mark details with emoticons of appropriate moods, such as *excited*, *amused*, *sad*, and so on. Name the moods and have students repeat them. **SUBSTANTIAL**
- Guide students to discuss the author's voice by using this sentence frame: *I can almost "hear" the author's voice when he says, ______. I think he feels ______ because he uses the word(s) ______.* **MODERATE**
- Provide these frames: *To tell about this event, the author chooses such words and phrases as ______. This language creates a ______ tone. So, I think that the author feels ______ about ______.* **LIGHT**

READING

Identify Author's Purpose

Tell students that as they read, they will determine the author's purpose, or reason for writing. Explain that thinking about how details are organized, and making inferences, or thoughtful guesses, about them can help.

Direct students' attention to paragraph 7. Then, use the following supports with students at varying proficiency levels:

- Help students locate and understand time-order phrases, such as *At age eleven* and *after three years*. Model how to list age numbers and key events. Explain why the author tells about events in order: He wants readers to know what his childhood was like before coming to the United States. **SUBSTANTIAL**
- Tell students they can use what the author says directly to figure out his purpose for writing. Ask: As you read each sentence, what do you find out? How are the boy's experiences like or unlike those of most children you know? So, what might the author want people to understand? **MODERATE**
- Have students identify the order of events. Then ask: What do the events show about the author's childhood? Ask students to express the author's message orally: *Most children ______, but I ______.* **LIGHT**

WRITING

Write a Summarizing Report

Set students up for success with the writing assignment by coaching them through the instructions on page 29 of their Student Edition.

Use the following supports with students at varying proficiency levels:

- Have students copy these lines: *Suppose you were forced to fight a war. Around the world, this is the reality for thousands of children. Many are under the age of 15.* Using the sample notes from the chart on page 28, model how to use details to create a summary. **SUBSTANTIAL**
- Provide sentence frames for writing the summaries. For example: *In the country of __________, child soldiers are ___________. U.S. resettlement efforts consist of __________.* **MODERATE**
- Have partners peer-edit each other's writing and ask about anything they did not understand. Invite volunteers to explain revisions they made. **LIGHT**

Connect to the ESSENTIAL QUESTION

In this personal essay, Ishmael Beah recalls the keen sense of difference he felt from his high school classmates in the United States. While they had a naïve innocence about violence that filtered into their speech and games, Beah had already survived war in Sierra Leone as a child soldier. The essay recounts his efforts to bridge the vast differences in their experiences and to connect with them as friends.

MENTOR TEXT

At the end of the unit, students will be asked to write a personal essay. "Unusual Normality" provides a model for how a writer can develop a personal experience into an insightful and cohesive account.

UNUSUAL NORMALITY

Personal Essay by **Ishmael Beah**

ESSENTIAL QUESTION:

How can we come together despite our differences?

LEARNING MINDSET

Setting Goals Explain to students that setting goals is an essential life skill that can help them succeed in school, future careers, and their personal lives. As they read this personal essay, have them think about the goals the author set for himself and how he tried to reach them. Then encourage students to set goals for themselves, perhaps starting with one goal for school (*get a better grade on the next test*), one goal for their future career (*explore requirements for a specific job*), and one goal for their personal lives (*eat healthier*).

QUICK START

The title of this personal essay, "Unusual Normality," is an **oxymoron**. The words *unusual* and *normal* have opposite meanings. What do you think the author meant by this title? Discuss your ideas with a small group. Can you think of any other common oxymorons, such as *open secret?*

ANALYZE PURPOSE AND MESSAGE

The **author's purpose** is the reason the writer has for writing a text. Authors may write to express thoughts or feelings, to persuade, to inform or explain, or to entertain. To determine the author's purpose in a personal essay, readers should:

- analyze the text structure. The author of this essay uses a chronological text structure to describe his experiences at one point in his life.
- analyze language, including voice and tone
- make inferences based on the author's style and message

The **message** is the central idea of the work, or what the author is trying to communicate to the audience. To determine central ideas and message in a personal essay, readers should:

- analyze the author's interpretations of events
- make inferences based on events and people the author describes

The **audience** is the people for whom the author is writing. To determine audience of a personal essay, readers should:

- analyze evidence in the text, including voice and tone
- make inferences based on details in the text and the author's message

GENRE ELEMENTS: PERSONAL ESSAY

- similar to memoirs but shorter and more focused
- explores the writer's experiences
- includes the author's feelings and reactions at the time
- written after the events in the story

ANALYZE VOICE AND TONE

Voice and tone are elements of an author's style.

Voice is a writer's unique use of language that allows a reader to "hear" a human personality in the writer's work. Elements of style that contribute to a writer's voice include sentence structure (or syntax), word choice (or diction), and tone.

Tone is the writer's attitude toward his or her subject. A writer communicates tone through choice of words and details.

LITERARY ELEMENT	EXAMPLE FROM "UNUSUAL NORMALITY"
Voice is created through sentence structure, word choice, and tone.	**And I thought to myself, *What a great omen. Fresh new start to everything.***
Tone is the writer's attitude toward his or her subject, conveyed through word choice and details.	**I learned a new American term for what they *did* find it. They were "weirded out" by the strange sense of humor that I had about this.**

As you read, note the voice of the author and the tone of the essay, and use them as clues to the essay's purpose, message, and audience.

TEACH

QUICK START

Give students a moment to jot down their thoughts about the title, "Unusual Normality," before they discuss their ideas with a small group. To help students think of other common oxymorons, share and discuss examples such as *jumbo shrimp, act naturally,* and *clearly confused*. Students might also enjoy creating their own oxymorons.

ANALYZE AUTHOR'S PURPOSE AND MESSAGE

Coach students to approach analyzing the author's purpose and message in a strategic way. One approach they might take as they read the selection is to keep in mind three questions:

- Why is the author writing about this?
- What big ideas is he trying to tell me?
- Who is the author writing this for?

These questions (or ones students generate on their own) can focus their reading as they annotate and take notes using the model on the next page as a guide.

ANALYZE VOICE AND TONE

Tell students that **voice,** the unique use of language, and **tone,** the writer's attitude, are both parts of a writer's style. Explain that by analyzing a writer's voice and tone, they'll be able to explain why his or her style is distinct and the techniques that make it so. Finally, remind students that by analyzing an author's style, particularly voice and tone, they'll also see how they can create their own distinct style and improve their own writing.

TEACH

CRITICAL VOCABULARY

Remind students to look for context clues in the questions that can help them write their answers. Encourage students to share their sentences with a partner and exchange ideas about each word's meaning.

Possible Answers:

1. *Rehabilitation for a broken leg would likely include physical therapy to retrain the leg muscles.*
2. *Grandfathers are the counterpart of grandmothers.*
3. *A stereotype might be a good thing if it helps people to better understand themselves and others.*
4. *A naïve belief is one that is too simple and probably not true, such as "it's easy for people to change their behavior."*

■ English Learner Support

Use Cognates Tell students that two of the Critical Vocabulary words have Spanish cognates: *rehabilitation/ rehabilitación* and *stereotype/estereotipo*. **ALL LEVELS**

LANGUAGE CONVENTIONS

Review the information about active and passive voice with students. Point out that writers often use both, although the active voice is often preferred. Explain that another advantage of writing in the active voice—particularly for students—is that it can help them to better understand what they're writing about, especially when responding to a question or prompt. Encourage students to note examples of the author's use of active and passive voice, and how each influences the reader's understanding.

ANNOTATION MODEL

Remind students of the annotation ideas in Analyze Voice and Tone on page 17, which includes noting examples of sentence structure, word choice, tone, and details. Point out that they may follow this suggestion or use their own system for marking up the selection in their write-in text. They may want to underline important ideas, circle key words and phrases, and color-code their annotations using highlighters. Their notes in the margin may include questions about ideas that are unclear or topics they want to learn more about.

GET READY

CRITICAL VOCABULARY

rehabilitation **counterparts** **stereotype** **naïve**

To see how many Critical Vocabulary words you already know, write a brief answer to these questions.

1. What might **rehabilitation** for a broken leg involve?
2. What might be the **counterparts** of grandmothers?
3. Can a **stereotype** ever be a good thing?
4. What is a **naïve** belief?

LANGUAGE CONVENTIONS

Active and Passive Voice In this lesson, you will learn about the use of active and passive voice in writing. In active voice, the subject performing the action comes before the verb. The direct object *follows* the verb.

The boys played a game. The subject *boys* is the focus of the action.

In passive voice, the order is reversed.

A game was played by the boys. The focus is on the *game*.

ANNOTATION MODEL

NOTICE & NOTE

As you read, note the author's purpose and his voice and tone in the essay. You can also mark up evidence that supports your own ideas. In the model, you can see one reader's notes about "Unusual Normality."

I came to New York City in 1998. I was seventeen.

I entered the United States with just a passport in my hand, because somehow the baggage that I'd checked when I boarded the flight from Ivory Coast (which was tattered in ways unimaginable) didn't make it.

I stood there at the luggage rack watching all these huge bags go by, and mine didn't come. This bag held all my possessions at this point: two pairs of pants and two shirts — one long-sleeved and one short. So I just started laughing, and I didn't even bother going to the lost-baggage section to claim it.

author's purpose- express thoughts and feelings

author's voice comes from his unusual diction

this detail of author's reaction creates tone

BACKGROUND

Ishmael Beah *(b. 1980) began to write about his experiences as a way of dealing with being forced to be a child soldier in Sierra Leone in Africa. After his family was killed when he was just 12 years old, Beah was threatened with death if he didn't fight with a rebel group that was trying to overthrow the country. An American working for UNICEF brought him to the United States. Today, he is a lawyer, author, and a UN Goodwill Ambassador helping others like him.*

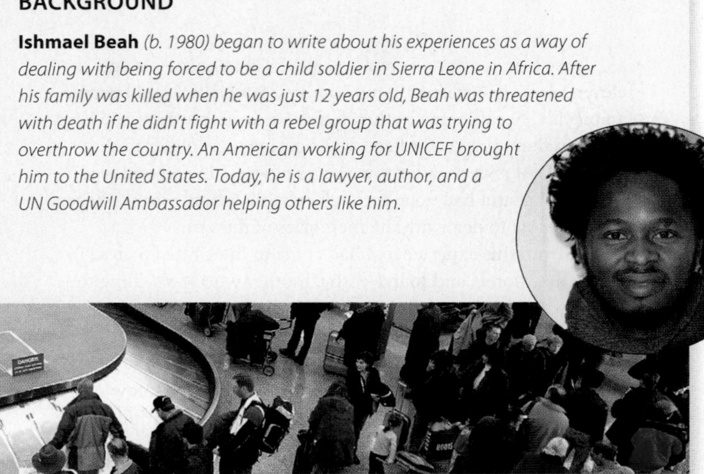

UNUSUAL NORMALITY

Personal Essay by Ishmael Beah

SETTING A PURPOSE

As you read, pay attention to the author's reflections on the person he once was, including how he tried to fit in with people in a new place.

1 I came to New York City in 1998. I was seventeen.

2 I entered the United States with just a passport in my hand, because somehow the baggage that I'd checked when I boarded the flight from Ivory Coast (which was tattered in ways unimaginable) didn't make it.

3 I stood there at the luggage rack watching all these huge bags go by, and mine didn't come. This bag held all my possessions at this point: two pairs of pants and two shirts—one long-sleeved and one short. So I just started laughing, and I didn't even bother going to the lost-baggage section to claim it.

4 I just walked right out to meet my new adoptive mother, who was standing there with a beaming smile, waiting for me. And I explained to her what had happened, and we laughed some more.

5 We left and went into Manhattan, and that evening we went to Kmart. (After we had Chinese food and a fortune cookie that said, "You're about to have new clothes.")

6 And I thought to myself, *What a great omen. Fresh new start to everything.*

Notice & Note

You can use the side margins to notice and note signposts in the text.

ANALYZE VOICE AND TONE

Annotate: Underline the author's thoughts, shown in italics. Circle two details in paragraphs 5–6 that caused these thoughts.

Analyze: How does the author's syntax and word choice reveal his attitude and outlook?

BACKGROUND

After students read the Background note, explain that UNICEF, the United Nations Children's Fund, is an organization that meets the emergency needs of children in 190 countries. Beah's adoptive mother, Laura Simms, was facilitating a storytelling project for UNICEF called Children's Voices when she first met him in 1996.

SETTING A PURPOSE

Direct students to use the Setting a Purpose prompt to focus their reading.

ANALYZE VOICE AND TONE

Remind students that **syntax** refers to the author's sentence structure and that **diction,** or word choice, refers to the words and phrase used. Both syntax and word choice shape the author's voice and tone as key elements of the author's style. (***Answer:*** *The author uses positive words to show his upbeat, resilient attitude. He uses sentence fragments to express excitement.)*

For **listening and speaking support** for students at varying proficiency levels, see the **Text X-Ray** on pages 16C–16D.

ENGLISH LEARNER SUPPORT

Practice Phonology Students whose primary language is Spanish, Cantonese, Korean, and Khmer may struggle with the pronunciation of the *v* sound at the beginning of the word *voice*. To provide some practice, direct students to paragraphs 1–6. Read aloud, and then have students repeat after you, these examples of words that contain the *v* sound: *seventeen, Ivory, even, adoptive, evening, everything*. Then share, and have students repeat, selection words that begin with *v*: *visa, village, very, violence*. Repeat words that seem to cause students trouble and encourage students as you see progress. **ALL LEVELS**

TEACH

For **reading support** for students at varying proficiency levels, see the **Text X-Ray** on page 16D.

MEMORY MOMENT

Remind students that in **nonfiction,** this signpost alerts readers to important events in a character's past. Prompt students to think about the question in a different way: If readers weren't given information about his early childhood, what questions might they have as they continue to read? (***Answer:*** *It explains why he is determined to have a normal life and suggests he will find the adjustment challenging.*)

LANGUAGE CONVENTIONS

Review with students that when the passive voice is used, the subject of the sentence receives the action expressed by the verb. In the active voice, the subject of the sentence performs the action. As students analyze paragraph 11 to identify the passive voice, coach them to focus on a sentence in which the author receives the action, rather than does the action. Encourage students to consider the difference in the effect of the author doing the action and the author receiving the action. Then have them answer the question. (***Answer***: *It emphasizes that even in his new life, Beah cannot control every event or its possible outcome.*)

English Learner Support

Language Conventions Tell students that as you read aloud paragraph 11, you will pause occasionally to ask them a question. Tell students to respond with thumbs up for yes, or thumbs down for no. Then, read aloud the paragraph pausing after each sentence to ask: Did the author perform the action? **SUBSTANTIAL/MODERATE**

CRITICAL VOCABULARY

rehabilitation: Most students will likely associate the word *rehabilitation* with helping a person recover from a physical injury. Encourage them to think of how the author uses this word to explain his recovery from war.

ASK STUDENTS to discuss how being a child soldier might affect someone and why rehabilitation would be needed. *(Because war can have traumatic effects on a person's physical, emotional, and mental health, rehabilitation would likely include treating the whole person, not just his or her physical injuries.)*

NOTICE & NOTE

rehabilitation
(rē´hə-bĭl´ĭ-tā´shən) *n.* the act of being restored to good health or condition

7 I was coming from a country called Sierra Leone. At age eleven, a war had started in my country. At twelve, I had become an orphan, because my mother, father, and two brothers had been killed in that war. At thirteen I was fighting as a soldier in that same war. At sixteen, after three years of war, I'd been removed from all that and had gone through **rehabilitation**, where I began learning how to deal with the memories of the war.

8 So from this experience, I had come to the United States. To have a new home, and to live with a mother who was willing to take me into her life when most people at the time were afraid of somebody like me.

9 It was a chance at living again, because all I had come to know, since I was eleven, was how to survive. I didn't know how to live. All I knew, really, up until this point in my life, was struggle. This was what I had come to expect from life, and I didn't trust in happiness or any kind of normality at all.

MEMORY MOMENT

Notice & Note: What words indicate that the author is finished relating information about his earlier childhood? Underline these words.

Infer: Why might this information about his earlier childhood be important to the rest of the essay?

LANGUAGE CONVENTIONS

Annotate: Mark a sentence in paragraph 11 that uses passive voice.

Respond: What is the effect of this use of passive voice?

10 So here I was in New York, with my new mother. We needed to step into that normality.

11 But we had a lot of things to deal with, and one of the most pressing ones was that I needed to get into school. You see, the visa that I had been given was a prospective-student visa. This meant that when I arrived in the United States, I had three months to get into a school. If I didn't, I would be returned to my war-torn country, Sierra Leone.

12 Now, when I arrived, it was in the summer, so all the schools were closed. But my mother got on the phone and called every school principal she could think of in Manhattan, and tried to get them to grant me an interview.

13 When I went to some of the interviews, I was immediately denied because of the following conversation:

14 "Do you have a report card to show that you had been in school?"

15 I would say, "No, but I know I have been in school."

16 And then my mother would interject to explain the context.

17 I would sit there thinking to myself, *What do these school principals think? Do they really think that when there's a war in your village or when your town is attacked, and people are gunned down in front of you, and you're running for your life, you're thinking to yourself, "You know, I must take my report card and put it in the back of my pocket."*

18 At some of these interviews, I was able to say some of these things, thinking that it would be funny. But the school principals didn't find it funny. I learned a new American term for what they *did* find it. They were "weirded out" by the strange sense of humor that I had about this.

19 So I decided that I was going to write an entrance essay about this, and the essay was simply titled "Why I Do Not Have a Report Card."

20 With this essay, along with exams that were given to me, I was accepted to the United Nations International School and placed in the eleventh grade.

21 Thus began my two years of high school and making other teenagers confused about who I was. You see, I didn't fit into any box. I didn't have the same worries about what shoes or clothes I wore. And so my teenage **counterparts** always wanted to find out why I was like that. Why I didn't worry about my essays or exams or things.

22 And of course I couldn't tell them, because I felt that they were not ready to hear the truth. What was I going to say?

23 During a break from class, "Hey, you know, I was a child soldier at thirteen. Let's go back to class now."

24 So I was silent, mostly. I didn't say much. I would just smile. And this made them more curious.

25 They would say to me, "You're such a weird kid."

26 And I would respond by saying, "No, no, no. I'm not weird. *Weird* has a negative connotation. I prefer the word *unusual.* It has a certain sophistication and gravitas[1] to it that suits my character."

27 And of course when I was finished saying this, they would look at me and say, "Why don't you speak like a normal person?"

28 The reason I spoke like this was because of my British-African English that I'd learned, which was the only formal English that I knew. So whenever I spoke, people felt ill at ease, particularly my fellow teenagers. They thought, *What is wrong with this fellow?*

29 Some of them, though, didn't find it as strange. They thought maybe my English was like this because I was from some royal African family.

30 So throughout my high-school years, I tried to make my English less formal, so that my friends would not feel disturbed by it. (However, I did not dispute the fact that I was from some royal African family or that I was a prince. Because, you see, sometimes some **stereotypes** have their benefits, and I certainly took advantage of that.)

31 But I needed to be silent about my background, because I also felt like I was being watched. When I got into the school, some of the other parents were not very happy that somebody with my background was in school with their children. And I realized that the way I conducted myself would determine whether they would ever let another child who had been through war into such a school.

[1] **gravitas** (grăv′ĭ-täs): seriousness, being solemn and respected.

counterparts
(koun′tər-pärts′) *n.* people or things that have the same characteristics and function as another

ANALYZE VOICE AND TONE

Annotate: Mark the author's word choices and syntax that create the tone of paragraphs 21–27.

Draw Conclusions: What attitude does the author have toward his teenaged counterparts?

stereotype
(stĕr′ē-ə-tīp′) *n.* one that is thought of as conforming to a set type or image

ANALYZE VOICE AND TONE

Review key elements that can help determine an author's **voice**—the unique use of language that lets a reader "hear" the human personality of the author—and the author's **tone**—the writer's attitude toward what he or she is writing about. Point out Beah's choice of words such as *unusual*, *sophistication*, and *gravitas* in paragraph 26 and how they contribute to his voice and tone. (***Answer:*** *He is sarcastic but playful toward them, joking about the differences between them. His word choice seems to reflect someone who is more worldly than a typical high schooler.)*

ENGLISH LEARNER SUPPORT

Use Content-Based Vocabulary Have students read paragraph 26 aloud. Then, allow time for them to look up the meaning of unfamiliar words, such as *unusual*, *sophistication*, and *gravitas*. Next, ask questions to give students the opportunity to demonstrate understanding. For example:

- What kind of animal would be an unusual pet? Why?
- Which has more sophistication, a video game or a game of catch? Why?
- At a public event to remember people who died in war, why might the speeches have gravitas?

LIGHT

WHEN STUDENTS STRUGGLE . . .

Analyze Author's Purpose Have partners review paragraphs 21–27. Provide them with a list of reasons for writing. (*express thoughts and feelings, persuade, inform, explain, entertain*) When students encounter clues to the author's reason for writing the essay, ask them to mark the words and suggest a reason from the list.

For additional support, go to the **Reading Studio** and assign the following **Level Up Tutorial: Author's Purpose.**

CRITICAL VOCABULARY

counterparts: Although the author considers the other students his counterparts, he also feels somewhat apart from them.

ASK STUDENTS why the author used *counterparts* rather than another word such as *classmates* or *friends*. (*The use of counterparts suggests his classmates are like him, but not in every way.)*

stereotype: The author wrote that he "took advantage" of a stereotype to put his friends at ease.

ASK STUDENTS to discuss the pros and cons of having others believe you fit a stereotype. (*People might treat you better, but they might also treat you worse.)*

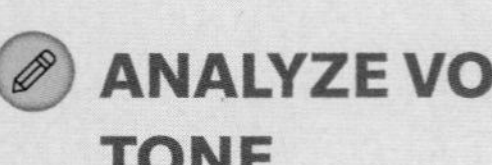

ANALYZE VOICE AND TONE

Mention that the author repeats some words. (*glorify, violence, enjoyed listening*) Point out that he also uses certain words and phrases that emphasize contrast (*pretend, lived in it, never really lived, actually experienced*) Have students consider how this affects their understanding of the author's voice and tone. Then have them answer the question. (**Answer:** *In Sierra Leone, Beah experienced real-life violence and actual war. The "tough kids" glorified violence and pretended to be tough, but they had never experienced violence for real.)*

ENGLISH LEARNER SUPPORT

Practice Newly Acquired Vocabulary Read paragraphs 39–40 aloud. Then use the following supports with students at varying proficiency levels:

- Write *glorify* on the board and draw lines to separate the syllables. Pronounce the word, with students repeating it after you. Point out the *gl-* consonant cluster. Provide definitions for *glorify*: "to praise" and "to make something seem better than it is." Point out the context clue (violence) to recognize that Beah uses the second definition. **SUBSTANTIAL**
- Explain that the verb *glorify* comes from the noun *glory*, meaning "praise." Display the frame: _____ *glorify violence*. (*Beah's classmates / The people who forced him to fight*). **MODERATE**
- Have students look up the word *glorify* in a dictionary. Ask them to use two different forms to write sentences and share their work with a partner. **LIGHT**

NOTICE & NOTE

32 But even with all of these attitudes, and with my silence, I started making friends. To them it was sufficient that I was just some kid who lived in the East Village, who was from an African country.

33 And these kids were tough (they told me). Because they lived in a tough city, New York. And therefore *they* were tough.

34 They had been to the Bronx. They had been to Bed-Stuy. They had taken the train there. They had gotten into fights and won.

35 So they would say things to me like, "If you want to survive the streets of New York City, we need to teach you a few things."

36 And I'd be like, "Okay, sure. I'm open to learning."

37 And they would tell me things about how to be tough and stuff, and I would say, "Well, thank you very much. I truly appreciate this advice that you're giving me."

38 They were like, "No worries, our African brother. Anytime, anytime."

39 Truth was, I'd been to some of these places that they spoke about, these neighborhoods, and I knew that the people who lived there didn't glorify violence the way they did. They didn't have time to pretend, because they lived in it, just like I had.

40 I noticed that these kids had a sort of *idea* of violence that they'd never really *lived*. They glorified it in a way, because they'd never actually experienced it at all.

41 When I walked with them, I observed that I paid more attention to the people who walked past us—how the person walked, which way they were coming from. I didn't take the same route twice, because I didn't want to develop a predictable path. These were all habits that were formed from my experiences, but I noticed that my

ANALYZE VOICE AND TONE

Annotate: In paragraphs 39–42, mark the words Beah uses to show the differences between himself and the "tough kids" of New York.

Compare: How does the violence of the "tough kids" differ from the violence the author has known?

TO CHALLENGE STUDENTS . . .

Explore Beah's Decision Give students an opportunity to express their ideas about Beah's decision to keep his childhood experiences a secret. To introduce the activity, ask: What are some reasons Beah listens to his classmates and does not share his own experiences? Tell students that they will explore what might happen if Beah speaks openly. Have small groups brainstorm and record possible reactions from his classmates. Then have all students reconvene to share some of their examples. Ask: Do you think it will bridge differences between Beah and his classmates if he speaks openly? Why or why not?

new friends didn't do that at all. So I knew they were just saying these things to seem tough to me.

42 Now, I did enjoy listening to my new friends that I had made. I enjoyed listening to them tremendously, because I wished, when I listened to them, that the only violence I knew was the violence that I imagined.

43 And listening to them allowed me to experience childhood in a way that I hadn't known was possible. It let me be a normal kid.

44 So I listened to them, and we hung out all the time, and through that I participated in what was left of my childhood.

45 I got to be a child again with them; the only worries that we had were when we went rollerblading without any protective gear. We took our brakes off, and sometimes we would avoid hitting an old lady by falling into a trash can on the street, and we laughed about it.

46 These things meant a lot to me.

47 After about a year of being friends with these boys, one of them decided to invite a group of us, about ten of us, to upstate New York. His family had property up there, and he said we were going there for the weekend to play a game called paintball.

48 I said, "Well, what is that?"

49 And he said, "Oh, man, you've never played paintball? You're gonna love it. It's a great game. The fellows and I, we always play it. And don't worry, we'll teach it to you, and we'll protect you.

50 "You use these balls of paint, and you shoot people," and he explained the basics of the game to me.

51 I said, "Okay, that sounds interesting."

52 And I thought, *If these guys who only pretend about violence can play it, it must not be that difficult a game*.

53 But of course I didn't say this. I just thought these things. So I went with them upstate to a humongous property that had trees and creeks that ran into a bigger river—this beautiful open place.

54 But as soon as we arrived, I began to memorize the terrain immediately, and this was from habit. I knew how many paces it took to get to the house, how many paces it took to the first tree, to the first bush, to the shed. I learned the spaces between the trees.

55 Overnight, while everybody was sleeping, I tried to replay some of these things in my head—to memorize the terrain.

56 And this was all out of habit, because where I came from, in my previous life, this kind of skill set could determine whether you lived or died.

57 In the morning, at breakfast, they were pumped up.

58 Everyone was saying, "Yeah, the game is gonna be awesome today."

59 And so after we finished breakfast, I was introduced to the game of paintball. They showed me the weapon, how you can shoot it. And I allowed them to teach me to shoot things.

AGAIN AND AGAIN

Notice & Note: Mark a thought about his friends that the author revisits, this time in a paintball game.

Predict: Based on this thought, make a prediction about what will happen during the paintball game.

AGAIN AND AGAIN

Explain that in a **personal essay,** an author may repeat an important idea. Remind students that earlier the author emphasized that for his classmates, violence is pretend. Then read aloud the dialogue in paragraphs 49–50. Ask students to identify phrases that show his classmates can only pretend about violence. (Possibilities include *You're gonna love it, a great game, we'll protect you,* and *shoot people.*) Then have students answer the question. (**Answer:** *The author's experiences of fighting in real battles will help him win the paintball game.*)

ENGLISH LEARNER SUPPORT

Use Cognates To help students better visualize the description in paragraphs 53–54 of where the paintball game is taking place, point out that several of the words the author uses have Spanish cognates: *property/propiedad* and *terrain/terreno*. Have students demonstrate their understanding of the words *property* and *terrain* by asking them the following questions:

- How does the author describe the property he went to with his friends?
- What does he mean when he says he memorized the terrain?

ALL LEVELS

ANALYZE PURPOSE AND MESSAGE

Remind students that one way to determine what the author wants to communicate to the audience is to make inferences based on an event (the paintball game) and the people the author describes (his classmates and himself). Ask: How do the comments and actions of Beah's classmates compare with his thoughts and actions? Based on what you already know, why do Beah and his classmates behave so differently? Then have students answer the questions. (***Answer:*** *He fights this way because of his real-life experiences as a child soldier. His message is that he understands war and violence in ways that his friends cannot.*)

English Learner Support

Make Inferences Provide students with a chart to help them make inferences about events before, during, and after the paintball game.

Event: ____	
I read that Beah ____.	I read that his classmates ____.
I also know that he ____.	I also know that they ____.
So, I think the author wants to communicate that ____.	

ALL LEVELS

NOTICE & NOTE

ANALYZE PURPOSE AND MESSAGE

Annotate: Mark words and phrases in paragraph 67–71 that reveal Beah's actions during paintball.

Interpret: Why does Beah fight the way he does during the paintball game? How does this help reveal the author's message?

60 They were very macho about it.

61 They said to me, "This is how you shoot, you aim like this."

62 I said, "Okay." I tried it a few times. I deliberately missed.

63 Then they showed me the camouflage and the combat gear and everything.

64 And then everybody was ready to go, and they were amped up, and all like, "Yeah, we're gonna go out! We're gonna DO THIS!!"

65 They decided we were going to play one-on-one. And then, after, we would play team games.

66 So they started painting their faces, getting into this idea of war that they knew.

67 I declined putting the face paint on, and I wanted to give them a hint about my past, but then I thought, *You know what? I'm going to have fun with this.*

68 So we went off into the bush, and when one of them shouted, "Yeah, let the war begin! I'm going to bring pain to all of you! I'm going to show you how it's done!" I thought to myself, *First rule of warfare, you never belittle your opponent.*

69 But I didn't say this. I went into the bushes. I already knew where to go, because I had memorized the layout of the place.

70 And so I would hide. I would wait for them. I would climb a tree here. I would hide under certain shrubs. And they would come rolling around, jumping, doing all kinds of things, things they'd probably seen in movies about how people act in war.

71 I would just wait for them. And after they were done exhausting themselves, I would come up behind them, and I would shoot the paintball at them.

72 This went on all day. And when we came back that night, during dinner, they talked about it.

73 You know: *How come you're so good? You're sure you've never played paintball before?*

74 I said, "No, I have never played paintball before. I'm just a quick learner, and you guys explained the game to me, and you are really great teachers. This is why I'm able to play so well."

75 But they said, "That can't be all."

76 Some of the kids' parents were there, and the kids said to them, "'This guy, he comes up on you. You can't even hear him coming at all."

77 And I said, "Well, you know, I grew up in a village. And I used to be a hunter when I was a boy, so I know how to blend into the forest, like a chameleon[2]. I know how to adapt to my environment."

[2] **chameleon** (kə-mēl′yən) *n.* a tropical lizard that can change color

IMPROVE READING FLUENCY

Targeted Passage Have students work in small groups to read paragraphs 60–68. First, return to the previous page and use paragraph 52 to model how to read a personal essay as students follow along. Point out that as you read, you're trying to reflect the author's tone, or attitude toward his friends, by using appropriate phrasing, pacing, and emphasis. Then, have students in their groups take turns reading each paragraph. Encourage students to support each other in pronouncing words so that they're comprehensible.

Go to the **Reading Studio** for additional support in developing fluency.

78 And they looked at me and said, "You're a very strange fellow, man. But you're *badass* at paintball."

79 I said, "Well, thank you. Thank you very, very much."

80 So this went on. We never got to play the group game. We played as individuals all throughout the weekend, because they wanted to beat me, and so they started to team up with each other. I would see them doing this, and then I would come up with a kind of watered-down version of another guerrilla tactic[3] just to play with them.

81 For example, sometimes I would walk backwards and then stand where my footsteps "began" and hide. They would follow my footprints, and then I would come up behind them.

82 Anyway, at some point I decided that I was going to sit out the game, just so that they could enjoy it. And I saw a sense of relief on all of their faces.

[3] **guerrilla tactic** (gə-rĭl′ə tăk′tĭk): warfare techniques practiced by small bands of native fighters harassing and surprising larger armies.

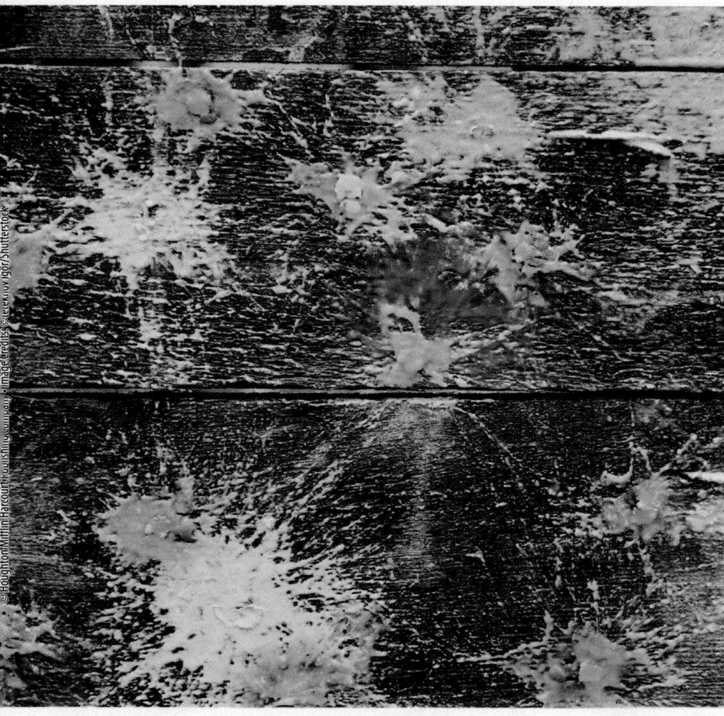

ENGLISH LEARNER SUPPORT

Expand Reading Skills Read paragraphs 80–82 aloud. Then use the following supports with students at varying proficiency levels:

- Write *guerrilla tactic* on the board and draw lines to separate the syllables. Pronounce the phrase several times, with students repeating it after you. Reinforce that a guerrilla is a fighter who belongs to a small group and that a tactic is an action fighters use to help win a war. Ask: Why does the author use a guerrilla tactic? (*to win the game*) Who do you think taught him about guerrilla tactics? (*other soldiers*) When? (*during the war in Sierra Leone*) **SUBSTANTIAL/MODERATE**
- Have students restate the footnote in their own words. Then ask: Do you think Beah's classmates use guerrilla tactics? (*no*) Why or why not? (*because they have never been fighters or soldiers in a war*) **LIGHT**
- Have students locate an example of a guerrilla tactic. Point out that Beah uses the adjective *watered-down* to describe this tactic. Have students look up the meaning of *watered-down*. Ask: How does this definition and the rest of the sentence help you understand why Beah uses a guerrilla tactic during a friendly game? (*He just wants to be competitive and have fun, not to hurt anyone.*) **ALL LEVELS**

APPLYING ACADEMIC VOCABULARY

☑ **enforce** ☐ **entity** ☐ **internal** ☑ **presume** ☐ **resolve**

Write and Discuss Have students turn to a partner to discuss the following questions. Guide students to include the academic vocabulary words *enforce* and *presume* in their responses. Ask volunteers to share their responses with the class.

- What rules, if any, did the paintball players **enforce** during their games? Why?
- What did the other paintball players **presume** about Beah as a paintball player?

ANALYZE VOICE AND TONE

Remind students that the author communicates his attitude through his voice, or his unique use of language. Ask: What does Beah find interesting to observe? (*how his friends perceive war*) How do Beah's classmates describe the weekend of paintball? (*awesome*) How does Beah compare to his friends? (*Beah's words make him seem older, wiser, or more serious than his friends.*) Then have students interpret the author's attitude toward his classmates. (***Answer:*** *He thinks they are childish, innocent, or less mature; he thinks paintball is only a game, but seems to wish his friends had acknowledged, or talked about, his part in it.*)

English Learner Support

Understand Voice Support students in recognizing the significance of Beah's word choices:

- Draw students' attention to the word *observe* in paragraph 88 and explain that to observe is to pay close attention to something or someone. Explain that a scientist gathers information through observation; he or she carefully observes details. **SUBSTANTIAL**
- Mention that the word *perceive* is similar in meaning to *understand*, but it is more formal. Explain that the way you perceive something is the way you think about it, or the ideas you have about it. Ask: Based on their description of the weekend, how do Beah's classmates perceive war? (*as a game*) **MODERATE**
- Have students locate the word *awesome* in paragraph 89. Ask: What does this word show about the way Beah's classmates use language? (*They are more informal than he is.*) What effect do Beah's word choices create? (*They make him seem serious or formal.*) **LIGHT**

NOTICE & NOTE

ANALYZE VOICE AND TONE

Annotate: Mark the words in paragraphs 88–90 that show the author's attitude towards his classmates and the paintball game.

Interpret: Describe the author's attitude toward his classmates and the paintball game in your own words.

83 They were like, *Oh, well, FINALLY!*

84 When I returned, I told my mother about this game. And my mother, being a mother, was immediately worried.

85 She said, "Oh, did that bring up something for you?"

86 And I said, "No, it didn't, absolutely."

87 Because I know the difference between pretend war and real war.

88 But it was interesting for me to observe how my friends perceived what war is.

89 The next day at school, these friends of mine talked about the awesome weekend of paintball we'd had. But they never said how I'd won all the games. And I said nothing at all.

90 They never invited me back to play paintball with them. And I didn't ask to be invited back.

91 I so wanted to talk to them about the war while we were playing the game. I wanted to explain certain things, but I felt that if they knew about my background, they would no longer allow me to be a child. They would see me as an adult, and I was worried that they would fear me.

92 My silence allowed me to experience things, to participate in my childhood, to do things I hadn't been able to do as a child.

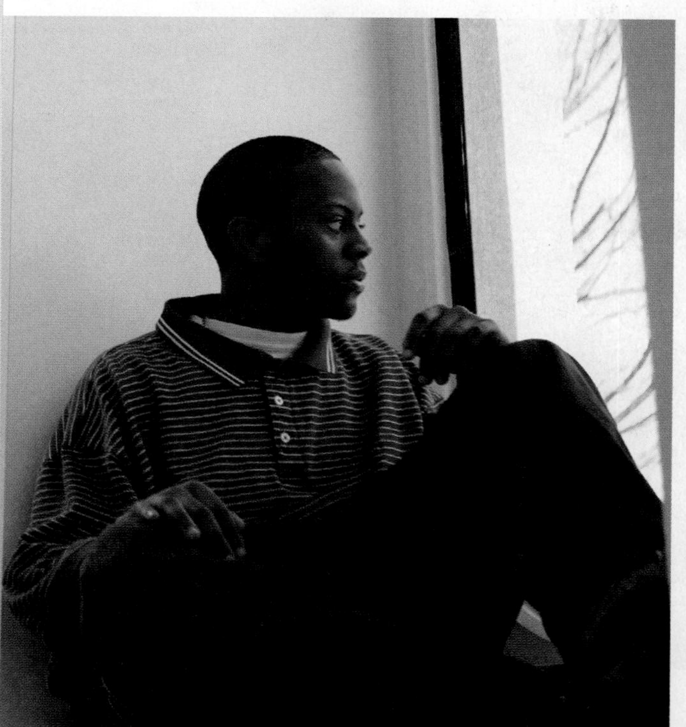

WHEN STUDENTS STRUGGLE . . .

Analyze Author's Style Have students work with partners to complete a chart similar to the one below to analyze paragraphs 91–93.

Element of Style	Definition	How It Is Expressed	Examples
Voice	Author's use of language	Through sentence structure, word choice, tone	I so wanted to talk to them about the war. . . . I wanted to explain. . . .
Tone	Author's attitude toward the subject	Through word choice and details	I was worried they would fear me. . . .

For additional support, go to the **Reading Studio** and assign the following **Level Up Tutorial: Author's Style**

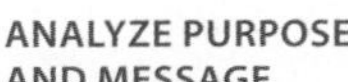

NOTICE & NOTE

93 It was only years later that they learned why I had won the game.

94 But I wish I had been able to tell them early on, because I wanted them to understand how lucky they were to have a mother, a father, grandparents, siblings.[4] People who annoyed them by caring about them so much and calling them all the time to make sure they were okay.

95 I wanted to tell them that they were so lucky to have this **naïve** innocence about the world. I wanted them to understand that it was extremely lucky for them to only play *pretend* war and never have to do the real thing. And that their **naïve** innocence about the world was something for which I no longer had the capacity.

[4] **siblings** (sĭb´lĭngs): *n.* brothers or sisters, individuals sharing one or more parents

ANALYZE PURPOSE AND MESSAGE

Annotate: Mark the sentences in paragraphs 92–95 that reveal the author's message.

Interpret: What is the author's message, and what does it reveal about the author's purpose for writing and who he sees as his audience?

naïve
(nī-ēv´) *adj.* lacking worldly experience or understanding

CHECK YOUR UNDERSTANDING

Answer these questions before moving on to the **Analyze the Text** questions on the following page.

1 Which of these best describes the purpose of the selection?

A To explain how the author became a great paintball player

B To show how people who think they are tough are really weak

C To explain how the past made the author appreciate his new life

D To describe how it was impossible for the author to escape his past

2 At the conclusion of the essay —

F the author's friends invite him to play paintball again

G the author tells his friends about his past

H the author finally gets into a good school

J the author explains what he wanted to tell his friends

3 Which of the following is not true about the author, Ishmael Beah?

A The author fought as a soldier in a war when he was a child.

B The author did not know how to play paintball before this story.

C The author is from a royal African family.

D The author took school very seriously.

ANALYZE PURPOSE AND MESSAGE

Have students explain **author's purpose** and **message** in their own words. Ask students to explain the strategies they've used to determine these, emphasizing that both depend on analyzing text details and **making inferences,** or logical guesses, based on those details. (***Answer:*** *The author's message is that his American friends are lucky to still have their innocence about the world, something that he lost and cannot explain to them. His purpose for writing is to inform readers about his past and how it affected his adjustment to American teen culture and to express his thoughts and feelings about living in two different worlds.)*

CHECK YOUR UNDERSTANDING

Have students answer the questions independently.

Answers:

1. *C*
2. *J*
3. *C*

If they answer any questions incorrectly, have them reread the text to confirm their understanding. Then they may proceed to ANALYZE THE TEXT on page 28.

CRITICAL VOCABULARY

naïve: The author describes his friends as having a naïve, or simple, unsuspecting view of the world.

ASK STUDENTS why the author feels he cannot ever again have naïve innocence. *(His war experiences prevent him from viewing the world this way.)*

ENGLISH LEARNER SUPPORT

Oral Assessment To assess students' comprehension and speaking skills, ask:

1. What is the author's purpose? Why did he write this essay? (*to show how his experience as a child soldier in Sierra Leone affected his new life as a high school student in New York*)
2. What does the author tell readers in the last paragraph? *(what he wanted to tell his friends, but couldn't)*
3. Which of the following statements is not true? (*The author is from a royal family. Some classmates thought he was royal because of the formal way he spoke.*) **SUBSTANTIAL/MODERATE**

APPLY

ANALYZE THE TEXT

Possible answers:

1. **DOK 2:** *Beah's voice may be described as observant and sophisticated, reflecting someone who is a careful observer of the world (which is reflected in his word choice and syntax in paragraph 41) and also sarcastic at times ("I'm going to have fun with this," paragraph 67). His tone may be described as detached ("I needed to be silent," paragraph 31) and wishful; he feels set apart from his peers based on his past experiences and wishes he had their innocence (paragraph 95).*
2. **DOK 3:** *Beah speaks differently than his classmates; is very guarded and cautious; and had first-hand experience with violence while most classmates did not. They have an innocence about the world that Beah has lost.*
3. **DOK 4:** *In this sentence, Beah notes that his behavior would determine how people viewed other children who had been child soldiers. He might have written this essay to help a wider audience understand and be more empathetic to former child soldiers like him.*
4. **DOK 4:** *A personal essay enabled Beah to use word choices, syntax, and other elements in ways that best reflected his personality. For example, his word choice shows humor and irony (paragraph 74). It also allowed him to share his true thoughts and feelings about his experiences as a child soldier and a high school student.*
5. **DOK 4:** *Beah is always aware of his surroundings, including the people and the terrain, based on skills learned as a child soldier (paragraphs 54–55 and 68–71). These skills and what he learned from his war experiences enabled him to win at paintball.*

RESEARCH

Remind students to use reliable sites to confirm information they find in their sources. Encourage them to review a website's "about" page, which often provides key information about the organizations and allows them to get a better sense of its reliability.

Connect Because many organizations work to rehabilitate and resettle child soldiers, guide students in avoiding researching the same organizations. For example, as a class, compile a list of organizations doing this work and then assign or have students choose different ones to research. Also encourage students to research reliable newspaper and magazine websites for details about the resettlement of individual soldiers in the United States.

RESPOND

ANALYZE THE TEXT

Support your responses with evidence from the text. NOTEBOOK

1. **Interpret** Ishmael Beah's use of language—his word choice and syntax—establishes an individual voice and tone. Describe the essay's voice and tone, citing examples from the selection.
2. **Cite Evidence** What are some of the ways that the author differs from his classmates? Cite evidence from the text in your answer.
3. **Analyze** Review the last sentence of paragraph 31. Use details in this sentence to help you infer a reason or purpose Beah might have had for writing this essay.
4. **Synthesize** How does the text structure—a personal essay—enable the author to deliver his message effectively? Explain your answer using examples from the text.
5. **Notice & Note** Think about the Memory Moments you noticed during this story. What skills and habits did the author learn as a child soldier that helped him both in New York and in the paintball game?

RESEARCH

RESEARCH TIP
At the end of an article, an author will often list the references he or she used to write the piece. Explore these links, which can reveal details that might lead to greater understanding of the topic.

Conflicts in the African nations of Sierra Leone, Sudan, and the Democratic Republic of the Congo brought the world's attention to children forced to serve as soldiers. Use these countries as well as terms such as "Lost Boys of Sudan" as keywords to find relevant sources about specific groups of child soldiers and the related conflicts. Verify that your sources are valid and your information is accurate. Record what you learn in the chart.

ARTICLE TITLE AND SOURCE	DETAILS OF CONFLICT
Democratic Republic of the Congo (Sources will vary.)	*Over 20 years of war; boys and girls exploited by fighting groups*
Sierra Leone (Sources will vary.)	*Thousands of children forced into the war; 50% under age of 15*
Sudan (Sources will vary.)	*Since 2012, estimated 16,000 children forced to fight*

Connect In the last paragraph of "Unusual Normality," the author discusses losing his naïve innocence. Continue your research about these child soldiers to learn about other children who have lost their childhood to war. Find out about the role of U.S. resettlement efforts, including details about individuals who escaped life as one of these child soldiers.

LEARNING MINDSET

Belonging Responding to a personal essay can generate a wide range of reactions in students, including strong emotions. Remind students that everyone's questions and comments, thoughts, and feelings are valuable and worthy of respect. By emphasizing that everyone is a valuable member of the classroom learning community, students will feel safer taking positive risks, such as sharing their responses in writing and with their classmates.

CREATE AND PRESENT

Write a Summarizing Report Write a three-to-four paragraph report in which you summarize your findings about child soldiers.

- ❑ Write about the facts and details you have learned about the topic, synthesizing information from a variety of sources. Compare sources to each other to reveal biases.
- ❑ As you write about U.S. resettlement efforts for refugees, include any specific stories or accounts of specific child soldiers.
- ❑ Maintain meaning and logical order as you write your report.

Debate with a Small Group Have a debate about what should be done about the problem of children forced to become soldiers.

- ❑ In your group, review the topic and the research individuals have done. Isolate the issues and areas of the topic that are controversial. Decide what your group position will be on the question.
- ❑ As you participate in the debate, use appropriate register (degree of formality), vocabulary, and tone to help convey your points. Listen actively to others' positions, respond appropriately, and adjust your responses when new evidence causes you to change your views.
- ❑ Review the ideas discussed in the debate, and summarize conclusions. Use evidence from your research sources to support your conclusions.

Go to the **Writing Studio** for more on writing an informative report.

Go to the **Speaking and Listening Studio** for help with holding a debate.

RESPOND TO THE ESSENTIAL QUESTION

How can we come together despite our differences?

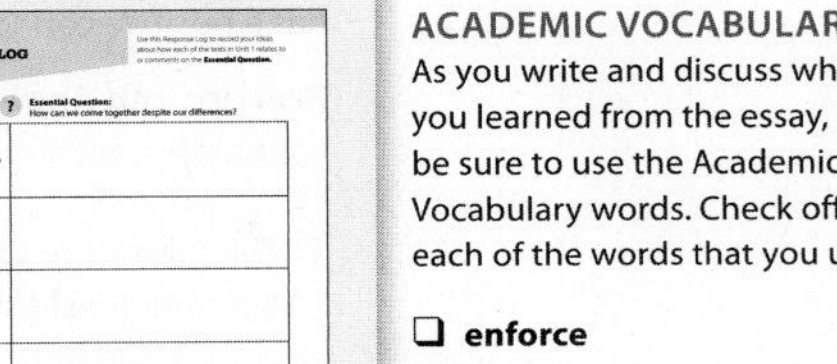

Gather Information Review your annotations and notes on "Unusual Normality." Then, add relevant information to your Response Log. As you determine which information to include, think about:

- how Beah's attitudes toward school reflect his background
- why and how Beah tries to fit in to his new environment and make friends
- what factors help Beah appreciate his new life

At the end of the unit, use your notes to help you write a personal essay.

ACADEMIC VOCABULARY

As you write and discuss what you learned from the essay, be sure to use the Academic Vocabulary words. Check off each of the words that you use.

- ❑ **enforce**
- ❑ **entity**
- ❑ **internal**
- ❑ **presume**
- ❑ **resolve**

CREATE AND PRESENT

Write a Summarizing Report Remind students that a summary involves extracting the main ideas and key details. Remind them that they will paraphrase in their report, or restate the information in their own words. Emphasize the importance of citing sources and using quotations properly to avoid plagiarism. Students may also want to exchange summaries with partners for peer-review feedback.

For **writing support** for students at varying proficiency levels, see the **Text X-Ray** on page 16D.

Debate with a Small Group Before students begin their debates, set some basic guidelines to ensure that everyone is able to fully participate. For example, students should agree to limit the time for speaking and to listen without interrupting the speaker. Assigning roles such as moderator, or facilitator, and timekeeper can help ensure productive, respectful debates.

■ English Learner Support

Adapt Language Discuss the concept of register with students, explaining that they should use more formal, or serious, words during a debate. Read the following word pairs to students, defining words as necessary and asking them to identify the words that convey a more formal tone: ***forced***/*pushed, used/****exploited, children****/kids, groups/* ***organizations.*** Help students practice pronouncing the more formal words and encourage them to try to incorporate them as they participate in the debate. **LIGHT**

RESPOND TO THE ESSENTIAL QUESTION

Allow time for students to add details from "Unusual Normality" to their Unit 1 Response Logs.

APPLY

CRITICAL VOCABULARY

Answers:

1. *b—nursing an injured animal; nursing restores the animal to good health*
2. *a—the governors of two neighboring states; they share the same characteristics and functions*
3. *a—tall people play basketball; this suggests conforming to a set type or belief*
4. *b—trusting a stranger with all your money; this reflects lack of worldly experience*

VOCABULARY STRATEGY: Denotative and Connotative Meanings

Answers:

1. ***denotation:*** *both words are similar—pulled apart into shreds;* ***connotation:*** *tattered—negative, suggesting the man was shabby and did not care about his looks; torn—suggests a neutral, matter-of-fact connotation*
2. ***denotation:*** *both words are similar—to express emotions with spontaneous sounds;* ***connotation:*** *laughing—generally suggests a neutral, matter-of-fact connotation; in this instance, it has a positive connotation because of the context of laughing at a joke; cackled—negative, suggesting a shrill or unpleasant laugh*
3. ***denotation:*** *both words are similar—odd, unusual, peculiar;* ***connotation:*** *weird—negative, suggesting something strange or bizarre; quirky—neutral or positive, suggesting something a bit unusual or interesting*

RESPOND

WORD BANK
rehabilitation
counterparts
stereotype
naïve

CRITICAL VOCABULARY

Practice and Apply Circle the letter of the best answer to each question. Then, explain your response.

1. Which of the following would be part of **rehabilitation**?
   - **a.** constructing something from new parts
   - **b.** nursing an injured animal
2. Which of the following are **counterparts**?
   - **a.** the governors of two neighboring states
   - **b.** the sky and the clouds floating through it
3. Which of the following is a **stereotype**?
   - **a.** tall people play basketball
   - **b.** I like music
4. Which of the following is a **naïve** action?
   - **a.** putting your money in a savings account
   - **b.** trusting a stranger with all your money

VOCABULARY STRATEGY: Denotative and Connotative Meanings

Some words have both a **denotative** and **connotative meaning**. A denotative meaning is the meaning of the word that you would find in a dictionary. A word's connotative meaning includes the feelings and ideas that people may connect with a word. For example, someone may be described as *slender* or *skinny*. The denotative meanings of the words are similar. But *skinny* implies that someone is too thin. It has a negative connotation, while *slender* has a positive connotation.

Go to the **Vocabulary Studio** for more on denotative and connotative meanings.

Practice and Apply Read these sentences. Then, state the denotative and connotative meanings of the boldfaced words.

1. The man wore **tattered** clothes to the mall. She had **torn** the sleeve on her favorite shirt.

   ____

2. She **laughed** at the joke. He **cackled** when she finished telling the story.

   ____

3. She had a **weird** way of talking. His songs were **quirky**.

   ____

ENGLISH LEARNER SUPPORT

Vocabulary Strategy To help students distinguish shades of meaning, use visual support and role play.

- For *torn* versus *tattered*, display a sheet of paper, make a tiny tear, and say, "*I have torn this paper, but it is still good enough to use.*" Then, make several long tears and say, "*Now the paper is too tattered to use.*"
- For *laugh* versus *cackle*, display and point to each word as you role play. Use brief, understated laughter for *laugh*. Then use an exaggerated, nasal or high-pitched *heh-heh-heh* for *cackle*.
- For *quirky* versus *weird*, mime putting on headphones and listening. Look amused and say, "*This sounds quirky and fun.*" Then, listen again, look uncomfortable, shudder, and say, "*This sounds weird.*"

SUBSTANTIAL

RESPOND

LANGUAGE CONVENTIONS: ACTIVE AND PASSIVE VOICE

Writers may use either active or passive voice in their writing. Active voice is easier to read and understand, flows more smoothly, and uses fewer words. Ishmael Beah uses active voice in the sentence below, with the subject *mother* first, and then the verb *called*, followed by the direct object *principal*.

But my mother got on the phone and called every school principal...

However, passive voice is appropriate when writers want to bring attention to the one receiving the action (the principal in the sentence above) instead of the one doing the action (the mother). The sentence could have been written as:

Every school principal was called by my mother on the phone.

Writers can choose to use passive voice for emphasis.

In "Unusual Normality," notice how Ishmael Beah uses both active and passive voice for different effects:

- Active: focus on the subject *I* not the direct object *term*.
  I learned a new American term for what they *did* find it.
- Passive: focus on the *visa*, not on who gave it to him.
  You see, the visa that I had been given was a prospective-student visa.

Practice and Apply Write your own sentences with active and passive voice. Your sentences can be about your own experiences in school or those of someone you know. When you have finished, share your sentences with a partner and compare your use of active and passive voice.

Go to the **Grammar Studio** for more on active and passive voice.

APPLY

LANGUAGE CONVENTIONS:
Active and Passive Voice

Review the distinction between active voice *(the subject of the sentence performs the verb's action)* and passive voice *(the subject of the sentence receives the action of the verb)*. Then, display and discuss the following list of pros and cons for each voice. Explain that *pros* are advantages, or things that are positive about something. Explain that *cons* are disadvantages, or things that are negative about something.

Active Voice: Pros

- Easier to read and understand.
- Flows more smoothly.
- Uses fewer words.
- Helps the writer focus attention on the subject that does the action.

Passive Voice: Pros

- Helps the writer focus attention on the action.
- Helps the writer focus attention on the object that receives the action.

Active Voice: Cons

- Writer may not want to focus attention on the subject.

Passive Voice: Cons

- Can be confusing.
- May sound awkward.
- Uses more words.

Practice and Apply Have partners take turns reading aloud each other's sentences. Then have them identify their partner's sentences that use the passive voice and those that use the active voice and then explain why. *(Students' sentences will vary.)* Encourage students to use the pro and con lists to discuss the reasons for their choices.

ENGLISH LEARNER SUPPORT

Active and Passive Voice Use the following supports with students of different proficiency levels:

- Display these sentence pairs: **(1)** *The boys played a game. The game was played by the boys.* **(2)** *Beah won every game. Every game was won by Beah.* Using the first pair, model saying the following terms as you mark the text: *subject, object, action, does the action, receives the action, passive voice, active voice*. Repeat the terms as you point to the examples. Then, help students say and point to the terms in the second sentence pair. **SUBSTANTIAL**
- Have students find and analyze two more sentences in the essay, one that uses active voice, one that uses passive voice. **MODERATE**
- Ask partners to each write two sentences about the paintball game, one using active voice and one using passive voice. Then, have partners compare sentences. Ask them to explain what makes the voice active or passive. **LIGHT**

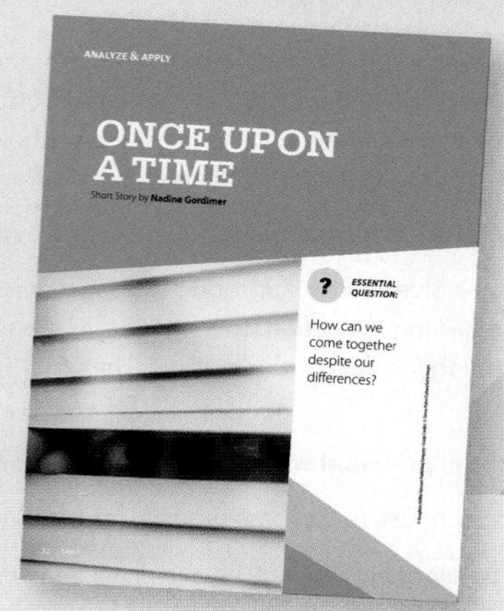

ONCE UPON A TIME

Short Story by Nadine Gordimer

GENRE ELEMENTS

SHORT STORY

Explain to students that a short story includes the basic elements of fiction—setting, characters, plot, conflict, and theme. Short stories differ from novels in that they center on one particular moment or event in life and they can be read in one sitting. Talk about how this element of the genre means that most short stories have a very clear theme or message that is developed over the course of relatively brief narrative.

LEARNING OBJECTIVES

- Analyze theme and setting in a short story.
- Conduct research on fairy tales.
- Write a modern fairy tale.
- Prepare and present a modern fairy tale.
- Use Latin roots to understand words.
- Use prepositional phrases effectively.
- **Language** Discuss with a partner the author's use of details using the key term *prepositional phrase.*

TEXT COMPLEXITY

Quantitative Measures	**Once Upon a Time**	Lexile: 1390L
Qualitative Measures	**Levels of Meaning/Purpose** Single level of complex meaning.	
	Structures Somewhat complex story concepts.	
	Language Conventionality and Clarity Complex and varied sentence structure.	
	Knowledge Demands Cultural and literary knowledge essential to understanding.	

Online 

RESOURCES

- Unit 1 Response Log
- Selection Audio
-  Close Read Screencasts: Modeled Discussions
-  Reading Studio: Notice & Note
-  Level Up Tutorial: Setting: Effect on Plot
-  Writing Studio: Writing Narratives
-  Speaking and Listening Studio: Giving a Presentation
-  Vocabulary Studio: Words from Latin
-  Grammar Studio: Module 3: Lesson 1: Prepositional Phrases
- "Once Upon a Time" Selection Test

SUMMARIES

English

In the first section of the short story (the subplot), a first-person narrator explains that she recently rejected an invitation to contribute to a collection of children's stories. However, she changes her mind and tells herself a bedtime story after a noise she fears is a burglar wakes her up in the night. The rest of the short story is the fairy tale that the narrator tells herself to fall back to sleep. In a seemingly perfect suburb, a family allows their fear of intruders to control their lives, resulting in a horrible incident involving barbed wire they had installed for protection.

Spanish

En la primera sección del cuento (el argumento secundario), una narradora en primera persona explica que recientemente rechazó una invitación para contribuir a una colección de cuentos infantiles. Sin embargo, cambia de parecer y se cuenta a sí misma un cuento para dormir luego de que la despierta un ruido que ella creyó que era un ladrón. El resto del cuento, es el cuento de hadas que la narradora se cuenta a sí misma para volverse a dormir. En un suburbio aparentemente perfecto, una familia permite que el miedo a los intrusos controle sus vidas, cosa que resulta en un horrible incidente con un alambre de púas que habían instalado para su propia protección.

SMALL-GROUP OPTIONS

Have students work in small groups and pairs to read and discuss the selection.

Jigsaw Discussion

- Form "expert" groups of 3–5 students.
- Provide a different section of the short story to each expert group (for example, paragraphs 1–8, 9–12, 13–16, 17–18) and a question for discussion related to that section and setting, plot, or theme. for example: How did the setting influence the plot?
- Set a time limit on the expert discussions; have all students take notes on the discussion.
- Reassign students to "teaching" groups, composed of one or two members from each expert group. Have students take turns presenting their analysis to the group.

Think-Write-Pair-Share

- After students have read and analyzed "Once Upon a Time" pose this question: What is the author's message about apartheid, and how do we know?
- Have students think about the question individually and write down their responses. If students struggle, prompt them to look at the difference in attitude and behavior between the narrator in the subplot and that of the family.
- Then have students join with a partner to discuss their ideas about the question.
- Finally, ask pairs to share a brief summary of their ideas with the class.

Text X-Ray: English Learner Support

for "Once Upon a Time"

Use the Text X-Ray and the supports and scaffolds in the Teacher's Edition to help guide students at different proficiency levels through the selection.

INTRODUCE THE SELECTION

DISCUSS FAIRY-TALE STRUCTURE

Tell students that the short story "Once Upon a Time" is actually two stories in one. The first story is an introduction in which the narrator, who is a writer, hesitates to write a children's story. The second story is a bedtime story the narrator tells herself when she can't sleep. Both stories explore how fear can affect both individuals and society.

Ask and discuss the following question:

- Discuss how different people respond to fear. Guide students to answer this question: How are fairy tales and other stories the same and different? *(Fairy tales and other stories are fiction, but a fairy tale is often a fantasy—or something that probably wouldn't happen, while other fiction stories describe things that realistically happen.)*

Explain and discuss that fairy tales often have common phrases, such as "once upon a time" or "happily every after." Fairy tales also have vividly described settings and good characters that are up against an evil force. In most fairy tales the characters learn a lesson in the end. Have students take notes as they read "Once Upon a Time" about the lesson that the characters learn. They can use their notes to help them discuss the theme(s).

CULTURAL REFERENCES

The following words or phrases may be unfamiliar to students:

- *in broad daylight* (paragraph 5): in the light of day
- *holiday* (paragraph 9): vacation
- *a wise old witch* (paragraph 9): an old woman who gives unwanted advice
- *inscribed in a medical benefit society* (paragraph 9): health insurance
- *Neighborhood Watch* (paragraph 9): an unofficial group of residents keeping a lookout for crime
- *hung about* (paragraph 13): to loiter
- *loafer* (paragraph 13): a lazy person

LISTENING

Identify Descriptive Language

Explain to students that descriptive language is used by writers to establish a **mood** and create **imagery**. Have students listen while you read aloud paragraphs 1–10. Cite two or three examples of descriptive language.

Use the following supports with students at varying proficiency levels:

- Ask students where the first story ends and the fairy-tale part begins. What mood is established in the first part of the story? **SUBSTANTIAL**
- Have students identify three or more instances of descriptive language in paragraphs 1–8 that prompted a sense of fear or dread while they were listening. (*Possible answers: creaking, murdered, strangled, knifed, threat*) **MODERATE**
- Have student listen while you read aloud paragraph 9. Ask students what mood is established in this paragraph. Have them cite that language that creates the mood. **LIGHT**

SPEAKING

Use Prepositional Phrases

Tell students that prepositional phrases can add rhythm and interest to a piece of writing as well as relevant detail. Have students reread paragraphs 9 and 16 of the selection.

Use the following supports with students at varying proficiency levels:

- Work with students to identify the prepositional phrases in the first sentence of paragraph 9. **SUBSTANTIAL**
- Ask students to describe a different setting, using the first sentence of paragraph 9 as a model. *(Example answer: in a tree, in an apple orchard, in the country)* **MODERATE**
- Have students read paragraph 16. Ask students to identify the prepositional phrases and summarize how they are used to describe how the neighborhood has changed. **LIGHT**

READING

Support Inferences About Theme

Explain that a story's **theme** is a message about life that the author wants to share. Traditional stories such as fairy tales often teach a lesson. Characters' actions and their consequences provide clues to the lesson or theme.

Have students reread the story and use the questions to infer its theme. Use the following supports with students at varying proficiency levels:

- Guide students to respond to questions such as the following: What is the family afraid of? *(They are afraid they will be robbed or even murdered by outsiders.)* **SUBSTANTIAL**
- Ask: Why didn't the author give the family a name or describe their race or religion? (*Fear does not discriminate; no one is exempt from its harmful effects.*) **MODERATE**
- Ask: What lesson can readers learn from what happened to the family? *(When we are overly fearful of others, we may end up hurting ourselves.)* **LIGHT**

WRITING

Write a Fairy Tale

To support students in writing their modern fairy tales (Student Edition page 43), provide an example of a story map for their narrative. It could include: setting, protagonists and antagonists, conflict, theme, and resolution.

Using the following supports, have students at varying proficiency levels create their own story maps :

- Allow students to map their story in their home language. Have students begin a basic story map of the setting under three labels: Where, When, Description of Setting. **SUBSTANTIAL**
- Have students work in pairs to create a simple story map. Break the story map into categories for Setting, Characters (protagonists and antagonists), and Plot (beginning, middle, ending). **MODERATE**
- Have students create a complete story map for their story that includes the following categories: Setting, Characters, Plot, Theme, Conflict, and Resolution. **LIGHT**

Connect to the
ESSENTIAL QUESTION

"Once Upon a Time" explores how differences in race and status lead people to be afraid of each other and separate themselves even further. However, the end of the story shows different people brought together, tragically, by shared grief.

ANALYZE & APPLY

ONCE UPON A TIME

Short Story by **Nadine Gordimer**

ESSENTIAL QUESTION:

How can we come together despite our differences?

32 Unit 1

LEARNING MINDSET

Growth MindSet Remind students that having a growth mindset means embracing the challenge of learning something new with enthusiasm. Encourage students to look for opportunities to set new goals and revise old ones. This might be their first encounter with a complex parallel plot structure and subplot. Encourage students to view this as an opportunity to take on the challenge of new material beyond their comfort zone.

QUICK START

What is something you fear? What is something that others in your family fear? Think about and discuss ways these fears shape and affect your lives.

ANALYZE SETTING AND THEME

The **setting** of a story is the time and place of the action of the story. Setting often shapes a story's events or plot, including the story's conflict.

The main message of a story is the **theme**, which can be enhanced or advanced by the setting. As you analyze "Once Upon a Time," make inferences, or logical guesses, about the theme by considering the details and symbols Gordimer includes. Pay particular attention to the characters' actions and motivations, as well as the setting—including the historical background—to help you infer the theme. Looking for the Signposts and asking questions about them as you read can also help you find the theme of a story.

LITERARY ELEMENT	EXAMPLES
A story's **setting** can shape the events of a story.	**In a house, in a suburb, in a city, there were a man and his wife….**
Look for clues to a story's **theme** throughout the story, such as changes in details of the setting.	So from every window and door in the house... they now saw the trees and sky through bars....

ANALYZE PLOT: SUBPLOTS

A **subplot** is an additional storyline that runs parallel to the main story. Sometimes subplots are used as framing devices at the beginning or end of a story.

Subplots may involve characters who are less important or another story that is happening outside the main, focused story. Subplots are usually linked to the main plot of the story in some way.

In "Once Upon a Time," the subplot involves the author's struggle to write a children's story. One night she is awakened by a noise and begins to imagine dangers in her home.

GENRE ELEMENTS: SHORT STORY

- includes the basic elements of fiction—setting, characters, plot, conflict, and theme
- centers on one particular moment or event in life
- can be read in one sitting

TEACH

QUICK START

Have students read the Quick Start question, and invite them to share things they fear. Build a class list of fears, getting as wide a variety of responses as possible. Responses may include common phobias, such as clowns or spiders, and others may be more abstract, such as the sudden loss of a loved one. Ask pairs of students to identify actions they or others take to avoid these fears. (*If someone is afraid of the dark, they may use a nightlight.*) Pairs can volunteer to share their ideas with the class.

ANALYZE SETTING AND THEME

Tell students that knowing the setting helps them understand the writer's message, or theme. Explain that writers often comment on the historical background of the setting, as Gordimer does in this story.

Review the literary elements in the table, and discuss or brainstorm how different settings could create or correspond to different themes.

Suggest that students use these questions to help them analyze setting and theme as they read and annotate the text:

- Where in the world is the story set?
- What is the historical background of the story?
- What is the writer's attitude toward the historical background?

ANALYZE PLOT: SUBPLOTS

Explain that "Once Upon a Time" has a subplot at the beginning of the story to frame the main story. Point out to students that the main story and subplot may be connected with similar themes. Subplots usually intersect or converge with the main plot at some point in the story, affecting the course of the action.

As with setting and theme, have students use these questions to help them analyze the relationship between the main plot and subplot:

- What is the subplot about?
- In what ways are the main plot and the subplot connected?
- When does the subplot intersect with the main plot? How does it affect the course of action?

TEACH

CRITICAL VOCABULARY

Have students read each sentence before deciding which word belongs in the sentence. Remind students to look at the context clues in the rest of the sentences to match the exact meaning of the word with the meaning of the sentence.

Answers:

1. *audacious*
2. *intrusion*
3. *intention*
4. *distend*
5. *serrated*

English Learner Support

Use Cognates Introduce these cognates to expand the vocabulary knowledge of Spanish-speaking students. The Spanish cognate for *audacious* is *audaz*, meaning daring or bold. The cognate for *intrusion* is the same as the English *intrusion*, or *intrusión*. *Intención* is the Spanish cognate for *intention*, meaning motive or an aim that guides an action. The cognate for *distend* is *distender*, meaning to expand or stretch. **ALL LEVELS**

LANGUAGE CONVENTIONS

Review the information about prepositional phrases. Note that prepositional phrases can be placed at the beginning, in the middle, or at the end of a sentence, depending on what detail the writer wishes to emphasize.

Read aloud the example sentences, then read them again without the prepositional phrases to emphasize the information they add to the sentence. *(The phrases give more detail and create a clearer image for the reader. They also emphasize the family's imprisonment.)*

ANNOTATION MODEL

Remind students of the guiding questions about setting, theme, and subplot on the previous page. Point out that they may want to color-code their annotations for setting, theme, and subplot using highlighters. Their notes in the margin may include questions about ideas that are unclear or topics they want to learn more about.

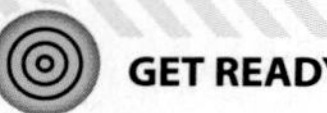

GET READY

CRITICAL VOCABULARY

distend **intention** **audacious** **intrusion** **serrated**

To see how many Critical Vocabulary words you already know, use them to complete the sentences.

1. The motorcyclist's stunt was terrifying and __________.
2. The thief's __________ in the middle of the night scared the whole family.
3. The businesswomen said it was her __________ to buy the company for cash.
4. The bacterial infection caused the baby's stomach to __________.
5. The knife was sharp because it was __________.

LANGUAGE CONVENTIONS

Prepositional Phrases are phrases consisting of a preposition and an object of the preposition, usually a noun or a pronoun. Prepositional phrases provide more information about the noun or verb in a sentence. Think about the information prepositional phrases add to the following sentences from the selection.

. . . she implored her employers to have burglar bars attached to the doors and windows of the house . . .

So from every window and door in the house where they were living happily ever after they now saw the trees and sky through bars . . .

ANNOTATION MODEL

NOTICE & NOTE

As you read, note the author's use of setting and subplots to advance the theme of the story. You can also mark up evidence that supports your own ideas. In the model, you can see one reader's notes about "Once Upon a Time."

I couldn't find a position in which my mind would let go of my body—release me to sleep again. So I began to tell myself a story; a bedtime story.

In a house, in a suburb, in a city, there were a man and his wife who loved each other very much and were living happily ever after.

This might be the end of a subplot, and the start of the main plot.

This is a very simple setting; I think it's going to get more complicated.

NOTICE & NOTE

BACKGROUND

Nadine Gordimer *(1923–2014) was born in South Africa. Her family was privileged and white in a country that practiced apartheid—an official policy of segregation of nonwhite South Africans. Gordimer became politically opposed to the policy. Her early works, such as* The Soft Voice of the Serpent *and* The Lying Days, *explore themes of exile and the effects of apartheid on life in South Africa. Before apartheid ended in 1994, some of Gordimer's writings were banned by the South African government. Gordimer was awarded many literary prizes, including the Nobel Prize for Literature in 1991.*

ONCE UPON A TIME

Short Story by Nadine Gordimer

SETTING A PURPOSE

As you read, pay attention to the way that the author builds a portrait of the suburb as a setting that should be safe but becomes something else.

1 Someone has written to ask me to contribute to an anthology of stories for children. I reply that I don't write children's stories; and he writes back that at a recent congress/book fair/seminar a certain novelist said every writer ought to write at least one story for children. I think of sending a postcard saying I don't accept that I "ought" to write anything.

2 And then last night I woke up—or rather was wakened without knowing what had roused me.

3 A voice in the echo chamber of the subconscious? Close Read

4 A sound.

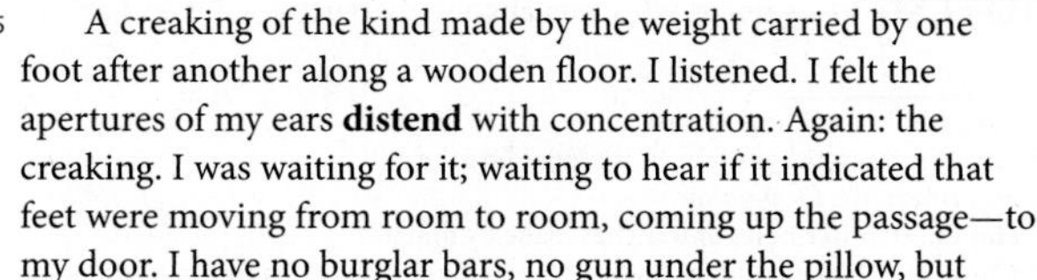

5 A creaking of the kind made by the weight carried by one foot after another along a wooden floor. I listened. I felt the apertures of my ears **distend** with concentration. Again: the creaking. I was waiting for it; waiting to hear if it indicated that feet were moving from room to room, coming up the passage—to my door. I have no burglar bars, no gun under the pillow, but

Notice & Note

You can use the side margins to notice and note signposts in the text.

LANGUAGE CONVENTIONS

Annotate: Mark the two prepositional phrases in paragraph 3.

Respond: What information do these prepositional phrases provide?

distend
(dĭ-stĕnd´) *v.*
to bulge or expand.

CLOSE READING SCREENCAST

Modeled Discussions In their eBook, have students view the Close Read Screencast, in which readers discuss and annotate the following key passages:

- introduction where the author explains how she came to write the story that follows (paragraphs 1–4).
- description of different classes, the unemployed, the trusted employee, and the sheltered family (paragraph 13, sentences 6–11).

As a class, view and discuss at least one video. Then have students pair up to do an independent close read of paragraph 17 (the description of a security measure the family takes). Students can record their answers on the Close Read Practice PDF.

Close Read Practice PDF

BACKGROUND

Have students read the background and information about the author. Tell students that when this story was published in 1989, South Africa was still under apartheid. White families lived in desirable neighborhoods while many nonwhite South Africans, Indians, and people of mixed race were forced to live in segregated areas called *townships* with poor living conditions. Nonwhites only came to white neighborhoods to work, for example, as housemaids and gardeners.

SETTING A PURPOSE

Direct students to use the Setting a Purpose prompt to focus their reading.

LANGUAGE CONVENTIONS

Remind students that prepositional phrases provide more information about the noun or verb in a sentence. (***Answer:*** *"in the echo chamber" tells where, and "of the subconscious" shows that this takes place in the author's mind.)*

For **listening support** for students at varying proficiency levels, see the **Text X-Ray** on page 32C.

CRITICAL VOCABULARY

distend: Explain that Gordimer uses this word figuratively here; the narrator's ears do not actually physically bulge or expand when concentrating on a sound.

ASK STUDENTS to make up a simile that explains what the narrator means when she writes that she "felt the apertures of my ears distend." *(Her ears would distend like a dog's ears perk up when it hears an interesting sound.)*

ANALYZE SUBPLOTS

Remind students that a **subplot** is an additional storyline that runs parallel to the main story. Tell students that **mood** is the atmosphere or general feeling conveyed by the details an author includes. Point out that the mood can refer to the entire work or to one particular part of a work or a subplot. The mood conveyed in the subplot has a direct effect on the mood of the main plot. *(**Answer:** The writer uses these words to create a mood of fear and tension.)*

ENGLISH LEARNER SUPPORT

Make Inferences About Theme Point out that the initial paragraphs of a text often give clues to the theme, or message, of the story. Read aloud the first paragraphs of the selection. Discuss with students their impressions of the details in paragraph 5. *(The theme has to do with fear and how different people in a community react to fear.)* Have students reread paragraph 5 and identify the reason the narrator is afraid and how she is similar to or different from others in her community. *(She is afraid someone is breaking into her home because she hears a creaking sound, and crimes have happened in her area. She does not have extra security in her home even though others do. However, she is explaining that she has the same fears as people who do have extra security.)* **MODERATE**

AHA MOMENT

Explain to students that this signpost is often used to show a character's realization of something that shifts their actions or understanding of themselves, others, or the world around them. Then have students answer the question to make inferences about why the writer has changed her mind. *(**Answer:** The strange sounds the author hears in the house give her the idea to write a story about reactions to fear.)*

For **speaking support** for students at varying proficiency levels, see the **Text X-Ray** on page 32D.

NOTICE & NOTE

I have the same fears as people who do take these precautions, and my windowpanes are thin as rime,[1] could shatter like a wineglass. A woman was murdered (how do they put it) in broad daylight in a house two blocks away, last year, and the fierce dogs who guarded an old widower and his collection of antique clocks were strangled before he was knifed by a casual laborer he had dismissed without pay.

ANALYZE SUBPLOTS
Annotate: Mark words and phrases in paragraphs 6 and 7 that tell how the author feels at this point in the story.
Analyze: What mood do these words create?

6 I was staring at the door, making it out in my mind rather than seeing it, in the dark. I lay quite still—a victim already—but the arrhythmia[2] of my heart was fleeing, knocking this way and that against its body-cage. How finely tuned the senses are, just out of rest, sleep! I could never listen intently as that in the distractions of the day; I was reading every faintest sound, identifying and classifying its possible threat.

7 But I learned that I was to be neither threatened nor spared. There was no human weight pressing on the boards, the creaking was a buckling, an epicenter[3] of stress. I was in it. The house that surrounds me while I sleep is built on undermined ground; far beneath my bed, the floor, the house's foundations, the stopes[4] and passages of gold mines have hollowed the rock, and when some face trembles, detaches, and falls, three thousand feet below, the whole house shifts slightly, bringing uneasy strain to the balance and counterbalance of brick, cement, wood, and glass that hold it as a structure around me. The misbeats of my heart tailed off like the last muffled flourishes on one of the wooden xylophones made by the Chopi and Tsonga[5] migrant miners who might have been down there, under me in the earth at that moment. The stope where the fall was could have been disused, dripping water from its ruptured veins; or men might now be interred there in the most profound of tombs.

AHA MOMENT
Notice & Note: Mark sentences that tell what caused the sudden change in the author's decision not to write a story for children.
Infer: Why did the author change her mind?

8 I couldn't find a position in which my mind would let go of my body—release me to sleep again. So I began to tell myself a story; a bedtime story.

9 In a house, in a suburb, in a city, there were a man and his wife who loved each other very much and were living happily ever after. They had a little boy, and they loved him very much. They had a cat and a dog that the little boy loved very much. They had a car and a caravan trailer for holidays, and a swimming pool which was fenced so that the little boy and his playmates would not fall in and drown. They had a housemaid who was absolutely trustworthy and an

[1] **rime** (rīm): a coating of frost
[2] **arrhythmia** (ə-rĭth´mē-ə): an irregular heartbeat
[3] **epicenter:** the focal point
[4] **stopes:** step-like holes or trenches made by miners
[5] **Chopi and Tsonga** (chō´pē and tsôn´ga): ethnic groups that live in Mozambique

ENGLISH LEARNER SUPPORT

Identify Figurative Language Explain that **similes** and **metaphors** are figures of speech comparing unlike things. Similes use the words *like* or *as*; metaphors do not. Have students reread paragraphs 5–7 and identify examples of simile and metaphor. *(**Simile:** "[My] windowpanes are thin as rime, could shatter like a wineglass." **Metaphor:** "[B]ut the arrhythmia of my heart was fleeing, knocking this way and that against its body-cage.")* **MODERATE**

itinerant[6] gardener who was highly recommended by the neighbors. For when they began to live happily ever after, they were warned by that wise old witch, the husband's mother, not to take on anyone off the street. They were inscribed in a medical benefit society, their pet dog was licensed, they were insured against fire, flood damage, and theft, and subscribed to the local Neighborhood Watch, which supplied them with a plaque for their gates lettered YOU HAVE BEEN WARNED over the silhouette of a would-be intruder. He was masked; it could not be said if he was black or white, and therefore proved the property owner was no racist.

10 It was not possible to insure the house, the swimming pool, or the car against riot damage. There were riots, but these were outside the city, where people of another color were quartered. These people were not allowed into the suburb except as reliable housemaids and gardeners, so there was nothing to fear, the husband told the wife. Yet she was afraid that some day such people might come up the street and tear off the plaque YOU HAVE BEEN WARNED and open the gates and stream in. . . . Nonsense, my dear, said the husband, there are police and soldiers and tear gas and guns to keep them away. But to please her—for he loved her very much and buses were being burned, cars stoned, and schoolchildren shot by the police in those quarters out of sight and hearing of the suburb—he had electronically controlled gates fitted. Anyone who pulled off the sign YOU HAVE BEEN WARNED and tried to open the gates would have to announce his **intentions** by pressing a button and speaking into a receiver relayed to the house. The little boy was fascinated by the device and used it as a walkie-talkie in cops and robbers play with his small friends.

11 The riots were suppressed, but there were many burglaries in the suburb and somebody's trusted housemaid was tied up and shut in a cupboard by thieves while she was in charge of her employers' house. The trusted housemaid of the man and wife and little boy was so upset by this misfortune befalling a friend left, as she herself often was, with responsibility for the possessions of the man and his wife and the little boy, that she implored her employers to have burglar bars attached to the doors and windows of the house, and an alarm system installed. The wife said, she is right, let us take heed of her advice. So from every window and door in the house where they were living happily ever after they now saw the trees and sky through bars, and when the little boy's pet cat tried to climb in by the fanlight[7] to keep him company in his little bed at night, as it customarily had done, it set off the alarm keening[8] through the house.

ANALYZE SETTING AND THEME

Annotate: What fear does the wife have? How does her husband reassure her that they are safe? Mark sentences in paragraph 10 that show the fear and the husband's reassurances.

Predict: What do you think will happen next?

intention
(ĭn-tĕn′shən) *n.* purpose or plan.

[6] **itinerant:** frequently traveling to different places
[7] **fanlight:** an arched window, usually over a door
[8] **keening:** wailing or crying

ANALYZE SETTING AND THEME

Remind students that Gordimer develops the theme, or the underlying message, through the details and symbols she includes in the story. Tell students to pay particular attention to the characters' actions and motivations, as well as the setting and historical background, to help them determine theme. The segregation and resulting racial tensions fuel the wife's fears of a break-in and robbery. Have students discuss how changes in the setting (the family's home and neighborhood) enhance the theme of the story. (***Answer:*** *The husband and wife's paranoia leads to a nightmarish existence inside the walls of their own making.)*

ENGLISH LEARNER SUPPORT

Describe Setting Read paragraph 10 aloud with students following along. Help students locate the words *house, riot, city,* and *suburb* in the text, and make sure they understand the meaning of each word. Then have students work in pairs to orally describe the setting to each other. Provide the following sentence frames to help start students' discussion about the setting:

- *The ______ is in the ______ of a large ______. (house, suburbs, city)*
- *There have been ______ in the city and the wife is afraid. (riots)* **MODERATE**

APPLYING ACADEMIC VOCABULARY

❑ enforce ❑ entity ☑ internal ☑ presume ❑ resolve

Write and Discuss Have students turn to a partner to discuss the following questions. Guide students to include the academic vocabulary words *internal* and *presume* in their responses. Ask volunteers to share their responses with the class.

- What is the narrator's **internal** struggle regarding safety and security?
- What does the family **presume** about people "of another color" from outside their neighborhood?

CRITICAL VOCABULARY

intention: The intercom system forces visitors to announce their presence and say why they are at the house—that is, they must state their intentions—before they can gain entry.

ASK STUDENTS what the real intention is of the intercom system. *(The intercom system gives the family a sense of control over who gains entry to the house.)*

ANALYZING SETTING AND THEME

Guide students to connect the characters' actions and motivations to the events taking place in South Africa during apartheid to help infer theme. (***Answer:*** *The conflict between the wife's desire to help and the family's fear shows that while there is hope in the society, because the wife cares, it is a hope that is being overwhelmed and crushed by fear.*)

English Learner Support

Understand Language Structures To help students understand how to infer the theme, model a think aloud. Read paragraph 13 aloud to the class. Then, use the following sentence frames to help students infer the theme:

The wife is conflicted because _________ .

The fear of the family gets worse because __________.

In the end, overwhelming fear causes the family to ________.

SUBSTANTIAL/MODERATE

CRITICAL VOCABULARY

audacious: The intruders' boldness in stopping to drink from the liquor cabinets showed that they were not afraid of being caught by the homeowners.

ASK STUDENTS why Gordimer included the detail about the intruders behaving audaciously. (*It shows that the security measures people put in their homes were not effective.*)

NOTICE & NOTE

audacious (ô-dā´shəs) *adj.* bold, rebellious.

ANALYZE SETTING AND THEME

Annotate: Mark the phrases and sentences in paragraph 13 that suggest the wife's desire to help is in conflict with the family's fear.

Analyze: How might this conflict relate to the author's theme, or message?

12 The alarm was often answered—it seemed—by other burglar alarms, in other houses, that had been triggered by pet cats or nibbling mice. The alarms called to one another across the gardens in shrills and bleats and wails that everyone soon became accustomed to, so that the din roused the inhabitants of the suburb no more than the croak of frogs and musical grating of cicadas'[9] legs. Under cover of the electronic harpies'[10] discourse intruders sawed the iron bars and broke into homes, taking away hi-fi equipment, television sets, cassette players, cameras and radios, jewelry and clothing, and sometimes were hungry enough to devour everything in the refrigerator or paused **audaciously** to drink the whiskey in the cabinets or patio bars. Insurance companies paid no compensation for single malt, a loss made keener by the property owner's knowledge that the thieves wouldn't even have been able to appreciate what it was they were drinking.

13 Then the time came when many of the people who were not trusted housemaids and gardeners hung about the suburb because they were unemployed. Some importuned for a job: weeding or painting a roof; anything, *baas*,[11] madam. But the man and his wife remembered the warning about taking on anyone off the street. Some drank liquor and fouled the street with discarded bottles. Some begged, waiting for the man or his wife to drive the car out of the electronically operated gates. They sat about with their feet in the gutters, under the jacaranda trees that made a green tunnel of the street—for it was a beautiful suburb, spoiled only by their presence—and sometimes they fell asleep lying right before the gates in the midday sun. The wife could never see anyone go hungry. She sent the trusted housemaid out with bread and tea, but the trusted housemaid said these were loafers and *tsotsis*,[12] who would come and tie her up and shut her in a cupboard. The husband said, she's right. Take heed of her advice. You only encourage them with your bread and tea. They are looking for their chance. . . . And he brought the little boy's tricycle from the garden into the house every night, because if the house was surely secure, once locked and with the alarm set, someone might still be able to climb over the wall or the electronically closed gates into the garden.

14 You are right, said the wife, then the wall should be higher. And the wise old witch, the husband's mother, paid for the extra bricks as her Christmas present to her son and his wife—the little boy got a Space Man outfit and a book of fairy tales.

[9] **cicadas** (sĭ-kā´ dəs): large, loud insects
[10] **harpies:** mythological creatures who were part woman and part bird
[11] **baas** (bäs): a white person in a position of authority in relation to nonwhites
[12] **tsotsis** (tsō´tsēs): dishonest, untrustworthy people

WHEN STUDENTS STRUGGLE . . .

Compare and Contrast Have individuals or partners use a chart like the one shown to compare the choices the narrator makes about her own security with the choices the family in her story make. Ask students to record their responses to these guiding questions on their charts: What do the narrator and the family have in common? (*They are both afraid of intruders.*) What do they do differently? (*The narrator chooses to live normally; she doesn't have extra security measures to protect herself. The family allows fear to dictate their life; they keep adding more and more "security" measures.*) What are the results for the narrator and the family? (*The narrator remains safe while the family is harmed by the very things that were meant to keep them safe.*)

	Similarities	Differences	Results
Narrator	Afraid of an intruder in the night	Lives normally, does not let fear control her life	Remains safe
Family	Afraid of intruders	Adds more security, lets fear control their lives	Harmed by their security measures

For additional support, go to the **Reading Studio** and assign the following  **Level Up Tutorial: Setting: Effect on Plot.**

NOTICE & NOTE

Getty Images

15 But every week there were more reports of **intrusion**: in broad daylight and the dead of night, in the early hours of the morning, and even in the lovely summer twilight—a certain family was at dinner while the bedrooms were being ransacked upstairs. The man and his wife, talking of the latest armed robbery in the suburb, were distracted by the sight of the little boy's pet cat effortlessly arriving over the seven-foot wall, descending first with a rapid bracing of extended forepaws down on the sheer vertical surface, and then a graceful launch, landing with a swishing tail within the property. The whitewashed wall was marked with the cat's comings and goings; and on the street side of the wall there were larger red-earth smudges that could have been made by the kind of broken running shoes, seen on the feet of unemployed loiterers, that had no innocent destination.

16 When the man and wife and little boy took the pet dog for its walk round the neighborhood streets they no longer paused to admire this show of roses or that perfect lawn; these were hidden

intrusion
(ĭn-tro͞o´ shən) *n.* act of trespass or invasion.

CONTRASTS AND CONTRADICTIONS

Notice & Note: Mark contrasts and contradictions between the "perfect" suburb and the walls and other protections that the neighbors have built.

Summarize: How has the suburb changed, and why?

CONTRASTS AND CONTRADICTIONS

Explain to students that this signpost is often used to show a sharp contrast between how we expect something to be and how it actually is. In this case, the suburb should be an ideal environment—beautiful, peaceful, safe—but instead it is the opposite. Then have students answer the question to **summarize** how the suburb has changed, and infer why the neighbors have made these changes and how they link to the theme. (***Answer:*** *The formerly "perfect" and beautiful suburb is now hidden behind barricades made threatening with spikes and broken glass. The neighbors' fear of burglary has prompted them to fortify their homes with these menacing features, showing that they have let fear control their lives.)*

English Learner Support

Analyze Descriptive Language Read the sentences in paragraph 16 describing the protections neighbors have built. Pause after each description and have students illustrate each one. Repeat each description as needed. After students have finished their drawings, ask: Do you think the people who live here are afraid? *(yes)* Do you think they want people visiting their neighborhood? *(no)* **MODERATE**

IMPROVE READING FLUENCY

Targeted Passage Use echo reading to help students read with appropriate pace and emphasis. First, read the first sentence of paragraph 15 aloud at a normal pace with expression and emphasis, pausing for effect at punctuation. Then have students read the same sentence aloud together, trying to imitate intonation, expression, emphasis, and pace. It may be helpful to use gestures on the first reading and repeat these gestures as the students imitate. Repeat this process for the remaining sentences in the paragraph. Remind students that when they are reading aloud, they should read aloud at a steady pace so the audience has time to understand what is being read to them.

 Go to the **Reading Studio** for additional support in developing fluency.

CRITICAL VOCABULARY

intrusion: Gordimer is referring to the act of burglars breaking into homes in the family's neighborhood.

ASK STUDENTS the difference between the cat jumping over the wall and a burglar entering the home. *(The cat is a family member and is welcome to come and go. The burglar is unwelcome, so entering the house is an intrusion.)*

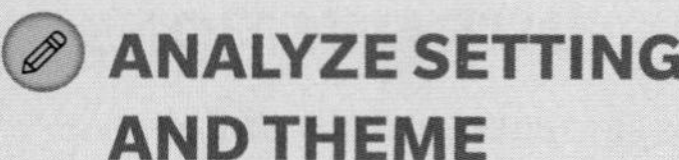

ANALYZE SETTING AND THEME

To help students infer the theme, prompt them to review the story from the beginning and to use their notes and annotations. Remind them to focus especially on the characters' actions and motivations and to consider the setting and historical background of the story. (***Answer:*** *The more people react to their fears by walling themselves off, the more likely that fear and a sense of threat will grow. The husband and wife try to protect their family, but in the end their little boy is hurt and possibly killed because of their efforts.*)

ENGLISH LEARNER SUPPORT

Discuss Environmental Print Read the last sentence in paragraph 16 aloud with students following along. Point out the text "Consult DRAGON'S TEETH The People For Total Security." Explain to students that the text is on a wall and that signs like these are called *environmental print*, or print that is found in the space that surrounds us.

Ask students to work with a partner to write a list of environmental print examples in the classroom and around the school. Have them share their findings with the class and as a group, discuss how environmental print helps guide people's actions. **ALL LEVELS**

For **reading support** for students at varying proficiency levels, see the **Text X-Ray** on page 32D.

NOTICE & NOTE

behind an array of different varieties of security fences, walls, and devices. The man, wife, little boy, and dog passed a remarkable choice: there was the low-cost option of pieces of broken glass embedded in cement along the top of walls, there were iron grilles ending in lance points, there were attempts at reconciling the aesthetics of prison architecture with the Spanish Villa style (spikes painted pink) and with the plastic urns of neoclassical facades (twelve-inch pikes finned like zigzags of lightning and painted pure white). Some walls had a small board affixed, giving the name and telephone number of the firm responsible for the installation of the devices. While the little boy and the pet dog raced ahead, the husband and wife found themselves comparing the possible effectiveness of each style against its appearance; and after several weeks when they paused before this barricade or that without needing to speak, both came out with the conclusion that only one was worth considering. It was the ugliest but the most honest in its suggestion of the pure concentration-camp style, no frills, all evident efficacy. Placed the length of walls, it consisted of a continuous coil of stiff and shining metal **serrated** into jagged blades, so that there would be no way of climbing over it and no way through its tunnel without getting entangled in its fangs. There would be no way out, only a struggle getting bloodier and bloodier, a deeper and sharper hooking and tearing of flesh. The wife shuddered to look at it. You're right, said the husband, anyone would think twice. . . . And they took heed of the advice on a small board fixed to the wall: Consult DRAGON'S TEETH The People For Total Security.

serrated
(sĕr´ā´tĭd) *adj.* having a jagged, saw-toothed edge.

17 Next day, a gang of workmen came and stretched the razor-bladed coils all round the walls of the house where the husband and wife and little boy and pet dog and cat were living happily ever after. The sunlight flashed and slashed off the serrations, the cornice of razor thorns encircled the home, shining. The husband said, Never mind. It will weather. The wife said, You're wrong. They guarantee it's rustproof. And she waited until the little boy had run off to play before she said, I hope the cat will take heed. . . . The husband said, Don't worry, my dear, cats always look before they leap. And it was true that from that day on, the cat slept in the little boy's bed and kept to the garden, never risking a try at breaching security.

ANALYZE SETTING AND THEME

Annotate: Mark the words that reveal the shocking ending of the story.

Connect: Think about the characters' actions and motivations that led to this ending. What can you infer about the theme, or message, of this story?

18 One evening, the mother read the little boy to sleep with a fairy story from the book the wise old witch had given him at Christmas. Next day, he pretended to be the prince who braves the terrible thicket of thorns to enter the palace and kiss the Sleeping Beauty back to life: he dragged a ladder to the wall, the shining coiled tunnel was just wide enough for his little body to creep in, and with the first fixing of its razor teeth in his knees and hands and head he screamed and struggled deeper into its tangle. The trusted housemaid and the itinerant gardener, whose "day" it was, came running, the first to see

TO CHALLENGE STUDENTS . . .

Write from Author's Perspective What does Nadine Gordimer think about the society of South Africa at the time the story was written? Explain that Gordimer is expressing her attitudes and beliefs through her writing. Challenge students to write a continuation or epilogue of the story that describes a conversation the parents have the next day about what has happened and what they are thinking (or have learned) about their security systems. Some students may find it intriguing to include the "wise old witch" character in their descriptions. Encourage students to try to write in the same tone and style as Gordimer. Give students the opportunity to share their writing in a small group or with the class.

CRITICAL VOCABULARY

serrate: Gordimer uses this word to describe the sharp, jagged edge of the wire used to make the wall secure.

ASK STUDENTS why a serrated edge would make the barricade more effective or dangerous. (*The jagged blades would cut a person if he or she tried to climb over the fence.*)

NOTICE & NOTE

and to scream with him, and the itinerant gardener tore his hands trying to get at the little boy. Then the man and his wife burst wildly into the garden and for some reason (the cat, probably), the alarm set up wailing against the screams while the bleeding mass of the little boy was hacked out of the security coil with saws, wire cutters, choppers, and they carried it—the man, the wife, the hysterical trusted housemaid, and the weeping gardener—into the house.

CHECK YOUR UNDERSTANDING

Answer these questions before moving on to the **Analyze the Text** section on the following page.

1 The author included the opening paragraph about not writing children's stories to —

A argue why children's stories are not important

B compare herself to other authors

C show how she came to write a fairy tale

D explain why her story is not like other children's stories

2 Which of the following is a central theme in the story?

F Private security measures are important for people's safety.

G Sometimes people must suppress the majority population.

H People shouldn't allow fear to dictate their actions and isolate them.

J Police and law enforcement can control robberies and intrusions.

3 The author's purpose for writing the selection was most likely to —

A warn about outsiders trying to invade your home

B explore different home security systems

C tell about a curse that was placed on a neighborhood

D show the dangers of fear and paranoia

CHECK YOUR UNDERSTANDING

Have students answer the questions independently.

Answers:

1. *C*
2. *H*
3. *D*

If they answer any questions incorrectly, have them reread the text to confirm their understanding. Then they may proceed to ANALYZE THE TEXT on page 42.

ENGLISH LEARNER SUPPORT

Oral Assessment Use the following questions to assess students' comprehension and speaking skills.

1. Why did the author include the first paragraph about not writing a story for children? *(The author included the opening paragraph to show how she came to write a fairy tale.)*
2. What is a central theme of the story? *(People should not allow fear to dictate their actions and isolate them).*
3. What is the author's purpose for writing this story? *(It is most likely the author's purpose to show the dangers of fear and paranoia.)*

MODERATE/LIGHT

APPLY

ANALYZE THE TEXT

Possible answers:

1. **DOK 4:** *Gordimer's story reveals her opposition to the attitudes and prejudices of people who support racial segregation. Text evidence should include how fear of outsiders threatens to destroy a family.*
2. **DOK 2:** *Gordimer does not reveal whether the boy lives or dies, but the reader can tell that they will be permanently affected by this incident. She mocks the idea of happily ever after by showing that despite all the protections and defenses the family builds, tragedy still strikes as a result of their reactions to fear.*
3. **DOK 2:** *The theme of this story relates to fear and the impulse to wall oneself off from others as a result. The people of the neighborhood fear outsiders, being "people of another color," and they build walls and use other security measures to keep others out. But at the end, they only hurt themselves and their little boy. Gordimer sets the story in a place much like South Africa during apartheid, where many white people tried to wall themselves off from people they feared.*
4. **DOK 2:** *The story uses language common in fairy tales, such as "once upon a time" and "happily ever after." The story also has characters who confront what they perceive as dangers. The subplot—the narrator's own story at the start of the text—foreshadows the theme of irrational fear.*
5. **DOK 4:** *The husband, wife, and neighbors keep looking to new security measures to keep people out of their homes and neighborhood. The fences turn into gates and walls with metal, glass, and other devices for protection. However, the family's impulse to isolate themselves does not make them safe; it hurts the family instead.*

RESEARCH

Remind students that they should look for a variety of fairy tales to get as many common characteristics as possible.

Connect Students may see a connection between these home security systems and conventions of fairy tales, such as the "DRAGON'S TEETH," or alarms going off so often they are not taken seriously, as in "The Boy Who Cried Wolf."

RESPOND

ANALYZE THE TEXT

Support your responses with evidence from the text. NOTEBOOK

1. **Connect** Nadine Gordimer wrote many stories about the injustices of apartheid. She was also active in bringing change to the political entities of South Africa. Even though her books were banned in South Africa for a time, she resolved to stay instead of living in exile. What do you learn about Gordimer's political point of view by reading this story? Explain your ideas using evidence from the story.
2. **Infer** Authors often leave things unstated in a story, leaving the reader with questions about the outcome. What can you infer about what Gordimer leaves unstated at the end of her story? How does it relate to her statements about the family living "happily ever after"?
3. **Infer** What is the theme of this story? Explain how Gordimer develops this theme through the story's setting.
4. **Identify Patterns** How is the structure of this story similar to a fairy tale? How does the story's subplot contribute to the structure? Cite details from the text to support your answer.
5. **Notice & Note** What actions do the husband, wife, and their neighbors do again and again because of their fear of outsiders? How does this reveal the story's theme?

RESEARCH

RESEARCH TIP
Search general terms like *fairy tale, tall tale,* and *bedtime story,* as well as the titles of these types that you encounter. Remember that each source will suggest other search terms that may or may not prove to be useful.

Fairy tales are one of the oldest forms of writing and originally came from oral stories passed down through cultures. Research and read a few well-known fairy tales, and write a summary for each fairy tale. Record what you learn in the chart, citing your sources. Then share your findings with a partner and discuss the structure and characteristics of each fairy tale.

FAIRY TALE AND SOURCE	SUMMARY
Cinderella—Grimm Brothers	*Cinderella is very poor. Then she goes to the ball and meets a handsome prince who marries her, and they live happily ever after.*
Jack and the Beanstalk—Old English Tale	*Jack climbs a magic beanstalk and steals from a giant who tries to eat him. He escapes and lives happily ever after.*

Connect In paragraph 7, Gordimer references a number of different home security systems. With a small group, discuss whether anyone knows about these protections or has seen them being used. Have them discuss what happens to the effectiveness of an alarm that falsely goes off too many times.

LEARNING MINDSET

Belonging Remind students that everyone in the classroom is part of a learning community. Everyone belongs—and everyone has something to contribute. When students partner with classmates to discuss the structure and characteristics of each fairy tale they have found in their research, encourage them to take advantage of the different perspectives and ideas each person offers. Working together, they'll be better able to help each other discover patterns in the structure and characteristics of the fairy tales.

CREATE AND PRESENT

Write a Fairy Tale With a partner create a modern fairy tale based on a community or school event that has happened already or you have observed.

- ❑ Introduce the setting and the characters.
- ❑ Include magical or made-up elements like talking animals or creative settings.
- ❑ Have the tale demonstrate some truth about life or a central message.

Present to the Class You and your partner should decide how you would like to present your fairy tale.

- ❑ You can rehearse it and then act it out.
- ❑ You can record it and then show the video.
- ❑ You can present the story and read it aloud or share illustrations.

If you encounter challenges in your process, change the presentation to fit your needs.

Go to the **Writing Studio** for more on writing narratives.

Go to the **Speaking and Listening Studio** for help with presenting a play or acting in a film.

RESPOND TO THE ESSENTIAL QUESTION

How can we come together despite our differences?

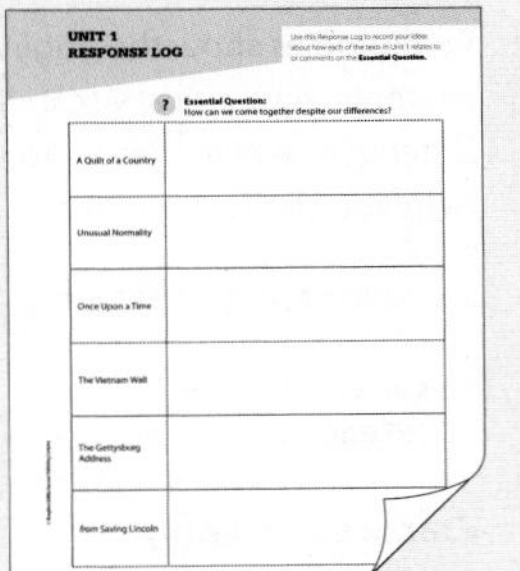

Gather Information Review your annotations and notes on "Once Upon a Time." Then, add relevant information to your Response Log. As you determine which information to include, think about:

- how the family becomes increasingly isolated
- what happens to a society when fear takes over people's lives
- what the cat might symbolize as the people in the story shut themselves off from others

At the end of the unit, use your notes to help you write a personal essay.

ACADEMIC VOCABULARY

As you write and discuss what you learned from the short story, be sure to use the Academic Vocabulary words. Check off each of the words that you use.

- ❑ **enforce**
- ❑ **entity**
- ❑ **internal**
- ❑ **presume**
- ❑ **resolve**

APPLY

CREATE AND PRESENT

Write a Fairy Tale Point out that students can use their research tables from page 42 to help decide on a central message or universal truth to present in their fairy tales. Also note that the directions in this section can serve as a guide for their work. Encourage students to use a graphic organizer to outline their work before they write.

ENGLISH LEARNER SUPPORT

Analyze Spelling Write the words *fairy, community,* and *fly* on the board. Read each word aloud and ask students what they notice. (*the* y *is pronounced differently*) Have students brainstorm other words with *y* at the end, for example, *shy, spy,* and *cry*. Point out that the *y* at the end of a word is often pronounced as a long /i/ sound. However, when words have more than one syllable, the *y* is usually pronounced as a long /e/ sound as in *fairy* and *community*. Review with students that the long /i/ sound and long /e/ sound at the end of words are often spelled with *y*. **SUBSTANTIAL**

For **writing support** for students at varying proficiency levels, see the **Text X-Ray** on page 32D.

Present to the Class Students should consider which of the three options is most appealing to them while planning their presentations. Images could include print photos or illustrations as well as digital images and videos. Point out that students in each pair can take a different role in the presentation to suit their strengths.

RESPOND TO THE ESSENTIAL QUESTION

Allow time for students to add details from "Once Upon a Time" to their Unit 1 Response Logs.

APPLY

CRITICAL VOCABULARY

Answers:

1. *a*
2. *b*
3. *a*
4. *a*
5. *b*

VOCABULARY STRATEGY: Words from Latin

Practice and Apply: Students should compare the English definitions to the Latin definitions:

1. ***distend****: The definitions are similar in that the Latin definition includes "extend" while the English means "expand."*
2. ***intention:*** *The English word* intention, *meaning "an aim or goal," is derivative of the Latin* intentiō, *meaning "a stretching out or effort."*
3. ***audacious****: Both the Latin and the English contain the concept of "bold." The definitions seem to suggest action.*
4. ***intrusion****: The definitions are not similar, but the English definition includes the idea of invasion, which is related to the idea of something being "thrust in" as in the Latin definition.*
5. ***serrate****: Both definitions include an idea of a saw, but the Latin is about the action of sawing while the English is about the form of a saw.*

RESPOND

WORD BANK
distend
intention
audacious
intrusion
serrated

CRITICAL VOCABULARY

Practice and Apply Choose which of the two situations best fits the word's meaning.

1. distend
a. After the Thanksgiving meal our stomachs were uncomfortably full.
b. Platters of food completely covered the holiday table.

2. intention
a. The soccer player showed his determination to shoot for the goal.
b. The soccer player's purpose was to play better in the next game.

3. audacious
a. The daring boy brought gum to the computer lab.
b. A teacher caught the mischievous boy.

4. intrusion
a. The newspaper talked about the girl's wrongful entrance into the clubhouse.
b. The girl's interruption of the conversation made the club members unhappy.

5. serrated
a. The edge of the paper was cut into a decorative pattern.
b. The toothed edge of the paper looked like a set of teeth.

VOCABULARY STRATEGY: Words from Latin

Go to the **Vocabulary Studio** for more on words from Latin.

Etymologies show the origin and historical development of a word. For example, the Critical Vocabulary word *distend* comes from the Latin word *distendere*, which means "to stretch." Exploring the etymology of words can help you clarify their precise meanings and expand your vocabulary.

WORD AND DEFINITION	ETYMOLOGY
surround "to enclose on all sides"	from the Latin *super-* + *unda* "to flow over in waves"

Practice and Apply
Follow these steps for each Critical Vocabulary word, using a chart like the one above:

- Find the etymology of each word in a dictionary. If you need help, in the front or the back of your dictionary there will be a section that explains how the etymology is noted and what the abbreviations mean.
- Compare the Latin definition of each word with the English definition. Are they the same? How does the English definition relate to the Latin meaning?

ENGLISH LEARNER SUPPORT

Confirm Understanding Use the following supports for students of varying proficiency levels:

- Write each critical vocabulary word on the board and draw lines to separate syllables. Pronounce the word several times, with students repeating after you. Then use drawings or images to illustrate the meaning of each word. Remind students that each of these words have Spanish cognates (*distender, intención, audaz, intrusión, serrado*). **SUBSTANTIAL**
- Have students pronounce each word, and help them correct errors as needed. Ask them to use each word in a sentence that demonstrates its meaning. Remind students that each of these words have Spanish cognates (*distender, intención, audaz, intrusión, serrado*). **MODERATE**
- Have students pronounce each word, correcting them as needed. Ask them to come up with a synonym for each word. Challenge students to explain the nuanced differences in the meanings of the vocabulary word and a synonym. **LIGHT**

RESPOND

LANGUAGE CONVENTIONS: Prepositional Phrases

Authors use different types of phrases to add variety and interest to their writing. **Prepositional phrases** are phrases that consist of a preposition and an object of the preposition, such as a noun or a pronoun. Here are some common prepositions and phrases that can be created with them.

PREPOSITION	OBJECT OF PREPOSITION	PREPOSITIONAL PHRASE
from	the street	from the street
before	the rain	before the rain
during	the game	during the game
until	her test	until her test
outside	the gate	outside the gate

Read the following sentence from the story.

> **In a house, in a suburb, in a city, there were a man and his wife who loved each other very much and were living happily ever after.**

Nadine Gordimer might have written the sentence this way:

> **In a suburban house, there were a man and his wife who loved each other very much and were living happily ever after.**

While the second sentence conveys the same meaning, it doesn't hold the same interest as the original sentence. In the original sentence, the author uses the prepositional phrases to create a unique sentence structure that adds variety and emphasis. The prepositional phrases used one after another, *in a house, in a suburb, in a city,* help the author change gears from a story about something that happened to her to a story about another family. The phrases mimic the way a storyteller might use a steady beat or rhythm to start a story.

Notice also that Gordimer used commas to set off each prepositional phrase to emphasize each prepositional phrase.

Examine another sentence from "Once Upon a Time":

> **One evening, the mother read the little boy to sleep with a fairy story from the book the wise old witch had given him at Christmas.**

Although Gordimer could have written several shorter sentences, this sentence with a series of prepositional phrases conveys the sense of a fairy tale. The prepositional phrases add details to the sentence.

Notice that here the prepositional phrases are not set off with commas.

Practice and Apply Rewrite the beginning of your modern fairy tale. Use prepositional phrases to add detail and enhance the storytelling rhythm. Use proper punctuation to set off prepositional phrases.

Go to the **Grammar Studio** for more on prepositional phrases.

APPLY

LANGUAGE CONVENTIONS: Prepositional Phrases

Review the information on prepositional phrases. Tell students that identifying prepositional phrases and what they modify can help them understand long sentences.

Note that prepositional phrases can come before or after the noun or verb they modify. Commas are used to set off prepositional phrases that come before what they describe but not for prepositional phrases that follow what they describe.

Point out that the choice of where to put the prepositional phrase in a sentence is up to the writer. Encourage students to try swapping the position of prepositional phrases to see how they change the meaning of the sentence.

Practice and Apply Have partners discuss whether there is the right amount of detail in the beginning of the modern fairy tale, and whether commas are used correctly and effectively. *(Students' answers will vary.)*

ENGLISH LEARNER SUPPORT

Use Prepositions and Prepositional Phrases Explain that in formal English, the prepositions *in*, *on*, and *at* may all describe location. For example, *in* describes a specific point or enclosed space, *on* refers to the surface of something, and *at* indicates a general area.

- Review the following sentences and ask students to identify the prepositional phrases:
  1. They took a ride in the car.
  2. She looked at the flowers on the table. *(in the car, at the flowers, on the table)* **SUBSTANTIAL**
- Ask students to highlight the prepositional phrases in this sentence from "Once Upon a Time": "And he brought the little boy's tricycle from the garden into the house every night, because if the house was surely secure, once locked and with the alarm set, someone might still be able to climb over the wall or the electronically closed gates into the garden." **MODERATE/LIGHT**

THE VIETNAM WALL

Poem by Alberto Ríos

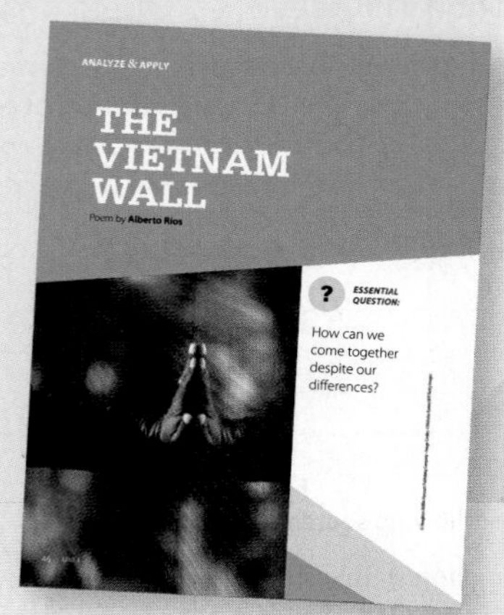

GENRE ELEMENTS

POETRY

Remind students that **poetry** is literature written in meter or verse. A **poem** often includes imagery that appeals to the senses and creates a mood. It may use sound devices such as rhyme, alliteration, assonance, consonance, and repetition to build upon the imagery. Tell students that poems express themes, or messages, about life. In this lesson, students will analyze figurative language and graphic elements to deduce the theme of "The Vietnam Wall."

LEARNING OBJECTIVES

- Analyze a poem's graphic elements and figurative language.
- Research images of the Vietnam Veterans Memorial.
- Create an image display based on the poem.
- Present and discuss image displays.
- **Language** Discuss text features in small groups.

TEXT COMPLEXITY

Quantitative Measures	**The Vietnam Wall**	**Lexile: N/A**
Qualitative Measures	**Ideas Presented** Mostly implied meaning due to figurative language.	
	Structures Used Text features graphic elements that create an image of the poem.	
	Language Used Mostly Tier II and III words.	
	Knowledge Required Text deals mostly with emotions involved at seeing a memorial.	

Online 

RESOURCES

- Unit 1 Response Log
- Selection Audio
-  Reading Studio: Notice & Note
-  Level Up Tutorial: Figurative Language
-  Writing Studio: Writing as a Process
- Speaking and Listening Studio: Participating in Collaborative Discussions
-  "The Vietnam Wall" Selection Test

SUMMARIES

English

The Vietnam Veterans Memorial was dedicated in 1982 to commemorate the 2.7 million military men and women who served in the Vietnam War. In the poem, the speaker describes visiting the memorial and uses figurative language to describe the sudden emotions seeing the wall of names evokes. The speaker walks easily along the wall at first because it is short, but soon the wall towers over him. The speaker feels as if he is trapped in a grave, but before escaping, he stops to look for the names of friends. The wall is a somber place of reflection.

Spanish

El Monumento a los Veteranos de Vietnam fue dedicado en 1982 para conmemorar a los 2.7 millones de militares que sirvieron en la Guerra de Vietnam. En el poema, la voz narrativa describe la visita al monumento y utiliza un lenguaje figurativo para describir las emociones súbitas que evoca el ver los nombres en el muro. La voz narrativa fácilmente pasea frente al muro porque este es bajo, pero pronto se da cuenta de que el muro descolla sobre él. La voz narrativa se siente como si estuviese atrapada en una tumba, pero antes de escapar, se detiene para buscar los nombres de sus amigos. El muro es un sombrío sitio de reflexión.

SMALL-GROUP OPTIONS

Have students work in small groups to read and discuss the selection.

Retelling

- Divide the poem into three parts (for example: lines 1–19, 20–29, 30–44).
- Have students form groups of three, and assign a part to each student in the group. Students read their section, then write two or three sentences summarizing it. Have them focus their summaries on the setting, what the speaker sees, and how the speaker feels.
- Students then read their sentences aloud in turn (or they can summarize orally their section).
- Guide students to discuss how the poem changes in each section. For example: What emotions are expressed in each section? Why do you think those emotions differ in each section? How are they similar in each section?

Questioning the Author

- Have students read the poem, then work in pairs to "question the author."
- Each student takes a turn asking a question about a segment of the poem of their choice, or one you assign to them. For example: *What is the meaning of line _____?*
- Partners in turn answer the question posed by first thinking about it from the perspective of the author. For example: *Why do you think the poet used the phrase _____?*
- To support students, ask for a volunteer to model with you the question-and-answer process before students begin.

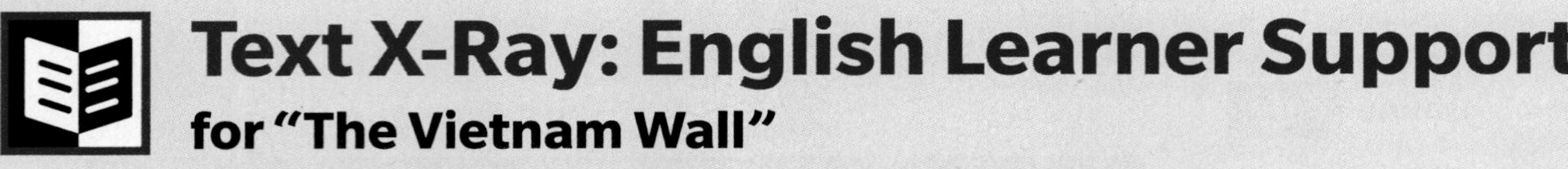

Text X-Ray: English Learner Support
for "The Vietnam Wall"

Use the Text X-Ray and the supports and scaffolds in the Teacher's Edition to help guide students at different proficiency levels through the selection.

INTRODUCE THE SELECTION

DISCUSS MEMORIALS

Explain to students that the Vietnam Veterans Memorial was built to honor or commemorate veterans who fought, died, or were missing in action during the Vietnam War. You may wish to discuss the following:

- A commemoration is a type of ceremony to honor the memory of someone or something. Ask students if they have attended a commemoration before. Can a poem be a form of commemoration?
- Archaeologists study human history by excavating or digging up sites and studying the objects they discover in their "digs." How is a memorial like a dig?
- The U.N. building in New York City, like the Vietnam Veterans Memorial, is a very unique design. Have students preview photographs of both structures to help them understand the comparison used in the poem. Note that the U.N. was founded following World War II to promote peace and security.

CULTURAL REFERENCES

The following words or phrases may be unfamiliar to students:

- *appendix* (line 9): a small organ in the abdomen, often removed surgically when inflamed
- *a shine the boys in the street want to give* (lines 15–16): a shoeshine given by boys who walk the streets looking for customers, which was common in the United States during the early to mid-1900s
- *headlocks* (line 32): someone holding an arm tightly around the head of a person so he or she can't move
- *St. Patrick's Day* (line 34): a holiday celebrating Irish culture, which includes the custom that people might be punished with a pinch for not wearing green

LISTENING

Understand the Central Idea

Read aloud the poem. As you read, discuss how lines 18–21 convey the poem's central idea.

Use the following supports with students at varying proficiency levels:

- Have students work in pairs to read aloud and mark sections of the poem that convey a message. Provide these frames: *The author is showing us* _____. *This represents* _____. **SUBSTANTIAL**
- Have students work in pairs to read aloud and mark sections of the poem that convey a message. Then, ask them to summarize the overall meaning of the poem. Provide these frames: *The author wants us to feel* _____. *The Vietnam Memorial is* _____. **MODERATE**
- Have students summarize their thoughts regarding the poem's central idea and then work with partners to explain what language brought them to their conclusion. Provide these frames: *When the author says* _____, *it makes me feel* _____. *This part reminded me of* _____. **LIGHT**

SPEAKING

Discuss Figurative Language

Draw students' attention to lines 1–10 of the poem. Tell students that figurative language makes a point by comparing two things that are dissimilar.

Use the following supports with students at varying proficiency levels:

- Model how to identify and annotate figurative language in lines 2–5. Have students underline "The magic" to "out of nowhere." Ask: What two things is the author comparing? Provide this frame: *The author is comparing _____ and _____.* **SUBSTANTIAL**
- Review similes, metaphors, and personification. Guide students in identifying metaphors the author uses in lines 6–10. *("scar," "skin of the ground," "black winding Appendix line")* **MODERATE**
- Have small groups reread lines 1–10 and discuss the author's use of figurative language. Provide sentence frames: *Have you considered _____? Adding to that, I felt_____.* **LIGHT**

READING

Analyze Graphic Elements

Draw students' attention to the indentation patterns and varying line lengths of the poem.

Use the following supports with students at varying proficiency levels:

- Present students with images of the Vietnam Wall. Then have them reread the poem. Have them use this sentence frame to express the way the author shapes the poem: *The poem looks like _____.* **SUBSTANTIAL**
- In pairs, have students discuss indentation patterns and line lengths in the poem. Provide sentence frames to help them share their thoughts: *In line _____, the author indents the poem to show _____.* **MODERATE**
- Have students discuss the poem's line lengths and graphic elements in small groups. Encourage students to reread the poem and paraphrase lines to confirm their understanding. **LIGHT**

WRITING

Create an Imagery Board

Work with students to read the imagery board assignment on Student Edition page 53.

Use the following supports with students at varying proficiency levels:

- Reread the poem as students follow along in the text. Have them mark two words that seem important to the topic. Then help them use these words as labels for their images. **SUBSTANTIAL**
- Provide these frames to help students write descriptions of their images: *This image shows _____. This image helps me understand _____.* **MODERATE**
- Have students work with a partner to search for images and write notes about whether the images they find can be tied to specific portions of the poem. **LIGHT**

Connect to the ESSENTIAL QUESTION

"The Vietnam Wall" explores the ways in which shared tragedy and loss can unite people of vastly different backgrounds in shared concern.

THE VIETNAM WALL

Poem by **Alberto Ríos**

ESSENTIAL QUESTION:

How can we come together despite our differences?

QUICK START

How much do you know about the Vietnam Veterans Memorial? List three things you think are true and three questions you have. Share your assumptions and questions with your group.

ANALYZE GRAPHIC ELEMENTS

Think of a few of the **graphic elements** you've seen in the texts you've read. Your list might include photos, headings, captions, sidebar features, charts, and words emphasized in boldfaced or italic type. Each graphic element is there for a specific purpose; it adds to your experience as a reader and contributes to what you know about the text.

Poets create graphic effects through the way they organize type on the page. The author of "The Vietnam Wall" made intentional decisions about graphic elements including line length, punctuation, capitalization, word position, and the overall shape of the poem on the page.

FROM "THE VIETNAM WALL"	GRAPHIC ELEMENTS
I **Have seen it** **And I like it: The magic,** **The way like cutting onions** **It brings water out of nowhere.**	• The word "I" by itself on line 1 focuses the reader's attention on the speaker. • Ending line 2 in the middle of a thought builds tension. • The colon in line 3 tells the reader that more information is coming about what the author likes and why.

In this poem, most lines are short, averaging about five words each. The narrator speaks in short, choppy phrases. This effect builds suspense and suggests that the narrator's experience of the wall is an emotional experience. As a whole, the poem visually resembles the physical structure of the wall.

GENRE ELEMENTS: POETRY

- includes imagery that appeals to the senses
- includes sound devices such as rhyme, alliteration, assonance, consonance, and repetition
- creates a mood
- expresses a theme, or message about life

TEACH

QUICK START

Have students answer and discuss the Quick Start question and clarify any misconceptions about the Vietnam Veterans Memorial. Students might remember that the memorial was designed by a young woman, Maya Lin, after winning a national competition. They may remember its location *(Washington, DC)*, that it is made of polished black stone, and has thousands of names of people who died or were missing in action in the Vietnam War.

ANALYZE GRAPHIC ELEMENTS

Review the information about graphic elements with students. Explain that words themselves can become graphic elements when their arrangement on the page contributes to or enhances their meaning. Help students recognize how these five lines from "The Vietnam Wall," by their gradually increasing length, reflect the shape of the monument itself.

TEACH

ANALYZE FIGURATIVE LANGUAGE

Remind students that poets combine precise literal terms with figurative language to convey complex ideas. Figurative language ignores the literal meaning of words in order to show or imply relationships between diverse things. It expresses images and emotions by using words in unusual contexts. Read aloud the example from "The Vietnam Wall." Discuss how the comparison of the wall to a scar emphasizes the healing process as well as the painful and divisive effects of the war.

ANNOTATION MODEL

Remind students of the annotation ideas in the Graphic Elements chart on page 47. Point out that they may follow these suggestions or use a system of their own for marking up the selection in their texts. They may choose to color-code their annotations by using highlighters. Their notes in the margin may include questions about ideas that are unclear or topics about which they want to learn more.

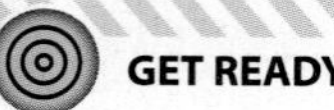

GET READY

ANALYZE FIGURATIVE LANGUAGE

A writer using literal language states the facts. **Figurative language** makes a point by comparing two things that are dissimilar. Examples of figurative language include similes, metaphors, and personification.

Similes and metaphors are the basic elements of figurative language. A **simile** uses *like* or *as* to compare two unlike things. A **metaphor** directly compares two things by saying that one thing *is* another. Figurative language creates mental pictures that help the reader visualize what the poet is describing.

WRITING STYLE	EXAMPLE
Literal Language	At seven feet, seven inches tall, basketball player Manute Bol was taller than his opponents.
Figurative Language	**Simile:** Manute Bol loomed over opponents like a grown man in a crowd of toddlers.
	Metaphor: To Bol, the opposing guards were the grass beneath his tremendous feet.

Authors use **personification** to give human qualities to an object, animal, or idea. Personification can emphasize an idea or create an emotional effect.

PERSONIFICATION IN "THE VIETNAM WALL"	EFFECT
Invisible from one side, a scar Into the skin of the ground From the other, a black winding Appendix line.	The author compares the memorial to a scar from an appendix operation. This **personification** helps readers understand that the Vietnam War left a "scar" on the American conscience.

As you read "The Vietnam Wall," watch for examples of graphic elements and figurative language. Notice what the author conveys through the use of these elements, and the effect they have on you.

ANNOTATION MODEL

NOTICE & NOTE

As you read, makes notes about the graphic elements and figurative language that are striking to you. Write your observations as well as your questions in the margins of your text. This model shows one reader's notes about lines 17–21 of "The Vietnam Wall."

One name. And then more
Names, long lines, lines of names until
They are the shape of the U.N. building
Taller than I am: I have walked
Into a grave.

"lines," "names" ⟶ repeated words for emphasis

metaphor compares seeing the wall to walking into a grave

NOTICE & NOTE

BACKGROUND

The Vietnam Veterans Memorial was dedicated in 1982 to commemorate the 2.7 million military men and women who served in the Vietnam conflict. There are approximately 58,272 names inscribed in the wall in chronological order from the first death, injury, or missing-in-action date to the last. The polished black granite V-shaped wall was designed by Maya Lin. **Alberto Ríos** *(b. 1952) grew up in the U.S.-Mexican border town of Nogales, Arizona. He has published numerous award-winning books of poetry, three books of short stories, and a memoir. In 2013, Ríos was named the first Poet Laureate of Arizona. He lives in Tempe and teaches at Arizona State University.*

THE VIETNAM WALL

Poem by Alberto Ríos

SETTING A PURPOSE

As you read, consider how the poem expresses the reaction of visitors to the Vietnam Veterans Memorial. Write down the questions and observations you generate as you read.

I
Have seen it
And I like it: The magic,
The way like cutting onions
It brings water out of nowhere.
Invisible from one side, a scar
Into the skin of the ground
From the other, a black winding
Appendix line.
 A dig.
 An archaeologist can explain.
The walk is slow at first
Easy, a little black marble wall
Of a dollhouse,

Notice & Note

You can use the side margins to notice and note signposts in the text.

ANALYZE GRAPHIC ELEMENTS

Annotate: Circle the one word in line 1.

Connect: Why do you think this is the only word in the first line?

TEACH

QUICK START

Explain that the Vietnam War, fought between 1964 and 1973, resulted in the deaths of more than 58,000 U.S. soldiers and more than a million Vietnamese (who refer to the conflict as "the American War"). The war sharply divided the people of the United States; massive protests erupted throughout the country, many of which were led by students and returning veterans. The Vietnam Veterans Memorial was designed to bring Americans together by avoiding disputes over the war and by honoring the Americans who lost their lives.

SETTING A PURPOSE

Direct students to use the Setting a Purpose prompt to focus their reading.

ANALYZE GRAPHIC ELEMENTS

Remind students that the positioning and organization of words in a poem can enhance its meaning. (***Answer:*** *It might emphasize the speaker's first-person experience at the memorial, or it may reinforce a pause to suggest that the speaker has carefully considered his or her reaction to the experience.)*

For **listening, speaking, and reading support** for students at varying proficiency levels, see the **Text X-Ray** on pages 46C–46D.

ENGLISH LEARNER SUPPORT

Understand Directionality Read lines 1–11 aloud. Have students follow along with their fingers, tapping the page every time they pass a period. Ask the following yes-or-no questions: Did your finger move from left to right as you followed along? *(yes)* Did it move from the top of the page to the bottom? *(yes)* Point out that poetry is read from left to right and top to bottom, just like other writing. Tell them that poets sometimes use punctuation differently from writers of prose. For example, point out that the periods in the poem do not always come at the end of sentences. **SUBSTANTIAL**

TEACH

ANALYZE FIGURATIVE LANGUAGE

Point out that **figurative language** often draws familiar comparisons to suggest certain feelings associated with a subject. Discuss the different types of feelings that the comparisons in lines 6–21 might suggest. *(Feelings might include pain, detachment, innocence, reflection, desire for peace, or despair.) (**Answer:** The poet uses metaphors to compare characteristics of the wall to a scar, an archaeological dig, a dollhouse wall, a shoeshine, the shape of the UN building, and a grave.)*

ANALYZE GRAPHIC ELEMENTS

Point out that indentations in poetry often signal changes in rhythm, tone, and perspective. *(**Answer:** Lines 23–25 indicate a change in the speaker's attitude, from subjective reflection to the sharp recognition of people categorized by their order of death that ends with "screaming." The indentation of line 36 emphasizes its ambiguity: it might refer to holiday behavior, why flowers are stuffed into the wall, or why the soldiers died.)*

NOTICE & NOTE

ANALYZE FIGURATIVE LANGUAGE

Annotate: Mark the use of figurative language in lines 6-21. What type of figurative language is this?

Interpret: What does the narrator compare the wall to in these lines?

ANALYZE GRAPHIC ELEMENTS

Annotate: Mark the lines that are indented on lines 23–25.

Interpret: Why do you think the author chose to indent these words? What other words or phrases did he indent, and why?

A smoothness, a shine
The boys in the street want to give.
One name. And then more
Names, long lines, lines of names until
They are the shape of the U.N. building[1]
Taller than I am: I have walked
Into a grave.
And everything I expect has been taken away, like that, quick:
  The names are not alphabetized.
  They are in the order of dying.
  An alphabet of—somewhere—screaming.
I start to walk out. I almost leave
But stop to look up names of friends,
My own name. There is somebody
Severiano Ríos.
Little kids do not make the same noise
Here, junior high school boys don't run
Or hold each other in headlocks.
No rules, something just persists
Like pinching on St. Patrick's Day
Every year for no green.
  No one knows why.
Flowers are forced
Into the cracks
Between sections
Men have cried
At this wall.
I have
Seen them.

[1] **U. N. Building:** headquarters of the United Nations in New York City.

WHEN STUDENTS STRUGGLE . . .

Analyze Figurative Language Have partners create a chart that lists examples of figurative language in the poem. Encourage them to circle the words *like* or *as* to help them identify similes. Then help them to identify the comparison that each example makes.

Example	Type of Figurative Speech
a little black marble wall / Of a dollhouse	*metaphor*
Like pinching on St. Patrick's day	*simile*

For additional support, go to the **Reading Studio** and assign the following **Level Up Tutorial: Figurative Language.**

NOTICE & NOTE

CHECK YOUR UNDERSTANDING

Answer these questions before moving on to the **Analyze the Text** section on the following page.

1 Which of the following is an example of figurative language used to describe the memorial?

A *The boys in the street want to give*

B *Names, long lines, lines of names*

C *My own name. There is somebody / Severiano Ríos.*

D *A scar into the skin of the ground*

2 The speaker compares the wall to —

F a dollhouse

G St. Patrick's Day

H his relative

J onions

3 At one point, the speaker starts to leave the memorial. Why does he decide to stay?

A To see why people are screaming

B To look for names he recognizes

C To leave flowers

D To visit the U.N. Building

TEACH

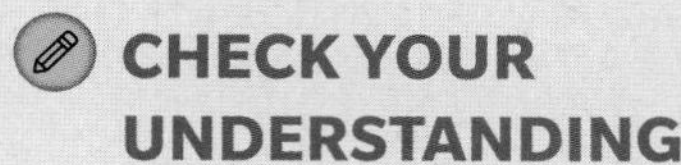

CHECK YOUR UNDERSTANDING

Have students answer the questions independently.

Answers:

1. *D*
2. *F*
3. *B*

If students answer any questions incorrectly, have them reread the text to confirm their understanding. Then they may proceed to ANALYZE THE TEXT on page 52.

ENGLISH LEARNER SUPPORT

Oral Assessment Use the following questions to assess students' comprehension and speaking skills.

1. How is the memorial like a scar? *(Both relate to healing.)*
2. Which does the speaker compare to the wall: a dollhouse, St. Patrick's Day, his name, or onions? *(a dollhouse)*
3. The speaker almost leaves the memorial. Why does he stay? *(The speaker stops "to look up names of friends" and his own name.)*
ALL LEVELS

APPLY

ANALYZE THE TEXT

Possible answers:

1. **DOK 2** *The speaker compares the experience of entering the memorial to walking into a grave. Gradually, he is overcome by the sheer number of names and what each name represents. The names seem to dissolve into a meaningless, screaming alphabet.*
2. **DOK 3** *The narrator initially "likes" the memorial. Then the mood becomes more solemn. He mentions tears and cites grown men crying. Seeing his own last name on the wall heightens his personal connection.*
3. **DOK 4** *The poem forms a sideways triangle. It looks like the V-shape of the memorial wall.*
4. **DOK 3** *The central idea is that the memorial has emotional impact on visitors as they contemplate those who died.*
5. **DOK 2** *The speaker repeats the words "lines" and "names." The former emphasizes the length of the wall and the thousands of names inscribed on it. The repetition of names draws attention to the human toll of war.*

RESEARCH

Model using advanced search options to filter image search results by image type, orientation, color, or source. Remind students to review images for credibility and bias and to cite sources. (*Students' sketches and thoughts will vary.*)

RESPOND

ANALYZE THE TEXT

Support your responses with evidence from the text. NOTEBOOK

1. **Interpret** Reread lines 20–25. What image is conveyed by the metaphor? How does that image express the speaker's emotions?
2. **Evaluate** Over the course of the poem, the author describes several responses to the wall. What are they? Cite text evidence for each.
3. **Analyze** The Vietnam Veterans Memorial forms a V-shape. How does the physical shape of the poem reflect the shape of the wall?
4. **Draw Conclusions** What is the central idea of the poem? How does the poet use his subject—the Vietnam Veterans Memorial—to convey that central idea?
5. **Identify Patterns** What words or images appear in this poem again and again? What is the effect of this repetition?

RESEARCH

Search for photos of the Vietnam Veterans Memorial. Look for images that depict different views of the wall and include people's reactions to it. Sketch two images that had an impact on you, and tell why.

SKETCH OF IMAGE	YOUR THOUGHTS

RESEARCH TIP
Be sure to use only reputable sources for your information, including sites you know and trust, those your teachers recommend, and those with *.edu*, *.org*, or *.gov* addresses.

WHEN STUDENTS STRUGGLE . . .

Reteaching: Analyze Figurative Language
Work with students to clarify key differences between similes and metaphors. Review how a simile uses the words *like* or *as* to compare two things, and a metaphor compares directly by stating how one thing *is* another. Have students work with a partner using the sentence frames to write their own simile and metaphor.

Simile: *I am* ____ *as a/an* ____.

Metaphor: *My* ____ *is a/an* ____.

For additional support, go to the **Reading Studio** and assign the following **Level Up Tutorial: Figurative Language.**

CREATE AND PRESENT

Create an Imagery Board With a partner or a small group, create an imagery board in which you find photos that relate to "The Vietnam Wall," to the memorial itself, or to images mentioned in the poem.

- ❑ Search online or draw pictures of at least 3–5 images from the poem.
- ❑ Match those images with specific lines from the poem.
- ❑ Take notes about the meanings of the images and how they enhance your understanding of both the Vietnam Veterans Memorial and the poem. Think about what each image conveys and how it appeals to different senses or emotions.

Present Your Work Share your imagery board with another group, or you may have a gallery walk with different image boards in the class.

- ❑ Describe each image and tell why you chose those images.
- ❑ Read the lines of the poem and interpret them for your classmates.
- ❑ Explain why you chose each of these images.
- ❑ Speak slowly and clearly and look at your audience as you share your ideas. Use language that is appropriate for your audience.
- ❑ Listen carefully as others present, and ask thoughtful questions. Point out differences in images and interpretations between groups.

Go to the **Speaking and Listening Studio** for help with having a group discussion.

RESPOND TO THE ESSENTIAL QUESTION

How can we come together despite our differences?

Gather Information Review your annotations and notes on "The Vietnam Wall" and add relevant details to your response log. As you determine which information to include, think about how memorials honoring the dead can bring people together.

At the end of the unit, you will use your notes to write a personal essay.

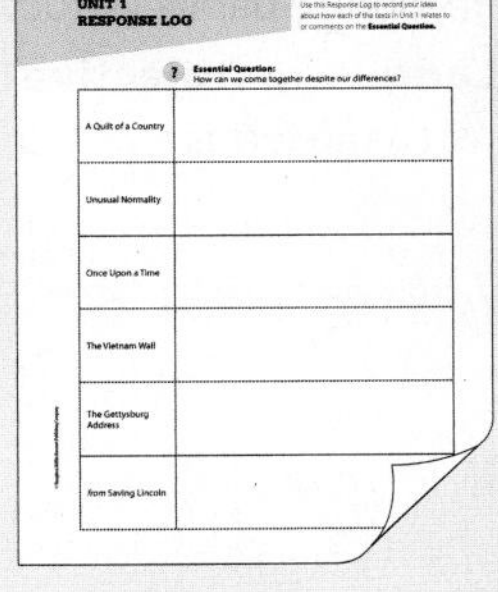

UNIT 1 RESPONSE LOG

Use this Response Log to record your ideas about how each of the texts in Unit 1 relates to or comments on the **Essential Question.**

Essential Question: How can we come together despite our differences?

A Quilt of a Country	
Unusual Normality	
Once Upon a Time	
The Vietnam Wall	
The Gettysburg Address	
from Saving Lincoln	

ACADEMIC VOCABULARY

As you write and discuss what you learned from the poem, be sure to use the Academic Vocabulary words. Check off each of the words that you use.

- ❑ **enforce**
- ❑ **entity**
- ❑ **internal**
- ❑ **presume**
- ❑ **resolve**

APPLY

CREATE AND PRESENT

Create an Imagery Board Explain that although poetry, drawing, and photography are different mediums, they all convey meaning and express ideas. Explain that like the poem, the drawings and photos on their imagery boards should be organized in a way that develops a message. Have students review the poem and note how the descriptions progress from the general to the specific. Discuss the effect of this organization and suggest that students consider organizing their imagery boards using this approach.

For **writing support** for students at varying proficiency levels, see the **Text X-Ray** on page 46D.

Present Your Work Encourage partners to plan and prepare notes for their presentations and to practice delivering it with each other. Suggest that they anticipate questions that the audience members might raise and develop appropriate responses.

RESPOND TO THE ESSENTIAL QUESTION

Allow students time to add details from "The Vietnam Wall" to their Unit 1 Response Logs.

THE GETTYSBURG ADDRESS

Speech by Abraham Lincoln

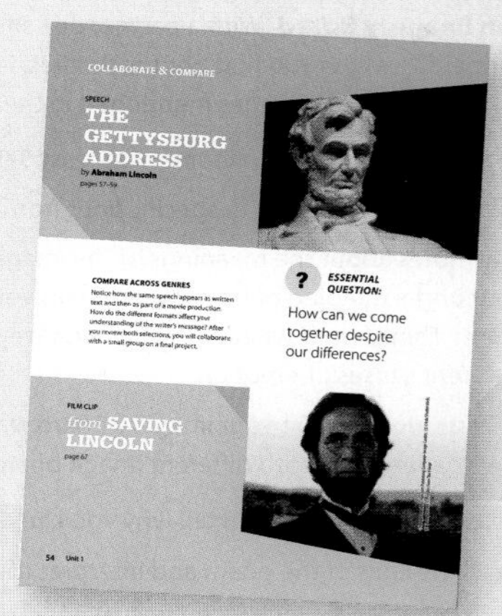

GENRE ELEMENTS

SPEECH

Remind students that a **speech** is used to send a clear message directly to its audience. In this lesson, students will analyze a speech to understand its purpose and its intended audience. Effective speeches typically include rhetorical devices—specific words and language structures that make a message memorable. Students will learn to recognize certain rhetorical devices and determine how they are used to achieve an author's purpose.

LEARNING OBJECTIVES

- Analyze a speech to determine the author's purpose, the audience, and rhetorical devices used.
- Conduct research about "The Gettysburg Address."
- Create and deliver an oral critique of "The Gettysburg Address."
- Participate in a small-group discussion as preparation for a critique.
- Determine the contextual meaning of multiple-meaning words.
- Recognize parallel structures and understand their effects.
- **Language Objective** Discuss rhetorical devices with a partner using the terms *repetition* and *parallelism*.

TEXT COMPLEXITY

Quantitative Measures	**The Gettysburg Address** Lexile: 1170L
Qualitative Measures	**Ideas Presented** Mostly literal, explicit meaning; one main purpose, but with two applications.
	Structures Used Text organization of main ideas and details is complex but clear.
	Language Used More complex sentence structure, with some allusive language.
	Knowledge Required Historical references require some specialized knowledge.

Online 

RESOURCES

- Unit 1 Response Log
- Selection Audio
- Reading Studio: Notice & Note
- Level Up Tutorial: Elements of an Argument
- Speaking and Listening Studio: Giving a Presentation
- Vocabulary Studio: Multiple-Meaning Words
- "The Gettysburg Address" Selection Test

SUMMARIES

English

President Abraham Lincoln presented "The Gettysburg Address" as part of the ceremony dedicating a burial ground at the site of the Battle of Gettysburg. Lincoln reminds his audience that the United States was founded on liberty and that the Civil War is now being fought to preserve the nation and its founding principles. He then charges his listeners to honor the sacrifices made by the war dead by dedicating themselves to preserving the nation and giving it "a new birth of freedom."

Spanish

El presidente Abraham Lincoln presentó el "Discurso de Gettysburg" como parte de una ceremonia dedicada al cementerio en el emplazamiento de la Batalla de Gettysburg. Lincoln le recuerda a su público que Estados Unidos fue una nación fundada sobre la base de la libertad y que la Guerra Civil está siendo librada para preservar la nación y sus principios fundadores. Luego ordena a sus oyentes que honren los sacrificios hechos por los muertos de la guerra dedicándose a preservar la nación y a darle "un nuevo nacimiento de libertad".

SMALL-GROUP OPTIONS

Have students work in small groups to read and discuss the selection.

Three-Minute Review

- After students have read "The Gettysburg Address" for the first time, direct students to form groups of two or three students each.
- Pose a question to guide a group review, such as "What is the main idea of Lincoln's speech?"
- Set the timer for three minutes. During that time, have students discuss possible answers to the question and then write at least one clarifying question to be handed in per group.
- Review the speech, or prepare students for a second reading, by discussing the clarifying questions.

Numbered Heads Together

- Have students form groups of four. Count off 1-2-3-4 to assign each student a number within a group.
- Pose a question to the class, such as "What was the importance of 'The Gettysburg Address'?" Alternatively, ask a question posed in Respond: Analyze the Text.
- Have students discuss responses to the question in their groups.
- Call a number from 1 to 4. Each student with that number responds for the group.

Text X-Ray: English Learner Support
for "The Gettysburg Address"

Use the Text X-Ray and the supports and scaffolds in the Teacher's Edition to help guide students at different proficiency levels through the selection.

INTRODUCE THE SELECTION

DISCUSS THE GETTYSBURG ADDRESS

In this lesson, students will discuss the historic speech in which President Abraham Lincoln helped dedicate a cemetery at the site of the Battle of Gettysburg. Read the Background note aloud and explain the following terms:

- In this context, an *address* is a speech.
- A *civil war* is a war fought between people or regions of the same country.
- *Gettysburg* is a town in the state of Pennsylvania.
- A *dedication* is a ceremony to honor and respect people, an event, or a place.

Have volunteers use the terms to complete these sentence frames:

- *President Lincoln delivered an* _____.
- *Soldiers died during the* _____ *on the battlefield at* _____.
- *Lincoln honored the dead at a ceremony of* _____.

CULTURAL REFERENCES

The following words or phrases may be unfamiliar to students:

- *score* (paragraph 1): a group of 20
- *our fathers* (paragraph 1): the men who founded, or set up, the United States as a new nation
- *all men are created equal* (paragraph 1): the idea that all people are born with equal rights to freedom and justice
- *final resting place* (paragraph 2): a cemetery, or a place where the dead are buried
- *fitting and proper* (paragraph 2): appropriate; correct
- *poor power* (paragraph 3): weak ability
- *gave the last full measure of devotion* (paragraph 3): died in support of their cause
- *in vain* (paragraph 3): for no purpose

LISTENING

Analyze an Audience

Direct students to *our* in paragraph 1 of the text and *we* in paragraph 2. Explain that the use of *our* and *we* helps the speaker connect with the audience and makes listeners feel included as partners.

Have students listen as you read aloud paragraphs 1–2. Explain footnotes as needed. Use the following supports with students at varying proficiency levels:

- Tell students to respond *yes* or *no* to questions about what they just heard. For example, ask: Was he speaking to politicians in Washington, DC? *(no)* Was he speaking to a crowd at Gettysburg? *(yes)* **SUBSTANTIAL**
- Have students respond to questions about the passage. For example, ask: What does Lincoln mean when he says, "we are engaged in a great civil war"? *(we are fighting a huge civil war)* Who is "we"? *(the crowd at Gettysburg)* **MODERATE**
- After listening to the passage, have partners discuss details that suggest the intended audience of the speech. **LIGHT**

SPEAKING

Discuss Rhetorical Devices

Have students use paragraph 3 to discuss the use of rhetorical devices in the text. Circulate around the room to make sure that students are using the terms correctly.

Use the following supports with students at varying proficiency levels:

- Read aloud paragraph 3 with students while clapping on repeated words and phrases. **SUBSTANTIAL**
- Have two volunteers read aloud the first sentence of paragraph 3. Ask students: What words were repeated? *(we cannot)* How many times do the words appear in that sentence? *(three)* What type of rhetorical device is used here? *(parallelism)* **MODERATE**
- Have partners read aloud sentences from paragraph 3, pausing after each sentence to discuss examples of repetition and parallelism. **LIGHT**

READING

Analyze an Argument

Explain to students that, in this context, an argument is not a disagreement; rather, it is writing that makes a claim and supports it with reasons and evidence. Refer students to paragraphs 2 and 3 of the text.

Review terms, reminding students that authors provide reasons to support a *claim*, or the author's position on an issue. Then use the following supports with students at varying proficiency levels:

- Read aloud paragraph 2. Have students complete this sentence stating the claim: *Dedicating a portion of the field to a burial ground is "altogether ______." (fitting and proper)* **SUBSTANTIAL**
- Have small groups identify the claim in paragraph 2. Then point to "they gave their last full measure of devotion" in paragraph 3. Have groups complete this sentence stem: *This statement is a reason that supports the claim because ______. (it tells why dedicating the burial ground is fitting and proper)* **MODERATE**
- Have partners reread paragraph 3 and then complete this sentence stem with a reason Lincoln provides in his speech to support his claim: *At the end, Lincoln claims that American democracy will survive if ______. (Americans become more dedicated to the cause for which the soldiers died)* **LIGHT**

WRITING

Write Notes for an Oral Presentation

Work with students to clarify and support their preparation for the oral presentation assignment on Student Edition page 61.

Review connecting terms with students. Then use the following supports with students at varying proficiency levels:

- Remind students of the purpose of connecting words, starting with *and*, *but*, and *or*. Have them choose the correct word to complete sentences. For example: *Many soldiers died at Gettysburg, ______ people gathered to honor them. (and)* **SUBSTANTIAL**
- Have partners choose a rhetorical device from the speech and write a sentence that uses the connecting word *because* to explain its effect. **MODERATE**
- Provide a list of connecting terms such as *because, since, so that,* and *when*. Urge students to include two of them in their notes. **LIGHT**

Connect to the ESSENTIAL QUESTION

The United States has struggled through several periods of divisiveness, but none so catastrophic as the Civil War (1861–1865). During that era, President Abraham Lincoln took on the daunting goal of reunifying the country. But was such a goal achievable, given the fact that viewpoints were so different, and so fervently held, that they had led to open warfare? Lincoln was devoted to the cause of having Americans come together again, and "The Gettysburg Address" was one of the ways in which he furthered that cause.

COMPARE ACROSS GENRES

Ask students if they have ever read a book and then seen a movie adaptation of that same book. Did the book help them to understand the movie? Did the movie reveal aspects of the text that they hadn't considered? Tell students that in this Collaborate & Compare lesson, they will read the text of Abraham Lincoln's "Gettysburg Address" and watch a clip from a film in which an actor portraying Lincoln delivers that speech.

COLLABORATE & COMPARE

SPEECH

THE GETTYSBURG ADDRESS

by **Abraham Lincoln**

pages 57–59

COMPARE ACROSS GENRES

Notice how the same speech appears as written text and then as part of a movie production. How do the different formats affect your understanding of the writer's message? After you review both selections, you will collaborate with a small group on a final project.

ESSENTIAL QUESTION:

How can we come together despite our differences?

FILM CLIP

from SAVING LINCOLN

page 67

LEARNING MINDSET

Growth Mindset Remind students that a *growth mindset* means believing that you can improve your skills and get smarter by taking on challenges and pushing yourself. Some students may find the language or style of "The Gettysburg Address" to be challenging. Encourage students to look at this speech—one of the most important speeches in American history—as an opportunity to set higher goals and stretch beyond their comfort zone.

The Gettysburg Address

QUICK START

During difficult times, good leaders address people with words that inspire and encourage them. What should a leader say when things are going wrong? With a group, discuss what a strong leader has said to you when you have been discouraged.

ANALYZE PURPOSE AND AUDIENCE

A person may write a speech for one or more reasons. These reasons are called the **author's purpose**. An author's purpose might be to inform or explain, to persuade, to express thoughts or feelings, or to entertain. Writers also craft their speeches for a particular **audience,** or group of people.

SPEAKER'S PURPOSE	INTENDED EFFECT ON AUDIENCE
Inform or explain	The audience gains new information from the speech.
Persuade	The audience is persuaded to adopt the speaker's position on an argument.
Express thoughts and feelings	The audience gets a better sense of who the speaker is and what he or she cares about.
Entertain	The audience is amused or experiences enjoyment.

As you read "The Gettysburg Address," note how Lincoln addresses his audience and how he achieves his purpose.

ANALYZE RHETORICAL DEVICES

To help advance a purpose, an author will often use **rhetorical devices**, or specific words and language structures that make a message memorable. Rhetorical devices to look for in "The Gettysburg Address" include:

- **Repetition:** the use of the same word or words more than once. Repetition is used to emphasize key ideas.
- **Parallelism:** a form of repetition in which a grammatical pattern is repeated. Parallelism is used to create rhythm and evoke emotions.
- **Understatement:** a technique of creating emphasis by saying less than is literally true. Understatement can be used for humorous effect, to create satire, or to achieve a restrained tone.

As you read "The Gettysburg Address," notice the repeated words and parallel clauses and phrases, such as *we are engaged, we are met, we have come.* Also look for statements that may downplay, or lessen, the seriousness of the situation. Think about how Lincoln uses repetition, parallelism, and understatement to advance his purpose.

GENRE ELEMENTS: SPEECH

- directly addresses and connects with audiences
- uses rhetorical devices to achieve specific purposes
- contains a clear message, stated near the beginning
- ends memorably

ENGLISH LEARNER SUPPORT

Apply Directionality Demonstrate the directionality of English using the Analyze Purpose and Audience chart. Explain that each column heading applies to the text in all the rows directly beneath it (a vertical direction). Model how to read the chart by tracing with your finger while reading the first example of Speaker's Purpose from the first row, top left, and then tracking to the right (a horizontal direction) to read the Intended Effect on Audience. Have students follow along with their finger as you read the text in the rest of the chart. Point out that the text within each column follows the same rules of directionality.

SUBSTANTIAL/MODERATE

QUICK START

Have students consider difficult circumstances made easier by the words and assistance of a "leader," whether a friend, coach, relative, or community member. As students discuss the Quick Start question, remind them that inspirational, encouraging words have value in a wide range of situations—for example, during sports competitions, at an accident scene or in a hospital, and in after-school clubs and activities.

ANALYZE PURPOSE AND AUDIENCE

As you guide students through the chart of purposes and audiences, note that "The Gettysburg Address" can be analyzed as an argument. Invite volunteers to suggest a title or topic for a speech written for each purpose listed in the chart. *(Informative: How to Start an Exercise Program; Entertain: My First Driving Lesson)* Point out that a speech may have more than one purpose but that one probably will dominate.

Explain that knowing the intended audience of a speech helps in determining the author's purpose. Ask students to discuss a speech they have heard. Who was the audience? What was the purpose of the speech?

ANALYZE RHETORICAL DEVICES

Guide students through the bulleted list of rhetorical devices. Explain that repetition, parallelism, and understatement appear in other types of writing but are frequently found in speeches, where they can drive home a message to an audience. Tell students that identifying rhetorical devices will help them to understand an author's message and purpose. Suggest that students use these questions to help them identify rhetorical devices and understand their meaning and purpose:

- What does this statement mean?
- How does it create emphasis?
- What is its effect on the audience?

TEACH

CRITICAL VOCABULARY

Remind students to read all the sentences before deciding which word best completes each one.

Answers:

1. *a. conceive*
2. *d. perish*
3. *c. resolve*
4. *b. detract*

■ English Learner Support

Use Cognates Tell students that three of the Critical Vocabulary words have Spanish cognates: *conceive/concebir, resolve/resolver, perish/perecer.* **ALL LEVELS**

LANGUAGE CONVENTIONS

Relate the information about parallel structure to the previous discussion of parallelism as a rhetorical device. Remind students that a **phrase** is a group of related words that does *not* contain both a subject and a predicate but that functions in a sentence as a single part of speech. (For example, a verb phrase functions as a verb, and a prepositional phrase usually functions as an adjective or an adverb.) By contrast, a **clause** is a group of words that contains both a subject and its predicate. Consider the following sentence:

The teacher called on me when I raised my hand.

The teacher called on me is an **independent clause** because it can stand on its own as a sentence. *When I raised my hand* is a **dependent clause** because it needs the independent clause to make its meaning clear.

ANNOTATION MODEL

Remind students that they may underline, circle, highlight, or otherwise mark details from the text that indicate the author's purpose, as well as mark examples of rhetoric. Their notes in the margin may include questions about ideas that are unclear or topics they want to learn more about.

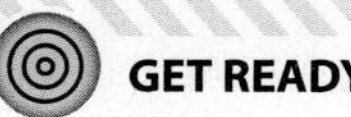

GET READY

CRITICAL VOCABULARY

To preview the Critical Vocabulary words, match the words to their definitions.

1. In a flash of inspiration, Michel was suddenly able to ___________ a brilliant plan to earn money.	a. conceive
2. When the mouse saw a cat about to pounce, the mouse feared she would ___________.	b. detract
3. After earning a poor grade on a math quiz, Asha would ___________ to study harder for the next quiz.	c. resolve
4. One faulty firework did not ___________ from an amazing fireworks show.	d. perish

LANGUAGE CONVENTIONS

One grammatical feature that makes Abraham Lincoln's rhetoric so effective is his use of **parallel structure**, or the repetition of grammatical forms within a sentence. The repetition can occur at the word, phrase, or clause level. Lincoln uses parallel structure as a rhetorical device to express and connect ideas that are related or equal in importance, and to create rhythm and evoke emotions. Here is an example of parallel words from "The Gettysburg Address":

The brave men, living and dead, who struggled here have consecrated it, far above our poor power to add or detract.

As you read "The Gettysburg Address," watch for repetition of words, phrases, and clauses.

ANNOTATION MODEL

NOTICE & NOTE 

Here is how you might annotate to identify the parallel structures Lincoln uses.

Four score and seven years ago our fathers brought forth on this continent, a new nation, conceived in liberty, and dedicated to the proposition that all men are created equal. Now we are engaged in a great civil war, testing whether that nation, or any nation so conceived and so dedicated, can long endure.	Lincoln sets a serious tone and purpose by talking about how America was founded based on the ideas of freedom and equality. parallel structure → "so conceived," "so dedicated"

TEACH

BACKGROUND

*President **Abraham Lincoln** (1809–1865) is considered an American hero for preserving the Union and emancipating the slaves. He was a skillful politician, leader, and orator. One of his most famous speeches was delivered at the dedication of the National Cemetery at Gettysburg, Pennsylvania, in 1863, site of one of the most deadly battles of the Civil War. The victory for the Union forces marked a turning point in the Civil War, but losses on both sides at Gettysburg were staggering: 28,000 Confederate soldiers and 23,000 Union soldiers were killed or wounded. Lincoln was assassinated by John Wilkes Booth in 1865. Lincoln's dedication to the ideals of freedom and equality continue to inspire people around the world.*

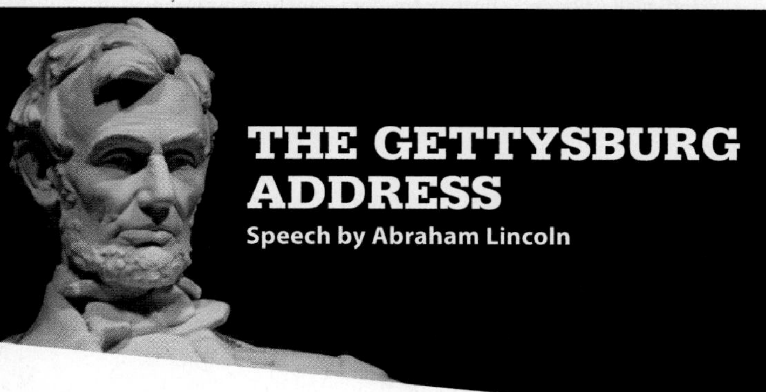

THE GETTYSBURG ADDRESS

Speech by Abraham Lincoln

PREPARE TO COMPARE

As you read, pay attention to how Lincoln's speech emphasizes the importance of ending the Civil War and reuniting the country. This information will help you compare this speech with the video that follows it. If you come across words or passages you do not understand, ask for help from your classmates or your teacher.

1 Four score and seven[1] years ago our fathers brought forth on this continent a new nation, **conceived** in liberty and dedicated to the proposition that all men are created equal.

2 Now we are engaged in a great civil war, testing whether that nation, or any nation so conceived and so dedicated, can long endure. We are met on a great battlefield of that war. We have come to dedicate a portion of that field, as a final resting place for those who here gave their lives that that nation might live. It is altogether fitting and proper that we should do this.

[1] **four score and seven:** eighty-seven.

NOTICE & NOTE

Notice & Note

You can use the side margins to notice and note signposts in the text.

conceive
(kən-sēv´) *v.* to form or develop in the mind; devise

ANALYZE PURPOSE AND AUDIENCE

Annotate: Underline a sentence that tells why the audience has gathered.

Respond: How does Lincoln's tone reflect the audience and occasion?

BACKGROUND

Have students read the Background note. Explain that the Civil War resulted from issues that were not resolved during the ratification of the U.S. Constitution in 1788–1789, particularly the constitutionality of slavery and the right of states to secede. At the end of the Civil War, the Union was preserved and slavery was abolished. The human cost, however was high: at least 620,000 soldiers died, and the economy of the South was devastated.

PREPARE TO COMPARE

Direct students to use the Prepare to Compare prompt to focus their reading.

ANALYZE PURPOSE AND AUDIENCE

Remind students that as authors prepare to write speeches, they think about their audience and the reason that its members will have gathered. This information helps authors select a purpose for writing. Before considering Lincoln's tone, have students think about the audience for this speech and the reason that its members have gathered. (***Answer:*** *Lincoln has a serious tone, which fits the occasion—honoring the soldiers who died at the location.)*

For **listening support** for students at varying proficiency levels, see the **Text X-Ray** on page 54C.

IMPROVE READING FLUENCY

Targeted Passage Read aloud the first two paragraphs of the speech while students follow along silently. Then have students choral read the same passage. Model appropriate pacing, intonation, and expression as you read.

Go to the **Reading Studio** for additional support in developing fluency.

CRITICAL VOCABULARY

conceive: Lincoln declares that the United States was built upon the foundation of a desire for liberty.

ASK STUDENTS to explain the relationship between a nation "conceived in liberty" and the reason that Lincoln was giving this speech. *(Although the nation was conceived in a desire for liberty, not all Americans were free because slavery still existed. It could be argued that the horrific Civil War battle that brought Lincoln to Gettysburg was fought to make it possible for all Americans to be free.)*

CONTRASTS AND CONTRADICTIONS

Have students identify the clue word in the sentence that signals a comparison. *(but)* Point out that Contrasts and Contradictions often reflect the **author's purpose** and help to emphasize one of the author's key points, which in this instance is the grave loss of the soldiers' lives. (***Answer:*** *Lincoln compares the soldiers' deaths, which will be remembered for a long time, with the words of the speech he is giving, which he says will soon be forgotten.)*

ANALYZE RHETORICAL DEVICES

Review that rhetorical devices are specific words and language structures that help to make a message memorable. Ask students to quietly read the sentences containing the repeated word *devotion* before answering the question. (***Answer:*** *Repeating the word emphasizes the importance of carrying on the mission to which the soldiers had been devoted.)*

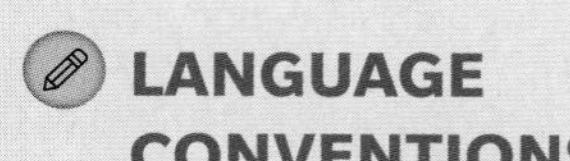

For **speaking and reading support** for students at varying proficiency levels, see the **Text X-Ray** on page 54D.

LANGUAGE CONVENTIONS

Remind students that writers use parallel structure to connect ideas that are related or equal in importance. Read the sentence that includes "of the people, by the people, and for the people," emphasizing its rhythms. Elicit that the word *people* appears at the end of in all three phrases and that its repetition makes an impact, as well. Encourage students to consider the emotions the sentence evokes before answering the question. (***Answer:*** *Lincoln reminds the audience that it is important for people to participate in the government that was created to help them.)*

NOTICE & NOTE

CONTRASTS AND CONTRADICTIONS

Notice & Note: Underline a sentence that shows a contrast or contradiction.

Interpret: What two things does Lincoln compare?

detract
(dĭ-trăkt´) *v.* to take away from

resolve
(rĭ-zŏlv´) *v.* to decide or become determined

perish
(pĕr´ĭsh) *v.* to die or come to an end

ANALYZE RHETORICAL DEVICES

Annotate: Underline the repeated word *devotion*.

Respond: What is the effect of this repetition?

LANGUAGE CONVENTIONS

Annotate: Mark the phrases "of the people, by the people, for the people."

Respond: What does Lincoln's use of parallel structure say about the importance of people's participation in government?

3 But in a larger sense, we cannot dedicate—we cannot consecrate[2]—we cannot hallow[3]—this ground. The brave men, living and dead who struggled here have consecrated it, far above our poor power to add or **detract**. The world will little note, nor long remember what we say here, but it can never forget what they did here. It is for us, the living, rather to be dedicated here to the unfinished work which they who fought here have thus far so nobly advanced. It is rather for us to be here dedicated to the great task remaining before us—that from these honored dead we take increased devotion to that cause for which they gave the last full measure of devotion—that we here highly **resolve** that these dead shall not have died in vain—that this nation, under God, shall have a new birth of freedom—and that government of the people, by the people, for the people shall not **perish** from the earth.

[2] **consecrate:** to dedicate as sacred.
[3] **hallow:** define as holy.

WHEN STUDENTS STRUGGLE . . .

Analyze Parallel Structure Point out that in the final sentence of the speech ("It is rather for us to be here dedicated . . ."), Lincoln uses parallel structure to expand upon the meaning of the "great task." Write "the great task remaining before us" on the board, followed by a list of four bullets. Work with students to identify what should come after each bullet by locating each of the four subordinate clauses that follow a dash and begin with *that*. Help students paraphrase each point in Lincoln's concluding statement.

For additional support, go to the **Reading Studio** and assign the following **Level Up Tutorial: Elements of an Argument.**

NOTICE & NOTE

CHECK YOUR UNDERSTANDING

Answer these questions before moving on to the **Analyze the Text** questions on the following page.

1 In the Gettysburg Address, Lincoln's main idea is that —

- **A** the soldiers died because of injustice
- **B** these men would not die in vain
- **C** the Civil War was over after the Battle of Gettysburg
- **D** America deserved independence and freedom

2 What historic event does Lincoln mention at the beginning of the speech?

- **F** The Emancipation Proclamation
- **G** The arrival of European colonists
- **H** The founding of the United States
- **J** The end of the Civil War

3 What does Lincoln want the audience to do?

- **A** Continue supporting the war effort
- **B** Reject the idea of war
- **C** End the Civil War
- **D** Enlist in the army

CRITICAL VOCABULARY

detract: Lincoln's use of a contrasting clue, the word *add*, helps to make the meaning of *detract* clear.

ASK STUDENTS how Lincoln might have detracted from the soldier's actions. *(possibly by criticizing them or in some other way minimizing their value)*

resolve: Lincoln wants his audience to *resolve*, or determine, that "the dead shall not have died in vain."

ASK STUDENTS how Lincoln's enemies might react to the way he has resolved to honor the dead. *(They might feel threatened by the intensity of his resolve and redouble their efforts to defeat the Union.)*

perish: Lincoln believes that there is a danger that the United States will come to an end.

ASK STUDENTS to discuss the connection between *conceive* in the first sentence of the speech and *perish* in the final sentence. *(What is conceived, or created, can also perish, or be destroyed.)*

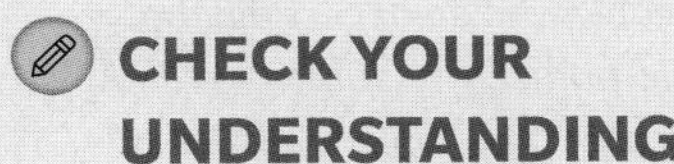

CHECK YOUR UNDERSTANDING

Have students answer the questions independently.

Answers:

1. *B*
2. *H*
3. *A*

If they answer any questions incorrectly, have them reread the text to confirm their understanding. Then they may proceed to ANALYZE THE TEXT on page 60.

ENGLISH LEARNER SUPPORT

Oral Assessment Use the following questions to assess students' comprehension and speaking skills.

1. What is the main idea in Lincoln's "Gettysburg Address"? *(The men who fought at Gettysburg died for a reason.)*
2. Lincoln mentions a historic event at the beginning of the speech. What event does he mention? *(Lincoln mentions the founding of the United States at the beginning of his speech.)*
3. What is Lincoln asking the audience to do? *(Lincoln is asking the people to keep supporting the war.)*

SUBSTANTIAL/MODERATE

APPLY

ANALYZE THE TEXT

Possible answers:

1. **DOK 4:** *Lincoln's two main purposes were to dedicate the cemetery at Gettysburg and to argue that the people of the United States must keep fighting for the nation. Lincoln directly states the first purpose in paragraph 2, by explaining why the audience has gathered. For the second purpose, he tells his listeners that they need to make sure that the "dead shall not have died in vain."*
2. **DOK 2:** *To dedicate means to give time to fulfill a certain purpose, or to honor people by naming something for them. Lincoln repeats this word because the cemetery will be dedicated in the soldiers' honor and because he wants to remind the audience that the soldiers have given their lives for a cause—a cause for which people should continue to fight.*
3. **DOK 2:** *Lincoln uses parallel structure to begin paragraph 3, with the clauses "we cannot dedicate—we cannot consecrate—we cannot hallow—this ground." He does this to make a point that they, the audience, cannot make the site important; the people who died there did that. Lincoln also uses a parallel phrase structure in the final sentence, with the phrases "of the people, by the people, for the people," to remind the audience that the country's government belongs to its people.*
4. **DOK 3:** *Students can name themes such as sacrifice, duty, or unity. Students should make connections between each theme and American values.*
5. **DOK 4:** *The Union triumphed at Gettysburg—although at great cost of life—and Lincoln wants his audience to believe that the Union is able to win the war.*

RESEARCH

Remind students to conduct research on credible web sites. Newspapers and government websites (*.gov*) also may have primary sources.

Connect Students may find conflicting reports from eyewitnesses. Encourage students to examine multiple sources in order to get a well-rounded picture of the response to Lincoln's speech.

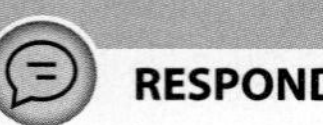

RESPOND

ANALYZE THE TEXT

Support your responses with evidence from the text. NOTEBOOK

1. **Analyze** Why did Lincoln write and deliver "The Gettysburg Address"? What were his two main purposes? Explain using evidence from the speech.
2. **Interpret** The word *dedicate* is repeated several times in the speech. What does *dedicate* mean? What idea does Lincoln emphasize with the repetition of this word?
3. **Identify Patterns** Identify two examples of parallel structure in the speech. How does Lincoln use parallel structure to persuade the audience to accept his message?
4. **Draw Conclusions** Seminal U.S. documents often refer to themes and ideals that are important to the audience they address. What is the **theme**, or underlying message, of "The Gettysburg Address"? Is this theme still important today? Explain the American ideals that the speech upholds.
5. **Notice & Note** Lincoln refers to a "great civil war" and notes that Gettysburg is "a great battlefield of that war." Why do you think Lincoln wanted his audience to believe Gettysburg was important and significant?

RESEARCH

RESEARCH TIP
Choose your sources carefully as you research this topic. Look for valid, reliable sources that cite historical documents. Message boards or presentations by other students may not be reliable sources.

At the time of Lincoln's speech, only the people physically gathered with him at Gettysburg would have heard it. Everyone else would have been aware of it only through word of mouth or through newspaper reports. Find out more about the people who were present to hear Lincoln speak. What were they doing at Gettysburg? What were their reactions? How did the media report on the speech?

RESEARCH QUESTIONS	DETAILS	URL/SOURCE
Who was the audience for the speech?	*Answers will vary, but should mention the large audience, that some people thought the speech was too short, and that media coverage differed on political lines.*	*Sources will vary.*
What was the audience's reaction to the speech?		
How did the media cover the speech?		

Connect Share what you learn in a panel discussion or brief presentation. Be sure to identify the source for each piece of information you use to support your ideas.

LEARNING MINDSET

Belonging Encourage students to ask for help from a classmate or from you, the teacher, if they are struggling with an Analyze the Text question. Remind students that they are all part of a learning community and should support each other as learners, celebrating their triumphs and learning from their mistakes.

CREATE AND PRESENT

Deliver an Oral Presentation "The Gettysburg Address" is one of the most famous speeches in U.S. history. Prepare an oral presentation in which you critique the speech for its effectiveness.

- ❑ Reread the speech silently to yourself, making notes about Lincoln's main points and the important ideas he emphasizes.
- ❑ Take notes about the rhetorical devices that Lincoln includes, such as repetition, parallelism, and understatement. Write down examples, describing the effect of each device.
- ❑ Make a list of points that you want to make about the speech.

Discuss with a Small Group To refine your presentation, discuss your ideas with a small group.

- ❑ Summarize the points you want to make. Choose a main idea and support it with specific examples from the speech.
- ❑ After revising your points and creating your presentation, practice your presentation with a partner or small group. Give each other feedback about eye contact, speaking rate, volume, and body language.
- ❑ Use the feedback from your partner or small group to deliver the presentation to your class. Acknowledge that different people may want to emphasize different words or phrases in the speech or may have different reactions to parts of the speech.

Go to the **Speaking and Listening Studio** for help with oral presentations.

RESPOND TO THE ESSENTIAL QUESTION

How can we come together despite our differences?

Gather Information Review your annotations and notes on "The Gettysburg Address." Highlight those that help answer the Essential Question. Then, add relevant details to your Response Log.

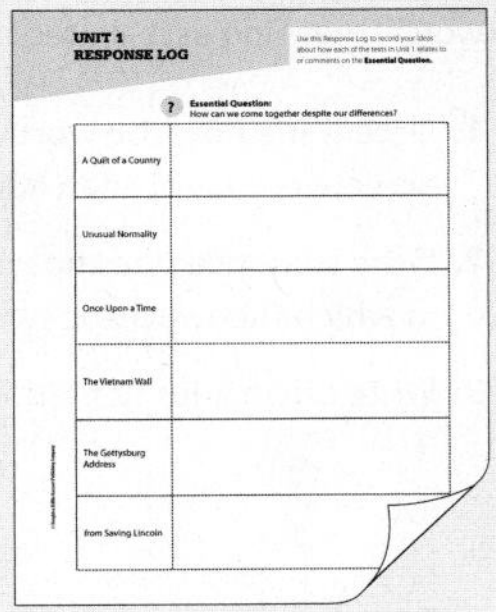

ACADEMIC VOCABULARY

As you write and discuss what you learned from the speech, be sure to use the Academic Vocabulary words. Check off each of the words that you use.

- ❑ **enforce**
- ❑ **entity**
- ❑ **internal**
- ❑ **presume**
- ❑ **resolve**

CREATE AND PRESENT

Deliver an Oral Presentation To critique the effectiveness of Lincoln's speech, refer students to their findings from the Research assignment on page 60 as well as to the notes they took while reading the selection.

For **writing support** for students at varying proficiency levels, see the **Text X-Ray** on page 54D.

Discuss with a Small Group Remind students that the summary should be a shortened version of the main points they want to make, backed by specific examples from the speech. Students may quietly rehearse their presentations before practicing them with a partner or group. Emphasize the importance of speaking slowly, clearly, and loudly enough for everyone to understand. Model for students natural gestures to accompany an oral presentation.

RESPOND TO THE ESSENTIAL QUESTION

Allow time for students to add details from "The Gettysburg Address" to their Unit 1 Response Logs.

APPLY

CRITICAL VOCABULARY

Answers:

1. *detract*
2. *resolve*
3. *conceive*
4. *perish*

VOCABULARY STRATEGY: Multiple-Meaning Words

1. *engaged: adj., occupied, busy*
2. *testing: v., showing*
3. *poor: adj., inadequate*
4. *measure: n., amount*

RESPOND

WORD BANK
conceive **resolve**
detract **perish**

CRITICAL VOCABULARY

Practice and Apply Choose which Critical Vocabulary word is most closely associated with the underlined word or phrase in each sentence.

1. Additional details in a speech sometimes <u>take away from</u> the whole message.
2. A special election can be used to <u>decide</u> a tie in the vote for the student body president.
3. It takes a creative person <u>to form an idea</u> in his or her mind about an important issue and then convey that message to an audience.
4. Sometimes organizations such as clubs <u>come to an end</u> when the members are no longer interested.

Go to the **Vocabulary Studio** for more on multiple-meaning words.

VOCABULARY STRATEGY: Multiple-Meaning Words

Words that have more than one definition are considered **multiple-meaning words**. To determine a word's appropriate meaning within a text, you need to look for context clues in the words, sentences, and paragraphs that surround it. Look at the word *fitting* in this sentence from the Gettysburg Address:

It is altogether <u>fitting</u> and proper that we should do this.

The word *fitting* can mean "the act of trying on clothes" or "a small part for a machine." However, the word *proper* is a context clue that tells you that the correct meaning of *fitting* in this sentence is "appropriate."

Practice and Apply Find these multiple-meaning words in the speech: *engaged* (paragraph 2), *testing* (paragraph 2), *poor* (paragraph 3), *measure* (paragraph 3). Working with a partner, use context clues to determine each word's meaning as it is used in the speech.

1. Determine how the word functions in the sentence. Is it a noun, an adjective, a verb, or an adverb?
2. If the sentence does not provide enough information, read the paragraph in which the word appears and consider the larger context of the speech.
3. Write down your definition.

ENGLISH LEARNER SUPPORT

Vocabulary Strategies Provide students with additional practice in understanding multiple-meaning words. Write on the board the following words and their placement in the speech: *great* (paragraph 2), *live* (paragraph 2), *note* (paragraph 3), *advanced* (paragraph 3), *vain* (paragraph 3). Have students work in pairs to determine each word's meaning as it is used in the speech by following the Practice and Apply steps in the Vocabulary Strategy lesson. Have students share their findings with the class. **MODERATE/LIGHT**

LANGUAGE CONVENTIONS
Parallel Structure

As you read "The Gettysburg Address," look for examples of **parallel structure** in Lincoln's words, phrases, and clauses. Then evaluate how this rhetorical device creates a poetic and rhythmic effect that helps make the words and ideas in this speech powerful and memorable.

Type of Structure	Example from the Gettysburg Address
parallel words	living and dead

Type of Structure	Example from the Gettysburg Address
parallel phrases	of the people, by the people, for the people

Type of Structure	Example from the Gettysburg Address
parallel clauses	we cannot dedicate—we cannot consecrate—we cannot hallow

Practice and Apply With a partner, look back at "The Gettysburg Address" and identify additional examples of parallel structure. Then imagine you were at Gettysburg on the day President Lincoln delivered his speech. Write a brief letter to Lincoln explaining how you were affected by his remarks. Use parallel structure at least twice in your letter. Exchange letters with a partner and discuss how effectively you each used parallel structure to communicate your message to Lincoln.

LANGUAGE CONVENTIONS:
Parallel Structure

Review the information about parallel structure, including the difference between a phrase and a clause. Tell students that the rhythmic effects of parallel structure come from the length of phrases, the placement of words within the phrases, and the repetition of sounds. Explain that when a speech is read aloud, parallel structure can make certain words, phrases, and clauses particularly memorable to an audience. When students use parallel structure in their own writing, they should read their sentences aloud to listen for a poetic or rhythmic effect. Encourage students to think about what they want people to remember in their speech and how they can use parallel structure.

To illustrate the use of parallel structure in other speeches, read the following examples from Patrick Henry's "Speech to the Virginia Convention" aloud to the class.

- "The battle, sir, is not to the strong alone; it is to the vigilant, the active, the brave."
- ". . . those who, having eyes, see not, and, having ears, hear not."

Practice and Apply Have partners discuss whether parallel structure was used twice in their letters. Ask partners to look for repeated words, phrases, and clauses and then to read the examples quietly aloud to assess their rhythms. Finally, have students offer their partners any ideas for improvement. *(Students' letters should describe their reactions to the speech and should include at least two examples of parallel structure at the word, phrase, or clause level.)*

ENGLISH LEARNER SUPPORT

Language Conventions Use the following supports with students at varying proficiency levels:

- Display sentences that demonstrate parallel structure. For example: *We believe in freedom for all people. We believe in justice. We believe in peace.* Have students approach the board and mark the phrase that indicates parallel structure. **SUBSTANTIAL**
- Display sentence frames that demonstrate parallel structure. Have students write and complete the sentences with parallel structure. Point out that one way they can check their work is to read each sentence aloud. For example: *We believe in freedom for all people. ___ justice.___ peace.* **MODERATE**
- Have students write three sentences that use parallel structure. Then have partners check their work by identifying the repeated words, phrases, and clauses. Ask partners to write an additional sentence that uses the repeated words, phrases, or clauses. **LIGHT**

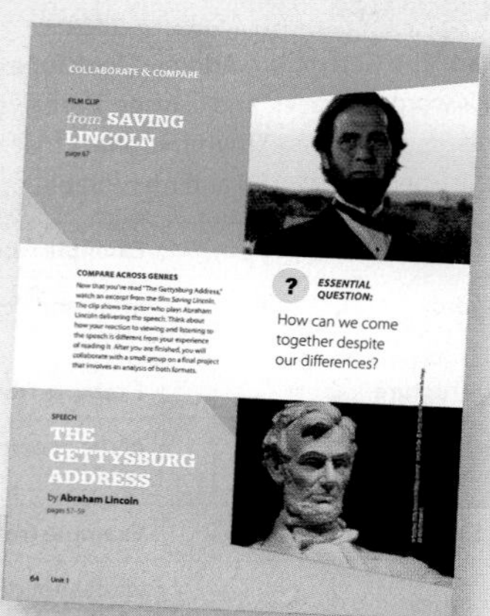

from SAVING LINCOLN

Film Clip

GENRE ELEMENTS

FILM

Tell students that a film—a digital text—is created for a specific purpose. In this lesson, students will analyze an excerpt from a biographical film, or "biopic," to understand how sets, costumes, props, camera shots, lighting, music, and computer-generated imagery work to achieve the director's purpose and convey meaning. The excerpt that students will watch focuses on actor Tom Amandes's portrayal of Abraham Lincoln delivering "The Gettysburg Address" to the audience at the burial ground's dedication ceremony. Students will then compare the text and film version of Lincoln's historic speech.

LEARNING OBJECTIVES

- Analyze a biographical film to determine how its use of computer-generated and practical effects achieve purpose and convey meaning.
- Conduct research on other audio and video interpretations of "The Gettysburg Address."
- Write a review of a biographical film that includes analysis of how the film affects moviegoers' understanding of a historical event.
- Compare text and media interpretations of a historic speech and collaborate to synthesize ideas from different formats of that speech.
- **Language Objective** Describe the film using terms such as *biopic, background,* or *special effect*.

TEXT COMPLEXITY

Quantitative Measures	**Saving Lincoln**	Lexile: N/A
Qualitative Measures	**Ideas Presented** Mostly literal, explicit meaning; more than one purpose.	
	Structures Used Organization of main ideas and details is complex but generally clear and sequential.	
	Language Used Complex sentence structure and some allusive language.	
	Knowledge Required References to historical events are easily envisioned.	

Online 

RESOURCES

- Unit 1 Response Log
-  Reading Studio: Notice & Note
-  Level Up Tutorial: Biographies and Autobiographies
-  Writing Studio: Writing Informative Texts
-  Speaking and Listening Studio: Giving a Presentation
- *Saving Lincoln* Selection Test

SUMMARIES

English

This clip from the biographical film *Saving Lincoln* offers a reenactment of Abraham Lincoln's presentation of "The Gettysburg Address." Actors, music, historical photographs, costuming, and other special effects combine to offer an interpretation of a speech and event that would become an important part of United States history.

Spanish

El clip de la película biográfica *Salvando a Lincoln* ofrece una recreación de cuando Abraham Lincoln dio su "Discurso de Gettysburg". Los actores, la música, las fotografías históricas, los disfraces y otros efectos especiales se combinan para ofrecer una interpretación de un discurso y evento que pasarían a formar parte esencial de la historia de Estados Unidos.

SMALL-GROUP OPTIONS

Have students work in small groups to view and discuss the selection.

Think-Pair-Share

- After viewing *Saving Lincoln*, pose a question to the class—for example, "How did the film's presentation of this speech compare with what you imagined when you read the text?"
- Ask students to consider the question individually and to jot down a response.
- Have students meet with partners and collaborate on a shared response.
- Optional: Student pairs may consult other pairs to reach a new consensus.
- Call upon pairs or larger groups to share and compare their responses in a whole-class discussion.

Focus on Details

- After students have viewed *Saving Lincoln* at least once, have students break into small groups.
- Assign each group a detail to focus on the next time they view the film clip: music, acting, costumes and makeup, camera work, scenery, sound effects, narration.
- As students watch the clip again, have them take notes on their assigned detail and the way in which it affects the movie as a whole.
- Afterward, allow students time to discuss their observations within the group and form a summary statement. Then have each group share its findings with the class.

Text X-Ray: English Learner Support

for *Saving Lincoln*

Use the Text X-Ray and the supports and scaffolds in the Teacher's Edition to help guide students at different proficiency levels through the selection.

INTRODUCE THE SELECTION

DISCUSS FILM TERMINLOLOGY

In this lesson, students will need to be able to discuss the use of special effects to convey meaning in a biographical film. Read the Analyze Digital Texts presentation aloud and explain the following terms:

- A *biopic* is the filmed story of someone's life.
- A *backdrop* is artwork or photography that shows on the background for a filmed scene.
- *Focus* is the clearness of the pictures taken by the movie camera.

Explain that students will use these terms and others to discuss the film clip—a part of the movie—from *Saving Lincoln*. Have students use the terms to complete these sentence frames:

- *A clear picture is in sharp _____.*
- Saving Lincoln *is a _____ that includes "The Gettysburg Address."*
- *The movie uses photographs for a _____ to show scenes behind the actors.*

CULTURAL REFERENCES

The following words or phrases may be unfamiliar to students:

- *score*: a group of 20
- *our fathers*: the men who founded, or set up, the United States as a new nation
- *all men are created equal*: the idea that all people are born with equal rights to freedom and justice
- *final resting place*: a cemetery, or a place where the dead are buried
- *fitting and proper*: appropriate; correct
- *poor power*: weak ability
- *gave the last full measure of devotion*: died in support of their cause
- *in vain*: for no purpose

LISTENING

Identify Special Effects

As students experience the film clip, focus their attention on the role of voice, music, and sound used in the film clip without the distraction of visuals.

Have students listen to the excerpt from *Saving Lincoln* without viewing the film. Use the following supports with students at varying proficiency levels:

- Have students hold up green cards (yes) and red cards (no) in response to questions after they listen to the film. Ask questions such as these: Did you notice any sounds before Lincoln's speech began? *(yes)* Was there any music in the film? *(yes)* **SUBSTANTIAL**
- Supply students with a numbered sheet of paper to record the types of sounds they hear, in order, throughout the film clip. Sounds include crowd murmurs, an announcer, and clapping. **MODERATE**
- Ask students to volunteer the different types of sounds they heard in the film. Ask follow-up questions. For example: Who do you think was clapping? **LIGHT**

SPEAKING

Discuss the Impact of a Film's Special Effects

Work with students to create a list of special effects often found in films. Encourage students to refer to the list as they participate in the panel discussion activity on Student Edition page 69.

Use the following supports with students at varying proficiency levels:

- Ask questions such as these about how students reacted to the effects: How did the music make you feel? How did the audience react during the speech? Invite students to use drawings and their home language to express concepts. **SUBSTANTIAL**
- Think aloud about the special effects in the film clip, such as commenting on the director's use of a green screen, and then then have students answer questions—for example: What did you see in the background? What does the setting look like? **MODERATE**
- Invite partners to use the list of effects to start a discussion. Then have partners answer these questions: What was the film's message? How did the digital and special effects help make that message clear? **LIGHT**

READING

Understand Background Notes

Explain to students that this film's narrator is someone important to Lincoln's story. Tell students that the Background helps to provide context, or a setting, for understanding the film.

Read aloud the Background note while students follow along. Use the following supports with students at varying proficiency levels:

- Preteach potentially difficult terms by showing pictures and discussing the following terms: *law partner, bodyguard, assassination, diaries, voiceover*. **SUBSTANTIAL**
- Provide students with a Main Idea/Details organizer to fill out while they reread the Background note. **MODERATE**
- Ask students guiding questions to understand the Background note: Why do you think a good friend of Lincoln's was chosen as the story's narrator? Why would these friends' diaries and letters help the filmmakers? **LIGHT**

WRITING

Write a Film Review

Work with students to clarify and support the writing assignment on Student Edition page 69.

Provide a word bank of terms students can use to describe the setting, actors, costumes, and special effects in the film clip. Provide a model film review for students. Use the following supports with students at varying proficiency levels:

- Have students draw pictures of the setting, costumes, and special effects. Then have them write an adjective describing each one using sentences frames such as these: *The setting was* _____. *The costumes were* _____. **SUBSTANTIAL**
- Have students complete sentence stems: *The setting was* _____. *The narrator was effective because* _____. *The actor made Lincoln's speech interesting when he* _____. **MODERATE**
- Provide a list of transitional words and phrases, such as *however, therefore,* or *as a result of*. Invite students to use at least three of them in their review. **LIGHT**

Connect to the
ESSENTIAL QUESTION

The excerpt from the film *Saving Lincoln* enables students to envision how Abraham Lincoln may have presented "The Gettysburg Address" in 1863. By hearing the text of the speech and watching the various members of the audience as they listen, students are reminded that powerful words can help people come together and move forward during a time of trouble.

COMPARE ACROSS GENRES

Have students take a few moments to reread or reflect upon their experience of reading "The Gettysburg Address." Ask students to keep the text version of the address in mind as they prepare to experience the speech in a different way. Let students know that they'll have an opportunity to take notes on the excerpt from *Saving Lincoln,* which will help them to compare the genres.

FILM CLIP
from SAVING LINCOLN
page 67

COMPARE ACROSS GENRES

Now that you've read "The Gettysburg Address," watch an excerpt from the film *Saving Lincoln*. The clip shows the actor who plays Abraham Lincoln delivering the speech. Think about how your reaction to viewing and listening to the speech is different from your experience of reading it. After you are finished, you will collaborate with a small group on a final project that involves an analysis of both formats.

ESSENTIAL QUESTION:

How can we come together despite our differences?

SPEECH
THE GETTYSBURG ADDRESS
by **Abraham Lincoln**
pages 57–59

GET READY

from Saving Lincoln

QUICK START

Nowadays, it seems like we have a video record of almost everything that happens. But actors on stage or on film can still retell events so that we see them in a new way. Think about a recent event in the news. How could actors portray that event to reveal the meaning of it? Discuss with a partner.

ANALYZE DIGITAL TEXTS

A film about the life of a famous person is often called a biopic (biography picture). Script writers and directors must do a great deal of research before filming a biopic. They have to find information about not just the famous person, but also the time period in which he or she lived. This information shapes decisions about settings and costumes.

In the biopic *Saving Lincoln,* director Salvador Litvak used a green screen stage, on which actors are filmed in front of a blank green screen. The director, editors, and special effects artists can then add details to the background to make it look like the actors are in any number of settings.

Litvak also used a technique of adding historical photographs as backdrops to the filmed action. As you watch the film, look to the background behind the actors. The images you see are real photographs laid behind the actors.

GENRE ELEMENTS: FILM

- created for a specific purpose or reason
- combines visual and sound techniques
- may use film techniques such as camera shots, lighting, music, and other special effects

TEACH

QUICK START

Help students complete the activity by noting that an actor (including the actor portraying Abraham Lincoln in the film clip) works with a director to make choices about how to portray a character. These choices—including pacing, tone of voice, eye contact with other actors, and gestures—affect the interpretation of the script. Have students think about the choices they would make as actors interpreting a real-life news event; then call on volunteers to share their ideas with the class.

ANALYZE DIGITAL TEXTS

Explain that both a biography and a biopic tell the story of a person's life, or an important part of his or her life. While a text biography uses words and perhaps photographs, a biopic will use dramatic interactions (sometimes including fictionalized details) and sophisticated visuals to help tell the story.

Have students pay special attention to the use of visuals in the film. Pause the film near the beginning to point out the backdrop of historical photographs. Note the sharp focus on the actors in contrast to the blurred backdrop. Ask students to consider how the backdrop affects viewers' thoughts about the dramatic portrayal of this historic moment.

ENGLISH LEARNER SUPPORT

Understand Meanings Display the word *biopic*. Ask a volunteer to identify the two parts of the word: *bio* and *pic*. Then explain that the word combines *bio*, which is short for *biography*, and *pic*, which is short for *picture*.

ALL LEVELS

ANALYZE SPECIAL EFFECTS

Ask a volunteer to explain why a fight scene is a special effect. *(Actors are not really harming one another; rather, stage fighting techniques, makeup to mimic injuries, and sound effects join to create the illusion of a real fight.)*

Next, hold a brainstorming session to help students understand how special effects are classified. Show the class a chart with the headings **Practical Effect** and **Computer-Generated Image (CGI)**. Invite volunteers to name examples of each type of effect. *(Additional examples for Practical Effect include puppets used for monsters, plastic snowflakes, wigs, air cannons, and other sound effects. Additional examples for Computer-Generated Image include actors encountering monsters, exploring other planets, and reacting to natural disasters.)*

■ English Learner Support

Use Cognates Read aloud the text's discussion of digital effects. Encourage students to ask for clarification of any unfamiliar words. Help students to understand that *special* means "distinct or different." Explain that *especial* is the Spanish cognate for *special*. Other Spanish cognates for terms in this lesson include *effect/efecto, practical/práctico, generate/generar,* and *image/imagen*.
SUBSTANTIAL/MODERATE

ANALYZE SPECIAL EFFECTS

In film and other digital texts, a **special effect** is an illusion created so that the audience "sees" something that is not happening naturally. Fight scenes, car crashes, mythical monsters—all of these details in a movie are put together by special effects artists.

Special effects in films are usually categorized into practical effects and computer-generated effects.

- A **practical effect** is any effect created without the help of a computer. For example, producers might sprinkle water while filming to make it look like it is raining or make up an actor to look like a zombie.
- Today, film crews have almost limitless capacities for creating **computer-generated imagery**, or CGI. By using computers, they can place actors in outer space, create fires and explosions, animate magical creatures, and even create computer-generated characters.

As you watch the clip from *Saving Lincoln,* notice how the director has made the scene resemble something from the past. Look at the costumes, props, and the set. List details in a chart like this and write whether you think the effects are physical or computer-generated.

FILM TECHNIQUE	PRACTICAL EFFECT OR CGI?	EFFECT ON AUDIENCE
Students' answers will vary, but should focus on costumes, props, sets, and how special effects impact the audience.		

BACKGROUND

Saving Lincoln is a biopic, released in 2013, that is partly about Abraham Lincoln. Saving Lincoln is told from the point of view of Ward Hill Lamon, who was Lincoln's law partner in Illinois and a longtime friend. When Lincoln became president, Lamon acted as his main bodyguard, preventing several assassination attempts. Saving Lincoln ends up telling part of Lamon's life story as well. In this way, it is a biopic of both men. Film director Salvador Litvak researched Lincoln and Lamon's friendship by reading through letters and diaries from both of them. In this excerpt from the film, a voiceover describes what Lamon thinks is Lincoln's purpose for delivering the speech. Then we watch and hear the address delivered by the actor playing Lincoln.

PREPARE TO COMPARE

As you watch the film, pay attention to how the actor playing Lincoln presents the speech. Note how he emphasizes certain words or phrases and uses body language to get his points across. NOTEBOOK

To view the video, log in online and select **"from SAVING LINCOLN"** from the unit menu.

As needed, pause the video to make notes about how the director and actors involved in the film created an interpretation of Lincoln's speech. Replay or rewind so that you can clarify anything you do not understand.

TEACH

BACKGROUND

Have students read the Background note. Point out that the biopic's narrator—Ward Hill Lamon, Lincoln's close friend—provides both a viewpoint and a way into the story, just as a fictional narrator does. Tell students that the letters and diaries of Lincoln and Lamon that were used to create the film are primary sources that give the film credibility.

For **reading support** for students at varying proficiency levels, see the **Text X-Ray** on page 64D.

PREPARE TO COMPARE

Direct students to use the Prepare to Compare prompt to focus their viewing and listening.

For **listening support** for students at varying proficiency levels, see the **Text X-Ray** on page 64C.

WHEN STUDENTS STRUGGLE . . .

Analyze Media Have students watch the film excerpt three times, focusing on something different each time. After the first viewing, ask students about their general impression of the excerpt. Before the second viewing, ask students to focus on the actor's interpretation of the speech. After the viewing, ask: Do you think the actor delivered the speech as Lincoln intended? Have students share their reactions. Then have students view the excerpt a third time, paying close attention to the special effects. After the viewing, have students share one observation about the special effects with a partner. Then have students discuss what they learned from focusing on different aspects of the excerpt for each viewing.

APPLY

ANALYZE THE TEXT

Possible answers:

1. **DOK 2:** *He explains that resistance to the war was growing and Lincoln was faced with explaining to the audience why the war must continue.*
2. **DOK 4:** *The audience is all dressed in somber dark clothing, as at a funeral. Some of them are holding portraits that may be of loved ones killed in the war. Some of the men in the audience are dressed in uniforms. They are paying close attention and look affected by Lincoln's words, but they seem surprised at how short the speech is.*
3. **DOK 2:** *Because Lamon worked as Lincoln's main bodyguard, the film probably focuses on his efforts to save Lincoln from harm.*
4. **DOK 4:** *The actors' costumes place the scene in the Civil War period. The director has used a historical photograph to create the background behind Lincoln. These effects recreate the crowd and physical site of Gettysburg as it was the day of the speech.*
5. **DOK 4:** *The director contrasts the tense, somber mood at the speech with the harsh, critical review. The scene shows the audience that not everyone was pleased with Lincoln's performance as president.*

RESEARCH

Remind students to use specific search terms to achieve the best results. For instance, urge them to consider including words such as *video, actor,* or *dramatization* to refine their notes.

Connect Help students consider the relationship between voice quality, spoken words, and image. Suggest that students think about radio or podcast personalities whose voices they are familiar with but whom they have never seen. Ask, "Do you have pictures in your mind of what they look like?" Point out that just as you might imagine someone's image based upon his or her voice, you might imagine someone's voice based upon his or her image.

RESPOND

ANALYZE MEDIA

Support your responses with evidence from the text. NOTEBOOK

1. **Summarize** How does the narrator, Ward Hill Lamon, provide context for the presentation of the speech?
2. **Analyze** How would you describe Lincoln's audience, as shown in the film? What is their response to the speech?
3. **Infer** Based on the title of the film and the background information you read, what do you think is the focus of *Saving Lincoln?*
4. **Evaluate** How does the director make use of special effects and costumes to create geographic and historical effects?
5. **Draw Conclusions** Why do you think the director included the scene where Lamon reads newspaper reactions to the speech? Consider what biographical information this adds to the movie.

RESEARCH

As one of the most famous speeches in the English language, "The Gettysburg Address" has been recorded and filmed by many actors and narrators. Find other interpretations—video or audio—of the speech online. Take notes on how each version gives you a different insight, or enables you to understand the speech's message in a new way.

RESEARCH TIP
Most search engines have options that allow you to view results in the form of images and videos. Further filter options let you view certain kinds of videos; for example, you can choose to view videos of certain lengths.

URL OF VIDEO OR AUDIO CLIP	NOTES ABOUT PRESENTATION OF SPEECH
Students' answers will vary.	

Connect At the time of Lincoln's speech, recording equipment had not been invented. Actors and readers today have to imagine what he sounded and looked like as he spoke to his audience. Think about the meaning of Lincoln's speech. How do you think he looked and sounded while speaking? Which interpretation most closely matches your vision?

WHEN STUDENTS STRUGGLE . . .

Reteaching: Analyze Digital Texts Work with students to create a list of features of a biopic, such as *based on the life of a famous person, researched by script writers,* or *featuring professional actors.*

Then ask students to explain how a biopic is different from films about fictional subjects.

For additional support, go to the **Reading Studio** and assign the following  **Level Up Tutorial: Biographies and Autobiographies**.

CREATE AND PRESENT

Review the Film Write a review of how the director of *Saving Lincoln* portrayed the Gettysburg Address.

- ❑ First, describe the setting and context of the film clip.
- ❑ Then, write your impressions of the actors, costumes, and special effects.
- ❑ Finally, state your opinion about how the director added to moviegoers' understanding of the historical event.

Hold a Panel Discussion Using your opinions from your review, as well as your notes about the other interpretations of Lincoln's speech, hold a panel discussion about the effectiveness of different interpretations of the speech.

- ❑ Before the discussion, make a list of points you would like to make about both *Saving Lincoln* and other recordings you have found. Cue up other recordings in case you need to play them for the rest of the panel.
- ❑ Establish rules for speaking. Will speakers go in order? When will the rest of the group be able to respond to a viewer's points?
- ❑ Hold the discussion with your panel. State your opinions about the different pieces of media and back them up with evidence. Listen and respond to your group members' opinions.

Go to the **Writing Studio** for help with writing informative texts.

Go to the **Speaking and Listening Studio** for help with holding a panel discussion.

RESPOND TO THE ESSENTIAL QUESTION

How can we come together despite our differences?

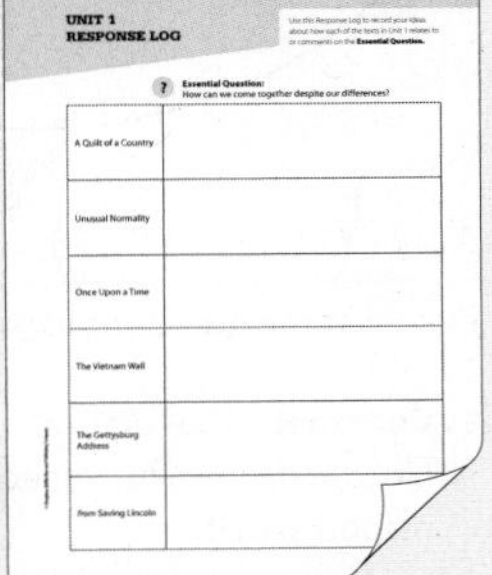

Gather Information Review your annotations and notes on the excerpt from *Saving Lincoln*. Think about Lincoln's message and how the audience is shown reacting to it. Then, add relevant details to your Response Log.

At the end of the unit, you will use your notes to write a personal essay.

ACADEMIC VOCABULARY

As you write and discuss what you learned about the film presentation of "The Gettysburg Address," be sure to use the Academic Vocabulary words. Check off each of the words that you use.

- ❑ **enforce**
- ❑ **entity**
- ❑ **internal**
- ❑ **presume**
- ❑ **resolve**

APPLY

CREATE AND PRESENT

Review the Film Have students review their notes on the film and its special effects. Before completing the task, invite students to locate and read reviews of a recently released movie to become familiar with the review format.

English Learner Support

Understand Information In addition to reviewing their notes, have students watch the film clip again. Encourage them to listen carefully to understand what is being said. Point out that they also can use the visual information in the film clip to help them make sense of what is being said. **MODERATE/LIGHT**

For **writing support** for students at varying proficiency levels, see the **Text X-Ray** on page 64D.

Hold a Panel Discussion Invite students to agree upon rules for conducting the discussion. They may wish to appoint a moderator to call on panel participants as needed, to keep their remarks within a time limit, and to invite questions from the audience.

Remind students to come to the discussion well prepared. Students may wish to review their list of talking points beforehand. Some students may find it easier to join in the discussion by summarizing and rehearsing their talking points. Remind students to participate fully, to listen actively, and to respond thoughtfully and with respect to others.

For **speaking support** for students at varying proficiency levels, see the **Text X-Ray** on page 64D.

RESPOND TO THE ESSENTIAL QUESTION

Allow time for students to add details from the excerpt from *Saving Lincoln* to their Unit 1 Response Logs.

TO CHALLENGE STUDENTS . . .

Write a Sidebar Challenge students to analyze the role of either the director of the film or the actor playing Lincoln in a sidebar critique to accompany their movie review. To critique acting, students should pay particular attention to the tone, gestures, enunciation, speech style, and body language, and how these factors contribute to the actor's portrayal of Lincoln. To critique the director, students may wish to evaluate camera angles, close-ups of individual actors in the "audience" throughout the speech, and other choices that affect the perception of the viewer.

COMPARE ACROSS GENRES

Emphasize that students should use the Venn diagram to compare how the speech and film formats affected their overall understanding of Lincoln's speech. As groups of students collaborate to complete the diagram, encourage students to refer to their notes and, if they wish, reread the text of "The Gettysburg Address" or to rewatch the film clip.

ANALYZE THE TEXTS

Possible answers:

1. **DOK 3:** *The voiceover tells the audience that the purpose of the speech was to encourage people to continue to support the war, but the immediate response shows that the speech was not well received at first.*
2. **DOK 4:** *Lincoln says that it is not up to him, or the audience in front of him, to "consecrate" the ground, as the soldiers had done so by giving their lives. Keeping the speech short helps Lincoln keep the attention off himself.*
3. **DOK 4:** *Students should explain what they visualized when reading the text and then should compare it to the director's portrayal.*
4. **DOK 4:** *Students may point out the actor's serious tone, how he looks around at the entire audience as he speaks, and how he gestures and emphasizes certain words such as cannot to make his point.*

Collaborate & Compare

COMPARE ACROSS GENRES

When you compare two or more presentations of the same material in different formats, you **synthesize** the information: You make connections and combine ideas, which deepens your understanding. It's easier to do this when the texts you're comparing are the same genre—for example, two poems. But sometimes you can get a more thorough understanding of the topic by experiencing the material in different ways—say, by reading a print version of it and watching actors perform it.

In a small group, complete the Venn Diagram with similarities and differences in how the written speech and the film affect your understanding of the material. One example is completed for you.

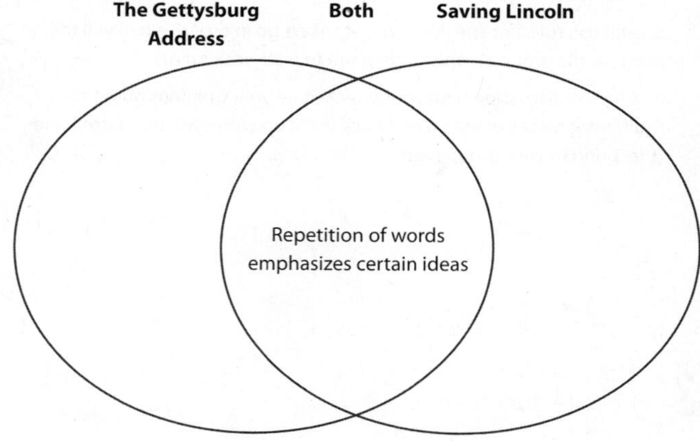

ANALYZE THE TEXTS

Discuss these questions in your group.

1. **Contrast** What do the introductory voiceover and the brief scene after Lincoln delivers his speech tell you about its purpose and the immediate response to it?
2. **Evaluate** An audience member in the film reacts to the speech by saying that it was unusually short. Evaluate why Lincoln might have kept the speech so short.
3. **Connect** What did you visualize when you were reading the text of the speech? Compare that to how the director staged the speech.
4. **Analyze** How does the actor playing Lincoln use voice and body language to communicate the message of the speech?

APPLYING ACADEMIC VOCABULARY

❑ enforce ❑ entity ☑ internal ☑ presume ☑ resolve

Write and Discuss Have students turn to a partner to discuss the following questions. Guide students to include the academic vocabulary words *internal, presume,* and *resolve* in their responses. Ask volunteers to share their responses with the class.

- What **internal** conflict might Lincoln have had about continuing to fight the war?
- What had Lincoln **resolved** about the soldiers who had died at Gettysburg?
- What values do you think Lincoln **presumed** about his audience?

DISCUSS AND PRESENT

You have developed an understanding of "The Gettysburg Address" through multiple avenues, including the printed text, several readings of the speech, and the film clip. Now, your group can discuss your overall understanding of the purpose and message of "The Gettysburg Address." Follow these steps:

1. **Synthesize Ideas** Review the different interpretations of the speech that you have studied—the transcript of the speech and the excerpt from the film as well as any performances or recordings you found online. How was the speech presented? How did each interpretation add to your understanding of the speech's purpose, meaning, and impact, as well as its audience?

Record your thoughts on the speech. You can use this framework to synthesize what you learn:

Information gained from written speech:	Information gained from film of speech:
Information gained from online source:	Information gained from class discussion:
My understanding of the speech's purpose:	
My understanding of the speech's meaning:	
My understanding of the speech's impact:	
My understanding of the speech's audience:	

2. **Listen and Share Ideas** In your group, state your understanding of the speech's purpose, meaning, and impact, as well as its actual audience. Use details from the sources to support your interpretation of the speech. Ask questions about words or phrases you don't understand.
3. **Come to a Consensus** Based on the discussion, can the group construct a statement about the speech, telling its purpose, meaning, and impact? Together, write a summary statement about "The Gettysburg Address" and its effect on the audience.

DISCUSS AND PRESENT

Tell students that they will review the various perspectives on "The Gettysburg Address," discuss them with a group, and come to a shared understanding about the purpose and meaning of the speech.

1. **Synthesize Ideas** Make sure that students have the notes they took on each source, including the class discussions. Emphasize that groups should cover the following elements:
   - **purpose**—the reasons for writing or producing a work *(Possible answer: Lincoln delivered the speech at Gettysburg both to dedicate the burial ground and to encourage Americans to keep fighting for their country.)*
   - **meaning**—the main idea, or message, stated directly or inferred *(Possible answer: Lincoln's meaning, or message, was that those who died at Gettysburg should be remembered and that the living should keep fighting for the ideals for which they had given their lives.)*
   - **impact**—the effect on an audience *(Possible answer: Immediate reaction to the speech was surprise that it was so short, and at least one newspaper criticized it as "flat" and "silly.")*
   - **audience**—the people who receive the message *(Possible answer: His audience was the crowd gathered at the ceremony to remember the dead and people who would read about the speech in newspapers.)*
2. **Listen and Share Ideas** Have groups decide how everyone should participate. For example, the person who is sharing holds a red pen while speaking. Each listener holds a pencil and may use it to take notes on the discussion. To share, students must trade their pencil for the red pen. Each student gets a turn to share.
3. **Come to a Consensus** Have students use their Listen and Share notes to create a group-written summary of "The Gettysburg Address." Remind students to include purpose, meaning, impact, and audience in the summary.

ENGLISH LEARNER SUPPORT

Express Ideas Help students speak and write about the speech's purpose, meaning, and effect on the audience. Use the following supports with students at varying proficiency levels:

- Write and choral read sentence frames: *The purpose of the speech is to _____. (inform, persuade, explain, entertain, express feelings)* **SUBSTANTIAL**
- Have partners use their own words to complete sentence frames and then use their opinions as discussion starters: *I think people who read or heard Lincoln's speech felt _____. When I read Lincoln's speech, I feel _____.* **MODERATE**
- Ask partners to use sentence stems to write about and discuss the speech's purpose, meaning, and effect on the audience—for example: *I think one purpose of the speech is to (inform, persuade, entertain, express feelings) because _____.* Tell students to use evidence to support their opinions. **LIGHT**

READER'S CHOICE

Setting a Purpose Have students review their Unit 1 Response Logs and think about what they've already learned about how we can come together despite our differences. As they choose their Independent Reading selections, encourage them to consider what more they want to know.

NOTICE & NOTE

Explain that some selections may contain multiple signposts; others may contain only one. And the same type of signpost can occur many times in the same text.

LEARNING MINDSET

Setting Goals Tell students that setting goals is an important part of having a learning mindset. Explain that setting goals for reading the self-selected texts outside of class—such as having a set reading time or set number of pages to read each night—can make the overall goal of completing the text much easier. Consider setting up a class progress report that students can use to track their goals.

INDEPENDENT READING

? *ESSENTIAL QUESTION:*

How can we come together despite our differences?

Reader's Choice

Setting a Purpose Select one or more of these options from your eBook to continue your exploration of the Essential Question.

- Read the descriptions to see which text grabs your interest.
- Think about which genres you enjoy reading.

Notice & Note

In this unit, you practiced asking **Big Questions** and noticing and noting two signposts: **Contrasts and Contradictions** and **Word Gaps**. As you read independently, these signposts and others will aid your understanding. Below are the anchor questions to ask when you read literature and nonfiction.

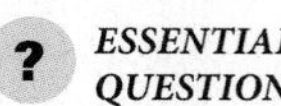

Reading Literature: Stories, Poems, and Plays		
Signpost	**Anchor Question**	**Lesson**
Contrasts and Contradictions	Why did the character act that way?	p. 419
Aha Moment	How might this change things?	p. 171
Tough Questions	What does this make me wonder about?	p. 494
Words of the Wiser	What's the lesson for the character?	p. 171
Again and Again	Why might the author keep bringing this up?	p. 170
Memory Moment	Why is this memory important?	p. 418

Reading Nonfiction: Essays, Articles, and Arguments		
Signpost	**Anchor Question(s)**	**Lesson**
Big Questions	What surprised me? What did the author think I already know? What challenged, changed, or confirmed what I already knew?	p. 248 p. 2 p. 84
Contrasts and Contradictions	What is the difference, and why does it matter?	p. 3
Extreme or Absolute Language	Why did the author use this language?	p. 85
Numbers and Stats	Why did the author use these numbers or amounts?	p. 249
Quoted Words	Why was this person quoted or cited, and what did this add?	p. 85
Word Gaps	Do I know this word from someplace else? Does it seem like technical talk for this topic? Do clues in the sentence help me understand the word?	p. 3

72 Unit 1

ENGLISH LEARNER SUPPORT

Develop Fluency Select a passage from a text that matches students' abilities. Read the passage aloud while students follow along silently.

- Echo read the passage by reading aloud one sentence and then having students repeat the sentence back to you. Then have students read the passage silently several times. Check their comprehension by asking yes/no questions about the passage. **SUBSTANTIAL**
- Have students read the passage silently several times. Without making them feel rushed, suggest that they try timing themselves. Explain that this will help them see how much they are improving. Remind students that the goal is to read at a steady pace, not to race or skip over any challenging parts. **MODERATE**
- Allow more fluent readers to select their own texts. Set a specific time for students to read silently. Then check their comprehension by asking them to write a brief summary. **LIGHT**

Go to the **Reading Studio** for additional support in developing fluency.

You can preview these texts in Unit 1 of your eBook.

Then, check off the text or texts that you select to read on your own.

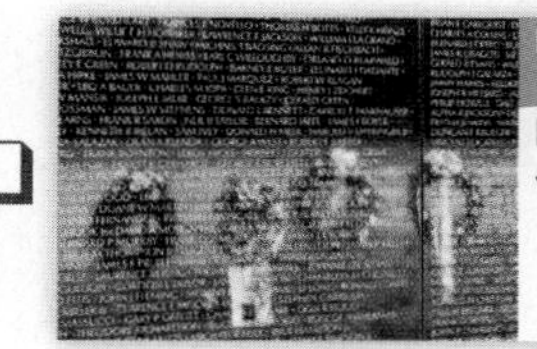

☐ POEM

Facing It
Yusef Komunyakaa

The narrator struggles with memories of fallen comrades as he contemplates the Vietnam Veterans memorial.

☐ BLOG

Making the Future Better, Together
Eboo Patel

Could George Washington's views about unity and diversity be relevant today?

☐ SPEECH

Oklahoma Bombing Memorial Address
Bill Clinton

President Bill Clinton takes a stand against the fear, hatred, and violence that can divide a nation.

☐ SHORT STORY

Night Calls
Lisa Fugard

A girl uses her gift of mimicking bird calls to create a bond with her emotionally distant father.

☐ POEM

Theme for English B
Langston Hughes

The poet who says he often does not "want to be a part of you" nevertheless acknowledges that we learn from each other.

Collaborate and Share Work with a partner to discuss what you learned from at least one of your independent readings.

- Give a brief synopsis or summary of the text.
- Describe any signposts that you noticed in the text and explain what they revealed to you.
- Describe what you most enjoyed or found most challenging about the text. Give specific examples.
- Decide if you would recommend the text to others. Why or why not?

Go to the **Reading Studio** for more resources on **Notice & Note.**

INDEPENDENT READING

MATCHING STUDENTS TO TEXTS

Use the following information to guide students in choosing their texts.

Facing It
Genre: poem
Overall Rating: Challenging

Making the Future Better, Together **Lexile: 1170L**
Genre: blog
Overall Rating: Accessible

Oklahoma Bombing Memorial Address **Lexile: 1060L**
Genre: speech
Overall Rating: Accessible

Night Calls **Lexile: 1110L**
Genre: short story
Overall Rating: Challenging

Theme for English B
Genre: poem
Overall Rating: Accessible

Collaborate and Share To assess how well students read the selections, walk around the room and listen to their conversations. Encourage students to be focused and specific in their comments.

for Assessment

- Independent Reading Selection Tests

Encourage students to visit the **Reading Studio** to download a handy bookmark of **NOTICE & NOTE** signposts.

WHEN STUDENT STRUGGLE . . .

Keep a Reading Log As students read their selected texts, have them keep a reading log for each selection to note signposts and their thoughts about them. Use their logs to assess how well they are noticing and reflecting on elements of their texts.

Reading Log for (title)		
Location	**Signpost I Noticed**	**My Notes about It**

UNIT 1 Tasks

- **WRITE A PERSONAL ESSAY**

MENTOR TEXT
UNUSUAL NORMALITY
Personal Essay by Ishmael Beah

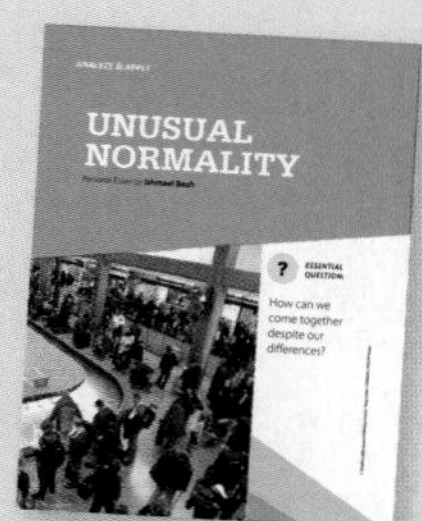

LEARNING OBJECTIVES

Writing Task

- Write a personal essay about how differences between people can be opportunities rather than obstacles.
- Use strategies to plan and organize ideas for a personal essay.
- Develop a focused, structured draft.
- Use the Mentor Text as a model for including dialogue and reflections about the topic of a personal essay.
- Revise drafts incorporating feedback from peers.
- Edit drafts to incorporate standard English conventions and the use of active and passive voice.
- Use a rubric to evaluate writing.
- Publish writing to share it with an audience.
- **Language** Write about a personal experience and reflection using transition words and phrases.

Assign the Writing Task in ***Ed.***

RESOURCES

- Unit 1 Response Log
- Reading Studio: Notice & Note
- Writing Studio: Narrative Context
- Grammar Studio: Module 6: Lesson 4: Active and Passive Voice

Language X-Ray: English Learner Support

Use the instruction below and the supports and scaffolds in the Teacher's Edition to help you guide students at different proficiency levels.

INTRODUCE THE WRITING TASK

Explain that a **personal essay** is a type of nonfiction writing in which the writer expresses an opinion on a topic or provides insight based on personal experience. Point out that the word *personal* is the same in Spanish and that in this case it means "related to one's own life, relationships, beliefs, and feelings." Make sure students understand that personal essays reveal the way an author thinks or feels based on real-life experiences or observations of the world.

Remind students that the selections in this unit deal with how people can come together despite their differences. Use sentence frames to help them articulate ideas—for example: I *learned that even though people are different, we* ____ . Provide assistance as students brainstorm words and phrases and record them on the board. Have pairs of students work together to write an original sentence about how differences can bring people together. Encourage students to use their sentences as models as they begin the writing task.

WRITING

Use Time-Order Transitions

Tell students that they will be writing about events in their own lives. Emphasize that it is important to describe events in chronological, or time, order to make them clear to readers.

Use the following supports with students at varying proficiency levels:

- Discuss the use of time-order transitions (for example, *first, next, at that moment,* and *finally*) when relating a personal experience. Have students write an original sentence or two with time-order transitions by dictating the sentences to you or a partner. **SUBSTANTIAL**
- Use sentence frames to help students practice using time-order transitions. For example: *When I was just* ____ *, I* ______ . **MODERATE**
- After students have completed their drafts, have them work with partners to determine whether they used time-order transitions effectively. **LIGHT**

SPEAKING

Use Active and Passive Voice

Provide oral practice for transforming sentences from the passive voice to the active voice.

Use the following supports with students at varying proficiency levels:

- Provide models on how to transform sentences from passive to active voice. For example: *Ishmael's luggage was lost by the airline. The airline lost Ishmael's luggage.* Have students repeat the sentences after you read them aloud. **SUBSTANTIAL**
- Have students orally identify the subject and verb in each of the model sentences above. Discuss how word order changes and affects the voice. **MODERATE**
- Have pairs of students orally identify examples of sentences in the passive and active voice from a unit selection other than "Unusual Normality." **LIGHT**

WRITE A PERSONAL ESSAY

Read the introductory paragraph with students and discuss the writing task with them. Encourage students to refer to the notes they recorded in the Unit 1 Response Log before they begin planning and writing a draft. Emphasize that the Response Log will contain a variety of ideas about the value of diversity based on their reading of the unit's selections. Encourage students to identify passages, examples, and other text elements they especially liked and may find useful as they write their personal essays.

USE THE MENTOR TEXT

Explain to students that their personal essays will be similar to "Unusual Normality" by Ishmael Beah. Like Beah's essay, their essays will be about a personal experience that provided them with an important insight into the value of diversity in the human experience.

WRITING PROMPT

Discuss the prompt with students. Encourage them to ask questions about any aspect of the assignment they find unclear. Emphasize that the purpose of their personal essay is to express an opinion or insight into how differences between people can provide opportunities for them to come together.

Review the list of key points that students should be sure to include in their personal essays.

WRITING TASK

Write a Personal Essay

Go to the **Writing Studio** for help writing your essay.

As you read this unit, you focused on how people from different backgrounds and with different experiences can come together as human beings. For this writing task, you will write a personal essay related to this topic. A personal essay is a short work of nonfiction in which the writer expresses an opinion or provides insight based on personal experiences. For an example of a well-written personal essay you can use as a mentor text, review the essay "Unusual Normality."

As you write your essay, you will want to look at the notes you made in your Response Log, which you filled out after reading the texts in this unit.

Writing Prompt

Read the information in the box below.

This is the topic or context for your essay.

> **Our differences can help us explore and understand more of the world and what it means to be human.**

This is the Essential Question for the unit. How would you answer this question, based on the texts in this unit and your personal experience?

Think carefully about the following question.

> **How can we come together despite our differences?**

Think about events in your own experience that relate to this topic.

Write a personal essay about how differences between people can be opportunities rather than obstacles.

Be sure to—

- ❑ write an introduction that catches the reader's attention and presents the topic of the essay
- ❑ write about an event from your own life or something you've noticed in the world around you
- ❑ use transitions to connect related ideas
- ❑ use appropriate register (level of formality), vocabulary, tone, and voice.
- ❑ end by sharing your insights about the value of diversity in a school, a community, or a country

Review these points as you write and again when you finish. Make any needed changes.

LEARNING MINDSET

Belonging Remind students that everyone in the classroom is a valuable member of a learning community and has something to contribute. Emphasize that students should be respectful of the perspectives and suggestions offered by others to improve their writing. Discuss how a personal essay is just that—a personal, individualized type of writing. Because it takes courage to write about oneself, emphasize the importance of making sure everyone feels valued and supported throughout the writing and presenting process.

1 Plan

Before you begin to write your personal essay, you need to have an idea of what you want to explore in your writing. In this case, you will write about an event or experience that helped you to understand something about the value of diversity. Your essay will be more interesting if you describe the challenges you faced in your experience, as the author did in "Unusual Normality."

You also need to think about what you hope to achieve in your essay and who you are writing it for—your purpose and your audience. One way to choose what to write about is to brainstorm. Use the chart below to help you. When you have finished filling out the chart, circle the event you would like to write about for this essay.

Personal Essay Brainstorming Chart

Experience or Event	What I Thought and Felt About It

Background Reading Review the notes you have taken in your Response Log after reading the texts in this unit. These texts provide background reading that will help you think about what you want to say in your essay.

Go to **Writing as a Process: Planning and Drafting** for help planning your essay.

Notice & Note

From Reading to Writing

As you plan your personal essay, apply what you've learned about signposts to your own writing. Remember that writers use common features, called signposts, to help convey their message to readers.

Think about how you can incorporate an **Aha Moment** into your essay.

Go to the **Reading Studio** for more resources on Notice & Note.

Use the notes from your Response Log as you plan your essay.

1 PLAN

Review the key points students should consider during the planning step—purpose, audience, and possible topics based on personal experiences. Allow time for students to complete the brainstorming chart for their personal essays.

English Learner Support

Learning Strategies Emphasize that the purpose of brainstorming at this stage of the prewriting process is to generate ideas, not to focus on grammar, spelling, or using formal language. Explain that brainstorming is a valuable thinking skill—and is used by professionals in all fields. By generating lots of ideas, writers are more likely to find one that most appeals to them and inspires their writing. You may wish to offer students alternatives to traditional brainstorming in English, such as drawing pictures that represent the personal narrative they wish to share or brainstorming in their home language. **ALL LEVELS**

NOTICE AND NOTE

From Reading to Writing Discuss the focus of the **Aha Moment** signpost, in which the writer realizes something about one's actions or an understanding of oneself and others in the world. Emphasize that an Aha Moment does not necessarily refer to an extraordinary event; rather, its focus is on the understanding of the world the writer draws from an experience.

Background Reading As students plan their personal essays, encourage them to review the notes in their Response Logs for Unit 1. Suggest that they briefly review the unit's selections to identify examples that might prove helpful in their writing.

WHEN STUDENTS STRUGGLE . . .

Use Small Group Brainstorming If students are struggling to come up with ideas for their personal essays, have them brainstorm in small groups. Have group members state a possible topic that comes to mind in two quick rotations (or provide prompts, such as *what you learned about getting along with others from a teacher or coach*, or *an experience you had as part of a team, club, or other group*). Then have students discuss and list their ideas.

Organize Your Ideas Emphasize to students the importance of doing preliminary planning before beginning to write a draft of their personal essays. Review the organization chart with students and guide them step by step in how to use it to make an outline. Ask: How should the body of your personal essay be organized? *(chronological order)*

Suggest that students consider using other graphic organizers, such as a T-chart, if they need more space to make detailed notes about the events they plan to describe and to help order them. Remind students that their introduction should clearly state the topic. Finally, discuss the conclusion of a personal essay, stressing that this is the place where the writer ties everything together and provides a clear explanation of what he or she learned from the experience.

2 DEVELOP A DRAFT

Remind students to follow their outlines as they draft their personal essays. Explain that an outline is preliminary and that they can makes changes to it if they think of better details or more interesting examples during the drafting process.

English Learner Support

Develop a Topic Statement Emphasize the importance of drafting a clear and concise topic statement. If students need more guidance, use the following sentence frames:

- *One important thing I learned about coming together is* _______.
- *I learned how important diversity is when I* _______.

SUBSTANTIAL/MODERATE

Organize Your Ideas After you have chosen an event to write about, you need to organize your ideas. First, write a statement of the topic you're going to explore. That will lead to the narrative part of the essay: telling about the event from your life that affected how you thought and felt about differences among people. In your conclusion, you will explain the insight you gained from the experience you just described. Use the chart below to help you organize your ideas. Then, use it to make an outline. If you find that you do not have enough to write about, you may need to go back to your brainstorming chart and choose a different event.

Personal Essay: Being True to Yourself
Topic Statement
Event from Your Life **How it started:** **What happened:** **How it ended:**
Conclusion

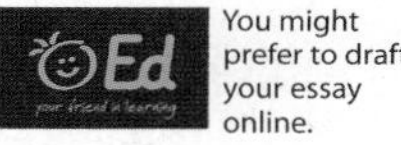

You might prefer to draft your essay online.

2 Develop a Draft

Once you have completed your planning activities, you will be ready to begin drafting your personal essay. Refer to your Graphic Organizer and the outline you have created, as well as any notes you took as you studied the texts in the unit. These will provide a kind of map for you to follow as you write. Using a word processor or online writing application makes it easier to make changes or move sentences around later when you are ready to revise your first draft.

WHEN STUDENTS STRUGGLE . . .

Learn Drafting Strategies If students are having difficulty starting their drafts, encourage them to think about what works best for them in terms of a starting point. For example, some students might find it helpful to start with the introduction and then move to the conclusion before tackling the body of their essay. For others, you might want to suggest that they look over their outlines for a small section they think might be easiest to write, such as writing about one of the examples they plan to include. Emphasize that once they "get the juices flowing," it usually becomes easier to continue drafting. Also point out that the immediate audience for a draft is the writer, not the eventual readers of the final version.

Use the Mentor Text

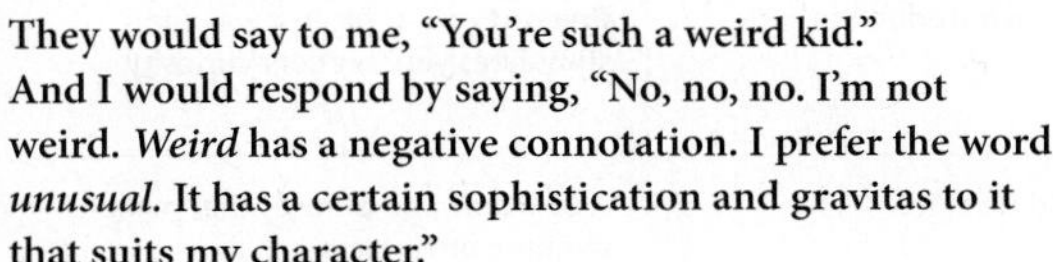

Author's Craft

As you draft your essay, be sure to communicate your thoughts, feelings, and responses to events. You also want to give the reader a sense of your personality. Note how Ishmael Beah uses dialogue to convey his friends' thoughts and feelings as well as his own.

> They would say to me, "You're such a weird kid." And I would respond by saying, "No, no, no. I'm not weird. *Weird* has a negative connotation. I prefer the word *unusual.* It has a certain sophistication and gravitas to it that suits my character."

The author uses dialogue to reveal his personality and view of the world.

Apply What You've Learned Use the techniques of narration, including dialogue, to convey thoughts and feelings.

Genre Characteristics

Your personal essay should describe your feelings at the time of the event or experience, as well as thoughts and insights that came later. Notice how Beah reflects on his decision not to tell his friends about his past in "Unusual Normality."

> But I wish I had been able to tell them early on, because I wanted them to understand how lucky they were to have a mother, a father, grandparents, siblings.

The author reflects on how he feels about choices he made in the past.

Apply What You've Learned As you describe your life experience, comment on its meaning for you in order to help the reader understand the reactions you had at the time and after it happened.

WHY THIS MENTOR TEXT?

"Unusual Normality" provides a good example of a personal essay. Use the instruction below to help students use the mentor text as a model for how to include dialogue and personal responses to events in their essays.

USE THE MENTOR TEXT

Author's Craft Have a volunteer read aloud the introduction to this section and the example from the mentor text. Discuss why it is important to express one's thoughts, feelings, and insights in a personal essay. Ask: Why do you think dialogue might be a good way to let the reader know how you think and feel about events? *(It engages the reader as if he or she is listening to you speak.)*

Genre Characteristics Discuss the introductory text. Ask a volunteer to read aloud the example of genre characteristics from Beah's essay. Ask: What information did Beah withhold from his new friends? *(that he had been a soldier in the civil war in Sierra Leone)* What does the example from this essay reveal about the author's ability to deal with the events he experienced? *(Beah wishes he could share details of his past with his new friends.)*

ENGLISH LEARNER SUPPORT

Use the Mentor Text Use the following supports with students at varying proficiency levels:

- Have groups of students reread the example under Author's Craft. Ask them to identify two words or phrases that seem surprisingly formal. *(any two: "negative connotation," "sophistication," "gravitas")* Briefly discuss how the formality shows an aspect of the author's personality. **SUBSTANTIAL**
- Have pairs of students reread the example under Author's Craft. Invite them to explain a word that they think describes them and to consider using that in their essay. **MODERATE**
- Have students reread the example under Genre Characteristics. Ask them to identify a verb that is in the present tense *(wish)*, a verb that is in the past tense *(wanted, were)*, and a verb that is in the past perfect tense *(had been)*. Remind students that since their personal essay will include both an event from the past and their current reflections upon that event, they almost certainly will need to use more than one tense. **LIGHT**

WRITING

3 REVISE

Have students evaluate their drafts by answering each question posed in the Revision Guide. Call on volunteers to model their revision techniques.

With a Partner Have students work with peer reviewers to evaluate their personal essay drafts. Use the following questions as a guide for their peer reviews:

- Does the introduction clearly state the topic and engage readers?
- Do all the details and dialogue used directly support the topic and give the reader a vivid picture of the event?
- Does the conclusion explain why the event described was important to the writer?

Encourage students to use their reviewer's comments to add interesting and relevant details, examples, and quotations to further develop their personal essays.

For **writing and speaking support** for students at varying proficiency levels, see the **Language X-Ray** on page 74B.

WRITING TASK

Go to **Writing as a Process: Revising and Editing** for help revising your essay.

3 Revise

On Your Own After you write your draft, you will use the process of revision to improve your essay. The Revision Guide will help you focus on specific elements to make your writing stronger.

REVISION GUIDE

Ask Yourself	Tips	Revision Techniques
1. Does my introduction present my topic in a way that makes people want to read my essay?	**Highlight** the introduction.	**Reword** your topic in a way that stimulates your readers' curiosity.
2. Have I told an event from my life in a clear, coherent way?	**Underline** time clues.	**Add** words and phrases that make the time order clear.
3. Have I used the active voice whenever possible?	**Note** any use of the passive voice.	**Change** passive voice to active voice if the active voice would be more effective.
4. Have I made the event feel real to the reader?	**Underline** dialogue and details that show where and with whom the experience happened.	**Add** dialogue and descriptive, sensory details about the place and the people.
5. Is the first-person point of view used consistently?	**Note** anywhere the point of view changes.	**Change** third-person pronouns to first-person pronouns as necessary.
6. Does my essay reveal why the experience was significant?	**Underline** comments you have made about the event.	**Add** statements that explain the event's importance and meaning to you.

ACADEMIC VOCABULARY

As you conduct your **peer review,** try to use these words. Ask questions if you do not understand any of the vocabulary words.

- ❑ **enforce**
- ❑ **entity**
- ❑ **internal**
- ❑ **presume**
- ❑ **resolve**

With a Partner After you have worked through the Revision Guide on your own, exchange papers with a partner. Evaluate each other's drafts in a peer review. Help your partner accomplish his or her purpose in writing. Ask questions about anything you did not understand. Explain how you think your partner's draft could be revised and what your specific suggestions for revision are.

When giving feedback to your partner, include praise for what he or she has done well.

ENGLISH LEARNER SUPPORT

Use Transitions Effectively Explain that to effectively relate the details of a personal experience, it is important to make clear to the reader exactly how the sequence of events unfolded. Note that a good way to do this is to use transition words and phrases that directly connect the details to the chronology of events. Display transition frames such as *"First, _______," Second, _______," and so on; "Next, _______," "Then, _______," and "Finally, _______"; and "It all began when _______," "Soon, _______," "At the same time, _______," and "In the end, _______,"* to help students keep the chronology of events clear. **ALL LEVELS**

4 Edit

Once you have addressed the organization, development, and flow of ideas in your essay, you can look to improve the finer points of your draft. Edit for the proper use of standard English conventions and make sure to correct any misspellings or grammatical errors.

Language Conventions

- **Active and Passive Voice** Most of the time, writers use active voice.
- **Active voice** indicates that the subject of the sentence is performing the action of the sentence. (*I baked the bread.*)
- **Passive voice** indicates that the subject of the sentence is being acted upon. (*The bread was baked.*)

! Go to **Active and Passive Voice** in the **Grammar Studio** to learn more.

The chart contains examples of active and passive voice verbs from "Unusual Normality."

VERB VOICE	EXAMPLE
Active	**So here I was in New York, with my new mother. We needed to step into that normality.**
Passive	**At age eleven, a war had started in my country.**

5 Publish

Finalize your essay and choose a way to share it with your audience. Consider these options:

- Present your essay as a speech to the class.
- Post your essay as a blog on a classroom or school website.

TO CHALLENGE STUDENTS . . .

Peer Reviews Before they publish their essays, have students work in small groups to review each group member's essay in turn. Instruct reviewers to write two positive comments and one suggestion for improvement. Authors can then discuss with the group the comments and suggestions before they decide whether and how to make any changes before publishing their final essays. Encourage students to look for and emphasize what they thought worked well and briefly explain why.

4 EDIT

Explain to students that reading the text aloud at a steady pace is an excellent strategy for determining how effectively they have presented ideas in their drafts. It will help them identify places where more transitions and additional details are needed. Emphasize that their personal essays should read smoothly, with ideas flowing naturally from one to the next. Short, choppy sentences or those that repeat words indicate that their drafts would benefit from additional revising.

LANGUAGE CONVENTIONS

Active and Passive Voice Discuss the definitions and examples of active and passive voice. Note that in the example of active voice, "I" is the subject that performs the action of "baked," the verb. In the example of passive voice, "bread" is the subject and "was baked" is the verb. Who or what is acting upon the bread is unknown, but an actor often is named (as in "The bread was baked by her").

Write the following examples on the board.

- Ishmael was made an orphan by the war in his country.
- Eventually, an American woman adopted him.

Elicit that the first sentence is in passive voice; then have students rephrase it in active voice. (*The war in his country made Ishmael an orphan.*) Explain that using the passive voice occasionally can be an effective way to create an important effect but that the active voice usually is clearer.

ENGLISH LEARNER SUPPORT

Check Subject-Verb Agreement Have students work with partners to check that their subject-verb agreement is used correctly. They can use the following sentence frame to check subject-verb agreement for selected sentences from their essays:

- *The subject* ________ *agrees/disagrees with the verb* _______ *because* _______.

MODERATE/LIGHT

5 PUBLISH

Students can present their essays as speeches to the class or post them on an appropriate website. Encourage everyone to listen carefully to each speech and to thoughtfully read each essay posted and then to ask questions and offer constructive feedback.

USE THE SCORING GUIDE

Have students read the scoring guide. Encourage them to ask questions they may have about any words, phrases, or ideas they find unclear. Tell partners to exchange their final personal essays and score them using the scoring guide. Each student reviewer should write a paragraph explaining the reason for the score he or she awarded for each of the three major categories.

WRITING TASK

Use the scoring guide to evaluate your essay.

WRITING TASK SCORING GUIDE: PERSONAL ESSAY			
	Organization/Progression	Development of Ideas	Use of Language and Conventions
4	• The organization is effective and appropriate to the purpose. • All ideas are focused on the topic specified in the prompt. • Transitions clearly show the relationship among ideas.	• The introduction catches the reader's attention, clearly states the topic. • The essay contains an appropriate, clearly narrated life experience. • The writer includes details and uses devices such as dialogue to make the event or experience vivid. • The conclusion effectively communicates the meaning and significance of the event.	• Language and word choice is purposeful and precise. • Verb tenses are correct and consistent. • Active voice is used whenever possible. • Spelling, capitalization, and punctuation are correct. • Grammar, usage, and mechanics are correct.
3	• The organization is, for the most part, effective and appropriate to the purpose. • Most ideas are focused on the topic specified in the prompt. • A few more transitions are needed to show the relationship among ideas.	• The introduction is semi-engaging. The topic is stated. • The essay contains a fairly appropriate and clearly narrated life experience. • The writer includes some details. • The conclusion explains the meaning of the event.	• Language is for the most part specific and clear. • Verb tenses are mostly correct and consistent. • Active voice is used most of the time. • Some spelling, capitalization, and punctuation mistakes are present. • Some grammar and usage errors occur.
2	• The organization is evident but is not always appropriate to the purpose. • Only some ideas are focused on the topic specified in the prompt. • More transitions are needed to show the relationship among ideas.	• The introduction is not engaging. The topic is stated, but not clearly. • The essay contains vaguely narrated life experience. • The writer includes insufficient details. • The conclusion tries to explain and connect the meaning of the event, but does not do it well.	• Language is somewhat vague. • There are occasional errors in verb tense. • Active voice is used more than passive voice. • Spelling, capitalization, and punctuation errors occur but do not make reading difficult. • Grammar and usage are often incorrect, but the writer's ideas are still clear.
1	• The organization is not appropriate to the purpose. • Ideas are not focused on the topic specified in the prompt. • No transitions are used, making the essay difficult to understand.	• The introduction is missing or confusing. • There are not details about the event or experience. • The writer does not convey the meaning of the experience. • The conclusion is missing.	• Language is inappropriate for the text. • Verb tenses are confused. • Active voice is rarely used. • Many spelling, capitalization, and punctuation errors are present. • Grammatical and usage errors confuse the writer's ideas.

Reflect on the Unit

In this writing task, you wrote about your own experience after reading about the experiences of others in the readings in this unit. Now is a good time to reflect on what you have learned.

SELECTIONS

- "Quilt of a Country"
- "Unusual Normality"
- "Once Upon a Time"
- "The Vietnam Wall"
- "The Gettysburg Address"
- from *Saving Lincoln*

Reflect on the Essential Question

- How can we come together despite our differences? How has your answer to this question changed since you first considered it when you started this unit?
- What are some examples from the texts you've read that show how our differences can be opportunities rather than obstacles?

Reflect on Your Reading

- Which selections were the most interesting or surprising to you?
- From which selection did you learn the most about the value of diversity?

Reflect on the Writing Task

- What difficulties did you encounter while working on your personal essay? How might you avoid them next time?
- What part of the essay was the easiest and hardest to write? Why?
- What improvements did you make to your essay as you were revising?

REFLECT

REFLECT ON THE UNIT

Read aloud the three main headings that indicate major points of reflection students are to undertake. Then ask students to work independently to write notes on how they would respond to each question. After they have completed this task, bring students together in small groups to discuss their reflections. Circulate around the room as the discussions take place, taking note of the questions that seem to be most engaging to students. Use these major discussion points as the basis for a whole-class discussion that wraps up the unit.

LEARNING MINDSET

Self-Reflection Point out that self-reflection can be a valuable tool for improving students' skills. Reflection can help students realize where they made mistakes and how to avoid making them again. Self-reflection can also help them identify what worked well for them and how to use those same successful strategies in the future. Emphasize that focusing on what went well is a sure way to build upon their successes—big and small—and to move toward proficiency and mastery of content and skills.

Instructional Overview and Resources

	Instructional Focus	Online  Resources
Unit Introduction **The Struggle for Freedom**	**Unit 2 Essential Question** **Unit 2 Academic Vocabulary**	**Stream to Start:** The Struggle for Freedom **Unit 2 Response Log**
ANALYZE & APPLY		
 **"I Have a Dream"** Speech by Martin Luther King Jr. **Lexile 1120L** **NOTICE & NOTE** READING MODEL **Signposts** • Big Questions • Extreme or Absolute Language • Quoted Words	**Reading** • Analyze Arguments • Analyze Rhetorical Devices **Writing:** Write a Response **Speaking and Listening:** Discuss with a Small Group **Vocabulary:** Antonyms **Language Conventions:** Repetition and Parallelism	 **Audio** **Close Read Screencasts:** Modeled Discussions **Reading Studio:** Notice & Note **Level Up Tutorial:** Figurative Language **Speaking and Listening Studio:** Collaborative Discussions **Vocabulary Studio:** Antonyms
 **"Interview with John Lewis"** NPR Podcast	**Reading** • Analyze a Podcast • Analyze Author's Purpose **Writing:** Create a Multimedia Presentation **Speaking and Listening:** Discuss with a Small Group	 **Audio** **Reading Studio:** Notice & Note **Speaking and Listening Studio:** Using Media in a Presentation; Collaborative Discussions
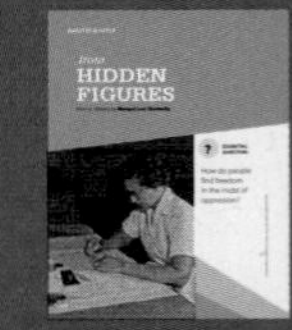 **Mentor Text** **from *Hidden Figures*** History Writing by Margot Lee Shetterly **Lexile 1140L**	**Reading** • Analyze Text Structure • Make Predictions **Writing:** Write a Blog Post **Speaking and Listening:** Discuss with a Small Group **Vocabulary:** Reference Sources **Language Conventions:** Pronoun-Antecedent Agreement	 **Audio** **Reading Studio:** Notice & Note **Level Up Tutorial:** Cause-and-Effect Organization **Writing Studio:** Writing Informative Texts **Speaking and Listening Studio:** Collaborative Discussions **Vocabulary Studio:** Reference Sources **Grammar Studio:** Module 5: Lesson 7: Pronoun-Antecedent Agreement
 **"The Censors"** Short Story by Luisa Valenzuela **Lexile 1200L**	**Reading** • Analyze Literary Devices • Analyze Setting and Theme **Writing:** Write a Letter **Speaking and Listening:** Discuss with Your Class **Vocabulary:** Suffixes That Form Nouns **Language Conventions:** Colons and Semicolons	 **Audio** **Close Read Screencasts:** Modeled Discussions **Reading Studio:** Notice & Note **Writing Studio:** Revising and Editing **Speaking and Listening Studio:** Collaborative Discussions **Vocabulary Studio:** Suffixes **Grammar Studio:** Module 11: Lesson 7: Semicolons

SUGGESTED PACING: 30 DAYS

Unit Introduction	I Have a Dream	Interview with John Lewis	*from* Hidden Figures	The Censors
1	2 3 4 5	6 7 8	9 10 11 12 13	14 15 16

English Learner Support		Differentiated Instruction	Online Ed Assessment
• Learn New Expressions • Learning Strategies			
• Text X-Ray • Understand Figurative Language • Use Cognates • Analyze Figurative Language • Understand Cultural/ Historical Background	• Discuss Historical/Cultural References • Oral Assessment • Discuss with a Small Group • Use Antonyms • Interpret Repetition and Parallelism	**When Students Struggle** • Use Strategies • Analyze Figurative Language	**Selection Test**
• Text X-Ray • Confirm Understanding • Oral Assessment • Create a Multimedia Presentation		**When Students Struggle** • Use Repeated Listening	**Selection Test**
• Text X-Ray • Visually Reinforce Text Structure • Use Cognates • Comprehend Language Structures	• Analyze Idioms • Comprehend Language Conventions • Use Capitalization • Oral Assessment • Spell Accurately • Use Reference Sources	**When Students Struggle** • Chart Cause-and-Effect Relationships **To Challenge Students** • Conduct Research	**Selection Test**
• Text X-Ray • Use Prereading Support • Use Cognates • Seek Clarification • Identify Base Words	• Retell Material • Oral Assessment • Write a Letter • Make Words with Suffixes • Use Colons and Semicolons in Sentences	**When Students Struggle** • Analyze Text Details **To Challenge Students** • Analyze Subversive Tactics	**Selection Test**

UNIT 2 Continued

	Instructional Focus	 Online Ed Resources
ANALYZE & APPLY		
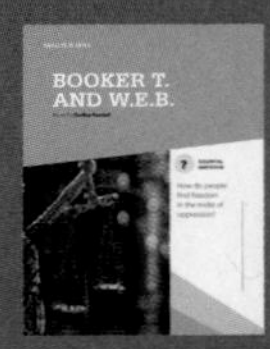 **"Booker T. and W.E.B."** Poem by Dudley Randall	**Reading** • Analyze Poetic Elements • Analyze Poetic Language **Writing:** Assess the Viewpoints **Speaking and Listening:** Conduct a Debate	**Audio** **Reading Studio:** Notice & Note **Level Up Tutorials:** Summarizing; Paraphrasing **Speaking and Listening Studio:** Giving a Presentation
COLLABORATE & COMPARE		
 **from *Reading Lolita in Tehran*** Memoir by Azar Nafisi **Lexile 1150L**	**Reading** • Analyze Rhetorical Devices • Analyze Setting and Purpose **Writing:** Create a Podcast **Speaking and Listening:** Present to a Small Group **Vocabulary:** Denotative and Connotative Meanings **Language Conventions:** Verb Tense	**Audio** **Reading Studio:** Notice & Note **Speaking and Listening Studio:** Using Media in a Presentation **Vocabulary Studio:** Denotative and Connotative Meanings **Grammar Studio:** Module 6: Lesson 3: Verb Tense
 **from *Persepolis 2: The Story of a Return*** Graphic Memoir by Marjane Satrapi	**Reading** • Analyze Multimodal Texts • Evaluate Print and Graphic Features **Writing:** Write an Argumentative Essay **Speaking and Listening:** Share and Discuss Opinions	**Audio** **Reading Studio:** Notice & Note **Level Up Tutorial:** Analyzing Visuals **Writing Studio:** Writing Arguments **Speaking and Listening Studio:** Participating in Collaborative Discussions
Collaborate and Compare	**Reading:** Compare Across Genres **Speaking and Listening:** Collaborate and Present	**Speaking and Listening Studio:** Participating in Collaborative Discussions

Online Ed INDEPENDENT READING

The Independent Reading selections are only available in the eBook.

Go to the Reading Studio for more information on Notice & Note.

"We Wear the Mask"
Poem by Paul Laurence Dunbar

"The Prisoner Who Wore Glasses"
Short Story by Bessie Head
Lexile 970L

END OF UNIT		
Writing Task: Write a Research Report **Speaking and Listening Task:** Create a Podcast **Reflect on the Unit**	**Writing:** Write a Research Report **Language Conventions:** Pronoun-Antecedent Agreement **Speaking and Listening:** Create a Podcast	**Unit 2 Response Log** **Mentor Text:** from *Hidden Figures* **Writing Studio:** Conducting Research **Reading Studio:** Notice & Note **Grammar Studio:** Module 5: Lesson 7: Pronoun-Antecedent Agreement **Speaking and Listening Studio:** Using Media in a Presentation

English Learner Support	Differentiated Instruction	Online Ed Assessment
• Text X-Ray • Use Prereading Support • Use Context Clues • Develop Vocabulary • Practice Using Imagery • Oral Assessment • Conduct a Debate	**When Students Struggle** • Compare and Contrast • Paraphrase Poetic Language **To Challenge Students** • Write a Dialogue Poem	**Selection Test**
• Text X-Ray • Use Cognates • Language Transfer: Varying Uses of *-s* at End of Words • Oral Assessment • Understand Connotative and Denotative Meanings • Language Conventions	**When Students Struggle** • Create a Podcast	**Selection Test**
• Text X-Ray • Use Cognates • Master Vocabulary • Oral Assessment • Share and Discuss Opinions	**When Students Struggle** • Demonstrate Print Features • Analyze Graphic Features **To Challenge Students** • Report on Comics and Graphic Novels	**Selection Test**
• Compare Selections	**To Challenge Students** • Create a Unique Graphic Novel	
"America's Women: Reforming the World" History Writing by Gail Collins **Lexile 1150L** from *Long Walk to Freedom* Autobiography by Nelson Mandela **Lexile 1200L**	"Eulogy for Martin Luther King Jr." Speech by Robert F. Kennedy **Lexile 1290L**	**Selection Tests**
• Language X-Ray • Understand Academic Language • Record Source Information • Analyze Text Structure • Use Subject and Object Pronouns • Check Pronoun-Antecedent Agreement • Adapt the Report	**When Students Struggle** • Small Group Brainstorming • Overcome "Writer's Block" • Collaborate on Partner and Small Group Podcasts	**Unit Test**

TEACH

Connect to the
ESSENTIAL QUESTION

Ask a volunteer to read aloud the Essential Question. Then allow students to reflect on the question for a moment. Have them discuss whether people in various communities might view what it means to be free or oppressed differently. Prompt them to give examples of past events where an oppressed group achieved freedom. Can freedom be reached the same way each time? Have them consider why that may or may not be possible.

English Learner Support

Learn New Expressions Make sure students understand the Essential Question. If necessary, explain the following terms:

- *Freedom* means "the power or right to act, speak, or think as one wants without restraint."
- *Midst* means "in the middle of something, or during the time when something is happening."
- *Oppression* means "cruel or unjust treatment of a person or group over a long period of time."

Help the students restate the question in simpler language: What can people do when they are being controlled?
ALL LEVELS

DISCUSS THE QUOTATION

Frederick Douglass (1818–1895) was an African American who escaped slavery and went on to become an abolitionist and social reformer. Douglass was well known for his strong oratorical and writing skills; he wrote multiple autobiographies that detailed his time in slavery and were influential in promoting freedom for enslaved people. Ask students to read the quotation and pause to reflect on it. Then have students discuss the message Douglass is conveying. Have they heard similar sentiments? What significance do these words from the past have for people today?

UNIT 2

THE STRUGGLE FOR FREEDOM

ESSENTIAL QUESTION:

How do people find freedom in the midst of oppression?

"If there is no struggle, there is no progress."

Frederick Douglass

LEARNING MINDSET

Curiosity Explain that curiosity—the desire to discover new things—is often what leads to deeper, more engaged learning and greater achievements. By exploring what they were curious about, for example, people from ancient times to today have generated new ideas, invented new products, and created new styles that have changed the world. Discuss how new ideas, products, and services often arise from people trying to find creative solutions to problems. As students read the selections in this unit, prompt them to think about what kinds of society and government allow curiosity to flourish. Encourage them to explore in more depth an idea or event they read or talk about that sparks their curiosity.

ACADEMIC VOCABULARY

Academic Vocabulary words are words you use when you discuss and write about texts. In this unit you will practice and learn five words.

☑ decline ☐ enable ☐ impose ☐ integrate ☐ reveal

Study the Word Network to learn more about the word **decline**.

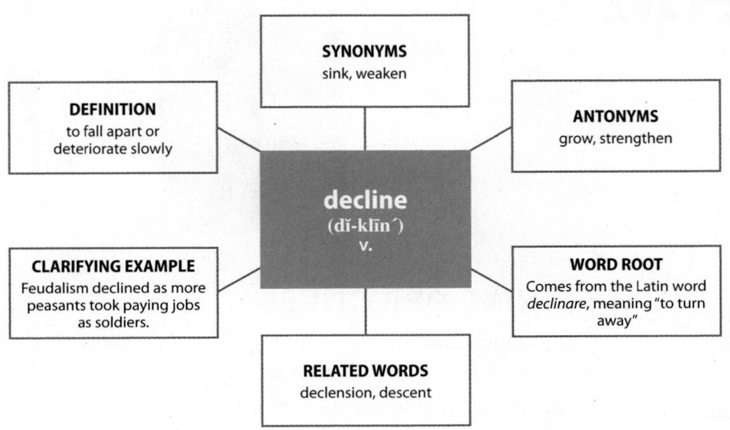

Write and Discuss Discuss the completed Word Network with a partner, making sure to talk through all of the boxes until you both understand the word, its synonyms, antonyms, and related forms. Then, fill out a Word Network for each of the four remaining words. Use a dictionary or online resource to help you complete the activity.

Go online to access the Word Networks.

RESPOND TO THE ESSENTIAL QUESTION

In this unit, you will explore the universal desire for freedom. As you read, you will revisit the **Essential Question** and gather your ideas about it in the **Response Log** that appears on page R2. At the end of the unit, you will have the opportunity to write a **research report** about the difficulties people have as they struggle for freedom. Filling out the Response Log will help you prepare for this writing task.

You can also go online to access the Response Log.

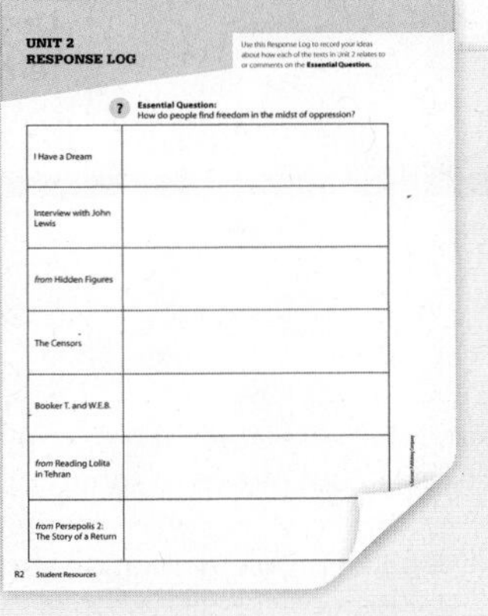

UNIT 2
RESPONSE LOG

Essential Question: How do people find freedom in the midst of oppression?

I Have a Dream	
Interview with John Lewis	
from Hidden Figures	
The Censors	
Booker T. and W.E.B.	
from Reading Lolita in Tehran	
from Persepolis 2: The Story of a Return	

R2 Student Resources

TEACH

ACADEMIC VOCABULARY

As students complete Word Networks for the remaining four vocabulary words, encourage them to include all the categories shown in the completed network if possible, but point out that some words do not have clear synonyms or antonyms.

decline (dĭ-klīn´) *v.* To fall apart or deteriorate slowly. (Spanish cognate: *declinar*)

enable (ĕ-nā´bəl) *v.* To give the means or opportunity.

impose (ĭm-pōz´) *v.* To bring about by force. (Spanish cognate: *imponer*)

integrate (ĭn´tĭ-grāt´) *v.* To pull together into a whole; unify. (Spanish cognate: *integrar*)

reveal (rĭ-vēl´) *v.* To show or make known. (Spanish cognate: *revelar*)

RESPOND TO THE ESSENTIAL QUESTION

Direct students to the Unit 2 Response Log. Explain that students will use it to record ideas and details from the selections that help answer the Essential Question. When they work on the writing task at the end of the unit, their Response Logs will help them think about what they have read and make connections between the texts.

ENGLISH LEARNER SUPPORT

Learning Strategies Use the following strategy to help students use their prior knowledge and experiences to understand meanings in English:

- Before reading a selection, prompt students to think about what they may already know about the topic, situation, conflict, and so on. Use prompting questions such as *What do you know about _______? What experience have you had with _______? Close your eyes and think of _________. What do you see? Hear? Feel?*
- For some selections, provide sentence stems that students can use with partners or in small groups to discuss what they may already know. For example:
  - *An experience I had with _________ was ______________.*
  - *I remember __________________.*
  - *A time I used (saw, heard, etc.) ___________ was when _________.*
- Encourage students to think about what they already know or may have experienced that connects to what they're reading.

ALL LEVELS

READING MODEL
I HAVE A DREAM
Speech by Martin Luther King Jr.

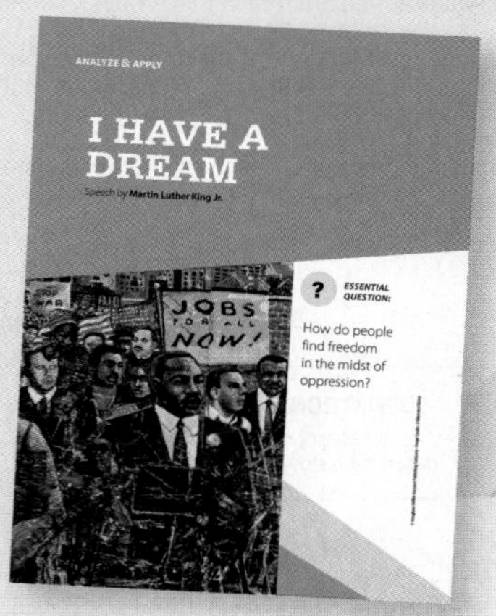

GENRE ELEMENTS
SPEECH

Remind students that a **speech** is meant to be delivered to an audience. It may convey information or present an argument; but regardless of its purpose, a speech will be effective only if it appeals to the people who are listening to it. To make an argumentative speech more persuasive and emotionally appealing, the author may use rhetorical devices. In this lesson, students will examine the structure of the argument in one of King's most famous speeches and analyze his use of repetition, parallelism, and figurative language.

LEARNING OBJECTIVES

- Analyze the structure of an argument and the rhetorical devices that can make it more persuasive.
- Locate an audio or video version of King's speech and compare its impact to that of the written version.
- Write a response to an audio or video recording of the speech.
- Discuss personal responses to King's speech.
- Use antonyms to increase understanding of vocabulary words.
- Analyze examples of repetition and parallelism and apply the techniques in writing.
- **Language** Discuss the main idea of a speech using the key term *claim*.

TEXT COMPLEXITY

Quantitative Measures	**I Have a Dream**	Lexile: 1120L
Qualitative Measures	**Ideas Presented** Mostly explicit, but moves to some implied meaning.	
	Structures Used Primarily explicit problem-solution structure; one perspective.	
	Language Used Vocabulary not defined in text; extensive use of figurative language and allusion.	
	Knowledge Required Many cultural and historical references; explores complex ideas.	

Online 

RESOURCES

- Unit 2 Response Log
- Selection Audio
- Close Read Screencasts: Modeled Discussions
-  Reading Studio: Notice & Note
-  Level Up Tutorial: Figurative Language
-  Speaking and Listening Studio: Participating in Collaborative Discussions
-  Vocabulary Studio: Antonyms
-  "I Have a Dream" Selection Test

SUMMARIES

English

King points out that although the Declaration of Independence and the U.S. Constitution promise "unalienable rights" to all citizens, African Americans in 1963 still do not enjoy these rights. Instead, they face segregation, discrimination, and poverty. King emphasizes that this problem must be addressed immediately, but with dignity and discipline rather than with violence. In spite of the struggles ahead, he envisions a future in which Americans of all ethnicities and faiths will join together as one people and share the benefits of freedom and justice.

Spanish

King señala que a pesar de que la Declaración de Independencia y la Constitución Americana prometen "derechos inalienables" a todos los ciudadanos, los afroamericanos en 1963 aún no gozan de estos derechos. En vez de eso, enfrentan segregación, discriminación y pobreza. King hace énfasis en que este problema debe ser enfrentado inmediatamente, pero con dignidad y disciplina en lugar de con violencia. A pesar de las luchas venideras, él prevé un futuro en el que los americanos de todas las etnias y fes se unirán como uno solo pueblo y compartirán los beneficios de la libertad y la justicia.

SMALL-GROUP OPTIONS

Have students work in small groups to read and discuss the selection.

Pinwheel Discussion

- Select four of the guided reading questions from Student Edition pages 89–94 for students to discuss after they have read the speech.
- Have students form groups of eight. Four students in each group stand in the center facing out. The other four stand facing in, each paired with a student facing out.
- Read the first question and have each pair discuss their answers.
- Have the outer group of students rotate to form new pairs. These pairs then discuss the second question. Repeat until all questions have been discussed.

Reciprocal Teaching

- Provide students with a list of question stems such as the following: *What does King think is wrong about ____? What does King mean by ____? How/Why does King think people should ____?*
- After students have read the speech, have them work individually to write three to five questions about it. Explain that they do not need to know the answers to their questions.
- Have students form pairs or small groups. Each student should then offer at least two of his or her questions for discussion.
- Ask students to reach a consensus on the answer to each question they discuss.

Text X-Ray: English Learner Support
for "I Have a Dream"

Use the Text X-Ray and the supports and scaffolds in the Teacher's Edition to help guide students at different proficiency levels through the selection.

INTRODUCE THE SELECTION

DISCUSS FREEDOM

In his speech, King says that in 1963 African Americans were still not free. Prepare students to understand what he means by "the manacles of segregation and the chains of discrimination" in paragraph 3 by sharing this information:

- *Segregation* means "separation." In the American South, black and white people were separated in public places, such as restaurants. Facilities for African Americans were usually of poorer quality.
- *Discrimination* means "treating one person or group differently from others." African Americans faced discrimination when they applied for jobs, schools, housing, and so on.

Discuss the ways in which segregation and discrimination take freedom away from people. Provide sentence frames such as the following:

- *If you are always segregated from other people, you are not free because* ______.
- *If people discriminate against you when you apply for a job, you are not free because*_______.

CULTURAL REFERENCES

The following words or phrases may be unfamiliar to students:

- *the Negro, black men, citizens of color* (paragraphs 3–5): various terms King uses to refer to African Americans
- *gradualism* (paragraph 6): the idea that change will happen slowly
- *blow off steam* (paragraph 7): express anger
- *soul force* (paragraph 8): the power of nonviolent, peaceful resistance
- *trials and tribulations* (paragraph 10): difficult, painful experiences
- *creative suffering* (paragraph 10): going through hard times in order to bring about positive change

LISTENING

Analyze Repetition

Tell students that the author of a speech may repeat certain words or phrases to emphasize important ideas. When spoken aloud, the repetition also creates a rhythm.

Write "I have a dream" on the board. Then read aloud paragraphs 11–12.

- Ask students to listen closely as you read and to raise their hands whenever they hear "I have a dream." **SUBSTANTIAL**
- Ask students whether King's repetition of "I have a dream" makes the paragraph more interesting for listeners, and have them explain why. **MODERATE**
- Have students consider all the ideas King introduces with "I have a dream." Then, have them summarize what his dream for the United States is. **LIGHT**

SPEAKING

Discuss the Author's Claim

Explain that in an **argument,** the author states a **claim,** or a position on a topic, and then supports the claim with reasons and evidence.

Use the following supports with students at varying proficiency levels:

- Display and read aloud this sentence: King's claim is that African Americans are not free. Have students repeat it several times. Then help them locate the first clause in paragraph 3, where the claim is stated. *("the Negro still is not free")* **SUBSTANTIAL**
- Have students answer these questions in complete sentences, using the word *claim:* What is the claim in an argument? What claim does King state at the beginning of paragraph 3? **MODERATE**
- Ask students to orally summarize paragraph 3, using the words *claim, support(s),* and *evidence.* **LIGHT**

READING

Comprehend the Text

King's speech uses some complex sentence structures and vocabulary that will be unfamiliar to many students.

Use the following supports with students at varying proficiency levels:

- Reread paragraphs 2–3 as students follow along. Tell students you will ask some questions about what they just heard. Model that they should give a thumbs up if the answer is yes, and a thumbs down for no. For example, ask: Did the Emancipation Proclamation free the slaves? *(yes.)* Is King happy with the way African Americans ("Negroes") are being treated in his time? *(no.)* **SUBSTANTIAL**
- Have students read paragraphs 1–4 in pairs, pausing to take notes about unfamiliar terms or phrases. Circulate to define unfamiliar terms and answer any questions they may have. **MODERATE**
- Distribute key words from paragraphs 1–4 among pairs of students (e.g., *momentous, captivity, poverty, prosperity, exile, unalienable*). Have students read and take notes about clues to the words' meanings in the text. Then have them look up the words and report the definitions to the class. **LIGHT**

WRITING

Write a Response

Work with students to read the writing assignment on Student Edition page 97.

Use the following supports with students at varying proficiency levels:

- Have students focus on a short section of the speech, such as paragraphs 11–14, that they comprehend well. After listening to the recording, work with students to write a few sentences about its emotional impact on the board. Have them copy these sentences into their notebooks. **SUBSTANTIAL**
- Provide sentence frames such as the following that students can use to write their responses: *Hearing the speech was (more/less) ____ than reading it. It helped me understand ____. When I heard the speech, I felt ____ because ____.* **MODERATE**
- Encourage students to use literary terms such as *repetition, parallelism,* and *metaphor* in their responses. **LIGHT**

EXPLAIN THE SIGNPOSTS

Explain that **NOTICE & NOTE Signposts** are significant moments in the text that help readers understand and analyze works of fiction or nonfiction. Use the instruction on these pages to introduce students to the signposts **Extreme or Absolute Language** and **Quoted Words,** and to asking **Big Questions** as they read. Then use the selection that follows to have students apply the signposts and Big Questions to a text.

For a full list of the fiction and nonfiction signposts, see p. 156.

BIG QUESTIONS

Explain to students that **Big Questions** involves asking questions as they read. Asking questions such as *What confirms, challenges, or changes what I already know? What do I agree with?* and *What do I disagree with?* can help readers understand and connect to a text.

Write or project the above questions on the board. Then read aloud the example passage and pause as you read to model for students how to use **Big Questions**. For example, say, "What does he mean when he says 'cash a check'? That language surprised me. At first I thought he was talking about money, but now I get it: King is talking about a promise—'a promissory note'—that is in the Constitution and the Declaration of Independence. He means that the founders of our country promised that all Americans would be treated equally. I know that about those documents. But King says that America has 'defaulted' on that promise. He means that the promise has been broken and people of color are not treated equally. That confirms what I know about the civil rights movement: King and others fought for equal rights."

Tell students that as they read, they should pause to think about how what King says challenges, confirms, or changes their thoughts about equality in the United States. **Comparing and contrasting** what they know or believe to what the author asserts will provide important insights into the topic. Guide students to use the chart to keep track of the questions they ask, the text that they are responding to, and the answers they produce as they read.

I HAVE A DREAM

For more information on these and other questions and signposts in Notice & Note, visit the **Reading Studio**.

You are about to read the speech "I Have a Dream." In it, you will notice and note questions and signposts that will give you clues about the topic of the speech and the intentions of the author. Here are three key signposts to look for as you read this speech and other works of nonfiction.

When you read a speech like this one, pause to **challenge, change, or confirm** what you know:

"At first I thought . . . , but . . ."

"I had to rethink . . ."

"My understanding changed when . . ."

"I was right/wrong about . . ."

Big Questions Whenever we read something, we start with what we already know. You probably have heard the words "I Have a Dream" and know that Martin Luther King Jr. said those words. As you read the speech this time, think about what those words truly mean. Ask yourself: **What challenged, changed, or confirmed what I knew?**

Imagine you have dropped a few items from a high point, including a feather, a paper clip, a magnet, a piece of paper, a balloon, and a pen. Which items hit the floor first? You know some facts about gravity and air resistance, but not everything will happen the way you expect. The rate at which some items fall may confirm what you already knew, while others may change or challenge your assumptions. The same thing happens when you read.

Read this part of "I Have a Dream" to see a student's annotation of a Big Question.

> So we've come here today to dramatize a shameful condition. In a sense we've come to our nation's capital to cash a check. When the architects of our republic wrote the magnificent words of the Constitution and the Declaration of Independence, they were signing a promissory note to which every American was to fall heir. This note was the promise that all men, yes, black men as well as white men, would be guaranteed the unalienable rights of life, liberty, and the pursuit of happiness.
>
> It is obvious today that America has defaulted on this promissory note insofar as her citizens of color are concerned.

What statements confirm, change, or challenge what you already know?	1. The Declaration of Independence says all men, regardless of the color of their skin, have the right to "life, liberty, and the pursuit of happiness."
	2. Dr. King says that America has "defaulted" on this promise for people of color.

Extreme or Absolute Language Imagine you are passionate about a subject and determined to persuade people that you are right. You might use absolute words such as "always" and "never" to emphasize your point. You might use powerful or exaggerated images to sway your audience's opinion.

This kind of strong language in a speech can influence the reader's thinking. **Extreme or Absolute Language** often reveals what is most important to a speaker. Pay attention to the speaker's language in order to identify and understand his or her point of view. Here's an example of a student underlining Extreme or Absolute Language:

> Now is the time to make real the promises of democracy; now is the time to rise from the dark and desolate valley of segregation to the sunlit path of racial justice; now is the time to lift our nation from the quicksands of racial injustice to the solid rock of brotherhood . . .

When you see **Extreme or Absolute Language** as you read, pause to note:

"This language shows . . . about the author."

"The author used this language because . . ."

"The language emphasizes the author's point by . . ."

Anchor Question
When you notice this signpost, ask: Why did the author use this language?

What statement sounds absolute or extreme to you?	"the dark and desolate valley of segregation to the sunlit path of racial justice"
Why did the author use this language?	He wants to help his audience picture the brutality and injustice of segregation.

Quoted Words Sometimes you need proof to persuade readers of your opinion or claim. You might cite the words of someone important to prove your point, or share the perspective of someone who was there. Quoting their words can strengthen your argument. Authors and speakers often use **Quoted Words** to reinforce important ideas. Quoted Words might include:

- the conclusions of someone who is an expert on the subject
- someone who witnessed an event

When you come across quoted words, ask yourself why this expert was quoted and what he or she helps you understand about the topic. In this example, a student underlined instances of Quoted Words:

> I say to you today, my friends, even though we face the difficulties of today and tomorrow, I still have a dream. … I have a dream that one day this nation will rise up and live out the true meaning of its creed, "We hold these truths to be self-evident; that all men are created equal."

When you see **Quoted Words** as you read, pause to note:

"This quote comes from . . ."

"This quote means . . ."

"The author uses these words to . . ."

"This quote reinforces the author's message by . . ."

Anchor Question
When you notice this signpost, ask: Why was this person quoted or cited, and what did this add?

What words are quoted?	"We hold these truths to be self-evident; that all men are created equal."
Why did Martin Luther King Jr. quote or cite this sentence?	It is from the Declaration of Independence. Dr. King says that this is the "creed" of our nation. It is an ideal that our country believes in firmly.

WHEN STUDENTS STRUGGLE . . .

Use Strategies If students are struggling to notice signposts, use the Poster strategy to help instill the habits of slowing down, rereading, taking notes, and questioning. Have students read a short passage from the selection. Then provide small groups with a sheet of flip-chart paper or large paper with the passage taped in the middle. Read aloud the passage and have group members write their reactions to the passage on their poster. They must be silent during the writing. Tell students that they may write whatever occurs to them. They may write about why they agree or disagree with something in the passage. They may list questions, draw their impressions, or respond to what others have written. After ten to twenty minutes, display the posters and discuss the ideas students wrote.

EXTREME OR ABSOLUTE LANGUAGE

Explain that **Extreme or Absolute Language** can give readers clues to the **main idea,** the author's **point of view,** and the author's **bias.**

Read aloud the example passage and pause at the underlined text. Note the strong negative image created by the words "dark and desolate valley of segregation." This image seems bleaker when the author sets up a contrast with "the sunlit path of racial justice." Ask students to consider what this signpost indicates about the author's purpose. What message does the author want to convey?

Tell students that when they spot an Extreme or Absolute Language signpost, they should pause, mark it in their consumable text, and ask themselves the anchor question: *Why did the author use this language?*

QUOTED WORDS

Explain that **Quoted Words** help to prove a point or appeal to a particular **audience**. Explain that quoting an expert or a respected source lends the voice of authority to an author's message.

Read aloud the example passage and pause at the underlined text. Point out that the author relies on the reader's prior knowledge to recognize these familiar words as a quotation from the Declaration of Independence. Ask students to consider why the author chose to use this quotation and how these words appeal to the audience.

Tell students that when they spot Quoted Words, they should pause, mark the quotation in their consumable text, and ask themselves the anchor question: *Why was this person quoted or cited, and what did this add?*

APPLY THE SIGNPOSTS

Have students use the selection that follows as a model text to apply the signposts and adopt a questioning stance. As students encounter signposts, prompt them to stop, reread, and ask themselves the anchor questions that will help them understand the topic of the speech and the intentions of the author.

Tell students to continue to look for these and other signposts as they read the other selections in the unit.

Connect to the ESSENTIAL QUESTION

In his powerful "I Have a Dream" speech, Martin Luther King Jr. galvanized Americans to join together in the struggle against oppression and make a forceful but peaceful stand for freedom and equality. Over the years, King's speech has continued to inspire oppressed people around the world to stand up for their rights.

I HAVE A DREAM

Speech by **Martin Luther King Jr.**

ESSENTIAL QUESTION:

How do people find freedom in the midst of oppression?

LEARNING MINDSET

Effort On the board, list different areas of interest that students have, such as sports, music, technology, the environment, community service, and so on. Discuss how effort—hard work—is needed for success in these areas. For example, talk about how a musician spends hours practicing a new song and how making a difference in the community takes a dedicated effort over time. Dispel the myth that all successful people are naturally gifted. Although true for a few people, perhaps, the vast majority of successful people have simply put in the time and effort—the hard work—that's required for success in any area and to achieve any worthwhile goal. Point students to the model of King, whose tireless efforts for racial justice still inspire us.

QUICK START

Have you ever been treated differently for any reason? How did it make you feel? Write a paragraph describing what happened and how you reacted.

ANALYZE ARGUMENTS

One way to analyze Martin Luther King Jr.'s speech is to look at it as an argument. To analyze an argument, you think about how each part works.

PART OF AN ARGUMENT	EXAMPLE FROM SPEECH
The central idea of an argument is the **claim**.	. . . the Negro still is not free; one hundred years later, the life of the Negro is still sadly crippled by the manacles of segregation and the chains of discrimination . . .
The author must support the claim with **evidence** and examples.	We can never be satisfied as long as the Negro is the victim of the unspeakable horrors of police brutality . . . we cannot be satisfied as long as the Negro's basic mobility is from a smaller ghetto to a larger one . . .
To persuade an audience of a claim, the author may **appeal** to the audience by connecting with their personal lives.	Some of you have come fresh from narrow jail cells. Some of you have come from areas where your quest for freedom left you battered by the storms of persecution and staggered by the winds of police brutality.
In the **conclusion**, the author sums up the claim with a strong statement about what the audience should believe.	I have a dream that my four little children will one day live in a nation where they will not be judged by the color of their skin, but by the content of their character.

ANALYZE RHETORICAL DEVICES

Rhetorical devices are techniques writers use to enhance their arguments and communicate more effectively. Rhetorical devices can evoke an emotional response in an audience and make the message memorable.

RHETORICAL DEVICES	EXAMPLE FROM SPEECH
Repetition repeats the same word(s) for emphasis.	Again and again we must rise to the majestic heights of meeting physical force with soul force.
Parallelism uses similar grammatical constructions to express related or equally important ideas. It often creates a rhythm.	Let freedom ring from Stone Mountain of Georgia; let freedom ring from Lookout Mountain of Tennessee; let freedom ring from every hill and molehill of Mississippi. "From every mountainside, let freedom ring."
An **extended metaphor** makes a lengthy comparison between two unlike things to emphasize an important idea.	Instead of honoring this sacred obligation, America has given the Negro people a bad check, a check which has come back marked "insufficient funds."

GENRE ELEMENTS: SPEECH

- directly addresses and connects with audiences
- uses rhetorical devices to achieve specific purposes
- contains a clear message, stated near the beginning
- ends memorably

TEACH

QUICK START

Have students read the Quick Start question, and suggest that they write about a time when they felt they were treated unfairly. Invite volunteers to share their experiences with the class. Then have the class discuss the most effective ways to respond to unfair treatment.

ANALYZE ARGUMENTS

Explain that the examples in the chart are direct quotations from Martin Luther King Jr.'s 1963 speech on civil rights. Point out that King makes a strong connection with his audience by **citing evidence** that his audience knows is true, based on their own experiences. Then, discuss how the different parts of King's speech work together to appeal to the emotions, ideals, and hopes of his audience.

ANALYZE RHETORICAL DEVICES

Read aloud each example from the chart and discuss how each type of rhetorical device enhances communication.

- **Repetition** emphasizes certain words and ideas, often conveying a sense of urgency or power.
- **Parallelism** creates a rhythm that is appealing to the ear, emphasizes an idea, and makes that idea memorable.
- An **extended metaphor** is developed through multiple comparisons throughout the text, creating a memorable mental image.

Tell students they can best appreciate and understand rhetorical devices by reading a text aloud or by listening to a recording of it.

ENGLISH LEARNER SUPPORT

Understand Figurative Language Students may be confused by the figurative language and higher-tier vocabulary used in the first text example (the claim) in the Analyze Arguments chart. Define the words *manacles* (handcuffs) and *chains*. Have students repeat and practice pronouncing the words after you and copy them into their notebooks. Tell students that the language is not literal: King uses a metaphor here to describe the lives of African Americans. While the physical chains of slavery may be gone, African Americans are still restrained, or "chained," by inequality. Help students restate this text excerpt in their own words: "African Americans are still not free; their lives are limited by segregation and discrimination."

SUBSTANTIAL/MODERATE

TEACH

CRITICAL VOCABULARY

Encourage students to read all the sentences before deciding which word best completes each one. Remind them to look for context clues that match the precise meaning of each word.

Answers:

1. *inextricably*
2. *default*
3. *desolate*
4. *redemptive*
5. *degenerate*

■ English Learner Support

Use Cognates Tell students that three of the Critical Vocabulary words have Spanish cognates: *inextricably/inextricablemente, desolate/desolado, degenerate/degenerar.* **ALL LEVELS**

LANGUAGE CONVENTIONS

Review the information about repetition and parallelism. Make sure that students understand that **repetition** involves exact words or phrases that are repeated throughout the text. **Parallelism,** on the other hand, involves a whole phrase or sentence structure that is repeated within a sentence or a paragraph—for example, *I couldn't eat, I couldn't sleep, I couldn't work, without thinking of my best friend in the hospital.* Tell students that the phrase "I couldn't" followed by a verb forms the parallel structure in this sentence. Read aloud the example of repetition but omit the repetition of the phrase "one hundred years later." Then read the passage aloud again, this time using the repetition. Discuss what the repetition adds to the speech. *(The repetition adds drama and emphasis.)*

ANNOTATION MODEL

Students can review the Reading Model introduction on pages 84–85 if they have questions about the signposts. Remind students to think about **Big Questions** as they read. Suggest that they underline important phrases or circle key words that help them identify signposts. They may want to color-code their annotations by using a different color highlighter for each signpost. Point out that they may follow this suggestion or use their own system for marking up the selections in their write-in texts.

GET READY

CRITICAL VOCABULARY

default **desolate** **degenerate** **inextricably** **redemptive**

To see how many Critical Vocabulary words you already know, use them to complete the sentences.

1. That story will always be __________ linked with childhood experiences.
2. If you __________ on a loan, your personal credit rating will be affected.
3. The moors are wide and __________, far from the noisy streets of London.
4. Calm music is __________, freeing my soul from worry.
5. Our talk will __________ into a fight if we don't find common ground.

LANGUAGE CONVENTIONS

Repetition and Parallelism Two devices King uses that make his rhetoric effective are repetition and parallelism—expressing related ideas using similar grammatical constructions. Using these devices, King creates a strong rhythm in his speech and links his ideas in listeners' minds.

Repetition

But one hundred years later, the Negro still is not free . . . one hundred years later, the Negro lives on a lonely island of poverty in the midst of a vast ocean of material prosperity; one hundred years later, the Negro is still languishing in the corners of American society and finds himself in exile in his own land.

Parallelism

. . . we will be able to work together, to pray together, to struggle together, to go to jail together, to stand up for freedom together . . .

ANNOTATION MODEL

NOTICE & NOTE

As you read, notice and note signposts, including **Big Questions, Extreme or Absolute Language,** and **Quoted Words.** In the model, you can see one reader's notes about "I Have a Dream."

I am happy to join with you today in what will go down in history as the greatest demonstration for freedom in the history of our nation.

Dr. King uses extreme language to emphasize the historical importance of the event.

BACKGROUND

On August 28, 1963, thousands of Americans marched on Washington, D.C., to urge Congress to pass a civil rights bill. Martin Luther King Jr. delivered his "I Have a Dream" speech on the steps of the Lincoln Memorial before more than 250,000 people. This momentous event was called the March on Washington. **Martin Luther King Jr.** *(1929–1968) came from a family of preachers. As pastor of a Baptist Church in Alabama, King honed his rhetorical skills. Preaching a philosophy of nonviolence, his leadership helped bring about the passage of the Civil Rights Act of 1964. Awarded the Nobel Peace Prize, King continued his work for justice and equality until he was assassinated in 1968.*

I HAVE A DREAM

Speech by Martin Luther King Jr.

SETTING A PURPOSE

As you read, monitor your comprehension by rereading and reviewing your background knowledge. Think about how this speech confirms, changes, or challenges what you know.

1 I am happy to join with you today in what will go down in history as the greatest demonstration for freedom in the history of our nation.

2 Five score[1] years ago, a great American, in whose symbolic shadow we stand today, signed the Emancipation Proclamation.[2] This momentous decree came as a great beacon light of hope to millions of Negro slaves who had been seared in the flames of withering injustice. It came as a joyous daybreak to end the long night of their captivity.

Notice & Note

You can use the side margins to notice and note signposts in the text.

[1] **five score:** 100; *score* means "twenty." (This phrasing recalls the beginning of Abraham Lincoln's Gettysburg Address: "Four score and seven years ago . . .")

[2] **Emancipation Proclamation:** a document signed by President Lincoln in 1863, during the Civil War, declaring that all slaves in states still at war with the Union were free.

BACKGROUND

Have students read the Background note and the biographical information about Martin Luther King Jr. Explain that in 1955 King led the greatest nonviolent demonstration of its kind in the United States—the Montgomery Bus Boycott against segregated busing. The boycott lasted for 382 days, ending when the Supreme Court ruled that segregated busing was (and is) unconstitutional. The ruling showed that nonviolent actions can achieve positive results. It also established King as the foremost leader of the civil rights movement.

SETTING A PURPOSE

Direct students to use the Setting a Purpose prompt to focus their reading.

For **reading support** for students at varying proficiency levels, see the **Text X-Ray** on page 84D.

WHEN STUDENTS STRUGGLE . . .

Analyze Figurative Language Have students use a chart to analyze figurative language in the speech. Tell students that figurative language makes a statement that is not literally true but conveys a feeling or idea, often by comparing two things or creating a mental picture. Model these steps: **1.** Write the first simile from paragraph 2 in the left column. **2.** Define any unknown words or terms. **3.** Think about the image of a "beacon light" and the feeling it suggests, and explain its meaning in your own words. Write this in the right column.

Then have students work in pairs to clarify the meaning of the second simile in paragraph 2. Have them continue to use the chart as they read.

Figurative Language	Meaning
"This momentous decree came as a great beacon light of hope to millions of Negro slaves. . . ."	*This important document gave welcome hope to millions of enslaved African Americans.*

For additional support, go to the **Reading Studio** and assign the following **Level Up Tutorial: Figurative Language.**

TEACH

ANALYZE ARGUMENTS

Explain to students that King uses **figurative language** to present his **claim**. He creates a mental picture of the situation of African Americans, and then he contrasts that picture with what the nation's founders promised for all Americans. ***(Answer:*** *King wants African Americans to be granted "the unalienable rights of life, liberty, and the pursuit of happiness.")*

For **speaking support** for students at varying proficiency levels, see the **Text X-Ray** on page 84D.

ENGLISH LEARNER SUPPORT

Analyze Figurative Language Read paragraph 3 aloud. Focus students' attention on "the Negro lives on a lonely island of poverty in the midst of a vast ocean of material prosperity."

Ask students to explain, in their own words, what King means. *(African Americans were poor and were prevented from sharing in the material wealth that other Americans enjoyed.)* Help students interpret other instances of figurative language in paragraphs 3–5.

ALL LEVELS

EXTREME OR ABSOLUTE LANGUAGE

Remind students that Extreme or Absolute Language may create powerful images and often reveals the **author's purpose.** ***(Answer:*** *King believes that injustice creates a reaction from oppressed people that no one can control; their revolt is like a "whirlwind." He warns that this revolt will "shake the foundations of," or deeply affect, the nation.)*

CRITICAL VOCABULARY

default: King says that the country has failed to honor its promises to African Americans.

ASK STUDENTS why King says that the country has defaulted on its promise to African Americans. *(The Constitution and the Declaration of Independence promise freedom and equality to Americans, but these rights have not been extended to African Americans.)*

desolate: King describes segregation as a dark and depressing valley.

ASK STUDENTS how a desolate person might feel. ***(Possible answers:*** *sad, lonely)*

NOTICE & NOTE

ANALYZE ARGUMENTS

Annotate: Underline King's claim. Mark details and evidence in paragraphs 3–5 that support his claim.

Analyze: What does King believe should happen?

3 But one hundred years later, the Negro still is not free; one hundred years later, the life of the Negro is still sadly crippled by the manacles of segregation and the chains of discrimination; one hundred years later, the Negro lives on a lonely island of poverty in the midst of a vast ocean of material prosperity; one hundred years later, the Negro is still languishing in the corners of American society and finds himself in exile in his own land. Close Read

4 So we've come here today to dramatize a shameful condition. In a sense we've come to our nation's capital to cash a check. When the architects of our republic wrote the magnificent words of the Constitution and the Declaration of Independence, they were signing a promissory note[3] to which every American was to fall heir. This note was the promise that all men, yes, black men as well as white men, would be guaranteed the unalienable rights of life, liberty, and the pursuit of happiness.

default
(dĭ-fôlt´) *v.* to fail to keep a promise to repay a loan.

5 It is obvious today that America has **defaulted** on this promissory note insofar as her citizens of color are concerned. Instead of honoring this sacred obligation, America has given the Negro people a bad check, a check which has come back marked "insufficient funds." But we refuse to believe that the bank of justice is bankrupt. We refuse to believe that there are insufficient funds in the great vaults of opportunity of this nation. And so we've come to cash this check, a check that will give us upon demand the riches of freedom and the security of justice.

6 We have also come to this hallowed spot to remind America of the fierce urgency of now. This is no time to engage in the luxury of cooling off or to take the tranquilizing drug of gradualism. Now is the time to make real the promises of democracy; now is the time to rise from the dark and **desolate** valley of segregation to the sunlit path of racial justice; now is the time to lift our nation from the quicksands of racial injustice to the solid rock of brotherhood; now is the time to make justice a reality for all of God's children. It would be fatal for the nation to overlook the urgency of the moment. This sweltering summer of the Negro's legitimate discontent will not pass until there is an invigorating autumn of freedom and equality. Close Read

desolate
(dĕs´ə-lĭt) *adj.* unhappy; lonely.

EXTREME OR ABSOLUTE LANGUAGE

Notice & Note: Mark examples of extreme or absolute language in paragraph 7.

Infer: What does King mean by "the whirlwinds of revolt"?

7 Nineteen sixty-three is not an end, but a beginning. And those who hope that the Negro needed to blow off steam and will now be content will have a rude awakening if the nation returns to business as usual. There will be neither rest nor tranquility in America until the Negro is granted his citizenship rights. The whirlwinds of revolt will continue to shake the foundations of our nation until the bright day of justice emerges.

[3] **promissory note:** a written promise to repay a loan.

CLOSE READ SCREENCAST

Modeled Discussions In their eBook, have students view the Close Read Screencasts, in which readers discuss and annotate the following key passages:

- King says that 100 years after the Emancipation Proclamation, African Americans still are not free (paragraph 3).
- King stresses the need for immediate action (paragraph 6).

As a class, view and discuss at least one video. Have student pairs do an independent close read of paragraph 9 and record their answers on the Close Read Practice PDF.

Close Read Practice PDF

8 But there is something that I must say to my people, who stand on the worn threshold which leads into the palace of justice. In the process of gaining our rightful place, we must not be guilty of wrongful deeds. Let us not seek to satisfy our thirst for freedom by drinking from the cup of bitterness and hatred. We must forever conduct our struggle on the high plain of dignity and discipline. We must not allow our creative protests to **degenerate** into physical violence. Again and again we must rise to the majestic heights of meeting physical force with soul force. The marvelous new militancy, which has engulfed the Negro community, must not lead us to a distrust of all white people. For many of our white brothers, as evidenced by their presence here today, have come to realize that their destiny is tied up with our destiny. And they have come to realize that their freedom is **inextricably** bound to our freedom. We cannot walk alone. And as we walk, we must make the pledge that we shall always march ahead. We cannot turn back.

degenerate
(dĭ-jĕn´ər-āt) *v.*
to decline morally.

inextricably
(ĭn-ĕk´strĭ-kə-blē) *adv.*
in a way impossible to untangle.

APPLYING ACADEMIC VOCABULARY

❑ decline ❑ enable ❑ impose ☑ integrate ☑ reveal

Write and Discuss Have students turn to a partner to discuss the following questions. Guide students to include the academic vocabulary words *integrate* and *reveal* in their responses. Ask volunteers to share their responses with the class.

- Does King believe **integration** is attainable?
- What does King **reveal** about his hopes and expectations regarding justice for African Americans?

CRITICAL VOCABULARY

degenerate: King beseeches activists not to allow the nonviolent protests to become violent.

ASK STUDENTS why King does not want the creative protests to degenerate. *(He thinks the protesters should be dignified and moral.)*

inextricably: King explains that many white Americans realize their freedom is tied to the freedom of African Americans.

ASK STUDENTS how the freedoms of white and black Americans might be inextricably bound. *(If the government is allowed to deny freedom to one group, there is nothing to prevent it from taking freedom away from other groups.)*

TEACH

LANGUAGE CONVENTIONS

Remind students that **parallelism** is the repeated use of a grammatical construction to express ideas that are equal in importance. Parallelism may use repetition of specific words or phrases. (***Answer:*** *It is like a chant that underscores the many ways African Americans are discriminated against. It emphasizes the urgency of the situation.*)

ENGLISH LEARNER SUPPORT

Understand Cultural/Historical Background Read aloud the parallelism in paragraph 10, beginning with "Go back to Mississippi." Explain that each place King names is a place where life has been especially difficult for African Americans. **MODERATE**

ANALYZE RHETORICAL DEVICES

Explain to students that King uses both **repetition** and **parallelism** in paragraphs 11–15. Encourage them to read the passage aloud or listen to a recording to better understand how the meaning of the repeated phrase changes. (***Answer:*** *Dr. King's dream for racial equality becomes more specific, vivid, and far-reaching.*)

For **listening support** for students at varying proficiency levels, see the **Text X-Ray** on page 84C.

CRITICAL VOCABULARY

redemptive: King assures African Americans that their suffering will not be in vain.

ASK STUDENTS in what way unjust suffering might be redemptive. (*It makes people stronger, and the injustice of it will eventually be apparent and lead to justice.*)

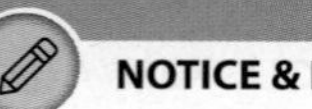

NOTICE & NOTE

LANGUAGE CONVENTIONS

Annotate: Underline the repetition and parallelism that King uses in paragraph 9.

Respond: Why is this use of repetition effective?

redemptive
(rĭ-dĕmp´tĭv) *adj.* causing freedom or salvation

ANALYZE RHETORICAL DEVICES

Annotate: Mark the phrase that is repeated throughout paragraphs 11–15.

Connect: How does the meaning of this phrase change and evolve?

9 There are those who are asking the devotees of civil rights, "When will you be satisfied?" We can never be satisfied as long as the Negro is the victim of the unspeakable horrors of police brutality; we can never be satisfied as long as our bodies, heavy with the fatigue of travel, cannot gain lodging in the motels of the highways and the hotels of the cities; we cannot be satisfied as long as the Negro's basic mobility is from a smaller ghetto to a larger one; we can never be satisfied as long as our children are stripped of their selfhood and robbed of their dignity by signs stating For Whites Only; we cannot be satisfied as long as the Negro in Mississippi cannot vote and a Negro in New York believes he has nothing for which to vote. No! No, we are not satisfied, and we will not be satisfied until "justice rolls down like waters and righteousness like a mighty stream."

10 I am not unmindful that some of you have come here out of great trials and tribulations. Some of you have come fresh from narrow jail cells. Some of you have come from areas where your quest for freedom left you battered by the storms of persecution and staggered by the winds of police brutality. You have been the veterans of creative suffering. Continue to work with the faith that unearned suffering is **redemptive**. Go back to Mississippi. Go back to Alabama. Go back to South Carolina. Go back to Georgia. Go back to Louisiana. Go back to the slums and ghettos of our Northern cities, knowing that somehow this situation can and will be changed. Let us not wallow in the valley of despair.

11 I say to you today, my friends, even though we face the difficulties of today and tomorrow, I still have a dream. It is a dream deeply rooted in the American dream. I have a dream that one day this nation will rise up and live out the true meaning of its creed, "We hold these truths to be self-evident; that all men are created equal." I have a dream that one day on the red hills of Georgia, sons of former slaves and the sons of former slave owners will be able to sit down together at the table of brotherhood. I have a dream that one day even the state of Mississippi, a state sweltering with the heat of injustice, sweltering with the heat of oppression, will be transformed into an oasis of freedom and justice. I have a dream that my four little children will one day live in a nation where they will not be judged by the color of their skin, but by the content of their character.

12 I have a dream today!

13 I have a dream that one day down in Alabama—with its vicious racists, with its Governor having his lips dripping with the words of interposition and nullification[4]— one day right there in Alabama,

[4] **Governor . . . nullification:** Rejecting a federal order to desegregate the University of Alabama, Governor George Wallace claimed that the principle of nullification (a state's alleged right to refuse a federal law) allowed him to resist federal "interposition," or interference, in state affairs.

NOTICE & NOTE 

little black boys and black girls will be able to join hands with little white boys and white girls as sisters and brothers.

14 I have a dream today!

15 I have a dream that one day every valley shall be exalted, and every hill and mountain shall be made low. The rough places will be plain and the crooked places will be made straight, "and the glory of the Lord shall be revealed, and all flesh shall see it together."

QUOTED WORDS

Notice & Note: Mark the quotation Dr. King uses in paragraph 15.

Analyze: What is he quoting from? Why is this effective?

TEACH

QUOTED WORDS

Remind students that this signpost is often used to appeal to an **audience.** If necessary, tell students that Dr. King is quoting from the Bible. (***Answer:*** *The language of the quotation is powerful, and it connects to both black and white listeners who are familiar with the scripture. It suggests that King is confident his dream will be achieved because it is right and good.)*

ENGLISH LEARNER SUPPORT

Discuss Historical/Cultural References Read aloud paragraph 11 and focus students' attention on "I have a dream that one day this nation will rise up and live out the true meaning of its creed, 'We hold these truths to be self-evident; that all men are created equal.'" Point out that the quotation is from the Declaration of Independence, the document in which the American colonies announced their separation from Great Britain and set forth the principles and standards by which the nation should be governed.

- Have small groups discuss why, according to King, the nation is failing to live up to its creed. Provide sentence frames to aid students' discussion:

The Declaration of Independence says that all people are ______. King says African Americans are not treated ______. King dreams that one day African Americans ______, as the Declaration of Independence promises. **SUBSTANTIAL**

- Have students discuss how the sources of the following quotations add to King's message.

—paragraph 4: ". . . life, liberty, and the pursuit of happiness." the Declaration of Independence (/)

—paragraph 16: "My Country, 'Tis of Thee" ("America"), patriotic song

—paragraph 18: "Free at Last," Negro spiritual **MODERATE/LIGHT**

ANALYZE RHETORICAL DEVICES

Point out that King uses repetition and parallelism to develop the extended metaphor in paragraphs 16 and 17.

In paragraph 16, King repeats the phrase "With this faith" to emphasize how the belief that one day all people will be treated as equals can help bring us together to work toward that goal, "to transform the jangling discords of our nation into a beautiful symphony." As he repeats the word *together*, he introduces lyrics from the song "My Country, 'Tis of Thee" to develop the metaphor of people singing harmoniously together.

Ask students to identify the parallelism in paragraph 17. Discuss how the repetition of "Let freedom ring" develops the metaphor of Americans singing together in freedom and builds rhythm and urgency in the speech. (***Answer:*** *In Dr. King's vision, he compares people in conflict to a discordant orchestra, and he imagines that they come together to create a "beautiful symphony." Songs of freedom and liberty would then ring from hilltops and mountains across the land.*)

NOTICE & NOTE

ANALYZE RHETORICAL DEVICES

Annotate Mark the extended metaphor King uses in paragraphs 16–17, including details that develop it.

Interpret: Explain Dr. King's vision in your own words.

16 This is our hope. This is the faith that I go back to the South with. With this faith we will be able to hew out of the mountain of despair a stone of hope. With this faith we will be able to transform the jangling discords of our nation into a beautiful symphony of brotherhood. With this faith we will be able to work together, to pray together, to struggle together, to go to jail together, to stand up for freedom together, knowing that we will be free one day. And this will be the day. This will be the day when all of God's children will be able to sing with new meaning, "My country 'tis of thee, sweet land of liberty, of thee I sing. Land where my fathers died, land of the pilgrims' pride, from every mountainside, let freedom ring." And if America is to be a great nation, this must become true.

17 So let freedom ring from the prodigious hilltops of New Hampshire; let freedom ring from the mighty mountains of New York; let freedom ring from the heightening Alleghenies of Pennsylvania; let freedom ring from the snowcapped Rockies of Colorado; let freedom ring from the curvaceous slopes of California. But not only that. Let freedom ring from Stone Mountain of Georgia; let freedom ring from Lookout Mountain of Tennessee; let freedom ring from every hill and molehill of Mississippi. "From every mountainside, let freedom ring."

18 And when this happens, and when we allow freedom to ring, when we let it ring from every village and every hamlet, from every state and every city, we will be able to speed up that day when all of God's children—black men and white men, Jews and Gentiles, Protestants and Catholics—will be able to join hands and sing in the words of the old Negro spiritual, "Free at last. Free at last. Thank God Almighty, we are free at last."

IMPROVE READING FLUENCY

Targeted Passage Use King's soaring words from paragraphs 17 and 18 to help students practice reading a speech. Remind them that a speech should be delivered with expression and with emphasis on repeated words and phrases, using punctuation marks as a guide to when to pause and when to begin a new thought.

First, model for students an effective reading of the speech, or show them a video of King delivering the specific lines they will be practicing. Then, read the passage again, pausing after each sentence or clause to have students echo read.

Go to the **Reading Studio** for additional support in developing fluency.

NOTICE & NOTE

CHECK YOUR UNDERSTANDING

Answer these questions before moving on to the **Analyze the Text** section on the following page.

1 Martin Luther King Jr.'s main purpose in "I Have a Dream" is to —

A celebrate the end of slavery and oppression of African Americans

B urge all people to peacefully work together for racial equality

C give a lecture about the Emancipation Proclamation

D describe his dreams and interpret them for his audience

2 In paragraph 5, King uses the extended metaphor of a check to —

F persuade demonstrators that they should avoid banks

G give an example of poverty in his community

H explain that America must keep its promise of freedom for all people

J ask the government to provide more financial assistance

3 How does King appeal to the emotions of his audience?

A He tells a story from the Christian Bible.

B He uses repetition and parallelism to create rhythm.

C He uses complicated, unfamiliar vocabulary.

D He interprets the Declaration of Independence.

TEACH

CHECK YOUR UNDERSTANDING

Have students answer the questions independently.

Answers:

1. *B*
2. *H*
3. *B*

If students answer any questions incorrectly, have them reread the text to confirm their understanding. Then they may proceed to ANALYZE THE TEXT on page 96.

ENGLISH LEARNER SUPPORT

Oral Assessment Use the following questions to assess students' comprehension and speaking skills.

1. Why did Dr. King give the "I Have a Dream" speech? *(He wanted to urge all people to peacefully work together for racial equality.)*
2. In paragraph 5, why does King compare a check to a promise? *(King compares a check to a promise to explain that America must keep its promise of freedom for all people.)*
3. What literary devices does Dr. King use to appeal to the emotions of his audience? *(King uses repetition and parallelism to create rhythm.)* **ALL LEVELS**

TEACH

ANALYZE THE TEXT

Possible answers:

1. **DOK 2:** *King's claim is that African Americans are not free in America because of racism and discrimination. He supports this claim by pointing out that segregation, discrimination, and poverty still exist for the majority of African Americans.*
2. **DOK 2:** *King's audience includes people who are fighting for equal treatment and rights. He urges them to demonstrate in a nonviolent way that does not "[drink] from the cup of bitterness and hatred." He tells them to "always march ahead. We cannot turn back."*
3. **DOK 4:** *King begins several clauses with "now is the time to. . . ." He urges his audience to rise from the "dark and desolate valley of segregation" and out of the "quicksands of racial injustice." This parallelism helps King convey the "fierce urgency of now" and explain to his audience why they must not hesitate to act.*
4. **DOK 4:** *King's speech is remembered because he raised important issues of race and discrimination that are still important and relevant today. He urged people to act rather than stand by in the face of inequality, and he criticized systemic unfairness and discrimination. He dreamed of a United States in which all the promises of freedom and human rights were kept, and he invited the nation's people to share that dream.*
5. **DOK 4:** *King uses extreme or absolute language such as "we shall always march ahead" (paragraph 8) and "we can never be satisfied" (paragraph 9). He wants to persuade his audience to keep going and never give up the fight for equal rights. This technique is effective because he describes a difficult fight that can be won only with persistence and determination.*

RESEARCH

Review the Research Tip with students. Suggest that they jot down their initial responses to the speech in audio or video form and then replay it to add more details to their charts.

Connect Suggest that students list the examples of injustice that King cites in paragraph 9. Remind them that Dr. King gave this speech in 1963 and have them consider how conditions in their own community or school might have changed since that time.

RESPOND

ANALYZE THE TEXT

Support your responses with evidence from the text. NOTEBOOK

1. **Summarize** The central point of an argument is the **claim**. What is King's claim in this speech? What evidence does he cite to support his claim?
2. **Interpret** Review paragraph 8. Who is King's audience in this paragraph? How does King want his audience to work toward racial justice? Explain your answer and cite evidence from the text.
3. **Analyze** Find examples of parallelism in paragraph 6. What effect does the parallel structure create? What point is King emphasizing?
4. **Evaluate** Why do you think King's "I Have a Dream" speech is remembered as one of the most significant speeches in American history? Explain what makes the speech memorable and how it contributes to the ideal of an American society.
5. **Notice & Note** Explain how King uses extreme or absolute language to persuade his audience. Give at least two examples. Do you think he uses this technique effectively? Explain.

RESEARCH TIP
The best search terms are very specific. Along with King's name, include the name of his speech and the form you want, such as text, image, or video, in order to find exactly what you are looking for.

RESEARCH

It's one thing to read a speech, but it's even better to listen to it or to be an audience member. Find a version of Martin Luther King Jr.'s speech in audio or video form. On the chart, explain what you noticed in the audio or video version, and how that is different from what you noticed in the text.

FORM OF SPEECH	WHAT I NOTICED	IMPACT ON ME
Text		
Audio/Video		

Connect In paragraph 9, Dr. King says that people ask civil rights activists, "When will you be satisfied?" Reread the paragraph and write a response about how his main idea in that part of the speech applies today. Share your response with a small group.

LEARNING MINDSET

Problem Solving If students get stuck while trying to respond to the Analyze the Text questions, suggest that they apply problem-solving strategies as they work through the questions. Encourage them to look at the question from a different angle or to try a different learning strategy. For example, they might ask themselves what part of the question is giving them trouble. If terms such as *claim* and *parallelism* are tripping them up, they can review the definitions and examples on Student Edition page 87.

CREATE AND DISCUSS

Write a Response Listen to a recording or watch a video of Martin Luther King Jr.'s "I Have a Dream" speech. Write a short response to describe how listening to the speech enhances your understanding of the topic.

- ❑ Listen to the recording or watch "I Have a Dream" at least twice. Follow along using the written speech.
- ❑ Annotate the written speech as you listen or watch. As you follow along, take notes on how hearing the speech changes your understanding of it. Is your emotional response different when you hear Dr. King read the speech?
- ❑ Summarize your overall response to the speech, including how your understanding of the speech changed as you listened to King speak.

Discuss with a Small Group Have a panel discussion to share personal thoughts and feelings about the speech.

- ❑ Review the text and decide which parts of the speech had a different impact as you listened to the recording.
- ❑ Have members prepare personal thoughts and feelings in response to the recording. Appoint a discussion leader to facilitate sharing.
- ❑ Have each group member share and discuss the impact of the recording on their understanding of the speech and how it affected them personally to hear King deliver the speech. All students should listen closely and respectfully before asking questions or making comments.
- ❑ Students can help one other define or describe terms or ideas when words in the text are unfamiliar.

Go to the **Speaking and Listening Studio** for help with having a group discussion.

RESPOND TO THE ESSENTIAL QUESTION

How do people find freedom in the midst of oppression?

Gather Information Review your annotations and notes on "I Have a Dream." Then, add relevant information to your Response Log. As you determine which information to include, think about:

- how Dr. King urged his audience to fight oppression
- how racial inequality can lead to injustice
- why it is important to understand that freedom takes many forms

At the end of the unit, use your notes to help you write a research report.

ACADEMIC VOCABULARY

As you write and discuss what you learned from the speech, be sure to use the Academic Vocabulary words. Check off each of the words that you use.

- ❑ **decline**
- ❑ **enable**
- ❑ **impose**
- ❑ **integrate**
- ❑ **reveal**

CREATE AND DISCUSS

Write a Response Remind students that when they summarize their response to the speech they can use the details they noted in their research charts as support. Have them consider what King's intonation and speaking style adds to their emotional response and to their understanding of what King feels is important.

For **writing support** for students at varying proficiency levels, see the **Text X-Ray** on page 84D.

Discuss with a Small Group Remind students that listening closely to their classmates' comments will allow them to ask appropriate questions that lead to a meaningful discussion. Encourage students to identify the lines in the speech that are most memorable or meaningful to them.

RESPOND TO THE ESSENTIAL QUESTION

Allow time for students to add details from "I Have a Dream" to their Unit 2 Response Logs.

ENGLISH LEARNER SUPPORT

Discuss with a Small Group Encourage students to ask for assistance as they discuss the speech in groups. Create a universal signal, such as a 3 x 5 card with a question mark on it. Allow students to hold up the card when they need clarification or assistance. Ask students to voice their question aloud to an English-speaking partner before resuming the discussion. Provide these sentence frames to help students ask questions and discuss the speech: *I have a question about* ____. *I felt* ____ *when I heard the speech.* **SUBSTANTIAL**

TEACH

CRITICAL VOCABULARY

Possible answers:

1. *King says that America has failed to keep a promise to guarantee people's rights.* Defaulted *carries the connotation that the American people have failed to keep a binding agreement.*
2. *Segregation is* desolate *because being separated from other citizens creates a feeling of loneliness and of not belonging.*
3. *King believes that avoiding violence is the dignified and moral path; therefore, to resort to violence would be to* degenerate.
4. *The freedom of all people is* inextricably *bound because if all Americans are not free, then no one's freedom is safe. If the government does not protect your neighbor's freedom, there's no guarantee it will protect yours, either.*
5. *A faithful person may suffer in this world, but the suffering is* redemptive *if the person is rewarded in heaven. Similarly, King suggests that people who suffer undeservedly while fighting for freedom will ultimately be rewarded.*

VOCABULARY STRATEGY:
Antonyms

Possible answers:

1. ***pay:*** *He will pay off the loan this year.*
2. ***improve:*** *Many people's lives would improve if racial inequality were eliminated.*
3. ***loosely:*** *In a secular regime, religion and politics are very loosely connected.*
4. ***destructive:*** *Their loss of freedom was destructive to their morale.*

RESPOND

WORD BANK
default
desolate
degenerate
inextricably
redemptive

CRITICAL VOCABULARY

Practice and Apply Answer the following questions in complete sentences, incorporating the Critical Vocabulary words and their meanings.

1. Look back at paragraph 5. Why does King say that America has **defaulted** on its promise?
2. Look back at paragraph 6. In what ways is segregation **desolate**?
3. Look back at paragraph 8. How is physical violence a good example of how protests might **degenerate**?
4. Look back at paragraph 8. How is the freedom of all people **inextricably** bound together?
5. Look back at paragraph 10. How and why does King use the word **redemptive** to link the concepts of freedom and religious faith?

VOCABULARY STRATEGY:
Antonyms

Go to the **Vocabulary Studio** for more on antonyms.

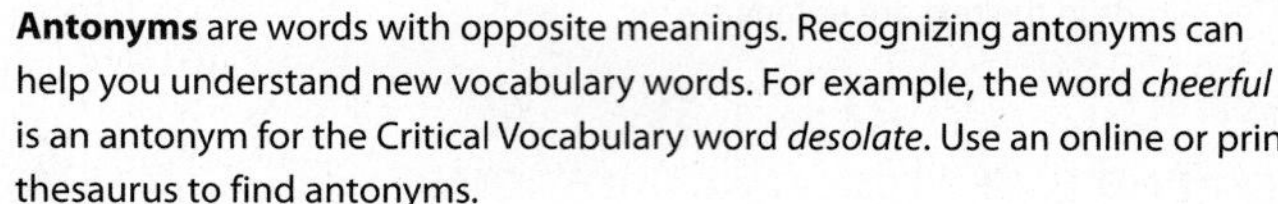

Antonyms are words with opposite meanings. Recognizing antonyms can help you understand new vocabulary words. For example, the word *cheerful* is an antonym for the Critical Vocabulary word *desolate*. Use an online or print thesaurus to find antonyms.

Practice and Apply Use a thesaurus to find an antonym for each of the remaining Critical Vocabulary words. Then, write sentences using each antonym.

1. **default**
2. **degenerate**
3. **inextricably**
4. **redemptive**

ENGLISH LEARNER SUPPORT

Use Antonyms Give students additional practice with antonyms.

- In a two-column chart with the headings *Academic Vocabulary* and *Antonyms*, have students list the academic vocabulary words *decline*, *integrate*, and *reveal*. Dictate antonyms for the right column in this order: *hide*, *rise*, *separate*. Then have partners draw lines connecting each academic vocabulary word with its antonym, checking the definitions in online or print resources. **SUBSTANTIAL/MODERATE**
- Adapt the above activity by having students work with partners to write an example sentence for each vocabulary word and each antonym. Then have pairs present their work. **LIGHT**

LANGUAGE CONVENTIONS: Repetition and Parallelism

Martin Luther King Jr. uses the techniques of repetition and parallelism to express his ideas. These patterns emphasize his important ideas and make his speech flow rhythmically. Through these techniques, he links ideas together and builds upon them.

Repetition refers to repeated words or phrases. Sometimes phrases are repeated throughout a sentence. Other times they are repeated throughout a paragraph, or between paragraphs. This is a way to link ideas together.

> **We can never be satisfied as long as the Negro is the victim of the unspeakable horrors of police brutality; we can never be satisfied as long as our bodies, heavy with the fatigue of travel, cannot gain lodging in the motels of the highways and the hotels of the cities . . .**

Here, Dr. King gives many reasons why "we can never be satisfied." He links his reasons together by repeating the same phrase again and again.

Parallelism refers to a similar sentence or phrase structure that is repeated within a sentence or paragraph. Speakers often use parallelism to highlight similarities or differences.

> **I have a dream that one day every valley shall be exalted, and every hill and mountain shall be made low. The rough places will be plain and the crooked places will be made straight . . .**

Here, Dr. King uses parallelism to highlight the contrasts, or differences in his imagery. Similar sentence structure is used in both phrases.

Practice and Apply Look back at the response you wrote to listening or watching the speech for Create and Discuss. Find two or three places where you can revise your wording to use the techniques of repetition or parallelism. Write your revised response below.

LANGUAGE CONVENTIONS: Repetition and Parallelism

Tell students that the examples on this page are just two of the many examples of repetition and parallelism in King's speech. Point out that many of the most famous lines in the speech use repetition and parallelism, and that this is one of the most important reasons for using these devices: they make an impact so that people remember the ideas.

Practice and Apply Students' revisions should focus on using repetition and parallelism to emphasize key words and phrases that clearly and forcefully express their responses to the speech.

ENGLISH LEARNER SUPPORT

Interpret Repetition and Parallelism Use the following supports with students at varying proficiency levels.

- Work with students to find and copy into their notes another example of repetition or parallelism in "I Have a Dream." **SUBSTANTIAL**
- Have students work with partners to identify an example of repetition or parallelism in "I Have a Dream." Have partners work together to create a word web that expresses how King's technique affects his audience. Invite pairs to share their webs with the class. **MODERATE**
- Ask students to locate one example of repetition and one example of parallelism in "I Have a Dream." Ask them to write a sentence describing the important idea that is expressed in each example. Invite them to share their sentences with the class and read aloud the examples from the speech. **LIGHT**

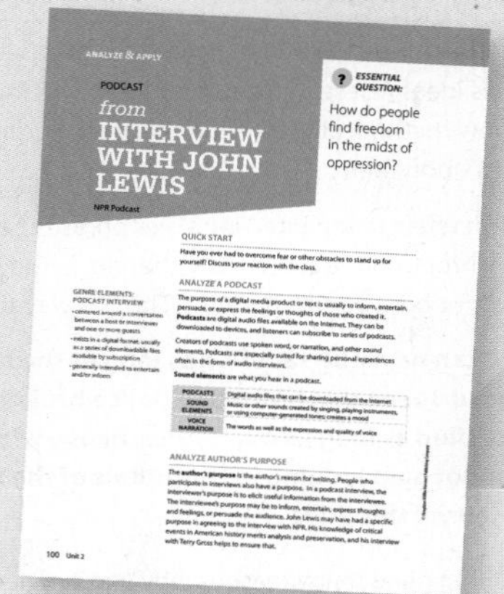

MEDIA

INTERVIEW WITH JOHN LEWIS

NPR Podcast

GENRE ELEMENTS

PODCAST INTERVIEW

Remind students that a **podcast interview** is a conversation between a host and one or more guests that exists in digital format. Podcasts are efficient, portable, and cost effective because they are available through different digital media instead of print. They also make it possible for people to listen to information or entertainment about specific topics that interest them. In this lesson, students will listen to a podcast interview and determine the interviewee's purpose for agreeing to be interviewed.

LEARNING OBJECTIVES

- Analyze elements of a podcast and various purposes for participating in a podcast.
- Conduct research about John Lewis's accomplishments and their effects.
- Create a multimedia presentation.
- Discuss with a small group how a podcast interview can inspire people to action.
- **Language** Express opinions about the podcast using specific details and complete sentences.

TEXT COMPLEXITY

Quantitative Measures	**Interview with John Lewis**	Lexile: N/A
Qualitative Measures	**Ideas Presented** Literal, explicit, and direct, with a clear purpose or stance.	
	Structures Used Primarily one perspective; may vary from simple chronological order.	
	Language Used Explicit, literal, contemporary, familiar language.	
	Knowledge Required Includes cultural or historical references but provides some explanation.	

Online 

RESOURCES

- Unit 2 Response Log
- Selection Audio
- Speaking and Listening Studio: Using Media in a Presentation
- Speaking and Listening Studio: Participating in Collaborative Discussions
- "Interview with John Lewis" Selection Test

SUMMARIES

English

In a 2009 radio interview, civil rights leader and Georgia congressman John Lewis speaks about encounters with discrimination and oppression during his youth in the then segregated South. He recounts how, inspired by Martin Luther King Jr. and Rosa Parks, he took part in civil rights marches and demonstrations. He persisted in his efforts despite being severely beaten in 1965—and he describes the joy he felt when the Voting Rights Act was finally introduced to Congress.

Spanish

En una entrevista de radio de 2009, el líder de los derechos civiles y congresista de Georgia, John Lewis, habla acerca de sus encuentros con la discriminación y opresión en su juventud, en el para entonces segregado Sur. Lewis narra cómo, inspirado por Martin Luther King Jr. y Rosa Parks, participó en marchas y protestas por los derechos civiles. Persistió en sus esfuerzos a pesar de ser severamente golpeado en 1965. Y describe la alegría que sintió cuando la Ley de Derecho al Voto fue finalmente introducida en el Congreso.

SMALL-GROUP OPTIONS

Have students work in small groups to discuss the selection.

Think-Pair-Share

- After students have listened to and analyzed the podcast, ask, "How can John Lewis's experiences and accomplishments serve as a model for people today?"
- Instruct students to think about the question individually and take notes about their response.
- Then have pairs discuss their ideas about the question and choose the two or three ideas that they consider most important.
- Invite pairs to share their responses with the class.

Send a Problem

- During a discussion about Lewis's interview, pose a question and call on a student to respond. For example, you might ask, "How do the examples John Lewis provides support his message?"
- If the student does not have a response after 11 seconds, he or she must name another student to answer the same question.
- The sending student should repeat the question for the second student.
- Monitor responses and redirect or ask another question at any time.

Text X-Ray: English Learner Support

for "Interview with John Lewis"

Use the Text X-Ray and the supports and scaffolds in the Teacher's Edition to help guide students at different proficiency levels through the selection.

INTRODUCE THE SELECTION

DISCUSS OPPRESSION

In this lesson, the topic of oppression may result in strong emotions and opinions from students:

- Help students define oppression. Have students use words such as *unjust, cruel, stereotype,* and *prejudice* to express their ideas about oppression. Record their ideas and guide them toward a general definition: *Prolonged cruel or unjust treatment*.
- Explain that while listening to the podcast, they may think of examples of oppression they have experienced and/or heard on the news or from family.
- As a group, brainstorm guidelines for discussions about "Interview with John Lewis." Encourage students to contribute in order to support talking about difficult subjects brought up in the podcast. Make a list that students can refer to. For example:
  - Listen carefully and don't interrupt.
  - Give everyone a chance to speak.
  - Ask questions to clarify ideas.
  - Focus on questioning ideas, not criticizing people.
  - Don't call people names.

CULTURAL REFERENCES

The following words or phrases (approximate time shown when occurring in podcast) may be unfamiliar to students:

- *National Book Award* (0:03): a set of annual U.S. literary awards
- *Selma* and *Montgomery* (0:23): cities in Alabama
- *sharecropper* (1:44): a tenant farmer who gives a share of the crops to the landlord instead of rent
- *AME Church* (3:58): African Methodist Episcopal Church
- *Voting Rights Act* (5:51): law passed to end barriers preventing African Americans from exercising their right to vote

English Learners may also need support with the following background knowledge:

- *NPR*, National Public Radio, is a privately and publicly funded non-profit U.S. media organization.
- *1960s Civil Rights Movement* was a social and political movement aimed at ending racial segregation and discrimination in the United States.

LISTENING

Understand the Central Idea

As they listen, draw students' attention to the key ideas of the podcast and the subject of the podcast, John Lewis winning the National Book Award.

Use the following supports with students at varying proficiency levels.

- Play the podcast, pausing at regular intervals to confirm students' comprehension. Ask questions such as: Were literacy tests used to prevent African Americans from voting? Have students use yes/no or thumbs up/thumbs downs to respond. **SUBSTANTIAL**
- Have students listen to the podcast to learn key points related to Lewis's literary background. As a group, discuss what made winning the National Book Award so significant. **MODERATE**
- Model how to take notes while listening to the first few minutes of the podcast. Explain that pausing while they listen and recording key points will help them comprehend. After listening, have partners compare notes and listen again to confirm important ideas. **LIGHT**

SPEAKING

Describe Reactions

Guide students to describe and support their reactions to what they learned from the podcast. Model how to identify and respectfully discuss their opinions.

Use the following supports with students at varying proficiency levels.

- Model how to support an opinion about the podcast, pointing out that opinions, or claims, need to be supported by reasons and evidence. Then, guide students to identify and explain their opinions. Provide sentence frames: *I liked/didn't like this part because ____. The ____ made me feel ____.* **SUBSTANTIAL**
- Model how to support an opinion about the podcast, for example: *In my opinion,_____. The detail about _____ in the podcast supports my opinion because_____.* Then, ask students to think about their opinions of Lewis's life overall or a specific incident and explain them in a few complete sentences. **MODERATE**
- Reference a specific part of the interview, such as when Lewis talks about peaceful marchers being beaten on the Edmund Pettus Bridge. Have students discuss and support their opinions of that part in small groups. **LIGHT**

LISTENING

Analyze a Podcast

Replay the podcast, asking students to keep in mind the podcast elements reviewed at the beginning of the selection (Student Edition page 100): sound elements and voice narration.

Use the following supports with students at varying proficiency levels.

- Review the podcast elements discussed in the beginning of the selection. Give examples for each one and check for understanding. For instance: *Sound elements can be full songs, but also single tones like horns or bird chirping.* **SUBSTANTIAL**
- As they listen, have students make a note whenever they hear one of the different elements used in the podcast. **MODERATE**
- In small groups, have students review the podcast elements and consider what elements were used most in this podcast. Then, have them discuss how effectively these were used. **LIGHT**

WRITING

Create a Multimedia Presentation

Help students choose an event or accomplishment described in the podcast that they would like to highlight in their presentation (Student Edition page 103).

Use the following supports with students at varying proficiency levels.

- Guide students in reviewing events in Lewis's life and his accomplishments, clarifying anything they find confusing. Ask leading questions to help them focus on a topic they find interesting. **SUBSTANTIAL**
- After they choose their topic, have students search for images that represent it. Provide sentence stems to help them write notes or captions for images: *This image supports my presentation because ____. The setting of my event is ____ and this image shows ____.* **MODERATE**
- Pair students and have them review each other's presentations. Tell them to write sentences and questions about their responses to the topic to use in discussions. Provide sentence stems: *This photo makes me think of ____. Did you include this because____?* **LIGHT**

Connect to the ESSENTIAL QUESTION

As Representative John Lewis (D-Georgia) explains in this interview, he had been taught as a child not to challenge the limitations of civil rights imposed on African Americans in the mid-20th century. In spite of this, he decided that finding freedom was more important than staying safe but oppressed.

QUICK START

Invite volunteers to share examples of times when they, or someone they admire, stood up for themselves. Prompt students to consider how they felt about the situation that challenged them and why they decided to make a stand. Have them also consider obstacles such as physical danger, disapproval of peers, embarrassment, or fear of failure.

ANALYZE A PODCAST

Have students read the information about podcasts. Then have them review the sound elements described in the chart. Ask them to give examples of each element based on their own experience of listening to podcasts or other media to which the elements apply.

Suggest that students use these questions to help them analyze the elements of the podcast interview:

- How does the interviewer introduce John Lewis?
- How do the interviewer's questions guide John Lewis to reveal important details about the topic?
- How do the tone and emotion in John Lewis's voice affect the listener's understanding of his experiences?

ANALYZE AUTHOR'S PURPOSE

Remind students that just as an author may have more than one reason for writing, a person may have more than one reason for taking part in a podcast interview. As students prepare to listen to the podcast, urge them to think carefully about what John Lewis wants to convey to his audience.

PODCAST

from INTERVIEW WITH JOHN LEWIS

NPR Podcast

ESSENTIAL QUESTION:

How do people find freedom in the midst of oppression?

QUICK START

Have you ever had to overcome fear or other obstacles to stand up for yourself? Discuss your reaction with the class.

ANALYZE A PODCAST

GENRE ELEMENTS: PODCAST INTERVIEW

- centered around a conversation between a host or interviewer and one or more guests
- exists in a digital format, usually as a series of downloadable files available by subscription
- generally intended to entertain and/or inform

The purpose of a digital media product or text is usually to inform, entertain, persuade, or express the feelings or thoughts of those who created it. **Podcasts** are digital audio files available on the Internet. They can be downloaded to devices, and listeners can subscribe to series of podcasts.

Creators of podcasts use spoken word, or narration, and other sound elements. Podcasts are especially suited for sharing personal experiences often in the form of audio interviews.

Sound elements are what you hear in a podcast.

PODCASTS	Digital audio files that can be downloaded from the Internet
SOUND ELEMENTS	Music or other sounds created by singing, playing instruments, or using computer-generated tones; creates a mood
VOICE NARRATION	The words as well as the expression and quality of voice

ANALYZE AUTHOR'S PURPOSE

The **author's purpose** is the author's reason for writing. People who participate in interviews also have a purpose. In a podcast interview, the interviewer's purpose is to elicit useful information from the interviewee. The interviewee's purpose may be to inform, entertain, express thoughts and feelings, or persuade the audience. John Lewis may have had a specific purpose in agreeing to the interview with NPR. His knowledge of critical events in American history merits analysis and preservation, and his interview with Terry Gross helps to ensure that.

ENGLISH LEARNER SUPPORT

Confirm Understanding To check students' understanding of key words and concepts, discuss the following terms after listening to the podcast:

polls **register to vote** **literacy test** **evict** **sharecroppers** **nonviolent**

Point out to students that context clues can help them understand meanings of unfamiliar terms. For example, *tenant farmers* is a synonym for *sharecroppers*. Encourage students to jot down unfamiliar words as they replay the podcast. In addition, guide discussion by asking vocabulary-related questions such as these: Why did so many educated African Americans fail the **literacy test**? Why was it important for the marchers in Selma to have a **nonviolent** protest? **ALL LEVELS**

BACKGROUND

John Lewis *(b. 1940) is one of the "Big Six" civil rights activists of the 1960s Civil Rights Movement, as well as a U.S. Representative in Congress. Lewis was born in Alabama in 1940, during a time when segregation was in full force. As a teen, he was inspired by Dr. Martin Luther King Jr. and Rosa Parks. He began college in 1957, and participated in civil rights marches, helping to plan the March on Washington in 1963. In 1965, he led the march from Selma, Alabama, with Hosea Williams and was beaten so badly by state troopers that his skull was fractured. His actions helped persuade President Johnson to enact the 1965 Voting Rights Act. The Act was intended to overcome legal barriers at the state and local levels that prevented African Americans from exercising their right to vote. Lewis's life in politics has been dedicated to voting rights, fighting poverty, and supporting public education. He has created a graphic novel series to teach young people about the marches for civil rights.*

SETTING A PURPOSE

Before listening, make a prediction about what John Lewis will discuss in the podcast, which was recorded in 2009. Afterward, check to see if your prediction was correct.

To listen to the podcast, log in online and select **"from INTERVIEW WITH JOHN LEWIS"** from the unit menu.

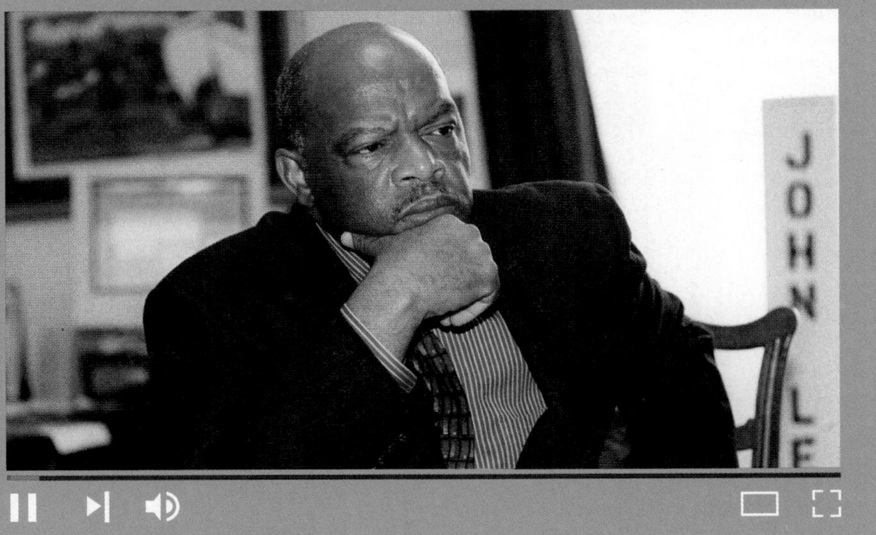

As needed, pause the recording to make notes about your predictions or what you might want to talk about later. Replay or rewind so that you can clarify anything you do not understand.

TEACH

BACKGROUND

After students read the Background note, ask them to consider how Lewis's life history relates to the Essential Question. What inspired him to act on his belief in freedom from oppression?

SETTING A PURPOSE

Direct students to use the Setting a Purpose prompt to focus their listening.

For **listening support** for students at varying proficiency levels, see the **Text X-Ray** on pages 100C and 100D.

WHEN STUDENTS STRUGGLE . . .

Use Repeated Listening Have students listen to the podcast with partners. Suggest that they play the podcast once without stopping and then discuss what they learned and what was unclear. Then, instruct them to play the podcast a second time, pausing between the interviewer's questions to jot down important ideas and any remaining questions. Finally, bring partners together in small groups to share and respond to one another's questions and to reflect upon Lewis's account.

APPLY

ANALYZE PODCASTS

Possible answers:

1. **DOK 2:** *Lewis says that Rosa Parks inspired him when she refused to move on the bus, and hearing the words of Dr. Martin Luther King Jr. on the radio convinced him that he, too, had to take risks and march for civil rights.*
2. **DOK 4:** *The interviewer's purpose is to have Lewis tell why he decided to become involved in the fight for voting rights. She begins by asking about Lewis's own experience with registering to vote, drawing him out about his family's fears and the failed attempts of many to register to vote. Then she probes the origins of his determination to fight for the right to vote.*
3. **DOK 3:** *Lewis saw that literate, highly educated African Americans were prevented from voting because they supposedly failed literacy tests. He recognized the unfairness of the situation. When he saw major figures in the African American community standing up for their rights, he knew that he, too, had to "make a contribution."*
4. **DOK 2:** *The "signs" to which Lewis refers are the signs preventing African Americans from having access to places where white people could go and receiving services that white people could receive. Lewis heard in Dr. King's message that the main goals were to get African Americans into jobs that were reserved for whites only and to break down the color barrier in Montgomery and the rest of the country.*
5. **DOK 3:** *Lewis's purpose in the interview seems to be to encourage people to take action, in a nonviolent way, even in the face of danger, to achieve true equality. He uses his own experiences as an example of how to take inspiration from the words and actions of others, such as Dr. King and Rosa Parks.*

RESEARCH

Review the Research Tip with students. Remind them that information on the Internet is not regulated for accuracy and that many websites—even some that purport to be devoted to "news"—contain inaccurate and undocumented stories. Urge students to check their findings in at least two sources to verify their accuracy.

Connect As students review the accomplishments and effects that they listed in their charts, point out that many rights and freedoms they take for granted resulted from Lewis's efforts. Encourage students to search local news outlets for stories that address community rights and freedoms.

RESPOND

ANALYZE PODCASTS

Support your responses with evidence from the podcast. NOTEBOOK

1. **Cause/Effect** The interviewer asks John Lewis about what caused him to go against his mother's wishes and get involved in civil rights marches. What does he say inspired him to organize and march with other activists?
2. **Analyze** What is the interviewer's purpose as she begins to ask questions of John Lewis? Describe the approach she takes to get Lewis to share his story.
3. **Draw Conclusions** What factors motivated John Lewis to fight for voting rights? Explain why Lewis felt that the risks were worth taking to change the society he lived in.
4. **Interpret** What does John Lewis mean when he says he focused on "bringing down those signs"? How does his story about listening to Dr. King talk about activism in Montgomery help you understand what his main goals were?
5. **Cite Evidence** What do you think was Lewis's purpose in agreeing to be interviewed? Cite evidence from the interview to support your answer.

RESEARCH TIP
Be sure to check the websites you use to ensure that they are reliable and credible sources of information. Sites of well-known news organizations are a good place to start, and sites with the suffix .org tend to be more reliable than commercial sites.

RESEARCH

John Lewis is a longtime member of Congress with a long list of civil rights achievements. Research Lewis's many accomplishments and their impact on others. Record what you learn in the chart.

ACCOMPLISHMENTS	EFFECTS
Created a graphic novel to teach young people about the Selma March	Inspires young people to understand the past and get involved in fighting for civil rights now

Connect In the interview, John Lewis says that he felt that Dr. King was speaking directly to him, saying that he, too, could "make a contribution." With a small group, discuss how John Lewis's contributions have had an impact on your own community's rights and freedoms.

ENGLISH LEARNER SUPPORT

Oral Assessment To gauge comprehension and speaking skills, conduct an informal assessment. Walk around the class, talking with students and asking these questions:

- What did John Lewis want to show by marching from Selma to Montgomery, Alabama, in 1965? *(that African Americans wanted to vote)* **SUBSTANTIAL**
- Why did it take great courage for Lewis and his group to decide to march to Montgomery? *(It was physically dangerous: peaceful demonstrators had been arrested and beaten; one had been killed.)* **MODERATE**
- How was the march to Montgomery both a failure and a success? *(It did not reach Montgomery, but it inspired the country to achieve voting rights for all.)* **LIGHT**

CREATE AND PRESENT

Create a Multimedia Presentation Using photos and images from your research on John Lewis, create a multimedia presentation about one aspect of Lewis's career. Present it to the class or post it online.

- ❑ Select photos and images that help to explain one aspect of John Lewis's career, such as an event in which he played a key role or one of his major accomplishments.
- ❑ Then, use presentation software to create a multimedia presentation about this aspect of Lewis's career. Prepare notes to guide you in speaking about the parts of the presentation. Choose language that suits your topic and purpose. Then, practice your presentation, noting when you should pause or change the volume of your voice for effect.
- ❑ Give your final presentation to the class in person and/or online.

Go to the **Speaking and Listening Studio** for more on creating a multimedia presentation.

Discuss with a Small Group Have a discussion about how information in "Interview with John Lewis" can help to inspire people to resist oppressive laws and fight for freedom.

- ❑ As a group, review the interview and decide which information is relevant to the discussion topic. Use the podcast player functions to replay important aspects of the interview and help you locate relevant information for the discussion.
- ❑ Have group members prepare ideas and details that relate to the topic.
- ❑ Review the ideas together and suggest which ones can help people fight when rights are denied. Listen closely and respectfully to all ideas.

Go to the **Speaking and Listening Studio** for more on participating in a collaborative discussion.

RESPOND TO THE ESSENTIAL QUESTION

How do people find freedom in the midst of oppression?

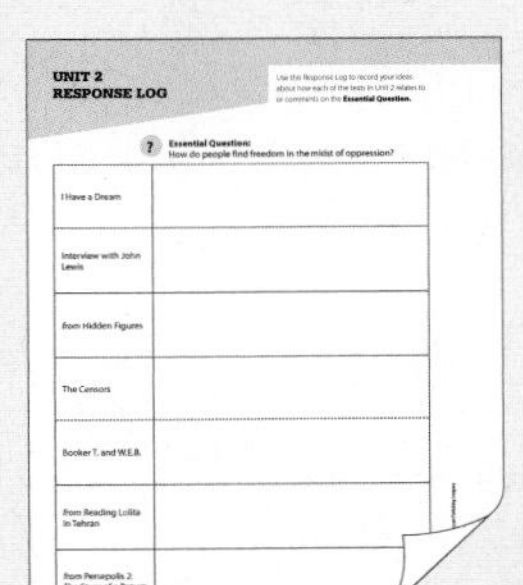

Gather Information Review your notes on "Interview with John Lewis." Then, add relevant information to your Response Log. As you determine which information to include, think about:

- the ways in which marginalized groups of people are oppressed
- what happens to people when they are denied their rights
- how oppressed people can fight for equal standing in their society

At the end of the unit, use your notes to help you write a research report.

ACADEMIC VOCABULARY

As you write and discuss what you learned from the podcast, be sure to use the Academic Vocabulary words. Check off each of the words that you use.

- ❑ **decline**
- ❑ **enable**
- ❑ **impose**
- ❑ **integrate**
- ❑ **reveal**

CREATE AND PRESENT

Create a Multimedia Presentation After individual students create their multimedia presentations, have them pair up to critique one another's presentations before presenting them to the class. In their critiques, suggest that partners do the following:

- Give specific ideas for improving presentations.
- Make sure that the text, graphics, images, and sound work together to convey the main idea.
- Check that the media elements create the desired tone and mood.

For **writing support** for students at varying proficiency levels, see the **Text X-Ray** on page 100D.

Discuss with a Small Group Instruct students to cite specific details from the interview. Suggest that as they review the interview they use a cluster diagram to note the details that relate to the topic. Encourage them to ask questions to clarify ideas and information.

For **speaking support** for students at varying proficiency levels, see the **Text X-Ray** on page 100D.

RESPOND TO THE ESSENTIAL QUESTION

Allow time for students to add details from "Interview with John Lewis" to their Unit 2 Response Logs.

ENGLISH LEARNER SUPPORT

Create a Multimedia Presentation Make sure students understand that their presentation will focus on just one aspect of John Lewis's career. Provide the following sentence frames to help students craft their presentation. Encourage them to note which sentence belongs with each photo or image in their presentation.

- *One of Lewis's most important accomplishments is ______.*
- *This part of Lewis's career is important because ______.*
- *John Lewis decided that ______.*
- *In this photograph, John Lewis ______.*
- *Because of the leadership of John Lewis, ______.* **SUBSTANTIAL/MODERATE**

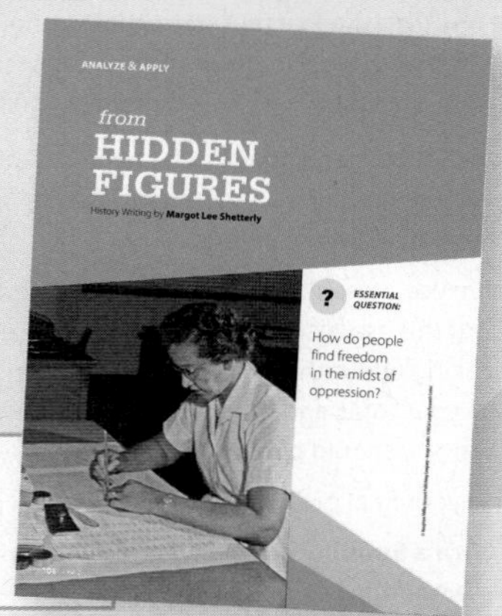

MENTOR TEXT

from HIDDEN FIGURES

History Writing by Margot Lee Shetterly

This nonfiction book excerpt serves as a **mentor text,** a model for students to follow when they come to the Unit 2 Writing Task: Write a Research Report.

GENRE ELEMENTS

HISTORY WRITING

Remind students that **history writing** chronicles a particular event, series of events, time period, or person's life. Like many informational texts, it contains text features such as headings and subheadings to help readers track information. It also includes evidence and explanations to support and clarify ideas. However, unlike other informational texts, it reads like a narrative in that it typically tells a story about real people, places, and events and presents events in chronological order.

LEARNING OBJECTIVES

- Analyze text structures and make predictions.
- Conduct research about African American women in World War II.
- Write a blog post about African American women at Langley.
- Discuss information that can help someone understand the history of segregation in the United States.
- Use reference sources to learn content-area vocabulary.
- Understand pronoun-antecedent agreement.
- **Language** Use transitions to discuss text structure.

TEXT COMPLEXITY

Quantitative Measures	**Hidden Figures** Lexile: 1140L
Qualitative Measures	**Ideas Presented** Mostly explicit, but some key ideas are left implied.
	Structures Used Text features help guide reading; narrative events are mostly in chronological order interspersed with information shared via cause-and-effect and main idea and details order.
	Language Used Mostly Tier II words with some Tier III words that are specific to the areas of law or government and aircraft engineering.
	Knowledge Required Most of the background knowledge needed to understand the text is provided prior to the text or embedded within the narrative.

Online 

RESOURCES

- Unit 2 Response Log
- Selection Audio
-  Reading Studio: Notice & Note
-  Level Up Tutorial: Cause-and-Effect Organization
-  Writing Studio: Writing Informative Texts
-  Speaking and Listening Studio: Participating in Collaborative Discussions
-  Vocabulary Studio: Reference Sources
-  Grammar Studio: Module 5: Lesson 7: Pronoun-Antecedent Agreement
- *from* Hidden Figures Selection Test

SUMMARIES

English

After the United States entered World War II, many men left to fight, so women were hired to do their jobs. By 1943, with a wartime boom in aviation technology, Langley Memorial Aeronautical Laboratory had a greater need for people to do mathematical computations than qualified white women could meet. Thus, the government began recruiting African American women for these jobs. Despite the discrimination they faced, these "hidden figures" were still proud to do such important work.

Spanish

Luego de que Estados Unidos entró en la Segunda Guerra Mundial, tantos hombres fueron a la guerra que las mujeres empezaron a ser contratadas para realizar los trabajos que los hombres habían dejado. En 1943, con un auge de tiempo de guerra en la tecnología de aviación, el Laboratorio Aeronáutico del Langley Memorial necesitaba de más "computadoras" humanas (gente que hiciera cálculos matemáticos) que el número de mujeres blancas calificadas que había disponible. De esa manera, el gobierno empezó a reclutar a mujeres afroamericanas para estos trabajos. Langley relegó a las mujeres a un antiguo almacén lejos de los trabajadores blancos, pero estas "figuras ocultas" seguían estando orgullosas de estar haciendo tan importante labor.

SMALL-GROUP OPTIONS

Have students work in small groups to read and discuss the selection.

Gallery Walk

- Tape large sheets of paper on the walls, writing a question, topic, or subheading from *Hidden Figures* at the top of each.
- Assign a small group to each sheet.
- Have each group discuss the topic, question, or subheading and write their ideas on the sheet.
- Once all groups have noted their ideas, signal groups to move to the next sheet.
- Discuss students' ideas once groups have completed the "gallery walk."

Read-Think-Pair-Share

- After students have read the selection, ask them to trace the events that had to take place before female African American mathematicians could work at Langley.
- Instruct individuals to skim the selection and make note of cause-effect relationships and facts that might help them trace key events.
- Have pairs discuss the information they found and put it into chronological order. Encourage students to use timelines or charts to do this.
- Ask pairs to share their findings with the class.

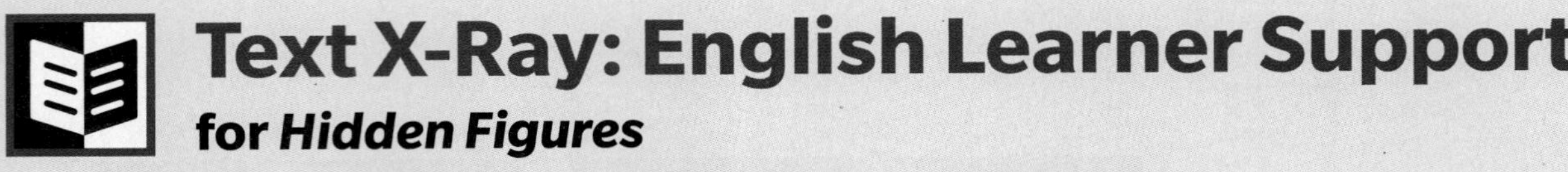

Text X-Ray: English Learner Support
for *Hidden Figures*

Use the Text X-Ray and the supports and scaffolds in the Teacher's Edition to help guide students at different proficiency levels through the selection.

INTRODUCE THE SELECTION
DISCUSS AIRCRAFT AND MATH

Read aloud the title. Point out that something *hidden* is something we cannot see and that *figures* can mean different things, including numbers and people. Explain that this selection is about female African American mathematicians who did important work in WWII. Ask students what the author may have meant by *hidden figures*. *(people who were hidden, math done in secret, or both)*

Tell students that these women worked at an aeronautical laboratory—where engineers design and test aircraft, or planes. Discuss why planes were important during WWII and how mathematicians could help build better planes. Provide these frames:

- *Planes were important because* ____ .
- *Mathematicians helped engineers* ____ *so that they could* ____ .

CULTURAL REFERENCES

Students might benefit from having the following put into a historical, cultural context:

- "a government agency dedicated to studying the science of flying" (paragraph 3): World War I had shown weaknesses in America's aviation technology. The United States was determined not to let that happen again.
- "in the 1940s, a computer was just someone whose job it was to do computations" (paragraph 11): Computing machines were just in development then, and hand-held electronic calculators didn't become available until the mid-1960s.

LISTENING

Understand Broader Effects

Ask students to consider the broader effects of passing laws to allow the integration of African Americans in federal government and defense industries.

Have students listen as you read aloud selected passages. Use the following supports with students at varying proficiency levels:

- Have students listen as you read aloud paragraph 13. Ask: Whom did the executive order help—African American women, or all African Americans? *(all African Americans)* **SUBSTANTIAL**
- Have students listen as you read aloud paragraph 13. Ask: Once signed, what did the executive order do? *(order desegregation of federal government and defense industry, create Fair Employment Practices Committee, open new jobs to African Americans)* **MODERATE**
- Read aloud paragraphs 13–14. Then have students summarize changes the federal government made that helped African Americans. **LIGHT**

SPEAKING

Discuss Text Structures

Note that historical texts often use chronological and cause-effect order. Review and list transitional words and phrases that are used to talk about chronological events and cause-and-effect relationships.

Use the following supports with students at varying proficiency levels:

- Have partners draw a simple cartoon of the events that led African American women to work at Langley. Then guide students to retell events by using words, phrases, and nonverbal responses. Coach them to use *first* and *next*. **SUBSTANTIAL**
- Provide these frames: *In 1943, ____ Langley needed ____ . Mathematicians were important because ____ .* Guide students to use them to retell why female African American mathematicians were needed at Langley. **MODERATE**
- Have partners discuss what they learned from paragraphs 6 and 7, using transitional words and phrases to order the steps involved. **LIGHT**

READING

Apply Reading Strategies

Work with students to reread and analyze paragraphs 1–5 for insights they can apply to their own writing.

Use the following supports with students at varying proficiency levels:

- Remind students that in informational text, the first and/or second sentence of a paragraph often states its topic. Guide students to identify the topic of paragraphs 1 and 2. **SUBSTANTIAL**
- Discuss how each paragraph provides information essential to understanding the next: paragraph 1 contains the text of an ad; paragraph 2 refers to that ad and puts it into historical context; paragraph 3 introduces the agency that placed the ad; paragraph 4 explains that agency's mission and its significance; paragraph 5 helps explain why the agency was recruiting workers. **MODERATE**
- Have pairs of students create an outline summarizing the key ideas in paragraphs 1–5. **LIGHT**

WRITING

Write a Blog Post

Work with students to help them develop and improve the blog posts assigned on Student Edition page 113.

Use the following supports with students at varying proficiency levels:

- Help students locate online images for their blog post. Then guide them to write captions and sequence the images in a meaningful way. **SUBSTANTIAL**
- Provide sentence frames such as the following for students to use when writing their blog posts: *Before/After [event], [description of situation].* **MODERATE**
- Remind students that the transitional words and phrases that help them recognize text structures are the same ones they can use to clarify the order of events and cause-effect relationships. Have them add these to their posts. **LIGHT**

Connect to the
ESSENTIAL QUESTION

In 1943, while most African Americans were prevented from doing anything but menial jobs, a small group of talented and well-educated African American women were invited to do intellectual work of great importance for the United States government. In this excerpt from *Hidden Figures,* Margot Lee Shetterly explains why and how these women gained a measure of freedom through access to jobs previously held predominantly by white males, even as most of their peers still labored at unskilled, manual jobs.

MENTOR TEXT

At the end of the unit, students will be asked to write a research report. This text from *Hidden Figures* models how to incorporate essential background information, explanations, and definitions of unfamiliar terms into history writing without impeding the natural flow of the text.

ANALYZE & APPLY

from HIDDEN FIGURES

History Writing by **Margot Lee Shetterly**

? ESSENTIAL QUESTION:

How do people find freedom in the midst of oppression?

LEARNING MINDSET

Effort Remind students that putting forth effort will help them achieve their goals. Look for opportunities to acknowledge students' efforts. For example, let students know when you saw them become frustrated but then reapply themselves to a task that was giving them difficulties. Offer specific, observation-based reinforcement to students for sustaining their efforts rather than just for succeeding. Remind students for whom sustained effort is not usually required that if—or *when*—they get "stuck," they should be patient with themselves and the process, make that extra effort, and ask for help.

QUICK START

What do you know about opportunities that were once closed to African Americans, women, or other minorities? Name some jobs a woman or an African American might not have been able to apply for in the past.

ANALYZE TEXT STRUCTURE

Authors use a variety of **text structures.** These include thesis or main idea and details; cause and effect; problem and solution; and chronology, or time order. Most historical texts are a combination of chronology, main idea, and cause and effect. Sometimes these organizational designs are intertwined.

As you read, keep track of the important events, the order in which they happen, any causal relationships, and key ideas.

TEXT STRUCTURES	EXAMPLE FROM *HIDDEN FIGURES*
Narration of an Event	By 1943, the American aircraft industry was the largest, most productive, and most sophisticated in the world, making three times more planes than the Germans, who were fighting on the other side of the war.
Cause and Effect	But in the spring of 1943, with World War II in full swing and many men off serving in the military . . . employers were beginning to hire women to do jobs that had once belonged *only* to men.
Thesis/Important Ideas	The NACA's mission was . . . to help the United States develop the most powerful and efficient airplanes in the world. . . . World leaders felt that the country that ruled the skies would win the war.

MAKE PREDICTIONS

To read historical text effectively, it is important to **make predictions** as you read. A prediction is an informed guess about what the author is about to say.

- Before you read, use text features such as the title, headings, and background information to make initial predictions about the text.
- As you read, use text structure as well as genre characteristics to correct your initial predictions and to predict what you will read about next.
- After you read, confirm your predictions. They may not always be correct. If the author surprises you, your predictions will help you evaluate and remember the unexpected information.

Use a chart like this one to help you make and evaluate your predictions:

WHAT I KNOW	MY PREDICTION	WAS IT CORRECT?

GENRE ELEMENTS: HISTORY WRITING

- uses chronological order
- is a form of informational text
- includes evidence to support ideas
- contains text features to help the reader absorb and retain information

QUICK START

Prompt students to recall the kinds of jobs African Americans, other minorities, and women have typically been limited to doing in the past. For example, suggest they think about jobs or roles shown on old TV shows and movies, who played those roles, and why. Discuss how producers and directors typically cast actors in roles based on what they thought society expected to see. Ask pairs of students to discuss how individuals and society as a whole are affected when certain groups of people are excluded from certain jobs or roles.

ANALYZE TEXT STRUCTURE

Note that transitional words and phrases are clues that can often help readers identify the structure of a text. Texts organized by main idea and details typically introduce each detail with words and phrases such as *for instance, for example, most importantly, first,* or *last.* Texts that are structured by cause and effect typically use words and phrases such as *consequently, as a result,* and *because.* In a narrative text, chronological order may be revealed by words and phrases that suggest the sequence of events, such as *first, next, later, after that,* and *last,* or by words and phrases that indicate time order or a particular time, such as *at dawn, by midday, later in the afternoon, the next day, that evening, the following week,* or even *years later.*

MAKE PREDICTIONS

Help students to apply the instruction by asking them to scan the selection's text features—title, headings, and background information. Ask students what predictions they might make about the content of the selection. Have students note their predictions in the chart on page 105. After students have read the selection, have them identify which of their predictions were correct and which were not. Discuss with students anything that surprised them and why this information might have come as a surprise.

ENGLISH LEARNER SUPPORT

Visually Reinforce Text Structure Explain that *structure* means how the parts of something are put together. For example, the structure of a human body includes a head, arms, and legs. Point out that when people talk about *text structure*, they are talking about the parts of a text and how those parts are organized, or put together. Display three graphic organizers: a sequence chart, a cause-and-effect chart, and a main idea and details chart. Provide familiar topics and use the graphic organizers to help students understand how a text on each topic might be organized—for example, "My first year of high school" *(sequence)*; "The best school activities" *(main idea and details)*; and "The benefits of playing on a team" *(cause and effect)*.
ALL LEVELS

TEACH

CRITICAL VOCABULARY

Suggest that students try out the words in each sentence before committing to their answers. Remind them that context clues may hint at the meaning of the missing word.

Answers:

1. *assess*
2. *analytical*
3. *maneuver*
4. *simulate*

English Learner Support

Use Cognates Tell students that three of the Critical Vocabulary words have a Spanish cognate: *analytical/analítico, maneuver/maniobrar,* and *simulate/simular.*
ALL LEVELS

LANGUAGE CONVENTIONS

Clarify that a pronoun antecedent is the noun or noun phrase that a pronoun refers to. If an antecedent is singular (e.g., *order*), then any pronoun used to refer to it needs to be singular (e.g., *it*). If an antecedent is plural (e.g., *opportunities*), then any pronoun referring to it needs to be plural (e.g., *they* or *them*). In the example provided, *them* is a plural pronoun that correctly agrees with, or matches, its plural antecedent, *African Americans*.

English Learner Support

Comprehend Language Structures In some Asian languages, including Cantonese and Korean, number agreement does not exist. When teaching students from these language backgrounds, you may need to spend a bit more time explaining the concept of number and emphasize that in English there is a grammar rule that one must match pronouns with their antecedents in number.
ALL LEVELS

ANNOTATION MODEL

Remind students that in Analyze Text Structure on page 105 they were urged to keep track of important events, the order in which those events happen, any cause-effect relationships, and key ideas. Point out that this reader did that by underlining, bracketing, and drawing arrows to important ideas and by writing explanatory notes in the side margin. Students can use these same kinds of annotations as they read.

GET READY

CRITICAL VOCABULARY

simulate **assess** **maneuver** **analytical**

To see how many Critical Vocabulary words you already know, use them to complete the sentences.

1. I always ____________ a new situation to determine its opportunities and dangers.
2. Someone with a(n) ______________ mind is usually a good problem solver.
3. It can be difficult to ______________ in a tight space.
4. Computers can now ___________________ the experience of flying an airplane.

LANGUAGE CONVENTIONS

Pronoun-Antecedent Agreement In this lesson, you will learn about the agreement of a pronoun with its antecedent. A singular pronoun replaces or refers to a singular noun, and a plural pronoun replaces a plural noun.

This executive order opened up new and exciting opportunities for African Americans, allowing them to work side by side with white people during the war.

In this sentence from the selection, the plural pronoun *them* refers back to the plural noun *African Americans*. Both words are plural, so they are in agreement.

ANNOTATION MODEL

NOTICE & NOTE

As you read, note the author's use of text structures, or organizational designs, in the article. Mark text that shows how the author used structure to organize the text. In the model, you can see one reader's notes about *Hidden Figures*.

A few years earlier, an ad like this would have been unthinkable—most employers never would have considered a woman for a job that had always been performed by a man. But in the spring of 1943, with [World War II in full swing] and [many men off serving in the military], the country needed all the help it could get. Employers were beginning to hire women to do jobs that had once belonged *only* to men.

time clues—helps set chronology

key idea about women and work

These details explain why the situation changed.

APPLYING ACADEMIC VOCABULARY

☐ decline ☑ enable ☐ impose ☐ integrate ☑ reveal

Write and Discuss Have students discuss the following questions with a partner. Instruct them to use the academic vocabulary words *enable* and *reveal* in their responses. Invite volunteers to share responses with the class.

- What is one strategy that might **enable** you to figure out antecedent of a particular pronoun?
- How will the number of a pronoun help **reveal** its antecedent?

BACKGROUND

Before World War II, most women did not work outside their homes. When the United States entered the war, the lack of working men created opportunities for women, including the women written about in Hidden Figures. **Margot Lee Shetterly** *(b. 1969) grew up in Hampton, Virginia, near the Langley Research Center. As she began to learn about the history of African American women mathematicians at Langley, she researched and wrote about them in a bestselling book, which has since been made into the popular movie* Hidden Figures.

History Writing by Margot Lee Shetterly

SETTING A PURPOSE

As you read, pay attention to the details that explain why the work African American women did at Langley was important to them and why it was important to the country.

1 The newspaper ad caught the attention of many women. It read: "Reduce your household duties! Women who are not afraid to roll up their sleeves and do jobs previously filled by men should call the Langley Memorial Aeronautical Laboratory."

2 A few years earlier, an ad like this would have been unthinkable—most employers never would have considered a woman for a job that had always been performed by a man. But in the spring of 1943, with World War II in full swing and many men off serving in the military, the country needed all the help it could get. Employers were beginning to hire women to do jobs that had once belonged *only* to men.

NOTICE & NOTE

Notice & Note

You can use the side margins to notice and note signposts in the text.

MAKE PREDICTIONS

Annotate: Mark at least two details in paragraphs 1 and 2 that help you predict what this article is about.

Predict: What do you think you will learn by reading this article?

TEACH

BACKGROUND

After students have read the Background note, prompt them to infer the cause for the "lack of working men" after the United States entered World War II and for the "opportunities" that resulted. *(Many men left their jobs to serve in the armed forces. The work still needed to be done, however, so women were hired to take the men's place—at least, until the war was over.)* Point out that this excerpt from *Hidden Figures* begins during that time period. Women had not entered the workforce in a significant way. Furthermore, a law had to be passed before African American women could work alongside white women. (If students have seen the movie *Hidden Figures*, you may wish to note that this excerpt from the book is set about twenty years before the setting in the movie but that the movie addresses some of the same challenges discussed in this excerpt.)

SETTING A PURPOSE

Direct students to use the Setting a Purpose prompt to focus their reading.

MAKE PREDICTIONS

Explain that we often base our **predictions** on cause-and-effect thinking. ("Because X happened, then Y probably will happen.") Remind students of the cause-and-effect thinking they did while discussing the Background note; then instruct them to look for causes and effects suggested in paragraphs 1 and 2. (***Answer:*** *The article probably will explain what it was like for women to enter the workforce during World War II and, more specifically, how women fared as workers at the Langley Memorial Aeronautical Laboratory.)*

For **reading support** for students at varying proficiency levels, see the **Text X-Ray** on page 104D.

ENGLISH LEARNER SUPPORT

Analyze Idioms Explain that an *idiom* is a phrase that conveys something other than its literal meaning. Point out the idioms *roll up their sleeves* in paragraph 1 and *in full swing* in paragraph 2. To clarify understanding of *roll up their sleeves*, pantomime the act of eagerly rolling up your sleeves and getting to work; then ask what your actions suggest about your attitude. *(readiness or eagerness to get to work)* For *in full swing*, ask students to consider the difference between just starting to swing on a swing set and being engaged in swinging fully and energetically—the latter being "in full swing." Then call on a volunteer to interpret what it would mean for World War II to be "in full swing." *(fully underway)* **SUBSTANTIAL/MODERATE**

 ANALYZE STRUCTURE

Remind students to look for terms that signal causal relationships, such as *as a result, because, therefore,* and *so.* (***Answer:*** *The statement is the sentence that ties President Roosevelt's belief in the importance of air power to his challenge for a major increase in the production of airplanes. It is important because it helps to explain why more workers—women workers—were needed.*)

 For **speaking support** for students at varying proficiency levels, see the **Text X-Ray** on page 104D.

ENGLISH LEARNER SUPPORT

Understand Language Structures Write a colon (:) on the board and have students locate the sentence containing the colon in paragraph 4. Explain that a colon can signal that a list, example(s), an explanation, or a long quotation follows. Also, what follows a colon usually clarifies or elaborates on the statement before the colon. Ask students which of these four—list, example(s), explanation, or quotation—comes after the colon in paragraph 4. *(explanation)* What does it help to clarify? *(the important and unique nature of the NACA's mission)* **MODERATE**

NUMBERS AND STATS

Point out that President Roosevelt called for a rapid change but that the change would still take time. Suggest that in paragraphs 4 and 5 students look for **numbers** that refer to dates as well as production numbers. (***Answer:*** *The numbers show that within two years, U.S. airplane production increased from 3,000 to 50,000 units per year and that 50,000 planes were three times more than the Germans were producing.*)

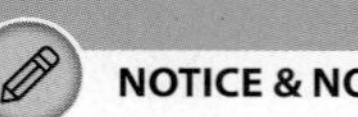

NOTICE & NOTE

ANALYZE STRUCTURE

Annotate: Mark the sentences in paragraph 4 that explain why the United States wanted better airplanes and wanted to make more of them.

Analyze: Find the cause and effect statement in this paragraph. Why is this important?

NUMBERS AND STATS

Notice & Note: Mark any numbers that tell you about how the United States increased military plane production for World War II.

Interpret: How do these numbers help you understand how much plane production increased in this time period?

simulate (sĭm´yə-lāt) *v.* to create in a controlled setting conditions similar to those a person or machine might face in the real world.

assess (ə-sĕs´) *v.* to determine the qualities or abilities of something.

maneuver (mə-no͞o´ vər) *v.* to make a series of controlled movements.

3 This particular ad was placed by the National Advisory Committee for Aeronautics (NACA), a government agency dedicated to studying the science of flying. The NACA shared a campus with the US Army Air Corps in Hampton, Virginia, a city in the southeastern part of the state, next to the Chesapeake Bay.

4 The NACA's mission was important and unique: to help the United States develop the most powerful and efficient airplanes in the world. Airplanes moved military troops, tracked enemies, and launched bombs. World leaders felt that the country that ruled the skies would win the war. President Franklin D. Roosevelt believed in the importance of air power, so two years earlier, in 1941, he had challenged the nation to increase its production of airplanes to fifty thousand units a year. At that time, the industry had manufactured only three thousand planes a year.

5 The NACA and private industry were up for the challenge. By 1943, the American aircraft industry was the largest, most productive, and most sophisticated in the world, making three times more planes than the Germans, who were fighting on the other side of the war.

"Victory through Air Power!"

6 Before manufacturers built the airplanes, the designs were developed, tested, and refined at the Langley Memorial Aeronautical Laboratory, which was where the NACA had first begun its operations, in 1917. The engineers created wind tunnels to **simulate**, or imitate, different conditions a plane could encounter when flying. This helped the engineers to test airplane parts as well as whole aircraft, examining them for any problems, like air disturbance and uneven wing geometry.

7 After that testing, pilots flew the planes, trying to **assess** how the machines handled in the air. Did the aircraft roll unexpectedly? Did it stall? Was it hard to guide or **maneuver**? Making small changes to the design added up to a difference in performance. Even tiny improvements in speed and efficiency multiplied over millions of pilot miles added to a difference that could tip the balance of the war.

8 People working at Langley knew that they were doing their part to win the war. "Victory through air power!" said Henry Reid, the engineer-in-charge of the Langley Laboratory. And the workers took their mission to heart.

WANTED: Female Mathematicians

9 Each of the engineers at the Langley Memorial Aeronautical Laboratory required the support of a number of other workers: craftsmen to build the airplane models, mechanics to maintain the test tunnels, and "number crunchers" to process the data that was collected during the tests. For the engineers, a plane was basically a complex physics experiment. Physics is the science of matter, energy, and motion. Physics meant math, and math meant mathematicians. At the Langley Laboratory, mathematicians meant women.

CRITICAL VOCABULARY

simulate: The engineers recreate weather conditions in the wind tunnels.

ASK STUDENTS why the engineers wanted to *simulate* weather conditions in wind tunnels. *(Doing so allowed them to test the likely in-flight performance of airplanes and airplane parts but without risk to a crew.)*

assess: In addition to wind-tunnel testing, the planes' actual performance in the air also needed to be checked.

ASK STUDENTS why the engineers wanted actual pilots to *assess* new planes' performance. *(They needed to test how the planes would do in real flying conditions.)*

maneuver: Pilots evaluated how well planes could be guided, or handled.

ASK STUDENTS to explain what the engineers hoped the pilots would be able to tell after *maneuvering* the planes. *(They hoped the pilots would be able to find out whether the planes would roll unexpectedly, stall, or prove difficult to guide in certain situations.)*

NOTICE & NOTE 

10 Female mathematicians had been on the job at Langley since 1935. And it didn't take long for the women to show that they were just as good or even better at computing than many of the male engineers. But few of the women were granted the title "mathematician," which would have put them on equal footing with some male employees. Instead, they were classified as "subprofessionals," a title that meant they could be paid less.

11 At Langley, the female mathematicians were called "computers." They did the computations to turn the results of the raw data gathered by the engineers into a more useful form. Today we think of computers as machines, but in the 1940s, a computer was just someone whose job it was to do computations, a flesh-and-blood woman who was very good with numbers.

12 In 1943, it was difficult for the Langley Laboratory to find as many qualified women as they needed. A recruiter from the National Advisory Committee for Aeronautics visited colleges in search of young women with **analytical** or mathematical skills.

The Human Computers

13 When the managers couldn't satisfy the demand with only white employees, the government decided to hire African Americans. A civil rights leader named A. Philip Randolph encouraged President Roosevelt to sign an executive order—a law that ordered the

LANGUAGE CONVENTIONS

Annotate: Underline the pronoun in the second sentence of paragraph 11. Then find the antecedent of the pronoun and circle it.

Respond: Why does the author use pronouns instead of repeating the same nouns?

analytical
(ăn´ə-lĭt´ĭ kəl) *adj.* able to analyze, or understand something by breaking it down into parts.

ANALYZE STRUCTURE

Annotate: In paragraph 13, sentence 1, underline the cause and circle the effect.

Infer: What does this cause-and-effect relationship explain about the decision to hire African American women as mathematicians at Langley?

Dorothy Vaughan

Katherine Johnson

Mary Jackson

TEACH

LANGUAGE CONVENTIONS

Review the meaning of *pronoun-antecedent agreement* and invite students to give examples of pronouns. When students identify *They* as the pronoun in sentence 2 of paragraph 11, elicit that since it is a plural pronoun, its antecedent also must be plural. In the previous sentence, there are two plural nouns. Explain that either *[the female] mathematicians* or *"computers"* can be called the antecedent in this case because the two terms are synonymous. (**Answer:** *The author uses pronouns to avoid unnecessary repetition and to make her writing sound more like natural speech.)*

■ English Learner Support

Comprehend Language Conventions In Spanish, subject pronouns are dropped in everyday speech and, because the verb conveys subject-verb agreement, the subject is understood after the first mention, without the need for a subject pronoun. Consequently, students whose home language is Spanish may struggle with subject pronouns in English. To help such students, reinforce the point that in English they will need to use nouns or subject pronouns such as *I, we, she, he,* and *they* to convey the subject of a sentence.

Ask students to write three sentences about the female mathematicians of Langley. Have students use a noun or noun phrase as the subject of the first sentence and pronouns as subjects of the next two sentences.
ALL LEVELS

ANALYZE STRUCTURE

In sentence 1 of paragraph 13, note that the words usually used to indicate cause-effect relationships are not present. The cause is a situation that came about, as indicated by *when*. (**Answer:** *Hiring African American women was a last resort—that is, a decision that the managers made only when they had no other options left.)*

CRITICAL VOCABULARY

analytical: The NACA wanted to hire women who could focus on small amounts of information and then relate it to other information.

ASK STUDENTS why *analytical* skills might have been helpful to female mathematicians who had to turn raw data into a more useful form. *(The ability to break down raw data into its parts would help them better understand the data and perform meaningful calculations with it.)*

WHEN STUDENTS STRUGGLE . . .

Chart Cause-and-Effect Relationships Distribute cause-and-effect graphic organizers to students. Have students reread sentence 1 of paragraph 13. Point out that in this sentence, the word *when* is used to signal a cause. Model how to record the cause and its related effect in the graphic organizer. *(Cause: When the managers couldn't satisfy the demand with only white employees; effect: the government decided to hire African Americans.)* Then encourage students to record other cause-and-effect relationships in the graphic organizer as they read the selection.

 For additional support, go to the **Reading Studio** and assign the following **Level Up Tutorial: Cause-and-Effect Organization.**

CITE EVIDENCE

Remind students that providing relevant and valid evidence to support an answer makes the answer stronger. Furthermore, a search for such evidence can help students verify that they have arrived at the correct answer. (**Answer:** *At that time in the South, African Americans were not permitted to attend colleges and universities open to white students. Consequently, they went to separate universities, such as the ones named in paragraph 14. If one of these names was listed on an applicant's résumé, recruiters could safely conclude that the applicant was an African American.)*

For **listening support** for students at varying proficiency levels, see the **Text X-Ray** on page 104C.

ENGLISH LEARNER SUPPORT

Use Capitalization Review with students that in English, when a word such as *college, university,* or *institute* is used as part of the official name of an educational institution, it is capitalized.

Ask students to use what they know about capitalization to locate the names of American colleges, universities, and institutes in paragraph 14. **SUBSTANTIAL**

CONTRASTS AND CONTRADICTIONS

Tell students that Contrasts and Contradictions are often signaled by words and phrases such as *on the other hand, in contrast,* or *however.* In paragraphs 15–17, however, the author does not use any of these words. Instead, she signals contrast in other ways. Direct students to the second sentence of paragraph 15. Ask them to explain how the author uses language to highlight the difference in treatment between blacks and whites. *(The phrases "East Area" and "West Area" and "all white" and "all black" emphasize the contrast in treatment between white and black workers.)* Explain that the author also lets the contrast in facts speak for themselves. Discuss why this might be a more powerful way to make readers aware of the contradictions between Langley's need for African Americans and its treatment of them. *(When words are not pointing out the contrast, readers are left to make the realization for themselves, which may have a more powerful effect.)* (**Answer:** *Although African American mathematicians were very needed at Langley, they were still treated as second-class citizens. This contrast matters because it is potentially infuriating to be needed and wanted and yet still be mistreated. It reveals that an unfair double standard existed at Langley at that time.)*

NOTICE & NOTE

desegregation of the federal government and defense industry and created the Fair Employment Practices Committee. This executive order opened up new and exciting opportunities for African Americans, allowing them to work side-by-side with white people during the war.

CITE EVIDENCE

Annotate: Mark the African American colleges listed in paragraph 14.

Connect: How did employers figure out which applicants were African Americans? Cite evidence to support your response.

14 The federal government also helped create special training classes at black colleges, where people could learn the skills they would need to be successful in the war jobs. Black newspapers like the *Norfolk Journal and Guide* published articles telling their readers to apply for these new job openings. And there were many applicants! The applications were not supposed to consider race—a recent law had done away with the requirement that the application must include a photo—but it wasn't hard for employers to figure out which job candidates were black. African Americans did not have access to white colleges and universities, so black applicants came from black colleges, such as West Virginia State University, Howard University, Hampton Institute, and Arkansas Agricultural, Mechanical & Normal College. Many of the African-American candidates had years of teaching experience as well as math and science degrees.

15 Once hired, the black mathematicians were assigned to a separate work space in the Warehouse Building on the west side of the Langley campus. The East Area Computers were all white; the West Area Computers were all black, except for the supervisor and her assistant, who were white women.

CONTRASTS AND CONTRADICTIONS

Notice & Note: Mark parts of the text in paragraphs 15–17 that show a contrast or contradiction between how much the African American female mathematicians were needed and how they were treated.

Analyze: What was the difference and why does it matter?

16 There had always been African-American employees at Langley, but they had worked as janitors, cafeteria workers, mechanic's assistants, and groundskeepers. Hiring black mathematicians—that was something new. For the most part, the engineers welcomed extra hands, even if those hands were black. The Langley Laboratory was operating around the clock to test airplanes to be flown by American soldiers in the war: everyone had a job to do.

17 Hampton, Virginia, where the Langley campus was located, was very much a southern town. State law and Virginia custom meant that African Americans did not ride the same buses or eat in the same cafeterias or use the same bathrooms as whites. The Langley staff had to prepare for the arrival of the African-American mathematicians. One of the tasks: creating metal bathroom signs that read "Colored Girls."

TO CHALLENGE STUDENTS . . .

Conduct Research Invite students to research how desegregation and segregation could co-exist at Langley at that time and report to the class what they learn. You might divide the activity into the following tasks and then review the results in a class discussion:

- See what NASA itself says about this topic. Encourage students to go to the NASA website and look for information about racial relations during the years 1941–1946.
- After the Civil War, southern states enacted laws referred to as Jim Crow laws to separate the races in every area of life. Langley, being located in Virginia, still had such laws. Research Jim Crow laws and consider their role in this story.
- Look into examples of what happens when state and federal laws clash.

NOTICE & NOTE

18 For the black women, the experience of working at a laboratory offered the chance to do interesting work that would help support the war effort. Walking into an unfamiliar environment wasn't easy for the women of the new West Area Computing Office, but each of them was eager for the opportunity to help their country and prove that they, too, could be excellent mathematicians.

CHECK YOUR UNDERSTANDING

Answer these questions before moving on to the **Analyze the Text** section on the following page.

1 The purpose of the National Advisory Committee for Aeronautics (NACA) during World War II was to —

- **A** train mathematicians
- **B** provide jobs for women
- **C** mass produce airplanes to be used in war
- **D** help the airline industry develop good airplanes

2 Female mathematicians had worked at Langley since —

- **F** it began its operations in 1917
- **G** 1935, a few years before the start of World War II
- **H** the beginning of World War II
- **J** just after World War II

3 Which idea is most important in the selection?

- **A** The U.S. needed good aircraft in World War II.
- **B** The first female mathematicians at Langley were white.
- **C** President Franklin Roosevelt believed in air power.
- **D** African American women were successful mathematicians at Langley.

CHECK YOUR UNDERSTANDING

Have students answer the questions independently.

Answers:

1. *C*
2. *G*
3. *D*

If they answer any questions incorrectly, have them reread the text to confirm their understanding. Then they may proceed to ANALYZE THE TEXT on page 112.

ENGLISH LEARNER SUPPORT

Oral Assessment Use the following questions to assess students' comprehension and speaking skills. Ask students to respond in short, complete sentences.

1. What was the purpose of the National Advisory Committee for Aeronautics (NACA) during World War II? *(Its purpose was to mass produce airplanes to be used in war.)*
2. Since when had female mathematicians worked at Langley? *(Women had worked there since 1935, several years before the start of World War II.)*
3. Which idea is the most important in the selection? *(African American women were successful mathematicians at Langley.)*

SUBSTANTIAL/MODERATE

APPLY

ANALYZE THE TEXT

Possible answers:

1. **DOK 2:** *Students may say that the headings helped them make accurate predictions by suggesting what the content of the selection would be about. They may also point out that knowing that history writing contains text features designed to help readers absorb and retain information helped them trust the text features to be accurate indicators of the selection's most important content. Some students may say that they incorrectly predicted that the selection would be about what it was like for all kinds of women to enter the workforce during World War II.*
2. **DOK 2:** *The U.S. entry into World War II was the main event that enabled women to get many jobs for the first time because it caused a shortage of workers—as men entered military service.*
3. **DOK 2:** *Engineers at Langley built wind tunnels that simulated different flight conditions and helped the engineers test plane parts for issues such as how well the planes responded to air disturbances. Pilots also flew planes to test how they maneuvered.*
4. **DOK 2:** *Women at Langley were treated unfairly because, although they were "just as good or even better at computing than many of the male engineers," they were classified as "subprofessionals," and as such were paid less than were their male counterparts. Langley engineers had welcomed the help of African American laborers but had not considered them employable in skilled positions until black mathematicians were hired. Since African Americans had to work in a separate area of the campus, under the supervision of white women, people at Langley must have considered them to be inferior to whites in some way.*
5. **DOK 4:** *"Unthinkable" suggests that people wouldn't have even imagined women being in the workplace.*

RESEARCH

Tell students that as they begin to type their questions into a search engine, suggestions for how to complete them will pop up. In subsequent searches, they might try using one of these "autofill" suggestions.

Extend Students will find that these posters portray women as being strong and ready to work rather than as frail or glamorous. Students may conclude that women felt strong and empowered to enter the workplace. Ask students what additional insights these posters and photographs bring to what they learned from reading the excerpt from *Hidden Figures.*

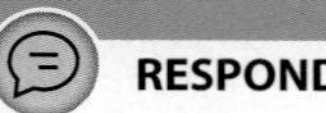

RESPOND

ANALYZE THE TEXT

Support your responses with evidence from the text. NOTEBOOK

1. **Predict** Review the predictions you made before and as you read. How did text features and the characteristics of history writing help you make correct predictions? Which predictions did you have to correct as you read?
2. **Cause/Effect** During the 1940s, women were able to get jobs for the first time in many industries. What event caused that to happen?
3. **Summarize** Review paragraphs 6–7. What tests and improvements performed at Langley helped the U.S. airplane industry? Give at least two examples.
4. **Infer** From the information given in paragraph 10, what inferences can you draw about attitudes towards woman at Langley? From the information given in paragraphs 15 and 16, what inferences can you draw about attitudes towards African Americans at Langley?
5. **Notice & Note** In paragraph 2, the author uses this extreme language: "... A few years earlier, an ad like this would have been unthinkable ...." How does the word "unthinkable" convey people's attitude toward women in the work place at the time?

RESEARCH

RESEARCH TIP
Frame your research in the form of a question. This will help you to make sure you include all the different keywords that you need to get a specific result.

African American women served in several important roles during World War II. Research the participation of African American women in the groups listed in the chart below. Record what you learn on the right side of the chart.

GROUP	CONTRIBUTION
Nurses	*African American nurses had to fight for the right to serve in WWII despite the fact that there was a nursing shortage.*
6888th Central Postal Battalion	*This was the only all-black, all-female battalion to serve overseas during WWII.*
Factory Workers	*African American women were usually given the most dangerous jobs and were still at the bottom of an unspoken hierarchy.*

Extend Find a poster or photograph of the World War II icon "Rosie the Riveter," which shows a white woman. Then find a photograph of a black "Rosie the Riveter." What do these posters show about the attitude of women entering the workplace during World War II? How does this help you understand *Hidden Figures*? Share your thoughts with a small group.

LEARNING MINDSET

Problem Solving Remind students that everyone runs into problems in the course of learning new things. Changing strategies or asking for help are both good ways to get past those problems. So, for example, developing a variety of strategies for conducting research can help students get past dead ends and irrelevant results in online searches. Asking a reference librarian for help also can lead to learning more about how to research a topic effectively. Encourage students to ask their classmates about the strategies they use to solve research problems and to keep a record of strategies to which they can refer.

CREATE AND DISCUSS

Write a Blog Post Write a three- to four-paragraph blog about the African American female mathematicians at Langley.

- ❏ Introduce the topic and express your main idea about the "human computers."
- ❏ Then, tell about the situation at Langley before and during the war.
- ❏ In your final paragraph, state your conclusion about the "Hidden Figures."

Go to the **Writing Studio** for more on writing an informative essay.

Discuss with a Small Group Have a discussion about how information in *Hidden Figures* can help someone understand the history of segregation in the United States.

- ❏ As a group, review the text and decide which information is relevant to the discussion topic. Use the headings to help you locate the information.
- ❏ Have group members prepare ideas and details that relate to the topic.
- ❏ Review the ideas together and generate questions about topics you might want to learn more about. Listen closely and respectfully to all ideas.

Go to the **Speaking and Listening Studio** for help with participating in a collaborative discussion.

RESPOND TO THE ESSENTIAL QUESTION

How do people find freedom in the midst of oppression?

Gather Information Review your annotations and notes on *Hidden Figures*. Then, add relevant information to your Response Log. As you determine which information to include, think about:

- the forms of discrimination the female mathematicians at Langley faced
- how they overcame discrimination
- how these mathematicians helped in the fight against oppression

At the end of the unit, use your notes to help you write a research report.

ACADEMIC VOCABULARY

As you write and discuss what you learned from the history, be sure to use the Academic Vocabulary words. Check off each of the words that you use.

- ❏ **decline**
- ❏ **enable**
- ❏ **impose**
- ❏ **integrate**
- ❏ **reveal**

APPLY

CREATE AND DISCUSS

Write a Blog Post Review the writing task with students. Point out that the main idea of the blog post should be something "supportable"; that is, it should hint at something that might cause readers to ask, "Why do you think that's true?" Suggest that students do some original research to supplement the material in the excerpt from *Hidden Figures*, and explain that the ethical use of the internet includes properly citing references. (If necessary, provide guidance about documenting sources.) Encourage students to work the idea of the workers' "hiddenness" into the blog post. Remind students that their conclusion should bring the reader back to the main idea of the blog post, stated in a memorable way.

For **writing support** for students at varying proficiency levels, see the **Text X-Ray** on page 104D.

Discuss with a Small Group Before students review the text, remind them that history writing uses chronological order, so they likely will find the events relevant to the history of segregation in the United States organized in time order. Also remind students to review, in particular, passages that use cause-effect organization because these will likely help them understand how and why the practice of segregation in the United States changed.

RESPOND TO THE ESSENTIAL QUESTION

Allow time for students to add details from *Hidden Figures* to their Unit 2 Response Logs.

ENGLISH LEARNER SUPPORT

Spell Accurately Remind students that spelling is part of communicating clearly in writing. Before sharing a piece of writing, such as a blog post, it is important to make sure that all words are spelled accurately. Knowing certain spelling rules can help students edit their work. Display and discuss the following rules and examples.

- Drop the *e* before adding a suffix beginning with a vowel or *y* to a word ending in a silent *e*. Example: compute / computing

Point out that the *e* at the end of *compute* is dropped to add the suffix *-ing*. Note that this rule doesn't always apply. For example, when a suffix is added to *courage*, the *e* remains, as in *courageous*.

- When a word that ends in *y* has a vowel before it, the *y* usually does not change to add a suffix. Example: employ / employed / employable

Point out that the *y* in *employ* does not change when the suffixes are added.

Ask pairs to review each others' blog posts and correct any spelling errors. Have them list words that they suspect aren't spelled correctly. Encourage them to apply the spelling rules above when applicable. In other cases, suggest that they consult a dictionary. **ALL LEVELS**

APPLY

CRITICAL VOCABULARY

Answers will vary. Make that students create scenes whose dialogue demonstrates the following activities:

- *simulating*
- *assessing*
- *maneuvering*
- *using analytical thinking or something else that is obviously analytical, such as an analytical process*

VOCABULARY STRATEGY: Reference Sources

Answers:

1. *improved in small ways or specified more precisely*
2. *designers of the airplanes and/or individual parts*
3. *the way in which a machine operates or functions*
4. *perform operations on data in order to gain meaning from it*

RESPOND

WORD BANK
simulate
assess
maneuver
analytical

CRITICAL VOCABULARY

Practice and Apply Work with a partner to write the dialogue for a brief scene that depicts the meaning of but does not mention each Critical Vocabulary word. Then swap your scene with another pair. Pairs will then analyze each other's scenes and identify the word that is being conveyed in each one. Here are some ideas:

- a character is **simulating** something
- a character **assessing** a situation or another character
- a character is **maneuvering** through a difficult space
- a situation requires **analytical** thinking

VOCABULARY STRATEGY: Reference Sources

Go to the **Vocabulary Studio** for more on reference sources.

When you read an informational text, looking up words or terms in print and digital **reference sources** such as dictionaries, glossaries or thesauruses can help you better understand the text. These resources help you clarify and validate your understanding of the precise and appropriate meaning of technical or discipline-based vocabulary.

Reference sources can be used along with context clues. You may encounter an unfamiliar word for which you are able to discover a meaning from the context in which the word appears. Here is a sentence from the selection:

The engineers created wind tunnels to <u>simulate</u>, or imitate, different conditions a plane could encounter when flying.

The word "imitate" and the context of "wind tunnels" and "different conditions" help you get the meaning of the word *simulate*. When you look the word up in a reference source to confirm the meaning, you may see a specific technical definition of the word. This will help clarify your understanding of the word's use in the text.

> **simulate** *v.* (sĭm´yə-lāt´) to produce the features of an event or process in a way that seems real but is not, usually for training or testing purposes.

Practice and Apply The words below are also used in *Hidden Figures*. Look them up in a dictionary, glossary, or thesaurus, using context clues from the text to help you choose the appropriate definition for the word. In the text margin, write the definition that fits the sentence.

1. refined (paragraph 6)
2. engineers (paragraph 6)
3. performance (paragraph 7)
4. process (paragraph 9)

ENGLISH LEARNER SUPPORT

Use Reference Sources Explain that before looking up a word in a reference source, it helps to know what part of speech the word is (for example, a noun or a verb). Guide students to locate and circle *refined* in paragraph 6 of *Hidden Figures*. Ask students what part of speech *refined* is and how they know. (*It is a verb. The subject of the sentence is* designs, *and* refined *follows the helping verb* were.) Point out that because *refined* is used as a verb, students should look up the verb form *(refine)* in the dictionary and choose a definition that describes an action relating to how airplane designs were created. **SUBSTANTIAL**

LANGUAGE CONVENTIONS: Pronoun-Antecedent Agreement

Pronouns take the place of nouns so that speakers and writers can avoid sounding repetitious. Pronouns can also make sentences clearer, but only if they agree with the nouns they replace—their antecedents.

A singular noun replaces a singular pronoun, and a plural noun replaces a plural pronoun. There are usually words, phrases, or even clauses between the antecedent and the pronoun, and those can sometimes be confusing. But you can simply look for the noun that the pronoun replaces and match the number of that noun.

Here are some examples of pronoun-antecedent agreement from *Hidden Figures*:

- These pronouns are separated from their antecedents by phrases and are in a new clause.

  People working at Langley knew that they were doing their part to win the war.

- The pronoun is in a new clause.

  President Franklin D. Roosevelt believed in the importance of air power, so two years earlier, in 1941, he had challenged the nation to increase its production of airplanes to fifty thousand units a year.

- The pronoun is in a new sentence.

  Did the aircraft roll unexpectedly? Did it stall?

Practice and Apply Write a paragraph about the female mathematicians described in *Hidden Figures*. Use at least three pronouns in your paragraph. Make sure that they agree with their antecedents.

Go to the **Grammar Studio** for more on pronoun-antecedent agreement.

LANGUAGE CONVENTIONS: Pronoun-Antecedent Agreement

Review the fact that speakers and writers use pronouns in place of nouns to avoid sounding repetitious. Remind students that an *antecedent* is the noun or noun phrase (or, sometimes, another pronoun) that a pronoun refers to and that a pronoun needs to agree with its antecedent in number (singular or plural) and gender, if singular. Also review the fact that pronouns may be separated from their antecedents by phrases, clauses, or even entire sentences. Caution students that allowing too many words, phrases, clauses, or sentences to come between a pronoun and its antecedent can make a pronoun's antecedent harder for readers to figure out.

Stress that when students use a pronoun, they should ask themselves which noun or noun phrase (or pronoun) it refers to and then make sure that the pronoun they intend to use agrees with that antecedent in number. If they cannot find an antecedent—or there is more than one possible antecedent—they should edit what they have written so that the antecedent is absolutely clear and specific.

Practice and Apply Have partners review one another's paragraphs and confirm that the pronouns agree in number with the nouns they replace.

ENGLISH LEARNER SUPPORT

Comprehend Language Conventions In Korean and Vietnamese, nouns are commonly repeated rather than substituted by pronouns. Consequently, students who speak these languages may need to be directed to substitute pronouns for nouns. To help these students work through the process of consciously avoiding such repetition, allow them to use the same noun repeatedly, but then have them circle each noun they have repeated. Next, pair students and have partners work through the process of deciding on appropriate pronouns to substitute for the circled nouns. **ALL LEVELS**

THE CENSORS

Short Story by Luisa Valenzuela

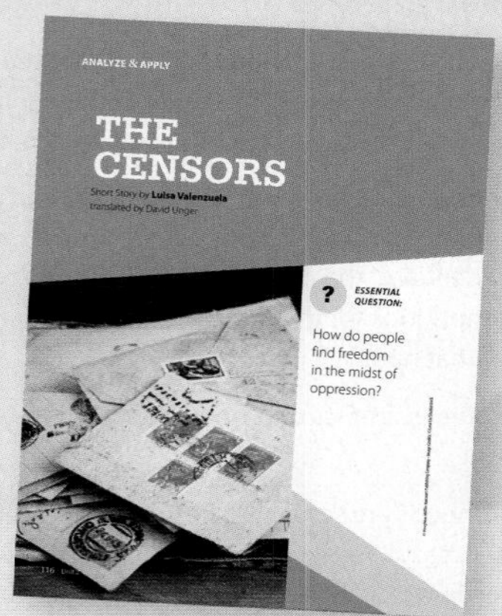

GENRE ELEMENTS

SHORT STORY

Remind students that a **short story** is a brief work of fiction that takes place in usually just one setting. Point out that the genre includes a conflict that propels a simple plot, and often only one or two main characters, who are generally not fully developed. Tell students that just as in novels, short stories have at least one theme or message about life, which the reader must usually infer through character traits and actions and through story events. Short stories may also be written from a first- or third-person point of view or from the point of view of an omniscient narrator, as is the case in "The Censors."

LEARNING OBJECTIVES

- Analyze how setting and an author's use of literary devices, including foreshadowing, idioms, and irony, develop a story's theme.
- Develop research questions around a central issue (censorship in U.S. history) and test them by locating relevant sources.
- Write a letter from the point of view of the character Juan and annotate it as a censor might.
- Use the letter students wrote to discuss censorship.
- Determine the meaning of nouns by analyzing base words and suffixes.
- Use colons and semicolons appropriately.
- **Language** Read a short story using a graphic organizer to track the plot.

TEXT COMPLEXITY

Quantitative Measures	**The Censors**	Lexile: 1200L
Qualitative Measures	**Ideas Presented** Multiple levels of meaning (multiple themes).	
	Structures Used Few, if any, shifts in point of view.	
	Language Used Contextual ambiguous language.	
	Knowledge Required Some cultural and literary knowledge useful.	

Online 

RESOURCES

- Unit 2 Response Log
- Selection Audio
-  Close Read Screencasts: Modeled Discussions
-  Reading Studio: Notice & Note
-  Level Up Tutorial: Reading for Details
-  Writing Studio: Revising and Editing
- Speaking and Listening Studio: Participating in Collaborative Discussions
-  Vocabulary Studio: Suffixes
-  Grammar Studio: Module 11: Lesson 7: Semicolons
-  "The Censors" Selection Test

SUMMARIES

English

Set in Argentina in the 1970s when a fascist dictatorship suppressed opposition, "The Censors" tells the story of Juan, a young man who discovers the address of his love interest, Mariana, and sends a letter to her in Paris. The contents of the letter are not revealed, only that they are harmless. Nevertheless, Juan becomes obsessed with fear that government censors will seize the letter and harm Mariana as a result. He determines to intercept the letter by becoming a censor. Over time, his task of looking for subtle messages in everyday correspondence consumes him and leads to his downfall.

Spanish

Ambientado en Argentina en los años 70, cuando una dictadura fascista suprimió a la oposición, "Los censores" cuenta la historia de Juan, un joven que descubre la dirección de su amada, Mariana, y le envía una carta a París. El contenido de la carta no es revelado, solo se dice que es inofensiva. Sin embargo, Juan se obsesiona por el miedo de que los censores del gobierno tomarían la carta y entonces le harían daño a Mariana. Se decide a interceptar la carta convirtiéndose en censor. Pero pronto su tarea de buscar mensajes sutiles en correspondencia diaria lo consume y ve sabotajes en todos lados. Cuando finalmente se encuentra con su propia carta, la censura sin piedad, llevándolo a su propio arresto y ejecución.

SMALL-GROUP OPTIONS

Have students work in small groups to read and discuss the selection.

Think-Pair-Share

- Pose a question to the class. For example: How effective was the author's use of literary devices? Cite examples from the text to support your response.
- Have students think about the question individually, writing down their responses.
- Have students pair up and discuss their responses to the question.
- Have students in a pair work with another pair to discuss responses and reach a consensus.
- Call on one student from each group to share the consensus response with the class.

Numbered Heads Together

- Have students work in groups of four and number off from 1 through 4 within each group.
- Pose a high-order discussion question to the class. For example: Is censorship ever justified? Why or why not?
- Ask group members to discuss the question.
- Call a number from 1 to 4 and have students with that number in each group respond to the question for the entire group.

Text X-Ray: English Learner Support
for "The Censors"

Use the Text X-Ray and the supports and scaffolds in the Teacher's Edition to help guide students at different proficiency levels through the selection.

INTRODUCE THE SELECTION
DISCUSS CENSORSHIP

On the board, write: *North Korea, Egypt, Iran, Saudi Arabia, China,* and *Syria*. Say that these are some of the countries that practice censorship. Ask students what they think this means. Ask guiding questions—for example, Can people who live in these countries read whatever they want? Write whatever they want? As needed, add these examples of censorship:

- journalists and bloggers are jailed or executed for writing anything seen as critical of the government
- websites are blocked
- users of the Internet are tracked
- emails from citizens are monitored and filtered
- people who try to get outside news are punished

Then ask students to read and paraphrase the first five sentences of paragraph 2. Explain that this story is about censorship (before the Internet), when people wrote letters to each other by hand and sent them through the post office.

CULTURAL REFERENCES

The following words or phrases may be unfamiliar to students:

- *censorship offices* (paragraph 2): parts of an organization that monitors communication for any content that it considers objectionable
- *ulterior motives* (paragraph 5): unspoken but true reasons for some action or behavior
- *festive air* (paragraph 6): a joyous quality
- *strike* (paragraph 7): when employees stop working to seek more pay or better working conditions
- *climbed a rung in the ladder* (paragraph 8): improved one's position in society or the workplace
- *zeal* (paragraph 11): enthusiastic devotion to a cause

English learners may also need support with the following background knowledge: In a *dictatorship,* the government is controlled by a dictator, someone who has absolute rule.

LISTENING

Analyze English Expressions

This story contains common, informal expressions that are also used in conversation. Students can understand changes in Juan by analyzing these expressions.

Use these expressions and the following supports for students at varying proficiency levels: "down in the dumps" (paragraph 2), "get to the bottom of the problem" (paragraph 3), "back on the right road" (paragraph 11), "lose his edge" (paragraph 11).

- Read aloud and translate each expression for students. Ask them to find the sentences where each expression occurs and read them aloud. **SUBSTANTIAL**
- Read aloud the sentences that contain each expression and ask students what they think they mean before providing translations. **MODERATE**
- Ask students to find each expression and underline it. In small groups, have students discuss what they probably mean before ensuring understanding. **LIGHT**

SPEAKING

Discuss Irony

Tell students that irony is a form of expression usually used to signify the opposite of the speaker's intent. Divide students into small groups and have them reread paragraph 12.

Use the following supports with students at varying proficiency levels:

- Model how to mark the ironic phrases in the passage. Then, discuss this question: How does the author use irony here? Provide sentence frames: *The irony makes me feel _____. The phrase _____ is ironic because _____.* **SUBSTANTIAL**
- In small groups, have students discuss irony in the passage. Provide sentence frames so that students build on each other's ideas: *I would like to add on to what you said. I also think that _____. I think differently because _____.* **MODERATE**
- Have students discuss the author's use of irony in the paragraph with partners or in small groups. Encourage students to paraphrase what they hear their peers say as a means of confirming understanding and seeking clarification. **LIGHT**

READING

Follow the Plot

A graphic organizer can help students follow the plot by dividing it into before Juan got the job, just after he got it, and his feeling about it at the end of the story.

- Tell students to make a two-column chart with this text in the left-hand rows: *At first, Juan is... When Juan gets hired, he is... By the end, Juan is...* Tell students to write a word or phrase in the right-hand column after reading paragraphs 1, 6, and 11. **SUBSTANTIAL**
- Using the same kind of chart, tell students to write each sentence starter but then to add *because*. As they read, tell them to fill in the chart after reading paragraphs 1, 6, and 11. **MODERATE**
- After reading paragraphs 1, 6, and 11, ask students to describe Juan and how he is changing. Tell them to cite lines of the story to support their answers. **LIGHT**

WRITING

Write a Letter

Work with students as they write the kind of letter that they think drives the plot of the story (Student Edition page 125).

Use these supports to help students at varying levels write and censor their letter:

- Model how to draft a letter and then provide sentence frames to help them write their ideas with increasing detail. Model how to identify and underline parts of the letter that might be censored. **SUBSTANTIAL**
- Provide guiding questions to help students decide what to censor in their letters, such as: Are there too many details about Juan's city? Could his questions about life in Paris be considered dangerous? **MODERATE**
- Have students review their censored letter and summarize why they censored sections of it as they did. **LIGHT**

Connect to the

ESSENTIAL QUESTION

"The Censors" explores one man's response to political oppression and the toll it takes on his psyche. Attempting to extract from government censors a letter that he had sent to a friend, Juan becomes a censor himself—and falls victim to his zeal to root out subversion.

THE CENSORS

Short Story by **Luisa Valenzuela**
translated by David Unger

ESSENTIAL QUESTION:

How do people find freedom in the midst of oppression?

116 Unit 2

LEARNING MINDSET

Persistence Remind students that learning requires taking on challenges. Point out that taking on a challenge requires working hard and putting forth real effort. You might use a sports analogy to make your point. Ask students what their favorite football, basketball, or soccer teams do when they are losing early in a game. Discuss how persistence and confidence—a sense that "I can do this"—propel athletes and sports teams to victory. Remind students that academic subjects, like sports, require that same level of confidence and persistence and a commitment to work hard. Just as athletes put in many hours of practice to hone their skills, completing homework and other assignments is, in essence, how students practice and improve upon their academic skills.

QUICK START

The short story you are about to read is about government censorship. Can you think of a situation in which it might be acceptable for a government to censor information? Discuss your thoughts with the class.

ANALYZE LITERARY DEVICES

Literary devices are techniques used by authors to communicate their experiences and ideas. Here are definitions of three literary devices used in "The Censors."

DEVICE	DEFINITION
Foreshadowing	**Foreshadowing** is a writer's use of clues to hint at events that will occur later in the story. It creates suspense, making readers eager to find out what will happen next.
Irony	**Irony** takes place when something happens that is the opposite of what readers would expect. **Verbal irony** is when what is said is the opposite of what is meant. **Situational irony** is when a character or reader expects one thing to happen but something else happens.
Idiom	An **Idiom** is a commonly-used expression that means something other than the literal meaning of its words.

ANALYZE SETTING AND THEME

The **setting**—the time and place in which a story occurs—can play an important role in developing the **theme,** or central message, of a story. Valenzuela wrote this story in Argentina in an atmosphere of censorship, suppression, and violence. She drew on the mood of fear and oppression to create the setting of this story and inform its theme.

As you read "The Censors," notice examples of how the story's cultural and social setting shape the theme.

GENRE ELEMENTS: SHORT STORY

- includes the basic elements of fiction—setting, characters, plot, conflict, and theme
- centers on one particular moment or event in the main character's life
- can be read in one sitting

TEACH

QUICK START

Ask students to read the Quick Start question, and then invite them to share their reactions. Ask students why governments might censor information, including personal letters or emails, during wartime. Then ask students if they think that censorship during wartime is warranted. Discuss why a government might extend censorship after wartime. Ask: Can you think of any reason why employing government censors in times of peace would be necessary?

ANALYZE LITERARY DEVICES

Explain that literary devices are techniques or tools that writers use to make their writing more interesting and to connect with readers. Explain each device in the chart and ask students for examples from books they've read or from movies or television shows they've seen. Point out that **foreshadowing** may include a mention of a person, place, or event and that in a television show or movie, it might also include background music that hints at events to come. Explain that like foreshadowing, **irony** can create suspense or tension that builds to an unlikely ending. Ask students to name movies or stories that contain endings that were the opposite of what was expected and discuss how the situational irony helped communicate a message or idea. Finally, discuss **idioms**, pointing out that they are phrases with meanings that do not follow from the words themselves—for example, *get over it* or *tongue in cheek*.

ANALYZE SETTING AND THEME

Review setting and theme, making sure that students understand what each term refers to. Then ask students for examples of stories in which the **setting** was particularly important—for example, a space adventure or a Civil War drama. Discuss how the setting in these stories helped develop the story's **theme** or message about life. Review the information about Valenzuela, and have students think about the following questions before they read:

- If Valenzuela believed her purpose was to witness and record the atrocities of the government, what might the theme of the story relate to?
- Why might Valenzuela have set the story in her native Argentina, even when it could have put her in great danger from government censors?

ENGLISH LEARNER SUPPORT

Use Prereading Support To help students understand what the theme of a story means, use music to introduce this concept. First, ask students to think of their favorite song and then to share it in a small group or with the whole class. Next, have students say what the song's theme or message is, either by drawing what they think it is or by completing a sentence frame such as: *The song "[Title]" says that* _____.

To support students in identifying the theme of the story, provide a graphic organizer such as a story map. Model how to use it to record important information, including details about the setting and what the main character did and said. As students read the story, have them work with a partner or small group to complete their graphic organizers. **ALL LEVELS**

TEACH

CRITICAL VOCABULARY

As a clue to determining meaning, point out that *irreproachable* includes the prefix *ir-*, meaning "not."

Answers:

1. *subversive*
2. *staidness*
3. *negligence*
4. *irreproachable*

English Learner Support

Use Cognates Tell students that three of the Critical Vocabulary words have Spanish cognates: *subversive/subversivo, negligence/negligencia,* and *irreproachable/irreprochable.* **ALL LEVELS**

LANGUAGE CONVENTIONS

Review the information about colons and semicolons. Note that semicolons separate independent clauses, or clauses that can stand alone; their use indicates a link between ideas in the two sentences.

Read aloud the example sentence using appropriate pauses indicated by the semicolon. Ask students why the author didn't use a comma or a period instead of a semicolon. *(A comma would have created a comma splice. A period would have been correct, but it would not have indicated the close connection between the ideas in the sentences.)*

ANNOTATION MODEL

Remind students of the annotation ideas in Analyze Setting and Theme on page 117, which suggest noting examples of how the story's cultural and social setting shapes the theme. Point out that students may want to underline or circle details about the setting. Suggest that they also mark examples of foreshadowing, irony, and idioms, perhaps using highlighters to color code the three literary devices.

GET READY

CRITICAL VOCABULARY

To see how many Critical Vocabulary words you already know, use them to complete the sentences.

irreproachable **staidness** **negligence** **subversive**

1. Rebel troops committed __________ acts against the government.
2. My father's love of routine makes many people accuse him of __________.
3. The auto company's __________ led to the faulty part on the car.
4. The mayor was considered very respectable and __________ in her character.

LANGUAGE CONVENTIONS

Colons and Semicolons In this lesson, you will learn about the effective use of colons and semicolons. Both types of punctuation indicate pauses in a sentence. Colons introduce related information. Semicolons show a connection between two separate ideas that are related in some way. Here is a sentence from the story:

. . . Juan didn't join in; after thinking it over, he reported him to his superiors . . . .

The semicolon emphasizes the contrast between the two ideas: not only did Juan not join in, but also he took the action of reporting the man to his superiors.

As you read, look for the author's use of colons and semicolons and how they contribute to the message.

ANNOTATION MODEL

NOTICE & NOTE 

As you read, mark passages that might foreshadow later events in the story. You can also note your thoughts and questions. This model shows one reader's notes from a passage in "The Censors."

Juan knows there won't be a problem with the letter's contents, that it's irreproachable, harmless. But what about the rest? He knows that they examine, sniff, feel, and read between the lines of each and every letter, and check its tiniest comma and most accidental stain. He knows that all letters pass from hand to hand and go through all sort of tests in the huge censorship offices and that, in the end, very few continue on their way. Usually it takes months, even years, if there aren't any snags; all this time the freedom, maybe even the life, of both sender and receiver is in jeopardy.

Who is doing this and why?

Why are there censorship offices?

What is putting their life in jeopardy? This sounds ominous.

ENGLISH LEARNER SUPPORT

Seek Clarification Use the following questions and sentence frames to prompt students to ask clarifying questions if they don't understand a word or phrase and to help them expand their vocabulary.

- Give students time to ask questions and let you know that they need help. For example, a pause can give them a chance to ask, "Would you please say that again more slowly?"
- Display sentence frames students can use to ask clarifying questions. For example: *Would you please repeat that? What does ______ mean here? Could you use ______ in a sentence to help me understand what it means?* **SUBSTANTIAL/MODERATE**

BACKGROUND

Luisa Valenzuela *(b. 1938) was born in Argentina and published her first story at the age of seventeen. After graduating from the University of Buenos Aires, she moved to Paris and traveled abroad for several years. She returned home in 1974 to find political turmoil and oppression. A fascist dictatorship, a system of government in which a leader suppresses opposition through violent means, now ruled Argentina. Despite threats of censorship and physical harm, she began using her writing to document the horrors of life under a dictator.*

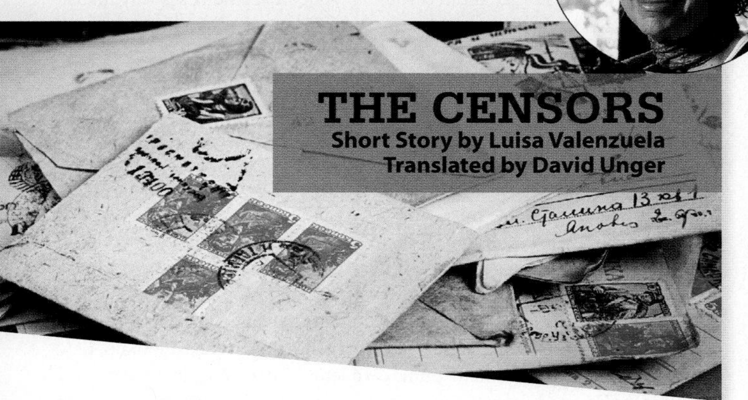

THE CENSORS

Short Story by Luisa Valenzuela
Translated by David Unger

SETTING A PURPOSE

As you read, pay attention to the clues that reveal how Juan's feelings about his work change.

1 Poor Juan! One day they caught him with his guard down before he could even realize that what he had taken as a stroke of luck was really one of fate's dirty tricks. These things happen the minute you're careless and you let down your guard, as one often does. Juancito let happiness—a feeling you can't trust—get the better of him when he received from a confidential source Mariana's new address in Paris and he knew that she hadn't forgotten him. Without thinking twice, he sat down at his table and wrote her a letter. *The* letter that keeps his mind off his job during the day and won't let him sleep at night (what had he scrawled, what had he put on that sheet of paper he sent to Mariana?).

NOTICE & NOTE

Notice & Note

You can use the side margins to notice and note signposts in the text.

ANALYZE LITERARY DEVICES

Annotate: Mark the idioms used by the author in paragraph 1.

Interpret: Explain the meaning of each idiom. What tone, or attitude toward the character and the audience, do the idioms create?

TEACH

BACKGROUND

Have students read the Background information. Explain that Argentina's "Dirty War," which began two years after Valenzuela returned to her country and continued until 1983, was a period of brutal military rule, during which thousands of people were killed and as many as 30,000 people "disappeared." Some of these victims were activists, but most were ordinary people. Family members of many of the "disappeared" continued to petition the government for information about their fate, and writers like Luisa Valenzuela continue to remind the world of the injustices.

SETTING A PURPOSE

Direct students to use the Setting a Purpose prompt to focus their reading.

ANALYZE LITERARY DEVICES

Remind students that an **idiom** is a familiar expression that signifies something other than the literal meaning of its words. Encourage students to speculate on the meaning of the idioms based on the context. ***(Answer:** "A stroke of luck"—a good thing that happens by chance; "let down your guard"—to relax and not be cautious; "let happiness get the better of him"—allow feeling happy to take control of him; "without thinking twice"—do it without hesitating.)*

Review with students that **tone** means the author's attitude toward his or her subject. Tone reflects the feelings of the writer and is communicated through word choice, details, and sometimes direct statements by the writer. ***(Answer:** The tone or attitude toward the character and audience is one of familiarity. The narrator is inviting the audience to share in Juan's experience by using language that is less formal.)*

For **listening support** for students at varying proficiency levels, see the **Text X-Ray** on page 116C.

WHEN STUDENTS STRUGGLE . . .

Analyze Text Details Have partners use a chart like the one below to ask each other questions and guide discussion.

Questions	Our Responses
What is Juan's plan?	*His plan is to get a job in the Censorship Division so that he can intercept his letter.*
What happens to Juan at work?	*He does his job and doesn't worry.*

For additional support, go to the **Reading Studio** and assign the following **Level Up Tutorial: Reading for Details.**

TEACH

ANALYZE SETTING AND THEME

Remind students that setting refers not only to the time and place of a story but also to cultural and social aspects of the time and place. **(*Answer:*** *Life is full of fear: if no one is safe anywhere in the world, if every letter is examined, then people are looking for subversive behavior, even where it doesn't exist.)*

ENGLISH LEARNER SUPPORT

Identify Base Words Review words and phrases related to *censor* in paragraph 2. Point out that the suffix *-ship* means "the skill or practice of." Help students list other words that have the suffix *-ship*. *(friendship, citizenship)*

Ask students to review paragraph 2 and then tell what they think *censorship* and *Censor's Secret Command* refer to. *("Censorship" is the practice of censoring. The "Censor's Secret Command" likely refers to a secret police force that arrested people identified by the censors.)*

Help students create a word web that includes *censor, censoring, censorship, censor's, censored, censorable*. Review the pronunciation and meaning of each word. **SUBSTANTIAL/MODERATE**

CRITICAL VOCABULARY

irreproachable: Juan knows that the letter he wrote is innocent and contains no secret messages.

ASK STUDENTS why Juan is concerned about the letter if he knows it is irreproachable. *(The censors closely examine all letters and find issues where there are none.)*

staidness: The calmness in the Censorship Division existed because of the serious work that took place there.

ASK STUDENTS what other buildings might have the same quality of staidness, and what kinds of buildings might have a "festive air." *(Government offices might have the quality of staidness, while a concert hall would seem more festive.)*

negligence: The employee was careless because he missed a signal that the envelope was sabotaged.

ASK STUDENTS if they think that Juan believes that his fellow worker lost his hand because of negligence. *(It is possible that there was negligence, although it is unlikely that anyone working in the explosives section would be careless.)*

NOTICE & NOTE

irreproachable
(ĭr′ĭ-prō′chə-bəl) *adj.* without fault or blame; perfect.

ANALYZE SETTING AND THEME
Annotate: Mark descriptions of setting in paragraph 2.
Synthesize: What is life like for people where Juan lives? How might this setting shape the author's theme, or message about life?

staidness
(stād′nĭs) *n.* the quality of being steady, calm, and serious.

negligence
(nĕg′lĭ-jəns) *n.* carelessness or failure to take normal precautions.

2 Juan knows there won't be a problem with the letter's contents, that it's **irreproachable**, harmless. But what about the rest? He knows that they examine, sniff, feel, and read between the lines of each and every letter, and check its tiniest comma and most accidental stain. He knows that all letters pass from hand to hand and go through all sorts of tests in the huge censorship offices and that, in the end, very few continue on their way. Usually it takes months, even years, if there aren't any snags; all this time the freedom, maybe even the life, of both sender and receiver is in jeopardy. And that's why Juan's so down in the dumps: thinking that something might happen to Mariana because of his letters. Of all people, Mariana, who must finally feel safe there where she always dreamed she'd live. But he knows that the *Censor's Secret Command* operates all over the world and cashes in on the discount in air rates; there's nothing to stop them from going as far as that hidden Paris neighborhood, kidnapping Mariana, and returning to their cozy homes, certain of having fulfilled their noble mission.

3 Well, you've got to beat them to the punch, do what everyone tries to do: sabotage the machinery, throw sand in its gears, get to the bottom of the problem so as to stop it.

4 This was Juan's sound plan when he, like many others, applied for a censor's job—not because he had a calling or needed a job: no, he applied simply to intercept his own letter, a consoling but unoriginal idea. He was hired immediately, for each day more and more censors are needed and no one would bother to check on his references.

5 Ulterior motives couldn't be overlooked by the *Censorship Division*, but they needn't be too strict with those who applied. They knew how hard it would be for those poor guys to find the letter they wanted and even if they did, what's a letter or two when the new censor would snap up so many others? That's how Juan managed to join the *Post Office's Censorship Division*, with a certain goal in mind.

6 The building had a festive air on the outside which contrasted with its inner **staidness**. Little by little, Juan was absorbed by his job and he felt at peace since he was doing everything he could to get his letter for Mariana. He didn't even worry when, in his first month, he was sent to *Section K* where envelopes are very carefully screened for explosives.

7 It's true that on the third day, a fellow worker had his right hand blown off by a letter, but the division chief claimed it was sheer **negligence** on the victim's part. Juan and the other employees were allowed to go back to their work, albeit feeling less secure. After work, one of them tried to organize a strike to demand higher wages for unhealthy work, but Juan didn't join in; after thinking it over, he reported him to his superiors and thus got promoted. Close Read

120 Unit 2

CLOSE READ SCREENCAST

Modeled Discussion In their eBook, have students view the Close Read Screencast, in which readers discuss and annotate the last sentence of paragraph 6 and all of paragraph 7 which describe the dangers of Juan's job.

As a class, view and discuss the video. Then have students pair up to do an independent close read of paragraph 10. Students can record their answers on the Close Read Practice PDF.

Close Read Practice PDF

Images/Alamy • (mail) ©Lena Lir/Shutterstock

8 You don't form a habit by doing something once, he told himself as he left his boss's office. And when he was transferred to *Section J*, where letters are carefully checked for poison dust, he felt he had climbed a rung in the ladder.

9 By working hard, he quickly reached *Section E* where the job was more interesting, for he could now read and analyze the letters' contents. Here he could even hope to get hold of his letter which, judging by the time that had elapsed, had gone through the other sections and was probably floating around in this one.

ANALYZE LITERARY DEVICES

Annotate: Mark instances of foreshadowing in paragraphs 6–8.

Analyze: Describe how the foreshadowing contributes to the story's tone.

ANALYZE LITERARY DEVICES

Remind students that **foreshadowing** occurs when the author gives hints or clues about future events. Point out that it is sometimes difficult to know when an author is using foreshadowing before knowing how the story will end. Explain that when a character notes something or when the mood or tone of the story changes, these elements can foreshadow future events. Remind students that **tone** refers to the author's attitude toward the subject and **mood** refers to the feeling that a piece of literature creates in the reader. ***(Answer:*** *The foreshadowing creates an ironic tone. Juan is slowly becoming part of the problem as he justifies his actions and comes to enjoy his job. Juan seems willing to be an informer in order to be promoted.)*

For **reading support** for students at varying proficiency levels, see the **Text X-Ray** on page 116D.

APPLYING ACADEMIC VOCABULARY

☑ decline ☑ enable ☐ impose ☐ integrate ☐ reveal

Write and Discuss Have students turn to a partner and discuss the following questions. Guide students to include the academic vocabulary words *decline* and *enable* in their responses. Ask volunteers to share their responses with the class.

- Why does Juan think that working in the Censorship Division will **enable** him to intercept his letter to Mariana?
- How does Juan's urgency to find his letter **decline** as he becomes obsessed with his job?

TEACH

ANALYZE LITERARY DEVICES

Remind students that **situational irony** occurs when characters or readers expect one thing to happen but then something else happens. Review with students Juan's reasons for becoming a censor. ***(Answer:*** *I would expect that Juan would be lenient, realizing that other people just want to communicate with loved ones as he did. Instead, he is imagining schemes to overthrow the government in innocent messages.)*

English Learner Support

Retell Material Help students recognize the situational irony in paragraph 10 by reviewing vocabulary, including *absorbing, noble, mission, pitilessly, shocked, subtle,* and *conniving.* Then have students take turns reading the paragraph aloud with a partner and retelling the events. **MODERATE**

LANGUAGE CONVENTIONS

Ask students to locate the colons in paragraph 11. Read the sentences aloud. The first one marks the start of the mother's talking. Ask students what an author typically does in this case. *(use quotation marks)* The author keeps us at a distance—contributes to a sense of alienation—by never using quotations or dialogue in this story. The colon in the second sentence separates independent clauses. The two clauses after the colon explain the clause before it.

NOTICE & NOTE

ANALYZE LITERARY DEVICES

Annotate: Mark instances of situational irony in paragraph 10.

Analyze: How would you expect Juan to do his job? Instead, how does he behave and think?

subversive
(səb-vûr´sĭv) *adj.* intending to undermine or overthrow those in power.

LANGUAGE CONVENTIONS

Annotate: Mark the colons that appear in paragraph 11.

Respond: Describe the effect of the colons in paragraph 11.

10 Soon his work became so absorbing that his noble mission blurred in his mind. Day after day he crossed out whole paragraphs in red ink, pitilessly chucking many letters into the censored basket. These were horrible days when he was shocked by the subtle and conniving ways employed by people to pass on **subversive** messages; his instincts were so sharp that he found behind a simple 'the weather's unsettled' or 'prices continue to soar' the wavering hand of someone secretly scheming to overthrow the Government. Close Read

11 His zeal brought him swift promotion. We don't know if this made him happy. Very few letters reached him in *Section B*—only a handful passed the other hurdles—so he read them over and over again, passed them under a magnifying glass, searched for microprint with an electronic microscope, and tuned his sense of smell so that he was beat by the time he made it home. He'd barely manage to warm up his soup, eat some fruit, and fall into bed, satisfied with having done his duty. Only his darling mother worried, but she couldn't get him back on the right road. She'd say, though it wasn't always true: Lola called, she's at the bar with the girls, they miss you, they're waiting for you. Or else she'd leave a bottle of red wine on the table. But Juan wouldn't overdo it: any distraction could make him lose his edge and the perfect censor had to be alert, keen, attentive, and sharp to nab cheats. He had a truly patriotic task, both self-denying and uplifting.

CRITICAL VOCABULARY

subversive: Juan believed that many of the letters contained undermining messages, although they seemed to be nonthreatening.

ASK STUDENTS to explain what the government believed might happen if these subversive messages were not intercepted. *(They might be the first step in overthrowing the government.)*

TO CHALLENGE STUDENTS . . .

Analyze Subversive Tactics Have students discuss the following prompt in small groups and then present their ideas to the class:

To *subvert* is to unsettle, disrupt, overturn, or corrupt. This short story is subversive—unsettling, rebellious—in many ways. How and what does it subvert? *(Possible answers include subverting our expectations of Juan; having a disconcerting ending; subverting our sense of normalcy; corrupting what patriotism means; and being openly rebellious toward censorship and authoritarianism.)*

12 His basket for censored letters became the best fed as well as the most cunning basket in the whole *Censorship Division*. He was about to congratulate himself for having finally discovered his true mission, when his letter to Mariana reached his hands. Naturally, he censored it without regret. And just as naturally, he couldn't stop them from executing him the following morning, another victim of his devotion to his work.

ANALYZE LITERARY DEVICES

Annotate: Mark an instance of situational irony that occurs twice in this paragraph.

Evaluate: What might this ironic statement foreshadow about Juan?

CHECK YOUR UNDERSTANDING

Answer these questions before moving on to the **Analyze the Text** section on the following page.

1 Why does Juan apply for the censorship job?

A His mother asked him to.

B He wants to intercept his letter.

C He thinks he would be good at it.

D He needs to make money.

2 Which of the following sentences explains how Juan feels when he is promoted to Section J?

F "He felt he had climbed a rung in the ladder."

G He felt he had "finally discovered his true mission."

H He felt "down in the dumps."

J "He felt at peace."

3 At the conclusion of the story, Juan —

A is promoted to head censor

B escapes to Paris

C has Mariana executed

D is executed

ANALYZE LITERARY DEVICES

Remind students that **situational irony** is when a character or reader expects one thing to happen but something else happens. ***(Answer:*** *The last two sentences are ironic because there is nothing natural about being so driven in your job that you censor your own letter to the point of being executed, and there is nothing natural about executing someone for an innocent letter.)*

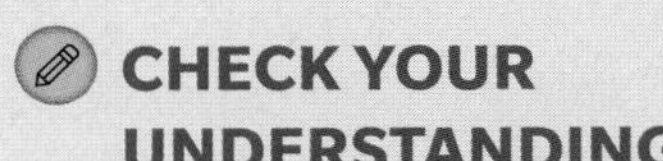

For **speaking and reading support** for students at varying proficiency levels, see the **Text X-Ray** on page 116D.

CHECK YOUR UNDERSTANDING

Have students answer the questions independently.

Answers:

1. *B*
2. *F*
3. *D*

If they answer any questions incorrectly, have them reread the text to confirm their understanding. Then they may proceed to ANALYZE THE TEXT on page 124.

ENGLISH LEARNER SUPPORT

Oral Assessment Use the following questions to assess students' comprehension and speaking skills. Ask students to respond in complete sentences.

1. Why does Juan become a censor? *(Juan becomes a censor to get the letter he sent to Mariana.)*
2. What does it mean when Juan "felt he had climbed a rung in the ladder?" *(He had received a promotion and was moving up to a more important position.)*
3. What happens at the end of the story? *(Juan is executed.)* **SUBSTANTIAL/MODERATE**

APPLY

ANALYZE THE TEXT

Possible answers:

1. **DOK 2** *The author's message is that people can begin to think that unnatural things—censorship and executions—are normal. The setting—a place oppressed by a government that censors everything—creates the ironic situation at the end. The author wants to show that censors themselves aren't safe from censorship: anyone could be a victim of an overzealous censor.*
2. **DOK 4** *The author increases the pace of events as Juan works at the Censorship Division. The phrase "little by little" shows how Juan is starting to change. As he moves up, phrases such as "day after day" show how quickly he is changing.*
3. **DOK 3** *For example, the author writes, "this was Juan's sound plan." This foreshadows that it is not a sound plan. Another example is "What's a letter or two when the new censor would snap up so many others?" This foreshadows the person Juan will become.*
4. **DOK 3** *Juan's original goal is to find his letter and pass it through so that Mariana receives it. Over time, Juan's goal is to be a perfect censor. The author includes details about the incremental steps that lead Juan to change. The work became "so absorbing to him that his noble mission blurred in his mind."*
5. **DOK 4** *Juan has come to believe that censorship is necessary and that he is doing his duty. His final action is an example of irony because originally, he wanted to find his letter and save it from the censors. Valenzuela is suggesting that the government in Argentina retains power by weakening the will of its people to resist, and in some cases, transforms them into the oppressors.*

RESEARCH

Remind students to paraphrase and summarize information in their own words to avoid plagiarism, and to check multiple sources as well.

Connect *In the story, everyone's mail was censored, and you could be executed for suspicion with no proof of illegal intent. In the U.S. the censorship offices closed after 1945, and mainly military mail was censored to prevent information from reaching the enemy. In both cases, the objective was to find hidden messages, especially if they were leaving the country.*

ANALYZE THE TEXT

Support your responses with evidence from the text. NOTEBOOK

1. **Infer** Revisit the final paragraph of the text. In your own words, what is the story's message, or **theme**? How is it influenced by the setting?
2. **Analyze** In his career as a censor, Juan moves from Section K to Section B. Describe the pacing or progression of his advancement. Besides the section letters, what devices and word choices does the author use to speed up or slow down the pace of the story?
3. **Cite Evidence** How does the author **foreshadow**, or hint at, the changes that will occur in Juan's personality and his life? Provide examples of foreshadowing along with the changes they foretell.
4. **Compare** Compare Juan's work goal or motivation near the beginning of the story with his goal or motivation near the end. How does the author communicate the way this change occurs?
5. **Evaluate** Why does Juan censor his own letter "without regret"? How is his final action as a censor an example of irony, or a seeming contradiction? How does this ending illustrate Valenzuela's point of view about the political situation in Argentina?

RESEARCH TIP
Remember to write ideas in your own words. When a direct quote is used, be sure to properly cite the source.

RESEARCH

During times of war, the U.S. government censored the postal system as well as other methods of communication. In a small group, brainstorm questions you have about censorship in U.S. history.

Record your questions in a chart like the one below. Then choose a topic for further research, and record your findings in the chart.

Summarize your research findings in a short informational report, including your citations. Share your findings with your group.

DEVELOP A QUESTION	MY QUESTIONS AND RESEARCH TOPICS
Brainstorm questions about this topic, including what you would like to know about how and why censorship occurred.	*What evidence of espionage did the censorship reveal? Who did the censoring? What methods of communication did they censor? Possible topics: Laws or acts that allowed censorship; wartime propaganda; reports from people censored.*
GATHER RESEARCH	**RESEARCH FINDINGS AND CITATIONS**
Research and take notes on one or more of the questions you developed. Make sure to properly cite sources.	*Students' notes should be about censorship in the United States during WWII, for example, the First War Powers Act and Executive Order 8985. Notes should be supported with specific documented sources.*

Connect How does the censorship described by Valenzuela in "The Censors" compare to ways in which the U.S. government censored communication in times of war?

LEARNING MINDSET

Problem Solving Point out that when they are conducting research on U.S. censorship, students might have trouble finding reputable sources. Remind students that there are a number of approaches they can try when faced with this problem or a similar one. They might change strategies—in this case, that might mean using a different search term. They could also ask a teacher, librarian, or classmate for help or clarification. Remind students that there are different approaches to try when solving any problem—rarely is there simply one path to a solution. Although the first attempt may not yield productive results, it often leads to new thinking and approaches that do. The key is to be patient—and persistent.

CREATE AND DISCUSS

Write a Letter In the character of Juan, write the one-page letter you imagine he wrote to Mariana at the beginning of the story.

- ❑ Write the letter to Mariana as Juan.
- ❑ Underline passages of the letter that a censor might conceal.
- ❑ Annotate the letter to explain why those passages would be censored.

Discuss with Your Class Share your letter with the class first without the annotations and then with the annotations.

- ❑ Read the letter to the class. Discuss what phrases or sentences they might censor and why.
- ❑ Share a copy of the letter with annotations. Discuss your annotations and your reasoning for censoring those sections.
- ❑ Review the phrases that you or your classmates would choose to censor. Discuss what they might have in common and what made you more likely to choose them.

Go to the **Speaking and Listening Studio** for more on participating in a collaborative discussion.

RESPOND TO THE ESSENTIAL QUESTION

How do people find freedom in the midst of oppression?

Gather Information Review your annotations and notes on "The Censor." Then, add relevant information to your Response Log. As you determine which information to include, think about:

- the impact that oppression has on individuals
- how choices are limited under oppression
- how freedom can grow or survive during times of oppression

At the end of the unit, use your notes to help you write a research report.

ACADEMIC VOCABULARY

As you write and discuss what you learned from the short story, be sure to use the Academic Vocabulary words. Check off the words that you use.

- ❑ **decline**
- ❑ **enable**
- ❑ **impose**
- ❑ **integrate**
- ❑ **reveal**

APPLY

CREATE AND DISCUSS

Write a Letter Note that the directions in this section can serve as a handy guide for students. Prompt them to review the first two paragraphs of the story for details about Mariana and where she lives; for clues about the relationship between Mariana and Juan; and for clues about his feelings for her. Then have students jot down a few ideas about what they think Juan wrote in the letter.

Before students write, remind them of the standard parts of a letter: heading, greeting, body, closing, and signature line. Encourage them to use their notes and some of the ideas they jotted down in their letters. Once students have completed their letters and reviewed them for spelling, grammar, and punctuation, suggest they think like a censor and look for hidden messages and subversive notes. Remind students that for the censors, anything as harmless as talking about the weather could activate the censors' red pens.

For **writing support** for students at varying proficiency levels, see the **Text X-Ray** on page 116D.

Discuss with Your Class Tell students to read aloud their letter at a steady rate and in a neutral tone of voice. Ask class members to listen closely, writing down any words, phrases, or ideas that they think might alert censors. As an alternative, students can make copies of their letters for peers to censor by hand; you can also project letters for students to view. Once students have compared the words, phrases, and ideas they identified with the annotated letter, discuss what information was most commonly singled out by students and why that information might arouse suspicion.

RESPOND TO THE ESSENTIAL QUESTION

Allow time for students to add details from "The Censors" to their Unit 2 Response Logs.

ENGLISH LEARNER SUPPORT

Write a Letter Assist students in writing their letters by first helping them to create a word bank. Direct students to review first two paragraphs of the selection and pick out words and phrases such as *"new address in Paris," "hadn't forgotten," and "where she'd always dreamed she'd live"* to add to their word bank. Then coach students in brainstorming words and clauses that could express Juan's feelings or describe his situation, such as *miss you, haven't received a letter from you, I am well, the weather is nice,* and so on. Next, guide students in adding a variety of connecting words to their word bank, such as *where, when, and, but, for, nor, yet,* and *although.* Once students have generated their word banks, provide them with a letter form that begins with *Dear Mariana* and ends with *Love, Juan*. Lastly, have students work in pairs to write their letters, using their word banks as a resource. **SUBSTANTIAL/MODERATE**

APPLY

CRITICAL VOCABULARY

Answers:

1. *a*
2. *a*
3. *a*
4. *b*

VOCABULARY STRATEGY:
Suffixes That Form Nouns

Possible Answers:

1. ***elegance:*** *from elegant (adj.) meaning graceful and stylish*

   idiocy: *from idiot (n.) meaning a foolish person*

   freedom: *from free (adj.) meaning not confined*

   childhood: *from child (n.) meaning a baby or very young person*

2. ***elegance:*** *the condition of being graceful and stylish*

   idiocy: *the state or condition of being foolish*

   freedom: *a state of not being confined*

   childhood: *the state or condition of being a baby or child*

3. *The hotel was decorated with* ***elegance*** *and refinement.*

   She thought it was ***idiocy*** *to drive in a snowstorm.*

   He did not want to get grounded again because he liked his ***freedom*** *too much.*

   Most of the photographs in the album were from her ***childhood.***

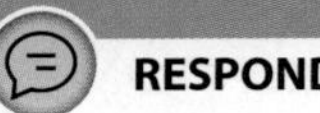

RESPOND

WORD BANK
irreproachable
staidness
negligence
subversive

CRITICAL VOCABULARY

Practice and Apply Circle the letter of the best answer to each question. Then, discuss your responses with a partner.

1. Which of the following shows **irreproachable** behavior?
   a. someone who returns money that was dropped on the street
   b. someone who tends to be private and shy at parties
2. Which of the following is a description of **staidness**?
   a. a person who speaks with a formal tone
   b. a person who speaks with great emotion
3. Which of the following demonstrates **negligence**?
   a. spilled water is left on the floor, causing someone to slip
   b. a small child gets angry and throws her toy
4. Which of the following is a **subversive** act?
   a. voting for a new mayor
   b. disrupting a peaceful protest

VOCABULARY STRATEGY:
Suffixes That Form Nouns

Go to the **Vocabulary Studio** for more on suffixes.

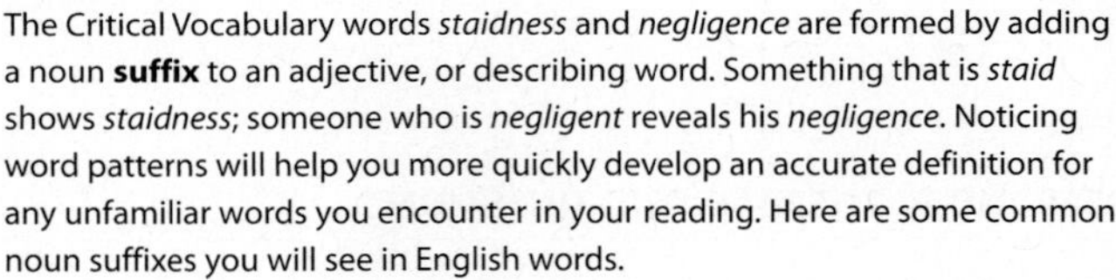

The Critical Vocabulary words *staidness* and *negligence* are formed by adding a noun **suffix** to an adjective, or describing word. Something that is *staid* shows *staidness*; someone who is *negligent* reveals his *negligence*. Noticing word patterns will help you more quickly develop an accurate definition for any unfamiliar words you encounter in your reading. Here are some common noun suffixes you will see in English words.

SUFFIXES	MEANINGS	EXAMPLES
-ance, -ence	act or condition of	radiance, excellence
-cy	state or condition of	sufficiency, redundancy
-dom	state, rank, or condition	officialdom, martyrdom
-hood	state or condition of	likelihood, childhood

Practice and Apply For each row of the chart, identify an additional example that uses the suffix shown. With each word you choose, follow these steps:

1. Identify the base—that is, the main word part without the suffix. Note the part of speech (adjective, verb, noun) and meaning of each base word.
2. Write a definition for each word you chose that incorporates the base word meaning and the suffix meaning.
3. Finally, use each word you chose in a sentence.

ENGLISH LEARNER SUPPORT

Make Words with Suffixes Give students additional practice in identifying nouns that are formed with suffixes. In pairs with differing skill levels, have students make a number of word cards, each containing a suffix or a word, for example: *-ence, -ance, -cy, -dom,* and *-hood*; *free, child, neighbor, resident, patient, infant, king,* and *resemble*. Then on new cards, have pairs form words by combining the suffixes with the words. Remind students that the spelling of some of the base words may have to be altered when the suffix is added. Prompt students to pronounce the resulting word. Provide (or have students look up) the definition in a dictionary or online source. Encourage students to use their suffix word cards to help them create useful nouns to use in their writing. **ALL LEVELS**

LANGUAGE CONVENTIONS:
Colons and Semicolons

An author's use of punctuation not only can help readers understand the message but also can help create meaning and tone. In "The Censors," Luisa Valenzuela uses colons and semicolons to great effect.

Read the following sentence from the story.

And that's why Juan's so down in the dumps: thinking that something might happen to Mariana because of his letters.

The author could instead have written the sentence this way:

Juan's down in the dumps from thinking that something might happen to Mariana because of his letters.

By setting up the sentence as she does, the author involves readers in making meaning. The two-part sentence provides readers with a question (What's bothering Juan?) followed by its answer (thinking that he's endangered Mariana). Readers naturally pause at the colon to prepare for what comes after it. Here are some other common uses of colons.

USES OF COLONS	
Purpose	Example
illustrate or provide an example of what was just stated	Argentina has seen much political turmoil: since World War II, the nation has endured numerous military coups and dictatorships.
introduce a quotation	Valenzuela is no stranger to censorship: "I wrote…thinking that I should write in illegible handwriting so that no one could read over my shoulder."
introduce a list	Valenzuela has lived in many places: Paris, New York, Barcelona, and Buenos Aires.

Valenzuela also uses semicolons effectively. For example, here is another sentence from "The Censors":

Usually it takes months, even years, if there aren't any snags; all this time the freedom, maybe even the life, of both sender and receiver is in jeopardy.

Valenzuela could have chosen to create two separate sentences; her use of the semicolon shows that the second idea results from the first.

Practice and Apply Look back at the letter you created in this selection's Create and Discuss. Revise the letter to add at least one colon and one semicolon. Then discuss with a partner how each punctuation mark you added clarified meaning or tone.

Go to the **Grammar Studio** for more on colons and semicolons.

LANGUAGE CONVENTIONS:
Colons and Semicolons

Review the uses of colons by referring to the chart. Remind students that colons have other uses, too, for example, in expressing time (12:00) and in stating the title and subtitle of a book *(America: A History)*. Point out, however, that when used in writing, colons always follow an independent clause and often draw attention to specific subject matter. What follows the colon is not necessarily a complete sentence. Discuss the example from the selection as well as the examples in the chart. Then talk about how the use of colons helps make writing clear and succinct, allowing the writer to avoid unnecessary words or weighty phrases.

Remind students that semicolons, like colons, are often used to connect independent clauses; that is, the clauses on each side of the semicolon are complete sentences, but the reader knows that they are closely connected through the use of the semicolon. Direct students' attention to the sentence containing a semicolon. Ask students why the author did not choose to use a comma and the conjunction *and* instead of a semicolon. Point out that semicolons, like colons, allow writers to avoid wordiness and complicated sentences.

Practice and Apply Have partners discuss whether the colons and semicolons are used correctly in their letters and what effect they have on the meaning or the tone.

ENGLISH LEARNER SUPPORT

Use Colons and Semicolons in Sentences Use the following supports with students at varying proficiency levels.

- Have students copy the following sentences, circle the semicolon and colon, and discuss why the usage is correct: The club had one rule: be kind to others. We played soccer today; our team won. **SUBSTANTIAL**
- Provide students with the following sentences, stripping away the semicolon or colon, and have them add the correct punctuation: Alyssa didn't finish her homework; she watched television instead. Javi's letter had one goal: he wanted to tell Lana how he felt. **MODERATE**
- Place students in pairs. Have each one come up with two related sentences (or provide pairs with sentences) and then have the partner combine them with a semicolon or colon, as appropriate. **LIGHT**

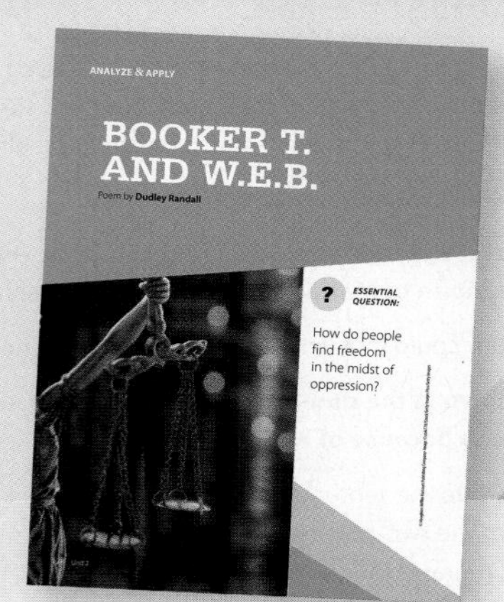

BOOKER T. AND W.E.B.

Poem by Dudley Randall

GENRE ELEMENTS

POETRY

Remind students that **poetry** uses language to appeal to the reader's emotions and imagination. Read aloud the Genre Elements note on Student Edition p. 129. Then list these terms on the board: *imagery, rhyme, alliteration, assonance, consonance, repetition, mood,* and *theme*. Invite students to draw upon their prior reading experiences to define and/or give examples (even silly ones) of each term. Provide that information for any terms that are not covered. (See the Index of Skills, in the appendix of this book, for definitions.) Encourage students to watch for these features of poetry as they read "Booker T. and W.E.B."

LEARNING OBJECTIVES

- Analyze poetic elements (rhythm, repetition, and rhyme) and language (diction, idiom, understatement).
- Conduct research to learn more about the views of Booker T. Washington and W.E.B. Du Bois.
- Analyze and assess information gained through research.
- Conduct a team debate about opposing ideas.
- **Language** Discuss and frame the kinds of statements common in a debate.

TEXT COMPLEXITY

Quantitative Measures	**Booker T. and W.E.B.**	Lexile: N/A
Qualitative Measures	**Ideas Presented** Contrasting ideas presented and challenged; mostly specific and direct.	
	Structures Used Alternating stanzas express opposing points of view to simulate an argument.	
	Language Used Mostly contemporary, casual, colloquial.	
	Knowledge Required Situations and subjects familiar or easily envisioned; some cultural and historical knowledge may be helpful.	

Online 

RESOURCES

- Unit 2 Response Log
- Selection Audio
- Reading Studio: Notice & Note
- Level Up Tutorials: Summarizing; Paraphrasing
- Speaking and Listening Studio: Giving a Presentation
- "Booker T. and W.E.B." Selection Test

SUMMARIES

English

In the poem "Booker T. and W.E.B.," two speakers—Booker T. Washington and W.E.B. Du Bois—argue about the most effective way for African Americans to achieve equality. Washington claims that education is the path to equality, while Du Bois argues that the only way for African Americans to be treated equally is to protest and fight for their rights.

Spanish

En el poema, Booker T. y W.E.B. (Booker T. Washington y W.E.B. Du Bois) discuten la manera más efectiva de que los afroamericanos logren la igualdad. Washington afirma que la educación es el camino a la igualdad, mientras que Du Bois argumenta que la única manera de que los afroamericanos sean tratados como iguales es protestando y luchando por sus derechos.

SMALL-GROUP OPTIONS

Have students work in small groups to read and discuss the selection.

Think-Write-Pair-Share

- After students have read and analyzed "Booker T. and W.E.B.," pose this question: Which of the speakers has the more convincing argument about the way for African Americans to achieve equality?
- Have students think about the question individually and then jot down notes about their responses.
- Then have pairs discuss their ideas about the question.
- Finally, ask pairs to share their responses with the class.

Jigsaw with Experts

- Have students form groups of four and then number off, 1-2-3-4, within the group.
- Have each student read and take notes about the stanza in "Booker T. and W.E.B." that corresponds with their number.
- After reading the stanza, have students form groups with other students who read the same stanza. Each expert group should discuss its stanza.
- Then have students form new groups with a representative for each stanza. These jigsaw groups should discuss the poem as a whole, including the short but decisive stanza 5.

Text X-Ray: English Learner Support

for "Booker T. and W.E.B."

Use the Text X-Ray and the supports and scaffolds in the Teacher's Edition to help guide students at different proficiency levels through the selection.

INTRODUCE THE SELECTION

DISCUSS IMAGINARY CONVERSATION

In this lesson, students will need to understand the concept of an "imaginary conversation."

- *Imaginary* identifies something as fictional; imaginary events occur only in the author's mind (imagination).
- *Conversation* describes two or more people talking to each other (conversing).

Remind students that while the conversation in the poem is imaginary, Booker T. Washington and W.E.B. Du Bois were actual leaders in the African American community with very different perspectives on achieving racial equality. Hold a group discussion to see what students already know and what more they would like to learn about African Americans' fight for racial equality following the end of the Civil War and the abolishment of slavery.

CULTURAL REFERENCES

The following words or phrases may be unfamiliar to students:

- *mighty lot of cheek* (line 2): a huge lack of respect
- *hoe the cotton* (line 5): dig up weeds among cotton plants
- *skill of hand* (line 13): physical ability
- *missed the boat* (line 18): made a mistake
- *uproar* (line 21): noisy excitement, confusion
- *civil rights* (line 21): rights of citizens, such as the right to vote
- *avail* (line 25): to be of use or value
- *trumped-up clause* (line 28): a false part of a document
- *A rope's as tight, a fire as hot* (line 29): references to common attacks on African Americans by white mobs

LISTENING

Identify Rhymes and Rhyming Patterns

Explain that some poets make use of rhymes and patterns of rhymes to guide readers and listeners in rhythm and pacing. Use the poem on Student Edition page 131 to give students practice in identifying rhymes and rhyme patterns.

Use the following supports with students at varying proficiency levels:

- Read lines 1–3 aloud several times. Coach students in identifying the words that rhyme. **SUBSTANTIAL**
- Read lines 1–5 aloud several times. Ask students to identify the words that rhyme. **MODERATE**
- Read lines 1–7 aloud several times. Ask students to identify the words that rhyme and explain why. **LIGHT**

SPEAKING

Give Opinions in a Debate

Help students prepare for participation in a debate as described on Student Edition page 135 by practicing statements and responses out loud.

Use the following supports with students at varying proficiency levels:

- Help students say their team's basic position statement using this frame: *We support the ideas of ___________ (Booker T. Washington/W.E.B. Du Bois).* **SUBSTANTIAL**
- Help students say their team's basic position statement and support it using this frame: *We support the ideas of ___________ (Booker T. Washington/W.E.B. Du Bois) because _____________.* **MODERATE**
- Help students prepare to respond to opposing opinions during a debate using this frame: *I understand __________ (opposing opinion), but I think _______ is more important.* **LIGHT**

READING

Identify Poetic Imagery

Explain that, like other writers, poets want to create vivid images with words. Students can practice identifying and understanding visual imagery.

Use the following supports with students at varying proficiency levels:

- Have students reread lines 13–16 and discuss the meaning of *cultivating land* and *cultivate the brain*. Have partners draw two images that illustrate these meanings. **SUBSTANTIAL**
- Have students reread lines 13–16 and answer any questions they may have about the lines' literal or figurative meanings. Have partners draw two images that illustrate these lines. **MODERATE**
- With partners, have students reread lines 13–16 and compare the meanings of the phrases *cultivating land* and *cultivate the brain*. **LIGHT**

WRITING

Summarize Views

Explain that summarizing a character's or person's views can help students compare them to others' views, as described in the activity on Student Edition page 135. Provide practice by having students summarize the views expressed in this poem.

Use the following supports with students at varying proficiency levels:

- Direct students to lines 1–7 and model how to write a summary sentence on the views of Booker T. Washington. Use these prompting questions: What does he think about studying books? What does he think about jobs on a farm or in a kitchen? **SUBSTANTIAL**
- Direct students to lines 1–7 and help them write a summary sentence on the views of Booker T. Washington with this frame. *Booker T. Washington thinks it's better to _________ than to _________*. **MODERATE**
- Have students reread lines 1–7 and write a summary sentence on the views of Booker T. Washington. **LIGHT**

Connect to the
ESSENTIAL QUESTION

The speakers in "Booker T. and W.E.B." express different attitudes and opinions about the best path forward for equality for African Americans in the face of continued racial oppression in the United States. Booker T. Washington believed that the pursuit of economic independence, rather than civil rights, would eventually lead African Americans to true equality. Meanwhile, W.E.B. Du Bois believed that the path to equality was through education and the pursuit of civil rights. Many of their ideas about how best to end class and racial injustice continue to be discussed and debated today.

ANALYZE & APPLY

BOOKER T. AND W.E.B.

Poem by **Dudley Randall**

? ESSENTIAL QUESTION:

How do people find freedom in the midst of oppression?

128 Unit 2

WHEN STUDENTS STRUGGLE . . .

Compare and Contrast To help prepare students to read and analyze the poem, have individuals or partners create a chart to record the key ideas of each speaker in the poem. Model how to summarize ideas in one's own words.

Booker T.		
W.E.B.		

For additional support, go to the **Reading Studio** and assign the following  **Level Up Tutorial: Summarizing.**

QUICK START

The poem you are about to read depicts an imaginary conversation between Booker T. Washington (1856–1915) and W.E.B. Du Bois (1868–1963), two men who had very different ideas about what African Americans should do to improve their lives in the late 19th and early 20th centuries. How much do you already know about these men? What questions do you have about them? Record what you know and want to know in the chart. After you read the poem, you'll do research to find out more about both of them.

BOOKER T. WASHINGTON	W.E.B. DU BOIS

ANALYZE POETIC ELEMENTS

Most poets try to create word pictures in their poems that help readers see, hear, feel, smell, and even taste the experiences they present. Such word pictures are called **imagery**. The imagery in a poem can help to describe things and to convey the feeling of the poem. When you read poems, pay attention to the how the poet's use of imagery affects you as a reader.

Underline the imagery that appeals to your sense of hearing in this excerpt from Edgar Allen Poe's poem "The Raven."

Once upon a midnight dreary, while I pondered, weak and weary,
Over many a quaint and curious volume of forgotten lore—
While I nodded, nearly napping, suddenly there came a tapping,
As of some one gently rapping, rapping at my chamber door.
"'Tis some visitor," I muttered, "tapping at my chamber door—
Only this and nothing more."

GENRE ELEMENTS: POETRY

- includes imagery that appeals to the senses
- includes sound devices such as rhyme, alliteration, assonance, consonance, and repetition
- creates a mood
- expresses a theme, or message about life

TEACH

QUICK START

Booker T. Washington and W.E.B. Du Bois were influential black leaders who promoted rival philosophies regarding social and economic progress for African Americans. For students who are unfamiliar with these men, explain that Washington suggested a more cautious approach while Du Bois argued for a more direct one. Ask students to think about what actions Washington might have proposed to help African Americans achieve greater equality. What actions might Du Bois have proposed?

ANALYZE POETIC ELEMENTS

Read aloud the excerpt from "The Raven" and ask students to identify imagery that appeals to their sense of hearing (*"rapping," "tapping"*). Ask students what kind of feeling or effect the poet is trying to convey to the reader. As they read the poem, invite students to consider how imagery reveals the thoughts and feelings of the speaker in the poem.

Next, point out the bulleted list of the elements of poetry. Explain that the poem students are about to read includes many sound devices, including rhythm and rhyme. Explain these terms:

- **Rhythm** is the emphasis, or stress, on certain words and syllables in a line.
- With **repetition**, a poet can create the sound of casual speech or formal poetry. A poet can also repeat certain words or lines for emphasis.
- **Rhyme** is the repetition of the accented vowel sound and all subsequent sounds in a word (*find/mind, history/mystery, wonder/thunder*).

Encourage students to read "Booker T. and W.E.B." aloud and to pay attention to the rhyming words. Ask them to consider whether repetition conveys the sound of casual speech or formal poetry and how the repetition of words and lines emphasizes important ideas.

ENGLISH LEARNER SUPPORT

Use Prereading Support Make sure students understand the difference between the vocabulary in the headings "Analyze Poetic Elements" and "Analyze Poetic Language." Review the meaning of the word *elements* by drawing students' attention to the list of poetic elements in the margin of Student Edition page 129. Point out that each bulleted entry in the list is an example of what makes poetry different from other kinds of literature. Next, explain that the three kinds of poetic language described on page 130 are techniques a poet uses to convey ideas. Finally, combine the meanings. (*analyze: "examine in detail"; poetic: "about poetry"; elements: "important parts"; language: "a system of communication"*) Ask students why it is so important to know about different poetic techniques. *(to better understand the ideas a poet wants to share)*
ALL LEVELS

TEACH

ANALYZE POETIC LANGUAGE

Encourage students to think about the poet's use of **diction**, or word choice, when they read "Booker T. and W.E.B." For example, when the poem's speakers refer to white employers, Booker T. uses a more formal address than W.E.B. does. Invite students to speculate on the tone, or attitude to the subject, that Booker T.'s formal diction might indicate.

Review the meaning of **idiom** and provide additional examples (or do a class brainstorming) to help familiarize students with this term. Some common idioms include *on the ball* (being competent or alert); *no pain, no gain* (results require effort); and *under the weather* (not feeling well).

Point out that **understatement** is often used to suggest that something is less important or severe than it actually is. This can be most effective in discussions of very serious topics. In "Booker T. and W.E.B.," "It seems to me" is an example of understatement. Discuss the effect of this repeated phrase. Encourage students to brainstorm other understatements that might be used to show polite disagreement. (Examples: "In my humble opinion," "But don't you think that," "This might not work but")

Explain how to use the chart on Student Edition page 130 to further support students in analyzing the poetic language of the poem.

ANNOTATION MODEL

Relate annotating text to the suggestion above regarding creating a chart to record examples and the effects of diction, idioms, and understatement in the poem. Then, point out the example of understatement and the idiom underlined in the model on this page. Discuss students' reactions to the reader's notes about the effect of these poetic language techniques. Have students add these examples to their chart, marking up the selection in their consumable text. Point out that they might want to color-code their annotations by using highlighters.

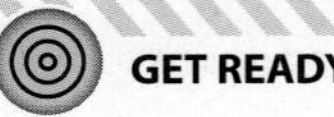

GET READY

ANALYZE POETIC LANGUAGE

"Booker T. and W.E.B." is an imaginary debate between two early leaders of the African American community. The leaders' conflicting perspectives are revealed through dialogue, as they attempt to change each other's mind. To this end, they employ several techniques to argue their points.

Diction includes the poet's choice of words as well as syntax—the way of arranging words in sentences. Diction may be formal or informal. Readers should pay close attention to a poet's word choice and syntax, and notice the mood and tone they create.

An **idiom** is an expression whose meaning differs from the actual meaning of the words. "Bought the farm" is an idiom that means someone has died.

Understatement is the technique of deliberately making a subject seem less important that it really is. Using understatement, a topic or idea is described with less force than expected. Understatement can allow an interaction to remain polite, despite the intensity of the disagreement.

As you read, use the chart to record examples of diction, idiom, and understatement. Think about how these techniques affect the tone, or attitude, of each speaker. Note connotations of each speaker's word choices.

DEVICES	EXAMPLES AND EFFECTS
diction	
idiom	
understatement	

ANNOTATION

NOTICE & NOTE 

As you read, note each speaker's diction and use of idiom and understatement.
This model shows a reader's notes about the first stanza of "Booker T. and W.E.B."

"It seems to me," said Booker T.,
"It shows a mighty lot of cheek
To study chemistry and Greek
When Mister Charlie needs a hand
To hoe the cotton on his land,
And when Miss Ann looks for a cook,
Why stick your nose inside a book?"

The speaker sounds as if he is being modest by saying "It seems to me." This might be an example of understatement.

He uses idioms like "mighty lot of cheek" to make W.E.B.'s ideas seem wrong-headed.

Why "Mister" Charlie, "Miss" Ann?

NOTICE & NOTE

BACKGROUND

Dudley Randall *(1914–2000) grew up in Detroit, Michigan. In 1981, he was named poet laureate of Detroit. In this poem, Randall depicts the title characters' clash over the path to equality for African Americans. Booker T. Washington believed that African Americans should work hard and save money to earn the equality they deserved. W.E.B. Du Bois advocated agitation and protest to demand equal treatment. Their dispute split the black community into a "conservative" side that supported Washington and a "radical" side that supported Du Bois.*

BOOKER T. AND W.E.B.

Poem by Dudley Randall

SETTING A PURPOSE

As you read, pay attention to the way the speakers talk to each other and argue their points.

(*Booker T. Washington and W.E.B. Du Bois*)
"It seems to me," said Booker T.,
"It shows a mighty lot of cheek[1]
To study chemistry and Greek
When Mister Charlie needs a hand
To hoe the cotton on his land,
And when Miss Ann looks for a cook,
Why stick your nose inside a book?"

"I don't agree," said W.E.B.,
"If I should have the drive to seek
Knowledge of chemistry or Greek,
I'll do it. Charles and Miss can look
Another place for hand or cook.

[1] **cheek:** rude or impertinent boldness; disrespect.

Notice & Note

You can use the side margins to notice and note signposts in the text.

ANALYZE POETIC LANGUAGE

Annotate: In line 11, mark the way W.E.B. refers to the people Booker T. calls "Mister Charlie" and "Miss Ann" in the first stanza.

Interpret: Why do the two men refer to these people in different ways? What does this reveal about the men and the way they see themselves in relation to Charles and Ann?

BACKGROUND

After students read the Background note, explain to them that both Booker T. Washington and W.E.B. Du Bois became adults after the Civil War had ended. At this time in U.S. history, all African Americans had become free, but their rights were often severely limited, and many were victims of discrimination and violence. Discuss the different paths to equality promoted by Washington and Du Bois and ask: Does freedom from oppression come from education and hard work, or through agitation and protest?

SETTING A PURPOSE

Direct students to use the Setting a Purpose prompt to focus their reading.

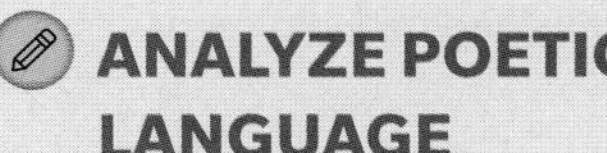

ANALYZE POETIC LANGUAGE

Discuss what the forms of address reveal about each speaker's attitude, or tone. Remind students that the speaker's attitude refers to how the speaker feels about the subject or topic. Word choices and the use of other techniques provide clues for understanding the speaker's feelings. (***Answer:*** *The men have different ideas about how these two white people should be treated. Booker T. treats them with deference by referring to them as* Mister Charlie *and* Miss Ann. *W.E.B refers to them as equals.)*

ENGLISH LEARNER SUPPORT

Develop Vocabulary Point out the words *cultivating* and *cultivate* on lines 14 and 16. Explain that the first use of the word applies to farming—developing land to grow crops. The second use has a similar meaning, but in this case it refers to what a person can do with his or her brain. Ask students what kinds of things a brain might cultivate. *(ideas or thoughts)* **MODERATE**

For **listening and reading support** for students at varying proficiency levels, see the **Text X-Ray** on pages 128C–128D.

ENGLISH LEARNER SUPPORT

Use Context Clues Remind students that they often can use context clues to help determine the meaning of idioms. Display these idioms: "needs a hand" (line 4), "stick your nose inside a book" (line 7), "have the drive" (line 9), "skill of hand" (line 13), and "missed the boat" (line 18). Organize students into small groups of students with mixed abilities. Assign each group one or more of the idioms and have them work together to use context clues to define it. Tell students to circle the idiom and then underline the context clues in their consumable text. Have groups present their definitions to the class and guide students in reaching a consensus of the correct definition. **ALL LEVELS**

ANALYZE POETIC ELEMENTS

Remind students that imagery is descriptive language that appeals to the senses (seeing, hearing, touching, tasting, smelling). Point out that line 29 ("A rope's as tight, a fire as hot") appeals to the senses of both sight and touch, while the phrase "speak soft" in line 31 appeals to the sense of hearing. Ask students to review the poem as a whole and note other words or phrases that appeal to the senses. For example: seeing—"stick your nose inside a book" (line 7) and hearing—"some men rejoice" (line 13) and "Who shout" (line 19). (**Answer:** *The images of the tight rope and hot fire in line 29, both of which appeal to the sense of sight as well as touch, emphasize the violence and oppression that African Americans suffered from white mobs. "Speak soft" is emphasizing W.E.B.'s view that trying to live quietly and peacefully won't be enough; only by legislating just laws can African Americans stop the cruel injustices of segregation and discrimination.)*

ENGLISH LEARNER SUPPORT

Practice Using Imagery Read aloud line 29 and have students identify the adjectives that appeal to the senses (*tight, hot*). On the board, create two columns using these words as headings. Encourage students to think of synonyms for the two words. Record students' responses in each column. Then reread line 29, substituting students' responses for the original adjectives. As a class, discuss whether these changes have a positive or a negative effect on the line's appeal to the senses. Repeat this activity with other examples of imagery from the poem. **MODERATE/LIGHT**

NOTICE & NOTE

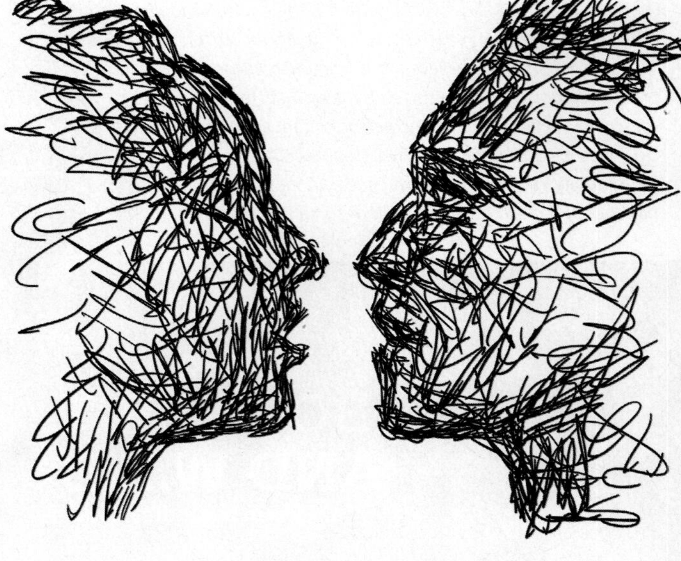

Some men rejoice in skill of hand,
And some in cultivating land,
But there are others who maintain
The right to cultivate the brain."

"It seems to me," said Booker T.,
"That all you folks have missed the boat
Who shout about the right to vote,
And spend vain days and sleepless nights
In uproar over civil rights.
Just keep your mouths shut, do not grouse,
But work, and save, and buy a house."

ANALYZE POETIC ELEMENTS

Annotate: Mark examples of imagery in lines 24-32.

Interpret: What sense or senses does the imagery appeal to? What ideas does it emphasize?

"I don't agree," said W.E.B.,
"For what can property avail
If dignity and justice fail?
Unless you help to make the laws,
They'll steal your house with trumped-up clause.
A rope's as tight, a fire as hot,
No matter how much cash you've got.
Speak soft, and try your little plan,

TO CHALLENGE STUDENTS . . .

Write a Dialogue Poem Invite students to write a poem mimicking the style of "Booker T. and W.E.B.," in which two or more speakers express opposing views about an important subject. In their poems, have students develop a specific diction and tone for each speaker. Encourage them to use idioms to capture the flavor of each speaker's personality. Finally, have them share their poems with a partner or read them to the class.

But as for me, I'll be a man."

"It seems to me," said Booker T.—

"I don't agree,"
Said W.E.B.

CHECK YOUR UNDERSTANDING

Answer these questions before moving on to the **Analyze the Text** section on the following page.

1 In the lines *Charles and Miss can look / Another place for hand or cook*, the word *hand* means —

- **A** applause
- **B** driver
- **C** laborer
- **D** ability

2 At the end of line 22, the word *grouse* means —

- **F** look for clues; investigate
- **G** ground-dwelling bird
- **H** complain; grumble
- **J** ability or talent

3 Which is the most accurate paraphrase of W.E.B. Du Bois's meaning in lines 31–32?

- **A** You try it your way. I'm going to keep fighting.
- **B** You are too soft-spoken to win an argument with me.
- **C** Your quiet approach is a good one. I will take your advice.
- **D** Your plan is too impractical to be successful.

CHECK YOUR UNDERSTANDING

Have students answer the questions independently.

Answers:

1. *C*
2. *H*
3. *A*

If they answer any questions incorrectly, have them reread the text to confirm their understanding. Then they may proceed to ANALYZE THE TEXT on page 134.

ENGLISH LEARNER SUPPORT

Oral Assessment Use the following questions to assess students' comprehension and speaking skills.

1. What does the word *hand* mean in the lines "Charles and Miss can look / Another place for hand or cook"? *("a worker or laborer")*
2. Reread line 22. What does the word *grouse* mean? *("to complain or grumble")*
3. In your own words, explain what lines 31–32 mean. *(They mean, "You can be polite, but I will fight.")* **MODERATE/LIGHT**

IMPROVE READING FLUENCY

Targeted Passage Have partners do a paired oral reading of the poem. Students should each read a stanza, taking on the personality of the speaker suggested by the language. Remind them to follow print cues such as punctuation and to pause briefly at the end of each line. Have partners take turns reading the stanzas.

Go to the **Reading Studio** for additional support in developing fluency.

TEACH

ANALYZE THE TEXT

Possible answers:

1. **DOK 4:** *It means that Booker T. believes W.E.B. is rude and inappropriate in his approach.*
2. **DOK 2:** *Mister Charlie and Miss Ann aren't real people. They stand for typical white employers. Booker T. thinks that people should do what Mister Charlie and Miss Ann pay them to do rather than to study all the time. His attitude may surprise students who might think that a person born into slavery would not be so respectful of white people.*
3. **DOK 2:** *The words* motivation *or* energy *could be substitutes. W.E.B. thinks that Booker T. isn't assertive enough or doesn't have as much motivation to improve his situation as W.E.B. does himself.*
4. **DOK 4:** *Booker T. thinks that the push for civil rights is a waste of time. He mentions "vain days and sleepless nights." Booker T. thinks that men like W.E.B. should stop complaining and "work, and save, and buy a house." W.E.B. thinks that unless you're in the government and "help to make the laws," people in power will "steal your house with trumped-up clause."*
5. **DOK 2:** *The rhyming and repetition highlight the debate the speakers are having while underscoring their different views. The understatement of "It seems to me" reflects Booker T.'s less assertive approach, whereas W.E.B.'s words "I don't agree" are more emphatic. The rhyming and repetition also build tension and show that the conflict between the men is heating up. They start off being polite to each other, but by the third and fourth stanzas, they are saying some pretty harsh things to each other. Booker T. tells W.E.B. that he and his "folks" should "keep their mouths shut" and W.E.B. says, "as for me, I'll be a man," showing he thinks that Booker T. isn't a real man.*

RESEARCH

Encourage students to use multiple websites that are reliable and credible to best ensure that they find accurate and sufficient information for both Washington and Du Bois. Point out that another benefit of using multiple sites is that students also are more likely to get additional perspectives or viewpoints on the two men.

Extend Students should look for at least two similarities and two differences between the subject matter in "Booker T. and W.E.B." and the poems they have found.

RESPOND

ANALYZE THE TEXT

Support your responses with evidence from the text. NOTEBOOK

1. **Analyze** Reread and paraphrase line 2, focusing on the word *cheek*. What does Booker T.'s choice of that word suggest to you about his opinion of W.E.B.?
2. **Infer** Reread lines 1–7. Who are "Mister Charlie" and "Miss Anne"? How does Booker T. think they should be treated? Does his attitude surprise you? Why or why not?
3. **Infer** Reread lines 8–11. What are some synonyms you could use in place of the word *drive* in line 9? What does W.E.B.'s choice of that word suggest to you about his opinion of Booker T.?
4. **Synthesize** Review the third and fourth stanzas. How do Booker T. and W.E.B.'s views of the fight for civil rights differ? Use evidence from the poem in your answer.
5. **Interpret** What is the effect of the use of rhyme and the repetition of the phrases "It seems to me" and "I don't agree"? What attitude does each phrase convey? How does this highlight the differences between the men? Use evidence from the poem in your answer.

RESEARCH

Find out more about the views of Booker T. Washington and W.E.B. Du Bois regarding the issues mentioned in the poem. Work with a partner to research their lives, influences, and points of view on those issues. Use what you learn to summarize their views in this chart.

ISSUE	BOOKER T. WASHINGTON	W.E.B. DU BOIS
What the focus of education should be	*Education should teach people to be useful and perform some necessary service.*	*People should have the right to choose what they study.*
What people should strive to achieve	*Get a practical education, get a job and work hard, earn and save money, and buy a house.*	*Seek power and equality; become part of the lawmaking class.*
How best to gain civil rights and political power	*You earn these by working hard and earning respect. The civil rights "movement" is a waste of time and won't work, at least not yet.*	*Civil rights and political power are not earned; they have to be demanded and fought for.*

RESEARCH TIP
When you conduct online research, be sure to evaluate the credibility of websites. Web addresses ending in .gov, .edu, or .org are the work of large groups. Because these sites are frequently reviewed, they are often more reliable and credible than other sites.

Extend Look for other poems by Dudley Randall and compare their subject matter to "Booker T. and W.E.B." What similarities do you notice? How are the poems different?

WHEN STUDENTS STRUGGLE . . .

Paraphrase Poetic Language Students may struggle with the diction in the poem—in particular, the syntax of some of the lines. (Review the meaning of *syntax*: how the words are arranged in a sentence.) To help students understand a key idea in the poem, read aloud lines 29–30. Point out that the syntax in line 29 is not common English syntax. Encourage students to work with a partner to paraphrase these lines. *(Even if you have a lot of money, you might still feel oppressed.)*

For more support, go to the **Reading Studio** and assign the following  **Level Up Tutorial: Paraphrasing.**

CREATE AND DEBATE

Assess the Viewpoints Expand on the chart you used in the research activity to define the pros and cons of each man's position on the issues listed.

- ❑ In your opinion, what are the strengths and weaknesses of each man's position on the issues of education, life goals, and civil rights/political power?
- ❑ How do you think each man would feel about the same issues if he were alive today?
- ❑ Conduct additional research as necessary.

Conduct a Debate Work with your classmates to conduct a team debate on the ideas of Booker T. Washington and W.E.B. Du Bois. Use the ideas and information you gathered and conduct additional research to prepare your arguments. Then hold your debate in front of your class.

- ❑ Speak in a loud, clear voice so everyone can hear and understand you. Use a formal tone and appropriate vocabulary.
- ❑ Stand up straight and make eye contact with your opponents and your audience. Use facial expressions and natural gestures to add emphasis to your words.
- ❑ Use evidence from your research to support your arguments. Adjust your views in light of persuasive evidence from your classmates.
- ❑ Listen actively while others are speaking, and don't interrupt.
- ❑ Evaluate your preparation for and participation in the debate.

Go to the **Speaking and Listening Studio** for more on giving a presentation.

RESPOND TO THE ESSENTIAL QUESTION

How do people find freedom in the midst of oppression?

Gather Information Review your annotations and notes on "Booker T. and W.E.B." Then add relevant information to your Response Log. As you determine which information to include, think about:

- What are some different paths to gaining freedom and equality?
- What are the effects of oppression?
- Must we change within ourselves before we can change society?

At the end of the unit, use your notes to help you write a research report.

ACADEMIC VOCABULARY

As you write and discuss what you learned from the poem, be sure to use the Academic Vocabulary words. Check off each of the words that you use.

- ❑ **decline**
- ❑ **enable**
- ❑ **impose**
- ❑ **integrate**
- ❑ **reveal**

TEACH

CREATE AND DEBATE

Assess the Viewpoints Point out that the chart on Student Edition page 134 can serve as an outline for students' ideas about the strengths and weaknesses of each man's position on the issues. Additional research might yield present-day examples to support the positions.

Conduct a Debate Review the debate guidelines with students. Remind students that both Booker T. Washington and W.E.B. Du Bois were expressing views within a particular historical context, and that their debate focused on the best course of action for African Americans to take in order to improve their lives and achieve equality at that time. Emphasize that when students conduct their own debate, they should broaden their scope to include Americans as a whole rather than limiting the debate to any one group of people. Students might focus their debate on whether it is better to earn equality indirectly or to seek it directly. Ask volunteers to provide examples of each approach. *(indirect means: getting a practical education, volunteering for leadership roles; direct means: protesting injustice, working to create fairer laws).*

Remind students of the importance of ensuring that all speakers have a chance to be heard. Encourage listeners to take notes and provide thoughtful feedback about the persuasiveness of the arguments as well as the effectiveness of the delivery.

For **speaking and writing support** for students at varying proficiency levels, see the **Text X-Ray** on page 128D.

RESPOND TO THE ESSENTIAL QUESTION

Allow time for students to add details from "Booker T. and W.E.B." to their Unit 2 Response Logs.

ENGLISH LEARNER SUPPORT

Conduct a Debate Have students prepare for their debate by recasting the assignment, using these question frames: *What are the pros (strengths or advantages) of each man's position on ________? What are the cons (weaknesses or disadvantages) of each man's position on ________?* Encourage students to refer to the answers they provided in the research activity. Then provide these sentence frames to help students formulate their ideas for the debate: *I liked ______'s ideas about ______. He believed that ______ was important because ______.*

MODERATE/LIGHT

from READING LOLITA IN TEHRAN

Memoir by Azar Nafisi

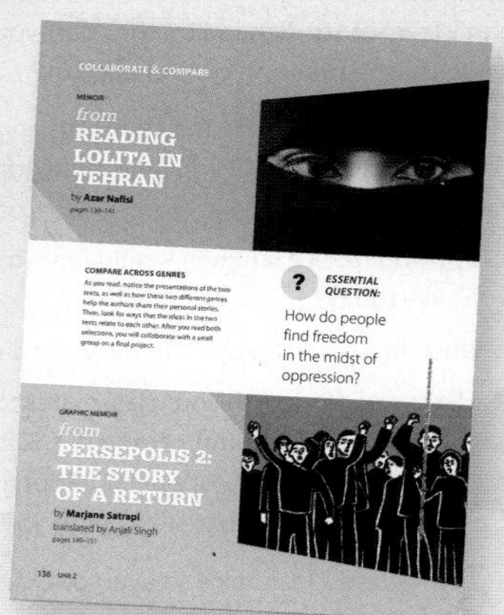

GENRE ELEMENTS

MEMOIR

Explain to students that a **memoir** is a way for an author to describe specific events and the author's reactions to them. It focuses on actual events the author experienced in the past and describes those events and the author's reactions using the author's unique point of view. Although the events are factual, the author provides personal observations and opinions about them, including their effect upon the author.

LEARNING OBJECTIVES

- Analyze rhetorical devices in a memoir, along with the memoir's setting and the author's purpose.
- Research Iranian government and society today.
- Create and present a podcast about Iran today.
- Identify denotative and connotative meanings of words.
- Analyze the effects of present and past tenses in verbs.
- **Language** Vary intonation to express declarative and interrogative intent.

TEXT COMPLEXITY

Quantitative Measures	***from* Reading Lolita in Tehran**	Lexile: 1150L
Qualitative Measures	**Ideas Presented** Requires weighing of multiple perspectives and author's purpose.	
	Structures Used Organization of main ideas and details is highly complex, not explicit, and must be inferred.	
	Language Used Clear, direct language.	
	Knowledge Required Requires understanding of moderately complex civics concepts.	

Online 

RESOURCES

- Unit 2 Response Log
- Selection Audio
- Reading Studio: Notice & Note
- Speaking and Listening Studio: Using Media in a Presentation
- Vocabulary Studio: Denotative and Connotative Meanings
- Grammar Studio: Module 6: Lesson 3: Verb Tense
- from *Reading Lolita in Tehran*/from *Persepolis 2* Selection Test

SUMMARIES

English

Azar Nafisi describes conditions for women in Tehran after the Iranian Revolution of the 1970s. Nafisi secretly teaches a literature class for women in her home and illustrates the repressive restrictions on women's appearance and their public conduct by imagining what it's like for one of her students to travel across Tehran after leaving Nafisi's house. Nafisi explores the woman's thoughts as well as the cultural demands on her—and the dangers she faces.

Spanish

Azar Nafisi describe las condiciones de las mujeres en Tehran después la revolución Iraní de los años 70. Nafisi da secretamente clases de literatura para mujeres en su casa e ilustra las restricciones represivas en su apariencia y conducta pública al seguir a una mujer mientras camina a su casa desde la casa de Nafisi. Nafisi explora los pensamientos de la mujer, así como las exigencias culturales con que tiene que cargar y los peligros que enfrenta.

SMALL-GROUP OPTIONS

Have students work in small groups and pairs to read and discuss the selection.

Pinwheel Discussion

- Form groups of 6 (or 8), with 3 (or 4) students facing out, each paired with a partner facing in.
- Provide a question about the selection and have pairs discuss it for a prescribed time.
- Randomly call on pairs to summarize their discussion for the class and answer questions.
- Have students in the outer circle rotate one person to the right to form a new pair. Repeat the process so that all students work with all others.
- Possible questions: Why do you think Nafisi left Iran? Do you think the small acts of rebellion by women were effective?

Think-Write-Pair-Share

- After students have read and analyzed the excerpt from *Reading Lolita in Tehran*, pose this question: Can restrictions like those used in Iran force people to change their opinions and attitudes? Why or why not?
- Have students think about the question individually and take notes.
- Then have pairs discuss their ideas about the question.
- Finally, ask pairs to share their responses with the class.

Text X-Ray: English Learner Support
for *Reading Lolita in Tehran*

Use the Text X-Ray and the supports and scaffolds in the Teacher's Edition to help guide students at different proficiency levels through the selection.

INTRODUCE THE SELECTION

DISCUSS OPPRESSIVE REGIMES

In this lesson, students will read about and discuss oppressive regimes. Explain the following terms:

- *Oppressive* is an adjective that refers to actions that prohibit people from speaking, acting, or thinking freely.
- A *regime* is a group that temporarily controls a government or organization.

Explain that not all *regimes* are *oppressive* and that some regimes offer freedoms to their people. Provide these frames to prompt discussion about *oppressive* laws and changing *regimes*:

- *The regime in the United States changes every ______ because of ______.*
- *Punishing people for ______ is oppressive.*

CULTURAL REFERENCES

The following words or phrases from the selection may be unfamiliar to students:

- *It is in her best interest* (paragraph 2): the results will be better for her
- *white Toyota patrols* (paragraph 2): a type of car used by Iranian militia to travel in the city
- *squeezed together like sardines* (paragraph 3): packed closely together like small fish in cans
- *stoning* (paragraph 4): an ancient type of punishment (sometimes fatal) in which a crowd attacks someone by throwing stones

LISTENING

Understand Important Ideas

Explain that you are going to read the Background paragraph on Student Edition page 139 aloud. Students can practice listening comprehension to ensure their understanding of key ideas and details.

Use the following supports with students at varying proficiency levels:

- As you read aloud the Background paragraph, pause after each sentence and have students rephrase it to confirm their understanding. **SUBSTANTIAL**
- Encourage students to note any clarifying questions they have as you read the Background paragraph aloud. When complete, have students ask their questions to confirm understanding. **MODERATE**
- After you read the Background paragraph aloud, confirm students' understanding by asking them to provide an oral summary statement of the paragraph. **LIGHT**

SPEAKING

Speak with Rhythm and Intonation

On Student Edition page 143, students will be asked to create a podcast in which they read a script aloud. Help them practice English rhythms and intonation to gain confidence in speaking.

Use the following supports with students at varying proficiency levels:

- Explain that English speakers often use a different rhythm and intonation for questions and declarative statements. Repeat the following question and response aloud and have students echo them, focusing on rhythm and intonation: How has Iran changed in recent years? It has changed in many ways. What is life there today like? I will do some research to find out. **SUBSTANTIAL**
- Ask students to say the following sentences aloud and assist them as necessary with rhythm and intonation: How has Iran changed in recent years? It has changed in many ways. What is life there today like? I will do some research to find out. **MODERATE**
- Have pairs write a question and a declarative statement about Iran and practice saying them aloud with proper rhythm and intonation. **LIGHT**

READING

Recognize and Analyze Rhetorical Questions

Explain that this author uses rhetorical questions (questions that do not require or expect an answer) to direct the reader's attention and to stir careful thought.

Have students reread paragraph 4 and number the sentences in their consumable text. Then use the following supports with students at varying proficiency levels:

- Instruct students to identify the punctuation mark that indicates a question. Ask them to count up the number of sentences that are questions compared to the number of statements. **SUBSTANTIAL**
- Have students focus on the first four sentences. Ask: What answers does the author supply for the rhetorical question in sentence 2? **MODERATE**
- Point out that sentence 2 is a rhetorical question. Ask: What is the purpose of the questions in sentences 5–7? **LIGHT**

WRITING

Use Varied and Complex Sentence Structures

Explain that interesting podcasts use a variety of sentence structures. Provide practice using independent and dependent clauses to combine sentences before students complete the activity on Student Edition page 143.

Use the following supports with students at varying proficiency levels:

- Provide assistance as necessary in combining the following sentences: Iran experienced a revolution in the late 1970s. It caused many changes. **SUBSTANTIAL**
- Ask students to combine these sentences using the modifier although: The government placed many restrictions on women. Many women rebelled against them. **MODERATE**
- Have students write two declarative sentences about Iran and then combine them into a complex sentence. **LIGHT**

Connect to the
ESSENTIAL QUESTION

The excerpt from *Reading Lolita in Tehran* is by a teacher who describes the challenges and worries faced by girls and women in Iran during the 1990s. In order to convey the ways in which the government restricted women during this period, she imagines and vividly describes the experience of one of the girls she taught in Tehran as she returns home from a literature class. The author suggests that, under such harsh government control, girls and women like herself could only find freedom through their imagination. Any outward expression of freedom would have very serious consequences.

COMPARE ACROSS GENRES

Point out that both excerpts—one from *Reading Lolita in Tehran* and one from *Persepolis 2*—are memoirs: they record actual events as seen or experienced by the author and include the author's feelings and learning from her own, unique point of view. However, Nafisi's account relies exclusively on words to communicate the events, feelings, and other details. Ask students if they form pictures or images in their heads as they read a selection like hers. Do these mental images help them better understand or picture the events?

MEMOIR

from READING LOLITA IN TEHRAN

by **Azar Nafisi**

pages 139–141

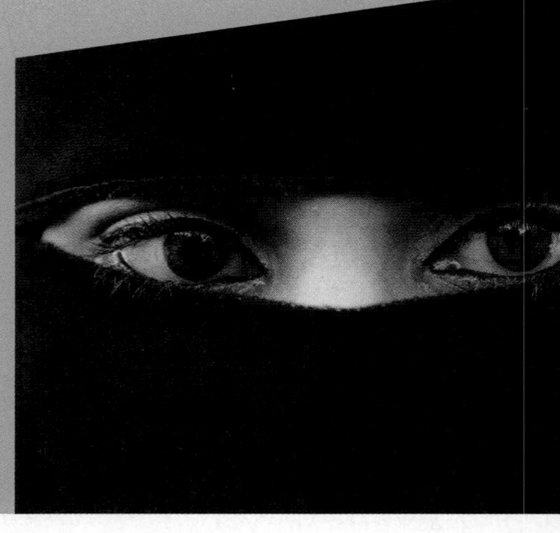

COMPARE ACROSS GENRES

As you read, notice the presentations of the two texts, as well as how these two different genres help the authors share their personal stories. Then, look for ways that the ideas in the two texts relate to each other. After you read both selections, you will collaborate with a small group on a final project.

ESSENTIAL QUESTION:

How do people find freedom in the midst of oppression?

GRAPHIC MEMOIR

from PERSEPOLIS 2: THE STORY OF A RETURN

by **Marjane Satrapi**

translated by Anjali Singh

pages 149–151

LEARNING MINDSET

Persistence Remind students that when they encounter a challenging work of literature, it's important not to give up but rather to tell themselves that they can understand it if they stick with it. In order to comprehend and respond to this memoir, students will need to understand its historical context, navigate its unusual text structure, use text details to empathize with the young women the author describes, and make inferences about the author's message and purpose. Emphasize that students will have multiple opportunities to engage with the text and respond to its content, and that their persistence will pay off in terms of helping them develop and deepen their understanding of the selection.

GET READY 

from Reading Lolita in Tehran

QUICK START

Throughout history and across cultures, women have experienced different treatment and faced different social expectations than men. With a group, discuss ways that males and females are treated differently in your culture.

ANALYZE RHETORICAL DEVICES

Azar Nafisi uses rhetorical questions to engage the audience and to make a point. **Rhetorical questions** are questions that do not require or expect an answer. Depending on the context, they are often posed for dramatic effect. For example:

RHETORICAL QUESTION FROM SELECTION	MEANING
How can I create this other world outside the room?	Nafisi uses the rhetorical question as an opener to explain why she creates an imaginary scene involving Sanaz.
Does she compare her own situation with her mother's when she was the same age?	The question engages readers and invites them to consider any background knowledge they have about Iran's history.
Is she aware, Sanaz, of her own power?	Nafisi uses the rhetorical question to provide dramatic effect and to give meaning to the questions that follow.

ANALYZE SETTING AND PURPOSE

The setting and purpose of a text reveal important information. As you analyze the effect of setting and purpose on *Reading Lolita in Tehran,* consider:

- **Setting:** The **setting** is where a text occurs. Iran requires women to live according to a specific set of laws that govern their dress and behavior.
- **Purpose:** The **purpose** reflects why an author wrote a text—what she hopes to communicate. In *Reading Lolita in Tehran*, Nafisi discusses how she taught a small group of women in her home in Tehran after she stopped teaching at an Iranian university.
- **Author's point of view:** The **author's point of view** is how an author thinks or feels about a subject. Azar Nafisi wrote her book after she left Iran to live abroad. Her perspective as a woman and scholar who had once lived under an oppressive regime influences how she approaches the topic and constructs the text.

Setting, purpose, and point of view all help shape the **main idea**, or message the author wants to convey. As you read the excerpt from *Reading Lolita in Tehran,* note how the writer uses the setting and point of view to accomplish her purpose and convey her feelings about her experiences.

GENRE ELEMENTS: MEMOIR

- records actual events based on the writer's observations
- dependent on the author's point of view
- looks back at specific event or series of events
- shares the author's feelings and what she has learned

ENGLISH LEARNER SUPPORT

Use Cognates Be sure that students understand the word *oppression* in the Essential Question. Point out the Spanish cognate *opresión* and define it in English: "prolonged cruel or unjust treatment". Compare it with the synonyms *repression* and *suppression*: "state of being stopped or prevented by force." Note that all refer to the use of force by a government to control people's actions. Note that all of these words have very negative connotations in the United States, where personal freedom usually has a high priority. **ALL LEVELS**

TEACH

QUICK START

If groups struggle to identify different treatment and social expectations for women, suggest that they identify situations and the different experiences men and women have in them. For example, they can look at businesses and jobs, schools, sports, entertainment, fashion and clothing, religion, politics, and government. They might extend the discussion by considering whether they think these differences have positive or negative effects or are essentially neutral (yet different). Point out that different levels of government and courts have been involved in this issue for many years.

ANALYZE RHETORICAL DEVICES

Discuss with students the fact that writers use rhetorical questions to convey ideas. These types of questions help keep the prose lively and interesting for readers, while also helping the author express a point of view. They are often used to provoke a reader or listener to think about and consider a subject from a different point of view. For example, the second question in the chart encourages the reader to compare Sanaz's situation with that of Sanaz's mother.

ANALYZE SETTING AND PURPOSE

Point out that setting provides limitations in a text as well as focus. For example, living in a rural area in Iran rather than urban Tehran would make the fictional main character's journey home different; there might not be taxis or buses, or militia patrolling the streets. Different time periods also frame and limit the story because of changes in culture and expectations.

An author's purpose and point of view are central to a story and combine with the setting to provide a theme. In this selection, the author wants to point out the pressures and obstacles for women under the oppressive regime in Tehran in the 1990s.

To emphasize how these factors affect a story, ask students to choose a setting, purpose, and point of view that are different from this one and discuss how they would affect the story. For example, they might choose their own hometown and imagine a story about a positive experience they have had.

TEACH

CRITICAL VOCABULARY

As a clue to determining meaning, point out that *irrelevant* includes the prefix *ir-*, which indicates "not" or "the opposite of." Point out that the second letter of the prefix *ir-* often changes to match the first letter of the attached word (for example, *illegal*).

Answers:

1. *Answers will vary but may include* separate.
2. *Answers will vary but may include* set aside.
3. *Answers will vary but may include* unnecessary.
4. *Answers will vary but may include* change.

■ English Learner Support

Use Cognates Tell students that several of the Critical Vocabulary words have Spanish cognates: *segregate/segregar, irrelevant/irrelevante, convert/convertir).*

ALL LEVELS

LANGUAGE CONVENTIONS: VERB TENSE

Review the information about verb tenses. Note that the use of the present tense places the reader in the exact time of the events described while past tense presents reflections after the events have occurred.

Have students practice by writing a few sentences using the same approach for present and past tenses. They can describe a person's actions at the beginning of a sporting, musical, or other event. *(She waits breathlessly for the star to appear.)* Then, add knowledge or reflections from after the event. *(Later, she realized that the music had changed her life.)*

ANNOTATION MODEL

Remind students of the ideas in Analyze Setting and Purpose on Student Edition page 137. The Annotation Model shows that the student chose to circle words that establish a writer's purpose and underline words that indicate setting. Point out that they may follow this model or use their own system for marking up the selection in their write-in text. They may want to color-code their annotations using highlighters. Their notes in the margin may also include questions about ideas that are unclear or topics they want to learn more about.

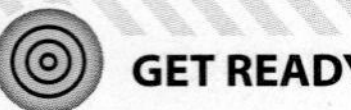

GET READY

CRITICAL VOCABULARY

segregate **allocate** **irrelevant** **convert**

To preview the Critical Vocabulary words, replace each boldfaced word with a different word or words that have the same meaning.

1. Be sure to (**segregate**) ____________ the different types of recycling into different waste containers.
2. The school decided to (**allocate**) ____________ some money to buy a new playground swing set.
3. She revised her paragraph to remove any (**irrelevant**) ____________ details.
4. We are free to keep our religious beliefs and not (**convert**) ____________ to another way of thinking.

LANGUAGE CONVENTIONS: VERB TENSE

In her memoir, Nafisi alternates between past and present tense, using each in a consistent way.

When she uses present tense, as in, "Let's imagine one of the girls, say Sanaz, leaving my house . . ." she focuses the reader's attention on the thoughts and feelings of that one student. When Nafisi uses past tense, as in, "They were never free of the regime's definition of them as Muslim women," she is reflecting more generally on the events and atmosphere of Iran.

As you read the excerpt from *Reading Lolita in Tehran*, watch for ways the author uses present and past tense verbs.

ANNOTATION MODEL

NOTICE & NOTE 

Here are one student's annotations about setting and purpose.

from **Reading Lolita in Tehran**

How can I create this other world outside the room? I have no choice but to appeal once again to your imagination. Let's imagine one of the girls, say Sanaz, leaving my house and let us follow her from there to her final destination. She says her good-byes and puts on her black robe and scarf over her orange shirt and jeans, coiling her scarf around her neck to cover her huge gold earrings.

The first sentence shows that the author's purpose for writing is to describe what life is like for Iranian women outside her study group.

The phrase "black robe and scarf" tells me that the text is set somewhere where women must completely cover themselves when outside.

NOTICE & NOTE

BACKGROUND

The Iranian Revolution in the late 1970s resulted in the overthrow of the pro-western Shah of Iran. Iranians established a theocracy, or religious government, based on the rule of Islam. The new government passed laws that segregate men and women and that force women to adhere to an Islamic dress code. Iranian women are required to wear veils that cover their hair and neck and coats that cover their arms and legs.

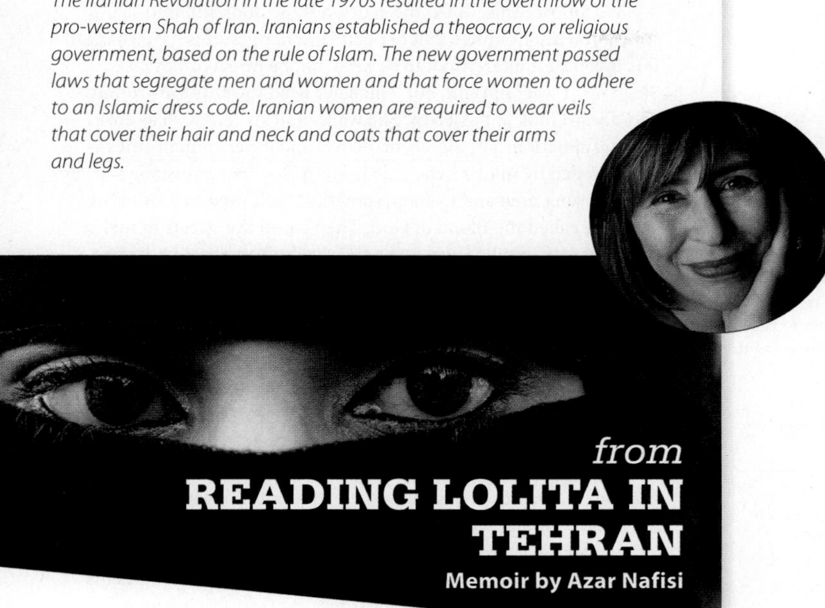

from READING LOLITA IN TEHRAN

Memoir by Azar Nafisi

Azar Nafisi *(b. 1947), an Iranian, taught English literature in Tehran from 1979 until 1995. Laws passed after the revolution made Nafisi's job difficult. Nafisi's university scrutinized novels that she taught, and she was chastised for not wearing a veil. In 1995, Nafisi left the university and began teaching a small group of women in her home, where they were free to discuss books, like* Lolita, *that were considered unacceptable by Iranian authorities. In 1997, she left Iran for the United States, where she now teaches.*

PREPARE TO COMPARE

As you read, make note of the kind of information included in a narrative memoir. You will compare this genre to Persepolis 2, *which is in the form of a graphic novel. If you encounter words or ideas you don't understand, ask your classmates or teacher for assistance.*

1 How can I create this other world outside the room? I have no choice but to appeal once again to your imagination. Let's imagine one of the girls, say Sanaz, leaving my house and let us follow her from there to her final destination. She says her goodbyes and puts on her black robe and scarf over her orange shirt and jeans, coiling her scarf around her neck to cover her huge gold earrings. She directs wayward strands of hair under the scarf, puts her notes into her large bag, straps it on over her

Notice & Note

You can use the side margins to notice and note signposts in the text.

LANGUAGE CONVENTIONS

Annotate: Underline examples of present tense verbs.

Respond: How do the present tense verbs help you understand the current living conditions of the women?

TEACH

BACKGROUND

Have students read the Background and information about the author. Tell students that in countries with oppressive regimes such as Iran's, openly protesting the government is very dangerous. This selection gives some details on the dangers. It also provides an Iranian woman's perspective on the challenges of living in a country under such a regime and how some girls and women respond.

For **listening support** for students at varying proficiency levels, see the **Text X-Ray** on page 136C.

PREPARE TO COMPARE

Direct students to use the Prepare to Compare prompt to focus their reading.

LANGUAGE CONVENTIONS

Authors may choose to use the present tense to draw the reader into the story. The author forces the reader to see things as if they were happening at the same time the reader is reading them. Note that in movies, viewers often see the events just as they are happening. Using the present tense can help readers visualize important events, as if they are seeing them on a movie screen. Have pairs of students compare the present tense verbs they underlined in paragraph 1. (***Answer:*** *The author describes the experience of one girl, Sanaz, so that readers can experience the living conditions of women through her eyes. The present-tense verbs give the details of Sanaz's experience—putting on the black robe and scarf and hiding her colorful clothes, hair, and nail polish—more immediacy and impact and make the scene more vivid, more real for modern readers.)*

APPLYING ACADEMIC VOCABULARY

- ☐ decline
- ☑ enable
- ☑ impose
- ☐ integrate
- ☐ reveal

Write and Discuss Have students turn to a partner to discuss the following questions. Guide students to include the academic vocabulary words *enable* and *impose* in their responses. Ask volunteers to share their responses with the class.

- How did the classes in Nafisi's home **enable** her students to continue learning about controversial ideas?
- What rules did the government **impose** on women and girls after the Iranian Revolution?

TEACH

ANALYZE SETTING AND PURPOSE

The setting for a memoir is not a writer's choice, since the memoir relates actual events. However, if the writer had a different purpose, he or she might choose a different setting and events to accomplish that purpose. For example, if Nafisi's purpose was to help people understand the richness of Iran's environment, she might have chosen a time from her childhood where she experienced its beauty. (***Answer:*** *The setting is Tehran, Iran. The author is writing to reveal the conditions under which the women of Iran are living.)*

For **reading support** for students at varying proficiency levels, see the **Text X-Ray** on page 136D.

EXTREME OR ABSOLUTE LANGUAGE

Certain **language** communicates an uncompromising, or firm, position. In this case, the slogans on the walls show an uncompromising position in their words and in the important location where they are displayed. Absolute certainty is shown in the first slogan with the definitive phrases "ARE U.S. LACKEYS" and "VEILING IS." The second slogan contains clear demands for certain behavior. Both slogans are displayed prominently on walls where they can't be missed. (***Answer:*** *The author quotes these slogans to help the reader understand these cultural messages better: that men who dress in Western ways are subservient to the United States; that women must be shielded from the world by veils; and that men must control themselves around women.)*

CRITICAL VOCABULARY

segregate: In Iran, women are kept separate from men in public.

ASK STUDENTS who ensures that women and men are segregated in Iran. *(Militia, named the Blood of God, patrol the streets to make sure that women don't appear in public with men who are not in their family.)*

allocate: The rear seats of the buses are designated for women.

ASK STUDENTS to discuss why the seats allocated to women are in the back of the bus and not the front or another location. *(so that the women are not seen by men and to indicate that women are second-class citizens)*

NOTICE & NOTE

ANALYZE SETTING AND PURPOSE

Annotate: Mark text evidence that discusses the setting.

Respond: What is the setting for this memoir? What do you think the author's purpose is for writing it?

EXTREME OR ABSOLUTE LANGUAGE

Notice & Note: Mark text that quotes messages conveyed by the culture in which the women live.

Interpret: Why might the author have included these quoted messages?

segregate
(sĕg´rĭ-gāt´) *v.* to cause people to be separated based on gender, race, or other factors.

allocate
(ăl´ə-kāt´) *v.* to assign or designate for.

shoulder and walks out into the hall. She pauses a moment on top of the stairs to put on thin lacy black gloves to hide her nail polish.

2 We follow Sanaz down the stairs, out the door and into the street. You might notice that her gait[1] and her gestures have changed. It is in her best interest not to be seen, not be heard or noticed. She doesn't walk upright, but bends her head towards the ground and doesn't look at passersby. She walks quickly and with a sense of determination. The streets of Tehran and other Iranian cities are patrolled by militia, who ride in white Toyota patrols, four gun-carrying men and women, sometimes followed by a minibus. They are called the Blood of God. They patrol the streets to make sure that women like Sanaz wear their veils properly, do not wear makeup, do not walk in public with men who are not their fathers, brothers or husbands. She will pass slogans on the walls, quotations from Khomeini[2] and a group called the Party of God: MEN WHO WEAR TIES ARE U.S. LACKEYS.[3] VEILING IS A WOMAN'S PROTECTION. Beside the slogan is a charcoal drawing of a woman: her face is featureless and framed by a dark chador.[4] MY SISTER, GUARD YOUR VEIL. MY BROTHER, GUARD YOUR EYES.

3 If she gets on a bus, the seating is **segregated**. She must enter through the rear door and sit in the back seats, **allocated** to women. Yet in taxis, which accept as many as five passengers, men and women are squeezed together like sardines, as the saying goes, and the same goes with minibuses, where so many of my students complain of being harassed by bearded and God-fearing men.

4 You might well ask, What is Sanaz thinking as she walks the streets of Tehran? How much does this experience affect her? Most probably, she tries to distance her mind as much as possible from her surroundings. Perhaps she is thinking of her brother, or of her distant boyfriend and the time when she will meet him in Turkey. Does she compare her own situation with her mother's when she was the same age? Is she angry that women of her mother's generation could walk the streets freely, enjoy the company of the opposite sex, join the police force, become pilots, live under laws that were among the most progressive in the world regarding women? Does she feel humiliated by the new laws, by the fact that after the revolution, the age of marriage was lowered from eighteen to nine, that stoning became once more the punishment for adultery and prostitution?

5 In the course of nearly two decades, the streets have been turned into a war zone, where young women who disobey the rules are hurled into patrol cars, taken to jail, flogged, fined, forced to wash the toilets and humiliated, and as soon as they leave, they go back

[1] **gait:** manner of walking.
[2] **Khomeini** (kō-mā´ nē): Ruhollah Khomeini (1902–1989), religious and political leader of Iran after the 1979 revolution.
[3] **U.S. lackeys:** people who serve United States policies. The Iranian government is hostile to the U.S. because it supported the former Shah of Iran.
[4] **chador** (chə´-dər): a long scarf that covers a Muslim woman's hair, neck, and shoulders.

ENGLISH LEARNER SUPPORT

Language Transfer: Varying Uses of -s at End of Words For native Vietnamese speakers, point out three different uses of -s at the end of words in paragraph 2. Have students practice pronouncing each word until they can distinguish and form the /s/ sound relatively easily.

- To form plural nouns: *gestures, patrols, fathers, brothers, husbands*
- To form present tense, third-person verbs: *bends, walks*
- To form possessives with an apostrophe: *WOMAN'S* **ALL LEVELS**

and do the same thing. Is she aware, Sanaz, of her own power? Does she realize how dangerous she can be when her every stray gesture is a disturbance to public safety? Does she think how vulnerable the Revolutionary Guards are who for over eighteen years have patrolled the streets of Tehran and have had to endure young women like herself, and those of other generations, walking, talking, showing a strand of hair just to remind them that they have not **converted**?

6 We have reached Sanaz's house, where we will leave her on her doorstep, perhaps to confront her brother on the other side and to think in her heart of her boyfriend.

7 These girls, my girls, had both a real history and a fabricated one. Although they came from very different backgrounds, the regime that ruled them had tried to make their personal identities and histories **irrelevant**. They were never free of the regime's definition of them as Muslim women.

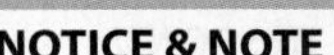

NOTICE & NOTE

ANALYZE RHETORICAL DEVICES

Annotate: Mark the rhetorical questions in paragraph 5.

Respond: What is the effect of these questions?

convert

(kən-vûrt´) *v.* to change one's system of beliefs.

irrelevant

(ĭr-rĕl´ə-vənt) *adj.* insignificant, unimportant.

CHECK YOUR UNDERSTANDING

Answer these questions before moving on to the **Analyze the Text** section on the following page.

1 This passage is mostly about —

- **A** the author's opinion of universities in Iran
- **B** the author's experience with her daughters
- **C** the author's opinion of the government of Iran
- **D** the author's experience with a female literature group

2 How does the genre of this selection allow the author to share her point of view?

- **F** In this informational text, the author notes specific facts about Iran.
- **G** In this memoir, the author shares her observations of situations she experienced in Iran.
- **H** In this informational text, the author provides her opinion about Iran.
- **J** In this memoir, the author tells a story based on historical events.

3 In the first paragraph, the description of Sanaz tells you that she —

- **A** openly disobeys laws governing how women in Iran must dress
- **B** has more freedom in how she dresses than other women in Iran
- **C** is interested in fashion even though she has to cover herself
- **D** is more concerned with what people think of her than she is with following the laws governing women

ENGLISH LEARNER SUPPORT

Oral Assessment Use the following questions to assess students' comprehension and speaking skills. Ask students to respond in complete sentences.

1. What is the main subject of this selection? *(The main subject is the author's view of the government of Iran, based on her and her students' experiences there.)*
2. How does the genre of this selection help the author achieve her purpose? *(The memoir allows the author to share events she experienced and her observations on them.)*
3. What does the description of Sanaz in the first paragraph tell you about her personality and interests? *(It shows that she is interested in fashion even though she has to cover herself.)*

ALL LEVELS

ANALYZE RHETORICAL DEVICES

Review with students that **rhetorical questions** do not require or expect a response. You might also point out that rhetoric is the art of using language effectively to achieve a certain purpose. Discuss with students what purpose the questions in paragraph 5 might serve for the author. (***Answer:*** *The rhetorical questions serve two purposes. First, the author uses the questions to speculate on what Sanaz might have thought. She also uses the questions to suggest that young women such as Sanaz have a power that they may or may not recognize. If a government has to work so hard to oppress young women, then it doesn't have as much control over them as it would like.)*

For **reading support** for students at varying proficiency levels, see the **Text X-Ray** on page 136C.

CRITICAL VOCABULARY

convert: The author points out that women can do small, subtle things to show that they do not share the beliefs of the Revolutionary Guards.

ASK STUDENTS why it would be difficult for women to "convert" to the thinking of the Iranian government. *(The government violates women's human rights. Women must submit to the laws but are not deterred from showing they do not agree.)*

irrelevant: The author is emphasizing that the regime's laws regarding women took away their ability to express themselves as individuals.

ASK STUDENTS how the regime's laws made personal histories irrelevant. *(By forcing all women to dress the same and not letting them express themselves publicly, the regime made it difficult for women to speak out against it.)*

CHECK YOUR UNDERSTANDING

Have students answer the questions independently.

Answers:

1. *C* **2.** *G* **3.** *C*

If they answer any questions incorrectly, have them reread the text to confirm their understanding. Then they may proceed to ANALYZE THE TEXT on page 142.

APPLY

ANALYZE THE TEXT

Possible answers:

1. **DOK 2:** *Details include Sanaz putting on her black robe over her orange shirt and jeans and coiling her scarf around her neck to cover her earrings. There also is a description of how Sanaz walks, with her head bent down, quickly and with determination. The author includes these details to help the reader visualize the "real" Sanaz.*
2. **DOK 4:** *Iranian authorities have imposed such stringent laws on women—such as the law that a woman cannot walk with a man who is not her father, brother, or husband—as a way to control them.*
3. **DOK 3:** *Sanaz and the other women obey the laws out of self-preservation, but they do not necessarily agree with them. The author suggests that a young woman like Sanaz may cope by trying "to distance her mind as much as possible from her surroundings."*
4. **DOK 4:** *When the author uses a rhetorical question such as "Is she angry that women in her mother's generation could walk the streets freely . . . ?" she reveals her own anger and frustration with Iran's regressive laws.*

RESEARCH

Remind students to list at least two online sources with relevant notes on paraphrased or quoted information. Also remind students that direct quotes should be identified by quotation marks.

Connect Help students prepare for their small-group discussion by directing them to formulate 1–3 summary sentences based on their research. Then have them prepare to support their statements using evidence from the research. Note that summarizing change in a culture can be tricky and that different sources may not agree. Encourage a respectful discussion even if research information fuels differing perspectives.

RESPOND

ANALYZE THE TEXT

Support your responses with evidence from the text. NOTEBOOK

1. **Infer** This excerpt opens with a clue to the author's purpose. What is it? How does she use details of setting to achieve her purpose? Cite text evidence in your response.
2. **Analyze** Why might Iranian authorities have imposed such stringent laws on women?
3. **Conclude** What can you determine about how Sanaz and the other women in the literature group cope with the laws about their behavior and appearance?
4. **Notice & Note** Nafisi repeatedly uses rhetorical questions. How are they effective in conveying her point of view? Explain with evidence from the text.

RESEARCH

RESEARCH TIP
Be sure to check the websites you use to ensure that they are reliable and credible sources of information. Sites of well-known news organizations are a good place to start, and sites with the suffix *.org* tend to be more reliable than commercial sites.

Find out more about how the Iranian government and society has or has not changed since 2003, when Nafisi's memoir was written. Research modern Iranian politics, society, and culture based on information from two or three reliable websites. Keep track of your sources in a chart like the one shown. Remember to use quotation marks around text taken word-for-word from your sources.

TITLE	URL/ SOURCE	PARAPHRASED OR QUOTED INFORMATION
Iran: Education	*Encyclopedia Britannica Online* *(URLs will vary.)*	*Universities in Iran often look at how religious applicants are.* *By 2000, more women than men were admitted to universities in Iran.*
Iran 30 Years after the Revolution	*National Public Radio Online* *(URLs will vary.)*	*In a radio program from 2009, some young Iranian women said the revolution brought independence.* *Many economic programs haven't worked well; life is hard for many.*

Connect What generalizations can you make about how Iranian government and society have changed since 2003? Discuss in a small group.

142 Unit 2

LEARNING MINDSET

Problem Solving Remind students that learning is not usually a smooth process. In most cases, there are struggles that include basic comprehension, understanding and using new skills, and working and sharing with others. Encourage students to use a variety of strategies to solve problems, including consulting reference sources and asking for help from adults and peers. Note that some educational thinkers believe that problem-solving skills are more important in achieving success than intelligence, learning background, or ability to retain information.

CREATE AND PRESENT

Create a Podcast With a partner, use what you've learned from this memoir and your research to create a podcast about Iran today.

- ❑ Start with an attention-getting anecdote.
- ❑ Present specific information about Iranian government and society. Support these statements with evidence you cited from your research.
- ❑ End with a summary of the information.

Present to a Small Group Take turns playing your podcast for your group and listening to others' podcasts.

Write a summary of what you have learned about modern-day Iranian society. Then reflect on what you have learned in order to answer these questions:

- ❑ In what ways do Iranian women today respond to the restrictions put on them?
- ❑ How do you think you would respond if the United States experienced societal change as dramatic as Iran's?

Go to the **Speaking and Listening Studio** for help using media in a presentation.

RESPOND TO THE ESSENTIAL QUESTION

How do people find freedom in the midst of oppression?

Gather Information Review your annotations and notes on *Reading Lolita in Tehran* and highlight those that help answer the Essential Question. Then, add relevant details to your Response Log.

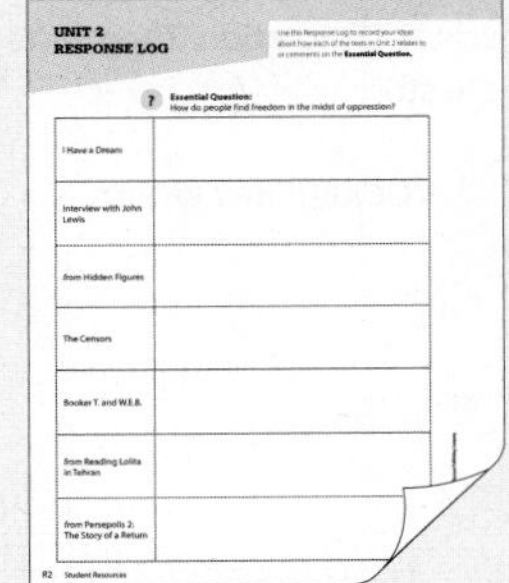

UNIT 2 RESPONSE LOG

Use this Response Log to record your ideas about how each of the texts in Unit 2 relates to or comments on the **Essential Question.**

Essential Question: How do people find freedom in the midst of oppression?

I Have a Dream	
Interview with John Lewis	
from Hidden Figures	
The Censors	
Booker T. and W.E.B.	
from Reading Lolita in Tehran	
from Persepolis 2: The Story of a Return	

R2 Student Resources

ACADEMIC VOCABULARY

As you write and discuss what you learned from the memoir *Reading Lolita in Tehran*, be sure to use the Academic Vocabulary words. Check off each of the words that you use.

- ❑ **decline**
- ❑ **enable**
- ❑ **impose**
- ❑ **integrate**
- ❑ **reveal**

APPLY

CREATE AND PRESENT

Create a Podcast For any students unfamiliar with the format and presentation of a podcast, suggest that they listen to one or two from appropriate sources. Also, provide a general range for length, such as 5–10 minutes, to help them focus their efforts. Partners should prepare an outline for their presentation using the steps listed before they begin work on actual production. Remind students that their podcasts should present facts supported by evidence, not personal opinions or disparaging remarks that others might find offensive.

For **speaking and writing support** for students at varying proficiency levels, see the **Text X-Ray** on page 136D.

Present to a Small Group Encourage students to note their thoughts as they listen to their own and others' presentations. Reinforce the process of summarizing information as isolating the most important facts and paraphrasing them into a few sentences.

Guide students to use the questions to frame their reflections. Note that the questions ask them to use their learning as a basis for drawing conclusions. Explain that informed opinions are based on evidence and research. Encourage students to note any ways that their research and presentations have changed their opinions or views on modern Iran.

RESPOND TO THE ESSENTIAL QUESTION

Allow time for students to add details from the excerpt from *Reading Lolita in Tehran* to their Unit 2 Response Logs.

WHEN STUDENTS STRUGGLE . . .

Create a Podcast Explain that an **anecdote** is a short, amusing, or interesting story about real events. Point out how an an anecdote can function in a presentation such as a podcast *(hook the reader's attention with a real story before presenting more general information)*. Explain that much of the excerpt from *Reading Lolita in Tehran* uses the anecdote of Sanaz's imagined return home to draw and keep the reader's attention. Help students identify anecdotes using these questions: What stories about real people have I found during research? Have I had an interesting experience related to the research, such as finding surprising facts? How have people's lives changed in big or surprising ways during this period? Once a subject is established, coach students on presenting the information as a narrative story that will interest their listeners.

APPLY

CRITICAL VOCABULARY

Possible answers:

1. *Since **irrelevant** means that something does not apply, friends' opinions can be irrelevant if the friends lack knowledge on a topic or experience with a given situation.*
2. *One way to **allocate** the money would be based on the membership and need of each club. Clubs that perform a community service would probably receive more funding than clubs that just support a student interest.*
3. *Children may be **segregated** by age in school because they have different learning needs.*
4. *Someone who believes fiercely in something is less likely to **convert** to another belief system, since the person already holds fast to one system of thinking.*

VOCABULARY STRATEGY:
Denotative and Connotative Meanings

Reinforce the idea that writers can deliberately choose words for their connotations to create a specific effect. In this selection, the use of the word *segregate* in connection with buses provides a very strong negative connotation. It brings to mind how, prior to the 1960s, many Americans were denied equal rights in transportation and other areas of life. As students complete the Practice and Apply activity on Student Edition page 144, remind them to locate each word in the selection and see how it is used. Explain that a word's context can help them determine its connotation.

RESPOND

WORD BANK
segregate
allocate
irrelevant
convert

CRITICAL VOCABULARY

Practice and Apply Use your understanding of the Critical Vocabulary words to answer the following questions.

1. Are your friends' opinions ever **irrelevant**? Explain.
2. If your job were to **allocate** money to the clubs or sports teams at school, how would you do it?
3. Why might you **segregate** children according to age?
4. Is someone who believes fiercely in something likely to **convert**? Explain.

Go to the **Vocabulary Studio** for more on denotative and connotative meanings.

VOCABULARY STRATEGY:
Denotative and Connotative Meanings

A word's denotation is its strict dictionary definition. But many words have slight nuances or differences in meaning. These nuances, or connotations, have associated meanings and emotions. Nafisi explains that in Iran, the buses are segregated. The Critical Vocabulary word segregate has a similar denotation to the word separate. They both mean "to set apart." But the word segregate has an altogether different connotation. To segregate suggests separating people or things forcefully, often in an unfair way.

Practice and Apply: For each Critical Vocabulary word below, write the word's denotation. Then write the connotation of the word as it appears in the story.

VOCABULARY WORD	DENOTATION	CONNOTATION
allocate	*to distribute for a particular purpose*	*to forcibly assign*
irrelevant	*not related or connected*	*not important or even valid*
convert	*to change one's mind, especially about religious beliefs*	*to change one's mind politically, to be brainwashed by the regime*

ENGLISH LEARNER SUPPORT

Understand Connotative and Denotative Meanings Help students understand connotations and practice using reference sources with the words listed in the activity. Direct them to find the three words *(allocate, irrelevant, convert)* in a dictionary or thesaurus and select at least 3 synonyms for each. Then ask them to work with a partner to note the different connotations for each. For example, they might select *immaterial*, *unrelated*, and *inappropriate* for the adjective *irrelevant*. Ask them to suggest a possible context for using each word. For example, *immaterial* might be used in a courtroom or a legal sense; *unrelated* might be used in discussing a scientific proof or experiment; and *inappropriate* is often used to describe behavior that is not suitable for the situation. **LIGHT**

LANGUAGE CONVENTIONS:
Verb Tense

In her memoir, Nafisi alternates between past and present tense, using each tense in a consistent way. When she uses **present tense**, Nafisi refers the reader to the actions taking place in the women's literature group, as if they are currently taking place. When the author uses **past tense**, she reflects on her time with the women, as well as on the events and atmosphere of Iran.

She doesn't walk upright, but bends her head towards the ground and doesn't look at passersby.	By using present tense as if the actions are currently taking place, the author creates a more vivid, immediate picture of her students.

These girls, my girls, had both a real history and a fabricated one.	By using past tense, the author reflects on the women in the literature group.

Practice and Apply Locate two additional sentences that use present tense verbs and two additional sentences that use past tense verbs. Write the sentences and describe how the author uses the verb tenses to make her point.

PRESENT TENSE	EFFECT OF THE VERB TENSE
1. *"We follow Sanaz down the stairs, out the door and into the street."*	*Brings readers into the scene with Sanaz*
2. *"She must enter through the rear door and sit in the back seats, allocated to women."*	*Lends immediacy to this vivid detail*

PAST TENSE	EFFECT OF THE VERB TENSE
1. *". . . the regime that ruled them had tried to make their personal identities and histories irrelevant."*	*Shows how all women were treated in this period*
2. *"They were never free of the regime's definitions of them as Muslim women."*	*Shows how Iranian laws affected the author's students*

LANGUAGE CONVENTIONS:
Verb Tense

Explain to students that in this context, the word tense comes from a Latin word *(tempus)* meaning "time." Simply put, *present tense* means "the time is now" and past tense means "the time was then." Most memoirs use the past tense almost exclusively because the author is remembering events that have already occurred. Nafisi, however, has chosen to use the present tense to describe past events that she imagines took place in order to make them more vivid. Discuss the first example with students, inviting comments about how the use of the present tense helps them feel as if they are watching the scene as it is happening. Then contrast that effect with the reflective effect in the second example.

Point out that there are a wide variety of other verb tenses in English that allow speakers and writers to convey their thoughts more precisely. For example, if you are completing an action, you might use the present progressive tense to say *I am finishing.* Note that many English speakers do not know the exact definitions of the tenses of the verbs they are using but use them naturally.

Practice and Apply

You may choose to ask partners to work together in identifying examples of various tenses and the effect of each chosen tense. They can consider the effect by changing the present to past tense or vice versa and identifying how the change produces a different overall effect.

ENGLISH LEARNER SUPPORT

Language Conventions Provide practice in using verb tenses by having students write and then speak sentences that have present and past tenses. Remind students to orally reread sentences to help them edit and check their writing for correct verb tenses. Note that some verbs are irregular when changing from present to past and that two verbs in a complex sentence usually agree in tense.

- Teach and model how to write and speak these sentences by changing the present tense to past and vice versa: I study the assignments before class. I tried to remember all the vocabulary words. **SUBSTANTIAL**
- Have pairs work together to write and speak these sentences by changing the present tense to past and vice versa: I feel excited before a test. I concentrated while I was learning the words. **MODERATE**
- Direct students to write and speak two simple sentences in which they change the present tense to past and vice versa. **LIGHT**

from PERSEPOLIS 2: THE STORY OF A RETURN

Graphic Memoir by Marjane Satrapi

GENRE ELEMENTS

GRAPHIC MEMOIR

Explain to students that a **graphic memoir** shares the basic characteristics of a **memoir** but uses a graphic novel format. It presents real-life events and the author's reactions to them. A graphic memoir includes personal observations on the events and the author's thoughts and feelings about them, combining graphic images with text to help communicate that information. Students may be familiar with print or digital **comic books,** which also rely on graphic images but usually tell a continuing story over several issues. A **graphic novel** usually tells one story and is presented as a single book.

LEARNING OBJECTIVES

- Analyze multimodal texts, especially the print and graphic features in graphic novels.
- Research ways in which graphic novels present information differently from print-only texts.
- Write an argumentative essay that presents a clear opinion on the importance of graphic novels compared to print-only texts.
- Discuss the value of reading graphic novels.
- **Language** Express reactions to a text orally and explain them with reasons.

TEXT COMPLEXITY

Quantitative Measures	***from*** **Persepolis 2: The Story of a Return**	Lexile: N/A
Qualitative Measures	**Ideas Presented** Single purpose, explicitly stated.	
	Structures Used Genre traits specific to graphic novels.	
	Language Used Some familiar language.	
	Knowledge Required Requires understanding of moderately complex civics concepts.	

Online 

RESOURCES

- Unit 2 Response Log
- Selection Audio
- Reading Studio: Notice & Note
- Level Up Tutorial: Analyzing Visuals
- Writing Studio: Writing Arguments
- Speaking and Listening Studio: Participating in Collaborative Discussions
- from *Reading Lolita in* Tehran/from *Persepolis 2* Selection Test

SUMMARIES

English

In *Persepolis 2: The Story of a Return*, Marjane Satrapi presents a memoir in a graphic novel format. This selection shows how, following the brutal reactions of the Iranian government to student protest demonstrations, Iranian women were forced to resort to more subtle forms of protest. The author highlights the fear and worries of women during this period and how this persistent anxiety crowds out thoughts about individual freedoms.

Spanish

En *Persepolis 2*, Marjane Satrapi presenta sus memorias en formato de novela gráfica. Esta selección realza las brutales reacciones del gobierno iraní a las protestas de los estudiantes antes de 1990, y cómo las mujeres se vieron forzadas a participar en formas más sutiles de protesta. El autor destaca el miedo y las preocupaciones de las mujeres durante este período y cómo esta persistente ansiedad desplaza los pensamientos acerca de las libertades individuales.

SMALL-GROUP OPTIONS

Have students work in small groups to read and discuss the selection.

Activate Academic Vocabulary

- Form groups of 5 students per group, or 5 groups with about an equal number of students.
- Review Academic Vocabulary words for the unit: *decline, enable, impose, integrate, reveal.*
- Assign each member of a group one or more of the words. Each student is responsible for providing a definition, a question related to the selection using the word, and a possible answer to the question using the word.
- Call on students or groups to share their work with the whole class. Then ask other students to create another question and answer using the word correctly.

Triple-Entry Journals

- Have pairs of students prepare by creating a three column notebook page for entries.
- Tell students to read the excerpt from *Persepolis 2*, noting important or interesting graphic elements or text details in the left column.
- Instruct partners to exchange journals and use the middle column to record questions or comments about the notes in the left column.
- Have partners exchange journals again and respond to the comments in the middle column.
- Ask pairs to share a few key ideas from their work with the class when complete.

Text X-Ray: English Learner Support

for *Persepolis 2: The Story of a Return*

Use the Text X-Ray and the supports and scaffolds in the Teacher's Edition to help guide students at different proficiency levels through the selection.

INTRODUCE THE SELECTION

DISCUSS "THE ERA OF GRAND REVOLUTIONARY IDEAS"

In this lesson, students will read the phrase "the era of grand revolutionary ideas." Explain the following terms:

- An *era* is a general period of time when a particular condition is common.
- *Grand revolutionary ideas* is a phrase that refers to theories about perfect ways to govern people, especially ways that differ from those of the current government.

Discuss the fact that *eras* can refer to a variety of conditions and characteristics and that *grand revolutionary ideas* relates not only to a time in Iran's history but also to the history of other countries. Use these frames to guide discussion:

- *Today, we live in an era when* __________ *is common.*
- *Leaders of many British colonies in North America discussed grand revolutionary ideas before* __________ *(historic change).*

CULTURAL REFERENCES

The following words or phrases from the selection may be unfamiliar to students:

- *as best we could* (panel 1): using the only methods available
- *the committee* (panel 5): the group responsible for enforcing rules about women's appearance
- *it's only natural* (panel 8): the expected result; the reasonable response
- *driving force* (panel 8): most important or powerful factor

LISTENING

Understand Graphic Features and Important Ideas

Read aloud the speech in panel 8 on Student Edition page 150. Students can practice listening comprehension to ensure their understanding of the graphic memoir genre and important information in the graphic memoir.

Use the following supports with students at varying proficiency levels:

- Read the text in panel 8 aloud. Explain that the speech bubble indicates that the character is speaking out loud. Ask students to identify who the character is speaking to. **SUBSTANTIAL**
- As you read the text in panel 8 aloud, have students make note of questions. When complete, have students identify who the character is speaking to and ask questions to confirm understanding. **MODERATE**
- Read the text in panel 8 aloud. Confirm students' understanding by asking them to provide an oral summary statement for the panel that includes who the character is speaking to. **LIGHT**

SPEAKING

Explain Reactions to Text

Students will be asked to share their reactions to different texts. Teach and model how to explain a reaction by providing one or more supporting reasons.

Use the following supports with students at varying proficiency levels:

- Explain that opinions on texts should be supported by reasons. Help students explain their reactions orally, using these sentence frames: *I liked/didn't like* Persepolis 2. *It was* ____________. **SUBSTANTIAL**
- Guide students in explaining their reactions with this sentence frame: *I liked/didn't like* Persepolis 2 *because* ____________. **MODERATE**
- Ask students to explain their reactions *to Persepolis 2* orally in a few complete sentences using *because* or *so*. **LIGHT**

READING

Recognize and Use Graphic Features

Explain that on Student Edition page 155, students will be asked to use the same graphic features as in this selection to construct their own graphic novels. These activities offer practice identifying and using these features.

Direct students to Student Edition page 150. Then use the following supports with students at varying proficiency levels:

- Instruct students to identify a speech bubble and then draw a panel of their own that uses a speech bubble. Emphasize that they can use a stick figure or simple drawing for the panel. **SUBSTANTIAL**
- Instruct students to identify a speech bubble and a thought balloon. Ask them to draw panels that use each one. Emphasize that they can use a stick figure or simple drawing for the panels. **MODERATE**
- Direct students to panel 2 and ask them to identify the emotion conveyed by the raised arms and closed fists in the panel. Discuss ideas for how to use graphic features to express this emotion and others. **LIGHT**

WRITING

Use Cause-and-Effect Statements

Direct students to Write an Argumentative Essay on Student Edition page 153. Point out the value of using cause-and-effect statements when giving and supporting opinions.

Use the following supports with students at varying proficiency levels:

- Define the terms *cause* and *effect* and have students identify the same in this sentence: *The game was canceled* [effect] *because it rained* [cause]. Work with students to revise this sentence to state a new cause and effect. **SUBSTANTIAL**
- Teach, model, and give students practice in writing cause-and-effect sentences. Provide sentence frames as needed: *This event,* __________*, resulted because* ________. **MODERATE**
- Model a cause-and-effect sentence that presents an opinion. Then have student pairs write a similar sentence, exchange sentences with another pair, and peer-review the sentences. **LIGHT**

TEACH

Connect to the ESSENTIAL QUESTION

Like the excerpt from *Reading Lolita in Tehran,* this excerpt from *Persepolis 2: The Story of a Return* is set in Iran in the 1990s. During this period, Iranians lived under an oppressive regime, and conditions for women were especially restrictive. Like the previous selection, *Persepolis 2* was created by a woman to explore Iranian women's reactions to governmental control, which extended to restrictions on the smallest details of their appearance and actions. Both selections show that women during this period found freedom only in their thoughts and in the way they hid forbidden fashions from the harsh gaze of authorities.

COMPARE ACROSS GENRES

Both selections share a common setting and similar points of view. They also address some of the same issues: restrictions on women's appearance during this period and how women reacted to those restrictions. Because of these similarities, students can focus on the differences in the genres and how each helps the author convey the precise information she wants.

COLLABORATE & COMPARE

GRAPHIC MEMOIR

from PERSEPOLIS 2 : THE STORY OF A RETURN

by **Marjane Satrapi**
translated by Anjali Singh
pages 149–151

COMPARE ACROSS GENRES

Now that you've read the excerpt from *Reading Lolita in Tehran*, read the excerpt from *Persepolis 2* and explore how this graphic memoir connects to some of the same ideas. As you read, think about how the graphic novel genre helps the author of *Persepolis 2* tell her personal story. After you are finished, you will collaborate with a small group on a final project that involves an analysis of both texts.

ESSENTIAL QUESTION:

How do people find freedom in the midst of oppression?

MEMOIR

from READING LOLITA IN TEHRAN

by **Azar Nafisi**
pages 139–141

TO CHALLENGE STUDENTS . . .

Report on Comics and Graphic Novels Explain that graphic novels are a relatively new type of literature and that people still don't agree on some basic definitions and characteristics. Ask students (or pairs) to research and prepare a short oral or multimedia report on the subject. They will need to choose a focus from this broad subject to limit their work, such as innovative comic strips and comic books, important examples of comics and graphic novels, the use of fine details in artwork, changing views of graphic novels, adaptations of comics and graphic novels to movies, or the significance of a particular graphic novel such as *Maus,* which won a Pulitzer Prize in 1992. They can give their presentation to the whole class or a small group when completed and should be prepared to respond to questions.

GET READY

from Persepolis 2: The Story of a Return

QUICK START

Throughout history, people have found ways to advocate for change. Whether it is students hoping to see change in their schools or citizens protesting against their governments, people possess the capability to effect change. With a group, discuss ways that people have protested against injustice throughout history.

ANALYZE MULTIMODAL TEXTS

Authors choose a format that tells their personal story in a compelling way. Different formats emphasize details that help to tell the story. The challenge for readers or viewers is to determine which details are emphasized and how those details convey the author's message.

A **graphic novel** tells a story or conveys information in a series of frames that show action, along with narrative text and the characters' words. In graphic novels, both words and images work together to convey the work's meaning and to advance the author's point of view, or how he or she feels about a subject. Where a comic book tells a continuing story over a series of issues that are published over time, perhaps once a month or four issues over the course of a year, a graphic novel tells a stand-alone story that is usually bound as a single book. Graphic novels also tend to be longer than comic books.

Graphic novels can be fiction, such as historical fiction, realistic fiction, and science fiction; nonfiction, such as history or informational text; fantasy; and many other types.

MAIN TYPES OF GRAPHIC NOVELS	
Manga	Manga is read from top to bottom and right to left, a traditional Japanese reading pattern
Personal Narratives	Autobiographical stories that tell about the author's experiences and observations
Nonfiction	Similar to a personal narrative, but the author tells a personal story to call attention to a social issue or cause

As you read this excerpt from *Persepolis 2,* notice how Marjane Satrapi tells her story through words and stark black and white images. In this excerpt, the author's perspective as a young woman out of place in a rigid and uncompromising society is reflected in the way the main character's face is drawn. It is also shown in panels revealing her thoughts and interactions with others.

GENRE ELEMENTS: GRAPHIC NOVEL

- uses sequential art to tell a story in different panels
- content can be fiction or nonfiction
- text appears in captions and in dialogue and thought balloons

ENGLISH LEARNER SUPPORT

Use Cognates An important word on Student Edition page 147 has a Spanish cognate. The root for the word *multimodal* (found in the subhead) is *mode/moda/modo*. For *multimodal*, begin by comparing it to the more commonly used *multimedia*. Break down the prefix and root word, and then apply the same prefix to the cognate *mode/moda/modo*. Supply students with a variety of words they may be familiar with that use the *multi-* prefix (or ask students to supply words themselves): *multidimensional, multipurpose, multiplex, multiuse, multinational.*

ALL LEVELS

TEACH

QUICK START

If groups struggle to identify protests throughout history, provide a few subjects that may spark their interest or memory. Also note that the term *injustice* can have several levels of meaning (or connotations), ranging from people who are starving, enslaved, or imprisoned to those who have been misled by advertisements or prevented from attending a particular event.

Some protests they might consider include those that were controversial at the time, including recent protests related to immigration, police tactics in certain communities, and profits for Wall Street investors as well as previous protests related to civil rights, continuation of the Vietnam War, women's right to vote, slavery, and taxes before the American Revolution.

ANALYZE MULTIMODAL TEXTS

Note that there are a variety of types of multimodal texts other than graphic novels. They use signs that communicate meaning in a variety of ways. Multimodal texts can include written and audio language, visual images, personal gestures, and spatial movement or arrangements. Some examples include web pages that combine written words with images, audio recordings, static images, and/or movies; live performances that combine music, gestures, and movement or dance; and graphic novels.

Strictly speaking, even modern print newspapers and magazines are multimodal in the ways that they combine visual images with printed words. But most often, the term is reserved for presentations that rely less on printed words and more heavily on other types of media or visual elements to convey meaning.

Graphic novels are one choice for communicating meaning and, like all genres, have certain strengths and weaknesses. For example, graphic novels may not be the best choice for including long or complicated thought processes or discussions because they have limited space for written words. On the other hand, they can communicate a scene or context very quickly and powerfully using images. Reinforce the idea that all writers, including students, can make choices about the best way to achieve their purpose in communicating to an audience.

TEACH

EVALUATE PRINT AND GRAPHIC FEATURES

Remind students that they are already familiar with texts that combine print and graphic features. Most books, magazines, and newspapers use some combination of print and graphic features to help them achieve their purpose in communicating.

Identify what makes a graphic novel different from a book with many pictures or other graphic features: a graphic novel uses the author's images as a **primary** way to communicate as opposed to images and effects that are used to support the text or even expand upon it.

Point out the list of print and graphic features and note that a printed text (such as this book) can use one or more of the graphic features listed to help get its message across. For example, the print and graphic features are listed on this page in a chart for easy reading and identification features. You can also direct students to Student Edition page 146 and ask them to identify the varying print and graphic features used there. *(large print, bold print, italics, different font sizes and types. colored print and backgrounds, a variety of punctuation including the question mark icon, a photograph)*

You may also point out the list of expected ways that graphic novels (and memoirs) represent text. These have been developed over many years and allow graphic authors to avoid using language constructions such as ". . . she thought" or ". . . she said" while clearly conveying those ideas to readers.

■ English Learner Support

Use Cognates Point out the multiple Spanish cognates that appear in the chart: *punctuation/puntuación, illustration/ilustración, graph/gráfico, map/mapa, photograph/fotografía, table/tabla.* **ALL LEVELS**

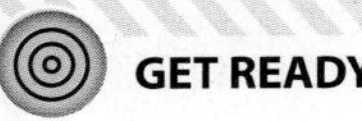

GET READY

EVALUATE PRINT AND GRAPHIC FEATURES

In graphic novels, authors integrate print and graphic features to achieve their purpose for writing. **Print features** help readers pay attention to important words. **Graphic features** help readers visualize or make pictures in their minds. Words or images alone do not fully communicate the author's message in a graphic novel.

PRINT FEATURES	GRAPHIC FEATURES
large print	illustrations
bold print	graphs
italics	maps
underlining	photographs
font size	charts/tables
font type	sketches
colored print	drawings
quotation marks	cartoons
punctuation	pictures

Careful readers must study details in the drawings, as well as read the captions, speech bubbles, and thought balloons, to understand the author's point of view.

Graphic novel authors may represent text in different ways.

- **Speech bubbles** show words that the characters are speaking directly.
- **Thought balloons** convey what is going on in characters' minds.
- **Captions** contain the narrative, allowing the author to speak directly to the reader.

As you read the excerpt from *Persepolis 2*, note how words and images work together to convey the author's message.

WHEN STUDENTS STRUGGLE . . .

Demonstrate Print Features Provide a computer demonstration of print features for any students struggling to understand the terms. You can provide help on a single classroom computer or on a projection screen when available. Open a word processing application and type a simple word or phrase. Then show how the word looks using each of the different print features in the chart. Help them consider and discuss how each feature might be used in a text and what effect this has compared to when the word appears without the feature.

BACKGROUND

Since the Iranian Revolution of the late 1970s, "morality police" ensure that people comply with the laws in Iran. People who do not comply may be taken to the morality police headquarters to be questioned, beaten, or jailed.

Marjane Satrapi *(b. 1969) was born in Iran. After the revolution, her parents sent her to school in Europe. Later, she studied illustration.* Persepolis 1 *tells the story of Satrapi's childhood in Iran, and* Persepolis 2 *tells the story of her adolescence in Europe and Iran and of her struggle to fit in.* Persepolis, *a movie based on both books, has won many awards. Satrapi lives in Paris.*

from PERSEPOLIS 2: THE STORY OF A RETURN

Graphic Novel by Marjane Satrapi
translated by Anjali Singh

PREPARE TO COMPARE

As you read, pay attention to how the author uses graphic novel elements to tell her personal story. Look for ways that Satrapi's story is similar to and different from that of Azar Nafisi. Write down any questions you generate as you read.

Notice & Note

You can use the side margins to notice and note signposts in the text.

TEACH

BACKGROUND

Have students read the Background and information about the author. Note that the setting is the same as for the previous selection and that the information concerning the harsh actions of the government during this period is confirmed in both selections.

Explain to students that Persepolis was a royal capital of ancient Iran, about 2,500 years ago. Ask students why they think Marjane Satrapi chose that for part of her title. *(Perhaps it recalls—either with sadness or with sarcasm—the glory of an Iran that once existed but that no longer exists.)* Then have students review the information about the author and ask how this affects the title of the graphic novel. *(The subtitle "The Story of a Return" indicates that Satrapi spent time away from Iran.)* You may ask volunteers, pairs, or small groups to speculate on how her time away might affect her feelings about Iran and the story she tells. *(She might feel the oppression of the regime very strongly after living in Europe, whose governments do not control people's lives so strongly.)*

PREPARE TO COMPARE

Direct students to use the Prepare to Compare prompt to focus their reading.

APPLYING ACADEMIC VOCABULARY

☐ **decline** ☐ **enable** ☐ **impose** ☑ **integrate** ☑ **reveal**

Write and Discuss Have students turn to a partner to discuss the following questions. Guide students to include the academic vocabulary words *integrate* and *reveal* in their responses. Ask volunteers to share their responses with the class.

- Do you think it will be hard for a girl to become **integrated** into a society like Iran's after living in Europe?
- Why would it be important for someone like Satrapi to avoid **revealing** many of her thoughts and feelings?

TEACH

ANALYZE MULTIMODAL TEXTS

Note that a graphic novel uses images to express things that a traditional text would use words to describe. Point out the lack of any background in the first panel and explain that graphic novels do not necessarily use fine, detailed artwork in their images. However, the author/artist must be able to convey action and strong feelings, such as in the second panel of people protesting and in the fifth panel of criticizing a pair of socks. (***Answer:*** *The woman is drawn folding her arms protectively, which suggests that she feels determined but perhaps also resigned. This matches her speech, where she says they stood up for themselves "as best we could." The author is conveying defiance from a position of relative powerlessness.)*

CONTRASTS AND CONTRADICTIONS

Explain that the author uses specific details to indicate this **contradiction** and emphasize it. Note the difference in the effect of using details compared to using a general statement such as "The regime watched everything about our appearance and actions." (You may wish to point out that the item in the panel that is identified as a "Walkman" was a portable music player that was very popular at the time of this narrative. Various models could play cassette tapes, CDs, or MP3s as well as AM/FM radio.) (***Answer:*** *It is surprising that a woman could get into trouble for showing her wrist, laughing loudly, or having a audio device. The author included this panel to help show just how oppressive and controlling this regime is.)*

EVALUATE PRINT AND GRAPHIC FEATURES

Point out the different conventions used for a thought balloon (circles from a balloon leading to the character), a speech bubble (pointed tail from a balloon leading to the character), and a caption (text separated above or below a panel that is not a character's speech or thought). Examine how these conventions save space and extra words and how they support both the author and the reader. (***Answer:*** *The caption tells what was going on in general society, while the speech bubbles allow the character to speak her thoughts directly to the reader.)*

For **listening and reading support** for students at varying proficiency levels, see the **Text X-Ray** on pages 146C–146D.

NOTICE & NOTE

ANALYZE MULTIMODAL TEXTS

Annotate: Make a checkmark on a panel in which emotion is shown.

Respond: How does the image pair with the words to convey the author's emotion about her experiences?

CONTRASTS & CONTRADICTIONS

Notice & Note: Mark with a star a panel that contradicts your view of how you would expect the world to be.

Interpret: Why might the author have presented you with this information?

EVALUATE PRINT AND GRAPHIC FEATURES

Annotate: Circle a speech bubble and underline a caption.

Respond: How do the speech bubble and the caption convey different types of information?

ENGLISH LEARNER SUPPORT

Master Vocabulary Teach or confirm understanding of the following words and phrases to assist comprehension. Ask volunteers or small groups to suggest, draw, or act out definitions and then guide discussion to an accurate understanding:

- discreet *(careful, quiet, attracting little attention)*
- hinged on *(depended on, involved)*
- subversion *(undermining the power and authority of those in control)*
- pretext *(a reason given for an action that is not the real reason)* **SUBSTANTIAL/MODERATE**

NOTICE & NOTE

CHECK YOUR UNDERSTANDING

Answer these questions before moving on to the **Analyze the Text** section on the following page.

1 This passage is mostly about —

- **A** how women tried to escape from Iran
- **B** how women tried to educate themselves in Iran
- **C** how women rebelled against oppression in Iran
- **D** how women sought to overthrow the government of Iran

2 How does the presentation of the text allow the author to share her point of view?

- **F** The realistic fiction text tells how life has changed for the author.
- **G** The informational text provides the reader with facts about life in Iran.
- **H** The graphic novel format allows the reader to learn about Iran's cultural history.
- **J** The graphic novel format allows the reader to visually see and read about the author's experiences.

3 How does the caption in the second panel add to the reader's understanding of the text?

- **A** The factual information in the caption explains why the revolution occurred.
- **B** The factual information in the caption provides historical background for the text.
- **C** The opinions in the caption help explain the author's point of view.
- **D** The opinions in the caption help explain why people demonstrated against the government.

CHECK YOUR UNDERSTANDING

Have students answer the questions independently.

1. *C*
2. *J*
3. *B*

If they answer any questions incorrectly, have them reread the text to confirm their understanding. Then they may proceed to ANALYZE THE TEXT on page 152.

ENGLISH LEARNER SUPPORT

Oral Assessment Use the following questions to assess students' comprehension and speaking skills. Ask students to respond in complete sentences.

1. What is the main subject of this selection? *(It is about ways the author and other young women rebelled against the oppressive regime in Iran.)*
2. How does the format of a graphic novel help the author share her point of view? *(Readers can read about and visually see the author's experiences.)*
3. How is the reader's understanding of the text helped by the caption in the second panel? *(It provides factual information so that the reader understands the historical background.)*
ALL LEVELS

APPLY

ANALYZE THE TEXT

Possible answers:

1. **DOK 2:** *The main character understands that she cannot openly oppose the regime. While she can rebel in small ways, she cannot change the oppressive system.*
2. **DOK 4:** *Panel 2 shows a large group of people waving their arms, and the caption explains that at first, Iranians openly protested the regime. Panel 3 shows a close-up of two young women and the caption explains that individuals began to rebel in subtler ways.*
3. **DOK 2:** *The red socks may have represented a refusal to follow the rules and conform.*
4. **DOK 2:** *The narrator looks unhappy, worried, and puzzled. The author points out that women are disturbed by what is happening but don't know how to make any real changes.*
5. **DOK 4:** *The seemingly unimportant acts of showing hair or wearing makeup become significant acts of rebellion against the government.*

RESEARCH

As students begin to make a research plan, suggest that they use the "5W + H" questions—*Who, What, Where, When, Why,* and *How*—to guide their thinking. Remind students to list at least two graphic novels and appropriate observations related to the images in each of them.

Extend If students struggle with identifying differences, direct them to identify one panel in the excerpt from *Persepolis 2* or one of the graphic novels they reviewed that is particularly memorable to them (for example, the 3rd panel of the selection on Student Edition page 150). Ask them to identify what the panel communicates to them and why it is different from straight text on the same subject. Then ask them to expand their thinking to include the graphic novel format rather than just one panel.

RESPOND

ANALYZE THE TEXT

Support your responses with evidence from the text. NOTEBOOK

1. **Infer** How does the main character in the text feel about any power she may possess? Does she feel powerful or powerless? Why?
2. **Analyze** Look at the second and third panels in the text. How does the author use both words and graphics to make a point about how the people's struggle has changed?
3. **Infer** The narrator says that she spent an entire day at the committee because of a pair of red socks. What might red socks have **symbolized**, or represented, to the committee?
4. **Interpret** The narrator's facial expression remains the same in each of the panels. How would you describe it? How does this visual consistency help reveal the author's point of view?
5. **Notice & Note** Reread the last part of the speech bubble in the final panel. What contrast or contradiction points to the author's larger message?

RESEARCH

RESEARCH TIP
It's always easier to begin a research project by creating a research plan. First, identify exactly what you want to learn. Then, think about sources that would be helpful to use.

Graphic novels can convey information about real or fictional events. They can also communicate information about characters' dress, attitude, and emotions. Look at several graphic novels, paying attention to what kinds of information are conveyed by the images alone. For example, images could convey details about the setting, what characters look like, their emotions, plot events, and even theme. Take notes on what kinds of information are included and how they are conveyed.

GRAPHIC NOVEL	INFORMATION AND HOW IT IS CONVEYED
Joe	*Detailed drawings convey setting and action. Story focuses on a bear who talks and travels.*
Dreamless	*Detailed drawings show setting and conveys dark, threatening mood.*

Extend Describe how the graphic novel structure can provide different information about a subject than is possible with a narrative format.

152 Unit 2

WHEN STUDENTS STRUGGLE . . .

Analyze Graphic Features Help students complete this chart with examples and analyses to build comprehension of the selection's graphic features:

Speech bubble	*Panel 1*	*Character speaks directly to the reader*
Thought balloon	*Panels 6–7*	*Reader sees/hears character's thoughts*
Caption	*Panel 2*	*Explains the historical context and reasons women are not outspoken*

For additional support, go to the **Reading Studio** and assign the following  **Level Up Tutorial: Analyzing Visuals.**

CREATE AND DISCUSS

Write an Argumentative Essay Write a three- to four-paragraph essay in which you address the genre of graphic novels.

- ❑ Introduce your essay by describing the format of graphic novels.
- ❑ Then, explain similarities and differences between graphic novels and other narrative formats. Think about how graphic novels are similar to and different from prose texts and plays.
- ❑ In your final paragraph, state whether you think graphic novels should be considered as important a genre as print-only texts.

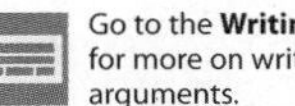

Go to the **Writing Studio** for more on writing arguments.

Share and Discuss Opinions With a small group, discuss graphic novels as a genre. How do you feel about reading graphic novels? Do you feel that they are an effective way of communicating information? Why or why not?

- ❑ Review the characteristics of a graphic novel. Discuss how graphic novels differ from comic books.
- ❑ Then, discuss graphic novels you have read. Note how the graphic novel may or may not have enhanced the author's ability to communicate her story.
- ❑ Finally, end by recommending a graphic novel and/or noting a graphic novel that you would like to read.

Go to the **Speaking and Listening Studio** for help with having a group discussion.

RESPOND TO THE ESSENTIAL QUESTION

How do people find freedom in the midst of oppression?

Gather Information Review your annotations and notes on *Persepolis 2*. Examine how the main character creates freedom for herself in the midst of oppression. Think about the character's actions, motivations, and traits as you respond. Then, add relevant details to your Response Log.

At the end of the unit, use your notes to write a research report.

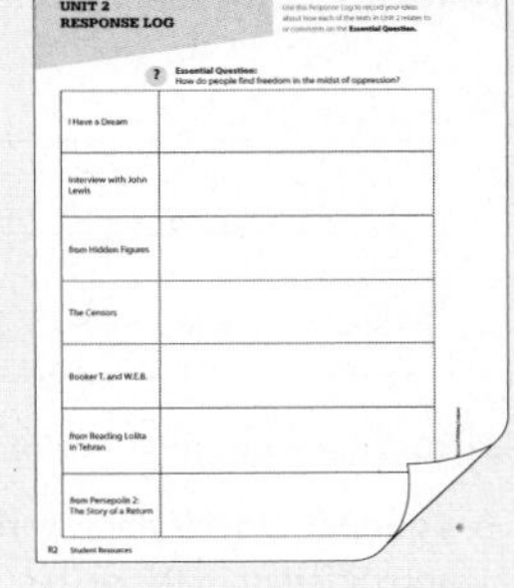

ACADEMIC VOCABULARY

As you write and discuss what you learned about *Persepolis 2*, be sure to use the Academic Vocabulary words. Check off each of the words that you use.

- ❑ **decline**
- ❑ **enable**
- ❑ **impose**
- ❑ **integrate**
- ❑ **reveal**

APPLY

CREATE AND DISCUSS

Write an Argumentative Essay Note that the process for writing the argumentative essay shown on this page may be slightly different from that of other argumentative essays. In this case, the main argument is not stated until the final paragraph. The previous paragraphs of this essay should provide information on graphic novels rather than strong opinions about them.

You might suggest that once students have finished the essay, they review it to see if their opinion in the final paragraph is supported by the information in previous paragraphs. For example, if they feel graphic novels should be considered as important as print-only texts, then the discussion of similarities and differences should note either strong similarities to print-only texts or unique differences that offset any weaknesses in their comparison. On the other hand, if their opinion suggests that graphic novels are less important, then the similarities and differences might highlight unique strengths of print-only texts or weaknesses of graphic novels.

For **writing support** for students at varying proficiency levels, see the **Text X-Ray** on page 136D.

Share and Discuss Opinions In preparing for the small-group discussion, remind students that informed opinions are based on specific evidence or details.

- In discussing differences in graphic novels and comic books, encourage students to identify one or more specific examples that illustrate a difference.
- When discussing how the format enhanced (or did not enhance) the author's ability to tell a story, they can identify a specific example and be prepared to explain their opinion.
- They can support their recommendation of a graphic novel or interest in a graphic novel by identifying and explaining something unique about it.

For **speaking support** for students at varying proficiency levels, see the **Text X-Ray** on page 136D.

RESPOND TO THE ESSENTIAL QUESTION

Allow time for students to add details from the excerpt from *Persepolis 2* to their Unit 2 Response Logs.

ENGLISH LEARNER SUPPORT

Share and Discuss Opinions Point out that in a small-group discussion, students can use less formal language—for example, the contraction *don't* instead of *do not*. Share these sentence frames and have students point out the contractions:

- *Graphic novels are different from comic books because they're* ______ .
- *I've read the graphic novel* ______ *. Its author could/couldn't communicate (feeling/theme/ details, etc.) as well as a print novelist could.*
- *I'd like to read the graphic novel* ______ *because* ______ .

SUBSTANTIAL/MODERATE

APPLY

COMPARE ACROSS GENRES

Before small groups begin work to fill in the chart, note that these two selections offer an excellent chance for comparison of genres since the setting, topic, and general type of text (memoir) are identical. Because of these similarities, effects of the specific genre can be more easily isolated.

ANALYZE THE TEXTS

Possible answers:

1. **DOK 4:** *Nafisi provides a full narrative and much descriptive language. Satrapi uses minimal word descriptions and narrative language, but she uses images to convey feelings and actions.*
2. **DOK 2:** *Both texts describe restrictions on women and girls following the Iranian Revolution, how they felt about their situation, and some of the small actions they took to protest the restrictions.*
3. **DOK 4:** *Each format has strengths and weaknesses. Satrapi uses the impact of visual images to convey certain feelings without words. Nafisi uses words to create vivid images from careful descriptions.*
4. **DOK 4:** *After the revolution, the Iranian government placed many restrictions on women. They could express their true feelings only in private or in their own thoughts. Because the consequences were so severe, women could protest their treatment only in symbolic ways.*

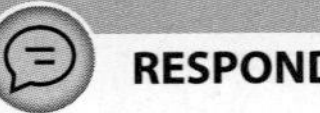

RESPOND

MEMOIR
from READING LOLITA IN TEHRAN
by Azar Nafisi

GRAPHIC MEMOIR
from PERSEPOLIS 2: THE STORY OF A RETURN
by Marjane Satrapi

Collaborate and Compare

COMPARE ACROSS GENRES

Both *Reading Lolita in Tehran* and *Persepolis* 2 discuss life in Iran following the Iranian Revolution of the 1970s. Even though the texts address a similar topic, they do so using different genres. Both print and graphic novel formats allow the author to communicate her story to the reader, but only one uses illustrations integrated with text.

In a small group, discuss the common elements in the two selections. Take notes in the chart below about the authors' purpose, message, and use of language. On your own, write a few sentences describing your personal reactions to reading about the same general topic in two genres. Which genre did you prefer? Why?

ELEMENTS	READING LOLITA IN TEHRAN	PERSEPOLIS 2
AUTHOR'S PURPOSE	*Share experience teaching women's literature group*	*Inform others about life after the Iranian Revolution*
AUTHOR'S MESSAGE	*Her students resisted the regime's control.*	*Women rebelled in small ways.*
USE OF LANGUAGE	*Rhetorical questions allow the reader to consider the points mentioned.*	*The questions show how dealing with small matters keeps people from addressing larger issues.*

Notes about my reactions to the two selections:

Reading Lolita in Tehran gets readers to empathize with Iranian women.

Persepolis 2 conveys the injustices of life after the Iranian Revolution.

ANALYZE THE TEXTS

Discuss these questions in your group.

1. **Connect** How is the way the authors communicate with readers similar and different in the texts?
2. **Compare** What information is presented in both texts?
3. **Analyze** What is the effect of using language only, as opposed to combining language and images? Are any aspects of the story gained by using images and/or lost by using fewer words in a graphic novel?
4. **Synthesize** What have you learned from these sources together about the status of women in Iran since the Iranian Revolution?

ENGLISH LEARNER SUPPORT

Compare Selections Use these questions to help students compare the selections.

1. What method does Nafisi use to describe the limitations, or rules about, clothing and appearance? What method does Satrapi use to describe the same things?
2. What is the character Sanaz in *Reading Lolita in Tehran* doing as she walks down the street? What is the character in *Persepolis 2* doing as she walks down the street?
3. What small, symbolic protests does Nafisi describe? What small, symbolic protests does Satrapi describe? **MODERATE/LIGHT**

COLLABORATE AND PRESENT

Now your group can continue exploring the ideas in these texts by collaborating to create a graphic novel version of the excerpt from *Reading Lolita in Tehran*. Follow these steps:

1. **Brainstorm** Imagine that Nafisi had written her memoir in the form of a graphic novel. Brainstorm how to recast the selection into a graphic novel. Think about how to create panels to convey the story.
2. **Create Storyboards** Create sequential storyboards to tell Nafisi's story.
   - ❑ **Illustrate** the panels with hand-drawn images or with computer-generated images.
   - ❑ **Decide** how to use speech bubbles and captions to convey the specific activities of the women's literature group and captions to describe the setting in Iran.
   - ❑ **Use** details from the memoir that you think advance the story.
3. **Discuss What You Have Learned** After partners or groups present their graphic novels to the class, discuss how effectively they convey Nafisi's message. Communicate and accept suggestions for improvement in a constructive manner. Think about how your graphic novel conveys the contrasts between what occurs in the women's literature group and what occurs in Iranian society as a whole.
4. **Reflect on Your Work** Evaluate your role in creating the graphic novel and in the group discussion. Jot down notes about your preparation for and participation in this activity. What were your main contributions?

PROJECT TIP

Plan your graphic novel as a group. Then divide the work equally among members of the group.

COLLABORATE AND PRESENT

Explain that communicating in the graphic novel genre does not require extreme artistic abilities (although some students may be very skilled in this area). Reinforce the idea that work within groups can be divided among members according to their interests and abilities. For students struggling with the idea of creating artwork, encourage the use of computer programs to ease the process. Establish a limit on length (such as one page, like the excerpt from *Persepolis 2*) and emphasize that their graphic novel should not try to include every bit of information from the text selection.

1. **Brainstorm** Brainstorming generates ideas for later consideration. One student can record ideas without comment or criticism. Suggest that students concentrate on the strongest mental images from the story. They can scan the selection during this process.
2. **Create Storyboards** Remind students that initial storyboards serve as an outline. Once there is agreement on what basic panels to include, work may be divided among group members, or the entire group can work to use graphic features in the best way.
3. **Discuss What You Have Learned** Note that there is not a single, correct way to create the assigned graphic novel. One group may find one part of Nafisi's message more important than what is favored by a different group. Be sure that the discussion stays respectful and that comments are framed positively.
4. **Reflect on Your Work** Emphasize that self-reflection involves honest consideration of both positives and negatives.

TO CHALLENGE STUDENTS . . .

Create a Unique Graphic Novel Encourage interested students to create a separate and unique graphic novel by choosing their own subject. They may choose a scene from a favorite book, focus on a favorite character, or create their own story or short novel. They may follow the steps outlined for the group or rely on their own creative process. For example, they might choose to write dialogue, captions, and thought balloons first and then work to illustrate the panels. Note that some graphic novels use almost no captions or words and rely on the illustrations to tell the story. Remind students that, as with any written or artistic work, they may need to create multiple versions and make many edits before achieving a final product.

INDEPENDENT READING

READER'S CHOICE

Setting a Purpose Have students review their Unit 2 Response Log and think about what they've already learned about how to find freedom amidst oppression. As they choose their Independent Reading selections, encourage them to consider what more they want to know.

NOTICE & NOTE

Explain that some selections may contain multiple signposts; others may contain only one. And the same type of signpost can occur many times in the same text.

LEARNING MINDSET

Curiosity Tell students that curiosity is a core skill to having a learning mindset. It's one of the first steps to overcoming any hurdles that accompany learning new skills or content. Have students focus on the Independent Reading selections that spark the most curiosity in them. Remind them not to get discouraged if the selection they choose is more challenging than they expected—greater challenges can lead to learning more, developing new perspectives, and strengthening skills.

INDEPENDENT READING

? *ESSENTIAL QUESTION:*

How do people find freedom in the midst of oppression?

Reader's Choice

Setting a Purpose Select one or more of these options from your eBook to continue your exploration of the Essential Question.

- Read the descriptions to see which text grabs your interest.
- Think about which genres you enjoy reading.

Notice & Note

In this unit, you practiced asking **Big Questions** and noticing and noting two signposts: **Extreme or Absolute Language** and **Quoted Words.** As you read independently, these signposts and others will aid your understanding. Below are the anchor questions to ask when you read literature and nonfiction.

Reading Literature: Stories, Poems, and Plays

Signpost	Anchor Question	Lesson
Contrasts and Contradictions	Why did the character act that way?	p. 419
Aha Moment	How might this change things?	p. 171
Tough Questions	What does this make me wonder about?	p. 494
Words of the Wiser	What's the lesson for the character?	p. 171
Again and Again	Why might the author keep bringing this up?	p. 170
Memory Moment	Why is this memory important?	p. 418

Reading Nonfiction: Essays, Articles, and Arguments

Signpost	Anchor Question(s)	Lesson
Big Questions	What surprised me? What did the author think I already knew? What challenged, changed, or confirmed what I already knew?	p. 248 p. 2 p. 84
Contrasts and Contradictions	What is the difference, and why does it matter?	p. 3
Extreme or Absolute Language	Why did the author use this language?	p. 85
Numbers and Stats	Why did the author use these numbers or amounts?	p. 249
Quoted Words	Why was this person quoted or cited, and what did this add?	p. 85
Word Gaps	Do I know this word from someplace else? Does it seem like technical talk for this topic? Do clues in the sentence help me understand the word?	p. 3

ENGLISH LEARNER SUPPORT

Develop Fluency Select a passage from a text that matches students' abilities. Read the passage aloud while students follow along silently.

- Have students choral read with you. Coach them in correct pronunciation and check comprehension by asking yes/no questions. **SUBSTANTIAL**
- Have the students read the text silently and mark unfamiliar words as they go. Help them find definitions for the words and practice pronouncing the word and stating the definition in their own words. Then ask them to read the passage again. **MODERATE**
- Allow more fluent readers to select their own texts. Then, have partners prepare and present a summary of the texts. **LIGHT**

Go to the **Reading Studio** for additional support in developing fluency.

You can preview these texts in Unit 2 of your eBook.

Then, check off the text or texts that you select to read on your own.

❑ POEM
We Wear the Mask
Paul Laurence Dunbar
The poem's speaker conceals great pain under "the mask" that "lies."

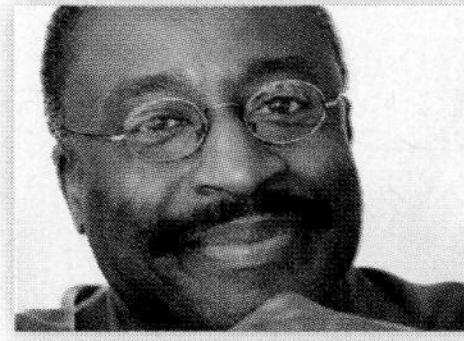

❑ SHORT STORY
The Prisoner Who Wore Glasses
Bessie Head
A political prisoner combines cleverness and courage to get the best of a brutal overseer.

❑ HISTORY WRITING
Reforming the World *from* America's Women
Gail Collins
Middle class women become radicalized as they fight for equality and the right to vote.

❑ AUTOBIOGRAPHY
from ***Long Walk to Freedom***
Nelson Mandela
Nelson Mandela shows fearlessness and humility as he devotes his life to ending apartheid in South Africa.

❑ SPEECH
Eulogy for Martin Luther King Jr.
Robert F. Kennedy
Robert Kennedy, as presidential candidate, delivers news that shocks the nation.

Collaborate and Share Get with a partner to discuss what you learned from at least one of your independent readings.

- Give a brief synopsis or summary of the text.
- Describe any signposts that you noticed in the text and explain what they revealed to you.
- Describe what you most enjoyed or found most challenging about the text. Give specific examples.
- Decide if you would recommend the text to others. Why or why not?

Go to the **Reading Studio** for more resources on **Notice & Note.**

INDEPENDENT READING

MATCHING STUDENTS TO TEXTS

Use the following information to guide students in choosing their texts.

We Wear the Mask
Genre: poem
Overall Rating: Accessible

The Prisoner Who Wore Glasses **Lexile: 970L**
Genre: short story
Overall Rating: Challenging

America's Women: Reforming the World **Lexile: 1150L**
Genre: history writing
Overall Rating: Accessible

***from* Long Walk to Freedom** **Lexile: 1200L**
Genre: autobiography
Overall Rating: Challenging

Eulogy for Martin Luther King Jr. **Lexile: 1290L**
Genre: speech
Overall Rating: Accessible

Collaborate and Share To assess how well students read the selections, walk around the room and listen to their conversations. Encourage students to be focused and specific in their comments.

for Assessment

- Independent Reading Selection Tests

Encourage students to visit the **Reading Studio** to download a handy bookmark of **NOTICE & NOTE** signposts.

WHEN STUDENTS STRUGGLE . . .

Keep a Reading Log As students read their selected texts, have them keep a reading log for each selection to note signposts and their thoughts about them. Use their logs to assess how well they are noticing and reflecting on elements of their texts.

Reading Log for (title)		
Location	**Signpost I Noticed**	**My Notes about It**

UNIT 2 Tasks

- **WRITE A RESEARCH REPORT**
- **CREATE A PODCAST**

MENTOR TEXT
HIDDEN FIGURES
History by Margot Lee Shetterly

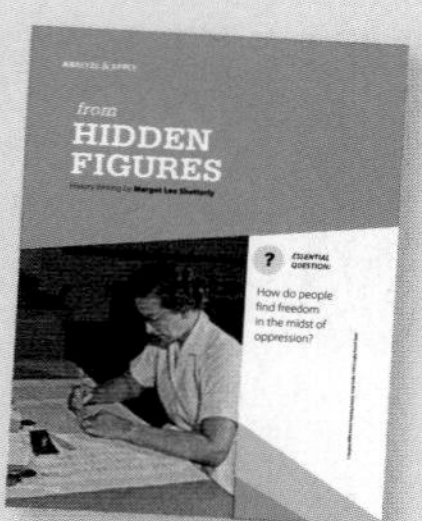

LEARNING OBJECTIVES

Writing Task

- Write a research report about an event or person(s) connected to the struggle for freedom.
- Use strategies to plan and organize ideas for a research report. Record accurate references to sources used for a research report.
- Develop a focused, structured draft of a research report. Use the Mentor Text as a model for a thesis statement and precise, vivid details.
- Revise drafts to incorporate feedback from peers. Edit drafts to incorporate standard English conventions. Use a rubric to evaluate writing.
- Publish writing to share it with an audience.
- **Language** Focus on a specific topic to guide research report writing.

Assign the Writing Task in ***Ed.***

RESOURCES

- Unit 2 Response Log
- Reading Studio: Notice & Note
- Writing Studio: Conducting Research
- Speaking and Listening Studio: Using Media in a Presentation
- Grammar Studio: Module 5: Lesson 7: Pronoun-Antecedent Agreement

Speaking and Listening Task

- Adapt a research report into a podcast.
- Present a research report podcast to an audience.
- Use appropriate verbal and nonverbal techniques.
- Listen actively to a podcast presentation.
- **Language** Practice identifying main ideas and supporting details in spoken language.

Language X-Ray: English Learner Support

Use the instruction below and the supports and scaffolds in the Teacher's Edition to help you guide students at different proficiency levels.

INTRODUCE THE WRITING TASK

Explain that in a **research report** the writer presents factual information about a specific topic. The introduction briefly explains the topic and expresses a position about it in the form of a thesis statement, or controlling idea. The body consists of paragraphs with main ideas and supporting details about the topic. The conclusion restates the writer's thesis, synthesizes key points, and may express new insights into the topic.

Note that the selections in this unit deal with people who struggle for "freedom" in a society that oppresses them, or treats them unfairly.

Use sentence frames such as these to help students explore the ideas related to oppression and freedom: *People are free when they* _______. *People who push for basic freedoms* _______. Provide phrases students can use when brainstorming, such as *can make decisions about their daily lives* and *must be brave and willing to suffer losses.* Have pairs of students work together to write an original sentence about the importance of fighting for individual freedoms in oppressive societies.

WRITING

Focus on a Specific Topic

Tell students that as they work on their research report, they will begin with a general topic and then narrow it to one that is manageable and can be expressed in a thesis statement.

Use the following supports with students at varying proficiency levels:

- List two broad topics related to the writing task—for example, *struggles for freedom* and *people who fight for freedom*. Model how to narrow each topic by asking questions such as "What are some problems people who are oppressed face?" List ideas on the board. **SUBSTANTIAL**
- Use sentence frames to promote specificity: ____ *fought for freedom when* ____. **MODERATE**
- After narrowing their topics, have partners work together to draft their thesis statements into one or two sentences. **LIGHT**

SPEAKING AND LISTENING

Identify Main Ideas and Supporting Details

Using the examples from the mentor text (Student Edition page 161), provide oral practice in which students identify main ideas and supporting details.

Use the following supports with students at varying proficiency levels:

- Read aloud the second example as students follow along. As you reread it, prompt students to circle the main idea. **SUBSTANTIAL**
- Read aloud the first example and prompt students to circle the main idea. Then ask students to listen again and mark details that connect to the main idea. **MODERATE**
- Assign pairs a paragraph from the text. Have one student read the paragraph aloud as the other listens for the main idea. Then reverse roles and have the listener identify two supporting details. **LIGHT**

WRITING

WRITE A RESEARCH REPORT

After reading the introductory paragraph with students, engage them in a discussion about the writing task. Encourage students to refer to the notes they recorded in the Unit 2 Response Log before they begin planning and writing a draft. Emphasize that the Response Log will contain a variety of ideas about how people find freedom in the midst of being oppressed based on their reading of the unit's selections. Note that these different perspectives will be useful in making their research reports more informative and interesting.

As students conduct Internet research, remind them to evaluate informational media messages carefully. Discuss methods of identifying valid online sources, and review the format for citing them properly.

USE THE MENTOR TEXT

Explain to students that their research reports will be similar to the excerpt from *Hidden Figures* by Margot Lee Shetterly. Emphasize that, like Shetterly's selection, their research reports will present accurate information drawn from valid sources about a specific historical person, event, or topic. Point out that their research report should include an engaging introduction with a thesis statement, several body paragraphs of well-organized information, a final paragraph that summarizes the information or draws a conclusion, and a list of research sources.

WRITING PROMPT

Discuss the prompt with students. Encourage them to ask clarifying questions about any part of the assignment they find unclear. Emphasize that the purpose of their research is to present information concerning a specific event, person, or topic related to the struggle for freedom.

Review the checklist of key points that students should include in their research reports.

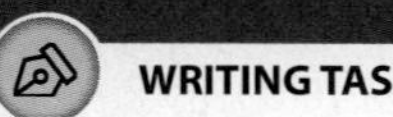

WRITING TASK

Write a Research Report

Go to the **Writing Studio** for help writing your report.

This unit focuses on how people find freedom in a society that oppresses them. For this writing task, you will write a research report. For a research report, you gather information from a number of different, valid sources about a specific topic and write about what you have discovered. For an example of a well-written research report you can use as a mentor text, review the selection *Hidden Figures*.

As you write your report, you will want to look at the notes you made in your Response Log after reading the texts in this unit. Include words and terms you learned from your research.

Writing Prompt

Read the information in the box below.

This is the general topic or context for your report.

> **Throughout history, people in many societies have fought for the freedom and equality they were denied.**

Think carefully about the following question.

This is the Essential Question for the unit. How would you answer this question, based on the texts in this unit?

> **How do people find freedom in the midst of oppression?**

Think about how you will find a specific topic for your report.

Write a research report about one event, or a person or group of people, connected to the struggle for freedom.

Be sure to—

Review these points as you write and again when you finish. Make any needed changes.

- ❑ research your topic using only valid sources and keep careful notes about your sources
- ❑ narrow your topic so that it is specific to one event, person, or group of people
- ❑ write an introduction that catches the reader's attention and clearly states your topic
- ❑ organize your information in a logical way
- ❑ connect related ideas effectively
- ❑ avoid plagiarism by paraphrasing or quoting sources
- ❑ write a final paragraph that summarizes your information or draws a conclusion
- ❑ cite your sources correctly at the end of the report

LEARNING MINDSET

Asking for Help Discuss with students how to ask for help when they feel "stuck" and unable to move forward with a task. Explain that, depending on the situation and task at hand, students should consider whether it would be best to ask a teacher, classmate, or parent or guardian for help. Reinforce that asking for help is not a sign of failure or "not being smart." Instead, tell them asking for help is a tried-and-true learning technique—and doing so is often a big help to others who have the same or a similar question.

1 Plan

Before you begin to write your research report, you need to research the topic of how people have fought for the freedom and equality they were denied. Be sure to use only valid, accurate sources for your research. Check sources for omissions, which may show bias. Also look for faulty reasoning, such as loaded language. While you are researching, narrow the topic to focus on one specific event, person, or group in the struggle for freedom, such as the first African American female doctor and challenges she faced, or Cesar Chavez and the struggle for migrant workers. Develop questions that you would like to answer through your research and write them down. Keep track of the sources you are using so that you can credit them appropriately in your report. When you have enough information, write a thesis statement to express your main idea. You also need to think about the purpose of your report and the audience you are writing it for. Use the chart below to help you organize your research.

Go to **Conducting Research: Starting Your Research** for help planning your report.

Research Report Planning Chart

Specific Research Topic	
Thesis Statement:	Source 1: Information:
Source 2: Information:	Source 3: Information:

Background Reading Review the notes you have taken in your Response Log after reading the texts in this unit. These texts provide key ideas that will help you think about what you want to say in your report.

Notice & Note

From Reading to Writing

As you plan your research report, apply what you've learned about signposts to your own writing. Remember that writers use common features, called signposts, to help convey their message to readers.

Think about how you can incorporate **Quoted Words** into your report.

Go to the **Reading Studio** for more resources on Notice & Note.

Use the notes from your Response Log as you plan your report.

1 PLAN

Review the key points students should consider during the planning stage—purpose, audience, topic, and research sources. Allow sufficient time for students to complete the planning chart.

English Learner Support

Understand Academic Language Make sure students understand words and phrases used in the chart such as *research topic*, *thesis statement*, and *source*. Encourage peer mentoring by pairing students who require substantial language learner support with students who are advanced, or proficient, English language users. **ALL LEVELS**

For **writing support** for students at varying proficiency levels, see the **Language X-Ray** on page 158B.

NOTICE & NOTE

From Reading to Writing Discuss the different types of **Quoted Words** that students may use in a research report. For example, a writer may quote the opinion or conclusion of someone who is an expert on the topic. Another powerful type of quotation involves citing the words of someone who was a direct witness to or participant in key historical events.

Background Reading As students plan their research reports, encourage them to review the notes in their Response Logs for Unit 2. Suggest that they briefly scan the unit's selections to identify examples of text elements they might use as models in their own writing.

WHEN STUDENTS STRUGGLE . . .

Use Small Group Brainstorming If students are struggling to come up with ideas for their research reports, suggest that they work together in small groups to brainstorm a list of general topics they can search online—for example, civil rights heroes, labor leaders, or innovative artists. Explain that their research should then move from general topics to specific ones by narrowing their searches—for example, famous women of the Civil Rights movement or notable Latina artists. Have students share and discuss their research results before deciding on specific topics of personal interest.

WRITING

Organize Your Ideas Emphasize the importance of organizing ideas in an outline before students begin a draft of their research reports. Review the organization of the Research Report planning chart.

Remind students that an introduction includes a clear thesis statement, or controlling idea, that expresses the central or main idea of the report and also captures the writer's position on the topic.

Discuss the different types of development a writer might use to organize the body of the research report—for example, chronological, narrative, or cause-and-effect organization. Explain that how they organize their report depends in part on the information being discussed and the writer's position toward the topic.

Remind students that a research report ends with a conclusion that restates the thesis and synthesizes the main points and key supporting evidence. A conclusion shows how all the elements of the research paper fit together in a way that supports the writer's goal.

For **speaking support** for students at varying proficiency levels, see the **Language X-Ray** on page 158B.

2 DEVELOP A DRAFT

Encourage students to use their outlines as they draft their research reports. However, remind students that an outline is a preliminary step and, if new ideas come to them during the drafting stage, they should make changes to their outlines.

ENGLISH LEARNER SUPPORT

Record Source Information Emphasize the importance of maintaining accurate information about sources consulted as students work on the research phase of their research reports. Model how to keep track of information and encourage students to work with a partner to support each other in this task. Coach students in recording all relevant information such as titles, authors, publishers, date of publication, and accurate URL addresses. **SUBSTANTIAL/MODERATE**

WRITING TASK

Go to **Writing as a Process: Planning and Drafting** to draft your report.

Organize Your Ideas After you have researched your topic, you need to organize your ideas. In your introduction, you will state your thesis. You will also introduce the event, person, or people you have chosen. The body of your report can be a narrative, told in chronological order. Or it can be several important ideas, supported by details. In your conclusion, you summarize your research. You might include a statement about the overall importance of your topic; or questions that remain unanswered.

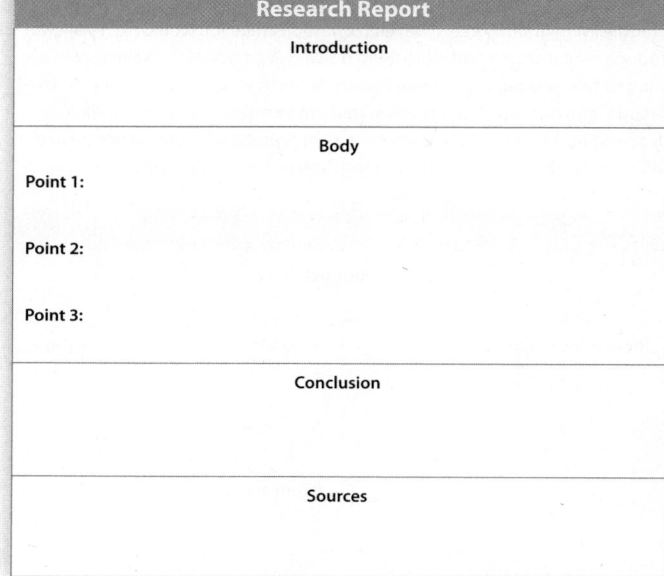

Research Report
Introduction
Body **Point 1:** **Point 2:** **Point 3:**
Conclusion
Sources

Go online to find examples of documentation that use the MLA or APA style. Choose one style and use it consistently for your sources.

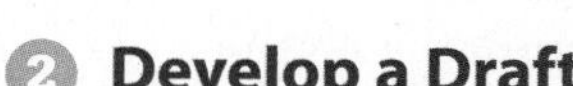

2 Develop a Draft

Once you have completed your planning activities, you will be ready to begin drafting your research report. Refer to your Graphic Organizer and the outline you have created, as well as any notes you took as you studied the selections in the unit. These will provide a kind of map for you to follow as you write. Use a word processing program or online writing app to make it easier to make changes or move sentences around. Finally, be sure to list your sources at the end of the report using a standard method of documentation such as that of the Modern Language Association (MLA) or the American Psychological Association (APA).

WHEN STUDENTS STRUGGLE . . .

Overcome "Writer's Block" Explain that it is common for writers to struggle when drafting a research report. Offer these tips to keep their writing momentum going:

- Have your brainstorming and planning notes in front of you when you begin.
- Review your notes and use them as a jumping off point. Start anywhere you want.
- Work in periods of 20 to 30 minutes without stopping and then take a break.
- Change your writing mode—from a computer, to paper and pencil, to a voice recording.
- Change the location where you are writing from time to time.

WRITING TASK

Use the Mentor Text

Author's Craft

A clearly stated thesis makes everything that follows clearer and easier to understand. Look at the way the author states the thesis in *Hidden Figures*.

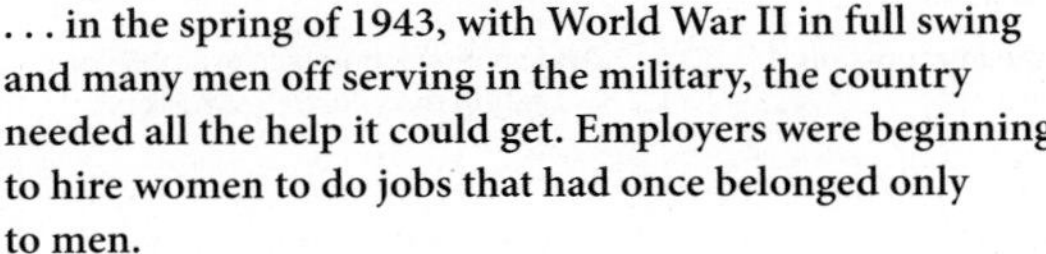

. . . in the spring of 1943, with World War II in full swing and many men off serving in the military, the country needed all the help it could get. Employers were beginning to hire women to do jobs that had once belonged only to men.

The author uses dates and other facts to state her thesis clearly and convincingly.

Apply What You've Learned State the thesis of your research report clearly. If you have trouble doing that, you may not have narrowed your topic sufficiently.

Genre Characteristics

One of the most important qualities of a good research report is clearly stated ideas, with precise use of language. Note the way the author explains why Langley needed so many people to do mathematical computations.

Each of the engineers at the Langley Memorial Aeronautical Laboratory required the support of a number of other workers: craftsmen to build the airplane models, mechanics to maintain the test tunnels, and "number crunchers" to process the data that was collected during the tests.

The author states her idea clearly and completely.

Apply What You've Learned Use precise language to state your ideas as your write your research report. If your language seems vague, try adding more specific details to make it more precise.

WHY THIS MENTOR TEXT?

The excerpt from *Hidden Figures* provides a good example of a research report. Use the instruction below to model how to write a clear thesis statement and how to include precise explanations in their research reports.

USE THE MENTOR TEXT

Author's Craft Have a volunteer read aloud the introduction to this section and the example from the mentor text. Ask: Why is it important to include factual details in a thesis statement? *(Details make the thesis statement specific and facts add validity to the author's point.)*

Genre Characteristics Ask a volunteer to read aloud the example of genre characteristics from Shetterly's text. Ask: What key idea do the details about the different kinds of workers at Langley support? *(Details about the different kinds of workers needed support the idea that "each of the engineers at Langley Memorial Aeronautical Laboratory required the support of a number of other workers. . . .")* What are the three types of workers the author provides as examples? *(craftsmen, mechanics, and "number crunchers")* Encourage students to take the time to consider which details to include to support their key points—and which ones might be unnecessary or even distracting to readers.

ENGLISH LEARNER SUPPORT

Analyze Text Structure Use the following supports with students at varying proficiency levels:

- Provide a visual that shows students how to use chronological order to narrate a sequence of events. Draw several lines in color to model the topic sentence followed by numbered lines (1, 2, 3) in a different color. **SUBSTANTIAL**
- Provide a visual that shows students how to organize a paragraph beginning with a main idea followed by supporting details. Draw several lines in color to model the topic sentence followed by lettered lines (A, B, C) in a different color. Repeat the procedure for a text structure using cause and effect. **MODERATE**
- Have groups of three students work as a team to find an example of a main idea supported by details in the excerpt from *Hidden Figures*. Have students determine the text structure in groups; then ask groups to share their examples and insights with other students during a class discussion. **LIGHT**

WRITING

3 REVISE

Have students evaluate their drafts by answering each question posed in the Revision Guide. Call on volunteers to model their revision techniques.

With a Partner Have students work with peer reviewers to evaluate their research report drafts. Use the following questions as a guide for peer review:

- Does the introduction include a clear and concise thesis statement?
- Does each body paragraph discuss a key idea in clear and logical ways?
- Is each key idea supported with relevant details, such as examples and quotations?

Encourage students to use their reviewer's comments to add specific details and revise for precise language as they further develop their research reports.

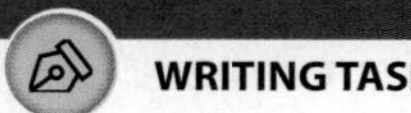

WRITING TASK

3 Revise

On Your Own Once you have written your draft, you will use the process of revision to turn that draft into an effective piece of writing. The Revision Chart will help you focus on specific elements to make your writing stronger.

Go to **Writing as a Process: Revising and Editing** for help revising your report.

REVISION GUIDE

Ask Yourself	Tips	Revision Techniques
1. Does my introduction grab the readers' attention?	**Highlight** the introduction.	**Add** an interesting fact, example, or quotation that illustrates the topic.
2. Does my introduction clearly state the thesis?	**Underline** the thesis statement.	**Reword** the thesis statement to make it clearer. If necessary, narrow the topic.
3. Are my main ideas organized in a clear and logical way?	**Highlight** each main idea. **Underline** transitions.	**Reorder** ideas so that each one flows easily to the next. **Add** appropriate transitions to connect ideas and clarify the organization.
4. Do I support each main idea with relevant details?	**Underline** each supporting fact, definition, example, or quotation.	**Add** facts, details, examples, or quotations to support ideas.
5. Do my pronouns consistently agree with their antecedents?	**Underline** any place where pronoun agreement is not clear.	**Change** pronouns to agree with their antecedents.
6. Have I used the correct format to cite information for my sources?	**Highlight** each source of information that you have used.	**Add** any information that you have omitted and correct format errors.

ACADEMIC VOCABULARY
As you conduct your peer review, try to use these words.

- ❑ **decline**
- ❑ **enable**
- ❑ **impose**
- ❑ **integrate**
- ❑ **reveal**

With a Partner After you have worked through the Revision Guide on your own, exchange papers with a partner. Evaluate each other's drafts in a **peer review.** Try to see how your partner could better accomplish his or her purpose in writing. Explain how you think your partner's draft should be revised and what your specific suggestions are.

When receiving feedback from your partner, listen carefully and take notes so that you can remember the revision suggestions.

ENGLISH LEARNER SUPPORT

Use Subject and Object Pronouns English language learners often need practice in differentiating between subject and object pronouns. Help students by providing model sentences in which the pronouns appear before and after the verb.

- Juan and Paolo ride bicycles. *They* ride bicycles. Juan and Paolo ride *them*.
- Maria borrowed the book from the library. *She* borrowed the book from the library. Maria borrowed *it* from the library.

Use sentences from the mentor text for additional practice and support.
SUBSTANTIAL/MODERATE

4 Edit

Once you have addressed the organization, development, and flow of ideas in your report, you can look to improve the finer points of your draft. Edit for the proper use of standard English conventions and make sure to correct any misspellings or grammatical errors.

Go to **Pronoun Antecedent Agreement** in the **Grammar Studio** to learn more.

Language Conventions

Pronoun-Antecedent Agreement An antecedent is the noun to which a pronoun refers. A pronoun must "agree with," or match, its antecedent.

- A **singular pronoun** must replace a singular noun.
- A **plural pronoun** must replace a plural noun.

The chart contains examples of pronoun-antecedent agreement from *Hidden Figures*.

PRONOUN TYPE	EXAMPLE
Singular pronoun	**President Franklin D. Roosevelt believed in the importance of air power, so two years earlier, in 1941, he had challenged the nation to increase its production of airplanes to fifty thousand units a year.**
Plural pronoun	**People working at Langley knew that they were doing their part to win the war.**

5 Publish

Finalize your report and choose a way to share it with your audience. Consider these options:

- Present your report as a speech to the class.
- Produce your report as a podcast to be posted on a classroom or school website.

ENGLISH LEARNER SUPPORT

Check Pronoun-Antecedent Agreement Have students work with partners to check that their pronouns agree with their antecedents. They can use the following sentence frame to summarize their findings for selected sentences from their research reports:

- *The pronoun ________ agrees/disagrees with its antecedent _______ because _________________________.* **SUBSTANTIAL/MODERATE**

4 EDIT

Suggest that students read their drafts aloud (to themselves or to a partner) multiple times to assess how effectively they have expressed their ideas. Tell them to listen first for short, choppy sentences and repeated words or phrases. During a second reading, have students determine whether they have used transitions effectively to connect their ideas. A third reading might focus on the use of precise, vivid language.

LANGUAGE CONVENTIONS

Pronoun-Antecedent Agreement Review the definitions of *pronoun* and *antecedent*. Note that a pronoun must agree in number with the noun, or antecedent, it replaces. Copy the sentences below on the board. Then have volunteers identify the noun and its number followed by the related pronoun and its number.

- *Sonya* practiced *her* speech. *(singular noun followed by singular pronoun)*
- The *students* rooted for *their* school's team. *(plural noun followed by plural pronoun)*

Point out that when nouns are joined by the word *and*, they form a compound noun and are considered plural.

- *Minjun and Ji-woo* made *their* presentation. *(compound noun followed by plural pronoun)*

Have students read aloud the model sentences from *Hidden Figures*. Note that these sentences contain more than one noun or noun phrase and that each has its own pronoun replacement. Ask: In the second sentence, how is the use of the pronoun *they* different from the use of the pronoun *their*? *(Both pronouns refer to* People. They *functions as a subject;* their *shows possession.)*

5 PUBLISH

Discuss the two publishing options suggested. Have students note the benefits and challenges that each method of publication may present. Ask: Can you think of other ways to publish your research report? Remind students that their final research reports must list detailed information about their sources.

USE THE SCORING GUIDE

Have students read the scoring guide. Encourage them to ask questions they may have about any ideas, sentences, phrases, or words they find unclear in the scoring guide. Tell partners to exchange their final research reports and score them using the scoring guide. Have each student reviewer write a paragraph explaining the reason for the score he or she awarded for each of the three major categories.

WRITING TASK

Use the scoring guide to evaluate your report.

WRITING TASK SCORING GUIDE: RESEARCH REPORT

	Organization/Progression	Development of Ideas	Use of Language and Conventions
4	• The organization is effective and appropriate to the purpose. • All ideas are focused on the topic specified in the prompt. • Transitions clearly show the relationship among ideas.	• The introduction catches the reader's attention, clearly states the topic. • The report contains a clear and insightful thesis statement. • The topic is well developed with clear main ideas supported by specific and well-chosen facts, details, examples, etc. • The report is based on multiple, valid research sources.	• Language and word choice is purposeful and precise. • Pronouns agree with their antecedents. • Spelling, capitalization, and punctuation are correct. • Grammar, usage, and mechanics are correct. • Research sources are cited correctly using a standard format.
3	• The organization is, for the most part, effective and appropriate to the purpose. • Most ideas are focused on the topic specified in the prompt. • A few more transitions are needed to show the relationship among ideas.	• The introduction could be more engaging. The topic is stated. • The report contains a clear thesis statement. • The development of ideas is clear because the writer uses specific and appropriate facts, details, examples, and quotations. • The report is based on at least two valid research sources.	• Language is for the most part specific and clear. • Pronoun-antecedent agreement is usually clear. • There are some spelling, capitalization, and punctuation mistakes. • Some grammar and usage errors occur. • Research sources are cited with some formatting errors.
2	• The organization is evident but is not always appropriate to the purpose. • Only some ideas are focused on the topic specified in the prompt. • More transitions are needed to show the relationship among ideas.	• The introduction is not engaging. The topic is not clear. • The thesis statement does not express a clear point. • The development of ideas is minimal. The writer uses facts, details, examples, etc. that are inappropriate or ineffectively presented. • The report is based on at least one valid research source.	• Language is somewhat vague and unclear. • There are occasional errors in pronoun-antecedent agreement. • Spelling, capitalization, and punctuation, as well as grammar and usage, are often incorrect but do not make reading difficult. • Research sources are cited using incorrect format.
1	• The organization is not appropriate to the purpose. • Ideas are not focused on the topic specified in the prompt. • No transitions are used, making the report difficult to understand.	• The introduction is missing or confusing. • The thesis statement is missing. • The development of ideas is weak. Supporting facts, details, examples, or quotations are unreliable, vague, or missing. • The report is not based on research sources, or the research sources cited are not valid.	• Language is inappropriate for the text. • Pronouns do not agree with their antecedents. • Many spelling, capitalization, and punctuation errors are present. • Grammatical and usage errors confuse the writer's ideas. • No research sources are cited.

Create a Podcast

You will now adapt your research report as a podcast that your classmates can listen and respond to. You also will listen to their podcasts, ask questions to better understand their ideas, and help them improve their work.

Go to **Using Media in a Presentation** in the **Speaking and Listening Studio** for help planning and crafting your presentation.

1 Adapt Your Report as a Podcast

Review your research report, and use the chart below to guide you as you adapt your report and follow instructions for creating a script and effects for your podcast. Ensure that the vocabulary, language, and tone of your podcast are appropriate for your audience. Also, make sure to link your ideas clearly using connecting words to transition smoothly from one idea to the next.

Podcast Planning Chart		
Title and Introduction	How will you revise your title and introduction to capture the listener's attention? Is there a catchier way to state your thesis? Consider putting your thesis in the form of a question that you can then answer.	
Audience	Who is your audience? What information will your audience already know? What information can you exclude? What should you add?	
Effective Language and Organization	Which parts of your report should be simplified? What can you change to strike a more informal voice and tone? Make sure you use standard language conventions so your ideas are clear to listeners.	
Sound	Think about whether you want to begin your podcast with music or sound effects. What kind of music is appropriate to the topic? Are there sound effects you can use that will help you create a mood?	

CREATE A PODCAST

Introduce students to the Speaking and Listening Task by discussing the differences between a podcast and a discussion. Explain that in their podcasts, students will present their research reports as audio files for others to listen to. Ask: How is listening to a research report different from reading it silently? Which type of a presentation do you think is more formal in tone, a written research report or a podcast? Why might it be necessary to adapt a research report when turning it into a podcast?

1 ADAPT YOUR REPORT AS A PODCAST

Have students read the questions for each major topic listed in the chart. Discuss some general principles for converting a written research report into a podcast. *(Examples: Use music and sound effects to introduce and highlight key ideas. Introduce, explain, and restate important ideas. Engage the audience's interest with examples, humor, and other techniques.)* Emphasize that being clear, concise, and engaging are essential hallmarks of a quality podcast.

ENGLISH LEARNER SUPPORT

Adapt the Report Use the following supports with students at varying proficiency levels:

- Model for students how to retell basic information from their reports, so that their actual podcast will sound more natural and fluid. Coach them in choosing key sentences and vocabulary they are comfortable speaking aloud. **SUBSTANTIAL**
- Have students work in small groups to review the questions in the chart and support each other in understanding and completing the task. Check in with each group to offer encouragement, provide support, and answer clarifying questions. **MODERATE**
- Have students form groups of four and assign one of the chart categories to each group (or let groups choose). After discussing that category, students can create their podcasts independently. **LIGHT**

2 PRACTICE WITH A PARTNER OR GROUP

Practice Effective Verbal Techniques Discuss the checklist items with students. Model the effective use of each verbal technique. Following the modeling activity, have student volunteers demonstrate how they would use the technique. Establish a recording location for students to practice microphone skills or demonstrate how they can practice using smartphones, tablets, or computers.

Create Your Podcast Have student volunteers read each of the checklist items. If students are using their classroom or the media center, or a special practice room in the school, be sure to set up a schedule and review any rules for proper equipment use. Teach and model the use of school or open source editing software before students prepare their podcasts. When considering music and sound effects to use, have students think about the mood they want to create with their musical selections.

Provide and Consider Advice for Improvement Discuss the focus students should have as an audience for the podcasts. Ask: What are the main ideas of this podcast? Are the ideas effectively presented? What are some of the other qualities of a good podcast that the presenter achieved? What parts of the podcast can be improved, and how? Which parts were most effective? What key ideas did I learn? What did I enjoy most about the podcast?

Encourage students to review the comments from other students about their podcasts. Ask: Which suggestions do you think would be most helpful in improving your podcast? What changes would you make to incorporate these suggestions? How can you build upon what went well the next time you make a presentation?

3 POST YOUR PODCAST

Set aside time for all students to post their podcasts and to listen to the podcasts made by other members of their group or other students in the class. Have students share how their classmates' feedback helped them improve their research reports, podcasts, and general presentation skills.

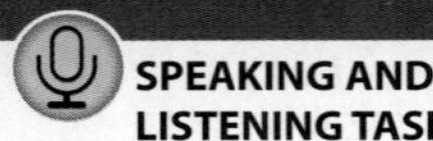

SPEAKING AND LISTENING TASK

As you work to improve your podcast and those of your classmates, follow these rules of constructive criticism:

- ❑ **Accept the other person's purpose and try to help them achieve it.**
- ❑ **Begin your comments with the strong points of the work.**
- ❑ **Remember that the best criticism is both kind and truthful.**

2 Practice with a Partner or Group

When your script is ready and you've decided on whether to have music and/or sound effects, practice before you record.

Practice Effective Verbal Techniques

- ❑ **Enunciation** Replace words that you stumble over, and rearrange sentences so that your delivery is smooth.
- ❑ **Voice Modulation and Register** Change the tone and pitch of your voice (louder, softer, higher, lower) to show enthusiasm and emphasis.
- ❑ **Speaking Rate** Speak slowly enough that listeners understand you. Pause briefly now and then to let them consider important points.
- ❑ **Microphone Skills** Practice to see how far your mouth should be from the microphone to record clearly without making distracting noises.

Create Your Podcast

- ❑ **Recording Location** If your school doesn't have a music practice room or a studio, find a room with as little outside sound as possible.
- ❑ **Editing** If your school has audio editing software, or if you can download an open source app, use that to clean up the start and finish of your podcast after you have recorded it.
- ❑ **Music** Find appropriate music free for your podcast from archive.org or the Library of Congress music collection. You can also use music from your own collection as long as you use it only for this school assignment.
- ❑ **Sound Effects** You can download free sound effects from many different sites online.

Provide and Consider Advice for Improvement

As an audience, listen closely to the podcast. Evaluate its impact, purpose, point of view, and any rhetorical devices used. Take notes about ways that podcasters can improve their presentations and more effectively present their ideas. Paraphrase and summarize each presenter's key ideas and main points to confirm your understanding and ask questions to clarify any confusing ideas.

As a podcaster, pay attention to feedback and consider ways to improve your podcast to make it more effective. Remember to ask for suggestions about your music and sound effects, if you chose to use them.

3 Post Your Podcast

Use the advice you received during practice to make final changes to your podcast. Then, make it available to your classmates.

WHEN STUDENTS STRUGGLE . . .

Collaborate on Partner and Small Group Podcasts Have students work in pairs or groups of three to present a joint podcast, with each student performing a specific role, such as writer, producer, or main speaker/narrator. Encourage each student to speak a few lines in the finished podcast. Give them additional time and support as they practice presenting their podcast and as they make revisions before finalizing it.

Reflect on the Unit

As you were planning your research report, you reviewed your thoughts about the reading you have done in this unit. Now is a good time to reflect on what you have learned.

Reflect on the Essential Question

- How do people find freedom in the midst of oppression? How has your answer to this question changed since you first considered it when you started this unit?
- What are some examples from the texts you've read that show how people find freedom?

Reflect on Your Reading

- Which selections were the most interesting or surprising to you?
- From which selection did you learn the most about finding freedom in the midst of oppression?

Reflect on the Writing Task

- What difficulties did you encounter while working on your research report? How might you avoid them next time?
- What part of the report was the easiest and hardest to write? Why?
- What improvements did you make to your report as you were revising?
- What changes did you need to make to your report to make it work as a podcast?

UNIT 2 SELECTIONS
- "I Have a Dream"
- "Interview with John Lewis"
- from *Hidden Figures*
- "The Censors"
- "Booker T. and W.E.B."
- from *Reading Lolita in Tehran*
- from *Persepolis 2: The Story of a Return*

REFLECT ON THE UNIT

Have students reflect on the questions independently and write some notes in response to each one. Then have students meet with partners or in small groups to discuss their reflections. Circulate during these discussions to identify the questions that are generating the liveliest conversations. Wrap up with a whole-class discussion focused on these questions.

LEARNING MINDSET

Problem Solving If students get stuck when trying to respond to questions posed in the Reflect on the Unit section, encourage them to apply problem-solving strategies as they work through the questions. For example, encourage students to look at the question from a different viewpoint by rephrasing it. Because students may be impatient or resistant when it comes to working through a problem instead of trying to ignore it, coach them to focus on each question one at a time: Take a few deep breaths, read the question carefully, pause to think about it, and then write down a response.

Instructional Overview and Resources

	Instructional Focus	Online Ed Resources
 **Unit Introduction** **The Bonds Between Us**	**Unit 3 Essential Question** **Unit 3 Academic Vocabulary**	**Stream to Start:** The Bonds Between Us **Unit 3 Response Log**
ANALYZE & APPLY		
 **"The Grasshopper and the Bell Cricket"** Short Story by Yasunari Kawabata **Lexile 1060L** **NOTICE & NOTE** READING MODEL **Signposts** • Again and Again • Aha Moment • Words of the Wiser	**Reading** • Analyze Setting and Theme • Make Inferences about Theme **Writing:** Write an Informal Letter **Speaking and Listening:** Discuss with a Small Group **Vocabulary:** Context Clues **Language Conventions:** Verb Phrases	**Audio** **Reading Studio:** Notice & Note **Level Up Tutorial:** Making Inferences **Writing Studio:** Writing as a Process **Speaking and Listening Studio:** Participating in Collaborative Discussions **Vocabulary Studio:** Context Clues **Grammar Studio:** Module 2: Lesson 8: Verb Phrases
 **"Monkey See, Monkey Do, Monkey Connect"** Science Writing by Frans de Waal **Lexile 1160 L**	**Reading** • Monitor Comprehension • Analyze Author's Claim **Writing:** Take a Position **Speaking and Listening:** Participate in a Debate **Vocabulary:** Words from Greek **Language Conventions:** Colons	**Audio** **Close Read Screencasts:** Modeled Discussions **Reading Studio:** Notice & Note **Level Up Tutorials:** Evidence; Analyzing Arguments **Writing Studio:** Building Effective Support **Speaking and Listening Studio:** Introduction: Collaborative Discussions **Vocabulary Studio:** Words from Greek **Grammar Studio:** Module 11: Lesson 8: Colons
"With Friends Like These..." Informational Text by Dorothy Rowe **Lexile 1070L**	**Reading** • Summarize and Paraphrase Texts • Evaluate Details **Writing:** Write a Personal Essay **Speaking and Listening:** Present a Scene **Vocabulary:** Print and Digital Resources **Language Conventions:** Adjective and Adverb Phrases	**Audio** **Reading Studio:** Notice & Note **Level Up Tutorial:** Comparison-Contrast Organization **Writing Studio:** Writing Narratives **Speaking and Listening Studio:** Giving a Presentation **Vocabulary Studio:** Print and Digital Resources **Grammar Studio:** Module 3: Lesson 2: Adjective Phrases and Adverb Phrases

SUGGESTED PACING: 30 DAYS

Unit Introduction	The Grasshopper and the Bell Cricket	Monkey See, Monkey Do, Monkey Connect	With Friends Like These...
1	2 3 4 5 6	7 8 9 10 11	12 13 14 15

 STUDIOS 

English Learner Support	Differentiated Instruction	Online Ed Assessment
• Learn New Expressions		
• Text X-Ray • Use Cognates • Identify Participles • Express Ideas • Understand Plural Nouns • Oral Assessment • Use Context Clues • Comprehend Language Structures	**When Students Struggle** • Use Syntax Surgery • Make Inferences	**Selection Test**
• Text X-Ray • Understand Directionality • Use Cognates • Determine Meaning • Determine Technical Meanings • Suffixes • Pronounce Words Correctly • Oral Assessment • Distinguish Intonation Patterns • Decode Words • Colons	**When Students Struggle** • Understand Reasons Versus Evidence • Hold a Discussion	**Selection Test**
• Text X-Ray • Note False Cognates • Learn Essential Language • Use Visual Support • Use Prepositions • Discuss Text Structure • Oral Assessment • Use Cognates • Use Adjective and Adverb Phrases • Comprehend Language Structures	**When Students Struggle** • Evaluate Details **To Challenge Students** • Conduct Research	**Selection Test**

UNIT 3 Continued

	Instructional Focus	Online Ed Resources
ANALYZE & APPLY		
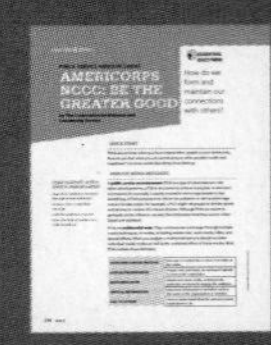 **"AmeriCorps NCCC: Be the Greater Good"** Public Service Announcement by The Corporation for National and Community Service	**Reading** • Analyze Media Messages **Writing:** Create a Public Service Announcement **Speaking and Listening:** Present a Public Service Announcement	**Reading Studio:** Notice & Note **Level Up Tutorial:** Analyzing Visuals **Writing Studio:** Producing and Publishing with Technology **Speaking and Listening Studio:** Using Media in a Presentation
COLLABORATE & COMPARE		
Mentor Text  **"Loser"** Short Story by Aimee Bender **Lexile 900L**	**Reading** • Analyze Plot • Analyze Characterization **Writing:** Freewrite **Speaking and Listening:** Discuss with a Small Group **Vocabulary:** Context Clues **Language Conventions:** Active and Passive Voice	 **Audio** **Reading Studio:** Notice & Note **Level Up Tutorial:** Plot: Sequence of Events **Writing Studio:** Planning and Drafting **Speaking and Listening Studio:** Participating in Collaborative Discussions **Vocabulary Studio:** Context Clues **Grammar Studio:** Module 6: Lesson 4: Active and Passive Voice
"At Dusk" Poem by Natasha Trethewey	**Reading** • Analyze Diction and Syntax • Create Mental Images **Speaking and Listening** • Present an Oral Reading • Discuss with a Small Group	**Audio** **Reading Studio:** Notice & Note **Level Up Tutorial:** Setting and Mood **Speaking and Listening Studio:** Giving a Presentation; Participating in Collaborative Discussions
Collaborate and Compare	**Reading:** Compare Themes **Speaking and Listening:** Collaborate and Present	**Speaking and Listening Studio:** Participating in Collaborative Discussions

INDEPENDENT READING

The Independent Reading selections are only available in the eBook.

Go to the Reading Studio for more information on Notice & Note.

"The Power of a Dinner Table"
Editorial by David Brooks
Lexile 1010L

"The Debt"
Poem by Tim Seibles

END OF UNIT		
Writing Task: Write a Short Story **Reflect on the Unit**	**Writing:** Write a Short Story **Language Conventions:** Spelling Plural Nouns	**Unit 3 Response Log** **Mentor Text:** "Loser" **Writing Studio:** Writing Narratives; Writing as a Process **Reading Studio:** Notice & Note **Grammar Studio:** Module 13: Lesson 2: Spelling Rules

Online Ed

English Learner Support	Differentiated Instruction	Assessment
• Text X-Ray • Recognize Directionality and Decode Words • Identify Purpose of Environmental Print • Oral Assessment	**When Students Struggle** • Analyze Media Messages	**Selection Test**
• Text X-Ray • Use Cognates • Compare Verb Forms • Analyze Antonyms • Develop Vocabulary • Analyze Characterization • Oral Assessment • Use Appropriate Language • Practice Phonology • Language Conventions	**When Students Struggle** • Track Plot Events **To Challenge Students** • Make Inferences	**Selection Test**
• Text X-Ray • Respond to Text • Clarify Vocabulary • Discuss Pronoun Referents • Use Cognates • Oral Assessment • Express Opinions	**When Students Struggle** • Understand Diction and Syntax	**Selection Test**
• Share Information	**When Students Struggle** • Compare Themes	
from *War* Informational Text by Sebastian Junger **Lexile 1150L** "A Worn Path" Short Story by Eudora Welty **Lexile 660L** "My Ceremony for Taking" Poem by Lara Mann		**Selection Tests**
• Language X-Ray • Understand Academic Language • Create a Storyboard • Identify Point of View • Discuss a Text	**When Students Struggle** • Brainstorm Story Ideas • Describe a Setting **To Challenge Students** • Hold a Staged Reading	**Unit Test**

TEACH

Connect to the ESSENTIAL QUESTION

Ask a volunteer to read aloud the Essential Question. Have students pause to reflect on the meaning of the question. Then ask them to consider the relationships they have with others. How did they form important relationships and how do they maintain them? Prompt students to compare ways they maintain relationships with their friends and family members. In what ways are they similar or different?

English Learner Support

Learn Vocabulary Make sure students understand the Essential Question. If necessary, explain the terms:

- *Form* means "to create something."
- *Maintain* means "to cause something to continue."
- *Connections* means "relationships."

Help students restate the question in simpler language: How do we make and keep relationships with others?
SUBSTANTIAL/MODERATE

DISCUSS THE QUOTATION

Provide students with background information. In 1901, after U.S. President William McKinley was assassinated, Theodore Roosevelt became president. Then ask students to read the quotation and prompt them to reflect on the meaning of the word *welfare*. Ask students to consider how their welfare is connected to the welfare of others. Then have them give examples of how their welfare affects their connections with others.

UNIT 

THE BONDS BETWEEN US

ESSENTIAL QUESTION:

How do we form and maintain our connections with others?

The welfare of each of us is dependent fundamentally upon the welfare of all of us.

Theodore Roosevelt

LEARNING MINDSET

Setting Goals Ask students to consider what goals they want to achieve during the school year. Whether they want to learn how to play a new instrument or strengthen a relationship, emphasize that setting goals can make their work easier. Explain that setting goals helps them track progress and divide work into more manageable tasks. Have students practice breaking down their main objective into smaller goals. Discuss how achieving these smaller goals over a period of time will be easier and more beneficial than trying to complete a large goal all at once. Remind students about the importance of setting goals that they are comfortable with, because everyone learns at different speeds and has unique needs.

ACADEMIC VOCABULARY

Academic Vocabulary words are words you use when you discuss and write about texts. In this unit, you will practice and learn five words.

☑ **capacity** ❑ **confer** ❑ **emerge** ❑ **generate** ❑ **trace**

Study the Word Network to learn more about the word **capacity**.

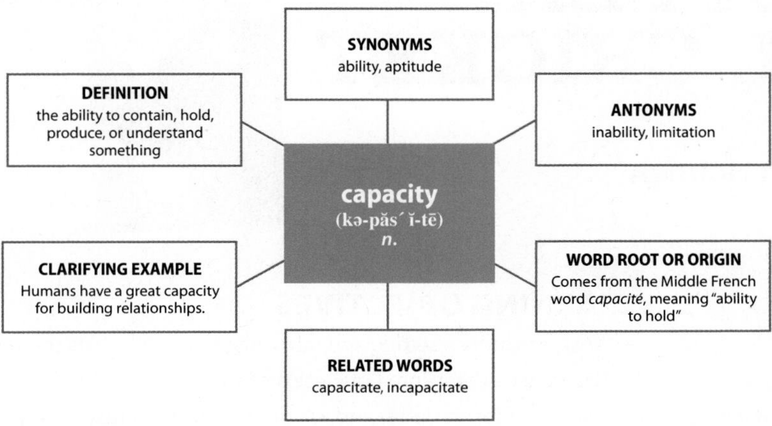

Write and Discuss Discuss the completed Word Network with a partner, making sure to talk through all of the boxes until you both understand the word, its synonyms, antonyms, and related forms. Then, fill out a Word Network for each of the remaining four words. Use a dictionary or online resource to help you complete the activity.

Go online to access the Word Networks.

RESPOND TO THE ESSENTIAL QUESTION

In this unit, you will read various genres that explore what links us to family, friends, pets, and community. As you read, you will revisit the **Essential Question** and gather your ideas about it in the **Response Log** that appears on page R3. At the end of the unit, you will have the opportunity to write a **short story** about interpersonal connections. Filling out the Response Log will help you prepare for this writing task.

You can also go online to access the Response Log.

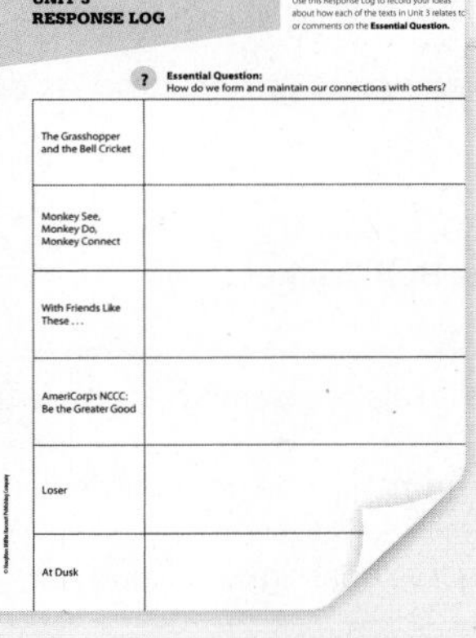

TEACH

ACADEMIC VOCABULARY

As students complete Word Networks for the remaining four vocabulary words, encourage them to include all the categories shown in the completed network if possible, but point out that some words do not have clear synonyms or antonyms. Some words may also function as different parts of speech—for example, *trace* can function as a noun or a verb.

capacity (kə-păs´ ĭ-tē) *n.* The ability to contain, hold, produce, or understand. (Spanish cognate: *capacidad*)

confer (kən-fûr´) *v.* To grant or give to. (Spanish cognate: *conferir*)

emerge (ĭ-mûrj´) *v.* To come forth, out of, or away from. (Spanish cognate: *emerger*)

generate (jĕn´ə-rāt´) *v.* To produce or cause something to happen or exist. (Spanish cognate: *generar*)

trace (trās) *v.* To discover or determine the origins or developmental stages of something.

RESPOND TO THE ESSENTIAL QUESTION

Direct students to the Unit 3 Response Log. Explain that students will use it to record ideas and details from the selections that help answer the Essential Question. When they work on the writing task at the end of the unit, their Response Log will help them think about what they have read and make connections between the texts.

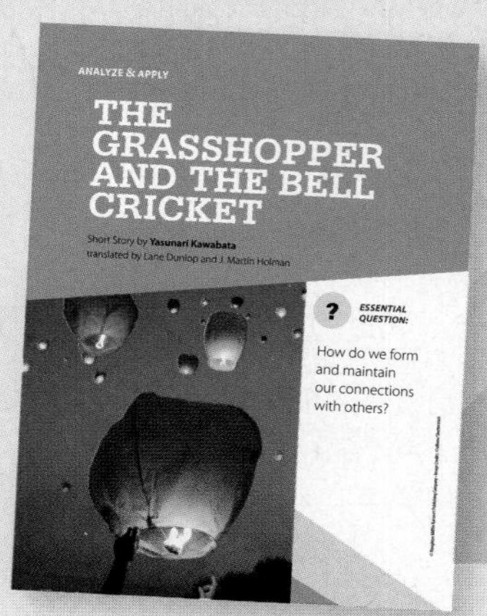

READING MODEL

THE GRASSHOPPER AND THE BELL CRICKET

Short Story by **Yasunari Kawabata**
translated by Lane Dunlop and J. Martin Holman

GENRE ELEMENTS

SHORT STORY

Remind students that a **short story** (fiction that is shorter than a novel) includes the four basic elements of fiction: setting, characters, plot, and theme. "The Grasshopper and the Bell Cricket" begins with a descriptive exposition that introduces the characters and the setting within which the action occurs. It then employs a conflict to build to an important moment, and also allows the narrator to express thoughts and feelings about the story's action. The story's main ideas and details point to a theme, or message.

LEARNING OBJECTIVES

- Analyze a story's setting and make inferences about its theme.
- Conduct research into Japanese art forms.
- Write an informal letter and ask questions about research.
- Discuss researched information and draw conclusions.
- Use context clues to understand unfamiliar words.
- Identify verb phrases and use them in writing for various purposes.
- **Language** Discuss differences between descriptive passages and dialogue in a story.

TEXT COMPLEXITY

Quantitative Measures	**The Grasshopper and the Bell Cricket**	Lexile: 1060L
Qualitative Measures	**Ideas Presented** Multiple levels of meaning (multiple themes) are evident.	
	Structures Used There is primarily one point of view—that of the narrator.	
	Language Used There is some unassigned dialogue.	
	Knowledge Required The theme is fairly complex. Knowledge of the author's cultural background is necessary for a full understanding.	

Online 

RESOURCES

- Unit 3 Response Log
-  Selection Audio
-  Reading Studio: Notice & Note
-  Level Up Tutorial: Making Inferences
-  Writing Studio: Writing as a Process
-  Speaking and Listening Studio: Participating in Collaborative Discussions
-  Vocabulary Studio: Context Clues
-  Grammar Studio: Module 2: Lesson 8: Verb Phrases
- "The Grasshopper and the Bell Cricket" Selection Test

SUMMARIES

English

One evening, the narrator hears the chirping of a bell cricket and follows the sound. He discovers a group of children on an insect chase, lighting their way with handmade lanterns. The narrator describes the children's artistry in making the lanterns. He then recounts a conversation in which one of the boys, Fujio, gives a bell cricket he has caught to Kiyoko, a girl. The narrator notices that the light from the two children's lanterns cast the image of their names on each other's clothing, unbeknownst to them. He considers that Kiyoko may be special, like a bell cricket, and he hopes that Fujio someday will choose a "bell cricket" kind of girl to love.

Spanish

Una noche, el narrador escucha el chirrido de un grillo y sigue su sonido. Descubre a un grupo que anda en busca de insectos; ellos iluminan su camino con faroles hechos a mano. El narrador describe la maestría de los niños al hacer los faroles. Luego recuenta la conversación en la cual uno de los niños, Fujio, le da uno de los grillos que había atrapado a Kiyoko, una niña. El narrador nota que la luz de los faroles de los dos niños proyecta la imagen de sus nombres en la ropa del otro, sin ellos saberlo. Él considera que Kiyoko puede ser especial, como un grillo, y espera que un día Fujio se enamore de una chica que sea como un "grillo".

SMALL-GROUP OPTIONS

Have students work in small groups to read and discuss the selection.

Pinwheel Discussions

- Place students in discussion groups of eight: four students seated facing in, four facing out.
- Instruct students in the inner circle to remain in place throughout the discussion and students in the outer circle to rotate to their right after discussing each of the following questions:
- Why do the children make new lanterns every day? What do you think the lanterns symbolize?
- What is the significance of Fujio's and Kiyoko's names being reflected on each other's clothing?
- How does the author use the grasshopper and the bell cricket to present a message to readers?

Activating Academic Vocabulary

- Provide students with a list of the Academic Vocabulary words: *capacity, confer, emerge, generate, trace.*
- Model the appropriate context and usage for each word.
- Have student pairs write sentences pertaining to "The Grasshopper and the Bell Cricket," using each Academic Vocabulary word.
- Have pairs share their sentences with the class for open discussion.

Text X-Ray: English Learner Support

for "The Grasshopper and the Bell Cricket"

Use the Text X-Ray and the supports and scaffolds in the Teacher's Edition to help guide students at different proficiency levels through the selection.

INTRODUCE THE SELECTION

DISCUSS OBSERVATIONS

In this lesson, students will need to be able to discuss the narrator's observations. Read paragraph 1 and the beginning of paragraph 2 with students, pointing out the following:

- An observation can be something that you hear. What does the narrator hear? *(an insect's voice)*
- An observation can be something that you see. What does the narrator see? *(white fence, playground, bushes, trees)*
- An observation can be something that you realize, based on what you see and hear. What does the narrator realize? *(There is a group of children hunting insects.)*

Provide these sentence frames to help students discuss their observations: *The narrator hears ____. The narrator sees ____. The narrator realizes that ____.*

CULTURAL REFERENCES

The following words or phrases may be unfamiliar to students:

- *insect cage* (paragraph 19): made from bamboo to house singing insects, such as bell crickets
- *kimono* (paragraph 23): a Japanese robe with wide sleeves and an obi (sash)
- *paper lanterns* (paragraph 2): a common sign of Japanese culture; used for celebrations and festivals
- *singing insects* (paragraph 3): thought to show the coming of winter or death in Japanese culture; therefore, they have a sad meaning

Other cultural references are explained in footnotes and on the first Get Ready page.

LISTENING

Understand Tone

Tell students that **tone** is an author's attitude toward the subject he or she writes about. A formal tone is serious and respectful, while an informal tone is like talking with a friend and may even be funny.

Have students listen as you read aloud paragraphs 1–3. Use the following supports with students at varying proficiency levels:

- Ask students whether they think the tone of the story is formal or informal. Have students nod or shake their heads in response to these questions: Is the tone informal? *(no)* Is the tone formal? *(yes)* **SUBSTANTIAL**
- Ask students if what they just listened to has a formal or informal tone. Then, ask them to recall words that helped them decide on the tone. **MODERATE**
- Remind students that word choice and sentence structure have an effect on tone. Ask students to work in pairs to discuss the words and sentence structures that contribute to the formal tone of the story. Have pairs share their ideas with the class. **LIGHT**

SPEAKING

Use Cultural Vocabulary

Display photos of a black cherry tree, simple Japanese lanterns, Japanese written characters, and a kimono. Have students use terms related to Japanese culture to discuss aspects of the story.

Use the following supports with students at varying proficiency levels:

- Read the following questions and answers aloud and have students repeat each word or phrase. Point to each photo as you say the answer. Ask: What is something that can be worn? (*a kimono*) What might grow in a Japanese garden? (*a black cherry tree*) What can be used to light a path? (*a lantern*) **SUBSTANTIAL**
- Use the following questions to discuss Japanese cultural elements from the story: How does the narrator express in paragraphs 2 and 3 that the homemade lanterns are nicer than the store ones? What words in paragraphs 16–21 show that the children like the bell cricket more than a grasshopper? **MODERATE**
- Point out to students that in paragraphs 2 and 3 the narrator describes the children's lanterns very carefully and talks about the "insect chase." Ask students to discuss why children in this culture might want to have both a lantern and an insect cage. **LIGHT**

READING

Contrast Descriptive Passages and Dialogue

Point out that the middle part of the story consists of dialogue. Discuss how this middle part of the story is different from the rest.

Use the following supports with students at varying proficiency levels:

- Help students examine dialogue and descriptive passages in paragraphs 5–21. Ask: Does dialogue have quotation marks? (*yes*) Do descriptive passages include characters talking with each other? (*no*) Have students point to dialogue in the paragraphs and then point to the descriptive passage. **SUBSTANTIAL**
- After students have read the story, have them complete these sentence frames: *During the dialogue, the boy _____. Before the dialogue, the narrator _____. After the dialogue, the narrator _____.* **MODERATE**
- After students have read the story, have them work in pairs to answer these questions: How do paragraphs 1–4 set the scene for the dialogue? How does the dialogue suggest the boy's feeling for the girl? How do paragraphs 22–27 allow the narrator to share his thoughts about what happened during the conversation? **LIGHT**

WRITING

Write an Informal Letter

Work with students to complete the writing assignment on Student Edition page 181.

Use the following supports with students at varying proficiency levels:

- Provide students with the parts of an informal letter, explaining each one. Allow students to write one paragraph, using these sentence frames: *I found out that some Japanese artists _____. I'm still wondering how the artists _____. Please write back to tell me what you know about _____.* **SUBSTANTIAL**
- Provide sentence frames that students can use as they draft their letter: *I think that [art form] is interesting because _____. I'm not sure that I understand _____.* **MODERATE**
- Remind students that language and sentence structure can affect tone. Ask: What is the tone of this letter? (*informal*) What kinds of words and sentence structures could you use to create an informal tone? (*words and sentence structures that people use in casual conversation*) Display students' answers to use as a resource while writing. **LIGHT**

EXPLAIN THE SIGNPOSTS

Explain that **NOTICE & NOTE Signposts** are significant moments in the text that help readers understand and analyze works of fiction or nonfiction. Use the instruction on these pages to introduce students to the signposts **Again and Again, Aha Moment,** and **Words of the Wiser**. Then use the selection that follows to have students apply the signposts and Big Questions to a text.

For a full list of the fiction and nonfiction signposts, see p. 236.

AGAIN AND AGAIN

Explain that, as the title suggests, the **Again and Again** signpost is all about **repetition**—words, phrases, images, details, or events that appear over and over again in a text. Point out that we tend to repeat something because we want to emphasize it and that the same is true in literature. To determine what is being emphasized in a text, students should think about the contexts in which previous appearances of the word, image, and so on were seen. Do those contexts have anything in common? Do differences in context change or add to the meaning of the repeated item? Questions like these can reveal insights into the author's ideas.

Read aloud the example passage. Use a Think Aloud to model the reader's recognition of the repeated question. Explain that the boy repeating the question helps readers see that he has a reason for waiting to give away the grasshopper. Have students read the final sentence of the passage; then elicit that the reason for his delay is that he wants to give the grasshopper to a particular girl. Use the example to show that analyzing an Again and Again signpost can help students understand characters and begin to make **inferences** about **theme**.

Tell students that when they spot an Again and Again signpost, they should pause, mark it in their consumable text, and ask themselves the anchor question: *Why might the author keep bringing this up?*

READING MODEL

For more information on these and other signposts to Notice & Note, visit the **Reading Studio**.

THE GRASSHOPPER AND THE BELL CRICKET

You are about to read the short story "The Grasshopper and the Bell Cricket." In it, you will notice and note signposts that provide clues about the story's setting and themes. Here are three key signposts to look for as you read this short story and other works of fiction.

When you see a word or phrase repeated several times in a text, pause to see if it is an **Again and Again**.

Again and Again Have you ever been reading a story when you begin to notice that a word, an event, or an image keeps popping up over and over? This isn't an accident or an oversight by the author. Pay attention—the author is trying to tell you something.

When a word, image or event in a story comes up **Again and Again**, you know it's important, but you might not immediately know *why* it's important. The repetition might give you clues about characters or setting, foreshadow an important event, or help you to understand the story's themes.

The paragraphs below illustrate a student's annotation within "The Grasshopper and the Bell Cricket" and a response to a Notice & Note signpost.

"Does anyone want a grasshopper?" A boy . . . suddenly straightened up and shouted . . . .

"Does anyone want a grasshopper? A grasshopper!"

"I do! I do!" Four or five more children came running up . . . . The boy called out a third time.

"Doesn't anyone want a grasshopper?"

Two or three more children came over.

"Yes. I want it."

It was a girl . . . The boy . . . thrust out his fist that held the insect at the girl.

Anchor Question When you notice this signpost, ask: *Why might the author keep bringing this up?*

What words are repeated?	"anyone want a grasshopper?"
What is the significance of the repetition?	The boy repeats his offer until the girl, the one he really wants to give the grasshopper to, says she'd like to have it.

Aha Moment Here's a familiar story: a detective snoops around and asks questions in order to solve a murder mystery. Using intuition and keen intelligence, the detective combs through the clues until they all fall into place and suddenly--aha! —mystery solved!

A character experiencing an **Aha Moment** may:

- reach a broader understanding about something or someone
- discover a way to resolve a conflict or problem
- soon begin to think or act differently

Read this part of "The Grasshopper and the Bell Cricket" to see a student's annotation of an Aha Moment:

21 By the light of his . . . lantern . . . [the boy] glanced at the girl's face.

22 Oh, I thought . . . How silly of me not to have understood his actions until now!

When you see phrases like these, pause to see whether it's an **Aha Moment**:

"All of a sudden..."

"for the first time..."

"and just like that..."

"I realized..."

Anchor Question
When you notice this signpost, ask: *How might this change things?*

What words tell you that something has changed?	Oh, I thought...How silly of me not to have understood his actions until now.
What might this realization tell you about the characters?	The boy likes the girl.

Words of the Wiser In this situation, a wiser character—who is often older—offers insight or advice about life to the main character. This insight comes from having life experiences that the main character has yet to have. The advice often suggests a theme. Here's an example of a student finding and marking an instance of **Words of the Wiser**:

25 Even if you have the wit to look by yourself in a bush away from the other children, there are not many bell crickets in the world. Probably you will find a girl like a grasshopper whom you think is a bell cricket.

When you see a phrase like this, pause to see if it is a **Words of the Wiser**:

"I have learned over the years . . ."

"I now realize . . ."

Anchor Question
When you notice this signpost, ask: *What's the lesson for the character?*

What kind of advice is the wiser character giving Fujio?	The wiser character is advising Fujio that there are only a few people in the world who will be special to him.
What's the life lesson?	The lesson is to seek people who capture your heart.

AHA MOMENT

Explain that **Aha Moments** are moments when a **character** experiences surprise and sudden understanding and that they provide insight into that **character** for readers. Point out the examples of phrases that can signal an Aha Moment. Then discuss the list of some of the results of such moments. If possible, share a memory about a time in which you experienced such a moment and explain how it changed the way you did or thought about something.

Call on a volunteer to read aloud the example passage. Invite students to explain that the marked statement in paragraph 22 is another way of saying, "Aha!" or "I get it!" Since this realization comes right after the detail in paragraph 21, it indicates that the realization indeed has something to do with the relationship between the boy and the girl.

Tell students that when they spot an Aha Moment, they should pause, mark it in their consumable text, and ask themselves the anchor question: *How might this change things?*

WORDS OF THE WISER

Ask students if they ever have received good advice from someone and how that advice was helpful. Then discuss the explanation of **Words of the Wiser**, pointing out that the wise words provide a lesson for the less-wise **character**—a lesson that may provide hints to the **theme**.

Read aloud the example passage and discuss the reader's comments. Tell students that the advice will become clearer when they see it in the full context of the story.

Tell students that when they spot Words of the Wiser, they should pause, mark it in their consumable text, and ask themselves the anchor question: *What's the lesson for the character?*

APPLY THE SIGNPOSTS

Have students use the selection that follows as a model text to apply the signposts. As students encounter signposts, prompt them to stop, reread, and ask themselves the anchor questions that will help them understand story details.

Tell students to continue to look for these and other signposts as they read the other selections in the unit.

WHEN STUDENTS STRUGGLE . . .

Use Syntax Surgery Some students may grasp material better if they can write and draw on a text. Explain that to use the Syntax Surgery strategy, students should look for ways in which one part of a text connects with another and then use arrows, lines, and other markings of their choice to connect them. Suggest that students use this strategy when they discover an Again and Again signpost in the text; it also can help some students mark the results of an Aha Moment or the effect of Words of the Wiser. This strategy can help students figure out context clues, as well. Invite students who use this strategy to share their thinking process with classmates who may be struggling.

Connect to the ESSENTIAL QUESTION

Author Yasunari Kawabata narrates "The Grasshopper and the Bell Cricket" from the point of view of an observer watching a group of children search for insects at night. The children's intricately designed lanterns cast a beautiful light on the scene. Kawabata uses artistic imagery to create a contemplative tone and a sense of wonder for the natural world. As he watches the innocent interplay between a boy and a girl in the group, deep emotions stir within him. He connects their sweet exchange to the broader spectrum of human experience—to the love, joy, loss, and sorrow that lie ahead of them.

ANALYZE & APPLY

THE GRASSHOPPER AND THE BELL CRICKET

Short Story by **Yasunari Kawabata**
translated by Lane Dunlop and J. Martin Holman

ESSENTIAL QUESTION:

How do we form and maintain our connections with others?

172 Unit 3

LEARNING MINDSET

Curiosity Remind students that curiosity leads to learning; it helps to expand human experience by exploring other realms. Encourage students to ask questions and to explore new ideas, books, and skills. Point out how they can use reading and writing to take them in new directions and ignite new interests. In conjunction with this selection, for example, suggest that students:

- Read more about Japanese culture and its influence on world literature.
- Explore the art of Japanese calligraphy, or artistic writing.

GET READY 

QUICK START

Nature is all around you. Every day, you experience nature in many ways—by feeling the sun on your face or the wind in your hair, or by smelling the ocean air. Take a moment to list the elements of nature you encounter each day and how they affect you. Then turn to a partner and share your thoughts.

ANALYZE SETTING AND THEME

The time and place of a short story's action is the setting. **Setting** can also include the social and cultural environment in which the action of the story takes place. "The Grasshopper and the Bell Cricket" was written in the early twentieth century by a Japanese author. Knowing some characteristics of Japanese culture will help you better understand the role of setting in the story and how the setting influences the theme.

- Traditionally nature is quite important in Japanese culture. The roots of this reverence for nature come from the Shinto religion, which honors all aspects of the natural world: water, rocks, trees, sun, birds, and insects.
- Instead of hoping to tame nature, Japanese culture aims to live in harmony with it. Japanese culture shows both respect and gratitude for nature.
- In Japan, as in other cultures, crickets are symbols of good luck. The bell cricket is an insect appreciated for its song, not its beauty.

As you read the story, pay attention to the details of setting and the atmosphere they create. Think about how this contributes to the mood of the story and helps reveal the story's **theme** or themes.

GENRE ELEMENTS: SHORT STORY

- includes the four basic elements of fiction—setting, characters, plot, and theme
- usually develops one major conflict
- can be read in one sitting

MAKE INFERENCES ABOUT THEME

The **theme** of a story, or its central idea, may express an attitude or an underlying message about life or human nature. Themes are seldom stated directly. Instead, you must make **inferences**, or logical guesses, about them using evidence in the text and your own common sense. To determine theme, think about the experiences story characters go through, and note key statements that say something about life or people in general. Then ask yourself, "What conclusions can I draw about theme using these details?"

The chart below shows three key subjects in "The Grasshopper and the Bell Cricket." As you read the story, record plot details related to these subjects. Then make inferences from these details and use your own knowledge to write three themes for the story.

KEY SUBJECTS	STORY EVIDENCE	THEMES
love		
nature		
finding someone special to you		

TEACH

QUICK START

Discuss with students how the examples make them feel, and urge them to go beyond responses of "happy" or "sad" (for example, feeling "comforted," "energized," or "refreshed"). Have partners discuss how items on their lists affect them, either positively or negatively. Invite partners to share their lists and conclusions with the class.

ANALYZE SETTING AND THEME

Have students read the information about **setting**. Tell students that an author's cultural background includes the values, beliefs, and customs of his or her society and family heritage. Drawing from his or her cultural background helps an author write with authenticity. Being familiar with an author's cultural background helps readers understand why an author's characters speak, act, and see the world as they do—all of which help point to the **theme** of a text.

Discuss the aspects of Japanese culture noted in the text. Tell students to watch for these aspects as they read "The Grasshopper and the Bell Cricket."

MAKE INFERENCES ABOUT THEME

Suggest that students think of a **theme** as a "lesson" for readers to learn. Give examples of common themes, such as "pride can lead to tragedy" or "courage means taking action even when afraid." Clarify the difference between a topic (subject) and a theme; for example, the topic of a story might be "pride" or "courage" or even "a quest for love," but none of those would be a theme. Invite students to name themes that they associate with books they have read.

Discuss the definition of **inference**. Explain that people frequently make inferences in daily life; for example, if someone comes into the house and shakes out a wet umbrella, it would be logical to infer that it is raining. Using this skill when reading involves applying prior knowledge and personal experience to details in the text. Discuss the inference-making steps; emphasize supporting inferences with textual evidence.

Encourage students to use the chart to develop their understanding of themes in "The Grasshopper and the Bell Cricket" and to provide support as they discuss and write about the story.

TEACH

CRITICAL VOCABULARY

Encourage students to read all five sentences before attempting to complete them. Remind students to look for context clues that point to the likely meaning of each Critical Vocabulary word.

Answers:

1. *sheepish*
2. *discernible*
3. *loiter*
4. *emanate*
5. *lozenge*

■ English Learner Support

Use Cognates Tell students that two of the Critical Vocabulary words have Spanish cognates: *discernible/discernible* and *emanate/emanar.* **ALL LEVELS**

LANGUAGE CONVENTIONS

Discuss the definition of **verb phrase** and the examples of verb phrases built on the main verb *read*. Also offer these examples of *to be, to have,* and *to do* as helping verbs:

- I **am reading** *Snow Country.*
- You **have read** it, too.
- **Did** you **read** *The Master of Go* instead?

As students read the story, encourage them to consider how verb phrases clarify meaning or show shifts in time.

ANNOTATION MODEL

As students read, they should review the Notice & Note coverage on Student Edition pages 170–171 if they have questions about any of the signposts. Suggest that they color-code their annotations with a different color for each signpost. They also may underline important phrases or mark key words about which they want to make comments or ask questions. Point out that students may follow this suggestion or use their own system for marking up the selections in their write-in texts.

GET READY

CRITICAL VOCABULARY

lozenge **loiter** **emanate** **sheepish** **discernible**

To see how many Critical Vocabulary words you already know, use them to complete the sentences.

1. Jason's ____________ expression showed that he had broken the vase.
2. The gravestone was so old that the writing on it was barely ____________.
3. The principal told us not to ____________ in the halls between classes.
4. Every morning, delicious smells ____________ from the corner bakery.
5. Louisa's new sweater has a large, red ____________ shape on it.

LANGUAGE CONVENTIONS

Verb Phrases In this lesson, you will learn that a sentence may have a single-word verb or a verb phrase. A **verb phrase** consists of a main verb and one or more helping verbs. Helping verbs can also be used to indicate ability or permission. Common helping verbs include all tenses of *to be, to have, to do.*

In a verb phrase, the helping verbs add meaning to the main verb.

- They can indicate the time of the main verb: I **will read** *Snow Country.*
- They can indicate obligation: You **should read** it too.
- They can indicate possibility: I **might read** *The Master of Go* instead.

ANNOTATION MODEL

NOTICE & NOTE

As you read, take notes about signposts you notice, including **Again and Again, Aha Moment**, and **Words of the Wiser**. Here is an example of how one reader responded to the opening of "The Grasshopper and the Bell Cricket."

Behind the white board fence of the school playground, from a dusky clump of bushes under the black cherry trees, <u>an insect's voice</u> could be heard. . . . One of the neighborhood children had heard an insect sing on this slope one night.

Insect → sound again and again

The narrator must love nature or bugs. Maybe the insect will be important in the story somehow.

NOTICE & NOTE

BACKGROUND

Yasunari Kawabata *(1899–1972) was born in Osaka, Japan, and became an orphan when he was quite young. This experience may have led to the themes of loneliness and death in much of his writing. He published his first story, "The Izu Dancer," in 1926, and he became a major author in Japan after his novel* Snow Country *was published in 1948. In 1968, he was awarded the Nobel Prize in Literature "for his narrative mastery, which with great sensibility expresses the essences of the Japanese mind."*

THE GRASSHOPPER AND THE BELL CRICKET

Short Story by Yasunari Kawabata
translated by Lane Dunlop and J. Martin Holman

SETTING A PURPOSE

As you read, consider the way the narrator talks about nature and describes his surroundings.

1 Walking along the tile-roofed wall of the university, I turned aside and approached the upper school. Behind the white board fence of the school playground, from a dusky clump of bushes under the black cherry trees, an insect's voice could be heard. Walking more slowly and listening to that voice, and feeling reluctant to part with it, I turned right so as not to leave the playground behind. When I turned to the left, the fence gave way to an embankment[1] planted with orange trees. At the corner, I exclaimed with surprise. My eyes gleaming at what they saw up ahead, I hurried forward with short steps.

2 At the base of the embankment was a bobbing cluster of beautiful varicolored lanterns, such as one might see at a festival in a remote country village. Without going any farther, I knew that it was a group of children on an insect chase among the bushes of the embankment. There were about twenty lanterns.

[1] **embankment:** a man-made elevated area of land used to prevent flooding or to raise a roadway.

Notice & Note

You can use the side margins to notice and note signposts in the text.

ANALYZE SETTING

Annotate: In paragraphs 1–2, mark the interactions between characters and nature.

Infer: What aspects of Japanese culture do these details illustrate?

ENGLISH LEARNER SUPPORT

Express Ideas Tell students that *motives* are the reasons that someone does something. Explain that to discuss motives, or reasons, students need to think about *why* and *because*. Provide these sentence starters and have students use them to explore motives in the beginning of the story: *The narrator changes the direction of his walk because _____. (he wants to find the insect he has heard). The children have gathered at the base of the embankment because _____. (they are on an insect hunt).* Coach students to consider characters' motives as they continue reading the story. **MODERATE/LIGHT**

TEACH

BACKGROUND

Have students read the biographical information about the author. Tell them that Kawabata's writing is strongly connected to traditional Japanese literature in its themes, mood of reflective sadness, and form. In addition, Kawabata was always interested in new literary movements and experimented with several different approaches in the early days of his career. He sought to express feeling in a way that was fresh and powerful. His style is characterized by precise and detailed images that imply meaning rather than explain it.

SETTING A PURPOSE

Direct students to use the Setting a Purpose statement to focus their reading.

ANALYZE SETTING

Remind students that traditional Japanese culture embraces living in harmony with nature. Tell students to look for details that not only describe the natural setting but also place human beings in that setting. *(**Answer:** The details illustrate an appreciation of and even reverence toward nature, especially regarding insects.)*

ENGLISH LEARNER SUPPORT

Identify Participles As students read or hear about the characters in this natural setting, have them mark words ending in *-ing*. Introduce or review the meaning of *participle*—a verb form that ends in *-ing* and that can be used as an adjective. Remind students that authors often use adjectives to help them describe the setting and characters in a story. Display paragraph 1 and point to the first sentence, showing that *walking* modifies *I*. Similarly, *walking* and *feeling* in the third sentence also modify *I*. Guide students to mark *gleaming* as a modifier of *eyes*, later in paragraph 1, and *bobbing* as a modifier of *cluster*, in paragraph 2. **MODERATE/LIGHT**

For **listening** and **reading support** for students at varying proficiency levels, see the **Text X-Ray** on pages 170C and 170D.

TEACH

MAKE INFERENCES ABOUT THEME

Explain that by describing what's in a character's imagination, an author can convey ideas that help readers understand the theme. Point out that the narrator is imagining all the details except those in the last sentence of paragraph 3. (***Possible answers:*** *People need to keep trying to achieve beauty. Expressing your unique vision is important.)*

AGAIN AND AGAIN

Remind students that the Again and Again signpost invites readers to consider the importance of **repeated words** or **images.** Ask: In paragraph 3, what appears again and again? *(the word* lantern *and images of lanterns)* Then ask students why they think the author has his narrator spend so much time describing the lanterns and the children's practice of making new ones each day. *(**Answer:** The author is showing an appreciation for the children's creativity and drive to create beauty.)*

English Learner Support

Understand Plural Nouns In several languages (including Cantonese, Hmong, Korean, Tagalog, and Vietnamese), nouns do not change form to indicate a plural. In English, most nouns are made plural by adding an *-s* to the end. Have student pairs find the plural forms of *window, carton, diamond,* and *lantern* in paragraph 3. Tell students that some nouns are irregular, and not made plural with *-s*. Challenge students to find the plural of *child.* Have partners practice spelling plurals by writing two sentences about paragraph 3. **SUBSTANTIAL/MODERATE**

CRITICAL VOCABULARY

lozenge: The narrator describes some openings in the lanterns as diamond-shaped.

ASK STUDENTS to explain the effect of having different-shaped openings in the lanterns. *(As the light from the candle shone out, it would create different patterns.)*

loiter: The narrator wants to stay just to watch.

ASK STUDENTS what the narrator observes as he loiters near the lanterns. *(Details include old-fashioned patterns, flower shapes, and the names of children who made them.)*

emanate: The narrator notices that some of the light comes from the lantern windows the children designed.

ASK STUDENTS what feelings might emanate from the narrator at this moment. *(**Possible answers:** nostalgia, joy, appreciation, wonderment, reverence)*

NOTICE & NOTE

MAKE INFERENCES ABOUT THEME

Annotate: Paragraph 3 takes place in the narrator's imagination. Mark text that expresses the narrator's admiration for the children.

Connect: Why do you think the author goes into such detail in an imaginary scene? What conclusions can you draw about theme using these details?

AGAIN AND AGAIN

Notice & Note: In paragraph 3, the narrator says that each day the children make new lanterns. Mark the explanation the narrator provides.

Connect: Why do you think the children do this?

lozenge
(lŏz´ĭnj) *n.* a diamond-shaped object.

loiter
(loi´tər) *v.* to stand or wait idly.

emanate
(ĕm´ə-nāt) *v.* to emit or radiate from.

Not only were there crimson, pink, indigo, green, purple, and yellow lanterns, but one lantern glowed with five colors at once. There were even some little red store-bought lanterns. But most of the lanterns were beautiful square ones that the children had made themselves with love and care. The bobbing lanterns, the coming together of children on this lonely slope—surely it was a scene from a fairy tale?

3 One of the neighborhood children had heard an insect sing on this slope one night. Buying a red lantern, he had come back the next night to find the insect. The night after that, there was another child. This new child could not buy a lantern. Cutting out the back and front of a small carton and papering it, he placed a candle on the bottom and fastened a string to the top. The number of children grew to five, and then to seven. They learned how to color the paper that they stretched over the windows of the cutout cartons, and to draw pictures on it. Then these wise child-artists, cutting out round, three-cornered, and **lozenge** leaf shapes in the cartons, coloring each little window a different color, with circles and diamonds, red and green, made a single and whole decorative pattern. The child with the red lantern discarded it as a tasteless object that could be bought at a store. The child who had made his own lantern threw it away because the design was too simple. The pattern of light that one had in hand the night before was unsatisfying the morning after. Each day, with cardboard, paper, brush, scissors, penknife, and glue, the children made new lanterns out of their hearts and minds. Look at my lantern! Be the most unusually beautiful! And each night, they had gone out on their insect hunts. These were the twenty children and their beautiful lanterns that I now saw before me.

4 Wide-eyed, I **loitered** near them. Not only did the square lanterns have old-fashioned patterns and flower shapes, but the names of the children who had made them were cut in squared letters of the syllabary.[2] Different from the painted-over red lanterns, others (made of thick cutout cardboard) had their designs drawn onto the paper windows, so that the candle's light seemed to **emanate** from the form and color of the design itself. The lanterns brought out the shadows of the bushes like dark light. The children crouched eagerly on the slope wherever they heard an insect's voice.

5 "Does anyone want a grasshopper?" A boy, who had been peering into a bush about thirty feet away from the other children, suddenly straightened up and shouted.

6 "Yes! Give it to me!" Six or seven children came running up. Crowding behind the boy who had found the grasshopper, they

[2] **syllabary** (sĭl´ə-bĕr-ē): A set of written characters for a language, with each character representing a syllable.

IMPROVE READING FLUENCY

Targeted Passage Use echo reading of paragraph 3 to help students use appropriate phrasing and emphasis in reading formal English. Begin by reading the paragraph aloud, emphasizing pauses and phrasing. Then have students echo your reading as you read it a second and third time, first by pausing after each phrase or clause and then reading it again with pauses after each sentence. You may choose to conclude with choral reading with everyone reading this complex paragraph aloud together.

Go to the **Reading Studio** for additional support in developing fluency.

peered into the bush. Brushing away their outstretched hands and spreading out his arms, the boy stood as if guarding the bush where the insect was. Waving the lantern in his right hand, he called again to the other children.

7 "Does anyone want a grasshopper? A grasshopper!"

8 "I do! I do!" Four or five more children came running up. It seemed you could not catch a more precious insect than a grasshopper. The boy called out a third time.

9 "Doesn't anyone want a grasshopper?"

10 Two or three more children came over.

11 "Yes. I want it."

12 It was a girl, who just now had come up behind the boy who'd discovered the insect. Lightly turning his body, the boy gracefully bent forward. Shifting the lantern to his left hand, he reached his right hand into the bush.

13 "It's a grasshopper."

14 "Yes. I'd like to have it."

15 The boy quickly stood up. As if to say "Here!" he thrust out his fist that held the insect at the girl. She, slipping her left wrist under the string of her lantern, enclosed the boy's fist with both hands. The boy quietly opened his fist. The insect was transferred to between the girl's thumb and index finger.

16 "Oh! It's not a grasshopper. It's a bell cricket." The girl's eyes shone as she looked at the small brown insect.

17 "It's a bell cricket! It's a bell cricket!" The children echoed in an envious chorus.

18 "It's a bell cricket. It's a bell cricket."

19 Glancing with her bright intelligent eyes at the boy who had given her the cricket, the girl opened the little insect cage hanging at her side and released the cricket in it.

20 "It's a bell cricket."

21 "Oh, it's a bell cricket," the boy who'd captured it muttered. Holding up the insect cage close to his eyes, he looked inside it. By the light of his beautiful many-colored lantern, also held up at eye level, he glanced at the girl's face.

22 Oh, I thought. I felt slightly jealous of the boy, and **sheepish**. How silly of me not to have understood his actions until now! Then I caught my breath in surprise. Look! It was something on the girl's breast that neither the boy who had given her the cricket, nor she who had accepted it, nor the children who were looking at them noticed.

AHA MOMENT

Notice & Note: In paragraphs 7–16, mark how the boy's behavior toward the girl is different from the way he acts toward the other children.

Compare: What can you infer about his feelings toward her?

LANGUAGE CONVENTIONS

Annotate: Mark the verb phrase that uses a form of the helping verb *have* in paragraph 21.

Connect: What is the effect of this verb phrase? What subtle shift in time does the verb phrase help express?

sheepish
(shē´pĭsh) *adj.* showing embarrassment.

AHA MOMENT

Explain to students that this signpost is characterized by a moment when a **character** has a sudden realization or finally understands something. Paragraphs 7–16 show the buildup to an Aha Moment. Ask students to identify the sentences that express the Aha Moment. *("Oh! It's not a grasshopper. It's a bell cricket.")* Remind students that a bell cricket is a symbol of good luck; then ask what the fact that the boy has given her something so special suggests. (***Answer:*** *The behavior of the boy toward the girl implies that he favors her over the other children and may have a crush on her.)*

For **speaking support** for students at varying proficiency levels, see the **Text X-Ray** on page 170D.

LANGUAGE CONVENTIONS

Point out that particular helping verbs add specific meanings to the main verb in a verb phrase. Sometimes, the "meaning" may show how actions are related in time. If students do not mention the term *past perfect tense* in their answer, you may wish to refer to the term before moving on. (***Answer:*** *The verb shows something that happened at an earlier time. The boy had captured the cricket before he realized it wasn't a grasshopper.)*

CRITICAL VOCABULARY

sheepish: The narrator feels foolish or embarrassed because he didn't immediately recognize the boy's reason for his actions.

ASK STUDENTS how someone who feels sheepish might look. *(The person might blush and avoid eye contact.)*

WHEN STUDENTS STRUGGLE . . .

Make Inferences Display an inference chart to increase comprehension of the boy's actions.

What I read	What I know	What I think
The boy asks, "Who wants a grasshopper?" but doesn't give it away at first. He finally gives it to the girl.	*He waited to give the grasshopper to the girl. I realize he wanted to give it to her all along.*	*The boy likes the girl.*

For additional support, go to the **Reading Studio** and assign the following **Level Up Tutorial: Making Inferences.**

ANALYZE SETTING AND THEME

As students review their annotations, ask: Whose name appears in red, and where does it appear? *(Kiyoko's name is in red, and it appears on Fujio's waist.)* Whose name appears in green, and where does it appear? *(Fujio's name is in green, and it appears on Kiyoko's breast.)* Point out that the narrator wonders whether this "interplay of red and green" is just an accident ("chance"). (***Answer:*** *The narrator sees that the boy likes the girl and that their names are shining from their lanterns onto each other's clothes. The narrator seems to believe that this means the two children are meant for each other or maybe that their innocence is a gift. It is important that the setting is evening: Earlier in the day, the lanterns would not be used, so the names would not be visible on the children's clothes.)*

NOTICE & NOTE

discernible
(dĭ-sûr´nə-bəl) *adj.* recognizable or noticeable.

23 In the faint greenish light that fell on the girl's breast, wasn't the name "Fujio" clearly **discernible**? The boy's lantern, which he held up alongside the girl's insect cage, inscribed his name, cut out in the green papered aperture, onto her white cotton kimono. The girl's lantern, which dangled loosely from her wrist, did not project its pattern so clearly, but still one could make out, in a trembling patch of red on the boy's waist, the name "Kiyoko." This chance interplay of red and green—if it was chance or play—neither Fujio nor Kiyoko knew about.

ANALYZE SETTING AND THEME

Annotate: In paragraphs 23 and 24, mark the places where the narrator talks about the red and green colors coming from the lanterns.

Analyze: What insight does the narrator have about the red and green colors coming from Fujio and Kiyoko's lanterns? Why is the time of day an important element of the setting?

24 Even if they remembered forever that Fujio had given her the cricket and that Kiyoko had accepted it, not even in dreams would Fujio ever know that his name had been written in green on Kiyoko's breast or that Kiyoko's name had been inscribed in red on his waist, nor would Kiyoko ever know that Fujio's name had been inscribed in green on her breast or that her own name had been written in red on Fujio's waist.

25 Fujio! Even when you have become a young man, laugh with pleasure at a girl's delight when, told that it's a grasshopper, she is given a bell cricket; laugh with affection at a girl's chagrin when, told that it's a bell cricket, she is given a grasshopper.

CRITICAL VOCABULARY

discernible: The narrator sees what the children have not noticed—the boy's name projected onto the girl's kimono.

ASK STUDENTS why this name might not be discernible to the children. *(They do not observe the interaction as closely as the narrator does; at that moment, they are more interested in observing the bell cricket.)*

APPLYING ACADEMIC VOCABULARY

☐ capacity ☑ confer ☑ emerge ☐ generate ☐ trace

Write and Discuss Have students turn to a partner to discuss the following questions based on paragraphs 23–24. Guide students to include the academic vocabulary words *confer* and *emerge* in their responses. Ask volunteers to share their responses with the class.

- According to paragraph 23, what do the lights from the lanterns **confer** upon the children?
- In paragraph 24, what realization about this moment **emerges** in the mind of the narrator? Who else—if anyone—might have this same realization?

26 Even if you have the wit to look by yourself in a bush away from the other children, there are not many bell crickets in the world. Probably you will find a girl like a grasshopper whom you think is a bell cricket.

27 And finally, to your clouded, wounded heart, even a true bell cricket will seem like a grasshopper. Should that day come, when it seems to you that the world is only full of grasshoppers, I will think it a pity that you have no way to remember tonight's play of light, when your name was written in green by your beautiful lantern on a girl's breast.

WORDS OF THE WISER

Notice & Note: In paragraphs 25–27, underline the references to grasshoppers and circle references to bell crickets.

Draw Conclusions: What is the narrator advising Fujio about?

CHECK YOUR UNDERSTANDING

Answer these questions before moving on to the **Analyze the Text** questions on the following page.

1 Which of the following is true?

- **A** The narrator is annoyed with the children.
- **B** A grasshopper is rare, and a bell cricket is common.
- **C** Fujio sees his name reflected onto Kiyoko's kimono.
- **D** The children are looking in some bushes for insects.

2 Where is Fujio when he finds the grasshopper?

- **F** He is climbing the embankment.
- **G** He is at a distance from the other children.
- **H** He is sitting next to the narrator.
- **J** He and Kiyoko are standing together.

3 What does the narrator see on the clothing of Fujio and Kiyoko?

- **A** A bell cricket
- **B** A grasshopper
- **C** The reflection of each others' names
- **D** Multicolored circle and diamond shapes

WORDS OF THE WISER

Remind students that this signpost signals that a character who is wiser than the main character is sharing insights or advice. These wise words often provide a lesson for the less-wise **character** that may suggest the **theme** of the story. In the case of "The Grasshopper and the Bell Cricket," the narrator is sharing insights on life and love. Ask: According to the story, which is more valuable: a grasshopper or a bell cricket? *(a bell cricket)* After students respond, point out that the narrator is not actually talking to Fujio; rather, he is imagining what he would like to say to Fujio. (***Answer:*** *The narrator wants Fujio to know that bell crickets are unique and not as easily found as grasshoppers; "there are not many bell crickets in the world." They represent the people who are special to another person. Grasshoppers, however, are common; "it seems that the world is only full of grasshoppers." They represent the people who do not capture a person's heart. The narrator is warning Fujio—from a distance—telling him that as he grows, he must appreciate a girl's thoughts and feelings and that finding a girl who truly will capture his heart may be very difficult.)*

CHECK YOUR UNDERSTANDING

Have students answer the questions independently.

Answers:

1. *D*
2. *G*
3. *C*

If they answer any questions incorrectly, have them reread the text to confirm their understanding. Then they may proceed to ANALYZE THE TEXT on page 180.

ENGLISH LEARNER SUPPORT

Oral Assessment Use the following questions to assess students' comprehension and speaking skills.

1. True or false: The narrator is annoyed with the children. *(false)* A grasshopper is rare, and a bell cricket is common. *(false)* Fujio sees his name reflected onto Kiyoko's kimono. *(false)* The children are looking in some bushes for insects. *(true)*
2. Where is Fujio when he finds the grasshopper? *(He is away from the other children.)*
3. What does the narrator see on the clothing of Fujio and Kiyoko? *(He sees the reflection of each other's names—light shining through cutouts on their lanterns.)* **SUBSTANTIAL/MODERATE**

APPLY

ANALYZE THE TEXT

Possible answers:

1. **DOK 3:** *The outside setting enables the author to use the Japanese cultural affinity for nature to develop his themes. The narrator's attentiveness to and appreciation of the natural world reveals this connection. The hunt for the relatively common grasshopper versus the rare bell cricket in this setting represents the theme of individuality and of the importance of being true to yourself and seeing the true self of others.*
2. **DOK 2:** *He appreciates the lanterns' colors, the care that goes into making them, and the ingenuity of the designs. The lanterns might symbolize each child's individuality or the innocence and creativity of youth. Each day the children make lanterns "out of their heart and minds," wanting their individual creation to be the most beautiful. The reflections of the lanterns are the children's spirits—all beautiful, detailed, unexpected, and glowing.*
3. **DOK 4:** *People desire things that are not common. The children are "envious" when a bell cricket is found. Understanding the value of bell crickets in Japanese culture allows readers to appreciate the children's envy.*
4. **DOK 2:** *The narrator expresses the thought that it is hard to find a person who is your bell cricket, uniquely special. Even if you are willing to go off the usual path, you are not guaranteed success—or you might fail to identify your bell cricket and settle for someone who is not your soulmate.*
5. **DOK 4:** *In the narrator's first Aha Moment, he realizes that Fujio keeps asking whether anyone wants the grasshopper because he wants Kiyoko to take it. Then the narrator sees the lighted names that appear on the two children and realizes that the children are connected in a special way that neither of them recognizes. After these realizations, the narrator's mood shifts; he becomes more pessimistic about what might lie ahead for Fujio.*

RESEARCH

Remind students to check information about the art forms in at least two reliable sources.

Extend Students may note that the children's colorful lanterns were intricately designed and had the children's names carved into them, so that the names became part of the artwork. The designs often were from nature but also included geometric elements. The children made new lanterns every day because they wanted to create lanterns that were more and more beautiful. The lanterns show the traditional Japanese reverence for nature and love of art. They also show an appreciation for individuality.

RESPOND

ANALYZE THE TEXT

Support your responses with evidence from the text. NOTEBOOK

1. **Cite Evidence** In what ways is setting important in this story? How does the setting connect to themes about love, nature, or being an individual?
2. **Interpret** The narrator spends a great deal of time observing and commenting on the children's lanterns in paragraphs 2–4. What does he appreciate about the lanterns? What could the lanterns symbolize? Cite evidence from the text to support your ideas.
3. **Analyze** In paragraphs 16–21, what opinions does the narrator express about people? Why is it important to understand the role of bell crickets in Japanese culture in order to understand the narrator's point of view? Explain using details from the story.
4. **Infer** Determine the **theme**, or underlying message, that the narrator expresses in paragraph 26 when he thinks, "Even if you have the wit to look by yourself in a bush away from the other children, there are not many bell crickets in the world. Probably you will find a girl like a grasshopper whom you think is a bell cricket."
5. **Notice & Note** The narrator experiences back-to-back Aha Moments beginning in paragraph 22. How does the story change after these Aha Moments? Cite text evidence to support your response.

RESEARCH

Japan is famous for its arts and crafts, including paper lanterns and origami. Conduct research to identify and explore the history of three Japanese art forms. Record what you learn in the chart and jot down other questions that come to you as you work.

ART FORM	INFORMATION ABOUT ART FORM AND ITS SIGNIFICANCE
Students' choices of art forms might include calligraphy, ceramics, and manga.	*Research findings will vary.*

Extend Think about the children's lanterns in the story and their qualities that impress the narrator. What do these details and the art forms you researched help you understand about Japanese culture?

LEARNING MINDSET

Try Again Remind students that the children in this story made new lanterns every day; they tried again and again to create a lantern whose beauty satisfied them. Similarly, if students find themselves dissatisfied with their follow-up work regarding this reading—for example, if they have trouble answering an Analyze the Text question or getting started on one of the activities—suggest that they try again, perhaps using a different approach or collaborating with a classmate. Encourage students to learn from their mistakes and false starts and to not give up because the effort they put in to learning is a key to understanding.

CREATE AND DISCUSS

Write an Informal Letter Write an informal letter to Fujio or Kiyoko in which you describe the results of your research on Japanese art forms and ask the questions that occurred to you during your research.

- ❑ Begin your letter with a greeting, usually "Dear . . ." and end your letter with a friendly closing such as "Sincerely," "Yours Truly," or "Regards."
- ❑ Include an introductory paragraph to explain your purpose for writing. Then write 1–3 paragraphs in the body of your letter. Go into detail about the ideas you mentioned in the introduction.
- ❑ Finally, write a concluding paragraph in which you restate your purpose for writing and add any final thoughts you may have.

Discuss with a Small Group Have a discussion on the information compiled about Japanese art forms and the questions generated during research.

- ❑ As a group, review what members learned about Japanese art forms. Discuss what these art forms might reveal about Japanese culture and connect these ideas with information in the story.
- ❑ Next, have group members share questions that came up during their research. Create a list of questions and any answers.
- ❑ Finally, review the conclusions about Japanese culture. Discuss ways it has influenced artistic and popular activities in the United States today. Remember to listen closely and respectfully to all ideas.

Go to the **Speaking and Listening Studio** for help with having a group discussion.

RESPOND TO THE ESSENTIAL QUESTION

How do we form and maintain our connections with others?

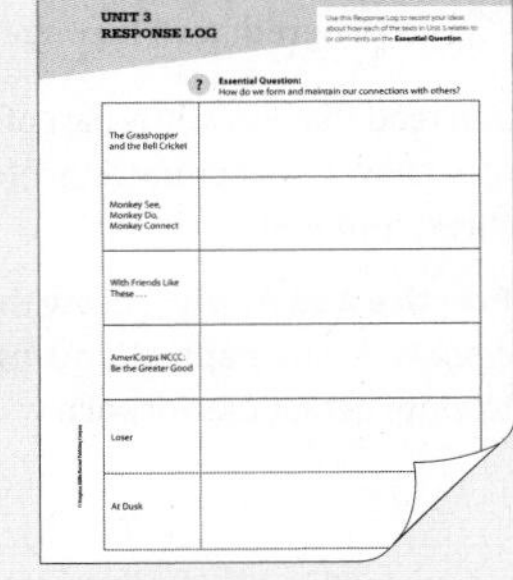

Gather Information Review your annotations and notes on "The Grasshopper and the Bell Cricket." Then add relevant information to your Response Log. As you determine which information to include, think about:

- the message in this story about connections between people
- the ways in which you form and maintain connection with friends
- how relationships with your closest friends are different from your connections with other friends and acquaintances

At the end of the unit, use your notes to help you write a short story.

ACADEMIC VOCABULARY

As you write and discuss what you learned from the short story, be sure to use the Academic Vocabulary words. Check off each of the words that you use.

- ❑ **capacity**
- ❑ **confer**
- ❑ **emerge**
- ❑ **generate**
- ❑ **trace**

APPLY

CREATE AND DISCUSS

Write an Informal Letter Have students review their findings from the Research activity. If necessary, review the parts of a friendly letter:

- heading (the writer's address, the date)
- greeting
- body (where the writer shares ideas and information)
- closing
- signature
- postscript (optional)

Remind students that they are presenting information and asking questions, but with a friendly, casual tone. You may wish to have students exchange letters and evaluate the writer's clarity and tone.

For **writing support** for students at varying proficiency levels, see the **Text X-Ray** on page 170D.

Discuss with a Small Group Before students gather into groups, suggest that they review their research and create one or two sentences about points that they want to contribute to the discussion. Students should use those points, their research notes, and notes that they made while reading the story in the group discussion. Have the group appoint someone to take notes and compile a list of questions that group members come up with. Urge students to be attentive when they are not talking and to keep the discussion positive in tone. You may wish to extend the activity by having a whole-group discussion, especially when it comes to connecting research to the story and to American interests today.

RESPOND TO THE ESSENTIAL QUESTION

Allow time for students to add details from "The Grasshopper and the Bell Cricket" to their Unit 3 Response Logs.

APPLY

CRITICAL VOCABULARY

Possible answers:

1. *You would be more likely to blush and grin because sheepish means to be embarrassed by a fault or mistake.*
2. *Yes, you can see the light because emanate means "to emit or give out."*
3. *Crayon would be more discernible because discernible means "able to be detected by one of the senses."*
4. *I hang around because loiter means "stay in a place without any obvious intent."*
5. *A kite is more lozenge-shaped than an egg would be; a kite has a diamond-like shape.*

VOCABULARY STRATEGY:
Context Clues

Possible answers:

- *discarded: got rid of something unwanted*
- *crouched: stooped or bent down*
- *inscribed: marked or wrote*

RESPOND

WORD BANK
lozenge
loiter
emanate
sheepish
discernable

CRITICAL VOCABULARY

Practice and Apply Answer the questions to show your understanding of the Critical Vocabulary words. Use a dictionary or thesaurus as needed.

1. Which would you be more likely to do if you are feeling **sheepish**: blush and grin or scowl and shout? Why?
2. If a room **emanates** light, can you see the light or not? Why?
3. Which would be more **discernible**, something written in crayon or in invisible ink? Why?
4. If I **loiter**, do I run away, or do I hang around? Why?
5. Which item has a **lozenge** shape: a kite or an egg? Why?

VOCABULARY STRATEGY:
Context Clues

Go to the **Vocabulary Studio** for more on context clues.

When you read, you can use **context clues** to understand unfamiliar words. **Context** is how a word relates to the overall meaning of a sentence, paragraph, or piece of writing.
Here are some types of context clues you may find in texts:

SYNONYMS OR DEFINITION	CONTRAST	EXAMPLES
The text may provide a definition or a synonym.	The text may give an antonym, or contrasting information.	The text may list examples of the word.

Look at this example from the story:

> **Then these wise child-artists, cutting out round, three-cornered, and lozenge leaf shapes in the cartons . . .**

You read that *lozenge* is part of a list of shapes, an example of a shape. You also know from contrasting information that a *lozenge* is not round or three-cornered.

Practice and Apply Locate these words in the story: *discarded* (paragraph 3), *crouched* (paragraph 4), and *inscribed* (paragraph 23). Then use context clues to write definitions for each word. Check your definitions in a dictionary.

ENGLISH LEARNER SUPPORT

Use Context Clues Provide students with additional practice in using context clues. Display the sentences with the following words: *reluctant* (paragraph 1), *bobbing* (paragraph 2), *tasteless* (paragraph 3), and *chagrin* (paragraph 25). Have students work in pairs to determine each word's meaning as it is used in the story by analyzing context clues and then checking their definition in a print or digital dictionary. Have partners meet with other partners to compare their work. **MODERATE**

LANGUAGE CONVENTIONS:
Verb Phrases

Verb phrases are a combination of one or more helping verbs and a main verb. In "The Grasshopper and the Bell Cricket," Yasunari Kawabata uses many verb phrases to express shifts in time.

By using the verb phrase *might see*, the author sets up a comparison—between the lanterns on the embankment and lanterns at a festival.

> **At the base of the embankment was a bobbing cluster of beautiful varicolored lanterns, such as one might see at a festival in a remote country village.**

Here, the author uses the verb phrase *had made* to show that the children made the lanterns in the past—prior to the narrator seeing them.

> **But most of the lanterns were beautiful square ones which the children had made themselves with love and care.**

Other words can interrupt the parts of a verb phrase. Here, *does* and *want* create the verb phrase, which is interrupted by the subject, a structure common with questions.

> **Does anyone want a grasshopper?**

The table shows some common helping verbs. You can use these verbs in their different forms in verb phrases.

COMMON HELPING VERBS IN VERB PHRASES		
be	can	am
do	have	may
might	shall	should
will	would	could

Practice and Apply With a partner, review the letters you created in response to the selection's Create and Discuss assignment. Note the use of verb phrases in your letters. Help each other revise verb phrases to make your writing more effective in showing shifts in time, or work together to create sentences that contain verb phrases. Remember to consider the tense of the verbs as you are revising.

Go to the **Grammar Studio** for more on verb phrases.

APPLY

LANGUAGE CONVENTIONS:
Verb Phrases

Discuss the information about verb phrases and the example of each usage. Reinforce these ideas by assigning groups of students one or more paragraphs from the story and having them list the verb phrases they find. Have them discuss how, in each case, the helping verb(s) clarify meaning, show a shift in time, or allow for a question to be asked. You may also want to point out that the story contains many verb phrases, used for a variety of purposes.

Practice and Apply When students complete their revisions, ask them to underline at least two verb phrases they added to their work. *(Students' revisions will vary.)*

ENGLISH LEARNER SUPPORT

Comprehend Language Structures Use the following supports with students at varying proficiency levels:

- Read the helping verbs aloud. Then read the examples, having students raise their hands when they hear a helping verb. **SUBSTANTIAL**
- Have pairs read the examples on the student page, identifying the helping verb in each underlined verb phrase. Then have pairs reread paragraph 24 and underline all verb phrases. **MODERATE**
- Explain that some helping verbs are called **modal verbs** because they signal modality—that is, likelihood, ability, permission, or obligation. For instance, in the first example, *might* signals that one is "likely" to see such lanterns at a village festival not "certain to." Share these common modal verbs: *can/could, may/might, must, will/would,* and *shall/should*. As a group, make distinctions among likelihood, ability, permission, and obligation. Then have pairs decide what each verb you shared expresses—likelihood, ability, permission, or obligation. **LIGHT**

MONKEY SEE, MONKEY DO, MONKEY CONNECT

Science Writing by Frans de Waal

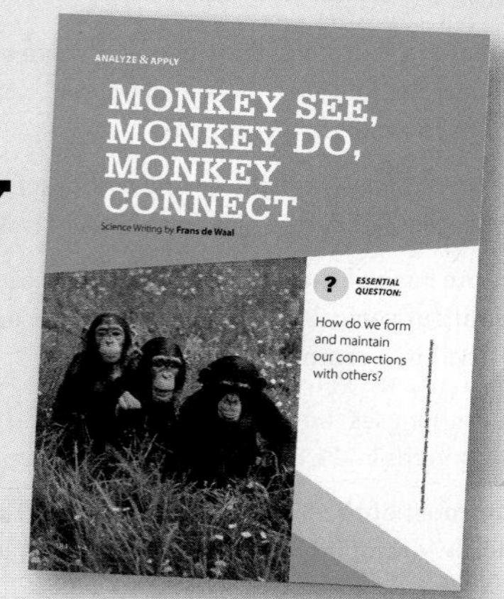

GENRE ELEMENTS

SCIENCE WRITING

Explain that a **claim** is the author's position on a topic or issue. The science article "Monkey See, Monkey Do, Monkey Connect" is an informational text that states a specific claim about the behavior of human beings. Although Frans de Waal is an expert on the topic, it is not enough for him to simply state his claim and expect readers to accept what he is saying. He must support his claim throughout the essay with **reasons**—declarations made to justify an action, decision or belief—and with **evidence** such as facts, details, and examples.

LEARNING OBJECTIVES

- Read complex subject matter using a variety of strategies.
- Identify a writer's claim and evaluate evidence used to back it up.
- Write a position statement that states a claim and support it with reasons and evidence.
- Research questions generated by the selection.
- Take part in a debate as part of a team.
- Use Greek roots to define words and understand related words.
- Use a colon to introduce a list, quotation, or independent clause.
- **Language** Use context clues to determine the meanings of scientific and domain-specific words.

TEXT COMPLEXITY

Quantitative Measures	**Monkey See, Monkey Do, Monkey Connect** Lexile: 1160L
Qualitative Measures	**Ideas Presented** Single level of complex meaning.
	Structures Used Organization of main ideas and details complex, but clearly stated and generally sequential.
	Language Used Many unfamiliar, academic, and domain-specific words.
	Knowledge Required Requires understanding of some science concepts.

RESOURCES

- Unit 3 Response Log
-  Selection Audio
-  Close Read Screencasts: Modeled Discussions
-  Reading Studio: Notice & Note
-  Level Up Tutorials: Evidence; Analyzing Arguments
-  Writing Studio: Building Effective Support
-  Speaking and Listening Studio: Introduction: Collaborative Discussions
-  Vocabulary Studio: Words from Greek
-  Grammar Studio: Module 11: Lesson 8: Colons
-  "Monkey See, Monkey Do, Monkey Connect" Selection Test

SUMMARIES

English

Frans de Waal presents the claim that humans, like other primates, learn by observing others. To support his claim, he cites numerous examples from the human and animal world. He references empathy, synchronization in the form of laughter and yawn contagion, the herd instinct, and mimicry (imitation) as key behaviors that lead to social bonding and connect human beings with one another.

Spanish

Frans de Waal presenta el argumento de que los primates y los humanos aprenden al observar a los demás. Para apoyar su argumento, cita muchos ejemplos del mundo humano y el mundo animal. Hace referencia a la empatía, a la sincronización de la risa y el contagio de los bostezos, el instinto de manada y la mímica (imitación) como comportamientos clave que llevan a la unión social y a la conexión que los humanos tienen unos con otros.

SMALL-GROUP OPTIONS

Have students work in small groups and pairs to read and discuss the selection.

Reciprocal Teaching

- After students have read "Monkey See, Monkey Do, Monkey Connect," provide them with a list of generic question stems. (For example: *What is the author's claim about _____? Why do you think _____? What does the phrase _____ mean? What is the main idea in paragraph X?*)
- Ask students to work independently to create at least two questions about the reading selection using the stems.
- Group students into teams of three or four. Ask each student to present their questions for group discussion.
- Guide groups to answer each question, using text evidence to support their answers.

Three-Minute Review

- After students have read the selection, facilitate a whole-class discussion about the author's claim.
- Ask students the following question: Has the author presented valid reasons and enough support for his claim?
- Direct students to work with a partner. Then set a timer for three minutes.
- Guide student pairs to review the selection and their notes, and then write clarifying questions in response to the prompt.
- When the three minutes are up, ask student pairs to share their thoughts with the class.

Text X-Ray: English Learner Support

for "Monkey See, Monkey Do, Monkey Connect"

Use the Text X-Ray and the supports and scaffolds in the Teacher's Edition to help guide students at different proficiency levels through the selection.

INTRODUCE THE SELECTION

DISCUSS TYPES OF EVIDENCE

Students will need to identify reasons and evidence the author presents to support a claim. Begin a discussion by asking students to distinguish between a fact and an opinion, such as: "The book is on the desk" versus "The book is interesting." As a class, review the various types of evidence that the author may use. Have students write the following definitions in their notebook:

- **fact:** information that is true because it can be proven
- **statistic:** numbers or amounts that people study to find patterns
- **example:** a particular object, situation, action, or person that explains or supports an idea
- **expert opinion:** the belief of a professional who has knowledge on a topic

Engage students' prior knowledge about types of evidence by using frames—for example:

- *If something can be proven, it is a* ____.
- *The percentage of high school students who graduate is a* ____.
- *What a doctor says about the flu season is an example of an* ____.

Encourage students to refer to this list as they read and discuss the selection.

CULTURAL REFERENCES

The following names and terms may be unfamiliar to students:

- *Yerkes Primate Center* (paragraph 2): a place where scientists do research using monkeys and apes
- *ghost box* (paragraph 11): a box that opens and closes without a person touching it
- *Wolfgang Köhler* (paragraph 15): German psychologist who studied chimpanzees

LISTENING

Use Context Clues

Discuss with students the value of using context clues to understand the meaning of complex language. Remind students that context clues can appear immediately before or after the unfamiliar word, in nearby sentences, or in a different paragraph.

Read aloud paragraph 16. Use the following supports with students at varying proficiency levels:

- Define *matriarch*. Help students copy *matriarch* and *family* onto notecards. Reread paragraph 16 aloud. Have students hold up the "matriarch" card when they hear that word and the "family" card when they hear words related to family. **SUBSTANTIAL**
- Define *matriarch*. Ask students whether the matriarch in the paragraph is a human or a female animal. *(a female animal—"an old monkey")* **MODERATE**
- Have students write down words and phrases they heard that helped them understand the word *matriarch*. *("her children started doing the same," "her grandchildren," "the entire family")* **LIGHT**

SPEAKING

Participate in a Debate

Work with student teams as they prepare for the debate activity presented on Student Edition page 195.

Use the following supports with students at varying proficiency levels:

- Model an opening statement for the debate. For example: *I/we believe that* ____. Coach students in creating their opening statements. **SUBSTANTIAL**
- Pair student teams. Have each student on a team practice giving the team's opening statement to the other team. Remind students to speak clearly and make eye contact with the audience. **MODERATE**
- Ask students to take turns stating supporting reasons and evidence. Have team members offer constructive criticism to improve delivery. **LIGHT**

READING

Analyze and Evaluate an Author's Claim

Tell students that authors of scientific articles may support a claim with multiple reasons and evidence in the form of facts, examples, explanations, definitions, direct quotations, and other details.

Work with students to reread paragraphs 16–18. Use the following supports with students at varying proficiency levels:

- Pantomime the actions of the chimp drinking and walking on his wrist (or find photos). Pair words such as *slurp, underarm,* and *hobble* with visuals. Have students do the same to understand the term *mimicry*. **SUBSTANTIAL**
- Guide students to find evidence to support the claim that we, and animals, learn by observing others. Draw their attention to the introductory phrases "For example" and "There is also the case." Ask: Which kind of evidence do these phrases indicate? **MODERATE**
- Ask students to locate three pieces of evidence and identify the type of evidence each represents. Have students underline the words or phrase that helped them know. **LIGHT**

WRITING

Take a Position

Review with students the writing activity on Student Edition page 195. Work with students as they write a position statement about the ways in which humans relate to one another as described in the article.

Use the following supports with students at varying proficiency levels:

- Ask questions to elicit language from students: Are humans separate or connected? *(connected)* Do humans learn alone or from one another? *(from one another)* Then guide students to write a position statement. *(Humans are connected to one another and learn from one another.)* **SUBSTANTIAL**
- Provide sentence frames such as the following that students can use as they write their position statement: *I agree/disagree with* ____. *The reason I believe* ____ *is* ____. *The facts that support my idea are* ____. *In my opinion,* ____. **MODERATE**
- Remind students that scientific writing often uses technical vocabulary. Encourage students to use technical terms in their writing and check that they are being used appropriately. **LIGHT**

Connect to the ESSENTIAL QUESTION

In this selection, Frans de Waal claims that humans, like other primates, are naturally influenced by what we see those around us do. This helps us understand and share other people's feelings and it helps us build and maintain connections with others.

Ask students to think about how their own actions are influenced by others, including friends, family members, and even people they don't know, such as celebrities. For example, ask: Have you ever watched a sports event during which you have imitated the actions of a certain player? Have you ever lip-synched (matched lip movements with) favorite songs or speeches? Encourage students to share personal examples of how they identify with or are influenced by other people. Ask if they think their behavior helped build a connection with another person or a group.

ANALYZE & APPLY

MONKEY SEE, MONKEY DO, MONKEY CONNECT

Science Writing by **Frans de Waal**

ESSENTIAL QUESTION:

How do we form and maintain our connections with others?

LEARNING MINDSET

Curiosity Remind students that curiosity leads to learning. This selection introduces scientific concepts—for example, yawn contagion and herd instinct—that students may not have heard of previously. Encourage students to ask questions about these concepts and any other unfamiliar terms and to seek out additional information about them using print and online resources.

QUICK START

Have you ever been with a group when one of you got the giggles, and soon no one could stop laughing? Share your experience with a partner or the class.

MONITOR COMPREHENSION

When you **monitor** comprehension, you check your own understanding as you read. You can do this by using strategies, including the ones below. You might have to modify the strategy you use to suit your own needs:

STRATEGY	WHAT IT MEANS
Use background knowledge	Consider what you already know as you read and how this helps you understand the text.
Reread	Read a paragraph, page, or section again to see what you missed or to clarify an idea.
Annotate	Mark important facts, key passages, or vocabulary you want to remember.
Ask questions	Look for answers to questions such as *what, why,* and *how* as you read the text.

GENRE ELEMENTS: SCIENCE WRITING

- introduces a key idea, sometimes a surprising one
- uses analogies or examples to illustrate concepts
- may use scientific terminology or refer to established theories
- generally sticks to facts, not opinions

ANALYZE AUTHOR'S CLAIM

A **claim** is the author's position on a topic or issue. The science article "Monkey See, Monkey Do, Monkey Connect" is an informational text that states a specific claim about the behavior of human beings. Although Frans de Waal is an expert on the topic, it is not enough for him to simply state his claim and expect readers to accept what he is saying. He must **support** his claim throughout the essay with reasons, or declarations made to justify an action, decision, or belief; and with **evidence**, such as facts, details, and examples. He should end with a convincing **conclusion**.

As a reader, it is your job to consider an author's claim and determine if the claim is valid.

First, identify the author's credibility, or if the author is a believable source.

- *Is the author an expert on the topic?*
- *What qualifications does the author have to speak about the topic?*

Next, note the reasons and evidence the author provides.

- *Do the reasons make sense? Are they logical?*
- *Is the evidence relevant?*

Finally, decide if you agree with the author's claim based on the reasons and evidence. You can either defend the author's claim or challenge it if the reasons and evidence do not lead you to the same conclusion. Either way, you will use text evidence to support your position.

TEACH

QUICK START

To get the conversation started, share a funny personal story, video, or joke with the class. See how many students you can get to giggle or laugh. If a lot of students begin to join in, ask if they believe the laughter was contagious. Then invite students to share their experiences with the class.

MONITOR COMPREHENSION

Discuss the strategies shown in the table and when and how students might apply them. Note that there is not a single preferred strategy. Some students may be most comfortable with annotating, others with notetaking or with freewriting, and many with using a combination of strategies. Point out that another way to check one's understanding of a text is to write a summary sentence for each paragraph after reading it. If students have trouble writing a sentence, they could also use the listed strategies until they can succinctly summarize the paragraph's meaning.

ANALYZE AUTHOR'S CLAIM

Review the terms *claim, reasons,* and *evidence*. Share this graphic organizer to show how ideas are organized in an argument:

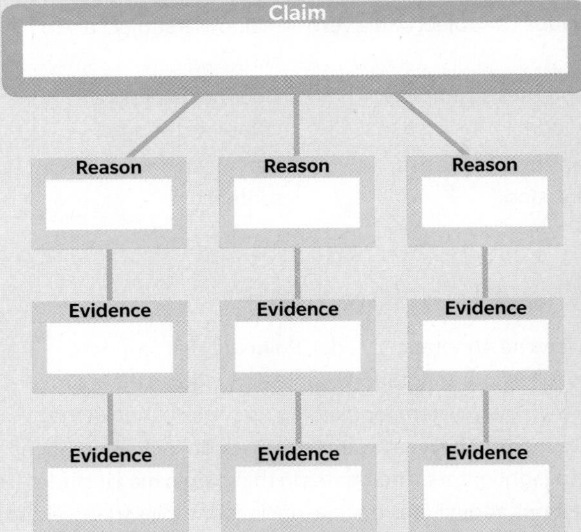

ENGLISH LEARNER SUPPORT

Understand Directionality Reinforce the directionality of English by reviewing how to read the Monitor Comprehension chart. Explain that each column heading applies to the text in all the rows beneath it. To read the chart, students should begin at the top left. The top row, left column introduces the first strategy—use background knowledge. After reading this strategy, students should track to the right to read a description of that strategy. Then they should move on to the middle row, left column. Ask students to trace with a finger the order in which a reader would read the information in the chart. **SUBSTANTIAL**

TEACH

CRITICAL VOCABULARY

Encourage students to read all the sentences before deciding which word best completes each one. Remind them to look for context clues that fit with the precise meaning of each word.

Answers:

1. *contagion*
2. *synchronization*
3. *cognition*
4. *empathy*
5. *implication*

English Learner Support

Use Cognates Tell students that all of the Critical Vocabulary words have Spanish cognates: *contagion/contagio, synchronization/sincronización, cognition/cognición, empathy/empatía, implication/implicatión*.
ALL LEVELS

LANGUAGE CONVENTIONS

Review the information about colons. Ask students if they know the difference between an independent and a dependent clause. If necessary, clarify using a chart like the following:

Independent Clause	Dependent Clause
Includes a subject and a verb	Includes a subject and a verb
Expresses a complete thought	Does not express a complete thought
Can stand alone as a sentence	Cannot stand alone as a sentence

ANNOTATION MODEL

Review the Annotation Model. Point out that students may follow the annotation suggestions shown there or use their own system for marking up the selection in their write-in text. They may want to color-code their annotations using highlighters. Their notes in the margin may include questions about ideas that are unclear or topics they want to learn more about.

GET READY

CRITICAL VOCABULARY

empathy **synchronization** **contagion** **cognition** **implication**

To see how many Critical Vocabulary words you already know, use them to complete the sentences.

1. When Catherine came to class with the flu, the __________ quickly spread.
2. I was impressed by the __________ of the swimmers' movements.
3. Humans can think through more difficult problems because they have a higher capacity for __________ than other primates.
4. __________ is the ability to understand what another person is feeling.
5. What is the __________ of the new dress code on outfits for picture day?

LANGUAGE CONVENTIONS

Colons A colon can introduce a list, explanation, or quotation; emphasize an idea; or connect ideas. Use a colon only after an independent clause.

correct	For french toast, you need five ingredients: eggs, bread, butter, cinnamon, and maple syrup.
incorrect	For french toast you need: eggs, bread, butter, cinnamon, and maple syrup.

As you read the article, note the author's use of colons and their function.

ANNOTATION MODEL

NOTICE & NOTE

As you read, note the author's claims and the reasons and evidence he gives to support them. Mark information that supports your own ideas; and record questions you have. In the model, you can see one reader's notes about "Monkey See, Monkey Do, Monkey Connect."

What intrigues me most about laughter is how it spreads. It's almost impossible not to laugh when everybody else is. There have been laughing epidemics, in which no one could stop and some even died in a prolonged fit. There are laughing churches and laugh therapies based on the healing power of laughter. The must-have toy of 1996—Tickle Me Elmo—laughed hysterically after being squeezed three times in a row. All of this because we love to laugh and can't resist joining laughing around us.

Is this going to be part of the author's claim?

People have died from laughing?

Is this a reason? Or evidence?

NOTICE & NOTE

BACKGROUND

Frans B.M. de Waal *(b. 1948) was born in the Netherlands. Trained in biology, de Waal analyzes the behaviors and social interactions of primates, an order of mammals that includes monkeys, chimpanzees, gorillas, lemurs, and homo sapiens, or humans. He is the director of The Living Links Center at the Yerkes National Primate Research Center in Lawrenceville, Georgia, and the author of numerous books including* Chimpanzee Politics.

MONKEY SEE, MONKEY DO, MONKEY CONNECT

Science Writing by Frans de Waal

SETTING A PURPOSE

As you read, monitor your comprehension by annotating, using background knowledge, rereading, and asking questions as appropriate.

1 What intrigues me most about laughter is how it spreads. It's almost impossible not to laugh when everybody else is. There have been laughing epidemics, in which no one could stop and some even died in a prolonged fit. There are laughing churches and laugh therapies based on the healing power of laughter. The must-have toy of 1996—Tickle Me Elmo—laughed hysterically after being squeezed three times in a row. All of this because we love to laugh and can't resist joining laughing around us. This is why comedy shows on television have laugh tracks and why theater audiences are sometimes sprinkled with "laugh plants": people paid to produce raucous laughing at any joke that comes along.

Notice & Note

You can use the side margins to notice and note signposts in the text.

MONITOR COMPREHENSION

Annotate: Mark context clues in paragraph 1 that suggest the meaning of the word *raucous.*

Infer: How would you define *raucous* as it is used in the last sentence of paragraph 1?

BACKGROUND

Have students read the Background note. Explain that chimpanzees share more genetic traits with humans than other primates do. In fact, humans and chimpanzees share about 98 percent of the same DNA. Researchers have been studying primate behavior for nearly a century; this research has taught us much about human beings as well as other primates.

SETTING A PURPOSE

Direct students to use the Setting a Purpose prompt to focus their reading.

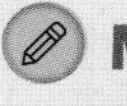

MONITOR COMPREHENSION

Remind students that **context clues** are words that are used in a sentence or surrounding sentences in a way that suggests the meaning of another word. This paragraph offers several context clues to the word *raucous*. One is that students may be familiar with laugh tracks from watching comedy shows, so they can imagine that type of laughter. Another clue is that Elmo laughs "hysterically," which is loud and manic. (***Answer:*** Raucous *means "loud, uproarious, and enthusiastic."*)

IMPROVE READING FLUENCY

Targeted Passage Use echo reading to help students practice appropriate phrasing and emphasis in reading paragraph 1. Begin by reading the paragraph aloud, emphasizing pauses and phrasing. Then have students echo your reading as you read it a second and third time, first by pausing after each phrase or clause and then by pausing after each sentence. You may choose to conclude with a choral reading, having all students read the paragraph aloud together.

Go to the **Reading Studio** for additional support in developing fluency.

TEACH

WORD GAPS

Model rereading the second sentence in paragraph 2 and thinking aloud. For example, "Hearing the chimps laugh probably makes the writer laugh, too. He says he 'cannot suppress a chuckle.' So *suppress* could mean "to stop doing something." Substituting the word "stop" makes sense. The writer could have written, 'When I hear the chimps laugh, I cannot stop a chuckle myself.'" (***Answer:*** *It could be used in everyday conversation, such as "to suppress anger when someone cuts in front of you in line" or "to suppress a desire to call out in the middle of class."*)

ENGLISH LEARNER SUPPORT

Determine Meaning Draw students' attention to the second sentence in paragraph 3. Then read footnote 1, which offers background information about the reference to Robinson Crusoe.

To help students understand the meaning of this reference, use the following supports with students at varying proficiency levels.

- Show an image of Crusoe, alone on the island, and talk about it using the words *alone* and *solitary*. Compare it to an image of a group of people laughing. **SUBSTANTIAL**
- Ask pairs of students to identify context clues to help them understand the contrast the author is making. *(the words "instead of" and "separate islands")* **MODERATE**
- Ask students to paraphrase the second sentence in paragraph 3. *(People aren't like Robinson Crusoe. We don't live all by ourselves, far away from other people. Instead, we are connected to one another through our bodies and our feelings.)* **LIGHT**

NOTICE & NOTE

WORD GAPS

Notice & Note: In paragraph 2, what clues from the sentence help you understand the word *suppress*?

Infer: Do you think this is a technical term, or could it be used in everyday conversation?

2 The infectiousness of laughter even works across species. Below my office window at the Yerkes Primate Center, I often hear my chimps laugh during rough-and-tumble games, and I cannot suppress a chuckle myself. It's such a happy sound. Tickling and wrestling are the typical laugh triggers for apes, and probably the original ones for humans. The fact that tickling oneself is notoriously ineffective attests to its social significance. And when young apes put on their play face, their friends join in with the same expression as rapidly and easily as humans do with laughter.

3 Shared laughter is just one example of our primate sensitivity to others. Instead of being Robinson Crusoes sitting on separate islands,[1] we're all interconnected, both bodily and emotionally. This may be an odd thing to say in the West, with its tradition of individual freedom and liberty, but *Homo sapiens*[2] is remarkably easily swayed in one emotional direction or another by its fellows.

[1] **Robinson Crusoes . . . islands:** Crusoe, the title character of Daniel Defoe's 1719 novel, was stranded alone on a tropical island.

[2] ***Homo sapiens*** (hō′mō sā′pē-ənz): the species of primates that includes humans.

WHEN STUDENTS STRUGGLE . . .

Understand Reasons Versus Evidence To help students understand the difference between reasons and evidence, explain that reasons usually answer the question "why" and evidence should answer the question "how," or "what proof is there?"

Claim: It is valuable to study the behavior of primates such as chimps and apes. **Reason:** It is valuable because we can learn a lot about human behavior, too. **Evidence:** All primates re-create the movements they see others do. Parents watching their child sing will mouth the words of the song; one ape observes and then imitates another's actions.

For additional support, go to the **Reading Studio** and assign the following  **Level Up Tutorial: Evidence.**

4 This is precisely where **empathy** and sympathy start—not in the higher regions of imagination, or the ability to consciously reconstruct how we would feel if we were in someone else's situation. It began much more simply, with the **synchronization** of bodies: running when others run, laughing when others laugh, crying when others cry, or yawning when others yawn. Most of us have reached the incredibly advanced stage at which we yawn even at the mere mention of yawning—as you may be doing right now!—but this is only after lots of face-to-face experience.

5 Yawn **contagion**, too, works across species. Virtually all animals show the peculiar "paroxystic respiratory cycle characterized by a standard cascade of movements over a five- to ten-second period," which is the way the yawn has been defined. I once attended a lecture on involuntary pandiculation (the medical term for stretching and yawning) with slides of horses, lions, and monkeys—and soon the entire audience was pandiculating. Since it so easily triggers a chain reaction, the yawn reflex opens a window onto mood transmission,

LANGUAGE CONVENTIONS

Annotate: Mark the sentence in paragraph 4 in which a colon introduces a list of examples.

Analyze: What does the list that follows the colon give examples of?

empathy (ĕm´pə-thē) *n.* the ability to understand and identify with another's feelings.

synchronization (sĭng-krə-nĭ-zā´shən) *n.* coordinated, simultaneous action.

contagion (kən-tā´jən) *n.* the spreading from one to another.

ENGLISH LEARNER SUPPORT

Determine Technical Meanings Draw students' attention to the technical word *pandiculation* in paragraph 5 and the definition the author provides: "stretching and yawning." Then point out the word *pandiculating* later in the same sentence, asking students to restate the sentence in which it appears in their own words. *(Soon the whole audience was stretching and yawning.)* Guide students to see that *pandiculating* is the verb form of *pandiculation*. **MODERATE/LIGHT**

TEACH

LANGUAGE CONVENTIONS

Remind students that although a **colon** is similar to a period, its usage differs. In the second sentence of paragraph 4, a colon is used after an independent clause in order to introduce a list. (***Answer:*** *The phrases that follow the colon are examples of ways in which people unconsciously synchronize their physical actions with the actions of others.)*

CRITICAL VOCABULARY

empathy: Human beings have the ability to imagine themselves in someone else's situation.

ASK STUDENTS how "running when others run" relates to empathy. *(Moving our bodies in the same way others do is the first stage of empathy, or being able to imagine how others feel.)*

synchronization: Humans and other primates tend to match the actions of other individuals.

ASK STUDENTS how synchronization explains some primate behavior. *(Humans and other primates laugh or yawn when others do so.)*

contagion: De Waal describes how yawning can spread from one individual to another like an infectious disease.

ASK STUDENTS how de Waal's story about the lecture on yawning illustrates the idea of contagion. *(Just looking at pictures of animals yawning caused people in the room to start yawning—the action spread through the entire audience.)*

TEACH

MONITOR COMPREHENSION

Have partners review paragraphs 4–6 and identify any references to yawning. Also have students reread the definition of *contagion* in the side note on page 189. Then ask students to use these clues to explain what the term *yawn contagion* means. (***Answer:*** *Yawn contagion is the tendency of a person or an animal to yawn after seeing another person or animal yawn.)*

ENGLISH LEARNER SUPPORT

Suffixes Learning the meanings of suffixes can help students unpack the meaning of many challenging but ultimately accessible words. On the board, write the suffixes *-al, -ive, -ous,* and *-tion/-ation*. After each suffix, note its meaning. (*-al: "act or process of"; -ive: "having the nature of"; -ous: "characterized by"; -tion/-ation: "state of being")*

Ask students to work in pairs to define these words from the selection: *ineffective, emotional, imagination,* and *various*. Discuss how the suffix helps them understand the meanings of these words.

MODERATE/LIGHT

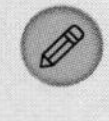

ANALYZE AUTHOR'S CLAIM

Remind students that **paraphrasing** means restating something the author said using other words. Encourage students to use their own words in addition to repeating words the author used. Tell students that paraphrasing what they read (and what they hear) is an effective way to ensure they understood what they read or heard.

(***Answer:*** *Paragraph 8 describes an example of the herd instinct, when a group of baboons in a zoo stood atop a rock staring in the same direction for a week. No one ever figured out why. Paragraph 9 describes British Prime Minister Tony Blair unconsciously imitating former President George W. Bush's cowboy swagger. Primate sensitivity is the tendency of primates to unconsciously imitate the movements, actions, and habits of nearby others of the same species.)*

NOTICE & NOTE

MONITOR COMPREHENSION

Annotate: Mark clues in paragraph 4–6 that hint at the meaning of *yawn contagion.*

Analyze: What is *yawn contagion?*

ANALYZE AUTHOR'S CLAIM

Annotate: Paragraphs 8 and 9 each provide an example supporting the author's claim that primates, including humans, share primate sensitivity. Mark lines that summarize each example.

Summarize: Paraphrase each example, then define *primate sensitivity.*

an essential part of empathy. This makes it all the more intriguing that chimpanzees yawn when they see others do so.

6 Yawn contagion reflects the power of unconscious synchrony, which is as deeply ingrained in us as in many other animals. Synchrony may be expressed in the copying of small body movements, such as a yawn, but also occurs on a larger scale, involving travel or movement. It is not hard to see its survival value. You're in a flock of birds and one bird suddenly takes off. You have no time to figure out what's going on: You take off at the same instant. Otherwise, you may be lunch.

7 Or your entire group becomes sleepy and settles down, so you too become sleepy. Mood contagion serves to coordinate activities, which is crucial for any traveling species (as most primates are). If my companions are feeding, I'd better do the same, because once they move off, my chance to forage will be gone. The individual who doesn't stay in tune with what everyone else is doing will lose out like the traveler who doesn't go to the restroom when the bus has stopped.

8 The herd instinct produces weird phenomena. At one zoo, an entire baboon troop gathered on top of their rock, all staring in exactly the same direction. For an entire week they forgot to eat, mate, and groom. They just kept staring at something in the distance that no one could identify. Local newspapers were carrying pictures of the monkey rock, speculating that perhaps the animals had been frightened by a UFO. But even though this explanation had the unique advantage of combining an account of primate behavior with proof of UFOs, the truth is that no one knew the cause except that the baboons clearly were all of the same mind.

Close Read

9 Finding himself in front of the cameras next to his pal President George W. Bush, former British prime minister Tony Blair—known to walk normally at home—would suddenly metamorphose into a distinctly un-English cowboy. He'd swagger with arms hanging loose and chest puffed out. Bush, of course, strutted like this all the time and once explained how, back home in Texas, this is known as "walking." Identification is the hook that draws us in and makes us adopt the situation, emotions, and behavior of those we're close to. They become role models: We empathize with them and emulate[3] them. Thus children often walk like the same-sex parent or mimic their tone of voice when they pick up the phone.

10 How does one chimp imitate another? Does he identify with the other and absorb its body movements? Or could it be that he doesn't need the other and instead focuses on the problem faced by the other? This can be tested by having a chimpanzee show another how to open a puzzle box with goodies inside. Maybe all that the

[3] **emulate:** to imitate or behave like.

CLOSE READ SCREENCAST

Modeled Discussions In their eBook, have students view the Close Read Screencast, in which readers discuss and annotate the following key passage:

- the discussion of the herd instinct (paragraph 8)

As a class, view and discuss this video. Then have students pair up to do an independent close read of an additional passage—the way our bodies and minds connect us in society (paragraph 19). Students can record their answers on the Close Read Practice PDF.

Close Read Practice PDF

watching ape needs to understand is how the thing works. He may notice that the door slides to the side or that something needs to be lifted up. The first kind of imitation involves reenactment of observed manipulations; the second merely requires technical know-how.

11 Thanks to ingenious studies in which chimps were presented with a so-called ghost box, we know which of these two explanations is correct. A ghost box derives its name from the fact that it magically opens and closes by itself so that no actor is needed. If technical know-how were all that mattered, such a box should suffice. But in fact, letting chimps watch a ghost box until they're bored to death—with its various parts moving and producing rewards hundreds of times—doesn't teach them anything.

12 To learn from others, apes need to see actual fellow apes: Imitation requires identification with a body of flesh and blood. We're beginning to realize how much human and animal cognition runs via the body. Instead of our brain being like a little computer that orders the body around, the body-brain relation is a two-way street. The body produces internal sensations and communicates with other bodies, out of which we construct social connections and an appreciation of the surrounding reality. Bodies insert themselves into everything we perceive or think. Did you know, for example, that physical condition colors perception? The same hill is assessed as steeper, just from looking at it, by a tired person than by a well-rested one. An outdoor target is judged as farther away than it really is by a person burdened with a heavy backpack than by one without it.

13 Or ask a pianist to pick out his own performance from among others he's listening to. Even if this is a new piece that the pianist has performed only once, in silence (on an electronic piano and without headphones on), he will be able to recognize his own play. While listening, he probably recreates in his head the sort of bodily sensations that accompany an actual performance. He feels the closest match listening to himself, thus recognizing himself through his body as much as through his ears.

14 The field of "embodied" **cognition** is still very much in its infancy but has profound **implications** for how we look at human relations. We involuntarily enter the bodies of those around us so that their movements and emotions echo within us as if they're our own. This is what allows us, or other primates, to re-create what we have seen others do. Body mapping is mostly hidden and unconscious, but sometimes it "slips out," such as when parents make chewing mouth movements while spoon-feeding their baby. They can't help but act the way they feel their baby ought to. Similarly, parents watching a singing performance of their child often get completely into it, mouthing every word. I myself still remember as a boy standing on the sidelines of soccer games and involuntarily making kicking or jumping moves each time someone I was cheering for got the ball.

ANALYZE AUTHOR'S CLAIM

Annotate: In paragraph 12, the author asserts the claim that "[our bodies and the bodies of others of our species] insert themselves into everything we perceive or think." He then gives three examples of ways we use our bodies to perceive the world. Mark those examples in paragraphs 12 and 13.

Analyze: Restate each example in your own words.

cognition
(kŏg-nĭsh′ən) *n.* the process or pattern of gaining knowledge.

implication
(ĭm-plĭ-kā′shən) *n.* consequence or effect.

ANALYZE AUTHOR'S CLAIM

Tell students that speakers and writers often include multiple examples to strengthen a **claim.** Discuss how examples and other evidence can make a claim more convincing. Explain that the examples the author provides in paragraphs 12 and 13 enrich and deepen our understanding of the author's claim. Point out that each example builds on the next. You might also point out that one example may be more helpful to a particular reader than another. (***Possible answer:*** *A hill seems more steep to someone who is tired; a walking or hiking goal seems farther away to a person carrying heavy gear; a pianist can identify a recording of his own performance based on the way his body reacts to the music.)*

ENGLISH LEARNER SUPPORT

Pronounce Words Correctly Native speakers of Spanish or Vietnamese may have trouble pronouncing the soft "g" as in *giant*; native Khmer speakers with the hard "g" as in *goat*; and native Hmong, Cantonese, or Korean speakers with both sounds. Many students may also struggle recognizing when a "g" is pronounced one way or the other. Have students write these words from pages 190–191 on index cards: *ingenious, ghost, got, contagion, beginning, cognition, magically, target, recognize*. Say each word aloud. Then have pairs sort the words into two columns by hard "g" and soft "g" and practice pronouncing the words. **ALL LEVELS**

CRITICAL VOCABULARY

cognition: De Waal believes the process of learning involves the body as much as the mind.

ASK STUDENTS to explain how "embodied" cognition explains some human and other primate behavior. *(Because of the body-brain connection, primates unconsciously copy the body movements of those around them.)*

implication: Studying how we learn through our bodies has had an effect on how we view human relationships.

ASK STUDENTS to explain what implications the study of "embodied" cognition might have. *(We will see how important social interactions are to the process of learning.)*

WHEN STUDENTS STRUGGLE . . .

Hold a Discussion The explanation of the "ghost box" studies in paragraphs 10–12 may be challenging for some students. First, ask students to reread paragraphs 10–12. Guide students to understand the reason for discussing the ghost box by asking the following:

- How is a ghost box different from a puzzle box? *(A ghost box opens and closes without manipulation by the ape.)*
- What did the ghost box experiments reveal? *(that apes do need to imitate their fellows in order to learn)*

For additional support, go to the **Reading Studio** and assign the following **Level Up Tutorial: Analyzing Arguments.**

MONITOR COMPREHENSION

Tell students that authors often use **synonyms**, or words with similar meanings, to make their writing less repetitive and to express subtle shades of meaning. Synonyms are one type of **context clue** that can help readers determine the meaning of another word.

(***Answer:*** body mapping *and* imitation *in paragraph 15;* synchrony, aping, *and* herd instinct *in paragraph 16.* Imitation *is the closest synonym;* imitation *and* mimicry *both mean "to copy the behavior of another."* Body mapping *refers more specifically to mimicking physical movements.* Synchrony *can refer to actions mirrored unconsciously.* Aping *can mean copying or imitating.* Herd instinct *refers to a general tendency to act in accordance with a group, rather than to mimick a specific act.)*

For **listening and reading support** for students at varying proficiency levels, see the **Text X-Ray** on pages 184C–184D.

NOTICE & NOTE

15 The same can be seen in animals, as illustrated in an old black-and-white photograph from Wolfgang Köhler's classic tool-use studies on chimpanzees. One ape, Grande, stands on boxes that she has stacked up to reach bananas hung from the ceiling, while Sultan watches intently. Even though Sultan sits at a distance, he raises his arm in precise synchrony with Grande's grasping movement. Another example comes from a chimpanzee filmed while using a heavy rock as a hammer to crack nuts. The actor is being observed by a younger ape, who swings his own (empty) hand down in sync every time the first one strikes the nut. Body mapping provides a great shortcut to imitation.

16 When I see synchrony and mimicry—whether it concerns yawning, laughing, dancing, or aping—I see social connection and bonding. I see an old herd instinct that has been taken up a notch. It goes beyond the tendency of a mass of individuals galloping in the same direction, crossing the river at the same time. The new level requires that one pay better attention to what others do and absorb how they do it. For example, I knew an old monkey matriarch with a curious drinking style. Instead of the typical slurping with her lips from the surface, she'd dip her entire underarm in the water, then lick the hair on her arm. Her children started doing the same, and then her grandchildren. The entire family was easy to recognize.

MONITOR COMPREHENSION

Annotate: Locate and mark the word *mimicry* in paragraph 16. Reread to identify several terms in the surrounding text that provide context clues for the meaning of *mimicry*.

Draw Conclusions: Summarize the meanings of the words you identified and determine which of them is closest in meaning to *mimicry*.

17 There is also the case of a male chimpanzee who had injured his fingers in a fight and hobbled around leaning on a bent wrist instead of his knuckles. Soon all of the young chimpanzees in the colony were walking the same way in single file behind the unlucky male. Like chameleons changing their color to match the environment, primates automatically copy their surroundings.

18 When I was a boy, my friends in the south of the Netherlands always ridiculed me when I came home from vacations in the north, where I played with boys from Amsterdam. They told me that I

APPLYING ACADEMIC VOCABULARY

☑ capacity ☐ confer ☑ emerge ☐ generate ☑ trace

Write and Discuss Have students turn to a partner to discuss the following questions. Guide students to include the academic vocabulary words *capacity, emerge,* and *trace* in their responses. Ask student volunteers to share their responses with the class.

1. How would you describe the **capacity** for empathy?
2. What surprising results have **emerged** from primate research?
3. Why is it possible for researchers to **trace** mimicry?

talked funny. Unconsciously, I'd return speaking a poor imitation of the harsh northern accent.

19 The way our bodies—including voice, mood, posture, and so on—are influenced by surrounding bodies is one of the mysteries of human existence, but one that provides the glue that holds entire societies together. It's also one of the most underestimated phenomena, especially in disciplines that view humans as rational decision makers. Instead of each individual independently weighing the pros and cons of his or her own actions, we occupy nodes within a tight network that connects all of us in both body and mind.

CHECK YOUR UNDERSTANDING

Answer these questions before moving on to the **Analyze the Text** section on the following page.

1 In the paragraph 2 sentence, *The fact that tickling oneself is notoriously ineffective attests to its social significance*, notoriously means —

A unfavorably

B humorously

C famously

D seriously

2 In paragraph 18, the author includes an anecdote, or brief story about himself. Its purpose is to —

F connect with readers who have had a similar experience

G support the author's claim about language and accents

H provide an example of unconscious synchrony

J show the herd mentality regarding human bullying

3 Which idea is supported by information throughout the selection?

A Humans unconsciously imitate the actions and behaviors of other humans.

B Laughter has a healing psychological effect on all primates, including humans.

C Humans learn best by imitating other humans.

D Sympathy and empathy are critical to the formation of meaningful human relationships.

CHECK YOUR UNDERSTANDING

Have students answer the questions independently.

Answers:

1. *C*
2. *H*
3. *A*

If they answer any questions incorrectly, have students reread the text to confirm their understanding. Then they may proceed to ANALYZE THE TEXT on page 194.

ENGLISH LEARNER SUPPORT

Oral Assessment Use the following questions to assess students' comprehension and speaking skills. Ask students to respond in short, complete sentences.

1. What does the word *notoriously* mean? *(It means famously.)*
2. Skim paragraph 18. Why did the author include this story about himself? *(He included the story to give an example of how people copy one another.)*
3. The author gives many examples of things humans do. What idea do these examples show? *(They show that humans imitate the actions of other humans.)* **MODERATE/LIGHT**

APPLY

ANALYZE THE TEXT

Possible answers:

1. **DOK 4:** *The author uses a light, conversational tone throughout the selection. His initial references to laughter establish that tone right away. In paragraph 1, he writes, "It's almost impossible not to laugh when everybody else is," and in paragraph 2, he writes, "I cannot suppress a chuckle myself."*
2. **DOK 3:** *The primary claim is that humans and primates learn by observing others. Supporting examples include mimicry, synchrony, yawn contagion, and the herd instinct.*
3. **DOK 2:** *The "herd instinct" is the tendency to follow what a crowd is doing without really considering why. People look to each other for inspiration and to emulate positive traits, and children imitate the behavior of their parents. The downside might include following a crowd down a dangerous path or making bad decisions based on what others do or think.*
4. **DOK 3:** *De Waal believes that interdependence—the fact that people need other people—is the glue that holds societies together. Students may cite the anecdote of one world leader imitating the walk of another as showing the deep level of connection among individuals and, ultimately, whole societies.*
5. **DOK 4:** *The high degree to which our bodies are influenced by those around us suggests that our behavior may be less controlled by our minds, or cognition, than we think.*

RESEARCH

Review the Research Tip with students. Point out that sites published by respected news organizations are other useful sources for reliable information. Encourage students to visit multiple websites to double-check and confirm facts and to find other perspectives on their questions.

RESPOND

ANALYZE THE TEXT

Support your responses with evidence from the text. NOTEBOOK

1. **Analyze** An author carefully chooses words and phrases to establish **tone**, or a particular attitude toward his or her subject. Some authors use formal language to convey a serious tone, while others use a more conversational style. What tone does de Waal establish in the opening paragraphs of his essay? What words and phrases create this tone?
2. **Cite Evidence** What is the primary claim that emerges in this essay? Provide evidence from the text to support your idea.
3. **Infer** What is the "herd instinct"? According to de Waal, what is the positive side of people watching and imitating one another? What might be a potential downside of this part of human nature?
4. **Draw Conclusions** What, according to de Waal, is the "glue that holds entire societies together"? What do you think are his strongest pieces of evidence in support of that claim?
5. **Notice & Note** Reread the final paragraph of the selection. How might the author's conclusions create an Aha Moment, causing the reader to see human behavior in a new light?

RESEARCH

Brainstorm at least three questions you have after reading the selection "Monkey See, Monkey Do, Monkey Connect." Are you curious about Dr. de Waal and his credentials? Do you want to learn more about an aspect of his or other scientists' research? The Yerkes Primate Center? Or something else? List your questions, put a star by the question that interests you most, then research its answer. Write down additional questions that occur to you during your research.

RESEARCH TIP
When you conduct online research, be sure to evaluate the credibility of websites. Web addresses that end in .gov, .edu, or .org are the work of large groups. Because these sites are frequently reviewed, they are often more reliable than other sites. Use them and other sites you trust, including those your teachers recommend.

INITIAL BRAINSTORM QUESTIONS	ADDITIONAL QUESTIONS
Questions will vary.	

LEARNING MINDSET

Try Again Remind students that taking chances shows strength and that no one is successful in every effort, every time. This selection asks students to take a position and participate in a debate with their classmates. Even if students think that they were unsuccessful in presenting or supporting their position during the debate, prompt them to consider what worked well, what didn't, and why. That will help them improve their performance the next time they take part in a debate. Encourage students to learn from their experiences as they continue challenging themselves both in and outside the classroom. And let them know that positive risk-taking—trying to learn a new skill or hobby, or develop a new interest, or take on a new role in class—benefits them cognitively and emotionally.

CREATE AND DEBATE

Take a Position The author of "Monkey See, Monkey Do, Monkey Connect" presents one view of the ways in which humans relate to one another. Do you agree with his view, or do you believe that people are, or should be, "Robinson Crusoes sitting on separate islands"?

- ❑ Review your notes and annotations, consider your own research, and reflect on what you already know.
- ❑ Write a position statement in which you state your claim clearly, using appropriate academic and content vocabulary.
- ❑ Create a list of reasons and evidence that support your claim using the article, your own research, and other logical reasons.

Participate in a Debate Choose sides for or against a stated claim and use reasons and evidence to support your position.

- ❑ As a class, choose a position statement to argue for or against.
- ❑ In teams, prepare an opening statement, a list of supporting reasons and evidence, and a concluding statement.
- ❑ Listen actively as the other team present arguments. Allow them to respond to each of your team's arguments with counter-arguments.

Go to the **Speaking and Listening Studio** for help having a group discussion.

RESPOND TO THE ESSENTIAL QUESTION

How do we form and maintain our connections with others?

Gather Information Review your annotations and notes on "Monkey See, Monkey Do, Monkey Connect." Then add relevant information to your Response Log. As you determine which information to include, think about:

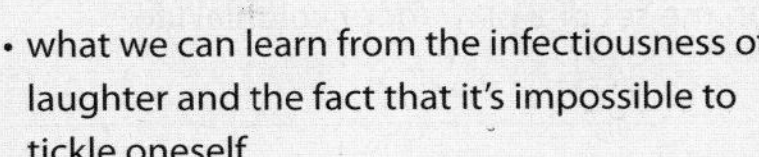

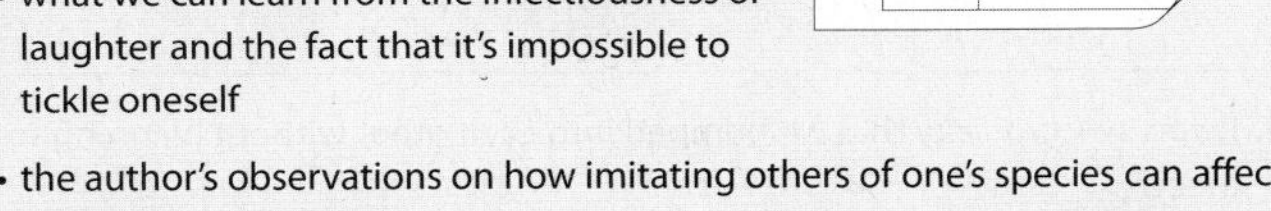

- what we can learn from the infectiousness of laughter and the fact that it's impossible to tickle oneself
- the author's observations on how imitating others of one's species can affect an individual's survival
- benefits an individual gains from the formation of lasting connections

At the end of the unit, use your notes to help you write a short story.

ACADEMIC VOCABULARY

As you write and discuss what you learned from the scientific article, be sure to use the Academic Vocabulary words. Check off each of the words that you use.

- ❑ **capacity**
- ❑ **confer**
- ❑ **emerge**
- ❑ **generate**
- ❑ **trace**

APPLY

CREATE AND DEBATE

Take a Position Review the terms *claim, reasons,* and *evidence*. Ensure that students also know the terms *argument* and *counterargument.*

For **writing support** for students at varying proficiency levels, see the **Text X-Ray** on page 184D.

Participate in a Debate To support students as they prepare to debate, discuss these points:

- Teams supporting de Waal's position on the social nature of learning should review the selection and make notes on the author's key reasons and evidence.
- Teams opposing de Waal's position should conduct research to gather evidence. They might use a search term such as "individual versus social learning" and then review the results for articles written at an appropriate level of complexity.
- Team members should share the results of their research and then work together to develop a clear position statement, or claim.
- Each team should discuss the opposing claims and reasons the other team is likely to present and prepare to respond with strong counterarguments or rebuttals.
- Teams should review the rules for debating and decide on time limits, who will speak first, who will respond to the other team's argument, and who will summarize the team's claim and strongest reasons at the end of the debate.

For **speaking support** for students at varying proficiency levels, see the **Text X-Ray** on page 184D.

RESPOND TO THE ESSENTIAL QUESTION

Allow time for students to add details from "Monkey See, Monkey Do, Monkey Connect" to their Unit 3 Response Logs.

ENGLISH LEARNER SUPPORT

Distinguish Intonation Patterns Use the debate to focus on English intonation. Practice the following patterns with students so they can listen for them during the debate.

- Falling intonation indicates a statement. (*I disagree with you.*)
- Rising, or rising and falling intonations, indicate questions. (*Would you repeat that? Have you ever considered...?*)

Have students create a T-chart labeled with rising and falling arrows (or a question mark and period). Read aloud paragraph 10. Have students put a mark in the appropriate column after hearing each sentence. **SUBSTANTIAL/MODERATE**

APPLY

CRITICAL VOCABULARY

Answers:

1. cognition, *which means "the process of gaining knowledge"*
2. implication, *because both refer to ideas that follow from other ideas or evidence*
3. empathy, *because to understand another person's feelings is to have empathy*
4. contagion, *because a disease can spread through contagion*
5. synchronization, *which means doing something in a coordinated or organized way*

VOCABULARY STRATEGY
Words from Greek

Tell students that a *root* is a word part that contains the core meaning of a word.

Possible answers:

1. *happening again and again for a long time*
2. *describe events in the order that they happened*
3. *out of place in time*
4. *coincidence*

Practice and Apply Students can create a chart similar to the one shown on page 196, or one of their own design. (***Possible answers:*** *The Greek root* pathos *refers to feeling or suffering;* pathetically—*The cat cried pathetically at the back door.* pathology—*Doctors study the pathology of a disease to learn how to treat it;* pathogenic—*The pathogenic bacteria caused the infection.)*

RESPOND

WORD BANK
empathy
synchronization
contagion
cognition
implication

CRITICAL VOCABULARY

Practice and Apply Explain which Critical Vocabulary word listed above is most closely associated with the familiar word shown below.

1. Which vocabulary word is associated with *thinking*?
2. Which vocabulary word is associated with *suggestion*?
3. Which vocabulary word is associated with *feeling*?
4. Which vocabulary word is associated with *disease*?
5. Which vocabulary word is associated with *coordination*?

VOCABULARY STRATEGY: Words from Greek

Go to the **Vocabulary Studio** for more on words from Greek.

Many English words contain Greek roots. The Critical Vocabulary word *synchronization* contains the prefix *syn-*, meaning "with or together," combined with the Greek root *chrono*, which means "time." *Chrono* is the basis of many other words in our everyday vocabulary.

THE GREEK ROOT *CHRONO*	
chronic	anachronistic
chronicle	synchronicity

Use your understanding of the root *chrono* and context clues in the sentences below to understand meaning of the words in the chart. Under each sentence, write down the meaning of the italicized word.

1. My sister has a *chronic* cough that has kept her awake for weeks.

____

2. The book will *chronicle* the history of our community.

____

3. A computer is *anachronistic* on the set of a play about colonial life.

____

4. It was *synchronicity* that we bumped into each other without planning to meet.

____

Practice and Apply The Critical Vocabulary word *empathy* contains the Greek root, *pathos*. Work with a partner to define *pathos* and create a chart of words that contain the root. Write sentences with the words you identify.

ENGLISH LEARNER SUPPORT

Decode Words Explain that students can use a combination of strategies to decode, or figure out word meanings. Have students read sentence 1 and circle the part of the word *chronic* that relates to time. *(chron)* Explain that in addition to using word roots, another decoding strategy is to ask questions. Model this strategy by asking the following questions about the word *chronic*: What does time have to do with the sister's cough? *(It kept her awake for weeks—that's a long time.)* So what might *chronic* mean? *(It's something that happens for a long time.)* Ask pairs to apply these decoding strategies to the other three sentences.
LIGHT

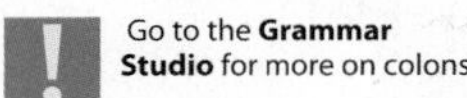

LANGUAGE CONVENTIONS: Colons

Authors use colons to add clarity to their writing. They also use colons for emphasis in order to draw attention to key ideas. In an essay, colons commonly introduce a list, quotation, or independent clause.

USE OF A COLON	EXAMPLE
In this sentence from the selection, notice how de Waal uses a colon to lead to a key idea, a definition of the term "laugh plants."	This is why comedy shows on television have laugh tracks and why theater audiences are sometimes sprinkled with "laugh plants": people paid to produce raucous laughing at any joke that comes along.
In this passage from the selection, the colon has a different purpose. It introduces a list.	It began much more simply, with the synchronization of bodies: running when others run, laughing when others laugh, crying when others cry, or yawning when others yawn.
Now read the same sentence without the colon. Consider how the sentence loses clarity without the colon to introduce the list.	It began much more simply, with the synchronization of bodies running when others run, laughing when others laugh, crying when others cry, or yawning when others yawn.
You can also use a colon to introduce a long quotation or a related independent clause. This sentence from the selection is an example.	They become role models: We empathize with them and emulate them.

When an independent clause follows a colon, should that clause begin with a capital letter? Experts disagree. If your assignment is to follow a certain style (APA, MLA, Chicago Manual of Style, and so on) be sure to look up the rule in that style manual. In general, it's up to the individual but it is important to be consistent.

Practice and Apply Write two paragraphs summarizing key points in the article, "Monkey See, Monkey Do, Monkey Connect." Use colons in at least three places. At least one colon should introduce a list and one should introduce a quotation or independent clause.

Go to the **Grammar Studio** for more on colons.

APPLY

LANGUAGE CONVENTIONS: Colons

Review the instruction and examples with students. Remind students that they can only use a colon after an independent clause, not a dependent clause or sentence fragment. If students need additional support, provide examples such as the following:

- My two cats are: an orange tabby and a calico.
- I have two cats: an orange tabby and a calico.

Ask students to determine whether or not each example is correct and explain why or why not. *(The first example is incorrect because "My two cats are" is a fragment; the second example is correct because "I have two cats" is an independent clause.")*

Practice and Apply After students finish writing, have them exchange summaries with a partner. Ask partners to locate each colon and check whether it's been used correctly. *(Students' paragraphs should demonstrate an understanding of the use of colons for introducing lists and for introducing quotations or independent clauses.)*

ENGLISH LEARNER SUPPORT

Colons Use the following supports with students at varying proficiency levels:

- Demonstrate the effectiveness of colons. Display a "list" sentence without a colon. (I have three cousins Emma, Diego, and Celia.) Read the sentence aloud, not pausing between "cousins" and "Emma." Then insert the colon and read the sentence again, demonstrating pausing after the colon. **SUBSTANTIAL**
- Have students find examples of sentences that use colons. Choral read the sentences, pausing after the colon. Ask: What does this colon introduce? A key idea, quotation, list, or independent clause? **MODERATE**
- Ask students to write their own sentences in which they use colons to introduce a key idea, a list, a quotation, and an independent clause. Have pairs check each other's work and read the sentences aloud. **LIGHT**

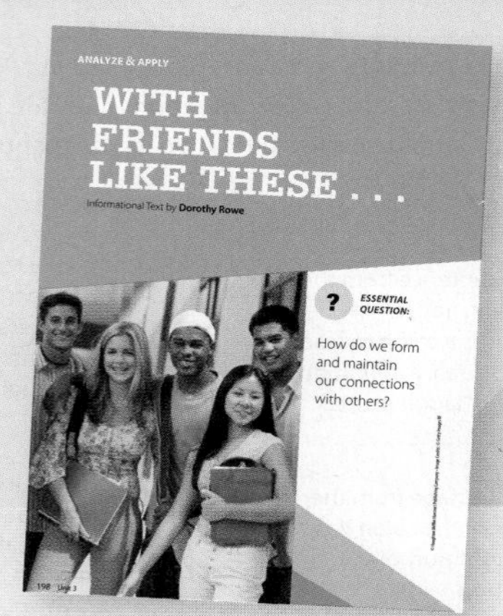

WITH FRIENDS LIKE THESE . . .

Informational Text by **Dorothy Rowe**

GENRE ELEMENTS

INFORMATIONAL TEXT

Remind students that **informational text** is written primarily to inform or explain something. It usually contains text features such as headings and subheadings to help readers absorb and retain information. In addition, a strong informational text is unbiased—that is, it relates factual information without attempting to persuade the reader to adopt a particular opinion about those facts. However, like a persuasive text, it does include evidence to support ideas.

LEARNING OBJECTIVES

- Summarize and paraphrase texts and evaluate details.
- Conduct research about friendship.
- Write a personal essay about how key ideas in "With Friends Like These . . ." and articles researched relate to students' friendships.
- Present a scene about two teenagers discovering the ideal friend.
- Use print and digital resources such as glossaries, encyclopedias, technical dictionaries, and print dictionaries to better understand the precise meaning of discipline-based vocabulary.
- Understand how to use adjective and adverb phrases.
- **Language** Demonstrate comprehension by retelling ideas in the text.

TEXT COMPLEXITY

Quantitative Measures	**With Friends Like These . . .** Lexile: 1070L
Qualitative Measures	**Ideas Presented** Mostly clear but abstract and likely to be somewhat unfamiliar.
	Structures Used Text features help guide reading; main ideas and supporting details organization.
	Language Used Mostly Tier II words with just a few Tier III words specific to psychology.
	Knowledge Required Explanations provided to understand psychological concepts in the text; students' past experiences will also help them grasp the concepts.

Online 

RESOURCES

- Unit 3 Response Log
- Selection Audio
- Reading Studio: Notice & Note
- Level Up Tutorial: Comparison-Contrast Organization
- Writing Studio: Writing Narratives
- Speaking and Listening Studio: Giving a Presentation
- Vocabulary Studio: Print and Digital Resources
- Grammar Studio: Module 3: Lesson 2: Adjective Phrases and Adverb Phrases
- "With Friends Like These . . ." Selection Test

SUMMARIES

English

Neuroscientists have determined that we interpret reality based on our experiences. From our interpretations, we derive our sense of self; explain past and present; and predict future events. Our emotions are nonverbal assessments of how safe our sense of self is. When our sense of who we are is safe, or validated, we feel secure and happy. When it's threatened, or invalidated, we may feel scared. Friends play a central role in maintaining our sense of self. They help us confirm our view of ourselves, which boosts our self-confidence. The more self-confident we feel, the less risk we perceive from others and the better able we are to accept change.

Spanish

Los neurocientíficos han determinado que uno interpreta la realidad según sus experiencias. De nuestras interpretaciones derivamos nuestro sentido de identidad; explicamos el pasado y el presente; y predecimos sucesos futuros. Nuestras emociones son análisis no verbales de qué tan seguro está nuestro sentido de identidad. Cuando nuestro sentido de quién somos está a salvo, o validado, nos sentimos seguros y felices. Cuando está amenazado, o invalidado, nos asustamos. Los amigos son clave para mantener nuestro sentido de identidad. Confirman nuestra percepción propia, cosa que nos da autoconfianza. Mientras más seguros estemos de nosotros mismos, menor es el riesgo que percibimos de los demás y mejor nos adaptamos a los cambios.

SMALL-GROUP OPTIONS

Have students work in small groups to read and respond to the selection.

Total Physical Response

Have small groups demonstrate by their movements, gestures, and body language what Rowe says would be emotional responses in these circumstances:

- Surrounded by true friends who confirm your sense of self *(happy, confident)*
- With someone who tells you that you aren't the kind of person you think you are *(threatened, fearful, sad, worried)*

Pinwheel Discussion

- Have students form an inner circle facing out and an outer circle facing in, so each student faces a partner.
- Tell partners to discuss questions such as: Why are friends important? Can we know reality directly? How do we react to our emotions? After a few minutes of discussion, have one circle shift so that each student has a new partner.
- Then ask a new question and repeat as time allows.

Text X-Ray: English Learner Support

for "With Friends Like These . . ."

Use the Text X-Ray and the supports and scaffolds in the Teacher's Edition to help guide students at different proficiency levels through the selection.

INTRODUCE THE SELECTION

DISCUSS FRIENDSHIPS

In this lesson, students will need to be able to discuss risks and rewards of friendship. Provide the following explanations:

- A *risk* is the possibility of suffering harm or loss.
- A *reward* is a positive result or benefit.

Have volunteers share examples of risks and rewards of friendship. Supply the following sentence frames:

- *A possible risk of friendship is* ____.
- *A possible reward of friendship is* ____.

CULTURAL REFERENCES

The following phrases may be unfamiliar to students:

- *"With Friends Like These . . ."* (title): the beginning of a saying that ends, "who needs enemies?"
- *the path of friendship, like love, rarely runs smooth* (paragraph 1): friendships often develop unevenly over time; an allusion to a quote from Shakespeare's play *A Midsummer Night's Dream* ("The course of true love never did run smooth.")

LISTENING

Understand Main Points of Spoken Language

Read aloud paragraphs 14–15.

Use the following supports with students at varying proficiency levels:

- Guide students to mark the first sentence of each paragraph. Ask: Do these sentences state a main idea that is supported by details in the paragraph?? *(yes)* **SUBSTANTIAL**
- Guide students to explain how the first sentence in each paragraph relates to the rest of the paragraph. Provide these frames: *In paragraph 14, the first sentence states* ____*, and the following sentences* _____*. In paragraph 15, the first sentence states* ____*, and the next sentence* ____. **MODERATE**
- Have partners work together to identify the main point of each paragraph. **LIGHT**

SPEAKING

Express Feelings

Work with students to read the presentation assignment on Student Edition page 207.

Use these supports with students at varying proficiency levels:

- Encourage students to participate in the scene presentation at a level in which they feel comfortable. For example, they may limit their dialogue to short phrases practiced ahead of time and focus on expressing feelings using facial expressions and gestures. **SUBSTANTIAL**
- Guide students to combine facial expressions, gestures, and dialogue to express feelings in their scenes. For example, have them practice smiling, putting their hand on their hearts, and saying *thank you so much* to express gratitude. **MODERATE**
- Have partners take turns rehearsing their actions and dialogue while the other partner observes. Tell students to provide their partner with feedback on how they might adjust their tone of voice or body language to express their feelings more effectively. **LIGHT**

READING

Demonstrate Comprehension by Retelling

Work with students to paraphrase the second sentence in paragraph 2.

Use the following supports with students at varying proficiency levels:

- Guide students to replace unknown words in the sentence with more familiar phrases. For example, replace *neuroscientists* with *people who study the brain* and replace *reveal* with *show.* **SUBSTANTIAL**
- Provide these frames to help students unpack the sentence and restate it as two sentences: *People who study the brain have proved that the brain does not show* ______. *Instead, the brain shows* ______.
  MODERATE
- Have students work in pairs to paraphrase the sentence, using reference sources as necessary to determine the meanings of unknown words. **LIGHT**

WRITING

Write a Personal Essay

Work with students to express details that support a key idea in order to prepare them for the writing assignment on Student Edition page 207.

Use the following supports with students at varying proficiency levels:

- Ask students yes/no questions about paragraph 1: Is friendship important? (*yes*) Is friendship always easy? (*no*). **SUBSTANTIAL**
- Have students identify the key idea of paragraph 1 and the details that support it. Guide them to break down the paragraph into a sentence stating a key idea, three supporting examples, and a restatement of the key idea. Tell them to use this same structure for a paragraph of their own about friendship.
  MODERATE
- Have students analyze paragraph 1 with a partner to identify its structure and use it as a model for a paragraph of their own about friendship. **LIGHT**

TEACH

Connect to the ESSENTIAL QUESTION

As psychologist Dorothy Rowe points out in this next article, friendships are vitally important—essential not only to our enjoyment of life but also to our sense of who we are as people. But, "the path of friendship, like love, rarely runs smooth." So, what do we do when a friend disappoints? What even enables us to form and maintain friendships? Discuss these questions with students, and ask volunteers to suggest examples of lessons people can learn from their friendships.

ANALYZE & APPLY

WITH FRIENDS LIKE THESE . . .

Informational Text by **Dorothy Rowe**

ESSENTIAL QUESTION:

How do we form and maintain our connections with others?

LEARNING MINDSET

Effort Prompt students to think about their own friendships while working on this lesson. Point out that the best friendships require effort by each person. For example, good communication between friends means both people work at listening to the other person and sharing their thoughts and feelings. Have students discuss their ideas about what goes into making and keeping healthy friendships. Encourage them to keep these ideas in mind as they read and analyze the selection—and as they think about their own friendships.

QUICK START

Why do certain people become your friends and not others? How do you stay friends? With a partner, discuss the factors that make you likely to become friends with someone and factors that determine whether the person becomes your long-term friend.

SUMMARIZE AND PARAPHRASE TEXTS

Two skills that will help you understand a text—and communicate your understanding to others—are **summarizing** and **paraphrasing**.

When you **summarize** a text, you briefly retell the main ideas in your own words, while maintaining meaning and logical order. The **central idea** is the main point that the author wants you to understand. To keep your summary **objective**, include only the author's ideas.

When you **paraphrase** a text, you restate its ideas in your own words. Paraphrasing helps you clarify the author's meaning because you must understand it before you can rephrase it. An effective paraphrase maintains both the author's meaning and the logical order in which the ideas are presented. As you read, makes notes about the key idea in each paragraph. This will help you grasp the central idea of the selection. When you come across a long or confusing sentence, take time to paraphrase it.

EVALUATE DETAILS

To determine key ideas in a text, you need to **evaluate details**. Authors of informational texts support their ideas with several types of details. These can include key words and terms, facts and examples, statistics, quotations or ideas from experts, and real-world anecdotes.

As you read each paragraph or section of an informational text, ask yourself what types of details the author includes. After you read, determine the key idea of the paragraph based on the details by asking yourself questions:

- How do these details relate to each other?
- What key idea do these details support?
- How reliable are the details? How clear and accurate are they?
- How well do the details support the main idea of the text?

Use a chart like this to organize the most important details and the key ideas:

PARAGRAPH NUMBER	MOST IMPORTANT DETAILS	KEY IDEA

GENRE ELEMENTS: INFORMATIONAL TEXT

- provides factual information
- includes evidence to support ideas
- may contains text features to organize ideas
- includes many forms, such as news articles and essays

QUICK START

To prepare for their discussions with a partner, encourage students to consider the following questions:

- How long has your longest friendship lasted?
- Why do you suppose you became friends?
- What do you suppose has kept you together?
- Why do you think other friendships didn't last?

SUMMARIZE AND PARAPHRASE TEXTS

To help students understand the difference between summarizing and paraphrasing, guide them to compare these in a Venn diagram or three-column chart. For example:

To Summarize	Both	To Paraphrase
• briefly retell only the text's main ideas in your own words	• maintain the author's meaning and logical order	• restate the text in your own words

EVALUATE DETAILS

Support students' understanding of the instruction by explaining that asking questions can help them evaluate details in order to determine key ideas. Remind students that authors use different types of details to develop their ideas. Review these examples of supporting details from the text:

- **Example:** "We may feel jealous of a friend's achievements when we want to feel happy for her" (paragraph 1). This example illustrates the idea that friendships are sometimes difficult.
- **Fact:** "Most of our brain's constructions are unconscious" (paragraph 3). This fact can be verified by checking published articles about the brain.

TEACH

CRITICAL VOCABULARY

Suggest that students try out the words in each sentence before committing to their answers. Remind them that context clues may hint at the meaning of the word that is missing.

Answers:

1. *assess*
2. *derive*
3. *validate*

■ English Learner Support

Note False Cognates Tell students that the Critical Vocabulary word *assess,* meaning "to evaluate," should not be confused with the Spanish word *asesar,* which means "to gain good judgment or common sense through experience." A closer synonym for *assess* in Spanish is *evaluar.*
ALL LEVELS

LANGUAGE CONVENTIONS

Remind students that adjectives and adjective phrases modify only nouns and pronouns. Adverbs and adverb phrases modify verbs, adjectives, and other adverbs by telling where, when, how, or to what extent.

■ English Learner Support

Learn Essential Language Remind students whose first language is Cantonese that there are no direct equivalents of English prepositions in Cantonese. If students tend to omit prepositions, display a list of common prepositions, such as: *at, by, for, from, in, on, to*. Remind them that these words are important for showing direction, location, and time.
ALL LEVELS

ANNOTATION MODEL

Review these suggestions for marking up the selection:

- Mark details the author uses to support her ideas.
- Note what types of details they are.
- Evaluate their effectiveness.
- Summarize key ideas.

Remind students that their notes in the margin may also include questions about ideas that are unclear or topics they want to learn more about.

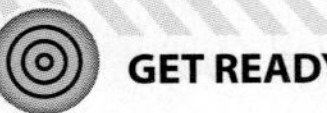

GET READY

CRITICAL VOCABULARY

validate **assess** **derive**

To see how many Critical Vocabulary words you already know, use them to complete the sentences.

1. We always ______________ the options on the menu before we try a new restaurant.
2. The popularity of those websites will always ______________ from their focus on celebrities.
3. The mayor hopes that re-election will ______________ her leadership.

LANGUAGE CONVENTIONS

Adjective and Adverb Phrases A **prepositional phrase** is a phrase that consists of a preposition, its object, and any modifiers of the object. Authors use prepositional phrases to add information and enhance a sentence. In this lesson, you will learn about two types of prepositional phrases: **adjective phrases** and **adverb phrases.** Here is an example from the selection of each:

We are constantly assessing how safe our sense of being a person is.

Friends are central to this all-important sense of validation.

The underlined phrase in the first sentence is an adjective phrase modifying the noun *sense*. The underlined phrase in the second sentence is an adverb phrase modifying the adjective *central*. As you read "With Friends Like These . . . ," note the author's use of adjective and adverb phrases.

ANNOTATION MODEL

NOTICE & NOTE 

As you read, mark the details the author uses to support her ideas. Note what types of details they are, and evaluate their effectiveness. When you finish the selection, summarize the main idea. Here is an example of how one reader responded to "With Friends Like These . . .":

We value friends, but the path of friendship, like love, rarely runs smooth.① We may feel jealous of a friend's achievements when we want to feel happy for her.② We might find it hard to give friends objective advice, unrelated to the person we want them to be.③ We can be reluctant to allow each other to change, sometimes falling out in a way that is painful for all involved. And yet friendships are vitally important, central to our enjoyment of life.	1, 2, and 3: examples of friendship not running smoothly; effective because anyone with friends can relate Key idea: friendships important but challenging

NOTICE & NOTE 

BACKGROUND

Dorothy Rowe *(b. 1930) is an Australian-born psychologist who has lived in England since 1968. During her career, she has studied the ways in which people make meaning and the biological basis of mental disorders. Rowe is the author of 16 books. In 2010, London's* Daily Telegraph *included Rowe on its list of the 100 most powerful women in Britain in business, academia, and politics.*

WITH FRIENDS LIKE THESE . . .

Informational Text by Dorothy Rowe

SETTING A PURPOSE

As you read, pay attention to whether the author appears to be drawing on scientific studies or personal experience to support her ideas.

1 We value friends, but the path of friendship, like love, rarely runs smooth. We may feel jealous of a friend's achievements when we want to feel happy for her. We might find it hard to give friends objective advice, unrelated to the person we want them to be. We can be reluctant to allow each other to change, sometimes falling out in a way that is painful for all involved. And yet, friendships are vitally important; central to our enjoyment of life.

2 More fundamentally, friendships are essential to our sense of who we are. Neuroscientists have shown that our brain does not reveal to us the world as it is, but rather as possible interpretations of what is going on around us, drawn from our past experience. Since no two people ever have exactly the same experience, no two people ever see anything in exactly the same way.

Notice & Note

You can use the side margins to notice and note signposts in the text.

SUMMARIZE AND PARAPHRASE TEXTS

Annotate: Mark a sentence that you find long or confusing in paragraphs 1–3.

Interpret: Paraphrase the sentence. How does the sentence you chose relate to the ideas in the first three paragraphs? Explain your answer.

BACKGROUND

After students have read the Background note on Rowe, point out that the 2010 *Daily Telegraph* list of powerful women recognized Rowe for her influential writings about psychology as well as for her role in establishing one of the first clinical psychology departments for public health in Britain. Lead a brief discussion about how the work of scientists and researchers can impact individuals' ideas and behavior as well as public policy.

SETTING A PURPOSE

Direct students to use the Setting a Purpose prompt to focus their reading.

 SUMMARIZE AND PARAPHRASE TEXTS

Guide students to paraphrase and explain the second sentence in paragraph 2 because it is a key idea that is potentially difficult to grasp. (***Possible answer:*** *People who study the brain, or neuroscientists, have shown that we don't really understand the world as something separate from ourselves. Our unique perception of the world is based on what we have experienced. This idea helps to explain what Rowe means in paragraph 3 by "our brain's constructions" and how our sense of who we are comes from those constructions.)*

For **reading support** for students at varying proficiency levels, see the **Text X-Ray** on page 198D.

 ENGLISH LEARNER SUPPORT

Use Visual Support Help students understand the metaphor of the stream and the whirlpool in paragraph 3. Use the following supports with students at varying proficiency levels.

- Point out that *conscious* means "aware," and that adding the prefix *un-* to this base word forms the word *unconscious*, meaning "not aware." Explain that the author uses the words *stream* and *constructions* to refer to our flow of thoughts. Work with students to label a drawing of a stream with the words *conscious thoughts* and *unconscious thoughts* flowing as if they were each a branch of the same stream, merging and swirling together to create a whirlpool, labeled *sense of being a person.* **SUBSTANTIAL**
- Have partners work together to label a drawing of a whirlpool forming in a stream with key phrases from paragraph 3. **MODERATE**
- Have students draw a whirlpool forming in a stream and then use the drawing to explain the main idea of paragraph 3. **LIGHT**

TEACH

CONTRASTS AND CONTRADICTIONS

Explain that contrasts are often introduced by transitional words and phrases, such as *however* or *on the contrary*. Encourage students to skim paragraph 5 for transitions. (***Answer:*** *The contrast reminds us that our experience of validation—feeling safe and reassured—is extremely different from how we feel when our sense of self is challenged or, worse, invalidated—which is when we say that we feel "shattered" or that we're "losing our grip."*)

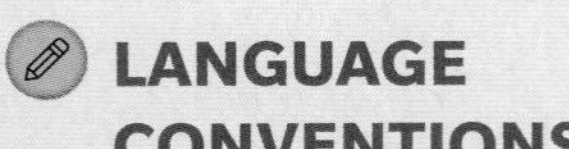

LANGUAGE CONVENTIONS

Model how to find and identify **adjective and adverb phrases** with the following example from paragraph 7:

> *We can be invalidated by events such as the bankruptcy of the firm that employs us. . . .*

Think aloud: "First I'll find and underline the prepositions." Underline *by* and *of.* "Next I'll look for the information introduced by each preposition and underline that." Underline *events such as the bankruptcy* and *the firm that employs us*.

Notice aloud: "Since *by events such as the bankruptcy* tells me how we can be invalidated, it must be an adverb phrase." Next, "Since *of the firm that employs us* tells me which one, it must be an adjective phrase." ***(Possible answers:*** *From paragraph 8, "of trust in the person she saw as her best friend" explains which loss, making it an adjective phrase. From paragraph 9, "as falling apart" tells how she described herself, making it an adverb phrase.)*

CRITICAL VOCABULARY

validate: When events prove, or confirm, that our ideas about ourselves are true, we feel secure.

ASK STUDENTS why people would prefer to have their ideas about themselves validated. *(People feel safer, more secure, more confident, and reassured that their view of themselves is accurate when events prove their ideas about themselves to be true.)*

assess: We are constantly evaluating how secure we feel in our sense of self.

ASK STUDENTS how our emotions help us assess how secure we feel in our sense of self. *(Positive emotions make us feel more secure, while negative emotions make us feel less secure.)*

NOTICE & NOTE

3 Most of our brain's constructions are unconscious. Early in our life our stream of conscious and unconscious constructions create, like a real stream, a kind of whirlpool that quickly becomes our most precious possession, that is, our sense of being a person, what we call "I", "me", "myself." Like a whirlpool, our sense of being a person cannot exist separately from the stream that created it.

4 Because we cannot see reality directly, all our ideas are guesses about what is going on. Thus our sense of being a person is made up of these guesses. All the time we are creating ideas about who we are, what is happening now, what has happened in our world, and what our future will be. When these ideas are shown by events to be reasonably accurate, that is, our ideas are **validated**, we feel secure in ourselves, but when they are proved wrong, we feel that we are falling apart.

validate
(văl´ĭ-dāt) *v.* to establish the value, truth, or legitimacy of

CONTRASTS AND CONTRADICTIONS

Notice & Note: What phrase indicates the author is introducing contrasting details in paragraph 5? Mark it in the text.

Interpret: How does the contrast in this paragraph illustrate the importance of validation?

5 Friends are central to this all-important sense of validation. When a friend confirms to us that the world is as we see it, we feel safer, reassured. On the other hand, when we say, "I'm shattered," or "I'm losing my grip," we might not be using clichés to describe a bad day but talking about something quite terrifying that we are experiencing: our sense of who we are is being challenged. So terrifying is this experience that we develop many different tactics aimed at warding off invalidation and defending ourselves against being annihilated as a person.

Emotional support

6 We are constantly **assessing** how safe our sense of being a person is. Our assessments are those interpretations we call emotions. All our emotions relate to the degree of safety or danger our sense of being a person is experiencing. So important are these interpretations to our survival that we do not need to put them into words, although of course we can. Our positive emotions are interpretations to do with safety, while the multitude of negative emotions define the particular kind of danger and its degree. Joy is: "Everything is the way I want it to be"; jealousy is: "How dare that person have something that is rightly mine."

assess
(ə-sĕs´) *v.* to evaluate

7 We can be invalidated by events such as the bankruptcy of the firm that employs us, but most frequently we are invalidated by other people.

8 A friend told me how her husband had used her password and pin to drain her bank account and fund his secret gambling habit. Losing her savings was a terrible blow, but far worse was her loss of trust in the person she saw as her best friend.

9 When she described herself as falling apart, I assured her that what was falling apart were some of her ideas. All she had to do was

LANGUAGE CONVENTIONS

ANNOTATE: Mark two adjective or adverb phrases in paragraphs 7–9.

ANALYZE: For each adjective or adverb phrase, describe how it adds information to the sentence.

WHEN STUDENTS STRUGGLE . . .

Evaluate Details Have partners use a chart to contrast the details in paragraph 5. Then have them discuss how these details relate to and support the main idea of the text.

	Validation	Invalidation
What It Is	*confirmation that the world is as we see it*	*having our sense of the world or who we are challenged*
How It Makes You Feel	*safe, reassured*	*shattered, terrified, like you're "losing your grip"*

For additional support, go to the **Reading Studio** and assign the following **Level Up Tutorial: Comparison-Contrast Organization.**

NOTICE & NOTE

ENGLISH LEARNER SUPPORT

Use Prepositions Direct students' attention to the photo on page 203. Encourage students to use and reuse prepositions such as *at, around, above, below, from, in,* and *of* in small-group discussions about what they see in this image and what the image seems to convey. **ALL LEVELS**

APPLYING ACADEMIC VOCABULARY

❑ **capacity** ❑ **confer** ☑ **emerge** ☑ **generate** ❑ **trace**

Write and Discuss Have students turn to a partner and discuss the questions below. Guide students to include the academic vocabulary words *generate* and *emerge* in their responses. Ask volunteers to share their responses with the class.

- As you study the image, what **emerges** as its central focus?
- What ideas and feelings might the photographer have hoped to **generate** with this image?

EVALUATE DETAILS

Analyze paragraph 10 with students by asking a volunteer to identify its topic sentence. *("Friendship can be rewarding but, like all relationships, it can also be risky.")* Review the fact that all the details in a paragraph usually elaborate on its key idea. Ask students to predict what the details in this paragraph should all elaborate on. *(the rewards and risks of friendship)* Write *Rewards* and *Risks* on the board. Ask students to identify each reward or risk they find in the paragraph. Write these beneath the appropriate heading. *(**Answer:** Friends can disappoint us, but they can also reinforce our sense of self.)*

English Learner Support

Discuss Text Structure Point to the columns of the completed Rewards/Risks chart on the board and review the meanings of the words *reward* and *risk*. Display these sentence frames: *This is a reward because ______. This is a risk because ______.* Point to each entry in the chart and ask volunteers to state their opinion using the appropriate sentence frame. **MODERATE**

NOTICE & NOTE

to endure a period of uncertainty until she could construct ideas that better reflected her situation.

10 Friendship can be rewarding but, like all relationships, it can also be risky. Other people can let us down, insult or humiliate us, leading us to feel diminished and in danger. Yet we need other people to tell us when we have got our guesses right, and, when we get things wrong, to help us make more accurate assessments. Live completely on your own and your guesses will get further and further away from reality.

EVALUATE DETAILS

Annotate: In paragraph 10, circle one example of how a friendship can be risky. Underline one example of how a friendship can be helpful.

Evaluate: How can the contrasting examples you marked be expressed as a key idea?

11 The degree of risk we perceive from our friends relates directly to the degree of self-confidence we feel. When confident of ourselves, we feel that we can deal with being invalidated; when lacking self-confidence, we often see danger where no danger need exist. Take jealousy, for example. Feeling self-confident, we can rejoice in our friend's success at a new job; feeling inferior, we see danger and try to defend ourselves with: "It's not fair." We can fail to see that our friendship should be more important to us than our injured pride.

12 Our levels of confidence also relate to how ready we are to accept change, and how able we are to allow our friends to change. To feel secure in ourselves, we need to be able to predict events reasonably accurately. We think we know our friends well, and so can predict what they will do. We create a mental image of our friends, and we want to keep them within the bounds of that image. Our need to do this can override our ability to see our friends in the way they see themselves. We do not want them to change because then we would have to change our image of them. Change creates uncertainty, and uncertainty can be frightening.

TO CHALLENGE STUDENTS . . .

Conduct Research Paragraph 10 ends with the unsupported assertion, "Live completely on your own and your guesses will get further and further away from reality." Challenge students to investigate the truth of this assertion via online research. Before individuals begin, review how to determine if a source is reliable (e.g., *website is from reliable source, author is an expert in field, information is current, information is verified by research*). Have students work in small groups to generate key words for their online search, such as "living completely on your own" (e.g., *social isolation*). Instruct students to individually research evidence to support the accuracy of the final remark. Then have groups reconvene to compare findings; decide which results were best supported by facts, studies, and expert opinions; and report these to the class.

NOTICE & NOTE

Falling out

13 However, an inability to allow change can lead to the end of a friendship. Falling out with a friend shows us that our image of them, from which we **derive** our predictions about that friend, is wrong; and if that is the case, our sense of being a person is threatened.

14 If we lose a friend, we have to change how we see ourselves and our life. Each of us lives in our own individual world of meaning. We need to find friends whose individual world is somewhat similar to our own so that we are able to communicate with one another.

15 The people who can validate us best are those we can see as equals, and with whom there can be mutual affection, trust, loyalty and acceptance. Such people give us the kind of validation that builds a lasting self-confidence despite the difficulties we encounter.

16 These are our true friends.

derive
(dĭ-rīv′) *v.* to obtain or extract from

SUMMARIZE AND PARAPHRASE TEXTS
Annotate: Mark two details in paragraphs 13–16 that indicate the selection's central idea.

Summarize: In two to four sentences, write an objective summary of the selection.

CHECK YOUR UNDERSTANDING

Answer these questions before moving on to the **Analyze the Text** section on the following page.

1 Many of the author's supporting details come from —

A sociology and television shows
B neuroscience and day-to-day life
C her own friendships in high school
D a documentary film about relationships

2 The author probably included the information in paragraph 6 to —

F explain why emotions are important to our survival
G demonstrate that joy is the key to friendship
H show that joy and jealousy cannot be put into words
J describe how emotions are connected to our sense of being a person

3 How does the author support the idea that the degree of perceived risk and the degree of self-confidence are related?

A By including an example about jealousy over a friend's new job
B By defining the qualities that lead to self-confidence
C By including examples of normal risks taken in healthy friendships
D By comparing two of her friends with varying degrees of self-confidence

SUMMARIZE AND PARAPHRASE TEXTS

Ask students to restate the text's central idea. Then have them identify details in paragraphs 14 and 15 that point to and support that central idea. (***Answer:*** *True friends are important to us because they validate our sense of who we are and how we interpret events, allowing us to feel safe and to build lasting self-confidence. When our sense of self is invalidated we may feel like we're falling apart because our ideas about our identity have been challenged. True friends help us to rebuild our sense of who we are and bolster our self-confidence—and the more self-confidence we have, the better we can withstand challenges to our self image and the more freely we can engage with the world.*)

For **listening support** for students at varying proficiency levels, see the **Text X-Ray** on page 198C.

CHECK YOUR UNDERSTANDING

Have students answer the questions independently.

Answers:

1. *B*
2. *J*
3. *A*

If they answer any questions incorrectly, have them reread the text to confirm their understanding. Then they may proceed to ANALYZE THE TEXT on page 206.

CRITICAL VOCABULARY

derive: We base our predictions about our friends from our images of them.

ASK STUDENTS to explain what they can derive from true friends. (*They can derive validation, affection, trust, loyalty, acceptance, and self-confidence.*)

ENGLISH LEARNER SUPPORT

Oral Assessment Use the questions below to assess students' comprehension and speaking skills. Ask students to respond in short, complete sentences.

1. Where does the author get many supporting details? (*The author gets many details from neuroscience and day-to-day life.*)
2. Why did the author include paragraph 6? (*She wants to show how emotions relate to a sense of safety or danger.*)
3. In paragraph 11, the author suggests that how we think about risk relates to our self-confidence. How does she support this idea? (*She describes how reactions to a friend's success can differ depending on how self-confident a person feels.*) **SUBSTANTIAL/MODERATE**

APPLY

ANALYZE THE TEXT

Possible answers:

1. **DOK 2:** *The first-person pronouns create a welcoming, friendly tone. By introducing the topic in this way, the author suggests that she understands her readers since she has had similar experiences.*
2. **DOK 4:** *She connects her explanation of how we develop constructs about reality and a sense of self to the role of friends by explaining that our sense of self is strengthened by validation, which friends can supply.*
3. **DOK 4:** *Paragraph 12 explains how our capacity to accept change relates to our self-confidence. This explanation helps readers understand the information in the "Falling out" section, which explains what can result from an inability to accept change.*
4. **DOK 3:** *The author provides an anecdote and explanation in paragraph 11 to support this. There she says that if we are self-confident, we do not feel threatened by a friend's accomplishments because they don't endanger our assessment of our self and our accomplishments; but if we lack confidence, our idea of our self may be threatened, causing us to feel jealousy and to try to defend ourselves against this perceived threat. In paragraph 12, she adds that to feel secure, we need to believe that we make accurate predictions about our friends. In paragraph 14, she explains what can happen when a friend isn't predictable. So, by paragraph 15, she has justified this claim by showing how someone who lacks these qualities could destroy our sense of self.*
5. **DOK 4:** *Accept all thoughtful answers. For example, students may note that they were surprised by the concept of emotions being assessments of how safe our sense of our self is and challenged by the idea that "an inability to allow change" can end a friendship.*

RESEARCH

Encourage students to use a dictionary or other reference source to determine the meanings of any technical terms in the article they find.

Connect Students may notice that the topics discussed in their article are similar to those in "With Friends Like These . . ." but that the ideas and explanations differ. Any alternative ideas, explanations, and analyses that are equally plausible to those offered by Rowe may cause them to adjust their views about friendship.

RESPOND

ANALYZE THE TEXT

Support your responses with evidence from the text. NOTEBOOK

1. **Infer** Reread the first paragraph. What **tone**, or attitude, is created by the author's use of the first-person pronouns *we* and *our*? Why do you think she chose to introduce her topic to readers in this way?
2. **Evaluate** In paragraphs 2–4, the author develops her ideas with details from the fields of neuroscience and psychology. How does she connect this information to the key idea that "friendships are essential to our sense of who we are"?
3. **Analyze** In paragraph 12, the author discusses people's capacity to accept change. Why does she introduce these ideas immediately before the section "Falling out"?
4. **Cite Evidence** In paragraph 15, the author makes this claim: "The people who can validate us best are those we can see as equals, and with whom there can be mutual affection, trust, loyalty and acceptance." What evidence does the author provide to support this claim? Is she justified in making it?
5. **Notice & Note** What information challenged, changed, or confirmed what you already knew about friendship? Paraphrase key ideas and details from the text in your answer.

RESEARCH

In paragraph 2 of "With Friends Like These . . ." Dorothy Rowe introduces concepts about friendship based on research by neuroscientists. Find another article about friendship and neuroscience. After you read the article, **freewrite**, or write your thoughts continuously without stopping, for 2 minutes. Record your thoughts about friendship in the chart below.

ARTICLE TITLE AND TOPIC	FREEWRITE
"Your Brain on Friendship" by Sarah Rose Cavanagh Ph.D. The presence of loved ones in threatening situations or just the belief that you do not have to face threats alone affects your brain and thereby your emotional and physical health.	Maybe this explains why we feel comforted by our parents' presence when we are ill and why people with lots of friends appear to be more cheerful and confident.

RESEARCH TIP
When researching an unfamiliar or complex topic, look for sources geared toward a general audience. Technical sources assume that the audience is knowledgeable about the terms and concepts of the academic field. Newspaper articles and books meant for the general reader will be easier to understand.

Connect Share your response to the article with a partner. Talk about ways in which the ideas in your article relate to the ideas in "With Friends Like These . . . ." Did anything in the second article cause you to change your views about friendship? Note details that caused you to adjust your perspective.

LEARNING MINDSET

Try Again Remind students that everyone makes mistakes—especially while learning new things. In fact, making a mistake can be a sign that we are trying to learn something that's unfamiliar or difficult. So, tell students that instead of feeling discouraged when they make a mistake, they should feel encouraged and just try again in a different way. For instance, students might slow down and follow instructions more closely. Alternatively, they might try to paraphrase something they are trying to understand or explain it to a classmate.

CREATE AND PRESENT

Write a Personal Essay Using your notes, charts, and marked-up selection, write a personal essay about how the key ideas in "With Friends Like These . . ." and in your self-selected article relate to your own friendships.

- ❑ Introduce the topic and tell readers how you relate to the key ideas overall. Cite evidence from both your own experiences and the texts.
- ❑ Refer to the characteristics of true friends listed in paragraph 15. Use synonyms if Rowe's wording is too technical.
- ❑ In your final paragraph, discuss how your approach toward friendship might change based on what you learned.

Go to the **Writing Studio** for more on writing a narrative.

Present a Scene With a partner, present a two- to three-minute scene in which two teenagers meet and discover the ideal friend.

- ❑ Share your essay with your partner. Based on your essays and notes, brainstorm a list of the qualities of an ideal friend.
- ❑ Write a script for your scene. Think about how to communicate your ideas through words, actions, and body language. Include a prop.
- ❑ Rehearse your scene. Practice speaking clearly and loudly, facing your audience, and pausing for dramatic effect. Use a synonym if you cannot remember an exact word from your script.

Go to the **Speaking and Listening Studio** for help with giving a presentation.

RESPOND TO THE ESSENTIAL QUESTION

How do we form and maintain our connections with others?

Gather Information Review your "With Friends Like These . . ." notes and annotations. Then, add relevant information to your Response Log. As you determine which information to include, think about:

- how friendships help create and validate our sense of self
- the role of self-confidence in perceiving risk and accepting change
- the conditions and characteristics that promote long, successful friendships

At the end of the unit, use your notes to help you write a short story.

ACADEMIC VOCABULARY

As you write and discuss what you learned from the informational text, be sure to use the Academic Vocabulary words. Check off each of the words that you use.

- ❑ **capacity**
- ❑ **confer**
- ❑ **emerge**
- ❑ **generate**
- ❑ **trace**

CREATE AND PRESENT

Write a Personal Essay Help students to understand the writing assignment by reviewing the following:

- Tell students that the topic of their essay and how their friendships relate to the key ideas of the texts can serve as the basis for their thesis statement. Evidence from their experiences and the texts should support this thesis.
- Remind students that referring to the characteristics of true friends in paragraph 15 does not mean stating all of these characteristics in a second paragraph of their own. They should also be providing their own insights and evidence to support their thesis.
- Explain that their final paragraph might identify a change in their way of being a friend or selecting friends or in the expectations they have of friends. Remind them that they should also restate their thesis here and the reasons they gave to support it.

For **writing support** for students at varying proficiency levels, see the **Text X-Ray** on page 198D.

Present a Scene Point out to students that their first step should be to read one another's essays and list the qualities of friendship that they agree on. Then, using this list as a description of the kind of person they should portray, they should act out a meeting in which they demonstrate these traits. Tell them to exaggerate these qualities in both dialogue and actions.

For **speaking support** for students at varying proficiency levels, see the **Text X-Ray** on page 198D.

RESPOND TO THE ESSENTIAL QUESTION

Allow time for students to add details from "With Friends Like These . . ." to their Unit 3 Response Logs.

APPLY

CRITICAL VOCABULARY

Answers will vary. Make sure that scenes demonstrate the following:

- *a character being validated*
- *a character assessing a situation or another character*
- *a character deriving an idea from an observation*

VOCABULARY STRATEGY
Print and Digital Resources

Possible answers:

1. *constructions: interpretations drawn from experience; The people who appear in my dreams are my brain's constructions of who they are.*
2. *unconscious: unaware; According to Rowe, we're mostly unconscious of the constructions we have formed to explain reality.*
3. *perceive: interpret; I get frustrated when people perceive my shy behavior as snobbishness.*

RESPOND

WORD BANK
validate
assess
derive

CRITICAL VOCABULARY

Practice and Apply Working with a partner, develop a brief scene that depicts the meaning of each Critical Vocabulary word but does not include the word. Swap your scenes with another pair. Pairs will then analyze each other's scenes and identify the Critical Vocabulary word that is being conveyed in each one. Start by briefly describing each idea below.

1. An experience makes a character feel **validated**. Idea for scene:

2. A character **assesses** a situation or another character. Idea for scene:

3. A character **derives** an idea from something he or she observes. Idea for scene:

Go to the **Vocabulary Studio** for more on print and digital sources.

VOCABULARY STRATEGY: Print and Digital Resources

Many informational texts include words and phrases that are specific to a particular discipline. Dorothy Rowe draws on psychology and neurology to support the ideas in "With Friends Like These . . . ." To clarify and validate your understanding of technical words, you can look them up in **print and digital resources** such as glossaries, encyclopedias, technical dictionaries, and print dictionaries. If you find more than one definition for a word, context clues can help you choose the appropriate definition.

Practice and Apply The words below appear in "With Friends Like These . . . ." Look up each word in a print or digital dictionary, glossary, or thesaurus. Then, use the word in an original sentence that demonstrates your understanding of the word as it is used in the text.

1. constructions

2. unconscious

3. perceive

ENGLISH LEARNER SUPPORT

Use Cognates Tell students that the Practice and Apply terms have Spanish cognates: *unconscious/inconsciente, perceive/percibir, construction/construcción*. Encourage Spanish-speaking students to use a Spanish dictionary, glossary, or thesaurus to help them determine the meanings of the words as they are used in the text.

ALL LEVELS

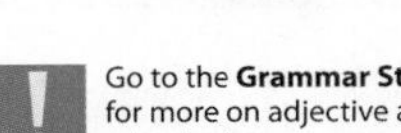

LANGUAGE CONVENTIONS:
Adjective and Adverb Phrases

A **prepositional phrase** is a phrase that consists of a preposition, its object, and any modifiers of the object. Prepositional phrases that modify nouns or pronouns are called **adjective phrases**. Prepositional phrases that modify verbs, adjectives, or adverbs are called **adverb phrases**.

"With Friends Like These . . ." opens with these sentences:

> **We value friends, but the path of friendship, like love, rarely runs smooth. We may feel jealous of a friend's achievements when we want to feel happy for her.**

The prepositional phrase *of friendship* functions as an adjective modifying *path*. The phrases *of a friend's achievements* and *for her* act as adverbs modifying *jealous* and *happy*. Notice how removing the adverb phrases makes the second sentence much less specific:

> **We may feel jealous when we want to feel happy.**

This chart shows sentences from the selection that use prepositional phrases as either adjectives or adverbs. Read each sentence carefully and note the relationship between the phrase and the word it modifies. There may be other words between the phrase and the word it modifies.

ADJECTIVE PHRASE	ADVERB PHRASE
Each of us lives in our own individual world of meaning. (modifies the noun *world*)	**More fundamentally, friendships are essential to our sense of who we are.** (modifies the adjective *essential*)

Practice and Apply Write a summary of the author's ideas about how friendships validate our sense of who we are. Then, revise your paragraph to include at least one of each kind of phrase shown in the chart—a prepositional phrase that functions as an adjective and a prepositional phrase that functions as an adverb.

Go to the **Grammar Studio** for more on adjective and adverb phrases.

LANGUAGE CONVENTIONS:
Adjective and Adverb Phrases

Review these common prepositions: *at, by, for, from, in, of, on, to,* and *with.* Remind students that a prepositional phrase is a phrase that consists of a preposition, its object, and any modifiers of the object. The object of a preposition is whatever the phrase is adding information about.

Note on the board for students' reference that if that information tells *which one, what kind, how much,* or *how many,* the prepositional phrase is modifying a noun or pronoun and acting as an **adjective phrase.** If it tells *where, when, how,* or *to what extent,* the prepositional phrase is modifying a verb, adjective, or adverb and acting as an **adverb phrase.**

Practice and Apply Students' summaries should contain one prepositional phrase that functions as an adjective and one that functions as an adverb. Have partners review one another's summaries to find these.

ENGLISH LEARNER SUPPORT

Use Adjective and Adverb Phrases Have pairs of students find one example each of an adjective phrase and an adverb phrase in the selection. Remind them that these phrases are types of prepositional phrases, which are made up of prepositions and accompanying words. Ask them to work together to write a new sentence using each phrase.

SUBSTANTIAL/MODERATE

ENGLISH LEARNER SUPPORT

Comprehend Language Structures In Cantonese and Korean, adverbs and adverb phrases usually come before verbs, as in this example:

> *More fundamentally, friendships are to our sense of who we are essential.*

Guide native Cantonese and Korean speakers to place adverb phrases after the verb, as in this example:

> *More fundamentally, friendships are essential to our sense of who we are.*

ALL LEVELS

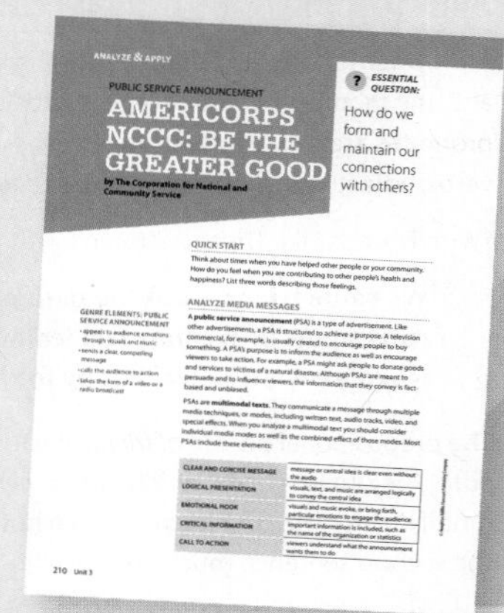

AMERICORPS NCCC: BE THE GREATER GOOD

Public Service Announcement by
The Corporation for National and Community Service

GENRE ELEMENTS

PUBLIC SERVICE ANNOUNCEMENT

Remind students that a public service announcement (PSA) usually has a dual purpose: to inform and/or explain something of importance and to persuade viewers to take a particular action. Since a PSA is designed to persuade, students should be aware that it often utilizes persuasive techniques such as loaded language, appeals to emotion, ethical appeals, as well as powerful visual images, attention-getting sounds, and music chosen to appeal to its target audience. Information in a PSA is usually based on facts. PSAs may take the form of video or radio broadcasts.

LEARNING OBJECTIVES

- Analyze a public service announcement to identify its primary purpose and evaluate the various techniques, or modes, it uses to accomplish that purpose.
- Conduct research to find, watch, and analyze other public service announcements.
- Create and present a public service announcement.
- **Language** Analyze and discuss media images using topic-related vocabulary.

TEXT COMPLEXITY

Quantitative Measures	**"AmeriCorps NCCC: Be the Greater Good"**	**Lexile: N/A**
Qualitative Measures	**Ideas Presented** Explicit and direct; purpose clear.	
	Structures Used Easily identified text structure; images help provide meaning.	
	Language Used Mostly Tier I words; metaphor used throughout.	
	Knowledge Required No background knowledge is needed for comprehension.	

Online 

RESOURCES

- Unit 3 Response Log
-  Reading Studio: Notice & Note
-  Level Up Tutorial: Analyzing Visuals
-  Writing Studio: Producing and Publishing with Technology
-  Speaking and Listening Studio: Using Media in a Presentation
- "AmeriCorps NCCC: Be the Greater Good" Selection Test

SUMMARIES

English

This Public Service Announcement is designed to recruit teenage volunteers into AmeriCorps NCCC. It does so by showing and describing ways in which volunteers serve the greater good through disaster response, environmental stewardship, and infrastructure and community projects. Energizing music and images of volunteers as well as those they serve help convey the sense of accomplishment and camaraderie that volunteers might feel.

Spanish

Este Anuncio de Servicio Público está diseñado para reclutar a adolescentes voluntarios para los AmeriCorps NCCC. Se muestra a jóvenes que están ayudando a otras personas; se les ve apilando sacos de arena y proveyendo agua potable); se ven sus sonrisas de satisfacción y su interconexión; y se sugiere que ellos se sentirán empoderados a través de las imágenes de gente tan joven abriendo un cortafuegos que pare los incendios forestales. Su atractivo es aún más efectivo por su ritmo rápido y energético, por su percusión y por la narración que anuncia a los espectadores qué son (y figurativamente, *quiénes* son) cuando son miembros del AmeriCorps NCCC. El hecho de que esta narración se entienda como poesía hablada es por seguro algo también atrayente para el público al que se dirige.

SMALL-GROUP OPTIONS

Have students work in small groups to read and respond to the selection.

Think-Pair-Share

Have pairs analyze and discuss images from the PSA:

- Have each student select an image from the PSA.
- Have partners discuss the images they chose. Encourage them to consider how the images appeal to the emotions of the audience. (*For example, images might suggest empowerment, connection, strength, personal efficacy, joy, or adventure.*)
- Ask volunteers to share their responses with the class.

Focus on Modes

After students have viewed the PSA and discussed the modes it uses, divide the class into three groups and assign each group one of the following:

- voiceover (word choice, style, tone, message)
- visuals (content, lighting, camera angles)
- sound and music (tempo, volume, style)

Have groups watch the PSA again, taking notes on their particular area of focus. Allow students time to discuss their observations. Then ask a volunteer from each group to share the group's findings.

Text X-Ray: English Learner Support

for "AmeriCorps NCCC: Be the Greater Good"

Use the Text X-Ray and the supports and scaffolds in the Teacher's Edition to help guide students at different proficiency levels through the selection.

INTRODUCE THE SELECTION

DISCUSS COMMUNITY SERVICE

In this lesson, students will need to be able to discuss ways in which people take action to help others. Point out that the public service announcement students will view was created by the Corporation for National and Community Service. Explain that *community service* refers to volunteer work that is done to help the public and that volunteers willingly give help for a cause without expectation of a reward.

Discuss examples of community service. In your discussion, note that *volunteer* can be used as a noun, an adjective, or a verb. Supply the following sentence frames:

- *We volunteer to* ____.
- *A group of volunteers organized* ____.
- *Volunteer workers helped* ____.

CULTURAL REFERENCES

The following words and phrases may be unfamiliar to students:

- *be the greater good* (title; 0:59): take action to benefit the community or the people as a whole
- *sand bag* (0:16): a bag filled with sand that is stacked with others to form a barrier against floodwater
- *forklift* (0:28): a vehicle with a power-operated platform that can be raised and lowered to lift and move items
- *chainsaw* (0:28): a portable saw with teeth linked to form a loop of chain
- *a line in the woods that fires can't cross* (0:42): an area that is cleared of trees and other vegetation in order to prevent the spread of fire

LISTENING

Listen to Media

Have students listen to the audio of the PSA without watching the video.

Use the following supports with students at varying proficiency levels:

- Instruct students to raise their hands whenever they hear *you're* in the voiceover. Then replay the PSA, telling them to write down at least two of the noun phrases that follow the contraction *you're*. **SUBSTANTIAL**
- Pause the audio after every sentence. Have students work in small groups to transcribe and punctuate each sentence. **MODERATE**
- Provide students with a three-column chart with the headings *voiceover, music,* and *pacing*. Have students note observations about each element in the chart as they listen to the PSA. **LIGHT**

SPEAKING

Analyze and Discuss Media Images

Have students analyze and discuss the images in the video.

Use the following supports with students at varying proficiency levels:

- Play the video for students, telling them to study the images of volunteers as you pause at various intervals. Ask yes/no questions such as: Do these volunteers look happy? Are they working hard? Are they working as a team? **SUBSTANTIAL**
- Have students list five adjectives to describe the mood of the PSA and the impact it has on their mood. Encourage them to point out visual details that help create that mood. **MODERATE**
- Ask students to discuss the audience for this PSA. What visual images do the videographers use to ensure that the PSA appeals to a broad audience? **LIGHT**

READING

Demonstrate Comprehension by Using Inferential Skills

Work with students to read the Background note on page 211.

Use the following supports with students at varying proficiency levels:

- Restate the Background information using simple sentences. Ask: Is AmeriCorps a community service program? *(yes)* Do you think this PSA will encourage people to join AmeriCorps? **SUBSTANTIAL**
- Have students use this frame to predict what the PSA will be about: *I predict that the PSA will _____ because the Background note says _____.* **MODERATE**
- Have partners use the Background information about PSAs, the agency that created the PSA, and AmeriCorps to infer the purpose of the PSA. **LIGHT**

WRITING

Use Grade-Appropriate Sentence Patterns

Work with students to read the writing assignment on Student Edition page 213.

Use the following supports with students at varying proficiency levels:

- Tell students that they can rely solely on images and music to convey their message and simply state that message in a sentence at the end. Point out that the subject is understood as *you* (the audience) in imperative sentences that urge a call to action, such as *Join Americorps NCCC*. Provide additional examples: *Protect (our parks). Stop (violence). Support (our school).* **SUBSTANTIAL**
- Provide these frames to help students plan their PSAs: *The topic of my PSA is _____. The audience for my PSA is _____. The purpose of my PSA is to encourage my audience to _____. My main message will be _____. Details that support my message include _____.* **MODERATE**
- Have students write their main point and supporting details on strips of paper. Then have them choose the most logical and effective organization to arrange the strips. **LIGHT**

TEACH

Connect to the ESSENTIAL QUESTION

The Public Service Announcement (PSA) about AmeriCorps NCCC promotes joining the group to help others. It also claims AmeriCorps participants form strong connections with their peers. In fact, the PSA makes such connections seem exhilarating and an inevitable outcome of joining AmeriCorps.

QUICK START

Help students begin this activity by brainstorming a list of situations and relationships in which they may have played a helping role. These might include helping a parent by doing chores at home; helping elderly relatives or neighbors with errands, gardening, or by bringing them books or movies from the library; helping a friend or sibling with homework; or contributing to a food drive or a bake sale to raise money for a worthwhile cause. Invite students to describe how they feel when they help others.

ANALYZE MEDIA MESSAGES

Have students read the information about analyzing media messages. Then ask them to share examples of the elements in the chart from other media messages they have viewed. Discuss the following questions:

- What was the central idea of the media message you viewed?
- How did visuals, text, and music work together to support the central message?
- What emotions did the media message evoke?
- What information about the topic did the media message include?
- What action did the media message want the audience to take?

ANALYZE & APPLY

PUBLIC SERVICE ANNOUNCEMENT

AMERICORPS NCCC: BE THE GREATER GOOD

by The Corporation for National and Community Service

? ESSENTIAL QUESTION:

How do we form and maintain our connections with others?

QUICK START

Think about times when you have helped other people or your community. How do you feel when you are contributing to other people's health and happiness? List three words describing those feelings.

ANALYZE MEDIA MESSAGES

GENRE ELEMENTS: PUBLIC SERVICE ANNOUNCEMENT

- appeals to audience emotions through visuals and music
- sends a clear, compelling message
- calls the audience to action
- takes the form of a video or a radio broadcast

A **public service announcement** (PSA) is a type of advertisement. Like other advertisements, a PSA is structured to achieve a purpose. A television commercial, for example, is usually created to encourage people to buy something. A PSA's purpose is to inform the audience as well as encourage viewers to take action. For example, a PSA might ask people to donate goods and services to victims of a natural disaster. Although PSAs are meant to persuade and to influence viewers, the information that they convey is fact-based and unbiased.

PSAs are **multimodal texts.** They communicate a message through multiple media techniques, or modes, including written text, audio tracks, video, and special effects. When you analyze a multimodal text you should consider individual media modes as well as the combined effect of those modes. Most PSAs include these elements:

CLEAR AND CONCISE MESSAGE	message or central idea is clear even without the audio
LOGICAL PRESENTATION	visuals, text, and music are arranged logically to convey the central idea
EMOTIONAL HOOK	visuals and music evoke, or bring forth, particular emotions to engage the audience
CRITICAL INFORMATION	important information is included, such as the name of the organization or statistics
CALL TO ACTION	viewers understand what the announcement wants them to do

ENGLISH LEARNER SUPPORT

Recognize Directionality and Decode Words Read aloud the information about the elements of PSAs in the chart, reinforcing students' understanding of directionality by pointing out that the information in the right column explains each element in the left column. Tell students that several of the terms in the chart have Spanish cognates: clear message/mensaje claro, logical presentation/presentatión lógico, emotion/emoción, critical information/información crítico, action/acción. Note that the suffix *-tion* in English functions similarly to the *-ción* suffix in Spanish by forming nouns. **ALL LEVELS**

BACKGROUND

A public service announcement (PSA) is a message usually produced for television or radio about a topic or issue of interest to the public. Media and news organizations distribute PSAs at no charge. This particular announcement is for a program that is part of the Corporation for National and Community Service, a federal agency that provides support to volunteer organizations and to individual volunteers around the country. The program, which is called AmeriCorps NCCC (National Civilian Community Corps), develops leaders and strengthens communities through team-based community service.

SETTING A PURPOSE

As you view the video, pay attention to how the visuals, music, and text contribute to the PSA's message. NOTEBOOK.

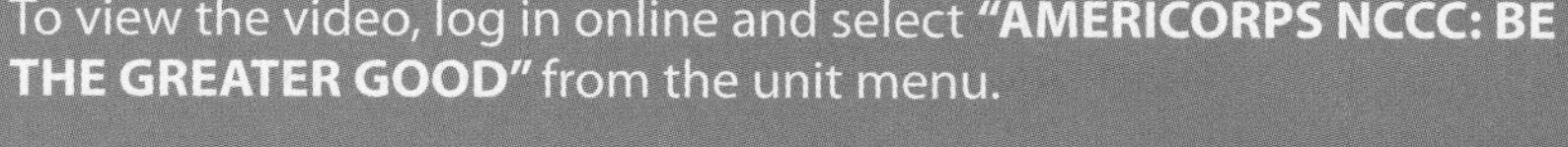

To view the video, log in online and select **"AMERICORPS NCCC: BE THE GREATER GOOD"** from the unit menu.

As needed, pause the video to make notes about how the visuals, music, and text work together to communicate each idea. Replay or rewind so that you can clarify anything you do not understand.

WHEN STUDENTS STRUGGLE . . .

Analyze Media Messages Explain that metaphors are figures of speech that directly compare two unlike things. Point out that the PSA uses the phrase *You're a* to compare the viewer to solutions to problems that AmeriCorps NCCC volunteers address. Have students view the PSA with partners, using a two-column chart with the headings *Metaphor* and *Images* to take notes on the images that relate to each metaphor. Then have partners discuss how the images help them understand the meaning of each metaphor and the overall message of the PSA.

For additional support, go to the **Reading Studio** and assign the following **Level Up Tutorial: Analyzing Visuals.**

TEACH

BACKGROUND

You may wish to share that Public Service Announcements have been used for decades. The first PSAs were released shortly before World War II. For example, "loose lips sink ships" was a message broadcast during WWII to warn people against speaking openly about information that could, if it was overheard by spies, jeopardize the success of war efforts. The goal of a PSA is usually to raise awareness about an issue or problem and provoke a feeling or reaction that will prompt a desired action.

ENGLISH LEARNER SUPPORT

Identify Purpose of Environmental Print Before students view the video, review what public service announcements aim to achieve. Have students look at the chart on page 210 and go over the Critical Information row. Explain that one way to convey critical information in a video is to use environmental print, or the print that people find around them every day. Signs, posters, logos, billboards, and labels are all forms of environmental print.

Encourage students to look for environmental print as they view the video and to pause the video to examine environmental print more closely. After viewing, have partners or small groups discuss the environmental print they saw in the video. Ask: What information did the environmental print give, and what was its purpose? *(The NCCC logos on shirts show that the people are working for the National Civilian Community Corps. The badges on the sleeves highlight that it is Americorps. The purpose is to show the connection between the work and workers to the organization.)*

MODERATE/LIGHT

SETTING A PURPOSE

Direct students to use the Setting a Purpose prompt to focus their viewing.

For **listening, speaking, and reading support** for students at varying proficiency levels, see the **Text X-Ray** on pages 210C–210D.

APPLY

ANALYZE MEDIA

Possible answers:

1. **DOK 2:** *Volunteers might help build or rebuild homes, pass out water after a disaster, lay sandbags to prevent flooding, use power tools and machines to clear areas and rebuild after a disaster, fight fires, and plant community gardens.*
2. **DOK 2:** *AmeriCorps wants the audience to feel excited and eager to be part of its team. Audio that says "You're a team member," combined with visuals of people smiling at one another and groups of volunteers walking, running, hugging, and sitting together, foster these feelings.*
3. **DOK 4:** *The music is upbeat and fast-paced; the beat of the music thumps like a hammer, reinforcing the image of pounding a nail with a hammer, and conveys the idea that the volunteers work hard and are driven to help others. The images are often lit by bright sunlight, while the camera angles are mid-range to close-up to focus on actions and connection. Together these elements communicate the joy of teamwork and helping others.*
4. **DOK 4:** *"Be the Greater Good" emphasizes helping others and solving problems. Each statement that begins with the phrase* You're a *supports this central message by identifying ways in which volunteers help others, such as by delivering water to help disaster victims.*
5. **DOK 4:** *This is an effective PSA for the following reasons: The hook shows people in need and workers meeting those needs. It shows enjoyable aspects of volunteering, including traveling and working with others. The pacing of the images and the upbeat music also help create a mood that might appeal to the audience. Toward the end, the narrator asks people to join the AmeriCorps NCCC, which is a clear and direct call to action. Finally, it ends with a powerful "Be the greater good" message.*

RESEARCH

Tell students to avoid search items that begin with the word *Ad* boxed in red before their content descriptions, as these are clearly paid advertisements.

Extend Although the text encourages students to analyze the PSA's techniques, remind students to consider the impact of each PSA as a whole.

RESPOND

ANALYZE MEDIA

Support your answers with evidence from the video. NOTEBOOK

1. **Summarize** In your own words, describe jobs that a volunteer for AmeriCorps NCCC might perform.
2. **Infer** How does AmeriCorps NCCC want the audience to feel about volunteering as part of a team? What audio and visuals in the PSA help communicate this? Cite specific words, scenes or images in your response.
3. **Integrate** Describe the music, lighting, camera angle and perspective used in the video. In what way do they support the purpose of the video?
4. **Synthesize** Explain the title and last line "Be the Greater Good." How does this phrase relate to the voiceover statements that begin "You're a . . ."?
5. **Critique** Think about the purpose of the PSA. Consider the hook, the call to action, and the techniques used to present information. Do you think "Be the Greater Good" is an effective PSA? Why or why not?

RESEARCH

In a small group, research two additional PSAs on topics people in your group care about. Compare and contrast the use of media elements, and determine the main message that each PSA sends.

RESEARCH TIP
When researching PSAs, watch out for advertisements that do not fit the genre. Navigate away from any video that appears biased, not based on facts, or focused on a commercial product. Review any accompanying notes that identify the creator, publication date, and purpose of the PSA. Find the website or the organization that sponsors the PSA; it is most likely reputable if its URL ends in *.org*, *.edu*, or *.gov*.

TITLE OF PSA	PSA 1	PSA 2
Voiceover: Language style and techniques	Students should accurately describe the elements of the PSAs they research.	
Visual techniques		
Sound/music techniques		
Special effects		
Message		

Extend Compare the two PSAs you researched. Which PSA communicates its main message more effectively? How?

ENGLISH LEARNER SUPPORT

Oral Assessment To gauge comprehension and speaking skills, conduct an informal assessment. Walk around the class, talking with students and asking these questions:

- Do AmericCorps NCCC volunteers help people affected by disasters? *(yes)* **SUBSTANTIAL**
- What types of jobs do AmericCorps NCCC volunteers perform? *(build homes, deliver supplies, maintain parks, plant gardens)* **MODERATE**
- How do AmericCorps NCCC volunteers serve communities? *(through disaster response and environmental and community projects)* **LIGHT**

CREATE AND PRESENT

Create a Public Service Announcement In a small group, create a PSA script or storyboard in which you send a message and deliver a call to action.

- ❏ Brainstorm a list of issues people in your group care about, then come to a consensus on a topic.
- ❏ Determine a compelling way to hook your audience. Think about how to best use audio, video, and voiceover text to achieve your purpose.
- ❏ Find factual information to include in your PSA. Credit your sources.
- ❏ Write the script and/or storyboard for your PSA to organize the multiple streams of information you want to present.

Go to the **Writing Studio** for more on producing and publishing with technology.

Present a Public Service Announcement Turn your plan into a finished product, which your group will present to the class.

- ❏ Choose the format for your presentation: audio (for a radio broadcast), video, or poster presentation.
- ❏ Make a list of equipment you will need, and consult with your teacher and media center about obtaining it.
- ❏ Assign specific roles and responsibilities to each group member so that all elements of your PSA are covered.
- ❏ When delivering your presentation, keep in mind the message and call to action that you want the audience to hear. Use speaking rate, volume, and pauses to emphasize your message.

Go to the **Speaking and Listening Studio** for more on using media in a presentation.

RESPOND TO THE ESSENTIAL QUESTION

How do we form and maintain our connections with others?

Gather Information Review your notes on "AmeriCorps NCCC: Be the Greater Good." Then, add relevant information to your Response Log. As you determine which information to include, think about:

- How helping people enhances your connection to them
- The benefits to working as part of a group to help others

At the end of the unit, use your notes to help you write a short story.

ACADEMIC VOCABULARY

As you write and discuss what you learned from the public service announcement, be sure to use the Academic Vocabulary words. Check off each of the words that you use.

- ❏ **capacity**
- ❏ **confer**
- ❏ **emerge**
- ❏ **generate**
- ❏ **trace**

APPLY

CREATE AND PRESENT

Create a Public Service Announcement Have students begin by discussing the PSAs they analyzed during their research activity. In particular, suggest that students share with one another the ways these PSAs hook their audience. Direct groups to identify what made the best hooks effective. Suggest that they consider not only the images but also audio, text, and voiceovers. Tell students that they can apply what they have discovered about strong hooks when creating their own PSAs.

For **writing support** for students at varying proficiency levels, see the **Text X-Ray** on page 210D.

Present a Public Service Announcement Explain to students who are creating audio and/or video broadcasts that they may need to allow time to connect the segments of audio or video they have created and to integrate music into their presentation. Remind students to:

- Choose engaging visuals that clearly support the message
- Assess the order of visuals, text, and sound elements to create a logical sequence
- Evaluate the pacing of the presentation to keep the message clear and the audience engaged

RESPOND TO THE ESSENTIAL QUESTION

Allow time for students to add details from "AmeriCorps NCCC: Be the Greater Good" to their Unit 3 Response Logs.

MENTOR TEXT

LOSER

Short Story by **Aimee Bender**

This short story serves as a **mentor text**, a model for students to follow when they come to the Unit 3 Writing Task: Write a Short Story.

GENRE ELEMENTS
SHORT STORY

Tell students that, like novels, **short stories** have characters, setting, and plot and can have elements of realism, fantasy, magic, or science fiction. Because of its length, a short story generally focuses on one main conflict that propels the plot to its conclusion.

LEARNING OBJECTIVES

- Analyze the plot of a short story, recognizing chronology and flashbacks, and the methods used to develop characterization.
- Conduct research on common themes in fiction.
- Write about theme and discuss theme with a small group.
- Use context clues to determine the meaning of words.
- Identify and use active-voice and passive-voice constructions.
- **Language Objective** Discuss examples of characterization using the term *evidence*.

TEXT COMPLEXITY

Quantitative Measures	**Loser** Lexile: 900L
Qualitative Measures	**Ideas Presented** Some implied meaning requires inferential reasoning. Use of symbolism.
	Structures Used Clear point of view. Mostly chronological order but with some deviation.
	Language Used Mostly explicit and conventional language, with some inference required.
	Knowledge Required Subject and situation somewhat unconventional but easily envisioned.

Online 

RESOURCES

- Unit 3 Response Log
- Selection Audio
- Reading Studio: Notice & Note:
- Level Up Tutorial: Plot: Sequence of Events
- Writing Studio: Planning and Drafting
- Speaking and Listening Studio: Participating in Collaborative Discussions
- Vocabulary Studio: Context Clues
- Grammar Studio: Module 6: Lesson 4: Active and Passive Voice
- "Loser"/ "At Dusk" Selection Test

SUMMARIES

English

"Loser" tells about a young man who was orphaned as a child. He later discovers a special talent for finding lost objects, which seem to call to him in a way that no one else can hear or sense. As a young man, he uses this gift to help others in his community. Sadly, his rare ability sets him apart and keeps him from forming meaningful connections with others. One day, a woman begs the young man to find her son, who has failed to return home from school. The young man finds the boy, but he then returns to his lonely room and thinks of finding his own lost parents.

Spanish

"Perdedor" cuenta la historia de un joven que quedó huérfano cuando era niño. Luego descubre su talento especial de encontrar objetos perdidos, que parecen llamarlo en una forma que nadie más puede escuchar o sentir. De joven, utiliza sus dones para ayudar a otros en su comunidad. Tristemente, su raro talento lo aparta de los demás y le impide formar conexiones significativas. Un día, una mujer le ruega que encuentre a su hijo menor, quien no ha vuelto a casa después de la escuela. El joven lo hace, pero regresa a su habitación solitaria y piensa sobre sus padres perdidos.

SMALL-GROUP OPTIONS

Have students work in small groups to read and discuss the selection.

Pinwheel Discussion

- Seat groups of six in a pinwheel pattern, with three students in the center facing out, and one student across from each facing in.
- Have students of the inner circle remain seated in place throughout the discussion.
- Have students in the outer circle move to their right after discussing each question.
- Read aloud a new question to the group for each rotation. For example:
  1. What was the conflict, or main problem, of the story?
  2. Was the young man in "Loser" a believable character? Explain.
  3. Why do you think that the author didn't give the young man a name?

Reciprocal Teaching

- After students have read "Loser" at least once, provide them with question stems, such as these: *Why did the author ______? How did the community ______? What was the young man's attitude toward ______? What was the purpose of ______?*
- Instruct students to work individually, using the stems to write questions about the story.
- In groups of two or three students, have each student offer two discussion questions. Make sure that questions are not duplicated.
- Have groups work together to answer each question and support it with text evidence.

Text X-Ray: English Learner Support
for "Loser"

Use the Text X-Ray and the supports and scaffolds in the Teacher's Edition to help guide students at different proficiency levels through the selection.

INTRODUCE THE SELECTION

DISCUSS ELEMENTS OF FANTASY

In this lesson, students will need to be able to discuss a work of fiction containing fantastical elements in an otherwise realistic setting. Explain the following:

- *Fiction* tells an imaginary story.
- *Realistic fiction* is an imaginary story that tells about ordinary life. Realistic fiction could be true.
- In *fantasy fiction,* the plot might involve the supernatural, or characters might have superhuman powers.

Discuss the differences between realism and fantasy in fiction, using these sentence frames:

- *______ is an example of a realistic setting.*
- *A character who can ______ has superhuman powers. Such a character might be found in a story that is an example of ______.*

CULTURAL REFERENCES

The following words or phrases may be unfamiliar to students:

- *to . . . sniff out* (paragraph 1): to detect and find, as a dog uses its nose to sniff and find things
- *burst into laughter* (paragraph 2): laughed suddenly and loudly
- *boom* (paragraph 2): an exclamation used to call attention to what has been described or said
- *watched him like a hawk* (paragraph 6): watched him closely, as a hawk stares intently at its prey
- *party trick* (paragraph 9): an act done mainly to impress
- *run with tears* (paragraph 19): worn out because of crying
- *to feel the scent of the boy* (paragraph 23): usually one smells a scent; feeling a scent indicates supernatural powers
- *fourteen houses back* (paragraph 32): a return trip the length of fourteen houses

LISTENING

Use Context Clues

Tell students they can find clues in the text to understand the meaning of unfamiliar words and phrases.

Have students listen as you read aloud paragraphs 1–2. Explain footnotes as needed. Use the following supports with students at varying proficiency levels, using explanations in Cultural References as needed:

- Use pictures and/or objects to support understanding of *swimming, ocean, sunglasses,* and other words in the text. After reading paragraph 1, ask: What does *sniff* mean? Read aloud paragraph 2, pausing after *young man's nose twitched* to ask the question again. **SUBSTANTIAL**
- Discuss questions about words and phrases in the passage. Ask: What does *sniff out lost sunglasses* mean? What clues did you hear? **MODERATE**
- Have students write down unfamiliar words as you read the passage. Discuss context clues that suggest the words' meanings. **LIGHT**

SPEAKING

Discuss Characterization

Have students discuss characterization using the term *evidence.*

Use the following supports with students at varying proficiency levels:

- Display and choral read the following sentence with students: *"Jenny's mother kissed the young man on the cheek but Jenny herself looked at him suspiciously all night long."* Point to the underscored words and say, "The way Jenny and her mother act tell us that some people trust the young man and others don't. Does Jenny's mother trust him?" *(yes)* "Does Jenny trust him?" *(no)* **SUBSTANTIAL**
- Have partners discuss the character's thoughts in the story. Provide sentence frames: *In paragraph 5, evidence of characterization includes ____. In paragraph 7, the young man's thoughts of ____ are evidence of characterization.* **MODERATE**
- Ask partners to read aloud and discuss paragraphs 11–20 using the phrase *evidence of characterization*. Have them discuss how each paragraph contributes to understanding the young man's characterization. **LIGHT**

READING

Analyze Plot

Explain that a **linear plot** follows events in the order in which the characters experience the events. A **non-linear plot** is not strictly chronological or sequential; it jumps backward and/or forward in time.

Use the following supports with students at varying proficiency levels;

- Display a curved plot line labeled *exposition* at its start, followed by the remaining stages in sequence. Write the words *yesterday, today, tomorrow* in sequence along the plot line. Trace the line and ask: Is this a linear plot? *(yes)* Reorder *yesterday, today,* and *tomorrow* to explain the term *non-linear plot*. **SUBSTANTIAL**
- Use questions to help students identify the story's order of events: How old is the boy at the beginning of the story? *(eight)* How do we know time is moving forward in paragraph 2? *(The boy is now a "young man.")* **MODERATE**
- Have student pairs read alternate paragraphs aloud, looking for evidence of a linear plot or a non-linear plot. Have them mark plot stages in the margin pf the text. **LIGHT**

WRITING

Write a Statement About Theme

Work with students to read the writing assignment on Student Edition page 223.

Use the following supports with students at varying proficiency levels:

- Display a web diagram with a theme in the center. Complete the web by adding examples from "Loser" that connect to the theme. Add words describing the connection on each spoke. **SUBSTANTIAL**
- Have students complete a web diagram; then use it to complete sentence starters: *One theme in "Loser" is ____. Evidence supporting this theme includes ____. The evidence connects to the theme because ____.* **MODERATE**
- Provide a list of transitional words, phrases, and clauses. Have students use at least three of them in the statement. **LIGHT**

Connect to the ESSENTIAL QUESTION

"Loser" describes one young man's unique talent and how it sets him apart from other people in his community. The story explores the way his talent helps him form and facilitate connections, while making him feel disconnected from people, too.

COMPARE THEMES

Tell students that in this Collaborate & Compare lesson, students will explore two selections—a short story and a poem—that express similar themes. Allow students time to preview the titles and the photographs that illustrate the two selections. Then read the Essential Question aloud. Ask students to volunteer any impressions or predictions they have about the two selections based on this information.

MENTOR TEXT

At the end of the unit, students will be asked to write a short story. "Loser" provides a model for how a writer can develop a short story that engages readers with descriptive details and maintains a consistent point of view.

SHORT STORY

LOSER

by **Aimee Bender**

pages 217–221

COMPARE THEMES

As you read, notice how authors working in two different genres address similar themes. What messages do these texts relate about the world in general? How do the authors express those messages? After you review both selections, you will collaborate with a small group on a final project.

ESSENTIAL QUESTION:

How do we form and maintain our connections with others?

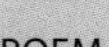

POEM

AT DUSK

by **Natasha Trethewey**

pages 229–231

LEARNING MINDSET

Effort Remind students that learning requires effort and that their abilities will increase as they work through problems. Encourage students to keep trying if they don't understand something right away. Remember to reinforce students for their efforts—for example: "You put a great deal of effort into your assignment. You may have struggled to get started, but you kept at it. Once you settled into your work, you kept going and that enabled you to finish everything successfully and on time."

Loser

QUICK START

Think about something you have lost that meant a lot to you. How did you try to find it? Would you have given up something else of value in order to get it back? Write for a few minutes about the thing you lost and what it meant to you.

ANALYZE PLOT

Authors usually write fictional stories in chronological, or **linear**, order. This means the author reveals plot events in the order that the characters experience them. Sometimes, however, an author will create a **non-linear plot**. They may use these literary devices:

- **Flashbacks:** the placement of earlier events into the present action, often by having a character recall something that happened in the past.
- **Foreshadowing:** a technique that warns readers of future events.
- **Subplots:** a device in which less important events happen at about the same time as the main plot, but in a separate place and to different characters.

As you read "Loser," notice the sequence of plot events and the author's use of flashbacks. How do the flashbacks help push the plot forward and help you better understand the story's characters and messages?

ANALYZE CHARACTERIZATION

The way a writer creates and develops characters' personalities is known as **characterization.** Authors develop complex yet believable characters by describing what they do, say, and think, as well as how they interact with other characters. These details about the characters often shape the story's themes. Use a chart like the one below to record text details that reveal the personality of this story's main character. Then, make an inference or ask a question about each detail.

TEXT EVIDENCE	EXAMPLES	INFERENCES AND QUESTIONS
Character's words and actions		
Character's thoughts and observations		
What others say to and about the character		

As you read "Loser," note how the author uses the main character's traits and experiences to relate messages about life.

GENRE ELEMENTS: SHORT STORY

- contains elements found in longer fiction, such as character, setting, and plot development
- usually focuses on a single idea and one or very few settings and moments in time
- can usually be read in one sitting

QUICK START

Before students write, share experiences about things you have lost and tried to recover. To help expand students' thinking, share stories about losing both material and non-material things. For example, you might share a story about losing a family heirloom and the efforts you underwent to recover it. You might also share a story about losing a friend over a misunderstanding and how you attempted to repair the relationship.

ANALYZE PLOT

Help students understand the difference between a *linear* and a *non-linear* plot. Use a student's class schedule, as in this example, to model a story told in chronological order.

7:30 A.M.: A student arrives at her first class of the day.

11:30 A.M.: The student is handed an exam that she didn't study for. She panics.

2:30 P.M.: The student heads home, smiling.

Next, use a timetable to tell the same story in a non-linear way, with a *flashback:*

11:30 A.M.: The student is handed an exam that she didn't study for. She panics. Then she notices the topic.

Flashback to last summer: Student remembers visiting Gettysburg and learning about the Gettysburg Address.

Use the same model to illustrate other plot devices.

Foreshadowing: During her walk to school, she passes a man delivering a speech to some tourists.

Subplot: She later learns that the man used to teach history at her school. She writes a story about him for the school newspaper.

ANALYZE CHARACTERIZATION

Point out that one character detail, by itself, is not enough to give an accurate portrayal of a character; instead, students should compare details as they read before drawing conclusions.

Remind students that in a work of fiction, a **theme** is the central idea or message about life. Use this frame to help students relate characterization to theme: *Because the main character is [brief description of the character], I think that the story's theme is about [possible theme].*

TEACH

CRITICAL VOCABULARY

Remind students to read all the sentences before deciding which word best completes each one.

Answers:

1. *skeptic*
2. *scam*
3. *insistent*
4. *knack*

■ English Learner Support

Use Cognates Tell students that two of the Critical Vocabulary words have Spanish cognates: *skeptic/escéptico* and *insistent/insistente.* **ALL LEVELS**

LANGUAGE CONVENTIONS: Active and Passive Voice

Tell students that using the active voice usually makes sentences shorter, more direct, and easier to understand. Use these examples to illustrate:

I read the story. (active voice)

The story was read by me. (passive voice)

Point out that the passive voice is useful, however, when the doer of the action is unknown or unimportant, as in *That house was built in 1860.*

■ English Learner Support

Compare Verb Forms Reinforce students' understanding of the passive voice by having them identify the passive-voice construction (underlined here) in each of the following pairs: *plan / is planned; designed / was designed; will be sung / will sing; has been explained / has explained; can tell / can be told.* Read each pair aloud and have students raise their hand when they hear the passive-voice construction. Point out the various forms of *be* in the passive-voice constructions. **SUBSTANTIAL/MODERATE**

ANNOTATION MODEL

Remind students that they may use highlighting or a variety of markings to note text details concerning plot devices, character traits, and inferences about theme as they read. Have them use the margins for questions, interpretations, and other comments about the text.

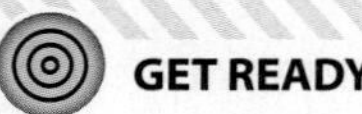

GET READY

CRITICAL VOCABULARY

knack **skeptic** **scam** **insistent**

To see how many Critical Vocabulary words you already know, use them to complete the sentences below.

1. I am a(n) ____________ and don't believe in ghosts or UFOs.
2. If an offer seems too good to be true, it could be a(n) ____________.
3. I didn't want another piece of pie, but my aunt was ____________.
4. Take the broken phone to Olivia, who has a(n) ________ for fixing them.

LANGUAGE CONVENTIONS
Active and Passive Voice

In a sentence in the **active voice**, the subject performs the action. In the sentence below from the selection, the subject (the neighbors) did the action (discovered):

The neighbors discovered his talent accidentally. . .

In the **passive voice**, the subject (his talent) is being acted upon:

His talent was discovered by the neighbors accidentally.

Writers usually use the active voice because it is clear and direct. They may use the passive voice to emphasize the object or the action, rather than who or what did it.

As you read "Loser," look for examples of sentences written in the active voice and in the passive voice.

ANNOTATION MODEL

NOTICE & NOTE

Here is how one student annotated plot developments in "Loser."

Once there was an orphan who had a knack for finding lost things. Both his parents had been killed when he was eight years old—they were swimming in the ocean when it turned wild with waves, and each had tried to save the other from drowning. The boy woke up from a nap, on the sand, alone. After the tragedy, the community adopted and raised him, and a few years after the deaths of his parents, he began to have a sense of objects even when they weren't visible. This ability continued growing in power through his teens and by his twenties, he was able to actually sniff out lost sunglasses, keys, contact lenses and sweaters.

The author starts the story with a flashback to tell about the day the boy became an orphan.

The story is set years later, when he is in his twenties.

NOTICE & NOTE

BACKGROUND

Aimee Bender *(b.1969) is an American writer whose short stories have been published in many magazines and journals, as well as read aloud on radio broadcasts and podcasts. Her five books, all collections of short stories, have won several awards. Bender often writes about realistic-seeming characters set in our real world, but with slightly magical or fantastical elements. The following story, "Loser," appeared in her book* The Girl in the Flammable Skirt, *which was first published in 1988. Bender lives with her family in Los Angeles, where she teaches creative writing at the University of Southern California.*

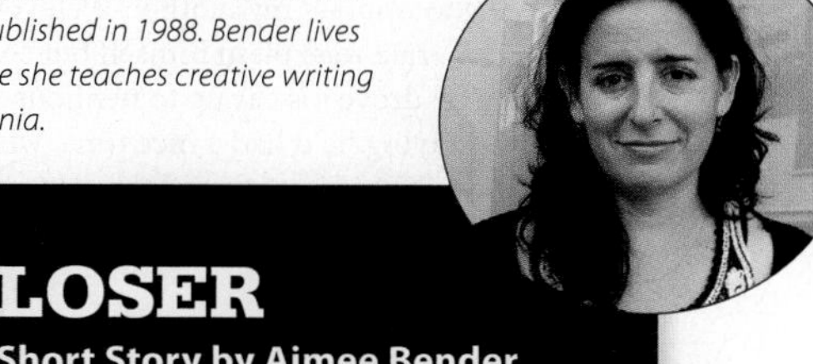

LOSER

Short Story by Aimee Bender

PREPARE TO COMPARE

As you read, think about how the characters' experiences connect to your own or to those of other characters you have read about. Ask yourself what the events tell you about the characters in this story.

1 Once there was an orphan who had a **knack** for finding lost things. Both his parents had been killed when he was eight years old—they were swimming in the ocean when it turned wild with waves, and each had tried to save the other from drowning. The boy woke up from a nap, on the sand, alone. After the tragedy, the community adopted and raised him, and a few years after the deaths of his parents, he began to have a sense of objects even when they weren't visible. This ability continued growing in power through his teens and by his twenties, he was able to actually sniff out lost sunglasses, keys, contact lenses and sweaters.

2 The neighbors discovered his talent accidentally—he was over at Jenny Sugar's house one evening, picking her up for a date, when Jenny's mother misplaced her hairbrush, and was walking around, complaining about this. The young man's nose twitched and he turned slightly toward the kitchen and pointed to the drawer where the spoons and knives were kept. His date burst into laughter. Now that would be quite a silly place to put

Notice & Note

You can use the side margins to notice and note signposts in the text.

knack
(năk) *n.* a special talent for doing something.

LANGUAGE CONVENTIONS

Annotate: Mark an example of passive voice in the first paragraph.

Respond: Why do you think the author started the story using passive voice?

BACKGROUND

Explain that a *fantastical element* is something that you would not expect to see in real life and that the fantastical element in "Loser" will be revealed early in the story. Point out that when authors mix fantasy with realism, they expect readers to accept the "unreal" elements as truth. At the same time, the "unreal" element may reveal something about a story's characters and help point to a story's theme.

PREPARE TO COMPARE

Direct students to use the Prepare to Compare prompt to focus their reading.

LANGUAGE CONVENTIONS

Remind students that passive voice combines the verb *to be* with another verb. After students identify the passive voice in the text, point out that some sentences would be difficult to recast in the active voice. (***Answer:*** *The passive voice keeps the narrative focus on the young boy.)*

For **listening and speaking support** for students at varying proficiency levels, see the **Text X-Ray** on pages 214C–214D.

WHEN STUDENTS STRUGGLE . . .

Track Plot Events Encourage students to trace the events of the story by using a two-column chart that lists story parts (which you may wish to review first) and provides space for writing details: **Exposition** [paragraphs 1–7], **Rising Action** [paragraphs 8–30], **Climax** [paragraph 31], **Falling Action** [paragraphs 32–35], and **Resolution** [paragraphs 36–38]. Instruct students to Include notes about flashbacks in the space for writing details.

For additional support, go to the **Reading Studio** and assign the following **Level Up Tutorial: Plot: Sequence of Events.**

CRITICAL VOCABULARY

knack: The boy's special talent was finding things that people had lost or misplaced.

ASK STUDENTS to find details in paragraph 1 that describe how the boy discovered that he had a knack for finding things. *(After his parents died, he realized that he could "sense" objects, such as "sunglasses, keys, contact lenses and sweaters," even if he could not see them.)*

ANALYZE PLOT

Help students understand the role of this *inciting event*—an event that sets into motion the tensions that will drive the plot. Before students make a prediction, ask them how they think they would react to knowing that a neighbor had this gift. (***Answer:*** *People may keep their distance, though some may take advantage of him because he can help them find things.)*

For **reading support** for students at varying proficiency levels, see the **Text X-Ray** on page 214D.

ANALYZE PLOT

Read aloud paragraphs 7 and 8. Listening to the story read aloud may help students identify the shift in time. (***Answer:*** *In paragraphs 1–7, the author gave information about the young man's past and his gift. Paragraph 8 begins with a specific time, which shifts the story into the present and to the story's main events.)*

CRITICAL VOCABULARY

skeptic: Some people doubted the young man's ability.

ASK STUDENTS how the skeptics behaved differently from the "appreciative ones." *(The "appreciative ones" gave him gifts; the skeptics suggested that he was a thief.)*

scam: The skeptics thought the young man had a plan to cheat them.

ASK STUDENTS to discuss the scam that one woman believed in. *(She thought that his scam was to hide things and then later find them, just to get attention.)*

insistent: The lost object kept trying to get his attention.

ASK STUDENTS how the object insists on the young man's attention. *(It repeatedly demands his attention, "like a child [tugging] at his sleeve," until he moves toward it and finds it.)*

NOTICE & NOTE

ANALYZE PLOT

Annotate: How do other people find out about the young man's gift? Mark the words that tell the reader.

Predict: How do you think people will treat the young man now that they know this?

skeptic (skĕp′tĭk) *n.* someone who doubts something.

scam (skăm) *n.* a plan to cheat others, often out of money.

insistent (ĭn-sĭs′tənt) *adj.* demanding that something happen or refusing to accept that it will not happen.

ANALYZE PLOT

Annotate: Mark words the author uses to establish time in this part of the story.

Analyze: How does the author shift from past events to the current or main events of the story?

the brush, she said, among all that silverware! and she opened the drawer to make her point, to wave with a knife or brush her hair with a spoon, but when she did, boom, there was the hairbrush, matted with gray curls, sitting astride the fork pile.

3 Jenny's mother kissed the young man on the cheek but Jenny herself looked at him suspiciously all night long.

4 You planned all that, didn't you, she said, over dinner. You were trying to impress my mother. Well you didn't impress me, she said.

5 He tried to explain himself but she would hear none of it and when he drove his car up to her house, she fled before he could even finish saying he'd had a nice time, which was a lie anyway. He went home to his tiny room and thought about the word lonely and how it sounded and looked so lonely, with those two l's in it, each standing tall by itself.

6 As news spread around the neighborhood about the young man's skills, people reacted two ways: there were the deeply appreciative and the **skeptics**. The appreciative ones called up the young man regularly. He'd stop by on his way to school, find their keys, and they'd give him a homemade muffin. The skeptics called him over too, and watched him like a hawk; he'd still find their lost items but they'd insist it was an elaborate **scam** and he was doing it all to get attention. Maybe, declared one woman, waving her index finger in the air, Maybe, she said, he steals the thing so we think it's lost, moves the item, and then comes over to save it! How do we know it was really lost in the first place? What is going on?

7 The young man didn't know himself. All he knew was the feeling of a tug, light but **insistent**, like a child at his sleeve, and that tug would turn him in the right direction and show him where to look. Each object had its own way of inhabiting space, and therefore messaging its location. The young man could sense, could smell, an object's presence—he did not need to see it to feel where it put its gravity down. As would be expected, items that turned out to be miles away took much harder concentration than the ones that were two feet to the left.

8 When Mrs. Allen's little boy didn't come home one afternoon, that was the most difficult of all. Leonard Allen was eight years old and usually arrived home from school at 3:05. He had allergies and needed a pill before he went back out to play. That day, by 3:45, a lone Mrs. Allen was wreck. Her boy rarely got lost—only once had that happened in the supermarket but he'd been found quite easily under the produce tables, crying; this walk home from school was a straight line and Leonard was not a wandering kind.

9 Mrs. Allen was just a regular neighbor except for one extraordinary fact—through an inheritance, she was the owner of a gargantuan[1] emerald she called the Green Star. It sat, glass-cased, in her kitchen, where everyone could see it because she insisted that

[1] **gargantuan** (gär-găn′cho͞o-ən): huge.

IMPROVE READING FLUENCY

Targeted Passage Cloze read paragraphs 8–9 with the class to help students read at an appropriate rate with good expression. Tell students you will read aloud while they follow the text silently. Let them know that from time to time you will pause before reading a random word, at which time they should read, together and aloud, the omitted word. Afterward, review the pronunciation of any multisyllabic words.

Go to the **Reading Studio** for additional support in developing fluency.

it be seen. Sometimes, as a party trick, she'd even cut steak with its beveled[2] edge.

10 On this day, she removed the case off the Green Star and stuck her palms on it. Where is my boy? she cried. The Green Star was cold and flat. She ran, weeping, to her neighbor, who calmly walked her back home; together, they gave the house a thorough search, and then the neighbor, a believer, recommended calling the young man. Although Mrs. Allen was a skeptic, she thought anything was a worthwhile idea, and when the line picked up, she said, in a trembling voice:

11 You must find my boy.

12 The young man had been just about to go play basketball with his friends. He'd located the basketball in the bathtub.

13 You lost him? said the young man.

14 Mrs. Allen began to explain and then her phone clicked.

15 One moment please, she said, and the young man held on.

16 When her voice returned, it was shaking with rage.

17 He's been kidnapped! she said. And they want the Green Star!

18 The young man realized then it was Mrs. Allen he was talking to, and nodded. Oh, he said, I see. Everyone in town was familiar with Mrs. Allen's Green Star. I'll be right over, he said.

19 The woman's voice was too run with tears to respond.

20 In his basketball shorts and shirt, the young man jogged over to Mrs. Allen's house. He was amazed at how the Green Star was all exactly the same shade of green. He had a desire to lick it.

21 By then, Mrs. Allen was in hysterics.

22 They didn't tell me what to do, she sobbed. Where do I bring my emerald? How do I get my boy back?

23 The young man tried to feel the scent of the boy. He asked for a photograph and stared at it—a brown-haired kid at his kindergarten graduation—but the young man had only found objects before, and lost objects at that. He'd never found anything, or anybody, stolen. He wasn't a policeman.

24 Mrs. Allen called the police and one officer showed up at the door.

25 Oh it's the finding guy, the officer said. The young man dipped his head modestly. He turned to his right; to his left; north; south. He got a glimmer of a feeling toward the north and walked out the back door, through the backyard. Night approached and the sky seemed to grow and deepen in the darkness.

[2] **beveled (bĕv´əld):** cut at sloping angles.

NOTICE & NOTE

ANALYZE CHARACTERIZATION

Annotate: Mark details that show what other characters think of the young man.

Analyze: What can you infer about the young man from what the neighbors say?

ANALYZE CHARACTERIZATION

Annotate: Mark information that the author tells you about the young man's actions.

Analyze: What do the young man's actions tell you about his character?

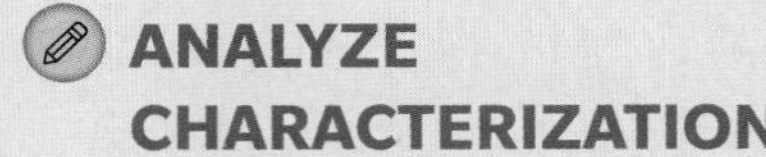

TEACH

ANALYZE CHARACTERIZATION

Have students scan paragraphs 10–11 to identify Mrs. Allen and her neighbor as the characters in question. Point out that these characters' ideas reflect the opinions held by the community at large. *(**Answer:** The neighbors are split between being skeptical of him [Mrs. Allen] and believing in him [her neighbor]. However, even a skeptic like Mrs. Allen will reach out to him because he is known to be a helpful person.)*

English Learner Support

Analyze Antonyms Read aloud the Analyze Characterization question on page 219. Have students find words in paragraph 10 that are opposites, or antonyms, and that show differences between Mrs. Allen and her neighbor. *(Mrs. Allen: ran, weeping; a skeptic; her neighbor: calmly walked; a believer)*

Ask: Based on what you know about each character, would Mrs. Allen or the neighbor be more likely to call the young man for help? *(Although Mrs. Allen reaches out to the young man, the neighbor is the one who first brings up the idea of calling him.)* **MODERATE/LIGHT**

ANALYZE CHARACTERIZATION

Remind students that readers often must make inferences about character traits. Pantomime dipping your head to make sure that students understand what that action looks like; then point out the adverb *modestly*. *(**Answer:** The young man is not arrogant about his abilities. He also may be a little embarrassed at being called "the finding guy," especially if thinks that the officer is belittling him.)*

ENGLISH LEARNER SUPPORT

Develop Vocabulary Use key words and phrases in the text to further students' understanding of the selection.

- Point to the illustration while reading aloud *a gargantuan emerald she called the Green Star* in paragraph 9. Ask: Is this the Green Star? *(yes)* Is it huge? *(yes)* Is it gargantuan? *(yes)* Have students repeat *gargantuan* after you. **SUBSTANTIAL**
- Have students circle unfamiliar words in the text. Monitor students as they discuss the meaning of each word in pairs or small groups. **MODERATE**
- Invite student pairs to take turns using challenging words from paragraphs 9–25 in their own phrases and sentences. Suggested words: *gargantuan, believer, skeptic, modestly, glimmer.* **LIGHT**

TEACH

ANALYZE PLOT

Point out that most of the story is written in the past tense and the flashbacks are about events that took place before other actions in the past. Remind students that the past perfect tense uses *had* with the past participle to express such actions—for example, *had said* and *had known* in the active voice and *had been told* and *had been taught* in the passive voice. (***Answer:*** *The author uses flashbacks to suggest mini-stories about objects that might otherwise seem unimportant. These details show that the young man feels a connection to the people and events that shaped the existence of the objects around him.)*

ANALYZE CHARACTERIZATION

Tell students to look for words and phrases that indicate the character's thoughts, feelings, and actions in paragraph 32. Remind students to consider all of these details as they answer the question. (***Answer:*** *The young man feels a connection to Leonard, seen in the way he holds the boy and smells his hair. His thoughts and feelings are seen in his failed hope that Leonard will talk to him and in what he would like to say to Leonard. The connection may come from the fact that Leonard is the same age that the young man was when his parents died. He wishes that he could connect with Leonard because he lost a connection to his parents at that age.)*

English Learner Support

Analyze Characterization

- Read paragraph 32 aloud, pausing after key phrases to clarify understanding with simple questions, such as *Did the young man smell the boy's hair?* (yes) **SUBSTANTIAL**
- Use sentence stems to encourage discussion about characterization. For example: *He smelled the boy's hair because ______.* **MODERATE**
- Call on volunteers to retell what happened in the paragraph. **LIGHT**

NOTICE & NOTE

ANALYZE PLOT

Annotate: Mark verbs that signal a flashback.

Analyze: How does the author use these flashbacks to connect to the young man's talent?

ANALYZE CHARACTERIZATION

Annotate: Mark details that tell you about the young man's character.

Explain: How does the author use the young man's actions and thoughts here to tell you about his character?

26 What's his name again? he called back to Mrs. Allen.

27 Leonard, she said. He heard the policeman pull out a pad and begin to ask basic questions.

28 He couldn't quite feel him. He felt the air and he felt the tug inside of the Green Star, an object displaced from its original home in Asia. He felt the tug of the tree in the front yard which had been uprooted from Virginia to be replanted here, and he felt the tug of his own watch which was from his uncle; in an attempt to be fatherly, his uncle had insisted he take it but they both knew the gesture was false.

29 Maybe the boy was too far away by now.

30 He heard the policeman ask: What is he wearing?

31 Mrs. Allen described a blue shirt, and the young man focused in on the blue shirt; he turned off his distractions and the blue shirt, like a connecting radio station, came calling from the northwest. The young man went walking and walking and about fourteen houses down he felt the blue shirt shrieking at him and he walked right into the backyard, through the back door, and sure enough, there were four people watching TV including the tear-stained boy with a runny nose eating a candy bar. The young man scooped up the boy while the others watched, so surprised they did nothing, and one even muttered: Sorry, man.

32 For fourteen houses back, the young man held Leonard in his arms like a bride. Leonard stopped sneezing and looked up at the stars and the young man smelled Leonard's hair, rich with the memory of peanut butter. He hoped Leonard would ask him a question, any question, but Leonard was quiet. The young man answered in his head: Son, he said, and the word rolled around, a marble on a marble floor. Son, he wanted to say.

33 When he reached Mrs. Allen's door, which was wide open, he walked in with quiet Leonard and Mrs. Allen promptly burst into tears and the policeman slunk out the door.

34 She thanked the young man a thousand times, even offered him the Green Star, but he refused it. Leonard turned on the TV and curled up on the sofa. The young man walked over and asked him

TO CHALLENGE STUDENTS . . .

Make Inferences Have partners work together to use their Analyze Characterization chart (see page 215) to make observations about supporting characters in the story, including Jenny, the police officer, and Mrs. Allen. Give partners the following discussion questions: Why do you think the author included this character? How does this character reflect the community in which the young man lives?

about the program he was watching but Leonard stuck a thumb in his mouth and didn't respond.

35 Feel better, he said softly. Tucking the basketball beneath his arm, the young man walked home, shoulders low.

36 In his tiny room, he undressed and lay in bed. Had it been a naked child with nothing on, no shoes, no necklace, no hairbow, no watch, he could not have found it. He lay in bed that night with the trees from other places rustling and he could feel their confusion. No snow here. Not a lot of rain. Where am I? What is wrong with this dirt?

37 Crossing his hands in front of himself, he held on to his shoulders. Concentrate hard he thought. Where are you? Everything felt blank and quiet. He couldn't feel a tug. He squeezed his eyes shut and let the question bubble up: Where did you go? Come find me. I'm over here. Come find me.

38 If he listened hard enough, he thought he could hear the waves hitting.

NOTICE & NOTE

AGAIN AND AGAIN

Notice & Note: Mark identical or similar words and phrases that repeat in the last two paragraphs.

Analyze: What do the words and phrases tell you about the young man's thoughts?

CHECK YOUR UNDERSTANDING

Answer these questions before moving on to the **Analyze the Text** section on the following page.

1 What happened to the young man's parents?

A They drowned.

B They abandoned him.

C They were kidnapped.

D They were in a car accident.

2 The neighbors discover the boy's talent when he finds —

F Leonard

G his parents

H a hairbrush

J the Green Star

3 What helps the young man find Leonard?

A The Green Star

B The boy's shirt

C The waves

D The trees

TEACH

AGAIN AND AGAIN

Explain that when students notice **repetition** they should ask themselves, "Why does this (word / phrase / action) keep coming up? How can it help me **analyze a character**?" Point out that repetition in this story, especially near the story's end, could offer important clues about who the young man is and what motivates him, as well as clues about the story's theme. (***Answer:*** *Although his parents are dead, the young man yearns to connect with them. He's lonely and in pain.)*

CHECK YOUR UNDERSTANDING

Have students answer the questions independently.

Answers:

1. *A*
2. *H*
3. *B*

If they answer any questions incorrectly, have them reread the text to confirm their understanding. Then they may proceed to ANALYZE THE TEXT on page 222.

ENGLISH LEARNER SUPPORT

Oral Assessment Use the following questions to assess students' comprehension and speaking skills.

1. Something happened to the young man's parents. What happened to them? *(They died.)*
2. The neighbors discover the boy's talent. What does he find? *(a hairbrush)*
3. What helps the young man find Leonard? *(the boy's shirt)* **SUBSTANTIAL/MODERATE**

APPLY

ANALYZE THE TEXT

Possible answers:

1. **DOK 4:** *The author assigns human traits to objects that the young man senses, such as the Green Star and the trees. For example, in paragraph 36 the young man can feel the trees' "confusion." The effect is to show the importance that objects have in the mind of the young man.*
2. **DOK 2:** *Leonard is silent and withdrawn. He doesn't seem to want to connect with the young man, who rescues him. In contrast, the young man is eager to connect with others and yearns to be with his parents, who are dead.*
3. **DOK 3:** *The author uses* loser *to refer to a person who has lost something. This meaning fits the story, which is about a young man who has an ability to find lost items. He himself has also lost something—his parents—and that loss has shaped his personality. In that way, he is a "loser."*
4. **DOK 4:** *The author uses an element of fantasy—the unusual gift of sensing and finding lost objects—to create a character who seems very human: vulnerable and complex. The extreme loneliness that stems from the young man's loss of his parents seems believable, as is the way his differences make the loneliness more acute.*
5. **DOK 4:** *The young man thinks back to his parents' drowning ("the waves hitting") as he tries to reunite with them in his mind. Although he can find other "lost" items and people, he cannot find his parents. The young man feels lonely and lost, suggesting that although people may be able to help others, they may not be able to help themselves.*

RESEARCH

Remind students that **theme** is the central idea or message in the story, a "lesson" about human life or behavior. *(Relevant themes may address loss, human connection, companionship, family, and loneliness. Make sure that students cite examples from the text for each theme.)*

Connect Students may work in pairs or small groups to brainstorm ideas for books, movies, and shows that address the various themes in their chart.

RESPOND

ANALYZE THE TEXT

Support your responses with evidence from the text. NOTEBOOK

1. **Analyze Personification** is the assigning of human traits to non-human objects. How does the author use personification for effect in this story?
2. **Compare** In fiction, a **foil** is a character whose personality and attitude contrast sharply with those of another character. How does the character of Leonard act as a foil for the young man?
3. **Evaluate** The word *loser* can be a cruel insult. It can also refer to someone who loses a competition. Why do you think the author used "Loser" as the story's title? Do you think it fits the story? Why or why not?
4. **Critique** Do you think the author has created a complex character in the young man? Is he a believable character, even with his unusual gift?
5. **Notice & Note** Reread the last paragraph. How does this Memory Moment—the young man's flashback—help you understand how the story explores the theme of loss?

RESEARCH

RESEARCH TIP
Use search terms such as *common themes* or *literature themes* to find lists of themes commonly used by authors. If a theme sounds like it might relate to "Loser," search for the specific theme to learn more about it.

Most works of fiction, including "Loser," explore multiple themes. Some themes are commonly found throughout literature and other works of fiction, such as plays and movies. Look online for lists of common fictional themes. Which themes do you think fit the story in "Loser"? List three themes that you think the author addresses. Cite evidence from the text that supports your choices.

THEME	HOW "LOSER" REFLECTS THIS THEME

Connect Add a column to your chart. List books, movies, and shows you know that address the themes you discovered.

LEARNING MINDSET

Try Again Encourage students to take advantage of their mistakes by learning from them. Explain that if they realize that they have made a mistake, they should try again, using a different approach. Invite students to share their mistakes and to tell what they learned from them. Regularly remind students to risk making a mistake because the effort is not wasted; trying again after making a mistake is one of the ways in which we learn and grow.

CREATE AND PRESENT

Freewrite Use the chart of themes you researched and evidence from the text that connects to those themes. You will write a statement about how the story explores the different themes. To get started, freewrite to develop your ideas.

- ❑ For each theme, write your understanding of what the theme says about human nature and life. Then write why you think this theme connects to "Loser."
- ❑ List examples from the text that support the presence of the theme.
- ❑ Use your freewriting to draft a three-paragraph statement about the theme in "Loser."

Discuss with a Small Group To refine your ideas, discuss them with a small group.

- ❑ Tell your group the three themes you believe are explored in "Loser." Explain your thinking by citing the evidence from the short story.
- ❑ Listen carefully and respond appropriately to your group members. Jot down the three themes each person lists and then listen as they explain why they chose each one.
- ❑ Ask questions about your group members' points to clarify what you don't understand. You may all have chosen different themes—after all, there are countless themes found in literature!

Go to the **Writing Studio** for more on drafting a statement.

Go to the **Speaking and Listening Studio** for help with participating in collaborative discussions.

RESPOND TO THE ESSENTIAL QUESTION

How do we form and maintain our connections with others?

Gather Information Review your annotations and notes on "Loser" and highlight those that help answer the Essential Question. Then, add relevant details to your Response Log.

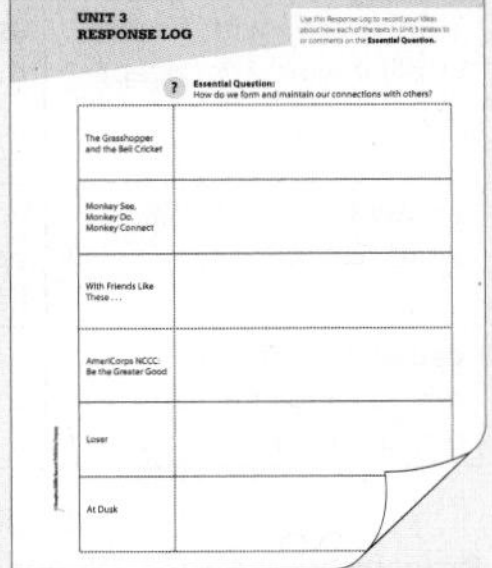

UNIT 3
RESPONSE LOG

Essential Question:
How do we form and maintain our connections with others?

The Grasshopper and the Bell Cricket	
Monkey See, Monkey Do, Monkey Connect	
With Friends Like These . . .	
AmeriCorps NCCC: Be the Greater Good	
Loser	
At Dusk	

ACADEMIC VOCABULARY

As you write and discuss what you learned from the short story, be sure to use the Academic Vocabulary words. Check off each of the words that you use.

- ❑ **capacity**
- ❑ **confer**
- ❑ **emerge**
- ❑ **generate**
- ❑ **trace**

CREATE AND PRESENT

Freewrite Remind students that they should not be overly concerned about "correct" grammar and sentence structure when they freewrite, for the purpose of freewriting is to generate several ideas in a short period of time. They may use only some of the ideas in their freewriting.

- Have students spend a few moments reviewing their charts before they begin freewriting.
- Give students five minutes to freewrite their ideas about how "Loser" explores each of the three themes they recorded during the Research activity.
- Use the freewrite material to create a statement that answers the following questions: What does the theme say about life and human nature? How does "Loser" express this theme?

For **writing support** for students at varying proficiency levels, see the **Text X-Ray** on page 214D.

Discuss with a Small Group Remind students to come to the discussion prepared with their statements and writing materials. Provide students with a graphic organizer in which to list the themes and supporting details covered in the discussion. Allow groups to decide how they will make sure everyone gets a turn to share their findings.

RESPOND TO THE ESSENTIAL QUESTION

Allow time for students to add details from "Loser" to their Unit 3 Response Logs.

ENGLISH LEARNER SUPPORT

Use Appropriate Language Display and read aloud the following sentences with students echo reading:

- The boy decided to help his neighbor find her son. He is able to locate lost items.
- The boy decided to help find his neighbor's son. He's able to find lost things.

Discuss formal and informal language, reviewing the idea that formal language is often used in writing and in presentations while informal language is more common in discussions. Ask: How does the first sentence compare to the second sentence? Which sentence is more formal? *(The first sentence is more formal because it does not use contractions and the word* locate *is more precise.)* Remind students that the way they express their ideas can affect how they are received by an audience. Ask: In a small group discussion, would it be appropriate to use contractions to help express ideas? *(yes)* Would using longer words make it easier or more difficult to convey thoughts about a text? *(Using longer words might confuse listeners and make it harder for the members of the group to understand each other.)* Encourage students to adapt their language during their small group discussion to make sure their ideas are clear. However, remind students that using informal language does not mean that it is acceptable to interrupt or talk over other people. **ALL LEVELS**

APPLY

CRITICAL VOCABULARY

Possible answers:

1. *I have a knack for fixing broken computers.*
2. *I was a skeptic when my parents told me that moving to a new city would be fun.*
3. *An email that makes a claim that seems too good to be true is likely a scam.*
4. *I am insistent that if I need extra help, I will seek it out.*

VOCABULARY STRATEGY:
Context Clues

Answers:

1. *matted:* adjective, *filled (in a messy way)*
2. *hysterics:* noun, *the state of reacting wildly emotionally*
3. *gesture:* noun, *an action performed to show one's feelings*

RESPOND

WORD BANK
knack **scam**
skeptic **insistent**

CRITICAL VOCABULARY

Practice and Apply Answer these questions to demonstrate your understanding of each Critical Vocabulary word.

1. What is something that you have a **knack** for doing?
2. When have you been a **skeptic** about something other people believe in?
3. How can you tell whether an email offer is a **scam**?
4. What are you **insistent** on doing during this school year?

VOCABULARY STRATEGY:
Context Clues

Go to the **Vocabulary Studio** for more on context clues.

The **context** of a word can give you important clues about the word's meaning, including both its denotation and connotation. Sometimes writers provide specific clues such as those shown in the chart.

SPECIFIC CONTEXT CLUES

Type of Clue	Key Words/Phrases	Example
Definition or restatement of the meaning of the word	or, which is, that is, in other words, also known as, also called	His first conjecture, **or guess**, was correct.
example following an unfamiliar word	such as, like, as if, for example, especially, including	She loved macabre stories, **such as those by Stephen King.**
comparison with a more familiar word or concept	as, like, also, similar to, in the same way, likewise	Despite his physical suffering, his mind was as **lucid** as any **rational** person's.
contrast with a familiar word or experience	unlike, but, however, although, on the other hand, on the contrary	Unlike her **clumsy** partner, she was an **agile** dancer.
cause-and-effect relationship in which one term is familiar	because, since, when, consequently, as a result, therefore	Because that perfume has a **sharp** scent, I chose a more **subtle** fragrance.

Practice and Apply Working with a partner, use context clues to define these words from "Loser": *matted* (paragraph 2), *hysterics* (paragraph 21) and *gesture* (paragraph 28). For each word, determine its part of speech in the sentence, write your understanding of the meaning of the word based on the context clues, then verify the meaning of the word in a dictionary.

ENGLISH LEARNER SUPPORT

Practice Phonology Students who are learning English may struggle with certain beginning consonant sounds—for example, the hard /c/ and the /s/ for speakers of Hmong, the hard /g/ for speakers of Cantonese and Korean, and the /r/ for speakers of Spanish and Haitian Creole. Offer students who struggle with those sounds additional practice. Write the following words from the chart on this page on the board: *conjecture, correct, guess, rational, subtle.* Point to each word and read it aloud with students. Then read aloud the sentence in which the word appears and have students repeat it after you. Supplement the practice with words such as *camera, galaxy, ribbon,* and *security.* **ALL LEVELS**

LANGUAGE CONVENTIONS: Active and Passive Voice

The **voice** of a verb tells whether its subject performs or receives the action expressed by the verb. When the subject performs the action, the verb is in the **active voice**. When the subject is the receiver of the action, the verb is in the **passive voice**.

You might think writers should always use active voice, as it makes the action clear. However, sometimes writers want to emphasize the receiver of the action. *I was hit by the car* is written in the passive voice to emphasize how the accident affected the subject, *I*. Writing *The car hit me* changes the emphasis to the car.

In other cases, writers cannot or do not want to specify the subject. For example, *Kate was elected president* is written in the passive voice. Rewriting the sentence in the active voice requires knowing who voted (for example, *The class elected Kate president; The students elected Kate president; The group elected Kate president*). The writer might not know who voted; or might want to keep the subject vague in order to focus on a more important point.

Look at the examples of sentences from "The Loser" written in the active and passive voice.

ACTIVE VOICE	PASSIVE VOICE
After the tragedy, the community adopted and raised him...	**Both of his parents had been killed when he was eight years old...**
Jenny's mother kissed the young man on the cheek but Jenny herself looked at him suspiciously all night long.	**...he'd been found quite easily under the produce tables...**

Practice and Apply Write a one-paragraph summary of the story "Loser," using only active voice. Then look through your paragraph. Which sentences could you rewrite in the passive voice? Rewrite your paragraph and evaluate which sentence structures make the paragraph easier to understand.

SUMMARY

____

____

____

____

Go to the **Grammar Studio** for more help with active and passive voice.

LANGUAGE CONVENTIONS: Active and Passive Voice

Remind students that the **subject** of a sentence is the person, place, thing, or idea that the sentence is about.

Discuss the chart of examples from "Loser." Demonstrate the role of the subject in active and passive voice by rewriting some of the example sentences and discussing the effect of the change:

- After the tragedy, he was adopted and raised by the community. (Discuss how changing the active voice to passive voice shifts the subject of the sentence from *community* to the boy, or *he*, and alters the focus of the sentence. It also makes the sentence longer and the style seem more formal and less direct.)
- Someone or something killed his parents when he was eight years old. (Discuss how changing the subject from the boy's *parents* to *someone or something* forces the writer to try to specify an unknown subject and shifts the focus away from the main point—that his parents died.)

Practice and Apply Remind students that their summaries should briefly retell the story in their own words. Have partners discuss whether sentences rewritten in the passive voice improved the summary. *(Students' summaries will vary.)*

ENGLISH LEARNER SUPPORT

Language Conventions Assist students in recognizing and using active voice and passive voice to summarize the selection. Use the following supports with students at varying proficiency levels:

- Choral read a passage with students and then model summarizing that passage in the active and passive voice. For example, write: *The community raised the orphan boy.* Ask: Is this active voice, or passive voice? *(active)* The orphan boy was raised by the community. *(passive)*
  SUBSTANTIAL
- Have students work in pairs to change sentences from the selection to the passive voice.
  MODERATE
- Provide sentence stems to help students summarize: *An eight-year-old boy _____. He discovered that _____. The community _____.* Have students identify the use of active and passive voice in a partner's summary and make suggestions for improvement.
  LIGHT

AT DUSK

Poem by Natasha Trethewey

GENRE ELEMENTS
POETRY

Tell students that in **poetry,** words are carefully chosen and arranged to create certain effects. Some poems tell a story while others focus on the speaker's personal thoughts and feelings—and some do both. Poets use sound devices (such as repetition), imagery, and figurative language (such as personification) to evoke pictures in readers' minds and to express emotions, ideas, and themes. In this lesson, students will use elements of poetry to explore themes in "At Dusk."

LEARNING OBJECTIVES

- Analyze the effects of poetic diction and syntax to create mental images.
- Research and compare poems set at dawn, dusk, and night by identifying their descriptive words and phrases.
- Present an oral reading of a poem with appropriate prosody.
- Critique classmates' poetry readings.
- **Language** Identify words and phrases that create mental imagery and discuss using the terms *diction* and *syntax*.

TEXT COMPLEXITY

Quantitative Measures	**At Dusk** Lexile: N/A
Qualitative Measures	**Ideas Presented** Multiple levels of meaning (multiple themes).
	Structures Used Free verse, with no particular patterns.
	Language Used Clear, direct language.
	Knowledge Required Everyday knowledge; familiarity with genre conventions required.

Online 

RESOURCES

- Unit 3 Response Log
- Selection Audio
-  Reading Studio: Notice & Note
-  Level Up Tutorial: Setting and Mood
-  Speaking and Listening Studio: Giving a Presentation; Participating in Collaborative Discussions
- "Loser"/ "At Dusk" Selection Test

SUMMARIES

English

The speaker in "At Dusk" observes a neighbor trying to call her cat home as night is falling. The cat, fascinated by a group of fireflies, does not come, and the neighbor gives up. The observation prompts the speaker to imagine the neighbor waiting at home to reconnect with her cat, and then to consider the possibility that she, the speaker, also might reach out to reestablish a lost connection.

Spanish

La narradora de "Al anochecer" ve a su vecina tratando de llamar a su gato mientras cae la noche. El gato, fascinado por un grupo de luciérnagas, no vuelve a casa y la vecina se rinde de momento. Esa visión lleva a la narradora a imaginar a su vecina esperando en casa para reconectarse con su gato, y luego considera la posibilidad de que ella, la narradora, también podría tenderle la mano para restablecer una conexión perdida.

SMALL-GROUP OPTIONS

Have students work in small groups to read and discuss the selection.

Think-Pair-Share

- After students have read and analyzed "At Dusk," ask: What story does the poem tell? What message about life does that story suggest?
- Have students work independently to freewrite ideas that answer the questions.
- Have students form pairs to discuss and create a shared response.
- Invite pairs to share their responses with the class.

Send a Problem

- Discuss "At Dusk" with the class. Pose a question to a volunteer, such as this: What mood is created by the line *leaning through her doorway / at dusk* (lines 2–3)?
- Wait up to 11 seconds for a response.
- If the student responds, continue the discussion. After a time, ask another question.
- A student without a response must repeat the question, call on another student by name, and "send" the question to that student.
- Monitor responses. Redirect and ask questions as desired.

Text X-Ray: English Learner Support
for "At Dusk"

Use the Text X-Ray and the supports and scaffolds in the Teacher's Edition to help guide students at different proficiency levels through the selection.

INTRODUCE THE SELECTION
DISCUSS OBSERVATIONS

In this lesson, students will discuss how in "At Dusk," the speaker makes an observation that leads her to reflect on her own life. Provide the following explanations of terms students can use to discuss the speaker's experience:

- When people make an **observation**, they notice something.
- When people **imagine** something, they see it in their mind.
- When people **wonder** about something, they think about it.

Provide frames like the following to allow students to practice using the terms: *Today I made an observation about* _____. _____ *makes me imagine* _____. *Sometimes I wonder about* ______.

CULTURAL REFERENCES

The following words or phrases may be unfamiliar to students:

- *here here* (line 7): often used in place of "come here," to call pets such as cats and dogs home
- *fall short* (line 8): are not enough, are insufficient, or are disappointing
- *lifts her ears* (line 10): a cat's ears rise and twitch to focus on sound
- *trails off* (line 20): becomes more and more quiet
- *over the lines* (line 27): possibly a reference to telephone lines, or wires, strung between tall poles, connecting people by voice

LISTENING

Create Mental Images

Tell students that creating images in their mind while they listen will help them to understand a poem's meaning.

Have students listen as you read aloud lines 1–8 of "At Dusk." Use the following supports with students at varying proficiency levels:

- Before reading, use labeled pictures to support understanding of *dusk, doorway, street lamps,* or other words that may be new to students. After reading, have students draw and label the mental image they created. **SUBSTANTIAL**
- Use sentence frames to describe mental images: *There was an image of* _____ *in my mind. I could see* _____ *and hear* _____. **MODERATE**
- Have students quickwrite about the mental images they created. **LIGHT**

SPEAKING

Present an Oral Reading

Work with students to prepare for the oral poetry reading assignment on Student Edition page. 233.

Use the following supports with students at varying proficiency levels:

- Choral read the poem. Then read it again and have students raise their hand to pause and review the pronunciation of unfamiliar words. **SUBSTANTIAL**
- Demonstrate the concept of expressive reading by showing what it is *not.* Read a few sentences from a text in a flat way and then in an over-the-top way. Invite comments. Then read it in a natural but expressive way. Urge students to aim for that "middle ground." **MODERATE**
- Tell students to think of oral reading as a form of storytelling. Have them read the first eight lines in pairs. Then have them read the lines again, imagining that they are telling a story. Ask them to discuss the differences between the readings. **LIGHT**

READING

Analyze Imagery

Tell students that poets create vivid images by using language that helps readers see, hear, and feel what is happening. Some images suggest interesting comparisons.

Display and choral read lines 3–4 and 12–13. Use the following supports with students at varying proficiency levels:

- Use Think Alouds to help students analyze imagery—for example: "The 'streetlamps just starting to hum' makes me think about warming up their voices. I can hear and see this image." Ask: What does a hum sound like to you? **SUBSTANTIAL**
- Help students understand the comparison in line 12. Explain that a *constellation* is a group of stars. Ask: How do shining stars look? *(They twinkle.)* How do shining fireflies look? *(They twinkle, too.)* **MODERATE**
- Ask volunteers to read aloud the lines displayed. Ask questions to tap into students' prior knowledge: What are the street lamps doing? *(humming)* What does humming sound like? What else can make this sound? **LIGHT**

WRITING

Take Notes

Tell students that taking good notes while they read or listen will improve their writing.

Use the following supports with students at varying proficiency levels:

- Supply a word bank to help students take notes about the selection or to complete a critique of a poetry reading. In addition to terms such as *imagery, mood, tone,* and *voice,* include words such as *dislike/like, feeling, happy, idea, lonely, quiet, sad,* and *serious.* **SUBSTANTIAL**
- In addition to a word bank, supply students with phrases such as these to help them take notes: *Sounds like; Reminds me of; This seems; I feel/think/wonder.* **MODERATE**
- Show students a model of marginal notes for "At Dusk" or a critique of a poetry reading. Have partners compare their marginal notes and critiques and then use them to write a statement that reflects their ideas. **LIGHT**

Connect to the

ESSENTIAL QUESTION

In her poem "At Dusk," the speaker describes a neighbor calling for her cat to come home as night falls. Like many poems, this one uses an image or event to explore related ideas, including our connections with others.

COMPARE THEMES

Tell students that they will now read and analyze a poem with themes similar to those in the short story "Loser." Invite students to review and share their impressions of "Loser." What ideas did Aimee Bender, the author of "Loser," explore through her story? How might a poem explore some of those ideas?

POEM

AT DUSK

by **Natasha Trethewey**

pages 229–231

COMPARE THEMES

Read "At Dusk" to explore how this poem addresses some of the same themes as the short story "Loser." As you read, ask yourself what ideas the author expresses about life or human nature and if those ideas overlap with the ideas in "Loser." After you are finished, you will collaborate with a small group on a final project that involves an analysis of both texts.

ESSENTIAL QUESTION:

How do we form and maintain our connections with others?

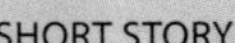

SHORT STORY

LOSER

by **Aimee Bender**

pages 217–221

At Dusk

QUICK START

Dusk is the time of day just after the sun has set, when the light on earth and in the sky grows dimmer. People have long associated that time of day with certain emotions. What feelings and memories do you have about dusk? What words would you use to describe this time of day? Discuss with a partner.

ANALYZE DICTION AND SYNTAX

Poets choose words and phrases to convey a specific **tone**—that is, an attitude toward a subject; a **mood**—the feeling or atmosphere; and a **voice**—use of language that creates a personality we can "hear."

Diction is an author's choice of words. **Syntax** is the arrangement of those words into phrases and sentences. The diction and syntax the author uses throughout "At Dusk" contribute to the poem's tone, mood, and voice.

The examples below show how these elements of the author's style contribute to the poem's theme, or message.

LINES FROM POEM	EFFECT ON TONE, MOOD, OR VOICE
the cat lifts her ears, turns first / toward the voice, then back / to the constellation of fireflies flickering / near her head. It's as if she can't decide/ whether to leap over the low hedge, /. . . or stay where she is.	Here, the poet has chosen to describe the cat's motions in detail—she "lifts her ears, turns first toward the voice . . . "—which creates a tone of fascination regarding the cat.
street lamps just starting to hum / the backdrop of evening	The poet uses the sensory details of the street lamps "starting to hum" to signal the darkening of the scene as evening falls. This creates a dark, quiet mood.
She's given up calling for now, left me / to imagine her inside the house waiting, / perhaps in a chair in front of the TV, / or walking around, doing small tasks;	The poet has the speaker wonder about what her neighbor is doing inside her house, and she lists several possibilities. This establishes the speaker's curious, imaginative voice.

As you read "At Dusk," make note of the author's diction and syntax choices. Use a chart like the one above to guide your interpretation of the effects of Trethewey's diction and syntax on tone, mood, and voice.

GENRE ELEMENTS: POETRY

- uses figurative language, including personification
- includes imagery that appeals to the senses and expresses emotions
- expresses a theme, or a message about life

QUICK START

Have partners discuss the mood and emotions that dusk evokes. Suggest questions such as these:

- What colors are in the sky at dusk?
- How do city streets change at that time?
- What sights and sounds of nature appear at dusk?
- What activities do you associate with that time of day?
- Does your energy level change at dusk—and, if so, how?

After partners meet, invite students to share with the class the words they used to describe dusk.

ANALYZE DICTION AND SYNTAX

As you discuss **tone, mood,** and **voice,** help students "hear" the effects of each by reading aloud the examples in the chart. Suggest that students ask these questions as they read:

- What is the speaker's attitude toward the subject? *(tone)*
- What feeling or atmosphere does the poem create? *(mood)*
- What personality can I "hear" in the poem? *(voice)*

Then help students distinguish **diction** from **syntax.**

- **Diction** is an author's choice of words: *the cat lifts her ears, turns first / toward the voice* (lines 10–11). Ask how students might change the diction of these lines. *(the kitty cat points her furry black ears and swivels / in the direction of the voice she heard)*
- **Syntax** reflects how words are ordered and arranged. Present this variation of lines 10–11: *the cat's ears lift / first she turns toward the voice.* Ask students what effect the change in syntax has on those lines. *(It changes the rhythm and the line breaks.)*

APPLY

CREATE MENTAL IMAGES

Begin by pointing out that we almost always create mental images of the characters and action we encounter as we read fiction. (If possible, give an example from a story that students have read this year.) Explain that we do so in poetry, too. The images that our minds create as we read poetry may not have the narrative flow inspired by fiction; still, poetic images can reinforce a poet's ideas and help make a poem memorable.

Have students work in pairs to list the images they visualize as they read the selected lines from "At Dusk." Ask one partner to read aloud slowly from the examples provided while the other listens, eyes closed, visualizing. Have the reader pause frequently to ask, "What is the mental image? What do you see?" The reader then notes the listener's response. After reading several lines, partners may swap roles and continue. In addition, point out that some of the details in the examples appeal to the sense of hearing; in other words, "visualizing" is about details that appeal to any of our senses, not just to what we see.

English Learner Support

Respond to Text Students probably will think about the mental images they make in terms of their primary language. Encourage them to make some initial notes about each excerpt from "At Dusk" in their primary language. Then have them meet in mixed-proficiency groups to discuss their responses and craft an English-language description of each image. **ALL LEVELS**

ANNOTATION MODEL

Remind students of the annotation suggestions on page 227 for noting the author's diction and syntax choices. Urge students also to mark words and phrases that evoke mental images or spark interest. In particular, point out that the comment in this model refers not only to details that the student "sees" but also to details that the student "hears." Remind students to use the margins for their own comments about the text and for questions they may want to ask during class discussion.

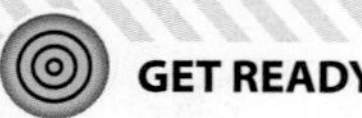

GET READY

CREATE MENTAL IMAGES

Poets use **imagery,** or descriptive words and phrases that recreate sensory experiences for the reader. These descriptions help you make **mental images** of what the poet wants you to visualize. Think of the pictures the words and phrases paint, and ask yourself how you would experience those scenes using your senses.

Review the excerpts from the poem in the chart on the previous page. As you read them the first time, you might have quickly pictured the scene. Now reread them in the chart below, and think more specifically: What did you visualize?

street lamps just starting to hum / the backdrop of evening
the cat lifts her ears, turns first / toward the voice, then back / to the constellation of fireflies flickering / near her head. It's as if she can't decide / whether to leap over the low hedge, / . . . or stay where she is
She's given up calling for now, left me / to imagine her inside the house waiting, / perhaps in a chair in front of the TV

As you read "At Dusk," make mental images of the scene to help you understand the poet's message.

ANNOTATION MODEL

NOTICE & NOTE

Here are annotations about mental images one student created based on the poem.

At first I think she is calling a child, my neighbor, leaning through her doorway at dusk, street lamps just starting to hum the backdrop of evening. Then I hear the high-pitched wheedling we send out to animals who know only sound, not the meanings of our words—*here here*— nor how they sometimes fall short.	I have a mental image of a neighborhood street that is pretty quiet—you can hear the street lamps humming—and a neighbor leaning out the door, calling as the speaker watches. The neighbor is whistling or making high-pitched sounds: the noises we make when we call for our pets.

ENGLISH LEARNER SUPPORT

Clarify Vocabulary Students cannot create mental images unless they understand the words in the text, so clarify students' understanding of the vocabulary in the examples from the Create Mental Images chart above..

- *first example:* Explain that in photography or in a stage play, a *backdrop* shows a scene behind the main action.
- *second example:* Explain that a *constellation* is a group of stars; that *flickering* happens when something (the flame of a candle, for example) appears and disappears rapidly; and that a *hedge* is row of bush-like plants that serves as a kind of fence.
- *third example:* Explain that to *give up* is to stop doing something because it seems useless. **SUBSTANTIAL**

NOTICE & NOTE

BACKGROUND

Natasha Trethewey *(b. 1966) was named United States Poet Laureate in 2012. Her role, she says, is "to be the biggest promoter of poetry; someone who's really got to do the work of bringing poetry to the widest audience possible." A native of Gulfport, Mississippi, Trethewey has published several collections of poetry and is a professor of English at Northwestern University in Evanston, Illinois. She has won many honors, including the Pulitzer Prize for poetry in 2007 for her book* Native Guard.

AT DUSK

Poem by Natasha Trethewey

PREPARE TO COMPARE

As you read, think about how the author uses language not just to convey a scene, but also to make a statement about life. What mood does the scene create for the reader? How do the tone, mood, and voice contribute to the poem's theme?

At first I think she is calling a child,
my neighbor, leaning through her doorway
at dusk, street lamps just starting to hum
the backdrop of evening. Then I hear
the high-pitched wheedling we send out
to animals who know only sound, not
the meanings of our words—here here—
nor how they sometimes fall short.
In another yard, beyond my neighbor's
sight, the cat lifts her ears, turns first
toward the voice, then back
to the constellation of fireflies flickering
near her head. It's as if she can't decide
whether to leap over the low hedge,
the neat row of flowers, and bound
onto the porch, into the steady circle

Notice & Note

You can use the side margins to notice and note signposts in the text.

AGAIN AND AGAIN

Notice & Note: Mark an example of repeated words.

Interpret: What is the effect of this repetition?

BACKGROUND

Have students read the Background note. Explain that Natasha Trethewey grew up feeling the prejudices of being a mixed-race child, having a white Canadian father and an African American mother. Trethewey's parents divorced when she was six, and her mother was murdered when Trethewey was in college. That tragedy prompted her to express her feelings and grief through poetry. Trethewey's poems often explore ideas related to experiences that shaped her youth, including her identity as both black and white.

PREPARE TO COMPARE

Direct students to use the Prepare to Compare prompt to focus their reading.

For **listening, reading, and writing support** for students at varying proficiency levels, see the **Text X-Ray** on pages 226C–226D.

AGAIN AND AGAIN

Remind students that when they see this signpost, they should look for language, images, or events that appear repeatedly in a text. Explain that when they notice **repetition**, students should ask themselves, *Why might the author bring this up again or use this word or phrase more than once?* Point out that the details and ideas that recur may offer insight into the poem's **theme.** *(**Answer:** Repeating "here" emphasizes how the neighbor wishes for the cat to come back to her—to connect with her again.)*

ENGLISH LEARNER SUPPORT

Discuss Pronoun Referents Clarify the pronoun referents in the poem.

- Read aloud lines 1–8. Point out the pronoun *she* (line 1). Ask: Who is *she? (my neighbor)* Point to *neighbor* in line 2. **SUBSTANTIAL**
- Point out the pronoun *she* (line 1) and the phrase *my neighbor* (line 2) and explain that sometimes the pronoun referent (which we usually call an antecedent) occurs after the pronoun. **MODERATE**
- Read aloud lines 9–19 and ask whether this use of *she* has the same referent as *she* in line 1. *(No; this time, the referent is the cat.)*

Have students identify the referent for *she* in the rest of the poem. *(the neighbor)* Ask students then to identify the referent for *they* in line 8 (*words*) and for *it* in line 27 (*voice*). You may wish to point out that sometimes a pronoun refers to a group of details (*It* in line 13) and sometimes may be understood even without a referent (*we* in line 5). **LIGHT**

ANALYZE DICTION AND SYNTAX

Remind students that poets, like fiction writers, sometimes choose words that help them to inhabit, or live inside of, their characters. In this part of "At Dusk," that character is a cat. Help students think about voice by looking for words and phrases in lines 9–19 that reveal the character's personality and interests. (***Answer:*** *The phrase "luminous possibility" reveals the poet's imagination as she considers how potential experiences might appear from the cat's point of view.)*

English Learner Support

Use Cognates Point out to students that both words in *luminous possibility* have Spanish cognates and that the expression in Spanish would be *posibilidad luminosa.*

ALL LEVELS

CREATE MENTAL IMAGES

Encourage students to reread this last part of "At Dusk" several times, giving their mental images opportunity to develop. Ask them to mark the specific words and phrases that elicit vivid images—perhaps familiar objects, such as the "chair in front of the TV" (line 23), or unusual phrases, such as "stitching here / to there" (lines 27–28). If necessary, guide students in making an inference by having them consider what the speaker wonders about. (***Answer:*** *The speaker may be pictured with an expression suggesting that she feels sad, alone, and perhaps a little hopeful. She wishes that she could call home "someone out there," just as her neighbor has tried calling for her cat.)*

NOTICE & NOTE

ANALYZE DICTION AND SYNTAX

Annotate: Mark the words and phrases the author uses to describe the cat's thoughts.

Analyze: How does the phrase "luminous possibility" convey the author's voice?

CREATE MENTAL IMAGES

Annotate: Mark language the poet uses to help you picture this scene.

Infer: How do you picture the expression of the speaker at the end of the poem? Why?

of light, or stay where she is: luminous
possibility—all that would keep her
away from home—flitting before her.
I listen as my neighbor's voice trails off.
She's given up calling for now, left me
to imagine her inside the house waiting,
perhaps in a chair in front of the TV,
or walking around, doing small tasks;
left me to wonder that I too might lift
my voice, sure of someone out there,
send it over the lines stitching here
to there, certain the sounds I make
are enough to call someone home.

IMPROVE READING FLUENCY

Targeted Passage Tell the class that everyone will read a passage in unison, paying attention to appropriate expression, rate, and phrasing. Choral read with the class one of the following passages: lines 1–8, lines 9–19, or lines 20–29. Then have partners take turns reading the same passage aloud to one another. Allow time for partners to discuss the meaning of the passage as a whole, as well as specific words and phrases that capture their attention and make them think. Afterward, call on volunteers to share their ideas about the meaning of the passage.

Go to the **Reading Studio** for additional support in developing fluency.

NOTICE & NOTE

CHECK YOUR UNDERSTANDING

Answer these questions before moving on to the **Analyze the Text** section on the following page.

1 Why is the neighbor calling out her door?

- **A** To greet the speaker
- **B** To ask for her children
- **C** To call her cat home
- **D** To ask for help

2 What does the speaker see in another neighbor's yard?

- **F** A light
- **G** A child
- **H** A cat
- **J** A TV

3 The poem ends with the speaker thinking about —

- **A** what the neighbor wants
- **B** what the cat will do
- **C** calling someone home
- **D** how to help the neighbor

ENGLISH LEARNER SUPPORT

Oral Assessment Use the following questions to assess students' comprehension and speaking skills.

1. The neighbor is at her door. Why? *(She is trying to get her cat to come home.)*
2. The speaker sees something in a neighbor's yard. What is it? *(a cat)*
3. What is the speaker thinking about at the end of the poem? *(calling out to someone to come home)* **SUBSTANTIAL/MODERATE**

TEACH

CHECK YOUR UNDERSTANDING

Have students answer the questions independently.

Answers:

1. *C*
2. *H*
3. *C*

If they answer any questions incorrectly, have them reread the text to confirm their understanding. Then they may proceed to ANALYZE THE TEXT on page 232.

APPLY

ANALYZE THE TEXT

Possible answers:

1. **DOK 2:** *The speaker might be referring to the difficulties that people sometimes have in communicating.*
2. **DOK 2:** *The cat's preoccupation with the fireflies in lines 11–13 and 17–19 delays her return. The fireflies represent a "luminous possibility," which may be the promise of the unexplored world beyond home.*
3. **DOK 4:** *The images of night ("street lamps just starting to hum / the backdrop of evening" in lines 3–4 and "the constellation of fireflies flickering" in line 11); loneliness ("I listen as my neighbor's voice trails off. . . . [she's] left me to imagine her inside the house waiting," in lines 20–22); and yearning ("luminous possibility–all that would keep her away from home—flitting before her" in lines 17–19) establish a bittersweet tone of longing.*
4. **DOK 3:** *Dusk is a time of transition, and the speaker implies that he or she is looking for some kind of change. Because the speaker has a wish to "call someone home" (line 29), perhaps he or she hopes to reconcile or reunite with another person or to end feelings of loneliness.*
5. **DOK 4:** *The speaker acknowledges a feeling of solitude and wonders whether he or she, too, might call out in some way to bring someone home. The speaker may work harder in the future to reach out to and connect with others.*

RESEARCH

Tell students that many poetry organizations have poetry search engines on their websites. Encourage students to use the search terms *poetry organization* or *poetry association*. After selecting an organization, they might use *dawn, dusk,* or *night* as search terms at that site. *(Poems will vary. Students should support their ideas about differences in mood with evidence from the poems.)*

Extend Once you have approved the choices of poems, suggest that students practice reading the poem aloud a few times before sharing it with their partner. Suggest that the partner also read aloud the same poem, or parts of it, to aid understanding of the poem's mood.

RESPOND

ANALYZE THE TEXT

Support your responses with evidence from the text. NOTEBOOK

1. **Interpret** The speaker talks about the cat not hearing meanings of our words "nor how they sometimes fall short" (line 8). What might this mean?
2. **Infer** What might keep the cat from returning home? What might the image of a "constellation of fireflies flickering" represent?
3. **Analyze** What is the tone of this poem? What words and phrases convey the tone?
4. **Draw Conclusions** Explain the significance of the title "At Dusk."
5. **Notice & Note** What realization does the speaker come to at the end of the poem, and how might this Aha Moment affect the speaker's actions in the future?

RESEARCH

The different times of the day, and the feelings that they evoke in people, are common subjects for poets. Go online and find another poem set at dusk, as well as poems set at dawn and at night. Compare the poems. How does the mood in each poem differ? Record words and phrases that contribute to the poems' moods and messages.

TIME OF DAY	POEM	DESCRIPTIVE WORDS AND PHRASES
Dawn		
Dusk		
Night		

RESEARCH TIP
Some poems might have the words *dawn, dusk,* or *night* in the title, but don't limit your search to those. You can also search, for example, "poems set at sunrise" or "poems about evening."

Extend Choose a poem about a time of day that is meaningful for you, and that you would like to read to the class. Have your teacher approve it, and then share it with a partner. Describe the mood of the poem to your partner.

WHEN STUDENTS STRUGGLE . . .

Understand Diction and Syntax Review the term *mood.* Explain that **diction,** or word choice, along with **syntax,** the arrangement of words into phrases and sentences, can help to create mood. Read aloud lines 20–29. Point out the repeated use of *[she's] left me* in the passage *(left me / to imagine; left me to wonder).* Discuss how diction and syntax work to create a melancholy mood here. Change lines 21–22 to *For now, she's stopped calling, so I think of her waiting in the house, instead.* Ask: How have diction and syntax changed the mood? *(The mood is lighter but less compelling.)*

For additional support, go to the **Reading Studio** and assign the following **Level Up Tutorial: Setting and Mood.**

CREATE AND PRESENT

Present an Oral Reading Using either "At Dusk", or a poem you discovered during your research, plan a poetry reading for your group. The focus of the poetry reading will be appropriate **prosody**, or expressive reading.

- ❑ Read the poem to yourself, making note of line breaks and punctuation. Determine how the poet means for the words to flow.
- ❑ Think about the tone, mood, and voice of the poem. This will determine how you use the elements of prosody—timing, phrasing, emphasis, and intonation—to interpret the poem for your listeners.
- ❑ Practice reading the poem aloud with a partner.

Discuss with a Small Group Hold a poetry reading with your group.

- ❑ Read your poem to your classmates. Use gestures and body language as needed, but focus on how your voice conveys the meaning and feeling of the poem.
- ❑ Listen carefully as the members of your group read their poems. Make mental images based on each poem's descriptive details. Take notes on the critique form given to you by your teacher. Answer any questions your classmates have about the poem's diction or meaning.
- ❑ After everyone has read, exchange information from your critique form with group members. Discuss how you gain a sense of the poets' voice, mood, and tone from hearing the poems read aloud.

Go to the **Speaking and Listening Studio** for help with presenting a recitation.

RESPOND TO THE ESSENTIAL QUESTION

How do we form and maintain our connections with others?

Gather Information Review your annotations and notes on "At Dusk" and highlight those that help answer the Essential Question. Then, add relevant details to your Response Log.

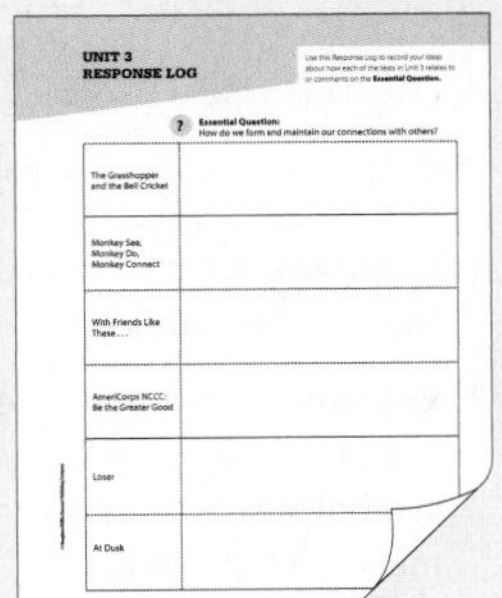

ACADEMIC VOCABULARY

As you write and discuss what you learned from the poem, be sure to use the Academic Vocabulary words. Check off each of the words that you use.

- ❑ **capacity**
- ❑ **confer**
- ❑ **emerge**
- ❑ **generate**
- ❑ **trace**

CREATE AND PRESENT

Present an Oral Reading Guide students to read poetry in a way that reflects the timing, phrasing, emphasis, and intonation that they think the poet intends.

- Model giving an oral reading of a poem of your choice. If possible, display the poem and point out where and why you chose certain timing, phrasing, emphasis, and intonation. Point out that another person might present the same poem with some differences in prosody, depending on what he or she wants to impress upon the audience.
- Suggest that students whisper-read their poem to themselves several times. Tell students that line breaks rarely require more than a very brief pause; in fact, in many poems (especially free-verse poems) sentences run from one line to the next, without a break.
- Encourage students to try out a variety of interpretations—again, whisper-reading—to find the appropriate elements of prosody for the poem. Students then should present the poem at a normal volume when practicing with partners.

For **speaking support** for students at varying proficiency levels, see the **Text X-Ray** on page 226D.

Discuss with a Small Group Either on your own or working with students, create a critique form that covers each element of prosody (timing, phrasing, emphasis, intonation) and includes a rubric for evaluating the oral readings. Remind students to offer useful, respectful criticism.

RESPOND TO THE ESSENTIAL QUESTION

Allow time for students to add details from "At Dusk" to their Unit 3 Response Logs.

ENGLISH LEARNER SUPPORT

Express Opinions Help students participate in an oral reading of a poem, followed by a small-group discussion.

- Model making choices by reading aloud a short poem several ways and then ask: Which reading did you like best? Why? **SUBSTANTIAL**
- Provide sentence frames for discussion: *When I hear that, I imagine _____ in my mind. The voice in the poem seems _____. The poem sounded best when _____.* **MODERATE**
- Guide students to form thoughtful opinions by having them make comparisons. Offer the following sentence frames: *When you read with that expression, it reminds me of _____. Your gestures are similar to _____.* **LIGHT**

APPLY

COMPARE THEMES

Before partners begin work on the chart, review the following terms. Note that these are elements that are more often associated with stories but that poems can have them too.

- **Characterization** is the way a writer creates and develops characters. It may be revealed through the physical description, thoughts, speech, and actions of a character. Comments made by the story's narrator or the poem's speaker can also reveal character.
- **Setting** is the time and place of the action.
- **Plot** is the series of events in which one or more characters try to solve a problem.

Urge students to be specific in recording their ideas, for they will need to draw upon their notes as they go on to talk about the themes of the two selections.

ANALYZE THE TEXTS

Possible answers:

1. **DOK 2:** *Both texts explore the themes of loneliness, human connection, and loss. The author of "Loser" seems more pessimistic about the possibility of making meaningful connections: Even though the young man tries to establish meaningful relationships with other people, he seems unable to do so. In "At Dusk," on the other hand, the speaker seems to believe that "I too might lift / my voice" and "call someone home." The poet's attitude appears to be more confident that efforts to make connections can combat loneliness.*
2. **DOK 4:** *In "Loser," Mrs. Allen has an emerald that she could exchange for her loved one. By contrast, the young man has no special object or power that will bring his parents back to him. In "At Dusk," the cat sees a "constellation of fireflies," which the speaker calls a "luminous possibility." A constellation shows connections among stars. The speaker may long for the connections and possibility that the fireflies represent.*
3. **DOK 4:** *Answers will vary. Students should cite mental images and descriptive language from each text.*
4. **DOK 4:** *Students' connections to the texts will vary but may include relating to feelings of loneliness expressed by both characters.*

RESPOND

LOSER
Short Story by Aimee Bender

AT DUSK
Poem by Natasha Trethewey

Collaborate & Compare

COMPARE THEMES

Now that you have read "Loser" and "At Dusk," you can compare how the authors developed themes in their work. You may have noticed some overlap in themes between the two texts, but the authors used different techniques and were working in different **genres**, or literary categories, to express those ideas.

Both authors rely on characterization, setting, plot, and use of language to communicate their themes. Review the texts with a partner. Use a chart like the one below to record your ideas about how the authors have used these elements to develop their themes. Cite specific text evidence where you can. You will **synthesize**, or combine, the information from your chart to draft a theme statement about both works.

Possible answers are shown.

	"LOSER"	"AT DUSK"
Characterization	*The theme of loneliness is seen in the young man's thoughts about the word loneliness as he lies in bed.*	*The lonely speaker wishes she could "call someone home" (line 29).*
Setting	*The young man is surrounded by objects that call to him—and by neighbors who are skeptical of him.*	*The street is quiet; only the speaker and the neighbor seem to be around. The neighbor goes indoors, leaving the speaker alone.*
Plot	*Characters experience loss—from people who have lost everyday objects, to Mrs. Allen losing her son, to the young man having lost his parents.*	*The narrator sees a neighbor calling for her cat and wishes that she, too, had someone to call.*
Use of Language	*The young man pleads, "Where did you go? Come find me. I'm over here. Come find me."*	*The speaker wonders whether if she calls out, "the sounds I make are enough to call someone home.*

ANALYZE THE TEXTS

Discuss these questions in your group.

1. **Compare** What themes did you discover in both "Loser" and "At Dusk"? How do the authors' attitudes toward those themes differ?
2. **Evaluate** Both authors use **symbols**—people, places, objects, or activities—that stand for something beyond themselves. Choose a symbol from each text and evaluate how the author uses it to add meaning to the text.
3. **Connect** How did creating mental images help you understand both texts? Cite examples from each text.
4. **Connect** The young man in "Loser" and the speaker in "At Dusk" share some qualities. Do you relate to either or both of their feelings or experiences? Explain.

WHEN STUDENTS STRUGGLE . . .

Compare Themes Provide a new chart that includes one assigned element, as in this example. Instruct partners to look for a specified number of examples from each genre.

	"Loser"	"At Dusk"
Use of Language	**1.** **2.**	**1.** **2.**

For additional support, go to the **Reading Studio** and assign the following **Level Up Tutorial: Analyzing Literature: Theme**.

COLLABORATE AND PRESENT

In your group, create a theme statement about "Loser" and "At Dusk." Your group will write a statement describing how the themes you found apply to both texts. You will also describe how the authors develop these themes using characterization, setting, plot, and language.

1. **Synthesize Ideas** Discuss the charts you used to compare the texts and other notes you took while reading. Where are the overlaps in theme between the texts? Collaborate to draft a statement with a description of themes the works share. Include an explanation of how each author developed those themes, citing text evidence and drawing on your own experiences and background knowledge.
2. **Present** Each group will present its statement to the class. As there are countless themes in literature, you may have focused on different ones. Listen to other groups' ideas and think about how the evidence in the texts supports different themes.
3. **Discuss and Reflect** A **theme** is an important idea about life or human nature. It is likely that the themes you have analyzed in both texts relate to your life or the lives of people around you. As a group, discuss how the themes in the texts enrich your understanding of the world around you.

COLLABORATE AND PRESENT

Tell students that they will meet in groups to compare themes in these two texts. First, each group will decide on some themes that everyone in the group agrees appear in both texts. Then, group members will work together to state those themes, choose text evidence that shows how each author developed the themes, and decide how to present that information to the class.

1. **Synthesize Ideas** Suggest that when students think they have identified an overlapping theme, they should stop and ask: *What happens in the story and in the poem to make me think of this theme?* If group members can produce text evidence, then they are well on their way to determining how each author developed that theme. When students have discussed two or three themes, have them work on crafting a statement that describes the shared themes.
2. **Present** Tell groups to decide how each member will have a part in the presentation. Remind students to make eye contact with the audience at logical moments during their presentation and to hold the audience's attention by speaking in a conversational way. When groups are part of the audience, remind them to listen to the presenters and to respond thoughtfully and respectfully.
3. **Discuss and Reflect** Help students begin a discussion by reviewing their themes. Tell them to circle key words in their theme statements, such as *loneliness, connect,* or *separate.* Then ask students to think of commonly experienced moments or situations that relate to these words—for example, the first day of school or the loss of a friendship. Finally, have students use their ideas to discuss how reading these texts might offer a deeper understanding of common experiences.

ENGLISH LEARNER SUPPORT

Share Information Help students discuss the selections' themes and supporting evidence. Use the following supports with students at varying proficiency levels:

- Ask yes/no questions about shared ideas and themes: Is the story "Loser" about loneliness? Is the poem about loneliness? *(yes)* Under the heading of *theme,* write *loneliness* on the board. Point to the word and ask: What is another way to say this? *(wanting to connect with someone)* **SUBSTANTIAL**
- Have partners use their charts to complete sentence frames and discuss their answers: *The theme of the story is ____. The theme of the poem is ____. The theme they share is ____.* **MODERATE**
- Provide students with questions such as these to answer in discussion: How does the author of "Loser" develop characterization? How does the author of "At Dusk" develop characterization? What do their characters have in common? What does this information say about a shared theme? **LIGHT**

INDEPENDENT READING

READER'S CHOICE

Setting a Purpose Have students review their Unit 3 Response Log and think about what they've already learned about maintaining connections with others. As they choose their Independent Reading selections, encourage them to consider what more they want to know.

NOTICE & NOTE

Explain that some selections may contain multiple signposts; others may contain only one. The same type of signpost may occur many times in the same text.

LEARNING MINDSET

Plan/Predict Tell students that planning is essential to completing work efficiently and exceptionally. Encourage students to create a plan for reading the self-selected texts. Also discuss the steps they can take to plan out how to complete an assignment, for example, mapping out steps and working from easier to harder parts of the task.

INDEPENDENT READING

ESSENTIAL QUESTION:

How do we form and maintain our connections with others?

Reader's Choice

Setting a Purpose Select one or more of these options from your eBook to continue your exploration of the Essential Question.

- Read the descriptions to see which text grabs your interest.
- Think about which genres you enjoy reading.

Notice & Note

In this unit, you practiced noticing and noting these signposts: **Words of the Wiser, Aha Moment,** and **Again and Again.** As you read independently, these signposts and others will aid your understanding. Below are the anchor questions to ask when you read literature and nonfiction.

Reading Literature: Stories, Poems, and Plays

Signpost	Anchor Question	Lesson
Contrasts and Contradictions	Why did the character act that way?	p. 419
Aha Moment	How might this change things?	p. 171
Tough Questions	What does this make me wonder about?	p. 494
Words of the Wiser	What's the lesson for the character?	p. 171
Again and Again	Why might the author keep bringing this up?	p. 170
Memory Moment	Why is this memory important?	p. 418

Reading Nonfiction: Essays, Articles, and Arguments

Signpost	Anchor Question(s)	Lesson
Big Questions	What surprised me? What did the author think I already knew? What challenged, changed, or confirmed what I already knew?	p. 248 p. 2 p. 84
Contrasts and Contradictions	What is the difference, and why does it matter?	p. 3
Extreme or Absolute Language	Why did the author use this language?	p. 85
Numbers and Stats	Why did the author use these numbers or amounts?	p. 249
Quoted Words	Why was this person quoted or cited, and what did this add?	p. 85
Word Gaps	Do I know this word from someplace else? Does it seem like technical talk for this topic? Do clues in the sentence help me understand the word?	p. 3

ENGLISH LEARNER SUPPORT

Develop Fluency Select a passage from a text that matches students' abilities. Read the passage aloud while students follow along silently.

- Choral read the passage by inviting students to read aloud with you. Repeat this until you have read the passage aloud with the students two or three times. Check their comprehension by asking yes/no questions. **SUBSTANTIAL**
- Cloze read the passage with the students by reading aloud and occasionally skipping a word as you read. Students must follow along closely so that they can read the skipped word out loud. **MODERATE**
- Allow more fluent readers to select their own texts. Have them read silently, marking any sentences that might give them trouble. Have them discuss the difficult parts and restate in their own words. Then ask them to reread the passage and reflect on whether their comprehension improved. **LIGHT**

Go to the **Reading Studio** for additional support in developing fluency.

INDEPENDENT READING

You can preview these texts in Unit 3 of your eBook.

Then, check off the text or texts that you select to read on your own.

☐ EDITORIAL
The Power of a Dinner Table
David Brooks
Close bonds form when a couple opens their home and hearts to local teens.

☐ POEM
The Debt
Tim Seibles
The poet explores how history can teach us to treat one another with more humanity.

☐ INFORMATIONAL TEXT
from *War*
Sebastian Junger
Under what circumstances would you give your life for someone else?

☐ SHORT STORY
A Worn Path
Eudora Welty
In this story set in the deep South, a woman overcomes harsh obstacles to take care of someone she loves.

☐ POEM
My Ceremony for Taking
Lara Mann
A poet finds a way to heal herself after her family splits apart.

Collaborate and Share Work with a partner to discuss what you learned from at least one of your independent readings.

- Give a brief synopsis or summary of the text.
- Describe any signposts that you noticed in the text and explain what they revealed to you.
- Describe what you most enjoyed or found most challenging about the text. Give specific examples.
- Decide whether you would recommend the text to others. Why or why not?

Go to the **Reading Studio** for more resources on **Notice & Note.**

INDEPENDENT READING

MATCHING STUDENTS TO TEXTS

Use the following information to guide students in choosing their texts.

The Power of a Dinner Table **Lexile: 1010L**
Genre: editorial
Overall Rating: Challenging

The Debt
Genre: poem
Overall Rating: Accessible

***from* War** **Lexile: 1150L**
Genre: informational text
Overall Rating: Challenging

A Worn Path **Lexile: 660L**
Genre: short story
Overall Rating: Accessible

My Ceremony for Taking
Genre: poem
Overall Rating: Accessible

Collaborate and Share To assess how well students read the selections, walk around the room and listen to their conversations. Encourage students to be focused and specific in their comments.

for Assessment

- Independent Reading Selection Tests

Encourage students to visit the **Reading Studio** to download a handy bookmark of **NOTICE & NOTE** signposts.

WHEN STUDENTS STRUGGLE . . .

Keep a Reading Log As students read their selected texts, have them keep a reading log for each selection to note signposts and their thoughts about them. Use their logs to assess how well they are noticing and reflecting on elements of their texts.

Reading Log for (title)		
Location	**Signpost I Noticed**	**My Notes About It**

UNIT 3 Task

• WRITE A SHORT STORY

MENTOR TEXT

LOSER

Short Story by Aimee Bender

LEARNING OBJECTIVES

Writing Task

- Write a short story that reveals something about how people connect with each other.
- Plan to incorporate an Aha Moment signpost into a short story.
- Use a chart to help plan and organize ideas for a short story.
- Develop a focused, structured draft of a short story.
- Use the Mentor Text as a model for writing a short story.
- Revise drafts for use of transitions and vivid details.
- Revise drafts incorporating feedback from peers.
- Edit drafts to incorporate standard English conventions.
- Use a rubric to evaluate writing.
- Publish writing to share it with an audience.
- **Language** Practice using transitions and spelling plural nouns correctly in a short story.

Assign the Writing Task in ***Ed***.

RESOURCES

- Unit 3 Response Log
-  Writing Studio: Writing Narratives; Writing as a Process
-  Grammar Studio: Module 13: Lesson 2: Spelling Rules

Language X-Ray: English Learner Support

Use the instruction below and the supports and scaffolds in the Teacher's Edition to help you guide students at different proficiency levels.

INTRODUCE THE WRITING TASK

Remind students that a **short story** is about made-up characters and events. Ask: Does a short story tell about real people? (*no*) Does a short story tell what happened in the real world? (*no*) Ask students to name a short story they have read this year.

Review that a **theme** is an idea about life that readers can learn from a story. Tell students that they will be writing a short story with a theme about connections between people. Point out that the English verb *connect* has a Spanish cognate, *conectar*.

Work with students to brainstorm phrases to complete these sentence frames: *People can connect by* ____. *You know that two people have a strong connection if they* ____. Have students keep these ideas in mind as they plan their short stories.

WRITING

Use Transitions

Tell students that the events in a story happen in a particular order. Transition words help readers understand the order of events.

Use the following supports with students at varying proficiency levels:

- Have students draw storyboard sketches of events in a narrative. Help them label each sketch with a transitional word, such as *first, then, next,* etc. **SUBSTANTIAL**
- Provide sentence frames to give students practice using transitions. For example: *At that moment,* ____. *Then,* ____. **MODERATE**
- Help students brainstorm a list of transitional words and phrases to use in their short stories. **LIGHT**

SPEAKING AND LISTENING

Use Plural Nouns

Use the Mentor Text, "Loser," to give students practice identifying, using, and spelling the plural forms of nouns.

Use the following supports with students at varying proficiency levels:

- Read aloud the first two sentences of paragraph 1 from the mentor text as students follow along. As you reread the sentences, prompt students to raise their hands when they hear a plural noun. **SUBSTANTIAL**
- Read aloud sentence 3 of paragraph 1. Ask students to raise their hands when they hear a singular noun. Then have students say the plural form. **MODERATE**
- Ask partners to review the mentor text and find examples of singular nouns whose plural forms end in *-s* and *-es*. Have one student identify the noun and the other correctly spell its plural aloud. Then, have student reverse roles. **LIGHT**

WRITE A SHORT STORY

Read the introductory paragraph with students and discuss the writing task. Encourage students to refer to the notes they recorded in their Unit 3 Response Logs before they begin planning and drafting their short stories. Explain that the Response Logs contain a variety of ideas about forming and maintaining connections with others, and by reviewing different perspectives on this topic, students will be able to clarify their own ideas.

USE THE MENTOR TEXT

Explain to students that their short stories will resemble "Loser" by Aimee Bender in several basic ways. Like Bender's, their stories will be set in a particular time and place and will have a narrator, a main character, and a central conflict that is resolved by the end of the story. Review the importance of effective transitions. Point to examples of transitions in the beginnings of paragraphs 8, 10, and 21 of "Loser" and discuss how they affect pacing as well as clarify the sequence of events.

WRITING PROMPT

Read and discuss the writing prompt. Elicit questions about the assignment and clarify any misunderstandings. Point out that the purpose of their short stories is to entertain readers with a narrative that demonstrates how we connect with others through what we see, hear, say, and do.

Review the checklist of key points that students should consider as they write their stories.

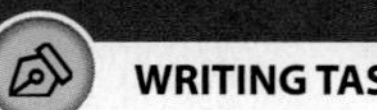

WRITING TASK

Write a Short Story

Go to **Writing Narratives** in the **Writing Studio** for help writing a short story.

This unit focuses on the connections each of us has with family, friends, pets, and community. For this writing task, you will write a short story that shows how we connect with others. Think about how the selections you have read use narrative techniques to explore interpersonal connections. For an example of a well-written short story you can use as a mentor text, review the story "Loser."

THE BONDS BETWEEN US

As you write your story, you will want to look at the notes you made in your Response Log after reading the texts in this unit.

Writing Prompt

Read the information in the box below.

This is the topic or context for your story.

We connect with others through what we see, hear, say, and do.

Think carefully about the following question.

This is the Essential Question for the unit. How would you answer this question, based on the text in this unit?

How do we form and maintain our connections with others?

Be sure to follow the instructions that explain exactly what you are supposed to write.

Write a short story about an event that reveals something about how we connect with each other.

Be sure to—

Review these points as you write and again when you finish. Make any needed changes.

- ❑ begin by introducing a setting, a narrator, and a main character
- ❑ have an engaging plot with a central conflict
- ❑ provide a clear progression of events, using transitions to connect paragraphs and ideas
- ❑ use a variety of narrative techniques to develop characters, plot, theme, and suspense or surprise
- ❑ include sensory language and descriptive details
- ❑ end with a logical and satisfying resolution to the conflict

LEARNING MINDSET

Seeking Challenges Explain to students that a willingness to take on the challenges of difficult learning tasks will help them develop a learning mindset. Point out that making mistakes is a natural part of the learning process. Remind students that when they encounter problems, seeking assistance from you and from their peers is an important strategy for success. Encourage students to think about areas in their lives in which they have taken on challenges, such as helping a friend with a problem or moving to a new school, and what they learned from the experience that can help them now and in the future.

1 Plan

Every short story begins with an idea. It may come from something you've seen, heard, or experienced. If you keep a journal, look it over for ideas. Look through a photo book or images online for inspiration. Think about things that connect people to one another, such as interests, beliefs, goals, ethnicity, neighborhood, or family. Building on one of these connections, write down ideas for characters, setting, plot, conflict, and theme. Use the chart below to help you plan your story.

Short Story Planning Chart

Type of Connection (interests, goals, family, etc.)	
Characters	Setting
Conflict	Plot
Theme	

Background Reading Review the notes you have taken in your Response Log after reading the texts in this unit. These texts provide background reading that will help you think about what you want to say in your short story.

Go to **Writing Narratives: Narrative Context** for help planning your short story.

Notice & Note

From Reading to Writing

As you plan your short story, apply what you've learned about signposts to your own writing. Remember that writers use common features, called signposts, to help convey their message to readers. Think about how you can incorporate an **Aha Moment** into your short story.

Go to the **Reading Studio** for more resources on **Notice & Note**.

Use the notes from your Response Log as you plan your short story.

1 PLAN

After reading the introductory text, review some of the resources students might use to develop ideas as they plan their short stories. Remind them that their stories should focus on a way that people connect with each other. Ask: What special connections do you have with your closest friends? What makes you feel connected to a favorite fictional character?

English Learner Support

Understand Academic Language Define and discuss the following academic terms from the planning chart: *characters, setting, conflict, plot,* and *theme*. As you discuss each term, ask volunteers to suggest examples from stories they have read. **ALL LEVELS**

NOTICE & NOTE

From Reading to Writing Discuss the Aha Moment signpost, in which a person realizes something about his or her actions or gains an insight about others. Emphasize that an Aha Moment need not involve an unusual or extraordinary event; rather, it occurs when a specific experience generates a new understanding of self or of the world. As students consider Aha Moments, encourage them to ask, "How might this moment change things?"

Background Reading Remind students to review the notes in their Unit 3 Response Logs as they plan their short stories. Suggest that they scan the unit's selections to find story elements and language that can serve as models for their own writing.

WHEN STUDENTS STRUGGLE . . .

Brainstorm Story Ideas Organize students into small groups and have them brainstorm ideas for stories. Once they have settled on several story ideas, let them use story starters like those below to develop interesting opening lines:

- *Our neighbor's dog kept* _____.
- *Walking along the road, I was surprised to find* _____.
- *I'm not sure what I was thinking when* _____.

After students have finished the brainstorming activity, have them freewrite about an event that might be part of their stories.

Organize Your Ideas Discuss the benefits of mapping out ideas before drafting a short story, and then introduce the diagram showing the five stages of plot development. Note how the stages rise to a high point, or climax, and then descend through the resolution of the main conflict and the final ending of the story, or dénouement.

Emphasize that the beginning of a short story introduces the main character and the setting in a way that engages the reader's attention.

As the plot develops, the reader learns more about the characters and the conflict as events unfold and build toward a climax, or moment of greatest tension.

After the climax, readers learn how the conflict will be resolved. The ending presents the story's outcome and shows its effect on the main character.

2 DEVELOP A DRAFT

Encourage students to consult their graphic organizers, planning notes, or other prewriting ideas as they draft their short stories. Explain that reviewing their outlines is their first step in drafting. The outlines can help them arrange their paragraphs in a logical progression. However, remind them that they should feel free to change their plans as new ideas arise during the drafting stage.

English Learner Support

Create a Storyboard Storyboards can help students visualize and arrange the progression of events in their short stories. Use the following supports with students at varying proficiency levels:

- Have students create storyboards. Provide a word bank of transitional words. Have students write a transitional word from the bank over each frame. **SUBSTANTIAL**
- Have students create storyboards. Then have them write captions over each frame that use transitions from a provided word bank. **MODERATE**

For **writing support** for students at varying proficiency levels, see the **Language X-Ray** on page 238B.

WRITING TASK

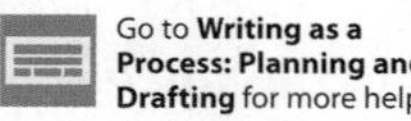

Go to **Writing as a Process: Planning and Drafting** for more help.

Organize Your Ideas Draw upon the techniques you identified in the texts as you organize your own ideas in an outline or graphic organizer. Consider these points:

- How can the beginning of your story engage readers?
- What is the story's plot? What is the central conflict?
- What is the progression of events? How do the events lead to a climax—a turning point or moment of greatest intensity?
- How is the conflict resolved? How does the story end?
- Which point of view will you use in your story?
- Create an outline or use this plot line to plan your story.

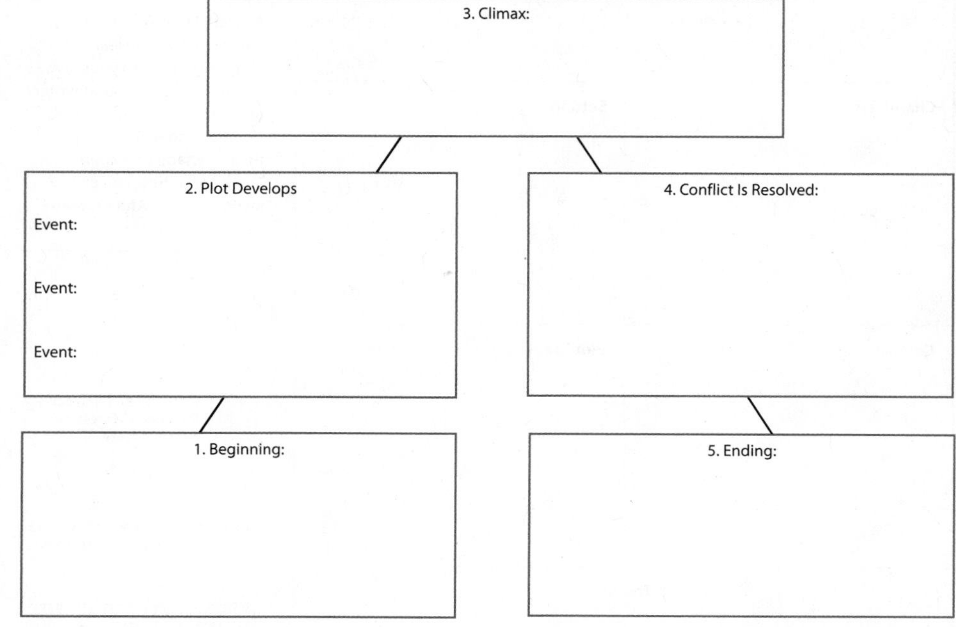

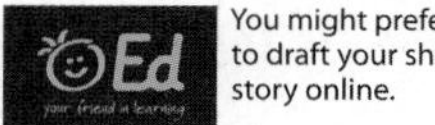

You might prefer to draft your short story online.

2 Develop a Draft

Once you have completed your planning activities, you will be ready to begin drafting your short story. Refer to your graphic organizer and/or the outline you have created, as well as any notes you took as you studied the texts in the unit. These will provide a kind of map for you to follow as you write. Use a word processor or online writing application to make it easier for you to make changes and move sentences around later when you are ready to revise your first draft.

WHEN STUDENTS STRUGGLE . . .

Describe a Setting Prepare sets of index cards that name a location, such as a desert island, a mountaintop, a beach, or a haunted house, on one side of each card. Have students in small groups each draw a card from the face-down set and then prepare a brief description of the setting on the card.

Explain that students cannot name the location. Instead, they must reveal the setting only through the vivid details in their descriptions. When students finish, ask them to share their descriptions with the group and let members guess the locations.

Use the Mentor Text

Author's Craft

Sensory and descriptive details can be very effective in drawing the reader into a story, even when the details seem to be small and unimportant. Note the way the author uses details in "Loser."

> … he walked right into the backyard, through the back door, and sure enough, there were four people watching TV including the tear-stained boy with a runny nose eating a candy bar.

The author makes the scene seem very real by giving vivid details about the boy's appearance.

Apply What You've Learned When describing your characters and setting, be creative in your use of sensory and descriptive details.

Genre Characteristics

"Loser" uses a consistent point of view. The entire story is told by a third-person narrator with a clear voice. The narrator is outside the story and can talk about the feelings and thoughts of all the characters. At the same time, the narrator focuses primarily on the unnamed young man at the center of the story.

> He went home to his tiny room and thought about the word lonely and how it sounded and looked so lonely, with those two l's in it, each standing tall by itself.

The narrator is telling exactly what is in the heart and mind of the young man.

Apply What You've Learned You can choose a third-person point of view like the one in "Loser," using pronouns like "he" and "she," or you can choose a first-person point of view, using the pronoun "I." First-person point of view is limited to the thoughts and feelings of one character but has a more personal feeling. Whichever one you choose, use it throughout your story.

WHY THIS MENTOR TEXT?

"Loser" provides a good example of a short story that explores the theme of forming and maintaining connections with others. It does so in part by describing how disconnected and alone the main character feels. Use the instruction below to model how sensory and descriptive details engage the reader and how point of view influences the description of characters and story events.

USE THE MENTOR TEXT

Author's Craft Ask volunteers to read aloud the introduction and the example from the mentor text. Ask: What vivid details does the author use to make this scene engaging to the reader? *(She describes the path the main character takes, the setting in which he finds the lost boy, and the boy's appearance.)*

Genre Characteristics Review the differences between first-person and third-person points of view, and distinguish between third-person omniscient and third-person limited points of view. Discuss the ways that the narrative voice can influence a story. Ask: How would "Loser" change if the young man told the story in his own voice, or if the story were told from the point of view of the lost child?

ENGLISH LEARNER SUPPORT

Identify Point of View Use the following supports with students at varying proficiency levels:

- Read aloud paragraph 1 of "Loser" and discuss its point of view. Ask: Who is the main character in this story? *(the orphan)* Is this character telling us the story? *(no)* **SUBSTANTIAL**
- Have small groups identify clues in the paragraph that indicate the story is told by a third-person narrator. Facilitate their recognition of pronouns (*he* and *him*) and phrases, such as "Once there was an orphan…." Help group members discuss their examples. **MODERATE**
- Have students work with a partner to rewrite paragraph 1 from a first-person point of view. Ask: Which details of paragraph 1 would you include in a first-person account? Which details would you leave out? What pronouns would you use in place of *he, him*, and *his*? **LIGHT**

WRITING

3 REVISE

As students determine how they can improve their drafts by answering each question posed in the Revision Guide, call on volunteers to model their revision techniques.

With a Partner In addition to considering the questions in the Revision Guide, suggest the following techniques to help students get ideas for improvement flowing:

- If a section of the draft needs something but students aren't sure what, tell them to try reading it aloud. They might "hear" the problem when reading it silently doesn't reveal it.
- The reviewer can ask specific questions to help the writer come up with more images or tweaks to the plot. For example, if the reviewer asks, "Is the main character in the grocery store or the yard at this point?" The writer would know that a key detail is missing.

Encourage students to use their reviewers' comments to add descriptive details and effective transitions as they continue to develop their stories.

WRITING TASK

Go to **Writing as Process: Revising and Editing** for help revising your short story.

3 Revise

On Your Own In your first draft, you put your ideas together and see how they work. Then, you can do important and creative work while revising, including bringing color to your story by introducing effective descriptions. Use sensory details, including well-chosen adjectives and vivid verbs. Also, make sure you use effective transitions between paragraphs. For example, you might mention something at the end of one paragraph and then refer back to it in the first sentence of the next paragraph. The Revision Guide will help you focus on specific elements to make your writing stronger.

REVISION GUIDE

Ask Yourself	Tips	Revision Techniques
1. Does the narrative begin in an engaging way and introduce characters, setting, conflict, and point of view?	**Underline** the opening and **mark** clues about the characters, setting, conflict, or point of view.	**Revise** your introduction to begin with action or dialogue, and **add** details about the characters, setting, or conflict.
2. Do narrative techniques and precise language bring the story to life?	**Underline** dialogue, sensory details, and vivid verbs.	**Add** dialogue, sensory details, and vivid verbs where they are lacking.
3. Does the plot build steadily, without getting slow or sluggish?	**Mark** important plot points.	**Make cuts** if the story goes on too long without advancing the plot.
4. Are suspense or surprise used effectively?	**Mark** passages that build tension or reveal a surprise.	**Add d**etails that build tension. **Add** a surprising event.
5. Is the narrative told from a consistent point of view?	**Note** any places where the point of view changes.	**Change** pronouns to make the point of view consistent.
6. Are there clear transitions between paragraphs?	**Note** any confusion moving from one paragraph to another.	**Revise** paragraph transitions to make them clearer.
7. Does the conclusion resolve the conflict in a logical way?	**Underline** the part where the conflict is or should be resolved	**Add** dialogue or narration that logically resolves the conflict.

ACADEMIC VOCABULARY

As you conduct your **peer review**, try to use these words.

- ❑ **capacity**
- ❑ **confer**
- ❑ **emerge**
- ❑ **generate**
- ❑ **trace**

With a Partner After you have worked through the Revision Guide on your own, exchange papers with a partner. Evaluate each other's drafts in a **peer review**. Begin by giving your partner praise for what he or she has done well. Then try to see how your partner could better accomplish his or her purpose in writing. Explain how you think your partner's draft should be revised and what your specific suggestions for revision are.

When receiving feedback from your partner, listen attentively and ask questions to make sure you fully understand the revision suggestions.

ENGLISH LEARNER SUPPORT

Discuss a Text Before students begin their peer-review evaluations, review the elements of a successful discussion and encourage active listening with the following sentence frames:

I like the way you used _____ to describe _____.

I think changing _____ to _____ might make the story more interesting.

What do you think of _____? Is there a way that I can improve it?

What if you tried _____?

Use the frames to model several statements and responses for the group. Then, if possible, pair English learners with fluent speakers to discuss their drafts. **MODERATE/LIGHT**

4 Edit

So that your readers can fully appreciate your story, edit for proper use of standard English conventions and make sure to correct any misspellings or grammatical errors.

Language Conventions

Spell Plural Nouns Most plural nouns are made by adding either *-s* or *-es.*

- To form the plural of **most nouns**, including those ending in *o*, add *-s.*
- To form the plural of **a few nouns that end in *o***, such as *hero, tomato, potato,* and *echo,* and all nouns that end in *s, sh, ch, x, or z,* add *-es.*
- When a singular noun ends in ***y* with a consonant** before it, change the *y* to *i* and add *-es.*
- When a singular noun ends in ***y* with a vowel** (*a, e, i, o, u*) before it, just add *-s.*

Go to **Spelling Rules** in the **Grammar Studio** to learn more.

The chart has examples of nouns from "Loser" and the correct plural spellings.

NOUNS	PLURALS
orphan, parent, neighbor, sweater, object, nose, kitchen, sleeve, location, case, marble	orphans, parents, neighbors, sweaters, objects, noses, kitchens, sleeves, locations, cases, marbles
hairbrush, search, watch	hairbrushes, searches, watches
tragedy, community, ability, twenty, allergy, party, candy	tragedies, communities, abilities, twenties, allergies, parties, candies
year, key, boy, guy	years, keys, boys, guys

5 Publish

Finalize your story and choose a way to share it with your audience. Consider these options:

- Present your story to the class by reading it aloud. Be sure to use different voices for different characters.
- Self-publish your story by printing it in a readable font and adding a cover with an illustration you draw yourself or download. Make the finished product available to other students.

TO CHALLENGE STUDENTS . . .

Hold a Staged Reading Challenge students to adapt their essays for a dramatic presentation. Explain that in a staged reading, actors read from scripts. Their movement, if any, is limited, and there are no costumes or scenery. Have students write scripts that retell their stories using only lines for characters and narrators. Form small groups in which students can revise their scripts and stage presentations.

4 EDIT

Suggest that during the first reading of their revised drafts, students should focus on vivid descriptive details. Encourage them to consider the following questions: Does the story include verbs, adjectives, and phrases that describe sensory experiences? Are the people, places, and events described in a lively and engaging way?

During their second reading, suggest that students look for transitions that make the flow of events and ideas clear to the reader. A third reading might focus on grammar, mechanics, and the correct spelling of plural nouns.

LANGUAGE CONVENTIONS

Spell Plural Nouns Review the four basic rules for forming plurals as presented in the text. Explain that these rules cover most English nouns. Review the examples of singular and plural nouns in the chart. As a challenge, have students find sentences in which these singular nouns appear and then rewrite the sentences using the plural forms.

Remind students that some common nouns have irregular plurals that do not follow any of these rules, for example, *foot/feet* and *woman/women*. Have volunteers suggest others. Ask: Can you think of other nouns that have irregular or special plural forms? *(**Sample responses:** child/children, person/people, mouse/mice, tooth/teeth)*

For **speaking and listening support** for students at varying proficiency levels, see the **Language X-Ray** on page 238B.

5 PUBLISH

Discuss possible publishing options and provide suggestions for dramatic readings. Ask: Why is it important to use different voices for different characters when reading a story aloud? Discuss ways to differentiate explanatory text, or exposition, from dialogue. Collect students' "published" stories and make them accessible in the classroom. Encourage students to review and recommend stories they like to others.

USE THE SCORING GUIDE

Discuss the organization of the scoring guide, noting the three major column heads. Allow students time to read the scoring guide, and encourage them to ask questions about anything they do not understand. Let partners exchange their final short stories and score them according to the guidelines. Ask each student reviewer to make notes that explain the reasons for the scores they awarded.

WRITING TASK

Use the scoring guide to evaluate your short story.

WRITING TASK SCORING GUIDE: SHORT STORY

	Organization /Progression	Development of Ideas	Use of Language and Conventions
4	• The organization is effective and appropriate to the purpose. • Events serve the plot and/or the character development. • The conflict of the story is presented, developed, and resolved. • The story is told from a consistent point of view.	• The beginning of the story catches the reader's attention and begins to introduce the conflict. • The theme emerges from the plot events and character development. • The conclusion resolves the conflict and supports the theme.	• Language and word choice is precise and descriptive. • Complex sentences are used well. • Spelling, capitalization, and punctuation are correct. • Grammar, usage, and mechanics are correct.
3	• The organization is, for the most part, effective and appropriate to the purpose. • Most events serve the plot and/or the character development. • The conflict of the story is presented, developed, and resolved fairly well. • The story is told from a mostly consistent point of view.	• The beginning of the story catches the reader's attention fairly well and begins to introduce the conflict. • For the most part, the theme emerges from the plot events and character development. • The conclusion resolves the conflict and supports the theme well enough for the story to be enjoyable.	• Language is for the most part specific and descriptive. • Complex sentences are used. • There are some spelling, capitalization, and punctuation mistakes. • Some grammar and usage errors occur.
2	• The organization is evident but is not always appropriate to the purpose. • Only some events serve the plot and/or the character development. • The conflict of the story needs to be better presented, developed, and resolved. • The story is told from an inconsistent point of view.	• The beginning of the story does not catch the reader's attention well and the introduction of the conflict is vague. • The theme does not emerge from the plot events and character development in a clear way, but it does exist. • The conclusion does not resolve the conflict and support the theme well.	• Language is somewhat vague and lacking in detail. • Spelling, capitalization, and punctuation, as well as grammar and usage, are often incorrect but do not make reading too difficult.
1	• The organization is not appropriate to the purpose. • Events do not serve the plot and/ or the character development. • The conflict of the story is not presented, developed, and resolved. • The story does not show evidence of a point of view.	• The beginning of the story does not catch the reader's attention and conflict is missing. • The theme does not emerge from the plot events and character development. • The conclusion does not resolve the conflict and support the theme.	• Language is inappropriate for the text. • Many spelling, capitalization, and punctuation errors are present. • Grammatical and usage errors confuse the writer's ideas.

Reflect on the Unit

You've encountered a lot of ideas about connection in this unit, and you've written a story that brings together some of those ideas with ideas of your own. Now is a good time to reflect on what you have learned.

Reflect on the Essential Question

- How do we form and maintain our connections with others? How has your answer to this question changed since you first considered it when you started this unit?

- What are some examples from the texts you've read that show how we form and maintain our connections with others?

Reflect on Your Reading

- Which selections were the most interesting to you? Which ones were the most moving?

- From which selection did you learn the most about making connections in a complex society?

Reflect on the Writing Task

- What difficulties did you encounter while working on your short story? How might you handle them differently next time?

- What part of the short story was the easiest and which part was the hardest to write? Why?

- What improvements did you make to your story as you were revising?

UNIT 3 SELECTIONS

- **"The Grasshopper and the Bell Cricket"**
- **"Monkey See, Monkey Do, Monkey Connect"**
- **"With Friends Like These . . ."**
- **"AmeriCorps NCCC: Be the Greater Good"**
- **"Loser"**
- **"At Dusk"**

REFLECT

REFLECT ON THE UNIT

Review the three major points of reflection. Then ask students to think about the questions and work independently to write a brief response to each one. Next, form small groups in which students can share their responses. Circulate among the groups and identify the questions that seem to stimulate the liveliest conversations. Use these questions to wrap up the unit with a whole-class discussion.

LEARNING MINDSET

Self-Reflection Emphasize that accurately identifying one's strengths and weaknesses is essential to developing a growth mindset. Improving our areas of weakness, obviously, helps us become more successful, but trusting our own strengths and abilities can help us succeed, too. Stress that we often face difficult challenges, and sometimes we don't meet them with complete success. Encourage students to recognize these situations as personal learning opportunities and to think about the positive lessons that they can take away from these experiences, including ideas about how they would do things differently next time.

Instructional Overview and Resources

	Instructional Focus	Online Ed Resources
Unit Introduction **Sweet Sorrow**	**Unit 4 Essential Question** **Unit 4 Academic Vocabulary**	**Stream to Start:** Sweet Sorrow **Unit 4 Response Log**
ANALYZE & APPLY		
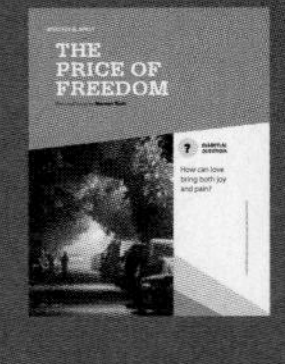 **"The Price of Freedom"** Personal Essay by Noreen Riols **Lexile 760L** **NOTICE & NOTE** READING MODEL **Signposts** • Big Questions • Numbers and Stats • Word Gaps	**Reading** • Analyze Text Meanings • Create Mental Images **Writing:** Write a Professional Letter **Speaking and Listening:** Discuss with a Small Group **Vocabulary:** Foreign Words **Language Conventions:** Sentence Variety	 **Audio** **Reading Studio:** Notice & Note **Level Up Tutorial:** Making Inferences **Writing Studio:** Formal Style **Speaking and Listening Studio:** Participating in Collaborative Discussions **Vocabulary Studio:** Decoding Foreign Words **Grammar Studio:** Module 1: Lesson 10: Classifying Sentences by Purpose
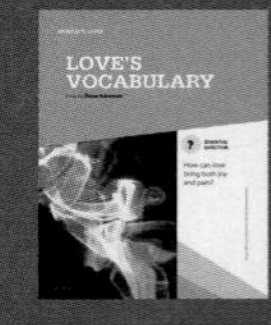 **Mentor Text** **"Love's Vocabulary"** Essay by Diane Ackerman **Lexile 1020L**	**Reading** • Analyze Informational Text • Generate Questions **Writing:** Discuss the Author's Statement **Speaking and Listening:** Present in a Panel Discussion **Vocabulary:** Synonyms **Language Conventions:** Participial Phrases	 **Audio** **Reading Studio:** Notice & Note **Level Up Tutorial:** Main Idea and Supporting Details **Speaking and Listening Studio:** Preparing for Discussion **Vocabulary Studio:** Synonyms **Grammar Studio:** Module 3: Lesson 4: Participial Phrases
 **"My Shakespeare"** Video and Poem by Kate Tempest	**Reading** • Analyze Multimodal Texts **Writing:** Write a Poem **Speaking and Listening:** Produce a Video	**Reading Studio:** Notice & Note **Level Up Tutorial:** Elements of Poetry **Speaking and Listening Studio:** Giving a Presentation
 ***The Tragedy of Romeo and Juliet*** Drama by William Shakespeare	**Reading** • Analyze Literary Devices • Analyze Parallel Plots **Writing:** Write a Journal Entry; Write a Eulogy **Speaking and Listening:** Discuss; Debate; Present to a Partner; Participate in a Dramatic Reading; Discuss with a Small Group **Vocabulary:** Shakespeare's Language **Language Conventions:** Parallel Structure	**Audio** **Close Read Screencasts:** Modeled Discussions **Reading Studio:** Notice & Note **Level Up Tutorials:** Listed at point of use **Speaking and Listening Studio:** Giving a Presentation; Participating in Collaborative Discussions **Vocabulary Studio:** Foreign Words

SUGGESTED PACING: 30 DAYS

Unit Introduction	The Price of Freedom	Love's Vocabulary	My Shakespeare
1	2 3 4 5	6 7 8 9	10 11

English Learner Support	Differentiated Instruction	Online Ed Assessment
• Learn Vocabulary		
• Text X-Ray • Express Concepts • Use Cognates • Analyze Figurative Language • Make Vocabulary Connections • Use Contractions • Use Context Clues • Oral Assessment • Write a Letter • Foreign Terms in English • Use Punctuation in Combined Sentences	**When Students Struggle** • Collaborate with Partners • Make Inferences **To Challenge Students** • Write a Memoir Episode	**Selection Test**
• Text X-Ray • Comprehend English Vocabulary • Comprehend Language Structures • Use Learning Strategies • Understand Language Structures • Oral Assessment • Vocabulary Strategy • Comprehend Language Conventions	**When Students Struggle** • Support Comprehension **To Challenge Students** • Compare Poems	**Selection Test**
• Text X-Ray • Analyze Multimodal Texts • Oral Assessment	**When Students Struggle** • Analyze Multimodal Texts **To Challenge Students** • Identify Allusions	**Selection Test**
• Text X-Ray • Ask and Answer Questions • Understand Puns • Summarize Events • Comprehend Figurative Language • Examine Dialogue • Restate Oxymorons • Listen and Answer Questions • Use Visual Support • Understand Inverted Word Order • Identify and Use Pronouns • Analyze Dialogue • Analyze Figurative Language • Oral Assessment • Identify Pronoun Antecedents • Use Visual Support	**When Students Struggle** • Reading Shakespearean Tragedy • Summarize a Scene • Make Inferences • Understand Historical Context • Analyze Cause and Effect • Cite Evidence • Compare and Contrast Characters • Analyze Character Motivation • Identify Sequence of Events • Understand Role of Chorus • Analyze Soliloquy **To Challenge Students** • Sketch and Analyze the Globe Theater	**Selection Test**

The Tragedy of Romeo and Juliet 12 13 14 15 16 17 18 19 20 21

Having It Both Ways/Superheart 22 23 24 25

Independent Reading 26 27

End of Unit 28 29 30

UNIT 4 Continued

	Instructional Focus	 Resources
ANALYZE & APPLY		
(continued)  ***The Tragedy of Romeo and Juliet*** *Drama* by William Shakespeare	**See previous page.**	**See previous page.**
COLLABORATE & COMPARE		
 **"Having It Both Ways"** Sonnet by Elizabeth Jennings **"Superheart"** Sonnet by Marion Shore	**Reading** • Analyze Poetry • Connect Ideas **Speaking and Listening:** Discuss the Poems; Create a Visual Response	**Audio** **Reading Studio:** Notice & Note **Level Up Tutorials:** Rhythm; Rhyme **Speaking and Listening Studio:** Participating in Collaborative Discussions
Collaborate and Compare	**Reading:** Compare Poems **Speaking and Listening:** Collaborate and Present	**Speaking and Listening Studio:** • Giving a Presentation

Online Ed INDEPENDENT READING

The Independent Reading selections are only available in the eBook.

 **Go to the Reading Studio for more information on Notice & Note.**

"Pyramus and Thisbe" from *Metamorphoses* Myth by Ovid

"Sonnet 71" Sonnet by Pablo Neruda

END OF UNIT

	Instructional Focus	Resources
Writing Task: Write a Literary Analysis **Reflect on the Unit**	**Writing:** Write a Literary Analysis **Language Conventions:** Capitalization	**Unit 4 Response Log** **Mentor Text:** "Love's Vocabulary" **Writing Studio:** Writing as a Process **Reading Studio:** Notice & Note **Grammar Studio:** Module 10: Capital Letters

English Learner Support	Differentiated Instruction	Online Ed Assessment
(continued) • Explain Characters' Actions • Rewrite Sentences with Negatives • Use Visual and Contextual Support • Use Cognates • Develop Vocabulary • Demonstrate Comprehension • Use Details to Make Inferences • Understand Idioms • Paraphrase to Demonstrate Comprehension • Read with Support • Learn Language Structures • Make Predictions • Summarize • Understand Language Structures • Make Inferences • Understand Homophones • Language Conventions	**When Students Struggle *(continued)*** • Understand Hyperbole • Analyze Character and Theme • Analyze Plot • Understand Author's Purpose • Compare and Contrast • Analyze Foreshadowing • Analyze Parallel Plots • Analyze Characters • Analyze Dramatic Irony **To Challenge Students *(continued)*** • Discuss the Function of a Scene • Analyze Poetic Form • Analyze Wordplay • Deliver a Soliloquy • Consider Alternate Plot Events • Analyze Dialogue • Analyze Plot • Compare Two Relationships • Explore Multimedia Adaptations • Analyze Shakespeare's Syntax • Explore Shakespearean Heroines • Reimagine a Scene	
• Text X-Ray • Preteach Vocabulary • Enhance Comprehension • Oral Assessment	**When Students Struggle** • Analyze Rhyme Scheme **To Challenge Students** • Analyze Diction and Syntax	**Selection Tests**
• Use Academic Language	**When Students Struggle** • Collaborate and Present	
"Why Love Literally Hurts" Science Writing by Eric Jaffe **Lexile 1260L**	"The Bass, the River, and Sheila Mant" Short Story by W.D. Wetherell **Lexile 1060L**	**Selection Tests**
• Language X-Ray • Understand Academic Language • Write a Group Literary Analysis • Use Precise Descriptive Language • Use Proper Adjectives	**When Students Struggle** • Use Writing Prompts • Improve Writing Fluency • Present Text Evidence	**Unit Test**

Connect to the *ESSENTIAL QUESTION*

Ask a volunteer to read aloud the Essential Question. Ask students to think of examples from books or movies that relate to the question. Was there love in these stories that caused characters both joy and pain? Have students recall and discuss the circumstances that caused characters to experience extreme emotions.

English Learner Support

Learn Vocabulary Make sure students understand the Essential Question. If necessary, explain the following terms:

- *Love* means "a feeling of deep affection; liking a lot."
- *Joy* means "happiness."
- *Pain* means "suffering."

Help students restate the question in simpler language: How can love cause someone both happiness and hurt? **SUBSTANTIAL/MODERATE**

DISCUSS THE QUOTATION

Tell students that Diane Ackerman (1948) is an American poet and essayist, who is known for her interest in natural science. Ask students to read the quotation and reflect on its meaning. If necessary, explain that something intangible is difficult to grasp, understand, or perceive. Do students agree with Ackerman's statement? Have them discuss the ways in which love may be intangible, or hard to understand.

UNIT 4

SWEET SORROW

ESSENTIAL QUESTION:

How can love bring both joy and pain?

"Love is the great intangible."

Diane Ackerman

LEARNING MINDSET

Effort Explain the importance of effort. In order to improve skills, students must apply the necessary amount of effort. Have students consider the amount of effort, or hard work, it takes for an athlete to compete in the Olympics. Talk about how continuous hard work can lead to one of the greatest accomplishments in athletics: being an Olympian. Prompt students to think of something they have become better at through hard work. Be sure to offer positive feedback to students for their continued effort.

ACADEMIC VOCABULARY

Academic Vocabulary words are words you use when you discuss and write about texts. In this unit, you will practice and learn five words.

☑ **attribute** ☐ **commit** ☐ **expose** ☐ **initiate** ☐ **underlie**

Study the Word Network to learn more about the word **attribute**.

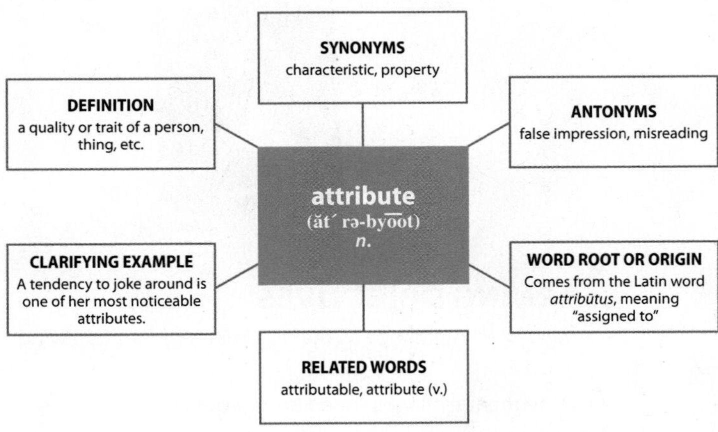

Write and Discuss Discuss the completed Word Network with a partner, making sure to talk through all of the boxes until you both understand the word, its synonyms, antonyms, and related forms. Then, fill out a Word Network for each of the remaining four words. Use a dictionary or online resource to help you complete the activity.

Go online to access the Word Networks.

RESPOND TO THE ESSENTIAL QUESTION

In this unit, you will explore the nature of love and the conflicts surrounding it. As you read, you will revisit the **Essential Question** and gather your ideas about it in the **Response Log** that appears on page R4. At the end of the unit, you will have the opportunity to write a **literary analysis**. Filling out the Response Log will help you prepare for this writing task.

You can also go online to access the Response Log.

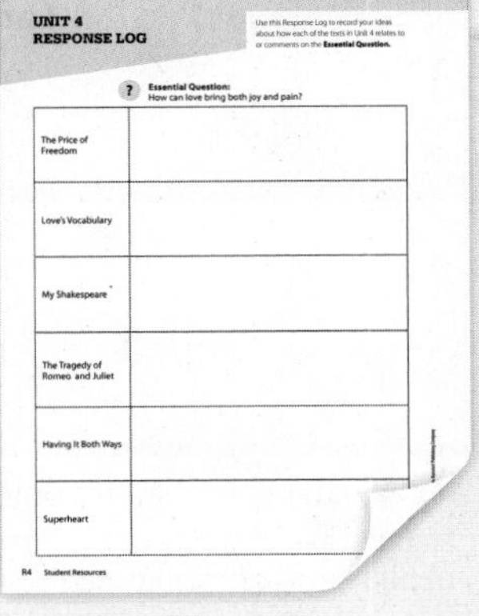

UNIT 4 RESPONSE LOG

Essential Question: How can love bring both joy and pain?

The Price of Freedom	
Love's Vocabulary	
My Shakespeare	
The Tragedy of Romeo and Juliet	
Having It Both Ways	
Superheart	

R4 Student Resources

ACADEMIC VOCABULARY

As students complete Word Networks for the remaining four vocabulary words, encourage them to include all the categories shown in the completed network if possible, but point out that some words do not have clear synonyms or antonyms. Some words may also function as different parts of speech—for example, *initiate* can be an adjective or noun.

attribute (ăt´rə-byo͞ot´) *n.* A quality or trait of a person, thing, etc. (Spanish cognate: *atributo*)

commit (kə-mĭt´) *v.* To carry out, engage in, or perform.

expose (ĭk-spōz´) *v.* To make visible or reveal. (Spanish cognate: *exponer*)

initiate (ĭ-nĭsh´ē-āt´) *v.* To start or cause to begin. (Spanish cognate: *iniciar*)

underlie (ŭn´dər-lī´) *v.* To be the basis or support of.

RESPOND TO THE ESSENTIAL QUESTION

Direct students to the Unit 4 Response Log. Explain that students will use it to record ideas and details from the selections that help answer the Essential Question. When they work on the writing task at the end of the unit, their Response Log will help them think about what they have read and make connections between the texts.

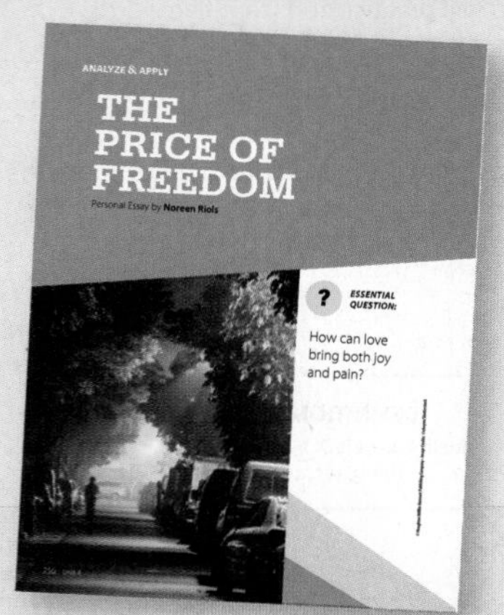

READING MODEL

THE PRICE OF FREEDOM

Personal Essay by Noreen Riols

GENRE ELEMENTS

INFORMATIONAL TEXT

Explain to students that a **personal essay** explores the writer's life experiences in ways that are similar to a **memoir.** A personal essay also includes the author's feelings and reactions at a particular time. However, a personal essay is much shorter and more tightly focused than a memoir. In this lesson, students will analyze text meanings and create mental images to help them explore the author's experiences of working with secret agents fighting the Nazis during World War II.

LEARNING OBJECTIVES

- Analyze text meanings by making inferences and drawing conclusions.
- Create mental images based on text details.
- Conduct research into the roles agents played during WWII.
- Write a professional application letter to a WWII agency.
- In small groups, discuss how to interview agency "applicants" from a recruiter's point of view.
- Determine the meaning of foreign terms from context.
- Write using longer sentences as well as fragments.
- **Language** Write to convey word meanings.

TEXT COMPLEXITY

Quantitative Measures	**The Price of Freedom**	Lexile: 760L
Qualitative Measures	**Ideas Presented** Somewhat explicit; inferential reasoning often required.	
	Structures Used Primarily explicit and chronological, with one perspective.	
	Language Used Often explicit; some figurative and historically contextual language used.	
	Knowledge Required Much of text is easily imagined; many cultural and historical references.	

Online 

RESOURCES

- Unit 4 Response Log
- Selection Audio
-  Reading Studio: Notice & Note
-  Level Up Tutorial: Making Inferences
-  Writing Studio: Formal Style
-  Speaking and Listening Studio: Participating in Collaborative Discussions
-  Vocabulary Studio: Decoding Foreign Words
-  Grammar Studio: Module 1: Lesson 10: Classifying Sentences by Purpose
- "The Price of Freedom" Selection Test

SUMMARIES

English

When she was 18 years old, author Noreen Riols was recruited into Winston Churchill's Special Operations Executive, a secret agency formed to combat the Nazis by training special agents to infiltrate enemy territory and commit acts of espionage and sabotage. As she writes about her first romance with a legendary agent, doomed to sacrifice his life for the cause of freedom, she describes the courage of these volunteers and makes the dangers they faced palpable.

Spanish

Cuando tenía 18 años, la autora Noreen Riols fue reclutada en la Dirección de Operaciones Especiales de Winston Churchill: una agencia secreta formada para combatir a los nazis mediante el entrenamiento de agentes especiales para tareas de infiltración en territorio enemigo y actos de espionaje y sabotaje. Mientras escribe sobre su primer romance con un agente legendario, condenado a sacrificar su vida por la causa de la libertad, la autora describe el valor de estos voluntarios y hace palpable el peligro que estos enfrentaron.

SMALL-GROUP OPTIONS

Have students work in small groups and pairs to read and discuss the selection.

Three-Minute Review

- After five minutes of reading the essay, instruct students to pause.
- Tell students to spend three minutes rereading any parts with unfamiliar terms or concepts and then to write questions about those passages.
- Give small groups several minutes to discuss their questions.
- Instruct students to read the rest of the essay with the remaining questions in mind.
- Hold a class discussion about the unanswered questions.

Key Word Prediction

- In pairs, tell students to make three columns on a sheet of paper and label these from left to right New Word, Our Prediction, and Text Definition.
- Choose five or six words in the essay that you think will be unfamiliar to students. Tell them to write these in the New Word column.
- Have pairs predict what each word means.
- Instruct students to read the essay and use context clues to define each word.
- Review terms with students to ensure they have arrived at correct definitions.
- Encourage students to reread sections of the essay with a fresh understanding of new terms.

Text X-Ray: English Learner Support
for "The Price of Freedom"

Use the Text X-Ray and the supports and scaffolds in the Teacher's Edition to help guide students at different proficiency levels through the selection.

INTRODUCE THE SELECTION

DISCUSS ESPIONAGE IN WWII

As a whole group:

- Discuss what *espionage* means. Create a word board of all the terms the group knows related to spying and ensure that everyone understands their meaning. Tell students to write words and definitions that are new to them in their notebooks.
- On the board, put together a timeline of what happens in order to become a spy for the Allies (recruitment, training, mission, debriefing; add details as students' interest and comprehension allow). Use this discussion to lay groundwork for understanding the scenes the author will describe in her essay.

Encourage students to refer to the word board and timeline as they read the selection and then write about or discuss it.

CULTURAL REFERENCES

The following words or phrases may be unfamiliar to students:

- *confidences* (paragraph 8): secrets
- *cool as cucumbers* (paragraph 24): appearing calm and in control
- *New Forest* (paragraph 27): a wooded area of southwest England, 80 miles from the French coast
- *pitch* (paragraph 28): British term for a work area
- *carried a lot of weight* (paragraph 33): had much influence; mattered a great deal
- *carry it off* (paragraph 40): succeed
- *breaking down* (paragraph 42): showing strong emotion; crying and losing control

LISTENING

Listen for Idioms

Note that every language includes **idioms**—expressions that don't mean what they seem to when taken literally. In this activity, have students listen for English idioms and use context to understand their meaning.

Have students listen as you or classmates read aloud paragraphs 23–24 of the essay. Then use the following supports with students at varying proficiency levels:

- Slowly read the paragraphs aloud. Tell students to hold up a card when they think they hear an idiom, such as "their nerves absolutely shattered, in shreds." Stop and discuss what each one means. **SUBSTANTIAL**
- Slowly read the paragraphs aloud. Tell students to hold up a card when they think they hear an idiom. Tell them to turn to a partner and discuss its meaning before you explain each one. **MODERATE**
- Instruct students to form pairs. One student reads the first paragraph but stops when the partner hears an idiom; they discuss it before continuing and switch roles for the second paragraph. **LIGHT**

SPEAKING

Use Perfect Tense Verb Forms

Help students understand the differences between present, past, and future perfect tenses and use them correctly in a conversation.

Use the following supports with students at varying proficiency levels, especially speakers of Vietnamese:

- Use a clock and the student lunch time to explain when to use these verb forms: "I have eaten my lunch" (present perfect); "I had eaten lunch early, at 11 o'clock" (past perfect); "I will have eaten lunch by 1 o'clock" (future perfect). **SUBSTANTIAL**
- Provide a couple of examples of present, past, and future perfect tense and discuss when to use them. Invite students to offer their own examples. **MODERATE**
- Provide examples and discuss present, past, and future perfect tense. Ask students to look for these in paragraphs 6, 34, 35, 36, 39 of the essay (all of which are examples of past perfect), mark them, and discuss. **LIGHT**

READING

Analyze Text Meanings

Tell students that the author of "The Price of Freedom" writes about 1940 in England. As they practice analyzing the meaning of her text, they should ask for help when they don't understand a historical or cultural reference.

Tell students to divide a piece of paper down the middle. On the left, have them copy quotes from the text; on the right, have them write their questions about the quotes. Then, use the following supports with students at varying proficiency levels:

- Preteach the meanings of *option, thrill,* and *seductive*. Ask students to follow along while you read paragraph 2 aloud. Pause after each sentence to paraphrase it or explain what it conveys. **SUBSTANTIAL**
- Ask students to read paragraph 1 and write down one word or phrase that confuses them, and why, in their charts. Discuss each point of confusion before doing the same for paragraphs 2 and 3. **MODERATE**
- Ask students to read paragraphs 1–3, writing down words or phrases that they are unsure of in their charts. Discuss each point of confusion. **LIGHT**

WRITING

Write to Convey Meaning, Explicitly and Implicitly

Help students to master the difference between conveying meaning explicitly and implicitly in writing as you may have begun to do with the activity on Teacher's Edition page 251.

Explain that an explicit statement states its main message directly, such as "I was thrilled!" In other words, it tells. An implicit statement conveys an idea or feeling without telling what it is, such as "I shouted and held the prize up high." This statement describes behavior but only implies that the narrator was happy. Use the following supports with students at varying proficiency levels:

- Write simple sentences that explicitly convey a feeling—for example, "I was scared," "He was angry," or "They were in love." Have students choose one statement to convey implicitly in a drawing. Let students discuss details that convey this message before drawing. **SUBSTANTIAL**
- Create a list of adjectives that describe emotions and display images of people showing such feelings. Have students explicitly state these feelings, using this frame: *[She/He/They] [is/are]* _____. Allow them to use adjectives from the word board. **MODERATE**
- Have students write and swap an explicit or implicit message. Then have recipients convert the message they received: if explicit, make it implicit; if implicit, state it explicitly. **LIGHT**

EXPLAIN THE SIGNPOSTS

Explain that **NOTICE & NOTE Signposts** are significant moments in the text that help readers understand and analyze works of fiction or nonfiction. Use the instruction on these pages to introduce students to asking **Big Questions** and to using the **Numbers and Stats** and **Word Gaps** signposts. Then use the selection that follows to have students apply the Big Questions and signposts to a text.

For a full list of the fiction and nonfiction signposts, see page 406.

BIG QUESTIONS

Explain that asking **Big Questions** such as *What surprised me?* can draw students into the text and foster their curiosity. Asking such questions can also raise their awareness of **facts, details,** or **comments** that don't align with their expectations or beliefs, prompting them to think more deeply about their assumptions.

Ask students to listen as you read the example passage aloud while keeping the Big Question—*What surprised me?*—in mind. Then ask volunteers to share what surprised them. *(Possible answers: that the radio operator would offer a precious keepsake to a stranger; that he lost every member of his family in a German concentration camp; that being remembered by anyone at all is a wish that someone in his situation would have.)* Then suggest to students that, when surprised, they should ask themselves this follow-up question: *What effect does this surprise have on me as a reader?* Discuss how in this case, the surprise helps readers sympathize with and care about the author.

Tell students that when they encounter a passage of text that is unexpected or intriguing, they should pause, mark it in their consumable text, and ask themselves this Big Question: *What surprised me?*

THE PRICE OF FREEDOM

For more information on these and other signposts to Notice & Note, visit the **Reading Studio**.

You are about to read the personal essay "The Price of Freedom." In it, you will notice and note signposts that will give you clues about the essay's claims and evidence. Here are three key signposts to look for as you read this essay.

Big Questions When listening to a narrative, you expect the unexpected. The point of telling a story is to entertain or inform the listener, and a key element of storytelling is surprise. Just when the audience thinks it knows what is going to happen, there's a twist that makes the story memorable. As you read this essay, think about the **Big Question:** What surprised me?

When authors introduce a surprising element, they are drawing the reader's attention to the story, as well as making a point about why this story is special. Authors offer the unexpected in a variety of ways:

- a story begins one way, the expected route, and then shifts suddenly
- a surprise lets the author take readers places they might not want to go
- a shift reveals hidden sides of a character and explores their abilities
- a plot twist teases the reader to guess the ending

The paragraphs below illustrate a student's annotation of "The Price of Freedom" and responses to the Big Question.

> During the evening he drew out of his pocket a small velvet box. And inside there was a gold chain with a Star of David and a dove of peace hanging on it.
> He said simply, "I'd like you to have this."
> "Thank you so much," I stammered. "I'm terribly touched, but I couldn't possibly accept it."
> He looked so sad. So disappointed.
> He said, "Please do, oh, please do. All my family in France has perished in a German concentration camp. I've nobody left in the world. And I'd like to think somebody remembers me. Somebody perhaps even thinks of me when I'm over there."

What surprised you in this passage? Why?	I was surprised that someone would offer a stranger such a precious gift. The author was surprised, too!
Why do you think the author included this incident in her essay?	Maybe she wanted to show an agent who had lost all his family, yet wanted to be remembered by someone.

Numbers and Stats A writer's use of specific numbers and statistics provides concrete detail in an essay. Numbers and statistics work along with words to give a clear picture of the facts for the reader.

If a writer states that there were "a lot of spies" in the war, it is up to the reader to imagine what "a lot of" means. But, if a specific number is used such as, "2,786 spies died," then readers can clearly visualize how many lives were lost. The same is true of statistics. A writer referring to an increase in missions leaves the reader wondering how much of an increase. If the writer specifies a 70% increase, readers can judge for themselves if the increase is significant. Here a student marked two examples of **Numbers and Stats**:

> . . . He needed nerves of steel, because once infiltrated, his life expectancy was six weeks . . . After all, he was an old man—he was almost thirty-five.

When you read and encounter phrases like these, see if it's a **Numbers and Stats** signpost:

"But on reaching the ripe old age of eighteen. . . .

". . . in and out of four languages."

". . . their long, tough, six-month training."

Anchor Question: When you notice this signpost, stop and ask: Why did the author use these numbers?

How does the author use a number to shock the reader with the possibility of death?	The author says a spy could die within six weeks of entering enemy territory.
How does the author use a nonspecific word and then a statistic to play off each other?	She says he was old. When she adds that he is thirty-five, I realized the agent was a young man, and she was even younger.

Word Gaps Authors will often mention terms that some readers will not know. Sometimes these include specialized or technical concepts, or familiar words used in an unusual way. A reader encountering a **Word Gap** can:

- Consider the context in which the word is used. What is it likely to mean?
- Ask if this seems like technical talk for experts on the subject.
- Define specialized words with a search engine, dictionary or thesaurus.

In this example, a student underlined two Word Gaps.

> He smiled and raised his hand to his red parachutist beret. A final salute.
>
> He was infiltrated that night.
>
> I never saw him again.
>
> The mission was successful, but he didn't return. And I was left with a little cameo of a perfect love.

When you notice one of the following while reading, pause to see if it's a **Word Gaps** signpost:

- Descriptive language
- Multiple meanings
- References to events, art, or ideas
- Rare words and technical talk

Anchor Question: When you notice this signpost, stop and ask: Do clues in the sentence help me understand the word?

What context clues explain the meaning of "parachutist beret"?	He raises his hand in a salute so his hand would go to his head touching a cap a parachutist would wear.
How does the word "cameo" sum up the type of relationship the author had?	A cameo is a small portrait, like a little picture, or an image, like their brief encounter.

WHEN STUDENTS STRUGGLE . . .

Collaborate with Partners Students may struggle to apply the Word Gaps signpost if the number of unfamiliar words is high. Place students in pairs and have them reread a paragraph containing words that are unfamiliar to one or the other student. Together, have them identify and discuss context clues and make notes about possible meanings. Model this method with a volunteer so that students can see how each teaches the other how to read more closely and thoughtfully as they figure out the meaning of words. When partners have finished with their unfamiliar words, they can see how close they got to the correct definition by dividing up the words and looking them up in a print or online dictionary.

NUMBERS AND STATS

In a personal essay about a specific time in history, **Numbers and Stats** serve the important function of enhancing the author's credibility. Because she provides a precise level of detail via amounts, ages, spans of time, percentages, and statistics, she comes across as a trustworthy authority on the topic she's writing about.

Explain to students that the numbers and stats in this essay also can help them **make inferences** as well as **draw conclusions.** Read aloud the example passage. Ask students what this means: "his life expectancy was six weeks." *(Once the radio operator successfully entered enemy territory, he was likely to die at the hands of the enemy within a month and a half.)* The amount "six weeks" is a succinct, compelling way to underscore the extreme bravery of this man.

Tell students that when they spot Numbers and Stats, they should pause, mark them in their consumable text, and ask themselves the anchor question: *Why did the author use these numbers?*

WORD GAPS

Students are likely to experience a number of **Word Gaps** in this essay, which uses foreign phrases, the jargon of WWII special agents, and terms that are relatively archaic. Consequently, encourage students to use **context clues** to take educated guesses at the meaning of unfamiliar terms.

Read aloud the example passage. Model considering the many context clues that reveal what a *parachutist beret* is. For example, a salute is a movement of a hand to the side of the head, and here he raises his hand. A *beret* is a kind of hat. *Parachutist* sounds a lot like the word *parachute;* it probably means someone like a skydiver who uses a parachute.

Tell students that when they spot a Word Gap, they should pause, mark it in their consumable text, and ask themselves the anchor question: *Do clues in the sentence help me understand this word?*

APPLY THE SIGNPOSTS

Have students use the selection that follows as a model text to apply the signposts. As students encounter signposts, prompt them to stop, reread, and ask themselves the anchor questions that will help them understand the author's argument.

Tell students to continue to look for these and other signposts as they read the other selections in the unit.

Connect to the ESSENTIAL QUESTION

Noreen Riols's personal essay describes an extraordinary time in her youth when she was recruited into Winston Churchill's Special Operations Executive (SOE). Through her experiences as a secret agent, the author explores the joy and pain that different kinds of love can bring—love of country during wartime as well as romantic love. The essay also touches on love of freedom, for which many heroes, in many times and places, have given their lives.

THE PRICE OF FREEDOM

Personal Essay by **Noreen Riols**

ESSENTIAL QUESTION:

How can love bring both joy and pain?

LEARNING MINDSET

Seeking Challenges Explain to students that taking risks and trying new things comes more naturally to some people than others; in fact, genetics can play a role in how people respond to novelty and risk. But seeking challenges is a key element of the learning mindset, and everyone can grow more capable of taking on challenges simply by taking them on, one at a time. As students read this essay about people who sought the challenge of defeating a wartime enemy, ask them to consider how they can seek and respond to academic challenges at school.

QUICK START

Secret agents are often portrayed as glamorous, daring characters in movies and books. Why do you think an agent's job might be dangerous and deadly? Write a few sentences about what you think happens to secret agents if they get caught.

ANALYZE TEXT MEANINGS

Most texts have both explicit, or openly stated, meanings; and implicit, or implied, meanings. Your job as a reader is to figure out these explicit and implicit meanings, using references from the text for support.

Follow these steps to determine a text's meanings.

1. Read the complete text without taking any notes.
2. Reread the text, focusing on the main ideas and the most important details. This time take notes, listing key words, main ideas with their supporting details, and quotations that make strong points.
3. Make an **inference**, or logical assumption, about key ideas in the text. Inferences are based on details in the text plus your own knowledge and experience.
4. Draw a **conclusion** about Riols's main message by reviewing key details in the text and the inferences you made. Ask yourself: What do most of the ideas and details have in common? What does Riols want her readers to know?

CREATE MENTAL IMAGES

Mental Images are pictures or scenes you create in your mind as you read. You become part of the creative process and "see" what you are reading. Mental images help you become more involved in what you are reading and as a result, pay closer attention to the details of the text. This helps to deepen your understanding and enjoyment of the text.

Write down mental images the author's words create in your mind in a chart similar to this one.

MENTAL IMAGES	EXAMPLE FROM THE SELECTION
A shocking, surprising vision	He was leaping like a demented kangaroo in and out of four languages.
A portrait of human emotion	For me it was a revelation to see their different reactions. Some returned with their nerves absolutely shattered, in shreds. Their hands were shaking uncontrollably as they lit cigarette after cigarette.
A snapshot of an intense moment	As I walked through the door, I turned. He was standing on the pavement, watching me. He smiled and raised his hand to his red parachutist beret. A final salute.

GENRE ELEMENTS: PERSONAL ESSAY

- similar to memoirs but shorter and more focused
- explores the writer's experiences
- includes the writer's feelings and reactions at the time

ENGLISH LEARNER SUPPORT

Express Concepts Offer support to students as they respond to the Quick Start prompt. Provide simpler vocabulary, such as *spy* instead of *secret agent, exciting* and *attractive* instead of *glamorous*, and *able to kill you* instead of *deadly*. For students who need additional support, ask yes-and-no questions about what might happen to a captured spy—for example: Would the spy go to jail? Would the spy be beaten in hopes of getting information from him or her? Would the spy be set free? **SUBSTANTIAL/MODERATE**

TEACH

QUICK START

After students write down their ideas on the fate of captured secret agents, call on a student to share one idea and ask students to raise their hands if they also wrote it down. Record the idea on the board. Invite volunteers to share until all possibilities are on the board. Which ideas were cited the most? The least? Suggest that students think about these class expectations as they read the essay to discover what might actually happen if a secret agent were captured.

ANALYZE TEXT MEANINGS

Review the terms **explicit** and **implicit** with students and ask for examples of each type of statement. Model this exercise by saying something like, "The secret agent was terrified." See if students recognize that this is an explicit statement. If they were to make it implicit, they could say, "The agent was sweating and his eyes were huge, like a cornered animal's." The clear implication is that the agent is terrified. To figure that out, they make an **inference**, or logical assumption, based on the details in the text and their prior knowledge of what a terrified person looks like. Instruct students to circle details in the text that help them to infer meaning and to write their inferences in the margin. By rereading their inferences and seeing how they connect, students can draw a conclusion about the author's message.

For **writing support** for students at varying proficiency levels, see the **Text X-Ray** on page 248D.

CREATE MENTAL IMAGES

Tell students that they may find themselves drawing upon scenes they remember from films and photographs of World War II to create **mental images** as they read this essay. Readers evoke images from all kinds of sources as they read; it is one of the reasons reading can be such a powerful experience. Encourage students to notice what mental images are stirred up for them as they read this essay and to take notes on what they see in their mind's eye as they fill in their charts.

TEACH

CRITICAL VOCABULARY

Encourage students to take a risk and guess at answers; remind them that they aren't expected to know all of the vocabulary already. Place students in pairs or trios to pool their ideas and refine their answers.

Possible answers:

1. *Something would be completely destroyed by an act intended to cause damage.*
2. *A seductive decoy would pretend to be something it's not in order to attract and trick an intended subject.*
3. *Large numbers of soldiers would fight madly, or as if out of their minds.*
4. *A person pretending to admire someone would gain their trust and more easily sneak in.*

■ English Learner Support

Use Cognates Tell students that many of the Critical Vocabulary words have Spanish cognates: *seductive/seductor, demented/demente, hordes/hordas, sabotage/sabotaje, infiltration/infiltración, adulate/adular, annihilate/aniquilar.* **ALL LEVELS**

LANGUAGE CONVENTIONS

Discuss with students how writers vary the length and structure of their sentences according to the effects they want to achieve. To give readers a sense of someone who is in a dangerous situation and who has to think quickly, they might keep the sentences short and staccato—perhaps even fragmented. The example sentence shows how the writer conveys sequential information. The gravity of the outcome is framed by placing it as an interruption to the main sentence; the reader's eye must take it in before continuing with the sequence of events.

ANNOTATION MODEL

Students can review the Notice & Note coverage on pages 248–249 if they have questions about any of the signposts. Suggest that they underline important phrases or circle key words that help them identify signposts. They may want to color-code their annotations by using a different color highlighter for each signpost. Point out that they may follow this suggestion or use their own system for marking up the selections in their write-in texts.

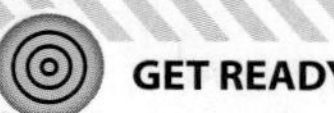

GET READY

CRITICAL VOCABULARY

seductive	demented	hordes	sabotage
infiltration	decoy	adulate	annihilate

To see how many Critical Vocabulary words you already know, write brief answers to these questions.

1. What does it mean to **annihilate** something with **sabotage**? __________
2. How would a **seductive decoy** operate? __________
3. How would **demented hordes** fight in battle? __________
4. How would pretending to **adulate** help **infiltration**? __________

LANGUAGE CONVENTIONS

Sentence Variety In this lesson, you will learn about using sentence variety for different effects. Writers often vary their writing by alternating short and long sentences. This creates a rhythm that keeps the reader interested. Notice how the long sentence below contains several facts in one clear statement.

Before they were returned to London at the end of their month in Beaulieu—and it was in London, in their country section, that their fate would be decided—each one had an interview with our commandant, Colonel Woolrych.

Sometimes writers will purposely create sentence fragments to emphasize an idea or image. In the second sentence below, the author stresses the man's unhappiness by using a different adjective in a fragment.

He looked so sad. So disappointed.

ANNOTATION MODEL

NOTICE & NOTE 

As you read, note the author's use of details that help you create mental images. Here is one reader's response to the first paragraphs of "The Price of Freedom."

But when I went to sign on, I was taken aside and closeted in a kind of windowless broom cupboard with a high-ranking army officer, who began asking me an awful lot of questions which had nothing to do with the navy.

He was leaping like a demented kangaroo in and out of four languages. And he seemed very surprised that I could keep up.

I can picture this—a tiny, dark office.

I can imagine how strange and funny the officer must have seemed.

My inference is that the officer is testing the author for skills as an agent.

NOTICE & NOTE

BACKGROUND

Noreen Riols *(b. 1926) was born in Malta in Italy to English parents. She now lives in a seventeenth-century house in a little town near Versailles in France. Among her many books is* The Secret Ministry of Ag. & Fish, *published in 2014 in several countries. Riols is a recipient of the Chevalier de la Legion d'Honneur, France's highest award. This essay is based on her service with The Special Operations Executive, a volunteer fighting force created by Winston Churchill to go behind German lines in Europe and blow up trains, bridges, and factories. He ordered them to "set Europe ablaze!"*

THE PRICE OF FREEDOM

Personal Essay by Noreen Riols

SETTING A PURPOSE

As you read, pay attention to the author's descriptions of the emotional suffering of agents she worked with. Compare it to the suffering the author herself experienced.

1 During World War II, I was a pupil at the French Lycée[1] in London. But on reaching the ripe old age of eighteen, I was obliged to abandon my studies and either join the armed forces or work in a munitions factory[2].

2 Well, that option did not thrill me. So I decided to become a member of the Women's Royal Naval Service. Because I liked the hat. I thought it was most **seductive**.

3 But when I went to sign on, I was taken aside and closeted in a kind of windowless broom cupboard with a high-ranking army officer, who began asking me an awful lot of questions which had nothing to do with the navy.

[1] **French Lycée** (li´-say'): secondary school in France.

[2] **munitions** (myo͝o-nĭsh´ənz) **factory**: a place where weapons and ammunition are manufactured.

Notice & Note

You can use the side margins to notice and note signposts in the text.

seductive
(sĭ-dŭk´tĭv) *adj.* tempting, alluring.

ANALYZE TEXT MEANINGS

Annotate: Mark the sentences in paragraphs 3–4 that describe the army officer's odd behavior.

Infer : What can you infer about his bizarre behavior? (Hint: he speaks several languages during their meeting.)

BACKGROUND

After students have read the Background note, explain that Winston Churchill was the Prime Minister of England during World War II. When France fell to Nazi Germany in 1940, all of Europe was in danger of a similar fate. Churchill created the Special Operations Executive (SOE) to train secret agents whose task was to conduct espionage—spying—and sabotage in countries occupied by Germany. The SOE played a significant role in defeating the Nazis. Its files became declassified in 2000, allowing Noreen Riols to tell her story at long last.

SETTING A PURPOSE

Direct students to use the Setting a Purpose prompt to focus their reading.

For **speaking and reading support** for students at varying proficiency levels, see the Text X-Ray on page 248D.

ANALYZE TEXT MEANINGS

Point out that there usually is no need for secrecy or a high-ranking officer to conduct a first interview. These clues help set the reader up for a surprise. In paragraph 4, the surprises continue as the officer continuously changes which language he is speaking—and the author understands him, in all four languages. (***Answer:*** *The officer is interviewing the author for a role that requires understanding several languages and quick thinking; he may also want to see how she handles a strange and stressful situation.)*

ENGLISH LEARNER SUPPORT

Analyze Figurative Language Explain that the phrase "leaping like a demented kangaroo" in paragraph 4 is a **simile,** or a way of comparing two things by using the word *like* and creating a mental image. Ensure that English learners know what a kangaroo is by showing them a picture. Explain that *demented* means "not thinking straight" or "crazy." Then ask students to complete this sentence: *In this sentence in the essay, "leaping like a demented kangaroo" means* ______________. Ask students to share their ideas for completing the sentence in small groups and then work together to create one sentence that they all agree best captures the meaning of the expression. **MODERATE**

CRITICAL VOCABULARY

seductive: The author thought the hat would be attractive—and thus make her attractive—to men.

ASK STUDENTS why they think the author says that she wants to join a branch of the military because the hat part of the uniform is seductive. *(The author is likely showing that she was a teenager looking for ways to get the attention of young men; she is also implying that her main goal was to avoid the boredom of factory work.)*

TEACH

NUMBERS AND STATS

Remind students to pause at numbers and statistics in a text and consider why this type of **factual information** is important. Prompt students as they read to think about how Numbers and Stats help establish the author's credibility and what additional insights into the essay these facts give them. (***Answer:*** *The statistic to note in paragraph 9 is that agents had only a 50 percent chance of returning. This means that they had a 50/50 chance of dying—a fact liable to create extreme fear.)*

ENGLISH LEARNER SUPPORT

Make Vocabulary Connections Ask students to find the word *courage* in paragraph 10 (and note that the Spanish cognate is *coraje*). Instruct students to make a list of the words they find in paragraphs 8–11 related to courage. Possibilities include *apprehension* (paragraph 8), *afraid* (paragraphs 9, 10), *brave* (paragraph 10), and *fear* (paragraphs 10, 11). **MODERATE**

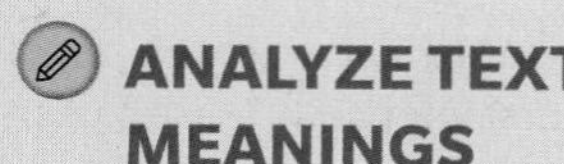

ANALYZE TEXT MEANINGS

Reread paragraph 13 with students. One phrase provides a concrete example of what makes this job so dangerous: "always with the Gestapo just a couple of steps behind him." (***Answer:*** *A radio operator would constantly be sending and receiving signals, which means that the enemy could track his movements.)*

CRITICAL VOCABULARY

demented: Because the author did not know why the interviewer kept switching languages, his behavior seemed abnormal and irrational.

ASK STUDENTS whether they think the author was intimidated by the officer's demented behavior. *(No; she understood him—kept up with him—no matter what he did.)*

horde: Central London was a very busy place, with large crowds of people constantly coming and going.

ASK STUDENTS why the author might mention hordes of people at this point in her story. *(At this point the author is just one of the unknowing public, oblivious to the secrets going on right in front of them.)*

NOTICE & NOTE

demented
(dĭ-mĕn´tĭd) *adj.* suffering from dementia, crazy, foolish.

horde
(hôrd) *n.* a large group or crowd, a swarm.

sabotage
(săb´ə-täzh) *n.* deliberate destruction of property; an act of damage to stop something.

infiltration
(ĭn-fĭl-trā´shən) *n.* the act or process of passing in secret through enemy lines.

NUMBERS AND STATS

Notice & Note: Mark a statistic that reveals how dangerous an agent's job is.

Interpret: How does this statistic account for the agent's fears?

ANALYZE TEXT MEANING

Annotate: Mark text that describes why the radio operator's job was the most dangerous.

Draw Conclusions: Why would a radio operator be easy for the Gestapo to find?

4 He was leaping like a **demented** kangaroo in and out of four languages. And he seemed very surprised that I could keep up.

5 He sent me to a large building in central London. Oh, I knew it well. But like the **hordes** of people who passed by every day, never had I imagined or even suspected that this was the headquarters of Churchill's secret army. And that behind those walls, members of every occupied country were organizing acts of **sabotage**, and the **infiltration** of secret agents into enemy territory at night, by parachute, fishing boat, felucca[3], and submarine.

6 Without realizing what had happened, I had been recruited into the hidden world of secret agents on special missions. (But I never got my seductive hat.)

7 I was assigned to "F" for France section. It was an exhausting but exciting, thrilling, exhilarating life, full of action and emotion. We lived some very intense moments.

8 I got to know an awful lot of agents. And I shared many confidences with those who were about to leave. They told me of their concerns for their families—many of them were married with young children—and of their own apprehension of torture and of death.

9 They knew they only had a 50 percent chance of coming back. And they were afraid.

10 Brave men are always afraid. Courage isn't the absence of fear. It's the willingness—the guts, if you like—to face the fear.

11 They faced their fears. And they left.

12 I remember one. He was a Jew. A radio operator. And he was going in on a second mission. Well, for a Jew to go in at all was extremely dangerous. But many did—we had quite a few Jewish agents. But a radio operator? A second mission?

13 A radio operator was the most stressful, hazardous, dangerous mission of all. He lived on his nerves. He could never relax. He was always on the run, always with the Gestapo[4] just a couple of steps behind him. He needed nerves of steel, because once infiltrated, his life expectancy was six weeks.

14 I was with this agent on the night before he left. Oh, there was no romantic association; I was just keeping him company. After all, he was an old man—he was almost thirty-five.

15 During the evening he drew out of his pocket a small velvet box. And inside there was a gold chain with a Star of David and a dove of peace hanging on it.

16 He said simply, "I'd like you to have this."

17 "Thank you so much," I stammered. "I'm terribly touched, but I couldn't possibly accept it."

18 He looked so sad. So disappointed.

[3] **felucca** (fə-lŭk´ə): a swift and narrow sailing vessel.
[4] **Gestapo** (gə-shtä´pō): German internal security police known for terrorist methods.

CRITICAL VOCABULARY *CONT.*

sabotage: People were preparing to destroy the enemy's wartime operations and property.

ASK STUDENTS what acts of sabotage they think the secret army was preparing to carry out. (***Possible answers:*** *destroying bridges, munitions factories, key roads, tanks, supply trucks, and enemy-occupied buildings)*

infiltration: This term is intentionally nonspecific, because the means of sneaking into enemy territory varied.

ASK STUDENTS what they think was needed for agents to successfully carry out their infiltration plans. (***Possible answers:*** *safe contacts in the enemy territory, knowledge of the terrain and language of the country being infiltrated, a convincing cover for being there, and a safe place to hide)*

NOTICE & NOTE

19 He said, "Please do, oh, please do. All my family in France has perished in a German concentration camp. I've nobody left in the world. And I'd like to think that somebody remembers me. Somebody perhaps even thinks of me when I'm over there."

20 So I took his little box, promising to look after it and give it back to him when he returned.

21 But he didn't return.

22 Those who did return were taken immediately for a debriefing[5], and I often accompanied the two debriefing officers.

23 For me it was a revelation to see their different reactions. Some returned with their nerves absolutely shattered, in shreds. Their hands were shaking uncontrollably as they lit cigarette after cigarette.

24 Others were as cool as cucumbers. And I realized then that we all have a breaking point. And we can never know until we're faced with the situation what that breaking point actually is. Perhaps that is why departing agents were strongly urged if arrested by the Gestapo to take the cyanide[6] pill, which was always hidden somewhere around their person, before they left. It would kill them within two minutes.

25 I grew up attending those debriefing sessions.

26 Many of those agents weren't very much older than I. Hearing their incredible stories, witnessing their courage, their total dedication, I changed almost overnight from a teenager to a woman.

27 One snowy Saturday evening in early February, I was told that I was to leave and go down to Beaulieu. Now, Beaulieu was the last of the many secret training schools. These training schools were dotted all over England. And the future agents attended each one in turn during their long, tough, six-month training. Beaulieu, or Group B

LANGUAGE CONVENTIONS

Annotate: Mark the long sentence in paragraph 24.

Respond: What details does the sentence convey? Why might the author have chosen to communicate this information in one long sentence rather than two or three shorter ones?

[5] **debriefing** (dē-brē´fĭng): the act or process of interviewing after an assignment to obtain information.

[6] **cyanide** (sī´ə-nīd): a powerful chemical poison.

For **listening support** for students at varying proficiency levels, see the **Text X-Ray** on page 248C.

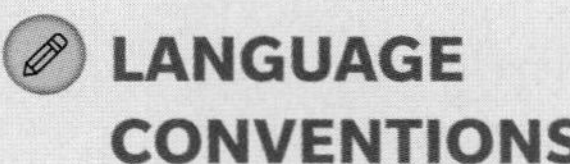

LANGUAGE CONVENTIONS

Call students' attention to the calibrated use of sentence variety in paragraph 24. The first sentence is short and simple; each sentence is successively longer and more complex, culminating in the fourth sentence; then the last sentence of the paragraph is again short and simple. ***(Answer:*** *The longest sentence conveys the most details and the most chilling information: how agents were to kill themselves if caught by the Gestapo. The successive lengthening of sentences up until this one builds the ominous tone.)*

ENGLISH LEARNER SUPPORT

Use Contractions Make sure that students understand that in paragraph 24, *we're* is a contraction of *we are* (not the past-tense verb *were*). Then give students practice with contractions by asking them to circle all of the contractions in paragraphs 19–21. Ask them to say what words each contraction is shortening; for example, *I've* means "I have." Point out that the apostrophe in a contraction is not pronounced (but that it may affect the pronunciation of the word, as in the difference between *we're* and *were*); then have students pronounce each word with a contraction clearly. Finally, ask students to either write or say each sentence that contains a contraction, substituting the noncontracted forms. "But he didn't return," for example, becomes "But he did not return." **SUBSTANTIAL**

WHEN STUDENTS STRUGGLE . . .

Make Inferences To help students make inferences, instruct them to create a two-column graphic organizer like the one below. Then complete a few entries together such as the ones below, modeling how to infer.

Hint	My Inference
"I've nobody left in the world."	The radio operator feels alone.
But he didn't return.	The Gestapo caught him, and he died.

For additional support, go to the **Reading Studio** and **Level Up Tutorial: Making Inferences.**

ENGLISH LEARNER SUPPORT

Use Context Clues When a text includes foreign expressions, technical, or dated terms, students can get a sense of their meaning by looking at the context. In paragraph 28, students may not understand the terms *decoy* or *pitch*. Show students how to look at the sentences before and after the ones with unknown terms in them to help them guess at meanings. They can infer, for example, that a *decoy* is a job of some kind, because the women were working in these places. *Pitch* must have something to do with the author's job as a decoy.

Ask students to use this rationale to figure out what *tête-à-tête* means in paragraph 32. *(a private and somewhat secretive get-together)*

MODERATE/LIGHT

CREATE MENTAL IMAGES

Forming mental images is one way that students become actively engaged with the text. Instruct students to allow their imaginations to create the scene that the text is describing. Paragraph 29 gives students ample opportunity to imagine student spies practicing skills essential to their work: watching without being seen, and disappearing when they have been spotted. ***(Answer:** Student responses will vary but should be relevant to the text. They might imagine secret agents-in-training trailing people or hiding from pursuers at locales mentioned in the paragraph—beach, town park, public benches, telephone booths, and tearooms.)*

CRITICAL VOCABULARY

decoy: The author helped figure out which agents might not have the discipline to keep their identity and mission secret.

ASK STUDENTS why the author is called a *decoy* when her task is to get agents to talk about their top-secret work. *(A decoy poses as something it isn't; in hunting, a duck decoy is a wooden model used to attract real ducks to land on the water. The author is posing as a resident of the town who happened to meet the agent and is attracted to him.)*

NOTICE & NOTE

as it was called, was in Hampshire, deep in the New Forest. Only six women worked there during the war, and I am the last survivor.

28 We were used as decoys. We worked in the neighboring seaside towns of Bournemouth and Southampton. My pitch was usually Bournemouth.

29 It was there that we taught future agents how to follow someone—find out where they were going, who they were seeing—without being detected. How to detect if someone were following *them* and throw them off. How to pass messages without any sign of recognition or even moving our lips. This took place on the beach, in the park, on benches in the town, in telephone booths, and in the tearooms above the Gaumont Cinema.

CREATE MENTAL IMAGES
Annotate: Mark the details about place in paragraph 29.
Synthesize: What mental images do they create for you?

30 The last exercise was reserved for those future agents whom the instructors thought might talk. Now, the instructors were with them all the time. They watched their every movement. They analyzed it all. And if they thought that they might talk, they would have a carefully prearranged setup meeting between a **decoy** and a future agent in one of the two grand hotels in Bournemouth.

decoy
(dē´koi) *n.* a means to trick or attract.

31 (Of course, if I had taken part in the earlier exercises, I couldn't take part in that one, because they would know me, and then one of the other women took over.)

32 The meeting would take place in the bar or the lounge, followed by an intimate dinner tête-à-tête. It was our job to get them to talk—to betray themselves, in fact.

33 The Brits didn't talk much. Foreigners sometimes did, especially young ones. Oh, I understood. They were lonely. They were far from their homes and their families. They didn't even know if they would *have* a home, or even a country, to go back to once the war was over. And it was flattering to have a young girl hanging on their every word. Before they were returned to London at the end of their month in Beaulieu—and it was in London, in their country section, that

APPLYING ACADEMIC VOCABULARY

☐ **attribute** ☑ **commit** ☑ **expose** ☐ **initiate** ☐ **underlie**

Write and Discuss Have students turn to a partner to discuss the following questions. Guide students to include the academic vocabulary words *commit* and *expose* in their responses. Ask volunteers to share their responses with the class.

- What do secret agents **commit** to when they agree to take on this work?
- What do you think the consequences are if secret agents **expose** their identities while they are in enemy territory?

their fate would be decided—each one had an interview with our commandant, Colonel Woolrych. (We called him Woolly Bags behind his back.) He had all the reports from the different training schools, and he made his final report that went back to London and carried a lot of weight.

34 Now, if they had talked, during the interview a door would open and I, or another decoy, would walk in.

35 Woolly Bags would say, "Do you know this woman?" And they would realize they'd been tricked . . . .

36 On the eve of my nineteenth birthday, I fell madly, hopelessly in love with an agent. He was one of our best agents. A crack. He'd just returned from a very successful second mission, and he was **adulated.** He was a legend in the section. I'd heard all about him, but I never thought I'd meet him.

adulate (ăj´ə-lāt) *v.* to praise or admire excessively.

37 Then, suddenly one evening, he was there. Our eyes locked across a crowded room. And it was as if a magnet drew us irresistibly towards each other.

38 I couldn't believe that he could love me. He was handsome. He was twelve years older than I. He was a hero.

39 He must have met many beautiful, sophisticated, elegant, gorgeous women. (Oh, he had—he told me. But he said he'd been looking for me.) Our idyll lasted three months, until he left on his next mission.

40 I was terrified. It was a very dangerous mission. They said only he could carry it off. I was so afraid. But he reassured me. He said he was a survivor. And he promised me that this would be his last mission, and when he came back, he'd never leave me again. We'd grow old together.

41 The day he left, we had lunch, just the two of us, in a little intimate restaurant. We both knew that it would be many months perhaps before we'd be together again.

WORD GAPS

Notice & Note: Mark any words in paragraph 39 whose meaning you are not sure about.

Analyze: How can you use context to determine meaning?

WORD GAPS

In paragraph 39, the word *idyll* may be unfamiliar to students. A helpful strategy here is to **use context** to understand the **author's purpose**. In this short paragraph, the author conveys how attractive and romantic the agent was. The sentence with *idyll* in it also describes the relationship's brevity. The author's purpose in using the word *idyll* is to sum up the whole experience. *(**Answer:** Given the context of the agent's choosing the author over many other highly desirable women, in a relationship that was only three months long, a reader can infer that the word* idyll *must mean something like "perfect" or "incredibly wonderful.")*

IMPROVE READING FLUENCY

Targeted Passage Tell students that this part of the essay invites a more dramatic reading than most nonfiction texts. Model reading paragraph 36 aloud with personal feeling but without exaggerating to the point of melodrama. Have students follow along in their books as you read. Then have pairs of students take turns reading paragraphs 37–40 aloud expressively. Encourage students to provide feedback to each other. Are they pausing for effect at the right moments? Are they emphasizing the words that show how poignant this experience was?

Go to the **Reading Studio** for additional support in developing fluency.

CRITICAL VOCABULARY

adulate: The agent incites intense admiration because he has successfully completed two extremely dangerous missions thanks to his superlative skills.

ASK STUDENTS why an agent worthy of being adulated would be beneficial to everyone in the section. *(The life-or-death nature of secret agent work created an extremely stressful environment. Celebrating a hero would boost morale and remind everyone that being well trained can result in successful missions and agents who come back alive.)*

LANGUAGE CONVENTIONS

This sentence offers an example of how the skillful use of a **complex sentence** enables the writer to convey a complex idea. In this case, the author sees the agent as the embodiment of the values upheld by the Allies and by the SOE; she connects his story to the larger theme of the essay. (***Answer:*** *The agent's courageous and ultimate sacrifice represents the sacrifice for freedom that was so often required as the Allies fought the Germans. This is the sentence in which the author begins to sum up her message, which she makes explicit in the rest of her essay.*)

Noreen Riols in France, 2014

42 We kept emotion out of our conversation. I think we were both afraid of breaking down. I know if we hadn't, I would have broken down, and I'd have begged him not to go.

43 I imagine you've all been in love. Can you picture what it's like to be terribly in love, and know that all you have is a few hours, this moment in time?

44 He took me back to the office, and we said good-bye at the bus stop. I don't think we even said "good-bye."

45 As I walked through the door, I turned. He was standing on the pavement, watching me. He smiled and raised his hand to his red parachutist beret. A final salute.

46 He was infiltrated that night.

47 I never saw him again.

48 The mission was successful, but he didn't return. And I was left with a little cameo of a perfect love. Perfect, perhaps, because it had been so brief.

49 When the news that I'd dreaded came through, they tried to comfort me. They told me I should be proud. He was incredibly courageous—a wonderful man, who realized that there was a force of

LANGUAGE CONVENTIONS

Annotate: Mark the longest sentence in paragraph 49.

Respond: How does this sentence link the man with the larger issues the author is writing about?

TO CHALLENGE STUDENTS . . .

Write a Memoir Episode Ask small groups of students to describe the characteristics of this writer's style as she relays the story of her romance in paragraphs 36–48. Instruct the group to list these characteristics. Then have each student write a fictional episode about these characters. It could be one more conversation before the agent is infiltrated, or it could be a description of an experience they had during their three months together. The goal is to imitate the writer's style as closely as possible.

Instruct students not to write their names on their episodes. Shuffle the finished episodes and pass them out to the group. Have each student read the episode aloud. Does it sound as if the author wrote it? Would students use their list of characteristics to describe it? Encourage students to point out nice similarities or jarring differences between the voice in the episode and Riols's actual voice. Finally, have the group vote on which episode sounds most as if the author actually wrote it.

evil in the world that had to be **annihilated**, but that freedom has a price tag. He paid that price with his life.

50 But I didn't want a dead hero. I didn't want a medal in a velvet box. I wanted Bill.

51 All those agents in the secret army were volunteers. They didn't have to go. But they went. Almost half of them never returned. Like Bill, they gave their youth, their joie de vivre, their hopes and dreams for the future.

52 They gave their all, for us.

53 They gave their todays, so that we might have our tomorrow.

annihilate (ə-nī´ə-lāt): *v.* to destroy completely.

CHECK YOUR UNDERSTANDING

Answer these questions before moving on to the **Analyze the Text** section on the following page.

1 The primary purpose of the selection is —

A to explain the sorts of things special agents did in Europe during WW II

B to have readers understand the sacrifices special agents made during WW II

C to encourage other citizens to make the ultimate sacrifice

D to tell a little-known tale of mystery and wartime intrigue

2 As the essay begins —

F the author tells about her difficulties caused by falling in love with the wrong guy

G the author explains the importance of patriotism when stopping evil

H the author demonstrates how agents had to be carefully screened

J the author describes how she came to work with secret agents

3 Which sentence invites the reader to make a personal connection with the author's story?

A *Courage isn't the absence of fear.*

B *I grew up attending those debriefing sessions.*

C *I imagine you've all been in love.*

D *They gave their todays so that we might have our tomorrows.*

CHECK YOUR UNDERSTANDING

Have students answer the questions independently.

Answers:

1. *B*
2. *J*
3. *C*

If they answer any questions incorrectly, have them reread the text to confirm their understanding. Then they may proceed to ANALYZE THE TEXT on page 260.

CRITICAL VOCABULARY

annihilate: The author chooses a word that comes from the Latin *annihilare,* which means "reduce to nothing." The agent believed that evil had to be so completely destroyed that nothing would be left.

ASK STUDENTS whether they think *annihilated* is also an appropriate word to describe what happens to the secret agent. *(Answers will vary; arguably, the agent's life is not reduced to nothing because it has been immortalized in this essay and lives on in the author's memory.)*

ENGLISH LEARNER SUPPORT

Oral Assessment Provide the following sentence frames to assess students' comprehension and speaking skills.

1. *The author's main purpose is to ______. (Possible answer: explain the work of special agents in World War II)*
2. *In the beginning of the essay, the author describes how she ______. (came to work with secret agents)*
3. *The author believes that most of her readers have had the experience of ______. (Possible answer: being in love)*

SUBSTANTIAL/MODERATE

APPLY

ANALYZE THE TEXT

Possible answers:

1. **DOK 4**: *Answers will vary but should cite specific details from the text to support the mental images students created.*
2. **DOK 2**: *In paragraph 24, the author says that agents might be arrested by the Gestapo; the reader implicitly understands that the agents would be tortured to the breaking point, which is when they might give up secret information.*
3. **DOK 2:** *Agents learned how to be radio operators (paragraph 13) as well as how to follow someone without detection, how to lose someone if they were followed, and how to pass secret messages (paragraph 29). They also learned how to infiltrate enemy territory and complete missions of sabotage (paragraph 5). These skills were useful for success in spying and sabotage as well as for agents' survival.*
4. **DOK 4**: *Answers will vary but should be supported with text evidence; some will note that accepting it gave the radio operator comfort.*
5. **DOK 4:** *Students should cite specific statistics from the text, such as the one in paragraph 9.*

RESEARCH

Tell students to type in the whole name of the agency they are researching rather than its acronym; that way they won't get unrelated websites in their search.

Extend The full name of the KGB is lengthy and Russian, so typing it is difficult. If students have trouble locating information about KGB agents fighting spies from other countries during the Cold War, suggest they research something more specific, such as Jack Barsky, a KGB agent who spied on America.

RESPOND

ANALYZE THE TEXT

Support your responses with evidence from the text. NOTEBOOK

1. **Connect** Describe two mental images you created as you read. What details in the text did you use to create the pictures in your mind?
2. **Infer** Make an inference about why special agents might have been encouraged to use their cyanide pill if captured. Identify where the text provides explicit information, and the implicit meaning that led to your inference.
3. **Interpret** What skills were special agents taught in secret training school? Why might they have been useful?
4. **Evaluate** Do you think the author was right to accept the necklace from the Jewish radio operator? Why or why not?
5. **Notice & Note** Which statistics persuaded you of the dangers secret agents faced?

RESEARCH TIP
Be careful when choosing sources for your research. Make sure the websites you use are reliable and relevant to your search.

RESEARCH

Several intelligence agencies formed in the United States and Great Britain during and after World War II. For example, in 1942 the Office of Strategic Services (OSS) was established in the United States. Research the jobs people did at these agencies. Record what you learn in the chart.

WORLD WAR II AGENCIES	JOBS EMPLOYEES PERFORMED
OSS (Office of Strategic Services)	*Gathered information about enemy troops and supplies, supervised resistance groups, rescued soldiers, spread misinformation, committed sabotage*
SOE (Special Operations Executive)	*Blew up trains, planes, and railroads; booby-trapped trains; created spy equipment; assassinated Nazis; used secret code to communicate by radio*
CIA (Central Intelligence Agency)	*Conduct counterintelligence, analyze cyber threats, analyze weapons, specialize in languages, collect intelligence*

Extend In 1954, the Soviet Union formed its own security agency, the KGB. With a partner, research how KGB agents operated against intelligence agents from other countries during the Cold War.

LEARNING MINDSET

Asking for Help Sometimes students may get bogged down when they are trying to understand a new concept or complete a difficult task, such as finding answers when conducting research. Remind students that asking for help is a good way to break the stalemate and start making progress again. Classmates, the teacher, and family members can all offer help. Assure students that everyone needs help from time to time and that asking for assistance or advice is a smart way to work.

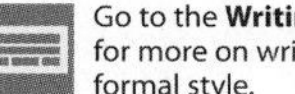

CREATE AND DISCUSS

Write a Professional Letter Imagine you live in the country where one of the agencies you researched has its headquarters. Write a one-page letter to the agency asking questions about their organization or expressing interest in working with them.

- ❑ Express your willingness to help your country and make sacrifices.
- ❑ Ask for more detailed information about the jobs available and what skills would be required.
- ❑ Use the words and terms you have learned while reading the essay and researching these agencies.

Go to the **Writing Studio** for more on writing using formal style.

Discuss with a Small Group Share your letters with your fellow budding secret agents.

- ❑ Determine the effectiveness of the letters.
- ❑ Think like a working spy who is looking to recruit new agents, just like the army officer who interviewed the author of the essay.
- ❑ Discuss which agency you would like to work for and why.

Go to the **Speaking and Listening Studio** for more on participating in collaborative discussions.

RESPOND TO THE ESSENTIAL QUESTION

How can love bring both joy and pain?

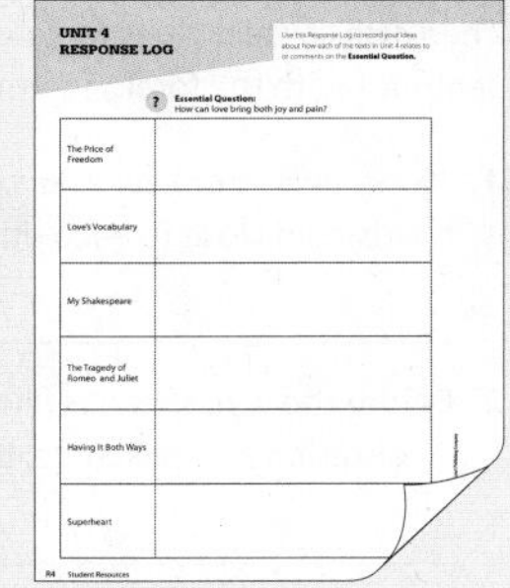

Gather Information Review your annotations and notes on "The Price of Freedom." Then, add relevant information to your Response Log. As you determine which information to include, think about how wartime might intensify both the joy and pain of love.

At the end of the unit, use your notes to help you write a literary analysis.

ACADEMIC VOCABULARY

As you write and discuss what you learned from the essay, be sure to use the Academic Vocabulary words. Check off each of the words that you use.

- ❑ **attribute**
- ❑ **commit**
- ❑ **expose**
- ❑ **initiate**
- ❑ **underlie**

APPLY

CREATE AND DISCUSS

Write a Professional Letter Point out that a professional letter is a type of business letter. Thus, the content should be formal in tone, and the format should include the components of a traditional business letter: the heading (the sender's address and the date of writing), the inside address (the address of the recipient), the greeting, the body, the close, and the signature. Then discuss the body of the letter in more detail, telling students that this is an opportunity to write a letter as if they are living during the time of WWII, if they choose a WWII-era agency. They can use the body of the letter to ask for the information specified in the prompt and can talk about the sacrifices they are prepared to make for the war effort.

Discuss with a Small Group Suggest that students write down questions they would ask in an interview if they were to meet with the writer of the letter. What questions would they ask, based on information in the letter? On the other hand, what would make them decide not to interview the letter writer?

RESPOND TO THE ESSENTIAL QUESTION

Allow time for students to add details from "The Price of Freedom" to their Unit 4 Response Logs.

ENGLISH LEARNER SUPPORT

Write a Letter To help English learners write a letter to one of the agencies that they researched, have these supports on hand:

- Familiarize students with the parts of a letter by preparing one that students can fill in. Include each letter section, such as Name of Agency, Street Address, City, and Country written out with blanks next to them for students to fill in. **SUBSTANTIAL**
- Instruct students to practice writing questions by asking them aloud with a partner first—for example, "What jobs are available at your agency?" **MODERATE**
- Ask students to write rough drafts of their letters. Then have them swap letters with a partner and do a peer edit before revising and writing the final draft. **LIGHT**

APPLY

CRITICAL VOCABULARY

Answers:

1. *b*
2. *a*
3. *a*
4. *a*

Explanations of responses will vary but must demonstrate understanding of the vocabulary terms.

VOCABULARY STRATEGY: Foreign Words

Answers:

1. ***tête-à-tête*** *Sentence should be about two people having an intimate conversation.*
2. ***joie de vivre*** *Sentence should be about someone having a joyful nature or excitement for living.*
3. ***pièce de résistance*** *Sentence should discuss something being the absolute best.*
4. ***je ne sais quoi*** *Sentence should be about someone having a mysterious appeal.*

RESPOND

WORD BANK
seductive
demented
hordes
sabotage
infiltration
decoy
adulate
annihilate

CRITICAL VOCABULARY

Practice and Apply Circle the letter of the best answer to each question. Then, explain your response.

1. Which of the following could be used when describing bees?
   a. decoy **b.** horde
2. Which of the following would be used when talking about heroes?
   a. adulate **b.** annihilate
3. Which of the following could be described as **seductive**?
   a. danger **a.** sadness
4. Which of the following would be used when seeking secret information about an enemy country?
   a. infiltration **b.** sabotage

VOCABULARY STRATEGY: Foreign Words

Go to the **Vocabulary Studio** for more on decoding foreign words.

The author of "The Price of Freedom" lived and worked in France so it's not surprising that she used many French words. **Foreign words and phrases** often appear in writing that has as its subject matter the cultures of different nations. Some foreign words and terms are commonly used in English, even though they retain their foreign spelling. You can find definitions in a dictionary. But often you can determine meaning through context.

Practice and Apply Underline the foreign word or phrase in each sentence. Then, use context clues to determine meaning. In your own words, write a sentence with the foreign term.

1. Alone, away from all others, the two lovebirds had a tête-à-tête with their heads held close to each other to listen to every word.

   ____

2. Before the war, she was filled with genuine joie de vivre that kept her celebrating her existence, but after the war, the world was a sad place.

   ____

3. The artist's studio had many beautiful paintings; but the pièce de résistance was the large, stunning self-portrait.

   ____

4. No one could explain her mysterious je ne sais quoi which left her admirers wondering, "I can't exactly say what is so appealing about her."

   ____

262 Unit 4

ENGLISH LEARNER SUPPORT

Foreign Terms in English In some cases, similarities between French and Spanish vocabulary can help students understand foreign expressions that are used in English. In French, *quoi*, or *what* in English, is close to the Spanish *que*, or *that* or *what*. *Vivre* in French, *to live* in English, is *vivir* in Spanish and thus a cognate. Sometimes these similarities don't help explain what an expression has evolved to mean in English. *Pièce* in French is *pieza* in Spanish, and both mean *piece* in English; but the expression *pièce de résistance* when used in English means *the best of the best*, while in French it means *main dish*. Ask English learners to write down each of the four French expressions that we use in English and discuss when translating into another Romance language whether it is or is not helpful for understanding its English use. **LIGHT**

LANGUAGE CONVENTIONS: Sentence Variety

Writers often use a variety of sentence lengths to create different effects in their work. Noreen Riols, author of "The Price of Freedom," sometimes combines complete sentences into one longer sentence. Notice the three underlined subjects and predicates in the sentence below.

> **I know if we hadn't, I would have broken down, and I'd have begged him not to go.**

Riols varies her style by using long sentences, short sentences, and even fragments—short, incomplete sentences. Fragments are complete thoughts but often lack subjects or predicates. Authors use fragments to create a more informal, conversational style. They also use fragments to call attention to a detail or idea.

> **But many did—we had quite a few Jewish agents. But a radio operator? A second mission?**

In the passage above, the author wants to emphasize the agent's willingness to risk his life in a second, hazardous mission.

In addition, Riols uses fragments to reveal her inner thoughts. The casual tone she uses to share her thoughts makes readers feel she is talking directly to them. Here is an example, using slang to reinforce the informal tone.

> **He was one of our best agents. A crack. He'd just returned from a very successful mission, and he was adulated.**

Practice and Apply Write a short passage about a topic that interests you. Try combining your own sentences into longer sentences. Also, practice writing fragments. When you have finished, share your writing with a partner and discuss how you incorporated variety into your writing by varying sentence length and structure.

Go to the **Grammar Studio** for more on sentence variety.

LANGUAGE CONVENTIONS: Sentence Variety

Explain to students that using a variety of sentences effectively requires a firm understanding of punctuation. Otherwise, lengthy sentences won't make sense. Examine each of the example sentences with these caveats in mind.

- Point out that the first example begins with an introductory element (itself a miniature complex sentence = *I know + [that] if we hadn't*), set off with a comma; then the two independent clauses that follow are separated by a comma and the conjunction *and*.
- In the second example, two independent clauses that are closely related are punctuated with an em dash. The two fragments that follow are posed as questions, causing the reader to pause for emphasis.
- In the third example, the fragment "a crack" is surrounded by complete sentences. Its spare use is another way to create emphasis—in this case, emphasizing the agent's skill. Point out that sentence fragments can be a great way to convey feeling and tone, but they, too, have to be used with care.

Practice and Apply When discussing each other's paragraphs, have partners suggest trying out a different form of punctuation. For example, how does the effect of a sentence change if a semicolon replaces a period or an em dash? What if a short sentence were reduced to a fragment? Encourage students to articulate the way these changes affect the voice and mood of the paragraph.

ENGLISH LEARNER SUPPORT

Use Punctuation in Combined Sentences Help students construct longer sentences by showing them how to use commas in some combined sentences. Discuss these examples and give students more short sentences to combine according to these models. Then have students construct their own sentences.

Short sentences	*It was dangerous.*	*He went anyway.*
Longer sentence	*It was dangerous, but he went anyway.*	
Short sentences	*He returned from a mission.*	*We were proud of him.*
Longer sentence	*When he returned from a mission, we were proud of him.*	

ALL LEVELS

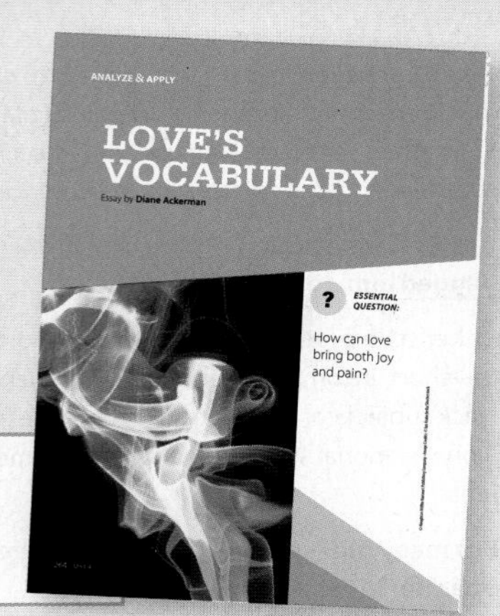

MENTOR TEXT

LOVE'S VOCABULARY

Essay by Diane Ackerman

This essay from a nonfiction book serves as a **mentor text,** a model for students to follow when they come to the Unit 4 Writing Task: Write a Literary Analysis.

GENRE ELEMENTS

ESSAY

Remind students that an **essay** is an informational text that delivers facts and details about a specific topic. Its characteristics include a thesis, supporting evidence that explains and clarifies the thesis, and a conclusion that summarizes the thesis.

Explain that an essay uses one or more organizational patterns, such as comparison and contrast, problem and solution, and cause and effect, to present information. While an essay is written to inform, it often also entertains or persuades.

LEARNING OBJECTIVES

- Analyze informational text by generating questions during reading.
- Research cultural expressions of love.
- Discuss connections between informational text and ideas in other texts and societies.
- Use synonyms to better understand content-area vocabulary.
- Use participial phrases correctly.
- **Language** Discuss with partners characteristics of informational text using the key terms *thesis* and *supporting evidence*.

TEXT COMPLEXITY

Quantitative Measures	**Love's Vocabulary**	Lexile: 1020L
Qualitative Measures	**Ideas Presented** Mostly explicit, but moves to some implied meaning.	
	Structures Used More complex, multiple perspectives presented.	
	Language Used Mostly Tier II words with a few Tier III words.	
	Knowledge Required Some references to other texts; text deals with common or easily imagined experience.	

Online Ed

RESOURCES

- Unit 4 Response Log
- Selection Audio
- Reading Studio: Notice & Note
- Level Up Tutorial: Main Idea and Supporting Details
- Speaking and Listening Studio: Preparing for Discussion
- Vocabulary Studio: Synonyms
- Grammar Studio: Module 3: Lesson 4: Participial Phrases
- "Love's Vocabulary" Selection Test

SUMMARIES

English

Love is difficult to define or understand. Just as a prism separates white light into a spectrum of colors, love is the white light of emotion. Love is a small word for such a big idea. We use the word in ways both important and trivial yet cannot agree on what it means. Our ideal of love is affected by culture and other factors. We often resort to using clichés, or expressions that quantify love. As a society, we are embarrassed by love. Yet we all recognize love when we see it, and, despite the variables, love itself is unchanging.

Spanish

El amor es difícil de definir o comprender. Como un prisma refracta la luz blanca en un espectro de colores, el amor es la luz blanca de las emociones. *Amor* es una palabra pequeña para tan gran idea. Utilizamos la palabra en formas importantes y triviales, pero no podemos ponernos de acuerdo en qué significa. Nuestra idea del amor es afectada por la cultura y otros factores. Tenemos clichés o expresiones que cuantifican el amor. Como sociedad, estamos avergonzados del amor. Pero todos reconocemos el amor cuando lo vemos y, a pesar de las variables, el amor es inmutable.

SMALL-GROUP OPTIONS

Have students work in small groups to read and discuss the selection.

Three-Minute Review

- Before a guided reading of "Love's Vocabulary," tell students that you will pause occasionally for review. Explain that during each pause, students will reread the passage and write clarifying questions.
- Next, begin the reading and pause after every two paragraphs. Each time you pause, set the timer for three minutes. Have students work independently.
- When the time is up, have students discuss their clarifying questions. Ask: What did you notice: when you reread the passage?

Numbered Heads Together

- After students have read "Love's Vocabulary," number off groups of four students 1-2-3-4 within the group.
- Ask a higher-order question about "Love's Vocabulary," such as a question from Analyze the Text on page 272.
- Have students discuss their responses within their groups.
- Call a number from 1 to 4.
- Have each student with that number respond for his or her group.
- Repeat the process until all four numbers have been called.

Text X-Ray: English Learner Support
for "Love's Vocabulary"

Use the Text X-Ray and the supports and scaffolds in the Teacher's Edition to help guide students at different proficiency levels through the selection.

INTRODUCE THE SELECTION

DISCUSS WORD CHOICES

Tell students that in this essay, the author begins by stating that love is difficult to define and then develops her ideas about love. Explain that in order to avoid using clichés, or overused expressions, she chooses her words very carefully. As a result, some word choices are unusual or unexpected.

Have students preview the first few paragraphs of the text and mark interesting word choices they notice, using two different colors to mark words they recognize and those that are unfamiliar. Ask students to share examples, and model using rereading and context clues to clarify understanding. Then discuss how the author's word choices relate to the idea that love is difficult to define.

CULTURAL REFERENCES

The following phrases from the selection may be unfamiliar to students:

- *fell in love* (paragraph 2): began to love
- *turned . . . to mush* (paragraph 3): caused to act more sensitive or weak
- *driven . . . mad* (paragraph 3): made to feel crazy
- *stealing a kiss* (paragraph 8): kissing somebody when you think no one is watching

LISTENING

Monitor Understanding

Have students practice listening comprehension and seek clarification as needed.

Use the following supports with students at varying proficiency levels:

- Read aloud the following sentences from paragraph 5: *"I love Ben & Jerry's Cherry Garcia ice cream"; "I really loved my high school boyfriend"; "Don't you just love this sweater?" "I'd love to go to the lake for a week this summer"; "Mommy loves you."* Pause after each sentence and ask students to give a thumbs up if they understand or thumbs down to seek clarification. **SUBSTANTIAL**
- Read aloud paragraph 4. Pause after each sentence to allow students to ask clarifying questions using sentence frames such as this: *I don't understand what the author means when she says ______.* **MODERATE**
- Read aloud paragraph 4. Confirm students' understanding by asking them to provide a summary statement for paragraph 4. **LIGHT**

SPEAKING

Speak Using Content-Area Vocabulary

Note that informational texts include a controlling idea, or **thesis**, and **supporting evidence**, such as examples and other details. Review these key terms.

Use the following supports with students at varying proficiency levels:

- Read aloud the first sentence of "Love's Vocabulary" and review the definition of the Critical Vocabulary word *intangible*. Then ask: Does the author's thesis state that love is difficult to explain, or easy? *(difficult)* **SUBSTANTIAL**
- Have partners read paragraphs 1–2. Then have them discuss the thesis and supporting evidence using these sentence frames: *In her thesis, the author states that _____. Evidence that supports the thesis includes ______.* **MODERATE**
- Have partners take turns restating the thesis. Then have them discuss which sentences in paragraphs 1–2 provide details that support the thesis, or controlling idea, and which sentences mainly restate it. **LIGHT**

READING

Expand Reading Skills

Work with students to reread and analyze paragraphs 1–6 for insights they can apply to their own writing.

Use the following supports with students at varying proficiency levels:

- Direct students' attention to paragraph 4. Have students point to and read words that are familiar or that they can figure out by decoding and using context clues. Provide support with pronunciation. **SUBSTANTIAL**
- Model asking these questions about paragraph 1: How does the author describe love? Why does the author mention hate in an essay about love? Then have students generate 2–3 questions about paragraphs 2–6. **MODERATE**
- Survey students about which paragraphs raise the most questions for them. Have them discuss their questions in small groups. **LIGHT**

WRITING

Write Using Acquired Vocabulary

Support students as they prepare for the discussion activity on Student Edition page 273.

Use the following supports with students at varying proficiency levels:

- Have students create or find images based on movies, books, or people's behaviors that relate to the author's statement about love. Then help them label each image with descriptive words and phrases. **SUBSTANTIAL**
- Have students create or find images based on movies, books, or people's behaviors that relate to the author's statement about love. Then have students write captions for each image to share in the discussion. **MODERATE**
- Have students work with a partner to write sentences expressing their views and opinions about the statement. **LIGHT**

Connect to the
ESSENTIAL QUESTION

In this excerpt from *A Natural History of Love*, Diane Ackerman explores one of the most elusive concepts—love. Starting from the idea that love is difficult to understand, Ackerman proceeds to analyze its many facets, including the variety of emotions it encompasses, the rich and contradictory meanings of the word, its cultural and literary connections, and its array of physical sensations. Through factual details and creative descriptions, Ackerman shows that while love comprises a world of variables, including joy and sorrow, its essence is unchanging.

MENTOR TEXT

At the end of the unit, students will be asked to write a literary analysis. "Love's Vocabulary" provides a model for how to structure an essay with a clearly stated thesis, supporting evidence, and a conclusion that restates the thesis and expresses a final thought.

ANALYZE & APPLY

LOVE'S VOCABULARY

Essay by **Diane Ackerman**

? ESSENTIAL QUESTION:

How can love bring both joy and pain?

264 Unit 4

LEARNING MINDSET

Questioning Discuss the benefits of asking questions with your students. Explain that asking questions is an important part of having a learning mindset because it reflects openness to new ways of thinking about things and an eagerness to understand. Remind them that asking questions is also one of the best ways to think through a problem because it engages the mind in looking for possible answers. Encourage students to share any questions they have about the selection.

QUICK START

The author of "Love's Vocabulary" calls love a concept that no one can define. Brainstorm with classmates words that define or describe love.

ANALYZE INFORMATIONAL TEXT

Informational text is nonfiction writing that delivers facts and details about a specific topic. The author's purpose usually is to inform, but the writing often also entertains or persuades. The characteristics and structural elements of expository informational text include:

- thesis or main idea, which is a statement of the author's purpose as well as the text's main idea
- supporting evidence, such as examples that explain or clarify the thesis
- text features, such as headings and subheadings, that organize ideas
- visual aids, such as pictures, graphs, charts, and timelines
- a conclusion that summarizes the thesis

Informational text also uses types of **organizational design** to frame the information the writer presents. Organizational patterns include:

- comparison and contrast
- problem and solution
- cause and effect

"Love's Vocabulary" is organized as an extended discussion of the meaning of a single word.

GENRE ELEMENTS: ESSAY

- explores and explains a single topic
- may include the writer's own thoughts or experiences
- provides factual information supported with evidence
- uses a specific organizational structure

GENERATE QUESTIONS

Asking questions is an important part of active reading. In order to understand main ideas and supporting details, readers should generate questions about what they are reading. As a reader, you should ask questions:

- to help eliminate confusion about a text
- to focus on parts of the text
- to seek answers by finding specific evidence
- to guide you to inferences about meaning and author's purpose
- to explore a topic and gain greater understanding

Use a chart similar to the one here to keep track of your questions while reading. You can also record your questions in your Response Log.

TEXT PASSAGE	REASON TO QUESTION	QUESTION	ANSWER

ENGLISH LEARNER SUPPORT

Comprehend English Vocabulary Make sure that students understand what is meant by *generate* in the skill title "Generate Questions." Tell students that *generate* has a Spanish cognate: *generar*. Pronounce the word several times for students and have them repeat it after you. Explain that *generate* means "to produce" or "to bring into being." To generate questions as they read, students should think about ideas in the text that they find interesting or confusing and then express their thoughts in the form of questions. Mention that students can generate a list of questions about the text by listing them in the chart and in the margins of the selection. **ALL LEVELS**

TEACH

QUICK START

Have students brainstorm a list of words. To help students get started, suggest they begin with the first adjectives that come to mind. If students seem uncomfortable expressing their personal ideas about love, have them consider how love is described or defined in popular culture. For example, ask students how they think someone who creates popular songs, fiction, movies, or other popular entertainment would define love. Afterward, invite volunteers to point out any pairs of words that express opposing ideas. Ask students what this activity says about trying to define or describe love.

ANALYZE INFORMATIONAL TEXT

Help students understand the terms and concepts related to analyzing an informational text. Emphasize that a thesis is not the topic. Clarify that a clear thesis reveals the author's purpose—the stated or implied reason for writing about the topic—and the main idea—the idea that the author most wants to convey. Explain that in an informational essay an author also supplies relevant facts and examples that support the thesis. To show how the structure of an essay reflects this, point out that from the introduction to the conclusion, each paragraph should provide evidence that supports the author's purpose and main idea.

Provide students with questions they can use to analyze informational text, such as these: How would you restate the author's thesis? Why do you think the author wrote this? What does she most want the reader to understand? What evidence supports your ideas?

GENERATE QUESTIONS

Tell students that asking questions before, during, and after they read will help them check their understanding and get more out of the selection. Help students apply the instruction by asking them to generate questions about the text, including:

- a question they will look to answer as soon as they begin reading
- questions about things that confuse them
- questions they think the text might answer as they continue reading

TEACH

CRITICAL VOCABULARY

Suggest that students try out the words in each sentence before committing to their answers. Remind them that context clues may hint at the meaning of the missing word.

Answers:

1. *supple*
2. *guise*
3. *gradation*
4. *intangible*
5. *increment*

LANGUAGE CONVENTIONS

Clarify that a participial phrase acts as an adjective and should be placed close to the noun or pronoun that it modifies. In the example provided, the participial phrase *Laughing wildly* is placed before the noun *lovers*. Point out that just as writers often use two adjectives in a row, a writer sometimes uses two participial phrases in a row.

■ English Learner Support

Comprehend Language Structures In the primary Haitian Creole, Hmong, Khmer, Spanish, and Vietnamese languages, adjectives commonly come after nouns. Explain to students whose first language is one of these five that in English an adjective is usually placed before the noun or pronoun it modifies. Since a participial phrase functions as an adjective, we apply the same general rule for placement before the noun or pronoun. **ALL LEVELS**

ANNOTATION MODEL

Remind students that in Analyze Informational Text on page 265 they learned about the characteristics and structural elements of an expository informational text. Point out that the Annotation Model shows how one reader identified and took notes on these elements. Point out that students may follow the model or use their own system for marking up the selection in their write-in text. They may want to color-code their annotations by using highlighters. Their notes in the margins may include questions about ideas that are unclear or topics they may want to learn more about.

GET READY

CRITICAL VOCABULARY

intangible **guise** **increment** **supple** **gradation**

To see how many Critical Vocabulary words you already know, use them to complete the sentences.

1. Gymnasts perform intense workouts so their bodies stay __________.
2. Thieves use the __________ of respectability to steal from victims.
3. If you look at the squirrel's fur you will see a __________ in the color.
4. The director's contributions to the play were __________ but important.
5. We were paid our salary in a daily__________ of ninety dollars each.

LANGUAGE CONVENTIONS

Participial Phrases Writers use many techniques to keep their writing vivid and interesting. Sometimes, they do this through sentence structure—for example, by using participial phrases.

Participial phrases use verbs as adjectives. Like adjectives, they modify nouns or pronouns. Notice that the participial phrase in this sentence describes what the young lovers are doing.

Laughing wildly, the young lovers ignored everyone else in the room.

The lovers are ignoring and laughing. But *laughing* is combined with the adverb *wildly* to become a phrase that describes them as more than just *young*. The participial phrase could be placed in other positions in the sentence and make sense. However, it is usually placed in front of, or close to the noun it describes.

ANNOTATION MODEL

NOTICE & NOTE

As you read, note how this essay reflects characteristics of informational text. Write questions in the margins. Here is one reader's notes on "Love's Vocabulary."

Love's Vocabulary

Love is the great intangible. In our nightmares, we can create beasts out of pure emotion. Hate stalks the streets with dripping fangs, fear flies down narrow alleyways on leather wings, and jealousy spins sticky webs across the sky. In daydreams, we can maneuver with poise, foiling an opponent, scoring high on fields of glory while crowds cheer, cutting fast to the heart of an adventure. But what dream state is love? Frantic and serene, vigilant and calm, wrung-out and fortified, explosive and sedate—love commands a vast army of moods.

The title and first sentence tell me the author's topic and her thesis.

She develops her thesis using examples and supporting details.

NOTICE & NOTE

BACKGROUND

Diane Ackerman *(b. 1948), author of* A Natural History of the Senses, An Alchemy of Mind, *and* The Zookeeper's Wife, *which was made into a film in 2017, weaves her love of science and natural history into her poetry, fiction, and nonfiction. Her memoir,* One Hundred Names for Love, *chronicles her husband's struggle to reclaim language after a stroke. In describing that time, Ackerman said, "I've always transcended best by pretending that I'm Margaret Mead viewing a scene for the first time or an alien from another planet regarding the spectacle of life on Earth and discovering how spectacular, unexpected, and beautiful it is."*

LOVE'S VOCABULARY

Essay by Diane Ackerman

SETTING A PURPOSE

As you read, imagine that the author is sitting beside you and you can ask her whenever you don't understand something. Write down your questions.

1 Love is the great **intangible**. In our nightmares, we can create beasts out of pure emotion. Hate stalks the streets with dripping fangs, fear flies down narrow alleyways on leather wings, and jealousy spins sticky webs across the sky. In daydreams, we can maneuver with poise, foiling an opponent, scoring high on fields of glory while crowds cheer, cutting fast to the heart of an adventure. But what dream state is love? Frantic and serene, vigilant and calm, wrung-out and fortified, explosive and sedate—love commands a vast army of moods. Hoping for victory, limping from the latest skirmish, lovers enter the arena once again. Sitting still, we are as daring as gladiators.

2 When I set a glass prism on a windowsill and allow the sun to flood through it, a spectrum of colors dances on the floor. What we call "white" is a rainbow of colored rays packed into a small space. The prism sets them free. Love is the white light

Notice & Note

You can use the side margins to notice and note signposts in the text.

intangible
(ĭn-tăn´jə-bəl) *n.* something that is difficult to grasp or explain.

LANGUAGE CONVENTIONS

Annotate: Mark the author's use of three participial phrases in paragraph 1.

Analyze: What is the effect of these phrases?

BACKGROUND

Discuss the reference to Margaret Mead. Explain that Mead was an influential anthropologist, or someone who studied human societies and cultures. Point out that Mead had many accomplishments, but she is best known for her work studying the psychology and culture of people in Oceania. Mead died in 1978.

SETTING A PURPOSE

Direct students to use the Setting a Purpose prompt to focus their reading.

For **speaking and reading support** for students at varying proficiency levels, see the **Text X-Ray** on page 264D.

LANGUAGE CONVENTIONS

Remind students that participial phrases use verbs as adjectives to modify nouns or pronouns. Reiterate the example from page 266: "Laughing wildly, the young lovers ignored everyone else in the room." (***Answer:*** *These participial phrases emphasize the contradictory experience of being in love.)*

ENGLISH LEARNER SUPPORT

Use Learning Strategies Provide students with a main-idea-and-details organizer. Ask them to work individually to record the controlling idea from the first sentence in paragraph 1. Then have pairs of students compare their organizers to confirm or adjust their statements. Next, have students work individually to identify supporting details as they read the selection. Afterward, have students compare their organizers and confirm which details support the controlling idea. Have students check their recorded details against the text for accuracy and create revised versions of their organizers as needed. **MODERATE**

CRITICAL VOCABULARY

intangible: The author uses the adjective *intangible* as a noun to state that love is difficult to define.

ASK STUDENTS to name other concepts that would be considered intangible. *(abstract qualities, such as leadership, bravery, and honesty)*

TEACH

QUOTED WORDS

Remind students that an author may use Quoted Words to include the observations of someone who is an expert on the topic. Then have students answer the question to explain how the quoted words relate to the author's **thesis** statement. ***(Answer:** The quoted words provide supporting evidence for the author's thesis that love is the great intangible, or difficult to define and describe. She emphasizes this by echoing the Quoted Words in the phrase "love did all the intangibles.")*

GENERATE QUESTIONS

Remind students that they can ask questions for many purposes, such as to find out more about something that interests them or to clear up confusion. ***(Answer:** Questions will vary but may include stems such as these: Why do you think . . . ? What do you mean by . . . ? Could you elaborate on the idea that. . . ?)*

For **listening support** for students at varying proficiency levels, see the **Text X-Ray** on page 264C.

CRITICAL VOCABULARY

guise: Ackerman says that the form in which love appears depends on many factors.

ASK STUDENTS to explain what factors might influence the guise in which love comes. *(The guises of love are influenced, among other things, by culture, background, and beliefs.)*

NOTICE & NOTE

QUOTED WORDS

Notice & Note: Mark the words in paragraph 2 that tell you the author is quoting a sports expert to support her beliefs on love.

Cite Evidence: How does this quotation relate to the author's thesis statement?

GENERATE QUESTIONS

Annotate: Mark the statements in paragraph 4 that show the author thinks love can be both a positive and a negative force.

Analyze: What would you like to ask the author about her attitude toward love?

guise
(gīz) *n.* form or outward appearance; outfit.

of emotion. It includes many feelings which, out of laziness and confusion, we crowd into one simple word. Art is the prism that sets them free, then follows the gyrations[1] of one or a few. When art separates this thick tangle of feelings, love bares its bones. But it cannot be measured or mapped. Everyone admits that love is wonderful and necessary, yet no one can agree on what it is. I once heard a sportscaster say of a basketball player, "He does all the intangibles. Just watch him do his dance." As lofty as the idea of love can be, no image is too profane to help explain it. Years ago, I fell in love with someone who was both a sport and a pastime. At the end, he made fade-away jump shots in my life. But, for a while, love did all the intangibles. It lets us do our finest dance.

3 *Love.* What a small word we use for an idea so immense and powerful it has altered the flow of history, calmed monsters, kindled works of art, cheered the forlorn, turned tough guys to mush, consoled the enslaved, driven strong women mad, glorified the humble, fueled national scandals, bankrupted robber barons, and made mincemeat of kings. How can love's spaciousness be conveyed in the narrow confines of one syllable? If we search for the source of the word, we find a history vague and confusing, stretching back to the Sanskrit *lubhyati* ("he desires"). I'm sure the etymology rambles back much farther than that, to a one-syllable word heavy as a heartbeat. Love is an ancient delirium, a desire older than civilization, with taproots[2] stretching deep into dark and mysterious days.

4 We use the word *love* in such a sloppy way that it can mean almost nothing or absolutely everything. It is the first conjugation[3] students of Latin learn. It is a universally understood motive for crime. "Ah, he was in love," we sigh, "well, that explains it." In fact, in some European and South American countries, even murder is forgivable if it was "a crime of passion." Love, like truth, is the unassailable defense. Whoever first said "love makes the world go round" (it was an anonymous Frenchman) probably was not thinking about celestial mechanics, but the way love seeps into the machinery of life to keep generation after generation in motion. We think of love as a positive force that somehow ennobles the one feeling it. When a friend confesses that he's in love, we congratulate him.

5 In folk stories, unsuspecting lads and lasses ingest love potions and quickly lose their hearts. As with all intoxicants, love comes in many **guises** and strengths. It has a mixed bouquet, and may include some piquant ingredients.[4] One's taste in love will have a lot to do with one's culture, upbringing, generation, religion, era, gender, and

[1] **gyrations** (jī-rā´shənz): spiral or circular movements.
[2] **taproots** (tăp´ro͞ots): the main roots of a tree or plant from which other roots grow.
[3] **conjugation** (kŏn-jə-gā´shən): in grammar, the various forms of a verb.
[4] **piquant** (pē´kənt) **ingredients:** components that make something pleasantly spicy.

WHEN STUDENTS STRUGGLE . . .

Support Comprehension Explain that just as the essay has a thesis, or controlling idea, each paragraph has a main idea. Then give students a strategy to use to understand how each paragraph develops the essay's thesis. Have partners track main ideas and supporting evidence for paragraphs 3–4 and continue doing so as they read.

Main Idea	Supporting Evidence
Love is a small word for a big idea.	It has "altered. . . history," "kindled . . . art," "fueled . . . scandals."

For additional support, go to the **Reading Studio** and assign the following **Level Up Tutorial: Main Idea and Supporting Details.**

so on. Ironically, although we sometimes think of it as the ultimate Oneness, love isn't monotone or uniform. Like a batik[5] created from many emotional colors, it is a fabric whose pattern and brightness may vary. What is my goddaughter to think when she hears her mother say: "I love Ben & Jerry's Cherry Garcia ice cream"; "I really loved my high school boyfriend"; "Don't you just love this sweater?"; "I'd love to go to the lake for a week this summer"; "Mommy loves you." Since all we have is one word, we talk about love in **increments** or unwieldy ratios. "How much do you love me?" a child asks. Because the parent can't answer *I* (verb that means unconditional parental love) *you,* she may fling her arms wide, as if welcoming the sun and sky, stretching her body to its limit, spreading her fingers to encompass all of Creation, and say: "This much!" Or: "Think of the biggest thing you can imagine. Now double it. I love you a hundred times that much!"

6 When Elizabeth Barrett Browning wrote her famous sonnet "How do I love thee?" she didn't "count the ways" because she had an arithmetical turn of mind, but because English poets have always had to search hard for personal signals of their love. As a society, we are embarrassed by love. We treat it as if it were an obscenity. We reluctantly admit to it. Even saying the word makes us stumble and blush. Why should we be ashamed of an emotion so beautiful and natural? In teaching writing students, I've sometimes given them the assignment of writing a love poem. "Be precise, be individual, and be descriptive. But don't use any clichés," I caution them, "or any curse words." Part of the reason for this assignment is that it helps them understand how inhibited we are about love. Love is the most important thing in our lives, a passion for which we would fight or die, and yet we're reluctant to linger over its name. Without a **supple** vocabulary, we can't even talk or think about it directly. On the other hand, we have many sharp verbs for the ways in which human beings can hurt one another, dozens of verbs for the subtle **gradations** of hate. But there are pitifully few synonyms for love. Our vocabulary of love and lovemaking is so paltry that a poet has to choose among clichés, profanities, or euphemisms. Fortunately, this has led to some richly imagined works of art. It has inspired poets to create their own private vocabularies. Mrs. Browning sent her husband a poetic abacus[6] of love, which in a roundabout way expressed the sum of her feelings. Other lovers have tried to calibrate their love in equally ingenious ways. In "The Flea," John Donne watches a flea suck blood from his arm and his beloved's, and rejoices that their blood marries in the flea's stomach.

7 Yes, lovers are most often reduced to comparatives and quantities. "Do you love me more than her?" we ask. "Will you love me less if I

[5] **batik** (bə-tēk´): colorful design created by applying different dyes and wax to fabric.
[6] **abacus** (ăb´ə-kəs): a device for performing calculations by manipulating beads strung on wires in a rectangular frame.

ANALYZE INFORMATIONAL TEXT

Annotate Mark the examples cited in paragraph 5.

Connect How do these sentences serve as supporting details for the author's thesis that love is "intangible," not easily defined?

increment
(ĭn´krə-mənt) *n.* an addition or increase by a standard measure of growth.

CONTRASTS AND CONTRADICTIONS

Annotate: Mark the sentences in paragraph 6 in which the author introduces the negative ideas people have about love.

Compare: Is the author contradicting herself? Explain.

supple
(sŭp´əl) *adj.* flexible or easily adaptable.

gradation
(grā-dā´shən) *n.* a slight, successive change in color, degree or tone.

ANALYZE INFORMATIONAL TEXT

Remind students that authors often use direct quotations as examples. (***Answer:*** *The examples show that love cannot be expressed in one specific, precise, or quantifiable way.)*

English Learner Support

Understand Language Structures Point out the sentence in paragraph 5 that begins, "What is my goddaughter to think . . . ." Have students circle the punctuation marks in the sentence. Explain that the author uses a colon to introduce the list of statements that a mother might say to her child and that the semicolons separate each statement that is enclosed in quotation marks. Guide students to complete this sentence frame: *The list of statements helps show that the word* love *is* _____. *(used in many different contexts)* **MODERATE**

CONTRASTS AND CONTRADICTIONS

Tell students that sometimes authors signal Contrasts and Contradictions by introducing ideas in one paragraph that oppose ideas expressed in the preceding paragraph. Have students mark sentences that express negative ideas about love in paragraph 6 and then **compare** them with the examples they marked in paragraph 5. (***Answer:*** *The author uses the contrast between the two sets of ideas to argue that everyone's ideas about love are contradictory.)*

CRITICAL VOCABULARY

increment: Ackerman says we try to convey the depth and extent of our love by expressing it little by little.

ASK STUDENTS to give examples of things that increase in increments. *(wages, costs, fares, voltages, taxes)*

supple: We need a supple, or flexible, vocabulary just to express ideas about love.

ASK STUDENTS to explain what a supple vocabulary of love would include. *(It would include words to describe many moods and emotions related to love.)*

gradation: Ackerman explains that we have many different verbs to express subtle degrees of hate.

ASK STUDENTS to name some words that describe gradations of hate. *(abhor, abominate, despise, loathe, repulse)*

APPLYING ACADEMIC VOCABULARY

❑ attribute ❑ commit ☑ expose ❑ initiate ☑ underlie

Write and Discuss Have students discuss the following questions with a partner. Instruct them to use the academic vocabulary words *expose* and *underlie* in their responses. Invite volunteers to share responses with the class.

- In paragraph 7, what does the author **expose** about people in regard to love? *(She exposes people's fear of love, as when she says, "We are afraid to face love head on.")*
- What feeling do you think **underlies** the author's interest in the topic? *(Possible responses: curiosity to have a deeper understanding of love; frustration over society's view of love)*

TEACH

GENERATE QUESTIONS

Remind students that generating questions can help a reader infer an **author's purpose** and can build on details in the text. ***(Answer:** Why does the author use a woman from ancient Egypt as an example? What aspects of love does the author think are universal? How does the author think the meaning of love has changed over time despite cultural differences?)*

WORD GAPS

Explain to students that nonfiction often includes **technical terms and other unfamiliar words** whose meanings most readers would not know. When encountering a technical term or other unfamiliar words, students should reread the sentence to find context clues. ***(Answer:*** A sistrum *is an ancient Egyptian instrument that is not common today, so the example helps emphasize that despite cultural differences, people throughout time have shared a "passion for music." Both the meaning and the rhythm of the word* phantasmagoria *help emphasize the idea that* love *is a loaded word.)*

NOTICE & NOTE

GENERATE QUESTIONS

Annotate: Mark the sentences in paragraph 8 where the author introduces a woman from ancient Egypt into the essay.

Evaluate: What questions could readers ask about why the author uses this example in a discussion of love?

WORD GAPS

Annotate: Mark two words in paragraph 8 that many readers might not know.

Interpret: Why do you think the author uses unusual words like these?

don't do what you say?" We are afraid to face love head on. We think of it as a sort of traffic accident of the heart. It is an emotion that scares us more than cruelty, more than violence, more than hatred. We allow ourselves to be foiled by the vagueness of the word. After all, love requires the utmost vulnerability. We equip someone with freshly sharpened knives; strip naked; then invite him to stand close. What could be scarier?

8 If you took a woman from ancient Egypt and put her in an automobile factory in Detroit, she would be understandably disoriented. Everything would be new, especially her ability to stroke the wall and make light flood the room, touch the wall elsewhere and fill the room with summer's warm breezes or winter's blast. She'd be astonished by telephones, computers, fashions, language, and customs. But if she saw a man and woman stealing a kiss in a quiet corner, she would smile. People everywhere and everywhen understand the phenomenon of love, just as they understand the appeal of music, finding it deeply meaningful even if they cannot explain exactly what that meaning is, or why they respond viscerally to one composer and not another. Our Egyptian woman, who prefers the birdlike twittering of a sistrum,[7] and a twentieth-century man, who prefers the clashing jaws of heavy metal, share a passion for music that both would understand. So it is with love. Values, customs, and protocols may vary from ancient days to the present, but not the majesty of love. People are unique in the way they walk, dress, and gesture, yet we're able to look at two people—one wearing a business suit, the other a sarong[8]—and recognize that both of them are clothed. Love also has many fashions, some bizarre and (to our taste) shocking, others more familiar, but all are part of a phantasmagoria[9] we know. In the Serengeti[10] of the heart, time and nation are irrelevant. On that plain, all fires are the same fire.

9 Remember the feeling of an elevator falling in your chest when you said good-bye to a loved one? Parting is more than sweet sorrow, it pulls you apart when you are glued together. It feels like hunger pains, and we use the same word, *pang.* Perhaps this is why Cupid is depicted with a quiver of arrows, because at times love feels like being pierced in the chest. It is a wholesome violence. Common as child birth, love seems rare nonetheless, always catches one by surprise, and cannot be taught. Each child rediscovers it, each couple redefines it, each parent reinvents it. People search for love as if it were a city lost beneath the desert dunes, where pleasure is the law, the streets are lined with brocade cushions, and the sun never sets.

[7] **sistrum** (sĭs´trəm): an ancient percussion instrument that sounds like a metal rattle.

[8] **sarong** (sə-rông´): a traditional Southeast Asian woman's garment made from a long piece of fabric that is wrapped around the body.

[9] **phantasmagoria** (făn-tăz-mə-gôr´ē-ə): a dreamlike sequence of surreal images or events.

[10] **Serengeti** (sĕr-ən-gĕt´ē): a vast plain in Tanzania known for its migratory animals.

TO CHALLENGE STUDENTS . . .

Compare Poems What is a "good" love poem? Have students read the two poems that Ackerman references in her essay: Elizabeth Barrett Browning's "How do I love thee?" and John Donne's "The Flea." Have students write a short response in which they take a position on which poem they consider more effective at creating a personal "vocabulary of love." Remind students to state their positions clearly and to cite supporting evidence from the text.

10 If it's so obvious and popular, then what is love? I began researching this book because I had many questions, not because I knew at the outset what answers I might find. Like most people, I believed what I had been told: that the idea of love was invented by the Greeks, and romantic love began in the Middle Ages. I know now how misguided such hearsay is. We can find romantic love in the earliest writings of our kind. Much of the vocabulary of love, and the imagery lovers use, has not changed for thousands of years. Why do the same images come to mind when people describe their romantic feelings? Custom, culture, and tastes vary, but not love itself, not the essence of the emotion.

NOTICE & NOTE

ANALYZE INFORMATIONAL TEXT

Annotate: Mark the sentence in paragraph 10 that acts as a conclusion to the essay.

Draw Conclusions: How does this sentence expand upon the author's thesis?

CHECK YOUR UNDERSTANDING

Answer these questions before moving on to the **Analyze the Text** section on the following page.

1 The author refers to Cupid in order to —

- **A** cite a reason why love is part of cultural mythology
- **B** suggest his arrows symbolize the pain of loved ones parting
- **C** quote an expert in the field of romance and passion
- **D** prove that love is timeless and is a part of every culture

2 Which sentence best conveys the difficulty of defining the word *love*?

- **F** *How can love's spaciousness be conveyed in the narrow confines of one syllable?*
- **G** *Love is an ancient delirium, a desire older than civilization, with taproots stretching deep into dark and mysterious days.*
- **H** *We think of love as a positive force that somehow ennobles the one feeling it.*
- **J** *As a society, we are embarrassed by love.*

3 Which of the following describes the essay's organizational design?

- **A** The author traces the history of love as recorded in art through societies.
- **B** The author discusses the problems love causes and solutions humans find.
- **C** The author explores many ways humans define the word *love*.
- **D** The author seeks the causes of love and its effects.

ANALYZE INFORMATIONAL TEXT

Remind students that a conclusion restates the controlling idea of a text. Explain that it also draws on the facts and statements the author has used throughout the essay to support her points and explore the controlling idea. **(*Answer:*** *The concluding sentence shows that even though love is intangible, or difficult to define, it is unchanging.)*

CHECK YOUR UNDERSTANDING

Have students answer the questions independently.

Answers:

1. *B*
2. *F*
3. *C*

If they answer any questions incorrectly, have them reread the text to confirm their understanding. Then they may proceed to ANALYZE THE TEXT on page 272.

ENGLISH LEARNER SUPPORT

Oral Assessment Provide students with the following sentence frames to assess their comprehension and speaking skills. Ask students to complete each sentence using a word or short phrase.

1. *Cupid is used to show that love can bring _________. (feelings of pain)*
2. *The word _______ is defined in many ways. (love)*
3. *The author shows the many ways people _________. (define the word* love*)*

ALL LEVELS

APPLY

ANALYZE THE TEXT

Possible answers:

1. **DOK 2:** *She means that love is difficult to define and describe. Students should cite details and examples such as "Love commands a vast army of moods"; "It includes many feelings which . . . we crowd into one simple word"; "Everyone admits that love is wonderful and necessary, yet no one can agree on what it is"; "As lofty as the idea of love can be, no image is too profane to help explain it."*
2. **DOK 3:** *She attributes to love the human ability to change the course of history and affect the emotions or fates of large groups of people. She creates a tone of amazement or awe at the power of love.*
3. **DOK 4:** *She cites the Sanskrit word* lubhyati *("he desires") but then adds that the etymology probably goes back much farther than that word. This supports her thesis that love is difficult to define or describe.*
4. **DOK 2:** *She means that despite historical and cultural differences, people everywhere and in all times recognize love. She says if you took a woman from ancient Egypt and put her in an automobile factory in Detroit, a disorienting experience, she would still understand the familiar sight of two people in love.*
5. **DOK 4:** *She uses these examples to support the idea that poets have sought to express love in highly personal ways. Quoted words can support the controlling idea of an informational text by elaborating on it or giving examples of it.*

RESEARCH

Tell students that when conducting research online, they should use search phrases that are as specific to the topic as possible. For example, after previewing possible sites for classroom appropriateness, show students the different outcomes that result when you research "Japanese culture" and "Japan cultural norms love." You may also wish to show students how to look up the word *love* in different languages, using a translation app or language-learning site.

Connect After students use a thesaurus to explore different ways to express love, have them compare the results to the types of examples Ackerman provides in her essay.

RESPOND

ANALYZE THE TEXT

Support your responses with evidence from the text. NOTEBOOK

1. **Infer** Ackerman begins by stating that "Love is the great intangible." What does she mean by this statement? What details and examples in the first two paragraphs help to support this thesis?
2. **Evaluate** In paragraph 3, what human qualities does Ackerman attribute to love? Describe the tone she creates by this use of personification.
3. **Analyze** In paragraph 3, what does the author say is the source of the word *love*? Why is this important information for the structure and purpose of the essay?
4. **Interpret** In paragraph 8, Ackerman writes, "Values, customs, and protocols may vary from ancient days to the present, but not the majesty of love." What does she mean by this statement? What example does she use to develop this idea?
5. **Notice & Note** Why does Ackerman include Quoted Words—references to Elizabeth Barrett Browning's poem "How Do I Love Thee?" and John Donne's poem "The Flea"? Why would you expect to see citations like this in an informational text?

RESEARCH TIP
If the initial results of your search are too general, refine it by using more specific terms.

RESEARCH

Diane Ackerman' essay explores many of the ways Americans define or demonstrate their love for each other. In other countries, love is expressed in different ways according to differing customs. Research how people from other countries and regions—for example, Latin America, France, and Japan—express their love and what is allowed or not allowed for those in love.

COUNTRY	DEFINITIONS AND CULTURAL EXPRESSIONS OF LOVE
Answers will vary.	*Answers will vary, but students should support their evidence by citing credible sources of fact-based information.*

Connect In the United States, people use a variety of words and phrases to say "I love you." Use a thesaurus to explore all the ways we say we love each other. Discuss the different connotations of these words and phrases.

LEARNING MINDSET

Asking for Help Remind students that being open to help is part of the learning process for everyone. For example, asking a peer for constructive feedback on the student's writing can lead to an improved final draft. Point out that this is a form of help. Other ways to ask for help include inviting peers to collaborate on a project or task and asking a speaker to repeat or clarify something he or she said. Encourage students to brainstorm additional ways that they can ask for help.

CREATE AND PRESENT

Discuss the Author's Statement Discuss in small groups Diane Ackerman's statement that as a society we are "embarrassed" and "inhibited" by love.

- ❏ Discuss the points the author makes in paragraph 6 to support her statement. Which points are valid? Which would you challenge?
- ❏ Do her descriptions match what you have observed in movies, books, or the behavior of people around you?
- ❏ Take notes about your views and those of others.

Go to the **Speaking and Listening Studio** for help with small-group discussions.

Present in a Panel Discussion Have representatives of each group assemble a formal panel discussion to present the results of each group. If possible, put together two panels with differing opinions. All speakers should use appropriate register (degree of formality), vocabulary, tone, and voice when they discuss.

- ❏ Have a representative summarize their group's critique of the author's statement, citing text evidence.
- ❏ Members should discuss their views and opinions about the statement, citing the text as well as their own observations.
- ❏ Each member should write a summary of the panel discussion that synthesizes how we discuss love as a society.

Go to the **Speaking and Listening Studio** for help with having a panel discussion.

RESPOND TO THE ESSENTIAL QUESTION

How can love bring both joy and pain?

Gather Information Review your annotations and notes on "Love's Vocabulary." Then, add relevant information to your Response Log. As you determine which information to include, think about:

- how Ackerman demonstrates the difficulties of defining love
- some of the joys she discusses in connection with love
- how she characterizes the pains of love

At the end of the unit, use your notes to help you write a literary analysis.

ACADEMIC VOCABULARY

As you write and discuss what you learned from the essay, be sure to use the Academic Vocabulary words. Check off each of the words that you use.

- ❏ **attribute**
- ❏ **commit**
- ❏ **expose**
- ❏ **initiate**
- ❏ **underlie**

CREATE AND PRESENT

Discuss the Author's Statement Have students note evidence the author provides in paragraph 6 to support her statement. Ask them to mark points they either don't agree with or feel deserve deeper exploration. As they discuss the topic, remind them that their feelings may change. When students reference movies, books, and people's behavior, encourage them to be specific. For example: How did a character in a movie express love? How did he or she react when another character showed love? How does a person behave when he or she feels embarrassed?

For **writing support** for students at varying proficiency levels, see the **Text X-Ray** on page 264D.

Present in a Panel Discussion Remind students that a panel discussion involves a group of people gathered to discuss a topic in front of an audience. You may wish to have the representative for each group guide the discussion, present the questions, and check that each panelist has had an opportunity to speak. After each group presents, invite students to ask questions and offer constructive feedback.

RESPOND TO THE ESSENTIAL QUESTION

Allow time for students to add details from "Love's Vocabulary" to their Unit 4 Response Logs.

APPLY

CRITICAL VOCABULARY

Answers:

1. *b. Unlike school supplies, which can be described objectively, encouragement is not easily described.*
2. *a. A costume can change someone's outward appearance, but a house still looks like a house, even when its color is changed.*
3. *b. The amount by which body temperature can increase is measured in increments of degrees on a thermometer.*
4. *a. A new branch is usually supple, because it is flexible, while a loaf of frozen bread is not flexible and does not bend.*
5. *b. Unlike an argument breaking out, a subtle shift in tone indicates a slight, successive change.*

VOCABULARY STRATEGY: Synonyms

Answers:

- *immense: huge*
- *ennobles: enriches*
- *monotone: invariable*
- *inhibited: reluctant*

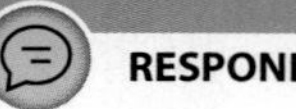

RESPOND

WORD BANK
intangible
guise
increment
supple
gradation

CRITICAL VOCABULARY

Practice and Apply Circle the letter of the best answer to each question. Then, explain your response.

1. Which of the following would be described as **intangible**?
   a. school supplies donated to a class
   b. encouragement given to students
2. Which of the following is a **guise**?
   a. a costume worn to a party
   b. a fresh coat of paint on a house
3. Which of the following is an example of an **increment**?
   a. exit ramps on a freeway
   b. a degree of body temperature on a thermometer
4. Which of the following is usually **supple**?
   a. a new branch on a sapling
   b. a loaf of frozen bread
5. Which of the following is an example of a **gradation**?
   a. an argument breaking out over an insult
   b. a subtle shift of tone in a conversation

VOCABULARY STRATEGY: Synonyms

Go to the **Vocabulary Studio** for more on synonyms.

When you encounter an unfamiliar word in an essay, you can often determine its meaning by substituting a **synonym**—a word with a similar meaning—for the unfamiliar word. For example, in the first line of the essay, Ackerman uses the Critical Vocabulary word *intangible*. The context clue "dream state" later in the paragraph indicates something unsubstantial. The synonym *unsubstantial* makes sense in the sentence.

Practice and Apply Work with a partner to locate these words in the essay: *immense* (paragraph 3), *ennobles* (paragraph 4), *monotone* (paragraph 5), *inhibited* (paragraph 6). Follow these steps:

1. Look for a context clue in the sentence or paragraph where the unfamiliar word occurs.
2. Use context clues to determine meaning and think of a synonym that fits.
3. Substitute your synonym for the unfamiliar word to see if it makes sense.
4. Consult a dictionary or a thesaurus to confirm the meaning.

ENGLISH LEARNER SUPPORT

Vocabulary Strategy Have students work in pairs to locate and record words by category, such as Negative Emotions, Lively Verbs, Vivid Adjectives, and so on. Then, have partners work together to write sentences using words from each targeted category. Next, invite students to share their words and sentences. Offer feedback as needed to help students clarify meanings or revise their sentences. **MODERATE/LIGHT**

LANGUAGE CONVENTIONS:
Participial Phrases

A **participle** is a verb form that functions as an adjective. Like adjectives, participles modify nouns and pronouns. Most participles are present-participle forms, ending in *-ing*, or past-participle forms, ending in *-ed* or *-en*. A **participial phrase** is a group of words that consists of either the present or past participle form of a verb and its modifiers. For example, the participial phrase in this sentence from "Love's Vocabulary" consists of a present participle (sitting) and an adverb (still):

Sitting still, we are as daring as gladiators.

The phrase *sitting still* modifies the pronoun *we*. The author could have conveyed the same information this way:

We are sitting still. We are as daring as gladiators.

However, the rhythm of these two sentences is choppy and uninteresting. Reread Ackerman's sentence and notice how her use of a participial phrase to combine the ideas adds variety and interest to her writing.

Several participial phrases may be used in one sentence to show different actions. Ackerman creates a sense of drama and builds interest by using participial phrases in combination to show several actions:

Hoping for victory, limping from the latest skirmish, lovers enter the arena once again.

Here, two participial phrases, separated by commas, modify the noun *lovers*. Ackerman could have written simply, "Lovers enter the arena once again." However, she includes participial phrases to tell us more about the lovers. She adds meaning by describing the lovers' states of mind and by presenting a dramatic visual image.

Participial phrases may be placed at the beginning, the middle, or the end of a sentence. When using participial phrases in your own writing, it is important to place them carefully and to use punctuation correctly for clarity.

Practice and Apply Look back at the summary of the discussion about love and embarrassment you wrote for this selection's Create and Present activity. Revise it to add at least three participial phrases. Then discuss with your group how the participial phrases improve the meaning or tone of the summary.

Go to the **Grammar Studio** for more on participial phrases.

LANGUAGE CONVENTIONS:
Participial Phrases

Review the fact that participial phrases function as adjectives and can be used to connect ideas.

Reinforce the difference between participles that end in *-ing* (present-participle forms) and participles that end in *-ed* or *-en* (past-participle forms). Have students recall examples of present-participle forms from the essay. Then, provide students with examples of past-participle forms, such as these: *Cleverly written and often quoted, the sonnet used the concept of measurement to express ideas about love.* Have students identify the adverbs *(cleverly, often)*, the past-participle forms *(written, quoted)*, and the noun *(sonnet)*.

Remind students that when using a participial phrase, they should position it close to the noun or pronoun that it modifies.

Practice and Apply Have partners review one another's discussion summaries and confirm that they correctly use at least three participial phrases. Then have partners discuss the effects of the participial phrases on their summaries, such as linking related ideas, creating a certain tone, or adding sentence variety.

ENGLISH LEARNER SUPPORT

Comprehend Language Conventions In Cantonese, Korean, and Vietnamese, adverbial clauses, such as participial phrases, are sometimes followed by a "balancing word" in the main clause. Display these sentences as examples: *Having discussed the selection, so Tran concluded that he disagreed with Kim. Politely disagreeing, but Kim pointed out that Ackerman cites evidence from different cultures.* Then cross out the words *so* and *but*. Read the sentences aloud without these balancing words and have students repeat after you. **ALL LEVELS**

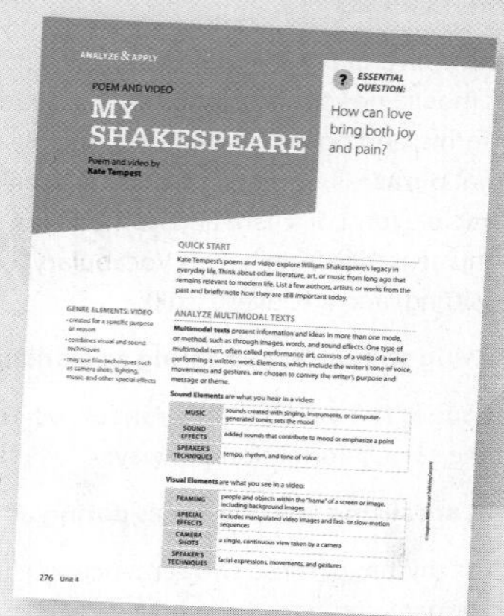

MY SHAKESPEARE

Video and Poem by Kate Tempest

GENRE ELEMENTS
POETRY AND VIDEO

Remind students that a **multimodal text** uses multiple communication modes, or methods, to convey meaning. For example, a video performance of a written work may incorporate the speaker's voice and movement techniques along with other visual and sound elements, such as camera shots, music, and special effects. These techniques can help reinforce an artist's tone, or attitude, toward his or her subject. In this lesson, students will consider how visual and sound elements in Kate Tempest's performance of her poem, "My Shakespeare," contribute to her overall tone and meaning.

LEARNING OBJECTIVES

- Analyze a multimodal text.
- Research the World Shakespeare Festival.
- Write a poem that expresses personal connections to a self-selected work, artist, or author.
- Produce a video performance of a poem.
- **Language** Analyze a multimodal text by listening for repeated words and varied intonation patterns.

TEXT COMPLEXITY

Quantitative Measures	**My Shakespeare**	Lexile: N/A
Qualitative Measures	**Ideas Presented** Single level of meaning requires some inferential reasoning.	
	Structures Used More complex structure with no regular patterns.	
	Language Used Mostly explicit; some figurative or allusive language.	
	Knowledge Required Cultural and literary references may make heavier demands.	

Online 

RESOURCES

- Unit 4 Response Log
-  Reading Studio: Notice & Note
-  Level Up Tutorial: Elements of Poetry
-  Speaking and Listening Studio: Giving a Presentation
- "My Shakespeare" Selection Test

SUMMARIES

English

Kate Tempest's free-verse poem uses allusions to Shakespeare's characters and examples of his influence on everyday speech to illustrate his enduring legacy. In Tempest's video performance of the poem, contemporary visual and sound effects in a modern urban setting emphasize the idea of creating new forms of expression inspired by artistic traditions.

Spanish

En su poema de verso libre, Kate Tempest utiliza alusiones a personajes de Shakespeare y ejemplos de su influencia en el habla común para ilustrar su legado. En la video presentación del poema, Tempest utiliza el ambiente moderno y urbano para hacer énfasis en la idea de crear nuevas formas de expresión inspiradas en tradiciones artísticas.

SMALL-GROUP OPTIONS

Have students work in small groups to read and discuss the selection.

Jigsaw with Experts

- Assign each student a numbered section of the video and poem: first, 00:00–00:47 (lines 1–17); second, 00:48–01:51 (lines 18–35); and third, 01:52–02:31 (lines 36–45).
- After viewing the video and reading the text, have students form groups with other students who viewed and read the same section. Each expert group should discuss its section and compare and contrast the video and poem.
- Then have students form new groups with a representative for each section. These groups should discuss all the sections and how they contribute to the video and poem overall.

Three-Minute Review

- After students have viewed and read "My Shakespeare," tell them that they will conduct a three-minute review in order to identify questions they still have.
- Set a timer for three minutes. Tell students to review the video and poem (along with their annotations and notes) and write clarifying questions.
- Have students share and discuss their questions in small groups.
- After groups have finished their discussions, invite them to share any questions they still have with the class.

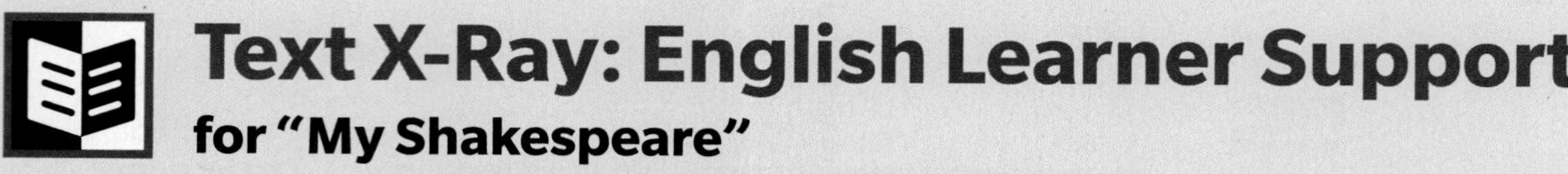

Text X-Ray: English Learner Support
for "My Shakespeare"

Use the Text X-Ray and the supports and scaffolds in the Teacher's Edition to help guide students at different proficiency levels through the selection.

INTRODUCE THE SELECTION

DISCUSS UNIVERSAL IDEAS

In this lesson, students will need to be able to discuss emotions and experiences that are universal and timeless. Display the video of "My Shakespeare" without sound, noting the quick cuts to the text insertion of the word *universal* (00:11, 00:17, 00:26, 01:51). Point out that *universal* is a Spanish, Portuguese, Italian, and French cognate that describes something that relates to or affects all people. Discuss types of universal ideas that writers, artists, and musicians explore, such as love, loss, power, or greed. Encourage students to suggest examples from favorite songs, TV shows, or movies.

Supply the following sentence frames:

- ______ *is an example of a universal idea.*
- ______ *is one artist/writer/work that explores* ______.

CULTURAL REFERENCES

The following idioms that derive from Shakespeare's writing may be unfamiliar to some students:

- *set your teeth on edge* (lines 18–19): make you feel annoyed
- *method in our madness* (line 20): plan that explains odd behavior
- *hair standing on end* (line 21): feeling afraid
- *our hearts were upon our sleeves* (lines 22–23): we showed our feelings openly
- *break the ice* (line 27): make people feel more relaxed
- *green eyed monster* (lines 27–28): envy
- *in a pickle* (line 28): in trouble

LISTENING

Analyze Sound and Intonation Patterns

Support students' listening comprehension of the video.

Use the following supports with students at varying proficiency levels:

- Since students may struggle to interpret Tempest's British accent and rapid rate of delivery, tell them to listen for repeated words and varied intonation patterns. Play the video for students and ask them to raise their hands when they hear the words *he's* and *every.* Ask: Does Tempest raise her tone of voice when she repeats the word *every? (yes)* **SUBSTANTIAL**
- Have students listen to the video in pairs, working together to identify words and phrases that Tempest repeats and emphasizes by varying her tone of voice. **MODERATE**
- Have students listen to the video in pairs, working together to identify words and phrases that Tempest repeats. Then have them discuss speaking techniques they heard Tempest use to add emphasis. **LIGHT**

SPEAKING

Produce a Video

Support students' participation in the video production activity on Student Edition page 281.

Use the following supports with students at varying proficiency levels:

- For students who are not ready to write poems in English, have them practice pronouncing words from the poem with clusters of three consonant sounds: *Shakespeare (ksp); squandering (skw); exactly (ktl); monster (nst); discretion (scr).* **SUBSTANTIAL**
- Have students highlight any words in their poems that they find difficult to pronounce. Then have students repeat the words after you model the correct pronunciation. **MODERATE**
- Have students practice reading aloud their poems to a partner. Have partners provide constructive feedback on their partner's pronunciation, volume, and rate. **LIGHT**

READING

Identify the Main Idea

Guide students to identify the main idea of the first stanza of "My Shakespeare."

Use the following supports with students at varying proficiency levels:

- Guide students to highlight the words *he's, in,* and *every* throughout the stanza. Explain that the phrases that follow the word *every* in lines 1–5 describe specific characters and conflicts from Shakespeare's plays. Explain that *unique* means "the only one of its kind" and that *common* means "seen everywhere." Ask: Are Shakespeare's characters and conflicts unique, or common? *(common)* **SUBSTANTIAL**
- Have students use this frame to summarize the main idea of the stanza: *Shakespeare exists in many ____. (different situations; types of art)* **MODERATE**
- Have partners write a sentence that states the main idea of the stanza. **LIGHT**

WRITING

Write a Poem

Support students' participation in the writing activity on Student Edition page 281.

Use the following supports with students at varying proficiency levels:

- Instead of writing a poem, guide students to think of words they have heard in poems that they like. Help in creating a list of these words; then have students practice writing them. Encourage students to focus on the words' sounds and the symbols that represent them. **SUBSTANTIAL**
- Have students work with a partner to brainstorm words and phrases that describe their topic and their personal connection to it. Review the following vowel and consonant sounds for students who wish to incorporate sound devices in their poems: toad/hose/toe/low; round/clown; tea/seed/me; pipe/sight; say/rain/whale/cake; when/win; boys/noise; giant/jump; cent/sorry; moon/blue/suit. **MODERATE**
- Encourage students to incorporate sound devices in their poems. Review the terms *alliteration, consonance,* and *assonance.* **LIGHT**

Connect to the ESSENTIAL QUESTION

"My Shakespeare" explores the idea that Shakespeare's works include archetypal characters who express universal themes relating to ideas such as love, hate, envy, sacrifice, and revenge. Tempest believes that Shakespeare's legacy endures because these characters and themes are common to people's everyday experiences, and they resurface and reappear in other works of art and literature.

QUICK START

Have students form pairs to discuss the Quick Start prompt. Then invite pairs to share examples of literature, art, or music from long ago that they think still remain relevant today. List students' responses on the board and then discuss qualities that these works share.

ANALYZE MULTIMODAL TEXTS

Have students read the information about multimodal texts. Then review the sound and visual elements described in the charts. Ask them to suggest examples of each element.

Suggest that students use these questions to help them analyze visual and sound elements in the video:

- How does the percussion music impact the mood?
- What are the effects of the rapid-fire cuts, flashes of color, and text insertions?
- How do Tempest's tone of voice and use of movements, facial expressions, and gestures add meaning?

VIDEO AND POEM

MY SHAKESPEARE

Video and poem by
Kate Tempest

? ESSENTIAL QUESTION:

How can love bring both joy and pain?

QUICK START

Kate Tempest's poem and video explore William Shakespeare's legacy in everyday life. Think about other literature, art, or music from long ago that remains relevant to modern life. List a few authors, artists, or works from the past and briefly note how they are still important today.

GENRE ELEMENTS: VIDEO
- created for a specific purpose or reason
- combines visual and sound techniques
- may use film techniques such as camera shots, lighting, music, and other special effects

ANALYZE MULTIMODAL TEXTS

Multimodal texts present information and ideas in more than one mode, or method, such as through images, words, and sound effects. One type of multimodal text, often called performance art, consists of a video of a writer performing a written work. Elements, which include the writer's tone of voice, movements and gestures, are chosen to convey the writer's purpose and message or theme.

Sound Elements are what you hear in a video:

MUSIC	sounds created with singing, instruments, or computer-generated tones; sets the mood
SOUND EFFECTS	added sounds that contribute to mood or emphasize a point
SPEAKER'S TECHNIQUES	tempo, rhythm, and tone of voice

Visual Elements are what you see in a video:

FRAMING	people and objects within the "frame" of a screen or image, including background images
SPECIAL EFFECTS	includes manipulated video images and fast- or slow-motion sequences
CAMERA SHOTS	a single, continuous view taken by a camera
SPEAKER'S TECHNIQUES	facial expressions, movements, and gestures

BACKGROUND

Kate Tempest *(b. 1985) is a London-born poet, playwright, and rapper. She began performing at age 16 and has performed all over the world, winning acclaim and awards at music festivals and poetry slams. Her first collection of poetry,* Everything Speaks in its Own Way, *was published in 2012 and includes a CD and a DVD along with the text. The Royal Shakespeare Company commissioned Kate to write and perform "My Shakespeare" for the World Shakespeare Festival in 2012. Thousands of artists from around the world participated in this festival. Her latest work,* Let Them Eat Chaos, *was nominated for the 2017 Mercury Prize for Album of the Year in the United Kingdom and Ireland.*

SETTING A PURPOSE

As you watch and read, pause to note any questions that you have. Then share your questions with a small group or with your teacher to clarify your understanding.

Notice & Note

You can use the side margins to notice and note signposts in the text.

To view the video, log in online and select **"MY SHAKESPEARE"** from the unit menu.

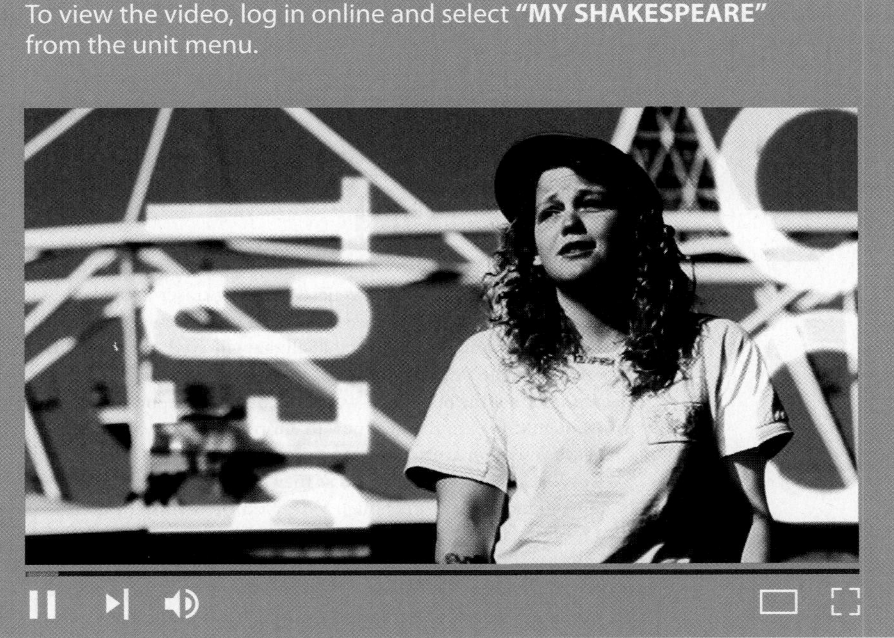

As needed, pause the video to make notes about Kate Tempest's performance of her poem "My Shakespeare," including how her performance techniques, sound effects, and camera shots engage the audience and add meaning to the poem. Replay or rewind to review anything you do not understand.

BACKGROUND

After students read the Background note, explain that like modern-day rappers, Shakespeare provided popular entertainment for all classes of people while serving to explore and illuminate themes that have fascinated people for centuries. Kate Tempest's poem, along with the work of hundreds of others in the World Shakespeare Festival, shows that the works of "The Bard" remain as inspirational and moving for young people today as they have for centuries. Note how Tempest's performance demonstrates her emotional involvement with Shakespeare's language and characters and the way in which she makes her connection clearly personal through the title and the last lines of the poem.

SETTING A PURPOSE

Direct students to use the Setting a Purpose prompt to focus their viewing and reading.

For **listening support** for students at varying proficiency levels, see the **Text X-Ray** on page 276C.

TO CHALLENGE STUDENTS . . .

Identify Allusions Point out that the first three stanzas of "My Shakespeare" include allusions to characters, themes, and scenarios from Shakespeare's plays. Have students work together in a small group to identify the characters and plays to which each allusion refers and explain the context, conducting research as needed to complete the task. When they have finished, invite students to present their findings to the class. *(first stanza: Romeo, Othello, Hamlet, Macbeth, Lear, Iago; second stanza: The Merry Wives of Windsor, Falstaff, A Midsummer Night's Dream; third stanza: Rosalind, Much Ado About Nothing, Lady Macbeth, Rosencrantz and Guildenstern)*

TEACH

ANALYZE MULTIMODAL TEXTS

Have students read the poem as they watch and listen to the video. Suggest that they pause and replay sections in which the speaker's words differ from the text of the poem. Encourage students to note these differences and consider what purpose they may serve. (***Answer:*** *The video may differ from the poem because the poet wished to express new thoughts that had occurred to her since writing the poem, because she felt like improvising, or because she thought her changes best suited the mode she was working in. The video adds the observation that people may not be aware when they are quoting Shakespeare. This observation elaborates on Tempest's theme.)*

For **reading support** for students at varying proficiency levels, see the **Text X-Ray** on page 276D.

NOTICE & NOTE

ANALYZE MULTIMODAL TEXTS

Annotate: Mark where the words in the written poem differ from the ones delivered in the video.

Infer: Why do you think the poet changed the words of the poem? How do the changes alter the meaning?

My Shakespeare

Performance by Kate Tempest

He's in every lover who ever stood alone beneath a window,
In every jealous whispered word,
in every ghost that will not rest.
He's in every father with a favorite,
Every eye that stops to linger
On what someone else has got, and feels the tightening in their chest.

He's in every young man growing boastful,
Every worn out elder, drunk all day;
muttering false prophecies and squandering their lot.
He's there—in every mix-up that spirals far out of control—and never seems to end,
even when its beginnings are forgot.

He's in every girl who ever used her wits. Who ever did her best.
In every vain admirer,
Every passionate, ambitious social climber,
And in every misheard word that ever led to tempers fraying,
Every pawn that moves exactly as the player wants it to,
And still remains convinced that it's not playing.

He's in every star crossed lover, in every thought that ever set your
teeth on edge, in every breathless hero, stepping closer to the ledge,
his is the method in our madness, as pure as the driven snow—his is
the hair standing on end, he saw that all that glittered was not gold.
He knew we hadn't slept a wink, and that our hearts were upon our
sleeves, and that the beast with two backs had us all upon our knees
as we fought fire with fire, he knew that too much of a good thing,
can leave you up in arms, the pen is mightier than the sword, still
his words seem to sing our names as they strike, and his is the milk
of human kindness, warm enough to break the ice—his, the green
eyed monster, in a pickle, still, discretion is the better part of valor,
his letters with their arms around each others shoulders, swagger
towards the ends of their sentences, pleased with what they've done,
his words are the setting for our stories—he has become a poet who
poetics have embedded themselves deep within the fabric of our
language, he's in our mouths, his words have tangled round our own
and given rise to expressions so effective in expressing how we feel,
we can't imagine how we'd feel without them.

WHEN STUDENTS STRUGGLE . . .

Analyze Multimodal Texts Have partners use a Venn diagram to compare and contrast the video and poem. Students should note similarities and differences between the spoken words of the video and the text of the poem; the effects of sound, visual, and literary elements; and the overall impact of both forms.

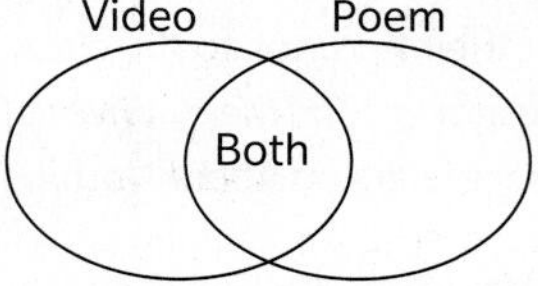

For additional support, go to the **Reading Studio** and assign the following  **Level Up Tutorial: Elements of Poetry.**

NOTICE & NOTE 

See—he's less the tights and garters—more the sons demanding answers from the absence of their fathers.
The hot darkness of your last embrace.
He's in the laughter of the night before, the tightened jaw of the morning after,
He's in us. Part and parcel of our Royals and our rascals.
He's more than something taught in classrooms, in language that's hard to understand,
he's more than a feeling of inadequacy when we sit for our exams,
He's in every wise woman, every pitiful villain,
Every great king, every sore loser, every fake tear.
His legacy exists in the life that lives in everything he's written.
And me. I see him everywhere. he's my Shakespeare.

ANALYZE MULTIMODAL TEXTS

Annotate: In the last two lines, underline words the poet emphasizes in her video delivery. Circle places where the poet pauses.

Connect: What does the poet's delivery of these lines add to the meaning of the poem? What is your personal reaction to these lines?

CHECK YOUR UNDERSTANDING

Answer these questions before moving on to the **Analyze the Text** section on the following page.

1 The speaker in the poem feels that Shakespeare's legacy belongs to her because —

A she understands the language he uses

B she has read many of his plays and can quote them

C she is following in his footsteps as a poet

D she recognizes his influence in the world around her

2 What is the phrase "tights and garters" used to represent?

F How people used to dress

G Something irrelevant to modern life

H Costumes designed for a theater production

J Clothing that is uncomfortable to wear

3 What is an important idea in the poem?

A Shakespeare's words have become part of everyday life.

B Shakespeare's works should be taught in every classroom.

C Shakespeare's understanding of the world was advanced for his time.

D Shakespeare's plays covered a wide range of topics and situations.

ANALYZE MULTIMODAL TEXTS

Tell students that the last two lines of the poem begin at approximately 02:20 in the video. Remind them that speakers may add emphasis through facial expressions, body movements, gestures, tone of voice, and volume. Encourage students to view Tempest's performance of the last two lines of the poem multiple times, each time focusing on just one aspect of her performance. (***Answer:*** *The author's delivery, gestures, and passionate facial expressions show that she deeply appreciates Shakespeare's words, which speak to universal human emotions and experiences, including her own. Students might note that Tempest's delivery encourages them to be more receptive to Shakespeare's works.)*

English Learner Support

Read aloud the last two lines of the poem, pausing between "everywhere" and "he's" (line 45). As you read aloud, also adjust your volume and tone of voice and use exaggerated gestures to emphasize "everything" (line 44), "everywhere" (line 45), and "my" (line 45). Then have students choral read the lines using the same speaking techniques. Finally, have students view Tempest's delivery of these lines. Ask students to complete these frames: *Tempest stresses the words ____. She pauses between ____.* **SUBSTANTIAL/MODERATE**

CHECK YOUR UNDERSTANDING

Have students answer the questions independently.

1. *D*
2. *G*
3. *A*

If students answer any questions incorrectly, have them reread the text to confirm their understanding. Then they may proceed to ANALYZE POEM AND VIDEO on page 280.

ENGLISH LEARNER SUPPORT

Oral Assessment Use the following questions to assess students' comprehension of the poem and speaking skills.

1. How does the speaker feel about Shakespeare? (*She feels that his ideas are universal and important.*)
2. The meaning of the phrase "tights and garters" is difficult to understand. Why? (*The phrase comes from a long-ago time.*)
3. What is one key idea in the poem? (*An important idea in the poem is that Shakespeare's words have become a part of everyday life.*) **ALL LEVELS**

APPLY

ANALYZE POEM AND VIDEO

Possible answers:

1. **DOK 2:** *The repetition signals that what follows is another allusion to one of Shakespeare's characters or themes. Tempest is conveying the message that Shakespeare's characters and themes connect to human emotions and experiences, which are so universal and timeless that we can recognize the same forces at work in ourselves and in the people around us.*
2. **DOK 3:** *Tempest is referring to the fact that many colorful phrases from Shakespeare's works have become such an accepted part of our everyday language that we use them without realizing that Shakespeare coined them. As evidence, Tempest lists phrases such as "star crossed lover" (line 18), "set your teeth on edge" (lines 18–19), and "the method in our madness" (line 20).*
3. **DOK 4:** *The text emphasizes that Shakespeare's works convey messages about life and human emotions with which we can all connect. In the video, Tempest's display of passion and sincerity combines with the contemporary style of her performance to drive home the idea of Shakespeare's continued relevance.*
4. **DOK 4:** *Tempest's delivery is impassioned and full of feeling. The opening music and quick pace of the camera shots add energy. She delivers the poem as an argument, claiming that ideas the audience may have about Shakespeare are mistaken. The background imagery includes an everyday setting in a modern city, reflecting the way that Shakespeare's words have come to be a part of everyday life.*
5. **DOK 4:** *The words "my Shakespeare" mean that Shakespeare and his works are not distant academic mysteries to her and other English speakers; rather, they have been internalized, whether we recognize it or not. Evidence from the poem includes the phrase "I see him everywhere" (line 45) and repetition of "He's in" and "every" throughout the poem.*

RESEARCH

Have students research their assigned topic and then share their results with their group. Remind students that sources may include the official event website as well as articles about the event and reviews of performances.

Extend Remind students to consider techniques the speaker uses to emphasize meaning as well as the impact of other visual and sound elements. Prompt them to discuss similarities and differences between the videos.

RESPOND

ANALYZE POEM AND VIDEO

Support your responses with evidence from the video and text. NOTEBOOK

1. **Infer** What does the repetition of the words "in every" throughout the poem signal to readers? What message does Tempest convey through these words?
2. **Cite Evidence** Explain the statement that Shakespeare is "in our mouths, his words have tangled round our own . . ." What evidence does the author provide to support this idea?
3. **Analyze** In the last stanza, Tempest acknowledges the negative ideas that today's young people might have about Shakespeare. How do the text and the video work together to refute these ideas?
4. **Synthesize** Explain how the poet uses visual elements, sound elements, and speaking techniques to develop the meaning of her poem through the video.
5. **Evaluate** What do the poem's final words, "my Shakespeare" mean? What evidence from the poem supports this meaning?

RESEARCH

RESEARCH TIP
When researching something from the past, look for accounts and information from that time. For example, search for newspaper articles about the event or reviews written about a performance.

Kate Tempest wrote the poem "My Shakespeare" for the World Shakespeare Festival in 2012. In a small group, research the 2012 World Shakespeare Festival and the productions it inspired. From the chart below, assign each group member a topic to research. Record your findings in the chart, and share them with the group.

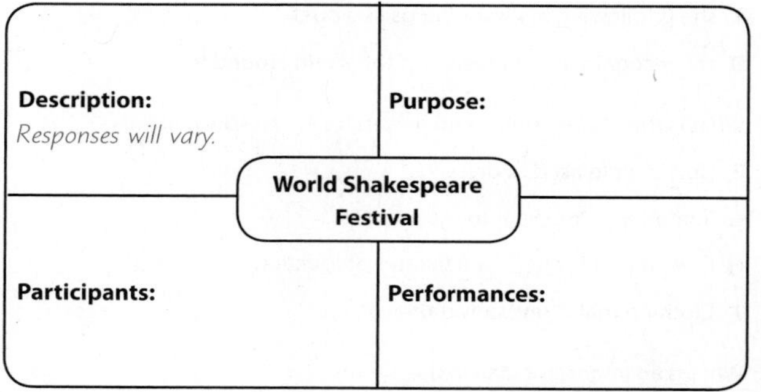

Extend Find another video of a performance from the World Shakespeare Festival. Think about what you see and hear in the video and how the images are arranged. With a partner, discuss how the video adds meaning to the text being performed.

ENGLISH LEARNER SUPPORT

Oral Assessment Conduct an informal assessment to gauge students' comprehension of the video and speaking skills. Ask students at varying proficiency levels the following questions:

- Demonstrate gestures, facial expressions, and intonation similar to those Tempest uses. Ask: Does this show feeling? What feeling? **SUBSTANTIAL**
- How does Tempest use speaking techniques to express meaning? *(Her facial expressions, gestures, and tone of voice show her strong feelings.)* **MODERATE**
- How do sound and visual elements add meaning in the video? *(Drum beats, quick cuts, flashes of light, and the city scene show strong feeling and connections to today.)* **LIGHT**

CREATE AND PRESENT

Write a Poem Write a three-to four-stanza poem about a work, artist, or author that has influenced you. Review your notes on the Quick Start activity before you begin.

- ❑ Think about the ideas you want to explore in your poem. For example, you might want to write about how the work, artist, or author has changed your view of yourself or of the world. Write a list of your ideas.
- ❑ Arrange your ideas in a logical or artistic order.
- ❑ Draft your poem using literary devices such as repetition to emphasize ideas. Use rhythm and a rhyme scheme that will best convey your thoughts and feelings.
- ❑ Revise and edit your poem as needed.

Produce a Video With a partner, create a video performance of your poem.

- ❑ Decide what your audience will see and hear in the video, including the speaking techniques, camera shots, music, and background images.
- ❑ Practice reading the poem aloud, emphasizing different words or phrases until it sounds the way you want it to.
- ❑ Record your video. You may want to use video editing software to arrange images and add audio and visual elements.
- ❑ Present your video to the class. Combine the videos into a class film about how artists affect our lives.

Go to the **Speaking and Listening Studio** for more on giving a presentation.

RESPOND TO THE ESSENTIAL QUESTION

How can love bring both joy and pain?

Gather Information Review your annotations and notes on "My Shakespeare." Then, add relevant information to your Response Log. As you determine which information to include, think about:

- why Shakespeare is still relevant today
- the role of love in the situations described in the poem
- how experiences of joy and pain are captured in the poem

At the end of the unit, use your notes to help you write a literary analysis.

ACADEMIC VOCABULARY

As you write and discuss what you learned from the poem, be sure to use the Academic Vocabulary words. Check off each of the words that you use.

- ❑ **attribute**
- ❑ **commit**
- ❑ **expose**
- ❑ **initiate**
- ❑ **underlie**

APPLY

CREATE AND PRESENT

Write a Poem Tell students that their poems should convey specific ways in which they make personal connections to a work, artist, or author of their choice. Students may write their poems in free verse, or they may choose a more formal structure. Point out that although free verse poems such as "My Shakespeare" lack conventional meter or rhyme scheme, they may still contain various rhythmic and sound effects, including repetition, alliteration, assonance, consonance, parallelism, and irregular rhyme.

For **writing support** for students at varying proficiency levels, see the **Text X-Ray** on page 276D.

Produce a Video Remind students to use speaking techniques such as volume, enunciation, rate, and purposeful gestures to emphasize meaning. Encourage students to consider the mood they want to convey as they select additional audio and visual elements to incorporate in their videos. After each video presentation, have students discuss which parts of the film they thought were most effective and why. Each student may provide a video clip for the class film on how artists affect our lives.

For **speaking support** for students at varying proficiency levels, see the **Text X-Ray** on page 276D.

RESPOND TO THE ESSENTIAL QUESTION

Allow time for students to add details from "My Shakespeare" to their Unit 4 Response Logs.

THE TRAGEDY OF ROMEO AND JULIET

Drama by William Shakespeare

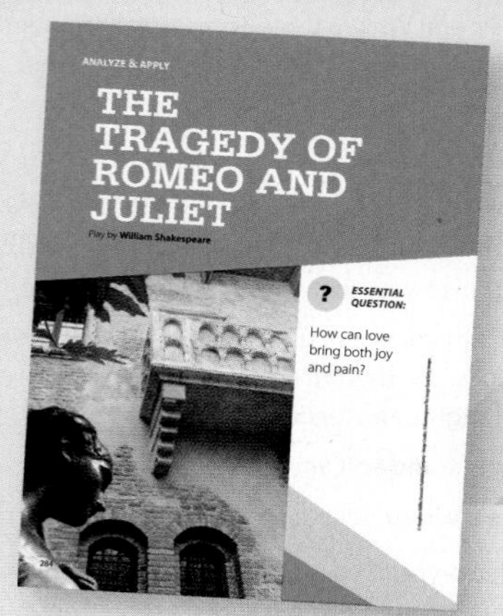

GENRE ELEMENTS

DRAMA

Remind students that a **drama** is written to be performed in front of an audience. It tells a story through the words and actions of the characters. Use resources in the Teacher's Edition to introduce the following terms:

- narrative elements: *setting, plot, conflict, characters*
- play divisions and graphic elements: *act, scene, stage directions*
- ways of speaking: *dialogue, monologue, soliloquy, aside*

LEARNING OBJECTIVES

- Analyze literary devices and parallel plots.
- Research other plays, films, musicals, songs, poems, and other works of art based on *The Tragedy of Romeo and Juliet.*
- Work with a partner to write a eulogy for Romeo and Juliet.
- Discuss in a small group the challenges of writing a eulogy.
- Analyze puns and foreign words in Shakespeare's language.
- Identify and use parallel structure.
- **Language** Use connecting words to discuss positive and negative character traits.

TEXT COMPLEXITY

Quantitative Measures	**The Tragedy of Romeo and Juliet**	Lexile: N/A
Qualitative Measures	**Ideas Presented** Explores complex ideas; multiple levels of meaning (multiple themes) are evident.	
	Structures Used The text uses complex structures such as parallel plots and parallel construction.	
	Language Used The text contains allusive, figurative, and ironic language that is often archaic and unfamiliar.	
	Knowledge Required Cultural and literary knowledge is essential for understanding.	

Online 

RESOURCES

- Unit 4 Response Log
- Selection Audio
- Close Read Screencasts: Modeled Discussions
-  Reading Studio: Notice & Note
-  Level Up Tutorials, listed at point of use
-  Speaking and Listening Studio: Giving a Presentation; Participating in Collaborative Discussions
- Vocabulary Studio: Foreign Words
- *The Tragedy of Romeo and Juliet* Selection Test

SUMMARIES

English

Romeo, son of the head of the Montague family, falls in love with Juliet, daughter of the head of the Capulet family. Despite the feud between these families, the young lovers are determined to be together. Friar Laurence marries them in secret, hoping to end the feud. After the wedding, however, Romeo kills Juliet's cousin and must flee the city. Juliet's parents, unaware of the wedding, arrange a marriage for her; to avoid it, Juliet works with Friar Laurence to fake her death and run away to be with Romeo. Miscommunication results in Romeo's belief that Juliet is dead, and he kills himself. Discovering Romeo's body, Juliet also commits suicide.

Spanish

Romeo, hijo del jefe de la familia Montesco, se enamora de Julieta, la hija del jefe de la familia Capuleto. A pesar de la enemistad entre las familias, los jóvenes amantes están decididos a estar juntos. El fraile Lorenzo los casa en secreto, con la esperanza de que esto termine la enemistad. Sin embargo, después de la boda, Romeo mata al primo de Julieta y debe huir de la ciudad. Ignorando la boda, los padres de Julieta arreglan su matrimonio; para evitarlo, el fraile Lorenzo y ella se las ingenian para que finja su muerte y huya para estar con Romeo. La falta de comunicación resulta en que Romeo cree que Julieta ha muerto y por esto se suicida. Al descubrir el cuerpo de Romeo, Julieta también se suicida.

SMALL-GROUP OPTIONS

Have students work in small groups to read and discuss the selection.

Jigsaw with Experts

- Have students count off from 1 to 5. Based on their number, have students review one of the five acts of the play.
- Have students form five groups based on their assigned number and discuss their act, becoming "experts" on it.
- Have students form new groups with one representative from each expert group and then discuss their acts and the play as a whole.

Double-Entry Journal

- Have students create a two-column chart, labeling the columns "Quotations from the Play" and "My Notes."
- In the left column, have students note significant events, important details, or puzzling passages from the play.
- In the right column, ask students to write their own interpretations and summaries, and any questions they might have.

Text X-Ray: English Learner Support

for *The Tragedy of Romeo and Juliet*

Use the Text X-Ray and the supports and scaffolds in the Teacher's Edition to help guide students at different proficiency levels through the selection.

INTRODUCE THE SELECTION

DISCUSS FEUDS AND FAMILY

In this lesson, students will need to be able to discuss the feud between the Montague and Capulet families. Read lines 1–8 of the Prologue to Act I (page 289) with students and point out the phrase *ancient grudge* in line 3. Provide these explanations:

- If you hold a **grudge,** you are angry about something someone did.
- A **feud** is a grudge that lasts a long time.

Point out that there is a feud between Romeo's family and Juliet's family. Ask: What makes a feud hard to end? Do you think the head of a family should make all of the important decisions? Provide frames to support students' responses:

A feud is hard to end because ______ .
I think that everyone in a family ______ .

CULTURAL REFERENCES

The following words or phrases may be unfamiliar to students:

- *page* (Cast, page 288): a person who runs errands
- *watchman* (Cast, page 288): a man paid to guard the streets
- *kinsman* (Act I, Scene 1, line 51): a male relative
- *cell* (Act II, Scene 2, line 189): a room where a friar or monk lives
- *banished* (Act III, Scene 2, line 69): sent away from a place
- *O woeful day!* (Act IV, Scene 5, line 49): Oh, what a sad day!

See also side glosses throughout the play.

LISTENING

Understand the Language of Shakespeare

Tell students that paraphrasing a passage of the text will improve their understanding of Shakespeare's language. Use Act II, Scene 3, lines 57–64, to illustrate.

Use the following supports with students at varying proficiency levels:

- Tell students to listen closely as you read to find out who is speaking and what the character wants. Read aloud lines 57–64 twice. Provide this frame for students to complete: ______ *asks the* ______ *to* ______. *(Romeo asks the friar to marry him to Juliet.)* **SUBSTANTIAL**
- Read aloud lines 57–64 . Then read aloud lines 57–58. Have students write a one-sentence paraphrase. *(I love Capulet's daughter.)* Next, read aloud from line 61 (beginning with When) through line 64. Have students write a brief paraphrase. *(I'll tell you everything about how we met and fell in love. But please tell me you will marry us today.)* **MODERATE**
- Read aloud lines 57–64 twice. The second time, pause after every complete thought. Have students write sentences paraphrasing what they hear. Then have partners compare what they wrote. **LIGHT**

SPEAKING

Use Connecting Words to Show Contrast

Review the discussion instructions on Student Edition page 391. Explain that transitions will help students contrast positive and negative character traits.

Use the following supports with students at varying proficiency levels:

- Help students create lists of positive and negative traits that describe Romeo and Juliet. Model how to say a sentence that combines both: *Romeo was fickle, but he was also loyal*. **SUBSTANTIAL**
- Provide sentence frames to help students discuss positive and negative character traits: *(Romeo/Juliet) _____, but (he/she) also _____. (Romeo/Juliet) _____; however, (he/she) also ____.* **MODERATE**
- Have pairs of students take turns using the words *but*, *although*, and *however* to join ideas as they discuss traits included in their eulogies. **LIGHT**

READING

Understand Figurative Language

Remind students that Shakespeare uses a lot of figurative language. Briefly review the meanings of **simile**, **metaphor**, and **personification**.

Use the following supports with students at varying proficiency levels:

- Have students read Act II, Scene 2, lines 2–3. Guide students to see that the comparison of Juliet to the sun is a metaphor because it does not contain *like* or *as*. **SUBSTANTIAL**
- Have students read Act II, Scene 2, lines 1–8. Then have them complete these frames: *Shakespeare uses a metaphor to compare Juliet to _____. He does this to show that she ___* **MODERATE**
- Have students read Act II, Scene 2, lines 1–8. Then have them explain the example of personification in lines 4–6. *(Romeo compares the moon to a woman. He says the moon is envious of Juliet because Juliet is more beautiful than the moon is.)* **LIGHT**

WRITING

Write a Eulogy

Work with students to prepare them for the writing assignment on Student Edition page 391.

Use the following supports with students at varying proficiency levels:

- Work with students to create a concept map that lists details about Romeo, Juliet, their love, and the future they wanted. Help students identify words and phrases to add to the concept map. Use the details to write a short eulogy on the board for students copy in their notebooks. **SUBSTANTIAL**
- Provide sentence frames for students' topic sentences: *Like every teenager, Romeo sometimes _____, but we will always remember him because _____. Like Romeo, Juliet sometimes _____, but she _____. Romeo and Juliet taught their families that _____.* **MODERATE**
- Remind students to use a mix of verb tenses in their eulogies. Point out they will mostly use past-tense verbs to talk about the lives of Romeo and Juliet, but they will also need to use some present-tense verbs and possibly future-tense verbs. Once they complete their draft, have students circle the verbs and check that they have used tenses correctly. **LIGHT**

CHARACTERISTICS OF SHAKESPEAREAN TRAGEDY

Characters

Remind students that drama develops character and plot through dialogue and action—through what they say and do, characters reveal their traits, motivations, thoughts, and feelings. Point out that the conflict, or struggle, between the antagonist and the protagonist, or hero, drives the action as the characters try to solve the complications resulting from it. Ask students if they can identify a tragic hero from another play they have read or seen. If so, ask them to identify the character's flaw; if not, ask them to speculate on what such a flaw might be. Explain also that Shakespeare's plays are populated with many minor characters and that a minor character often serves as a foil to the hero.

Dramatic Conventions

To familiarize students with the dramatic conventions in the chart, use these activities:

- Have volunteers improvise dialogue for a soliloquy and an aside. Prompt them by suggesting that their character feels discouraged about a difficult class assignment or hopeful about being nominated for a class officer position.
- Have students give examples of comic relief or dramatic irony from television shows, online videos, or movies.
- As a class, discuss what each dramatic convention adds to the drama.

THE LANGUAGE OF SHAKESPEARE

Blank Verse

Read aloud the line of **iambic pentameter** shown at the bottom of Student Edition page 282 (from Act I, Scene 1, line 168). Then read the line a second time, clapping on the stressed syllables, and have students count the number of stresses in each line.

SHAKESPEAREAN DRAMA

Shakespeare's 38 plays may be more popular today than they were in Elizabethan times. While Shakespeare's comedies and histories remain crowd-pleasing classics, his tragedies are perhaps his most powerful works. One of the most famous, *The Tragedy of Romeo and Juliet*, relates the tale of two love-struck teens caught in the tensions between their feuding families.

CHARACTERISTICS OF SHAKESPEAREAN TRAGEDY

A **tragedy** is a drama that results in a catastrophe for the main characters. Shakespearean tragedies offer more than just despair; they provide comic moments that counter the underlying tension of the plot. Before you read, familiarize yourself with some character types and dramatic conventions of Shakespearean tragedy.

Characters	Dramatic Conventions
Tragic Hero • the protagonist, or central character • usually fails or dies because of a character flaw or a cruel twist of fate	**Soliloquy** • a speech given by a character alone • exposes a character's thoughts and feelings to the audience
Antagonist • the adversary or hostile force opposing the protagonist • can be a character, a group of characters, or a nonhuman entity	**Aside** • a character's remark that others on stage do not hear • reveals the character's private thoughts
Foil • a character whose personality and attitude contrast sharply with those of another character • emphasizes another character's attributes and traits	**Dramatic Irony** • when the audience knows more than the characters; helps build suspense **Comic Relief** • a humorous scene or speech meant to relieve tension; the contrast can heighten the seriousness of the action

THE LANGUAGE OF SHAKESPEARE

Blank Verse Shakespeare wrote his plays primarily in blank verse: unrhymed lines of **iambic pentameter**, a meter that contains five unstressed syllables (˘), each followed by a stressed syllable (´). Read the following line aloud, emphasizing each stressed syllable:

Here's much to do with hate but more with love.

WHEN STUDENTS STRUGGLE . . .

Reading Shakespearean Tragedy Briefly review plot stages and point out how the plot is typically developed in a Shakespearean drama: Act I: exposition, conflict; Act II: rising action, complications; Act III: turning point (which determines play's direction); Act IV: falling action; Act V: climax, conclusion. Have students keep this organization in mind as they read each act. Also encourage them to summarize key ideas about the characters and plot after each scene.

For additional support, go to the **Reading Studio** and assign the following  **Level Up Tutorial: Elements of Drama.**

While this pattern forms the general rule, variations in the rhythm prevent the play from sounding monotonous. As you read, pay close attention to places where characters speak in rhyming poetry instead of unrhymed verse.

Allusion An allusion is a reference to a literary or historical person or event that the audience is expected to know. Shakespeare's audience was familiar with Greek and Roman mythology and the Bible, so his plays include many references to these works. For example, Mercutio refers to the mythological god of love when he says, "Borrow Cupid's wings and soar with them . . ." (Act I, Scene 4).

ELIZABETHAN THEATER

A Wide Audience Though acting companies toured throughout England, London was the center of the Elizabethan stage. One reason that London's theaters did so well was that they attracted an avid audience of rich and poor alike. In fact, Elizabethan theaters were among the few forms of entertainment available to working class people, and one of the only places where people of all classes could mix.

The Globe In 1599, Shakespeare and other shareholders of The Lord Chamberlain's Men built the Globe Theater, a three-story wooden structure with an open courtyard at its center where the actors performed on an elevated platform. The theater held 3,000 people, with most of them standing near the courtyard stage in an area known as the pit. The pit audience paid the lowest admission fee—usually just one penny. Theater-goers willing and able to pay more sat in the covered inner balconies that surrounded the courtyard.

Staging Elizabethan theater relied heavily on the audience's imagination. Most theaters had no curtains, no lighting, and very little scenery. Instead, props, sound effects, and certain lines of dialogue defined the setting of a scene. While the staging was simple, the scenes were hardly dull. Flashing swords, brightly colored banners, and elegant costumes contributed to the spectacle. The costumes also helped audience members imagine that women appeared in the female roles, which were actually performed by young men. In Shakespeare's time, women could not belong to theater companies in England—Elizabethan society considered it highly improper for a woman to appear on stage.

TEACH

Allusion

Clarify the concept of an **allusion** by pointing out that Romeo himself has become an allusion. Tell students that a male in love or pining away for a woman is referred to as a Romeo. Make sure that students are aware of the difference between *allusion* and *illusion* both in spelling and meaning. Explain that an *illusion* is a false perception.

ELIZABETHAN THEATER

A Wide Audience

Ask a volunteer to read aloud the section about Shakespearean audiences. Discuss the pressure that a playwright would face writing a play that had to appeal to such a diverse audience. Tell students that *Romeo and Juliet* has something for everyone: romance, action, tragedy, and humor.

The Globe

Have students read the description of the Globe Theater. If possible, display sketches of the original Globe or photographs of the rebuilt Globe, to help students visualize its structure. Explain that members of the audience in the courtyard had to stand throughout the play; that enabled more spectators to crowd in. It also meant that the rowdiest audience members were very close to the actors, an incentive for the actors to do their best.

Staging

As a class, define these terms: *scenery, props, sound effects, costumes.* Have students explain how these elements of staging were used in Elizabethan theater. Then, clarify for students that Shakespeare belonged to a theater company. The members of this company were the actors for each of the plays they put on. That is one of the reasons that Shakespeare's plays have many characters; he wrote a part for each of his fellow actors.

TO CHALLENGE STUDENTS . . .

Sketch and Analyze the Globe Theater What was it like to see a play in Shakespeare's day? Have students work in small groups to create a sketch of the Globe Theater as it might have appeared at the time. Suggest they do a cutaway view to allow them to show the inside of the theater. Encourage students to use the details of the structure included on this page as well as additional sources, such as reliable online sources. Have them label these details and other parts of their sketches, such as the stage, pit, courtyard, and covered balcony seating.

Ask students to present their sketches to the class. Have them explain the impact of the three-sided stage on the staging of plays, citing both its pros and cons.

Connect to the ESSENTIAL QUESTION

The Tragedy of Romeo and Juliet by William Shakespeare is the archetypal story of star-crossed lovers. Desperately in love, but forbidden by their feuding families to see each other, Juliet seeks the advice of Friar Laurence. Together Juliet and the friar devise a plan that will enable Romeo and Juliet to marry and be together for the rest of their lives. But the plan goes terribly awry, and both teenagers end up killing themselves. How can such passionate love turn into such a tragedy? This classic drama suggests the fragility of human emotions and the unreliability of human circumstances. Had reason and logic intervened, the story may have had a different ending. Or did fate have a hand to play in the tragic outcome?

THE TRAGEDY OF ROMEO AND JULIET

Drama by **William Shakespeare**

? ESSENTIAL QUESTION:

How can love bring both joy and pain?

LEARNING MINDSET

Seeking Challenges Remind students that a growth mindset means believing you can get smarter by taking on challenges and pushing yourself. Explain that having a growth mindset means taking risks, trying new things, and not being afraid to fail (or even look a little silly) in front of friends. Encourage students to think of a complex text, such as *The Tragedy of Romeo and Juliet*, as a challenge. Remind students that confronting and overcoming challenges is key to developing new skills and building on existing ones. Assure them that they are not expected to be perfect and that making mistakes is part of the learning process. By taking risks and trying different strategies, students can learn to overcome challenges.

284 Unit 4

QUICK START

Sketch a scene or image that you associate with the story of Romeo and Juliet.

ANALYZE LITERARY DEVICES

Shakespeare uses a variety of literary devices in *The Tragedy of Romeo and Juliet* to create complex and believable characters, establish mood and setting, and develop suspense. As you read the play, start a word wall of any terms or phrases you find interesting or challenging. Add to this word wall as you continue to read.

Characters In creating his characters, Shakespeare often uses a **foil**, a character who contrasts with one of his major characters. Mercutio is one of the most famous foils in literature, his ironic wit contrasting with Romeo's romanticism and his fierce family pride contrasting with Romeo's desire for peace between the Montagues and the Capulets.

Setting Since Shakespearean theaters did not have stage sets with false trees and painted walls, the playwright had to create a sense of where the characters were by using **descriptive dialogue**. It's difficult to make that dialogue sound natural, but Shakespeare does it in this line from Act I, Scene 5: "More light, you knaves! and turn the tables up, / And quench the fire, the room is grown too hot."

Mood Shakespeare is brilliant at varying moods and building tension. Then he breaks that tension with such devices as **comic relief**, in which he uses word play. For example, Shakespeare's **puns** make use of a word's multiple meanings, or they play on its sound. One of Shakespeare's most powerful literary devices for mood building is the **soliloquy**, in which a character who is alone—or thinks he or she is alone—speaks his or her innermost thoughts and feelings. The overlapping soliloquies in the balcony scene of *The Tragedy of Romeo and Juliet* (Act II, Scene 2), which gradually become a dialogue, create a mood of romance and longing. Other literary devices Shakespeare uses include **oxymorons**, expressions containing an apparent contradiction ("parting is such sweet sorrow"); and **similes** ("My bounty is as boundless as the sea, / My love as deep; the more I give to thee, / The more I have, for both are infinite.").

Suspense Shakespeare builds suspense even when the audience is so familiar with a story that it knows how the play ends. One device he uses is **dramatic irony**, in which the audience knows what one or more of the people on stage does not know. For example, Juliet pours out her heart in the balcony scene, not knowing that Romeo is listening. Another important device for building suspense is **foreshadowing**. At several points in the play characters refer, often unknowingly, to what will happen in the future.

GENRE ELEMENTS: DRAMA

- written to be performed by actors in front of an audience
- tells a story through characters' words and actions
- includes stage directions with important details that explain what's happening
- may be divided into acts, which are in turn divided into scenes
- may show that the time or place of the action has changed by starting a new act or scene

TEACH

QUICK START

Ask students what comes foremost to mind when they think of the story of Romeo and Juliet. Then have students sketch a scene or image that they associate with the story. Ask for volunteers to share their sketches with the class.

ANALYZE LITERARY DEVICES

Review the various literary devices that Shakespeare uses in *The Tragedy of Romeo and Juliet*.

Call on students to read each description aloud and discuss each term, its meaning, and the examples.

To reinforce students' understanding of the terms, have groups do as many of the following as they can in 10 minutes (or assign one task per group):

- Come up with their own examples of a **foil**, of **comic relief**, and of **foreshadowing** from popular movies or TV programs.
- Identify a program that includes a character who talks directly to the camera and then list how that is like and unlike a **soliloquy**.
- Draft a few lines of **descriptive dialogue** to convey a scene that is set at a school, assuming no physical props are available.
- Write original examples of an **oxymoron** and a **simile**.
- Turn to Act 1, Scene 4, lines 14–15 (on page 303) and write the **pun** Romeo uses there. *("Not I, believe me. You have dancing shoes / With nimble soles; I have a soul of lead / So stakes me to the ground I cannot move.")*

Then invite groups to share their results.

Tell students to keep these literary devices in mind as they read the play and to mark them as they come across them. Add notes to the margin. Have students start a word wall and add to it as they read the play.

TEACH

ANALYZE PARALLEL PLOTS

Point out that although the play has several parallel plots, the first two shown in the chart are the most important. The central plot is the story of Romeo and Juliet, but the feud between the Montagues and Capulets is also very important. Explain that although the other plots are less significant, they still reveal important insights into the characters. As students read the play, have partners complete story maps, with one student in each pair focusing on one of the two main plots and making note of its characters, central conflict, and major events. After students have read each act, convene the class to discuss how the two plots interact. Ask: How are the events in one story affecting the other story? How do the plots contrast with each other?

LANGUAGE CONVENTIONS

Explain to students that using parallel structure adds rhythm and flow to writing. Point out that repetition and parallelism are closely related because parallelism often involves the repetition of certain words. Repetition can bring an idea into focus and make it more persuasive. Explain, however, that parallelism also involves the repetition of a grammatical structure such as a string of nouns, verbs, or similarly constructed phrases or clauses.

Discuss the structure and effect of the example of parallel structure, pointing out how the parallelism of the structure and the repetition of the word *past* amplifies the pain and hopelessness expressed. Then encourage students to mark instances of parallel structure as they read the play.

ANNOTATION MODEL

Review the Annotation Model with students. Remind students that they can use their own system for marking up the selection as they read. They may want to color-code their annotations by using highlighters; for example, instead of marking up all literary devices in the same way, they could use yellow for comic relief, green for oxymorons, blue for puns, and so on.

Encourage students to add notes in the margin, including questions about ideas that are unclear or topics they want to learn more about.

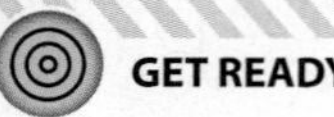

GET READY

ANALYZE PARALLEL PLOTS

Romeo and Juliet is not a simple love story with a **linear**, or straightforward, plot. It is a complex drama featuring **parallel plots**, separate story lines that happen at the same time and are linked by common characters and themes. The chart can help you identify the parallel plots in the play.

PLOT	PURPOSE
The love story of Romeo and Juliet	How does this main plot intertwine with the other parallel plots?
The feud between the Capulets and the Montagues	How does this plot contribute to the drama of the play?
Romeo's unrequited love for Rosaline	What does this show us about Romeo?
Juliet's marriage proposal from Paris	What do we learn about Juliet and her relationship with her family?

LANGUAGE CONVENTIONS

Parallel structure is the repetition of certain words, phrases, or grammatical structures. It adds emphasis or improves the rhythm of a piece of writing. Here is a line from the play with parallel structure underlined.

"O, shut the door! And when thou hast done so, / Come weep with me— past hope, past cure, past help!"

ANNOTATION MODEL

NOTICE & NOTE

As you read, note clues about the setting, plot, and characters of *The Tragedy of Romeo and Juliet*. This model shows one reader's notes about the Prologue.

Two households, both alike in dignity,
In fair Verona, where we lay our scene,
From ancient grudge break to new mutiny,
Where civil blood makes civil hands unclean.
From forth the fatal loins of these two foes,
A pair of star-crossed lovers take their life,
Whose misadventured piteous overthrows
Doth with their death bury their parents' strife.

These two families must have been fighting for a long time.

This foreshadows the way the play ends.

BACKGROUND

William Shakespeare *(1564–1616) has long been considered the greatest writer in the English language—and perhaps the greatest playwright of all time. Four hundred years after their premier performances, his plays remain more popular than ever, and they have been produced more often and in more countries than those of any other author. Despite Shakespeare's renown, we have relatively few details about his life and career as an actor, poet, and playwright.*

THE TRAGEDY OF ROMEO AND JULIET

Drama by William Shakespeare

Shakespeare came from Stratford-upon-Avon, a small village about 90 miles northwest of London, and was probably born in 1564. Though no records exist, we assume that he attended the local grammar school. In 1582, he married Anne Hathaway, the daughter of a farmer. The couple's first child arrived in 1583, and twins, a boy and a girl, followed two years later.

We know nothing about the next seven years of Shakespeare's life, but he likely left his family behind and joined a traveling theater troupe. His trail resurfaces in London, where he had become a successful poet and playwright. He wrote for and acted with The Lord Chamberlain's Men, a popular theater troupe. By 1597, the year that The Tragedy of Romeo and Juliet *was published, he had become a shareholder of the theater company. As his popularity grew, Shakespeare also became part owner of London's Globe Theater. In 1603, King James I became a patron of the Globe Theater, and the theater troupe became known as The King's Men.*

In 1609, Shakespeare published his sonnets, a series of poems that received wide popular acclaim. Shakespeare then began to take advantage of his wealth and fame, spending more time in Stratford-upon-Avon and retiring there permanently around 1612. He would write no more plays after that year. No records confirm the cause or date of his death; a monument marking his gravesite indicates that he died on April 23, 1616. Although we have little data documenting his life, more pages have been written about Shakespeare than about any author in the history of Western civilization.

TEACH

BACKGROUND

Have students read the biographical information on William Shakespeare. Tell students that Shakespeare is considered the finest playwright in the English language. Explain to them that even though Shakespeare only attended grammar school, his education would have exposed him to the classics and enabled him to draw plot ideas from ancient stories as well as make literary allusions, or indirect references to earlier works. He most likely studied Latin grammar, Latin literature, and rhetoric.

The Tragedy of Romeo and Juliet is one of Shakespeare's earlier works, and it is considered by many to be the greatest love story of all time. It probably was first performed in the mid-1590s, when Shakespeare would have been about thirty years old. As was the custom at that time, Shakespeare based his play on a story that already existed. Point out that many modern plays, stories, and films are based on his works, including the popular Broadway and movie musical *West Side Story.*

Tell students that Shakespeare contributed many words, phrases, and expressions to the English language. Some words were his own invention—for example, *assassination, bump,* and *lonely.* Explain that many of his expressions have become "household words"—a term first used in Shakespeare's play *Henry V.* For example, the following sayings are actually quotations from Shakespeare's plays: "dead as a doornail" (*Henry VI, Part 2*); "laughingstock" (*The Merry Wives of Windsor*); and "for goodness' sake" (*Henry VIII*).

TEACH

SETTING A PURPOSE

Direct students to use the Setting a Purpose prompt to focus their reading.

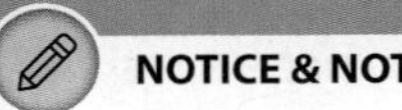

NOTICE & NOTE

Notice & Note

You can use the side margins to notice and note signposts in the text.

SETTING A PURPOSE

Look for clues that reveal the personalities of Romeo and Juliet. Write down any questions you generate during reading.

THE TIME: The 14th century

THE PLACE: Verona (və-rō´nə) and Mantua (măn´cho͞o-ə) in northern Italy

CAST

The Montagues

Lord Montague (mŏn´tə-gyo͞o)
Lady Montague
Romeo, son of Montague
Benvolio (bĕn-vō´lē-ō), nephew of Montague and friend of Romeo
Balthasar (bäl´thə-sär), servant to Romeo
Abram, servant to Montague

The Capulets

Lord Capulet (kăp´yo͞o-lĕt)
Lady Capulet
Juliet, daughter of Capulet
Tybalt (tĭb´əlt), nephew of Lady Capulet
Nurse to Juliet
Peter, servant to Juliet's nurse
Sampson, servant to Capulet
Gregory, servant to Capulet
An Old Man of the Capulet family

Others

Prince Escalus (ĕs´kə-ləs), ruler of Verona
Mercutio (mĕr-kyo͞o´shē-ō), kinsman of the prince and friend of Romeo
Friar Laurence, a Franciscan priest
Friar John, another Franciscan priest
Count Paris, a young nobleman, kinsman of the prince
Apothecary (ə-pŏth´ĭ-kĕr-ē)
Page to Paris
Chief Watchman
Three Musicians
An Officer
Chorus
Citizens of Verona, **Gentlemen** and **Gentlewomen** of both houses, **Maskers**, **Torchbearers**, **Pages**, **Guards**, **Watchmen**, **Servants**, and **Attendants**

ENGLISH LEARNER SUPPORT

Ask and Answer Questions Direct students to the cast of characters on page 288. Point out how the names are organized into three groups—two families and other characters. Read each name aloud, pausing to allow students to repeat it. Draw their attention to the phonetic pronunciations given for the more difficult names. Point out the details about how the characters are related to each other. Then have pairs take turns quizzing each other to familiarize themselves with the characters and to practice saying names and titles. For example, a student might say, "She is Romeo's mother. What's her name?" while his or her partner responds, "Lady Montague" or "Her name is Lady Montague," depending on their proficiency level. **Moderate/Light**

NOTICE & NOTE 

Prologue

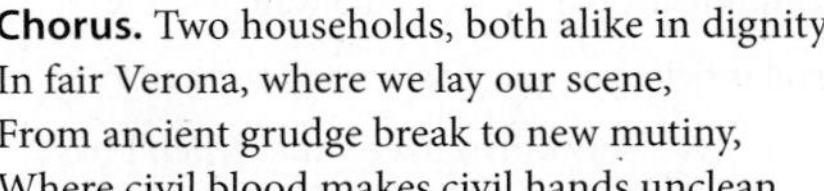

[*Enter* Chorus.]

Chorus. Two households, both alike in dignity,
In fair Verona, where we lay our scene,
From ancient grudge break to new mutiny,
Where civil blood makes civil hands unclean.
From forth the fatal loins of these two foes,
A pair of star-crossed lovers take their life,
Whose misadventured piteous overthrows
Doth with their death bury their parents' strife.
The fearful passage of their death-marked love,
And the continuance of their parents' rage,
Which, but their children's end, naught could remove,
Is now the two hours' traffic of our stage,
The which if you with patient ears attend,
What here shall miss, our toil shall strive to mend.

[*Exit.*]

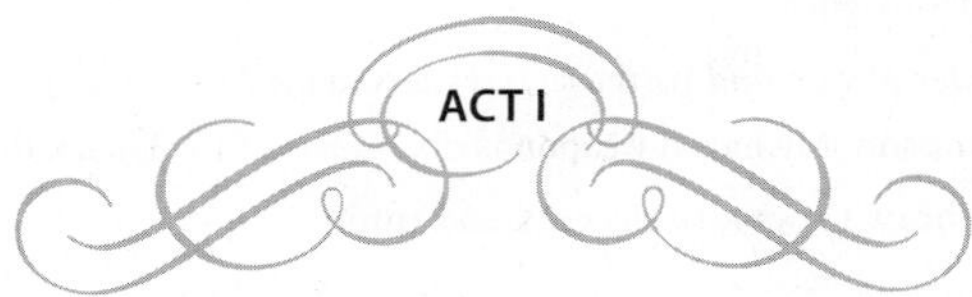

Scene 1 *A public square in Verona.*

[*Enter* Sampson *and* Gregory, *servants of the house of Capulet, armed with swords and bucklers* (*shields*).]

Sampson. Gregory, on my word, we'll not carry coals.

Gregory. No, for then we should be colliers.

Sampson. I mean, an we be in choler, we'll draw.

Gregory. Ay, while you live, draw your neck out of collar.

Sampson. I strike quickly, being moved.

Gregory. But thou art not quickly moved to strike.

Sampson. A dog of that house of Montague moves me.

Gregory. To move is to stir, and to be valiant is to stand. Therefore, if thou art moved, thou runnest away.

Sampson. A dog of that house shall move me to stand. I will take the wall of any man or maid of Montague's.

Gregory. That shows thee a weak slave, for the weakest goes to the wall.

3–4 ancient . . . unclean: A new outbreak of fighting (**mutiny**) between families has caused the citizens of Verona to have one another's blood on their hands.

6 star-crossed: doomed. The position of the stars when the lovers were born was not favorable. In Shakespeare's day, people took astrology very seriously.

7 misadventured: unlucky.

11 but: except for; **naught:** nothing.

14 what . . . mend: The play will fill in the details not mentioned in the prologue.

1–2 we'll not carry coals: we won't stand to be insulted; **colliers:** those involved in the dirty work of hauling coal, who were often the butt of jokes.

3–4 in choler: angry; **collar:** a hangman's noose.

11 take the wall: walk. People of higher rank had the privilege of walking closer to the wall, to avoid any water or garbage in the street.

ENGLISH LEARNER SUPPORT

Understand Puns Explain that the play opens with two Capulet servants (Sampson and Gregory) insulting each other through the use of puns, or plays on the multiple meanings of words. Ask students to underline instances of the word *move* in lines 5–11. Explain that in these lines, *move* is used to mean several different things. Have students look up the word *move* in a dictionary.

Then have partners work together to review lines 5–11. For each use of *move*, have students explain the word's meaning in context. Ask students to record their notes in a chart like this one:

line 5	*being moved* = when I'm angry
line 6	*moved to strike* = caused to strike
line 7	*a dog . . . moves me* = makes me angry
line 8	*to move is to stir* = change position
line 9	*if thou art moved* = made fearful
line 10	*a dog . . . shall move me to stand* = will cause me to fight

LIGHT

CLOSE READ SCREENCAST

Modeled Discussion In their eBook, have students view the Close Read Screencast, in which readers discuss and annotate the Prologue to Act I.

As a class, view and discuss the video.

 **Close Read Practice PDF**

TEACH

ANALYZE PARALLEL PLOTS

Remind students that in a full-length, complex drama, such as this one, there is often more than one story line. These **parallel plots** develop simultaneously along with the main plot—in this play, the love story of Romeo and Juliet. Explain that parallel plots often complicate the characters' lives and hinder their efforts to resolve the central conflict, or problem. Remind students that the feud between the Montagues and the Capulets is an important parallel plot.

Instruct students to reread lines 27–48 and the marginal notes. Ask: What does Sampson do when he sees the Montague servants? Why? *(In line 30 he pulls out his sword in anticipation of a fight. He bites his thumb at them [line 36], which is an insult. He wants to provoke them to fight.)* Why does he take back his gesture? *(He realizes that he could get into trouble if he is the first one to start the fight.)* What do the servants' actions reveal about the conflict between the two families? *(It is serious and may include bloodshed; it is a matter of pride; it involves everyone with a connection to the families.)* *(**Answer:** The parallel plot provides a backdrop of violence against which Romeo and Juliet's love will seem even more doomed.)*

English Learner Support

Summarize Events Display a two-column chart. In each row of the left column, write one of the sentences from this brief summary of lines 30–65: Gregory and Sampson start a fight by insulting Abram. Benvolio stops the fight. Tybalt arrives and fights with Benvolio.

Ask pairs or groups of students to match the sentence of the summary to the lines in the play that show each event taking place. Have students identify the words in the original text that helped them make their match. **MODERATE**

NOTICE & NOTE

14–24 Sampson's tough talk includes boasts about his ability to overpower women.

28 poor-John: a salted fish, considered fit only for poor people to eat.

33 marry: a short form of "by the Virgin Mary" and so a mild exclamation.

34–44 Gregory and Sampson decide to pick a fight by insulting the Montague servants with a rude gesture (**bite my thumb**).

ANALYZE PARALLEL PLOTS

Annotate: The storyline of the feud between the Capulets and Montagues runs parallel to the storyline of Romeo and Juliet. Mark the line(s) where the argument between the servants of the two households begins.

Predict: How might this parallel plot affect the main plot of the "star-crossed lovers"?

Sampson. 'Tis true; and therefore women, being the weaker vessels, are ever thrust to the wall. Therefore push I will Montague's men from the wall and thrust his maids to the wall.

Gregory. The quarrel is between our masters and us their men.

Sampson. 'Tis all one. I will show myself a tyrant. When I have fought with the men, I will be cruel with the maids: I will cut off their heads.

Gregory. The heads of the maids?

Sampson. Ay, the heads of the maids, or their maidenheads. Take it in what sense thou wilt.

Gregory. They must take it in sense that feel it.

Sampson. Me they shall feel while I am able to stand; and 'tis known I am a pretty piece of flesh.

Gregory. 'Tis well thou art not fish; if thou hadst, thou hadst been poor-John. Draw thy tool! Here comes two of the house of Montagues.

[*Enter* Abram *and* Balthasar, *servants to the Montagues.*]

Sampson. My naked weapon is out. Quarrel! I will back thee.

Gregory. How? turn thy back and run?

Sampson. Fear me not.

Gregory. No, marry. I fear thee!

Sampson. Let us take the law of our sides; let them begin.

Gregory. I will frown as I pass by, and let them take it as they list.

Sampson. Nay, as they dare. I will bite my thumb at them; which is disgrace to them, if they bear it.

Abram. Do you bite your thumb at us, sir?

Sampson. I do bite my thumb, sir.

Abram. Do you bite your thumb at us, sir?

Sampson [*aside* to Gregory]. Is the law of our side if I say ay?

Gregory [*aside* to Sampson]. No.

Sampson. No, sir, I do not bite my thumb at you, sir; but I bite my thumb, sir.

Gregory. Do you quarrel, sir?

Abram. Quarrel, sir? No, sir.

Sampson. But if you do, sir, I am for you. I serve as good a man as you.

WHEN STUDENTS STRUGGLE . . .

Summarize a Scene To increase students' understanding of what happens in this scene, ask for volunteers to represent the four servants, Benvolio, and Tybalt. Begin with the four servants "on the stage." Explain that Benvolio will enter the scene after line 50 and Tybalt will enter after line 58. Have students mark their lines. Then have student actors read their lines aloud, beginning with line 30. Cue students playing Benvolio and Tybalt to enter the "stage" at the proper time.

Ask students to work in pairs to write a brief summary of what happens in this scene. Have them explain how this scene helps them understand more about the feud between the two families.

Abram. No better.

Sampson. Well, sir.

[*Enter* Benvolio, *nephew of Montague and first cousin of Romeo.*]

Gregory [*aside* to Sampson]. Say "better." Here comes one of my master's kinsmen.

Sampson. Yes, better, sir.

Abram. You lie.

Sampson. Draw, if you be men. Gregory, remember thy swashing blow.

[*They fight.*]

Benvolio. Part, fools! [*beats down their swords*]
Put up your swords. You know not what you do.

[*Enter* Tybalt, *hot-headed nephew of Lady Capulet and first cousin of Juliet.*]

Tybalt. What, art thou drawn among these heartless hinds?
Turn thee, Benvolio! look upon thy death.

Benvolio. I do but keep the peace. Put up thy sword,
Or manage it to part these men with me.

Tybalt. What, drawn, and talk of peace? I hate the word
As I hate hell, all Montagues, and thee.
Have at thee, coward!

[*They fight.*]

[*Enter several of both houses, who join the fray; then enter* Citizens *and* Peace Officers, *with clubs.*]

Officer. Clubs, bills, and partisans! Strike! beat them down!

Citizens. Down with the Capulets! Down with the Montagues!

[*Enter old* Capulet *and* Lady Capulet.]

Capulet. What noise is this? Give me my long sword, ho!

Lady Capulet. A crutch, a crutch! Why call you for a sword?

Capulet. My sword, I say! Old Montague is come
And flourishes his blade in spite of me.

[*Enter old* Montague *and* Lady Montague.]

Montague. Thou villain Capulet!—Hold me not, let me go.

Lady Montague. Thou shalt not stir one foot to seek a foe.

[*Enter* Prince Escalus, *with attendants. At first no one hears him.*]

59 heartless hinds: cowardly servants.

63 drawn: with your sword out.

65 have at thee: Defend yourself.

66 bills, and partisans: spears.

69 A crutch . . . sword: You need a crutch more than a sword.

APPLYING ACADEMIC VOCABULARY

☐ attribute ☐ commit ☑ expose ☐ initiate ☑ underlie

Write and Discuss Have students turn to a partner to discuss the questions shown below. Guide students to include the academic vocabulary words *expose* and *underlie* in their responses. Ask volunteers to share their responses with the class.

- Review the conversation between Sampson and Gregory in Act I, Scene 1, lines 50–56. What does it **expose** about the servants' involvement?
- What do you think are the causes that **underlie** this feud between the families?

NOTICE & NOTE

74–81 The prince is furious about the street fighting caused by the feud. He orders the men to drop their weapons and pay attention.

77 pernicious: destructive.

82–90 Three… peace: The prince holds Capulet and Montague responsible for three recent street fights, each probably started by an offhand remark or insult (**airy word**). He warns that they will be put to death if any more fights occur.

***Exeunt*:** the plural form of *exit*, indicating that more than one person is leaving the stage.

97 Who … abroach: Who reopened this old argument?

99 adversary: enemy.

100 ere: before.

107 on part and part: some on one side, some on the other.

110 fray: fight.

113 drave: drove.

115 rooteth: grows.

Prince. Rebellious subjects, enemies to peace,
Profaners of this neighbor-stained steel—
Will they not hear? What, ho! you men, you beasts,
That quench the fire of your pernicious rage
With purple fountains issuing from your veins!
On pain of torture, from those bloody hands
Throw your mistempered weapons to the ground
And hear the sentence of your moved prince.
Three civil brawls, bred of an airy word
By thee, old Capulet, and Montague,
Have thrice disturbed the quiet of our streets
And made Verona's ancient citizens
Cast by their grave beseeming ornaments
To wield old partisans, in hands as old,
Cankered with peace, to part your cankered hate.
If ever you disturb our streets again,
Your lives shall pay the forfeit of the peace.
For this time all the rest depart away.
You, Capulet, shall go along with me;
And, Montague, come you this afternoon,
To know our farther pleasure in this case,
To old Freetown, our common judgment place.
Once more, on pain of death, all men depart.

[*Exeunt all but* Montague, Lady Montague, *and* Benvolio.]

Montague. Who set this ancient quarrel new abroach?
Speak, nephew, were you by when it began?

Benvolio. Here were the servants of your adversary
And yours, close fighting ere I did approach.
I drew to part them. In the instant came
The fiery Tybalt, with his sword prepared;
Which, as he breathed defiance to my ears,
He swung about his head and cut the winds,
Who, nothing hurt withal, hissed him in scorn.
While we were interchanging thrusts and blows,
Came more and more, and fought on part and part,
Till the Prince came, who parted either part.

Lady Montague. O, where is Romeo? Saw you him today?
Right glad I am he was not at this fray.

Benvolio. Madam, an hour before the worshiped sun
Peered forth the golden window of the East,
A troubled mind drave me to walk abroad,
Where, underneath the grove of sycamore
That westward rooteth from the city's side,

ENGLISH LEARNER SUPPORT

Comprehend Figurative Language Remind students that they can sometimes use the context of a figurative phrase to help define it. Ask students to underline the phrase "neighbor-stained steel" in line 75.

Then read aloud the side note and have pairs of students circle words and phrases, either in the side note or in the drama, that are clues to the meaning of this phrase. Call on a pair to explain the phrase. *(The phrase probably means "swords" because swords are made of steel, and the swords were used to fight other citizens of Verona.)* Ask students to underline each of the following phrases, circle context clues, and explain the phrase's meaning: "quench the fire" in line 77 *(show your anger)*; "purple fountains" in line 78 *(spurts of blood)*; "mistempered weapons" in line 80 *(swords used in anger)*; "cankered hate" in line 88 *(feud, diseased hate)*. Encourage students to use the same strategy to determine the meanings of other figurative expressions as they continue reading. **LIGHT**

So early walking did I see your son.
Towards him I made, but he was ware of me
And stole into the covert of the wood.
I—measuring his affections by my own,
Which then most sought where most might not be found,
Being one too many by my weary self—
Pursued my humor, not pursuing his,
And gladly shunned who gladly fled from me.

117–123 made: moved; **covert:** covering. Romeo saw Benvolio coming and hid in the woods. Benvolio himself was seeking solitude and did not go after him.

Montague. Many a morning hath he there been seen,
With tears augmenting the fresh morning's dew,
Adding to clouds more clouds with his deep sighs;
But all so soon as the all-cheering sun
Should in the farthest East begin to draw
The shady curtains from Aurora's bed,
Away from light steals home my heavy son
And private in his chamber pens himself,
Shuts up his windows, locks fair daylight out,
And makes himself an artificial night.
Black and portentous must this humor prove
Unless good counsel may the cause remove.

124–135 Romeo has been seen wandering through the woods at night, crying. At dawn he returns home and locks himself in his room. Montague feels that his son needs guidance.

129 Aurora's bed: Aurora was the goddess of the dawn.

134 portentous: indicating evil to come; threatening.

Benvolio. My noble uncle, do you know the cause?

Montague. I neither know it nor can learn of him.

Benvolio. Have you importuned him by any means?

138 importuned: asked in an urgent way.

Montague. Both by myself and many other friends;
But he, his own affections' counselor,
Is to himself—I will not say how true—
But to himself so secret and so close,
So far from sounding and discovery,
As is the bud bit with an envious worm
Ere he can spread his sweet leaves to the air
Or dedicate his beauty to the sun.
Could we but learn from whence his sorrows grow,
We would as willingly give cure as know.

140 his own affections' counselor: Romeo keeps to himself.

143–148 so far from . . . know: Finding out what Romeo is thinking is almost impossible. Montague compares his son to a young bud destroyed by the bite of a worm before it has a chance to open its leaves. Montague wants to find out what is bothering Romeo so he can help him.

[*Enter* Romeo *lost in thought.*]

Benvolio. See, where he comes. So please you step aside,
I'll know his grievance, or be much denied.

Montague. I would thou wert so happy by thy stay
To hear true shrift. Come, madam, let's away.

152 shrift: confession.

[*Exeunt* Montague *and* Lady.]

Benvolio. Good morrow, cousin.

Romeo. Is the day so young?

Benvolio. But new struck nine.

153 cousin: any relative or close friend. The informal version is *coz.*

WHEN STUDENTS STRUGGLE . . .

Make Inferences Explain to students that as a friend and relative of Romeo, Benvolio plays an important part. Ask students to reread lines 149–150 of Act I, Scene 1. What offer does Benvolio make to Lord Montague? What can students infer about why he makes it? *(Benvolio offers to find out what is wrong with Romeo. Benvolio has already shown himself to be sensitive and caring; his offer to find out what is wrong with Romeo is motivated by his concern for his cousin and for Lord and Lady Montague, who are very worried about their son.)*

For additional support, go to the **Reading Studio** and assign the following **Level Up Tutorial: Making Inferences About Characters.**

NOTICE & NOTE

Romeo. Ay me! sad hours seem long.
Was that my father that went hence so fast?

Benvolio. It was. What sadness lengthens Romeo's hours?

Romeo. Not having that which having makes them short.

Benvolio. In love?

Romeo. Out—

Benvolio. Of love?

Romeo. Out of her favor where I am in love.

Benvolio. Alas that love, so gentle in his view,
Should be so tyrannous and rough in proof!

Romeo. Alas that love, whose view is muffled still,
Should without eyes see pathways to his will!
Where shall we dine?—O me! What fray was here?—
Yet tell me not, for I have heard it all.

162–165 love: references to Cupid, the god of love, typically pictured as a blind boy with wings and a bow and arrow. Anyone hit by one of his arrows falls in love instantly.

ENGLISH LEARNER SUPPORT

Examine Dialogue Explain to students that in a conversation between friends, the speakers may not use complete sentences and may interrupt each other. Read aloud lines 155–167 as students follow along. Then have students:

- Underline incomplete sentences.
- Circle dashes.

Ask students to identify the function of the dashes based on their use in this passage. *(to indicate an interruption)* Then ask them how the incomplete sentences affect the sound of the dialogue. (*They make the dialogue seem rushed and emotional.*) **LIGHT**

Here's much to do with hate, but more with love.
Why then, O brawling love! O loving hate!
O anything, of nothing first create!
O heavy lightness! serious vanity!
Misshapen chaos of well-seeming forms!
Feather of lead, bright smoke, cold fire, sick health!
Still-waking sleep, that is not what it is!
This love feel I, that feel no love in this.
Dost thou not laugh?

Benvolio. No, coz, I rather weep.

Romeo. Good heart, at what?

Benvolio. At thy good heart's oppression.

Romeo. Why, such is love's transgression.
Griefs of mine own lie heavy in my breast,
Which thou wilt propagate, to have it prest
With more of thine. This love that thou hast shown
Doth add more grief to too much of mine own.
Love is a smoke raised with the fume of sighs;
Being purged, a fire sparkling in lovers' eyes;
Being vexed, a sea nourished with lovers' tears.
What is it else? A madness most discreet,
A choking gall, and a preserving sweet.
Farewell, my coz.

Benvolio. Soft! I will go along.
An if you leave me so, you do me wrong.

Romeo. Tut! I have lost myself; I am not here:
This is not Romeo, he's some other where.

Benvolio. Tell me in sadness, who is that you love?

Romeo. What, shall I groan and tell thee?

Benvolio. Groan? Why, no;
But sadly tell me who.

Romeo. Bid a sick man in sadness make his will.
Ah, word ill urged to one that is so ill!
In sadness, cousin, I do love a woman.

Benvolio. I aimed so near when I supposed you loved.

Romeo. A right good markman! And she's fair I love.

Benvolio. A right fair mark, fair coz, is soonest hit.

Romeo. Well, in that hit you miss. She'll not be hit
With Cupid's arrow. She hath Dian's wit,
And, in strong proof of chastity well armed,
From Love's weak childish bow she lives unharmed.

ANALYZE LITERARY DEVICES

Annotate: Romeo, confused and upset about love, describes his feelings using oxymorons, or contradictory expressions. Mark some of these expressions.

Analyze: How do these oxymorons help show the complexity of what Romeo is feeling?

176–182 Benvolio expresses his sympathy for Romeo. Romeo replies that this is one more problem caused by love. He now feels worse than before because he must carry the weight of Benvolio's sympathy along with his own grief.

184 purged: cleansed (of the smoke).

185 vexed: troubled.

187 gall: something causing bitterness or hate.

188 soft: Wait a minute.

192 sadness: seriousness.

201–204 She'll … unharmed: The girl isn't interested in falling in love. She is like Diana, the goddess of chastity.

ANALYZE LITERARY DEVICES

Remind students that an **oxymoron** is a phrase that is made up of contradictory terms. Have students discuss each oxymoron in lines 168–176 and how it makes sense in context. Then ask students to share their ideas about how Shakespeare's use of oxymorons affects the audience's understanding of Romeo's emotions. (***Answer:*** *The oxymorons show that Romeo is mystified by love. The love that he thought would bring him joy is causing him misery instead.*)

English Learner Support

Restate Oxymorons Read aloud lines 168–176 to students. Explain that Romeo is describing what it feels like to be in love with someone who doesn't love him back. Point out that love can make someone happy and confused at the same time, and that's why Romeo uses oxymorons, or phrases that include words with opposite meanings.

- Ask students which of these phrases are oxymorons: *cold snow* (*no*), *cold fire* (*yes*), *feather of lead* (*yes*), *heavy weights* (*no*), *heavy lightness* (*yes*). **SUBSTANTIAL**
- Display these frames and ask students to use them to explain the oxymorons *heavy lightness* (line 171), *bright smoke* (line 173), and *cold fire* (line 173): *The phrase _____ is an oxymoron because _____ and ____ have opposite meanings. _____ means _____, and _____ means _____.* **MODERATE**
- Ask pairs or small groups to find and list oxymorons in lines 168–176. Then have students write the meaning of each word or phrase in the oxymoron and the idea it conveys. **LIGHT**

The Tragedy of Romeo and Juliet: Act I, Scene 1 295

TEACH

NOTICE & NOTE

205–207 She will not ... gold: She is not swayed by Romeo's love or his wealth.

212–213 for beauty . . . posterity: She wastes her beauty, which will not be passed on to future generations.

215–216 to merit ... despair: The girl will reach heaven (**bliss**) by being so virtuous, which causes Romeo to feel despair; **forsworn to:** sworn not to.

221–222 'Tis ... more: That would only make me appreciate my own love's beauty more.

223 Masks were worn by Elizabethan women to protect their faces from the sun.

227–229 Show me . . . fair: A woman who is exceedingly (passing) beautiful will only remind me of my love, who is even prettier.

231 I'll pay . . . debt: I'll convince you you're wrong, or die trying.

1 bound: obligated.

4 reckoning: reputation.

6 what say . . . suit: Paris is asking for Capulet's response to his proposal to marry Juliet.

She will not stay the siege of loving terms,
Nor bide the encounter of assailing eyes,
Nor ope her lap to saint-seducing gold.
O, she is rich in beauty; only poor
That, when she dies, with beauty dies her store.

Benvolio. Then she hath sworn that she will still live chaste?

Romeo. She hath, and in that sparing makes huge waste;
For beauty, starved with her severity,
Cuts beauty off from all posterity.
She is too fair, too wise, wisely too fair
To merit bliss by making me despair.
She hath forsworn to love, and in that vow
Do I live dead that live to tell it now.

Benvolio. Be ruled by me: forget to think of her.

Romeo. O, teach me how I should forget to think!

Benvolio. By giving liberty unto thine eyes:
Examine other beauties.

Romeo. 'Tis the way
To call hers (exquisite) in question more.
These happy masks that kiss fair ladies' brows,
Being black, puts us in mind they hide the fair.
He that is strucken blind cannot forget
The precious treasure of his eyesight lost.
Show me a mistress that is passing fair,
What doth her beauty serve but as a note
Where I may read who passed that passing fair?
Farewell. Thou canst not teach me to forget.

Benvolio. I'll pay that doctrine, or else die in debt.

[*Exeunt.*]

Scene 2 *A street near the Capulet house.*

[*Enter* Capulet *with* Paris, *a kinsman of the Prince, and* Servant.]

Capulet. But Montague is bound as well as I,
In penalty alike; and 'tis not hard, I think,
For men so old as we to keep the peace.

Paris. Of honorable reckoning are you both,
And pity 'tis you lived at odds so long.
But now, my lord, what say you to my suit?

Capulet. But saying o'er what I have said before:
My child is yet a stranger in the world,
She hath not seen the change of fourteen years;

WHEN STUDENTS STRUGGLE . . .

Understand Historical Context Ask students to summarize the two main plots of the drama. *(the love story of Romeo and Juliet and the feud between the Montagues and Capulets)* Point out that another plot—one involving Romeo—was introduced in Scene 1 and that a fourth plot is introduced in Scene 2, line 6. Have partners work together to summarize these four parallel plots and record their notes in a chart such as the one shown on the next page.

Let two more summers wither in their pride
Ere we may think her ripe to be a bride.

Paris. Younger than she are happy mothers made.

Capulet. And too soon marred are those so early made.
The earth hath swallowed all my hopes but she;
She is the hopeful lady of my earth.
But woo her, gentle Paris, get her heart;
My will to her consent is but a part.
An she agree, within her scope of choice
Lies my consent and fair according voice.
This night I hold an old accustomed feast,
Whereto I have invited many a guest,
Such as I love, and you among the store,
One more, most welcome, makes my number more.
At my poor house look to behold this night
Earth-treading stars that make dark heaven light.
Such comfort as do lusty young men feel
When well-appareled April on the heel
Of limping Winter treads, even such delight
Among fresh female buds shall you this night
Inherit at my house. Hear all, all see,
And like her most whose merit most shall be;
Which, on more view of many, mine, being one,
May stand in number, though in reck'ning none.
Come, go with me. [*to* Servant, *giving him a paper*]
Go, sirrah, trudge about
Through fair Verona; find those persons out
Whose names are written there, and to them say,
My house and welcome on their pleasure stay.

[*Exeunt* Capulet *and* Paris.]

Servant. Find them out whose names are written here! It is written that the shoemaker should meddle with his yard and the tailor with his last, the fisher with his pencil and the painter with his nets; but I am sent to find those persons whose names are here writ, and can never find what names the writing person hath here writ. I must to the learned. In good time!

[*Enter* Benvolio *and* Romeo.]

Benvolio. Tut, man, one fire burns out another's burning;
One pain is lessened by another's anguish;
Turn giddy, and be holp by backward turning;
One desperate grief cures with another's languish.
Take thou some new infection to thy eye,
And the rank poison of the old will die.

10 Let two more summers . . . pride: let two more years pass.

14 The earth . . . she: All my children are dead except Juliet.

16 woo her: try to win her heart.

18–19 An . . . voice: I will give my approval to the one she chooses.

20 old accustomed feast: a traditional or annual party.

29–33 among . . . none: Tonight at the party you will see the loveliest girls in Verona, including Juliet. When you see all of them together, your opinion of Juliet may change.

34 sirrah: a term used to address a servant.

38–43 The servant cannot read. He confuses the craftsmen and their tools, tapping a typical source of humor for Elizabethan comic characters.

44–49 Tut, man . . . die: Benvolio says Romeo should find a new love—that a "new infection" will cure the old one.

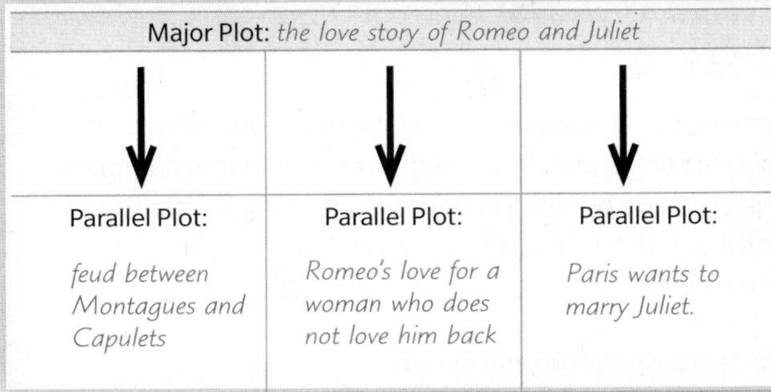

NOTICE & NOTE

55 God-den: good evening. Romeo interrupts his lament to talk to the servant.

56 God gi' go-den: God give you a good evening.

69 Rosaline: This is the woman that Romeo is in love with. Mercutio, a friend of both Romeo and the Capulets, is also invited to the party.

72 whither: where.

81 crush a cup of wine: slang for "drink some wine."

Romeo. Your plantain leaf is excellent for that.

Benvolio. For what, I pray thee?

Romeo. For your broken shin.

Benvolio. Why, Romeo, art thou mad?

Romeo. Not mad, but bound more than a madman is;
Shut up in prison, kept without my food,
Whipped and tormented and—God-den, good fellow.

Servant. God gi' go-den. I pray, sir, can you read?

Romeo. Ay, mine own fortune in my misery.

Servant. Perhaps you have learned it without book. But I pray, can you read anything you see?

Romeo. Ay, if I know the letters and the language.

Servant. Ye say honestly. Rest you merry!

[Romeo's *joking goes over the clown's head. He concludes that* Romeo *cannot read and prepares to seek someone who can.*]

Romeo. Stay, fellow; I can read. [*He reads.*]
"Signior Martino and his wife and daughters;
County Anselmo and his beauteous sisters;
The lady widow of Vitruvio;
Signior Placentio and his lovely nieces;
Mercutio and his brother Valentine;
Mine uncle Capulet, his wife, and daughters;
My fair niece Rosaline and Livia;
Signior Valentio and his cousin Tybalt;
Lucio and the lively Helena."
[*gives back the paper*]
A fair assembly. Whither should they come?

Servant. Up.

Romeo. Whither?

Servant. To supper, to our house.

Romeo. Whose house?

Servant. My master's.

Romeo. Indeed I should have asked you that before.

Servant. Now I'll tell you without asking. My master is the great rich Capulet; and if you be not of the house of Montagues, I pray come and crush a cup of wine. Rest you merry!

[*Exit.*]

Benvolio. At this same ancient feast of Capulet's
Sups the fair Rosaline whom thou so lovest,
With all the admired beauties of Verona.

Effect/Cause: *Benvolio vows to cheer Romeo up by taking him to the party.*

Cause: *Romeo loves a woman who does not return his love.*

Effect/Cause: *Romeo is depressed.*

Effect/Cause: *Romeo will see Rosaline and meet Juliet.*

WHEN STUDENTS STRUGGLE . . .

Analyze Cause and Effect To guide students' comprehension of the cause-and-effect relationship that drives the action of this part of the plot, have them work together to complete a chart similar to the one shown. Prompt students by filling in one or more of the boxes. Then have them review from line 175 in Scene 1 to line 101 in Scene 2 to complete the chart. Have students add to the chart as they read further.

For additional support, go to the **Reading Studio** and assign the following **Level Up Tutorial: Plot: Sequence of Events.**

Go thither, and with unattainted eye
Compare her face with some that I shall show,
And I will make thee think thy swan a crow.

Romeo. When the devout religion of mine eye
Maintains such falsehood, then turn tears to fires;
And these, who, often drowned, could never die,
Transparent heretics, be burnt for liars!
One fairer than my love? The all-seeing sun
Ne'er saw her match since first the world begun.

Benvolio. Tut! you saw her fair, none else being by,
Herself poised with herself in either eye;
But in that crystal scales let there be weighed
Your lady's love against some other maid
That I will show you shining at this feast,
And she shall scant show well that now shows best.

Romeo. I'll go along, no such sight to be shown,
But to rejoice in splendor of mine own.

[*Exeunt.*]

85 unattainted: unbiased; unprejudiced.

88–91 When . . . liars: If the love I have for Rosaline, which is like a religion, changes because of such a lie (that others may be more beautiful), let my tears be turned to fire and my eyes be burned.

94–99 Tut . . . best: You've seen Rosaline alone; now compare her with some other women.

100–101 Romeo agrees to go to the party, but only to see Rosaline.

Scene 3 *Capulet's house.*

[*Enter* Lady Capulet *and* Nurse.]

Lady Capulet. Nurse, where's my daughter? Call her forth to me.

Nurse. Now, by my maidenhead at twelve year old,
I bade her come. What, lamb! what, ladybird!
God forbid! Where's this girl? What, Juliet!

[*Enter* Juliet.]

Juliet. How now? Who calls?

Nurse. Your mother.

Juliet. Madam, I am here. What is your will?

Lady Capulet. This is the matter—Nurse, give leave awhile,
We must talk in secret. Nurse, come back again;
I have remembered me, thou's hear our counsel.
Thou knowest my daughter's of a pretty age.

Nurse. Faith, I can tell her age unto an hour.

Lady Capulet. She's not fourteen.

Nurse. I'll lay fourteen of my teeth—
And yet, to my teen be it spoken, I have but four—
She's not fourteen. How long is it now
To Lammastide?

Lady Capulet. A fortnight and odd days.

8–11 give leave . . . counsel: Lady Capulet seems nervous, not sure whether she wants the nurse to stay or leave; **of a pretty age:** of an attractive age, ready for marriage.

14 teen: sorrow.

16 Lammastide: August 1, a religious feast day. It is two weeks (**a fortnight**) away.

ENGLISH LEARNER SUPPORT

Listen and Answer Questions Explain that in Scene 2, Romeo and Benvolio meet a servant in the street. He has been sent out to invite people to a party, but he can't read the names on the invitation. Romeo reads the invitation for him and then asks for the name of the person for whom the servant works.

Ask students to listen as you read aloud lines 79–81. Then have students identify the servant's master. *(Lord Capulet, Juliet's father)* Then ask: What has Lord Capulet sent his servant to do? *(to invite people to a dinner party)*

Tell students to listen for the reason why Benevolio thinks Romeo should go to the party. Read aloud Benevolio's dialogue in lines 82–87. *(Rosaline will be at the party. Benevolio thinks that Romeo won't be so in love with Rosaline if there are other beautiful girls at the party.)*

MODERATE/LIGHT

NOTICE & NOTE

17–49 The nurse babbles about Juliet's childhood. Her own daughter, Susan, was the same age as Juliet, and died in infancy, leaving the nurse available to become a wet nurse (that is, breastfeed) to Juliet. An earthquake happened on the day she stopped breastfeeding Juliet (**she was weaned**).

27 laid wormwood to my dug: applied a plant with a bitter taste to her breast to discourage the child from breastfeeding.

33 tetchy: cranky.

34–35 Shake . . . trudge: When the dove house shook, I knew enough to leave.

37 by the rood: by the cross of Christ (a mild oath).

39 broke her brow: cut her forehead.

42–49 "Yea," . . . "Ay": The nurse's husband made a crude joke, asking the baby whether she'd fall the other way (on her back) when she was older. Although Juliet didn't understand the question, she stopped crying (**stinted**) and answered "Yes." The nurse finds the story so funny that she can't stop retelling it.

Nurse. Even or odd, of all days in the year,
Come Lammas Eve at night shall she be fourteen.
Susan and she (God rest all Christian souls!)
Were of an age. Well, Susan is with God;
She was too good for me. But, as I said,
On Lammas Eve at night shall she be fourteen;
That shall she, marry; I remember it well.
'Tis since the earthquake now eleven years;
And she was weaned (I never shall forget it),
Of all the days of the year, upon that day.
For I had then laid wormwood to my dug,
Sitting in the sun under the dovehouse wall.
My lord and you were then at Mantua—
Nay, I do bear a brain—But, as I said,
When it did taste the wormwood on the nipple
Of my dug and felt it bitter, pretty fool,
To see it tetchy and fall out with the dug!
Shake, quoth the dovehouse! 'Twas no need, I trow,
To bid me trudge.
And since that time it is eleven years,
For then she could stand alone; nay, by the rood,
She could have run and waddled all about;
For even the day before, she broke her brow;
And then my husband (God be with his soul!
'A was a merry man) took up the child.
"Yea," quoth he, "dost thou fall upon thy face?
Thou wilt fall backward when thou has more wit,
Wilt thou not, Jule?" And, by my holidam,
The pretty wretch left crying, and said "Ay."
To see now how a jest shall come about!
I warrant, an I should live a thousand years,
I never should forget it. "Wilt thou not, Jule?" quoth he,
And, pretty fool, it stinted, and said "Ay."

Lady Capulet. Enough of this. I pray thee hold thy peace.

Nurse. Yes, madam. Yet I cannot choose but laugh
To think it should leave crying and say "Ay."
And yet, I warrant, it had upon its brow
A bump as big as a young cock'rel's stone;
A perilous knock; and it cried bitterly.
"Yea," quoth my husband, "fallst upon thy face?
Thou wilt fall backward when thou comest to age,
Wilt thou not, Jule?" It stinted, and said "Ay."

Juliet. And stint thou too, I pray thee, nurse, say I.

WHEN STUDENTS STRUGGLE . . .

Cite Evidence Tell students that although it seems rambling, the nurse's speech in Act I, Scene 3, lines 17–49, serves to reveal character traits of the nurse and her relationship to Juliet. Explain that the nurse is another minor character who plays an important role. Read the nurse's long speech with students. Have students describe how the nurse feels about Juliet and cite evidence to support their inference. *(The nurse thinks of Juliet as her own child. She has detailed memories of important events in Juliet's childhood [lines 24–34].)* Ask students what they can infer about the nurse's character from what she says and how she says it. *(The nurse is very down-to-earth and coarse. She has a good sense of humor— she laughs at the recollection of how Juliet fell for her husband's joke [lines 36–49].)*

Nurse. Peace, I have done. God mark thee to his grace!
Thou wast the prettiest babe that e'er I nursed.
An I might live to see thee married once,
I have my wish.

Lady Capulet. Marry, that "marry" is the very theme
I came to talk of. Tell me, daughter Juliet,
How stands your disposition to be married?

Juliet. It is an honor that I dream not of.

Nurse. An honor? Were not I thine only nurse,
I would say thou hadst sucked wisdom from thy teat.

Lady Capulet. Well, think of marriage now. Younger than you,
Here in Verona, ladies of esteem,
Are made already mothers. By my count,
I was your mother much upon these years
That you are now a maid. Thus then in brief:
The valiant Paris seeks you for his love.

Nurse. A man, young lady! lady, such a man
As all the world—why he's a man of wax.

Lady Capulet. Verona's summer hath not such a flower.

Nurse. Nay, he's a flower, in faith—a very flower.

Lady Capulet. What say you? Can you love the gentleman?
This night you shall behold him at our feast.
Read o'er the volume of young Paris' face,

64 Marry . . . "marry": two different usages of the same word—the first meaning "by the Virgin Mary" and the second meaning "to wed."

73–74 I was . . . maid: I was your mother at about your age, yet you are still unmarried.

77 a man of wax: a man so perfect he could be a wax statue, of the type sculptors once used as models for their works.

82–89 Read . . . cover: Lady Capulet uses an extended metaphor that compares Paris to a book that Juliet should read.

ENGLISH LEARNER SUPPORT

Use Visual Support Remind students that images can add to their understanding of characters. Have students study the image from the 1968 film version of the play. Ask them to work in small groups of varied English levels to discuss these questions:

- What words could describe Juliet's attitude toward her mother in this image? Why? *(Possible answer: fearful, respectful, afraid—Juliet is not smiling and is looking serious.)*
- What does the image show about how the nurse and Juliet feel about each other? Explain. *(Possible answer: The nurse protects Juliet. Juliet feels close to the nurse. The nurse has her arm around Juliet, and Juliet is standing right next to her.)*
- Look at the face of each character and decide what each character is like and why. (The nurse is happy and funny; she is laughing. Juliet is young and serious. Lady Capulet is stern and strict; she is not smiling.)

Have groups share their answers to the questions.
ALL LEVELS

WHEN STUDENTS STRUGGLE . . .

Understand Historical Context Provide the following background information to help students understand the exchange between Juliet and her mother.

- Because people's lifespans were shorter, girls usually married in their early teens.
- The marriages of girls of wealthy or noble parents were arranged, often before the girls were even of marriageable age. Marrying a daughter into another influential family created powerful alliances and brought political and material advantages.

Ask students to predict whether Paris' hopes of marrying Juliet will complicate things for Romeo and Juliet.

The Tragedy of Romeo and Juliet: Act I, Scene 3 301

NOTICE & NOTE

84 every several lineament: each separate feature (of Paris's face).

87 margent . . . eyes: She compares Paris's eyes to the margin of a page, where notes are written to explain the content.

88–91 This . . . hide: This beautiful book (Paris) needs only a cover (wife) to become even better. He may be hiding even more wonderful qualities inside.

96 Women get bigger (pregnant) when they marry.

98–100 I'll look . . . fly: I'll look at him with the intention of liking him, if simply looking can make me like him; **endart**: look deeply, as if penetrating with a dart.

103–104 extremity: great confusion; **straight**: immediately.

105 the County stays: Count Paris is waiting for you.

1–10 What, shall this . . . be gone: Romeo asks whether they should send a messenger announcing their arrival at the party. Benvolio says that they'll dance one dance (**measure them a measure**) and then leave.

And find delight writ there with beauty's pen;
Examine every several lineament,
And see how one another lends content;
And what obscured in this fair volume lies
Find written in the margent of his eyes.
This precious book of love, this unbound lover,
To beautify him only lacks a cover.
The fish lives in the sea, and 'tis much pride
For fair without the fair within to hide.
That book in many's eyes doth share the glory,
That in gold clasps locks in the golden story;
So shall you share all that he doth possess,
By having him making yourself no less.

Nurse. No less? Nay, bigger! Women grow by men.

Lady Capulet. Speak briefly, can you like of Paris' love?

Juliet. I'll look to like, if looking liking move;
But no more deep will I endart mine eye
Than your consent gives strength to make it fly.

[*Enter a* Servingman.]

Servingman. Madam, the guests are come, supper served up, you called, my young lady asked for, the nurse cursed in the pantry, and everything in extremity. I must hence to wait. I beseech you follow straight.

Lady Capulet. We follow thee. [*Exit* Servingman.] Juliet, the County stays.

Nurse. Go, girl, seek happy nights to happy days.

[*Exeunt.*]

Scene 4 *A street near the Capulet house.*

[*Enter* Romeo, Mercutio, Benvolio, *with five or six other* Maskers; Torchbearers.]

Romeo. What, shall this speech be spoke for our excuse?
Or shall we on without apology?

Benvolio. The date is out of such prolixity.
We'll have no Cupid hoodwinked with a scarf,
Bearing a Tartar's painted bow of lath,
Scaring the ladies like a crowkeeper;
Nor no without-book prologue, faintly spoke
After the prompter, for our entrance;
But let them measure us by what they will,
We'll measure them a measure, and be gone.

WHEN STUDENTS STRUGGLE . . .

Compare and Contrast Characters Display a Venn diagram on the board. Then ask students to reread Lord Capulet's comments to Paris in Scene 2, lines 13–33, as well as what Lady Capulet says in Scene 3, lines 80–95. Have students work together to identify ways in which Lord and Lady Capulet's attitudes about Juliet's marriage to Paris are the same and different. *(Lord Capulet: does not want Juliet to marry too early; believes early mothers are marred. Both: wish for Juliet's happiness; hope that she will be agreeable to the plan. Lady Capulet: feels it is time Juliet is married; thinks Paris is a good husband for Juliet.)*

For additional support, go to the **Reading Studio** and assign the following **Level Up Tutorial: Character Traits.**

Romeo. Give me a torch. I am not for this ambling;
Being but heavy, I will bear the light.

Mercutio. Nay, gentle Romeo, we must have you dance.

Romeo. Not I, believe me. You have dancing shoes
With nimble soles; I have a soul of lead
So stakes me to the ground I cannot move.

Mercutio. You are a lover. Borrow Cupid's wings
And soar with them above a common bound.

Romeo. I am too sore enpierced with his shaft
To soar with his light feathers, and so bound
I cannot bound a pitch above dull woe.
Under love's heavy burden do I sink.

Mercutio. And, to sink in it, should you burden love—
Too great oppression for a tender thing.

Romeo. Is love a tender thing? It is too rough,
Too rude, too boist'rous, and it pricks like thorn.

Mercutio. If love be rough with you, be rough with love.
Prick love for pricking, and you beat love down.
Give me a case to put my visage in.
A visor for a visor! What care I
What curious eye doth quote deformities?
Here are the beetle brows shall blush for me.

Benvolio. Come, knock and enter, and no sooner in
But every man betake him to his legs.

Romeo. A torch for me! Let wantons light of heart
Tickle the senseless rushes with their heels;
For I am proverbed with a grandsire phrase,
I'll be a candle-holder and look on;
The game was ne'er so fair, and I am done.

Mercutio. Tut, dun's the mouse, the constable's own word!
If thou art Dun, we'll draw thee from the mire
Of, save your reverence, love, wherein thou stickst
Up to the ears. Come, we burn daylight, ho!

Romeo. Nay, that's not so.

Mercutio. I mean, sir, in delay
We waste our lights in vain, like lamps by day.
Take our good meaning, for our judgment sits
Five times in that ere once in our five wits.

Romeo. And we mean well in going to this masque;
But 'tis no wit to go.

12 heavy: sad. Romeo makes a joke based on the meanings of *heavy* and *light*.

14–32 Romeo continues to talk about his sadness, while Mercutio jokingly makes fun of him to try to cheer him up.

29–32 Give . . . for me: Give me a mask for an ugly face. I don't care if people notice my appearance. Here, look at my bushy eyebrows.

34 betake . . . legs: dance.

35–38 Let . . . look on: Let playful people tickle the grass (**rushes**) on the floor with their dancing. I'll follow the old saying (**grandsire phrase**) and just be a spectator.

40–43 Tut . . . daylight: Mercutio jokes, using various meanings of the word dun, which sounds like Romeo's last word, done. He concludes by saying they should not waste time (**burn daylight**).

ENGLISH LEARNER SUPPORT

Understand Inverted Word Order Explain that Shakespeare occasionally uses inverted word order in his sentences, putting the verb before the subject. Tell students that rearranging the subject and verb may help them understand the line more easily. Ask pairs of students to rewrite these lines, putting the subject first: Scene 3, line 94: "So shall you share all that he doth possess." *(You shall share all that he doth possess.)*; Scene 4, line 22: "Under love's heavy burden do I sink." *(I do sink under love's heavy burden.)* Encourage students to rearrange the word order when they see other inverted sentences. **MODERATE**

ENGLISH LEARNER SUPPORT

Identify and Use Pronouns Direct students to the side note for lines 53–95. Read the note aloud. Then direct students to the long speech Mercutio makes in lines 53–95. Explain that in long text passages such as this one, it is helpful to pay attention to the pronouns because the pronouns offer clues about who or what is being described. Have pairs or small groups skim lines 53–95 and circle the pronouns that show that Mercutio is describing Queen Mab. Point out that because Queen Mab is female, they should look for the pronouns *she*, *her*, and *hers*. Once students have identified pronouns in lines 53–95, have students write two sentences about Mercutio and two sentences about Queen Mab, using the correct pronoun to match the antecedent.
MODERATE

NOTICE & NOTE

53–95 Mercutio talks of Mab, queen of the fairies, a folktale character well-known to Shakespeare's audience. His language includes vivid descriptions, puns, and satires of people; and ultimately he gets caught up in his own wild imaginings.

55 agate stone: jewel for a ring.

57 atomies: tiny creatures.

59 spinners' legs: spiders' legs.

61 traces: harness.

Mercutio. Why, may one ask?
Romeo. I dreamt a dream tonight.
Mercutio. And so did I.
Romeo. Well, what was yours?
Mercutio. That dreamers often lie.
Romeo. In bed asleep, while they do dream things true.
Mercutio. O, then I see Queen Mab hath been with you.
She is the fairies' midwife, and she comes
In shape no bigger than an agate stone
On the forefinger of an alderman,
Drawn with a team of little atomies
Athwart men's noses as they lie asleep;
Her wagon spokes made of long spinners' legs,
The cover, of the wings of grasshoppers;
Her traces, of the smallest spider's web;

Her collars, of the moonshine's wat'ry beams;
Her whip, of cricket's bone; the lash, of film;
Her wagoner, a small grey-coated gnat,
Not half so big as a round little worm
Pricked from the lazy finger of a maid;
Her chariot is an empty hazelnut,
Made by the joiner squirrel or old grub,
Time out o' mind the fairies' coachmakers.
And in this state she gallops night by night
Through lovers' brains, and then they dream of love;
O'er courtiers' knees, that dream on curtsies straight;
O'er lawyers' fingers, who straight dream on fees;
O'er ladies' lips, who straight on kisses dream,
Which oft the angry Mab with blisters plagues,
Because their breaths with sweetmeats tainted are.
Sometime she gallops o'er a courtier's nose,
And then dreams he of smelling out a suit,
And sometime comes she with a tithe-pig's tail
Tickling a parson's nose as 'a lies asleep,
Then dreams he of another benefice.
Sometime she driveth o'er a soldier's neck,
And then dreams he of cutting foreign throats,
Of breaches, ambuscadoes, Spanish blades,
Of healths five fathom deep; and then anon
Drums in his ear, at which he starts and wakes,
And being thus frighted, swears a prayer or two
And sleeps again. This is that very Mab
That plaits the manes of horses in the night
And bakes the elflocks in foul sluttish hairs,
Which once untangled much misfortune bodes.
This is the hag, when maids lie on their backs,
That presses them and learns them first to bear,
Making them women of good carriage.
This is she—

Romeo. Peace, peace, Mercutio, peace!
Thou talkst of nothing.

Mercutio. True, I talk of dreams;
Which are the children of an idle brain,
Begot of nothing but vain fantasy;
Which is as thin of substance as the air,
And more inconstant than the wind, who woos
Even now the frozen bosom of the North
And, being angered, puffs away from thence,
Turning his face to the dew-dropping South.

68 joiner: carpenter.

77–78 Sometimes she . . . suit: Sometimes Mab makes a member of the king's court dream of receiving special favors.

81 benefice: a well-paying position for a clergyman.

84 ambuscadoes: ambushes; **Spanish blades:** high-quality Spanish swords.

89 plaits: braids.

96–103 True . . . South: Mercutio is trying to keep Romeo from taking his dreams too seriously.

TO CHALLENGE STUDENTS . . .

Discuss the Function of a Scene Have students review Scene 4. Point out that this scene does not seem to advance the plot. Ask students: Is Scene 4 merely an amusing digression, or does it fulfill a greater purpose? Have students discuss the question in small groups and be prepared to share their conclusions with the class. Have them consider whether this scene:

- contributes to an essential understanding of any character
- expresses important themes through the speeches and interactions of the characters
- affects the pacing of the play
- conveys mood

For additional support, go to the **Reading Studio** and assign the following **Level Up Tutorial: Elements of Drama.**

The Tragedy of Romeo and Juliet: Act I, Scene 4 305

NOTICE & NOTE

Benvolio. This wind you talk of blows us from ourselves.
Supper is done, and we shall come too late.

106–111 Romeo, still depressed, fears that some terrible event caused by the stars will begin at the party. Remember the phrase "star-crossed lovers" from the prologue.

Romeo. I fear, too early; for my mind misgives
Some consequence, yet hanging in the stars,
Shall bitterly begin his fearful date
With this night's revels and expire the term
Of a despised life, closed in my breast,
By some vile forfeit of untimely death.
But he that hath the steerage of my course
Direct my sail! On, lusty gentlemen!

Benvolio. Strike, drum.

[*Exeunt.*]

Scene 5 *A hall in Capulet's house; the scene of the party.*

[Servingmen *come forth with napkins.*]

1–13 These opening lines are a comic conversation among three servants as they work.

2 trencher: wooden plate.

6–7 plate: silverware and silver plates; **marchpane**: marzipan, a sweet made from almond paste.

First Servingman. Where's Potpan, that he helps not to take way? He shift a trencher! he scrape a trencher!

Second Servingman. When good manners shall lie all in one or two men's hands, and they unwashed too, 'tis a foul thing.

First Servingman. Away with the joint-stools, remove the court-cupboard, look to the plate. Good thou, save me a piece of marchpane and, as thou lovest me, let the porter let in Susan Grindstone and Nell. Anthony, and Potpan!

Second Servingman. Ay, boy, ready.

First Servingman. You are looked for and called for, asked for and sought for, in the great chamber.

Third Servingman. We cannot be here and there too. Cheerly, boys! Be brisk awhile, and the longer liver take all.

[*Exeunt.*]

14–27 Capulet welcomes his guests and invites them all to dance. He alternates talking with his guests and telling the servants what to do.

17–18 She that . . . corns: Any woman too shy to dance will be assumed to have corns, ugly and painful growths on the toes.

20 visor: mask.

[Maskers *appear with* Capulet, Lady Capulet, Juliet, *all the* Guests, *and* Servants.]

Capulet. Welcome, gentlemen! Ladies that have their toes
Unplagued with corns will have a bout with you.
Ah ha, my mistresses! which of you all
Will now deny to dance? She that makes dainty,
She I'll swear hath corns. Am I come near ye now?
Welcome, gentlemen! I have seen the day
That I have worn a visor and could tell
A whispering tale in a fair lady's ear,
Such as would please. 'Tis gone, 'tis gone, 'tis gone!

ENGLISH LEARNER SUPPORT

Analyze Dialogue Ask students to listen as you read aloud lines 14–31. Have partners make the following annotations:

- Underline the lines Lord Capulet speaks to his guests.
- Box the lines he directs to the servants and musicians.
- Circle the lines he speaks to his cousin.

Ask students how the actor playing this part would show to whom he was speaking. Point out that in the written text, cues such as "gentlemen" help to identify the person being spoken to.
MODERATE/LIGHT

You are welcome, gentlemen! Come, musicians, play.
A hall, a hall! give room! and foot it, girls.

[*Music plays and they dance.*]

More light, you knaves! and turn the tables up,
And quench the fire, the room is grown too hot.
Ah, sirrah, this unlooked-for sport comes well.
Nay, sit, nay, sit, good cousin Capulet,
For you and I are past our dancing days.
How long is't now since last yourself and I
Were in a mask?

Second Capulet. By'r Lady, thirty years.

Capulet. What, man? 'Tis not so much, 'tis not so much!
'Tis since the nuptial of Lucentio,
Come Pentecost as quickly as it will,
Some five-and-twenty years, and then we masked.

Second Capulet. 'Tis more, 'tis more! His son is elder, sir;
His son is thirty.

Capulet. Will you tell me that?
His son was but a ward two years ago.

Romeo [*to a* Servingman]. What lady's that, which doth enrich
the hand
Of yonder knight?

Servant. I know not, sir.

Romeo. O, she doth teach the torches to burn bright!
It seems she hangs upon the cheek of night
Like a rich jewel in an Ethiop's ear—
Beauty too rich for use, for earth too dear!
So shows a snowy dove trooping with crows
As yonder lady o'er her fellows shows.
The measure done, I'll watch her place of stand
And, touching hers, make blessed my rude hand.
Did my heart love till now? Forswear it, sight!
For I ne'er saw true beauty till this night.

Tybalt. This, by his voice, should be a Montague.
Fetch me my rapier, boy. What, dares the slave
Come hither, covered with an antic face
To fleer and scorn at our solemnity?
Now, by the stock and honor of my kin,
To strike him dead I hold it not a sin.

Capulet. Why, how now, kinsman? Wherefore storm you so?

Tybalt. Uncle, this is a Montague, our foe;

28–38 Capulet and his relative watch the dancing as they talk of days gone by.

33 nuptial: marriage.

44–45 Ethiop's ear: the ear of an Ethiopian (African); **for earth too dear:** too precious for this world.

52–57 Tybalt recognizes Romeo's voice and tells his servant to get his sword (**rapier**). He thinks Romeo has come to make fun of (**fleer**) their party.

ENGLISH LEARNER SUPPORT

Analyze Figurative Language Read lines 42–51 aloud. Explain important words and phrases that may be unfamiliar to students, such as *torches*. Point out that Romeo's dialogue contains a lot of figurative language, including similes and hyperbole. Review with students that **hyperbole** is exaggeration. For example, the statement "You're the best friend on the planet!" is hyperbole. Remind students that a **simile** is a comparison between two unlike things using as or *like*.

- Ask students: Is the line "she doth teach the torches to burn bright!" (line 42) an example of hyperbole, or simile? *(hyperbole)* Are the lines "It seems she hangs upon the cheek of night / Like a rich jewel in an Ethiop's ear—" an example of hyperbole, or simile? *(simile)* **SUBSTANTIAL**
- Ask pairs of students to review lines 42–51 and locate at least one example of hyperbole and one example of a simile. Then have partners compare what they found with another pair of students and discuss the ideas or feelings that the figurative language conveys in each case. **MODERATE/LIGHT**

IMPROVE READING FLUENCY

Targeted Passage Use echo reading to help students use appropriate phrasing and emphasis in reading formal English in Scene 5, lines 42–51. Begin by reading the paragraph aloud, emphasizing pauses and phrasing. Then have students echo your reading as you read it a second and third time, first by pausing after each line, and then reading it again with pauses after each line. You may choose to conclude with choral reading as all students read this complex verse aloud together.

Go to the **Reading Studio** for additional support in developing fluency.

NOTICE & NOTE

A villain, that is hither come in spite
To scorn at our solemnity this night.

Capulet. Young Romeo is it?

Tybalt. 'Tis he, that villain Romeo.

Capulet. Content thee, gentle coz, let him alone.
'A bears him like a portly gentleman,
And, to say truth, Verona brags of him
To be a virtuous and well-governed youth.
I would not for the wealth of all this town
Here in my house do him disparagement.
Therefore be patient, take no note of him.
It is my will; the which if thou respect,
Show a fair presence and put off these frowns,
An ill-beseeming semblance for a feast.

Tybalt. It fits when such a villain is a guest.
I'll not endure him.

64 portly: dignified.

68 do him disparagement: speak critically or insultingly to him.

72 semblance: outward appearance.

WHEN STUDENTS STRUGGLE . . .

Analyze Character Motivation Point out to students that a character's motivations can often be inferred from details in the text. With students, read and reread lines 63–72.

Ask students how Lord Capulet reacts to Romeo's presence at the ball and why he does so. *(Surprisingly, Lord Capulet is content to have Romeo stay. He does not anticipate that Romeo will cause any trouble. He also does not want Tybalt to be responsible for harm coming to Romeo on Capulet's own property after the Prince's warning to avoid conflict with the Montagues.)*

For additional support, go to the **Reading Studio** and assign the following  **Level Up Tutorial: Character Motivation.**

Capulet. He shall be endured.
What, goodman boy? I say he shall. Go to!
Am I the master here, or you? Go to!
You'll not endure him? God shall mend my soul!
You'll make a mutiny among my guests!
You will set cock-a-hoop! You'll be the man.

Tybalt. Why, uncle, 'tis a shame.

Capulet. Go to, go to!
You are a saucy boy. Is't so, indeed?
This trick may chance to scathe you. I know what.
You must contrary me! Marry, 'tis time.—
Well said, my hearts!—You are a princox—go!
Be quiet, or—More light, more light!—For shame!
I'll make you quiet; what!—Cheerly, my hearts!

Tybalt. Patience perforce with willful choler meeting
Makes my flesh tremble in their different greeting.
I will withdraw; but this intrusion shall,
Now seeming sweet, convert to bitter gall.

[*Exit.*]

Romeo. If I profane with my unworthiest hand
This holy shrine, the gentle fine is this:
My lips, two blushing pilgrims, ready stand
To smooth that rough touch with a tender kiss.

Juliet. Good pilgrim, you do wrong your hand too much,
Which mannerly devotion shows in this;
For saints have hands that pilgrims' hands do touch,
And palm to palm is holy palmers' kiss.

Romeo. Have not saints lips, and holy palmers too?

Juliet. Ay, pilgrim, lips that they must use in prayer.

Romeo. O, then, dear saint, let lips do what hands do!
They pray; grant thou, lest faith turn to despair.

Juliet. Saints do not move, though grant for prayers' sake.

Romeo. Then move not while my prayer's effect I take.
Thus from my lips, by thine my sin is purged.

[*kisses her*]

Juliet. Then have my lips the sin that they have took.

Romeo. Sin from my lips? O trespass sweetly urged!
Give me my sin again.

[*kisses her*]

75 goodman boy: a term used to address an inferior; **Go to:** Stop, that's enough!

79 set cock-a-hoop: cause everything to be upset.

82–83 scathe: harm; **I know ... contrary me:** I know what I'm doing! Don't you dare challenge my authority.

84–86 Capulet intersperses his angry speech to Tybalt with comments to his guests and servants.

87–90 Patience . . . gall: Tybalt says he will restrain himself, but his suppressed anger (**choler**) makes his body shake.

91–108 Romeo and Juliet are in the middle of the dance floor, with eyes only for each other. They touch the palms of their hands. Their conversation revolves around Romeo's comparison of his lips to pilgrims who have traveled to a holy shrine. Juliet goes along with the comparison.

105 purged: washed away.

ENGLISH LEARNER SUPPORT

Analyze Figurative Language Tell students that the words that Romeo and Juliet speak to each other when they first meet develop an extended metaphor. Remind students that a metaphor is a comparison made between two things that are not alike but have something in common. Have students view the photo from the film *Romeo and Juliet* on page 308. Check that students understand the word *palm*. Then read aloud lines 91–108 and the related side note. Explain the terms *shrine*, *pilgrim*, *devotion*, *saint*, and *purged*. Then display these frames and have students complete them orally:

Romeo compares Juliet's hand to a_____. (shrine)

He compares his lips to two_____. (pilgrims)

A _____ is a holy place. (shrine)

A _____ is a person who goes to a place to pay religious _____. (pilgrim, devotion)

Romeo and Juliet use religious words because _____. (they have strong feelings for one another)

SUBSTANTIAL/MODERATE

TO CHALLENGE STUDENTS . . .

Analyze Poetic Form Have students copy lines 91–104, omitting each character's name but preserving the line arrangement. Have pairs or small groups analyze the lines as a poem.

- First, ask them to identify the rhyme scheme of the lines. *(a, b, a, b, c, b, c, b, d, e, d,e, f, f)*
- Then have them explain what type of poem these lines create when put together. *(sonnet)*
- Next, have students consider the sound and literary devices, the punctuation, and the meaning that is brought out by combining the lines. Ask students if there is still an understanding of two speakers, even with their names omitted. Have pairs or groups contribute their insights to class discussion.

For additional support, go to the **Reading Studio** and assign the following **Level Up Tutorial: Elements of Poetry.**

TEACH

ANALYZE LITERARY DEVICES

Remind students that a playwright may use **foreshadowing,** or hinting at what may happen in the future, to maintain the audience's interest in his or her plot. Ask students what line or lines they marked. *("If he be married / My grave is like to be my wedding bed.")* Then discuss what they seem to foreshadow. (***Answer:*** *They suggest that Juliet's death will be linked to her marriage to Romeo.)*

NOTICE & NOTE

108 kiss by the book: Juliet could mean "You kiss like someone who has practiced." Or she could be teasing Romeo, meaning "You kiss coldly, as though you had learned how by reading a book."

109 At the nurse's message, Juliet walks to her mother.

115 shall have the chinks: shall become rich.

116 my life . . . debt: my life belongs to my enemy.

120 towards: coming up.

ANALYZE LITERARY DEVICES

Annotate: Foreshadowing is the use of hints or clues to suggest events that will happen later in the story. Mark the line(s) where Juliet's words foreshadow what will come later in the play.

Analyze: What do these lines suggest about Juliet's fate?

137–138 Too early . . . too late: I fell in love with him before I learned who he is; **prodigious:** abnormal; unlucky.

Juliet. You kiss by the book.

Nurse. Madam, your mother craves a word with you.

Romeo. What is her mother?

Nurse. Marry, bachelor,
Her mother is the lady of the house.
And a good lady, and a wise and virtuous.
I nursed her daughter that you talked withal.
I tell you, he that can lay hold of her
Shall have the chinks.

Romeo. Is she a Capulet?
O dear account! my life is my foe's debt.

Benvolio. Away, be gone, the sport is at the best.

Romeo. Ay, so I fear; the more is my unrest.

Capulet. Nay, gentlemen, prepare not to be gone;
We have a trifling foolish banquet towards.

[*They whisper in his ear.*]

Is it e'en so? Why then, I thank you all.
I thank you, honest gentlemen. Good night.
More torches here! [*Exeunt* Maskers.] Come on then, let's to bed.
Ah, sirrah, by my fay, it waxes late;
I'll to my rest.

[*Exeunt all but* Juliet *and* Nurse.]

Juliet. Come hither, nurse. What is yond gentleman?

Nurse. The son and heir of old Tiberio.

Juliet. What's he that now is going out of door?

Nurse. Marry, that, I think, be young Petruchio.

Juliet. What's he that follows there, that would not dance?

Nurse. I know not.

Juliet. Go ask his name.—If he be married,
My grave is like to be my wedding bed.

Nurse. His name is Romeo, and a Montague,
The only son of your great enemy.

Juliet. My only love, sprung from my only hate!
Too early seen unknown, and known too late!
Prodigious birth of love it is to me
That I must love a loathed enemy.

WHEN STUDENTS STRUGGLE . . .

Identify Sequence of Events To guide students' comprehension of plot, have them work in pairs to create a timeline charting the events that have happened since the Capulets' party. Have students identify approximately when each of these events takes place to help them see how compressed, or full of events, this part of the plot is.

Ask students to present their completed timelines to the class. Clarify differences between individual timelines. Then create a class version to display and add to during Act II.

For additional support, assign the following **Level Up Tutorial: Plot: Sequence of Events.**

NOTICE & NOTE

Nurse. What's this? what's this?

Juliet. A rhyme I learnt even now
Of one I danced withal.

[*One calls within, "Juliet."*]

Nurse. Anon, anon!
Come, let's away; the strangers all are gone.

[*Exeunt.*]

CHECK YOUR UNDERSTANDING

Answer these questions before moving on to the selection activities.

1 What role does Benvolio play in the fights that occur in Scene 1?

- **A** He starts the fights.
- **B** He runs away from the fights.
- **C** He tries to break up the fights.
- **D** He encourages others to fight.

2 Romeo's parents are concerned about him because —

- **F** they think his friend Mercutio is a bad influence on him
- **G** they're afraid he'll be arrested for fighting in the streets
- **H** they don't want him to be on friendly terms with the Capulets
- **J** they know something is bothering him but don't know what it is

3 Where do Romeo and Juliet first meet?

- **A** In a tavern
- **B** In a public square
- **C** At a costume party
- **D** At the Montagues' house

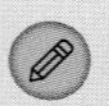

CHECK YOUR UNDERSTANDING

Answers:

1. *C*
2. *J*
3. *C*

If students answer any questions incorrectly, have them reread the text to confirm their understanding. Then they may proceed to ANALYZE THE TEXT on page 312.

ENGLISH LEARNER SUPPORT

Oral Assessment Use the following questions to assess students' comprehension and speaking skills.

1. How is Benvolio involved in the fights in Scene 1? *(He tries to break up the fights.)*
2. Why are Romeo's parents worried about him? *(They know something is bothering him.)*
3. Where do Romeo and Juliet first meet? *(They meet at a costume party.)*

SUBSTANTIAL/MODERATE

APPLY

ANALYZE THE TEXT

Possible answers:

1. **DOK 2:** *Act I's Prologue establishes the fate of the main characters by telling the audience exactly what they are going to see: a play about two "star-crossed lovers" who will die by the end of the play. The lovers are from feuding families, and the families will reconcile, but it will be too late. Shakespeare reveals the fate of the main characters in the Prologue to show that they will struggle against something that has already been decided and also to heighten the tragedy of the story. The audience will understand that it is the failure of the two families to make peace that will lead to the deaths of Romeo and Juliet.*
2. **DOK 2:** *Paraphrases will vary. If students review the line in context, they may point out that Juliet is suggesting that if she can't marry Romeo (because he is already married), then she will die single. The passage hints at Juliet's death, which comes soon after her marriage.*
3. **DOK 4:** *Tybalt and Benvolio are foils. Tybalt is brash and combative; Benvolio is reserved and contemplative. Romeo and Mercutio can also be seen as foils. Romeo is an impulsive romantic, and Mercutio, who is realistic and values common sense, often ridicules Romeo's dreamy romanticism.*
4. **DOK 1:** *The beginning of Act I, Scene I, is humorous as the Capulet servants trade puns using the words* coals, colliers, choler, *and* collar. *In Act 1, Scene 2, there is a funny exchange when another servant assumes Romeo cannot read. In Act 1, Scene 3, the nurse can't stop herself from telling an inappropriate story that is sure to amuse the audience.*
5. **DOK 4:** *Once Romeo realizes that Juliet is a member of the Capulet family, he feels conflicted. He is in love with her, yet his family's hatred of the Capulets means that he must also think of her as an enemy. Romeo will have to decide whether to continue to pursue Juliet.*

CREATE AND PRESENT

Speaking Activity: Discussion Remind students to ask clarifying questions of other group members if they do not understand a comment. The process of asking and answering questions can help everyone understand an issue more clearly and take the discussion in new directions.

After students have written summaries of the most important points of their discussion, ask volunteers to read them aloud or post them for the class.

RESPOND

ANALYZE THE TEXT

Support your responses with evidence from the text. NOTEBOOK

1. **Interpret** An important **theme**, or message, in *Romeo and Juliet* is the struggle against fate, or forces that determine how a person's life will turn out. Explain how Act I's Prologue establishes the fate of the main characters and introduces the struggles they will face. Why do you think Shakespeare tells the audience the fate of the main characters before the play begins?
2. **Predict** Review the foreshadowing in Scene 5, line 133, where Juliet says: "My grave is like to be my wedding bed." Paraphrase this line, then predict what event it foreshadows.
3. **Analyze** A **foil** is a character who highlights, through sharp contrast, the qualities of another character. Identify two sets of characters in Act I who are foils for each other. What do you learn about the characters by seeing them contrasted to one another?
4. **Identify** *Romeo and Juliet* is a play that deals with serious and tragic events, yet Shakespeare weaves in jokes and comical situations throughout Act I. One example is the conversation among the servants at the beginning of Scene 5. Identify other examples of **comic relief** in the first act.
5. **Notice & Note** In Act 1, Scene 5, there is an Aha Moment when Romeo realizes that Juliet is a Capulet (lines 116–117). How might this change the direction of the plot?

CREATE AND PRESENT

Speaking Activity: Discussion In *Romeo and Juliet*, characters are motivated by passion and strong emotions.

- ❑ Notice that throughout Act I, Shakespeare contrasts themes of love and hate through characters' words and actions.
- ❑ Work with a partner to identify passages that express love or hate. Often these emotions are expressed using the dramatic conventions of asides and soliloquies.
- ❑ Read the passages aloud with your partner. Read with feeling to express the emotions that underlie the words. Ask questions about any words or language you do not understand.
- ❑ Discuss what dramatic effect Shakespeare creates by pairing these two emotions in the first act of the play. Listen closely and respectfully to your partner's ideas.
- ❑ Write a summary that outlines the main points of your discussion.

Go to the **Speaking and Listening Studio** for more on participating in collaborative discussions.

SETTING A PURPOSE

Look for words and phrases that reveal the developing relationship between Romeo and Juliet and the intensity of their feelings for each other. Write down any questions you generate during reading.

Prologue

[*Enter* Chorus.]

Chorus. Now old desire doth in his deathbed lie,
And young affection gapes to be his heir.
That fair for which love groaned for and would die,
With tender Juliet matched, is now not fair.
Now Romeo is beloved, and loves again,
Alike bewitched by the charm of looks;
But to his foe supposed he must complain,
And she steal love's sweet bait from fearful hooks.
Being held a foe, he may not have access
To breathe such vows as lovers use to swear,
And she as much in love, her means much less
To meet her new beloved anywhere;
But passion lends them power, time means, to meet,
Temp'ring extremities with extreme sweet.

[*Exit.*]

1–4 Now . . . fair: Romeo's love for Rosaline (**old desire**) is now dead. His new love for Juliet (**young affection**) replaces the old.

7 but . . . complain: Juliet, a Capulet, is Romeo's supposed enemy, yet she is the one to whom he must plead (**complain**) his love.

14 Temp'ring . . . sweet: moderating great difficulties with extreme delights.

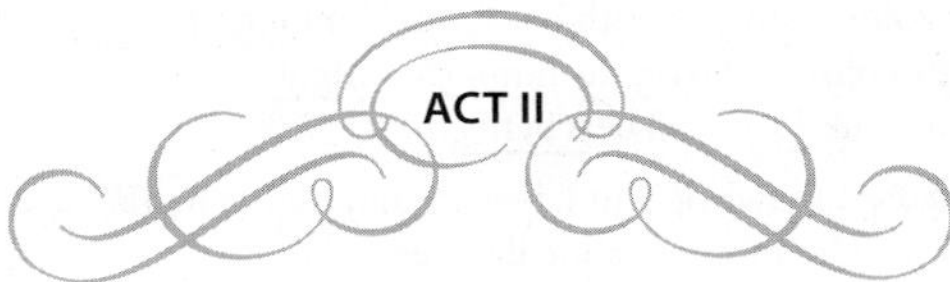

Scene 1 *A lane by the wall of Capulet's orchard.*

[*Enter* Romeo *alone.*]

Romeo. Can I go forward when my heart is here?
Turn back, dull earth, and find thy center out.

[*climbs the wall and leaps down within it*]

[*Enter* Benvolio *with* Mercutio.]

Benvolio. Romeo! my cousin Romeo! Romeo!

Mercutio. He is wise,
And, on my life, hath stol'n him home to bed.

Benvolio. He ran this way, and leapt this orchard wall.
Call, good Mercutio.

Mercutio. Nay, I'll conjure too.

1–2 Can . . . out: How can I leave when Juliet is still here? My body (**dull earth**) has to find its heart (**center**).

6 conjure: use magic to call him.

SETTING A PURPOSE

Direct students to use the Setting a Purpose prompt to focus their reading.

ENGLISH LEARNER SUPPORT

Identify Pronoun Antecedents Remind students that in English, each pronoun must agree in gender and number with its antecedent—the word or words to which the pronoun refers. Read aloud the Prologue. Have students circle each pronoun, underline each antecedent, and draw an arrow from the pronoun to its antecedent. Then work with students to summarize this information in a chart like the one here.

Pronoun	Antecedent
his (lines 1, 2)	*old desire (Rosaline)*
his / he (lines 7, 9)	*Romeo*
she / her (lines 8, 11, 12)	*Juliet*
them (line 13)	*Romeo and Juliet*

SUBSTANTIAL

WHEN STUDENTS STRUGGLE . . .

Understand the Role of the Chorus Point out that the Chorus (lines 1–14) has the dual function of summarizing the action from the previous act and giving an overview of what is to come. Ask students to discuss the conflict Romeo and Juliet will encounter in the pursuit of their love. *(As enemies, they will not find it easy to see each other.)* What lines support the idea that love will find a way? *(lines 13–14: "But passion lends them power, time means, to meet, / Temp'ring extremities with extreme sweet.")*

For additional support, go to the **Reading Studio** and assign the following **Level Up Tutorial: Elements of Drama.**

TEACH

ANALYZE LITERARY DEVICES

Remind students that a **foil** is a character whose personality and attitude contrast sharply with those of another character, serving to emphasize the other character's attributes and traits.

Point out that the most notorious foil in *The Tragedy of Romeo and Juliet* is Mercutio. He is Romeo's best friend and also Romeo's foil. He's quick and witty and fun to be around, but he can be volatile and push things too far. As neither a Montague or a Capulet, Mercutio is free to socialize with both households. He is related to both Prince Escalus and Count Paris.

Explain that in this scene, Mercutio contrasts with Benvolio. Point out Mercutio's lengthy speeches in contrast to Benvolio's short dialogue. Note that the name Mercutio is related to *mercurial,* which means "changeable." In one instant he is joking; in the next, he is fighting. Benvolio's name, on the other hand, is similar to *benevolent,* which can be traced to the Latin *bene,* meaning "good."

Ask students what Benvolio's responses in lines 16–43 of Scene 1 reveal about him and how he acts as a foil to Mercutio. (***Answer:*** *Benvolio's thoughtful responses are a sharp contrast to Mercutio's colorful language. They make Mercutio's behavior seem even more outlandish.)*

NOTICE & NOTE

8–21 Appear . . . us: Mercutio jokes about Romeo's lovesickness.

ANALYZE LITERARY DEVICES

Annotate: Character foils have contrasting traits. Read the exchange between Mercutio and Benvolio in lines 16–42 and mark Benvolio's responses.

Analyze: How does Benvolio act as a foil to Mercutio in this scene?

23–29 'Twould . . . raise up him: It would anger him if I called a stranger to join his beloved (**mistress**), but I'm only calling Romeo to join her.

31 To be . . . night: to keep company with the night, which is as gloomy as Romeo is.

34 medlar: a fruit that looks like a small brown apple.

39 truckle bed: trundle bed, a small bed that fits beneath a bigger one.

Romeo! humors! madman! passion! lover!
Appear thou in the likeness of a sigh;
Speak but one rhyme, and I am satisfied!
Cry but "Ay me!" pronounce but "love" and "dove";
Speak to my gossip Venus one fair word,
One nickname for her purblind son and heir,
Young Adam Cupid, he that shot so trim
When King Cophetua loved the beggar maid!
He heareth not, he stirreth not, he moveth not;
The ape is dead, and I must conjure him.
I conjure thee by Rosaline's bright eyes,
By her high forehead and her scarlet lip,
By her fine foot, straight leg, and quivering thigh,
And the demesnes that there adjacent lie,
That in thy likeness thou appear to us!

Benvolio. An if he hear thee, thou wilt anger him.

Mercutio. This cannot anger him. 'Twould anger him
To raise a spirit in his mistress' circle
Of some strange nature, letting it there stand
Till she had laid it and conjured it down.
That were some spite; my invocation
Is fair and honest and in his mistress' name
I conjure only but to raise up him.

Benvolio. Come, he hath hid himself among these trees
To be consorted with the humorous night.
Blind is his love, and best befits the dark.

Mercutio. If love be blind, love cannot hit the mark.
Now will he sit under a medlar tree
And wish his mistress were that kind of fruit
As maids call medlars when they laugh alone.
Oh, Romeo, that she were, O, that she were
An open et cetera, thou a pop'rin pear!
Romeo, good night. I'll to my truckle bed;
This field-bed is too cold for me to sleep.
Come, shall we go?

Benvolio. Go then, for 'tis in vain
To seek him here that means not to be found.

[*Exeunt.*]

314 Unit 4

Scene 2 *Capulet's orchard.*

[*Enter* Romeo.]

Romeo. He jests at scars that never felt a wound.

[*Enter* Juliet *above at a window.*]

But soft! What light through yonder window breaks?
It is the East, and Juliet is the sun!
Arise, fair sun, and kill the envious moon,
Who is already sick and pale with grief
That thou her maid art far more fair than she.
Be not her maid, since she is envious;
Her vestal livery is but sick and green,
And none but fools do wear it; cast it off.
It is my lady; O, it is my love!
O that she knew she were!
She speaks, yet she says nothing. What of that?
Her eye discourses; I will answer it.
I am too bold; 'tis not to me she speaks.
Two of the fairest stars in all the heaven,
Having some business, do entreat her eyes
To twinkle in their spheres till they return.
What if her eyes were there, they in her head?
The brightness of her cheek would shame those stars
As daylight doth a lamp; her eyes in heaven
Would through the airy region stream so bright
That birds would sing and think it were not night.
See how she leans her cheek upon her hand!
O that I were a glove upon that hand,
That I might touch that cheek!

Juliet. Ay me!

Romeo. She speaks.
O, speak again, bright angel! for thou art
As glorious to this night, being o'er my head,
As is a winged messenger of heaven
Unto the white-upturned wond'ring eyes
Of mortals that fall back to gaze on him
When he bestrides the lazy-pacing clouds
And sails upon the bosom of the air.

Juliet. O Romeo, Romeo! wherefore art thou Romeo?
Deny thy father and refuse thy name!
Or, if thou wilt not, be but sworn my love,
And I'll no longer be a Capulet.

1 He jests . . . wound: Romeo has overheard Mercutio and comments that Mercutio makes fun of love because he has never been wounded by it.

13–14 Her eye . . . speaks: Romeo shifts back and forth between wanting to speak to Juliet and being afraid.

15–22 Two of . . . not night: Romeo compares Juliet's eyes to stars in the sky.

25 Juliet begins to speak, not knowing that Romeo is nearby.

26–32 thou art . . . of the air: He compares Juliet to an angel (**winged messenger of heaven**) who stands on (**bestrides**) the clouds.

33 wherefore: why. Juliet asks why Romeo is who he is—someone from her enemy's family.

WHEN STUDENTS STRUGGLE . . .

Analyze Soliloquy Remind students that Shakespeare often makes use of the dramatic form of speech called a **soliloquy.** In a soliloquy, the character is alone and, unrestrained by the presence of others, speaks his or her innermost thoughts. Ask a student volunteer to read Romeo's soliloquy aloud. Ask students what provokes Romeo to speak aloud. *(He thinks he sees Juliet in the window and cannot restrain his emotion.)* What does this soliloquy reveal about his thoughts? *(It shows that he is enraptured by Juliet's beauty, that he idealizes her, and that he is uncertain about how to communicate with her.)*

For additional support, go to the **Reading Studio** and assign the following **Level UpTutorial: Elements of Drama.**

TEACH

ANALYZE PARALLEL PLOTS

Review the basic conflict that stands in the way of Romeo and Juliet's relationship, eliciting from students that it is their families' feud. Explain that in Act II, Scene 2, lines 38–49, Juliet considers the implications of Romeo's being a Montague, her family's enemy.

Organize students into pairs and assign each pair two or three lines to paraphrase. Call on pairs to write their paraphrases on the board in order. Read them together as a class.

Ask students to express Juliet's main idea in this speech. Make sure that students note the idea that a name does not hold the essence of a person; it is just a superficial formality. Then have students share their ideas about how the parallel plot of the feud between the two families is affecting the plot of Romeo and Juliet's love story. (***Answer:*** *It raises the stakes in the scene and heightens the tension because the reader knows that Romeo could die for visiting Juliet.)*

NOTICE & NOTE

43–47 Juliet tries to convince herself that a name is just a meaningless word that has nothing to do with the person. She asks Romeo to get rid of (**doff**) his name.

52–53 Juliet is startled that someone hiding (**bescreened**) nearby hears her private thoughts (**counsel**).

ANALYZE PARALLEL PLOTS

Annotate: Mark the words in lines 62–67 that refer to the feud between the Capulets and Montagues.

Analyze: How does the parallel plot of the feud affect the romance between Romeo and Juliet?

66–69 With . . . me: Love helped me climb (**o'erperch**) the walls. Neither walls nor your relatives are a hindrance (**let**) to me.

72–73 Look . . . enmity: Smile on me, and I will be defended against my enemies' hatred (**enmity**).

Romeo [*aside*]. Shall I hear more, or shall I speak at this?

Juliet. 'Tis but thy name that is my enemy.
Thou art thyself, though not a Montague.
What's Montague? It is nor hand, nor foot,
Nor arm, nor face, nor any other part
Belonging to a man. O, be some other name!
What's in a name? That which we call a rose
By any other name would smell as sweet.
So Romeo would, were he not Romeo called,
Retain that dear perfection which he owes
Without that title. Romeo, doff thy name;
And for that name, which is no part of thee,
Take all myself.

Romeo. I take thee at thy word.
Call me but love, and I'll be new baptized;
Henceforth I never will be Romeo.

Juliet. What man art thou that, thus bescreened in night,
So stumblest on my counsel?

Romeo. By a name
I know not how to tell thee who I am.
My name, dear saint, is hateful to myself,
Because it is an enemy to thee.
Had I it written, I would tear the word.

Juliet. My ears have yet not drunk a hundred words
Of that tongue's utterance, yet I know the sound.
Art thou not Romeo, and a Montague?

Romeo. Neither, fair saint, if either thee dislike.

Juliet. How camest thou hither, tell me, and wherefore?
The orchard walls are high and hard to climb,
And the place death, considering who thou art,
If any of my kinsmen find thee here.

Romeo. With love's light wings did I o'erperch these walls;
For stony limits cannot hold love out,
And what love can do, that dares love attempt.
Therefore thy kinsmen are no let to me.

Juliet. If they do see thee, they will murder thee.

Romeo. Alack, there lies more peril in thine eye
Than twenty of their swords! Look thou but sweet,
And I am proof against their enmity.

IMPROVE READING FLUENCY

Targeted Passage Point out that Scene 2 contains the famous balcony scene, with soliloquies delivered by both Romeo and Juliet. Remind students that a **soliloquy** is a speech given by a character alone onstage which reveals the character's thoughts or feelings. Read lines 1–51 aloud with appropriate emphasis and emotion. Then have students take turns reading lines 1–51 to a partner. As one partner reads, encourage the other partner to mark poetic language, including similes and metaphors. Have pairs of students share their annotations and discuss how Shakespeare's language makes this scene so memorable.

Go to the **Reading Studio** for additional support in developing fluency.

Juliet. I would not for the world they saw thee here.

Romeo. I have night's cloak to hide me from their sight;
And but thou love me, let them find me here.
My life were better ended by their hate
Than death prorogued, wanting of thy love.

Juliet. By whose direction foundst thou out this place?

Romeo. By love, that first did prompt me to enquire.
He lent me counsel, and I lent him eyes.
I am no pilot, yet, wert thou as far
As that vast shore washed with the farthest sea,
I would adventure for such merchandise.

78 than death . . . love: than my death postponed (**prorogued**) if you don't love me.

ENGLISH LEARNER SUPPORT

Use Visual Support Direct students to the movie still on page 317. Ask students to identify who is in the photo. (*Juliet and Romeo*) Have students point to the balcony. Remind students that a balcony is an area upstairs and outside a building where people can sit or stand. Ask students how Romeo got to the balcony. *(He climbed up there.)* Then ask students: Do Juliet's parents know that Romeo is there? *(no)* Is Romeo in danger there? *(yes)* Why? *(Their families are fighting.)* Why is Romeo there if it is so dangerous? *(He wanted to see Juliet.)* Have students suggest words that describe how Romeo and Juliet look in this photo. *(Students may suggest words such as worried or sad.)* **SUBSTANTIAL/MODERATE**

NOTICE & NOTE

85–89 Thou . . . compliment: Had I known you were listening, I would have gladly (**fain**) behaved more properly, but now it's too late for good manners (**farewell compliment**).

92–93 At . . . laughs: Jove, the king of the gods, laughs at lovers who lie to each other.

95–101 Or if . . . strange: You might think I've fallen in love too easily and that I'm too outspoken. But I'll be truer to you than those who play games to hide their real feelings (**be strange**).

117 I have . . . contract: I am concerned about this declaration of love (**contract**).

Juliet. Thou knowest the mask of night is on my face;
Else would a maiden blush bepaint my cheek
For that which thou hast heard me speak tonight.
Fain would I dwell on form—fain, fain deny
What I have spoke; but farewell compliment!
Dost thou love me? I know thou wilt say "Ay";
And I will take thy word. Yet, if thou swearst,
Thou mayst prove false. At lovers' perjuries,
They say Jove laughs. O gentle Romeo,
If thou dost love, pronounce it faithfully.
Or if thou thinkst I am too quickly won,
I'll frown, and be perverse, and say thee nay,
So thou wilt woo; but else, not for the world.
In truth, fair Montague, I am too fond,
And therefore thou mayst think my 'havior light;
But trust me, gentleman, I'll prove more true
Than those that have more cunning to be strange.
I should have been more strange, I must confess,
But that thou overheardst, ere I was ware,
My true love's passion. Therefore pardon me,
And not impute this yielding to light love,
Which the dark night hath so discovered.

Romeo. Lady, by yonder blessed moon I swear,
That tips with silver all these fruit-tree tops—

Juliet. O, swear not by the moon, the inconstant moon,
That monthly changes in her circled orb,
Lest that thy love prove likewise variable.

Romeo. What shall I swear by?

Juliet. Do not swear at all;
Or if thou wilt, swear by thy gracious self,
Which is the god of my idolatry,
And I'll believe thee.

Romeo. If my heart's dear love—

Juliet. Well, do not swear. Although I joy in thee,
I have no joy of this contract tonight.
It is too rash, too unadvised, too sudden;
Too like the lightning, which doth cease to be
Ere one can say "It lightens." Sweet, good night!
This bud of love, by summer's ripening breath,
May prove a beauteous flow'r when next we meet.

WHEN STUDENTS STRUGGLE . . .

Understand Hyperbole Point out that Romeo and Juliet frequently use **hyperbole**, or exaggerated language, to express their love. Have students identify examples of hyperbole in Juliet's dialogue in Act II, Scene 2, lines 131–136. *("My bounty is as boundless as the sea, / My love as deep"; "both are infinite")* Ask students to explain the effect of that hyperbole. *(It shows how strong Juliet's feelings are for Romeo.)*

For additional support, go to the **Reading Studio** and assign the following **Level Up Tutorial: Figurative Language.**

Good night, good night! As sweet repose and rest
Come to thy heart as that within my breast!

Romeo. O, wilt thou leave me so unsatisfied?

Juliet. What satisfaction canst thou have tonight?

Romeo. The exchange of thy love's faithful vow for mine.

Juliet. I gave thee mine before thou didst request it;
And yet I would it were to give again.

Romeo. Wouldst thou withdraw it? For what purpose, love?

Juliet. But to be frank and give it thee again.
And yet I wish but for the thing I have.
My bounty is as boundless as the sea,
My love as deep; the more I give to thee,
The more I have, for both are infinite.
I hear some noise within. Dear love, adieu!

[Nurse *calls within.*]

Anon, good nurse! Sweet Montague, be true.
Stay but a little, I will come again.

[*Exit.*]

Romeo. O blessed, blessed night! I am afeard,
Being in night, all this is but a dream,
Too flattering-sweet to be substantial.

[*Re-enter* Juliet, *above.*]

Juliet. Three words, dear Romeo, and good night indeed.
If that thy bent of love be honorable,
Thy purpose marriage, send me word tomorrow,
By one that I'll procure to come to thee,
Where and what time thou wilt perform the rite;
And all my fortunes at thy foot I'll lay
And follow thee my lord throughout the world.

Nurse [*within*]. Madam!

Juliet. I come, anon.—But if thou meanst not well,
I do beseech thee—

Nurse [*within*]. Madam!

Juliet. By-and-by I come.—
To cease thy suit and leave me to my grief.
Tomorrow will I send.

Romeo. So thrive my soul—

Juliet. A thousand times good night! [*Exit.*]

ANALYZE LITERARY DEVICES

Annotate: Mark the lines that contain foreshadowing.

Analyze: How do these lines foreshadow what may come later?

150–151 But if . . . thee: Juliet is still worried that Romeo is not serious.

ANALYZE LITERARY DEVICES

Remind students that authors sometimes use **foreshadowing**, or hinting that something is going to happen, in order to keep readers interested in the plot. Shakespeare uses foreshadowing in *The Tragedy of Romeo and Juliet* to create dramatic irony, tension, and suspense, building up to the dramatic ending of the "star-crossed lovers." Foreshadowing also helps to buffer the emotional trauma a reader might experience from the tragic deaths of the young lovers.

Read aloud the Analyze Literary Devices prompt and ask partners to locate an example of foreshadowing as Romeo and Juliet say "goodnight." *(Romeo says, "I am afeard, / Being in night, all this is but a dream, / Too flattering-sweet to be substantial.")* Ask students what this foreshadows. (***Answer:*** *Romeo's fear that his experience may be a dream foreshadows that his romance with Juliet is doomed.)*

APPLYING ACADEMIC VOCABULARY

❑ **attribute** ☑ **commit** ❑ **expose** ☑ **initiate** ❑ **underlie**

Write and Discuss Have students turn to a partner to discuss the questions below. Guide students to include the academic vocabulary words *commit* and *initiate* in their responses. Ask volunteers to share their responses with the class.

- How must Romeo show that he is willing to **commit** to Juliet?
- Why does Shakespeare have each character overhear the other as a way to **initiate** their relationship?

ANALYZE LITERARY DEVICES

Remind students that figurative language is a powerful way to express emotions and ideas without wordy explanations. **Similes** are comparisons between two unlike things using *as* or *like*.

Highlight some examples of similes in *The Tragedy of Romeo and Juliet*. For example, in Act I, Scene 4, lines 25–26, Romeo compares love to a thorn: "Is love a tender thing? it is too rough, / Too rude, too boist'rous, and it pricks like thorn." Romeo uses another simile in Act I, Scene 5, lines 43–44. Referring to Juliet, he says: "It seems she hangs upon the cheek of night / Like a rich jewel in an Ethiop's ear."

Then call on a student to identify the simile in Act II, Scene 2, lines 156–157, and explain what it compares. (***Answer:*** *Lovers and schoolboys: Lovers meet as eagerly as schoolboys leave their books; lovers separate with the sadness of boys going to school.)*

ANALYZE LITERARY DEVICES

Remind students that an **oxymoron** is a figure of speech that combines contradictory words. Ask students if they can come up with some oxymorons on their own and share them with the class. Give them a couple of examples such as "seriously funny" or "open secret." Then call on volunteers to share their examples. Encourage students to keep a list of oxymorons from *The Tragedy of Romeo and Juliet* as they continue to read.

Direct students to the Analyze Literary Devices question at the bottom of page 320. Have partners compare responses. Then invite students to share their ideas with the class. (***Answer:*** *The oxymoron shows that Juliet feels both the sweetness of Romeo's love and the sorrow of parting from him. It foreshadows the sorrow that each will feel at the other's death.)*

NOTICE & NOTE

ANALYZE LITERARY DEVICES
Annotate: Underline the simile in lines 156–157.

Interpret: What is being compared?

158–163 Hist . . . name: I wish I could speak your name as loudly as a falconer calls his falcon (**tassel-gentle**), but because of my parents I must whisper. **Echo** was a nymph in Greek mythology whose unreturned love for Narcissus caused her to waste away till only her voice was left.

177–182 I would . . . liberty: I know you must go, but I want you close to me like a pet bird that a thoughtless child (**wanton**) keeps on a string.

ANALYZE LITERARY DEVICES
Annotate: Mark the expression in lines 183–186 that is an oxymoron.

Analyze: How does this oxymoron foreshadow the fates of both Romeo and Juliet?

189 ghostly father: spiritual adviser or priest.

Romeo. A thousand times the worse, to want thy light!
Love goes toward love as schoolboys from their books;
But love from love, towards school with heavy looks.

[*Enter* Juliet *again, above.*]

Juliet. Hist! Romeo, hist! O for a falc'ner's voice
To lure this tassel-gentle back again!
Bondage is hoarse and may not speak aloud;
Else would I tear the cave where Echo lies,
And make her airy tongue more hoarse than mine
With repetition of my Romeo's name.
Romeo!

Romeo. It is my soul that calls upon my name.
How silver-sweet sound lovers' tongues by night,
Like softest music to attending ears!

Juliet. Romeo!

Romeo. My sweet?

Juliet. What o'clock tomorrow
Shall I send to thee?

Romeo. By the hour of nine.

Juliet. I will not fail. 'Tis twenty years till then.
I have forgot why I did call thee back.

Romeo. Let me stand here till thou remember it.

Juliet. I shall forget, to have thee still stand there,
Rememb'ring how I love thy company.

Romeo. And I'll still stay, to have thee still forget,
Forgetting any other home but this.

Juliet. 'Tis almost morning. I would have thee gone—
And yet no farther than a wanton's bird,
That lets it hop a little from her hand,
Like a poor prisoner in his twisted gyves,
And with a silk thread plucks it back again,
So loving-jealous of his liberty.

Romeo. I would I were thy bird.

Juliet. Sweet, so would I.
Yet I should kill thee with much cherishing.
Good night, good night! Parting is such sweet sorrow,
That I shall say good night till it be morrow.

[*Exit.*]

Romeo. Sleep dwell upon thine eyes, peace in thy breast!
Would I were sleep and peace, so sweet to rest!
Hence will I to my ghostly father's cell,

His help to crave and my dear hap to tell.
[*Exit.*]

Scene 3 *Friar Laurence's cell in the monastery.*

[*Enter* Friar Laurence *alone, with a basket.*]

Friar Laurence. The grey-eyed morn smiles on the frowning night,
Chequ'ring the Eastern clouds with streaks of light;
And flecked darkness like a drunkard reels
From forth day's path and Titan's fiery wheels.
Now, ere the sun advance his burning eye
The day to cheer and night's dank dew to dry,
I must upfill this osier cage of ours
With baleful weeds and precious-juiced flowers.
The earth that's nature's mother is her tomb,
What is her burying grave, that is her womb;
And from her womb children of divers kind
We sucking on her natural bosom find;
Many for many virtues excellent,
None but for some, and yet all different.
O, mickle is the powerful grace that lies
In plants, herbs, stones, and their true qualities;
For naught so vile that on the earth doth live
But to the earth some special good doth give;
Nor aught so good but, strained from that fair use,
Revolts from true birth, stumbling on abuse.
Virtue itself turns vice, being misapplied,
And vice sometimes by action dignified.
Within the infant rind of this small flower
Poison hath residence, and medicine power;
For this, being smelt, with that part cheers each part;
Being tasted, slays all senses with the heart.
Two such opposed kings encamp them still
In man as well as herbs—grace and rude will;
And where the worser is predominant,
Full soon the canker death eats up that plant.

[*Enter* Romeo.]

Romeo. Good morrow, father.

Friar Laurence. Benedicite!
What early tongue so sweet saluteth me?
Young son, it argues a distempered head
So soon to bid good morrow to thy bed.
Care keeps his watch in every old man's eye,
And where care lodges sleep will never lie;

190 dear hap: good fortune.

4 Titan is the god whose chariot pulls the sun into the sky each morning.

7 osier cage: willow basket.

9–12 The earth . . . find: The same earth that acts as a tomb is also the womb, or birthplace, of various useful plants that people can harvest.

15–18 mickle: great. The friar says that nothing from the earth is so evil that it doesn't do some good.

28 grace and rude will: good and evil. Both exist in people as well as in plants.

31 Benedicite (bĕ-nĕ-dĭ´sĭ-tē´): God bless you.

33–42 it argues . . . tonight: Only a disturbed (**distempered**) mind could make you get up so early. Old people may have trouble sleeping, but it is not normal for someone as young as you. Or were you up all night?

WHEN STUDENTS STRUGGLE . . .

Analyze Character and Theme Tell students that Friar Laurence is another minor character who plays a significant role in the plot. Read aloud the Friar's speech in Act II, Scene 3, lines 1–30, or invite volunteers to read lines aloud. Then discuss these questions with the class:

- Reread lines 9–10 and the related side notes. What does Friar Laurence mean when he calls the earth a womb and a tomb? *(The earth gives life, but it is also the final resting place when living things die.)* Is he talking only about garden plants? *(No; he also is talking about how people live and die.)*
- Reread lines 28–30 and the related side notes. How might this warning hint at future events in the play? *(When there is more evil than good in plants or in people, death often occurs.)* What might this suggest about the theme, or central idea, of the play? *(It might suggest that too much evil can result in tragedy, even for good people such as Romeo and Juliet.)*

For additional support, go to the **Reading Studio** and assign the following  **Level Up Tutorial: Theme.**

ENGLISH LEARNER SUPPORT

Use Visuals to Draw Inferences Have students examine the image of Romeo and Friar Laurence from the 1968 film *Romeo and Juliet*. Provide these frames:

Romeo is ______ing.
I think he ______.

Friar Laurence is ______ing.
I think he ______.

Guide students to describe what Romeo and Friar Laurence are doing and how they seem to feel toward each other. Allow students to pantomime actions they don't yet have vocabulary for, such as kneeling, and list any unfamiliar terms on the board. *(Possible responses: Romeo is kneeling. I think he respects Friar Laurence; Friar Laurence is laughing. I think he is happy for Romeo.)*

SUBSTANTIAL/LIGHT

NOTICE & NOTE

But where unbruised youth with unstuffed brain
Doth couch his limbs, there golden sleep doth reign.
Therefore thy earliness doth me assure
Thou art uproused with some distemp'rature;
Or if not so, then here I hit it right—
Our Romeo hath not been in bed tonight.

Romeo. That last is true, the sweeter rest was mine.

Friar Laurence. God pardon sin! Wast thou with Rosaline?

Romeo. With Rosaline, my ghostly father? No.
I have forgot that name, and that name's woe.

Friar Laurence. That's my good son! But where hast thou been
then?

Romeo. I'll tell thee ere thou ask it me again.
I have been feasting with mine enemy,
Where on a sudden one hath wounded me
That's by me wounded. Both our remedies
Within thy help and holy physic lies.
I bear no hatred, blessed man, for, lo,
My intercession likewise steads my foe.

Friar Laurence. Be plain, good son, and homely in thy drift.
Riddling confession finds but riddling shrift.

Romeo. Then plainly know my heart's dear love is set
On the fair daughter of rich Capulet;
As mine on hers, so hers is set on mine,
And all combined, save what thou must combine
By holy marriage. When, and where, and how
We met, we wooed, and made exchange of vow,
I'll tell thee as we pass; but this I pray,
That thou consent to marry us today.

Friar Laurence. Holy Saint Francis! What a change is here!
Is Rosaline, that thou didst love so dear,
So soon forsaken? Young men's love then lies
Not truly in their hearts, but in their eyes.
Jesu Maria! What a deal of brine
Hath washed thy sallow cheeks for Rosaline!
How much salt water thrown away in waste,
To season love, that of it doth not taste!
The sun not yet thy sighs from heaven clears,
Thy old groans ring yet in mine ancient ears.
Lo, here upon thy cheek the stain doth sit
Of an old tear that is not washed off yet.
If e'er thou wast thyself, and these woes thine,
Thou and these woes were all for Rosaline.
And art thou changed? Pronounce this sentence then:
Women may fall when there's no strength in men.

Romeo. Thou chidst me oft for loving Rosaline.

Friar Laurence. For doting, not for loving, pupil mine.

Romeo. And badest me bury love.

Friar Laurence. Not in a grave
To lay one in, another ought to have.

49–56 Romeo tries to explain the situation, asking for help both for himself and his "foe" (Juliet). The friar does not understand Romeo's convoluted language and asks him to speak clearly so that he can help.

69 brine: salt water— that is, the tears that Romeo has been shedding for Rosaline.

80 Women . . . men: If men are so weak, women may be forgiven for sinning.

81–82 chidst: scolded. The friar replies that he scolded Romeo for being lovesick, not for loving.

The Tragedy of Romeo and Juliet: Act II, Scene 3 323

WORDS OF THE WISER

Ask students to think of an older friend or relative that they often go to for comfort and advice. This is the sort of role Friar Laurence plays to Romeo. Explain to students that this signpost often occurs in literature when a wiser character is alone with the main character and shares wisdom in an effort to help him or her. Point out that Friar Laurence is fond of Romeo and wants to help him, but he recognizes the possible consequences of what Romeo is about to do. The relationship between Romeo and Friar Laurence gives the reader deeper insight into Romeo's behavior. Friar Laurence also plays a key role in advancing the plot. ***(Answer:** Friar Laurence is trying to tell Romeo to slow down and be careful, or else things will go wrong.)*

ENGLISH LEARNER SUPPORT

Explain Characters' Actions Read aloud the Words of the Wiser question and the final line of Scene 3 with students. Review that to do something *wisely* means to think about something carefully and to make a good decision. Explain that *stumble* means that you place your foot wrong when you are walking or running and you almost fall down. Tell students that "They stumble that go fast" is a proverb—a short, often imaginative saying that expresses a truth about life. Ask students to restate the proverb in their own words. *(People who act too quickly can have problems.)* Ask students why Friar Laurence gives Romeo this advice. Provide a sentence frame to support students' responses:

Friar Laurence tells Romeo to _____ because he doesn't want _____. (Friar Laurence tells Romeo to think carefully and go slowly because he doesn't want Romeo to have problems.)

NOTICE & NOTE

85–88 She whom . . . spell: Romeo says that the woman he loves feels the same way about him. That wasn't true of Rosaline. The friar replies that Rosaline knew that he didn't know what real love is.

91–92 For this . . . prove: this marriage may work out so well; **rancor**: bitter hate.

WORDS OF THE WISER

Notice & Note: Mark Friar Laurence's advice to Romeo in the last line of Scene 3.

Respond: What is Friar Laurence trying to make Romeo understand?

3 man: servant.

6–12 Tybalt . . . dared: Tybalt, still angry with Romeo, has sent a letter challenging Romeo to a duel. Benvolio says that Romeo will accept Tybalt's challenge and fight him.

15 blind bow-boy's butt-shaft: Cupid's dull practice arrow. Mercutio suggests that Romeo fell in love with very little work on Cupid's part.

18–24 More than . . . *hay:* Prince of Cats refers to a cat in a fable, named Tybalt. Mercutio makes fun of Tybalt's new style of dueling, comparing it to singing (**pricksong**). ***Passado, punto reverso***, and ***hay*** were terms used in the new dueling style.

Romeo. I pray thee chide not. She whom I love now
Doth grace for grace and love for love allow.
The other did not so.

Friar Laurence. O, she knew well
Thy love did read by rote, that could not spell.
But come, young waverer, come go with me.
In one respect I'll thy assistant be;
For this alliance may so happy prove
To turn your households' rancor to pure love.

Romeo. O, let us hence! I stand on sudden haste.

Friar Laurence. Wisely, and slow. They stumble that run fast.

[*Exeunt.*]

Scene 4 *A street.*

[*Enter* Benvolio *and* Mercutio.]

Mercutio. Where the devil should this Romeo be?
Came he not home tonight?

Benvolio. Not to his father's. I spoke with his man.

Mercutio. Why, that same pale hard-hearted wench, that Rosaline,
Torments him so that he will sure run mad.

Benvolio. Tybalt, the kinsman to old Capulet,
Hath sent a letter to his father's house.

Mercutio. A challenge, on my life.

Benvolio. Romeo will answer it.

Mercutio. Any man that can write may answer a letter.

Benvolio. Nay, he will answer the letter's master, how he dares, being dared.

Mercutio. Alas, poor Romeo, he is already dead! stabbed with a white wench's black eye; shot through the ear with a love song; the very pin of his heart cleft with the blind bow-boy's butt-shaft; and is he a man to encounter Tybalt?

Benvolio. Why, what is Tybalt?

Mercutio. More than Prince of Cats, I can tell you. O, he's the courageous captain of compliments. He fights as you sing pricksong—keeps time, distance, and proportion; rests me his minim rest, one, two, and the third in your bosom! the very butcher of a silk button, a duelist, a duelist! a gentleman of the very first house, of the first and second cause. Ah, the immortal *passado!* the *punto reverso!* the *hay!*

Benvolio. The what?

WHEN STUDENTS STRUGGLE . . .

Analyze Plot Have students work in pairs to create a timeline charting the events that have happened since the Capulets' party. Have them identify approximately when each of these events takes place to help them see how compressed this part of the plot is. Ask students to present their completed timelines to the class. Clarify any discrepancies and create a class timeline to display and add to during the rest of Act II.

For additional support, go to the **Reading Studio** and assign the following **Level Up Tutorial: Plot: Sequence of Events.**

NOTICE & NOTE

Mercutio. The pox of such antic, lisping, affecting fantasticoes—these new tuners of accent! "By Jesu, a very good blade! a very tall man! a very good whore!" Why, is not this a lamentable thing, grandsire, that we should be thus afflicted with these strange flies, these fashion-mongers, these perdona-mi's, who stand so much on the new form that they cannot sit at ease on the old bench? O, their bones, their bones!

[*Enter* Romeo, *no longer moody.*]

Benvolio. Here comes Romeo! here comes Romeo!

Mercutio. Without his roe, like a dried herring. O, flesh, flesh, how art thou fishified! Now is he for the numbers that Petrarch flowed in. Laura, to his lady, was but a kitchen wench (marry, she had a better love to berhyme her), Dido a dowdy, Cleopatra a gypsy, Helen and Hero hildings and harlots, Thisbe a grey eye or so, but not to the purpose. Signior Romeo, bon jour! There's a French salutation to your French slop. You gave us the counterfeit fairly last night.

Romeo. Good morrow to you both. What counterfeit did I give you?

Mercutio. The slip, sir, the slip. Can you not conceive?

Romeo. Pardon, good Mercutio. My business was great, and in such a case as mine a man may strain courtesy.

Mercutio. That's as much as to say, such a case as yours constrains a man to bow in the hams.

Romeo. Meaning, to curtsy.

Mercutio. Thou hast most kindly hit it.

Romeo. A most courteous exposition.

Mercutio. Nay, I am the very pink of courtesy.

Romeo. Pink for flower.

Mercutio. Right.

Romeo. Why, then is my pump well-flowered.

Mercutio. Well said! Follow me this jest now till thou hast worn out thy pump, that, when the single sole of it is worn, the jest may remain, after the wearing, solely singular.

Romeo. Oh, single-soled jest, solely singular for the singleness!

Mercutio. Come between us, good Benvolio! My wits faint.

Romeo. Switch and spurs, switch and spurs! or I'll cry a match.

Mercutio. Nay, if our wits run the wild-goose chase, I am done; for thou hast more of the wild goose in one of thy wits than, I

26–32 The pox . . . their bones: Mercutio continues to make fun of people who embrace new styles and new manners of speaking.

ANALYZE LITERARY DEVICES

Annotate: Mercutio refers to Petrarch, a poet, and uses literary and classical allusions to make fun of Romeo's lovesickness. Mark the allusions in Mercutio's speech.

Analyze: What is Mercutio's point in using these comparisons to mock Romeo's love?

39–44 *bon jour:* "Good day" in French; **There's . . . last night:** Here's a greeting to match your fancy French trousers (**slop**). You did a good job of getting away from us last night. (A piece of counterfeit money was called a **slip**.)

55 pump: shoe; **well-flowered:** Shoes with flowerlike designs.

61 Switch . . . match: Keep going, or I'll claim victory.

TO CHALLENGE STUDENTS . . .

Analyze Wordplay What's in a pun? Invite students to work in pairs to analyze the play on the word *goose* in lines 60–76 of Scene 4. Before they begin, tell students that it refers both to someone who is a silly fool and to the water bird. In Shakespeare's time, a goose was a staple meat dish. Alive, geese can be aggressive, hissing and biting at people who trespass near their nests.

Have pairs explain their analysis of the pun. Then ask them how this play on words builds their understanding of the character of Mercutio and shows what Romeo is like when he is not burdened by unrequited love.

ANALYZE LITERARY DEVICES

Review with students that an **allusion** is an indirect reference to a famous person, place, event, or literary work. For example, if a teen was moping over a girl, his friends might say, "Cheer up, Romeo!" That would be an allusion to this play. Explain that by using allusions, authors are able to convey meaning briefly, in a kind of "cultural shorthand." Remind students of the allusion that Mercutio makes to the folklore character Queen Mab in Act I, Scene 4. Tell students that often they can identify allusions by looking for capitalized names that do not refer to characters in the work they are reading and also by checking the marginal notes, which sometimes explain the reference.

Once students mark allusions that Mercutio makes in lines 34–41 of Act II, Scene 4, ask them to compare their annotations with those of a partner. Ask students what they marked. *(Petrarch, Laura, Dido, Cleopatra, Helen, Hero, and Thisbe)* Explain that Petrarch was a famous Italian poet from the 14th century who wrote more than 300 love sonnets to a mysterious woman named Laura. Explain that Petrarch's poems inspired the sonnets of Shakespeare. You might also explain that Dido, Helen, and Hero were all heroines in Greek legends, while Thisbe was the heroine of a Babylonian love story. Point out that Cleopatra was an actual queen of Egypt and that her relationship with the Roman general Mark Antony became the subject of another of Shakespeare's tragedies.

Ask students why Mercutio might mention all of these great heroines to his friend Romeo. ***(Answer:*** *Mercutio is jesting that Romeo's feelings for Rosaline are so intense that the great loves in literature could never measure up.)*

TEACH

LANGUAGE CONVENTIONS

Remind students that a **parallel construction** is a grammatical structure that is repeated. Have students identify the parallel construction in lines 77–80. *(Now art thou ______.)* Point out that what makes this a parallel construction is not only that certain words are repeated (*now, art,* and *thou*), but that the structure—or way in which the words are used—is repeated. In this case, the repeated structure is an entire clause: *Now art thou* (*something*). Discuss how this use of parallel construction provides a meaningful way for Mercutio to emphasize his point. ***(Answer:** This parallel construction gives Mercutio's speech a rhythmic cadence, and it adds emphasis to Mercutio's point that Romeo is more fun when he isn't lovesick.)*

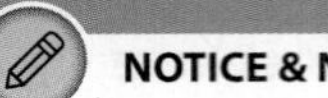

NOTICE & NOTE

64–65 Was . . . goose: Have I proved that you are a foolish person?

73 cheveril: kidskin, which is flexible. Mercutio means that a little wit stretches a long way.

LANGUAGE CONVENTIONS

Annotate: Underline the parallel construction in lines 77–80.

Analyze: What is the effect of this parallel construction?

80–81 great natural: an idiot, like a jester or clown who carries a fool's stick (**bauble**).

am sure, I have in my whole five. Was I with you there for the goose?

Romeo. Thou wast never with me for anything when thou wast not there for the goose.

Mercutio. I will bite thee by the ear for that jest.

Romeo. Nay, good goose, bite not!

Mercutio. Thy wit is a very bitter sweeting; it is a most sharp sauce.

Romeo. And is it not, then, well served in to a sweet goose?

Mercutio. O, here's a wit of cheveril, that stretches from an inch narrow to an ell broad!

Romeo. I stretch it out for that word "broad," which, added to the goose, proves thee far and wide a broad goose.

Mercutio. Why, is not this better now than groaning for love? Now art thou sociable, now art thou Romeo; now art thou what thou art, by art as well as by nature. For this driveling love is like a great natural that runs lolling up and down to hide his bauble in a hole.

Benvolio. Stop there, stop there!

Mercutio. Thou desirest me to stop in my tale against the hair.

Benvolio. Thou wouldst else have made thy tale large.

Mercutio. O, thou art deceived! I would have made it short; for I was come to the whole depth of my tale, and meant indeed to occupy the argument no longer.

[*Enter* Nurse *and* Peter, *her servant. He is carrying a large fan.*]

Romeo. Here's goodly gear!

Mercutio. A sail, a sail!

Benvolio. Two, two! a shirt and a smock.

Nurse. Peter!

Peter. Anon.

Nurse. My fan, Peter.

Mercutio. Good Peter, to hide her face; for her fan's the fairer of the two.

Nurse. God ye good morrow, gentlemen.

Mercutio. God ye good-den, fair gentlewoman.

Nurse. Is it good-den?

Mercutio. 'Tis no less, I tell ye, for the bawdy hand of the dial is now upon the prick of noon.

Nurse. Out upon you! What a man are you!

Romeo. One, gentlewoman, that God hath made himself to mar.

Nurse. By my troth, it is well said. "For himself to mar," quoth'a? Gentlemen, can any of you tell me where I may find the young Romeo?

Romeo. I can tell you; but young Romeo will be older when you have found him than he was when you sought him. I am the youngest of that name, for fault of a worse.

Nurse. You say well.

Mercutio. Yea, is the worst well? Very well took, i' faith! wisely, wisely.

Nurse. If you be he, sir, I desire some confidence with you.

Benvolio. She will endite him to some supper.

Mercutio. A bawd, a bawd, a bawd! So ho!

Romeo. What hast thou found?

Mercutio. No hare, sir; unless a hare, sir, in a lenten pie, that is something stale and hoar ere it be spent.

[*sings*]

"An old hare hoar,
And an old hare hoar,

88–89 goodly gear: something fine to joke about; **a sail:** Mercutio likens the nurse in all her petticoats to a huge ship coming toward them.

93 Fans were usually carried only by fine ladies. The nurse is trying to pretend that she is more than a servant.

112–113 confidence: The nurse means *conference;* she uses big words without understanding their meaning; **endite:** Benvolio makes fun of the nurse by using this word rather than *invite.*

114–124 Mercutio calls the nurse a **bawd,** or woman who runs a house of prostitution. His song uses the insulting puns **hare,** a rabbit or prostitute, and **hoar,** old.

The Tragedy of Romeo and Juliet: Act II, Scene 4 327

NOTICE & NOTE

Is very good meat in Lent.
But a hare that is hoar,
Is too much for a score
When it hoars ere it be spent."
Romeo, will you come to your father's? We'll to dinner thither.

Romeo. I will follow you.

Mercutio. Farewell, ancient lady. Farewell, [*sings*] lady, lady, lady.

[*Exeunt* Mercutio *and* Benvolio.]

Nurse. Marry, farewell! I pray you, sir, what saucy merchant was this that was so full of his ropery?

128 ropery: roguery, or jokes.

Romeo. A gentleman, nurse, that loves to hear himself talk and will speak more in a minute than he will stand to in a month.

Nurse. An 'a speak anything against me, I'll take him down, an 'a were lustier than he is, and twenty such Jacks; and if I cannot, I'll find those that shall. Scurvy knave! I am none of his flirt-gills; I am none of his skainsmates. [*turning to* Peter] And thou must stand by too, and suffer every knave to use me at his pleasure?

133–134 The nurse is angry that Mercutio treated her like one of his loose women (**flirt-gills**) or his gangsterlike friends (**skainsmates**).

Peter. I saw no man use you at his pleasure. If I had, my weapon should quickly have been out, I warrant you. I dare draw as soon as another man, if I see occasion in a good quarrel, and the law on my side.

Nurse. Now, afore God, I am so vexed that every part about me quivers. Scurvy knave! Pray you, sir, a word; and as I told you, my young lady bade me enquire you out. What she bid me say, I will keep to myself; but first let me tell ye, if ye should lead her into a fool's paradise, as they say, it were a very gross kind of behavior, as they say; for the gentlewoman is young; and therefore, if you should deal double with her, truly it were an ill thing to be offered to any gentlewoman, and very weak dealing.

142–147 The nurse warns Romeo that he'd better mean what he said about marrying Juliet.

Romeo. Nurse, commend me to thy lady and mistress. I protest unto thee—

148 commend me: give my respectful greetings.

Nurse. Good heart, and i' faith I will tell her as much. Lord, Lord! she will be a joyful woman.

Romeo. What wilt thou tell her, nurse? Thou dost not mark me.

Nurse. I will tell her, sir, that you do protest, which, as I take it, is a gentlemanlike offer.

Romeo. Bid her devise
Some means to come to shrift this afternoon;
And there she shall at Friar Laurence' cell
Be shrived and married. Here is for thy pains.

155–159 Romeo tells the nurse to have Juliet come to Friar Laurence's cell this afternoon, using the excuse that she is going to confess her sins (**shrift**). There she will receive forgiveness for her sins (**be shrived**) and be married.

Nurse. No, truly, sir; not a penny.

WHEN STUDENTS STRUGGLE . . .

Understand Author's Purpose Remind students that Act II, Scene 4, began with Tybalt's challenge to Romeo. Have pairs of students review lines 88–109. Ask students to describe the mood of this encounter with the nurse. *(The nurse's mannerisms and the way Romeo, Mercutio, and Benvolio tease her are humorous.)* Have students contrast this mood with the mood at the beginning of the scene. Ask: Why does Shakespeare structure his play in this way? *(He is showing the youthful liveliness of the characters and their capacity for joy in order to give the audience a break from the tension and to intensify the tragedy of what happens later.)*

For additional support, go to the **Reading Studio** and assign the following  **Level Up Tutorial: Author's Purpose.**

Romeo. Go to! I say you shall.

Nurse. This afternoon, sir? Well, she shall be there.

Romeo. And stay, good nurse, behind the abbey wall.
Within this hour my man shall be with thee
And bring thee cords made like a tackled stair,
Which to the high topgallant of my joy
Must be my convoy in the secret night.
Farewell. Be trusty, and I'll quit thy pains.
Farewell. Commend me to thy mistress.

Nurse. Now God in heaven bless thee! Hark you, sir.

Romeo. What sayst thou, my dear nurse?

Nurse. Is your man secret? Did you ne'er hear say,
Two may keep counsel, putting one away?

Romeo. I warrant thee my man's as true as steel.

Nurse. Well, sir, my mistress is the sweetest lady. Lord, Lord! when 'twas a little prating thing—O, there is a nobleman in town, one Paris, that would fain lay knife aboard; but she, good soul, had as lief see a toad, a very toad, as see him. I anger her sometimes, and tell her that Paris is the properer man; but I'll warrant you, when I say so, she looks as pale as any clout in the versal world. Doth not rosemary and Romeo begin both with a letter?

Romeo. Ay, nurse, what of that? Both with an R.

Nurse. Ah, mocker! that's the dog's name. R is for the—No; I know it begins with some other letter; and she hath the prettiest sententious of it, of you and rosemary, that it would do you good to hear it.

Romeo. Commend me to thy lady.

Nurse. Ay, a thousand times. [*Exit* Romeo.] Peter!

Peter. Anon.

Nurse. Peter, take my fan, and go before, and apace.

[*Exeunt.*]

164–165 tackled stair: rope ladder; **topgallant:** highest point.

167 quit thy pains: reward you.

174–177 The nurse begins to babble about Paris' proposal but says that Juliet would rather look at a toad than at Paris.

179–186 clout: old cloth; **the versal world:** the entire world; **Doth not . . . hear it:** The nurse tries to recall a clever saying that Juliet made up about Romeo and rosemary, the herb, but cannot remember it. She is sure that the two words couldn't begin with *R* because this letter sounds like a snarling dog; **sententious:** The nurse means *sentences*.

190 apace: quickly.

Scene 5 *Capulet's orchard.*

[*Enter* Juliet.]

Juliet. The clock struck nine when I did send the nurse;
In half an hour she promised to return.
Perchance she cannot meet him. That's not so.
O, she is lame! Love's heralds should be thoughts,
Which ten times faster glide than the sun's beams

4–6 Love's . . . hills: Love's messengers should be thoughts, which travel ten times faster than sunbeams.

The Tragedy of Romeo and Juliet: Act II, Scene 5 329

NOTICE & NOTE

7 nimble-pinioned . . . Love: Swift-winged doves pull the chariot of Venus, goddess of love.

14 bandy: toss.

16 feign as: act as if.

21–22 The nurse teases Juliet by putting on a sad face as if the news were bad.

25–26 give me . . . I had: Leave me alone for a while. I ache all over because of the running back and forth I've been doing.

36 I'll . . . circumstance: I'll wait for the details.

38 simple: foolish.

Driving back shadows over lowering hills.
Therefore do nimble-pinioned doves draw Love,
And therefore hath the wind-swift Cupid wings.
Now is the sun upon the highmost hill
Of this day's journey, and from nine till twelve
Is three long hours; yet she is not come.
Had she affections and warm youthful blood,
She would be as swift in motion as a ball;
My words would bandy her to my sweet love,
And his to me.
But old folks, many feign as they were dead—
Unwieldy, slow, heavy, and pale as lead.
[*Enter* Nurse *and* Peter.] O God, she comes! O honey nurse, what news?
Hast thou met with him? Send thy man away.

Nurse. Peter, stay at the gate.

[*Exit* Peter.]

Juliet. Now, good sweet nurse—O Lord, why lookst thou sad?
Though news be sad, yet tell them merrily;
If good, thou shamest the music of sweet news
By playing it to me with so sour a face.

Nurse. I am aweary, give me leave awhile.
Fie, how my bones ache! What a jaunce have I had!

Juliet. I would thou hadst my bones, and I thy news.
Nay, come, I pray thee speak. Good, good nurse, speak.

Nurse. Jesu, what haste! Can you not stay awhile?
Do you not see that I am out of breath?

Juliet. How art thou out of breath when thou hast breath
To say to me that thou art out of breath?
The excuse that thou dost make in this delay
Is longer than the tale thou dost excuse.
Is thy news good or bad? Answer to that.
Say either, and I'll stay the circumstance.
Let me be satisfied, is't good or bad?

Nurse. Well, you have made a simple choice; you know not how to choose a man. Romeo? No, not he. Though his face be better than any man's, yet his leg excels all men's; and for a hand and a foot, and a body, though they be not to be talked on, yet they are past compare. He is not the flower of courtesy, but, I'll warrant him, as gentle as a lamb. Go thy ways, wench; serve God. What, have you dined at home?

Juliet. No, no. But all this did I know before.
What say he of our marriage? What of that?

WHEN STUDENTS STRUGGLE . . .

Analyze Plot Make sure students understand Romeo's instructions to the nurse by having them reread lines 155–168 in Act II, Scene 4. Then, work with them to complete these sentence starters:

1. Immediately, the nurse must tell Juliet to . . . *(go to Friar Laurence's cell in the afternoon to meet Romeo).*
2. In one hour, the nurse must meet a man behind the abbey to . . . *(get a rope ladder).*
3. Later that night, Romeo will use . . . *(the rope ladder to get to Juliet's room).*

For additional support, go to the **Reading Studio** and assign the following **Level Up Tutorial: Plot: Sequence of Events.**

Nurse. Lord, how my head aches! What a head have I!
It beats as it would fall in twenty pieces.
My back o' t'other side—ah, my back, my back!
Beshrew your heart for sending me about
To catch my death with jauncing up and down!

Juliet. I' faith, I am sorry that thou art not well.
Sweet, sweet, sweet nurse, tell me, what says my love?

Nurse. Your love says, like an honest gentleman, and a courteous, and a kind, and a handsome, and, I warrant, a virtuous—Where is your mother?

Juliet. Where is my mother? Why, she is within.
Where should she be? How oddly thou repliest!
"Your love says, like an honest gentleman,
'Where is your mother?'"

Nurse. O God's Lady dear!
Are you so hot? Marry come up, I trow.
Is this the poultice for my aching bones?
Hence forward do your messages yourself.

Juliet. Here's such a coil! Come, what says Romeo?

Nurse. Have you got leave to go to shrift today?

Juliet. I have.

Nurse. Then hie you hence to Friar Laurence' cell;
There stays a husband to make you a wife.
Now comes the wanton blood up in your cheeks:
They'll be in scarlet straight at any news.
Hie you to church; I must another way,
To fetch a ladder, by the which your love
Must climb a bird's nest soon when it is dark.
I am the drudge, and toil in your delight;
But you shall bear the burden soon at night.
Go; I'll to dinner; hie you to the cell.

Juliet. Hie to high fortune! Honest nurse, farewell.

[*Exeunt.*]

Scene 6 *Friar Laurence's cell.*

[*Enter* Friar Laurence *and* Romeo.]

Friar Laurence. So smile the heavens upon this holy act
That after-hours with sorrow chide us not!

Romeo. Amen, amen! But come what sorrow can,
It cannot countervail the exchange of joy

50–51 Beshrew . . . down: Curse you for making me endanger my health by running around.

60–61 Marry . . . bones: Control yourself! Is this the treatment I get for my pain?

63 coil: fuss.

70–72 The nurse will get the ladder that Romeo will use to climb to Juliet's room after they are married.

1–2 So smile . . . us not: May heaven so bless this act that we won't regret it in the future (**after-hours**).

4 countervail: outweigh.

WHEN STUDENTS STRUGGLE . . .

Compare and Contrast Discuss with students how both Friar Laurence and the nurse facilitate the marriage of Romeo and Juliet. To help students see how Friar Laurence and the nurse are the same and different, have them complete a Venn diagram similar to the one shown.

Encourage students to refer to Scene 3, Scene 5, and Scene 6 for details to include in their diagrams.

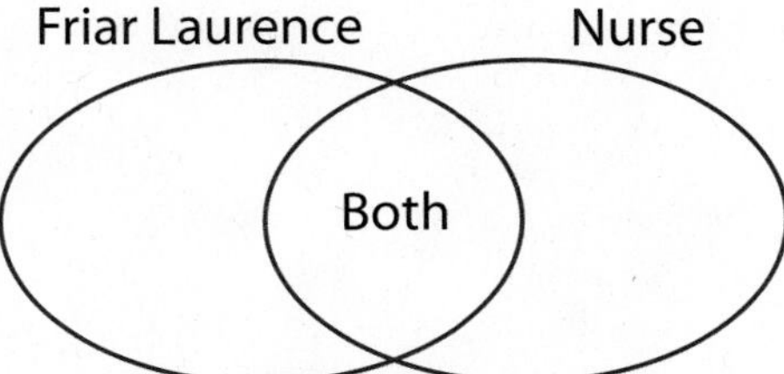

For additional support, go to the **Reading Studio** and assign the following **Level Up Tutorial: Character Traits.**

NOTICE & NOTE

That one short minute gives me in her sight.
Do thou but close our hands with holy words, 
Then love-devouring death do what he dare—
It is enough I may but call her mine.

Friar Laurence. These violent delights have violent ends
And in their triumph die, like fire and powder,
Which, as they kiss, consume. The sweetest honey
Is loathsome in his own deliciousness
And in the taste confounds the appetite.
Therefore love moderately: long love doth so;
Too swift arrives as tardy as too slow.

[*Enter* Juliet.]

Here comes the lady. O, so light a foot
Will ne'er wear out the everlasting flint.
A lover may bestride the gossamer
That idles in the wanton summer air,
And yet not fall; so light is vanity.

Juliet. Good even to my ghostly confessor.

Friar Laurence. Romeo shall thank thee, daughter, for us both.

Juliet. As much to him, else is his thanks too much.

Romeo. Ah, Juliet, if the measure of thy joy
Be heaped like mine, and that thy skill be more

9–15 These . . . slow: The friar compares Romeo's passion to gunpowder and the fire that ignites it—both are destroyed—then to honey, whose sweetness can destroy the appetite. He reminds Romeo to practice moderation in love.

23 As much to him: I give the same greeting to Romeo that he offers to me.

24–29 if the measure . . . encounter: If you are as happy as I am and have more skill to proclaim it, then sweeten the air by singing of our happiness to the world.

CLOSE READ SCREENCAST

Modeled Discussion In their eBook, have students view the Close Read Screencast, in which readers discuss and annotate Act II, Scene 6, lines 6–15.

As a class, view and discuss the video.

 **Close Read Practice PDF**

To blazon it, then sweeten with thy breath
This neighbor air, and let rich music's tongue
Unfold the imagined happiness that both
Receive in either by this dear encounter.

Juliet. Conceit, more rich in matter than in words,
Brags of his substance, not of ornament.
They are but beggars that can count their worth;
But my true love is grown to such excess
I cannot sum up sum of half my wealth.

Friar Laurence. Come, come with me, and we will make short work;
For, by your leaves, you shall not stay alone
Till Holy Church incorporate two in one.

[*Exeunt.*]

30–31 Conceit . . . ornament: True understanding (**conceit**) needs no words.

CHECK YOUR UNDERSTANDING

Answer these questions before moving on to the **Analyze the Text** questions on the following page.

1 Why is Friar Laurence pleased that Romeo has fallen in love with Juliet?

- **A** He never liked Rosaline and is glad Romeo found someone new to love.
- **B** He thinks it means the feud between the Montagues and Capulets will end.
- **C** He's sure that Romeo has made a careful and thoughtful decision.
- **D** He hopes that by marrying Juliet, Romeo will finally grow up.

2 Which of the following is a central theme in Act 2?

- **F** Love can transcend society's boundaries.
- **G** Older people are always wiser than younger people.
- **H** Any serious situation can be lightened by a few jokes.
- **J** Venturing outside one's social group can be dangerous.

3 As the act ends, Romeo and Juliet —

- **A** change their minds about marriage
- **B** make up after a lovers' quarrel
- **C** discuss their fears about the future
- **D** are about to be married

CHECK YOUR UNDERSTANDING

Have students answer the questions independently.

Answers:

1. *B*
2. *F*
3. *D*

If they answer any questions incorrectly, have them reread the text to confirm their understanding. Then they may proceed to ANALYZE THE TEXT on page 334.

ENGLISH LEARNER SUPPORT

Oral Assessment Use the following questions to assess students' comprehension and speaking skills.

1. Friar Laurence is happy that Romeo is in love with Juliet. Why? *(He hopes that if they marry, the Montagues and Capulets will end their feud.)*
2. What is the main theme in Act II? *(Love is stronger than people's differences.)*
3. How does Act II end? *(Romeo and Juliet are about to be marriedby Friar Laurence.)* **SUBSTANTIAL/MODERATE**

APPLY

ANALYZE THE TEXT

Possible answers:

1. **DOK 4:** *Juliet is saying that just as it doesn't matter what a rose is called, it shouldn't matter that Romeo's last name is Montague. She is trying to convince herself of this because the Montagues are her family's enemies.*
2. **DOK 3:** *Friar Laurence is suspicious of Romeo's declaration of love for Juliet because he knows that Romeo has been in love with Rosaline. He probably suspects that Romeo is fickle and his feelings aren't deep. Still, he agrees to marry Romeo and Juliet because he sees that it may unite the feuding Montagues and Capulets.*
3. **DOK 3: Soliloquy** *—In Act II, Scene 2, Juliet delivers a soliloquy from her balcony. She muses that it's only Romeo's last name of Montague that makes him an enemy and wishes that he would get rid of that name. Her speech shows that she is in love with Romeo but concerned about his familial ties.* **Aside** *—In Act II, Scene 2, Romeo overhears Juliet's soliloquy, in which she expresses her feelings for him. In an aside in line 37, he says, "Shall I hear more, or shall I speak at this?" Romeo is eager to respond but he isn't sure that he should.*
4. **DOK 3:** *Romeo is moody and depressed before he meets Juliet; he thinks he is in love with Rosaline, but she is not interested in him. After meeting Juliet at Capulet's party, Romeo becomes instantly joyful and elated. Shakespeare has shown that Romeo is impulsive and emotional. He is someone who rushes into love without thinking things through. Being overwhelmed by his love for Juliet clouds his judgment and causes him to get himself into dangerous situations.*
5. **DOK 4:** *The second line in Act II, Scene 2 refers to light: "What light through yonder window breaks?" In the next line, Romeo refers to Juliet as "the sun." Romeo speaks of Juliet in terms of "light" throughout the soliloquy; in lines 15–17, he compares her eyes to the brightest stars in the heavens. By calling Juliet "the sun," he means that her beauty is overpowering; her beauty and brightness contrast with the darkness of the night and the garden. Later, in Act II, Scene 3, line 5, the sun appears again in Friar Laurence's speech as something that brings "cheer" to the day.*

CREATE AND PRESENT

Debate Remind students to keep in mind the essential characteristics of both Friar Laurence and Mercutio as revealed through their speech. Encourage students to draw from what their character says to express their character's point of view in the debate over Romeo's plans.

RESPOND

ANALYZE THE TEXT

Support your responses with evidence from the text. NOTEBOOK

1. **Analyze** In Act II, Scene 2, Juliet says, "What's in a name? That which we call a rose / By any other name would smell as sweet" (lines 43–44). What does she mean? How does this comparison relate to one of the conflicts in her life?
2. **Cite Evidence** In Scene 3, why is Friar Laurence suspicious of Romeo's declaration of love for Juliet? What is his motivation for agreeing to marry Romeo and Juliet, despite his reservations?
3. **Draw Conclusions** Identify at least one soliloquy and one aside in Act II. Explain what each example reveals about the character who speaks it.
4. **Compare** Compare Romeo's behavior before he meets Juliet with his behavior after they declare their love for each other. What do you learn about Romeo's character from the change in his behavior?
5. **Notice & Note** In literature, a **motif** is a repeated image, idea, or theme. Explain the light/dark or day/night motif in Romeo's speech at the beginning of Act II, Scene 2. What does he mean when he refers to Juliet as "the sun"? Where else in Act II does this Again and Again motif appear?

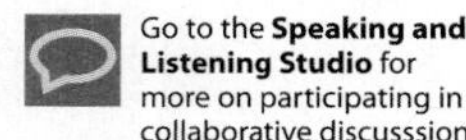

Go to the **Speaking and Listening Studio** for more on participating in collaborative discusssions.

CREATE AND PRESENT

Debate Both Friar Laurence and Mercutio have personal attributes that put them at odds with Romeo's passion. Analyze their differences and hold a debate in which each character presents his point of view.

- ❑ Working with two other students, discuss the characteristics of Friar Laurence, Mercutio, and Romeo. What differences do these three demonstrate in Act II?
- ❑ With each person in your group taking the point of view of one of these characters, debate Romeo's plan to marry Juliet.
- ❑ Work together to write a summary of your debate.

NOTICE & NOTE

SETTING A PURPOSE

Notice how events begin to shift in a more ominous or dangerous direction in this act. Write down any questions you generate during reading.

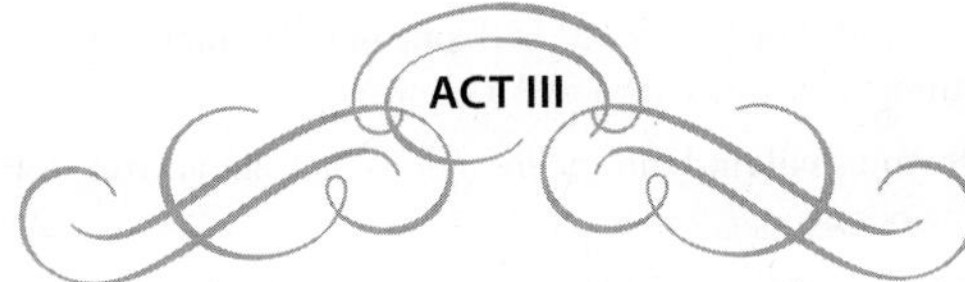

Scene 1 *A public place.*

[*Enter* Mercutio, Benvolio, Page, *and* Servants.]

Benvolio. I pray thee, good Mercutio, let's retire.
The day is hot, the Capulets abroad,
And if we meet, we shall not scape a brawl,
For now, these hot days, is the mad blood stirring.

Mercutio. Thou art like one of those fellows that, when he enters the confines of a tavern, claps me his sword upon the table and says "God send me no need of thee!" and by the operation of the second cup draws him on the drawer, when indeed there is no need.

Benvolio. Am I like such a fellow?

Mercutio. Come, come, thou art as hot a Jack in thy mood as any in Italy; and as soon moved to be moody, and as soon moody to be moved.

Benvolio. And what to?

Mercutio. Nay an there were two such, we should have none shortly, for one would kill the other. Thou! why, thou wilt quarrel with a man that hath a hair more or a hair less in his beard than thou hast. Thou wilt quarrel with a man for cracking nuts, having no other reason but because thou hast hazel eyes. What eye but such an eye would spy out such a quarrel? Thy head is as full of quarrels as an egg is full of meat; and yet thy head hath been beaten as addle as an egg for quarreling. Thou hast quarreled with a man for coughing in the street, because he hath wakened thy dog that hath lain asleep in the sun. Didst thou not fall out with a tailor for wearing his new doublet before Easter? with another for tying his new shoes with old riband? And yet thou wilt tutor me from quarreling!

Benvolio. An I were so apt to quarrel as thou art, any man should buy the fee simple of my life for an hour and a quarter.

Mercutio. The fee simple? O simple!

[*Enter* Tybalt *and others.*]

3–4 we shall . . . stirring: We shall not avoid a fight, since the heat makes people ill-tempered.

7–8 by the . . . drawer: feeling the effects of a second drink, is ready to fight (**draw on**) the waiter who's pouring the drinks (**drawer**).

12–13 as soon moved . . . to be moved: as likely to get angry and start a fight.

ANALYZE LITERARY DEVICES

Annotate: Mark one or more lines in which Mercutio teases his friend by insisting that Benvolio is quick to pick a fight.

Respond: How is Mercutio's teasing an example of irony?

25 doublet: jacket.

26 riband: ribbon or laces.

28–29 An I . . . quarter: If I picked fights as quickly as you do, anybody could own me for the smallest amount of money.

SETTING A PURPOSE

Direct students to use the Setting a Purpose prompt to focus their reading.

ANALYZE LITERARY DEVICES

Tell students that **verbal irony** is a type of irony in which someone knowingly exaggerates or says one thing and means another. Explain that in Mercutio's speeches in lines 5–27, he uses verbal irony to tease Benvolio, saying that Benvolio is something that he definitely is not.

Have partners review Act III, Scene 1, lines 1–30, and compare the line or lines they identified in which Mercutio teases Benvolio about being quick to pick a fight. Ask students how they know the lines they chose are examples of verbal irony. *(In lines 1–4, Benvolio tells Mercutio that he wants to go home because it's hot and the Capulets might be around; he clearly doesn't want to pick a fight.)* Discuss how Mercutio's use of irony helps readers see the differences in their characters. Have students point out an additional irony in Mercutio's saying that Benvolio is quick to pick a fight. *(It isn't Benvolio but Mercutio himself who is more likely to pick a fight.)* (**Answer:** *Mercutio is saying that Benvolio likes to start fights, but Benvolio is a calm person who doesn't like violence.)*

WHEN STUDENTS STRUGGLE . . .

Analyze Foreshadowing Reiterate that Benvolio and Mercutio have been talking about fighting and that their discussion seems to foreshadow a real fight. Then have students recall Tybalt's and Romeo's relationship up to this point in the play. Ask: How does Tybalt's entrance at this point create tension and suspense? *(His entrance creates suspense because the audience knows he wants to fight Romeo.)* What does his entrance foreshadow? *(an actual fight)* How do Benvolio and Mercutio respond to Tybalt's entrance? *(Benvolio is worried; Mercutio is defiant.)*

For additional support, go to the **Reading Studio** and assign the following **Level Up Tutorial: Suspense and Foreshadowing.**

ENGLISH LEARNER SUPPORT

Rewrite Sentences with Negatives Remind students that Shakespeare often inverts, or reverses, common word order. Read aloud lines 31–32 and explain that Benvolio and Mercutio see a group of Capulets coming toward them. Point out that Benvolio is worried but Mercutio isn't. Write line 32 on the board: "By my heel, I care not." Underline "I care not." Model rewriting this using the word do. *(I do not care.)* Explain that by saying, "By my heel," Mercutio is showing that he doesn't care about the Capulets at all—it's a kind of insult. Then write lines 59–60 on the board. Explain that a *villain* is a bad person and that *thou knowst* was a way to say "you know" in Shakespeare's time. Have pairs of students rewrite the lines as complete sentences using the proper word order. *(line 59: I am no villain; line 60: I see you do not know me.)* **SUBSTANTIAL/MODERATE**

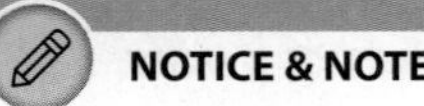
NOTICE & NOTE

Benvolio. By my head, here come the Capulets.

Mercutio. By my heel, I care not.

Tybalt. Follow me close, for I will speak to them. Gentlemen, good den. A word with one of you.

Mercutio. And but one word with one of us? Couple it with something; make it a word and a blow.

Tybalt. You shall find me apt enough to that, sir, an you will give me occasion.

Mercutio. Could you not take some occasion without giving?

Tybalt. Mercutio, thou consortest with Romeo.

Mercutio. Consort? What, dost thou make us minstrels? An thou make minstrels of us, look to hear nothing but discords. Here's my fiddlestick; here's that shall make you dance. Zounds, consort!

Benvolio. We talk here in the public haunt of men.
Either withdraw unto some private place
And reason coldly of your grievances,
Or else depart. Here all eyes gaze on us.

Mercutio. Men's eyes were made to look, and let them gaze.
I will not budge for no man's pleasure, I.

40–44 consortest: are friends with; Mercutio pretends to misunderstand him, assuming that Tybalt is insulting him by calling Romeo and him a **consort**, a group of traveling musicians. He then refers to his sword as his **fiddlestick**, the bow for a fiddle.

TO CHALLENGE STUDENTS . . .

Deliver a Soliloquy Dramatic text is most appreciated when it is heard. Have students choose a soliloquy or major speech in this act and then follow these instructions:

- On a copy of the text you chose, highlight or underline punctuation, words to emphasize, and places to look at the audience or show a particular expression.
- Practice reading your speech with a partner. Partners should offer constructive feedback on strengths and weaknesses of the delivery.
- Deliver your speech to the class. After the speeches have been presented, discuss how hearing them read aloud contributed to their meaning.

NOTICE & NOTE 

[*Enter* Romeo.]

Tybalt. Well, peace be with you, sir. Here comes my man.

Mercutio. But I'll be hanged, sir, if he wear your livery.
Marry, go before to field, he'll be your follower!
Your worship in that sense may call him man.

Tybalt. Romeo, the love I bear thee can afford
No better term than this: thou art a villain.

Romeo. Tybalt, the reason that I have to love thee
Doth much excuse the appertaining rage
To such a greeting. Villain am I none.
Therefore farewell. I see thou knowst me not.

Tybalt. Boy, this shall not excuse the injuries
That thou hast done me; therefore turn and draw.

Romeo. I do protest I never injured thee,
But love thee better than thou canst devise
Till thou shalt know the reason of my love;
And so, good Capulet, which name I tender
As dearly as mine own, be satisfied.

Mercutio. O calm, dishonorable, vile submission!
Alla stoccata carries it away.

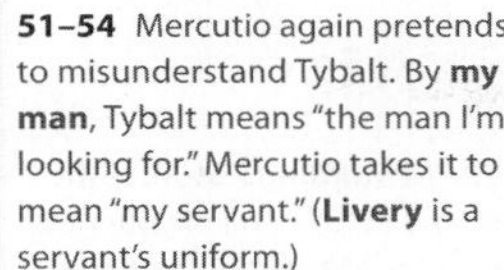

51–54 Mercutio again pretends to misunderstand Tybalt. By **my man**, Tybalt means "the man I'm looking for." Mercutio takes it to mean "my servant." (**Livery** is a servant's uniform.)

57–59 I forgive your anger because I have reason to love you.

61 Boy: an insulting term of address.

66 tender: cherish.

68–70 Mercutio assumes that Romeo is afraid to fight. ***Alla stoccata*** is a move used in sword fighting.

ENGLISH LEARNER SUPPORT

Use Visual and Contextual Support Direct students to the photograph from the movie *Romeo and Juliet* on pages 336–337. Point out Tybalt in red on page 336 and Mercutio in black on page 337. Ask students to point to Romeo (to the left of Tybalt). Build context by asking students these questions:

- Is Romeo a Montague or a Capulet? *(Montague)*
- Who is his friend? *(Mercutio)*
- What family is Tybalt from? *(the Capulets)*
- Why does Tybalt want to fight Romeo? *(He is angry that Romeo attended the Capulets' party uninvited.)*

Then read aloud lines lines 51–69 as students follow along in their books. Pantomime that the phrase *turn and draw* means to turn and pull out a sword. Ask: Does Romeo want to fight Tybalt? *(no)* If students need visual cues, point again to the photo of Romeo. Ask: Why doesn't Romeo want to fight? *(Tybalt is a member of Juliet's family.)*

Ask students to reread lines 63–67 and summarize them. *(Romeo tells Tybalt that he loves him more than he realizes. He asks Tybalt to be satisfied with that and not try to fight.)* Ask students to draw on clues in the photo to predict whether Romeo will fight Tybalt. *(Possible response: No, in the photo Mercutio is fighting Tybalt.)*
SUBSTANTIAL/MODERATE

WHEN STUDENTS STRUGGLE . . .

Analyze Parallel Plots Remind students that The Tragedy of *Romeo and Juliet* contains parallel plots, or separate storylines that happen at the same time. Scene 1 centers on the feud between the Capulets and the Montagues. Events in this scene will determine whether the ending of the play is happy or tragic. Ask students to create cause-and-effect charts. Provide the events shown in the Cause column and have partners complete the Effect column to show how each event in the scene causes another to happen.

Cause:	Effect:
Tybalt challenges Romeo.	*Mercutio fights Tybalt.*
Romeo holds Mercutio back.	*Tybalt kills Mercutio.*
Tybalt kills Mercutio.	*Romeo seeks revenge on Tybalt.*

 For additional support, go to the **Reading Studio** and assign the following **Level Up Tutorial: Plot: Sequence of Events.**

TEACH

ANALYZE LITERARY DEVICES

Remind students that **rhythm** is a pattern of stressed (accented) and unstressed (unaccented) syllables in a line or lines of poetry or drama. Ask a volunteer to read aloud lines 90–96 and then ask: How would you describe the rhythm and tone of Mercutio's words? *(a short, accented rhythm; an angry tone)* Discuss with students why Shakespeare wrote Mercutio's lines this way and what the effect is. *(**Answer:** Mercutio is dying, and it's as if he is spitting the words into Romeo's face. He is furious at Romeo for not fighting, and as he is dying, his words turn staccato—short and accented.)*

ENGLISH LEARNER SUPPORT

Understand Puns Display this joke: Why *was the baker sad? He had no dough*. Underline "He had no dough" and explain that it is a pun, or a play on words. Circle the word *dough*. Explain that it has two meanings: *dough* can mean either a mixture of flour and water, or money.

Remind students that Shakespeare uses many puns. Read aloud lines 91–92. Ask students to circle the word *grave*. Explain that *grave* can mean either "serious" or "a place in the ground where a dead person is put." Guide students to explain the pun that Mercutio is making. Provide these frames:

Mercutio is dying, so he says, "Ask for me tomorrow, and you shall find me ______." *(a grave man)*

That means he will be ______ tomorrow. *(dead)*

However, it's also a pun. Mercutio usually jokes, so he's saying after he dies he will be _______. *(serious)*

MODERATE/LIGHT

NOTICE & NOTE

72–74 nothing but . . . eight: I intend to take one of your nine lives (as a cat supposedly has) and give a beating to the other eight.

79 *passado:* a sword fighting maneuver.

80–84 Romeo wants Benvolio to help him stop the fight. They are able to hold back Mercutio.

83 bandying: fighting.

85 A plague . . . sped: I curse both the Montagues and the Capulets. I am destroyed.

ANALYZE LITERARY DEVICES

Annotate: Mark the section in lines 90–96 where Mercutio uses rhythm to express his feelings.

Analyze: Why does Mercutio speak to Romeo in such a rhythmic way at this moment?

[*draws*]

Tybalt, you ratcatcher, will you walk?

Tybalt. What wouldst thou have with me?

Mercutio. Good King of Cats, nothing but one of your nine lives. That I mean to make bold withal, and, as you shall use me hereafter, dry-beat the rest of the eight. Will you pluck your sword out of his pilcher by the ears? Make haste, lest mine be about your ears ere it be out.

Tybalt. I am for you.

[*draws*]

Romeo. Gentle Mercutio, put thy rapier up.

Mercutio. Come, sir, your *passado!*

[*They fight.*]

Romeo. Draw, Benvolio; beat down their weapons.
Gentlemen, for shame! forbear this outrage!
Tybalt, Mercutio, the Prince expressly hath
Forbid this bandying in Verona streets.
Hold, Tybalt! Good Mercutio!

[Tybalt, *under* Romeo's *arm, thrusts* Mercutio *in, and flies with his* Men.]

Mercutio. I am hurt.
A plague o' both your houses! I am sped.
Is he gone and hath nothing?

Benvolio. What, art thou hurt?

Mercutio. Ay, ay, a scratch, a scratch. Marry, 'tis enough.
Where is my page? Go, villain, fetch a surgeon.

[*Exit* Page.]

Romeo. Courage, man. The hurt cannot be much. 

Mercutio. No, 'tis not so deep as a well, nor so wide as a church door; but 'tis enough, 'twill serve. Ask for me tomorrow, and you shall find me a grave man. I am peppered, I warrant, for this world. A plague o' both your houses! Zounds, a dog, a rat, a mouse, a cat, to scratch a man to death! A braggart, a rogue, a villain, that fights by the book of arithmetic! Why the devil came you between us? I was hurt under your arm.

Romeo. I thought all for the best.

Mercutio. Help me into some house, Benvolio,
Or I shall faint. A plague o' both your houses!

CLOSE READ SCREENCAST

Modeled Discussion In their eBook, have students view the Close Read Screencast, in which readers discuss and annotate lines 89–101, which include Mercutio's dying words.

As a class, view and discuss the video.

 **Close Read Practice PDF**

They have made worms' meat of me. I have it,
And soundly too. Your houses!

[*Exit, supported by* Benvolio.]

Romeo. This gentleman, the Prince's near ally,
My very friend, hath got this mortal hurt
In my behalf—my reputation stained
With Tybalt's slander—Tybalt, that an hour
Hath been my kinsman, O sweet Juliet,
Thy beauty hath made me effeminate
And in my temper softened valor's steel!

[*Reenter* Benvolio.]

Benvolio. O Romeo, Romeo, brave Mercutio's dead!
That gallant spirit hath aspired the clouds,
Which too untimely here did scorn the earth.

Romeo. This day's black fate on more days doth depend;
This but begins the woe others must end.

[*Reenter* Tybalt.]

Benvolio. Here comes the furious Tybalt back again.

Romeo. Alive in triumph, and Mercutio slain?
Away to heaven respective lenity,
And fire-eyed fury be my conduct now!
Now, Tybalt, take the "villain" back again
That late thou gavest me, for Mercutio's soul
Is but a little way above our heads,
Staying for thine to keep him company.
Either thou or I, or both, must go with him.

Tybalt. Thou, wretched boy, that didst consort him here,
Shalt with him hence.

Romeo. This shall determine that.

[*They fight.* Tybalt *falls.*]

Benvolio. Romeo, away, be gone!
The citizens are up, and Tybalt slain.
Stand not amazed. The Prince will doom thee death
If thou art taken. Hence, be gone, away!

Romeo. O, I am fortune's fool!

Benvolio. Why dost thou stay?

[*Exit* Romeo.]

[*Enter* Citizens.]

102–108 This gentleman . . . valor's steel: My friend has died protecting my reputation against a man who has been my relative for only an hour. My love for Juliet has made me less manly and brave.

110 aspired: soared to.

112–113 This day's . . . must end: This awful day will be followed by more of the same.

116 respective lenity: considerate mildness.

CONTRASTS AND CONTRADICTIONS

Notice & Note: Mark the section in lines 115–122 where Romeo says something out of character.

Analyze: What causes the sudden change in Romeo's character?

124 The sword fight probably goes on for several minutes, till Romeo runs his sword through Tybalt.

129 I am fortune's fool: Fate has made a fool of me.

CONTRASTS AND CONTRADICTIONS

Remind students that noticing a character acting in a way that either **contrasts** with what you would expect or **contradicts** how the character has acted before can reveal a character's internal conflict. Draw students' attention to Romeo's sudden change in character. Ask: Why does he act this way? (***Answer:*** *The death of his friend Mercutio by Tybalt's hand makes Romeo furious, so he decides to kill Tybalt. Previously, Romeo had professed his love for Tybalt and wished him no harm.)*

Explain that Shakespearean drama usually has a turning point, or the event in the plot that determines how the rest of the play will unfold. Ask students why Tybalt's death is the play's turning point. Have them consider all of the implications of this event. *(By killing Tybalt, Romeo will now have to face the civil punishment handed out by Prince Escalus, possibly death. Additionally, he has killed Juliet's relative. This event makes the possibility of a happy ending unlikely.)*

TO CHALLENGE STUDENTS . . .

Consider Alternate Plot Events Ask: Did Mercutio's ignorance of Romeo's involvement with Juliet lead to his death? Point out to students that Mercutio dies without knowing of Romeo's marriage to Juliet. Ask students to consider these questions:

- Would Mercutio's actions or attitude have been different if he had known?
- Might he have avoided the duel that killed him?

Have students write a paragraph or two in response, citing details to support their position. Invite students to compare their analyses in small groups.

NOTICE & NOTE

Citizen. Which way ran he that killed Mercutio?
Tybalt, that murderer, which way ran he?

Benvolio. There lies that Tybalt.

Citizen. Up, sir, go with me.
I charge thee in the Prince's name obey.

[*Enter* Prince *with his* Attendants, Montague, Capulet, *their* Wives, *and others.*]

Prince. Where are the vile beginners of this fray?

135–136 Benvolio says he can tell (**discover**) what happened.

Benvolio. O noble Prince, I can discover all
The unlucky manage of this fatal brawl.
There lies the man, slain by young Romeo,
That slew thy kinsman, brave Mercutio.

141–142 as thou . . . Montague: If your word is good, you will sentence Romeo to death for killing a Capulet.

Lady Capulet. Tybalt, my cousin! O my brother's child!
O Prince! O cousin! O husband! O, the blood is spilled
Of my dear kinsman! Prince, as thou art true,
For blood of ours shed blood of Montague.
O cousin, cousin!

Prince. Benvolio, who began this bloody fray?

146–147 Romeo, that . . . was: Romeo talked calmly (**fair**) and told Tybalt to think how trivial (**nice**) the argument was.

150–151 could . . . peace: could not quiet the anger of Tybalt, who would not listen to pleas for peace.

156–157 whose dexterity retorts it: whose skill returns it.

159–160 his agile . . . rushes: He rushed between them and pushed down their swords.

164 entertained: thought of.

Benvolio. Tybalt, here slain, whom Romeo's hand did slay.
Romeo, that spoke him fair, bid him bethink
How nice the quarrel was, and urged withal
Your high displeasure. All this—uttered
With gentle breath, calm look, knees humbly bowed—
Could not take truce with the unruly spleen
Of Tybalt deaf to peace, but that he tilts
With piercing steel at bold Mercutio's breast;
Who, all as hot, turns deadly point to point,
And, with a martial scorn, with one hand beats
Cold death aside and with the other sends
It back to Tybalt, whose dexterity
Retorts it. Romeo he cries aloud,
"Hold, friends! friends, part!" and swifter than his tongue,
His agile arm beats down their fatal points,
And 'twixt them rushes; underneath whose arm
An envious thrust from Tybalt hit the life
Of stout Mercutio, and then Tybalt fled,
But by-and-by comes back to Romeo,
Who had but newly entertained revenge,
And to't they go like lightning; for, ere I
Could draw to part them, was stout Tybalt slain;
And, as he fell, did Romeo turn and fly.
This is the truth, or let Benvolio die.

WHEN STUDENTS STRUGGLE . . .

Analyze Plot To help students understand that Tybalt's death is a turning point—a crucial event in the plot of the play—work with them to draw a simple plot diagram on the board. Place Tybalt's death at the peak.

Tybalt's death

Then ask students what direction the action will probably take after Tybalt's death. *(Romeo and Juliet's situation will probably become more desperate when Romeo is banished. The newlyweds may do something foolish that will lead to their downfall.)*

For additional support, go to the **Reading Studio** and assign the following **Level Up Tutorial: Plot Stages.**

Lady Capulet. He is a kinsman to the Montague;
Affection makes him false, he speaks not true.
Some twenty of them fought in this black strife,
And all those twenty could but kill one life.
I beg for justice, which thou, Prince, must give.
Romeo slew Tybalt; Romeo must not live.

Prince. Romeo slew him; he slew Mercutio.
Who now the price of his dear blood doth owe?

Montague. Not Romeo, Prince; he was Mercutio's friend;
His fault concludes but what the law should end,
The life of Tybalt.

Prince. And for that offense
Immediately we do exile him hence.
I have an interest in your hate's proceeding,
My blood for your rude brawls doth lie a-bleeding;
But I'll amerce you with so strong a fine
That you shall all repent the loss of mine.
I will be deaf to pleading and excuses;
Nor tears nor prayers shall purchase out abuses.
Therefore use none. Let Romeo hence in haste,
Else, when he is found, that hour is his last.
Bear hence this body, and attend our will.
Mercy but murders, pardoning those that kill.

[*Exeunt.*]

178–179 Romeo is guilty only of avenging Mercutio's death, which the law would have done anyway.

179–190 The prince banishes Romeo from Verona. He angrily points out that one of his own relatives is dead because of the feud and declares that Romeo will be put to death unless he flees immediately.

Scene 2 *Capulet's orchard.*

[*Enter* Juliet *alone.*]

Juliet. Gallop apace, you fiery-footed steeds,
Toward Phoebus' lodging! Such a wagoner
As Phaëton would whip you to the West,
And bring in cloudy night immediately.
Spread thy close curtain, love-performing night,
That runaways' eyes may wink, and Romeo
Leap to these arms, untalked of and unseen.
Lovers can see to do their amorous rites
By their own beauties; or, if love be blind,
It best agrees with night. Come, civil night,
Thou sober-suited matron, all in black,
And learn me how to lose a winning match,
Played for a pair of stainless maidenhoods.
Hood my unmanned blood bating in my cheeks

2–3 Phoebus: Apollo, the god of the sun; **Phaëton:** a mortal who lost control of the sun's chariot when he drove it too fast.

14–16 Hood . . . modesty: Juliet asks that the darkness hide her blushing cheeks on her wedding night.

ENGLISH LEARNER SUPPORT

Use Cognates Read aloud the Prince's decision in lines 179–180. Tell students that the verb *exile* (line 180) has a Spanish cognate, *exiliar.* Ask Spanish-speaking students if they can use what they know about the word *exiliar* to figure out the meaning of *exile* in English. If necessary, point out that *exile* means "to send away from one's home or country." Ask: Why does the Prince exile Romeo? *(He exiles Romeo because Romeo killed Tybalt.)*

Then read aloud the side notes for lines 179–190. Ask students to find and circle a word that means the same thing as *exiles*. *(banishes)* **ALL LEVELS**

WHEN STUDENTS STRUGGLE . . .

Analyze Parallel Plots Tell students that as Act III, Scene 2 opens, Juliet is eager to see Romeo for their wedding night. Help students identify the dramatic irony in this scene: Ask: What does the audience know that Juliet does not? What is the effect of this knowledge? *(The audience knows that Mercutio and Tybalt are dead and that Romeo is banished. This knowledge makes the audience feel sorry for Juliet, who is completely unaware of this tragedy, which is about to change her world.)*

Ask students what effect Juliet's mention of death in lines 21–25 has on the audience. *(Juliet is awaiting her wedding night. She is filled with anticipation and joy. However, her mention of death is chilling to the audience, who knows that the lovers will ultimately die tragically. It increases the audience's pity for Juliet.)*

For additional support, go to the **Reading Studio** and assign the following **Level Up Tutorial: Plot: Sequence of Events.**

TEACH

LANGUAGE CONVENTIONS

Review with students the term **parallel structure**, or the repetition of certain words, phrases, or grammatical structures. Have partners work together to take turns reading aloud lines 1–35 from Juliet's soliloquy, while the other partner marks examples of repeated words and grammatical structures in these lines. Have student pairs discuss what they think is the effect of the repetition. (***Answer:*** *The repetition emphasizes Juliet's impatience for the night to come so that she can be with Romeo.)*

NOTICE & NOTE

LANGUAGE CONVENTIONS

Annotate: Mark the places in Juliet's speech (lines 1–35) where Shakespeare uses parallel structure—repetition of certain words, phrases, or grammatical structures for emphasis or other effects.

Analyze: How does parallel construction enhance what Juliet is saying in this section?

26–27 I have . . . possessed it: Juliet protests that she has gone through the wedding ceremony (**bought the mansion**) but is still waiting to enjoy the rewards of marriage.

34 the cords: the rope ladder.

37–42 well-a-day: an expression used when someone has bad news. The nurse wails and moans without clearly explaining what has happened, leading Juliet to assume that Romeo is dead.

45–50 Juliet's "I" means "aye," or "yes." A **cockatrice** is a mythological beast whose glance kills its victims.

51 my weal or woe: my happiness or sorrow.

53–56 God . . . mark: an expression meant to scare off evil powers, similar to "Knock on wood"; **corse:** corpse; **swounded:** fainted.

With thy black mantle; till strange love, grown bold,
Think true love acted simple modesty.
Come, night; come, Romeo, come; thou day in night;
For thou wilt lie upon the wings of night
Whiter than new snow on a raven's back.
Come, gentle night; come, loving, black-browed night;
Give me my Romeo; and, when he shall die,
Take him and cut him out in little stars,
And he will make the face of heaven so fine
That all the world will be in love with night
And pay no worship to the garish sun.
O, I have bought the mansion of a love,
But not possessed it; and though I am sold,
Not yet enjoyed. So tedious is this day
As is the night before some festival
To an impatient child that hath new robes
And may not wear them. Oh, here comes my nurse,

[*Enter* Nurse, *wringing her hands, with the ladder of cords in her lap.*]

And she brings news; and every tongue that speaks
But Romeo's name speaks heavenly eloquence.
Now, nurse, what news? What hast thou there? the cords
That Romeo bid thee fetch?

Nurse. Ay, ay, the cords.

Juliet. Ay me! what news? Why dost thou wring thy hands?

Nurse. Ah, well-a-day! he's dead, he's dead, he's dead!
We are undone, lady, we are undone!
Alack the day! he's gone, he's killed, he's dead!

Juliet. Can heaven be so envious?

Nurse. Romeo can,
Though heaven cannot. O Romeo, Romeo!
Who ever would have thought it? Romeo!

Juliet. What devil art thou that dost torment me thus?
This torture should be roared in dismal hell.
Hath Romeo slain himself? Say thou but "I,"
And that bare vowel "I" shall poison more
Than the death-darting eye of a cockatrice.
I am not I, if there be such an "I,"
Or those eyes shut, that make thee answer "I."
If he be slain, say "I," or if not, "no."
Brief sounds determine of my weal or woe.

Nurse. I saw the wound, I saw it with mine eyes,
(God save the mark!) here on his manly breast.
A piteous corse, a bloody piteous corse;

Pale, pale as ashes, all bedaubed in blood,
All in gore blood. I swounded at the sight.

Juliet. O, break, my heart! poor bankrout, break at once!
To prison, eyes; ne'er look on liberty!
Vile earth, to earth resign; end motion here,
And thou and Romeo press one heavy bier!

Nurse. O Tybalt, Tybalt, the best friend I had!
O courteous Tybalt! honest gentleman!
That ever I should live to see thee dead!

Juliet. What storm is this that blows so contrary?
Is Romeo slaughtered, and is Tybalt dead?
My dear-loved cousin, and my dearer lord?
Then, dreadful trumpet, sound the general doom!
For who is living, if those two are gone?

Nurse. Tybalt is gone, and Romeo banished;
Romeo that killed him, he is banished.

Juliet. O God! Did Romeo's hand shed Tybalt's blood?

Nurse. It did! it did! alas the day, it did!

Juliet. O serpent heart, hid with a flow'ring face!
Did ever dragon keep so fair a cave?
Beautiful tyrant! fiend angelical!
Dove-feathered raven! wolvish-ravening lamb!
Despisèd substance of divinest show!
Just opposite to what thou justly seemst,
A damnèd saint, an honorable villain!
O nature, what hadst thou to do in hell
When thou didst bower the spirit of a fiend
In mortal paradise of such sweet flesh?
Was ever book containing such vile matter
So fairly bound? O, that deceit should dwell
In such a gorgeous palace!

Nurse. There's no trust,
No faith, no honesty in men; all perjured,
All forsworn, all naught, all dissemblers.
Ah, where's my man? Give me some aqua vitae.
These griefs, these woes, these sorrows make me old.
Shame come to Romeo!

Juliet. Blistered be thy tongue
For such a wish! He was not born to shame.
Upon his brow shame is ashamed to sit;
For 'tis a throne where honor may be crowned
Sole monarch of the universal earth.

57–60 Juliet say her heart is broken and bankrupt (**bankrout**). She wants to be buried with Romeo, sharing his burial platform (**bier**).

ANALYZE LITERARY DEVICES

Annotate: Mark examples of oxymorons in lines 73–85.

Respond: How do these oxymorons help make Juliet a complex yet believable character?

81 bower . . . fiend: give a home to the spirit of a demon.

86–87 all perjured . . . dissemblers: All are liars and pretenders.

88 aqua vitae: brandy.

ANALYZE LITERARY DEVICES

Direct students' attention to the range of emotions that Juliet experiences in this scene, once she finds out that Romeo has killed Tybalt. Remind students that an **oxymoron** is a phrase consisting of contradictory elements.

Ask students to describe Juliet's first reaction once she understands what has happened. Why does she feel this way? *(She is furious at Romeo, yet she still loves him. The oxymorons she uses to describe him—such as "beautiful tyrant" and "fiend angelical"—reveal how conflicted she feels. She is grief-stricken over Tybalt and cannot believe that Romeo could do such a thing.)* Discuss whether Juliet's response is believable, reminding students to consider the cultural and historical context of the play. (***Answer:*** *Her expression of contradictory, paradoxical feelings makes her seem more like a real person and less like a simplistic fictional character.)*

ENGLISH LEARNER SUPPORT

Develop Vocabulary Read aloud Scene 2, lines 69–85. Write the phrase *beautiful tyrant* on the board. Explain that if someone is *beautiful*, the person is good or good to look at. Explain that a *tyrant* is a cruel king. Point out that *beautiful tyrant* is an oxymoron; it contains words with opposite, or contradictory, meanings.

Have students say the word *contradictory* after you. (It may help to have students clap out each of the five syllables, placing more emphasis on the third syllable.) Provide this frame and ask students to use it to explain the oxymoron:

"_____" is an oxymoron because _____ means _____ and _____ means _____. Those meanings are _____ .

Have pairs or small groups review lines 69–85 and circle other oxymorons. Circulate as they work and coach them to use a learner's dictionary to find meanings of unfamiliar terms. Once students have identified oxymorons from the passage, invite volunteers to list them on the board. Then have students explain each oxymoron, using the frame as necessary.

MODERATE/LIGHT

IMPROVE READING FLUENCY

Targeted Passage Point out that Scene 2 opens with a soliloquy, a speech given by a character alone onstage that reveals the character's thoughts or feelings. Read lines 1–31 aloud with appropriate emphasis and emotion. Then have students take turns reading lines 1–31 to a partner. As one partner reads, encourage the other partner to mark poetic language, including similes and metaphors, in Juliet's soliloquy. Have pairs of students share their annotations and discuss how Shakespeare's language conveys Juliet's emotions.

 Go to the **Reading Studio** for additional support in developing fluency.

O, what a beast was I to chide at him!

Nurse. Will you speak well of him that killed your cousin?

Juliet. Shall I speak ill of him that is my husband?
Ah, poor my lord, what tongue shall smooth thy name
When I, thy three-hours' wife, have mangled it?
But wherefore, villain, didst thou kill my cousin?
That villain cousin would have killed my husband.
Back, foolish tears, back to your native spring!
Your tributary drops belong to woe,
Which you, mistaking, offer up to joy.
My husband lives, that Tybalt would have slain;
And Tybalt's dead, that would have slain my husband.
All this is comfort; wherefore weep I then?
Some word there was, worser than Tybalt's death,
That murdered me. I would forget it fain;
But O, it presses to my memory
Like damned guilty deeds to sinners' minds!
"Tybalt is dead, and Romeo—banished."
That "banished," that one word "banished,"
Hath slain ten thousand Tybalts. Tybalt's death
Was woe enough, if it had ended there;
Or, if sour woe delights in fellowship
And needly will be ranked with other griefs,
Why followed not, when she said "Tybalt's dead,"
Thy father, or thy mother, nay, or both,
Which modern lamentation might have moved?
But with a rearward following Tybalt's death,
"Romeo is banished"—to speak that word
Is father, mother, Tybalt, Romeo, Juliet,
All slain, all dead. "Romeo is banished"—
There is no end, no limit, measure, bound,
In that word's death; no words can that woe sound.
Where is my father and my mother, nurse?

Nurse. Weeping and wailing over Tybalt's corse.
Will you go to them? I will bring you thither.

Juliet. Wash they his wounds with tears? Mine shall be spent,
When theirs are dry, for Romeo's banishment.
Take up those cords. Poor ropes, you are beguiled,
Both you and I, for Romeo is exiled.
He made you for a highway to my bed;
But I, a maid, die maiden-widowed.
Come, cords; come, nurse. I'll to my wedding bed;
And death, not Romeo, take my maidenhead!

Nurse. Hie to your chamber. I'll find Romeo

102–106 Juliet is uncertain whether her tears should be of joy or of sorrow.

114–127 If the news of Tybalt's death had been followed by the news of her parents' deaths, Juliet would have felt grief. To follow the story of Tybalt's death with the news of Romeo's banishment creates a sorrow so deep it cannot be expressed in words.

132 beguiled: cheated.

135–137 I . . . maidenhead: I will die a widow without ever really having been a wife. Death, not Romeo, will be my husband.

APPLYING ACADEMIC VOCABULARY

☑ **attribute** ☐ **commit** ☐ **expose** ☐ **initiate** ☑ **underlie**

Write and Discuss Have students turn to a partner to discuss the questions below. Guide students to use the academic vocabulary words *attribute* and *underlie* in their responses. Ask volunteers to share their responses with the class.

- What are the nurse's **attributes** as a servant and friend to Juliet? How would you describe her character?
- What idea **underlies** Juliet's words in lines 122–126?

NOTICE & NOTE

To comfort you. I wot well where he is.
Hark ye, your Romeo will be here at night.
I'll to him; he is hid at Laurence' cell.

Juliet. O, find him! give this ring to my true knight
And bid him come to take his last farewell.

[*Exeunt.*]

Scene 3 *Friar Laurence's cell.*

[*Enter* Friar Laurence.]

Friar Laurence. Romeo, come forth; come forth, thou fearful man.
Affliction is enamored of thy parts,
And thou art wedded to calamity.

[*Enter* Romeo.]

Romeo. Father, what news? What is the Prince's doom?
What sorrow craves acquaintance at my hand
That I yet know not?

Friar Laurence. Too familiar
Is my dear son with such sour company.
I bring thee tidings of the Prince's doom.

Romeo. What less than doomsday is the Prince's doom?

Friar Laurence. A gentler judgment vanished from his lips—
Not body's death, but body's banishment.

Romeo. Ha, banishment? Be merciful, say "death";
For exile hath more terror in his look,
Much more than death. Do not say "banishment."

Friar Laurence. Hence from Verona art thou banished.
Be patient, for the world is broad and wide.

Romeo. There is no world without Verona walls,
But purgatory, torture, hell itself.
Hence banished is banish'd from the world,
And world's exile is death. Then "banishment,"
Is death misterm'd. Calling death "banishment,"
Thou cuttst my head off with a golden axe
And smilest upon the stroke that murders me.

Friar Laurence. O deadly sin! O rude unthankfulness!
Thy fault our law calls death; but the kind Prince,
Taking thy part, hath rushed aside the law,
And turned that black word death to banishment.
This is dear mercy, and thou seest it not.

Romeo. 'Tis torture, and not mercy. Heaven is here,
Where Juliet lives; and every cat and dog

139 wot: know.

2 Affliction . . . parts: Trouble loves you.

4 doom: sentence.

9 doomsday: death.

10 vanished: came.

17–23 There is . . . murders me: Being exiled outside Verona's walls is as bad as being dead. And yet you smile at my misfortune.

WORDS OF THE WISER

Notice & Note: Mark the line(s) where Friar Laurence gives insight into Romeo's predicament.

Infer: What lesson is Friar Laurence trying to teach Romeo?

TEACH

WORDS OF THE WISER

Remind students that in fiction—as in life—advice from an older, wiser person is worth listening to. Ask: What roles has Friar Laurence played so far? *(He performed the wedding of Romeo and Juliet; he is a friend to Romeo and wants to help him.)* Have students **summarize** the advice Friar Laurence gives to Romeo in Act III, Scene 3. Discuss whether they think his words are convincing, and why. (***Answer:*** *Friar Laurence wants Romeo to understand that Romeo is overreacting to the news of banishment: Romeo could have been sentenced to death for his crime, but the Prince chose to banish him, or send him away, instead. The friar wants Romeo to see the banishment as good news, not bad.)*

WHEN STUDENTS STRUGGLE . . .

Analyze Parallel Plots Help students understand how Scene 3 parallels Scene 2. Remind students to note specific details and examples from the text in their story maps. *(Romeo experiences a range of emotions similar to Juliet's and must be comforted by Friar Laurence, just as the nurse attempted to comfort Juliet. Romeo, like Juliet, says he prefers death to being away from his love.)*

For additional support, go to the **Reading Studio** and assign the following **Level Up Tutorial: Plot: Sequence of Events.**

NOTICE & NOTE

33–35 More validity . . . than Romeo: Even flies that live off the dead (**carrion**) will be able to get closer to Juliet than Romeo will.

And little mouse, every unworthy thing,
Live here in heaven and may look on her;
But Romeo may not. More validity,
More honorable state, more courtship lives
In carrion flies than Romeo. They may seize
On the white wonder of dear Juliet's hand
And steal immortal blessing from her lips,
Who, even in pure and vestal modesty,

WHEN STUDENTS STRUGGLE . . .

Analyze Characters Have students recall Romeo's early appearances in the play and consider what they learned about his character previously. Have students discuss whether the portrayal of Romeo in Act III, Scene 3, is consistent with what they already know about him. Ask them to explain their answers. *(Romeo's character has always been emotional and dramatic; he uses language extravagantly to express his feelings. He does the same here, reacting with his heart rather than his head.)*

For additional support, go to the **Reading Studio** and assign the following  **Level Up Tutorial: Character Traits.**

Still blush, as thinking their own kisses sin;
But Romeo may not—he is banished.
This may flies do, when I from this must fly;
They are free men, but I am banished.
And sayst thou yet that exile is not death?
Hadst thou no poison mixed, no sharp-ground knife,
No sudden mean of death, though ne'er so mean,
But "banished" to kill me—"banished"?
O friar, the damned use that word in hell;
Howling attends it! How hast thou the heart,
Being a divine, a ghostly confessor,
A sin-absolver, and my friend professed,
To mangle me with that word "banished"?

Friar Laurence. Thou fond mad man, hear me a little speak.

Romeo. O, thou wilt speak again of banishment.

Friar Laurence. I'll give thee armor to keep off that word;
Adversity's sweet milk, philosophy,
To comfort thee, though thou art banished.

Romeo. Yet "banished"? Hang up philosophy!
Unless philosophy can make a Juliet,
Displant a town, reverse a prince's doom,
It helps not, it prevails not. Talk no more.

Friar Laurence. O, then I see that madmen have no ears.

Romeo. How should they, when that wise men have no eyes?

Friar Laurence. Let me dispute with thee of thy estate.

Romeo. Thou canst not speak of that thou dost not feel.
Wert thou as young as I, Juliet thy love,
An hour but married, Tybalt murdered,
Doting like me, and like me banished,
Then mightst thou speak, then mightst thou tear thy hair,
And fall upon the ground, as I do now,
Taking the measure of an unmade grave.

[Nurse *knocks within.*]

Friar Laurence. Arise; one knocks. Good Romeo, hide thyself.

Romeo. Not I; unless the breath of heartsick groans
Mist-like infold me from the search of eyes.

[*knock*]

Friar Laurence. Hark, how they knock! Who's there? Romeo, arise;
Thou wilt be taken.—Stay awhile!—Stand up;

[*knock*]

44–46 Hadst . . . to kill me: Couldn't you have killed me with poison or a knife instead of with that awful word *banished*?

52 fond: foolish.

54–56 The friar offers philosophical comfort and counseling (**adversity's sweet milk**) as a way to overcome hardship.

63 dispute: discuss; **estate:** situation.

72–73 Romeo will hide only if his sighs create a mist and shield him from sight.

ENGLISH LEARNER SUPPORT

Demonstrate Comprehension Have pairs of students read lines 52–70. Then have them work together to paraphrase what Romeo tells Friar Laurence in line 64 and discuss why he says this.

Once students have discussed the line in pairs, call on a volunteer to paraphrase line 64. *(You can't talk about something that you've never felt yourself.)* Ask: Why does Romeo say this? *(Romeo thinks that the friar, as a religious man, has never been in love, killed someone, or been banished. Therefore, because the friar has never experienced these things, he can't understand Romeo's feelings or give him appropriate advice.)*

LIGHT

WHEN STUDENTS STRUGGLE . . .

Analyze Plot Review the definitions of **internal conflict** and **external conflict**. Remind students that the plot is driven by the main characters' conflicts and efforts to resolve them.

Ask students what conflicts Romeo is experiencing. *(He is banished from Verona, which is an external conflict—character versus society. He will be separated from Juliet, which is creating internal conflict for him.)*

For additional support, go to the **Reading Studio** and assign the following **Level Up Tutorial: Characters and Conflict.**

NOTICE & NOTE

84–85 he is even . . . her case: He is acting the same way that Juliet is.

90 into so deep an O: into such deep grief.

96 blood . . . from her own: the blood of a close relative of hers.

98 concealed lady: secret bride.

102 that name: the name Romeo.

106–108 in what vile part . . . mansion: Romeo asks where in his body (**anatomy**) his name can be found so that he can cut the name out.

108–125 Hold thy . . . bedeck thy shape, thy love, thy wit: You're not acting like a man. Would you send your soul to hell by committing suicide (**doing damned hate upon thyself**)? Why do you curse your birth, heaven, and earth? You are refusing to make good use of your advantages, just as a miser refuses to spend his money.

Run to my study.—By-and-by!—God's will,
What simpleness is this.—I come, I come!

[*knock*]

Who knocks so hard? Whence come you? What's your will?

Nurse [*within*]. Let me come in, and you shall know my errand.
I come from Lady Juliet.

Friar Laurence. Welcome then.

[*Enter* Nurse.]

Nurse. O holy friar, O, tell me, holy friar,
Where is my lady's lord, where's Romeo?

Friar Laurence. There on the ground, with his own tears made drunk.

Nurse. O, he is even in my mistress' case,
Just in her case! O woeful sympathy!
Piteous predicament! Even so lies she,
Blubb'ring and weeping, weeping and blubbering.
Stand up, stand up! Stand, an you be a man.
For Juliet's sake, for her sake, rise and stand!
Why should you fall into so deep an O?

Romeo [*rises*]. Nurse—

Nurse. Ah sir! ah sir! Well, death's the end of all.

Romeo. Spakest thou of Juliet? How is it with her?
Doth not she think me an old murderer,
Now I have stained the childhood of our joy
With blood removed but little from her own?
Where is she? and how doth she? and what says
My concealed lady to our canceled love?

Nurse. O, she says nothing, sir, but weeps and weeps;
And now falls on her bed, and then starts up,
And Tybalt calls; and then on Romeo cries,
And then down falls again.

Romeo. As if that name,
Shot from the deadly level of a gun,
Did murder her; as that name's cursed hand
Murdered her kinsman. O tell me, friar, tell me,
In what vile part of this anatomy
Doth my name lodge? Tell me, that I may sack
The hateful mansion.

[*draws his dagger*]

Friar Laurence. Hold thy desperate hand.
Art thou a man? Thy form cries out thou art;
Thy tears are womanish, thy wild acts denote

TO CHALLENGE STUDENTS . . .

Analyze Dialogue Remind students that in previous scenes, the nurse's speeches have been written in prose. In Act III, Scene 3, lines 84–90, however, she speaks in blank verse. Have students evaluate her lines. Ask them to discuss the following points in small groups:

- why Shakespeare might have changed her speech pattern
- whether Shakespeare is being inconsistent in portraying her character

Have groups summarize the main ideas of their discussions and share them with another group.

NOTICE & NOTE 

The unreasonable fury of a beast.
Unseemly woman in a seeming man!
Or ill-beseeming beast in seeming both!
Thou hast amazed me. By my holy order,
I thought thy disposition better tempered.
Hast thou slain Tybalt? Wilt thou slay thyself?
And slay thy lady too that lives in thee,
By doing damnèd hate upon thyself?
Why railst thou on thy birth, the heaven, and earth?
Since birth and heaven and earth, all three do meet
In thee at once; which thou at once wouldst lose.
Fie, fie, thou shamest thy shape, thy love, thy wit,
Which, like a usurer, aboundst in all,
And usest none in that true use indeed
Which should bedeck thy shape, thy love, thy wit.
Thy noble shape is but a form of wax,
Digressing from the valor of a man;
Thy dear love sworn but hollow perjury,
Killing that love which thou hast vowed to cherish;
Thy wit, that ornament to shape and love,
Misshapen in the conduct of them both,
Like powder in a skilless soldier's flask,
Is set afire by thine own ignorance,
And thou dismembered with thine own defense.
What, rouse thee, man! Thy Juliet is alive,
For whose dear sake thou wast but lately dead.
There art thou happy. Tybalt would kill thee,
But thou slewest Tybalt. There art thou happy.
The law, that threatened death, becomes thy friend
And turns it to exile. There art thou happy.
A pack of blessings light upon thy back;
Happiness courts thee in her best array;
But, like a misbehaved and sullen wench,
Thou poutst upon thy fortune and thy love.
Take heed, take heed, for such die miserable.
Go get thee to thy love, as was decreed,
Ascend her chamber, hence and comfort her.
But look thou stay not till the watch be set,
For then thou canst not pass to Mantua,
Where thou shalt live till we can find a time
To blaze your marriage, reconcile your friends,
Beg pardon of the Prince, and call thee back
With twenty hundred thousand times more joy
Than thou wentst forth in lamentation.
Go before, nurse. Commend me to thy lady,
And bid her hasten all the house to bed,
Which heavy sorrow makes them apt unto.

LANGUAGE CONVENTIONS

Annotate: Mark the places in Friar Laurence's speech (lines 108–144) where Shakespeare uses parallel construction.

Analyze: What is the effect of parallel construction in this speech?

126–134 The friar explains how by acting as he is, Romeo is misusing his shape (his outer form or body), his love, and his wit (his mind or intellect).

148–149 look . . . Mantua: Leave before the guards take their places at the city gates; otherwise you will not be able to escape.

151 blaze . . . friends: announce your marriage and get the families (**friends**) to stop feuding.

TEACH

LANGUAGE CONVENTIONS

Read aloud Act III, Scene 3, lines 108–144, while students mark the repeated elements in these lines. Have partners compare the lines they marked. Then call on some students to share their annotations with the rest of the class. Discuss the patterns that Shakespeare uses. Point out that in a couple of cases he repeats a list of three things (for example, "thy birth, the heaven, and earth" and "thy shape, thy love, thy wit") and that he also repeats a clause three times: "There art thou happy." Ask students what impact this use of parallel structure has in this speech. *(By repeating these words and structures, Shakespeare makes the words spoken by Friar Laurence come across as more urgent and emphatic. It's as if by repeating these words and structures, Friar Laurence is trying to get Romeo to listen to him and understand all of the reasons he should rouse himself and be happy.)*

WHEN STUDENTS STRUGGLE . . .

Analyze Character Have students read Friar Laurence's speech (lines 108–144) carefully to determine what he says to Romeo in an effort to bring him to his senses. Have students explain Friar Laurence's tone in the first part of the speech. Ask: What words and phrases convey this tone? *(In lines 109–113, the friar's tone is disgusted and angry. He tells Romeo that his tears are womanish and that he is acting like a beast, not a man.)* Why does the friar begin his speech in this way? *(He is trying to shame Romeo into summoning his inner strength.)* How does he reinforce this purpose in lines 143–145? *(He returns to his original tone, telling Romeo he is acting like a "misbehaved and sullen wench.")*

For additional support, go to the **Reading Studio** and assign the following **Level Up Tutorial: Character Motivation.**

NOTICE & NOTE

162 bid . . . chide: Tell Juliet to get ready to scold me for the way I've behaved.

166–171 and here . . . here: Either leave before the night watchmen go on duty, or get out at dawn in a disguise. Stay awhile in Mantua. I'll find your servant and send messages to you about what good things are happening here.

1–2 Things have . . . our daughter: Such terrible things have happened that we haven't had time to persuade (**move**) Juliet to think about your marriage proposal.

8 Sad times are not good times for talking of marriage.

11 Tonight she is locked up with her sorrow.

12 desperate tender: bold offer.

Romeo is coming.

Nurse. O Lord, I could have stayed here all the night
To hear good counsel. O, what learning is!
My lord, I'll tell my lady you will come.

Romeo. Do so, and bid my sweet prepare to chide.

[Nurse *offers to go and turns again.*]

Nurse. Here is a ring she bid me give you, sir.
Hie you, make haste, for it grows very late.

[*Exit.*]

Romeo. How well my comfort is revived by this!

Friar Laurence. Go hence; good night; and here stands all your
state:
Either be gone before the watch be set,
Or by the break of day disguised from hence.
Sojourn in Mantua. I'll find out your man,
And he shall signify from time to time
Every good hap to you that chances here.
Give me thy hand. 'Tis late. Farewell; good night.

Romeo. But that a joy past joy calls out on me,
It were a grief so brief to part with thee.
Farewell.

[*Exeunt.*]

Scene 4 *Capulet's house.*

[*Enter* Capulet, Lady Capulet, *and* Paris.]

Capulet. Things have fall'n out, sir, so unluckily
That we have had no time to move our daughter.
Look you, she loved her kinsman Tybalt dearly,
And so did I. Well, we were born to die.
'Tis very late; she'll not come down tonight.
I promise you, but for your company,
I would have been abed an hour ago.

Paris. These times of woe afford no time to woo.
Madam, good night. Commend me to your daughter.

Lady Capulet. I will, and know her mind early tomorrow;
Tonight she's mewed up to her heaviness.

[Paris *offers to go and* Capulet *calls him again.*]

Capulet. Sir Paris, I will make a desperate tender
Of my child's love. I think she will be ruled
In all respects by me; nay more, I doubt it not.

WHEN STUDENTS STRUGGLE . . .

Analyze Plot Have partners review the plan Friar Laurence's proposes in Act III, Scene 3, and create a chart summarizing it. Ask students to insert the line numbers of the details they include. Then have students discuss whether the plan sounds as if it will work, and why or why not.

Romeo's Responsibilities	Friar Laurence's Jobs
comfort Juliet (lines 146–147)	*announce the marriage and reconcile friends and family (line 151)*
go to Mantua (lines 148–150 and 167–169)	*try to get Prince Escalus to pardon Romeo (line 152)*
await messages from Friar Laurence and the call to return to Verona (lines 150–154)	*keep Romeo informed and eventually bring him back to Verona (lines 169–171)*

For additional support, go to the **Reading Studio** and assign the following **Level Up Tutorial: Plot: Sequence of Events.**

NOTICE & NOTE

Wife, go you to her ere you go to bed;
Acquaint her here of my son Paris' love
And bid her (mark you me?) on Wednesday next—
But, soft! what day is this?

Paris. Monday, my lord.

Capulet. Monday! ha, ha! Well, Wednesday is too soon.
A Thursday let it be—a Thursday, tell her,
She shall be married to this noble earl.
Will you be ready? Do you like this haste?
We'll keep no great ado—a friend or two;
For hark you, Tybalt being slain so late,
It may be thought we held him carelessly,

ANALYZE PARALLEL PLOTS

Annotate: In this scene, Shakespeare continues the parallel plot of Paris's marriage proposal to Juliet. Mark the spot in lines 12–21 where Lord Capulet says that he will convince Juliet to marry Paris.

Predict: How will this parallel plot affect the main plot of Romeo and Juliet's romance?

23 no great ado: no big festivity.

TEACH

ANALYZE PARALLEL PLOTS

Point out to students that as Scene 4 unfolds, the audience is aware of intense dramatic irony. Ask: What do we know about Juliet that her parents do not? *(The audience knows that Juliet is already married to Romeo.)* What do the Capulets believe is the reason for Juliet's sadness? *(Her parents think Juliet is sad over Tybalt's death, but the audience knows she is grieving Romeo's banishment.)*

Prompt students to discuss how this dramatic irony creates suspense in the play and how the Capulets' decision to make Juliet marry Paris will affect Juliet. (***Answer:*** *It will increase the pressure on Juliet, who is already secretly married to Romeo and cannot marry another man.)*

ENGLISH LEARNER SUPPORT

Use Details to Make Inferences Have students underline the stage directions that tell where Scene 5 takes place and who is in the scene. *(Capulet's orchard. Enter* Romeo *and* Juliet *above, at the window.)* Ask: Where are Romeo and Juliet at the beginning of Scene 5? *(They are standing near the window that has a view of the Capulets' orchard, or backyard.)*

Ask pairs of students to review lines 1–11 for clues that suggest what time of day it is. Tell students that the clues may include metaphors—comparisons between two things that are basically unlike but share one or more things in common. After pairs have reviewed the passage, ask volunteers to share the clues they found. *(It was the lark, the herald of the morn; what envious streaks / Do lace the severing clouds in yonder East; Night's candles are burnt out, and jocund day / Stands tiptoe on the misty mountain tops.)* Ask students to explain the clues they found. Support them with any unfamiliar terms.

Point out that a nightingale and a lark are two birds: one sings at night and the other in the morning. Ask: When they hear a bird, why does Juliet tell Romeo, "Believe me, love, it was the nightingale." *(She doesn't want Romeo to leave. She wants it still to be nighttime, not morning.)*

MODERATE/LIGHT

NOTICE & NOTE

34–35 it is . . . by-and-by: It's so late at night that soon we'll be calling it early in the morning.

2 It was . . . lark: The nightingale sings at night; the lark sings in the morning.

9 Night's candles: stars.

12–25 Juliet continues to pretend it is night to keep Romeo from leaving. Romeo says he'll stay if Juliet wishes it, even if it means death.

20 Cynthia's brow: Cynthia is another name for Diana, the Roman goddess of the moon. She was often pictured with a crescent moon on her forehead.

26 Romeo's mention of death frightens Juliet, and she urges him to leave quickly.

Being our kinsman, if we revel much.
Therefore we'll have some half a dozen friends,
And there an end. But what say you to Thursday?

Paris. My lord, I would that Thursday were tomorrow.

Capulet. Well, get you gone. A Thursday be it then.
Go you to Juliet ere you go to bed;
Prepare her, wife, against this wedding day.
Farewell, my lord.—Light to my chamber, ho!
Afore me, it is so very very late
That we may call it early by-and-by.
Good night.

[*Exeunt.*]

Scene 5 *Capulet's orchard.*

[*Enter* Romeo *and* Juliet *above, at the window.*]

Juliet. Wilt thou be gone? It is not yet near day.
It was the nightingale, and not the lark,
That pierced the fearful hollow of thine ear.
Nightly she sings on yond pomegranate tree.
Believe me, love, it was the nightingale.

Romeo. It was the lark, the herald of the morn;
No nightingale. Look, love, what envious streaks
Do lace the severing clouds in yonder East.
Night's candles are burnt out, and jocund day
Stands tiptoe on the misty mountain tops.
I must be gone and live, or stay and die.

Juliet. Yond light is not daylight; I know it, I.
It is some meteor that the sun exhales
To be to thee this night a torchbearer
And light thee on thy way to Mantua.
Therefore stay yet; thou needst not to be gone.

Romeo. Let me be ta'en, let me be put to death.
I am content, so thou wilt have it so.
I'll say yon grey is not the morning's eye,
'Tis but the pale reflex of Cynthia's brow;
Nor that is not the lark whose notes do beat
The vaulty heaven so high above our heads.
I have more care to stay than will to go.
Come, death, and welcome! Juliet wills it so.
How is't, my soul? Let's talk; it is not day.

Juliet. It is, it is! Hie hence, be gone, away!
It is the lark that sings so out of tune,
Straining harsh discords and unpleasing sharps.

NOTICE & NOTE 

Some say the lark makes sweet division;
This doth not so, for she divideth us.
Some say the lark and loathed toad changed eyes;
O, now I would they had changed voices too,
Since arm from arm that voice doth us affray,
Hunting thee hence with hunt's-up to the day!
O, now be gone! More light and light it grows.

Romeo. More light and light—more dark and dark our woes!

[*Enter* Nurse, *hastily.*]

Nurse. Madam!

Juliet. Nurse?

Nurse. Your lady mother is coming to your chamber.
The day is broke; be wary, look about.

[*Exit.*]

29 division: melody.

31–34 I wish the lark had the voice of the hated (**loathed**) toad, since its voice is frightening us apart and acting as a morning song for hunters (**hunt's-up**).

ENGLISH LEARNER SUPPORT

Analyze Figurative Language Use the following supports with students at varying proficiency levels:

- Direct students to Act III, Scene 5, line 36: "More light and light—more dark and dark our woes!" Read the line aloud with students and have them echo read it. Explain that *woes* are problems, or things that make people sad. Ask: Does light mean night or morning? *(morning)* Is morning good or bad for Romeo and Juliet? *(bad)* Can Romeo stay with Juliet? *(no)* When Romeo says "more dark and dark our woes!" does he mean things are getting better or things are getting worse? *(They're getting worse.)* Why? *(He has to leave Verona.)* **SUBSTANTIAL**
- Have pairs of students paraphrase line 36. *(Romeo means that as the day breaks and light grows, the couple's troubles grow darker, or become more serious.)* **MODERATE**
- Have students work in small groups to review lines 1–36 and discuss how images of light and dark relate to the characters' conflict. *(Romeo and Juliet both want it to be nighttime because as soon as it becomes light, it will be morning and Romeo will have to leave. Usually light means hope, but in this case, light brings more darkness, because they will have to separate and their problems will increase.)* **LIGHT**

WHEN STUDENTS STRUGGLE . . .

Analyze Plot Have students create timelines showing the chronology of events in Act III.

- First, have students review their timelines from Act II.
- Help students identify the key events to place on their timelines for Act III. *(deaths of Mercutio and Tybalt, the announcement of Romeo's exile, Romeo and Juliet's wedding night, Romeo's departure for Mantua, planned wedding of Juliet to Paris)*
- Discuss the timeframe in which these events take place. *(Monday and Monday night, Tuesday morning, Thursday for planned wedding)*

Have students compare their timelines in small groups.

 For additional support, go to the **Reading Studio** and assign the following **Level Up Tutorial: Plot: Sequence of Events.**

NOTICE & NOTE

46 much in years: very old.

54–56 I have . . . tomb: Juliet sees an evil vision of the future.

59 Dry . . . blood: People believed that sorrow drained the blood from the heart, causing a sad person to look pale.

60–62 fickle: changeable in loyalty or affection. Juliet asks fickle Fortune why it has anything to do with Romeo, who is the opposite of fickle.

67 What . . . hither: What unusual reason brings her here?

72–73 have . . . wit: Stop crying (**have done**). A little grief is evidence of love, while too much grief shows a lack of good sense (**want of wit**).

Juliet. Then, window, let day in, and let life out.

Romeo. Farewell, farewell! One kiss, and I'll descend.

[*He starts down the ladder.*]

Juliet. Art thou gone so, my lord, my love, my friend?
I must hear from thee every day in the hour,
For in a minute there are many days.
O, by this count I shall be much in years
Ere I again behold my Romeo!

Romeo. Farewell!
I will omit no opportunity
That may convey my greetings, love, to thee.

Juliet. O, thinkst thou we shall ever meet again?

Romeo. I doubt it not; and all these woes shall serve
For sweet discourses in our time to come.

Juliet. O God, I have an ill-divining soul!
Methinks I see thee, now thou art below,
As one dead in the bottom of a tomb.
Either my eyesight fails, or thou lookst pale.

Romeo. And trust me, love, in my eye so do you.
Dry sorrow drinks our blood. Adieu! adieu!

[*Exit.*]

Juliet. O Fortune, Fortune! all men call thee fickle.
If thou art fickle, what dost thou with him
That is renowned for faith? Be fickle, Fortune,
For then I hope thou wilt not keep him long
But send him back.

Lady Capulet. [*within*]. Ho, daughter! are you up?

Juliet. Who is't that calls? It is my lady mother.
Is she not down so late, or up so early?
What unaccustomed cause procures her hither?

[*Enter* Lady Capulet.]

Lady Capulet. Why, how now, Juliet?

Juliet. Madam, I am not well.

Lady Capulet. Evermore weeping for your cousin's death?
What, wilt thou wash him from his grave with tears?
An if thou couldst, thou couldst not make him live.
Therefore have done. Some grief shows much of love;
But much of grief shows still some want of wit.

Juliet. Yet let me weep for such a feeling loss.

Lady Capulet. So shall you feel the loss, but not the friend

TO CHALLENGE STUDENTS . . .

Analyze Plot Tell students that this farewell scene in Act III, Scene 5, presents multiple contrasts that add to its emotional impact on the audience. Have students reread Romeo and Juliet's first farewell in Act II, Scene 2. Have students work in small groups to discuss how this parting is different from the one in Act II. *(The first scene promised future happiness. They were optimistic in their young love for each other. As they say goodbye here, they face uncertainty about whether they will ever see each other again.)* In small groups, have students contrast the two scenes and analyze each one's effect on the audience.

Which you weep for.

Juliet. Feeling so the loss,
I cannot choose but ever weep the friend.

Lady Capulet. Well, girl, thou weepst not so much for his death
As that the villain lives which slaughtered him.

Juliet. What villain, madam?

Lady Capulet. That same villain Romeo.

Juliet [*aside*]. Villain and he be many miles asunder.—
God pardon him! I do, with all my heart;
And yet no man like he doth grieve my heart.

Lady Capulet. That is because the traitor murderer lives.

Juliet. Ay, madam, from the reach of these my hands.
Would none but I might venge my cousin's death!

Lady Capulet. We will have vengeance for it, fear thou not.
Then weep no more. I'll send to one in Mantua,
Where that same banished runagate doth live,
Shall give him such an unaccustomed dram
That he shall soon keep Tybalt company;
And then I hope thou wilt be satisfied.

Juliet. Indeed I never shall be satisfied
With Romeo till I behold him—dead—
Is my poor heart so for a kinsman vexed.
Madam, if you could find out but a man
To bear a poison, I would temper it;
That Romeo should, upon receipt thereof,
Soon sleep in quiet. O, how my heart abhors
To hear him named and cannot come to him,
To wreak the love I bore my cousin Tybalt
Upon his body that hath slaughtered him!

Lady Capulet. Find thou the means, and I'll find such a man.
But now I'll tell thee joyful tidings, girl.

Juliet. And joy comes well in such a needy time.
What are they, I beseech your ladyship?

Lady Capulet. Well, well, thou hast a careful father, child;
One who, to put thee from thy heaviness,
Hath sorted out a sudden day of joy
That thou expects not nor I looked not for.

Juliet. Madam, in happy time! What day is that?

Lady Capulet. Marry, my child, early next Thursday morn
The gallant, young, and noble gentleman,
The County Paris, at Saint Peter's Church,

81–102 In these lines Juliet's words have double meanings. To avoid lying to her mother, she chooses her words carefully. They can mean what her mother wants to hear—or what Juliet really has on her mind.

89 runagate: runaway.

90 unaccustomed dram: poison.

93–102 dead: This could refer either to Romeo or to Juliet's heart. Juliet says that if her mother could find someone to carry a poison to Romeo, she would mix (**temper**) it herself.

WHEN STUDENTS STRUGGLE . . .

Analyze Dramatic Irony Remind students that Lady Capulet does not know that Juliet is already married to Romeo. This dramatic irony enables the audience to appreciate Juliet's skill in maintaining her loyalty to Romeo while saying the right things to her mother. Model how to read Juliet's speech in lines 93–102, while students echo-read with you.

Prompt students to explain what Juliet means in lines 93–95 versus what her mother thinks. *(Juliet is saying that she shall never be happy until she sees Romeo. Her heart is dead at the thought of her kinsman [Romeo] suffering. Her mother believes she is saying she wants Romeo dead.)*

Ask: What is Juliet actually saying in lines 96–99? *(Juliet wants to send Romeo a sleeping potion that would give him rest and peace, but her mother thinks Juliet is saying she wants to poison Romeo.)*

For additional support, go to the **Reading Studio** and assign the following **Level Up Tutorial: Irony.**

The Tragedy of Romeo and Juliet: Act III, Scene 5 355

ENGLISH LEARNER SUPPORT

Understand Idioms Tell students that idiomatic expressions mean something different from the literal meaning of the words. Point out "take it at your hands" in line 125. Have students work in pairs or small groups and use the context in which the phrase occurs to define it. *(see how he will react to hearing the news from you)*

Ask students how they think Juliet's parents will respond to Juliet's refusal to marry Paris. *(Her parents will be upset with her for disobeying their wishes.)*

LIGHT

NOTICE & NOTE

Shall happily make thee there a joyful bride.

Juliet. Now by Saint Peter's Church, and Peter too,
He shall not make me there a joyful bride!
I wonder at this haste, that I must wed
Ere he that should be husband comes to woo.
I pray you tell my lord and father, madam,
I will not marry yet; and when I do, I swear
It shall be Romeo, whom you know I hate,
Rather than Paris. These are news indeed!

Lady Capulet. Here comes your father. Tell him so yourself,
And see how he will take it at your hands.

[*Enter* Capulet *and* Nurse.]

127 the sunset . . . son: the death of Tybalt.

129–137 conduit: fountain. Capulet compares Juliet to a boat (**bark**), an ocean, and the wind because of her excessive crying.

Capulet. When the sun sets the air doth drizzle dew,
But for the sunset of my brother's son
It rains downright.
How now? a conduit, girl? What, still in tears?
Evermore show'ring? In one little body
Thou counterfeitst a bark, a sea, a wind:
For still thy eyes, which I may call the sea,
Do ebb and flow with tears; the bark thy body is,
Sailing in this salt flood; the winds, thy sighs,
Who, raging with thy tears and they with them,
Without a sudden calm will overset
Thy tempest-tossed body. How now, wife?
Have you delivered to her our decree?

Lady Capulet. Ay, sir; but she will none, she gives you thanks.
I would the fool were married to her grave!

141 take me with you: let me understand you.

Capulet. Soft! take me with you, take me with you, wife.
How? Will she none? Doth she not give us thanks?
Is she not proud? Doth she not count her blest,
Unworthy as she is, that we have wrought
So worthy a gentleman to be her bridegroom?

146–148 Not proud . . . meant love: I'm not pleased, but I am grateful for your intentions.

Juliet. Not proud you have, but thankful that you have.
Proud can I never be of what I hate,
But thankful even for hate that is meant love.

149–157 Capulet calls Juliet a person who argues over fine points (**choplogic**) and a spoiled child (**minion**). He tells her to prepare herself (**fettle your fine joints**) for the wedding or he'll haul her there in a cart for criminals (**hurdle**). He calls her a piece of dead flesh (**green-sickness carrion**) and a coward (**tallow-face**).

Capulet. How, how, how, how, choplogic? What is this?
"Proud"—and "I thank you"—and "I thank you not"—
And yet "not proud"? Mistress minion you,
Thank me no thankings, nor proud me no prouds,
But fettle your fine joints 'gainst Thursday next
To go with Paris to Saint Peter's Church,
Or I will drag thee on a hurdle thither.
Out, you green-sickness carrion! out, you baggage!

WHEN STUDENTS STRUGGLE . . .

Analyze Characters Explain that characters, like people in real life, react to stress in different ways. Point out that Juliet's parents are enraged and surprised that their daughter refuses to marry Paris. Juliet has always been respectful and cooperative, and they are shocked at her defiance.

Have students discuss what other emotions might be motivating the Capulets' outburst at Juliet. Remind them that the Capulets' nephew was just killed. *(The Capulets may want to see Juliet safe and settled before anything else happens.)*

Ask: Do you think the Capulets' reaction is realistic? Is it justified? *(Their treatment of Juliet seems harsh to contemporary readers, but it may have seemed justified in its historical context. Children were expected to follow their parents' plans for their future, including an arranged marriage.)*

For additional support, go to the **Reading Studio** and assign the following  **Level Up Tutorial: Making Inferences About Characters.**

You tallow-face!

Lady Capulet. Fie, fie; what, are you mad?

Juliet. Good father, I beseech you on my knees,

[*She kneels down.*]

Hear me with patience but to speak a word.

Capulet. Hang thee, young baggage! disobedient wretch!
I tell thee what—get thee to church a Thursday
Or never after look me in the face.
Speak not, reply not, do not answer me!
My fingers itch. Wife, we scarce thought us blest
That God had lent us but this only child;
But now I see this one is one too much,
And that we have a curse in having her.
Out on her, hilding!

Nurse. God in heaven bless her!
You are to blame, my lord, to rate her so.

Capulet. And why, my Lady Wisdom? Hold your tongue,
Good Prudence. Smatter with your gossips, go!

Nurse. I speak no treason.

Capulet. O, God-i-god-en!

Nurse. May not one speak?

Capulet. Peace, you mumbling fool!
Utter your gravity o'er a gossip's bowl,
For here we need it not.

Lady Capulet. You are too hot.

Capulet. God's bread! it makes me mad. Day, night, late, early,
At home, abroad, alone, in company,
Waking or sleeping, still my care hath been
To have her matched; and having now provided
A gentleman of princely parentage,
Of fair demesnes, youthful, and nobly trained,
Stuffed, as they say, with honorable parts,
Proportioned as one's thought would wish a man—
And then to have a wretched puling fool,
A whining mammet, in her fortunes tender,
To answer "I'll not wed, I cannot love;
I am too young, I pray you pardon me"!
But, an you will not wed, I'll pardon you.
Graze where you will, you shall not house with me.
Look to't, think on't; I do not use to jest.
Thursday is near; lay hand on heart, advise:
An you be mine, I'll give you to my friend;

164 My fingers itch: I feel like hitting you.

168 hilding: a good-for-nothing person.

171 smatter: chatter.

174 Utter . . . bowl: Save your words of wisdom for a gathering of gossips.

179 matched: married.

184 puling: crying.

185 mammet: doll.

189–195 Capulet swears that he'll kick Juliet out and cut her off financially if she refuses to marry.

ENGLISH LEARNER SUPPORT

Paraphrase to Demonstrate Comprehension Work with students to paraphrase Capulet's speech in Act III, Scene 5, lines 176–196. Read aloud groups of lines, along with any related side notes. Then guide students to restate them orally, supplying explanations as necessary for any key words and phrases. Record students' paraphrases on the board:

- **lines 176–179** *(It drives me crazy! All the time I'm thinking about how to find her a good husband.)*
- **lines 179–183** *(And now I have found a good man from a good family.)*
- **lines 184–187** *(And then to hear my daughter complaining about her bad luck and telling me "I can't marry him because I can't love him; I am too young; please forgive me!)"*
- **lines 188–189** *(Oh, sure, I'll forgive you if you don't marry Paris. But you won't live in my house or eat my food anymore.)*
- **lines 190–196** *(If you are my daughter, I will give you in marriage to Paris. But if you are not my daughter, you can die on the streets because I won't break my promise.)*

MODERATE/LIGHT

ENGLISH LEARNER SUPPORT

Read with Support Have students read the exchange between Capulet and the nurse in lines 167–172. Ask students what the nurse means in lines 168–169. *(She is defending Juliet. She is saying that Capulet is wrong to say that it is a curse to have Juliet for a daughter.)*

Point to Capulet's words "Hold your tongue" in line 170. Invite a volunteer to explain that idiom, or provide an explanation yourself. *(Do not speak.)* Read aloud line 172. Point out that the word *treason* has a Spanish cognate. Ask if any Spanish-speaking students know what the Spanish cognate is. *(traición)*

Explain that to "speak treason" means to be disloyal to someone or to speak against someone.

Ask students what the nurse means when she says, "I speak no treason." *(She is saying that she has a right to speak and that what she is saying is fair.)* Why does Nurse speak up for Juliet? *(She cares for Juliet; she thinks that Juliet's parents are too harsh; she knows that Juliet is already married.)*

MODERATE/LIGHT

NOTICE & NOTE

196 I'll not be forsworn: I will not break my promise to Paris.

207–211 Juliet is worried about the sin of being married to two men. She asks how heaven can play such tricks (**practice stratagems**) on her.

222 beshrew: curse.

223–225 This new marriage will be better than the first, which is as good as over.

229 Amen: I agree—that is, curse your heart and soul.

An you be not, hang, beg, starve, die in the streets,
For, by my soul, I'll ne'er acknowledge thee,
Nor what is mine shall never do thee good.
Trust to't. Bethink you. I'll not be forsworn.

[*Exit.*]

Juliet. Is there no pity sitting in the clouds
That sees into the bottom of my grief?
O sweet my mother, cast me not away!
Delay this marriage for a month, a week;
Or if you do not, make the bridal bed
In that dim monument where Tybalt lies.

Lady Capulet. Talk not to me, for I'll not speak a word.
Do as thou wilt, for I have done with thee.

[*Exit.*]

Juliet. O God!—O nurse, how shall this be prevented?
My husband is on earth, my faith in heaven.
How shall that faith return again to earth
Unless that husband send it me from heaven
By leaving earth? Comfort me, counsel me.
Alack, alack, that heaven should practice stratagems
Upon so soft a subject as myself!
What sayst thou? Hast thou not a word of joy?
Some comfort, nurse.

Nurse. Faith, here it is.
Romeo is banish'd; and all the world to nothing
That he dares ne'er come back to challenge you;
Or if he do, it needs must be by stealth.
Then, since the case so stands as now it doth,
I think it best you married with the County.
O, he's a lovely gentleman!
Romeo's a dishclout to him. An eagle, madam,
Hath not so green, so quick, so fair an eye
As Paris hath. Beshrew my very heart,
I think you are happy in this second match,
For it excels your first; or if it did not,
Your first is dead—or 'twere as good he were
As living here and you no use of him.

Juliet. Speakst thou this from thy heart?

Nurse. And from my soul too; else beshrew them both.

Juliet. Amen!

Nurse. What?

Juliet. Well, thou hast comforted me marvelous much.
Go in; and tell my lady I am gone,
Having displeased my father, to Laurence' cell,

WHEN STUDENTS STRUGGLE . . .

Analyze Character By the end of this act, everyone who has come into contact with Juliet has turned against her. Juliet's father has ordered her to marry Paris and has threatened to disown her if she does not comply. Lady Capulet sides with her husband and is "done" (line 204) with Juliet. Juliet's nurse advises Juliet to marry Paris, since Romeo is banished and as good as dead anyway. Explain that Shakespeare created complex characters who often have more than one motivation. Write these possible motivations on the board: family obligation, anger, fear, misunderstanding, anxiety, control, despair.

Have students work in pairs to match the nurse, Lord Capulet, and Lady Capulet with one or more of the motivations on the board (or another of their choosing) to explain why that character acts as he or she does in this scene. Have them explain how the motivation drives the behavior of the character.

For additional support, go to the **Reading Studio** and assign the following  **Level Up Tutorial: Character Motivation.**

NOTICE & NOTE 

To make confession and to be absolved.

Nurse. Marry, I will; and this is wisely done.

[*Exit.*]

Juliet. Ancient damnation! O most wicked fiend!
Is it more sin to wish me thus forsworn,
Or to dispraise my lord with that same tongue
Which she hath praised him with above compare
So many thousand times? Go, counselor!
Thou and my bosom henceforth shall be twain.
I'll to the friar to know his remedy.
If all else fail, myself have power to die.

[*Exit.*]

236–238 Ancient damnation: old devil; **dispraise:** criticize.

241 Thou . . . twain: I'll no longer tell you my secrets.

CHECK YOUR UNDERSTANDING

Answer these questions before moving on to the **Analyze the Text** section on the following page.

1 When the act begins, Benvolio is —

A trying to persuade Mercutio to avoid the Capulets

B arguing with Mercutio about how best to help Romeo

C explaining why he is eager to get into a brawl

D joking about how Mercutio always wants to fight

2 What is a sign in Act III that the story of Romeo and Juliet is turning into a tragedy?

F Juliet begs the Nurse to tell her what happened to Romeo.

G Romeo breaks his vow to love Tybalt and not to fight with him.

H Friar Laurence gets frustrated with how Romeo is acting.

J Lord and Lady Capulet become furious with Juliet.

3 In Scene 5, lines 1–35, Juliet wants the darkness to continue because —

A she is playfully trying to hide from Romeo

B she and Romeo are trying to escape together

C she wants Romeo to stay with her a little longer

D she knows she may not live to see the morning

CHECK YOUR UNDERSTANDING

Have students answer the questions independently.

Answers:

1. *A*
2. *G*
3. *C*

If they answer any questions incorrectly, have them reread the text to confirm their understanding. Then they may proceed to ANALYZE THE TEXT on page 360.

ENGLISH LEARNER SUPPORT

Oral Assessment Use the following questions to assess students' comprehension and speaking skills.

1. What is Benvolio doing when Act III begins? *(He is trying to get Mercutio to avoid the Capulets so that there will not be a fight.)*
2. What is a sign in this act that the story is turning into a tragedy? *(Romeo breaks his vow to love Tybalt and fights with him.)*
3. Reread Scene 5, lines 1–35. Why does Juliet want the darkness to continue? *(She wants Romeo to stay with her a little longer.)* **SUBSTANTIAL/MODERATE**

APPLY

ANALYZE THE TEXT

Possible answers:

1. **DOK 2:** *The "houses" are those of the Capulet and Montague families, whose rivalry led to his death. Mercutio's remark foreshadows the grief that will come to both families through Romeo and Juliet's tragedy. Another moment of foreshadowing comes when Juliet tells Romeo about a frightening vision in Scene 5, lines 55–57: "Methinks I see thee, now thou art below, / As one dead in the bottom of a tomb."*
2. **DOK 4:** *Romeo is motivated by rage when Tybalt kills Mercutio. Romeo loses control; and while his anger and grief are justifiable, it was probably unwise to kill a member of the Capulet family. This action will only cause more violence and create more problems for him and Juliet.*
3. **DOK 3:** *Since they both behave emotionally and irrationally, they need older and wiser people to guide them and help them to solve problems. For example, in Scene 3, lines 110–111, Friar Laurence says, "thy wild acts denote / The unreasonable fury of a beast."*
4. **DOK 4:** *He is thinking only of himself and not acting in a rational, open-minded manner. A likely consequence is driving his daughter away or somehow putting her in danger.*
5. **DOK 4:** *The nurse seems to contradict herself when she tells Juliet to marry Paris and forget Romeo (Scene 5, lines 213–226). Although the nurse offers this as sensible advice, Juliet feels betrayed and abandoned. This is revealed in Scene 5, lines 237–240, when Juliet says, "Ancient damnation! O most wicked fiend! / Is it more sin to wish me thus forsworn, / Or to dispraise my lord with that same tongue / Which she hath praised him with above compare / So many thousand times?"*

CREATE AND PRESENT

Write a Journal Entry Discuss the writing task on page 360. Have students review each scene, jotting down details of dialogue that reveal each character's feelings. Remind them that the journal entries will be written from the first-person point of view.

Present to a Partner Circulate around the room as students share their entries and help them compare perspectives.

ANALYZE THE TEXT

Support your responses with evidence from the text. NOTEBOOK

1. **Interpret** What is the meaning of Mercutio's repeated curse, "A plague o' both your houses!" (Scene 1, lines 85, 93)? What might this curse foreshadow? What other moments in Act III have similar foreshadowing?
2. **Evaluate** What is Romeo's motivation for killing Tybalt? Is his action justified or a mistake? Explain your response.
3. **Cite Evidence** In what ways do Romeo and Juliet need the help of Friar Laurence and the Nurse in order to save their love and to move forward? Support your response with evidence from the text.
4. **Analyze** In Scene 5, Lord Capulet becomes enraged when Juliet says she will not marry Paris. In what way are his words and actions in this scene like those of Romeo and Juliet? What are the likely consequences of his actions?
5. **Notice & Note** In Scene 5, how and why does the Nurse's behavior contrast with or contradict her earlier behavior? How does this contrast or contradiction affect Juliet? Explain, citing details from the text.

CREATE AND PRESENT

Write a Journal Entry Explore the parallel feelings of despair that Romeo and Juliet feel in Act III by writing a journal entry for each character. Base your journal entries on evidence from the text.

- ❑ Write a one-page journal entry from the point of view of Juliet when she learns of the death of Tybalt.
- ❑ Write a one-page journal entry from the point of view of Romeo when he is awaiting exile at the friar's cell.
- ❑ If you don't know the word for something or the way to express an idea, ask for assistance from your teacher or peers.

Present to a Partner Share your journal entries by reading them aloud to a partner.

- ❑ Read clearly, at an appropriate volume, and with proper expression.
- ❑ Listen carefully to your partner's journal entries.
- ❑ Ask questions about anything you do not understand.

SETTING A PURPOSE

Note the details of the plan Juliet and Friar Laurence initiate in this act. Pay attention to the reactions of other characters as the plan unfolds. Write down any questions you generate during reading.

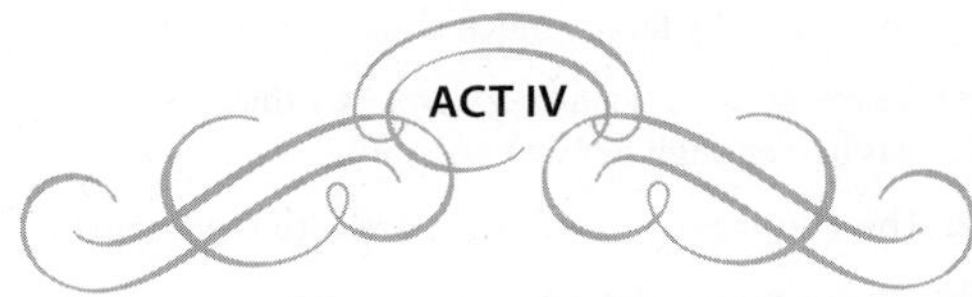

Scene 1 *Friar Laurence's cell.*

[*Enter* Friar Laurence *and* Paris.]

Friar Laurence. On Thursday, sir? The time is very short.

Paris. My father Capulet will have it so,
And I am nothing slow to slack his haste.

Friar Laurence. You say you do not know the lady's mind.
Uneven is the course; I like it not.

Paris. Immoderately she weeps for Tybalt's death,
And therefore have I little talked of love;
For Venus smiles not in a house of tears.
Now, sir, her father counts it dangerous
That she do give her sorrow so much sway,
And in his wisdom hastes our marriage
To stop the inundation of her tears,
Which, too much minded by herself alone,
May be put from her by society.
Now do you know the reason of this haste.

Friar Laurence [*aside*]. I would I knew not why it should be
slowed.—
Look, sir, here comes the lady toward my cell.

[*Enter* Juliet.]

Paris. Happily met, my lady and my wife!

Juliet. That may be, sir, when I may be a wife.

Paris. That may be must be, love, on Thursday next.

Juliet. What must be shall be.

Friar Laurence. That's a certain text.

Paris. Come you to make confession to this father?

Close Read

Juliet. To answer that, I should confess to you.

Paris. Do not deny to him that you love me.

2–3 My . . . haste: Capulet is eager to have the wedding on Thursday and so am I.

4–5 You . . . course: You don't know how Juliet feels about this. It's a very uncertain (**uneven**) plan.

13–14 Which . . . society: which, thought about too much by her in privacy, may be put from her mind if she is forced to be with others.

ANALYZE LITERARY DEVICES

Annotate: Mark two instances of dramatic irony in lines 18–25.

Analyze: What information does the audience have that a character doesn't? How does this information create suspense?

SETTING A PURPOSE

Direct students to use the Setting a Purpose prompt to focus their reading.

ANALYZE LITERARY DEVICES

Remind students that **dramatic irony** occurs when the audience knows something that a character on stage does not. Shakespeare uses dramatic irony as a way to build **suspense**—a feeling of growing tension and excitement. Even though we know that the play is a tragedy, and that both Romeo and Juliet die (as revealed in the Prologue to Act I), we can still feel suspense and wonder about how the events in the story will play out.

Have students explain the dramatic irony in this scene between Friar Laurence, Paris, and Juliet. Ask: What do Friar Laurence and Juliet know that Paris does not? *(They know Juliet is already married to Romeo.)* Why does Paris think Juliet's been crying? *(because of Tybalt's death)* How does Juliet speak in half-truths without completely lying to Paris? *(She says she will be happy when she may be a wife, and Paris thinks that's after the two of them are married; she says she should confess to Paris, and the audience knows that such a confession would tell him the truth about Romeo.)* Point out that Juliet's half-truths heighten the dramatic irony. Ask students to explain how this dramatic irony creates suspense. (***Answer:*** *The audience knows that Juliet is already married and that her wedding to Paris should not be sped up, but stopped. The use of dramatic irony causes the audience to feel suspense: readers are not sure how the conflict can be solved.)*

CLOSE READ SCREENCAST

Modeled Discussion In their eBook, have students view the Close Read Screencast, in which readers discuss and annotate lines 23–36, in which Juliet encounters Paris.

As a class, view and discuss the video.

Close Read Practice PDF

ENGLISH LEARNER SUPPORT

Learn Language Structures Read aloud lines 44–45: "O, shut the door! And when thou has done so, / Come weep with me—past hope, past cure, past help!" Ask students to listen for a word that repeated three times. *(past)* Remind students that when a writer repeats the same word, phrase, or grammatical structure, the writer is creating **parallelism**. Write each parallel phrase from lines 44–45 in a list on the board:

past hope
past cure
past help

Then use the following supports with students at varying proficiency levels:

- Have students read the phrases aloud chorally. Ask how Juliet feels when she says these words. *(sad, hopeless, helpless)* Explain that by repeating the word *past* and using the same structure (*past* + something good), Shakespeare could emphasize how sad and hopeless Juliet feels. **SUBSTANTIAL**
- Elicit two or three other positive nouns, such as *joy* and *happiness*. Have students add to the list of parallel structures, using these nouns. *(past joy, past happiness)* **MODERATE**
- Explain that writers can use different kinds of parallel structures, but to be parallel, they need to share the same pattern. Model adding *now* to the end of the first phrase to create *past hope now*. Then have students add *now* at the end of each line to keep the lines parallel. *(past hope now, past cure now, past help now)* Repeat by having students add *long* before each phrase. *(long past hope now, long past cure now, long past help now)* **LIGHT**

NOTICE & NOTE

Juliet. I will confess to you that I love him.

Paris. So will ye, I am sure, that you love me.

Juliet. If I do so, it will be of more price,
Being spoke behind your back, than to your face.

Paris. Poor soul, thy face is much abused with tears.

Juliet. The tears have got small victory by that,
For it was bad enough before their spite.

Paris. Thou wrongst it more than tears with that report.

Juliet. That is no slander, sir, which is a truth;
And what I spake, I spake it to my face.

Paris. Thy face is mine, and thou hast slandered it.

Juliet. It may be so, for it is not mine own.
Are you at leisure, holy father, now,
Or shall I come to you at evening mass?

Friar Laurence. My leisure serves me, pensive daughter, now.
My lord, we must entreat the time alone.

Paris. God shield I should disturb devotion!
Juliet, on Thursday early will I rouse ye.
Till then, adieu, and keep this holy kiss.

[*Exit.*]

Juliet. O, shut the door! and when thou hast done so,
Come weep with me—past hope, past cure, past help!

Friar Laurence. Ah, Juliet, I already know thy grief;
It strains me past the compass of my wits.
I hear thou must, and nothing may prorogue it,
On Thursday next be married to this County.

Juliet. Tell me not, friar, that thou hearest of this,
Unless thou tell me how I may prevent it.
If in thy wisdom thou canst give no help,
Do thou but call my resolution wise
And with this knife I'll help it presently.
God joined my heart and Romeo's, thou our hands;
And ere this hand, by thee to Romeo's sealed,
Shall be the label to another deed,
Or my true heart with treacherous revolt
Turn to another, this shall slay them both.
Therefore, out of thy long-experienced time,
Give me some present counsel; or, behold,
'Twixt my extremes and me this bloody knife
Shall play the umpire, arbitrating that
Which the commission of thy years and art

30–31 The tears . . . spite: The tears haven't ruined my face; it wasn't all that beautiful before they did their damage.

35 Paris says he owns Juliet's face (since she will soon marry him). Insulting her face, he says, insults him, its owner.

47–48 compass: limit; **prorogue:** postpone.

52–53 If in . . . wise: If you can't find a way to help me, at least agree that my plan is wise.

56–67 And ere this hand . . . of remedy: Before I sign another wedding agreement (**deed**), I will use this knife to kill myself. If you, with your years of experience (**long-experienced time**), can't help me, I'll end my sufferings (**extremes**) and solve the problem myself.

TO CHALLENGE STUDENTS . . .

Compare Two Relationships Discuss the chemistry between Juliet and Paris. Point out that, as far as the audience knows, this meeting between Juliet and Paris is the first time they have exchanged words. Ask students to compare this encounter with Romeo and Juliet's meeting at the party in Act I, Scene 5.

- Have students organize their comparison in a graphic organizer.
- Ask them to examine tone, figures of speech, and ideas.
- Have them draw conclusions about the character of Paris based on their comparison.
- Ask them to share their comparisons and conclusions in small groups.

NOTICE & NOTE

TEACH

Could to no issue of true honor bring.
Be not so long to speak. I long to die
If what thou speak'st speak not of remedy.

Friar Laurence. Hold, daughter, I do spy a kind of hope,
Which craves as desperate an execution
As that is desperate which we would prevent.
If, rather than to marry County Paris,
Thou hast the strength of will to slay thyself,
Then is it likely thou wilt undertake
A thing like death to chide away this shame,
That copest with death himself to scape from it;
And, if thou darest, I'll give thee remedy.

Juliet. O, bid me leap, rather than marry Paris,
From off the battlements of yonder tower,
Or walk in thievish ways, or bid me lurk
Where serpents are; chain me with roaring bears,
Or shut me nightly in a charnel house,
O'ercovered quite with dead men's rattling bones,
With reeky shanks and yellow chapless skulls;
Or bid me go into a new-made grave
And hide me with a dead man in his shroud—
Things that, to hear them told, have made me tremble—
And I will do it without fear or doubt,
To live an unstained wife to my sweet love.

Friar Laurence. Hold, then. Go home, be merry, give consent
To marry Paris. Wednesday is tomorrow.
Tomorrow night look that thou lie alone:

71–76 If, rather than . . . remedy: If you are desperate enough to kill yourself, then you'll be daring enough to try the deathlike solution that I propose.

77–88 Juliet lists the things she would do rather than marry Paris. **charnel house:** a storehouse for bones; **reeky shanks:** stinking bones; **chapless:** without jaws.

IMPROVE READING FLUENCY

Targeted Passage Direct students' attention to the exchange between Friar Laurence and Juliet in lines 68–88. First, read aloud the lines, pausing at each end stop (period) and have students echo read them. Model how to read the lines with expression and use the punctuation to guide your phrasing. Then, have partners take turns reading aloud each speech—the Friar's (lines 68–76) or Juliet's (lines 77–88). Encourage students to provide feedback and support for expression and phrasing. If time allows, have students either read the lines again, incorporating feedback, or swap roles and read the other character's lines.

 Go to the **Reading Studio** for additional support in developing fluency.

NOTICE & NOTE

93 vial: small bottle.

96–106 humor: liquid; **no pulse . . . pleasant sleep:** Your pulse will stop (**surcease**), and you will turn cold, pale, and stiff, as if you were dead; this condition will last for 42 hours.

111–112 same ancient vault . . . lie: same ancient tomb where all members of the Capulet family are buried.

114 drift: plan.

119–120 inconstant toy: foolish whim; **abate thy valor:** weaken your courage.

Let not the nurse lie with thee in thy chamber.
Take thou this vial, being then in bed,
And this distilled liquor drink thou off;
When presently through all thy veins shall run
A cold and drowsy humor; for no pulse
Shall keep his native progress, but surcease;
No warmth, no breath, shall testify thou livest;
The roses in thy lips and cheeks shall fade
To paly ashes, thy eyes' windows fall
Like death when he shuts up the day of life;
Each part, deprived of supple government,
Shall, stiff and stark and cold, appear like death;
And in this borrowed likeness of shrunk death
Thou shalt continue two-and-forty hours,
And then awake as from a pleasant sleep.
Now, when the bridegroom in the morning comes
To rouse thee from thy bed, there art thou dead.
Then, as the manner of our country is,
In thy best robes uncovered on the bier
Thou shalt be borne to that same ancient vault
Where all the kindred of the Capulets lie.
In the meantime, against thou shalt awake,
Shall Romeo by my letters know our drift;
And hither shall he come; and he and I
Will watch thy waking, and that very night
Shall Romeo bear thee hence to Mantua.
And this shall free thee from this present shame,
If no inconstant toy nor womanish fear
Abate thy valor in the acting it.

Juliet. Give me, give me! O, tell me not of fear!

Friar Laurence. Hold! Get you gone, be strong and prosperous
In this resolve. I'll send a friar with speed
To Mantua, with my letters to thy lord.

Juliet. Love give me strength! and strength shall help afford.
Farewell, dear father.

[*Exeunt*]

1–8 Capulet is having a cheerful conversation with his servants about the wedding preparations. One servant assures him that he will test (**try**) the cooks he hires by making them taste their own food (**lick their fingers**).

Scene 2 *Capulet's house.*

[*Enter* Capulet, Lady Capulet, Nurse, *and* Servingmen.]

Capulet. So many guests invite as here are writ.

[*Exit a* Servingman.]

Sirrah, go hire me twenty cunning cooks.

Servingman. You shall have none ill, sir; for I'll try if they can lick their fingers.

WHEN STUDENTS STRUGGLE . . .

Analyze Parallel Plots Tell students that Friar Laurence's plan is central to the action of the remaining scenes of the play. Have pairs of students reread Act IV, Scene 1, lines 89–120. Then, have them create sequence diagrams to map out his plan. As a class, discuss the potential problems that might arise with this plan. *(Friar Laurence has said more than once that courage is needed to carry it out. The danger might be that the dose will be too great and Juliet won't wake up, or that she will wake up too soon.)* What is an essential part of the plan? *(that Romeo gets word of the plan and will be there when she wakes up)*

For additional support, go to the **Reading Studio** and assign the following **Level Up Tutorial: Plot: Sequence of Events.**

NOTICE & NOTE

Capulet. How canst thou try them so?

Servingman. Marry, sir, 'tis an ill cook that cannot
lick his own fingers. Therefore he that cannot lick his
fingers goes not with me.

Capulet. Go, begone.

[*Exit a* Servingman.]

We shall be much unfurnished for this time.
What, is my daughter gone to Friar Laurence?

Nurse. Ay, forsooth.

Capulet. Well, he may chance to do some good on her.
A peevish self-willed harlotry it is.

[*Enter* Juliet.]

Nurse. See where she comes from shrift with merry look.

Capulet. How now, my headstrong? Where have you been
gadding?

Juliet. Where I have learnt me to repent the sin
Of disobedient opposition
To you and your behests, and am enjoined
By holy Laurence to fall prostrate here
To beg your pardon. Pardon, I beseech you!
Henceforward I am ever ruled by you.

Capulet. Send for the County. Go tell him of this.
I'll have this knot knit up tomorrow morning.

Juliet. I met the youthful lord at Laurence' cell
And gave him what becomed love I might,
Not stepping o'er the bounds of modesty.

Capulet. Why, I am glad on't. This is well. Stand up.
This is as't should be. Let me see the County.
Ay, marry, go, I say, and fetch him hither.
Now, afore God, this reverend holy friar,
All our whole city is much bound to him.

Juliet. Nurse, will you go with me into my closet
To help me sort such needful ornaments
As you think fit to furnish me tomorrow?

Lady Capulet. No, not till Thursday. There is time enough.

Capulet. Go, nurse, go with her. We'll to church tomorrow.

[*Exeunt* Juliet *and* Nurse.]

Lady Capulet. We shall be short in our provision.
'Tis now near night.

Capulet. Tush, I will stir about,

10 unfurnished: unprepared.

14 A silly, stubborn girl she is.

19 behests: orders; **enjoined:** commanded.

24 I'll have this wedding scheduled for tomorrow morning.

36–39 Lady Capulet urges her husband to wait until Thursday as originally planned. She needs time to get food (**provision**) ready for the wedding party.

39–46 Capulet is so set on Wednesday that he promises to make the arrangements himself.

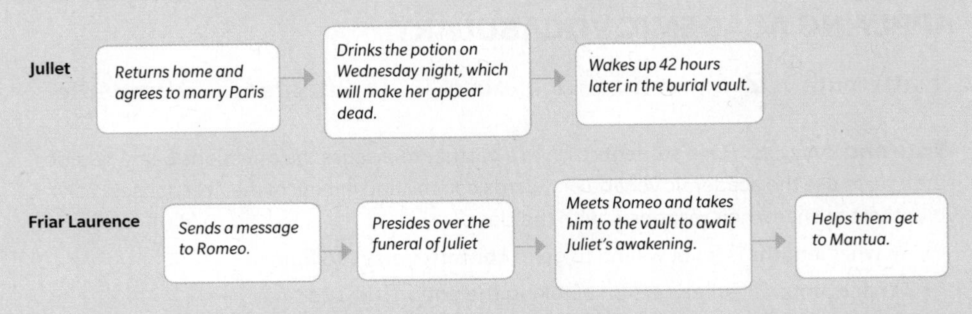

The Tragedy of Romeo and Juliet: Act IV, Scene 2 365

TEACH

ANALYZE PARALLEL PLOTS

Remind students that much of the suspense and drama in the play occurs when the play's separate story lines—or **parallel plots**—intersect. One such story line is Paris's plan to marry Juliet. Call on volunteers to review the main events in this story line that take place in Scene 2. *(Juliet accepts Paris's proposal even though she is legally married to Romeo. Capulet decides to move up the wedding by one day.)*

Ask students to discuss the contrasting emotions as Scene 2 ends. *(Juliet's parents are thrilled that their daughter has changed her mind and become obedient again; as Capulet says, "My heart is wonderous light" [line 46]. But their joy contrasts with Juliet's own sadness and worry over whether Friar Laurence's plan will succeed.)* How does Juliet's wedding to Romeo contrast with her upcoming wedding to Paris? *(**Answer:** The wedding to Romeo was held secretly and with love. The wedding to Paris will be held openly but without love.)*

ANALYZE LITERARY DEVICES

Tell students that Shakespeare uses **foreshadowing** to provide hints about future events in the play. Have a volunteer give an example of foreshadowing in Juliet's soliloquy in Scene 3. *(**Answer:** Juliet's sense of foreboding serves as foreshadowing that her plan may not turn out the way she wants and that tragedy awaits her.)*

English Learner Support

Make Predictions Remind students that when you make a **prediction,** you use text clues to make a reasonable guess about what will happen next in a story.

Review with students that at this point in the play, the day is Tuesday. List these questions on the board:

- Will Juliet take the potion?
- Will Juliet marry Paris on Wednesday?
- Will Romeo get the message from Friar Laurence?
- Will Romeo get back to Verona before Juliet wakes up?
- Will Friar Laurence's plan work?

Have partners take turns asking and answering the questions in order to share their own predictions about what will happen next in the story. **MODERATE**

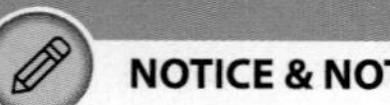

NOTICE & NOTE

ANALYZE PARALLEL PLOTS

Annotate: Mark evidence of Lord Capulet's feelings regarding Juliet's wedding to Paris.

Compare: How does Shakespeare contrast Juliet's wedding to Romeo with her upcoming wedding to Paris?

And all things shall be well, I warrant thee, wife.
Go thou to Juliet, help to deck up her.
I'll not to bed tonight; let me alone.
I'll play the housewife for this once. What, ho!
They are all forth; well, I will walk myself
To County Paris, to prepare him up
Against tomorrow. My heart is wondrous light,
Since this same wayward girl is so reclaimed.

[*Exeunt.*]

Scene 3 *Juliet's bedroom.*

[*Enter* Juliet *and* Nurse.]

Juliet. Ay, those attires are best; but, gentle nurse,
I pray thee leave me to myself tonight;
For I have need of many orisons
To move the heavens to smile upon my state,
Which, well thou knowest, is cross and full of sin.

3 orisons: prayers.

[*Enter* Lady Capulet.]

Lady Capulet. What, are you busy, ho? Need you my help?

Juliet. No madam; we have culled such necessaries
As are behooveful for our state tomorrow.
So please you, let me now be left alone,
And let the nurse this night sit up with you;
For I am sure you have your hands full all
In this so sudden business.

7–8 we have . . . tomorrow: We have picked out (**culled**) everything appropriate for the wedding tomorrow.

Lady Capulet. Good night.
Get thee to bed and rest, for thou hast need.

[*Exeunt* Lady Capulet *and* Nurse.]

Juliet. Farewell! God knows when we shall meet again.
I have a faint cold fear thrills through my veins
That almost freezes up the heat of life.
I'll call them back again to comfort me.
Nurse!—What should she do here?
My dismal scene I needs must act alone.
Come, vial.
What if this mixture do not work at all?
Shall I be married then tomorrow morning?
No, no! This shall forbid it. Lie thou there.

[*lays down a dagger*]

What if it be a poison which the friar
Subtly hath ministered to have me dead,
Lest in this marriage he should be dishonored
Because he married me before to Romeo?

ANALYZE LITERARY DEVICES

Annotate: Mark an instance of foreshadowing in the text.

Analyze: What does this detail imply about how Juliet's plan will ultimately result?

23 This shall forbid it: A dagger will be her alternative means of keeping from marrying Paris.

24–58 Juliet lists her various doubts and fears about what she is about to do.

APPLYING ACADEMIC VOCABULARY

☐ attribute ☑ commit ☐ expose ☑ initiate ☐ underlie

Write and Discuss Have students turn to a partner to discuss the questions below. Guide students to use the academic vocabulary words *commit* and *initiate* in their responses. Ask volunteers to share their responses with the class.

- To what lengths is Juliet willing to go to **commit** herself to Romeo?
- What events will Juliet's action of taking the potion **initiate**?

NOTICE & NOTE

I fear it is; and yet methinks it should not,
For he hath still been tried a holy man.
How if, when I am laid into the tomb,
I wake before the time that Romeo
Come to redeem me? There's a fearful point!
Shall I not then be stifled in the vault,
To whose foul mouth no healthsome air breathes in,
And there die strangled ere my Romeo comes?
Or, if I live, is it not very like
The horrible conceit of death and night,
Together with the terror of the place—
As in a vault, an ancient receptacle
Where for this many hundred years the bones
Of all my buried ancestors are packed;
Where bloody Tybalt, yet but green in earth,
Lies fest'ring in his shroud; where, as they say,
At some hours in the night spirits resort—
Alack, alack, is it not like that I,
So early waking—what with loathsome smells,
And shrieks like mandrakes torn out of the earth,
That living mortals, hearing them, run mad—
O, if I wake, shall I not be distraught,
Environed with all these hideous fears,
And madly play with my forefathers' joints,
And pluck the mangled Tybalt from his shroud,
And, in this rage, with some great kinsman's bone

36–43 Juliet fears the vision (**conceit**) she might have on waking in the family tomb and seeing the rotting body of Tybalt.

45–54 She fears that the smells together with the sounds of ghosts screaming might make her lose her mind and commit bizarre acts. Mandrake root was thought to look like the human form and to scream when pulled from the ground.

TO CHALLENGE STUDENTS . . .

Explore Multimedia Adaptations Challenge students to research adaptations of *Romeo and Juliet* in film, music, or the visual arts—for example, Franco Zeffirelli's 1968 film adaptation (stills from which are featured with this selection), Baz Luhrmann's 1996 *Romeo + Juliet*, Tchaikovsky's *Romeo and Juliet*, or Leonard Bernstein's *West Side Story*. Have students choose an adaptation to explore and instruct them to answer these questions:

- Why do you think Shakespeare's tragedy appeals to artists as a source for adaptation?
- How does the adaption you researched differ from the original? How is it similar? Consider the choice of media, the setting, the costumes, the theme or message of the adaptation, and so on.
- What new "spin," or point of view, does the adaptation offer?

Have students write a short essay that describes the adaptation they have chosen. In addition to addressing the questions above, they should consider these questions: Who is the author/artist/composer, and when was the piece created? How effective is the adaptation? Does the adaptation convey the same theme or message of Shakespeare's *Romeo and Juliet*? In what ways does the adaptation depart from Shakespeare's original?

NOTICE & NOTE

As with a club dash out my desp'rate brains?
O, look! methinks I see my cousin's ghost
Seeking out Romeo, that did spit his body
Upon a rapier's point. Stay, Tybalt, stay!
Romeo, I come! this do I drink to thee.

[*She drinks and falls upon her bed within the curtains.*]

57 stay: stop.

Scene 4 *Capulet's house.*

[*Enter* Lady Capulet *and* Nurse.]

Lady Capulet. Hold, take these keys and fetch more spices, nurse.

Nurse. They call for dates and quinces in the pastry.

2 pastry: the room where baking is done.

[*Enter* Capulet.]

Capulet. Come, stir, stir, stir! The second cock hath crowed,
The curfew bell hath rung, 'tis three o'clock.
Look to the baked meats, good Angelica;
Spare not for cost.

5 Angelica: In his happy mood, Capulet calls the nurse by her name.

Nurse. Go, you cot-quean, go,
Get you to bed! Faith, you'll be sick tomorrow
For this night's watching.

6 cot-quean: a "cottage quean," or housewife. This is a joke about Capulet doing women's work (arranging the party).

Capulet. No, not a whit. What, I have watched ere now
All night for lesser cause, and ne'er been sick.

Lady Capulet. Ay, you have been a mouse-hunt in your time;
But I will watch you from such watching now.

[*Exeunt* Lady Capulet *and* Nurse.]

Capulet. A jealous hood, a jealous hood!

11–13 Lord and Lady Capulet joke about his being a woman chaser (**mouse-hunt**) as a young man. He makes fun of her jealousy (**jealous hood**).

[*Enter three or four* Servants, *with spits and logs and baskets.*]

Now, fellow,
What is there?

First Servant. Things for the cook, sir; but I know not what.

Capulet. Make haste, make haste. [*Exit* Servant.] Sirrah, fetch drier logs.
Call Peter; he will show thee where they are.

Second Servant. I have a head, sir, that will find out logs
And never trouble Peter for the matter.

Capulet. Mass, and well said, merry whoreson, ha!
Thou shalt be loggerhead. [*Exit* Servant.] Good faith, 'tis day.
The County will be here with music straight,
For so he said he would. [*music within*] I hear him near.
Nurse! Wife! What, ho! What, nurse, I say!

[*Reenter* Nurse.]

20–23 The joking between Capulet and his servants includes the mild oath **Mass**, short for "by the Mass," and **loggerhead**, a word for a stupid person as well as a pun, since the servant is searching for drier logs. **straight:** right away.

368 Unit 4

WHEN STUDENTS STRUGGLE . . .

Analyze Dramatic Irony Review the definition of **dramatic irony.** *(The audience knows something the characters do not.)* Then display a two-column chart on the board with the headings "What the Characters Know" and "What the Audience Knows."

Have students work together to explain what the audience knows about each of these situations. Guide students to see that dramatic irony results from the contrast between what the characters know and what the audience knows.

For additional support, go to the **Reading Studio** and assign the following **Level Up Tutorial: Irony.**

What the Characters Know	What the Audience Knows
Juliet is apparently dead.	*Juliet has taken a potion that makes her seem dead.*
Juliet will not marry Paris on Wednesday.	*Juliet cannot marry Paris because she is already married to Romeo. She is planning to escape with Romeo when she wakes up.*

Go waken Juliet; go and trim her up.
I'll go and chat with Paris. Hie, make haste,
Make haste! The bridegroom he is come already:
Make haste, I say.

[*Exeunt.*]

Scene 5 *Juliet's bedroom.*

[*Enter* Nurse.]

Nurse. Mistress! what, mistress! Juliet! Fast, I warrant her, she.
Why, lamb! why, lady! Fie, you slugabed!
Why, love, I say! madam! sweetheart! Why, bride!
What, not a word? You take your pennyworths now,
Sleep for a week; for the next night, I warrant,
The County Paris hath set up his rest
That you shall rest but little. God forgive me,
Marry and amen, how sound is she asleep!
I needs must wake her. Madam, madam, madam!
Aye, let the County take you in your bed,
He'll fright you up, i' faith. Will it not be?

1–11 The nurse chatters as she bustles around the room. She calls Juliet a **slugabed**, or sleepyhead, who is trying to get her **pennyworths**, or small portions, of rest now, since after the wedding Paris won't let her get much sleep.

[*opens the curtains*]

What, dressed and in your clothes and down again?
I must needs wake you. Lady! lady! lady!
Alas, alas! Help, help! my lady's dead!
O well-a-day that ever I was born!
Some aqua vitae, ho! My lord! my lady!

[*Enter* Lady Capulet.]

Lady Capulet. What noise is here?

Nurse. O lamentable day!

17 lamentable: filled with grief.

Lady Capulet. What is the matter?

Nurse. Look, look! O heavy day!

Lady Capulet. O me, O me! My child, my only life!
Revive, look up, or I will die with thee!
Help! help! Call help.

[*Enter* Capulet.]

Capulet. For shame, bring Juliet forth; her lord is come.

Nurse. She's dead, deceased; she's dead! Alack the day!

Lady Capulet. Alack the day, she's dead, she's dead, she's dead!

Capulet. Ha! let me see her. Out alas! she's cold,
Her blood is settled, and her joints are stiff;
Life and these lips have long been separated.
Death lies on her like an untimely frost

The Tragedy of Romeo and Juliet: Act IV, Scene 5 369

NOTICE & NOTE

Upon the sweetest flower of all the field.

Nurse. O lamentable day!

Lady Capulet. O woeful time!

Capulet. Death, that hath ta'en her hence to make me wail,
Ties up my tongue and will not let me speak.

[*Enter* Friar Laurence *and* Paris, *with* Musicians.]

Friar Laurence. Come, is the bride ready to go to church?

Capulet. Ready to go, but never to return.
O son, the night before thy wedding day
Hath death lain with thy wife. See, there she lies,
Flower as she was, deflowered by him.
Death is my son-in-law, Death is my heir;
My daughter he hath wedded. I will die
And leave him all. Life, living, all is Death's.

40 Life . . . Death's: My life, my possessions, and everything else of mine belongs to Death.

Paris. Have I thought long to see this morning's face,
And doth it give me such a sight as this?

Lady Capulet. Accursed, unhappy, wretched, hateful day!
Most miserable hour that e'er time saw
In lasting labor of his pilgrimage!
But one, poor one, one poor and loving child,
But one thing to rejoice and solace in,
And cruel Death hath catched it from my sight!

46–48 But one . . . my sight: I had only one child to make me happy, and Death has taken (**catched**) her from me.

Nurse. O woe! O woeful, woeful, woeful day!
Most lamentable day, most woeful day
That ever, ever I did yet behold!
O day! O day! O day! O hateful day!
Never was seen so black a day as this.
O woeful day! O woeful day!

Paris. Beguiled, divorced, wronged, spited, slain!
Most detestable Death, by thee beguiled,
By cruel, cruel thee quite overthrown!
O love! O life! not life, but love in death!

55 Beguiled: tricked

Capulet. Despised, distressed, hated, martyred, killed!
Uncomfortable time, why camest thou now
To murder, murder our solemnity?
O child! O child! my soul, and not my child!
Dead art thou, dead! alack, my child is dead,
And with my child my joys are buried!

60–61 why . . . solemnity: Why did Death have to come to murder our celebration?

Friar Laurence. Peace, ho, for shame! Confusion's cure lives not
In these confusions. Heaven and yourself
Had part in this fair maid! now heaven hath all,
And all the better is it for the maid.

370 Unit 4

WHEN STUDENTS STRUGGLE . . .

Analyze Figurative Language Remind students that figurative language is a powerful way to express emotions and ideas. Review the meanings of **metaphor, simile,** and **personification**.

Ask students what Capulet compares Death to in lines 28–29 and what type of figurative language that is. *(Capulet uses a simile when he says that Death is like a frost.)* Ask what Capulet compares Juliet to. *(a flower)* Ask students what ideas and feelings are conveyed through these examples of figurative language. *(Capulet is expressing the idea that Juliet's death was sudden and that she died before her time. He also expresses sadness over losing a beloved daughter by describing her as "the sweetest flower of all the field.")* What is personified in lines 34–40? *(Capulet personifies Death as Juliet's husband and his son-in-law)* How does Shakespeare's use of personification add to the emotional impact of the scene? *(The audience feels Capulet's pain over the apparent death of his daughter, especially since we know that Juliet will actually die by the end of the play.)*

For additional support, go to the **Reading Studio** and assign the following **Level Up Tutorial: Figurative Language.**

NOTICE & NOTE 

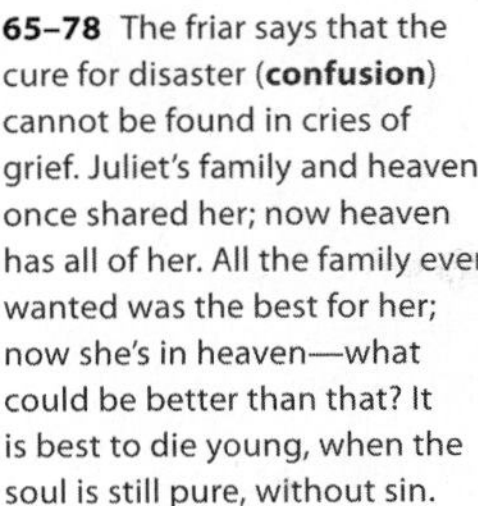

Your part in her you could not keep from death,
But heaven keeps his part in eternal life.
The most you sought was her promotion,
For 'twas your heaven she should be advanced;
And weep ye now, seeing she is advanced
Above the clouds, as high as heaven itself?
O, in this love, you love your child so ill
That you run mad, seeing that she is well.
She's not well married that lives married long,
But she's best married that dies married young.
Dry up your tears and stick your rosemary
On this fair corse, and, as the custom is,
In all her best array bear her to church;
For though fond nature bids us all lament,
Yet nature's tears are reason's merriment.

Capulet. All things that we ordained festival
Turn from their office to black funeral—
Our instruments to melancholy bells,
Our wedding cheer to a sad burial feast;
Our solemn hymns to sullen dirges change;
Our bridal flowers serve for a buried corse;
And all things change them to the contrary.

Friar Laurence. Sir, go you in; and, madam, go with him;
And go, Sir Paris. Every one prepare
To follow this fair corse unto her grave.
The heavens do lower upon you for some ill;
Move them no more by crossing their high will.

65–78 The friar says that the cure for disaster (**confusion**) cannot be found in cries of grief. Juliet's family and heaven once shared her; now heaven has all of her. All the family ever wanted was the best for her; now she's in heaven—what could be better than that? It is best to die young, when the soul is still pure, without sin.

79–80 stick . . . corse: Put rosemary, an herb, on her corpse.

82–83 though . . . merriment: Though it's natural to cry, common sense tells us we should rejoice for the dead.

84 ordained festival: intended for the wedding.

88 sullen dirges: sad, mournful tunes.

94–95 The heavens . . . will: The fates (**heavens**) frown on you for some wrong you have done. Don't tempt them by refusing to accept their will (Juliet's death).

TO CHALLENGE STUDENTS . . .

Analyze Shakespeare's Syntax Discuss with students how Shakespeare inverts word order for dramatic effect, for emphasis, and for conformity to his poetic meter.

Ask students to examine lines 56, 60, 63, 65, and 73. Have them explain why each line is inverted. *(The inversions in lines 56 and 65 conform to meter. The inversion in line 60 creates a dramatic effect. The inversion in line 63 creates emphasis [on dead]. The inversion in line 73 creates emphasis [on weep and now].)*

The Tragedy of Romeo and Juliet: Act IV, Scene 5 371

NOTICE & NOTE

113 pate: top of the head.

[*Exeunt* Capulet, Lady Capulet, Paris, *and* Friar.]

First Musician. Faith, we may put up our pipes, and be gone.

Nurse. Honest good fellows, ah, put up, put up,
For well you know this is a pitiful case.

[*Exit.*]

Second Musician. Aye, by my troth, the case may be amended.

[*Enter* Peter.]

Peter. Musicians, oh, musicians, "Heart's ease, heart's ease." Oh, an you will have me live, play "Heart's ease."

First Musician. Why "Heart's ease"?

Peter. Oh, musicians, because my heart itself plays "My heart is full of woe." Oh, play me some merry dump, to comfort me.

First Musician. Not a dump we, 'tis no time to play now.

Peter. You will not, then?

First Musician. No.

Peter. I will then give it you soundly.

First Musician. What will you give us?

Peter. No money, on my faith, but the gleek. I will give you the minstrel.

First Musician. Then will I give you the serving creature.

Peter. Then will I lay the serving creature's dagger
on your pate. I will carry no crotchets. I'll re you,
I'll fa you, do you note me?

First Musician. An you re us and fa us, you note us.

Second Musician. Pray you put up your dagger, and put out your wit.

Peter. Then have at you with my wit! I will drybeat
you with an iron wit, and put up my iron dagger.
Answer me like men:
"When griping grief the heart doth wound
And doleful dumps the mind oppress,
Then music with her silver sound—
Why "silver sound"? Why "music with her silver sound"? What say you, Simon Catling?

First Musician. Marry, sir, because silver hath a sweet sound.

Peter. Pretty! What say you, Hugh Rebeck?

Second Musician. I say "silver sound" because musicians sound for silver.

Peter. Pretty too! What say you, James Soundpost?

Third Musician. Faith, I know not what to say.

WHEN STUDENTS STRUGGLE . . .

Analyze Plot Have students create a timeline showing the chronology of events in this act. First, review timelines from Act III. Work with students to review the key events of Act IV. *(Paris meets with Friar Laurence to discuss his wedding to Juliet; Juliet expresses to the friar her desperation to avoid marrying Paris; the friar makes a plan to have Juliet take a potion that will put her to sleep so that everyone thinks she has died, and then he will send to Romeo to have him take Juliet away to Mantua; Juliet returns home and says she will marry Paris, and in response her father moves up the wedding to Wednesday; Juliet takes the potion; Juliet is discovered in the morning and is believed to be dead; the Capulets prepare to bury Juliet.)* Discuss the timeframe in which these events take place. *(Tuesday and Tuesday night, Wednesday morning)* Have students compare their timelines in small groups.

For additional support, go to the **Reading Studio** and assign the following  **Level Up Tutorial: Plot: Sequence of Events.**

NOTICE & NOTE 

Peter. Oh, I cry you mercy, you are the singer. I will say for you. It is "music with her silver sound" because musicians have no gold for sounding.

"Then music with her silver sound
With speedy help doth lend redress."

[*Exit.*]

First Musician. What a pestilent knave is this same!

Second Musician. Hang him, Jack! Come, we'll in here. Tarry for the mourners, and stay dinner.

[*Exeunt.*]

136 pestilent: bothersome; irritating.

CHECK YOUR UNDERSTANDING

Answer these questions before moving on to the **Analyze the Text** section on the following page.

1 What two possibilities does Juliet worry about when she goes to drink from the vial from Friar Laurence?

- **A** That she will have to marry Paris or that her marriage to Romeo will be revealed
- **B** That Paris will learn of her plan or that Friar Laurence will tell her father about it
- **C** That she won't see her mother or her nurse again
- **D** That the potion will either do nothing or kill her

2 The playwright has Nurse and Lady Capulet repeat "She's dead" throughout lines 23–24 in Scene 5 order to —

- **F** make sure the audience knows what happened
- **G** demonstrate the depth of the characters' grief
- **H** provide context for the following scene
- **J** symbolize the finality of death

3 Which statement best summarizes the interaction between Peter and the musicians?

- **A** Peter tries to get the musicians to play but they refuse.
- **B** Peter tries to get the musicians to leave but they stay.
- **C** The musicians try to get Peter to pay them but he leaves.
- **D** The musicians try to get Peter to join them but he refuses.

CHECK YOUR UNDERSTANDING

Have students answer the questions independently.

Answers:

1. *D*
2. *G*
3. *A*

If they answer any questions incorrectly, have them reread the text to confirm their understanding. Then they may proceed to ANALYZE THE TEXT on page 374.

ENGLISH LEARNER SUPPORT

Oral Assessment Use the following questions to assess students' comprehension and speaking skills.

1. Juliet worries about what will happen when she drinks the potion. What two things does she worry will happen? *(She worries that it will do nothing or that it will kill her.)*
2. The nurse and Lady Capulet repeat the words "She's dead" in Scene 5. Why? *(Repeating these words shows how sad they are.)*
3. *What does Peter ask the musicians to do? How do the musicians respond? (Peter tries to get the musicians to play, but they refuse.)*

SUBSTANTIAL/MODERATE

APPLY

ANALYZE THE TEXT

Possible answers:

1. **DOK 4:** *Based on the dialogue, they do not seem like a good match. Paris cannot match Juliet's wordplay, nor can he understand that she does not love him. As the son of a rich man, he is used to getting everything he wants. He even tells Juliet, "Thy face is mine" (line 35). Juliet would probably not have fallen in love with a man who treated her as a possession.*
2. **DOK 1:** *Paris comments that Juliet's excessive weeping is because of Tybalt's death (Scene 1, line 6) but the audience knows she cries over Romeo's exile and her impending marriage to Paris. Capulet praises Friar Laurence—"this reverend holy friar, / All our whole city is much bound to him" (Scene 2, lines 31–32)—not realizing that the Friar is plotting to undermine the wedding.*
3. **DOK 4:** *Capulet is so pleased that Juliet has agreed to marry Paris that he moves the date from Thursday back to Wednesday (lines 23–24). This increases the pace and the tension for the audience because events have already been unfolding very quickly, and the dangerous plan that Juliet and the friar have devised may fail now that there is less time for all of its elements to fall into place.*
4. **DOK 3:** *At the beginning of the play, Juliet is sheltered and doesn't openly challenge her parents. Now she is taking control of her own destiny.*
5. **DOK 4:** *Shakespeare uses humor to provide the audience with some comic relief after an intense, tragic scene. The contrasting scene relieves some of the tension and grief, and it conveys the message that life still goes on in the midst of tragedy.*

CREATE AND DISCUSS

Participate in a Dramatic Reading Review the steps students will take to prepare for their dramatic reading. Tell students, as they read their lines, to think about what the character is saying and how the character would feel saying those lines. Suggest that students write words in the margin such as *excited, sad, thoughtful,* or *confused* to help them remember how to read the lines with the proper expression. Point out that students can also make notes about what facial expressions or gestures they could make. Have group members perform staged readings of the dialogue. Evaluate students based on their expression, speaking rate and pauses for effect, volume, enunciation, and purposeful gestures.

RESPOND

ANALYZE THE TEXT

Support your responses with evidence from the text. NOTEBOOK

1. **Analyze** Review Juliet's dialogue with Paris in Scene 1. If Juliet had never met Romeo, might she have fallen in love with Paris? Explain your response.
2. **Identify** Shakespeare often employs a literary technique known as dramatic irony. **Dramatic irony** exists when the reader or viewer knows something that one or more of the characters does not. For example, when Paris asks Juliet to confess to Friar Laurence that she loves him, she carefully avoids denying it. We know that Juliet loves Romeo, not Paris. Identify two other examples of dramatic irony in Act IV. Explain how these ironic moments contribute to the building tension in the play.
3. **Analyze** In Scene 2, how does Shakespeare increase the pace of the plot even further? What effect is this likely to have on the audience?
4. **Compare** Juliet drinks the sleeping potion, despite her fears. What does this reveal about her character? Has she changed from the beginning of the play, before she met Romeo? Explain your response.
5. **Notice & Note** Shakespeare includes **comic relief,** a humorous exchange between Peter and the musicians, at the end of Act IV just after Juliet's family discovers her body. What is the impact of this choice on the audience? What message is conveyed by contrasting a humorous scene with a tragic one?

CREATE AND DISCUSS

Participate in a Dramatic Reading In a small group, prepare a dramatic reading of a scene from *The Tragedy of Romeo and Juliet*, Act IV.

- ❑ Choose a scene and assign roles to each member of the group. Include the role of a narrator to read the stage directions.
- ❑ Highlight or underline your character's lines. Mark notes beside the lines to indicate how you think each line should be read. Think about when you might change your tone, adjust your voice, or read more quickly or slowly.
- ❑ Practice reading through the scene as a group a few times until readers chime in smoothly with their lines. Then perform the dramatic reading for the rest of the class.

SETTING A PURPOSE

Notice the unexpected events, misunderstandings, and instances of poor timing that bring the play to its tragic end. Write down any questions you generate during reading.

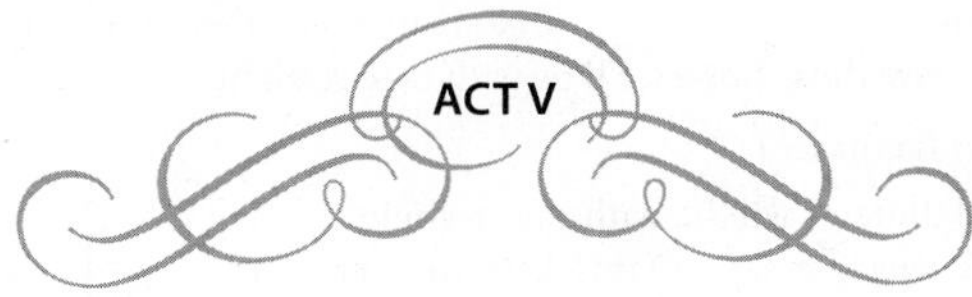

Scene 1 *A street in Mantua.*

[*Enter* Romeo.]

Romeo. If I may trust the flattering truth of sleep,
My dreams presage some joyful news at hand.
My bosom's lord sits lightly in his throne,
And all this day an unaccustomed spirit
Lifts me above the ground with cheerful thoughts.
I dreamt my lady came and found me dead
(Strange dream that gives a dead man leave to think!)
And breathed such life with kisses in my lips
That I revived and was an emperor.
Ah me! how sweet is love itself possessed,
When but love's shadows are so rich in joy!

[*Enter Romeo's servant,* Balthasar, *booted.*]

News from Verona! How now, Balthasar?
Dost thou not bring me letters from the friar?
How doth my lady? Is my father well?
How fares my Juliet? That I ask again,
For nothing can be ill if she be well.

Balthasar. Then she is well, and nothing can be ill.
Her body sleeps in Capels' monument,
And her immortal part with angels lives.
I saw her laid low in her kindred's vault
And presently took post to tell it you.
O, pardon me for bringing these ill news,
Since you did leave it for my office, sir.

Romeo. Is it e'en so? Then I defy you, stars!
Thou knowst my lodging. Get me ink and paper
And hire posthorses. I will hence tonight.

Balthasar. I do beseech you, sir, have patience.
Your looks are pale and wild and do import
Some misadventure.

17–19 Balthasar replies that Juliet is well, since although her body lies in the Capulets' (**Capels'**) burial vault, her soul (**her immortal part**) is with the angels.

21 presently took post: immediately rode (to Mantua).

23 you did . . . office: you gave me the duty of reporting important news to you.

24 I . . . stars: Romeo angrily challenges fate, which has caused him so much grief.

28–29 import some misadventure: suggest that something bad will happen.

SETTING A PURPOSE

Direct students to use the Setting a Purpose prompt to focus their reading.

ENGLISH LEARNER SUPPORT

Summarize Use the following activities to provide varying levels of support to help students summarize the events of Act IV before they read Act V. Begin by listing these characters on the board (list Juliet twice): Romeo, Paris, Friar Laurence, Juliet, Lord Capulet, Lady Capulet, Juliet.

- Point to each character and ask one or more yes/no or short answer questions to review recent events. For example: Is Romeo in Verona? *(no)* Where is Romeo? *(in Mantua)* Does Paris want to marry Juliet? *(yes)* Can Juliet marry Paris? *(no)* What does Friar Laurence give Juliet? *(a potion)* Will the potion kill Juliet? *(no)* Will it make her sleep? *(yes)* Drawing on students' responses, create a simple sequence chart summarizing events in Act IV. **SUBSTANTIAL**
- Have pairs of students use the list of characters' names as sentence starters to create a sequence diagram summarizing the key events in Act IV. **MODERATE**
- Have pairs or small groups of students orally summarize the events in each scene in Act IV. Then have students create a sequence diagram that captures the key events in each scene. **LIGHT**

NOTICE & NOTE

Romeo. Tush, thou art deceived.
Leave me and do the thing I bid thee do.
Hast thou no letters to me from the friar?

Balthasar. No, my good lord.

Romeo. No matter. Get thee gone
And hire those horses. I'll be with thee straight.

[*Exit* Balthasar.]

Well, Juliet, I will lie with thee tonight.
Let's see for means. O mischief, thou art swift
To enter in the thoughts of desperate men!
I do remember an apothecary,
And hereabouts he dwells, which late I noted
In tattered weeds, with overwhelming brows,
Culling of simples. Meager were his looks,
Sharp misery had worn him to the bones;
And in his needy shop a tortoise hung,
An alligator stuffed, and other skins
Of ill-shaped fishes; and about his shelves
A beggarly account of empty boxes,
Green earthen pots, bladders, and musty seeds,
Remnants of packthread, and old cakes of roses
Were thinly scattered, to make up a show.
Noting this penury, to myself I said,
"An if a man did need a poison now
Whose sale is present death in Mantua,
Here lives a caitiff wretch would sell it him."
O, this same thought did but forerun my need,
And this same needy man must sell it me.
As I remember, this should be the house.
Being holiday, the beggar's shop is shut.
What, ho! apothecary!

[*Enter* Apothecary.]

Apothecary. Who calls so loud?

Romeo. Come hither, man. I see that thou art poor.
Hold, there is forty ducats. Let me have
A dram of poison, such soon-speeding gear
As will disperse itself through all the veins
That the life-weary taker may fall dead,
And that the trunk may be discharged of breath
As violently as hasty powder fired
Doth hurry from the fatal cannon's womb.

35–40 Let's . . . means: Let me find a way (to join Juliet in death); **apothecary:** pharmacist; **tattered weeds:** ragged clothes; **culling of simples:** selecting herbs.

47 cakes of roses: rose petals pressed together to create a perfume.

49 penury: poverty.

50–52 "An if a man . . . sell it him": Though it is a crime to sell poison in Mantua, the apothecary is such a miserable (**caitiff**) wretch that he would probably do it for the money.

59 ducats: gold coins.

60–65 Romeo wants fast-acting (**soon-speeding**) poison that will work as quickly as gunpowder exploding in a cannon.

WHEN STUDENTS STRUGGLE . . .

Analyze Character Motivations Have students consider what they know of Romeo's character. As they read lines 34–57, have them think about how those traits are or are not illustrated in the decisions that he makes. Ask students what Romeo means in line 34. *(Romeo intends to kill himself so that he can be with Juliet in death.)* Have them discuss whether he considers his options or plunges immediately into action. Ask: Is his approach consistent with the way he has acted in the past? Why or why not? *(As he has in the past, Romeo plunges into action without thinking of possible options, such as consulting Friar Laurence, or consequences, such as what will happen when he returns to Verona.)*

For additional support, go to the **Reading Studio** and assign the following **Level Up Tutorial: Character Motivation.**

APPLYING ACADEMIC VOCABULARY

☐ **attribute** ☐ **commit** ☑ **expose** ☐ **initiate** ☑ **underlie**

Write and Discuss Have students turn to a partner to discuss the questions below. Guide students to use the academic vocabulary words *expose* and *underlie* in their responses. Ask volunteers to share their responses with the class.

- What important themes do the events in Act V, Scene 1, **expose?**
- Support your interpretation of the meaning that **underlies** these events with details from the text.

ENGLISH LEARNER SUPPORT

Use Contextual Support Read lines 85–86 aloud and have students read along with you. Point out that the word *cordial* (line 85) has a Spanish cognate, *el cordial.* Then read aloud the side note for line 85. Check comprehension by asking students: Why did people take a cordial? *(They thought it was good for the heart.)* Is Romeo really buying a cordial? *(no)* What is he buying? *(poison)*

Point out that when Romeo says, "Come, cordial and not poison" (line 85) he is using a metaphor. Remind students that a metaphor compares two unlike things that share something in common. Ask: What is Romeo comparing a poison to? *(a cordial)* How are a cordial and a poison different? *(A cordial might help people, but a poison probably would kill them.)* Romeo thinks that the poison will help him. Why? *(The poison will end his pain. It will bring him death so that he can be with Juliet.)*

SUBSTANTIAL/MODERATE

NOTICE & NOTE

67 any . . . them: any person who dispenses or sells them.

72–74 Romeo urges the apothecary to improve his situation by breaking the law and selling him the poison.

75 I'm doing this for the money, not because I think it's right.

79 dispatch you straight: kill you instantly.

85 Romeo refers to the poison as a cordial, a drink believed to be good for the heart.

5–12 Friar John asked another friar (**barefoot brother**) to go with him to Mantua. The health officials of the town, believing that the friars had come into contact with a deadly plague (**infectious pestilence**), locked them up to keep them from infecting others.

13 bare: carried (bore).

Apothecary. Such mortal drugs I have; but Mantua's law
Is death to any he that utters them.

Romeo. Art thou so bare and full of wretchedness
And fearest to die? Famine is in thy cheeks,
Need and oppression starveth in thine eyes,
Contempt and beggary hangs upon thy back;
The world is not thy friend, nor the world's law,
The world affords no law to make thee rich;
Then be not poor, but break it and take this.

Apothecary. My poverty but not my will consents.

Romeo. I pay thy poverty and not thy will.

Apothecary. Put this in any liquid thing you will
And drink it off, and if you had the strength
Of twenty men, it would dispatch you straight.

Romeo. There is thy gold—worse poison to men's souls,
Doing more murder in this loathsome world,
Than these poor compounds that thou mayst not sell.
I sell thee poison; thou hast sold me none.
Farewell. Buy food and get thyself in flesh.
Come, cordial and not poison, go with me
To Juliet's grave; for there must I use thee.

[*Exeunt.*]

Scene 2 *Friar Laurence's cell in Verona.*

[*Enter* Friar John.]

Friar John. Holy Franciscan friar, brother, ho!

[*Enter* Friar Laurence.]

Friar Laurence. This same should be the voice of Friar John.
Welcome from Mantua. What says Romeo?
Or, if his mind be writ, give me his letter.

Friar John. Going to find a barefoot brother out,
One of our order to associate me,
Here in this city visiting the sick,
And finding him, the searchers of the town,
Suspecting that we both were in a house
Where the infectious pestilence did reign,
Sealed up the doors, and would not let us forth,
So that my speed to Mantua there was stayed.

Friar Laurence. Who bare my letter, then, to Romeo?

Friar John. I could not send it—here it is again—
Nor get a messenger to bring it thee,

CLOSE READ SCREENCAST

Have students pair up to do an independent close read of lines 72–84, the exchange between Romeo and the apothecary. Students can record their answers on the Close Read Practice PDF.

Close Read Practice PDF

So fearful were they of infection.

Friar Laurence. Unhappy fortune! By my brotherhood,
The letter was not nice, but full of charge,
Of dear import, and the neglecting it
May do much danger. Friar John, go hence,
Get me an iron crow and bring it straight
Unto my cell.

Friar John. Brother, I'll go and bring it thee.

[*Exit.*]

Friar Laurence. Now must I to the monument alone.
Within this three hours will fair Juliet wake.
She will beshrew me much that Romeo
Hath had no notice of these accidents;
But I will write again to Mantua,
And keep her at my cell till Romeo come—
Poor living corse, closed in a dead man's tomb!

[*Exit.*]

Scene 3 *The cemetery that contains the Capulets' tomb.*

[*Enter* Paris *and his* Page *with flowers and a torch.*]

Paris. Give me thy torch, boy. Hence, and stand aloof.
Yet put it out, for I would not be seen.
Under yond yew tree lay thee all along,
Holding thine ear close to the hollow ground.
So shall no foot upon the churchyard tread
(Being loose, unfirm, with digging up of graves)
But thou shalt hear it. Whistle then to me,
As signal that thou hearst something approach.
Give me those flowers. Do as I bid thee, go.

Page [*aside*]. I am almost afraid to stand alone
Here in the churchyard; yet I will adventure.

[*withdraws*]

Paris. Sweet flower, with flowers thy bridal bed I strew

[*He strews the tomb with flowers.*]

(O woe! thy canopy is dust and stones)
Which with sweet water nightly I will dew;
Or, wanting that, with tears distilled by moans.
The obsequies that I for thee will keep
Nightly shall be to strew thy grave and weep.

[*The* Page *whistles.*]

NOTICE & NOTE 

18–20 The letter wasn't trivial (**nice**) but contained a message of great importance (**dear import**). The fact that it wasn't sent (**neglecting it**) may cause great harm.

21 iron crow: crowbar.

25–26 She . . . accidents: She will be furious with me when she learns that Romeo doesn't know what has happened.

ANALYZE LITERARY DEVICES

Annotate: Mark the oxymoron in line 29. Note that the word *corse* means "corpse."

Analyze: What emotional effect does this oxymoron create?

1 aloof: some distance away.

ANALYZE PARALLEL PLOTS

Annotate: Mark the transition between parallel plots that happens on this page.

Analyze: As the play comes to a close, Shakespeare brings together some parallel plots and the characters associated with them. What is the impact of Paris's entrance at this point in the play?

12–17 Paris promises to decorate Juliet's grave with flowers and sprinkle it with either perfume (**sweet water**) or his tears. He will perform these honoring rites (**obsequies**) every night.

TEACH

ANALYZE LITERARY DEVICES

Remind students that an **oxymoron** is a word or an expression that contains a contradiction. Ask a volunteer to identify the oxymoron in line 29. *(living corpse [corse])* Discuss the effect of this oxymoron on readers. (***Answer:*** *This oxymoron creates an eerie effect. Juliet is alive and merely sleeping, but she appears to be dead [a corpse], and she is entombed in a place of the dead.)*

ANALYZE PARALLEL PLOTS

Review that in a drama, each scene presents an episode of the play's plot, often at a single place and time. Explain that in a play with multiple parallel plots, tracking stage directions as characters enter and exit the scene can signal plot shifts.

Review the stage directions for Scenes 2 and 3 with students. Ask: Where did Scene 2 take place? *(Friar Laurence's cell)* Where does Scene 3 take place? *(cemetery where the Capulets' tomb is)* Ask: Which parallel plot was the focus of Scene 2? *(plot of Romeo and Juliet)* Which plot appears to be the focus of Scene 3? *(plot of Paris and Juliet)* Discuss with students what is revealed about Paris's character here. *(He has flowers, which suggests that the has come to leave them for Juliet. He may have had real affection for her, or his words may be melodramatic.)* Then discuss the impact of Paris's entrance at this point in the play. (***Answer:*** *Paris's entrance complicates the plot and increases the play's tension. The audience knows that if the potion works, Juliet will wake up soon. So the audience wonders if Paris will see that she is not dead.)*

Point out that in Act V, Scene 3, Shakespeare brings several parallel plots together. Have students read through line 24 on page 380 and identify stage directions that signal that two plots are about to converge. *([Enter Romeo and Balthasar with a torch . . .])*

WHEN STUDENTS STRUGGLE . . .

Analyze Plot Review the significance of Friar Laurence's letter to Romeo. Ask: Why did Friar John fail to deliver the letter? *(He was stopped for possibly carrying a plague. Believing the letter to be infected as well, messengers refused to carry it further.)* Point out that the failure of Friar John to deliver Friar Laurence's letter is another complication in the plot. Explain that it has effects on other events in the play. Have pairs or small groups of students complete a cause-and-effect diagram similar to the one shown in order to capture the immediate effects and possible later effects of this plot complication.

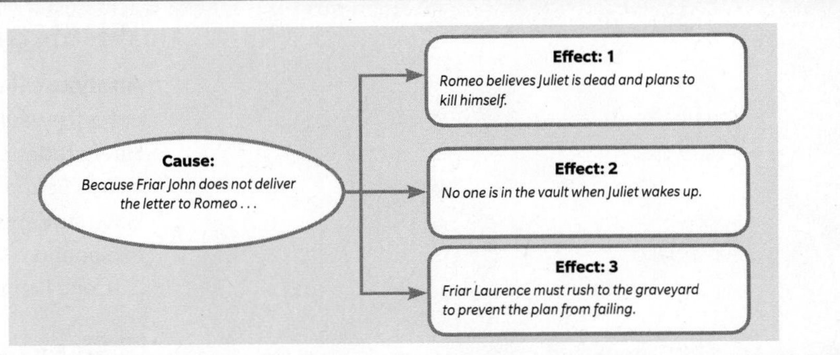

ENGLISH LEARNER SUPPORT

Understand Language Structures Use these activities to help students at varying levels of proficiency understand Paris's role in this final scene:

- Read aloud line 49. Ask students to underline the word *This*. Then have them circle the person or thing that *This* refers to. *(Romeo in the stage directions)* Have students draw an arrow from *This* to *Romeo*. Explain that lines 49–57 are about Romeo. Read those lines aloud. Stop after every couple of lines to paraphrase them, review key terms (such as *banish'd*), and explain any unfamiliar vocabulary (such as *villainous* and *apprehend*). Then ask yes/no questions to check comprehension. For example: Is Paris angry at Romeo? *(yes)* Does Paris know that Romeo killed Tybalt? *(yes)* Does Paris think that Juliet died because she was sad about Tybalt? *(yes)* Does Paris blame Romeo for Juliet's death? *(yes)*

  SUBSTANTIAL

- Display these questions and prompts:

1. What does Paris blame Romeo for? Circle text clues.
2. What does Paris think Romeo is doing at the tomb? Underline text clues.
3. What is Paris going to do? Bracket [ ] text clues.

Have pairs work together to answer each question and identify the text that helped them understand each question. (**1.** *Paris blames Romeo for killing Tybalt and for making Juliet die of grief.* **2.** *Paris thinks that Romeo is there to "do some villainous shame / To the dead bodies." That may mean he thinks that Romeo will vandalize, or do damage, to the graves because the Capulet family is buried there.* **3.** *Paris says he's going to catch Romeo.)*

MODERATE/LIGHT

NOTICE & NOTE

20 cross: interfere with.

21 muffle: hide.

mattock . . . iron: an ax and a crowbar.

32 in dear employment: for an important purpose.

33 jealous: curious.

37–39 Romeo's intention is more unstoppable (**inexorable**) than hungry (**empty**) tigers or the waves of an ocean.

45–48 Romeo addresses the tomb as though it were devouring people. He calls it a hateful stomach (**detestable maw**) that is filled (**gorged**) with Juliet, the **dearest morsel of the earth**.

49–53 Recognizing Romeo, Paris speaks these first few lines to himself. He is angry with Romeo, believing that Romeo's killing Tybalt caused Juliet to die of grief.

The boy gives warning something doth approach.
What cursed foot wanders this way tonight
To cross my obsequies and true love's rite?
What, with a torch? Muffle me, night, awhile.

[*withdraws*]

[*Enter* Romeo *and* Balthasar *with a torch, a mattock, and a crow of iron.*]

Romeo. Give me that mattock and the wrenching iron.
Hold, take this letter. Early in the morning
See thou deliver it to my lord and father.
Give me the light. Upon thy life I charge thee,
Whate'er thou hearest or seest, stand all aloof
And do not interrupt me in my course.
Why I descend into this bed of death
Is partly to behold my lady's face,
But chiefly to take thence from her dead finger
A precious ring—a ring that I must use
In dear employment. Therefore hence, be gone.
But if thou, jealous, dost return to pry
In what I farther shall intend to do,
By heaven, I will tear thee joint by joint
And strew this hungry churchyard with thy limbs.
The time and my intents are savage-wild,
More fierce and more inexorable far
Than empty tigers or the roaring sea.

Balthasar. I will be gone, sir, and not trouble you.

Romeo. So shalt thou show me friendship. Take thou that.
Live, and be prosperous; and farewell, good fellow.

Balthasar [*aside*]. For all this same, I'll hide me hereabout.
His looks I fear, and his intents I doubt.

[*withdraws*]

Romeo. Thou detestable maw, thou womb of death,
Gorged with the dearest morsel of the earth,
Thus I enforce thy rotten jaws to open,
And in despite I'll cram thee with more food.

[Romeo *opens the tomb.*]

Paris. This is that banish'd haughty Montague
That murdered my love's cousin—with which grief
It is supposed the fair creature died—
And here is come to do some villainous shame
To the dead bodies. I will apprehend him.
Stop thy unhallowed toil, vile Montague!
Can vengeance be pursued further than death?

WHEN STUDENTS STRUGGLE . . .

Analyze Character Point out that in this speech to Balthasar, Romeo explains why he must enter the vault. Remind students to consider what they know about Romeo's true intentions. Have students explain the two reasons that Romeo states for entering the tomb. *(In lines 28–32, he tells Balthasar that he wants to see Juliet's face one last time and take a ring from her finger.)* Have students read lines 34–44. Ask students whether Balthasar is convinced by Romeo's explanation. Why or why not? *(He is not convinced. He says: "I'll hide me hereabout. / His looks I fear, and his intents I doubt.")*

For additional support, go to the **Reading Studio** and assign the following **Level Up Tutorial: Character Motivation.**

Condemned villain, I do apprehend thee.
Obey, and go with me; for thou must die.

Romeo. I must indeed; and therefore came I hither.
Good gentle youth, tempt not a desp'rate man.
Fly hence and leave me. Think upon these gone;
Let them affright thee. I beseech thee, youth,
Put not another sin upon my head
By urging me to fury. O, be gone!
By heaven, I love thee better than myself.
For I come hither armed against myself.
Stay not, be gone. Live, and hereafter say
A madman's mercy bid thee run away.

Paris. I do defy thy conjuration
And apprehend thee for a felon here.

Romeo. Wilt thou provoke me? Then have at thee, boy!

[*They fight.*]

Page. O Lord, they fight! I will go call the watch.

[*Exit.*]

Paris. O, I am slain! [*falls*] If thou be merciful,
Open the tomb, lay me with Juliet.

[*dies.*]

Romeo. In faith, I will. Let me peruse this face.
Mercutio's kinsman, noble County Paris!
What said my man when my betossed soul
Did not attend him as we rode? I think
He told me Paris should have married Juliet.
Said he not so? or did I dream it so?
Or am I mad, hearing him talk of Juliet,
To think it was so? O, give me thy hand,
One writ with me in sour misfortune's book!
I'll bury thee in a triumphant grave.
A grave? O, no, a lantern, slaughtered youth,
For here lies Juliet, and her beauty makes
This vault a feasting presence full of light.
Death, lie thou there, by a dead man interred.

[*lays* Paris *in the tomb.*]

How oft when men are at the point of death
Have they been merry! which their keepers call
A lightning before death. O, how may I
Call this a lightning? O my love! my wife!

68 I reject your appeal.

LANGUAGE CONVENTIONS
Annotate: Parallel structure is the repetition of words, phrases, or grammatical structures to add emphasis or to improve the sound and rhythm of text. Mark the syllable that Romeo repeats several times in his parting speech in lines 74 to 120.

Analyze: What is Shakespeare's purpose in using parallel structure here? What is its impact?

82 Romeo notes that, like himself, Paris has been a victim of bad luck.

84–87 Romeo will bury Paris with Juliet, whose beauty fills the tomb with light. Paris' corpse (**Death**) is being buried (**interred**) by a dead man in that Romeo expects to be dead soon.

TEACH

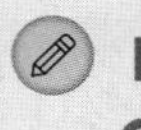

LANGUAGE CONVENTIONS

Review with students the term **parallel structure,** or the repetition of certain words, phrases, or grammatical structures. Have partners work together to take turns reading aloud lines 74–120 of Romeo's parting speech. Ask students to identify a word that's repeated eight times in those lines. Once students have read through the lines and marked the text, call on a student to tell what that word is. *(O)* Point out that *O* is an interjection used to express surprise or strong emotion. Explain that in modern English, the same interjection is spelled *Oh*. Have student pairs discuss what they think is the purpose and the effect of the repetition. (***Answer:*** *Shakespeare's purpose in repeating the word O is to emphasize Romeo's deep emotion and to create drama as Romeo addresses various audiences. For example, he says:*
"O, give me thy hand" to Paris; "O my love" to Juliet; "O you" to Juliet's lips; "O true apothecary" to the poison he drinks. The repetition contributes to the tragic, dramatic, passionate tone

ENGLISH LEARNER SUPPORT

Write a Summary Have pairs or small groups of students review Act V, Scene 3, lines 72–120. Then have them work together to write a summary of Romeo's final moments. Provide the following list of verbs and line references:

kills (lines 72–73)

lays (lines 87–88)

looks at (lines 90–96)

calls out (lines 97–100)

asks for (line 101)

tells (lines 108–112)

hugs (lines 113–114)

drinks (lines 119–120)

Have students review each set of lines in parentheses and then use the verb shown to write a single sentence summarizing Romeo's action(s). Once students have completed their summaries, ask one or two groups to read their summaries aloud.

SUBSTANTIAL/MODERATE

NOTICE & NOTE

94 ensign: sign

98–100 O, what . . . enemy: I can best repay you (Tybalt) by killing your enemy (myself) with the same hand that cut your youth in two (**twain**).

102–105 Romeo can't get over how beautiful Juliet still looks. He asks whether Death is loving (**amorous**) and whether it has taken Juliet as its lover (**paramour**).

111–112 shake . . . flesh: rid myself of the burden of an unhappy fate (**inauspicious stars**).

115 dateless: eternal; never-ending. Romeo means that what he is about to do can never be undone.

117–118 Romeo compares himself to the pilot of a ship (**bark**) who is going to crash on the rocks because he is so weary and sick.

Death, that hath sucked the honey of thy breath,
Hath had no power yet upon thy beauty.
Thou art not conquered. Beauty's ensign yet
Is crimson in thy lips and in thy cheeks,
And death's pale flag is not advanced there.
Tybalt, liest thou there in thy bloody sheet?
O, what more favor can I do to thee
Than with that hand that cut thy youth in twain
To sunder his that was thine enemy?
Forgive me, cousin! Ah, dear Juliet,
Why art thou yet so fair? Shall I believe
That unsubstantial Death is amorous,
And that the lean abhorred monster keeps
Thee here in dark to be his paramour?
For fear of that I still will stay with thee
And never from this palace of dim night
Depart again. Here, here will I remain
With worms that are thy chambermaids. O, here
Will I set up my everlasting rest
And shake the yoke of inauspicious stars
From this world-wearied flesh. Eyes, look your last!
Arms, take your last embrace! and, lips, O you
The doors of breath, seal with a righteous kiss
A dateless bargain to engrossing death!
Come, bitter conduct; come, unsavory guide!
Thou desperate pilot, now at once run on
The dashing rocks thy seasick weary bark!
Here's to my love! [*drinks*] O true apothecary!
Thy drugs are quick. Thus with a kiss I die.

[*falls*]

[*Enter* Friar Laurence, *with lantern, crow, and spade.*]

Friar Laurence. Saint Francis be my speed! how oft tonight
Have my old feet stumbled at graves! Who's there?

Balthasar. Here's one, a friend, and one that knows you well.

Friar Laurence. Bliss be upon you! Tell me, good my friend,
What torch is yond that vainly lends his light
To grubs and eyeless skulls? As I discern,
It burneth in the Capels' monument.

Balthasar. It doth so, holy sir; and there's my master,
One that you love.

Friar Laurence. Who is it?

Balthasar. Romeo.

IMPROVE READING FLUENCY

Targeted Passage Have students read lines 88–120 of Romeo's final soliloquy aloud to a partner. Prompt students to review the margin notes for any unfamiliar words or concepts before they begin their readings. Encourage students to provide each other with feedback and support for pronouncing multisyllabic words.

Go to the **Reading Studio** for additional support in developing fluency.

Friar Laurence. How long hath he been there?

Balthasar. Full half an hour.

Friar Laurence. Go with me to the vault.

Balthasar. I dare not, sir.
My master knows not but I am gone hence,
And fearfully did menace me with death
If I did stay to look on his intents.

Friar Laurence. Stay then; I'll go alone. Fear comes upon me.
O, much I fear some ill unthrifty thing.

Balthasar. As I did sleep under this yew tree here,
I dreamt my master and another fought,
And that my master slew him.

Friar Laurence. Romeo!

[*stoops and looks on the blood and weapons*]

Alack, alack, what blood is this which stains
The stony entrance of this sepulcher?
What mean these masterless and gory swords
To lie discolored by this place of peace?

[*enters the tomb*]

Romeo! O, pale! Who else? What, Paris too?
And steeped in blood? Ah, what an unkind hour
Is guilty of this lamentable chance!
The lady stirs.

[Juliet *rises.*]

Juliet. O comfortable friar! where is my lord?
I do remember well where I should be,
And there I am. Where is my Romeo?

Friar Laurence. I hear some noise. Lady, come from that nest
Of death, contagion, and unnatural sleep.
A greater power than we can contradict
Hath thwarted our intents. Come, come away.
Thy husband in thy bosom there lies dead;
And Paris too. Come, I'll dispose of thee
Among a sisterhood of holy nuns.
Stay not to question, for the watch is coming.
Come, go, good Juliet. I dare no longer stay.

Juliet. Go, get thee hence, for I will not away.

[*Exit* Friar Laurence.]

132–134 My master . . . intents: My master told me to go away and threatened me with death if I watched what he did.

136 unthrifty: unlucky.

140–143 Alack . . . place of peace? Why are these bloody swords lying here at the tomb (**sepulcher**), a place that should be peaceful? (The swords are also **masterless**, or without their owners.)

148 comfortable: comforting.

153–154 A greater . . . intents: A greater force than we can fight (**contradict**) has ruined our plans (**thwarted our intents**).

156–157 I'll dispose . . . nuns: I'll find a place for you in a convent of nuns.

ENGLISH LEARNER SUPPORT

Make Inferences Remind students that they can use clues in the text and their own knowledge and experience to make inferences about how characters are feeling and why they feel that way. Then use the following supports with students at varying proficiency levels:

- Have pairs of students read lines 121–139. Ask them to mark what Balthasar says that causes Friar Laurence to fear that something bad has happened to Romeo. *("My master knows not but I am gone hence, / And fearfully did menace me with death / If I did stay to look on his intents.")* Then have students complete this frame: *Friar Laurence feels _____ because _____. (afraid; Romeo sent Balthasar away)*
  MODERATE
- Ask pairs or small groups of students to use clues in the text to make inferences about the following:
  - In line 130, why does Friar Laurence ask, "How long hath he been here?" *(Balthasar tells the friar that the torch that's burning belongs to his master, Romeo.)* What inference can you make about how the friar is feeling? Why? *(He is worried about Romeo because Romeo may have found Juliet and thought she was dead.)*
  - In line 135, what causes Friar Laurence to say, "Fear comes upon me"? *(Balthasar tells him that Romeo told Balthasar to leave and said he would kill Balthasar if he returned. This causes Friar Laurence to fear that Romeo is going to do something terrible, such as kill himself.)* **LIGHT**

The Tragedy of Romeo and Juliet: Act V, Scene 3 383

TO CHALLENGE STUDENTS . . .

Explore Shakespearean Heroines Shakespeare created many memorable heroines in addition to Juliet, and not all his heroines faced tragic endings. Some famous Shakespearean women who experienced happy endings include Viola in *Twelfth Night,* Portia in *The Merchant of Venice,* Titania in *A Midsummer Night's Dream,* and Rosalind in *As You Like It.*

Direct students to research a heroine from one of Shakespeare's comedies. Students may choose a heroine from among those listed above, or choose another heroine. Have students read a synopsis of the comedy that provides useful information on the heroine. Then have them write a paragraph or two based on their research. Ask them to describe their heroine and explain her motivation(s). Have students compare their findings with those of other students.

What's here? A cup, closed in my true love's hand?
Poison, I see, hath been his timeless end.
O churl! drunk all, and left no friendly drop
To help me after? I will kiss thy lips.
Haply some poison yet doth hang on them
To make me die with a restorative.

[*kisses him*]

Thy lips are warm!

Chief Watchman [*within*]. Lead, boy. Which way?

Juliet. Yea, noise? Then I'll be brief. O happy dagger!

[*snatches Romeo's dagger*]

This is thy sheath; there rust, and let me die.

[*She stabs herself and falls.*]

[*Enter* Watchmen *with the* Page *of Paris.*]

Page. This is the place. There, where the torch doth burn.

Chief Watchman. The ground is bloody. Search about the churchyard.
Go, some of you; whoe'er you find attach.

[*Exeunt some of the* Watch.]

Pitiful sight! here lies the County slain;
And Juliet bleeding, warm, and newly dead,
Who here hath lain this two days buried.
Go, tell the Prince; run to the Capulets;
Raise up the Montagues; some others search.

[*Exeunt others of the* Watch.]

We see the ground whereon these woes do lie,
But the true ground of all these piteous woes
We cannot without circumstance descry.

[*Reenter some of the* Watch, *with* Balthasar.]

Second Watchman. Here's Romeo's man. We found him in the churchyard.

Chief Watchman. Hold him in safety till the Prince come hither.

[*Reenter* Friar Laurence *and another* Watchman.]

Third Watchman. Here is a friar that trembles, sighs, and weeps.
We took this mattock and this spade from him
As he was coming from this churchyard side.

Chief Watchman. A great suspicion! Stay the friar too.

[*Enter the* Prince *and* Attendants.]

162 timeless: happening before its proper time.

163 churl: miser.

165 Haply: perhaps.

173 attach: arrest.

178 Raise up: awaken.

179–181 We see . . . descry: We see the earth (**ground**) these bodies lie on. But the real cause (**true ground**) of these deaths is yet for us to discover (**descry**).

182–187 The guards arrest Balthasar and Friar Laurence as suspicious characters.

EL ENGLISH LEARNER SUPPORT

Develop Vocabulary Read aloud lines 161–170. Have students circle the words *churl* (line 163) and *restorative* (line 167). Direct students to consult the side note for the definition of *churl* ("miser"). Point out that today, people use the word *miser*; they don't use the word *churl*, as people did in Shakespeare's time.

Have pairs of students look up the words *miser* and *restorative*, preferably in a learner's dictionary. For each word, ask students to choose the definition that makes the best sense for the context. Then have students write each definition on a sheet of paper and complete each of these sentence frames:

Romeo is a churl, *or miser, because* ______ .
Juliet calls the poison a restorative *because* ______ .

Call on students to share their definitions and example sentences. **ALL LEVELS**

WHEN STUDENTS STRUGGLE . . .

Analyze Plot Tell students that the threads of various plots that have run through the play are tied up in this final scene. Work with students to summarize how the feud between the two families determined the outcome of the relationship between Romeo and Juliet. *(The feud between the families meant that Romeo and Juliet could not marry openly. Their secret marriage and Romeo's banishment led to their deaths.)* Who else suffered as a result of the fighting between the Montagues and Capulets? *(Mercutio, Tybalt, and Paris also died because the feud.)*

For additional support, go to the **Reading Studio** and assign the following **Level Up Tutorial: Plot Stages.**

ENGLISH LEARNER SUPPORT

Develop Vocabulary Direct students to Act V, Scene 3, lines 226–227. Read the lines aloud. Ask students to circle the words *impeach* and *purge* in line 226 and underline the words *condemned* and *excused* in line 227.

Have students read the side notes for lines 223–227 and use them to determine whether the words *impeach* and *purge* are synonyms or antonyms. Remind students that **synonyms** are words that mean the same thing and **antonyms** are words with opposite meanings. *(The words* impeach *and* purge *are antonyms.* Impeach *means "to accuse," and* purge *means "to clear of guilt.")*

Have pairs of students look up *condemn* in a learner's dictionary. Then have them determine which pairs of circled and underlined words are synonyms and which are antonyms. *(*Impeach *and* condemn *are synonyms;* purge *and* excuse *are synonyms;* impeach *and* purge *are antonyms;* condemn *and* excuse *are antonyms.)*

Then, have students apply what they have learned about these words to complete these sentence frames, based on their understanding of the play:

Friar Laurence should be condemned *because he ______. (gave Juliet a potion that made her seem dead)*

Friar Laurence should be excused *because he ______. (didn't mean for Romeo or Juliet to die)*

SUBSTANTIAL/MODERATE

NOTICE & NOTE

Prince. What misadventure is so early up,
That calls our person from our morning rest?

[*Enter* Capulet, Lady Capulet, *and others.*]

Capulet. What should it be, that they so shriek abroad?

Lady Capulet. The people in the street cry "Romeo,"
Some "Juliet," and some "Paris"; and all run,
With open outcry, toward our monument.

Prince. What fear is this which startles in our ears?

194 startles: causes alarm.

Chief Watchman. Sovereign, here lies the County Paris slain;
And Romeo dead, and Juliet, dead before,
Warm and new killed.

Prince. Search, seek, and know how this foul murder comes.

Chief Watchman. Here is a friar, and slaughtered Romeo's man,
With instruments upon them fit to open
These dead men's tombs.

Capulet. O heavens! O wife, look how our daughter bleeds!
This dagger hath mista'en, for, lo, his house
Is empty on the back of Montague,
And it missheathed in my daughter's bosom!

203–205 This dagger . . . in my daughter's bosom: This dagger has missed its target. It should rest in the sheath (**house**) that Romeo wears. Instead it is in Juliet's chest.

Lady Capulet. O me! this sight of death is as a bell
That warns my old age to a sepulcher.

[*Enter* Montague *and others.*]

Prince. Come, Montague; for thou art early up
To see thy son and heir now early down.

Montague. Alas, my liege, my wife is dead tonight!
Grief of my son's exile hath stopped her breath.
What further woe conspires against mine age?

210 liege: lord.

Prince. Look, and thou shalt see.

Montague. O thou untaught! what manners is in this,
To press before thy father to a grave?

214–215 what manners . . . grave: What kind of behavior is this, for a son to die before his father?

Prince. Seal up the mouth of outrage for a while,
Till we can clear these ambiguities
And know their spring, their head, their true descent;
And then will I be general of your woes
And lead you even to death. Meantime forbear,
And let mischance be slave to patience.
Bring forth the parties of suspicion.

216–221 Seal . . . patience: Stop your emotional outbursts until we can find out the source (**spring**) of these confusing events (**ambiguities**). Wait (**forbear**) and be patient, and let's find out what happened.

Friar Laurence. I am the greatest, able to do least,
Yet most suspected, as the time and place
Doth make against me, of this direful murder;
And here I stand, both to impeach and purge

WHEN STUDENTS STRUGGLE . . .

Analyze Plot Have students create a timeline showing the chronology of events in this act. Together, identify the key events to place on their timelines for Act V. *(Romeo hears that Juliet is dead and buys poison; Paris visits Juliet's tomb; Romeo arrives at the cemetery; Romeo kills Paris; Romeo kills himself; Friar Laurence sees Romeo and Paris dead; Juliet wakes and learns that Romeo is dead; Juliet kills herself; watchmen arrive with the Capulets, the Montagues, and the prince; Friar Laurence explains what happened; the Capulets and Montagues decide to put aside their feud.)* Then have students review their timelines and summarize these events in one or two sentences.

For additional support, go to the **Reading Studio** and assign the following **Level Up Tutorial: Plot: Sequence of Events.**

Myself condemned and myself excused.

Prince. Then say at once what thou dost know in this.

Friar Laurence. I will be brief, for my short date of breath
Is not so long as is a tedious tale.
Romeo, there dead, was husband to that Juliet;
And she, there dead, that Romeo's faithful wife.
I married them; and their stol'n marriage day
Was Tybalt's doomsday, whose untimely death
Banish'd the new-made bridegroom from this city;
For whom, and not for Tybalt, Juliet pined.
You, to remove that siege of grief from her,
Betrothed and would have married her perforce
To County Paris. Then comes she to me
And with wild looks bid me devise some mean
To rid her from this second marriage,
Or in my cell there would she kill herself.
Then gave I her (so tutored by my art)
A sleeping potion; which so took effect
As I intended, for it wrought on her
The form of death. Meantime I writ to Romeo
That he should hither come as this dire night
To help to take her from her borrowed grave,
Being the time the potion's force should cease.
But he which bore my letter, Friar John,
Was stayed by accident, and yesternight
Returned my letter back. Then all alone
At the prefixed hour of her waking
Came I to take her from her kindred's vault;
Meaning to keep her closely at my cell
Till I conveniently could send to Romeo.
But when I came, some minute ere the time
Of her awaking, here untimely lay
The noble Paris and true Romeo dead.
She wakes; and I entreated her come forth
And bear this work of heaven with patience;
But then a noise did scare me from the tomb,
And she, too desperate, would not go with me,
But, as it seems, did violence on herself.
All this I know, and to the marriage
Her nurse is privy; and if aught in this
Miscarried by my fault, let my old life
Be sacrificed, some hour before his time,
Unto the rigor of severest law.

Prince. We still have known thee for a holy man.
Where's Romeo's man? What can he say in this?

223–227 Friar Laurence confesses that he is most responsible for these events. He will both accuse (**impeach**) himself and clear (**purge**) himself of guilt.

236 It was Romeo's banishment, not Tybalt's death, that made Juliet so sad.

248 borrowed: temporary.

254 kindred's: family's.

265–269 and to . . . law: Her nurse can bear witness to this secret marriage. If I am responsible for any of this, let the law punish me with death.

The Tragedy of Romeo and Juliet: Act V, Scene 3 387

NOTICE & NOTE

273 in post: at full speed.

279–280 The Prince asks for Paris' servant, who notified the guards (**raised the watch**). Then he asks the servant why Paris was at the cemetery.

283–285 Anon . . . call the watch: Soon (**anon**) someone with a light came and opened the tomb. Paris drew his sword, and I ran to call the guards.

292–295 See what . . . punished: Look at the punishment your hatred has brought on you. Heaven has killed your children (**joys**) with love. For shutting my eyes to your arguments (**discords**), I have lost two relatives. We have all been punished.

297–298 jointure: dowry, the payment a bride's father traditionally made to the groom. Capulet means that no one could demand more of a bride's father than he has already paid.

301 at such rate be set: be valued so highly.

303–304 Capulet promises to do for Romeo what Montague will do for Juliet. Their children have become sacrifices to their hatred (**enmity**).

Balthasar. I brought my master news of Juliet's death;
And then in post he came from Mantua
To this same place, to this same monument.
This letter he early bid me give his father,
And threatened me with death, going in the vault,
If I departed not and left him there.

Prince. Give me the letter. I will look on it.
Where is the County's page that raised the watch?
Sirrah, what made your master in this place?

Page. He came with flowers to strew his lady's grave;
And bid me stand aloof, and so I did.
Anon comes one with light to ope the tomb;
And by-and-by my master drew on him;
And then I ran away to call the watch.

Prince. This letter doth make good the friar's words,
Their course of love, the tidings of her death;
And here he writes that he did buy a poison
Of a poor 'pothecary, and therewithal
Came to this vault to die and lie with Juliet.
Where be these enemies? Capulet, Montague,
See what a scourge is laid upon your hate,
That heaven finds means to kill your joys with love!
And I, for winking at your discords too,
Have lost a brace of kinsmen. All are punished.

Capulet. O brother Montague, give me thy hand.
This is my daughter's jointure, for no more
Can I demand.

Montague. But I can give thee more;
For I will raise her statue in pure gold,
That whiles Verona by that name is known,
There shall no figure at such rate be set
As that of true and faithful Juliet.

Capulet. As rich shall Romeo's by his lady's lie—
Poor sacrifices of our enmity!

Prince. A glooming peace this morning with it brings.
The sun for sorrow will not show his head.
Go hence, to have more talk of these sad things;
Some shall be pardoned, and some punished;
For never was a story of more woe
Than this of Juliet and her Romeo.

[*Exeunt.*]

TO CHALLENGE STUDENTS . . .

Reimagine a Scene Who is missing from Act V, Scene 3? Point out to students that the nurse and Benvolio are not present in this last scene. Discuss how this omission is particularly striking since the nurse is the person closest to Juliet and Benvolio is Romeo's best friend.

Have students collaborate with a partner to decide how the two might have been incorporated into the scene and what they might have said.

Ask students to share their ideas with the class. Then invite students to explain their thoughts on why Shakespeare might have chosen to exclude the two from the scene.

CHECK YOUR UNDERSTANDING

Answer these questions before moving on to the **Analyze the Text** section on the following page.

1 The apothecary's role in Act V is to —

A serve as a foil to Friar John

B foreshadow the fight between Romeo and Paris

C give Romeo a practical way to carry out a plan

D fuel the feud between the Montagues and the Capulets

2 Which line contains an oxymoron?

F *Under yond yew tree lay thee all along*

G *Sweet flower, with flowers thy bridal bed I strew*

H *Nightly shall be to strew thy grave and weep.*

J *Thou detestable maw, thou womb of death*

3 What important idea does Prince Escalus state at the end of the play?

A It is dangerous to make assumptions.

B A person can have only one true love.

C The body is mortal, but the soul is immortal.

D Hate between families can lead to tragedy.

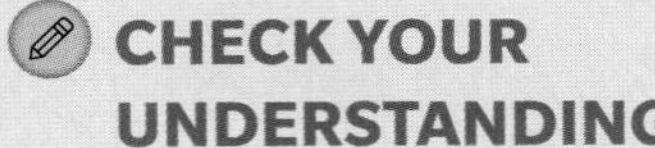

CHECK YOUR UNDERSTANDING

Have students answer the questions independently.

Answers:

1. *C*
2. *J*
3. *D*

If they answer any questions incorrectly, have them reread the text to confirm their understanding. Then they may proceed to ANALYZE THE TEXT on page 390.

ENGLISH LEARNER SUPPORT

Oral Assessment Use the following questions to assess students' comprehension and speaking skills.

1. Why is the Apothecary important to Act V? *(He sells Romeo the poison that will help Romeo carry out his plan.)*
2. Which line includes an oxymoron: *Thou detestable maw, thou womb of death*, or *Sweet flower, with flowers thy bridal bed I strew?* *(Thou detestable maw, thou womb of death)*
3. What does Prince Escalus say at the end of the play? *(Hate between families can lead to tragedy.)* **SUBSTANTIAL/MODERATE**

APPLY

ANALYZE THE TEXT

Possible answers:

1. **DOK 2:** *Romeo dreams of Juliet finding him dead and then reviving him with kisses. The former part of the dream foreshadows events in Act V, Scene 3.*
2. **DOK 4:** *Examples of oxymorons include "sweet sorrow," "brawling love," "loving hate," "heavy lightness," and "fiend angelical." Answers should discuss how the device contributes to complex characterizations and a view of life more nuanced and ambiguous and less black and white.*
3. **DOK 4:** *Juliet wants to please her mother by considering Paris, suggesting that she is obedient and trusting of her parents' judgment. Romeo, by contrast, is wildly romantic in his despair over Rosaline—an emotion that immediately dissipates when he sees Juliet. Juliet, transformed by the love she feels from their first meeting, becomes more independent, and also more like Romeo: passionate and willing to do anything to be with the person she loves.*
4. **DOK 4:** *Romeo's tragic flaw is that he is too impulsive and fails to think things through, qualities that often lead him astray. Juliet's tragic flaws include her naïveté and her willingness to go along with Romeo.*
5. **DOK 4:** *Friar Laurence fears what Romeo will do if he believes that Juliet is dead. At this moment, their elaborate plan begins to go tragically awry.*

RESEARCH

Direct students to hone their research by using search phrases such as "songs inspired by Romeo and Juliet" or "Romeo and Juliet artwork." Encourage students to explore historical and contemporary adaptations of *Romeo and Juliet* in their research. Remind students that they can use secondary sources to collect information about a longer original work.

Extend If students are having trouble locating an interview with an artist who based his or her work on a Shakespeare play, direct students to research the development of the popular 20th-century musical *West Side Story*. A number of sites give information about the genesis of this adaptation of Shakespeare's *Romeo and Juliet*, which features unlucky lovers with ties to two rival New York City street gangs in the 1950s.

RESPOND

ANALYZE THE TEXT

Support your responses with evidence from the text. NOTEBOOK

1. **Interpret** What dream does Romeo describe at the beginning of Act V, Scene 1? What part of his dream foreshadows events to come?
2. **Synthesize** *Romeo and Juliet* contains many **oxymorons**, expressions that bring together contradictory terms. Choose at least five instances in the play; then explain how this device deepens the play's themes.
3. **Connect** Recall Juliet's response when her mother suggests the idea of marrying Paris (Act I, Scene 3, lines 98–100). What does this reveal about Juliet's character before she meets Romeo? How does this contrast with Romeo's behavior in the parallel plot involving Rosaline? By Act V, how has Juliet changed?
4. **Evaluate** In a tragedy, a hero or heroine's character flaw is usually the cause of his or her downfall. Do you believe Romeo or Juliet has a character flaw that leads to his or her death? Support your response with evidence from the play.
5. **Notice & Note** In Scene 2, why is Friar Laurence in a panic when he finds out that his letter was not delivered to Romeo? Why is this Aha Moment a key turning point in the plot?

RESEARCH TIP
For a brief research task that involves long literary works, look for **secondary sources,** which summarize or interpret original works. For example, if you are researching *Warm Bodies*, a young-adult novel (and later a movie) based on *Romeo and Juliet*, you can search "warm bodies novel summary" to find sources that address the questions of the research task.

RESEARCH

Artists in many media have based works on *The Tragedy of Romeo and Juliet*. Research three of these works—songs, poems, plays, visual works of art, or musicals. Use the chart below to note how these adaptations remain true to Shakespeare's story and how they depart from it or put a different spin on it.

Extend Locate an interview with an artist who based a work of art or literature or art on a Shakespeare play. What was it about Shakespeare's work that spoke to the artist? In what way did the artist seek to transform, emphasize, or extend Shakespeare's message?

TITLE OF WORK	GENRE OF WORK	HOW IS IT TRUE TO SHAKESPEARE?	HOW DOES IT DEPART FROM SHAKESPEARE?
Students' responses will vary, based on the adaptations they research.			

LEARNING MINDSET

Asking for Help Remind students to ask peers, teachers, and other adults at school for help as they analyze and respond to the play. Explain that asking for help from others can help students get "unstuck" and move forward. Tell students that asking for help does not equal failure. Rather, seeking help is a way of "trying smarter." Also encourage students to think of other people in their lives whom they can trust and ask for help with academic as well as personal issues, such as family members, friends' parents or other relatives, and adults in the school community.

CREATE AND DISCUSS

Write a Eulogy With a partner, write a one-page collective eulogy—a tribute to someone who has died—for Romeo and Juliet.

- ❑ Brainstorm important details about Romeo, Juliet, their lives, and their relationship. Think about what motivates them, how they fall in love, the challenges they face, and how they change each other. Share information from your annotations and notes on the play.
- ❑ Craft your eulogy, highlighting key details about the characters of the two young people. Support your ideas with evidence from the play.
- ❑ If you have difficulty finding the right words to describe a character or express an idea, ask your peers or your teacher for help.

Discuss with a Small Group Share your eulogies with another pair. Discuss the challenges of casting tragic figures in a positive light—as is necessary in a eulogy—despite the fact that their own flaws contributed to their downfall.

- ❑ Make a collective list of the character traits your eulogies highlighted.
- ❑ What character traits or plot events did you omit or gloss over in your eulogies and why? Consider the audience of a eulogy, and talk about the challenge of capturing someone's life in a way that is flattering to him or her. Listen respectfully to the contributions of all group members.
- ❑ Reflect on your role in this activity. Make notes about what you did well and on areas for improvement.

Go to the **Speaking and Listening Studio** for help with having a small-group discussion.

RESPOND TO THE ESSENTIAL QUESTION

How can love bring both joy and pain?

Gather Information Review your annotations and notes on *The Tragedy of Romeo and Juliet*. Then, add relevant information to your Response Log. As you determine which information to include, think about:

- the joy and pain that come to Shakespeare's characters as they experience love
- the metaphors of love that Shakespeare uses in the play
- the lessons about love implied by Romeo and Juliet's tragic end

At the end of the unit, use your notes to help you write a literary analysis.

ACADEMIC VOCABULARY

As you write and discuss the ideas in the play, be sure to use the Academic Vocabulary words. Check off each of the words that you use.

- ❑ **attribute**
- ❑ **commit**
- ❑ **expose**
- ❑ **initiate**
- ❑ **underlie**

APPLY

CREATE AND DISCUSS

Write a Eulogy Explain that a eulogy is a formal speech often delivered at a funeral service. It is usually given by a friend or family member of the deceased, and its purpose is to praise the subject's positive qualities and to acknowledge the mourners' grief.

Have partners create a list of Romeo's and Juliet's positive attributes and then locate episodes from the play where they exhibit those attributes. The resulting anecdotes will provide content for their eulogies. Encourage students to decide on a pattern of organization before beginning to write. Then have partners decide how they will share the task of writing—for example, they could divide the task by paragraphs or by topics. Once students have drafted their parts of the eulogy, have them take turns reading their parts aloud and exchanging feedback.

For **writing support** for students at varying proficiency levels, see the **Text X-Ray** on page 282D.

Discuss with a Small Group Remind students that while eulogies are meant to be caring and respectful, and may sometimes come across as flattering, they should also be based in fact. Was it difficult to cast Romeo's and Juliet's lives in a positive light? Why or why not? Was it possible to highlight Romeo's and Juliet's best qualities, while also acknowledging their human limitations and failings? If so, how? Make sure group members share their opinions in a constructive and positive manner.

For **speaking support** for students at varying proficiency levels, see the **Text X-Ray** on page 282D.

RESPOND TO THE ESSENTIAL QUESTION

Allow time for students to add details from *The Tragedy of Romeo and Juliet* to their Unit 4 Response Logs.

APPLY

VOCABULARY STRATEGY: Shakespeare's Language

Find additional examples throughout the drama if students need more help understanding the play on words. Before pairs of students begin creating their own puns, brainstorm possible words as a class, listing them on the board for students' reference.

Possible answers:

1. *This pun uses homophones,* sole *and* soul, *to make a contrast between the lightness of spirit implied by dancing and the heaviness that Romeo feels in his heart.*
2. *The pun is on the word* grave, *which can mean "somber" as well as "a burial site."*

RESPOND

VOCABULARY STRATEGY: Shakespeare's Language

It takes time to get used to Shakespeare's language, but learning to unlock its layers will help you understand his continued popularity and influence. Shakespeare was a master of clever word play, including the use of **puns**. He also used many **foreign words** to add meaning and color to his writing.

A **pun** is a joke built upon multiple meanings of a word or upon two words that sound similar but have different meanings. Near the end of Act IV, Peter challenges the musicians to help him develop a pun based on a verse.

Peter. "When griping grief the heart doth wound
And doleful dumps the mind oppress,
Then music with her silver sound—

Why "silver sound"? Why "music with her silver sound"? What say you, Simon Catling?

First Musician. Marry, sir, because silver hath a sweet sound.

Peter. Pretty! What say you, Hugh Rebeck?

Second Musician. I say "silver sound" because musicians sound for silver.

Peter. Pretty too! What say you, James Soundpost?

Third Musician. Faith, I know not what to say.

Peter. Oh, I cry you mercy, you are the singer. I will say for you. It is "music with her silver sound" because musicians have no gold for sounding.

The English language is filled with words of foreign origin, but Shakespeare takes this a step further and includes words and phrases that many English speakers do not know. Once translated, these lend extra depth of meaning to his work. Here are some examples from *Romeo and Juliet:*

ambuscadoes (Spanish for "ambushes"), Act I, Scene 4

benedicite (Latin for "God bless you"), Act II, Scene 3

passado, punto reverso, hay, and *alla stoccata* (foreign terms for sword-fighting moves), Act II, Scene 4; Act III, Scene 1

aqua vitae (Latin for "water of life," signifying brandy), Act III, Scene 2

Practice and Apply With a partner, locate and explain the puns below. Then brainstorm a few words that you could use in original puns. Write a brief dialogue like the one between Peter and the musicians that uses your puns.

1. "You have dancing shoes / With nimble soles; I have a soul of lead / So stakes me to the ground I cannot move." (Act I, Scene 4, lines 14–16)
2. "Ask for me tomorrow, and you/shall find me a grave man." (Act III, Scene 1, lines 91–92)

Now review the word wall that you began in Act I. Which words on your wall are foreign? How do these words enhance your experience of reading Shakespeare?

ENGLISH LEARNER SUPPORT

Understand Homophones Introduce the homophones *soul* and *sole*. Write each word on the board, say the word aloud, and have students say the word with you. Point out that each word contains a long-*o* sound. Then write a definition beside each word: A person's *soul* includes the person's mind and feelings. The *sole* of a person's foot or shoe is the bottom of the foot or shoe.

Display the following cloze lines from the play (Act I, Scene 4, lines 14–16):

"You have dancing shoes
With nimble ______; I have a ______ of lead
So stakes me to the ground I cannot move."

Provide the following definitions: If someone or something is *nimble*, the person or thing moves quickly and easily. *Lead* is a metal, so something made of lead is heavy. If something *stakes* you to the ground, it pins you to the ground or ties you to the ground.

Then read lines 14–16 aloud and have students complete it with the proper homophone—*soul* or *sole*. (*"With nimble soles"; "I have a soul of lead"*)
SUBSTANTIAL/MODERATE

RESPOND

LANGUAGE CONVENTIONS: Parallel Structure

Parallel structure is the repetition of words, phrases, or grammatical structures in order to add emphasis or to improve the sound and rhythm of a piece of writing. Shakespeare regularly makes use of parallel structure to create cadence, or a balanced, rhythmic flow of words. Here is an example from Act II, Scene 1, lines 8–11:

> **Appear thou in the likeness of a sigh;**
> **Speak but one rhyme, and I am satisfied!**
> **Cry but "Ay me!" pronounce but "love" and "dove";**
> **Speak to my gossip Venus one fair word . . .**

Shakespeare repeats the structure of a verb followed by *but*: "Speak but . . . Cry but . . . pronounce but . . ." The parallel grammatical structures give equal weight to each phrase. Any one of these three tiny gestures from Rosaline, Mercutio jokes, would cause lovesick Romeo to rejoice. Read the passage aloud to hear the cadence that the parallel structures lend to the verse.

This example from Act I, Scene 5, lines 10–11 contains a series of four past-tense verbs, each followed by the word *for*.

> **You are looked for and called for, asked for**
> **and sought for, in the great chamber.**

In this case, the speaker (a servant) sounds rather ridiculous, as if he is trying to use flowery language to deliver a simple message.

In the next example, from Act IV, Scene 1, lines 102–103, Shakespeare repeats three parallel adjectives:

> **Each part, deprived of supple government,**
> **Shall, stiff and stark and cold, appear like death;**

Friar Laurence uses these grim adjectives to describe what Juliet's body will be like once she drinks the potion. The repetition gives his speech a somber rhythm, like a funeral march.

Practice and Apply Write a paragraph about how the themes, events, or characters of *Romeo and Juliet* relate to your life or to the life of someone you know. Include at least two examples of parallel structure in your paragraph. Share your work with a partner and discuss how the parallel structure increases the power and clarity of your language.

APPLY

LANGUAGE CONVENTIONS: Parallel Structure

Review the instruction and the examples with students. Remind students that repetition and parallelism are closely related and that parallelism often involves the repetition of certain words. However, the key to parallelism is the repetition of a grammatical structure.

Read the first example (lines 8–11 of Act II, Scene 1) with students. Have students underline three parallel structures. Call on a student to read them aloud. Explain that in this context the word *but* means "just" or "merely." Point out that in this example, the parallel structures are entire clauses (a verb in the imperative, followed by *but,* followed by an object).

Read through the second example, have students underline the parallel structures, and call on a student to read them aloud. Point out that the four parallel structures in this example passage are all verb phrases. Repeat this process with the last passage; point out that the repeated structure is three parallel adjectives.

Practice and Apply Invite volunteers to write examples of parallel structure from their paragraphs on the board. As a class, discuss what makes them parallel. Then analyze the impact of parallelism in the writing. Allow students to return to their own paragraphs to rework any sentences to include or edit parallel structures. *(Students' responses will vary but should include at least two examples of parallel structure.)*

ENGLISH LEARNER SUPPORT

Language Conventions Use the following supports with students at varying proficiency levels:

- Have students work with a partner to identify the examples of parallel structure used in Act III, Scene 5, Lines 43–45. *(my lord, my love, my friend)* Then have partners write three more phrases using the same structure and copy them into their notebooks. **SUBSTANTIAL**
- Have students imagine a "happy ending" in which Juliet wakes up just as Romeo arrives in the vault. Ask pairs of students to write several lines of dialogue that the two might say to one another. Have students include examples of parallel structure in their dialogue. **MODERATE**
- Have students write several lines of dialogue between Romeo's and Juliet's parents in which they apologize for their behavior. Have students include several examples of parallel structure. Then ask students to read their dialogue to a partner and discuss how the use of parallel structure increases the power and clarity of their writing and writing in general. **LIGHT**

HAVING IT BOTH WAYS

Sonnet by **Elizabeth Jennings**

SUPERHEART

Sonnet by **Marion Shore**

GENRE ELEMENTS

LYRIC POETRY

Tell students that a **lyric poem** is a short poem in which a single speaker expresses personal thoughts and feelings in a melodic or even songlike way. Lyric poetry comes in several forms, including sonnets, and addresses many aspects of the human experience.

LEARNING OBJECTIVES

- Analyze sonnet structures and characteristics, including rhyme scheme and rhythm, and connect ideas between sonnets.
- Conduct research to identify other sonnets and their themes.
- Discuss messages in sonnets.
- Create a visual response to poetry.
- Collaborate with a group to create a sonnet.
- **Language** Use content-area terms to discuss connections between sonnets.

TEXT COMPLEXITY

Quantitative Measures	**Having It Both Ways**	Lexile: N/A
	Superheart	Lexile: N/A
Qualitative Measures	**Ideas Presented** Implied meaning, some ambiguity; requires inferential reasoning.	
	Structures Used Traditional sonnet structures with both perfect and imperfect rhymes.	
	Language Used Both explicit and figurative or allusive language.	
	Knowledge Required Largely familiar popular culture references.	

Online 

RESOURCES

- Unit 4 Response Log
- Selection Audio
- Reading Studio: Notice & Note
- Level Up Tutorials: Rhythm; Rhyme
- Speaking and Listening Studio: Collaborative Discussions; Giving a Presentation
- "Having It Both Ways"/"Superheart" Selection Test

SUMMARIES

English

"Having It Both Ways" is a Petrarchan sonnet about the push and pull of emotions that love inspires. The speaker revels in the freedom and stability that one experiences when not being in love but also longs to be in love.

"Superheart" takes the form of a Shakespearean sonnet. Its pop culture imagery—Superman and his amazing powers—illustrates the speaker's will to resist the allure of love. The speaker then admits that she, like the superhero, has a fatal weakness: Her "kryptonite" is a new love.

Spanish

"Teniéndolo de ambas formas" es un soneto petrarquista acerca de la atracción y empuje de las emociones que inspira el amor. El narrador se deleita en la libertad y estabilidad que se experimenta al no estar enamorado pero también anhela estarlo.

"Supercorazón" toma la forma de un soneto shakesperiano. Sus imágenes de la cultura pop (Supermán y sus maravillosos poderes) ilustran la voluntad del narrador a resistirse al encanto del amor. El narrador luego admite que ella, como el superhéroe, tiene una debilidad fatal: su "kriptonita" es un nuevo amor.

SMALL-GROUP OPTIONS

Have students work in small groups to read and discuss the selection.

Think-Pair-Share

- After reading "Having It Both Ways" and "Superheart," pose a question to the class about one or both of the poems—for example, "What is the speaker's tone, or attitude, toward love?"
- Have students consider the question individually and jot down a response.
- Have pairs work together to arrive at a shared response.
- Optional: student pairs may consult other pairs to reach a new consensus.
- Call upon pairs or larger groups to share their responses with the entire class.

Reciprocal Teaching

- After students have read each sonnet at least once, provide them with question frames such as: *Why do you think the poem's speaker said ______? In line ______, what is the effect of ______ on the poem's structure? How does the image of ______ affect the poem's meaning?*
- Have students work individually, using the stems to complete questions about the sonnets.
- In groups of two or three students, have each student offer two discussion questions. Make sure that questions are not duplicated.
- Have groups work together to answer each question and support it with text evidence.

Text X-Ray: English Learner Support
for "Having It Both Ways" and "Superheart"

Use the Text X-Ray and the supports and scaffolds in the Teacher's Edition to help guide students at different proficiency levels through the selection.

INTRODUCE THE SELECTION
DISCUSS LOVE RELATIONSHIPS

In this lesson, students will need to be able to discuss love relationships and the range of emotions that love inspires. Explain the following:

- A *relationship* is a connection between people.
- An *emotion* is a feeling, such as sadness, joy, or anger.

Help students discuss love relationships and emotions. Supply these sentence frames:

- *A mother-child relationship is probably the first* _____ *that most people have.*
- *For long-term loving relationships to last, people should* _____.
- *When you are in love, you sometimes feel* _____ *because* _____ *and sometimes feel* _____ *because* _____.

CULTURAL REFERENCES

The following words or phrases from "Having It Both Ways" may be unfamiliar to students:

- *out of love* (line 1): not in a romantic relationship
- *In step with it* (line 4): moving at the same time
- *All virtues vices* (line 6): all good traits become faults

The following words or phrases from "Superheart" may be unfamiliar to students:

- *fortress in the north* (line 4): Superman's Fortress of Solitude, a headquarters and retreat
- *A fragment of his long-lost planet Krypton* (line 7)*; my kryptonite* (line 14): Superman's fictional home planet is Krypton. Contact with a broken-off piece of the planet, known as kryptonite, has the potential to kill Superman.

LISTENING

Analyze Sonnet Form

Tell students they can listen for the rhythm of stressed and unstressed syllables and rhyming sounds that give the sonnet structure.

Have students listen as you read aloud "Superheart," emphasizing the sonnet's stressed syllables and end rhymes. Use the following supports with students at varying proficiency levels:

- Repeat a set of end rhymes from the poem, emphasizing the parts of the words that rhyme: *p-**owers**/Ea-**rth**/t-**owers**/no-**rth***. Ask: Does "powers" rhyme with "Earth"? *(no)* Which sounds are rhyming sounds? *(p**owers**/t**owers** and Ea**rth**/no**rth**)* **SUBSTANTIAL**
- Reread the poem aloud while students nod at the stressed syllables and give a thumbs-up when they notice a rhyme. Pause after the first four lines and ask: What rhyming sounds did you hear? **MODERATE**
- Ask students to count the number of stressed syllables they hear in each line of the poem. Have them identify a perfect rhyme *(powers/towers)* and an imperfect rhyme *(Earth/north)*. **LIGHT**

SPEAKING

Discuss Connecting Ideas

Have students use content-area words, connecting words, and basic vocabulary to discuss both sonnets and their connections to each other as well as society.

Display a bank of content-area terms and basic vocabulary to use for discussion. Use the following supports with students at varying proficiency levels:

- Ask students questions that can be answered in a phrase: Which is freedom—being in love or out of love? **SUBSTANTIAL**
- Have students repeat an observation about the sonnets, such as *Both poems share ideas about love*. Provide sentence starters to stimulate further discussion: *Being in love is . . . . Being out of love is. . . .* **MODERATE**
- Have students take notes about ideas that connect the poems to each other and society and then use their notes to discuss the connections with a partner. **LIGHT**

READING

Understand Imagery and Ideas

Help students visualize details to comprehend the meaning of a poem.

Choral read "Superheart." Then, use the following supports with students at varying proficiency levels:

- Use pictures and discussion to preteach vocabulary and imagery. Show pictures of Superman, Earth, a fortress, and so on. Have students pause during choral reading to point to the correct picture. Invite students to create their own drawings to summarize the poem's ideas. **SUBSTANTIAL**
- Ask guiding questions to help students use their background knowledge to understand imagery. For example: Describe steel. What is a "heart of steel"? Why would someone want a heart of steel? **MODERATE**
- Have students use a graphic organizer to record the poem's images and their meanings. Then, use the information to identify a main idea. **LIGHT**

WRITING

Write a Sonnet

Work with students to read the writing assignment on Student Edition page 405.

Display both selections as models. Number each line and color code rhyming sounds to emphasize structure. Use the following supports with students at varying proficiency levels:

- Have students draw pictures of the imagery they want to use in their poems. Have students work with peers to suggest words that reflect those images. **SUBSTANTIAL**
- Supply students with a bank of rhyming words. Model using the words in a rhyming couplet. Have students write a rhyming couplet about love. **MODERATE**
- Guide students to write similes using sentence frames: _____ *is as beautiful as* _____. *Love is like a* _____. **LIGHT**

Connect to the
ESSENTIAL QUESTION

It may seem unlikely that anything can bring both joy and pain, yet the poets who have created "Having It Both Ways" and "Superheart" explore these opposing yet undeniably real aspects of love. Both poets have chosen the sonnet form—a classic poetic vehicle for expressions of love—to consider how people sometimes welcome love for the joy that it brings and sometimes try to shield themselves from it because of its potential for pain.

COMPARE POEMS

Tell students that they are about to explore two poems that may initially seem quite similar—same number of lines, lines that are approximately the same length, and a focus on the topic of love. Allow students time to preview the titles and images that illustrate each work. Read the Essential Question aloud. Have volunteers share any impressions or predictions they have about the two selections based on their preview. Then encourage students to look for similarities in the poems but also to be on the alert for the differences between them.

SONNET
HAVING IT BOTH WAYS

by **Elizabeth Jennings**

pages 397–399

ESSENTIAL QUESTION:

How can love bring both joy and pain?

COMPARE POEMS

As you read, notice the structure and graphic elements of the poems. Then, think about elements the poems share. After you read both poems, you will collaborate with a small group on a final project.

SONNET
SUPERHEART

by **Marion Shore**

pages 400–401

LEARNING MINDSET

Questioning Discuss the value of asking questions with students. Reinforce that asking questions demonstrates openness to new ideas and a desire to learn. In addition, if students have a question, it's likely others have a similar one. Encourage students to ask questions as they read the poems, and suggest various strategies for them to find answers, including rereading or asking a classmate.

GET READY

QUICK START

Love, in all its forms, is one of the most powerful feelings that humans experience. Whether it is the love between parent and child, a couple, or friends, the emotion of love leaves an indelible mark on everyone who experiences it. Think about examples of love that you have read about or witnessed in movies or in your life. How did those relationships affect the people involved? Share your thoughts and impressions with your group.

ANALYZE POETRY

A **sonnet** is a lyric poem composed of fourteen lines, usually written in **iambic pentameter.** An iamb is a pair of syllables, the first one stressed and the second one unstressed. The pair make up what's called a metrical foot. The *penta* in pentameter tells you there are five iambs, or syllable pairs, per line. Like this:

What liberty we have when out of love.

A sonnet follows a prescribed form and rhyming pattern. You will see different types of rhymes as you read sonnets. Traditional, or "perfect" rhymes are easy to identify. Other rhymes, called off rhymes or slant rhymes, are more subtle. For example:

Like Superman with all his super powers,	**A**
Cruising at lightning speed around the Earth,	**B**
Or leaping from Metropolis's towers,	**A**
Or soaring toward his fortress in the north,	**B**

In this stanza, *powers* and *towers* are a traditional, or perfect rhyme. But *Earth* and *north* are a rhyme as well. This type of slant rhyme is often called an eye rhyme, because the letters at the ends of the words mirror each other—they rhyme as much because they look alike as because of the way they sound.

The purpose of a sonnet is to set up a contrast between two things that are related but different, like love and vulnerability. That difference is often emphasized with a contextual twist called a *volta*, or turn. The poet can introduce the volta at any point. Often it comes near the rhyming couplet at the end—like the surprise twist at the end of a movie.

GENRE ELEMENTS: LYRIC POETRY

- usually short to convey strong emotions
- written using first-person point of view to express the speaker's thoughts and feelings
- often uses repetition and rhyme to create a melodic quality
- includes many forms, such as sonnets, odes, and elegies

TEACH

QUICK START

Have students read the Quick Start. Briefly discuss ways in which love is manifested in the relationships mentioned. Then have students brainstorm a list of examples of love, both fictional and factual, drawing from history (for example, the many marriages of King Henry VIII), literature (for example, the romance of Romeo and Juliet), popular culture (for example, the friendship of Harry Potter and Hermione Granger), and personal experience (for example, love for a younger sibling). Consider how each relationship could be described as "joyful," as "painful," or as "both." Discuss which relationships lasted, which did not, and why.

ANALYZE POETRY

Introduce the genre elements of lyric poetry and then the **sonnet** in particular. Help students hear the pattern of stressed and unstressed syllables of **iambic pentameter** by reading aloud these lines from "Superheart," with stresses as shown:

Like Súpěrmán wĭth áll hĭs súpěr pówěrs,
Crúisiňg ăt líghtnĭng spéed ăróund thĕ Eárth,

Explain that poets sometimes vary or reverse the stresses (as Marion Shore does with "*Cruising*") in order to emphasize certain words but also to keep the rhythms interesting to both hear and feel. Read the lines aloud again while clapping at each stressed syllable. Ask students to count the number of stressed syllables in each line. Tell students that reading a poem aloud, or whispering it to themselves, will help them recognize the stressed and unstressed syllables. You also may wish to point out that most of *The Tragedy of Romeo and Juliet*, earlier in this unit, was also written in iambic pentameter (unrhymed iambic pentameter, known as **blank verse**).

Explain that sonnets are often classified as Petrarchan or Shakespearean. A **Petrarchan** sonnet, named after the Italian poet Petrarch, sets up a contrast between the first eight lines, or octave, and the final six lines, or sestet. A **Shakespearean** sonnet consists of three quatrains, or four-line units, and a final couplet, with a typical rhyme scheme of *abab cdcd efef gg*. Note that poets often change or adapt these forms to suit their style and purpose.

ENGLISH LEARNER SUPPORT

Preteach Vocabulary Prepare students to understand the poems by preteaching meanings and pronunciations of words that are likely to be unfamiliar to them: *liberty, nerves, unstrung, tease, yearnings, nobly, encroachment, obdurate, hankering, prowess, invulnerable,* and *subdued*. Aid students whose primary language is Spanish by pointing out the following cognates: *liberty/libertad, nerve/nervio, noble/noble,* and *invulnerable/invulnerable*. Note that the suffix *-ly* forms the adverb *nobly*.
SUBSTANTIAL/MODERATE

CONNECT IDEAS

Review the information about making **connections** with students. Discuss ways in which readers might make connections to their own personal experiences, to ideas in other texts, and to society. Then call on volunteers to share examples of connections they noticed between two texts they recently read. In addition to theme, style, and text structure, suggest additional literary elements students might compare, such as setting, character, and conflict.

As you discuss the idea that many writers often draw inspiration from past writers, display and read aloud one of Shakespeare's sonnets, such as Sonnet 18 ("Shall I compare thee to a summer's day?"). Invite students to comment on the sonnet's structure and theme, and encourage them to consider these ideas as they read "Having It Both Ways" and "Superheart."

ANNOTATION MODEL

Encourage students to highlight rhyming words as a way to identify each poem's rhyme scheme. Invite them to mark unstressed (˘) and stressed (´) syllables to help them recognize the use of iambic pentameter. Remind students to use the margins for questions and comments about each text's ideas, themes, and any other points of interest.

GET READY

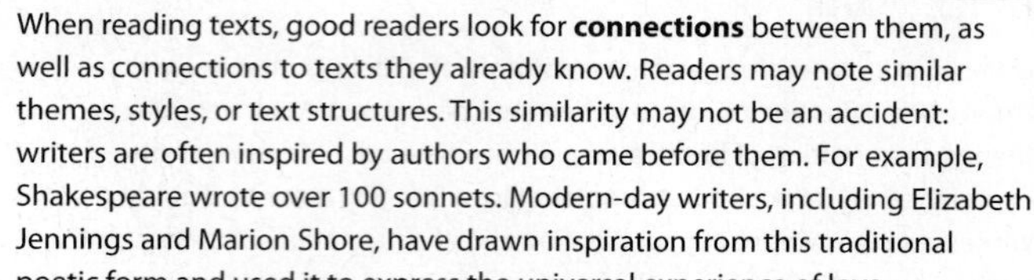

CONNECT IDEAS

When reading texts, good readers look for **connections** between them, as well as connections to texts they already know. Readers may note similar themes, styles, or text structures. This similarity may not be an accident: writers are often inspired by authors who came before them. For example, Shakespeare wrote over 100 sonnets. Modern-day writers, including Elizabeth Jennings and Marion Shore, have drawn inspiration from this traditional poetic form and used it to express the universal experience of love.

ANNOTATION MODEL

NOTICE & NOTE

As you read, notice the poetic elements each writer uses. In this model, you can see one reader's notes about "Having It Both Ways."

What liberty we have when out of love, Our heart's back in its place, our nerves unstrung, Time cannot tease us, and once more we move In step with it. Out of love we're strong,	Lines 1 and 3 end in the near-rhymes "love" and "move." Lines 2 and 4 also end in near-rhymes that end in an "ng" sound. I also notice that the syllables of of these lines alternate between unstressed and stressed.

396 Unit 4

BACKGROUND

Elizabeth Jennings *(1926–2001) is known as a traditional poet who excelled at the use of meter and rhyme. She spent most of her life in Oxford, England, and published her first book of poetry at age 27. Over her lifetime, Jennings published more than twenty-five books of poetry for which she received numerous awards. She said that while her life did influence her writing, her poetry is not autobiographical.*

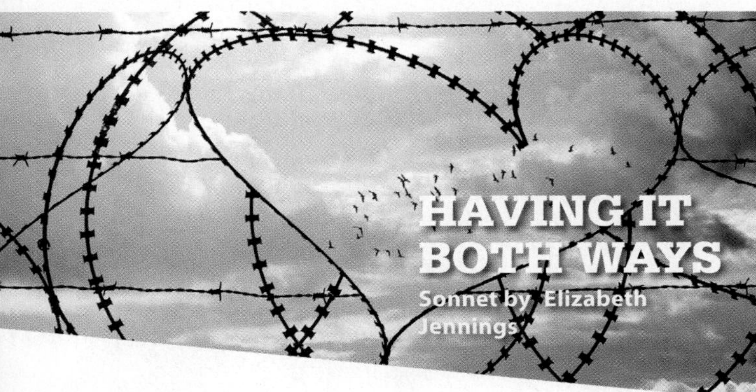

PREPARE TO COMPARE

As you read, note how the poet makes language choices to communicate message and tone. Specifically, think about how she uses diction and syntax to give voice to thoughts and feelings about love.

What liberty we have when out of love,
Our heart's back in its place, our nerves unstrung,
Time cannot tease us, and once more we move
In step with it. Out of love we're strong,

Without its yearnings and the way it makes
All virtues vices. Steady liberty
Is our element and no heartbreaks
Can touch or take us. We are nobly free.

NOTICE & NOTE

Notice & Note

You can use the side margins to notice and note signposts in the text.

CONNECT IDEAS

Annotate: Underline the first stanza.

Respond: What do you think the poet is saying in this part of the poem? How does it connect to experiences with love that you may have read about or observed?

TEACH

BACKGROUND

Have students read the Background note. Explain that although writers often draw from their personal experiences, they also find inspiration in what they observe in the world around them to create literature that many readers can identify with and understand. Also note that the poem's title comes from the expression "You can't have it both ways," which means that you have to make a choice between two things, even if neither option is ideal.

PREPARE TO COMPARE

Direct students to use the Prepare to Compare prompt to focus their reading.

CONNECT IDEAS

Have students work with partners to understand meaning and connect ideas. Suggest that partners read aloud one line or one sentence of the poem at a time and then consider possible interpretations. Use a Think Aloud to model how students might discuss the first line: The word *liberty* means "freedom," but it's the kind of freedom that people seek through revolution or after imprisonment. Maybe the speaker is equating love with a harsh ruler or a jailer.

Students may work individually or in pairs to connect their ideas about the poem to other texts or personal observations. (***Answer:*** *People feel free, at ease, and stable or stronger when they are not in love. They don't wear their heart on their sleeve, but back inside the body where it belongs. Nerves are calm, time no longer stands still, and people are synchronized with "real life" and the rest of the world. Connections to personal experiences will vary.)*

For **speaking support** for students at varying proficiency levels, see the **Text X-Ray** on page 394D.

ENGLISH LEARNER SUPPORT

Enhance Comprehension Choral read the poem with students. Then, use the following supports with students at varying proficiency levels:

- Provide students with adapted text that summarizes the meaning of each line or stanza. Ask questions to confirm understanding: Is the first line about being free from love? *(yes)* Are we stronger when we're not in love? *(yes)* **SUBSTANTIAL**
- Have students circle unfamiliar words in the poem. Discuss the meaning of each word in pairs or small groups. Then, read adapted text to confirm comprehension. **MODERATE**
- Have students discuss with peers any questions they have about specific words and the meaning of the poem. **LIGHT**

CONTRASTS AND CONTRADICTIONS

Explain that presenting Contrasts and Contradictions is one way in which a writer can point to a text's **theme**—that is, its central message or idea. Have students check their understanding of the line they marked by **paraphrasing** it in a way that connects it to the first eight lines of the poem. (***Example:*** *Even though we have more freedom when we are not in love, how long do we really want to live without love?)*

Then read aloud lines 9–14. Ask students to think about the contrasts and contradictions in the last line: "Begging for freedom, hankering for love." Remind students that when they notice contrasts and contradictions, they should ask themselves, *What is the difference, and why does it matter?* Guide students to identify the two opposing elements or ideas that the poet has expressed. (***Answer:*** *The poet is revealing the tension between the excitement and pleasure of being in love versus the feeling of safety and strength from not feeling subjected to the sometimes stressful feelings of being in love.)*

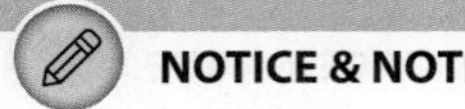

NOTICE & NOTE

CONTRASTS AND CONTRADICTIONS

Notice and Note: Underline the first line of the third stanza.

Respond: What internal contrast or contradiction about her feelings is the poet revealing?

But how long can we live within this state?
Don't we miss the slow encroachment of
Possessive passion? Don't we half-await

Its cruel enchantments which no longer have
Power over us? O we are obdurate,
Begging for freedom, hankering for love.

TO CHALLENGE STUDENTS . . .

Analyze Diction and Syntax In order to understand the effects of diction and syntax, ask students to study Elizabeth Jennings's choice of words and how they are arranged. Invite students to work individually or in pairs to rewrite the poem. Tell students to use synonyms and alternative phrasing, arriving as close as possible to the poem's meaning. Challenge students to adhere to the sonnet form in their rewrites. Students may share their work as part of a class discussion on diction, syntax, and rhythm.

NOTICE & NOTE 

CHECK YOUR UNDERSTANDING

Answer these questions about "Having It Both Ways" before moving on to the next selection.

1 In the second stanza, the poet is explaining —

- A how it feels when one sets off on a new adventure
- B how it feels when one is unencumbered by fluctuating emotions
- C how it feels when one reaches a goal before setting a new one
- D how it feels when one is constantly desiring what he does not have

2 In the fourth stanza, the poet uses the word obdurate to show —

- F how people repeatedly make choices that are not always wise
- G how people stubbornly pursue relationships that are not always pleasurable
- H how people repeatedly try to obtain possessions that cost too much money
- J how people stubbornly stay in relationships longer than they should

3 An important message in "Having It Both Ways" is —

- A the connection between the freedom of being able to do what you want and living by the rules of a relationship
- B the tension between wanting your partner to understand the intensity of your feelings for them and not wanting to overpower them
- C the virtuousness of liberty versus the vices of romantic love
- D the conflicting desires for emotional freedom and the feelings of being in love

TEACH

CHECK YOUR UNDERSTANDING

Have students answer the questions independently.

Answers:

1. *B*
2. *G*
3. *D*

If they answer any questions incorrectly, have them reread the text to confirm their understanding. Then, after reading "Superheart," they may proceed to ANALYZE THE TEXTS on page 402.

ENGLISH LEARNER SUPPORT

Oral Assessment Use the following simple, yes-or-no questions to assess students' comprehension and speaking skills.

1. According to the poet, do people feel free when they are not in love? *(yes)*
2. According to the poet, do people who are not in love want to find love again? *(yes)*
3. According to the poet, can people have it both ways—feel independent and in love? *(no)* **SUBSTANTIAL/MODERATE**

TEACH

BACKGROUND

Have students read the Background note. Students may be interested to know that translating poetry can be extremely challenging. Translators, like Marion Shore, must pay special attention to diction and syntax so that the translation preserves as many of the original poem's aesthetic qualities as possible. In "Superheart," students will see that Shore takes the same kind of care when crafting her own poetry.

PREPARE TO COMPARE

Direct students to use the Prepare to Compare prompt to focus their reading.

WORD GAPS

Remind students that Word Gaps are unfamiliar words, or words used in unfamiliar ways. Tell students that when they come across an unfamiliar word, such as *invulnerable,* they should try to understand its meaning from its context and word parts. Note that the prefix *in-* means "not," and *vulnerable* means "able to be harmed." Invite students to name some of the powers of the pop culture superhero Superman (for example, speed, strength, and X-ray vision); then focus on the fact, noted in lines 5–8, that nothing can stop him except kryptonite. (***Answer:*** *Superman is an invulnerable superhero, or person who cannot be hurt—someone with "mighty prowess."*)

ANALYZE POETRY

Point out that this poem follows the structure of a Shakespearean sonnet with its use of alternating rhyme to build toward a final **couplet,** or rhymed pair of lines that work together to make a point or to express an idea. Guide students to identify variations in the sonnet's iambic pentameter and rhyme scheme. Then discuss the effects of these variations on the poem's meaning. (***Answer:*** *The couplet draws attention to the revelation of the speaker's weakness: falling in love.*)

For **listening and reading support** for students at varying proficiency levels, see the **Text X-Ray** on pages 394C–394D.

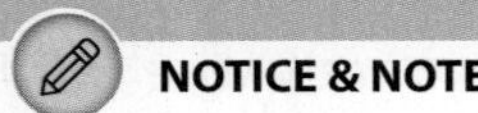

NOTICE & NOTE

BACKGROUND

Marion Shore *(b. 1952) is an award-winning American poet and translator. Her poems—and her translations of the work of other poets—have appeared in numerous journals and anthologies. Shore's first book of original poetry,* Sand Castle, *was published in 2010. A native of Queens, New York, she lives in Belmont, Massachusetts, with her husband and two sons.*

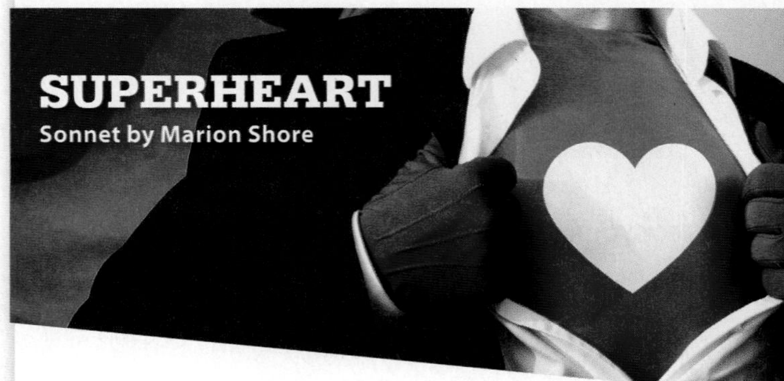

SUPERHEART

Sonnet by Marion Shore

Notice & Note

You can use the side margins to notice and note signposts in the text

WORD GAPS

Notice and Note: Underline the word that means "in total control" or "strong" in Line 10.

Respond: How does the use of that word reinforce the imagery of Superman?

ANALYZE POETRY

Annotate: Underline the words that help you determine the rhyming pattern of the final two lines of the poem.

Respond: How does this rhyming pattern reinforce the shift introduced in these lines?

PREPARE TO COMPARE

As you read, look for how the poet uses contemporary pop culture references to communicate the age-old experience of being in love.

Like Superman with all his super powers,
Cruising at lightning speed around the Earth,
Or leaping from Metropolis's towers,
Or soaring toward his fortress in the north,
His mighty prowess never falling victim
To any weapon save for (strangely enough)
A fragment of his long-lost planet Krypton,
Wounded by what he could not help but love,
So I too had lately come to feel
Invulnerable, the enemy subdued,
The bullets bouncing off my heart of steel,
Safe in its arctic fortress of solitude,
Or rising up in solitary flight —
And then you came along: my kryptonite.

WHEN STUDENTS STRUGGLE . . .

Analyze Rhyme Scheme Help students identify rhyme scheme by completing this chart.

	Last Word of Line	Rhyming Sounds	Pattern
1.	*powers*	*owers*	*a*
2.	*Earth*	*rth*	*b*
3.	*towers*		
4.	*north*		

For additional support, go to the **Reading Studio** and assign the following **Level Up Tutorials: Rhythm; Rhyme.**

NOTICE & NOTE

CHECK YOUR UNDERSTANDING

Answer these questions before moving on to the **Analyze the Texts** section on the following page.

1 In Lines 1 through 4, the poet —

- **A** asks the reader to believe that she really is a superhero
- **B** starts to build a simile between a superhero and the speaker
- **C** contrasts herself to a superhero who can do anything
- **D** describes how a superhero struggles to meet expectations

2 The author uses pop-culture references to —

- **F** explain how being in love makes people feel like a superhero
- **G** illustrate the theme of vulnerability in love
- **H** try to get graphic novel readers to read poetry
- **J** explain how writing makes her feel like a superhero

3 How does the last line of the poem contrast with what has come before?

- **A** The description of outlandish behavior at the beginning of the poem contrasts with the everyday activities at the end of the poem.
- **B** The calming tone at the beginning of the poem contrasts with the feelings of action at the end of the poem.
- **C** The discussion of a superhero at the beginning of the poem contrasts with the description of a villain at the end of the poem.
- **D** The image of a being who cannot be wounded contrasts with the image of one who is vulnerable.

CHECK YOUR UNDERSTANDING

Have students answer the questions independently.

Answers:

1. *B*
2. *G*
3. *D*

If they answer any questions incorrectly, have them reread the text to confirm their understanding. Then they may proceed to ANALYZE THE TEXTS on page 402.

ENGLISH LEARNER SUPPORT

Oral Assessment Use the following questions to assess students' comprehension and speaking skills.

1. To whom does the speaker of the poem compare herself? *(Superman)*
2. Based on what the speaker says in lines 9–13, does she feel she can be hurt? *(no)*
3. Based on the last line of the poem, does the speaker feel that she can be affected by love? *(yes)* **SUBSTANTIAL/MODERATE**

APPLY

ANALYZE THE TEXTS

Possible answers:

1. **DOK 4:** *The first eight lines confidently assert the benefits of freedom from romantic entanglements. The questions undercut that confidence, thus creating the turn in the sonnet toward acknowledging the pull of romantic love.*
2. **DOK 2:** *The author may want to show how a traditional poetic form can support contemporary images and ideas.*
3. **DOK 2:** *Continuing a thought from one line to the next keeps the sonnet to its traditional structure of alternating unstressed and stressed syllables.*
4. **DOK 4:** *The first-person plural establishes an intimate tone. It supports the author's attitude that everyone shares the speaker's thoughts and feelings.*
5. **DOK 4:** *The effect is rather comic, as the breathless buildup of the Superman image collapses into the revelation of the speaker's vulnerability.*

RESEARCH

Guide students to use search terms such as *modern sonnets, Shakespearean sonnets,* or *love sonnets,* according to their interests. Some websites offer "translations," or interpretations, of Shakespearean language that may help students grasp Shakespeare's meanings.

Extend Allow students time to compare and contrast the sonnets in their charts. Then have them form groups to share their ideas about how the sonnet form helps each poet to express a message. Invite group representatives to share ideas that the class can use to create an explanation of the connection between structure and theme.

RESPOND

ANALYZE THE TEXTS

Support your responses with evidence from the text. NOTEBOOK

1. **Analyze** In "Having It Both Ways," lines 9-13 consist of a series of questions. How do these questions represent a shift in thought from the ideas stated in the first eight lines?
2. **Interpret** What message do you think the author of "Superheart" is trying to communicate by combining the sonnet form with a modern-day pop culture **allusion,** or reference, to Superman?
3. **Explain** In "Having It Both Ways," why does the poet extend some thoughts across two lines, rather than completing them on one line?
4. **Analyze** The author of "Having It Both Ways" uses "we" and "our" as she describes contrary desires for romantic love and independence. What is the effect of this choice on the sonnet's tone?
5. **Notice & Note** What is the effect in "Superheart" of the first 13 lines building toward one image, only to be contradicted by the last line?

RESEARCH

Poets first began to write sonnets in Italy in the 1200s. Since then, countless poets have used sonnets to communicate their messages.

Read "Having It Both Ways" and "Superheart" aloud. Then, find at least three other sonnets. Read each of them aloud several times, paying attention to **prosody**—the timing, phrasing, emphasis, and intonation appropriate to each poem. Briefly describe the theme of each. Use the chart below for your notes.

TITLE	POET	THEME
Having It Both Ways	Elizabeth Jennings	People struggle with wanting to be in love yet wanting the peace that comes with an easy relationship.
Superheart	Marion Shore	Romantic relationships make people vulnerable.
Answers will vary.		

Extend Think about how the sonnets are similar to and different from each other. With a group, discuss how the form of the sonnet affects the message the poet is trying to communicate.

LEARNING MINDSET

Asking for Help Some students may be reluctant to ask for help in understanding a text or completing an assignment. Encourage students to ask for help whenever they are feeling "stuck." Explain that asking for help does not signal failure; rather, finding help is a way of "trying smarter." Remind students that help can come from peers, teachers, or adults at home. Sometimes a quick discussion about a problem or idea is enough to get "unstuck."

CREATE AND DISCUSS

Discuss the Poems Have a group discussion about the messages conveyed in the two sonnets.

- ❑ Think about what each poet says about love.
- ❑ Reflect on whether you agree or disagree with each poet's feelings about love. Explain why you feel that way.
- ❑ As a group, discuss what messages society communicates to us about love and relationships.

Create a Visual Response With your group, create a visual response to the messages that society communicates to us about love and relationships.

- ❑ With your group, locate five images that reflect messages society sends about love and relationships.
- ❑ Note what each image says and explain why you chose it.

Go to the **Speaking and Listening Studio** for help having a group discussion.

RESPOND TO THE ESSENTIAL QUESTION

How can love bring both joy and pain?

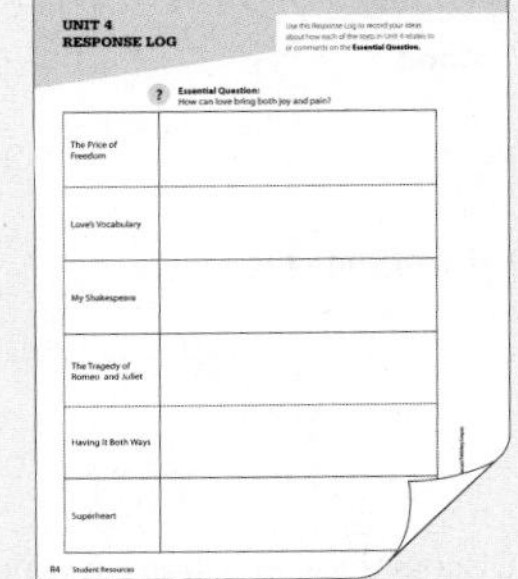

Gather Information Review your annotations and notes on "Having It Both Ways" and "Superheart" and highlight those that help answer the Essential Question. Then, add relevant details to your Response Log.

As you determine which evidence to include, think about:

- what each poem says about being in love
- how each poet uses the sonnet form to communicate her message

At the end of the unit, you will use your notes to write a literary analysis.

ACADEMIC VOCABULARY

As you write and discuss what you learned from the poems, be sure to use the Academic Vocabulary words. Check off each of the words that you use.

- ❑ **attribute**
- ❑ **commit**
- ❑ **expose**
- ❑ **initiate**
- ❑ **underlie**

APPLY

CREATE AND DISCUSS

Discuss the Poems Have students refer to their research notes and notes that they took while reading and discussing these two poems for this group discussion.

- Instruct students to sit or stand in a circle. Moving around the circle, have each student offer an idea about what "Having It Both Ways" says about love. Then go around the circle again for ideas about what "Superheart" says about love.
- Begin at a different student in the circle, but use the same process as above to express opinions about each poem's stance on love.
- To help students begin a discussion on messages about love from society, guide students to consider the various ways in which society communicates its messages—through movies and TV, music, person-to-person, schools, public forums, and so on. Ask them to consider the messages transmitted in these ways.

Create a Visual Response To locate images, students may search online or in a library. If time allows, students may bring images from home or take photos appropriate to the task. Depending on the size of the group, students may wish to assign each group member the task of finding one image. Remind students to provide source information about their photographs as they explain why they chose the images.

RESPOND TO THE ESSENTIAL QUESTION

Allow time for students to add details from "Having It Both Ways" and "Superheart" to their Unit 4 Response Logs.

APPLY

COMPARE POEMS

Before students work on the chart, review these terms:

- **Tone** is the speaker's attitude toward a subject.
- **Mood** is the feeling or atmosphere that is created by the words and imagery.
- **Diction** is an author's choice of words.
- **Syntax** is an author's arrangement of words into phrases and sentences.
- **Figures of speech** communicate meanings beyond the literal meanings of words. Poets use figurative language to create effects, emphasize ideas, and stir readers' emotions. Such language may include hyperbole, metaphor, personification, simile, and allusion.

Instruct students in how to use the chart to help them analyze and compare how elements of poetry are used to express theme in each sonnet.

ANALYZE THE TEXTS

Possible answers:

1. **DOK 3:** *The speakers in both poems are realistic about the positives and negatives of love. The tone of "Superheart" is lighter and more comical than the tone of "Having It Both Ways," which is more resigned and ironic.*
2. **DOK 2:** *"Having It Both Ways" discusses the tension of wanting freedom yet also wanting to be in love: "Begging for freedom, hankering for love." "Superheart" addresses the vulnerability that comes with being in love, as noted in the final line: "And then you came along: my kryptonite."*
3. **DOK 3:** *Students should support their opinions with examples from the chosen poem.*
4. **DOK 4:** *Some students will argue that "Having It Both Ways" is a more accurate depiction of human behavior and conflicting desires. Others may argue that "Superheart" is more truthful because it focuses on how one person (the "kryptonite") can change another's resolve to guard against falling in love.*

RESPOND

Collaborate & Compare

COMPARE POEMS

Both "Having It Both Ways" and "Superheart" are poems about love. Even though the sonnets share a topic, they may express different themes, or messages about life. They may also differ in tone and mood. Finally, the poets may use language—diction, syntax, and figures of speech, for instance—to convey their particular messages.

Complete the chart below to examine the two poems. Be sure to support your ideas with text evidence.

	HAVING IT BOTH WAYS	SUPERHEART
Theme, or Message about Life		
Tone		
Mood		
Use of Language		

ANALYZE THE TEXTS

Discuss these questions in your group.

1. **Compare** Both poems address the highs and lows of love. Compare the **mood,** the feeling or atmosphere created; and the **tone,** or attitude, each writer takes toward the topic of love. In what ways are they similar or different?
2. **Interpret** What is the theme of each poem? Try to state each theme in one sentence. Cite text evidence in your discussion.
3. **Critique** Discuss the language that each poet uses to convey her message. Which poem do you think uses language more effectively? Why? Use text evidence to support your opinion.
4. **Evaluate** Does one poem tell the "truth" about love better than the other? Discuss this question using text evidence as well as what you have observed or read about love.

ENGLISH LEARNER SUPPORT

Use Academic Language To help students compare the selections, provide the following:

- Review words and phrases that students can use to point out similarities (*similarly, likewise,* and *both*) and differences (*on the other hand, by contrast, but,* and *unlike*).
- Then provide students with the following sentence frames and model how to use them: *Both poems _____ , but only [name of poem] _____. In [name of poem], the speaker _____. On the other hand, in [name of poem], the speaker _____. The [tone/mood/theme] in [name of poem] is _____. By contrast, the [tone/mood/theme] in [name of poem] is _____.*

MODERATE/LIGHT

COLLABORATE AND PRESENT

Your group can continue exploring the ideas in these texts by collaborating on a sonnet. Follow these steps:

1. **Decide on the Topic** With your group, decide what aspect of love you would like to address. Think about how your group can bring a fresh interpretation to an age-old feeling and experience.
2. **Freewrite** Individually, take some time to freewrite about the topic. You can begin in poetic form, bullet points, or prose.
3. **Develop a Plan** Share your drafts, building on ideas from each group member to develop a final plan.
4. **Plan your sonnet** Review the elements of a sonnet:
   - 14 lines
   - Repetition of unstressed and stressed syllables
   - Often introduces a turn of thought near the end

   Decide what ideas you want to address in which stanzas, or groups of lines.
5. **Compose** Work together to write your sonnet. Your group may want to work individually or in pairs on separate stanzas or work together on the entire poem.
6. **Polish and Present** Make any needed revisions to the sonnet and share it with the class.

Go to the **Speaking and Listening Studio** for help with giving a presentation.

COLLABORATE AND PRESENT

Guide students to collaborate on creating and presenting a sonnet.

1. **Decide on the Topic** Invite groups to brainstorm on the topic of love. Ask them to consider the various approaches to the topic encountered throughout the lesson, including the sonnets they explored in the research project.
2. **Freewrite** Give students a set amount of time (perhaps five minutes) to freewrite on their chosen topic.
3. **Develop a Plan** Provide students with a "Comments" section to attach to their drafts for peer review. Remind students that comments should be encouraging and helpful and should include specific suggestions for improvement.
4. **Plan Your Sonnet** Use draft comments to continue planning the sonnet. Invite students to refer to published sonnets as a resource during the process.
5. **Compose** Encourage students to use figurative language in their works by providing examples of hyperbole, metaphor, personification, simile, and allusion. Allow groups to decide how they will collaborate, either by starting individually, by working as a group throughout, or by choosing some other configuration.
6. **Polish and Present** Have students take turns reading the sonnet aloud within their group and then making changes as necessary to improve the rhythm, rhyme, and other poetic elements. Work with groups to create a format for sharing the finished sonnets.

For **writing support** for students at varying proficiency levels, see the **Text X-Ray** on page 394D.

WHEN STUDENTS STRUGGLE . . .

Collaborate and Present Use the following supports to help students participate in small groups.

- Recast each step of the process as a question, followed by a sentence frame—for example, *What kind of love sonnet should we write? Let's write a sonnet about* _____.
- Provide graphic organizers to assist freewriting. Provide sentence starters for headings (such as *Love makes me feel* _____.) followed by bullet points.
- Display a list of content terms, including *couplet, rhyme, rhythm, sonnet*, and *stressed/unstressed syllable*, for students to use in their discussions. Model using the words as part of a discussion: This line should begin with an unstressed syllable.
- Provide sentence starters for commenting on drafts—for example, *I like this line because* _____.

INDEPENDENT READING

READER'S CHOICE

Setting a Purpose Have students review their Unit 4 Response Log and think about what they've already learned about how love can bring both joy and pain. As they choose their Independent Reading selections, encourage them to consider what more they want to know.

NOTICE  NOTE

Explain that some selections may contain multiple signposts; others may contain only one. The same type of signpost can occur many times in the same text.

INDEPENDENT READING

ESSENTIAL QUESTION:

How can love bring both joy and pain?

Reader's Choice

Setting a Purpose Select one or more of these options from your eBook to continue your exploration of the Essential Question.

- Read the descriptions to see which text grabs your interest.
- Think about which genres you enjoy reading.

Notice & Note

In this unit, you practiced asking **Big Questions** and noticing and noting two signposts: **Word Gap** and **Numbers and Stats.** As you read independently, these signposts and others will aid your understanding. Below are the anchor questions to ask when you read literature and nonfiction.

Reading Literature: Stories, Poems, and Plays		
Signpost	**Anchor Question**	**Lesson**
Contrasts and Contradictions	Why did the character act that way?	p. 419
Aha Moment	How might this change things?	p. 171
Tough Questions	What does this make me wonder about?	p. 494
Words of the Wiser	What's the lesson for the character?	p. 171
Again and Again	Why might the author keep bringing this up?	p. 170
Memory Moment	Why is this memory important?	p. 418

Reading Nonfiction: Essays, Articles, and Arguments		
Signpost	**Anchor Question(s)**	**Lesson**
Big Questions	What surprised me? What did the author think I already knew? What challenged, changed, or confirmed what I already knew?	p. 248 p. 2 p. 84
Contrasts and Contradictions	What is the difference, and why does it matter?	p. 3
Extreme or Absolute Language	Why did the author use this language?	p. 85
Numbers and Stats	Why did the author use these numbers or amounts?	p. 249
Quoted Words	Why was this person quoted or cited, and what did this add?	p. 85
Word Gaps	Do I know this word from someplace else? Does it seem like technical talk for this topic? Do clues in the sentence help me understand the word?	p. 3 p. 249

LEARNING MINDSET

Persistence Tell students that persistence is about not giving up when tasks become challenging. Explain that the way we grow and improve our skills is by continually putting in effort. Provide students with examples of positive thinking that show persistence, for example, "I know I can understand this as long as I keep trying."

ENGLISH LEARNER SUPPORT

Develop Fluency Select a passage from a text that matches students' abilities. Read the passage aloud while students follow along silently.

- Echo read the passage by reading aloud one sentence and then having students repeat the sentence back to you. Check their comprehension by asking yes/no questions. **SUBSTANTIAL**
- Have students read along with you and then reread the passage silently by themselves. Have them time their reading to track improvements. **MODERATE**
- Read the text aloud and ask students to follow along. As you read, occasionally substitute a word for a similar word. For example, say *pen* when the text says *pencil*. Instruct students to mark the mismatched words as they hear them. Then ask students to summarize the text, gauging whether they were able to comprehend what they read despite hearing the wrong words. **LIGHT**

Go to the **Reading Studio** for additional support in developing fluency.

You can preview these texts in Unit 4 of your eBook.

Then, check off the text or texts that you select to read on your own.

☐ MYTH

Pyramus and Thisbe from *Metamorphoses*
Ovid

Pyramus and Thisbe have grown up as neighbors, but their families despise each other. When Pyramus and Thisbe fall in love, the result is tragedy.

☐ SONNET

Sonnet 71
Pablo Neruda

The poet explores how we can't love in a vacuum. The world creeps into and affects our relationships.

☐ SCIENCE WRITING

Why Love Literally Hurts
Eric Jaffe

Older couples who have been together for a long time frequently die within months or even days of each other. What does love have to do with that?

☐ SHORT STORY

The Bass, the River, and Sheila Mant
W.D. Wetherell

What will a person sacrifice for love? Is the sacrifice always worth it?

Collaborate and Share With a partner, discuss what you learned from at least one of your independent readings.

- Give a brief synopsis or summary of the text.
- Describe any signposts that you noticed in the text and explain what they revealed to you.
- Describe what you most enjoyed or found most challenging about the text. Give specific examples.
- Decide whether you would recommend the text to others. Why or why not?

Go to the **Reading Studio** for more resources on **Notice & Note.**

INDEPENDENT READING

MATCHING STUDENTS TO TEXTS

Use the following information to guide students in choosing their texts.

Pyramus and Thisbe from *Metamorphoses*
Genre: myth
Overall Rating: Challenging

Sonnet 71
Genre: sonnet
Overall Rating: Accessible

Why Love Literally Hurts **Lexile: 1260L**
Genre: science writing
Overall Rating: Challenging

The Bass, the River, and Sheila Mant **Lexile: 1060L**
Genre: short story
Overall Rating: Challenging

Collaborate and Share To assess how well students read the selections, walk around the room and listen to their conversations. Encourage students to be focused and specific in their comments.

for Assessment

- Independent Reading Selection Tests

Encourage students to visit the **Reading Studio** to download a handy bookmark of **NOTICE & NOTE** signposts.

WHEN STUDENTS STRUGGLE . . .

Keep a Reading Log As students read their selected texts, have them keep a reading log for each selection to note signposts and their thoughts about them. Use their logs to assess how well they are noticing and reflecting on elements of their texts.

Reading Log		
Location	**Signpost I Noticed**	**My Notes About It**

UNIT 4 Task

- **WRITE A LITERARY ANALYSIS**

MENTOR TEXT
LOVE'S VOCABULARY
Essay by Diane Ackerman

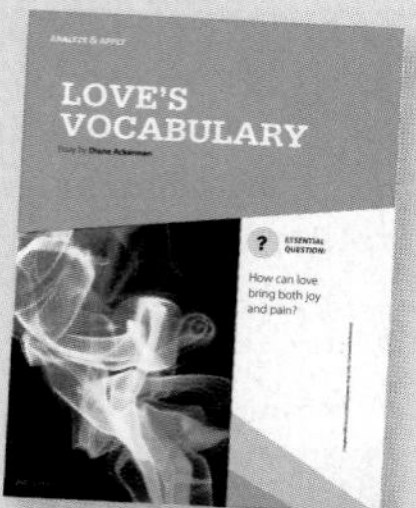

LEARNING OBJECTIVES

Writing Task

- Write a literary analysis that compares and contrasts the portrayal of love in two selections.
- Use strategies to plan and organize ideas for a literary analysis.
- Develop a focused, structured draft of a literary analysis.
- Use the Mentor Text as a model for a literary analysis.
- Revise drafts for organization and use of transitions and to incorporate feedback from peers.
- Edit drafts to incorporate standard English conventions.
- Use a rubric to evaluate writing.
- Publish writing to share it with an audience.
- **Language** Help partners identify and correctly capitalize proper nouns and proper adjectives.

Assign the Writing Task in ***Ed.***

RESOURCES

- Unit 4 Response Log
- Reading Studio: Notice & Note
- Writing Studio: Writing as a Process
- Grammar Module 10: Capital Letter

Language X-Ray: English Learner Support

Use the instruction below and the supports and scaffolds in the Teacher's Edition to help you guide students at different proficiency levels.

INTRODUCE THE WRITING TASK

Explain that a **literary analysis** takes a close look at certain details in one or more texts. For this writing task, students will compare how two different authors write about love.

Note that the unit's selections address how love can bring both joy and pain. Use sentence frames to explore ideas related to this theme. For example: *Love is* ____. *Love is not* ____ . Help students brainstorm phrases to complete the frames, such as *thinking about someone else rather than yourself,* or *[not] about your feelings, but the feelings of your loved one.*

WRITING

Organize Ideas

Tell students to introduce the thesis statement with an interesting quotation or detail. Review different types of openings that they might use.

Use the following supports with students at varying proficiency levels:

- In "Love's Vocabulary," have students find examples of words with short and long vowel sounds and list them in separate columns. Examples include *when, back, place, time, tease, step,* and *strong.* Model using some of these words in opening sentences. **SUBSTANTIAL**
- Ask partners to choose an important event or response in one of the selections. Tell them to write a sentence about the event that grabs the reader's attention. **MODERATE**
- Have each student write a sentence summarizing a personal anecdote that they could use to introduce a thesis statement. **LIGHT**

SPEAKING AND LISTENING

Use Proper Nouns and Adjectives

Provide practice for identifying proper nouns and adjectives and capitalizing them correctly.

Use the following supports with students at varying proficiency levels:

- Have students follow as you read paragraph 4 of "Love's Vocabulary" aloud. Tell students to raise their hands when they hear a proper noun or proper adjective. Have students repeat the proper nouns and adjectives they identify. **SUBSTANTIAL**
- Ask partners to underline capitalized titles, names, and proper adjectives in "Love's Vocabulary," paragraphs 5 and 6. Let them take turns using these words in new spoken sentences. **MODERATE**
- Have students find sentences with proper nouns and adjectives used in other selections. Form small groups in which students take turns reading their sentences aloud while other members identify words that should be capitalized. **LIGHT**

WRITING

WRITE A LITERARY ANALYSIS

Ask a volunteer to read the introductory paragraph, and then discuss the writing task with the class. Remind students to review the notes they recorded in their Unit 4 Response Logs before they begin work. Explain that the Response Log will contain ideas about different portrayals of love that students may find useful as they plan their literary analyses.

USE THE MENTOR TEXT

Tell students that their literary analyses will be similar to "Love's Vocabulary" by Diane Ackerman. Like Ackerman's essay, theirs will begin with an engaging introduction that includes a thesis statement defining the topic. The body of the analysis will develop the central idea in logically structured paragraphs that contain textual evidence and connect ideas with clear transitions. In a concluding paragraph, the analysis will summarize and synthesize main ideas. Remind students to use words, tone, and voice that are appropriate to the essay's formal purpose.

WRITING PROMPT

Discuss the prompt with students and encourage them to ask questions about any part of the assignment they do not completely understand. Emphasize that the purpose of the literary analysis is to discuss similarities and differences in the portrayal of love in two selections from the unit.

Discuss the checklist of key points and encourage students to keep them in mind as they write.

WRITING TASK

Go to the **Writing Studio** for help writing your literary analysis.

Write a Literary Analysis

This unit explores the many facets of love—joy, pain, passion, and conflict— to name just a few. For this writing task, you will write a literary analysis on a topic based on this idea. Look back at the texts in the unit and consider the aspects or characteristics of love that are represented in each text. Synthesize your ideas by writing a literary analysis. For an example of a well-written analytical text you can use as a mentor text, review the essay "Love's Vocabulary." You can also use the notes you made in your Response Log after reading the texts in this unit.

Writing Prompt

Read the information in the box below.

This is the topic or context for your literary analysis.

> **Love is an emotion that is easy to feel but sometimes difficult to endure.**

Think carefully about the following question.

Circle the two most important words, phrases, or ideas in the prompt.

> **How can love bring both joy and pain?**

Think about the ideas about love you have encountered in this unit and how they are similar to and different from one another.

Write a literary analysis comparing two selections in this unit. Explain how the portrayal of love is similar and different in each text.

Review these points as you write and again when you finish. Make any needed changes.

Be sure to—

- ❑ provide an introduction that catches the reader's attention, clearly states the topic, and includes a clear controlling idea or thesis statement
- ❑ develop a comparison using examples from the texts
- ❑ organize central ideas in a logically structured body
- ❑ use appropriate register, vocabulary, tone, and voice
- ❑ use transitions to create connections between sections of your analysis
- ❑ end by summarizing ideas or drawing an overall conclusion that synthesizes the comparisons you made

LEARNING MINDSET

Belonging Point out that the classroom is a learning community in which every student is a valued member. Emphasize the importance of participating actively in class discussions and activities. Note that everyone, from time to time, experiences difficulties with learning tasks, and each student should feel comfortable asking other students and you for assistance. Encourage students to consider helping others as an opportunity to "pay back" the help they have received from others.

1 Plan

Preparation is crucial in writing a literary analysis. Review each of the selections you plan to write about. Then start to analyze similarities and differences in the way they portray the topic of love.

- What ideas about love are explored in each text?
- Take notes on how the portrayal of love is similar and different in each. In your notes, list details, examples, and quotations that support your points.

As you prepare, keep in mind your purpose and your audience. Use the chart below to help you in planning your draft.

Literary Analysis: The Nature of Love		
Aspect or Characteristic of Love:		
Text Title	**Ideas about Love**	**Details, Examples, and Quotations**
First Text:		
Second Text:		

Background Reading Review the notes you have taken in your Response Log after reading the texts in this unit. These texts provide background reading that will help you think about what you want to say in your analysis.

Go to **Writing as a Process: Introduction** for help planning your literary analysis.

Notice & Note

From Reading to Writing

As you plan your literary analysis, apply what you've learned about signposts to your own writing. Remember that writers use common features, called signposts, to help convey their message to readers.

Think about how you can incorporate **Contrasts and Contradictions** into your literary analysis.

Go to the **Reading Studio** for more resources on **Notice & Note.**

Use the notes from your Response Log as you plan your analysis.

1 PLAN

Read the introductory text and review examples of evidence—details, examples, and quotations—that students should consider as they explore topics and texts for their literary analyses. Remind them to focus on similarities and differences between two selections.

Brainstorm the different aspects of love that selections have touched upon, such as selflessness and taking risks. Have students scan the unit for details, examples, and quotations that support each characteristic. To model questions for evaluation, ask: How is the language in two selections similar or different? Do the selections present positive or negative views of love?

English Learner Support

Understand Academic Language Review the headings in the planning chart and discuss examples to guide students before they begin working independently. Remind them that the details and examples they list as evidence should reflect both similarities and differences.

After students complete their charts, have them join small groups to discuss possible topics and ideas for their literary analyses. **ALL LEVELS**

NOTICE & NOTE

From Reading to Writing Discuss the focus of the Contrasts and Contradictions signpost, in which the writer notes a difference between two ideas or situations and helps readers see why the difference is significant. Emphasize phrases that often signal contrasts and contradictions, such as *on the one hand, however,* and *another viewpoint*.

Background Reading As students plan their literary analyses, encourage them to review the notes in their Unit 4 Response Logs. Suggest that they look back at the unit selections to identify information that can help them select an appropriate topic.

WHEN STUDENTS STRUGGLE . . .

Use Writing Prompts Introduce writing prompts to help students formulate main ideas for their essays. Present the sentence frames below and make sure students understand what is required to complete them. Model how to generate a thesis statement using two unit selections.

- *Both [title] and [title] portray love as ___________. (similarity)*
- *In [title] love appears ___________. [Title], however, shows love as ___________. (differences)*

Let students work in small groups to brainstorm ideas, draft thesis statements, and provide peer feedback and suggestions on how to make their statements more precise.

Organize Your Ideas Stress the importance of organizing ideas into an outline before writing. Tell students that the outline should include a section for the introduction, one section for each body paragraph, and one for the conclusion. Provide the following sample based on the chart:

I. Introduction: Interesting Detail/Quotation and Thesis Statement

II. Body Paragraph 1: Key Idea/Text Evidence

III. Body Paragraph 2: Key Idea/Text Evidence

IV. Conclusion: Restatement or Synthesis of the Main Idea Expressed in the Thesis Statement

Remind students that they can outline body paragraphs using evidence from the selections they have chosen.

For **writing support** for students of varying proficiency levels, see the **Language X-Ray** on page 408B.

2 DEVELOP A DRAFT

Remind students to follow their outlines as they draft their literary analyses. Emphasize that the outline is only a general guide to the writing process; they should feel free to change their plans as new ideas come up during the drafting stage.

English Learner Support

Write a Group Literary Analysis Work with small groups of students who require direct support. Work together to write an analysis that responds to the writing prompt. Begin by drafting a thesis statement that reflects the writing task and will serve as a guidepost for their literary analysis. **SUBSTANTIAL/MODERATE**

WRITING TASK

Go to **Writing as a Process: Planning and Drafting** for more help.

Organize Your Ideas After you have examined your chosen texts for ideas and evidence, organize them using the chart below. Write a clear thesis statement about how a particular aspect of love is depicted in each text. Search for an interesting quotation or detail to introduce your thesis statement. Then decide which organizational pattern you will use for the body, or middle section, of your literary analysis. You might present all your ideas about one text first, and then write about the second text. Or, you could discuss the similar ideas both texts, followed by a discussion of their differences. In the last box, write down some ideas for what you want to say in your concluding section.

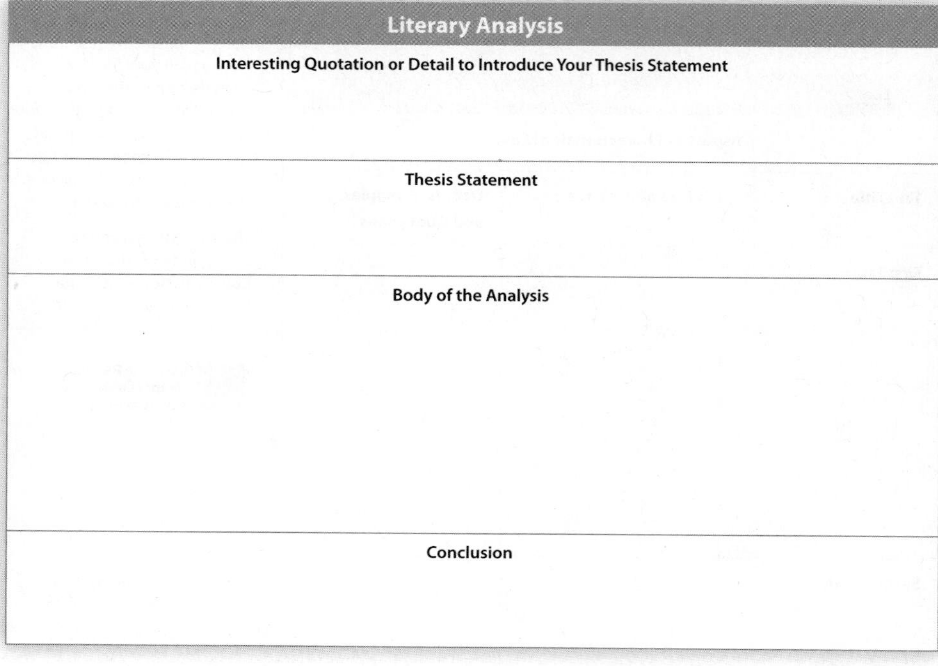

Literary Analysis
Interesting Quotation or Detail to Introduce Your Thesis Statement
Thesis Statement
Body of the Analysis
Conclusion

You might prefer to draft your analysis online.

2 Develop a Draft

Once you have completed your planning activities, you will be ready to begin drafting your literary analysis. Refer to your Graphic Organizers, as well as any notes you took as you studied the texts in the unit. Remember to present your ideas in logically ordered paragraphs, with one central idea for each paragraph. Use transitions to create clear connections between paragraphs and ideas. Using a word processor or online writing application makes it easier to make changes or move sentences around later when you are ready to revise your first draft.

WHEN STUDENTS STRUGGLE . . .

Improve Writing Fluency Explain that writers often get stuck when they begin drafting a text. Provide tips to help students get started and to keep their writing momentum moving.

- Keep your logs, brainstorming notes, and outlines close at hand for easy reference.
- Begin writing at any point of your outline. Don't feel obligated to start with the introduction and proceed straight to the end.
- Work in periods of 20 to 30 minutes without stopping. Take a break after each writing session and reread your work.
- Set aside a regular time and place to write.
- If you begin to feel boxed in, mix things up. Try using different methods of composition, such as a computer, paper and pencil, or audio recording.

WRITING

Use the Mentor Text

Genre Characteristics

In a literary analysis, you need to support your statements with examples and evidence. Note how the author of "Love's Vocabulary" uses this example to support her statement that poets have had to "create their own private vocabularies" for love.

Mrs. Browning sent her husband a poetic abacus of love, which in a roundabout way expressed the sum of her feelings.

The author gives an example of how Elizabeth Barrett Browning found a unique way to describe love in her poetry.

Apply What You've Learned In order to support your thesis statement, choose clear examples from the texts you are analyzing.

Author's Craft

The ideas you're presenting deserve your best efforts to express them clearly. To do that, you will need to use precise and descriptive language. Notice how the author of "Love's Vocabulary" uses language that is both expressive and exact.

Love is the white light of emotion. It includes many feelings which, out of laziness and confusion, we crowd into one simple word.

The author uses a vivid analogy ("white light") to describe love; and she identifies two specific factors ("laziness and confusion") in our misuse of the word "love."

Apply What You've Learned State your ideas clearly, using precise language.

WHY THIS MENTOR TEXT?

"Love's Vocabulary" by Diane Ackerman provides a good example of analytical writing. The author presents evidence from texts and from experience to compare different emotional responses associated with love. Use the instruction below to model how interesting language and text structures can be effective for comparing and analyzing literature.

USE THE MENTOR TEXT

Genre Characteristics Discuss the introductory paragraph and ask a volunteer to read aloud the example from the mentor text. Ask: Why do you think Ackerman chose the word *abacus* to describe Elizabeth Barrett Browning's collection of love sonnets? Why does she include the word *sum*? Encourage students to refer to paragraph 6 of "Love's Vocabulary" as they discuss their answers. *(Ackerman alludes to the first line of Browning's famous sonnet: "How do I love thee? Let me count the ways." An abacus is used to count and calculate, and the word* sum *refers to the results of an addition problem.)*

Author's Craft Read and discuss the opening paragraph and example. Then have the class reread the first sentence of the excerpt: "Love is the white light of emotion." Ask: In what ways is this statement both expressive and precise? Have students read paragraph 2 of "Love's Vocabulary" to find evidence to support their answers. *(Love is an overpowering emotion that can't be ignored, just as a bright, white light cannot be ignored. While we are overwhelmed, we often miss the subtleties of love, just as we miss the many colors of the spectrum that make up white light.)*

ENGLISH LEARNER SUPPORT

Use Precise Descriptive Language Use the following supports with students at varying proficiency levels:

- Read aloud paragraph 1 of "Love's Vocabulary" on page 277. Help students name some of the images that the writer evokes. *(monsters, bats, spiders, a sports arena)* Form small groups in which students underline descriptive words that help create these images. *(dripping fangs, leather wings, sticky webs, fields of glory)* **SUBSTANTIAL**
- Have students work in small groups. Assign one or two paragraphs from "Love's Vocabulary" to each group. Give students time to read the paragraphs and identify examples of vivid descriptive language. Let groups share their best examples with the class. **MODERATE**
- Discuss how writers use comparisons to describe abstract ideas such as love, hope, sorrow, joy, and suffering. Have students work in pairs to write sentences that explain an abstract idea by comparing it to something else. Let partners share and discuss their examples with other pairs. **LIGHT**

3 REVISE

To help students determine how they can improve their drafts, have them answer each question posed in the Revision Guide. Call on volunteers to model their revision techniques.

With a Partner Have students work with peer reviewers to evaluate the drafts of their literary analyses. Use the following questions as a guide for peer review:

- Does the introduction to the literary analysis grab the reader's attention with an engaging detail, example, or quotation?
- Does the introduction include a clear thesis statement?
- Has the writer provided text evidence from the selections?
- Does the literary analysis contain precise descriptive language?
- Are there clear connections, or transitions, between ideas?
- Does the conclusion sum up ideas contained in the thesis statement?

Encourage students to carefully evaluate their reviewers' comments as they further develop their literary analyses.

WRITING TASK

3 Revise

Go to **Writing as a Process: Revising and Editing** for help revising your literary analysis.

On Your Own A draft is where you get your ideas down on paper. It is the process of revision that turns that draft into a powerful piece of writing that really communicates what you're trying to say. The Revision Guide will help you focus on specific elements to make your writing stronger.

REVISION GUIDE

Ask Yourself	Tips	Revision Techniques
1. Does my introduction use an example or detail to introduce my thesis statement and make people want to read my analysis?	**Mark** the introduction.	**Add** an interesting example or detail from one of the texts you are analyzing.
2. Have I stated my thesis in a clear, coherent way?	**Underline** the thesis statement.	**Reword** the statement to make the central idea clearer.
3. In the body of the text, have I presented my key ideas in a logical, organized way?	**Mark** the sentence that introduces each important idea.	**Reorganize** your ideas to make the structure more logical.
4. Have I used effective details and examples from the literary texts to support my ideas?	**Underline** details and examples that support each idea.	**Add** more support for your ideas if necessary.
5. Are appropriate and varied transitions used to connect and contrast ideas?	**Note** transitions from paragraph to paragraph.	**Add** transition words and phrases to provide continuity.
6. Does the conclusion give the reader something to think about?	**Underline** the concluding insight offered to readers.	**Add** a final, thought-provoking statement about love.

ACADEMIC VOCABULARY

As you conduct your **peer review**, try to use these words.

- ❑ **attribute**
- ❑ **commit**
- ❑ **expose**
- ❑ **initiate**
- ❑ **underlie**

With a Partner After you have worked through the Revision Guide on your own, exchange papers with a partner. Evaluate each other's drafts in a **peer review**. Give constructive feedback to help your partner better accomplish his or her purpose in writing. Explain how you think your partner's draft should be revised and what your specific suggestions are.

WHEN STUDENTS STRUGGLE . . .

Present Text Evidence Discuss two types of text evidence that students might employ in a literary analysis.

- **Direct Quotation** Remind students that the purpose of a direct quote is not just to engage, but also to support a key idea. Quoting from more than one selection often provides an effective way to drive home similarities and differences in authors' views.
- **Summary/Paraphrase** When comparing or contrasting ideas from texts, writers often summarize or restate information. This lets the writer quickly highlight and connect information that supports the main ideas.

Ask students to find examples of both types of evidence in "Love's Vocabulary." Use these examples as the basis for further class discussion.

4 Edit

The final step in writing your literary analysis is editing for the proper use of standard English conventions and correcting any misspellings or grammatical errors. This process helps to ensure that readers will not be confused and will be able to understand your ideas and insights.

Language Conventions

Capitalization Capitalizing certain kinds of nouns is important to provide clarity and ease of reading. In a literary analysis, there are important capitalization conventions to pay attention to.

- In **titles of literary works**, capitalize the first and last words and all other important words. Do not capitalize conjunctions, articles, and prepositions shorter than five letters.
- Capitalize the first letters of names and titles used before names.
- Capitalize the first letters of adjectives made from proper nouns.

Go to Capital Letters in the **Grammar Studio** to learn more about capitalization.

The chart contains examples of properly capitalized names and titles.

Capitalization Type	Example
Titles	"**T**he **P**rice of **F**reedom" *The Tragedy of Romeo and Juliet* "**W**hy **L**ove **L**iterally **H**urts"
Names and titles	**P**rofessor **S**usan **H**olmes **D**octor **K**im **H**ong **F**riar **L**aurence
Proper Adjectives	**S**hakespearean **B**ritish **E**lizabethan

5 Publish

Finalize your literary analysis and choose a way to share it with your audience. Consider these options:

- Present your analysis as a speech to the class.
- Post your analysis as a blog on a classroom or school website.

ENGLISH LEARNER SUPPORT

Use Proper Adjectives Ask students to write sentences that contain proper nouns. Then have partners rewrite their sentences using proper adjectives. Provide the following sentences as a model:

My cousin from Canada will visit next week.

My Canadian cousin will visit next week.

When partners finish, have them share their sentence with the class. Help students compile a classroom glossary of proper adjectives. **MODERATE/LIGHT**

4 EDIT

Tell students that improving their literary analyses will involve reading their drafts several times. During their first reading, encourage students to focus on the clarity of their ideas and the evidence they use to support them. In the second reading, suggest that they look for places to add precise and vivid descriptions. For the third reading, suggest that students check for effective transitions that connect ideas and examples.

LANGUAGE CONVENTIONS

Capitalization Review the three categories of capitalization rules discussed in this section. Remind students that proper capitalization helps readers understand a text.

Have volunteers read the rules and then discuss the examples that appear in the chart. Review the use of lowercase prepositions and conjunctions within titles. Point out that while these examples include titles of literary works, the rule applies to all titles, including movies and songs. Then ask: What does *title* refer to in the second row? *(It refers to the professional titles of people.)* Ask volunteers to suggest examples of other personal titles. (***Possible responses:*** *President, King, Queen, Senator)*

Explain the difference between a proper noun and a proper adjective. Point out that these adjectives are made by adding endings, such as *-ian/-ean/-an* and *-ic/-ese/-ish,* to proper nouns. Review the examples in the chart and ask volunteers to cite other proper adjectives that contain these endings. *(**Possible responses:** Italian, Korean, American, Hispanic, Chinese, Spanish)*

For **speaking and listening support** for students of varying proficiency levels, use the **Language X-Ray** on page 408B.

5 PUBLISH

Discuss the suggested publishing options. If possible, have students post their literary analyses as blog posts on a school website. Encourage other students to read the literary analysis blogs and write meaningful comments and helpful suggestions. If students deliver their work in a speech, review the guidelines for successful oral presentations.

USE THE SCORING GUIDE

Allow students time to read the scoring guide. Encourage them to ask questions about any ideas, sentences, phrases, or words that they find unclear. Tell partners to exchange their final literary analyses and to score them using the guidelines. Have each student reviewer write a paragraph explaining the reason for the score he or she awarded for each major category.

WRITING TASK

Use the scoring guide to evaluate your literary analysis.

WRITING TASK SCORING GUIDE: LITERARY ANALYSIS

	Organization/Progression	Development of Ideas	Use of Language and Conventions
4	• The organization is effective and appropriate to the purpose. • All ideas are focused on the topic specified in the prompt. • Transitions clearly show the relationship among ideas.	• The introduction catches the reader's attention and clearly states the central insight. • The body of the analysis compares key ideas from two texts in a clear and logical way. • The ideas are well supported by examples and details from the literary texts. • The conclusion presents a thought-provoking statement about the topic.	• Language and word choice is purposeful and precise. • The style is appropriately formal. • Spelling, capitalization, and punctuation are correct. • Grammar, usage, and mechanics are correct.
3	• The organization is, for the most part, effective and appropriate to the purpose. • Most ideas are focused on the topic specified in the prompt. • A few more transitions are needed to show the relationship among ideas.	• The introduction could be more engaging. The central insight is stated. • The body of the analysis compares key ideas from two texts in a fairly logical way. • The ideas are supported by examples and details. • The conclusion presents a statement about the topic.	• Language is for the most part specific and clear. • The style is formal, for the most part. • Some spelling, capitalization, and punctuation mistakes are present. • Some grammar and usage errors occur.
2	• The organization is evident but is not always appropriate to the purpose. • Only some ideas are focused on the topic specified in the prompt. • More transitions are needed to show the relationship among ideas.	• The introduction is not engaging. The central insight is stated, but not clearly. • The body of the analysis compares key ideas from two texts, but not in a logical way. • The ideas are supported by a few examples and details. • The statement in the conclusion is not clearly related to the topic.	• Language is somewhat vague and unclear. • The style is often informal. • Spelling, capitalization, and punctuation are often incorrect but do not make reading difficult. • Grammar and usage are often incorrect, but the writer's ideas are still clear.
1	• The organization is not appropriate to the purpose. • Ideas are not focused on the topic specified in the prompt. • No transitions are used, making the analysis difficult to follow.	• The introduction is missing or confusing. • The body of the text does not effectively compare ideas from two texts. • The conclusion is missing.	• Language is inappropriate for the text. • The style is too informal. • Many spelling, capitalization, and punctuation errors are present. • Many grammatical and usage errors confuse the writer's ideas.

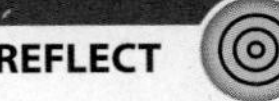

Reflect on the Unit

The literary analysis that you created pulls together and expresses your thoughts about two texts in this unit. Now is a good time to reflect on what you have learned.

Reflect on the Essential Question

- How can love bring both joy and pain? How has your answer to this question changed since you first considered it when you started this unit?
- What are some examples from the texts you've read that show how love affects our lives?

Reflect on Your Reading

- Which selections were the most interesting or surprising to you?
- From which selection did you learn the most about the nature of love?

Reflect on the Writing Task

- What difficulties did you encounter while working on your literary analysis? How might you avoid them next time?
- What part of the literary analysis was the easiest and what part was the hardest to write? Why?
- What improvements did you make to your analysis as you were revising?

UNIT 4 SELECTIONS

- **"The Price of Freedom"**
- **"Love's Vocabulary"**
- **"My Shakespeare"**
- ***The Tragedy of Romeo and Juliet***
- **"Having It Both Ways"**
- **"Superheart"**

REFLECT

REFLECT ON THE UNIT

Have students reflect independently on the questions that appear under each heading and write notes in response to each one. When students finish, have them join small groups to discuss their responses. During these discussions, circulate through the classroom and identify the questions that stimulate the liveliest conversations. Use these questions as the basis of a whole-class discussion to wrap up the unit.

LEARNING MINDSET

Try Again Tell students that people often think they know the answer to a question, only to find out that the answer is incorrect. Emphasize that in such cases, the key to successful learning is to return to the original question, reread it carefully, and determine what was misunderstood the first time around. Explain that when tackling a new task, it is not unusual for someone to try several times before succeeding.

Instructional Overview and Resources

	Instructional Focus	Online Ed Resources
Unit Introduction **A Matter of Life or Death**	**Unit 5 Essential Question** **Unit 5 Academic Vocabulary**	**Stream to Start:** A Matter of Life or Death **Unit 5 Response Log**
ANALYZE & APPLY		
"The Leap" Short Story by Louise Erdrich **Lexile 1260L** **NOTICE & NOTE** READING MODEL **Signposts** • Memory Moment • Again and Again • Contrasts and Contradictions	**Reading** • Analyze Plot • Make Inferences **Writing:** Write a Research Summary **Speaking and Listening:** Discuss with a Group **Vocabulary:** Prefixes **Language Conventions:** Relative Clauses	**Audio** **Reading Studio:** Notice & Note **Level Up Tutorial:** Plot: Sequence of Events **Writing Studio:** Writing Informative Texts **Speaking and Listening Studio:** Participating in Collaborative Discussions **Vocabulary Studio:** Prefixes **Grammar Studio:** Module 4: Lesson 2: The Adjective Clause
Mentor Text **"Is Survival Selfish?"** Argument by Lane Wallace **Lexile 1140L**	**Reading** • Analyze Arguments • Analyze Rhetorical Devices **Writing:** Prepare for Discussion **Speaking and Listening:** Class Discussion **Vocabulary:** Synonyms **Language Conventions:** Commas	**Audio** **Reading Studio:** Notice & Note **Level Up Tutorial:** Analyzing Arguments **Speaking and Listening Studio:** Participating in Collaborative Discussions **Vocabulary Studio:** Synonyms **Grammar Studio:** Module 11: Lesson 6: Commas with Sentence Interrupters
"The End and the Beginning" Poem by Wisława Szymborska	**Reading** • Analyze Poetic Language • Analyze Poetic Structure **Writing:** Write Photo Captions **Speaking and Listening:** Share with a Group	**Audio** **Close Read Screencasts:** Modeled Discussions **Reading Studio:** Notice & Note **Level Up Tutorial:** Tone **Speaking and Listening Studio:** Giving a Presentation

SUGGESTED PACING: 30 DAYS

Unit Introduction	The Leap	Is Survival Selfish?	The End and the Beginning
1	2, 3, 4, 5, 6, 7	8, 9, 10, 11, 12, 13	14, 15, 16

English Learner Support	Differentiated Instruction	Online Ed Assessment
• Build Vocabulary		
• Text X-Ray • Pronounce Vocabulary • Preteach Sequence Words and Phrases • Understand Contrasts • Learn Basic Vocabulary • Employ Inferential Skills • Oral Assessment • Use Cognates • Understand Language Structures	**When Students Struggle** • Use Strategies • Visualize Plot Events • Analyze Non-linear Plot **To Challenge Students** • Interpret Point of View	**Selection Test**
• Text X-Ray • Use Cognates • Use Questions and Question Marks • Oral Assessment • Use Cognates and Synonyms • Understand Language Structures	**When Students Struggle** • Analyze Arguments • Review an Argument	**Selection Test**
• Text X-Ray • Look for Patterns in Language • Confirm Understanding • Oral Assessment	**When Students Struggle** • Analyze Poetic Language **To Challenge Students** • Make Connections	**Selection Test**

from **Night**/*from* **The Pianist** — 17 18 19 20 21 22 23 24 25

Independent Reading — 26 27

End of Unit — 28 29 30

UNIT 5 Continued

	Instructional Focus	Online Ed Resources
COLLABORATE & COMPARE		
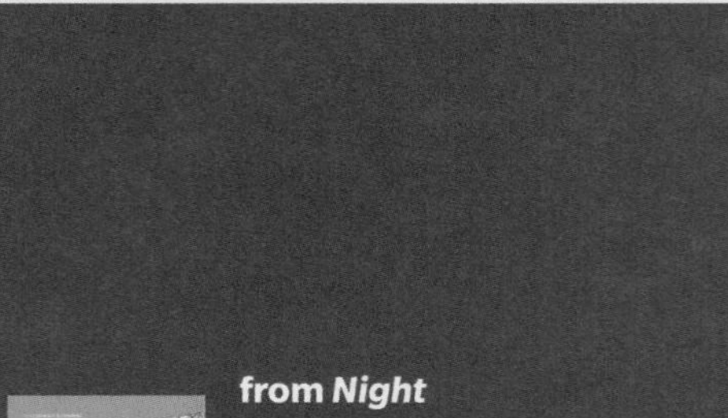 **from *Night*** Memoir by Elie Wiesel **Lexile 440L** **from *The Pianist*** Memoir by Władysław Szpilman **Lexile 910L**	**Reading** • Analyze Memoirs • Analyze Word Choice **Writing:** Write an Introduction **Speaking and Listening:** Discuss with a Small Group **Vocabulary:** Multiple-Meaning Words **Language Conventions:** Clauses	**Audio** **Close Read Screencasts:** Modeled Discussions **Reading Studio:** Notice & Note **Level Up Tutorials:** Analyzing Visuals; Reading for Details **Writing Studio:** Conducting Research **Speaking and Listening Studio:** Participating in Collaborative Discussions **Vocabulary Studio:** Multiple-Meaning Words **Grammar Studio:** Module 4: Lesson 1: Kinds of Clauses
Collaborate and Compare	**Reading:** Compare Memoirs **Speaking and Listening:** Collaborate and Present	**Speaking and Listening Studio:** Giving a Presentation

INDEPENDENT READING

The Independent Reading selections are only available in the eBook.

Go to the Reading Studio for more information on Notice & Note.

"Adventurers Change. Danger Does Not."
Article by Alan Cowell
Lexile 1160L

from *An Ordinary Man*
Memoir by Paul Rusesabagina
Lexile 980L

END OF UNIT

	Instructional Focus	Resources
Writing Task: Write an Argument **Speaking and Listening Task:** Present and Respond to an Argument **Reflect on the Unit**	**Writing:** Write an Argument **Language Conventions:** Transition Words **Speaking and Listening:** Present and Respond to an Argument	**Unit 5 Response Log** **Mentor Text:** "Is Survival Selfish?" **Writing Studio:** Writing Arguments **Reading Studio:** Notice & Note **Grammar Studio:** Module 2: Lesson 12: Conjunctions and Interjections **Speaking and Listening Studio:** Giving a Presentation

English Learner Support	Differentiated Instruction	Online Ed Assessment
• Text X-Ray • Talk and Write About Tone and Mood • Use Cognates • Produce Sounds of Newly Acquired Vocabulary • Preteach Vocabulary • Analyze a Symbol • Oral Assessment • Understand Language Structures • Analyze Writer's Craft • Double Conjunctions • Vocabulary Strategy • Comprehend Language Conventions	**When Students Struggle** • Clarify Historical Setting • Analyze Visuals	**Selection Tests**
• Match Comfort Level to Contribution	**When Students Struggle** • Think-Pair-Share	
"Who Understands Me But Me" Poem by Jimmy Santiago Baca "Truth at All Costs" Speech by Marie Colvin **Lexile 1080L**	from *Deep Survival* Informational Text by Laurence Gonzales **Lexile 960L**	**Selection Tests**
• Language X-Ray • Generate Ideas • Choose a Position • Use the Mentor Text • Formal Language • Use Connecting Words • Adapt the Argument • Give Feedback	**When Students Struggle** • Explore Ideas • Understand Academic Language • Use Transitions	**Unit Test**

TEACH

Connect to the
ESSENTIAL QUESTION

Ask a volunteer to read aloud the Essential Question. Have students pause to reflect. Prompt them for examples of recent environmental crises they've seen in the news, such as hurricanes, wildfires, or tornadoes. How did people endure those events? What might it take to survive a crisis of a different nature?

English Learner Support

Build Vocabulary Make sure students understand the Essential Question. If necessary, explain the following terms:

- *Survive* means "to continue to live despite hardship."
- *Crisis* means "a crucial point in a difficult or unstable situation involving change."

Help students restate the question in simpler language: What helps us live through a difficult time? **SUBSTANTIAL/MODERATE**

DISCUSS THE QUOTATION

Tell students that a proverb is "a short, pithy saying in frequent and widespread use that expresses a basic truth or practical precept." Ask students to read the quotation carefully and to take a moment to reflect. What do they take away from the proverb? Have them try restating it without using the repeated forms of "endure." Then have students discuss their new version of the proverb. How does the message change? Does it still have the same impact?

UNIT 

A MATTER OF LIFE OR DEATH

ESSENTIAL QUESTION:

What does it take to survive in a crisis?

"To endure what is unendurable is true endurance."

Japanese proverb

LEARNING MINDSET

Plan Tell students that planning is essential to completing work efficiently and exceptionally. Explain that developing planning skills helps them learn discipline, which will make completing tasks easier in the future. Have students think about what they do when they make plans to do something with friends. Is it easier when they decide ahead of time where they are going, what time to get there, and what to bring? Prompt them to apply those same types of planning skills to their assignments. Give them examples of how to plan, such as mapping out steps, setting goals, and using a calendar to track progress.

ACADEMIC VOCABULARY

Academic Vocabulary words are words you use when you discuss and write about texts. In this unit you will practice and learn five words.

☑ **dimension** ☐ **external** ☐ **statistic** ☐ **sustain** ☐ **utilize**

Study the Word Network to learn more about the word **dimension**.

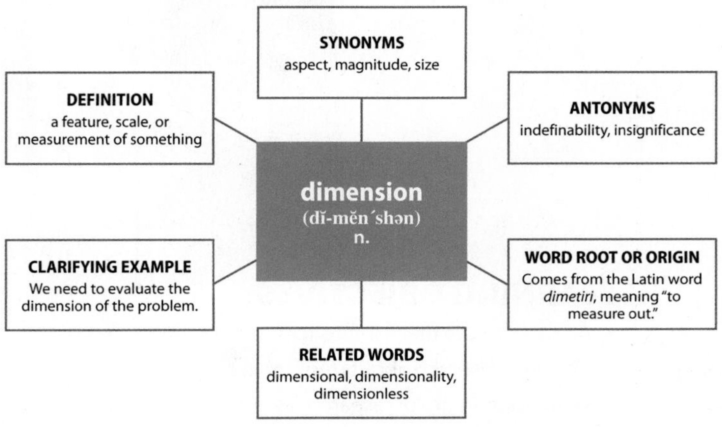

Write and Discuss Discuss the completed Word Network with a partner, making sure to talk through all of the boxes until you both understand the word, its synonyms, antonyms, and related forms. Then, fill out Word Networks for the remaining four words. Use a dictionary or online resource to help you complete the activity.

Go online to access the Word Networks.

RESPOND TO THE ESSENTIAL QUESTION

In this unit, you will explore how different people survive a crisis. As you read, you will revisit the **Essential Question** and gather your ideas about it in the **Response Log** that appears on page R5. At the end of the unit, you will have the opportunity to write an **argument** about whether or not survival is selfish. Filling out the Response Log will help you prepare for this writing task.

You can also go online to access the Response Log.

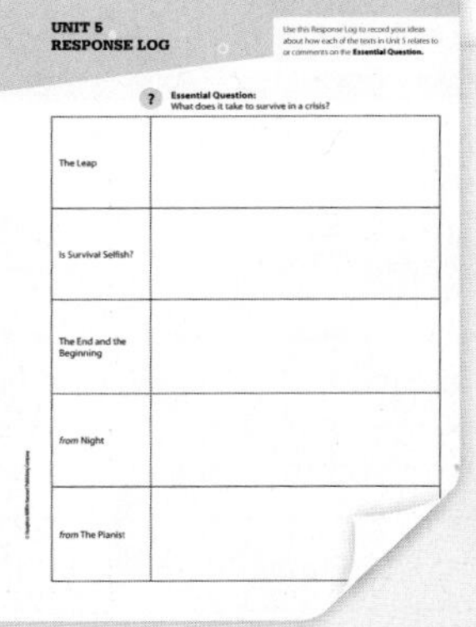

ACADEMIC VOCABULARY

As students complete Word Networks for the remaining four vocabulary words, encourage them to include all the categories shown in the completed network if possible, but point out that some words do not have clear synonyms or antonyms.

dimension (dĭ-mĕn´shən) *n.* A feature, scale, or measurement of something. (Spanish cognate: *dimensión*)

external (ĭk-stûr´nəl) *adj.* Related to, part of, or from the outside. (Spanish cognate: *externo*)

statistic (stə-tĭs´tĭk) *n.* A piece of numerical data. (Spanish cognate: *estadística*)

sustain (sə-stān´) *v.* To support or cause to continue. (Spanish cognate: *sostener*)

utilize (yo͞ot´l-īz´) *v.* To make use of. (Spanish cognate: *utilizar)*

RESPOND TO THE ESSENTIAL QUESTION

Direct students to the Unit 5 Response Log. Explain that students will use it to record ideas and details from the selections that help answer the Essential Question. When they work on the writing task at the end of the unit, their Response Logs will help them think about what they have read and make connections between the texts.

READING MODEL

THE LEAP

Short Story by Louise Erdrich

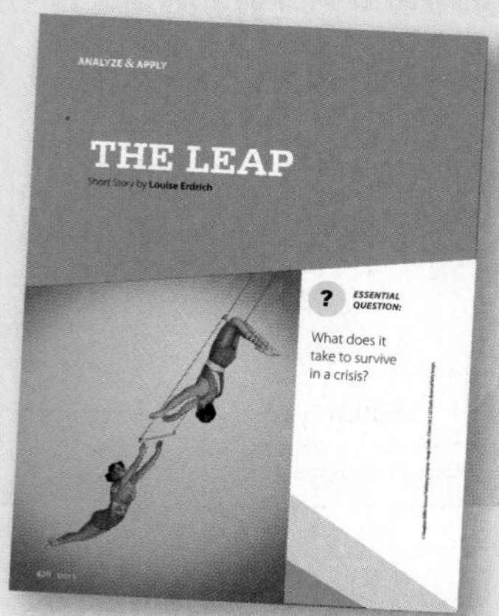

GENRE ELEMENTS

SHORT STORY

Remind students of the basic elements of a work of **fiction**—setting, characters, plot, conflict, and theme. A **short story** includes all these elements in a condensed format and often focuses on a particular event or moment in the life of the main character. Generally, a short story has one main conflict that keeps the story moving and stimulates readers' interest. In this lesson, students will explore the impact of Erdrich's use of flashback on the development of the story's theme.

LEARNING OBJECTIVES

- Analyze plot to make inferences about theme.
- Conduct research about traditional circuses.
- Write a summary of research results about circuses.
- Discuss research results about circuses.
- Use prefixes to understand complex words.
- Use relative clauses correctly.
- **Language** Discuss and provide feedback for research presentations.

TEXT COMPLEXITY

Quantitative Measures	**The Leap**	Lexile: 1260L
Qualitative Measures	**Ideas Presented** Mostly explicit, but some implied meaning.	
	Structures Used Deviates from chronological order with use of flashback and flash-forward.	
	Language Used Mostly explicit, some figurative language.	
	Knowledge Required More complexity in theme.	

Online 

RESOURCES

- Unit 5 Response Log
- Selection Audio
- Reading Studio: Notice & Note
- Level Up Tutorial: Plot: Sequence of Events
- Writing Studio: Writing Informative Texts
- Speaking and Listening Studio: Participating in Collaborative Discussions
- Vocabulary Studio: Prefixes
- Grammar Studio: Module 4: Lesson 2: The Adjective Clause
- "The Leap" Selection Test

SUMMARIES

English

After moving back home to care for her vision-impaired, elderly mother, the narrator of "The Leap" reflects on three ways in which she owes her existence to her mother. Through flashbacks, the narrator recounts the times her mother survives a trapeze accident, meets and falls in love with the narrator's father, and rescues the narrator from a house fire.

Spanish

Luego de mudarse de nuevo a casa para cuidar de su madre anciana y ciega, la narradora de "El salto" reflexiona sobre tres maneras en las que le debe su existencia a su madre. A través de flashbacks, la narradora recuenta la vez en la que su madre sobrevive un accidente en un trapecio, conoce y se enamora de su padre y rescata a la narradora de un incendio.

SMALL-GROUP OPTIONS

Have students work in small groups to read and discuss the selection.

Read-Think-Pair-Share

- After students have read "The Leap," ask them to create a timeline of the events in chronological order.
- Prompt students to answer this question: What do these events tell us about the narrator and her mother? Instruct individuals to skim the selection for details that reveal the relationship between the two.
- Tell pairs to discuss their ideas about the question and the information they found as support.
- Have pairs share their responses with the class.

Three-Minute Review

- As students read "The Leap," have them pause periodically to take notes. Encourage them to write down a variety of thoughts: what stands out to them, what confuses them, what details answer their questions, and so on.
- After they have read the story, set a timer for three minutes. During that time, students should skim the text and review the notes they made while reading.
- When the timer sounds, briefly discuss students' notes. Ask questions like the ones below to guide the discussion:
  — What did you notice as you reviewed this text?
  — What questions do you have about the text?
  — What in this text seems especially important?
  — What do you think is the theme of the text?

Text X-Ray: English Learner Support
for "The Leap"

Use the Text X-Ray and the supports and scaffolds in the Teacher's Edition to help guide students at different proficiency levels through the selection.

INTRODUCE THE SELECTION

DISCUSS INSTINCTS

In this lesson, students will need to be able to discuss instincts. Review the following:

- Explain that instincts are behaviors that people rely on naturally; they do not need to be learned through experience. For instance, a main character in "The Leap" relies on her survival instinct during a life-threatening disaster.
- Stories about survival often involve people relying on their instincts to get through a situation. Ask students to discuss other survival stories they have read or seen on TV or in movies. What details show that a character is using his or her instincts?

CULTURAL REFERENCES

The following words or phrases may be unfamiliar to students:

- *trapeze act* (paragraph 1): an acrobatic performance by a person or group using short horizontal bars suspended in air by two parallel ropes or wires
- *cataracts* (paragraph 1): clouding of the lens of the eye, causing blurred vision or loss of vision
- *commemorates* (paragraph 3): honors the memory of a person or event
- *Arabians* (paragraph 4): a breed of horse known for its endurance and the ability to learn quickly
- *ringmaster* (paragraph 4): a person in charge of performances in a circus ring
- *rekindle* (paragraph 18): to relight a fire
- *drawers* (paragraph 24): underpants

LISTENING

Monitor Understanding

Have students listen for clues to the order of plot events as you read aloud paragraphs 1–6.

Use the following supports with students at varying proficiency levels:

- Tell students to listen for time-order signal phrases such as *The first was when* (paragraph 3) and *That afternoon* (paragraph 6). Confirm comprehension with questions such as this: Is the narrator describing an event that occurred in the past? *(yes)* **SUBSTANTIAL**
- Tell students to listen for and mark verbs in the present and past tense, such as *is* and *was*. Provide frames for discussion: *Today, the narrator's mother* _____ *. In her youth, she* _____ *.* **MODERATE**
- Have students discuss the chronological order of events with a partner. Provide leading questions and sentence stems: When does the disaster take place? When does her mother go blind? *Did you notice the detail* _____ *? I took the transition phrase* _____ *to mean* _____ *.* **LIGHT**

SPEAKING

Share Information

Work with students to read the discussion assignment on Student Edition page 433.

Use the following supports with students at varying proficiency levels:

- Have students share labeled images of traditional circuses. **SUBSTANTIAL**
- Provide frames such as these of clarifying questions students might ask in their discussion: *I understood this to mean _____, but could you clarify _____ for me?* **MODERATE**
- Encourage students to use transition words and phrases such as *also* and *in addition* as they elaborate on group members' ideas. **LIGHT**

READING

Use Inferential Skills

Work with students to reread and analyze paragraph 24. Then have students practice using context clues to derive meaning from other parts of the text.

Use the following supports with students at varying proficiency levels:

- Read aloud paragraph 24 as students follow along. Have students pantomime the mother's actions of tapping gently on a window and smiling. Then have them act out how they think someone else might act in a similar situation. Does the mother seem relaxed? *(yes)* Is this how you would expect someone to act in this situation? *(no)* **SUBSTANTIAL**
- Provide these sentence frames to help students identify a contrast: *Based on the description of the mother's actions, she seems _____. (relaxed) In contrast, other people in a similar situation might act _____. (frantic)* **MODERATE**
- Have partners work together to identify text evidence that helps them make inferences about the mother's demeanor. Then have them contrast this with how they would expect others to behave in a similar situation. **LIGHT**

WRITING

Explain with Increasing Detail

Work with students to read the writing assignment on Student Edition page 433.

Use the following supports with students at varying proficiency levels:

- Have students add labels and captions to pictures they found of traditional circuses. **SUBSTANTIAL**
- Provide sentence frames to help students organize their writing: *Early circuses were _____. Popular acts included _____.* **MODERATE**
- Have students work with partners to review their summaries. Tell them to discuss their reactions to the topic and ask questions for clarification. Provide sentence stems: *What does the part about _____ mean? Why did you include _____?* **LIGHT**

EXPLAIN THE SIGNPOSTS

Explain that **NOTICE & NOTE Signposts** are significant moments in the text that help readers understand and analyze works of fiction or nonfiction. Use the instruction on these pages to introduce students to the **Memory Moment, Again and Again,** and **Contrasts and Contradictions** signposts. Then use the selection that follows to have students apply the signposts to a text.

For a full list of the fiction and nonfiction signposts, see page 480.

MEMORY MOMENT

Explain that **Memory Moments** often interrupt the flow of a narrative to give readers information needed to understand a character's present situation or to explain why a character acts or feels a certain way. Authors use Memory Moments to develop characters, which helps readers understand relationships between the **characters** and **plot.**

Read aloud the example passage. Note that the word *memory* in the first sentence signals that the passage is a signpost for a Memory Moment. Point out that the narrator draws a comparison between her mother's lasting memories and her own.

Tell students when they spot a Memory Moment, they should pause, mark it in their consumable text, and ask themselves the anchor question: *Why might this memory be important?*

READING MODEL

For more information on these and other signposts to Notice & Note, visit the **Reading Studio**.

THE LEAP

You are about to read the short story "The Leap." In it, you will notice and note signposts that provide clues about the story's characters and themes. Here are three key signposts to look for as you read this story and other works of fiction.

When you see phrases like these, pause to see if it's a **Memory Moment** signpost:

"I remember when . . ."

"That reminded me of . . ."

"This is just like when . . ."

"My mother used to tell me . . ."

Memory Moment You're telling a friend a great story about your weekend. You realize you need to tell about something that happened earlier, so your friend will get the point of the story. An author does the same thing in a Memory Moment, interrupting the narrative to tell readers a story from the past.

When an author introduces a blast from the past, it's for a good reason. Paying attention to a **Memory Moment** can:

- provide insight into the current situation
- explain character motivation, either now or in a situation still to come
- offer insight into theme
- explain one aspect of a relationship between character and plot

The paragraph below illustrates a student's annotation within "The Leap" and a response to a Memory Moment signpost.

> I would, in fact, tend to think that all memory of double somersaults and heartstopping catches had left her arms and legs were it not for the fact that sometimes, as I sit sewing in the room of the rebuilt house in which I slept as a child, <u>I hear the crackle, catch a whiff of smoke from the stove downstairs and suddenly the room goes dark</u>, the stitches burn beneath my fingers, and I am sewing with a needle of hot silver, a thread of fire.

Anchor Question When you notice this signpost, ask: Why might this memory be important?

What memory is introduced?	The narrator remembers a house fire that occurred when she was a child.
Why do you think this memory is important to the story? What might it tell us about characters or plot?	The narrator, an adult, still remembers a childhood fire. That tells her that her mother still remembers her earlier life as a trapeze artist. The fire connects the mother and daughter in some way, but we don't yet know how.

Again and Again When something happens over and over in a text, pay attention to it. There is a reason the author chose to repeat that element, and a message you as the reader should take from it.

- Look for a recurring word, phrase, image, or event.
- If it provides insight into character motivation or theme, it may be an important element in the story.
- Ask yourself: Why might the author keep bringing this up?

Here a student marked an instance of Again and Again:

> I owe her [the narrator's mother] my existence three times. The first was when . . .

Pause to see if it's an **Again and Again** signpost when you see repetition of:

- words
- phrases
- colors
- images

Anchor Question When you notice this signpost, ask: Why might the author keep bringing this up?

What does the narrator recognize?	three times her mother saved her or did something that led to her "existence"
What do you think this could mean? How might it change things?	These events could explain the mother/daughter relationship and why they're together now. The story may provide details about some or all of the events.

Contrasts And Contradictions What if your good friend met you every day at the same time and place to walk to class together—then one day she does not show up and she is not answering your texts. You would probably wonder what was going on: Is she okay? Is she mad at me?

A shift in a character's behavior—or a disconnect between what you expect to happen and what actually does—can grab your attention in a story the same way it does in real life. When a character thinks or does something unexpected, take the time to figure out what it means. In this example a student marked a Contrast and Contradiction.

> . . . she shows so little of the drama or flair one might expect from a performer that I tend to forget the Flying Avalons. She has kept no sequined costume, no photographs, no fliers or posters from that part of her youth.

When you see phrases like these, pause to see if it's a **Contrasts and Contradictions** signpost:

"This seems different from . . ."

"This is puzzling because . . ."

"This goes against . . ."

"This surprised me because . . ."

Anchor Question When you notice this signpost, ask: Why would the character act or feel this way?

What contradiction is expressed here?	The narrator's mother was once a highly skilled performer in a glamorous circus act. She doesn't talk about that part of her life and has kept no mementos of that time.
What insight might this provide about the narrator's mother?	Maybe something happened while she was in the circus that she wants to forget.

AGAIN AND AGAIN

Explain that **Again and Again** refers to the repetition of images, events, or words to grab readers' attention. The author may want to hint at the importance of events in the **plot** and offer insight into a **character.**

Read aloud the example passage. Point out that the narrator hints at three ways in which she owes her existence to her mother. The phrase "The first was when . . ." signals a **flashback,** or an interruption in the sequence of events, in which the narrator will describe the first way in which she owes her existence to her mother. Readers can infer that the narrator's recollection of the three ways in which her mother saved her will be used to develop the **theme,** or central message of the story.

Tell students when they spot an Again and Again signpost, they should pause, mark it in their consumable text, and ask themselves the anchor question: *Why might the author keep bringing this up?*

CONTRASTS AND CONTRADICTIONS

Explain that **Contrasts and Contradictions** show readers important aspects of **character** and **plot.** This information encourages readers to analyze character motivations and the **theme** of a narrative.

Read aloud the example passage. Model for students how to determine that the underlined sentence is a signpost for a Contrast and Contradiction. Point out that people might expect a performer to have a glamorous style, but the narrator's mother shows no evidence of this. Ask students to consider how this signpost may indicate something about the **plot.** What might this story be about?

Tell students that when they spot a Contrast and Contradiction, they should pause, mark it in their consumable text, and ask themselves the anchor question: *Why would the character act or feel this way?*

APPLY THE SIGNPOSTS

Have students use the selection that follows as a model text to apply the signposts. As students encounter signposts, prompt them to stop, reread, and ask themselves the anchor questions that will help them understand the story's characters, plot, and theme.

Tell students to continue to look for these and other signposts as they read the other selections in the unit.

WHEN STUDENTS STRUGGLE . . .

Use Strategies Visualizing can help students identify and understand signposts. If students show that they are having difficulty understanding the significance of a Memory Moment or a Contrast and Contradiction, suggest that they use the Sketch to Stretch strategy to visualize what is happening in the text. Have them reread the confusing passage and sketch what they picture happening. If the signpost is a Contrast and Contradiction, suggest that they also sketch what they would expect to happen. Finally, have students share and discuss their drawings with a partner.

Connect to the ESSENTIAL QUESTION

In "The Leap," the narrator describes her mother's reactions during times of crisis. Thanks to her quick thinking, the mother survives an accident during a circus performance and rescues her daughter from a house fire.

THE LEAP

Short Story by **Louise Erdrich**

ESSENTIAL QUESTION:

What does it take to survive in a crisis?

LEARNING MINDSET

Grit Remind students that our brains are muscles; the more we work them, the stronger they become. Tell them this means approaching problems as opportunities to learn and improve. Rather than praising students for arriving at a correct answer, offer encouragement that emphasizes their effort or approach. This kind of positive feedback will help students build confidence in their efforts to persist and not get discouraged if they don't immediately see the results they're after. It also reinforces the message that effort and hard work are keys to learning and achieving goals.

QUICK START

Examine the photographs that accompany the selection. Then read the first paragraph and predict what the story will be about. Note your prediction in the margin of your text so you can check it after you finish the story.

ANALYZE PLOT

The **plot** is the sequence of events in a work of fiction. A typical plot is linear—it evolves in chronological order in fairly predictable stages. "The Leap" has a non-linear plot that begins at the end: the adult daughter has moved home to care for her blind, elderly mother. Events that lead up to this situation are revealed in a series of **flashbacks**—interruptions in the chronological narrative—that describe events at different points in the past.

As the narrator's flashbacks reveal events in "The Leap," use a chart like this one to record events. When you finish the story, number the events in chronological order and write a summary of events in the order they occurred.

EVENTS BEFORE NARRATOR'S BIRTH	EVENTS DURING NARRATOR'S CHILDHOOD	EVENTS DURING NARRATOR'S ADULTHOOD

GENRE ELEMENTS: SHORT STORY

- includes the basic elements of fiction—setting, characters, plot, conflict, and theme
- centers on a particular moment or event in life
- can be read in one sitting

MAKE INFERENCES

In a short story, the **theme,** or underlying message, usually emerges through inference**.** An **inference** is a logical conclusion based on what you already know plus what the text tells you. To uncover themes in "The Leap," first examine the story's title. You might note, for example, that the speaker's mother would have made many fairly spectacular leaps in her career as a trapeze artist. But could *leap* also have one or more figurative meanings? Then, look for clues in the story that hint at its meaning. For example, character or plot developments may help reveal a story's themes.

As you read, use a chart like the one below to track your ideas and inferences about the story's themes.

STORY ELEMENTS OR CLUES	MY INFERENCES	POSSIBLE THEME
1		
2		
3		

TEACH

QUICK START

Prompt students to read the Quick Start activity. Before students read the first paragraph of the story, ask them to predict what the story will be about based only on their preview of the photographs. Then have them read the paragraph and discuss any changes in their predictions with a partner.

ANALYZE PLOT

Make sure students understand that a **flashback** is an account of a conversation, an episode, or an event that happened before the beginning of a story. Discuss how starting a narrative in the present and hinting at events in the past can allow readers to first see the results of events and then, through flashbacks, gradually learn what led to the present circumstances. To identify flashbacks, tell students to look for shifts in verb tense from the present to the past or past perfect. Point out that they should also look for words that signal a shift in time, such as *once, remember,* and *when*.

MAKE INFERENCES

Review that a **theme** is a central idea about life or human nature that a writer wants the reader to understand. Explain that in most cases, themes are not stated directly but implied. Readers must make inferences about a story's theme based on clues in the text as well as their own prior knowledge and experience. Discuss types of clues that might help readers infer a story's theme, such as details about how characters change or what they learn.

Suggest that students use these questions to help them make inferences about the story's theme:

- Who is the main focus in the story?
- What challenges does this character face?
- How does the character overcome challenges?
- What points of view does the narrator share with readers?

TEACH

CRITICAL VOCABULARY

Encourage students to reference a dictionary or thesaurus as needed to answer the questions. Then have students discuss their answers with partners.

Possible answers:

1. *No, the neighbor isn't happy, because your hedge is growing into his or her yard.*
2. *The neighbor hopes the fence will contain the overgrowth of the hedge, keeping it off his or her property.*
3. *No, it wasn't easy.* Extricate *suggests removal that is complicated or drawn out in some way.*
4. *Zach might be fired from the band, because he doesn't follow, or comply with, the rehearsal schedule.*
5. *No, since the plan is tentative, it may or may not happen.*

English Learner Support

Pronounce Vocabulary Model pronouncing the vocabulary words, telling students to listen carefully to the consonant clusters *cr, str,* and *pl,* the digraph *ch,* and the long and short vowel sounds. Point out the silent letter *e* in *extricate* and *tentative.* Have students echo your pronunciation of each word, multiple times, and provide correct feedback as necessary.

ALL LEVELS

LANGUAGE CONVENTIONS

Review the information about relative clauses. Explain that a relative clause is a type of subordinate clause, meaning that it contains a subject and a verb but cannot stand alone as a sentence.

Read aloud the example sentence. Explain that the relative pronoun *that* signals the relative clause. Ask a volunteer to identify the noun that the relative clause describes. *(disaster)*

ANNOTATION MODEL

Students can review the Reading Model introduction if they have questions about any of the signposts. Suggest that they underline important phrases or circle key words that help them identify signposts. They may want to color-code their annotations by using a different color highlighter for each signpost. Point out that they may follow this suggestion or use their own system for marking up the selections in their write-in texts.

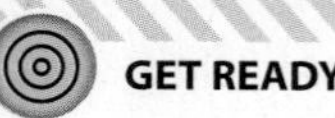

GET READY

CRITICAL VOCABULARY

encroach **extricate** **constrict** **comply** **tentative**

Answer the questions, using a dictionary or thesaurus as needed. Make sure answers reflect understanding of each Critical Vocabulary word's meaning.

1. My backyard hedge is beginning to **encroach** upon my neighbor's yard. Is my neighbor happy about this? Why or why not?
2. My neighbor wants to install a fence to **constrict** the growth of my hedge. What does my neighbor hope that fence will do?
3. The defendant had to **extricate** herself from the crush of news reporters and photographers outside the courthouse. Was this easy to do? Why?
4. Zach is a great bass player, but he doesn't **comply** with the band's rehearsal schedule. What might happen as a result?
5. We have **tentative** plans to visit the Grand Canyon this summer. Are we sure we're going to go? How do you know this?

LANGUAGE CONVENTIONS

Relative Clauses In this lesson you will learn about the **relative clause.** Relative clauses function as an adjective and describe a noun. A relative clause begins with a signal word: a relative pronoun *(that, which, who, whom, whose)* or a relative adverb *(when, where, why).* In this sentence from "The Leap," the relative clause is underlined:

It commemorates the disaster that put our town smack on the front page of the Boston and New York tabloids.

As you read "The Leap," look for the signal words that indicate a relative clause may follow a noun or noun phrase.

ANNOTATION MODEL

NOTICE & NOTE 

As you read, note your own questions and observations, and signposts, including **Memory Moment, Again and Again,** and **Contrasts and Contradictions.** Here is one reader's response to the first paragraph of "The Leap."

My mother is the surviving half of a blindfold trapeze act, not a fact I think about much even now that she is sightless, the result of encroaching and stubborn cataracts. She walks slowly through her house here in New Hampshire. . . . She has never upset an object or as much as brushed a magazine onto the floor. She has never lost her balance or bumped into a closet door left carelessly open.

"Surviving" means the mother's partner is dead. Trapeze accident?

"The mother is blind, but has never bumped into anything" Contradiction?

NOTICE & NOTE

BACKGROUND

Louise Erdrich *(b. 1954) is best known for exploring the Native American experience in her novels, poetry, and children's books. Born in Little Falls, Minnesota, she grew up in North Dakota. Of German American and Ojibwa (Chippewa) descent, her writing reflects a fascination with the influence of family and heritage on individuals and community. She lives in Minneapolis, Minnesota, where she owns a bookstore and continues to write. Her best-known works include the novels* Love Medicine, The Beet Queen, *and* The Round House.

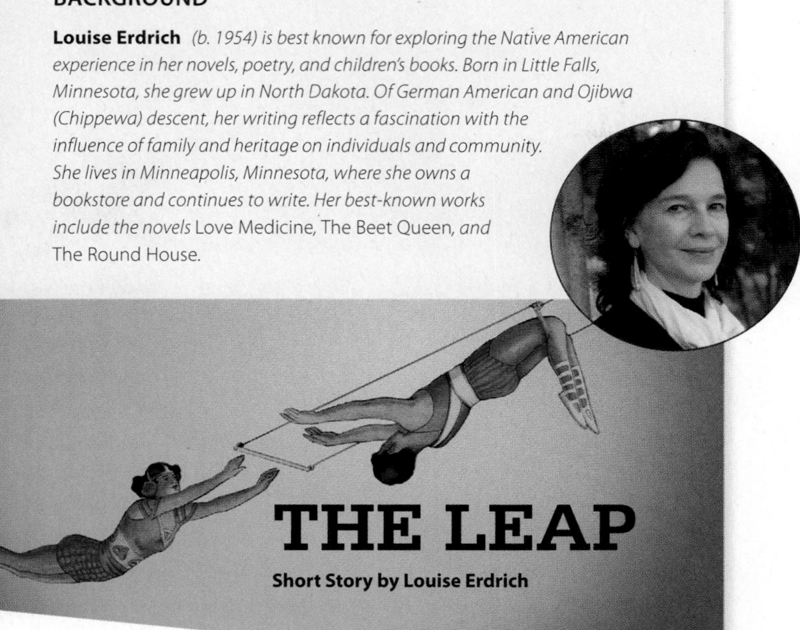

THE LEAP

Short Story by Louise Erdrich

SETTING A PURPOSE

Unraveling the truth about the past and deciding how the past informs the present are often steps of a journey. As you read "The Leap," consider how this story illustrates those steps in the speaker's journey.

1 My mother is the surviving half of a blindfold trapeze act, not a fact I think about much even now that she is sightless, the result of **encroaching** and stubborn cataracts. She walks slowly through her house here in New Hampshire, lightly touching her way along walls and running her hands over knickknacks, books, the drift of a grown child's belongings and castoffs. She has never upset an object or as much as brushed a magazine onto the floor. She has never lost her balance or bumped into a closet door left carelessly open.

2 It has occurred to me that the catlike precision of her movements in old age might be the result of her early training, but she shows so little of the drama or flair one might expect from a performer that I tend to forget the Flying Avalons. She has kept no sequined costume, no photographs, no fliers or posters from that part of her youth. I would, in fact, tend to think that all memory of double somersaults and heartstopping catches had

Notice & Note

You can use the side margins to notice and note signposts in the text.

encroach
(ĕn-krōch´) *v.* to gradually intrude upon or invade.

CONTRASTS AND CONTRADICTIONS

Notice & Note: What mementos from her past life does the narrator's mother keep?

Analyze: Why do you think this might be the case?

BACKGROUND

Have students read the Background note about the author. Tell students that although Erdrich grew up in North Dakota, she attended Dartmouth College in New Hampshire, the state where the story is set. "The Leap" was first published in 1990.

SETTING A PURPOSE

Direct students to use the Setting a Purpose prompt to focus their reading.

CONTRASTS AND CONTRADICTIONS

Explain that authors sometimes place words or phrases that describe different ideas or attitudes near each other to highlight contrasts or contradictions meant to surprise the reader. In this passage, the narrator explores links as well as disconnects between her mother's identity in old age and her experiences as a youth. (***Possible answer:*** *The mother keeps essentially nothing from her past life as a circus performer, possibly because she wants to avoid reminders of a painful or unpleasant experience.)*

ENGLISH LEARNER SUPPORT

Preteach Sequence Words and Phrases To help students understand the shifts in time, review words and phrases that signal the sequence of plot events. Display examples such as the following on a word wall: *once, when, then, that day/week/year*. Have students keep a list of sequence words and phrases they encounter in the text. Guide students to identify those that show a time change from present to past or from past to present.
SUBSTANTIAL/MODERATE

CRITICAL VOCABULARY

encroach: The narrator's mother loses her eyesight because of advancing cataracts.

ASK STUDENTS how the mother has adapted to her loss of sight due to encroaching cataracts. *(She is able to navigate well in her own home by walking slowly and carefully.)*

ANALYZE PLOT

Remind students to look for time-order signal words and shifts in verb tense to identify the **flashback**. For example, point out the phrase *when she saved herself* at the beginning of paragraph 3. Have students read the rest of the paragraph to identify additional clues that suggest when the flashback takes place. (***Answer:*** *Because the narrator gets her information from old newspapers and historical records, readers can infer that the event took place many years ago, likely before the narrator was born.)*

For **listening support** for students at varying proficiency levels, see the **Text X-Ray** on page 418C.

NOTICE & NOTE

left her arms and legs were it not for the fact that sometimes, as I sit sewing in the room of the rebuilt house in which I slept as a child, I hear the crackle, catch a whiff of smoke from the stove downstairs and suddenly the room goes dark, the stitches burn beneath my fingers, and I am sewing with a needle of hot silver, a thread of fire.

ANALYZE PLOT

Annotate: Mark the clue in paragraph 3 that tells you about when this flashback took place.

Cite Evidence: When did this scene take place? How do you know?

3 I owe her my existence three times. The first was when she saved herself. In the town square a replica tent pole, cracked and splintered, now stands cast in concrete. It commemorates the disaster that put our town smack on the front page of the Boston and New York tabloids. It is from those old newspapers, now historical records, that I get my information. Not from my mother, Anna of the Flying Avalons, nor from any of her in-laws, nor certainly from the other half of her particular act, Harold Avalon, her first husband. In one news account it says, "The day was mildly overcast, but nothing in the air or temperature gave any hint of the sudden force with which the deadly gale would strike."

4 I have lived in the West, where you can see the weather coming for miles, and it is true that out here we are at something of a disadvantage. When extremes of temperature collide, a hot and cold front, winds generate instantaneously behind a hill and crash upon you without warning. That, I think, was the likely situation on that day in June. People probably commented on the pleasant air, grateful that no hot sun beat upon the striped tent that stretched over the

APPLYING ACADEMIC VOCABULARY

❑ dimension ☑ external ❑ statistic ❑ sustain ☑ utilize

Write and Discuss Have students discuss the following question with a partner. Instruct them to use the academic vocabulary words *external* and *utilize* in their responses. Invite volunteers to share responses with the class.

- What **external** sources did the narrator **utilize** to learn about the disaster involving the Flying Avalons?

NOTICE & NOTE 

entire center green. They bought their tickets and surrendered them in anticipation. They sat. They ate caramelized popcorn and roasted peanuts. There was time, before the storm, for three acts. The White Arabians of Ali-Khazar rose on their hind legs and waltzed. The Mysterious Bernie folded himself into a painted cracker tin, and the Lady of the Mists made herself appear and disappear in surprising places. As the clouds gathered outside, unnoticed, the ringmaster cracked his whip, shouted his introduction, and pointed to the ceiling of the tent, where the Flying Avalons were perched.

5 They loved to drop gracefully from nowhere, like two sparkling birds, and blow kisses as they threw off their plumed helmets and high-collared capes. They laughed and flirted openly as they beat their way up again on the trapeze bars. In the final vignette[1] of their act, they actually would kiss in midair, pausing, almost hovering as they swooped past one another. On the ground, between bows, Harry Avalon would skip quickly to the front rows and point out the smear of my mother's lipstick, just off the edge of his mouth. They made a romantic pair all right, especially in the blindfold sequence.

6 That afternoon, as the anticipation increased, as Mr. and Mrs. Avalon tied sparkling strips of cloth onto each other's face and as they puckered their lips in mock kisses, lips destined "never again to meet," as one long breathless article put it, the wind rose, miles

MAKE INFERENCES

Annotate: In paragraph 6, mark lines that reveal the daughter's feelings about her mother.

Infer: What does she admire about her mother?

[1] **vignette:** (vĭn-yĕt´) a brief scene.

TEACH

MAKE INFERENCES

To make inferences about what the narrator admires about her mother, tell students to consider the details the narrator uses to describe her mother's actions and physical appearance. Ask volunteers to identify words and phrases that suggest the narrator's feelings about her mother. Then have students answer the question by explaining how these descriptions might suggest admiration. (***Answer:*** *The narrator is impressed with her mother's ability to feel comfortable in extreme situations, whether flying through the air while pregnant or becoming accustomed to blindness.)*

WHEN STUDENTS STRUGGLE . . .

Visualize Plot Events Explain that the use of visualization can aid students' understanding of plot events. After students read the description of the circus scene in paragraphs 4–8, have them turn to a partner and describe what they visualized: the tent, the audience, the trapeze performance, and what happened to the Flying Avalons when lightning struck. Encourage students to include additional sensory details that help them visualize the scene. Have partners help each other classify events and add details.

For additional support, go to the **Reading Studio** and assign the following **Level Up Tutorial: Plot: Sequence of Events.**

CONTRASTS AND CONTRADICTIONS

Remind students that Contrasts and Contradictions can be signaled by words and phrases such as *on the other hand*, *instead*, or *however*. Have them reread paragraph 9 and mark the observation the mother makes. Demonstrate **signal words** by pointing out that "perhaps" is used to signal the narrator's memory of how she first interpreted her mother's advice. This is followed by the signal phrase "but I also think" which shows an additional interpretation. (***Answer:*** *The narrator's mother told her she'd be amazed at how many things a person can do within the act of falling. It might be the mother's way of helping her daughter prepare to handle life's challenges. The mother knows this because she experienced a serious fall and had time, as she fell, to decide how to respond.)*

English Learner Support

Understand Contrasts Explain that contrasts set ideas in opposition in order to show differences. Model examples for students, such as *The rope was thin but strong*. Explain that describing a rope as thin might lead to the belief that it is also weak. The "but" in the sentence signals the contrasting idea that the rope is actually strong despite its thinness. Do the same modeling with *Although the pole was strong, it cracked.* Once students understand how to use signal words to find contrasting ideas, guide them to reread paragraph 9 and identify the signal phrase *But I also think.*

ALL LEVELS

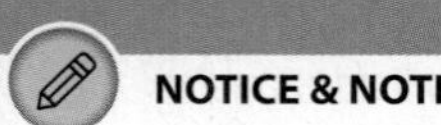

NOTICE & NOTE

off, wrapped itself into a cone, and howled. There came a rumble of electrical energy, drowned out by the sudden roll of drums. One detail not mentioned by the press, perhaps unknown—Anna was pregnant at the time, seven months and hardly showing, her stomach muscles were that strong. It seems incredible that she would work high above the ground when any fall could be so dangerous, but the explanation—I know from watching her go blind—is that my mother lives comfortably in extreme elements. She is one with the constant dark now, just as the air was her home, familiar to her, safe, before the storm that afternoon.

7 From opposite ends of the tent they waved, blind and smiling, to the crowd below. The ringmaster removed his hat and called for silence, so that the two above could concentrate. They rubbed their hands in chalky powder, then Harry launched himself and swung once, twice, in huge calibrated[2] beats across space. He hung from his knees and on the third swing stretched wide his arms, held his hand out to receive his pregnant wife as she dove from her shining bar.

8 It was while the two were in midair, their hands about to meet, that lightning struck the main pole and sizzled down the guy wires, filling the air with a blue radiance that Harry Avalon must certainly have seen through the cloth of his blindfold as the tent buckled and the edifice toppled him forward, the swing continuing and not returning in its sweep, and Harry going down, down into the crowd with his last thought, perhaps, just a prickle of surprise at his empty hands.

CONTRASTS AND CONTRADICTIONS

Notice & Note: In paragraph 9, what observation does the daughter reveal that the mother has shared?

Analyze: Why would the mother say this? How does she know?

9 My mother once said that I'd be amazed at how many things a person can do within the act of falling. Perhaps, at the time, she was teaching me to dive off a board at the town pool, for I associated the idea with midair somersaults. But I also think she meant that even in that awful doomed second one could think, for she certainly did. When her hands did not meet her husband's, my mother tore her blindfold away. As he swept past her on the wrong side, she could have grasped his ankle, the toe-end of his tights, and gone down clutching him. Instead, she changed direction. Her body twisted toward a heavy wire and she managed to hang on to the braided metal, still hot from the lightning strike. Her palms were burned so terribly that once healed they bore no lines, only the blank scar tissue of a quieter future. She was lowered, gently, to the sawdust ring just underneath the dome of the canvas roof, which did not entirely settle but was held up on one end and jabbed through, torn, and still on fire in places from the giant spark, though rain and men's jackets soon put that out.

10 Three people died, but except for her hands my mother was not seriously harmed until an overeager rescuer broke her arm in **extricating** her and also, in the process, collapsed a portion of the

extricate
(ĕk´strĭ-kāt) *v.* to release or disentangle from.

[2] **calibrated:** checked or determined by comparison with a standard.

ENGLISH LEARNER SUPPORT

Learn Basic Vocabulary Explain that homophones are words that sound alike but have different meanings and often different spellings. Display these homophones and have students repeat after you as you pronounce the words: *to/too/two, meet/meat, their/there/they're, seen/scene, through/threw.* Review the meaning of each word and have students follow along and listen for the underlined homophones in the list as you read paragraph 8 aloud. Then have partners work together to create charts that illustrate the meanings of the homophones. **SUBSTANTIAL**

CRITICAL VOCABULARY

extricate: A bystander frees the mother from the circus tent.

ASK STUDENTS why the mother needs to be extricated. *(The mother is stuck under the collapsed, still-flaming canvas of the tent.)*

tent bearing a huge buckle that knocked her unconscious. She was taken to the town hospital, and there she must have hemorrhaged,[3] for they kept her, confined to her bed, a month and a half before her baby was born without life.

11 Harry Avalon had wanted to be buried in the circus cemetery next to the original Avalon, his uncle, so she sent him back with his brothers. The child, however, is buried around the corner, beyond this house and just down the highway. Sometimes I used to walk there just to sit. She was a girl, but I rarely thought of her as a sister or even as a separate person really. I suppose you could call it the egocentrism[4] of a child, of all young children, but I considered her a less finished version of myself.

12 When the snow falls, throwing shadows among the stones, I can easily pick hers out from the road, for it is bigger than the others and in the shape of a lamb at rest, its legs curled beneath. The carved lamb looms larger as the years pass, though it is probably only my eyes, the visions shifting, as what is close to me blurs and distances sharpen. In odd moments, I think it is the edge drawing near, the edge of everything, the unseen horizon we do not really speak of in the eastern woods. And it also seems to me, although this is probably an idle fantasy, that the statue is growing more sharply etched, as if, instead of weathering itself into a porous mass, it is hardening on the hillside with each snowfall, perfecting itself.

13 It was during her confinement in the hospital that my mother met my father. He was called in to look at the set of her arm, which was complicated. He stayed, sitting at her bedside, for he was something of an armchair traveler and had spent his war quietly, at an air force training grounds, where he became a specialist in arms and legs broken during parachute training exercises. Anna Avalon had been to many of the places he longed to visit—Venice, Rome, Mexico, all through France and Spain. She had no family of her own and was taken in by the Avalons, trained to perform from a very young age. They toured Europe before the war, then based themselves in New York. She was illiterate.

14 It was in the hospital that she finally learned to read and write, as a way of overcoming the boredom and depression of those weeks, and it was my father who insisted on teaching her. In return for stories of her adventures, he graded her first exercises. He bought her her first book, and over her bold letters, which the pale guides of the penmanship pads could not contain, they fell in love.

15 I wonder if my father calculated the exchange he offered: one form of flight for another. For after that, and for as long as I can remember, my mother has never been without a book. Until now, that is, and it remains the greatest difficulty of her blindness. Since

[3] **hemorrhaged** (hĕm´ər-ĭjd): bled heavily.
[4] **egocentrism:** belief in the primary or sole importance of the self.

LANGUAGE CONVENTIONS

Annotate: Mark the two relative clauses in paragraph 13.

Analyze: How and why did the speaker's mother meet her second husband?

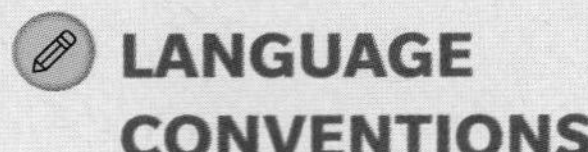

LANGUAGE CONVENTIONS

Remind students that **relative clauses** function as adjectives and begin with signal words such as *that, who, which, when, where,* or *why*. (You may wish to point out that these words can introduce other kinds of subordinate clauses, too; therefore, students should consider the function of the clause and not just the presence of a signal word.) Have students mark the relative clauses in paragraph 13 and identify the noun phrases they modify. *(The clause "which was complicated" modifies "the set of her arm." The clause beginning "where he became" modifies "air force training grounds.")* (**Answer:** *The narrator's mother met her second husband when, as an expert in broken bones, he was called into the hospital to look at the set of the mother's arm.)*

IMPROVE READING FLUENCY

Targeted Passage Read aloud paragraphs 13–14 as students follow along in their books. Point out how you use punctuation as a guide for phrasing, and model appropriate rate, accuracy, and prosody. Then have partners take turns reading the paragraphs to each other. Remind them to pay attention to punctuation cues, and encourage students to provide feedback to their partners.

 Go to the **Reading Studio** for additional support in developing fluency.

AGAIN AND AGAIN

Remind students that repetition is often used in fiction as a way to focus the reader's attention on **theme**. Explain that in some cases, repetition is clear, but students may often need to look deeper to notice repeated images or ideas. Have students read paragraph 17. Ask them to mark phrases that they have previously noticed in the story or those that call to mind images or events that have already occurred. Then, invite students to share their findings. Students may notice that the narrator again mentions how she owes her mother her existence or that the imagery of hanging on dearly to life reflects how her mother hung onto the wire to save herself during the accident. (***Possible answer:*** *Paragraph 17 contributes to the existing theme of the bond of love between a mother and her daughter. A new theme might be the human will to survive—none of us asks to be here, but once we are, "we hang on so dearly."*)

MAKE INFERENCES

Tell students that writers often try to show how their characters feel through their actions, rather than telling readers outright. As students read paragraph 20, have them note the narrator's actions during the fire. Have students consider what they already know about how the narrator's mother handles a crisis. Combining their background knowledge of the mother with their knowledge of the daughter's reaction to the fire, students should be able to make inferences about characteristics the two may share. (***Possible answer:*** *The narrator is like her mother in that she remembers everything she's been trained to do and she is calm and level-headed in a crisis.*)

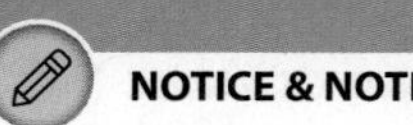

NOTICE & NOTE

my father's recent death, there is no one to read to her, which is why I returned, in fact, from my failed life where the land is flat. I came home to read to my mother, to read out loud, to read long into the dark if I must, to read all night.

16 Once my father and mother married, they moved onto the old farm he had inherited but didn't care much for. Though he'd been thinking of moving to a larger city, he settled down and broadened his practice in this valley. It still seems odd to me, when they could have gone anywhere else, that they chose to stay in the town where the disaster had occurred, and which my father in the first place had found so **constricting**. It was my mother who insisted upon it, after her child did not survive. And then, too, she loved the sagging farmhouse with its scrap of what was left of a vast acreage of woods and hidden hay fields that stretched to the game park.

constrict
(kən-strĭkt´) *v.* to limit or impede growth.

17 I owe my existence, the second time then, to the two of them and the hospital that brought them together. That is the debt we take for granted since none of us asks for life. It is only once we have it that we hang on so dearly.

AGAIN AND AGAIN

Notice & Note: The ideas in paragraph 17 suggest at least one theme. Mark the relevant ideas.

Infer: What is one theme suggested here? What other theme might be suggested?

18 I was seven the year the house caught fire, probably from standing ash. It can rekindle, and my father, forgetful around the house and perpetually exhausted from night hours on call, often emptied what he thought were ashes from cold stoves into wooden or cardboard containers. The fire could have started from a flaming box, or perhaps a buildup of creosote[5] inside the chimney was the culprit. It started right around the stove, and the heart of the house was gutted. The baby-sitter, fallen asleep in my father's den on the first floor, woke to find the stairway to my upstairs room cut off by flames. She used the phone, then ran outside to stand beneath my window.

19 When my parents arrived, the town volunteers had drawn water from the fire pond and were spraying the outside of the house, preparing to go inside after me, not knowing at the time that there was only one staircase and that it was lost. On the other side of the house, the superannuated[6] extension ladder broke in half. Perhaps the clatter of it falling against the walls woke me, for I'd been asleep up to that point.

20 As soon as I awakened, in the small room that I now use for sewing, I smelled the smoke. I followed things by the letter then, was good at memorizing instructions, and so I did exactly what was taught in the second-grade home fire drill. I got up, I touched the back of my door before opening it. Finding it hot, I left it closed and stuffed my rolled-up rug beneath the crack. I did not hide under my bed or crawl into my closet. I put on my flannel robe, and then I sat down to wait.

MAKE INFERENCES

Annotate: Mark lines in paragraph 20 that describe the daughter's reaction to the fire.

Infer: How is the narrator like her mother? What characteristics do they share?

[5] **creosote:** a flammable, oily byproduct of burning carbon-based fuels like coal, peat, and wood.

[6] **superannuated:** obsolete; ready for retirement.

CRITICAL VOCABULARY

constrict: The narrator's father thought the town felt limiting, but they settled there anyway.

ASK STUDENTS why a small town might have felt constricting to the narrator's father, while her mother felt at home there. (*The father envisioned settling in a larger city, perhaps to further his career aspirations or because he wanted to enjoy the different types of cultural activities that a city might provide. The mother likes the farmhouse and felt attached to the place where she had lost her first husband and daughter.*)

WHEN STUDENTS STRUGGLE . . .

Analyze Non-linear Plot The story's time sequence moves back and forth frequently, but each event is important to ushering in the next one. To help struggling students follow the sequence of events and understand their significance, have them write each major event in the story on an index card or sticky note. When they are finished reading, have them arrange their notes to reflect chronological order.

For additional support, go to the **Reading Studio** and assign the following **LevelUp Tutorial: Plot: Sequence of Events.**

21 Outside, my mother stood below my dark window and saw clearly that there was no rescue. Flames had pierced one side wall, and the glare of the fire lighted the massive limbs and trunk of the vigorous old elm that had probably been planted the year the house was built, a hundred years ago at least. No leaf touched the wall, and just one thin branch scraped the roof. From below, it looked as though even a squirrel would have had trouble jumping from the tree onto the house, for the breadth of that small branch was no bigger than my mother's wrist.

22 Standing there, beside Father, who was preparing to rush back around to the front of the house, my mother asked him to unzip her dress. When he wouldn't be bothered, she made him understand. He couldn't make his hands work, so she finally tore it off and stood there in her pearls and stockings. She directed one of the men to lean the broken half of the extension ladder up against the trunk of the tree. In surprise, he **complied**. She ascended. She vanished. Then she could be seen among the leafless branches of late November as she made her way up and, along her stomach, inched the length of a bough that curved above the branch that brushed the roof.

23 Once there, swaying, she stood and balanced. There were plenty of people in the crowd and many who still remember, or think they do, my mother's leap through the ice-dark air toward that thinnest extension, and how she broke the branch falling so that it cracked in her hands, cracked louder than the flames as she vaulted with

NOTICE & NOTE 

ANALYZE PLOT

Annotate: Mark the mother's assessment of the situation outside the daughter's window.

Draw Conclusions: Based on what you know about the mother's character, what do you think she is going to do?

comply
(kəm-plī´) *v.* to obey an instruction or command.

ANALYZE PLOT

Point out how the description of the tree branch evokes imagery of circus high wires. Tell students to use details about the fire scene along with what they have already learned about the mother from earlier descriptions to draw conclusions about what will happen next. (***Possible answer:*** *The mother is going to try to save her anyway, perhaps by climbing the big tree and jumping to the window.)*

English Learner Support

Employ Inferential Skills Guide students to make inferences about the mother's character using these sentence frames: *The mother's ability to find her way around her house after losing her vision shows that she is _____. (adaptable, careful, precise) The mother's skill as a trapeze artist shows that she is _____. (athletic, coordinated, agile) The mother's survival of the circus disaster shows that she is _____. (quick-thinking, adaptable, determined)* Then guide students to use the character traits they generate to predict how the mother might try to save her daughter before they go on to read paragraphs 22–25. **MODERATE/LIGHT**

CRITICAL VOCABULARY

comply: The narrator describes how the firefighters obeyed her mother's request to lean the broken ladder against the tree for her.

ASK STUDENTS why it is important to the story that we know the firefighter complied with the narrator's mother. *(It shows how her mother must have taken charge in her determination to save her daughter.)*

CONTRASTS AND CONTRADICTIONS

Ask students how they would expect someone to act in a situation similar to that described in paragraph 24. Discuss how their response contrasts with Anna's behavior. (***Answer:*** *The mother's calm, relaxed demeanor is unusual because the situation is frantic and potentially deadly. She demonstrates careful foresight in bringing the stick along to prop open the window and in her efforts to help her daughter remain calm. These actions demonstrate her exceptional ability to remain calm and level-headed in a disaster.)*

For **reading support** for students at varying proficiency levels, see the **Text X-Ray** on page 418D.

MEMORY MOMENT

Explain that a Memory Moment occurs when a character describes events or feelings from the past. It will usually halt the action of the story to draw the reader's attention back to a previous event and provide key information to develop the **plot**, **theme**, or **characters**. Have students mark the moment in paragraph 26 when the narrator recalls what her mother once told her. Encourage students to use the context in which the narrator recalls this to gain insight into the theme. (***Answer:*** *She remembers her mother telling her that as you fall, there is time to think—and realizes that her mother's observation was correct. She wonders what would happen if she and her mother missed the circle or bounced out of it. She also takes note of a wide variety of sensations, including the cries of the crowd and their looming faces, the feel of the hot wind at her and her mother's backs, and the sound of her mother's beating heart.)*

CONTRASTS AND CONTRADICTIONS

Notice & Note: What is unusual about the mother's demeanor in paragraph 24?

Evaluate: Why does the mother react this way? What does her demeanor tell you about her character?

tentative (tĕn´tə-tĭv) *adj.* with caution and without confidence.

MEMORY MOMENT

Notice & Note: In paragraph 26, what does the narrator remember about something her mother once told her?

Evaluate: What does the daughter think about during her fall toward the firefighters' net?

it toward the edge of the roof, and how it hurtled down end over end without her, and their eyes went up, again, to see where she had flown.

24 I didn't see her leap through air, only heard the sudden thump and looked out my window. She was hanging by the backs of her heels from the new gutter we had put in that year, and she was smiling. I was not surprised to see her, she was so matter-of-fact. She tapped on the window. I remember how she did it, too. It was the friendliest tap, a bit **tentative**, as if she was afraid she had arrived too early at a friend's house. Then she gestured at the latch, and when I opened the window she told me to raise it wider and prop it up with the stick so it wouldn't crush her fingers. She swung down, caught the ledge, and crawled through the opening. Once she was in my room, I realized she had on only underclothing, a bra of the heavy stitched cotton women used to wear and step-in, lace-trimmed drawers. I remember feeling light-headed, of course, terribly relieved, and then embarrassed for her to be seen by the crowd undressed.

25 I was still embarrassed as we flew out the window, toward earth, me in her lap, her toes pointed as we skimmed toward the painted target of the fire fighter's net.

26 I know that she's right. I knew it even then. As you fall, there is time to think. Curled as I was, against her stomach, I was not startled by the cries of the crowd or the looming faces. The wind roared and beat its hot breath at our back, the flames whistled. I slowly wondered what would happen if we missed the circle or bounced out of it. Then I wrapped my hands around my mother's hands. I felt the brush of her lips and heard the beat of her heart in my ears, loud as thunder, long as the roll of drums.

CRITICAL VOCABULARY

tentative: The mother cautiously taps on her daughter's window.

ASK STUDENTS why the narrator's mother might tentatively alert her daughter to her presence outside the window. *(The mother probably wants to avoid frightening her daughter.)*

TO CHALLENGE STUDENTS . . .

Interpret Point of View Ask students what a former trapeze artist might be thinking in an emergency that threatens the survival of a family member. Point out that first-person narration limits the reader's knowledge of what other characters experience. Have students rewrite the scene of the mother's rescuing the daughter from the house using either first-person narration from the mother's point of view or a third-person, omniscient voice. Encourage students to consider how the mother felt when she came home and realized her daughter was trapped in the burning house and what she saw and experienced as she acted to rescue her. Have students share and compare their finished narratives. Encourage students to discuss the new connections they made to the story by considering the mother's perspective.

CHECK YOUR UNDERSTANDING

Answer these questions before moving on to the **Analyze the Text** section on the following page.

1 Which of these is true about Harold Avalon?

A He is the narrator's father.

B He is killed in combat.

C He is buried near his uncle, founder of the Flying Avalons.

D He is a doctor who specializes in setting broken bones.

2 Chronologically, which of these events happens first?

F Anna Avalon's first child is stillborn.

G The narrator moves back into her childhood home in New Hampshire.

H The narrator's father dies.

J Ashes ignite a fire in the New Hampshire farmhouse.

3 Which of these statements is true about a character in "The Leap"?

A The father achieves a daring act of bravery.

B The mother achieves a daring act of bravery.

C The narrator loses her eyesight.

D The narrator does not get along with her mother.

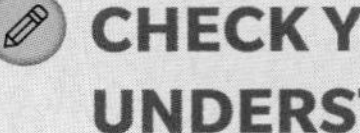

CHECK YOUR UNDERSTANDING

Have students answer the questions independently.

Answers

1. *C*
2. *F*
3. *B*

If they answer any questions incorrectly, have them reread the text to confirm their understanding. Then they may proceed to ANALYZE THE TEXT on page 432.

ENGLISH LEARNER SUPPORT

Oral Assessment Use the following questions to assess students' comprehension and speaking skills. Ask students to respond in short, complete sentences.

1. Which describes Harold Avalon: the narrator's father, killed in combat, buried near his uncle, or a doctor? *(Harold Avalon is buried near his uncle.)*
2. Which event happens first: Anna Avalon's child is stillborn, the narrator moves home, the narrator's father dies, or the house catches fire? *(Anna Avalon's child is stillborn.)*
3. Which event occurs in the story: the narrator's father achieves a daring act of bravery, Anna Avalon achieves a daring act of bravery, the narrator loses her eyesight, or the narrator does not get along with her mother? *(Anna Avalon achieves a daring act of bravery.)* **SUBSTANTIAL/MODERATE**

APPLY

ANALYZE THE TEXT

Possible answers:

1. **DOK 2:** *Reaching for her husband would mean choosing to die with him as he fell to the ground. By reaching for the wire, Anna chooses life, which shows her fierce devotion to living. One can infer that the "leap" may refer to a leap toward life.*
2. **DOK 2:** *The first is the literal leap to the hot wire during the circus accident. A second may be the figurative leap of falling in love with the doctor, followed by the literal leaps from the tree to the rooftop and from the window to the firefighters' net.*
3. **DOK 2:** *As the narrator is rescued, she learns the value of love, trust, and faith, especially in extreme circumstances. The experience suggests the theme that life and love may require us to take some big and potentially perilous "leaps." We risk getting hurt, but if we remain calm, self-possessed, and resourceful, we can make the best of whatever comes.*
4. **DOK 3:** *In both instances, Anna bravely attempts to save her child: an unborn child the first time, and then the narrator as a young child. Both scenes offer evidence of the mother's bravery, resourcefulness, and devotion.*
5. **DOK 4:** *Her mother saves herself from falling off the trapeze. Rather than despair following the tragedy, her mother opens her heart, falls in love, marries, and has a child (the narrator). Finally, her mother risks her life to save her daughter from the house fire. Each instance is revealed through flashback.*

RESEARCH

Remind students that using specific search terms will help them research more efficiently. Point out that students can use the results of general searches to determine time periods and names of specific circuses that will help them focus their research.

RESPOND

ANALYZE THE TEXT

Support your responses with evidence from the text. NOTEBOOK

1. **Infer** In paragraph 9, Anna decides to reach for the hot braided metal rather than for her husband as he falls. What does this reveal about her character?
2. **Interpret** Identify the leaps in the story. Which leaps are literal? Which are figurative?
3. **Infer** Reread paragraph 26. What does the narrator learn? What inferences can you make about the story's theme or themes?
4. **Compare** Compare the description of the trapeze accident with the description of the house fire. What do these descriptions reveal about the mother's character?
5. **Notice & Note** The narrator speaks of the three ways that she owes her existence to her mother. Identify the three ways and the plot-related literary technique used to reveal them.

RESEARCH

RESEARCH TIP
The best online search terms are specific, but it's hard to be specific when you're not sure what you are looking for. You might start with one of your questions, a specific circus act, or something like "early circus images" and a guess at a decade. Not sure how to spell something? Use an online dictionary or reference work. As you find articles you want to pursue, continue refining your search results.

How much do you know about traditional circuses? Research images of vintage circuses as well as any circus-related terms from the text that you are curious about or unfamiliar with. Record what you learn in a graphic organizer. Then reread the story, this time noting instances of circus imagery and how each instance contributes to character, theme, or another aspect of the story.

CIRCUS TERM OR IMAGE	WHAT RESEARCH REVEALS
Circus trapeze acrobats 1940s	
Early circus clowns	
20th-century circus tent	

LEARNING MINDSET

Questioning Remind students that asking questions helps them develop the kind of curiosity that leads to learning new things and improving current skills. Encourage students to feel comfortable asking questions about the class material. Demonstrate useful questions they can ask when they get stuck or don't understand something new: How did I get this answer? Can I approach this in a different way? What is the meaning of ______? Be sure to offer positive feedback for asking questions, for such reinforcement will encourage students to do it more often.

CREATE AND DISCUSS

Write a Research Summary Write a four- to five-paragraph summary of your research results.

- ❑ Introduce the topic and share the goals of your research.
- ❑ Decide on an organizational strategy, then in your two to three body paragraphs, share what your questions were and the details of what you learned.
- ❑ In your final paragraph, state your conclusion about the use of circus imagery in "The Leap."

Discuss with a Group Have a group discussion about the topics and terms you and your group members chose to research and the information you discovered.

- ❑ First, share what questions you and your group members researched. If another student researched a question similar to yours, you may choose to collaborate with that student for a portion of the discussion.
- ❑ As a group, decide on the order in which you and your group members will present your results.
- ❑ Keep your presentation brief, and listen closely as others share theirs. Write down at least one relevant question or meaningful observation you might contribute to each presentation.

Go to the **Writing Studio** for more on writing a research summary.

Go to the **Speaking and Listening Studio** for help having a group discussion.

RESPOND TO THE ESSENTIAL QUESTION

What does it take to survive in a crisis?

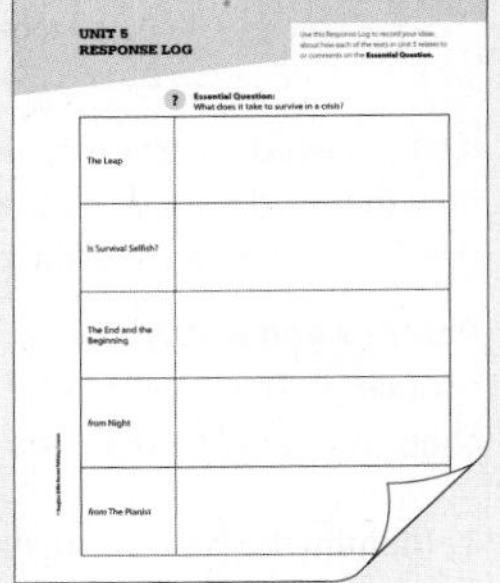

Gather Information Review your annotations and notes on "The Leap." Then, add relevant information to your Response Log. As you determine which information to include, think about:

- What crises the narrator faces and how she handles them
- What crises the mother faces and how she handles them
- What you know about responding to a crisis

At the end of the unit, use your notes to help you write an argument.

ACADEMIC VOCABULARY

As you write and discuss the short story, be sure to use the Academic Vocabulary words. Check off the words that you use.

- ❑ **dimension**
- ❑ **external**
- ❑ **statistic**
- ❑ **sustain**
- ❑ **utilize**

APPLY

CREATE AND DISCUSS

Write a Research Summary Have students use the terms and images they put in their graphic organizer to write a research summary about traditional circuses. Point out that students don't need to organize their summary in the same way they organized information in their chart. They should strategically order their topics in a way that best summarizes the information. As they write their conclusions, remind students to explain how their research results relate to the circus imagery in "The Leap."

For **writing support** for students at varying proficiency levels, see the **Text X-Ray** on page 418D.

Discuss with a Group In small groups, have students share and discuss their research results. Prompt students to listen carefully as the other members of their group present. Have them write down any comments or questions that would help elaborate on or clarify information.

For **speaking support** for students at varying proficiency levels, see the **Text X-Ray** on page 418D.

RESPOND TO THE ESSENTIAL QUESTION

Allow time for students to add details from "The Leap" to their Unit 5 Response Logs.

APPLY

CRITICAL VOCABULARY

Possible answers:

1. *No, hesitating in response to an advancing forest fire might limit a rescue crew's ability to save those who need help.*
2. *Yes, always going along with others' wishes would feel confining because it would limit opportunities for self-expression.*
3. *You would want to free yourself from having to drive in dangerous conditions.*

VOCABULARY STRATEGY: Prefixes

Students should follow the steps using a word based on each prefix in the chart. Check that students identify base words correctly and that their sentences convey a clear understanding of the words based on accurate definitions.

Sample answer:

1. *The base word of* enable *is* able.
2. *Enable: to supply with the means, knowledge, or opportunity to do something*
   Able: having sufficient power or resources to accomplish something
3. *Anna's experience as a trapeze artist enabled her to make the leap from the tree to the roof of her burning house.*

RESPOND

WORD BANK
encroach
extricate
constrict
comply
tentative

CRITICAL VOCABULARY

Practice and Apply Answer these questions, using a dictionary or thesaurus as needed. Make sure your answers reflect your understanding of each Critical Vocabulary word's meaning.

1. Should a rescue crew provide a **tentative** response to an **encroaching** forest fire? Why or why not?
2. Would it feel **constricting** to always **comply** with the wishes of others? Explain.
3. Why would you **extricate** yourself from a planned road trip upon learning of an approaching blizzard?

VOCABULARY STRATEGY: Prefixes

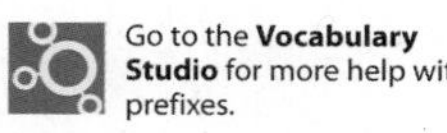

Go to the **Vocabulary Studio** for more help with prefixes.

The Critical Vocabulary words *encroach, extricate, constrict*, and *comply* all contain a **prefix,** an affix added to the beginning of a base word. Knowing the meaning of common prefixes, such as *en-, ex-, con-*, and *com-*, will help you clarify the meaning of unknown words. Here are the meanings of some common prefixes and examples of other words that contain the prefixes:

PREFIXES	MEANINGS	EXAMPLES
en-	to go into or onto	encapsulate, encircle
ex-	out of or away from	exchange, exterminate
con-	together, with, jointly	consensus, congenial

If a base word is unfamiliar, use your knowledge of the word's prefix and how the word is used in context to clarify its meaning. If necessary, consult a dictionary to determine the precise meaning of the word.

Practice and Apply For each prefix in the chart, identify one word that contains it. The word may be in the text, or it may be a word of your own choosing. For each word you choose, follow these steps:

1. Identify the base word, the main word part. For example, the base word of *exchange* is *change*
2. Write a definition for each word that incorporates the prefix meaning and the base word meaning. Use a dictionary to check your definition. Make changes if needed.
3. Finally, write a sample sentence for each word you choose.

ENGLISH LEARNER SUPPORT

Use Cognates Tell students that the prefixes *con-, com-*, and *ex-* have Spanish cognates. Have Spanish-speaking students follow the Practice and Apply steps in English and Spanish using the following cognates: *contradict/contradecir, compose/componer, compare/comparar, export/exportar, expose/exponer*. **ALL LEVELS**

LANGUAGE CONVENTIONS: Relative Clauses

A **clause** is a group of words that contains a subject and a predicate. **Relative clauses** describe nouns and function as adjectives. Here are the characteristics of a relative clause:

- It begins with a signal word: a relative pronoun (*that, which, who, whom, whose*) or a relative adverb (*when, where, or why*).
- It follows a noun or a noun phrase.
- It provides extra information about a noun or a noun phrase, or it answers the questions *What kind? How many? Which one?*

Authors use relative clauses not only to convey specific meanings, but also to add interest and variety to their work. Read this sentence from "The Leap":

> **It commemorates the disaster that put our town smack on the front page of the Boston and New York tabloids.**

The clause contains all the elements of a relative clause: it begins with a relative pronoun—*that;* it follows a noun—*disaster*; it answers the question *Which one?*—the disaster that put the town in the tabloids.

Erdrich could have expressed the same ideas this way:

> **It commemorates the disaster. The disaster put our town smack on the front page of the Boston and New York tabloids.**

Notice how the sentence with the relative clause is smoother and easier to read. Here are some other examples of relative clauses from the "The Leap":

RELATIVE CLAUSES		
SIGNAL WORD	EXAMPLE IN SELECTION	WORDS MODIFIED
which	He was called in to look at the set of her arm, which was complicated.	"the set of her arm"
who	...and it was my father who insisted on teaching her.	"father"
where	...they chose to stay in the town where the disaster had occurred...	"town"

Practice and Apply Look back at the summary you created in response to this selection's Write a Research Summary task. Revise your summary to include at least two relative clauses. With a partner, discuss your revised summaries. Then work together to identify three or four more relative clauses in "The Leap" that are not included as examples in this lesson.

APPLY

LANGUAGE CONVENTIONS: Relative Clauses

Review the characteristics of relative clauses, stressing that they function as adjectives that modify a noun. Then, review the examples in the chart and make sure students understand how each one illustrates the use of relative clauses. Invite students to explain what type of information is provided in each case.

Practice and Apply Ask students to look for ways to add relative clauses to their summaries, and encourage them to identify sentences they might combine to improve style and sentence effectiveness. Tell them to also think about ways in which they might develop ideas by providing additional information using relative clauses. Have partners discuss their revisions and then work together to find any relative clauses from "The Leap" that are not included in the examples from this lesson. *(Examples include "which did not entirely settle" in paragraph 9 and "who still remember" in paragraph 23.)*

ENGLISH LEARNER SUPPORT

Understand Language Structures To help students understand the examples and complete the Practice and Apply activity, use the following supports with students at varying proficiency levels:

- Review the parts of speech with students and then guide them to label parts of speech in the examples. **SUBSTANTIAL**
- Have students work with partners to mark the signal word, clause, and noun modified in the additional examples of relative clauses they find in "The Leap." **MODERATE**
- Have students categorize the additional examples of relative clauses they find in "The Leap" based on the type of information the clauses provide. **LIGHT**

MENTOR TEXT

IS SURVIVAL SELFISH?

Argument by Lane Wallace

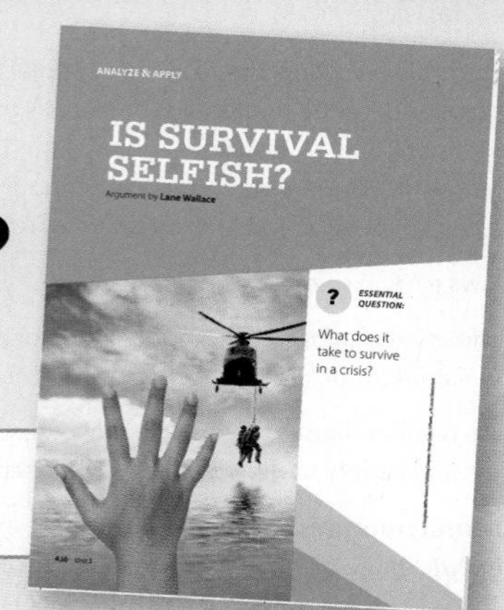

This article serves as a **mentor text**, a model for students to follow when they come to the Unit 5 Writing Task: Write an Argument.

GENRE ELEMENTS

ARGUMENT

An **argument** is a vehicle for presenting a point of view and persuading an audience to agree with that point of view, or claim. An argument presents reasons or evidence to support the claim, and it may make use of persuasive strategies and rhetorical devices.

LEARNING OBJECTIVES

- Analyze an argument by examining a claim and evidence.
- Conduct research into stories of survivors.
- Prepare for and hold a class discussion to share research and conclusions.
- Use analysis of synonyms to understand complex words.
- Use commas to distinguish and divide main and subordinate clauses.
- **Language** Identify and restate an argument's claim.

TEXT COMPLEXITY

Quantitative Measures	**Is Survival Selfish?** Lexile: 1140L
Qualitative Measures	**Ideas Presented** More than one purpose; implied, easily identified from context.
	Structures Used Organization of main ideas and details complex but mostly explicit; multiple perspectives presented.
	Language Used Some academic, unfamiliar, or domain-specific words.
	Knowledge Required Some specialized knowledge required.

Online 

RESOURCES

- Unit 5 Response Log
- Selection Audio
- Reading Studio: Notice & Note
- Level Up Tutorial: Analyzing Arguments
- Speaking and Listening Studio: Participating in Collaborative Discussions
- Vocabulary Studio: Synonyms
- Grammar Studio: Module 11: Lesson 6: Commas with Sentence Interruptors
- "Is Survival Selfish?" Selection Test

SUMMARIES

English

Lane Wallace uses historical events, anecdotes, and examples to answer the question of whether survivors of danger are selfish. After examining the idea that fleeing from danger is a basic survival instinct, she notes that some people seem to override this instinct in order to carry out dangerous rescues. She concludes that there is no one answer to the question because people respond differently to survival situations.

Spanish

Lane Wallace utiliza eventos históricos, anécdotas y ejemplos para responder preguntas de si los supervivientes de peligros son egoístas. Luego de examinar la idea de que huir del peligro es un instinto de supervivencia básico, afirma que ciertas personas aparentemente hacen caso omiso de estos instintos para realizar rescates peligrosos. Concluye que no hay una respuesta a la pregunta porque la gente reacciona diferentemente a las situaciones de supervivencia.

SMALL-GROUP OPTIONS

Have students work in small groups to read and discuss the selection.

Pinwheel Discussion

- Form groups of eight members, with four students seated facing in, and four students seated facing out.
- Have students in the inner circle remain stationary during the discussion while those in the outer circle move to the right after discussing each question.
- Guide the discussion by providing a question for each rotation.

Numbered Heads Together

- Form students into groups of four and assign numbers 1-2-3-4 within the group.
- Pose a higher-order discussion question to the group or class.
- After students discuss their responses in their groups, call a number from 1 to 4.
- The "numbered" student responds for the group.

Text X-Ray: English Learner Support
for "Is Survival Selfish?"

Use the Text X-Ray and the supports and scaffolds in the Teacher's Edition to help guide students at different proficiency levels through the selection.

INTRODUCE THE SELECTION
DISCUSS SURVIVORS

In this lesson, students will need to be able to discuss whether people who act to ensure their own survival instead of helping others are selfish.

- Start a Venn diagram on the board with the word *Survivors* in the middle. Add the details *Save Only Themselves* and *Save Others* in separate ovals extending from the middle. Work with students to list common ways in which people might describe each type of survivor, such as *selfish, lucky, cowardly (Save Only Themselves)* and *honorable, heroic, brave (Save Others).*
- Discuss the complex factors involved in making decisions during disasters or life-threatening events, pointing out how some people are able to remain calm in emergency situations and others panic.

CULTURAL REFERENCES

The following phrases may be unfamiliar to students:

- *"women and children first" protocol* (paragraph 2): a code of behavior in which men ensure that women and children are rescued from an emergency before they act to save themselves
- *kick in* (paragraph 6): get started
- *number one* (paragraph 6): most important
- *hold it together* (paragraph 6): maintain control
- *fall apart* (paragraph 6): lose one's ability to cope
- *"fight or flight" impulse* (paragraph 13): a reflexive reaction to danger or stress in which the body automatically produces hormones that enhance strength and speed so that a person or animal can either fight an attacker or flee from danger
- *there is a fine line* (paragraph 15): it is difficult to distinguish

LISTENING

Visualize

Explain that visualizing helps readers understand unfamiliar situations. Have students study the image on page 441. Then read aloud paragraph 1, encouraging students to use the image to visualize the scene that Ismay described.

Use the following supports with students at varying proficiency levels:

- Tell students to respond *yes* or *no* to questions about what they just heard. For example: Did J. Bruce Ismay say he saved women and children before saving himself? *(yes)* Did the general public think Ismay was a hero? *(no)* Did Ismay lose his job? *(yes)* **SUBSTANTIAL**
- Work with students to complete this sentence: *The description of Ismay helps readers understand that people in emergency situations must act _____. (quickly, impulsively)* **MODERATE**
- Have partners identify another image of the event they can visualize before expressing their opinions of Ismay's decision to climb aboard the lifeboat. **LIGHT**

SPEAKING

Share and Discuss Opinions

Work with students to read the discussion assignment about survivors' actions on page 445.

Use the following supports with students at varying proficiency levels:

- As partners review the examples they researched, model how students may take turns asking about and expressing their opinions about the survivors: Do you think this survivor's actions were selfish? I think this survivor's actions were/weren't selfish. **SUBSTANTIAL**
- Provide these frames for students to express opinions about survivors: *I think/I don't think survivors ____. This survivor ____, so I think that shows ____. I agree with the idea that ____.* **MODERATE**
- Suggest that students use expressions such as the following to discuss their ideas with other group members: *I agree with your point about ____, but I also think that ____.* **LIGHT**

READING

Monitor Comprehension

Point out that evidence in an argument may include descriptions of an author's personal experience. Then read aloud paragraphs 5–6 as students follow along.

Use the following supports with students at varying proficiency levels:

- Ask questions such as the following to support comprehension: Did the author act fast? *(yes)* Did the crowd do the right thing? *(no)* **SUBSTANTIAL**
- Guide students to contrast the reactions of Wallace and her friend with others in the crowd using this frame: *Wallace and her friend remained ____, but other people ____. (calm; panicked)* **MODERATE**
- Have students work in pairs to identify details about Wallace's personal experience in paragraph 5 that support the main idea of paragraph 6. **LIGHT**

WRITING

Explain Key Ideas

Work with students to respond to the Analyze Arguments note on page 440 and to prepare them to respond to Analyze the Text Item 1 on page 444.

Use the following supports with students at varying proficiency levels:

- Read aloud the sentence beginning "It's a complex question" in paragraph 3. Explain to students that *complex* means "complicated" or "hard to understand." Then provide this frame for students to copy and complete: *Wallace thinks it is ____ (easy/difficult) to determine whether survival is selfish.* **SUBSTANTIAL**
- Provide this frame to help students restate Wallace's claim: *It is difficult to judge whether survival is selfish because ____.* **MODERATE**
- Have students work with partners to review the claim in paragraph 3, the evidence Wallace provides to support her claim, and her conclusions at the end of the argument. Then have them work together to restate Wallace's overall claim. **LIGHT**

TEACH

Connect to the
ESSENTIAL QUESTION

"Is Survival Selfish?" by Lane Wallace explores how people act in life-threatening situations and how others might judge their actions. Her argument examines whether people who act to ensure their own survival instead of helping others are selfish, smart—or something else.

MENTOR TEXT

At the end of the unit, students will be asked to write an argument. "Is Survival Selfish?" provides a model for how to structure an argument with a clearly stated thesis, supporting evidence, and a conclusion that restates the thesis and expresses a final thought.

ANALYZE & APPLY

IS SURVIVAL SELFISH?

Argument by **Lane Wallace**

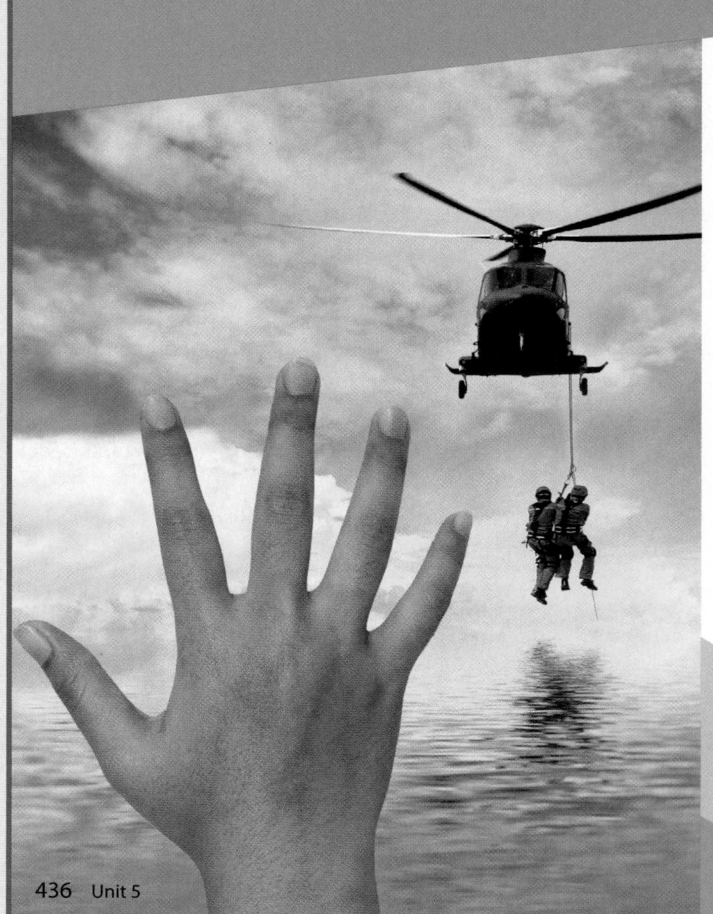

? ***ESSENTIAL QUESTION:***

What does it take to survive in a crisis?

QUICK START

Most people have either read or heard about life-threatening situations. What survival stories can you tell? Share them with the class.

ANALYZE ARGUMENTS

In an **argument,** an author expresses a position on an issue and then attempts to support that position. A successful argument persuades readers to agree with the author's claim, or position. To analyze arguments, you must first outline its basic parts.

- The **claim** is the author's position on the topic or issue. It is the central idea around which the argument is structured.
- **Reasons** are explanations that support the claim by answering the question. Why does the author hold that opinion? An author's reasoning must be clear and logical to create a valid argument.
- **Evidence** includes facts, statistics, personal experiences, statements by experts, and other information. The evidence supports the reasons and, ultimately, the author's claim.
- The argument ends with a persuasive **conclusion,** which revisits the claim.

Most arguments begin by stating a claim and presenting reasons and evidence for it. To be persuasive, an argument must include evidence that is valid, relevant, and sufficient. Facts must be true and provable through research. Opinions are beliefs, but do not support reasons and aren't evidence.

GENRE ELEMENTS: ARGUMENT

- presents a claim or position on an issue
- includes reasons or evidence that support the claim
- may include rhetorical devices or other persuasive strategies

ANALYZE RHETORICAL DEVICES

Authors often use **rhetorical devices** when they write arguments. Some devices, such as **rhetorical questions,** are intended to engage the audience and make a point. In other cases, an author may rely on faulty logic or rhetorical devices meant to deceive the audience. Always read arguments critically in order to assess the accuracy and validity of the author's argument. In particular, be on the lookout for instances and effects of logical fallacies or **faulty reasoning**, which are errors in reasoning.

TECHNIQUE	EXAMPLE	EXPLANATION
False Cause and Effect	I ate shrimp last night and feel sick today. The shrimp must have been bad.	A connection between two ideas does not always mean that one causes the other.
Circular Reasoning	Ms. Vasquez is a great teacher because she does a great job teaching.	Circular reasoning restates the argument as a reason to support it.
Overgeneralization	I saw three shooting stars this past winter. Shooting stars appear in winter.	Generalizations based on limited data may not be accurate. Stereotypes are a form of generalization.
Straw Man	My opponent believes all state laws are unnecessary.	Misstating an opposition's position so it is easy to attack or tear down.
Red Herring	Although we are meeting to talk about club rules, let's discuss upcoming projects.	Bringing up a topic that distracts from the real topic.
Begging the Question	Everyone will agree that my position is valid.	Assumption by the writer that a claim or other statement is true.

TEACH

QUICK START

After students have read the Quick Start question, ask them to recall survivor stories that they have seen or read about in the news, movies, or books. Ask volunteers to share stories with the class; as they do so, invite comments about the various survivors' actions.

ANALYZE ARGUMENTS

To help students understand the basic components of an author's argument, have them consider these points:

- The author's **claim** is a position about which people can have differing opinions.
- A **reason** for supporting a position is a general statement that can use the word *because* to answer the question "Why does the author believe that?"
- The information, or **evidence,** used to support a claim may be of different types, depending on the subject of the claim. A claim about environmental protection would require facts, statistics, and expert testimony for support. A claim about an opinion of a movie or a concert, however, would use anecdotes, quotations, and personal experiences for support.
- An effective **conclusion** restates the claim; it also may ask an intriguing question that invites the reader to look at the issue in a new way.

ANALYZE RHETORICAL DEVICES

Review the rhetorical techniques, examples, and explanations in the chart. Tell students that being able to identify false arguments not only will help them become better readers, it will help them in everyday life, as well. False arguments are used in persuasive messages in many spheres of human interaction, including advertising, politics, business, and even personal relationships.

TEACH

CRITICAL VOCABULARY

Encourage students to incorporate the definitions of the Critical Vocabulary words in their responses.

Possible responses:

1. *They would give her compliments on her work and/or give her an award.*
2. *Something interesting, unusual, or fascinating might cause a person to become motionless with awe.*
3. *The fire would be burning something completely, leaving only a pile of ashes.*
4. *You would be criticizing or scolding the person.*
5. *The intent of an edict is to force people to obey certain rules.*

■ English Learner Support

Use Cognates Tell students that two of the Critical Vocabulary words have Spanish cognates: *consume/consumir, edict/edicto.* **ALL LEVELS**

LANGUAGE CONVENTIONS

Review the information about commas and point out that by signaling where to pause, commas help to clarify sentences that might otherwise be confusing.

 ANNOTATION MODEL

Remind students of the elements of argument in Analyze Arguments and Analyze Rhetorical Devices on page 437. Point out that students may follow the example in the Annotation Model for noting these elements or use their own system for marking up the selection in their write-in text. They may want to color-code their annotations by using highlighters. Their notes in the margin may include questions about ideas that are unclear or topics they want to learn more about.

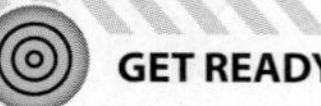

GET READY

CRITICAL VOCABULARY

berate **consume** **edict** **laud** **transfix**

To see how many Critical Vocabulary words you know, discuss answers to the questions below.

1. If fans **laud** an actor for her roles, what would they do?
2. What might **transfix** a person?
3. If a fire were to **consume** something, what would be happening?
4. If you **berate** another person, what would you be doing?
5. When someone delivers an **edict**, what is the intent?

LANGUAGE CONVENTIONS

Commas Authors use commas to achieve two purposes. First, commas show where the reader should pause. If the text were being read aloud, the reader would hesitate at each comma. Authors also use commas to signal a break in thought and make the sentence easier to read.

ANNOTATION MODEL

NOTICE & NOTE 

As you read, note the author's claim and her use of rhetorical devices. Here you can see one reader's notes about "Is Survival Selfish?"

The "women and children first" protocol of the *Titanic* may not be as strong a social stricture as it was a century ago. But we still tend to laud those who risk or sacrifice themselves to save others in moments of danger or crisis and look less kindly on those who focus on saving themselves, instead.

But is survival really selfish and uncivilized? Or is it smart? And is going in to rescue others always heroic? [Or is it sometimes just stupid?] . . .

In July 2007, I was having a drink with a friend in Grand Central Station when an underground steam pipe exploded just outside.

the author is preparing to make her claim

the author uses loaded language; she calls survival stupid

author backs up her claim with facts from a personal experience

BACKGROUND

Lane Wallace *is an author, speaker, and adventurer. She writes for* The Atlantic *magazine,* The New York Times, *and many aviation magazines. She survived a horrible car crash at age 20 in New Zealand, and after nearly dying, she quit her job in hospital administration and became an airplane pilot. She decided to combine a passion for writing, exploring, and seeking adventures. She has gone wreck-diving in the South Pacific, has flown a spy plane 70,000 feet above Earth, and has flown relief missions into Africa. She is the author of* Surviving Uncertainty *and* Unforgettable.

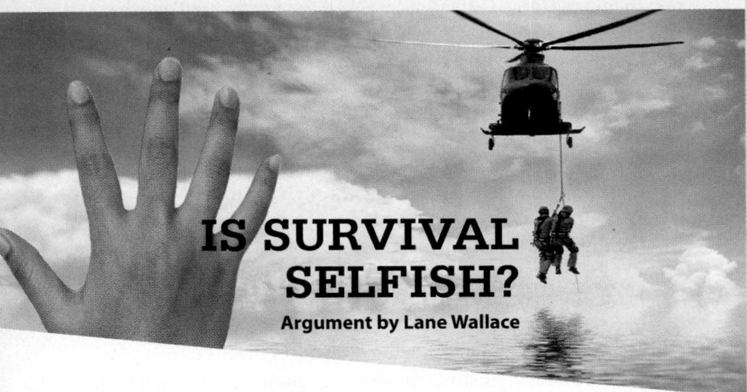

IS SURVIVAL SELFISH?

Argument by Lane Wallace

SETTING A PURPOSE

As you read, think about how you would react in a life-threatening situation. Would you save yourself? Or would you save others, and risk your own life?

1 When the ocean liner *Titanic* sank in April of 1912, one of the few men to survive the tragedy was J. Bruce Ismay, the chairman and managing director of the company that owned the ship. After the disaster, however, Ismay was savaged by the media and the general public for climbing into a lifeboat and saving himself when there were other women and children still on board. Ismay said he'd already helped many women and children into lifeboats and had only climbed in one himself when there were no other women or children in the area and the boat was ready to release. But it didn't matter. His reputation was ruined. He was labeled an uncivilized coward and, a year after the disaster, he resigned his position at White Star.

2 The "women and children first" protocol of the *Titanic* may not be as strong a social stricture[1] as it was a century ago. But we

[1] **social stricture:** behavioral restriction placed on society.

Notice & Note

Use the side margins to notice and note signposts in the text.

ANALYZE ARGUMENTS

Annotate: In paragraph 1, underline the topic the author introduces with an anecdote.

Analyze: Consider the title of this selection. Why might the author have chosen to begin her argument with this example?

TEACH

BACKGROUND

After students read the Background note, discuss how Lane Wallace's personal experiences might inform the argument she makes about survivors of disaster.

SETTING A PURPOSE

Direct students to use the Setting a Purpose prompt to focus their reading.

 ANALYZE ARGUMENTS

Point out that in an argument, an author must decide the most effective way to present ideas and support for a **claim,** or position on the issue. Discuss how the anecdote the author uses in the introduction relates to the title of the argument. (***Answer:*** *Using an example or anecdote helps draw the reader into the ideas that the author wants to present. Here the author wants the reader to think about the question presented in the title, "Is Survival Selfish?" The anecdote and the title suggest that Ismay might have been selfish for surviving the tragedy, as many people thought that he was. The author's argument explores whether people who survive a disaster should be judged harshly when others did not survive.)*

 For **listening support** for students at varying proficiency levels, see the **Text X-Ray** on page 436C.

WHEN STUDENTS STRUGGLE . . .

Analyze Arguments To help students manage the ambiguities of Wallace's argument, guide them to identify her claim in paragraph 3 that the answer to the title question is "It's a complex question, because there are so many factors involved, and every survival situation is different." Have individuals or partners record the author's claim in a chart. Then, as they read, have them identify and track reasons and evidence that support the claim.

 For additional support, go to the **Reading Studio** and assign the following **Level Up Tutorial: Analyzing Arguments.**

TEACH

ANALYZE ARGUMENTS

Tell students that **loaded language** is the use of words that have strong positive or negative connotations and is intended to influence a reader's attitude. ***(Answer:** By contrasting the negative words* uncivilized *and* stupid *with the positive words* smart *and* heroic, *the author is setting up a claim that will tend more toward survival being a healthy and prudent instinct.)*

For **writing support** for students at varying proficiency levels, see the **Text X-Ray** on page 436D.

LANGUAGE CONVENTIONS

Discuss how the first three clauses in the sentence list ways in which people responded to the explosion. Point out that the author could have used a comma to separate the third clause from the coordinating conjunction *but*, but the ellipsis signals that the examples are an incomplete list of people's reactions. ***(Answer:** The first two commas separate main clauses; the next two commas signal pauses; the comma after* survival *separates ideas; the last comma signals a pause.)*

For **reading support** for students at varying proficiency levels, see the **Text X-Ray** on page 436D.

ANALYZE RHETORICAL DEVICES

To help students identify the rhetorical device the author uses, suggest that they review the chart on page 437. ***(Answer:** She uses rhetorical questions. They are effective because they cause the reader to think about how they would answer them and to reflect on the alternatives being discussed.)*

CRITICAL VOCABULARY

laud: People who risk their own safety to save others are highly thought of and praised by our society.

ASK STUDENTS what the author implies by saying that society lauds people who risk themselves for others. *(She implies that society sometimes judges survivors too harshly.)*

transfix: The author and her friend saw people standing still and watching a problem.

ASK STUDENTS why the author was surprised that people were transfixed. *(It was an emergency, and people should have been moving away.)*

consume: Fire and smoke destroyed the plane.

ASK STUDENTS why the woman had to act quickly to get out as the plane was consumed. *(The intense fire consumed the inside of the plane faster than most people were able to get out.)*

berate: People who survive often criticize themselves for not having done more to help others.

ASK STUDENTS why some people berate themselves for surviving a crisis. *(People feel guilty and question whether they should have done things differently.)*

NOTICE & NOTE

laud
(lôd) *v.* to praise.

ANALYZE ARGUMENTS
Annotate: In paragraph 3, underline a statement the author can build on to create a full claim.
Analyze: How do the rhetorical devices in the questions that precede the statement set up the author's claim?

LANGUAGE CONVENTIONS
Annotate: Mark the commas in the last sentence of paragraph 5.
Analyze: What is the purpose of these commas?

transfix
(trăns-fĭks´) *v.* to captivate or make motionless with awe.

consume
(kən-so͞om´) *v.* to completely destroy or eradicate.

ANALYZE RHETORICAL DEVICES
Annotate: In paragraph 8, mark the question the author poses.
Evaluate: What rhetorical device is she using? Is it effective?

berate
(bĭ-rāt´) *v.* to criticize or scold.

still tend to **laud** those who risk or sacrifice themselves to save others in moments of danger or crisis and look less kindly on those who focus on saving themselves, instead.

3 But is survival really selfish and uncivilized? Or is it smart? And is going in to rescue others always heroic? Or is it sometimes just stupid? It's a complex question, because there are so many factors involved, and every survival situation is different.

4 Self-preservation is supposedly an instinct. So one would think that in life-and-death situations, we'd all be very focused on whatever was necessary to survive. But that's not always true. In July 2007, I was having a drink with a friend in Grand Central Station[2] when an underground steam pipe exploded just outside. From where we sat, we heard a dull "boom!" and then suddenly, people were running, streaming out of the tunnels and out the doors.

5 My friend and I walked quickly and calmly outside, but to get any further, we had to push our way through a crowd of people who were staring, **transfixed,** at the column of smoke rising from the front of the station. Some people were crying, others were screaming, others were on their cell phones . . . but the crowd, for the most part, was *not* doing the one thing that would increase everyone's chances of survival, if in fact a terrorist bomb with god knows what inside it had just gone off—namely, moving away from the area.

6 We may have an instinct for survival, but it clearly doesn't always kick in the way it should. A guy who provides survival training for pilots told me once that the number one determining factor for survival is simply whether people hold it together in a crisis or fall apart. And, he said, it's impossible to predict ahead of time who's going to hold it together, and who's going to fall apart.

7 So what is the responsibility of those who hold it together? I remember reading the account of one woman who was in an airliner that crashed on landing. People were frozen or screaming, but nobody was moving toward the emergency exits, even as smoke began to fill the cabin. After realizing that the people around her were too paralyzed to react, she took direct action, crawling over several rows of people to get to the exit. She got out of the plane and survived. Very few others in the plane, which was soon **consumed** by smoke and fire, did. And afterward, I remember she said she battled a lot of guilt for saving herself instead of trying to save the others.

8 Could she really have saved the others? Probably not, and certainly not from the back of the plane. If she'd tried, she probably would have perished with them. So why do survivors **berate** themselves for not adding to the loss by attempting the impossible? Perhaps it's because we get very mixed messages about survival ethics.

[2] **Grand Central Station:** a large commuter-rail and subway terminal in New York City.

NOTICE & NOTE

Survivors of the *Titanic* disaster in a lifeboat.

9 On the one hand, we're told to put our own oxygen masks on first, and not to jump in the water with a drowning victim. But then the people who ignore those **edicts** and survive to tell the tale are lauded as heroes. And people who do the "smart" thing are sometimes criticized quite heavily after the fact.

10 In a famous mountain-climbing accident chronicled in the book and documentary *Touching the Void*, climber Simon Yates was attempting to rope his already-injured friend Joe Simpson down a mountain in bad weather when the belay[3] went awry. Simpson ended up hanging off a cliff, unable to climb up, and Yates, unable to lift him up and losing his own grip on the mountain, ended up cutting the rope to Simpson to save himself. Miraculously, Simpson survived the 100 foot fall and eventually made his way down the mountain. But Yates was criticized by some for his survival decision, even though the alternative would have almost certainly led to both of their deaths.

11 In Yates' case, he had time to think hard about the odds, and the possibilities he was facing, and to realize that he couldn't save anyone but himself. But what about people who have to make more instantaneous decisions? If, in fact, survivors are driven by instinct not civilization, how do you explain all those who choose

edict
(ē´dĭkt) *n.* an official rule or proclamation.

CONTRASTS AND CONTRADICTIONS

Notice & Note: Mark the sentence in paragraph 10 that shows something unexpected that happened.

Respond: Does this unexpected event support or refute the author's claim?

[3] **belay:** the securing of a rope to a cleat or another object.

CONTRASTS AND CONTRADICTIONS

Point out that introducing an unexpected event can encourage the reader to reconsider previously held ideas about an **argument.** Discuss what students would expect to happen in the situation described in paragraph 10. (***Answer:*** *The event strengthens the author's claim that survival situations are complex and that people face tough decisions that don't necessarily make them selfish: If Yates had not cut the rope, both climbers probably would have died.)*

IMPROVE READING FLUENCY

Targeted Passage Use paragraphs 3–5 to model how to read an argument with appropriate rate, accuracy, and prosody. Remind students that when they read aloud an argument, they should adjust their volume and tone to emphasize key ideas. Have students follow along as you read aloud the text, using punctuation as a guide for pausing and varying your tone and pitch in the interrogative and declarative sentences. Then, have students echo read the paragraphs with you. Provide feedback and support for appropriate rate and expression.

 Go to the **Reading Studio** for additional support in developing fluency.

CRITICAL VOCABULARY

edict: There are often rules of behavior that are in place to help people survive.

ASK STUDENTS why society has a positive view about people who ignore the edicts about safety procedures to help others. *(Society praises as heroes people who break rules to save others.)*

ENGLISH LEARNER SUPPORT

Use Questions and Question Marks Tell students to mark the questions in paragraph 11. Explain that these are rhetorical questions: instead of requiring a reply (as direct questions do), they push readers to consider possible answers. Then use the following supports with students at varying proficiency levels:

- Tell students that the question mark (?) is a punctuation mark used at the end of a sentence that asks a question. Model framing direct questions for students: "What is your name?" and "Where do you live?" **SUBSTANTIAL**
- Point out to students that the first two questions ask readers to consider how people react when they do not have time to think about a decision. Model paraphrasing the remaining questions as a single question: Are people who risk their life to rescue people from icy water, subway tracks, or a battlefield more civilized, brave, or noble than others? Then help students to orally reframe the question as an answer that expresses an opinion: *I think that people who risk their life to rescue others [are/aren't] more [civilized/brave/noble] than others because* ____. Remind all students that paraphrasing and reframing questions can help them comprehend what they are reading. **MODERATE/LIGHT**

ANALYZE RHETORICAL DEVICES

Have students recall the examples of the woman who escaped the burning plane and the mountain climber who cut the rope. Point out that these examples support the idea that when faced with a crisis, people will make the rational decision to save themselves. (***Answer:*** *The statement that sometimes our instincts cause us to endanger ourselves to help others seems to contradict the idea that people make conscious decisions about whether to save themselves.)*

NOTICE & NOTE

otherwise? Who would dive into icy waters or onto subway tracks or disobey orders to make repeat trips onto a minefield to bring wounded to safety? Are they more civilized than the rest of us? More brave? More noble?

ANALYZE RHETORICAL DEVICES

Annotate: In paragraph 12, mark the sentence that appears to contradict the author's argument about how people behave in a crisis.

Analyze: Why is this an example of a false cause and effect as far as confirming the author's claim about bravery vs. selfishness?

12 It sounds nice, but oddly enough, most of the people who perform such impulsive rescues say that they didn't really think before acting. Which means they weren't "choosing" civilization over instinct. If survival is an instinct, it seems to me that there must be something equally instinctive that drives us, sometimes, to run into danger instead of away from it.

13 Perhaps it comes down to the ancient "fight or flight" impulse. Animals confronted with danger will choose to attack it, or run from it, and it's hard to say which one they'll choose, or when. Or maybe humans are such social herd animals, dependent on the herd for survival, that we feel a pull toward others even as we feel a contrary pull toward our own preservation, and the two impulses battle it out within us . . . leading to the mixed messages we send each other on which impulse to follow.

14 Some people hold it together in a crisis and some people fall apart. Some people might run away from danger one day, and toward

442 Unit 5

APPLYING ACADEMIC VOCABULARY

☐ **dimension** ☑ **external** ☑ **statistic** ☐ **sustain** ☐ **utilize**

Write and Discuss Have students turn to a partner to discuss the following questions. Guide students to include the academic vocabulary words *external* and *statistic* in their responses. Ask volunteers to share their responses with the class.

- Why might people's judgments about survivors be influenced by **external** factors?
- Would the use of **statistics** be useful in supporting Wallace's claim? Why or why not?

it the next. We pick up a thousand cues in an instant of crisis and respond in ways that even surprise ourselves, sometimes.

But while we laud those who sacrifice themselves in an attempt to save another, there is a fine line between brave and foolish. There can also be a fine line between smart and selfish. And as a friend who's served in the military for 27 years says, the truth is, sometimes there's no line at all between the two.

CHECK YOUR UNDERSTANDING

Answer these questions before moving on to the **Analyze the Text** section on the following page.

1 How does the author support her claim that people are sometimes blamed for saving themselves?

- **A** By arguing that some people are heroes and other people are not
- **B** By asking the reader questions that force them to assign blame
- **C** By giving examples of what happened during and after a crisis
- **D** By showing that it takes selfishness to want to save yourself

2 The author included the information in paragraph 7 to —

- **F** demonstrate that in some circumstances saving your life is the right action
- **G** argue that this woman cost other people their lives by her actions
- **H** offer an example of what you should do in an airplane fire
- **J** criticize the other passengers for not trying to save themselves

3 The author concludes her argument with —

- **A** recommendations for what you should do in a live-or-die situation
- **B** another example that explains what being selfish in a crisis means
- **C** a story about a friend who says you have to be brave and foolish
- **D** generalizations arguing that the issue is not so simple

CHECK YOUR UNDERSTANDING

Have students answer the questions independently.

Answers:

1. *C*
2. *F*
3. *D*

If students answer any questions incorrectly, have them reread the text to confirm their understanding. Then they may proceed to ANALYZE THE TEXT on page 444.

ENGLISH LEARNER SUPPORT

Oral Assessment Use the following questions to assess students' comprehension and speaking skills.

1. How does the author show that survivors are sometimes blamed for saving themselves? *(The author gives examples of how people sometimes have been treated that way.)*
2. What message about survival does the author give in paragraph 7? *(In some situations, saving your own life is the best thing to do.)*
3. What is the author's conclusion? *(The issue is not simple and there is no "correct" answer.)*

SUBSTANTIAL/ MODERATE

APPLY

ANALYZE THE TEXT

Possible answers:

1. **DOK 4:** *Survivors cannot be labeled as either selfish or unselfish because human behavior is influenced by many factors and each survival situation is unique.*
2. **DOK 4:** *This is an example of a reason. It explains one of the factors that influence human behavior. As evidence for this reason, in paragraph 7 the author describes how a woman who stayed calm after a plane crash survived while many others did not.*
3. **DOK 3:** *The author uses rhetorical questions (the title; paragraphs 2, 7, 8, and 11) and false cause and effect (paragraph 12). The author's uses of the devices support her claim that survival situations involve complex factors.*
4. **DOK 4:** *This paragraph is valid and relevant; it addresses the author's claim by supporting the idea that instinct drives our actions. People who perform rescues instead of ensuring their own survival do not actually choose their actions; they simply act before thinking. This responds to the question in the previous paragraph about whether people are more civilized if they choose to help others, rather than "selfishly" saving themselves. It supports the idea that survivors cannot be labeled selfish or unselfish, because they act instinctively.*
5. **DOK 4:** *She means that in a life-threatening situation, the same action on the part of a survivor could be interpreted as either selfish or smart, but more likely it is both. This restates her initial claim that the actions of people in crisis result from a complex set of factors and cannot be neatly categorized as selfish or heroic. In paragraph 3, she states, "It's a complex question, because there are so many factors involved, and every survival situation is different."*

RESEARCH

Review the Research Tip with students. Advise students to include the following information under the heading "Survivor Experience":

- What was the life-threatening event?
- Who survived? Who did not survive?
- What action did the survivor take?
- How does the survivor feel?

Remind students that the ethical use of the internet includes citing sources appropriately and making sure that quotations are accurate.

Extend Have students explore and discuss treatment for post-traumatic stress disorder (PTSD) on the U.S. Department of Veterans Affairs website, National Center for PTSD.

RESPOND

ANALYZE THE TEXT

Support your responses with evidence from the text. NOTEBOOK

1. **Synthesize** Lane Wallace begins her argument with a series of questions to get her readers thinking about what is selfish and what is heroic. In your own words, state the claim that she expresses in paragraph 3. Take into account the information she presents in the rest of her argument, including her conclusions at the end.
2. **Analyze** Wallace writes that "the number one determining factor for survival is simply whether people hold it together in a crisis or fall apart." Is this an example of a claim, a reason, or evidence? Explain with an example from the text.
3. **Critique** Review the list of rhetorical devices in the Get Ready section of this selection. Identify at least two that Wallace uses in her argument. Are they effective in advancing her argument? Explain.
4. **Evaluate** Reread paragraph 12. As evidence for Wallace's claim, is this paragraph valid and relevant? Explain.
5. **Notice & Note** In the final paragraph, Wallace writes that there can be "a fine line between smart and selfish," and that "sometimes there's no line at all between the two." What does she mean by this apparent contradiction? How does her conclusion restate her claim? Note the sentence at the beginning of the selection that states this claim.

RESEARCH

RESEARCH TIP
If you are having trouble finding enough information on a topic, research a related topic and expand your search to include other aspects.

Accounts of different individuals who have lived through life-threatening or even deadly crises often provide very different tales of survival. With a partner, research stories of survivors and take notes in first column of the chart below.

SURVIVOR EXPERIENCE	MY RESPONSE TO SURVIVOR'S ACTION
Students' responses will vary based on their research findings.	

Extend Explore the recent work being done to treat victims of Post-Traumatic Stress Disorder (PTSD), which has been recognized as the psychiatric reaction to surviving a life-threatening experience.

WHEN STUDENTS STRUGGLE . . .

Review an Argument To help students analyze Wallace's argument, have them review in small groups the claim, reasons, and evidence they recorded in their charts as they read. Have groups discuss which reasons and evidence they found most compelling and why.

For additional support, go to the **Reading Studio** and assign the following  **Level Up Tutorial: Analyzing Arguments.**

CREATE AND DISCUSS

Prepare for Discussion Review the examples you researched. With your partner, discuss whether or not you would describe each survivor's actions as selfish. Fill in the second column of the chart on the previous page.

Class Discussion Hold a class discussion on the issues of survival introduced in the selection.

Review the author's claim and her evidence and reason. Then use your charts to further the discussion about how issues of saving oneself versus saving others play out in specific circumstances.

- ❑ As a group, set rules and guidelines. Decide on your goals, taking votes on key issues. During your discussion, use appropriate content-area vocabulary. Allow members to express their views, responding thoughtfully.
- ❑ Have group members ask clarifying questions and respond to other's questions. Be sure to build on the ideas of others as you participate in the discussion.
- ❑ Review your discussion to determine any points of group consensus.

Go to the **Speaking and Listening Studio** for help with having a group discussion.

RESPOND TO THE ESSENTIAL QUESTION

What does it take to survive in a crisis?

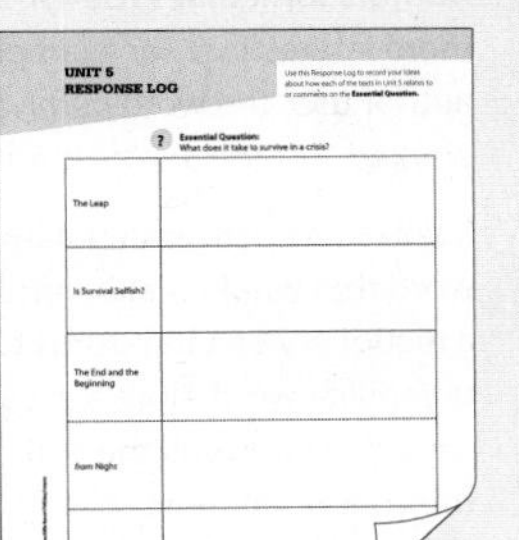

Gather Information Review your annotations and notes on "Is Survival Selfish?" Then, add relevant information to your Response Log. As you determine which information to include, think about:

- what characteristics enable survivors to survive
- what role luck or fate plays in surviving disaster
- why a person would feel guilt for surviving a life-threatening situation

At the end of the unit, use your notes to help you write an argument.

ACADEMIC VOCABULARY

As you write and discuss what you learned from the argument, be sure to use the Academic Vocabulary words. Check off each of the words that you use.

- ❑ **dimension**
- ❑ **external**
- ❑ **statistic**
- ❑ **sustain**
- ❑ **utilize**

APPLY

CREATE AND DISCUSS

Prepare for Discussion Tell students to consider all the evidence before they decide whether to describe survivors' actions as selfish or unselfish. Ask them to cite examples from their research that support their opinions and encourage them to draw upon ideas from the selection.

Class Discussion At the end of the discussion, have students consider points of agreement and disagreement. Ask volunteers to summarize the group's consensus on issues of survival.

For **speaking support** for students at varying proficiency levels, see the **Text X-Ray** on page 436D.

RESPOND TO THE ESSENTIAL QUESTION

Allow time for students to add details from "Is Survival Selfish?" to their Unit 5 Response Logs.

APPLY

CRITICAL VOCABULARY

Answers:

Explanations will vary but should reflect understanding of Critical Vocabulary definitions.

1. *a*
2. *a*
3. *b*
4. *a*
5. *b*

VOCABULARY STRATEGY: Synonyms

Possible answers: *Sentences will vary but should convey an understanding of Critical Vocabulary definitions. In choosing the best synonyms to exchange for Critical Vocabulary words, students may need to use a dictionary or a thesaurus to identify the nuances of each synonym.*

Critical Vocabulary	Synonyms
laud	*praise, honor*
transfix	*paralyze, fascinate*
consume	*destroy, devastate*
berate	*scold, reproach*
edict	*rule, decree*

RESPOND

WORD BANK
laud
transfix
consume
berate
edict

CRITICAL VOCABULARY

Practice and Apply Circle the letter of the best answer to each question. Then, explain your response.

1. Which of the following would be something you might **laud**?
   a. a supreme accomplishment **b.** a failure to complete
2. If something were to **transfix** you, how would you react?
   a. stand in awe **b.** run in fear
3. Which of the following would be likely to **consume** something?
   a. a cloud of fog **b.** a forest fire
4. If I **berate** another person, how would that person feel?
   a. humiliated **b.** delighted
5. If a king issued an **edict**, what would it be like?
   a. an opinion **b.** a law

VOCABULARY STRATEGY: Synonyms

Go to the **Vocabulary Studio** for more on synonyms.

Words that share the same or nearly the same meaning are called **synonyms**. Authors sometimes use synonyms to vary word choice and make their writing more interesting. For example, in paragraph 7 of "Is Survival Selfish?" the author uses the word *paralyzed*. The synonym *transfixed* might also have worked, but the author had already used it in paragraph 5.

If you come across an unfamiliar word in a text, try to think of another word that would make sense in the context of the sentence. Then check a dictionary or a thesaurus to see if your word is truly a synonym for the unfamiliar word. Note any subtle differences between the synonyms and try to understand why the author chose that precise word. Ask yourself whether the context sentence has the same or a slightly different meaning with your synonym as with the author's original word.

Practice and Apply Use a print or online thesaurus to complete this activity.

1. Create a two-column chart. In the first column, write the Critical Vocabulary words. In the second column, write at least two synonyms for each word.
2. Write a sentence using each Critical Vocabulary word.
3. For each sentence you write, exchange the Critical Vocabulary word for one of its synonyms. Work together with a partner to choose the best synonym for each sentence. Discuss whether using a synonym changes the meaning of each original sentence.

ENGLISH LEARNER SUPPORT

Use Cognates and Synonyms Explain that students can use cognates and synonyms to understand unfamiliar words. For example, if students do not know the meaning of the word *uncivilized* in paragraph 1, they might look up the word in a thesaurus and find the synonym *savage,* which has the Spanish cognate *salvaje*. Point out that the following synonyms for the Critical Vocabulary words have Spanish cognates: *honor/honor (laud), paralyze/paralizar (transfix), fascinate/fascinar (transfix), destroy/destruir (consume), reproach/reproche (berate), decree/decreto (edict).* **ALL LEVELS**

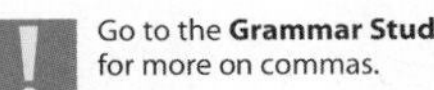

LANGUAGE CONVENTIONS: Commas

A writer's use of punctuation not only helps readers to understand the writer's message, but it also signals how the writer wants the text to be read. In your writing, you can use commas to signal a break or a pause to the reader. When you write, read your sentences out loud, noticing where you pause. The parts where you pause probably need to be punctuated by a comma. Commas are also used to distinguish and divide main and subordinate clauses. Look at these examples from "Is Survival Selfish?"

> **Simpson ended up hanging off a cliff, unable to climb up, and Yates, unable to lift him up and losing his own grip on the mountain, ended up cutting the rope to Simpson to save himself.**
>
> **If she'd tried, she probably would have perished with them.**

Read the two sentences out loud, noticing where you pause. The commas after "cliff" and "up" in the first sentence signal to the reader to pause. The comma after "mountain" signals a break in thought and makes the sentence easier to understand. The comma after "tried" in the second sentence separates a subordinate clause from the main clause.

Additional examples from "Is Survival Selfish" are shown in the following chart.

PURPOSE OF COMMA	EXAMPLE FROM THE SELECTION
to signal a break in thought	**And afterward, I remember she said she battled a lot of guilt for saving herself instead of trying to save the others.**
to signal the reader to pause	**He was labeled an uncivilized coward and, a year after the disaster, he resigned his position at White Star.**
to divide main and subordinate clauses	**If survival is an instinct, it seems to me that there must be something equally instinctive that drives us, sometimes, to run into danger instead of away from it.**

Practice and Apply These sentences include words, phrases, and clauses that need to be punctuated with commas. Rewrite the sentences, inserting the needed punctuation. If you get stuck, try reading the sentence out loud.

1. Yes I absolutely want to survive.
2. Beyond saving your own life people expect you to be a hero and save others.
3. If you survive people think you should have saved others.
4. If she'd tried to help others she probably would have perished with them.
5. Surviving danger what everyone hopes for changes the rest of a person's life.

Go to the **Grammar Studio** for more on commas.

APPLY

LANGUAGE CONVENTIONS: Commas

As a class, review the examples of comma usage in the chart. Model reading the examples aloud, slightly emphasizing the pauses indicated by the commas. Remind students to consider how they use commas in their own writing.

Practice and Apply

1. *Yes, I absolutely want to survive.*
2. *Beyond saving your own life, people expect you to be a hero and save others.*
3. *If you survive, people think you should have saved others.*
4. *If she'd tried to help others, she probably would have perished with them.*
5. *Surviving danger, what everyone hopes for, changes the rest of a person's life.*

ENGLISH LEARNER SUPPORT

Understand Language Structures Remind students that commas often set off phrases and clauses that come before a main clause. Explain that a main clause contains a subject and a verb and expresses a complete thought. Use the following supports with students at varying proficiency levels:

- Guide students to label the main clauses in the Practice and Apply sentences. Confirm comprehension of comma usage by asking students where commas should be placed in the sentences. **SUBSTANTIAL**
- Have students work independently to label the main clauses in the Practice and Apply sentences. Then have partners work together to read the sentences aloud and discuss the correct punctuation. **MODERATE**
- Have students work independently to rewrite the sentences in the Practice and Apply with correct punctuation. Then have them discuss their answers with a partner. **LIGHT**

THE END AND THE BEGINNING

Poem by Wisława Szymborska

GENRE ELEMENTS

LYRIC POETRY

Remind students that a **lyric poem** is a short poem in which the poet expresses thoughts and feelings through a single speaker. Lyric poetry takes a variety of forms, from rhymed sonnets to unrhymed free verse. The author uses poetic language and structure to convey impressions, emotions, and ideas related to themes about life. In this lesson, students will analyze the literary effect of the author's choices of poetic language and structure.

LEARNING OBJECTIVES

- Cite evidence to support analysis of poetic language and structure.
- Research images of the aftermath of war.
- Write captions using figurative and literal language.
- Discuss literal and figurative interpretations of images.
- **Language** Use adjectives to describe tone.

TEXT COMPLEXITY

Quantitative Measures	**The End and the Beginning**	Lexile: N/A
Qualitative Measures	**Ideas Presented** Mostly explicit, but moves to some implied meaning.	
	Structures Used Uses free verse, with no particular patterns.	
	Language Used Uses some figurative language.	
	Knowledge Required Experiences might be less familiar to many.	

Online 

RESOURCES

- Unit 5 Response Log
- Selection Audio
-  Close Read Screencasts: Modeled Discussions
-  Reading Studio: Notice & Note
-  Level Up Tutorial: Tone
-  Speaking and Listening Studio: Giving a Presentation
- "The End and the Beginning" Selection Test

SUMMARIES

English

The poet uses vivid imagery and figurative language to describe and reflect on the aftermath of war. As the speaker describes the tasks required for cleanup, the horror and devastation of the conflict are revealed. The speaker's speculation about the possibility of a peaceful future is tinged by the specter of the cyclical nature of conflict.

Spanish

La poeta utiliza imágenes vívidas y lenguaje figurativo para describir y reflexionar sobre las repercusiones de la guerra. Mientras el narrador describe las tareas requeridas para limpiar los escombros, el horror y la devastación del conflicto se revelan. La especulación del narrador acerca de la posibilidad de un futuro pacífico se ve amenazada por el espectro de la naturaleza cíclica de los conflictos.

SMALL-GROUP OPTIONS

Have students work in small groups to read and discuss the selection.

Reciprocal Teaching

- After students have read the poem, present them with a list of generic question stems.
- Instruct students to work independently to write three to five questions about the poem, using the question stems. They do not need to know the answers.
- Group students into teams of three and have each student offer two questions for group discussion.
- Guide groups to reach consensus on the answer to each question and cite text evidence that supports the answer.

Read Aloud

- Read the poem aloud to model rhythm, tone, and pronunciation.
- Make sure students understand the overall meaning of the poem.
- Have groups of up to four students read the poem aloud, alternating stanzas.
- Encourage students to pause after each stanza to clarify meaning, pronunciation, and understanding.

Text X-Ray: English Learner Support
for "The End and the Beginning"

Use the Text X-Ray and the supports and scaffolds in the Teacher's Edition to help guide students at different proficiency levels through the selection.

INTRODUCE THE SELECTION

DISCUSS HISTORIC INFLUENCE

In this lesson, the topic of war may result in strong emotions from students, so review guidelines for having respectful discussions. Then offer these supports:

- Explain that Poland, where Szymborska was born in 1923, was devastated by World War II. Hitler invaded Poland in 1939, causing Britain and France to officially declare war on Germany. Poland remained occupied until liberated by the USSR in 1945. During this time, the populace was persecuted—at least 3 million Polish Jews were executed and roughly 2 million Slavic Poles were deported or killed in an effort to eliminate Polish culture.
- Before reading, have students discuss how the experience of the Polish people during WWII may have influenced Szymborska's writing and affected the poem's message.

CULTURAL REFERENCES

The following words or phrases from the Background note and poem may be unfamiliar to students:

- *Socialist Realism* (Background): a movement promoting the development of a classless society through the use of literature, art, and music
- *Nobel Prize in Literature* (Background): an international prize awarded annually for outstanding achievement in the field of literature
- *straighten themselves up* (line 4): make themselves organized or tidy
- *rubble* (line 5): a loose mass of rock or masonry fragments, crumbled by natural or human forces
- *mired* (line 9): entrapped or entangled
- *scum* (line 10): discarded material or worthless matter
- *girder* (line 14): a beam used as a main horizontal support in a building or bridge
- *glaze* (line 16): to fit with glass

LISTENING

Understand the Central Idea

Read the poem aloud for students. As you read, emphasize lines that could be best used in a summary of the poem.

Use the following supports with students at varying proficiency levels:

- Point out lines that are essential to understanding the poem's meaning, such as lines 1–2 and 18–21. Ask yes/no questions—for example: Do these lines emphasize the destruction of war? **SUBSTANTIAL**
- Have students work in pairs to mark lines that convey ideas that they consider important to the poem's overall meaning. Then have them summarize the central idea of the poem. Provide sentence stems: *This part makes me think of ____. The author wants us to feel ____.* **MODERATE**
- Once students have summarized the meaning, have them work together to explain what language or structures brought them to that conclusion. Provide sentence stems: *The use of the words ____ made me feel ____.* **LIGHT**

SPEAKING

Discuss Text Features

Tell students that, due to the short length of most poetry, a poet's choice of language is often a key text feature. Poets make careful word choices in order to convey their message(s).

Use the following supports with students at varying proficiency levels:

- Point out the "Tone" section of the chart on page 449. Have students repeat after you as you model with expression examples of how words convey specific tones: *slap* has a harsh tone, *parade* implies loud and exciting tones. **SUBSTANTIAL**
- Review the examples covered above, explaining that the way a word or phrase is read can influence its tone. For example, say the word *slap* in a happy voice and then in an angry voice. Ask students to describe how the tone of your voice changes their interpretation of the word. **MODERATE**
- Have students read the poem with a partner, alternating between stanzas. Encourage students to use inflection to convey tone. As one student reads, the other should note the words and phrases that stand out. Then have partners discuss how the language helps convey the tone, or the author's attitude toward the subject. **LIGHT**

READING

Examine Poetic Structure

Explain that one text feature poets rely on to convey meaning is poetic structure.

Use the following supports with students at varying proficiency levels:

- Before students read, tell them that repetition is the use of a word or phrase two or more times. Encourage them to underline examples of repetition as they read. **SUBSTANTIAL**
- Have students read the first four stanzas and look for repetition. Encourage them to write down a word or phrase when it appears more than once and to place tally marks beside it every time it repeats. **MODERATE**
- With a partner, have students discuss the effect of the repetition in the poem. Ask students to consider why the author chooses to repeat the phrase "someone has to" and how repeating a different phrase might affect the poem. **LIGHT**

WRITING

Write Photo Captions

Work with students to help them research and caption the photos they choose in the activities on Student Edition pages 454–455.

Use the following supports with students at varying proficiency levels:

- Help students develop key phrases to use when searching the Internet for photos, such as *People after World War II images*. Remind them to use the terms *images* or *photographs* to find visual information. Adding words, such as *Poland*, to their search terms will give them more specific search results. **SUBSTANTIAL**
- After students have chosen their images, but before they write captions, review the difference between literal and figurative language. Have small groups collaborate on writing captions for two or three images. **MODERATE**
- Have students write a short explanation of how they chose literal and figurative captions. **LIGHT**

Connect to the
ESSENTIAL QUESTION

In "The End and the Beginning," people are coping with the aftermath of one type of destructive crisis—war. The necessary acts of cleaning up and rebuilding reflect the practicality, determination, and hope needed to survive a crisis.

ANALYZE & APPLY

THE END AND THE BEGINNING

Poem by **WISŁAWA SZYMBORSKA**

ESSENTIAL QUESTION:

What does it take to survive in a crisis?

QUICK START

Think about the aspects of daily life that are disrupted by war or mass violence. What kinds of challenges do people face in the aftermath of such events?

ANALYZE POETIC LANGUAGE

"The End and the Beginning" is a **lyric poem,** one in which a single speaker expresses his or her personal ideas and feelings. Lyric poetry can take many forms and can address all types of topics, from everyday experiences to complex ideas. Most poems—except narrative poems, which tell a story—are lyric poems.

Poetry is highly concentrated as far as language used, so poets must be precise and economical about the words they choose and how they use them. As Szymborska said in her Nobel Prize acceptance speech, "every word is weighed." Analyzing an author's language choices—and the literary effect of those choices—can deepen your understanding of a poem. You can analyze Wisława Szymborska's poetic language in "The End and the Beginning" by looking at the elements outlined in the chart below.

TONE	IMAGERY	DICTION/SYNTAX
Tone refers to the author's attitude toward the subject. Authors shape a work's tone through topics they choose to explore, word choices, and images those words create. Recognizing tone in literature is essential to gaining meaning, just as recognizing a person's tone of voice is essential to understanding what is said and meant. Elements to consider when evaluating tone include: • words with positive or negative connotations • use of informal language, such as idioms or colloquial expressions • repetition of significant words or phrases	Poets often use **imagery,** or descriptive words and phrases that create sensory experiences for the reader. Imagery usually appeals to one or more of the five senses to help readers imagine exactly what is being described. For example, the striking image of "corpse-filled wagons" passing through rubble-lined roads calls to mind photographs that most readers will have seen of war-torn, bombed-out cities. The image helps the reader envision what the speaker observes. Look for other images in the poem that engage your senses and evoke a strong emotional response.	Two closely related elements of an author's style that affect the tone of their work are diction and syntax. **Diction** is the writer's choice of specific words, and **syntax** is the way those words are arranged into phrases and sentences. A writer's choices regarding diction and syntax can reflect a tone that is formal or informal, concrete or abstract, or literal or figurative. Look for the specific words the author chose for the poem and how she chose to arrange them. What tone do those carefully chosen words create?

GENRE ELEMENTS: LYRIC POETRY

- usually short to convey strong emotions
- written using first-person point of view to express the speaker's thoughts and feelings
- often uses repetition and rhyme to create a melodic quality
- includes many forms, such as sonnets, odes, and elegies

QUICK START

After students read the Quick Start question, prompt them to discuss how war or mass violence might affect a neighborhood, a city, or a nation. Ask students to list the different kinds of challenges people would face in these three scenarios.

ANALYZE POETIC LANGUAGE

Make sure students understand the terms and concepts related to **tone, imagery, diction,** and **syntax.** Ask volunteers to summarize the important points in each column of the chart. Then provide students with the following questions to consider as they read and analyze the poem:

- What do the author's word choices reveal about her attitude toward the subject? What words might describe this attitude—the tone of the poem?
- What are the most striking images in the poem? How do they make the reader feel?
- How does the arrangement of words and ideas convey the author's attitude, or tone?

For **speaking support** for students at varying proficiency levels, see the **Text X-Ray** on page 448D.

TEACH

ANALYZE POETIC STRUCTURE

Point out that **repetition** uses the *same* word or phrase two or more times, while **parallelism** uses *different* words arranged in a similar (or parallel) structure. Read aloud the example stanzas, emphasizing the repeated words and parallel structures. Make sure students understand the difference between repetition and parallelism:

- Repetition: *Someone has to*
- Parallelism: *has to get mired, has to drag in a girder, has to glaze a window*

ANNOTATION MODEL

Discuss the annotations in the model, asking students to read the stanzas and volunteer additional observations about the tone, sensory imagery, or diction and syntax. If students have questions about the annotations, suggest that they review the material about poetic structure and language and then reread the stanzas. Encourage them to underline important phrases or circle key words and color-code their annotations by using a different color highlighter to help them distinguish between examples of the language and structure in the poem. Point out that they may follow this suggestion or use their own system for marking up the selections in their write-in texts.

GET READY

ANALYZE POETIC STRUCTURE

Poets use rhetorical devices such as repetition and parallelism to convey meaning. **Repetition** is the use of a word or phrase two or more times. **Parallelism** is the use of the same grammatical or metrical structure within and across lines and verses. Parallelism can provide rhythmic symmetry and balance to a piece, and often shows that two or more ideas are similar or connected. Repetition and parallelism are often used together.

Below are the third and fourth stanzas of "The End and the Beginning." Find and underline examples of repetition and parallelism.

Someone has to get mired
in scum and ashes,
sofa springs,
splintered glass,
and bloody rags.

Someone has to drag in a girder
to prop up a wall.
Someone has to glaze a window,
rehang a door.

As you read "The End and the Beginning," look for the use of repetition and parallelism. Think about the effect of these and other elements of the author's style; and how that style conveys information about the speaker and message.

ANNOTATION MODEL

NOTICE & NOTE

As you read, note your observations about the poem's tone, the use of sensory imagery, and the author's choice of diction and syntax. Here is how one reader responded to the first stanzas of "The End and the Beginning."

After every war someone has to clean up. Things won't straighten themselves up, after all. Someone has to push the rubble to the side of the road, so the corpse-filled wagons can pass.	There have been multiple wars. This suggests a cycle. Calling the aftereffects of war "cleaning up" and "straightening" seems ironic. Rubble = debris from bombed-out buildings? I see powerful language: "corpse-filled."

APPLYING ACADEMIC VOCABULARY

❑ **dimension** ❑ **external** ❑ **statistic** ☑ **sustain** ☑ **utilize**

Write and Discuss Have students turn to a partner to discuss the following questions. Guide students to include the academic vocabulary words *sustain* and *utilize* in their responses. Ask volunteers to share their responses with the class.

- What activities might **sustain** people during difficult times?
- How might people **utilize** scrap materials from ruined buildings?

NOTICE & NOTE

BACKGROUND

Wisława Szymborska *(1923–2012) was born in Poland. Her first two published volumes of poetry, written in post-World War II Communist-dominated Poland, were written in the style of Socialist Realism. Szymborska later disowned these works. Her disillusionment with communism was reflected in* Calling Out to Yeti, *published in 1957. Her poems, noted for their unique, ironic tone, have been translated into many languages. Szymborska won the Nobel Prize in Literature in 1996.*

THE END AND THE BEGINNING

Poem by Wisława Szymborska

SETTING A PURPOSE

As you read, think about the aspects of daily life that are disrupted by a war or mass violence. What kind of challenges do people confront in the immediate aftermath of such an event? Note your observations and any questions you have as you read.

After every war
[someone has to clean up.]
Things won't
straighten themselves up, after all.

[Someone has to push the rubble]
to the side of the road,
so the corpse-filled wagons
can pass.

[Someone has to get mired]
in scum and ashes,
sofa springs,
splintered glass,
and bloody rags.

Close Read

Notice & Note

You can use the side margins to notice and note signposts in the text.

ANALYZE POETIC LANGUAGE

Annotate: Underline words and phrases in lines 1–13 that appeal to the reader's senses.

Interpret: What general picture do these words or phrases create in your mind?

The End and the Beginning 451

TEACH

BACKGROUND

Have students read the biographical information about Wisława Szymborska (vēs-wävä shim-bôrskə). Explain that she was about 17 when World War II began, and in this poem she is almost certainly drawing upon her postwar experiences in Kraków, Poland. Szymborska lived there both during and after the war. Where there was once a notorious slave labor camp called Plaszow, today there is a grassland eerily reminiscent of the image at the poem's end.

SETTING A PURPOSE

Direct students to use the Setting a Purpose prompt to focus their reading.

For **reading support** for students at varying proficiency levels, see the **Text X-Ray** on page 448D

ANALYZE POETIC LANGUAGE

Tell students that poets use precise words and phrases to create powerful images that appeal to the reader's sense of sight, sound, smell, touch, and taste. Tell them to consider the overall effect of the sensory imagery in these lines. (***Possible answer:*** *a city destroyed by war)*

CLOSE READ SCREENCAST

Modeled Discussion In their eBook, have students view the Close Read Screencast, in which readers discuss and annotate the following key passage:

- Lines 9–17, which begin with "Someone has to get mired . . ." and end with "Someone has to glaze a window, / rehang a door."

As a class, view and discuss the video. Then have students work in pairs to perform a close read of lines 26–36.

Close Read

Close Read Practice PDF

TEACH

ANALYZE POETIC STRUCTURE

Point out that the structure of a poem is one way that poets convey meaning and express their ideas about the subject of the poem. **Repetition** and **parallelism** can provide not only rhythm and balance to a piece, but can emphasize an idea, tone, or mood that the poet wants to express. (***Answer:*** *The repetition of "someone" and the parallel structure "Someone has to . . ." reinforces the sense of how much work has to be done, as well as the difficult and repetitious nature of the work. The lines support a tone of resignation and a dark mood.)*

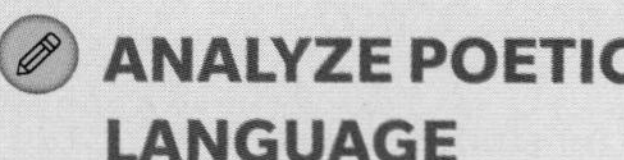

ANALYZE POETIC LANGUAGE

Remind students that **figurative language** is language that communicates meanings beyond the literal meanings of the words. In figurative language, words may be used to symbolize ideas and concepts in striking and unusual ways. (***Answer:*** *The "rusted-out arguments" are old ways of thinking that people figuratively drag out into the daylight and carry to the trash.)*

ENGLISH LEARNER SUPPORT

Confirm Understanding The word *photogenic* and the informal, colloquial sentence structure in lines 18–19 may be confusing to students.

- Help students use the Spanish cognate *fotogénico* and the context clue *cameras* in line 20 to understand that *photogenic* refers to something that looks attractive in photographs. **SUBSTANTIAL/MODERATE**
- Read stanza 5 aloud and direct students' attention to lines 18–19. Explain that this is an example of informal language that uses inverted word order to create emphasis. Invite volunteers to restate the lines in standard English, as a complete sentence. *(It's not photogenic, and [it] takes years.)* **MODERATE/LIGHT**

NOTICE & NOTE

ANALYZE POETIC STRUCTURE
Annotate: Mark the use of repetition and parallelism in the first four stanzas of the poem.
Interpret: What is the effect of these devices?

Someone has to drag in a girder
to prop up a wall.
Someone has to glaze a window,
rehang a door.

Photogenic it's not,
and takes years.
All the cameras have left
for another war.

We'll need the bridges back,
and new railway stations.
Sleeves will go ragged
from rolling them up.

Someone, broom in hand,
still recalls the way it was.
Someone else listens
and nods with unsevered[1] head.
But already there are those nearby
starting to mill about[2]
who will find it dull.

ANALYZE POETIC LANGUAGE
Annotate: Mark the use of figurative language in lines 33–36.
Interpret: Reread lines 26–42. What might people be figuratively throwing on garbage piles along with the rubble of war?

From out of the bushes
sometimes someone still unearths
rusted-out arguments
and carries them to the garbage pile.

[1] **unsevered:** not cut off; not separated.
[2] **mill about:** move idly or aimlessly.

ENGLISH LEARNER SUPPORT

Look for Patterns in Language Help students recognize and appreciate the poet's use of repetition and parallelism to convey meaning. Point out that the repetition of "someone has to" in lines 2–17 creates a string of sentences with parallel grammatical structures. The repetition emphasizes that all the statements are related—they all describe tasks associated with cleaning up after a war. The repetition also emphasizes the repetitive nature of the tasks. Ask pairs to practice reading this section of the poem aloud to each other to hear the effect of the repetition. **ALL LEVELS**

Those who knew
what was going on here
must make way for
those who know little.
And less than little.
And finally as little as nothing.

In the grass that has overgrown
causes and effects,
someone must be stretched out
blade of grass in his mouth
gazing at the clouds.

NOTICE & NOTE

CONTRASTS AND CONTRADICTIONS

Notice & Note: Mark the passages in lines 37-42 that tell what the speaker thinks needs to happen.

Interpret: Why should "those who knew" make way for "those who know little"?

CHECK YOUR UNDERSTANDING

Answer these questions before moving on to the **Analyze the Text** section on the following page.

1 The tone of the poem's speaker is best described as —

A grateful and relieved—she's happy to be alive

B resolute and enthusiastic—she's ready to get on with the rebuilding

C angry and harsh—she's bitter about what has happened

D ironic—she notices people's tendency to forget about war

2 The word mired in line 9 means —

F permanently stuck

G at a disadvantage

H deeply sunk into

J dirty or slimy

3 What is an important idea in the poem?

A The cyclical nature of war and recovery from it

B The abuse of government power

C The excitement of war makes a good news story.

D The importance of antiwar protests

TEACH

CONTRASTS AND CONTRADICTIONS

Remind students that Contrasts and Contradictions is a technique used by authors to show aspects of a situation that go beyond what is immediately apparent. The contrasts shown in this stanza refer to how quickly memories of war change between those who experienced it and those who did not. (***Answer:*** *The author is describing the passage of time and the shift of war-related memory to an increasingly older generation.*)

For **listening support** for students at varying proficiency levels, see the **Text X-Ray** on page 448C.

CHECK YOUR UNDERSTANDING

Have students answer the questions independently.

Answers:

1. *D*
2. *H*
3. *A*

If they answer any questions incorrectly, have them reread the text to confirm their understanding. Then they may proceed to ANALYZE THE TEXT on page 454.

ENGLISH LEARNER SUPPORT

Oral Assessment Use the following questions to assess students' comprehension and speaking skills.

1. An ironic tone refers to an attitude that is expressed with words that say something different from their literal meaning. At the end of the poem, how does the speaker convey an ironic tone? *(The speaker describes people's tendency to forget about war.)*
2. In line 9, what is the meaning of the word *mired? (deeply sunk into; covered in)*
3. What is an important idea from the poem about when war happens and what happens after a war? *(Possible answer: War happens over and over, and each time it is hard to recover.)* **SUBSTANTIAL/MODERATE**

APPLY

ANALYZE THE TEXT

Possible answers:

1. **DOK 4:** *The language is informal, helping the reader identify with the speaker. Examples include "clean up" (line 2), "straighten themselves up" (line 4), "drag in a girder" (line 14), and "Photogenic it's not" (line 18). The speaker is focused on the task at hand but is also jaded; he or she describes work that must be done "after every war" and is aware that somewhere "another war" probably has begun. Beginning in line 30, the tone grows more hopeful as the speaker recognizes a gradual healing and the future for a younger generation unaffected by war.*
2. **DOK 2:** *The use of "someone" emphasizes that war is a universal tragedy, not limited to just one country or generation. The poet also may have been commenting on what those who survive the war have lost, including their past selves. Along with their innocence, their individual identities have been erased.*
3. **DOK 2:** *The phrase refers to the arduous, dirty work necessary to rebuild the country. Images such as "corpse-filled wagons" (line 7) and "scum and ashes, sofa springs, splintered glass, and bloody rags" (lines 10–13) reinforce the horror; and the mention of a need for new girders, bridges, and railway stations shows the enormous scope of the destruction.*
4. **DOK 2:** *The grass symbolizes regeneration and growth, literally covering over the visible scars of war and figuratively covering up the causes of the war. The idle person in line 45, not burdened with reconciling the past, has never experienced the horrors of war.*
5. **DOK 4:** *The people "who knew" are the ones who experienced the war and are doing the work of rebuilding. These people are followed by generations who haven't experienced war and its aftermath. On the surface it seems that this lack of knowledge is a good thing; but through repetition and the way the lines are structured, the poet gives the impression that it isn't always a good thing for people not to remember.*

RESEARCH

Review the Research Tip with students. Advise students that because Web pages may change or disappear without notice it is important to immediately record all the relevant information about the images they find. If they plan to return to a site to record the details, they may find that the site has changed.

ANALYZE THE TEXT

Support your responses with evidence from the text. NOTEBOOK

1. **Analyze** Answer these questions to explore how Szymborska creates the tone of the poem. Cite words and phrases from the poem to support your answers.
   - Does the speaker use formal or informal language? What is the effect of this choice?
   - What is the speaker's attitude toward the situation he or she is describing?
   - How does the tone of the poem change beginning with line 30?
2. **Infer** Notice the repetition of the word "someone" throughout the poem. What statement is the speaker making by using an indefinite pronoun rather than referring to a specific person?
3. **Interpret** In line 18, the speaker says that the aftermath of war is not "photogenic." What images in the poem reinforce this idea about war? How does the poet show the extent of the devastation?
4. **Interpret** Reread the last stanza of the poem. What does the grass symbolize, or represent? What does the speaker mean when she describes this "someone" as being "stretched out / blade of grass in his mouth / gazing at the clouds"?
5. **Notice & Note** In lines 37–42, the speaker contrasts "those who knew" with those who know "as little as nothing"? How are these two groups of people different from each other?

RESEARCH

Research at least three images of people in the aftermath of war. If you have a particular area of interest, pursue it. If not, search for images of the aftermath of World War II from a city in Europe or Asia. Later, you'll write photo captions that incorporate literal and figurative language. As you search, use a chart like the one below to track your results.

RESEARCH TIP
The information on the Internet is not regulated for accuracy. Be sure to use only credible sources for your information, including sites you know and trust, those your teachers recommend, and those with .edu, .org, or .gov addresses.

WHAT I LOOKED FOR	WHAT I FOUND	WHERE I FOUND IT	WHAT I LEARNED ABOUT IT
Students' responses will vary.			

454 Unit 5

WHEN STUDENTS STRUGGLE . . .

Analyze Poetic Language Remind students that the connotations, or emotional associations, of words that an author chooses reveal the tone, or the author's attitude toward the subject. Have pairs identify at least five striking words or images in the poem and use a graphic organizer to record the emotional associations suggested by each word or image. Then have students use the details in their graphic organizers to describe the poem's overall tone.

For additional support, go to the **Reading Studio** and assign the following  **Level Up Tutorial: Tone.**

CREATE AND PRESENT

Write Photo Captions In "The End and the Beginning," Wisława Szymborska describes scenes of the aftermath of war using language that works at two levels: literal and figurative.

- ❑ Gather the photos you found in your research. Think of words that describe those images literally, as well as words that evoke figurative meanings.
- ❑ Write captions for up to three of your images, describing each image in both literal and figurative language. You may choose to write one literal and one figurative caption per image or combine them in some creative way.

Share with a Group Have a group discussion about the images, your captions, and the literal and figurative interpretations of those images.

- ❑ As a group, decide on the order in which you and your group members will present your images and captions. Will you share all three of your images or choose just one or two?
- ❑ Share your research experience and caption-writing thought process in a brief presentation. Point out the ways in which your caption(s) suggest both literal and figurative interpretations of those images.
- ❑ Listen closely as others share their work. For each presentation, write down at least one question that you would like to follow up with research.

Go to **Giving a Presentation** in the **Speaking and Listening Studio** to learn more.

RESPOND TO THE ESSENTIAL QUESTION

What does it take to survive in a crisis?

Gather Information Review your annotations and notes on "The End and the Beginning." Then, add relevant information to your Response Log. As you determine which information to include, think about:

- what it must be like to live in the aftermath of war
- the cleaning up and rebuilding of physical surroundings required of people
- the emotional rebuilding and recovery required of survivors

At the end of the unit, use your notes to help you write an argument.

ACADEMIC VOCABULARY

As you write and discuss what you learned from the poem, be sure to use the Academic Vocabulary words. Check off each of the words that you use.

- ❑ **dimension**
- ❑ **external**
- ❑ **statistic**
- ❑ **sustain**
- ❑ **utilize**

APPLY

CREATE AND PRESENT

Write Photo Captions Have students work in pairs or triads to compile lists of descriptive words with literal and figurative meanings. To help them distinguish between literal and figurative words, advise them to ask these questions about each photo:

- Literal: What is happening in this photo? What does the viewer see?
- Figurative: What feelings or ideas might this photo evoke in the viewer?

For **writing support** for students at varying proficiency levels, see the **Text X-Ray** on page 448D.

Share with a Group Ask students to use formal language in their presentations. Remind them to use complete sentences in the correct tense and to maintain clear pronunciation and appropriate volume as they present. Encourage partners to practice presenting their photos and captions smoothly, without distractions or technical problems.

RESPOND TO THE ESSENTIAL QUESTION

Allow time for students to add details from "The End and the Beginning" to their Unit 5 Response Logs.

TO CHALLENGE STUDENTS . . .

Make Connections Provide students with the following quotation attributed to writer George Santayana: "Those who do not remember the past are condemned to repeat it." Have pairs discuss how the following images relate to Santayana's message:

- "Those who knew. . . . as little as nothing." (lines 37–42)
- "the grass that has overgrown / causes and effects" (lines 43–44)
- "someone . . . gazing at the clouds." (lines 45–47)

Have pairs come together in groups and discuss their responses.

from NIGHT

Memoir by **Elie Wiesel**

from THE PIANIST

Memoir by **Władysław Szpilman**

GENRE ELEMENTS
MEMOIR

Remind students that a **memoir** is a type of autobiographical writing in which the writer provides a first-person account of real events. A memoir may serve as an important account of historical events. It usually has a tighter focus than an autobiography. As a result, memoir writers usually describe key events in detail, include personal observations and feelings, explore possible causes, and reflect upon their own motives and those of others. They often craft their text to convey a particular theme, or message.

LEARNING OBJECTIVES

- Analyze and compare memoirs, including authors' word choices.
- Conduct research to write an introduction to a memoir.
- Write and present historical contexts for WWII memoirs.
- Synthesize information about Jews surviving in Poland during World War II.
- Determine the meaning of multiple-meaning words.
- Analyze and use independent and dependent clauses.
- **Language** Discuss with a partner word choices that help to create the mood and convey the tone of each memoir.

TEXT COMPLEXITY

Quantitative Measures	***from* Night**	Lexile: 440L
	***from* The Pianist**	Lexile: 910L
Qualitative Measures	**Ideas Presented** Mostly explicit; some key ideas are implied but are easy to infer.	
	Structures Used Mostly in chronological order; some cause/effect or main idea/details order.	
	Language Used Mostly Tier II words with some Tier III and foreign words footnoted and/or defined.	
	Knowledge Required Most background knowledge needed to understand both texts is provided.	

SPEAKING

Understand Mood and Tone

Have students discuss the overall mood and tone of each memoir and some of the words from each selection that contribute to mood and reveal tone.

Use the following supports with students at varying proficiency levels:

- Display the word *anxiously*, which is in both selections. Help students understand how this word shapes mood and tone by sharing a real or imaginary anecdote about a time you did something anxiously (for example, entering a classroom for the first time). Then guide students in creating oral sentences that use *anxiously* to appropriately describe an action in a moment of uncertainty or fear. **SUBSTANTIAL**
- Encourage students to work with partners to identify two or three words in each memoir that convey mood and tone, and explain their impact. **MODERATE**
- Have small groups discuss the mood of each selection , paying attention to the author's diction, and read aloud to one another passages that they found particularly affecting. **LIGHT**

READING

Identify Main Ideas

Have students reread parts of the selections for the purpose of identifying main ideas.

Use the following supports with students at varying proficiency levels:

- Have students freewrite in their home language about the dangers people faced during World War II. Then instruct small groups to find one example, in either selection, of a danger and how the author responded to it. **SUBSTANTIAL**
- Have students read to find out how the authors address their physical needs. Allow time for sharing responses in a small-group discussion. **MODERATE**
- Suggest that students read to learn the authors' thoughts about survival. Have students meet with partners to compare their findings. **LIGHT**

WRITING

Write History

Work with students to help them draft the introduction they have been assigned to write on Student Edition page 475.

Use the following supports with students at varying proficiency levels:

- Direct students to arrange facts in chronological order. Have small groups list words they can use to indicate time order and/or sequence. (You may wish to start the list with words and phrases such as in [*year*], *next, later,* and *finally*.) **SUBSTANTIAL**
- Give students the option to paraphrase the existing Background paragraph for use as the basis of their introduction and then add one piece of information from the Research activity to it. **MODERATE**
- Remind students that an introduction should be objective. Instruct students to exchange drafts with a partner and read the draft they receive for signs of bias. **LIGHT**

Connect to the ESSENTIAL QUESTION

Two young Jewish men do what they must to survive different yet equally desperate circumstances in World War II Poland. In an excerpt from *Night,* Elie Wiesel describes how he and fellow concentration camp prisoners psyched themselves up to pass the dreaded "selection," a process by which their German captors decided who would live and who, having become too weak to work, would be put to death. In the excerpt from *The Pianist,* Wladyslaw Szpilman chronicles his practical and methodical approach to staying alive and sane in the bombed-out city of Warsaw; there, German snipers, exposure to cold, and starvation were all very real threats to his survival. From these accounts, students may begin to draw some tentative conclusions about what it takes to survive in a crisis.

You may wish to guide students in pronouncing the authors' names:
Elie Wiesel: EL-ee vee-SEL
Wladyslaw Szpilman: VWAH-dee-swahv SHPEEL-mahn

COMPARE MEMOIRS

Discuss with students the characteristics that memoirs have in common. (*Examples include a first-person point of view and content that includes not only factual details about an event but also personal observations, opinions, and feelings about that event.*) Then point out that both of the upcoming selections have the same general topic—being persecuted by the Nazis during World War II. Ask students to suggest how memoirs arising from the same general experience might differ. (*The specifics of the experiences probably differ; in addition, the authors might have different feelings about what they experienced, both at the time and as they look back.*) Encourage students to consider such similarities and differences as they read and make notes about the texts.

COLLABORATE & COMPARE

MEMOIR

from NIGHT

by **Elie Wiesel**

pages 459–465

Drawings by former concentration camp inmates.

COMPARE MEMOIRS

As you read, notice similarities in the settings, characters, points of view, and author's purpose in two memoirs set during the same time period and country. Think about how each author's use of language contributes to the tone of each text. After you read both selections, you will collaborate with a small group on a final project.

ESSENTIAL QUESTION:

What does it take to survive in a crisis?

MEMOIR

from THE PIANIST

by **Władysław Szpilman**

pages 466–473

LEARNING MINDSET

Grit Explain to students that the part of our brain that we use to plan and set goals, maintain our commitment to those goals, and persevere in working to achieve them is like a muscle, which can be strengthened with use. In other words, everyone can develop more *grit,* or the ability to persist in working hard toward long-term goals and to ignore potential distractions. So even if they have procrastinated in the past, students should not label themselves "procrastinators" and give up on trying to achieve their goals. Instead, they should flex that mental muscle again and again until they develop enough grit to get jobs done. You might also have small groups share and discuss the strategies they use to ignore distractions and remain on task.

QUICK START

In school and through different texts and works of art, you have learned about World War II and the European front. What do you know about the plight of Jewish communities in Europe shortly before and during the war? Talk with a partner about your understanding of the Holocaust and other atrocities during that time.

ANALYZE MEMOIRS

A **memoir** is an autobiographical account of a person's experiences and observations of an event. As you read the following memoirs, use these questions to help you think about both authors' purposes for writing:

- What is the historical context for the memoir? About what significant events and people is the author sharing memories?
- What perspective do you understand from reading a first-person account?
- What makes the author a reliable authority on writing about these events?
- Who is the audience for the memoir?
- What do you learn about the impact on people of the historical events described?

GENRE ELEMENTS: MEMOIR

- records actual events based on the writer's observations
- reveals the writer's feelings
- provides historical context for the events described

ANALYZE WORD CHOICE

The **tone** of a work is the author's attitude toward the subject. A writer's tone may be described by a single word, such as formal, informal, serious, angry, or lighthearted. The **mood** of a work is the emotional atmosphere the writer creates. Writers shape tone and mood through word choice. Similar words can describe both tone and mood—for example, *fear*, *dread*, *amusement*—but mood relates to how the author's words affect the reader. Which words help create the tone or mood?

TONE OR MOOD	EXAMPLE FROM SELECTIONS
Tone: Fear and dread	**One more hour. Then we would know the verdict: death or reprieve.**
Tone: Despair	**He felt time was running out. He was speaking rapidly, he wanted to tell me so many things. His speech became confused, his voice was choked.**
Mood: Suspense	**There was no time to stop and think: my last hiding place in this building had been discovered, and I must leave it at once.**

As you read the excerpts from *Night* and from *The Pianist*, identify specific words that contribute to each text's tone and mood.

TEACH

QUICK START

Before partnering students for private discussions, draw a blank KWL chart for the class. Invite volunteers to help you fill in the chart in the "K" column, beginning with facts they already know about European Jewish communities before and during World War II. Then ask students to share what they "Want to Know" in the "W" column. Finally, after students have read the selections, revisit the chart. Record and discuss what students learned and add to the "What We Learned" column. Prompt students to also revisit the "Want to Know" column and add what else they want to learn about next.

ANALYZE MEMOIRS

Before students embark on analyzing the memoirs, review the four basic purposes for writing and the fact that a writer may write to accomplish more than one:

- To express thoughts or feelings
- To inform or explain
- To persuade
- To entertain

Also mention that Elie Wiesel made it one of his lifelong goals to bear witness to what had happened during the Holocaust so that the world would never forget. In his opinion, to forget the Holocaust would be to kill the victims again. Discuss which purpose for writing most closely corresponds to "bearing witness" *(to inform)*.

ANALYZE WORD CHOICE

Help students to distinguish **tone** from **mood** by guiding them in a class discussion to complete a three-column chart such as this one:

Tone	Both	Mood
The author's attitude toward the subject	May be described by words that express emotions	The emotional atmosphere of the story
May be created by author's comments and observations	Created by word choices	May be created by imagery and figurative language

For **speaking support** for students at varying proficiency levels, see the **Text X-Ray** on page 456D.

ENGLISH LEARNER SUPPORT

Talk and Write About Tone and Mood Explain that when talking or writing about tone and mood in English, people often refer to the *text's* tone or mood rather than the *author's* tone, although both are acceptable. Then give students these sentence frames for talking and writing about tone and mood in a text:

- *The tone of the text is ______. I inferred this from words such as ______.*
- *The mood of the text is ______. The author achieves this by using ______.*
- *The author [takes/uses] a(n) _____ tone when writing about [subject].*
- *The _____ mood of this text is created by images such as ______.*
- *The [part of text] creates a mood of _____ by ______.* **ALL LEVELS**

TEACH

CRITICAL VOCABULARY

Suggest that students try out the words in each sentence before committing to their answers. Remind them that context clues may hint at the meaning of the missing word.

Answers:

1. *din*
2. *isolation*
3. *emaciated*
4. *Conscientiously*
5. *naïve*
6. *reprieve*
7. *execute*
8. *decisive*
9. *deprecating*

English Learner Support

Use Cognates Tell students that several of the Critical Vocabulary words have a Spanish cognate: *execute/ejecutar, decisive/decisivo, conscientiously/concienzudamente.*

ALL LEVELS

LANGUAGE CONVENTIONS

After reviewing the information about dependent clauses, find the subject and verb in the dependent clause added to the first example *(we, did)*. Next, read the first example aloud, pausing between the end of the independent clause and the beginning of the dependent one and stressing the word *as*. Explain that it is the word *as* that makes the second clause unable to stand alone. Point out that without *as*, the second clause could stand alone as a second sentence: *We did every day.* Invite a volunteer to identify the word in the second example that makes the dependent clause unable to stand alone *(where)*.

ANNOTATION MODEL

Remind students that in Analyze Word Choice on page 457, they were told to keep track of word choices and the tone and mood these words help to create. Point out that this reader did that by underlining significant words and phrases and writing notes about them in the side margin. Urge students to use underlining or circling to mark words that strike them as significant as they read, and then, in the side column, record their thoughts about what they have marked.

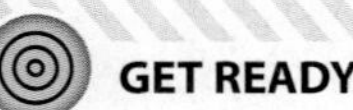

GET READY

CRITICAL VOCABULARY

reprieve	**emaciated**	**execute**	**decisive**	**din**
isolation	**conscientiously**	**deprecating**	**naïve**	

To preview the Critical Vocabulary words, use the words to complete the sentences.

1. I could not hear him over the __________ of the music.
2. The __________ of being home alone all day was starting to bother me.
3. After we found the __________ stray cat, we immediately gave it food.
4. __________ checking over the test for mistakes, I felt confident that I had aced it.
5. It is __________ to trust someone who keeps betraying you.
6. All day, I dreaded the teacher's punishment, but I received a(n) ________ .
7. Which steps do I need to follow to __________ the task properly?
8. The boxing match lasted a long time, but one boxer finally landed a(n) __________ blow that ended it.
9. My __________ tone as I criticized his work discouraged him.

LANGUAGE CONVENTIONS

A **dependent clause** has a subject and verb, but can not stand alone as a sentence. Read the following sentences from the texts. How do the dependent clauses add meaning to these sentences from the selection?

> **We had risen at dawn, as we did every day.**
>
> **I was wandering among the walls of totally burnt-out buildings where there could not possibly be any water or remnants of food, or even a hiding place.**

As you read the texts, notice how the authors use dependent clauses to express meaning and add interest.

ANNOTATION MODEL

NOTICE & NOTE 

In the model, see one student's notes about the first part of *Night*.

The SS offered us a beautiful present for the new year. We had just returned from work. As soon as we passed the camp's entrance, we sensed something out of the ordinary in the air. The roll call was shorter than usual. The evening soup was distributed at great speed, swallowed as quickly. We were anxious.	Wiesel is using the word "beautiful" ironically; he is describing the SS using a sarcastic tone. The prisoners sense that something is different and they are "anxious" about it.

ENGLISH LEARNER SUPPORT

Produce Sounds of Newly Acquired Vocabulary Students may find it difficult to pronounce English words with silent letters and consonant clusters. To help them with their pronunciation, remind them of the following:

- In *reprieve, execute, decisive,* and *naïve,* the final *e* is silent.
- The word parts *-tion, -ciated, -scien,* and *-tious* all begin with the *sh* sound as in *shoe*.

Then have pairs of students practice pronouncing the following Critical Vocabulary words aloud to one another, correcting their partner's pronunciation as needed: *reprieve, isolation, emaciated, conscientiously, execute, decisive,* and *naïve.*

SUBSTANTIAL/MODERATE

NOTICE & NOTE

BACKGROUND

Elie Wiesel *(1928–2016) was a teacher, writer, and Nobel Peace Prize winner. Born in Romania, Wiesel and his family were among millions of European Jews deported to concentration camps during the Holocaust. In 1944, the Nazis sent the family to Auschwitz, where Wiesel's mother and sister perished. Months later, when Wiesel and his father were moved to Buchenwald concentration camp, his father also died. Buchenwald was eventually liberated, and Wiesel went on to write about his experience. His many works include* Dawn *and* The Accident, *both sequels to* Night.

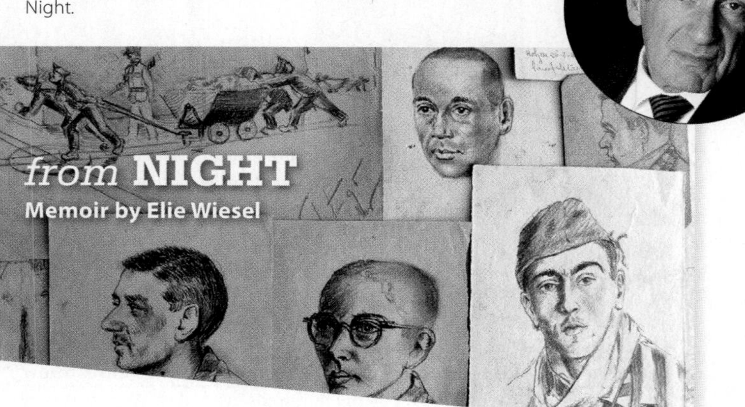

from NIGHT

Memoir by Elie Wiesel

PREPARE TO COMPARE

As you read, make note of Wiesel's point of view and possible purpose for writing this memoir. Notice details that help you understand the setting, characters, and events in this excerpt from Night. *Additionally, pay attention to how Wiesel uses word choice to achieve a certain tone.*

Notice & Note

You can use the side margins to notice and note signposts in the text.

1 The SS[1] offered us a beautiful present for the new year. We had just returned from work. As soon as we passed the camp's entrance, we sensed something out of the ordinary in the air. The roll call was shorter than usual. The evening soup was distributed at great speed, swallowed as quickly. We were anxious.

2 I was no longer in the same block as my father. They had transferred me to another Kommando,[2] the construction one, where twelve hours a day I hauled heavy slabs of stone. The head of my new block was a German Jew, small with piercing eyes. That evening he announced to us that henceforth no one was allowed to leave the block after the evening soup. A terrible word began to circulate soon thereafter: selection.

[1] **SS:** abbreviation of *Schutzstaffel*, German for "defense force"; an armed unit of the Nazi Party that controlled concentration camps.

[2] **Kommando** (kə-măn′dō): German for "command," a small-group organization for laborers in the camps.

TEACH

BACKGROUND

At the end of this Collaborate & Compare lesson, students will be asked to expand the Background note that precedes the excerpt from either *Night* or *The Pianist*. If you wish to ready students for this later activity, direct them to mark facts in each Background note and ask at least one question about each fact—for example:

- (1928–2016): How and where did Wiesel die?
- Teacher: What did Wiesel teach?
- Nobel Peace Prize winner: When was he awarded that prize, and for what reason?
- Born in Romania: Where in Romania was he born? Does the town still exist? Did he ever go back?
- Among millions of European Jews deported to concentration camps: Why were the Jews deported? Did they resist going? Who deported them?

Before students begin reading the selection, tell them that Wiesel was 15 years old when he and his family were deported to the Auschwitz concentration camp. At 15, he was just old enough to be kept alive as a worker; one had to be at least 14 years of age and fit enough to work in order to be spared from the gas chamber. Young children and people who were perceived to be too old, weak, or infirm to work were often condemned to death upon their arrival.

PREPARE TO COMPARE

Direct students to use the Prepare to Compare prompt to focus their reading.

ENGLISH LEARNER SUPPORT

Preteach Vocabulary Many of the words Wiesel uses to describe the setting of the prison camp are military terms; as such, English learners may not have encountered them in everyday conversation. Preview these words and their definitions, encouraging students to visualize what each term describes as you share its definition:

- *block* (paragraph 2): a group of barracks or buildings for sleeping
- *inmates* (paragraph 3): prisoners
- *veterans* (paragraph 4): former soldiers or those made wise by longtime experience
- *ration* (paragraph 43): a fixed or limited amount of food a person is allowed to have
- *form ranks* (paragraph 54): stand in orderly lines

ALL LEVELS

TEACH

WORDS OF THE WISER

Remind students that this signpost often shows one or more experienced characters giving advice to someone who does not yet understand a situation. This signpost often points to the **theme, the internal conflict,** and the relationship between the main character and events in a narrative (which may be either fiction or nonfiction).

Prepare students to better understand why the veterans' tales upset Wiesel by seeking clarification about what is implied by "good for the crematorium" in paragraph 3. *(Since crematoriums are places in which dead bodies are burned in large ovens, this statement means "sentenced to die.")* (**Answer**: *By having the veterans voice what went on in the camp before Wiesel arrived, the author helps readers understand the monstrous crimes that took place in concentration camps. Wiesel's reaction, which is to beg the veterans to be quiet, shows that he is terrified of what they are saying and is desperate to make them stop before his fear overwhelms him. His reaction contributes to a tone of shocked horror.)*

NOTICE & NOTE

WORDS OF THE WISER

Notice & Note: Underline what the author learns from the veteran inmates.

Respond: How does Wiesel use the words of the inmates to provide context for the reader? How does his reaction to the advice contribute to the tone of the text?

reprieve
(rĭ-prēv´) *n.* the cancellation or postponement of punishment.

3 We knew what it meant. An SS would examine us. Whenever he found someone extremely frail—a "Muselman" was what we called those inmates—he would write down his number: good for the crematorium.

4 After the soup, we gathered between the bunks. The veterans told us: "You're lucky to have been brought here so late. Today, this is paradise compared to what the camp was two years ago. Back then, Buna[3] was a veritable hell. No water, no blankets, less soup and bread. At night, we slept almost naked and the temperature was thirty below. We were collecting corpses by the hundreds every day. Work was very hard. Today, this is a little paradise. The Kapos[4] back then had orders to kill a certain number of prisoners every day. And every week, selection. A merciless selection . . . Yes, you are lucky."

5 "Enough! Be quiet!" I begged them. "Tell your stories tomorrow, or some other day."

6 They burst out laughing. They were not veterans for nothing.

7 "Are you scared? We too were scared. And, at that time, for good reason."

8 The old men stayed in their corner, silent, motionless, hunted-down creatures. Some were praying.

9 One more hour. Then we would know the verdict: death or **reprieve**.

10 And my father? I first thought of him now. How would he pass selection? He had aged so much. . . .

11 Our *Blockälteste*[5] had not been outside a concentration camp since 1933. He had already been through all the slaughterhouses, all the factories of death. Around nine o'clock, he came to stand in our midst:

12 "*Achtung!*"[6] **Close Read**

[3] **Buna** (bo͝o´nə): a section of the concentration camp at Auschwitz.
[4] **Kapos** (kä´pōs): prisoners who performed certain duties for the guards.
[5] **Blockälteste** (blŏk ĕl´təs-tə): a rank of Kapos; a prisoner designated by the Nazis to be the leader or representative of a block, or group of barracks.
[6] **Achtung!** (äk´to͝ong): German command for "Attention!"

CRITICAL VOCABULARY

reprieve: In just an hour, the men would be assessed to see who would be judged as only "good for the crematorium" and who would receive a postponement of that fate.

ASK STUDENTS why they think Wiesel used the word *reprieve* here instead of a word like *salvation*. *(A reprieve is a temporary cancellation; salvation is permanent. Wiesel implies that another selection will take place eventually and that someday a reprieve will not be available.)*

CLOSE READ SCREENCAST

Modeled Discussion In their eBook, have students view the Close Read Screencast, in which readers discuss and annotate paragraphs 11–16.

As a class, view and discuss the video. Then have students pair up to do an independent close read of paragraphs 27–29. Students can record their answers on the Close Read Practice PDF.

Close Read Practice PDF

13 There was instant silence.

14 "Listen carefully to what I am about to tell you." For the first time, his voice quivered. "In a few moments, selection will take place. You will have to undress completely. Then you will go, one by one, before the SS doctors. I hope you will all pass. But you must try to increase your chances. Before you go into the next room, try to move your limbs, give yourself some color. Don't walk slowly, run! Run as if you had the devil at your heels! Don't look at the SS. Run, straight in front of you!"

15 He paused and then added:

16 "And most important, don't be afraid!"

17 That was a piece of advice we would have loved to be able to follow.

18 I undressed, leaving my clothes on my cot. Tonight, there was no danger that they would be stolen.

19 Tibi and Yossi, who had changed Kommandos at the same time I did, came to urge me:

20 "Let's stay together. It will make us stronger."

21 Yossi was mumbling something. He probably was praying. I had never suspected that Yossi was religious. In fact, I had always believed the opposite. Tibi was silent and very pale. All the block inmates stood naked between the rows of bunks. This must be how one stands for the Last Judgment.

22 "They are coming!"

23 Three SS officers surrounded the notorious Dr. Mengele,[7] the very same who had received us in Birkenau. The *Blockälteste* attempted a smile. He asked us:

24 "Ready?"

[7] **Dr. Mengele** (mĕn-gə´lə): Josef Mengele (1911–1979), Nazi physician at Auschwitz known for conducting cruel experiments on prisoners.

APPLYING ACADEMIC VOCABULARY

☑ **dimension** ☐ **external** ☐ **statistic** ☑ **sustain** ☐ **utilize**

Write and Discuss Have students turn to a partner to discuss the following questions. Guide students to include the academic vocabulary words *dimension* and *sustain* in their responses. Ask volunteers to share their responses with the class.

- What might you do or learn about to better understand the **dimension** of the Holocaust?
- How do you think the prisoners were able to **sustain** themselves—not only physically, but also mentally and emotionally?

TEACH

ANALYZE MEMOIRS

Get students thinking about the kinds of details they should look for by reminding them of the ways that the older Wiesel could characterize his younger self:

- making direct comments about himself from the perspective of his older, narrator-author self
- describing his physical appearance
- presenting thoughts, speech, and actions of his that are indicative of his character
- presenting the thoughts, speech, and actions of others that show how they regard him

(***Answer:*** *At the time of the selection, Wiesel was relieved and happy. The passage of time, however, has allowed him to recognize that his joy was at the cost of the prisoners who had been selected and perhaps that he now regards his younger self as lacking in compassion.)*

For **listening support** for students at varying proficiency levels, see the **Text X-Ray** on page 456C.

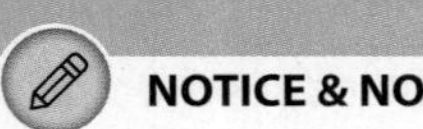

NOTICE & NOTE

25 Yes, we were ready. So were the SS doctors. Dr. Mengele was holding a list: our numbers. He nodded to the *Blockälteste*: we can begin! As if this were a game.

26 The first to go were the "notables" of the block, the *Stubenälteste*,[8] the Kapos, the foremen, all of whom were in perfect physical condition, of course! Then came the ordinary prisoners' turns. Dr. Mengele looked them over from head to toe. From time to time, he noted a number. I had but one thought: not to have my number taken down and not to show my left arm.

27 In front of me, there were only Tibi and Yossi. They passed. I had time to notice that Mengele had not written down their numbers. Someone pushed me. It was my turn. I ran without looking back. My head was spinning: you are too skinny . . . you are too weak . . . you are too skinny, you are good for the ovens . . . The race seemed endless; I felt as though I had been running for years . . . You are too skinny, you are too weak . . . At last I arrived. Exhausted. When I had caught my breath, I asked Yossi and Tibi:

28 "Did they write me down?"

29 "No," said Yossi. Smiling, he added, "Anyway, they couldn't have. You were running too fast . . ."

ANALYZE MEMOIRS

Annotate: Mark details that help you better understand Wiesel's character at the time of the events.

Evaluate: How has the passage of time given Wiesel insight into what he experienced at the end of the "selection"?

30 I began to laugh. I was happy. I felt like kissing him. At that moment, the others did not matter! They had not written me down.

31 Those whose numbers had been noted were standing apart, abandoned by the whole world. Some were silently weeping.

32 THE SS OFFICERS left. The *Blockälteste* appeared, his face reflecting our collective weariness.

33 "It all went well. Don't worry. Nothing will happen to anyone. Not to anyone . . ."

emaciated
(ĭ-mā´shē-āt id) *adj.* made extremely thin and weak.

34 He was still trying to smile. A poor **emaciated** Jew questioned him anxiously, his voice trembling:

35 "But . . . sir. They *did* write me down!"

36 At that, the *Blockälteste* vented his anger: What! Someone refused to take his word?

37 "What is it now? Perhaps you think I'm lying? I'm telling you, once and for all: nothing will happen to you! Nothing! You just like to wallow in your despair, you fools!"

38 The bell rang, signaling that the selection had ended in the entire camp.

39 With all my strength I began to race toward Block 36; midway, I met my father. He came toward me:

40 "So? Did you pass?"

41 "Yes. And you?"

42 "Also."

43 We were able to breathe again. My father had a present for me: a half ration of bread, bartered for something he had found at the depot, a piece of rubber that could be used to repair a shoe.

[8] **Stubenälteste** (shtyōō´bə-nĭl-tŭs -tə): a rank of Kapos; prisoners designated by the Nazis to be the leaders of their barracks, or rooms.

CRITICAL VOCABULARY

emaciated: A thin and weak prisoner is concerned about the fact that the SS doctors wrote down his number.

ASK STUDENTS why becoming emaciated was dangerous for the prisoners. *(If they were too thin and weak to work, they would likely be killed.)*

IMPROVE READING FLUENCY

Targeted Passage Tell students that when they read a text aloud, they should watch for helpful print cues. Point out that punctuation, such as commas and periods, tell them when to pause and when to stop. Question marks and exclamation points also tell them when to vary their intonation. Model reading paragraphs 38–44 aloud. Then assign pairs to read paragraphs 45–48 aloud to one another by alternating paragraphs. Invite students to share their reactions to these passages.

Go to the **Reading Studio** for additional support in developing fluency.

NOTICE & NOTE 

44 The bell. It was already time to part, to go to bed. The bell regulated everything. It gave me orders and I **executed** them blindly. I hated that bell. Whenever I happened to dream of a better world, I imagined a universe without a bell.

45 A FEW DAYS passed. We were no longer thinking about the selection. We went to work as usual and loaded the heavy stones onto the freight cars. The rations had grown smaller; that was the only change.

46 We had risen at dawn, as we did every day. We had received our black coffee, our ration of bread. We were about to head to the work yard as always. The *Blockälteste* came running:

47 "Let's have a moment of quiet. I have here a list of numbers. I shall read them to you. All those called will not go to work this morning; they will stay in camp."

48 Softly, he read some ten numbers. We understood. These were the numbers from the selection. Dr. Mengele had not forgotten.

49 The *Blockälteste* turned to go to his room. The ten prisoners surrounded him, clinging to his clothes:

50 "Save us! You promised . . . We want to go to the depot, we are strong enough to work. We are good workers. We can . . . we want . . ."

51 He tried to calm them, to reassure them about their fate, to explain to them that staying in the camp did not mean much, had no tragic significance: "After all, I stay here every day . . ."

52 The argument was more than flimsy. He realized it and, without another word, locked himself in his room.

53 The bell had just rung.

54 "Form ranks!"

55 Now, it no longer mattered that the work was hard. All that mattered was to be far from the block, far from the crucible[9] of death, from the center of hell.

56 I saw my father running in my direction. Suddenly, I was afraid.

57 "What is happening?"

58 He was out of breath, hardly able to open his mouth.

[9] **crucible:** a vessel used for melting materials at high temperatures.

execute
(ĕk´sĭ-kyo͞ot) *v.* to carry out, or accomplish.

LANGUAGE CONVENTIONS

Annotate: Underline the dependent clause in paragraph 44.

Analyze: How does this complex sentence contribute to the tone of the paragraph?

LANGUAGE CONVENTIONS

Remind students that a **dependent clause** has a subject and a verb but cannot stand alone as a complete sentence. As students read the Analyze question, review the fact that **tone** is the author's attitude toward the subject. Ask them to identify the subject of paragraph 44 *(the bell)* and then have them identify Wiesel's attitude toward it *(resentment toward it for being a hateful, relentless taskmaster)*. (***Answer:*** *This complex sentence intensifies Wiesel's tone of resentment. He hates the bell so much that he refuses to let it into his dreams.)*

ENGLISH LEARNER SUPPORT

Analyze a Symbol Have students reread Wiesel's comments about the bell in paragraph 44. Explain that whenever a character's reaction to something seems excessive, that thing probably has come to represent something more than itself; that is, it may be a **symbol**. Ask: "Could this bell be a symbol? What might it represent?" *(As a constant reminder to Wiesel that his life is not his own to direct, it might represent the Nazis. It also might represent inhumane, unsympathetic treatment since it limits his personal interactions and directs his daily activities.)*
LIGHT

CRITICAL VOCABULARY

execute: A bell signals when it is time for the prisoners to carry out the next task or activity of the day.

ASK STUDENTS what the word *execute* tells them about life in the camp. *(Every moment of the prisoners' lives is about obeying, or executing, orders.)*

ANALYZE WORD CHOICE

Remind students that word choices help to convey the author's attitude toward his subject and to create a mood. Ask students what is happening in this part of the memoir and what mood they think that situation would create. *(Wiesel learns that his father's name was written down during the selection. As they meet now, both he and his father realize that they may never see each other again. The mood in such a situation probably would be sad, confused, and frightened, even panicked.)*

Then discuss the meaning of *inheritance*: "the material possessions or wealth passed from one generation to the next." Ask students what receiving an inheritance implies. *(Life will go on; because of your parents, you will now have more than you did.)* (***Answer:*** *The word inheritance contributes to the poignant and somewhat bitter or ironic tone of the passage because it is a word that a son would usually use to describe wealth, property, and possessions—not a mere knife and spoon—and so underscores the bleakness of their existence. An inheritance also suggests that life and the family line will continue, but death appears to be inevitable and imminent for both father and son.)*

CRITICAL VOCABULARY

decisive: The first selection wasn't conclusive because a second one is going to take place.

ASK STUDENTS why the fact that a second, more decisive selection is being done stirs both hope and dread in Wiesel and his father. *(The prospect of there being a second, more decisive selection means that the first one, which had doomed Wiesel's father to death, might not be permanent after all. However, it also means that whether he continues to live will be determined that day, so this may be their last meeting.)*

din: The military music sounds like loud noise to the young Wiesel.

ASK STUDENTS why they suppose military music, which is usually precise and harmonious, sounds to Wiesel like a din. *(The music announces his imminent departure and blots out the words his father may have tried to call to him.)*

NOTICE & NOTE

59 "Me too, me too . . . They told me too to stay in the camp."

60 They had recorded his number without his noticing.

61 "What are we going to do?" I said anxiously.

62 But it was he who tried to reassure me:

63 "It's not certain yet. There's still a chance. Today, they will do another selection . . . a **decisive** one . . ."

decisive
(dĭ-sī′sĭv) *adj.* final or concluding.

64 I said nothing.

65 He felt time was running out. He was speaking rapidly, he wanted to tell me so many things. His speech became confused, his voice was choked. He knew that I had to leave in a few moments. He was going to remain alone, so alone . . .

66 "Here, take this knife," he said. "I won't need it anymore. You may find it useful. Also take this spoon. Don't sell it. Quickly! Go ahead, take what I'm giving you!"

ANALYZE WORD CHOICE
Annotate: Mark words in this section that contribute to the tone of the text.
Analyze: How does the word *inheritance* communicate the author's tone?

67 My inheritance . . .

68 "Don't talk like that, Father." I was on the verge of breaking into sobs. "I don't want you to say such things. Keep the spoon and knife. You will need them as much as I. We'll see each other tonight, after work."

69 He looked at me with his tired eyes, veiled by despair. He insisted:

70 "I am asking you . . . Take it, do as I ask you, my son. Time is running out. Do as your father asks you . . ."

71 Our Kapo shouted the order to march.

The Kommando headed toward the camp gate. Left, right!

72 I was biting my lips. My father had remained near the block, leaning against the wall. Then he began to run, to try to catch up with us. Perhaps he had forgotten to tell me something . . . But we were marching too fast . . . Left, right!

73 We were at the gate. We were being counted. Around us, the **din** of military music. Then we were outside.

din
(dĭn) *n.* loud noise.

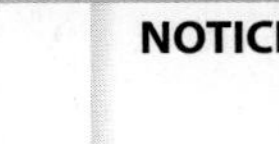

NOTICE & NOTE

74 ALL DAY, I PLODDED AROUND like a sleepwalker. Tibi and Yossi would call out to me, from time to time, trying to reassure me. As did the Kapo who had given me easier tasks that day. I felt sick at heart. How kindly they treated me. Like an orphan. I thought: Even now, my father is helping me.

75 I myself didn't know whether I wanted the day to go by quickly or not. I was afraid of finding myself alone that evening. How good it would be to die right here!

76 At last, we began the return journey. How I longed for an order to run! The military march. The gate. The camp. I ran toward Block 36.

77 Were there still miracles on this earth? He was alive. He had passed the second selection. He had still proved his usefulness . . . I gave him back his knife and spoon.

CHECK YOUR UNDERSTANDING

Choose the best answer to each question.

1 The guards separate the inmates by —

- **A** age
- **B** occupation
- **C** physical condition
- **D** observance of authority

2 After the first selection, why doesn't the author mind his work assignment?

- **F** It is easier than what he had been doing.
- **G** It gives him a chance to be with his father.
- **H** It keeps his mind occupied.
- **J** It means he has been spared.

3 What does Wiesel's father give him?

- **A** Coins
- **B** Letters
- **C** His watch and comb
- **D** A spoon and knife

TEACH

CHECK YOUR UNDERSTANDING

Have students answer the questions independently.

Answers:

1. *C*
2. *J*
3. *D*

If they answer any questions incorrectly, have them reread the text to confirm their understanding. Then, after reading the excerpt from *The Pianist*, they may proceed to ANALYZE THE TEXT on page 474.

ENGLISH LEARNER SUPPORT

Oral Assessment Use the following questions to assess students' comprehension and speaking skills. Ask students to respond in short, complete sentences.

1. How do the guards separate the inmates? *(They separate the inmates by their physical condition.)*
2. After the first selection, the author is given a work assignment. Why doesn't he mind the work? *(The fact that he has been given work means he is not going to be killed.)*
3. What does Wiesel's father give him? *(His father gives him a spoon and a knife).*
ALL LEVELS

Night 465

TEACH

BACKGROUND

To help students envision the selection's setting, consider playing for them the official trailer for the movie *The Pianist,* mentioned in the Background note.

Then, before students begin reading the text, familiarize them with the geography of Warsaw so that they can better envision Szpilman's orientation to the Vistula River mentioned in the excerpt and the location of the ongoing fighting. Also make sure that students understand that a *ghetto* is a part of a city in which most of the people have the same background and live with discrimination and poverty. Some cities develop ghettos on their own; the ghetto in this memoir was established by the Nazis, as they did in many cities that they captured.

PREPARE TO COMPARE

Direct students to use the Prepare to Compare prompt to focus their reading.

ANALYZE MEMOIRS

Discuss the impact of the opening three words: "I was alone," pointing out that even that simple statement suggests a bleak setting. Note that the contrasts between what the city once was and what it now is dramatically underscore the mood of the text. Then invite volunteers to share the details they underlined. ***(Answer:*** *The repetition of the word* alone *and the details of the city's ruin create a mood of isolation and despair. The sensory detail of* dreadful stench *also lends to a sense of horror.)*

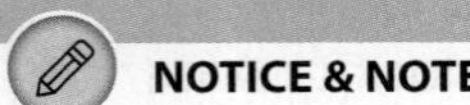

NOTICE & NOTE

BACKGROUND

Władysław Szpilman *(1911–2000) was a Polish musician and composer who lived through the atrocities of the Holocaust. Before the war, Szpilman had been a professional pianist who performed on Polish radio and in front of large crowds. Since he was of Jewish descent, he was confined to a ghetto in Warsaw after Germany invaded Poland in 1939. Szpilman's family was taken away to the death camps; afterward, the Nazis assigned him to work groups in Warsaw. After a rebel uprising, Szpilman managed to hide in a series of abandoned buildings, constantly searching for food and water while evading Nazi patrols. After the war, Szpilman lived a long life, during which he published his memoir,* The Pianist, *which was turned into an award-winning film in 2002.*

from

THE PIANIST

Memoir by Władysław Szpilman

Notice & Note

You can use the side margins to notice and note signposts in the text.

ANALYZE MEMOIRS

Annotate: Mark details Szpilman uses to establish setting.

Analyze: How does Szpilman's description of the setting contribute to the mood of the text?

PREPARE TO COMPARE

As you read, make note of how Szpilman establishes setting and character. Notice how his descriptions compare to those of Wiesel. Also pay attention to how Szpilman's word choices reveal his attitudes about the events he experiences.

1 I was alone: alone not just in a single building or even a single part of a city, but alone in a whole city that only two months ago had a population of a million and a half and was one of the richer cities of Europe. It now consisted of the chimneys of burnt-out buildings pointing to the sky, and whatever walls the bombing had spared: a city of rubble and ashes under which the centuries-old culture of my people and the bodies of hundreds of thousands of murdered victims lay buried, rotting in the warmth of these late autumn days and filling the air with a dreadful stench. . .

ENGLISH LEARNER SUPPORT

Understand Language Structures Write a colon on the board and explain that writers use colons to signal that a long quotation, list, example(s), explanation, or elaboration follows. Also, the text following the colon often clarifies the statement that precedes the colon. Ask students to locate the colon in the first sentence of paragraph 1 and identify its purpose. *(It introduces an elaboration on what the author means by "I was alone.")* **SUBSTANTIAL/MODERATE**

2 The first day of November was approaching, and it was beginning to get cold, particularly at night. To keep myself from going mad in my **isolation**, I decided to lead as disciplined a life as possible. I still had my watch, the pre-war Omega I treasured as the apple of my eye, along with my fountain pen. They were my sole personal possessions. I **conscientiously** kept the watch wound and drew up a timetable by it. I lay motionless all day long to conserve what little strength I had left, putting out my hand only once, around midday, to fortify myself with a rusk[1] and a mug of water sparingly portioned out. From early in the morning until I took this meal, as I lay there with my eyes closed, I went over in my mind all the compositions I had ever played, bar by bar. Later, this mental refresher course turned out to have been useful: when I went back to work I still knew my repertory and had almost all of it in my head, as if I had been practising all through the war. Then, from my midday meal until dusk, I systematically ran through the contents of all the books I had read, mentally repeating my English vocabulary. I gave myself English lessons, asking myself questions and trying to answer them correctly and at length.

3 When darkness came I fell asleep. I would wake around one in the morning and go in search of food by the light of matches—I had found a supply of them in the building, in a flat that had not been entirely burnt out. I looked in cellars and the charred[2] ruins of the flats, finding a little oatmeal here, a few pieces of bread there, some dank[3] flour, water in tubs, buckets and jugs. I don't know how many times I passed the charred body on the stairs during these expeditions. He was the sole companion whose presence I need not fear. Once I found an unexpected treasure in a cellar: half a litre of spirits.[4] I decided to save it until the end of the war came. . .

4 What tormented me most was not knowing what was happening in the battle areas, both on the front and among the rebels. The Warsaw rebellion itself had been put down. I could cherish no illusions about that. But perhaps there was still resistance outside the city, in Praga on the other side of the Vistula. I could still hear artillery fire over there now and then, and shells would explode in the ruins, often quite near me, echoing harshly in the silence amidst the burnt-out buildings. What about resistance in the rest of Poland? Where were the Soviet troops? What progress was the Allied offensive making in the west? My life or death depended on the answer to these questions, and even if the Germans did not discover my hiding place it was soon going be my death—of cold if not starvation. . .

[1] **rusk:** sweet biscuit or bread.
[2] **charred:** burned.
[3] **dank:** damp in an unpleasant way.
[4] **spirits:** alcoholic beverages.

NOTICE & NOTE

isolation
(ī-sə-lā´shən) *n.* the condition of being alone or apart from others.

conscientiously
(kŏn-shē-ĕn´shəs-ly) *adj.* doing something thoroughly.

ANALYZE WORD CHOICE

Annotate: Mark the author's description of the body on the stairs.

Interpret: How does the word *companion* contribute to the tone of the text?

WHEN STUDENTS STRUGGLE . . .

Clarify Historical Setting Be sure students understand the geography of Warsaw and the events that affect the story. Share the following information (possibly in conjunction with the Background note on Student Edition page 466) about the Warsaw Uprising that Szpilman calls the "Warsaw rebellion": On August 1, 1944, hopeful of soon being joined by Soviet troops (which were located on the east bank of the Vistula River) in a fight to liberate their city, Poland's home army and Polish resistance fighters started a rebellion to liberate Warsaw from the Nazis. They fought for nine weeks but were ultimately defeated and left with a decimated city.

ANALYZE WORD CHOICE

Remind students that **tone** is an author's attitude toward his or her subject. Establish that the subject of this text is the author's daily life and circumstances as well as the war itself. Then ask students to discuss the tone of the text thus far. *(practical, matter-of-fact, realistic, resolute)* Point out that this tone contrasts with the chaos of the ruins around him. (***Answer:*** *The way that Szpilman uses the word* companion *to refer to the charred body suggests that his attitude is rather matter-of-fact—that he has mentally adapted to his new circumstances. The tone is also ironic, for a dead person cannot truly be a companion, but it is the only human connection that Spzilman need not be afraid of in that setting.)*

CRITICAL VOCABULARY

isolation: He is so alone that he wonders whether he will go crazy.

ASK STUDENTS to describe what Szpilman does each day to keep his sanity in his isolation. *(He leads a disciplined life by following a daily routine. He also reviews the music he knows and books he's read, and he gives himself English lessons.)*

conscientiously: The author notes that he reliably and carefully keeps his watch wound.

ASK STUDENTS why they think he so conscientiously winds his watch. *(It is a part of his daily routine; in particular, he needs an accurate timepiece to keep him on the schedule he has established for himself. Also, he treasures the watch and wants to take care of it.)*

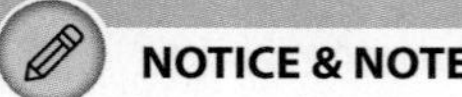

NOTICE & NOTE

5 Today the SS were driving a group of men in civilian clothing to work on the hospital. It was nearly ten in the morning, and I was lying flat on the steep roof when I suddenly heard a volley of firing quite close to me, from a rifle or machine pistol: it was a sound between whistling and twittering, as if a flock of sparrows were flying overhead, and shots fell around me. I looked round: two Germans were standing on the hospital roof opposite, firing at me. I slid back down into the attic and ran to the trapdoor, ducking. Shouts of, 'Stop, stop!' pursued me as bullets flew overhead. However, I landed in the stairway safely.

6 There was no time to stop and think: my last hiding place in this building had been discovered, and I must leave it at once. I raced down the stairs and out into Sędziowska Street, ran along the road and plunged into the ruins of the bungalows that had once been the Staszic estate.[5]

[5] **the ruins of the bungalows that had once been the Staszic estate:** referring to the housing complex owned by the family of Stanislaw Staszic, a prominent Polish scholar from the 19th century. Staszic was in favor of forcible assimilation of Jews into Polish society.

ENGLISH LEARNER SUPPORT

Analyze Writer's Craft Point out Szpilman's use of colons in paragraphs 5 and 6. Begin by having students read the relevant sentences aloud. Then ask:

- In paragraph 5, what information is provided by the part of the sentence after the first colon? *(It is primarily a description of what the gunshots sounded like.)*
- In paragraph 6, what information is provided by the part of the sentence after the colon? *(It is a brief explanation of why Szpilman had no time to stop and think.)*

Point out that in both cases, the colon is used to introduce information that elaborates on the information preceding the colon. Invite partners to create and share a sentence related to this memoir in which a colon introduces some kind of elaboration. **MODERATE/LIGHT**

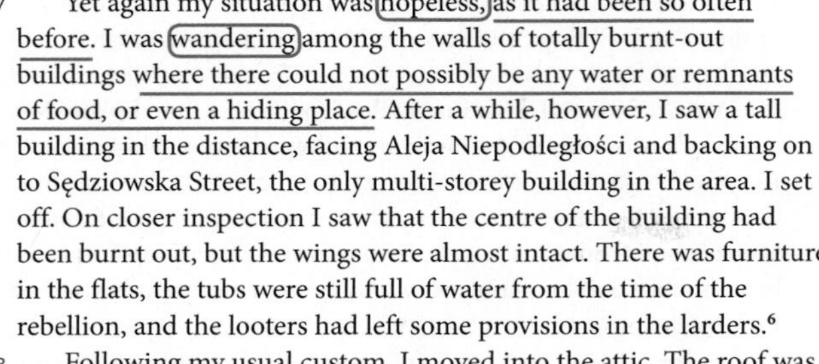

7 Yet again my situation was hopeless, as it had been so often before. I was wandering among the walls of totally burnt-out buildings where there could not possibly be any water or remnants of food, or even a hiding place. After a while, however, I saw a tall building in the distance, facing Aleja Niepodległości and backing on to Sędziowska Street, the only multi-storey building in the area. I set off. On closer inspection I saw that the centre of the building had been burnt out, but the wings were almost intact. There was furniture in the flats, the tubs were still full of water from the time of the rebellion, and the looters had left some provisions in the larders.[6]

8 Following my usual custom, I moved into the attic. The roof was quite intact, with just a few holes left in it by splinters of shrapnel. It was much warmer here than in my previous hiding place, although flight from it would be impossible. I could not even escape into death by jumping off the roof. There was a small stained-glass window on the last mezzanine floor of the building, and I could observe the neighbourhood through it. Comfortable as my new surroundings

[6] **larders:** places where food is stored.

NOTICE & NOTE

LANGUAGE CONVENTIONS

Annotate: Underline the dependent clauses in the first two sentences of paragraph 7.

Analyze: How do these clauses contribute to Szpilman's message?

ANALYZE WORD CHOICE

Annotate: Mark words in paragraphs 7 and 8 that reveal Szpilman's thoughts and feelings.

Analyze: What do these words tell you about Szpilman's thoughts and feelings at this moment?

LANGUAGE CONVENTIONS

Remind students that dependent clauses usually act as modifiers and quite often begin with one of the following words: *as if, as, since, than, that, though, until, whenever, where, while, who,* or *why.* These words link the dependent clause to its independent clause and indicate the relationship between the clauses. (***Answer:*** *His life was full of empty, lonely repetition, and he was running out of options.)*

English Learner Support

Double Conjunctions In complex sentences in Cantonese, Korean, and Vietnamese, a coordinating conjunction may be placed before the independent (main) clause. This additional conjunction is looked upon as a "balancing word." Consequently, students whose primary language is one of these three may have difficulty understanding why there is no conjunction preceding an independent clause in some of the complex sentences they see in this text. (It may not be an issue in sentences in which the independent clause comes first, but it may cause confusion when the dependent clause comes first.) Be sure to explain that English does not use "balancing words" as some other languages do. **ALL LEVELS**

ANALYZE WORD CHOICE

Remind students that an author's word choices can affect both the **tone** and **mood** of the writing. Point out that the word choices in paragraphs 7 and 8 reinforce the author's attitude toward his situation (his tone) as matter-of-fact and realistic in the face of the bleakest circumstances. However, most readers will react emotionally to the story and find that the mood created includes repressed horror and desperation. (***Answer:*** *Words such as* hopeless *and* wandering *show that the author has no plan or belief in any positive changes. The phrase* escape into death *makes it clear that the author is desperate enough to possibly welcome his own death.)*

CONTRASTS AND CONTRADICTIONS

Review what students have noticed about the **mood** and **tone** of this selection. *(The mood is one of isolation and despair; the tone is matter-of-fact—a disciplined approach to devastating circumstances.)* Remind students that Szpilman, before this war, was a concert pianist and must have played music beautifully on impeccable instruments. Then direct them to talk about what is conveyed in paragraph 21 and what Szpilman is contrasting. *(The contrast here is between the eerily distorted piano music and the silence dotted with feral imagery of a cat's meow and the sound of a gunshot. However, it is also, by implication, between the world as it was and as it is now.)* *(**Answer:** The contrast further establishes the fact that the world in this new set of circumstances is distorted and gloomy; even music is unsatisfying and unable to lift the gloom of the flat.)*

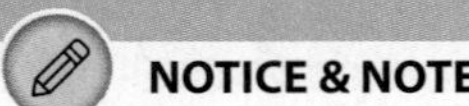

NOTICE & NOTE

were, I did not feel at ease here—perhaps just because I was now used to the other building. All the same, I had no choice: I must stay here. . .

9 After two days, I went in search of food. This time I planned to lay in a good supply so that I did not have to leave my hiding place too often. I would have to search by day, since I did not know this building well enough to find my way around it by night. I found a kitchen, and then a larder containing several cans of food and some bags and boxes. Their contents would have to be carefully checked. I untied strings and lifted lids. I was so absorbed in my search that I never heard anything until a voice right behind me said, 'What on earth are you doing here?'

10 A tall, elegant German officer was leaning against the kitchen dresser, his arms crossed over his chest.

11 'What are you doing here?' he repeated. 'Don't you know the staff of the Warsaw fortress commando unit is moving into this building any time now?'

12 I slumped on the chair by the larder door. With the certainty of a sleepwalker, I suddenly felt that my strength would fail me if I tried to escape this new trap. I sat there groaning and gazing dully at the officer. It was some time before I stammered, with difficulty, 'Do what you like to me. I'm not moving from here.'

13 'I've no intention of doing anything to you!' The officer shrugged his shoulders. 'What do you do for a living?'

14 'I'm a pianist.'

15 He looked at me more closely, and with obvious suspicion. Then his glance fell on the door leading from the kitchen to the other rooms. An idea seemed to have struck him.

16 'Come with me, will you?'

17 We went into the next room, which had obviously been the dining room, and then into the room beyond it, where a piano stood by the wall. The officer pointed to the instrument.

18 'Play something!'

19 Hadn't it occurred to him that the sound of the piano would instantly attract all the SS men in the vicinity? I looked enquiringly at him and did not move. He obviously sensed my fears, since he added reassuringly, 'It's all right, you can play. If anyone comes, you hide in the larder and I'll say it was me trying the instrument out.'

20 When I placed my fingers on the keyboard they shook. So this time, for a change, I had to buy my life by playing the piano! I hadn't practised for two and a half years, my fingers were stiff and covered with a thick layer of dirt, and I had not cut my nails since the fire in the building where I was hiding. Moreover, the piano was in a room without any window panes, so its action was swollen by the damp and resisted the pressure of the keys.

21 I played Chopin's Nocturne in C sharp minor. The glassy, tinkling sound of the untuned strings rang through the empty flat and the stairway, floated through the ruins of the villa on the other side of the street and returned as a muted, melancholy echo. When I had

CONTRASTS AND CONTRADICTIONS

Notice & Note: Mark the contrast Szpilman sets up in paragraph 21.

Evaluate: How does this contrast contribute to the memoir's tone?

IMPROVE READING FLUENCY

Targeted Passage Tell students that when they read a text aloud, they should watch for helpful print cues. Point out that punctuation, such as commas and periods, tell them when to pause and when to stop. Question marks and exclamation points also tell them when to vary their intonation. Model reading paragraphs 21–31 aloud. Then assign groups of three to read aloud the same paragraphs, alternating who reads the narrative, the officer's dialogue, and the narrator's dialogue. Invite students to share their reactions to these passages.

Go to the **Reading Studio** for additional support in developing fluency.

NOTICE & NOTE 

finished, the silence seemed even gloomier and more eerie than before. A cat mewed in a street somewhere. I heard a shot down below outside the building—a harsh, loud German noise.

22 The officer looked at me in silence. After a while he sighed, and muttered, 'All the same, you shouldn't stay here. I'll take you out of the city, to a village. You'll be safer there.'

23 I shook my head. 'I can't leave this place,' I said firmly.

24 Only now did he seem to understand my real reason for hiding among the ruins. He started nervously.

25 'You're Jewish?' he asked.

26 'Yes.'

27 He had been standing with his arms crossed over his chest; he now unfolded them and sat down in the armchair by the piano, as if this discovery called for lengthy reflection.

28 'Yes, well,' he murmured, 'in that case I see you really can't leave.'

29 He appeared to be deep in thought again for some time, and then turned to me with another question. 'Where are you hiding?'

30 'In the attic'

31 'Show me what it's like up there.'

32 We went upstairs. He inspected the attic with a careful and expert eye. In so doing he discovered something I had not yet noticed: a kind of extra floor above it, a loft made of boards under the roof valley and directly above the entrance to the attic itself. At first glance

WHEN STUDENTS STRUGGLE . . .

Analyze Visuals Point out the image on Student Edition pages 468–469. Ask: What does this image show? *(ruined buildings and desperate people fighting and trying to hide)* Ask the same question about the image on Student Edition page 471. *(someone playing a piano)* How do these images help tell the author's story? *(They emphasize the devastation and the danger for the author and how different the conditions are from the time he could play the piano.)*

 For additional support, go to the **Reading Studio** and assign the following **Level Up Tutorial: Analyzing Visuals.**

TEACH

ANALYZE MEMOIRS

Remind students that details that reveal character may include the following:

- direct comments from the narrator
- descriptive details of the character's appearance
- actions, words, thoughts, and feelings of the character
- actions, words, thoughts, and feelings of other characters about or toward the character

Direct students to look for these types of details to underline. Then discuss what they underline.

In paragraph 41, ask students to explain what the detail "jam wrapped in greaseproof paper" suggests about the officer. *(Since the jam is a thoughtful addition to the bread and is carefully wrapped to keep it from leaking out onto the bread, this detail suggests that the officer has empathy for the pianist and might be a kind, thoughtful, respectful person.)*

In paragraph 45, discuss the details about the officer's tone of voice and possible reasons for this description. *(He is choked with emotion and likely is masking with anger an impulse to implore the pianist to survive because he is so passionate about wanting to save this man and thereby prevent a horrible wrong from being committed.)*

Then remind students that since all of these details are communicated by the narrator, Szpilman, they reflect how Szpilman views the officer. (***Answer:*** *Szpilman communicates his view of the officer by identifying in detail what the officer brings to him, what he says and how he says it, and by noting that the officer has refused to take his only treasure. He also communicates his own feeling of gratitude toward the officer by sharing his personal feelings in paragraph 51: "I had long been racking my brains for some way of showing him my gratitude."*)

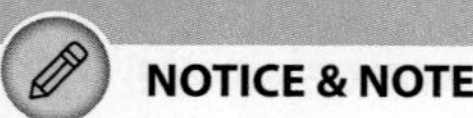

NOTICE & NOTE

you hardly noticed it because the light was so dim there. The officer said he thought I should hide in this loft, and he helped me look for a ladder in the flats below. Once I was up in the loft I must pull the ladder up after me.

33 When we had discussed this plan and put it into action, he asked if I had anything to eat.

34 'No,' I said. After all, he had taken me unawares while I was searching for supplies.

35 'Well, never mind,' he added hastily, as if ashamed in retrospect of his surprise attack. 'I'll bring you some food.'

36 Only now did I venture a question of my own. I simply could not restrain myself any longer. 'Are you German?

37 He flushed, and almost shouted his answer in agitation, as if my question had been an insult. 'Yes, I am! And ashamed of it, after everything that's been happening.'

38 Abruptly, he shook hands with me and left.

39 Three days passed before he reappeared. It was evening, and pitch dark, when I heard a whisper under my loft. 'Hello, are you there?'

40 'Yes, I'm here,' I replied.

41 Soon afterwards something heavy landed beside me. Through the paper, I felt several loaves and something soft, which later turned out to be jam wrapped in greaseproof paper. I quickly put the package to one side and called, 'Wait a moment!'

42 The voice in the dark sounded impatient. 'What is it? Hurry up. The guards saw me come in here, and I mustn't stay long.'

43 'Where are the Soviet troops?'

44 'They're already in Warsaw, in Praga on the other side of the Vistula. Just hang on a few more weeks—the war will be over by spring at the latest.'

45 The voice fell silent. I did not know if the officer was still there, or if he had gone. But suddenly he spoke again, 'You must hang on, do you hear?' His voice sounded harsh, almost as if he were giving an order, convincing me of his unyielding belief that the war would end well for us. Only then I did hear the quiet sound of the attic door closing . . .

46 On 12 December, the officer came for the last time. He brought me a larger supply of bread than before and a warm eiderdown. He told me he was leaving Warsaw with his detachment, and I must on no account lose heart, since the Soviet offensive was expected any day now.

47 'In Warsaw?'

48 'Yes.'

49 'But how will I survive the street fighting?' I asked anxiously.

50 'If you and I survived this inferno for over five years,' he replied, 'it's obviously God's will for us to live. Well, we have to believe that, anyway.'

51 'We had already said goodbye, and he was about to go, when an idea came to me at the last moment. I had long been racking

ANALYZE MEMOIRS

Annotate: Underline details that help you understand the character of the officer.

Describe: Describe how Szpilman views the officer. How does he communicate this feeling to the reader?

NOTICE & NOTE 

my brains for some way of showing him my gratitude, and he had absolutely refused to take my only treasure, my watch.

52 'Listen!' I took his hand and began speaking urgently. 'I never told you my name—you didn't ask me, but I want you to remember it. Who knows what may happen? You have a long way to go home. If I survive, I'll certainly be working for Polish Radio again. I was there before the war. If anything happens to you, if I can help you then in any way, remember my name. Szpilman, Polish Radio.'

53 He smiled his usual smile, half **deprecating**, half shy and embarrassed, but I felt I had given him pleasure with what, in the present situation, was my **naïve** wish to help him.

deprecating
(dĕp′rĭ-kāt-ing) *adj.* belittling or downplaying something.

naïve
(nī-ēv′) *adj.* lacking in experience and everyday knowledge.

CHECK YOUR UNDERSTANDING

Answer these questions before moving on to the **Analyze the Text** section on the following page.

1 Why does the narrator have to move to new hiding places?

A Other refugees needs to hide there.

B The Germans have found him.

C The corpse is bothering him.

D He has run out of food.

2 When the officer finds the narrator he asks him to —

F play the piano

G turn himself in

H hand over his watch

J inform him of anyone else hiding

3 How does the narrator keep his mind occupied while hiding?

A Helping others

B Spying on the Germans

C Writing poems and stories

D Going over compositions in his head

TEACH

CHECK YOUR UNDERSTANDING

Have students answer the questions independently.

Answers:

1. *B*
2. *F*
3. *D*

If they answer any questions incorrectly, have them reread the text to confirm their understanding. Then they may proceed to ANALYZE THE TEXT on page 474.

CRITICAL VOCABULARY

deprecating: The officer smiles in a way that suggests he's downplaying something.

ASK STUDENTS why they think that the officer's smile is usually half deprecating in addition to being shy and embarrassed. *(He probably feels that he doesn't deserve the narrator's gratitude or help because it doesn't even begin to offset all that his people have done to the Jews.)*

naïve: The pianist would like to help the officer, but he lacks the experience and everyday knowledge of the officer's circumstances to offer anything practical at that moment.

ASK STUDENTS why Szpilman, in retrospect, characterizes his offer of help as naïve? *(Most likely, after the war, Szpilman must have realized that his offer, although genuine, must have seemed like an offering a child would make to an adult—a child who realized nothing about the brutal realities of what would come next and the unlikelihood that the officer would survive.)*

ENGLISH LEARNER SUPPORT

Oral Assessment Use the following questions to assess students' comprehension and speaking skills. Ask students to respond in short, complete sentences.

1. Why does the narrator have to move to new hiding places? *(The Germans have found him.)*
2. When the officer finds the narrator, what does he ask the narrator to do? *(He asks the narrator to play the piano.)*
3. The narrator tries to keep his mind occupied while hiding. What does he do? *(He reviews musical compositions in his head.)* **SUBSTANTIAL/MODERATE**

APPLY

ANALYZE THE TEXT

Possible answers:

1. **DOK 2:** *The words* silent, motionless, hunted down, *and* creatures *have strong connotations. They create an image of people who have become like fearful, abused animals. They underscore the inhumanity of their treatment.*
2. **DOK 4:** *Wiesel repeats these thoughts to goad himself to go beyond his limits of endurance and thereby perform well enough to survive. His frenzied repetition of them helps the reader to understand that Wiesel feels panicked and focused solely on ensuring his survival.*
3. **DOK 4:** *Wiesel is a reliable authority because he experienced this life firsthand. He incorporates statements and perspectives from prisoners who have been there longer to show readers the scope of the atrocities; the other prisoners' perspectives legitimize Wiesel's fears.*
4. **DOK 4:** *Szpilman's detailed descriptions of his thoughts and routines help the reader imagine what it would be like to survive in isolation. Szpilman creates a tension, in which the reader wonders if Szpilman will be found.*
5. **DOK 4:** *Szpilman is paralyzed with the exhaustion of surviving when he encounters the officer. The tone suggests resignation. However, the officer's reaction is surprising. He doesn't want to harm Szpilman; in fact, he eventually helps him. Szpilman may have included this character to show the complexities of war and that not everyone believed in the position of the side for which they were fighting.*

RESEARCH

In a brainstorming session, compile a list of possible topics inspired by the two texts. Point out that an Internet search may yield many "hits" but that not all come from reliable sources.

Connect When critiquing a source, students should skim the text for instances of loaded language or other signs of bias, examine the author's credentials or experiences, and seek to verify the accuracy of a few facts.

RESPOND

ANALYZE THE TEXT

Support your responses with evidence from the text. NOTEBOOK

1. **Infer** In paragraph 8 of *Night*, Wiesel writes "The old men stayed in their corner, silent, motionless, hunted-down creatures. Some were praying." Which words in this quotation have strong connotations? How do these words convey the tone and mood of Wiesel's narrative?
2. **Analyze** Look back at the scene in which Wiesel must run before the SS doctors during selection. Why does Wiesel repeat his thoughts, "you are too skinny, you are too weak"? How do these words—and Wiesel's frenzied repetition of them—help the reader relate to Wiesel's experience?
3. **Analyze** What makes Wiesel a reliable authority on life in the prison camp? From what other prisoners does he incorporate statements and perspectives and why do you think he includes them in his memoir?
4. **Evaluate** In *The Pianist*, Szpilman writes about a great deal of time he spent in isolation, without interacting with anyone else. How does he draw the reader into the experience without the benefit of dialogue or much action?
5. **Notice & Note** Reread *The Pianist*, paragraphs 10–18. What is the tone of Szpilman's description of the German officer and of the dialogue between the two men? Why do you think Szpilman included the dialogue with the officer in his memoir?

RESEARCH

Both memoirs are set within the historical events of World War II and the Holocaust. Find a detail or event in one of the texts that you would like to know more about. What questions do you have about it? Search for answers to your questions and record your findings in a chart like the one below.

QUESTIONS: *When and how was Buchenwald liberated?*	
Findings: *On April 11, 1945, prisoners took over the camp just before U.S. forces arrived. A resistance movement obstructed German orders and saved many lives.*	Source: *website of the United States Holocaust Memorial Museum*

Connect Share your findings with a partner and show the sources you used. Critique each other's sources, keeping the following questions in mind:

- Do the authors of the source have credibility and the expertise to address this topic? What is their point of view, or perspective, on the topic?
- Do other sources back up the accuracy of their information? Does the source appear to offer a balanced view, or is it biased?

LEARNING MINDSET

Questioning Remind students that asking questions is as important as knowing the answers to those questions. Questioning shows engagement with the subject at hand, and it is an effective way to learn. Because some students may hesitate to ask questions, provide them with different ways of doing so, such as having a "parking lot" where they can post their questions and others can respond to them.

CREATE AND DISCUSS

Write an Introduction Reread the Background paragraph that appears before each selection. With a group, expand one of them into a longer introduction, using information from your research.

- ❑ Choose the Background for either *Night* or *The Pianist*.
- ❑ Share information group members gathered during their research time. Discuss how this information adds context to the author's experiences.
- ❑ Work individually to incorporate the pieces of information into an expanded introduction that could appear before the memoir.

Go to the **Writing Studio** for more on using research in your writing.

Discuss with a Small Group Now that you've used each other's research to write individual introductions to the text, share what you've written.

- ❑ Take turns reading aloud your texts.
- ❑ As a group, reflect on how you incorporated the research in different ways. How do the different introductions provide the reader with helpful context?

Go to the **Speaking and Listening Studio** for help with sharing ideas as a group.

RESPOND TO THE ESSENTIAL QUESTION

What does it take to survive in a crisis?

Gather Information Review your annotations and notes on *Night* and *The Pianist* and highlight those that help answer the Essential Question. Then, add relevant details to your Response Log.

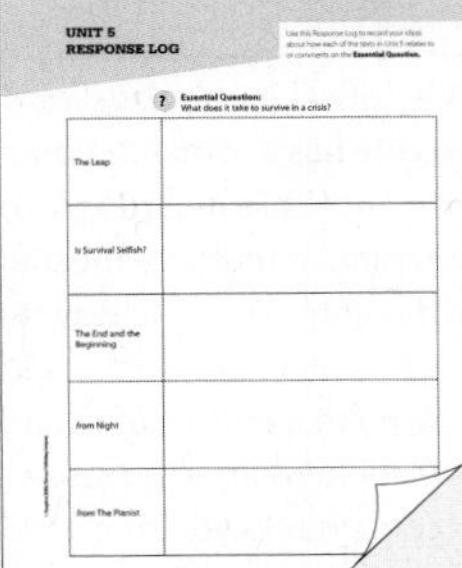

ACADEMIC VOCABULARY

As you write and discuss what you learned from the memoirs, be sure to use the Academic Vocabulary words. Check off each of the words that you use.

- ❑ **dimension**
- ❑ **external**
- ❑ **statistic**
- ❑ **sustain**
- ❑ **utilize**

APPLY

CREATE AND DISCUSS

Write an Introduction Remind students that the information they add should be accurate and help readers understand something about the author that is relevant to the selection. Explain that information is probably relevant if it answers one or more of the following questions:

- Will the information help readers better understand the author's perspective on the events he is describing?
- Will the information give readers a deeper understanding of the author's circumstances and/or events in the account?
- Will the information answer questions the reader is likely to be left wondering about after reading the selection?

For **writing support** for students at varying proficiency levels, see the **Text X-Ray** on page 456D.

Discuss with a Small Group Remind students to listen actively and to speak using appropriate discussion rules, maintaining an awareness of verbal and nonverbal cues. Also remind them to respond thoughtfully and tactfully. If students disagree with the accuracy or interpretations of facts that other groups present, encourage them to summarize what they disagree with and provide their reasons for disagreeing. Encourage students to begin their comments with phrases such as "Our group thought," "Based on the facts we gathered, I thought," or "According to our sources."

RESPOND TO THE ESSENTIAL QUESTION

Allow time for students to add details from *Night* and *The Pianist* to their Unit 5 Response Logs.

APPLYING ACADEMIC VOCABULARY

❑ **dimension** ❑ **external** ☑ **statistic** ❑ **sustain** ☑ **utilize**

Write and Discuss Have students use the following questions to respond to one another's introduction. Guide students to include the academic vocabulary words *statistic* and *utilize* in their responses.

- What kinds of **statistics** did you come across in your research?
- How did you decide which details and pieces of information to **utilize** in your writing?

APPLY

CRITICAL VOCABULARY

Possible answers:

1. *The prisoner looks extremely thin and unhealthy.*
2. *Wiesel knows that because of the latest ruling, there will not be another selection for a while.*
3. *No; they don't complain because Wiesel performs his work tasks properly and efficiently.*
4. *The music sounds like loud noise.*
5. *The prisoners hope for a postponement of death.*
6. *Szpilman's isolation ends when he meets the German officer.*
7. *He wants to be careful with the watch because he treasures it and wants to keep it working well.*
8. *Such a smile reveals that the officer does not think much of himself; in fact, he may be angry with himself.*
9. *Spzilman's offer is unrealistic because it is unlikely that both of them will survive the war, much less find each other again.*

VOCABULARY STRATEGY: Multiple-Meaning Words

Answers:

1. *present: a gift*
2. *block: a unit of buildings*
3. *mad: insane*
4. *flat: apartment*

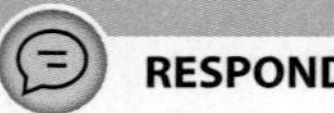

RESPOND

WORD BANK
emaciated
decisive
execute
din
reprieve
isolation
conscientiously
deprecating
naïve

CRITICAL VOCABULARY

Practice and Apply Use your knowledge of the Critical Vocabulary words to respond to each question.

1. Wiesel describes one of the prisoners as **emaciated**. What does the prisoner look like?
2. When Wiesel's father passes the second **decisive** selection, Wiesel is relieved. Explain why.
3. While a prisoner, Wiesel **executes** his work tasks. Do the guards likely have a complaint about his work? Explain.
4. The narrator can hear the **din** of military music in the background. What does the music sound like?
5. The prisoners at the concentration camp hope for a **reprieve** from death. What do they hope will happen?
6. Szpilman spends a lot of time in **isolation**. What ends that isolation?
7. Why do you think Szpilman treats the watch **conscientiously**?
8. The officer smiles in a **deprecating** way. What does that reveal about his view of himself?
9. What makes Szpilman's offer to help the officer **naïve?**

VOCABULARY STRATEGY: Multiple-Meaning Words

Go to the **Vocabulary Studio** for more on multiple-meaning words.

The Critical Vocabulary word *execute* means "to accomplish or carry out fully." *Execute* has another definition, "to put to death." Like *execute*, many words have **multiple meanings**. Use the strategies below to determine or clarify the meaning of multiple-meaning words.

- Use context, or the way the word is used in a sentence or paragraph, to determine meaning. Look at the words and sentences around the unknown word to clarify its meaning. For example, look at the following sentence: *Mountain climbing was her passion, and she wanted to scale every peak.* The context tells you that *scale* refers to climbing.
- Consult general and specialized reference materials, particularly glossaries and dictionaries, to determine or clarify the precise meaning of a word. Dictionary entries provide all the definitions of a word, as well as its part of speech, so select the definition that makes sense.

Practice and Apply Work in a group to locate these words from *Night*: *present* (paragraph 1) and *block* (paragraph 2), and these words from *The Pianist: mad* (paragraph 2) and *flat* (paragraph 3). Use context clues or reference materials to determine the precise meaning for each word.

ENGLISH LEARNER SUPPORT

Vocabulary Strategy As students consider the various meanings of each word, use the following supports with students at varying proficiency levels:

- Encourage students to write down the definitions they know and/or draw pictures to represent each definition. **SUBSTANTIAL**
- Tell students to check the accuracy of their responses by restating each sentence with a synonym for the word that they think is correct. Explain that if the synonym does not make sense in context, then the meaning they have selected may be incorrect as well. **MODERATE/LIGHT**

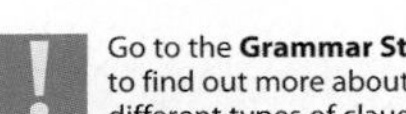

LANGUAGE CONVENTIONS
Clauses

A **clause** is a group of words with a subject and a verb. There are two types of clauses: an **independent clause** can stand alone as a sentence; a **dependent clause** cannot. Instead, dependent clauses act as modifiers, adding meaning to independent clauses. Dependent clauses often begin with these words: *as if, as, since, than, that, though, until, whenever, where, while, who,* and *why.* These words are subordinating conjunctions that clarify the connection between the clauses.

Read the following sentence from *Night*:

They had transferred me to another Kommando, the construction one, where twelve hours a day I hauled heavy slabs of stone.

This sentence contains one independent clause and one dependent clause. Notice how the independent clause *They had transferred me to another Kommando, the construction one* forms a complete thought and can stand alone as a sentence. The dependent clause, which is underlined, provides additional information about the independent clause, but it cannot stand alone.

The two types of clauses function together to convey the author's meaning. Without the clause, the author's ideas might be presented this way:

They had transferred me to another Kommando, the construction one. The Kommando was where twelve hours a day I hauled heavy slabs of stone.

These simple sentences are choppy, repetitive, and less interesting to read. Here are more examples of effective independent and dependent clauses from *The Pianist*. The dependent clauses are underlined.

He obviously sensed my fears, since he added reassuringly, "It's all right, you can play."

When I had finished, the silence seemed even gloomier and more eerie than before.

Practice and Apply Write three to four sentences, each with at least one independent and one dependent clause, about your reaction to the two memoirs. Try to use different subordinating conjunctions in your sentences.

Go to the **Grammar Studio** to find out more about different types of clauses.

LANGUAGE CONVENTIONS: Clauses

Remind students that writers often use a dependent clause to provide additional details or clarify something in the independent clause to which it is attached. Discuss the list of words that often begin dependent clauses, inviting volunteers to suggest short sentences that use each one.

Practice and Apply If students need help beginning this activity, suggest that they write a simple sentence first and then add a dependent clause to it that provides additional detail about something in that original sentence. Share examples, such as the following:

Snow began to fall.

While I was waiting for the bus, snow began to fall.

I got the autobiography from the library.

I got the autobiography from the library because the excerpt fascinated me.

Point out that if a dependent clause begins a sentence, it usually is followed by a comma. If a dependent clause follows the independent clause, there usually is no comma preceding it.

ENGLISH LEARNER SUPPORT

Comprehend Language Conventions In Vietnamese, relative pronouns are not required; in Hmong, the same form of a relative pronoun is used for both animate and inanimate antecedents. Consequently, students for whom Vietnamese is the primary language may need to be reminded to insert a relative pronoun when needed at the beginning of a dependent clause. Students for whom Hmong is the primary language may need to be reminded that in English we use different relative pronouns for animate and inanimate antecedents. For this latter group of students, you might provide the following example:

Incorrect: The math problem who gave me the most trouble was this one.

Correct: The math problem that gave me the most trouble was this one.

Work with students to write two sentences, one with an inanimate antecedent and one with an animate antecedent. **ALL LEVELS**

APPLY

COMPARE MEMOIRS

Instruct group members to share information, support their ideas with evidence, and adjust their responses as warranted. Remind students that authors often have more than one purpose when writing a text.

For **reading support** for students at varying proficiency levels, see the **Text X-Ray** on page 456D.

ANALYZE THE TEXTS

Possible answers:

1. **DOK 4:** *Szpilman describes only one other person, the officer who helps him. Szpilman uses this character to show how complicated war is. Both the officer and Szpilman work to retain their humanity, in spite of the horrendous circumstances. Wiesel includes the perspectives of the camp's guards, who are resentful of their responsibilities; the veteran prisoners, who have been hardened by spending so much time in the camp; and his father, who tries to guide and comfort his son through an unimaginable situation. These characters' reactions to events in the camp show that people, though they try, cannot hold on to their prewar identities.*

2. **DOK 3:** *Wiesel often writes with short, choppy sentences, reflecting the tense and confusing experience of being held in a concentration camp. On the other hand, Szpilman includes several long paragraphs and sentences, reflecting the long periods of time he had alone with his thoughts, going through the repetitive motions of keeping himself alive.*

3. **DOK 3:** *Both memoirs explore themes of morality, freedom, overcoming suffering, and maintaining one's humanity.*

4. **DOK 4:** *Students should note that they learned more about what European Jews experienced during World War II both in concentration camps and city ghettos. They also may say that they have learned that not all German officers approved of what the Nazis did.*

RESPOND

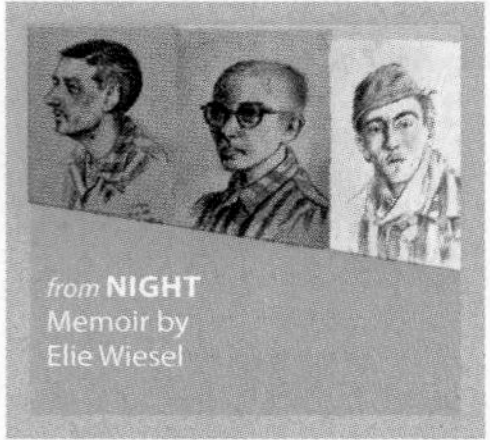

from **NIGHT**
Memoir by
Elie Wiesel

from **THE PIANIST**
Memoir by
Wladyslaw Szpilman

Collaborate & Compare

COMPARE MEMOIRS

When you compare two or more texts on the same topic, you **synthesize** the information: you make connections and extend key ideas. It's easier to do this when the texts you're comparing are the same genre, or type of writing.

In a small group, complete the chart with details from both memoirs. Some of these details are easy to find in the text. For others, you will need to make inferences or draw conclusions using the details that do appear in the text. Discuss elements the memoirs share. Support your ideas with specific evidence from the texts. After hearing other views, you may want to adjust the responses in your chart.

LITERARY ELEMENT	*NIGHT*	*THE PIANIST*
Setting	*the Buchenwald concentration camp*	*two hiding places in burnt-out Warsaw*
Point of View	*Wiesel's first-person point of view*	*Szpilman's first-person point of view*
How the Narrator Reacts to His Circumstance	*He focuses on not being "selected" for execution.*	*He works to keep his mind occupied while hiding.*
Characterization	*Wiesel's father tries to still be a parent to him.*	*The officer is ashamed of Nazi actions.*
Author's Purpose	*to show the atrocities in concentration camps*	*to show his experiences and reactions*
Word Choice	*phrases (e.g., silently weeping) show despair*	*repetition of alone conveys isolation*
Tone	*sarcastic and resigned*	*matter-of-fact and resigned*

ANALYZE THE TEXTS

Discuss these questions in your group.

1. **Analyze** Both authors describe characters other than themselves. How do these different characters' perspectives add to the texts' meanings?
2. **Contrast** What differences do you notice between the authors' styles and tones?
3. **Compare** What themes do the two texts share?
4. **Synthesize** What have you learned from these memoirs about the events of World War II and the Holocaust?

WHEN STUDENTS STRUGGLE . . .

Think-Pair-Share Have students work with a partner to answer the Analyze the Texts questions, breaking questions into parts they can answer step by step. For example, to tackle the first question, they might break it down like this:

- Which characters does Wiesel describe other than himself? How do their perspectives add to the memoir?
- Whom does Szpilman describe other than himself? What does this character's perspective add to the memoir?

For additional support, go to the **Reading Studio** and assign the following  **Level Up Tutorial: Reading for Details.**

RESPOND

COLLABORATE AND PRESENT

With your group, present your findings as you compared the memoirs. Use the information in your charts to plan a presentation to the rest of the class about how the memoirs have some common elements but differ in other ways.

1. **Plan Your Presentation** As a group, choose the most important ideas that you discussed, and write a summary of each. Use the following questions to prepare your presentation:
   - ❑ In what order will we present these ideas?
   - ❑ What will each group member say?
   - ❑ How will we conclude our presentation?
   - ❑ How can we use precise vocabulary and language, with evidence from the texts, to help the audience understand our points?
2. **Present and Discuss** Deliver your presentation to the rest of the class and listen to the other presentations. Then, with your group, discuss whether you think that the memoir is an appropriate genre for both writers to use to explore the events of the Holocaust. Explain your thinking.
3. **Reflect** On your own, write your thoughts on how you helped your group prepare and present the material.

COLLABORATE AND PRESENT

1. **Plan Your Presentation** Emphasize that in this comparison, students are asked to share how these selections are alike *and* how they differ. Remind students that a summary includes the key information from the original source but not every detail. Encourage all students in the group to contribute in creating the summaries and in making decisions about the presentation. Likewise, every student in the group should play a part in the presentation itself.
2. **Present and Discuss** Remind presenters to speak loudly, clearly, and slowly enough for listeners to absorb what they are saying. Then, before the discussion, review with students the elements of a memoir.
3. **Reflect** Suggest that students begin by recording the ways in which they participated in the activity. Then tell them to reflect on their contributions to determine such things as whether they did their fair share of the preparations, how they felt about the quality of what they did, and how else they helped their group (for example, by listening actively and respectfully or by encouraging the more quiet members of the group to share their ideas). You may not wish to have students share their reflections with the class, but do encourage students to use their thoughts to set personal goals for their next major activity.

ENGLISH LEARNER SUPPORT

Match Comfort Level to Contribution Allow English learners to contribute to their group's presentation in the ways they feel most comfortable. However, do remind them that by going a little beyond their comfort zone they will push themselves to improve.

- Allow students to contribute images rather than speaking publicly. **SUBSTANTIAL**
- Encourage less fluent speakers in each group to contribute to the presentations by rehearsing passages from the texts that support the group's main ideas and reading these aloud when called upon during the presentation. **SUBSTANTIAL**
- Pair English learners of mixed proficiency to help each other with pronunciations of English words. **SUBSTANTIAL/MODERATE**
- Encourage students to comb through their group's presentation to find overused words and phrases and replace these with fresh, appropriate synonyms. **LIGHT**

INDEPENDENT READING

READER'S CHOICE

Setting a Purpose Have students review their Unit 5 Response Log and think about what they've already learned about surviving in a crisis. As they choose their Independent Reading selections, encourage them to consider what more they want to know.

NOTICE & NOTE

Explain that some selections may contain multiple signposts; others may contain only one. And the same type of signpost can occur many times in the same text.

LEARNING MINDSET

Seeking Challenges Tell students that having a learning mindset about challenges means being willing to take risks and try new things despite the fear of failure. Trying hard is important, but so is trying things that *are* hard. Encourage students to focus on an Independent Reading selection that they might normally avoid because it seems like something they would struggle to understand.

INDEPENDENT READING

ESSENTIAL QUESTION:

What does it take to survive in a crisis?

Reader's Choice

Setting a Purpose Select one or more of these options from your eBook to continue your exploration of the Essential Question.

- Read the descriptions to see which text grabs your interest.
- Think about which genres you enjoy reading.

Notice & Note

In this unit, you practiced noticing and noting these signposts and strategies: **Memory Moment, Again and Again,** and **Contrasts and Contradictions**. As you read independently, these signposts and others will aid your understanding. Below are the anchor questions to ask when you read literature and nonfiction.

Reading Literature: Stories, Poems, and Plays		
Signpost	**Anchor Question**	**Lesson**
Contrasts and Contradictions	Why did the character act that way?	p. 419
Aha Moment	How might this change things?	p. 171
Tough Questions	What does this make me wonder about?	p. 494
Words of the Wiser	What's the lesson for the character?	p. 171
Again and Again	Why might the author keep bringing this up?	p. 170
Memory Moment	Why is this memory important?	p. 418

Reading Nonfiction: Essays, Articles, and Arguments		
Signpost	**Anchor Question(s)**	**Lesson**
Big Questions	What surprised me? What did the author think I already knew? What challenged, changed, or confirmed what I already knew?	p. 248 p. 2 p. 84
Contrasts and Contradictions	What is the difference, and why does it matter?	p. 3
Extreme or Absolute Language	Why did the author use this language?	p. 85
Numbers and Stats	Why did the author use these numbers or amounts?	p. 249
Quoted Words	Why was this person quoted or cited, and what did this add?	p. 85
Word Gaps	Do I know this word from someplace else? Does it seem like technical talk for this topic? Do clues in the sentence help me understand the word?	p. 3

480 Unit 5

ENGLISH LEARNER SUPPORT

Develop Fluency Introduce students to strategies they can use to help them understand a text that they are reading to themselves:

- Read a passage from a text aloud while students follow along. Have them raise their hands to indicate that a word or phrase is unfamiliar. Explain or act out the meaning. **SUBSTANTIAL**
- Have students read a passage silently. Then work together to summarize the passage. Encourage them to summarize passages as they read independently to check their understanding. **MODERATE**
- Have partners read the same passage independently. Then have them discuss the meaning of the passage and what strategies they use to comprehend the material. **LIGHT**

Go to the **Reading Studio** for additional support in developing fluency.

INDEPENDENT READING

You can preview these texts in Unit 5 of your eBook.

Then, check off the text or texts that you select to read on your own.

ARTICLE

Adventurers Change. Danger Does Not.
Alan Cowell

Which is more important—to reach the summit of Mount Everest or to save the life of a fellow climber in trouble?

MEMOIR

from *An Ordinary Man*
Paul Rusesabagina

A Rwandan hotel owner of mixed Hutu and Tutsi descent saves more than a thousand refugees and survives the 1994 genocide.

POEM

Who Understands Me But Me
Jimmy Santiago Baca

When a young man is sentenced to prison, he loses a lot but gains even more.

SPEECH

Truth at All Costs
Marie Colvin

Is it worth the risk to report from a war zone? Do war correspondents make a difference?

INFORMATIONAL TEXT

from *Deep Survival*
Laurence Gonzales

Is a positive mental attitude really the key to survival? The author explores how disaster survivors manage to beat the odds.

Collaborate and Share Work with a partner to discuss what you learned from at least one of your independent readings.

- Give a brief synopsis or summary of the text.
- Describe any signposts that you noticed in the text and explain what they revealed to you.
- Describe what you most enjoyed or found most challenging about the text. Give specific examples.
- Decide whether you would recommend the text to others. Why or why not?

Go to the **Reading Studio** for more resources on **Notice & Note.**

INDEPENDENT READING

MATCHING STUDENTS TO TEXTS

Use the following information to guide students in choosing their texts.

Adventurers Change. Danger Does Not. **Lexile: 1160L**
Genre: article
Overall Rating: Challenging

***from* An Ordinary Man** **Lexile: 980L**
Genre: memoir
Overall Rating: Challenging

Who Understands Me But Me
Genre: poem
Overall Rating: Accessible

Truth at All Costs **Lexile: 1080L**
Genre: speech
Overall Rating: Challenging

***from* Deep Survival** **Lexile: 960L**
Genre: informational text
Overall Rating: Accessible

Collaborate and Share To assess how well students read the selections, walk around the room and listen to their conversations. Encourage students to be focused and specific in their comments.

Online Ed **for Assessment**

- Independent Reading Selection Tests

Encourage students to visit the **Reading Studio** to download a handy bookmark of **NOTICE & NOTE** signposts.

WHEN STUDENTS STRUGGLE. . .

Keep a Reading Log As students read their selected texts, have them keep a reading log for each selection to note signposts and their thoughts about them. Use their logs to assess how well they are noticing and reflecting on elements of their texts.

Reading Log for (Title)		
Location	**Signpost I Noticed**	**My Notes About It**

UNIT 5 Tasks

- **WRITE AN ARGUMENT**
- **PRESENT AND RESPOND TO AN ARGUMENT**

MENTOR TEXT
IS SURVIVAL SELFISH?
Argument by LANE WALLACE

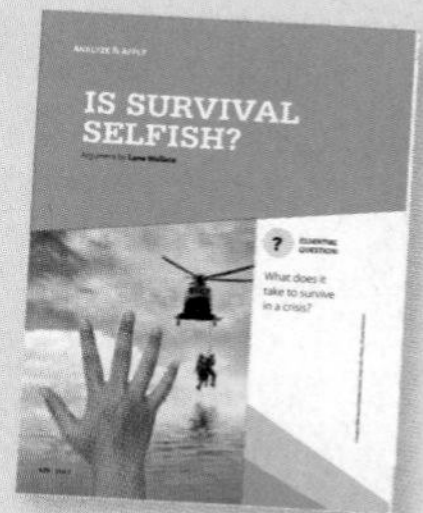

LEARNING OBJECTIVES

Writing Task

- Write an argument about whether or not survival requires selfishness.
- Use strategies to plan and organize reasons and evidence to support a thesis statement.
- Develop a focused, structured draft of an argument.
- Use the Mentor Text as a model for creating a strong introduction and using transitions effectively.
- Revise drafts, incorporating peers' suggestions.
- Edit drafts to incorporate transitions.
- Use a rubric to evaluate writing.
- Publish writing to share it with an audience.
- **Language** Revise writing with transitions and other connecting words.

Speaking and Listening Task

- Adapt an argument for an oral presentation.
- Deliver an argument to an audience.
- Listen actively to a presentation.
- **Language** Identify a claim by completing this sentence stem: *The author believes that the best way to ____ is to ____.*

Assign the Writing Task in ***Ed.***

RESOURCES

- Unit 5 Response Log
- Reading Studio: Notice & Note
- Writing Studio: Writing Arguments
- Speaking and Listening Studio: Giving a Presentation
- Grammar Studio: Module 2: Lesson 12: Conjunctions and Interjections

Language X-Ray: English Learner Support

Use the instruction below and the supports and scaffolds in the Teacher's Edition to help you guide students at different proficiency levels.

INTRODUCE THE WRITING TASK

Explain that an **argument** is a kind of writing in which the writer takes a position on a topic. In the first part of an argument, the writer states his or her position in a thesis. He or she then supports that position with reasons and evidence. Point out that the word *argument* is related to the Spanish *argumento*, which means "a statement for or against something." Give some examples of real-life arguments: "My brother and I argued about who would do the dishes." "The friends argued about who was the best player on the team."

Provide sentence frames to help students explore the unit theme—surviving a crisis and, in particular, whether survival is a selfish activity. For example: *To survive when lost in the wilderness, one must* ____. Assist students as they brainstorm words and phrases such as *find shelter* or *signal for help.* Have pairs of students work together to draft an original thesis statement with a claim that expresses a clear position on whether surviving a crisis requires selfishness.

WRITING

Write Claims and Counterclaims

Explain that a claim takes a position on a topic, and a counterclaim offers an opposing position.

Use the following supports with students at varying proficiency levels:

- Display and define vocabulary students can use in a claim about the topic, such as *help, danger, stranger, decision,* and *disaster.* Have students practice writing claims by completing sentence frames such as the following: *It is important to* ____ *during a* ____. **SUBSTANTIAL**
- Have partners work together. Instruct each partner to write a claim about survival; then have partners work together to write statements that express a counterclaim. **MODERATE**
- Have students write a brief paragraph including a claim and a counterclaim. Then ask them to exchange papers and offer constructive feedback. **LIGHT**

SPEAKING AND LISTENING

Use Connecting Words, or Transitions

Provide speaking and listening practice in which students identify and use connecting words, or transitions.

Use the following supports with students at varying proficiency levels:

- Display a list of transitions. Read aloud the first paragraph of "Is Survival Selfish?" Ask students to raise their hands when they hear these connecting words. **SUBSTANTIAL**
- Have partners take turns asking and answering questions about dangerous events using transitions from a word bank or ones displayed on the board. **MODERATE**
- Tell partners to use transitions in a conversation about a dangerous event or situation. These transitions might show contrast *(also, like, another, although, but, however,* and *instead)* or sequence *(before, after, next, finally).* **LIGHT**

WRITING

WRITE AN ARGUMENT

Have a volunteer read aloud the introductory paragraph and then discuss the writing task with students. Encourage them to review the notes they made in the Unit 5 Response Log before they begin planning and writing their drafts.

USE THE MENTOR TEXT

Explain to students that their arguments will have the same key features found in "Is Survival Selfish?" Their arguments also will present and develop a clear specific claim, offer valid reasons and evidence to support it, and anticipate and refute counterclaims. In the conclusion, students should briefly restate their claim and the main thrust of the evidence presented in their arguments.

WRITING PROMPT

Review the prompt with students. Encourage them to ask questions about any part of the assignment that is unclear. Emphasize that the purpose of their argument is to answer the question by making and supporting a claim about whether it is sometimes necessary to be selfish to survive.

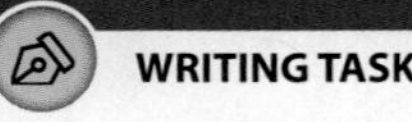

Write an Argument

Go to the **Writing Studio** for help writing your argument.

This unit explores the idea of survival and what it takes to endure an extreme situation. Look back at the texts you read, and think about the events that place the people and characters in danger and what their reactions are. Then decide for yourself whether the desire for survival can be selfish. Write an argument that explains your position, using evidence from at least two texts in this unit. For an example of a well-written argumentative text you can use as a mentor text, review Lane Wallace's "Is Survival Selfish?"

As you write your argument, you will want to look at the notes you made in your Response Log.

Writing Prompt

Read the information in the box below.

This is the topic or context for your argument. → **Survival may be instinctive, but it is not simple.**

Think carefully about the following question.

This is the essential question for the unit. → **What does it take to survive in a crisis?**

Mark the question you must answer in your essay. → **Write** an argument stating your position on the question "Does survival require selfishness?"

An effective argument:

Review these points as you write and again when you finish. Make any needed changes.

- ❑ makes a clear, specific claim
- ❑ develops the claim with valid reasons and relevant evidence
- ❑ anticipate and address counterclaims, or opposing arguments, by providing counterarguments
- ❑ includes a logically structured body, including transitions
- ❑ concludes with an effective summary of the claim
- ❑ demonstrates an appropriate, clear use of language, maintaining a formal style (register), voice, and tone through the use of standard academic English

LEARNING MINDSET

Try Again Discuss with students how completing assignments and other tasks often requires overcoming challenges and picking yourself up after a stumble, misstep, or mistake. Acknowledge that facing up to a challenge or fixing a mistake can be frustrating. Help students understand how important it is not to let frustrations build or become an even bigger hurdle to overcome. Suggest that they acknowledge their frustrations but then promptly move into an action-oriented perspective so that they can try again and keep moving forward. At the completion of the assignment or task, have them take time to reflect and learn from their experiences. Remind students that they are all valuable members of a learning community and that they should encourage each other to keep trying.

1 Plan

Writing an argument involves a lot of thought and planning. Think about the selections you've read in this unit and the questions they raise about what it takes to survive. Is a focus on saving oneself selfish, or is it a healthy, even smart, human instinct? Does it depend on the circumstances? Use the word web below to help you explore your thoughts and feelings about survival. Include ideas from the unit texts.

You also need to think about what you hope to achieve in your argument and for whom you are writing—your purpose and your audience.

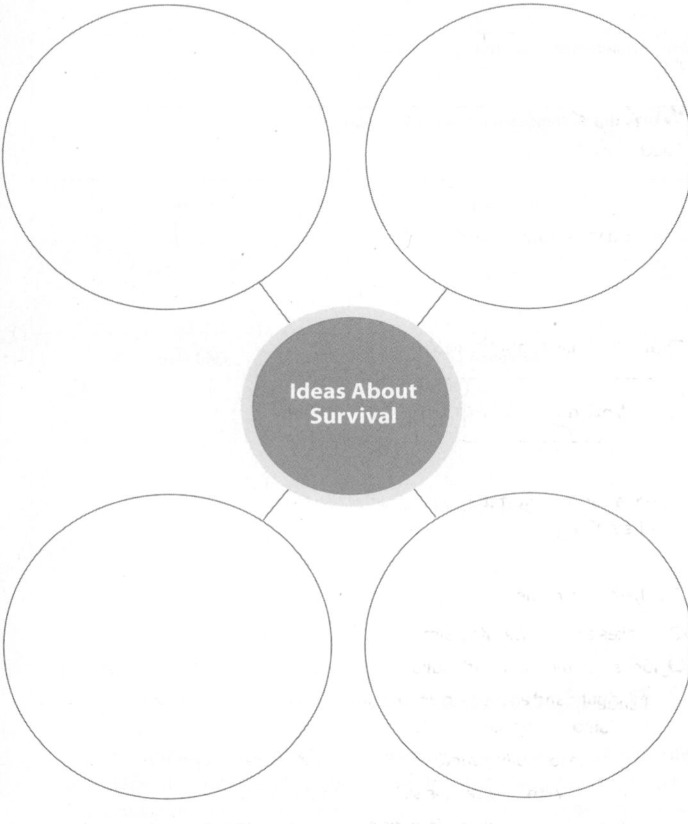

Background Reading To find evidence for your argument, go back to the notes you have taken in your Response Log for this unit. If needed, do additional research.

Go to **Writing Arguments: Planning and Drafting** for help planning your argument.

Notice & Note

From Reading to Writing

As you plan your argument, apply what you've learned about signposts to your own writing. Remember that writers use common features, called signposts, to help convey their message to readers.

Think about how you can incorporate **Quoted Words** into your argument.

Go to the **Reading Studio** for more resources on **Notice & Note**.

Use the notes from your Response Log as you plan your argument.

WHEN STUDENTS STRUGGLE . . .

Explore Ideas Before students begin to respond to the writing prompt, have them identify three selections in the unit that explore what it takes to survive a crisis. Then guide them to identify the main idea of each selection.

Selection	Main Idea About Survival
Selection #1	
Selection #2	
Selection #3	

Invite students to share their ideas with a partner or small group.

1 PLAN

Read the introductory text. Have volunteers offer questions about survival that the unit's selections have raised. For example, what makes a genuine crisis? Is survival possible in every crisis? Does survival always involve positive outcomes? Have students record some of the key words that arise during the discussion.

Point out the word web. Explain that students should feel free to use some or all parts of the web as they note their thoughts and feelings about survival, or even add parts if necessary. Before students begin their independent work on the word web, remind them to think about the purpose and audience for their argument.

English Learner Support

Generate Ideas Review the word web and discuss possible examples to guide students in generating ideas about survival before they begin working independently. Provide sentence frames to help them come up with ideas to complete the web, such as these: *Survival is based on ______. Some people who survive a crisis are ______. Sometimes thinking about ______ is most important to survival.* Encourage students to share their ideas with a partner. **ALL LEVELS**

NOTICE & NOTE

From Reading to Writing Remind students that they can use **Quoted Words** to include the opinions or conclusions of an expert or a participant in or a witness to an event. When deciding whether they should use a quotation, students should ask, "How are this person's words important to exploring the idea of survival?" Remind students to format direct quotations correctly and to give credit to the source.

Background Reading As they plan their arguments, remind students to review the notes in their Response Logs for Unit 5. They may also review the selections to find additional evidence to support ideas they want to include in their writing. For students doing additional research, guide them in finding reliable sources.

WRITING

Organize Your Ideas When planning their argument, students must first determine a claim based on the question and then write a thesis statement expressing their position. Discuss the different positions a writer might take in response to the question "Does survival require selfishness?"

Tell students that the writer of an effective argument can strengthen his or her claim by acknowledging counterclaims. Explain that a counterclaim is an opposing claim to the one being supported in the argument. A writer should respond to a counterclaim by offering counterpoints, or factual statements, as evidence.

Before students begin drafting their arguments, discuss the importance of organizing their ideas in an outline. Review the chart headings and explain that students can use their outlines as the basis for a five-paragraph argument. Connect the ideas in the planning chart with a traditional outline, such as the one below:

I. Introduction: Claim and Counterclaim

II. Body of Argument

   A. Reason 1 with Evidence

   B. Reason 2 with Evidence

   C. Reason 3 with Evidence

III. Conclusion: Summary of Argument

For **writing support** for students at varying proficiency levels, see the **Language X-Ray** on page 482B.

2 DEVELOP A DRAFT

Remind students that an outline is only a preliminary step in the writing process and is subject to change. Tell students that during the drafting stage they should feel free to make changes to their plans if they come up with new ideas or find new evidence to support their argument.

English Learner Support

Choose a Position Determine whether students understand the meaning of the word *selfish*. Remind students that in the thesis statement of an argument, the writer takes a position on the topic. (In Spanish, the cognate for the word *position* is *posición*.) If students need more guidance in stating their position, ask: Should people always help each other? Why or why not? Have students discuss their responses with a partner and write a statement of their position. **SUBSTANTIAL/MODERATE**

WRITING TASK

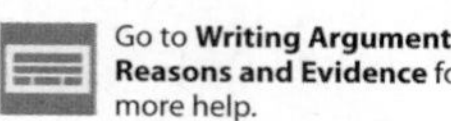

Go to **Writing Arguments: Reasons and Evidence** for more help.

Organize Your Ideas Organize the ideas for your argument in the chart below. Write a clear claim, or thesis statement. Acknowledge a counterclaim, or opposing view, that you will address by providing a counterargument. Then, clearly organize your reasons and relevant details, examples, and evidence, progressing logically from one reason to the next. Refer to at least three of the selections in the unit. When you write your conclusion, summarize your position in a persuasive way.

Argument: Does Survival Require Selfishness?		
Claim, or thesis statement		
Why the audience might not agree (counterclaim)		
Why the audience should agree with you		
Reason 1	Reason 2	Reason 3
Evidence	Evidence	Evidence
Conclusion		

2 Develop a Draft

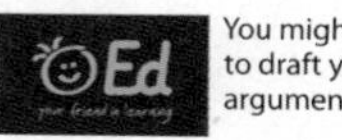

You might prefer to draft your argument online.

Write a well-organized draft of your argument, keeping your purpose and audience in mind as you write. Introduce your argument in a memorable way. Use formal language and a respectful tone. Refer to your graphic organizers and the outline you have created, as well as any notes you took as you studied the texts in the unit. These will provide a kind of map for you to follow as you write. Using a word processor or online writing application makes it easier to make changes or move sentences around later when you are ready to revise your first draft.

WHEN STUDENTS STRUGGLE . . .

Understand Academic Language Use the definitions provided below as the basis for a class discussion.

claim: a statement that can be argued about, answering the question "What do I think?"

reason: a statement in support of your claim, answering the question "Why do I think this?"

evidence: facts that support your claim, answering the question "How do I know this?" or "What do I know?"

Have students work in small groups to generate specific examples of claims, reasons, and evidence that might be used in connection with their arguments about survival.

Use the Mentor Text

Genre Characteristics

Introduce your argument in a memorable way that will grab your reader's attention. You want your readers to be involved in what you have to say from the very beginning. Note how the opening lines of "Is Survival Selfish?" capture the reader's attention.

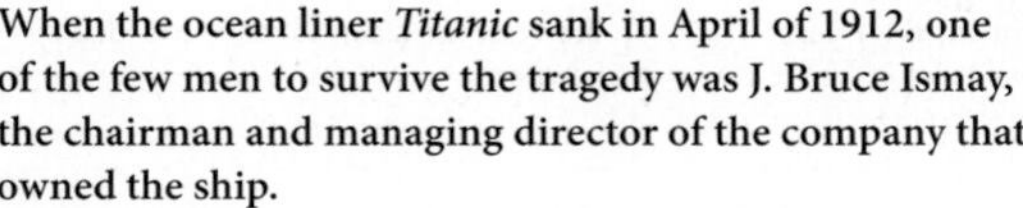

When the ocean liner *Titanic* sank in April of 1912, one of the few men to survive the tragedy was J. Bruce Ismay, the chairman and managing director of the company that owned the ship.

The writer uses a surprising and intriguing fact to immediately draw in the reader.

Apply What You've Learned Draw your reader into your argument quickly with an interesting fact or example.

Author's Craft

It's important to help your reader move smoothly through your argument. One way to do that is to use transitions—words that connect reasons and evidence to the claim and express the relationship between words, sentences, and paragraphs.

<u>In Yates' case</u>, he had time to think hard about the odds, and the possibilities he was facing, and to realize that he couldn't save anyone but himself. <u>But</u> what about people who have to make more instantaneous decisions?

See how this example makes smooth transitions from one idea to the next.

Apply What You've Learned Use transitions effectively in your argument.

WHY THIS MENTOR TEXT?

Lane Wallace's "Is Survival Selfish?" provides a good example of an argument. Use the instruction below to model how to incorporate a memorable fact or engaging detail to grab readers' attention in the introduction to an argument. Note how effective transitions can help readers follow the development of an argument's main points.

USE THE MENTOR TEXT

Genre Characteristics Ask a volunteer to read aloud the example of an engaging introduction. Discuss the details that capture the reader's attention and ask: What makes this detail interesting to you? *(Possible response: Ismay's wealth and connection to the company that owned the Titanic)* What question does this detail raise about Ismay's survival? *(Possible response: Did Ismay receive special treatment because of who he was?)* Discuss strategies students might use to find and incorporate an intriguing fact or idea into their introductions.

Author's Craft Have a volunteer read aloud the introduction to this section and the example from the mentor text. Ask: How does the opening phrase help make a smooth transition in this example? *(The opening phrase, "In Yates' case," introduces the idea that his decision was different from that of survivors who don't have time to weigh the odds.)*

ENGLISH LEARNER SUPPORT

Use the Mentor Text Use the following supports with students at varying proficiency levels:

- Point out the word *transitions* in Author's Craft. Tell students that they already know some transitions—connecting words like *and* and *but*. Read aloud the excerpt and have students raise their hands when they hear a connecting word. **SUBSTANTIAL**
- Have students discuss their ideas about survival using transitions such as *however, because, then, also, next,* and *so*. **MODERATE**
- Have students work independently to write a brief paragraph about survival that uses transitions to connect related ideas. Have students share their paragraphs with partners or group members and ask for peer feedback. **LIGHT**

WRITING

3 REVISE

Have students review the questions, tips, and revision techniques presented in the Revision Guide to determine how they can improve their drafts. Model responses for students who need additional support.

With a Partner Encourage students to carefully evaluate reviewer's comments as they further develop their arguments. Suggest that they follow the tips and apply the techniques suggested in the Scoring Guide to revise their writing.

WRITING TASK

Go to **Writing Arguments: Revising and Editing** for more help.

3 Revise

On Your Own Getting your ideas down on paper is the purpose of a draft. Revising that draft is where your ideas are polished and improved. The Revision Guide will help you focus on specific elements to make your writing stronger.

REVISION GUIDE

Ask Yourself	Tips	Revision Techniques
1. Does my introduction include a clearly stated claim?	**Underline** the introduction. **Highlight** the claim.	**Reword** the claim to make the idea clearer.
2. Do at least two valid reasons support the claim? Is each reason supported by relevant and sufficient evidence?	**Highlight** each reason. **Underline** each piece of evidence.	**Add** reasons or revise existing ones to make them more valid. **Insert** relevant evidence to ensure that your support is sufficient.
3. Have I addressed one or more counterclaims?	**Mark** both the counterclaims and your responses to them.	**Add** a counterclaim and counterargument that addresses the counterclaim.
4. Do I maintain a formal style throughout the argument?	**Highlight** slang and informal language.	**Reword** text to replace informal language with formal language.
5. Are appropriate and varied transitions used to connect reasons and evidence to the claim?	**Mark** each transition.	**Add** transition words and phrases to provide continuity.
6. Does the conclusion effectively summarize my argument?	**Underline** the summary of your argument.	**Add** or **reword** sentences to strengthen your summary.

ACADEMIC VOCABULARY

As you conduct your **peer review**, try to use these words.

- ❑ **dimension**
- ❑ **external**
- ❑ **statistic**
- ❑ **sustain**
- ❑ **utilize**

With a Partner After you have addressed all the points in the Revision Guide, exchange papers with a partner. Evaluate each other's drafts in a **peer review**. Look for places that need transitions and be ready to make suggestions of connecting words that might help. Pay attention to the style of the writing and notice any language that is too informal. As you make your suggestions for changes, be sure to bring up things your partner did well.

When you are receiving feedback, listen respectfully and consider your partner's points thoughtfully.

ENGLISH LEARNER SUPPORT

Formal Language Explain that students use informal language in conversation, with friends, but that with some kinds of writing designed for a different audience—such as arguments—they should use formal vocabulary. Give them the following examples:

Formal Vocabulary	obtain	object	cannot/is unable to	will not
Informal Vocabulary	get	thing	can't	won't

Have partners speak using formal and informal words. Then encourage students to write using newly acquired formal vocabulary. **MODERATE**

4 Edit

Once you have addressed the organization, development, and flow of ideas in your essay, you have one last step to take. Edit for the proper use of standard English conventions and make sure to correct any misspellings or grammatical errors.

Language Conventions

Look for places in your argument where you can use **transition words**, also known as **connecting words**, to link ideas, events, or reasons.

- **Contrast** Connecting words and phrases can show that two ideas are being contrasted. Some examples include *but, on the one hand, conversely, however, but then, nonetheless, in spite of, in contrast to.*
- **Sequence** Connecting words and phrases can also show time relationships between ideas. Some examples include *then, when, first, second, next, last, finally*. Dates are also sequence connectors.

Other types of connecting words indicate cause and effect, reasons, examples, and comparison. The chart contains examples of connecting words from "Is Survival Selfish?" and *Deep Survival* (in the online Independent Reading).

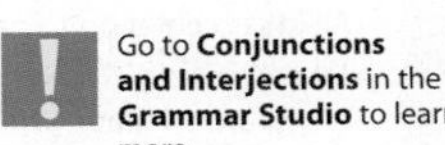

Go to **Conjunctions and Interjections** in the **Grammar Studio** to learn more.

Connecting words showing sequence	In July 2007, I was having a drink with a friend in Grand Central Station when an underground steam pipe exploded just outside. From where we sat, we heard a dull "boom!" and then suddenly, people were running, streaming out of the tunnels and out the doors.
Connecting words showing contrast	Survivors aren't fearless. They *use* fear: they turn it into anger and focus. Conversely, searchers are always amazed to find people who have died while in possession of everything they needed to survive.

5 Publish

Finalize your argument and choose a way to share it with your audience. Consider these options:

- Deliver your argument to your class.
- Present your argument as a letter to the editor. Submit it to your school or community newspaper or an online magazine.

4 EDIT

Explain to students that after they have revised their arguments, they should look for ways to improve the finer points of their drafts. Have students edit for the proper use of standard English conventions, including grammar, usage, punctuation, and spelling. Next, they will focus on using transition words to connect their ideas.

LANGUAGE CONVENTIONS

Use Transition Words Review the purpose for using transition words, also known as connecting words, as students revise and improve their arguments.

Contrast/Sequence Have a volunteer read aloud the introductory text and examples of transitions from the mentor text and *Deep Survival*. Discuss each of the underlined words and phrases. Ask: In what ways can transitions help clarify a writer's ideas? *(Transitions help to show how ideas differ and indicate the order in which ideas or events are presented. They also can show why and how things happen and compare ideas and events.)*

■ English Learner Support

Use Connecting Words Discuss the connecting words that can be used to show contrast and sequence, and encourage students to use these words as they edit their arguments. **MODERATE/LIGHT**

5 PUBLISH

Discuss the suggested publishing options. Encourage students who listen to, watch, or read other students' arguments to make notes and offer constructive comments about things they liked and suggestions they have for improvement. Encourage those who write to the editor of a newspaper or magazine to post their letters to a class website.

WHEN STUDENTS STRUGGLE . . .

Use Transitions Discuss examples of common transitional words and phrases such as the following:

Emphasis: *in this case, for example, in fact, namely, especially*
Contrast: *however, different from, on the one (other) hand*
Addition/Similarity: *and, in addition, like, also, as well as*
Cause and effect: *if ... then, therefore, because, since, as a result of*
Summary: *in conclusion, in fact, therefore, usually, finally*
Sequence: *first, after, later, since, when, meanwhile*

Prompt students to think of other transitional phrases and model their appropriate use.

USE THE SCORING GUIDE

Allow students time to read the scoring guide. Encourage them to ask questions about any ideas, sentences, phrases, or words they find unclear. Tell partners to exchange their final arguments and score them using the guidelines. Have each student reviewer write a paragraph explaining the reason for the score he or she awarded in each major category.

WRITING TASK

Use the scoring guide to evaluate your argument.

WRITING TASK SCORING GUIDE: ARGUMENT

	Organization/Progression	Development of Ideas	Use of Language and Conventions
4	• The organization is effective and appropriate to the purpose. • All ideas center on a specific claim. • Transitions clearly show the relationships among ideas.	• The introduction catches the reader's attention and clearly states the claim. • Reasons are compelling and supported by evidence including quotations and facts. • A counterclaim is effectively presented and addressed. • The conclusion synthesizes the ideas, effectively summarizes the argument, and provides a thought-provoking insight.	• Language and word choice is purposeful and precise. • The style is appropriately formal. • Spelling, capitalization, and punctuation are correct. • Grammar and usage are correct.
3	• The organization is, for the most part, effective and appropriate to the purpose. • Most ideas are focused on the claim. • A few more transitions are needed to show the relationship among ideas.	• The introduction could be more engaging. The claim is stated. • Appropriate reasons for the claim are supported by relevant evidence. • A counterclaim is presented and addressed. • The conclusion summarizes the argument effectively.	• Language is for the most part specific and clear. • The style is generally formal. • Minor spelling, capitalization, and punctuation mistakes do not interfere with the message. • Some grammar and usage errors occur but do not cause confusion.
2	• The organization is evident but is not always appropriate to the purpose. • Only some ideas are focused on the claim presented in the thesis. • Relationships among ideas are sometimes unclear.	• The introduction is not engaging. A vague claim is stated. • One or more reasons may be provided but lack sufficient evidence. • A counterclaim may be hinted at or not adequately addressed. • The conclusion merely restates the claim.	• Language is somewhat vague and unclear. • The style is often informal. • Spelling, capitalization, and punctuation are often incorrect. • Several errors in grammar and usage appear.
1	• The organization is not apparent. • Ideas are often tangential to a claim. • No transitions are used, making the argument difficult to understand.	• The introduction is missing or fails to make a claim. • Reasons are irrelevant or unsupported by evidence. • A counterclaim is either absent or not addressed. • The conclusion is missing.	• The style of language is inappropriate for the text. • Many spelling, capitalization, and punctuation errors make reading difficult. • Grammatical and usage errors cause significant confusion.

Present and Respond to an Argument

You will now prepare to deliver your argument as an oral presentation.

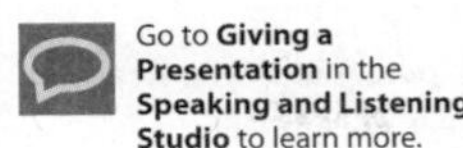
Go to **Giving a Presentation** in the **Speaking and Listening Studio** to learn more.

1 Adapt Your Argument for Presentation

Review your argument, thinking about how you can condense and clarify it for presentation. Use the chart below as you adapt your argument.

Argument Presentation Planning Chart		
Title and Introduction	How will you revise your title and introductory paragraph to capture the listener's attention and make a powerful statement of your claim?	
Audience	What information will your audience already know? What will they think about your claim? What counterclaims could they make?	
Effective Language and Organization	Which parts of your argument should be simplified? Where can you add connecting words such as "first, second, third" to clarify your main points?	
Visuals	What images could you use to illustrate your points or make your argument more convincing?	

2 Practice with a Partner or Group

After you have adapted your argument for presentation, practice with a partner or group to improve both the argument and your delivery. Remember to use appropriate content and academic vocabulary, and ask for help if you do not know the words to express your ideas.

Practice Effective Verbal Techniques

- ❑ **Enunciation** Practice saying difficult words aloud. If there are words that you stumble over, consider replacing them.
- ❑ **Voice Modulation and Pitch** Raise and lower your voice to emphasize points and make your arguments persuasive.

PRESENT AND RESPOND TO AN ARGUMENT

Introduce students to the Speaking and Listening task. Discuss ways in which oral arguments differ from written ones. Note that a reader has opportunities to adjust reading speed and to improve comprehension by rereading. Discuss techniques such as notetaking and preparing questions that students can use to improve their listening comprehension.

1 ADAPT YOUR ARGUMENT FOR PRESENTATION

Review the Argument Presentation Planning Chart. Discuss the four sections in the left-hand column. Have volunteers read aloud the question(s) for each major section and use them as the basis for a class discussion. Provide students with opportunities to ask additional questions about each topic. For example, when discussing the section on Effective Language and Organization, refer students to the previous discussion about connecting words used to show contrast and sequence.

For **speaking and listening support** for students at varying proficiency levels, see the **Language X-Ray** on page 482B.

ENGLISH LEARNER SUPPORT

Adapt the Argument Use the following supports with students at varying proficiency levels:

- Help students identify the claim of their arguments. With a partner, have them identify two connecting words to link ideas. **SUBSTANTIAL**
- Review the questions in the chart to confirm student comprehension of key ideas. Then have students practice pronouncing difficult words in their answers. If they stumble over the words, help them find replacements. **MODERATE**
- Have students discuss the questions in the chart with a partner before they begin writing their answers independently. **LIGHT**

2 PRACTICE WITH A PARTNER OR GROUP

Review the information and tips with the class, ensuring that all the terms and ideas are clear. Remind students that the purpose of practicing their presentations is to gain useful feedback from their peers. Emphasize that speaking before a group makes most people feel nervous, so everyone should be as supportive and helpful as possible.

Provide and Consider Advice for Improvement Read the introductory text. Ask: How can taking notes be useful in the follow-up discussion after listening to a presentation? *(to check comprehension of key ideas and provide specific comments and suggestions for improvement)* After practice is completed, have students generate a list of general suggestions that all students should keep in mind during their final presentations.

Discuss the rhetorical appeals and give examples. Suggest that students incorporate at least one of these appeals in their presentations.

3 DELIVER YOUR ARGUMENT

Remind students that it is up to them to decide which suggestions from others they will incorporate in their final presentations. Be sure to present students with a timetable that informs them of the day and duration of their presentations.

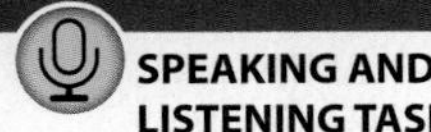

SPEAKING AND LISTENING TASK

As you work to improve your own delivery and that of your classmates, follow these discussion rules:

- ❑ **point out strengths as well as weaknesses**
- ❑ **only contribute information that is relevant to the discussion**
- ❑ **avoid generalizations like, "It was good," or "It could be better."**
- ❑ **include suggestions for improvement in a considerate and tactful manner**

- ❑ **Speaking Rate** Speak slowly enough that listeners understand you. Speak fast enough so that listeners don't fall asleep.
- ❑ **Volume** Have your partner or a group member go to the back of the room to see whether you can be heard.

Practice Effective Nonverbal Techniques

- ❑ **Eye Contact** Try to make eye contact with everyone in your audience at least once.
- ❑ **Facial Expression** Practice using facial expressions that mirror the emotions to which you are appealing with your argument.
- ❑ **Gestures** Gesture naturally with your hands, your shoulders, and your head, in ways that add meaning and interest to your delivery.

Provide and Consider Advice for Improvement

As a listener, pay close attention and listen respectfully. Take notes about ways that presenters can improve their deliveries and verbal and nonverbal techniques. Paraphrase and summarize each presenter's key ideas and main points, and ask questions to clarify ideas.

As a presenter, listen closely to questions and consider ways to revise your delivery to make sure your points are clear and logically sequenced. Remember to ask for suggestions about how you might make your delivery clearer and more interesting.

3 Deliver Your Argument

Use the advice you received during practice to make final changes to your argument. Then, using effective verbal and nonverbal techniques, present it to your classmates.

Listen for rhetorical appeals presenters use to support a claim. These strategies appeal to the reader's logic, ethics, or emotions. When writers use emotional appeals, they should offer evidence. Notice persuasive techniques presenters may use to manipulate your emotions:

- **Bandwagon** (everyone is doing it)
- **Personal attack** (discrediting an idea by attacking the person who expressed it)
- **Transfer** (connecting feelings about one thing to something else)
- **Loaded language** (choosing words that elicit strong feelings)
- **Understatement** (deliberately saying less than you mean)
- **Overstatement** (purposefully exaggerating or hyping)
- **Ad Hominem** (an argument directed against a person rather than an issue)
- **Testimonial** (relying on endorsements by well-known people)

ENGLISH LEARNER SUPPORT

Give Feedback Use the following supports with students at varying proficiency levels:

- After listening to the presentation, have students ask questions to clarify ideas. **SUBSTANTIAL**
- Have students take notes during the presentation and then give presenters feedback about verbal and nonverbal techniques. Explain whether these supported or detracted from their argument. **MODERATE**
- Discuss the list of rhetorical appeals. As they listen to the presentation, encourage students to pay attention to appeals speakers use to present a claim. When giving feedback to the speaker, have them explain why the appeal was or was not effective. **LIGHT**

Reflect on the Unit

In this writing task, you wrote about survival in the light of ideas and insights from the readings in this unit. Now is a good time to reflect on what you have learned.

Reflect on the Essential Question

- What does it take to survive in a crisis? How has your answer to this question changed since you first considered it when you started this unit?
- What are some examples from the texts you've read that show what it takes to survive in a crisis?

Reflect on Your Reading

- Which selections were the most interesting or surprising to you?
- From which selection did you learn the most about survival and survivors?

Reflect on the Writing Task

- What difficulties did you encounter while working on your argument? How might you avoid them next time?
- What part of the argument was the easiest and what part was the hardest to write? Why?
- What improvements did you make to your argument as you were revising?

UNIT 5 SELECTIONS

- **"The Leap"**
- **"Is Survival Selfish?"**
- **"The End and the Beginning"**
- **from *Night***
- **from *The Pianist***

REFLECT ON THE UNIT

Have students reflect independently on the questions and write notes on how they would respond. After students have completed these tasks, have them form small groups to discuss their responses. During these discussions, circulate about the classroom and note questions that seem to produce the liveliest conversations. Use these questions as the basis for a whole-class discussion that wraps up the unit.

LEARNING MINDSET

Questioning Prompt students to think about what being open to new ideas and trying new things means to them. Encourage students to think about ideas related to being flexible and open-minded. Point out that the key to these ideas is asking questions. Rather than letting themselves get stuck or frustrated, remind students that asking questions can spark creative thinking and generate new solutions to problems. Suggest to students that asking questions be their first strategy to try when they face a roadblock. Encourage them to help build a classroom climate that enables everyone to feel supported in asking questions and exploring new ideas and solutions.

Instructional Overview and Resources

	Instructional Focus	Online Ed Resources
 **Unit Introduction** **Heroes and Quests**	**Unit 6 Essential Question** **Unit 6 Academic Vocabulary**	**Stream to Start:** Heroes and Quests **Unit 6 Response Log**
ANALYZE & APPLY		
from *The Odyssey* Epic Poem by **Homer** **NOTICE & NOTE** READING MODEL **Signposts** • Tough Questions • Again and Again • Contrasts and Contradictions	**Reading** • Epic Heroes • Epic Poetry **Writing:** Write a Narrative **Speaking and Listening:** Deliver a Presentation **Vocabulary:** Words from Latin **Language Conventions:** Absolute Phrases	**Audio** **Close Read Screencasts:** Modeled Discussions **Reading Studio:** Notice & Note **Level Up Tutorial:** Plot: Sequence of Events **Writing Studio:** Writing Narratives **Speaking and Listening Studio:** Using Media in a Presentation **Vocabulary Studio:** Greek and Latin Word Roots **Grammar Studio:** Module 3: Lesson 4: Participial Phrases
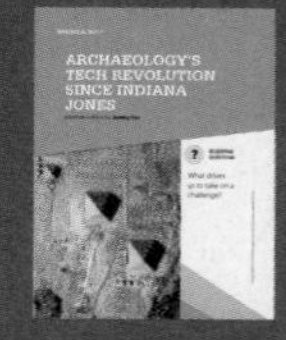 **Mentor Text** **"Archaeology's Tech Revolution Since Indiana Jones"** Informational Text by Jeremy Hsu **Lexile 1330L**	**Reading** • Make Predictions • Analyze Technical Texts **Writing:** Write a Summary **Speaking and Listening:** Present a Slideshow **Vocabulary:** Using References **Language Conventions:** Using Appositives Effectively	**Audio** **Reading Studio:** Notice & Note **Level Up Tutorials:** Main Idea and Supporting Details; Drawing Conclusions **Writing Studio:** Using Textual Evidence **Speaking and Listening Studio:** Using Media in a Presentation **Vocabulary Studio:** Using References **Grammar Studio:** Module 3: Lesson 8: Appositives and Appositive Phrases

SUGGESTED PACING: 30 DAYS

Unit Introduction	*from* The Odyssey	Archaeology's Tech Revolution Since Indiana Jones
1	2 3 4 5 6 7 8 9 10 11	12 13 14 15 16

English Learner Support	Differentiated Instruction	Online Ed Assessment
• Learn New Vocabulary		
• Text X-Ray • Expand Vocabulary • Practice Pronouncing Phonetically • Rephrase Unfamiliar Vocabulary • Analyze the Language of Foreshadowing • Practice Sequencing • Clarify Grammar Transfer Issues • Visualize Text Details • Practice Phonology • Oral Assessment • Spanish Cognates • Distinguish Two Uses of Participles	**When Students Struggle** • Use Strategies • Pronounce Greek Names • Chart the Sequence of Events **To Challenge Students** • Write a Scene	**Selection Test**
• Text X-Ray • Use Cognates • Understand Complex Syntax • Learning Strategies • Language Conventions • Identify Context Clues • Oral Assessment • Present a Slideshow • Vocabulary Strategy	**When Students Struggle** • Use Prereading Support • Draw Conclusions **To Challenge Students** • Research Archaeology of Native American Sites	**Selection Test**

UNIT 6 Continued

	Instructional Focus	Online Ed Resources
COLLABORATE & COMPARE		
from *The Cruelest Journey: 600 Miles to Timbuktu* Travel Writing by Kira Salak **Lexile 1030L**	**Reading** • Analyze Travel Writing • Evaluate Graphic Features **Writing:** Create Directions **Speaking and Listening:** Give and Receive Directions; Discuss the Directions **Vocabulary:** Foreign Words **Language Conventions:** Sentence Variety	**Audio** **Reading Studio:** Notice & Note **Level Up Tutorial:** Reading for Details **Vocabulary Studio:** Foreign Words Used in English **Grammar Studio:** Module 1: Lesson 10: Classifying Sentences by Purpose
"The Journey" Poem by Mary Oliver	**Reading** • Analyze Language • Make Connections **Writing:** Create a Visual Response **Speaking and Listening:** Discuss Visuals and Theme	**Audio** **Reading Studio:** Notice & Note **Level Up Tutorial:** Figurative Language **Writing Studio:** Task, Purpose, Audience **Speaking and Listening Studio:** Listening and Responding
Collaborate and Compare	**Reading:** Compare Theme and Main Idea **Speaking and Listening:** Collaborate and Present	**Speaking and Listening Studio:** Participating in Collaborative Discussions

Online Ed INDEPENDENT READING

The Independent Reading selections are only available in the eBook.

Go to the Reading Studio for more information on Notice & Note.

from *The Odyssey*
Epic Poem by Homer

"Siren Song"
Poem by Margaret Atwood

END OF UNIT

Writing Task: Write an Explanatory Essay **Speaking and Listening Task:** Participate in a Collaborative Discussion **Reflect on the Unit**	**Writing:** Write an Explanatory Essay **Language Conventions:** Spelling Commonly Confused Words **Speaking and Listening:** Participate in a Collaborative Discussion	**Unit 6 Response Log** **Mentor Text:** "Archaeology's Tech Revolution Since Indiana Jones" **Writing Studio:** Writing Informative Texts; Writing as a Process **Reading Studio:** Notice & Note **Grammar Studio:** Module 13: Lesson 6: Commonly Misspelled Words **Speaking and Listening Studio:** Participating in Collaborative Discussions

English Learner Support	Differentiated Instruction	Online Ed Assessment
• Text X-Ray • Build Academic Language Proficiency • Use Cognates • Use Pronouns • Recognize Informal English • Derive Meaning from Signs • Confirm Understanding • Use Learning Strategies • Oral Assessment • Use Direction Words • Use Text Features • Language Conventions	**When Students Struggle** • Analyze Travel Writing **To Challenge Students** • Reflect on Personal Motivations • Investigate Details	**Selection Test**
• Text X-Ray • Practice Personification • Use Linguistic Support • Oral Assessment • Provide Language Supports	**When Students Struggle** • Reteaching: Analyze Language	**Selection Test**
	When Students Struggle • Compare Texts **To Challenge Students** • Write or Create a Work with a Similar Theme	
from *The Odyssey: A Dramatic Retelling of Homer's Epic* Drama by Simon Armitage "Ilse, Who Saw Clearly" Short Story by E. Lily Yu **Lexile 830L**	"The Real Reasons We Explore Space" Argument by Michael Griffen **Lexile 1170L**	**Selection Tests**
• Language X-Ray • Discuss Academic Language • Use Transitions • Use the Mentor Text • Use Quotations • Ask Questions	**When Students Struggle** • Narrow a Topic • Choose an Organizational Pattern • Take Notes **To Challenge Students** • Create a Homophone Handbook	**Unit Test**

Connect to the ESSENTIAL QUESTION

Ask a volunteer to read aloud the Essential Question. Have students pause to reflect. Prompt them to discuss things they view as challenging, such as learning a new sport or going alone to an unfamiliar place. What are some of the factors that drive them to take on a challenge? Have them consider how much they are driven by rewards they expect to receive if they meet the challenge.

English Learner Support

Learn New Vocabulary Make sure students understand the Essential Question. If necessary, explain the following terms:

- *Drive* means "to push, compel, or press onward forcibly."
- *Take on* means "to begin to do a task or job."
- *Challenge* means "a task or job that is difficult to do."

Help students restate the question in simpler language: What makes us try things that are difficult?
SUBSTANTIAL/MODERATE

DISCUSS THE QUOTATION

Tell students that Kira Salak is an American journalist and adventurer, well known for her explorations of some of the world's most remote or inhospitable places. Ask students to read the quotation carefully and to take a moment to reflect. Prompt them to think about how a journey might teach them something about themselves. Then have them return to the Essential Question. Are we driven to take on challenges because we want to learn something about ourselves?

UNIT 6

HEROES AND QUESTS

ESSENTIAL QUESTION:

What drives us to take on a challenge?

If a journey doesn't have something to teach you about yourself, then what kind of journey is it?

Kira Salak

LEARNING MINDSET

Growth Mindset Remind students that people who believe they can improve their skills will be more successful than people who believe they're "just not good at" certain subjects or skills. Emphasize the importance of *yet*. They may not understand something *yet*, but with continued effort over time, they will eventually grasp the concept. Learning takes effort and it can be challenging, but in order to "grow" their brains they must continue to work hard. Assure students that although they may make mistakes as they work, mistakes are a sign of progress; they help people learn. Model how to reflect on a mistake and learn from it.

ACADEMIC VOCABULARY

Academic Vocabulary words are words you use when you discuss and write about texts. In this unit you will practice and learn five words.

- [x] motivate
- [ ] objective
- [ ] pursuit
- [ ] subsequent
- [ ] undertake

Study the Word Network to learn more about the word **motivate**.

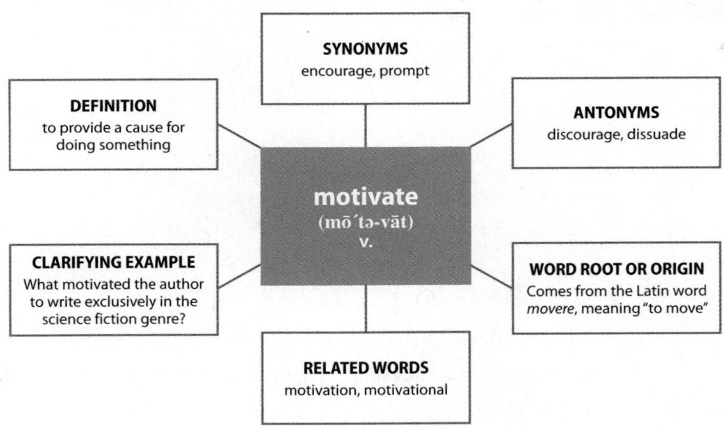

Write and Discuss Discuss the completed Word Network with a partner, making sure to talk through all of the boxes until you both understand the word, its synonyms, antonyms, and related forms. Then, fill out a Word Network for each of the four remaining words. Use a dictionary or online resource to help you complete the activity.

Go online to access the Word Networks.

RESPOND TO THE ESSENTIAL QUESTION

In this unit, you will explore what motivates people to take on a challenge. As you read, you will revisit the **Essential Question** and gather your ideas about it in the **Response Log** that appears on page R6. At the end of the unit, you will have the opportunity to write an **explanatory essay** exploring the human need for challenges. Filling out the Response Log will help you prepare for this writing task.

You can also go online to access the Response Log.

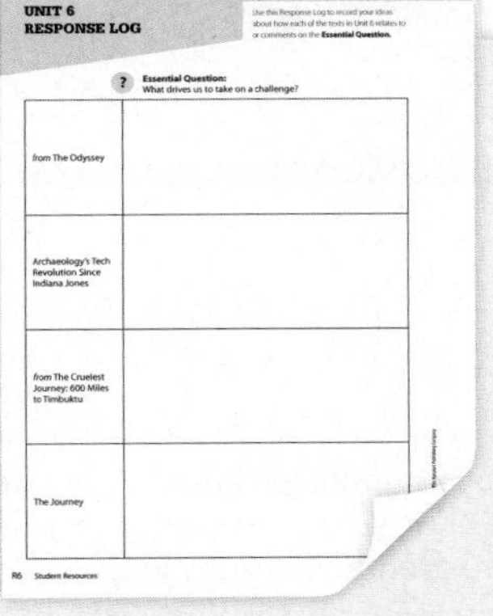

UNIT 6 RESPONSE LOG

Use this Response Log to record your ideas about how each of the texts in Unit 6 relates to or comments on the **Essential Question.**

Essential Question: What drives us to take on a challenge?

from The Odyssey	
Archaeology's Tech Revolution Since Indiana Jones	
from The Cruelest Journey: 600 Miles to Timbuktu	
The Journey	

R6 Student Resources

ACADEMIC VOCABULARY

As students complete Word Networks for the remaining four vocabulary words, encourage them to include all the categories shown in the completed network if possible, but point out that some words do not have clear synonyms or antonyms. Some words may also function as different parts of speech—for example, *objective* can also be an adjective.

motivate (mō´tə-vāt´) *v.* To provide a cause for doing something. (Spanish cognate: *motivar*)

objective (əb-jĕk´tĭv) *n.* An intention, purpose, or goal. (Spanish cognate: *objetivo*)

pursuit (pər-so͞ot´) *n.* The action of chasing or following something.

subsequent (sŭb´sĭ-kwĕnt´) *adj.* Coming after or following. (Spanish cognate: *subsecuente*)

undertake (ŭn´dər-tāk´) *v.* To assume responsibility for or take on a job or course of action.

RESPOND TO THE ESSENTIAL QUESTION

Direct students to the Unit 6 Response Log. Explain that students will use it to record ideas and details from the selections that help answer the Essential Question. When they work on the writing task at the end of the unit, their Response Logs will help them think about what they have read and make connections between the texts.

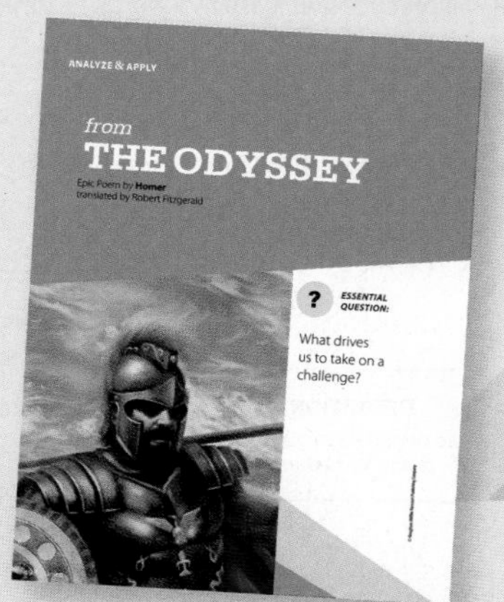

READING MODEL

from THE ODYSSEY

Epic Poem by **Homer**
translated by **Robert Fitzgerald**

GENRE ELEMENTS

EPIC POEM

Explain to students that **epic poetry** is one of the oldest forms of narrative. With *The Odyssey,* Homer took a story that had been sung for centuries and wrote it down. In so doing, he created a style and form that other Greek and Latin poets followed and that have characterized epic poetry ever since.

As students read excerpts from *The Odyssey,* they will become familiar with many of these characteristics. They will also start recognizing them in modern tales—for the action-packed adventures of heroes who embody values we admire are as compelling now as they were to the ancient Greeks.

LEARNING OBJECTIVES

- Identify characteristics of epic poetry and epic heroes.
- Research and evaluate the effectiveness of audio recordings of *The Odyssey*.
- Create a multimodal presentation of a narrative written from the perspective of a character other than Odysseus in *The Odyssey*.
- Recognize the Latin roots of common English vocabulary.
- Develop proficiency in using absolute phrases when composing sentences.
- **Language** Identify types of sensory imagery in *The Odyssey*.

TEXT COMPLEXITY

Quantitative Measures	**The Odyssey**	Lexile: N/A
Qualitative Measures	**Ideas Presented** Many key ideas are left implied; requires some inferential reasoning.	
	Structures Used Narrative events are mostly in chronological order interspersed with flashbacks.	
	Language Used Figurative and allusive language, often archaic and formal; complex sentence structures.	
	Knowledge Required More complex themes; experiences may be less familiar to many. Cultural or historical references may make heavier demands.	

Online 

RESOURCES

- Unit 6 Response Log
- Selection Audio
- Close Read Screencasts: Modeled Discussions
-  Reading Studio: Notice & Note
-  Level Up Tutorial: Plot: Sequence of Events
-  Writing Studio: Writing Narratives
-  Speaking and Listening Studio: Using Media in a Presentation
-  Vocabulary Studio: Greek and Latin Word Roots
-  Grammar Studio: Module 3: Lesson 4: Participial Phrases
-  from *The Odyssey* Selection Test

SUMMARIES

English

Excerpt, Book 9: The Cyclops

Odysseus and his men explore a cave where a Cyclops lives. They are trapped when the Cyclops heaves a slab of stone across the entrance. The Cyclops devours some of the men. Odysseus uses his cunning and bravery to escape.

Excerpt, Book 12: The Sirens

Odysseus follows the goddess Circe's instructions to plug his oarsmen's ears with beeswax and have them tie him to the mast to safely hear the Sirens' songs. Odysseus listens and begs to be untied, but the oarsmen tie him more tightly until the danger is passed.

Spanish

Pasaje, libro 9: El cíclope

Odiseo y sus hombres exploran una cueva donde vive un cíclope. Se ven atrapados cuando el cíclope atraviesa un pedazo de roca en la entrada. El cíclope devora a algunos de los hombres. Odiseo se vale de su astucia y valentía para escapar.

Pasaje, libro 12: Las sirenas

Odiseo sigue las instrucciones de la diosa Circe de tapar los oídos de sus remeros con cera de abejas y hacer que estos lo aten al mástil para escuchar de manera segura los cantos de las sirenas. Odiseo escucha y ruega ser desatado, pero los remeros lo atan más fuertemente hasta que el peligro pasa.

SMALL-GROUP OPTIONS

Have students work in small groups to read and discuss the selection.

Ask a Question

- Read a short section of the selection aloud while students follow in their texts.
- Ask a question about the section to confirm students' understanding and choose a student to respond.
- If the student does not respond in 11 seconds, the student poses the question again and calls on another student to respond.
- Once the question is answered, read the next short section of the poem and ask another key question about the text.

Reading Jigsaw

- After students have read the selection, divide them into groups of four.
- Give each group a topic to discuss and become "experts" on—for example, analyzing a character (Odysseus or the Cyclops); the Cyclops's daily routine; how to escape the Sirens.
- Reconfigure groups to make new jigsaw groups that include at least one expert on each topic.
- Each expert takes a turn making a brief presentation and answering questions from their jigsaw group. Then, each group discusses the selection as a whole.

Text X-Ray: English Learner Support

for the excerpt from *The Odyssey*

Use the Text X-Ray and the supports and scaffolds in the Teacher's Edition to help guide students at different proficiency levels through the selection.

INTRODUCE THE SELECTION

DISCUSS THE CHARACTERS

Display images of Odysseus and the Cyclops, Odysseus and the Sirens, and the ship of Odysseus. Ask students to describe what they see in each picture to assess their prior knowledge. Then introduce these characters from Greek mythology:

- Odysseus: the warrior hero and main character of *The Odyssey*
- Cyclops: a one-eyed giant
- Sirens: creatures who are part birds, part women, whose songs lure men to their deaths

As time allows and to provide context, introduce students to such major Greek gods and goddesses as Zeus, Athena, Apollo, and Poseidon.

Explain that today the word *odyssey* means a long adventurous trip; the word comes from the name Odysseus. Ask students what a hero or heroine would need in order to complete an odyssey. Supply these frames: *A hero/heroine would need to be ______. He/She would need to ______.*

CULTURAL REFERENCES

The Odyssey depicts a time and culture very different from our own and uses many unfamiliar terms. Encourage students to keep and refer to their own glossary of words that are specific to this epic poem, as in these examples from Book 9:

rowlocks (line 23): devices to hold oars in place
sheepfold (line 29): a pen for sheep
earthfast (line 30): held in the ground
goatskin (line 41): a pouch to hold liquid, made from sewing the skin of a goat together
Apollo's holy grove (line 43): a grove of trees dedicated to the god Apollo
ewes (line 86): female sheep
rogues (line 103): dishonest, unpredictable people

LISTENING

Learn New Vocabulary

Provide a range of supports for students to assimilate new vocabulary as they listen to and talk about epic poetry throughout the lesson.

Have students listen to selected lines from Book 9. Use the following supports with students at varying proficiency levels:

- Read aloud lines 419–422. Pause after each line to answer clarifying questions and define terms. **SUBSTANTIAL**
- Read aloud lines 404–413, beginning with "There." Instruct students to hold up a red card when they hear an unfamiliar word. Write each word on the board and discuss after the excerpt is read aloud. **MODERATE**
- Read aloud lines 404–418. As you read the excerpt, instruct students to mark words they don't know. Then, in small groups, tell them to look up the unfamiliar words. **LIGHT**

SPEAKING

Read Poetry Aloud

Model and teach students to read the poem so that its sound devices, such as meter and rhythm, are heightened and increase the listener's appreciation.

Use the following supports with students at varying proficiency levels:

- Tell students that the rhythm of lines 419–422 in Book 9 suggests sadness and reflection. Read them aloud and then have students read aloud with you. **SUBSTANTIAL**
- Choral read lines 419–422. Model how to identify stressed words. *(Example: the words "all day long")* Ask students how the sounds of stressed words add to meaning. *(Example: Stressing these three words in a row slows the rhythm, imitating the feeling of a long day.)* **MODERATE**
- Discuss the somber, thoughtful mood and tone of lines 419–422. Have students read the lines aloud. Ask students how the meter can help convey mood and tone with pauses and by stressing certain words. **LIGHT**

READING

Recognize Poetic Devices

Help students develop familiarity with sensory imagery through a close reading of excerpts from *The Odyssey*.

Use the following supports with students at varying proficiency levels:

- Ask student pairs to mark the visual imagery in Book 9, lines 30–31. *(tall trunks of pine, rugged towering oak trees)* Then have them mark the imagery in lines 53–54 and tell which senses are evoked. *(taste, scent)* **SUBSTANTIAL**
- Have students make a graphic organizer like the one below and find sensory images in a passage of their choice from Book 12. Discuss how these images enrich their ability to imagine the scene.

Lines	Sight	Hearing	Touch	Smell	Taste
40–47	dropped under the sea rim	singing dwindled away	laid thick		

MODERATE

- Pass out slips of paper. Ask each student to write down one or more examples of sensory imagery from Book 9, lines 136–155. Collect the slips, mix them up, and redistribute. Have students read the examples aloud and discuss how the imagery helps them imagine the scene. **LIGHT**

WRITING

Write a Narrative

Work with students as they approach the writing assignment on Student Edition page 521.

Use the following supports with students at varying proficiency levels:

- Ask students to draw a sequence of pictures depicting an event from the epic. Then support students as they write a caption for each image. **SUBSTANTIAL**
- Have partners choose a character or creature from *The Odyssey*. Ask them to retell aloud an event from that character's or creature's point of view. Then have them write their narrative. **MODERATE**
- Have students choose a narrator other than Odysseus and make a list of sensory details that their narrator would notice. Then have them write their narrative using those details. **LIGHT**

EXPLAIN THE SIGNPOSTS

Explain that **NOTICE & NOTE Signposts** are significant moments in the text that help readers understand and analyze works of fiction or nonfiction. Use the instruction on these pages to introduce students to the **Tough Questions, Again and Again,** and **Contrasts and Contradictions** signposts as they read. Then use the selection that follows to have students apply the signposts to a text.

For a full list of the fiction and nonfiction signposts, see page 562.

TOUGH QUESTIONS

Struggling to answer **Tough Questions** is a universal experience. Moments of self-doubt or remorse elicit them as well as moments of pain, indecision, or confusion. Odysseus asks tough questions for all of these reasons over the course of *The Odyssey.*

Explain to students that in a work of fiction, a tough question can reveal a character's **internal conflict.** It's another way of saying that the character is wrestling with an issue or is bothered by a situation, a choice, or the actions of another character. How the tough question gets answered—or not—is often the crux of the story.

Read aloud the example text. Students will notice that no actual question is asked; remind them that the tough question is not always explicit. In this sentence, "find out" is a cue for what the question is, and it can be posed in several ways. The first example annotation shows two tough questions that one reader identified based on Odysseus's situation. The second annotation shows a third question based on Odysseus's decision to take only a few people with him. A characteristic of tough questions is that they generate more questions for the reader. Ask students to frame the tough question differently. What other questions spring to mind for them?

Tell students that when they spot a Tough Questions signpost, they should pause, mark it in their consumable text, and ask themselves the anchor question: *What does this make me wonder about?*

READING MODEL

from THE ODYSSEY

For more information on these and other signposts to Notice & Note, visit the **Reading Studio**.

You are about to read a selection from the epic poem *The Odyssey*. In it, you will notice and note signposts that will give you clues about the poem's characters and themes. Here are three signposts to look for as you read this epic poem and other works of fiction.

When you read an epic poem, pause to see if the hero is facing a **Tough Question:**

"What could I could possibly do . . ."

"I am not sure what the right decision is . . ."

"How will I ever understand why . . ."

"Never have I been so confused about . . ."

Tough Questions Have you ever faced a difficult choice and asked a friend or yourself, "What should I do?" Questions such as these have no simple answers but make us consider our options.

When a character of a poem or story asks a tough question when facing a difficult choice, it reveals an internal conflict that the character is struggling to resolve. Authors may have characters ask an explicit question, or the question may be implied in a statement that suggests confusion or doubt.

One of the characteristics of an epic hero is the ability to respond to tough questions by taking swift action to overcome dangerous situations. Odysseus must prove his cleverness in facing tough choices many times throughout the course of *The Odyssey*. The lines below illustrate a student's annotation and a response to a **Tough Questions** signpost.

'Old shipmates, friends,
the rest of you stand by; I'll make the crossing
in my own ship, with my own company,
and find out what the mainland natives are—
for they may be wild savages, and lawless, or
hospitable and god fearing men.'

Anchor Question When you notice this signpost, ask: What does this make me wonder about?

What tough questions does Odysseus face here?	Are the natives dangerous or hospitable? Who should go find out?
What does Odysseus' decision make you wonder about?	Is it wise for Odysseus to go with only a few people?

Again and Again Song lyrics tend to include repetitive words and phrases which help us remember them. Songwriters use repeated words to enhance rhythm and rhyme and emphasize ideas and themes. Poets and authors create patterns by using situations, objects, and words or phrases **Again and Again** to make a point. Paying attention to instances of repetition can:

- provide insight into character, theme, or conflict
- reveal symbols or events being foreshadowed
- emphasize important ideas
- display literary artistry, such as rhyme, rhythm, or imagery

In this example, a student underlined an instance of Again and Again.

> When Dawn spread out her finger tips of rose
> the rams began to stir, moving for pasture . . .

When you see a word, phrase, or image appearing **Again and Again** as you read, pause to note:

"The author is repeating this phrase because . . ."

"This repeated phrase seems odd at this moment because . . ."

"Again the author is bringing up the image of . . ."

Anchor Question When you notice this signpost, ask: Why might the author keep bringing this up?

What is occurring again and again?	the reference to Dawn spreading out her "finger tips of rose"
Why do you think the author keeps using this phrase?	to add rhythm and incorporate imagery that describes the dawn

Contrasts and Contradictions Imagine watching a movie with a character who has been a bully, but is suddenly acting kind. You wonder why the character actions contradict previous behavior. Use **Contrasts and Contradictions** to draw conclusions and make predictions about characters. Authors often use Contrasts and Contradictions to:

- create complex characters
- show character development and growth
- build mystery and tension
- develop conflict
- provide insight into themes

Here a student marked a Contrast and Contradiction.

> He seized and drained the bowl, and it went down
> so fiery and smooth he called for more:
> 'Give me another, thank you kindly. Tell me, how are you called?
> I'll make a gift will please you.

When you see **Contrasts and Contradictions** as you read, pause to note:

"Until now, the character has acted . . ."

"I expected the character to . . ."

"This character is very different than . . ."

Anchor Question When you notice this signpost, ask: Why did the character act that way?

What is the contrast or contradiction?	Suddenly the Cyclops is being polite and friendly
Why is the character acting this way? What does this tell you about the character?	He wants more wine. I can infer that the Cyclops has a weakness, and Odysseus can manipulate him.

WHEN STUDENTS STRUGGLE . . .

Use Strategies Some students may struggle with the many unfamiliar names, creatures, places, and modes of expression in *The Odyssey.* The Somebody Wanted But So strategy gives them a means of following the narrative thread and recognizing signposts. Across the top of a page, students should write the following headers: *Somebody* (the main character of the scene), *Wanted* (What did this character want?), *But* (What got in the way?), *So* (What ended up happening?). Model how this works with one scene, emphasizing the need to reread the section to find out the answers, which students should write below each heading. This strategy also teaches students how to summarize, rather than retell. Invite students who use this strategy to share their thinking process with classmates who may be struggling.

AGAIN AND AGAIN

The **Again and Again** signpost asks students to notice repetition—words, phrases, images, details, or events that reappear in a text. In epic poetry, repetition serves as a kind of refrain; remind students that originally, epic poems were sung to an audience. Repetition also gives the poem structure, without which a poem of this length would be difficult to navigate.

Read aloud the example passage. The phrase about Dawn and "her finger tips of rose," also translated as "rosy-fingered Dawn," appears several times and is one of the most well-known phrases of *The Odyssey.* With repetition, it gathers significance. Homer uses it to signal a beginning, a starting afresh, a chance to get out of a predicament. Use the example to show that analyzing an Again and Again signpost can help students understand **setting** and the **symbolism** of the text.

Tell students that when they spot an Again and Again signpost, they should pause, mark it in their consumable text, and ask themselves the anchor question: *Why might the author keep bringing this up?*

CONTRASTS AND CONTRADICTIONS

When students see the behavior of a **character** suddenly change to be inconsistent with previous thoughts and actions, they have just encountered a **Contrasts and Contradictions** signpost. It often occurs as the result of a plot twist or a change in another character.

Read aloud the example passage. Odysseus has taken a different tack with the Cyclops by offering him something potent and unfamiliar. Odysseus is well aware of its effects, and his ploy works perfectly. A contrast in the behavior of Odysseus creates another contrast in the behavior of Cyclops.

Tell students that when they spot a Contrasts and Contradictions signpost, they should pause, mark it in their consumable text, and ask themselves the anchor question: *Why did the character act that way?*

APPLY THE SIGNPOSTS

Have students use the selection that follows as a model text to apply the signposts. As students encounter signposts, prompt them to stop, reread, and ask themselves the anchor questions that will help them understand the themes, characters, and conflicts of *The Odyssey.*

Tell students to continue to look for these and other signposts as they read the other selections in the unit.

CHARACTERISTICS OF THE EPIC

Ask volunteers to read aloud each section of the Elements of the Epic chart. As they read, tell students to jot down notes about characters, books, shows, or stories that the bullet points remind them of. For example, a "long, strange journey" full of "strange creatures" might remind students of *The Lord of the Rings* trilogy; an **epic hero** possessing superhuman strength could describe Superman or Wonder Woman. Pause after volunteers read each section to give students time to think and make notes.

Briefly discuss each section of the chart. Note that epic heroes have flaws and frailties as well as extraordinary abilities; nevertheless, they mostly embody admirable qualities. These heroes prove their heroic traits by contending with obstacles and challenges on their journeys. When discussing epic themes, remind students that **theme** is the message about life that the poet conveys through the characters and plot.

Start five lists on the board, one for each section of the chart. Call on students to offer the examples of characters, books, TV shows, or movies that they wrote down. Then organize students into groups of four. Their task is to look carefully at the chart and consider which of the examples on the board meet all of the criteria for an epic. They will need to discuss each bullet point to arrive at their decision.

Give each group the opportunity to state its decision and reasoning, and allow other groups to respond. As needed, assure students that there is no one right answer; there is room for different opinions. At the end of the discussion, ask students whether they think that any example meets all of the requirements of a true epic.

This process ensures that students become familiar with the elements of the epic while also drawing upon their personal experience. By the end of this activity, students will realize that the epic as a form is alive and well—and that they might actually be fans of it.

THE EPIC

Extraordinary heroes in pursuit of hideous monsters. Brutal battles fought and perilous quests undertaken. Spectacular triumphs and crushing defeats. The epic, still very much alive in today's novels and movies, began thousands of years ago in the oral tradition of ancient Greece. There, listeners gathered around poet-storytellers to hear the daring exploits of the hero Odysseus. Across storm-tossed seas, through wild forests, amid countless dangers and subsequent narrow escapes, the hero, motivated by a singular focus on his objective, prevails against all odds. It's no wonder that Homer's Odyssey *remains one of the most beloved epics in Western literature. It captivates us and carries us off into a time and place quite different from—yet somehow similar to—our own.*

CHARACTERISTICS OF THE EPIC

An **epic** is a long narrative poem. It recounts the adventures of an epic hero, a larger-than-life figure who undertakes great journeys and performs deeds requiring remarkable bravery and cunning. As you begin your own journey through Homer's epic, you can expect to encounter the following elements.

ELEMENTS OF THE EPIC	
Epic Hero • Possesses superhuman strength, craftiness, and confidence • Helped or harmed by gods or fate • Embodies qualities valued by the culture • Overcomes perilous situations	**Archetypes** Characters and situations recognizable across times and cultures • brave hero • sea monster • suitors' contest • evil temptress • loyal servant • buried treasure
Epic Plot Depicts a long, strange journey filled with such complications as • strange creatures • treacherous weather • divine intervention • large-scale events	**Epic Themes** Reflect universal concerns, such as • courage • loyalty • beauty • the fate of a nation • life and death • a homecoming
Epic Setting • Includes fantastic or exotic lands • Involves more than one nation or culture	

THE LANGUAGE OF HOMER

The people of ancient Greece who first experienced *The Odyssey* heard it sung in a live performance. The poet, or another performer, used epic similes, epithets, and allusions to help keep the audience enthralled.

- A **simile** is a comparison between two unlike things, using the word *like* or *as*. Homer often employs the **epic simile**, a comparison developed at great length over several lines. For example, the epic simile in the passage on the right compares an angry Odysseus to a roasting sausage.

> His rage
> held hard in leash, submitted to his mind,
> while he himself rocked, rolling from side to side,
> as a cook turns a sausage, big with blood
> and fat, at a scorching blaze, without a pause,
> to broil it quick: so he rolled left and right, . . .

- An **epithet** renames a person or thing with a descriptive phrase. To maintain the meter of the poem or complete a line of verse, the poet would often use an epithet containing the necessary number of syllables. For example, Homer often refers to Odysseus by such epithets as "son of Laertes" and "raider of cities."
- An **allusion** is a reference to a literary or historical person, place, event, or composition. For example, when Telemachus, Odysseus' son, beholds the palace of Menelaus, he exclaims, "This is the way the court of Zeus must be." Every listener in Greece immediately understood the allusion to Zeus, the ruler of the gods.

EXAMINING THE HOMERIC EPICS

Considered the greatest masterpieces of the epic form, *The Iliad* and *The Odyssey* present high drama and intense emotions. In both books, important plot elements include the interference of gods in human affairs, the epic heroism of the central characters, and the saga of the Trojan War and its aftermath.

THE TROJAN WAR The legendary conflict between Greece (or Achaea) and Troy began around 1200 BC. Paris, a Trojan prince, kidnapped Helen, the wife of Menelaus, king of Sparta. Menelaus recruited the armies of allied kingdoms to attack Troy and recover his wife. For ten years the Greek forces held Troy under siege, but they could not penetrate the walls of the city.

Finally, Odysseus, king of Ithaca, came up with a plan to break the stalemate. He ordered his men to build a giant wooden horse. One morning the people of Troy awoke to find that horse outside the city gates—and no Greeks in sight. Assuming the Greeks had retreated and had left the horse as a peace offering, they brought the horse inside the gates. They soon discovered, too late, that the horse was filled with Greek soldiers and that their city was doomed.

HEROISM *The Odyssey* recounts Odysseus' adventures as he struggles to make his way home from post-war Troy, along with the conflicts that arise in Ithaca just before and after his return. He prevails against gruesome monsters, enchanting women, and greedy rivals intent on preventing him from reaching his objective. Odysseus employs cleverness and guile to get out of difficult situations.

TEACH

THE LANGUAGE OF HOMER

Students have encountered **similes** in other literary works; the difference here is that an **epic simile** is more complex and lengthy than a simile in a short poem. Tell students to notice the nature of the simile as well. If someone's voice is compared to an angelic harp, for example, that's different from being compared to a screaming siren.

To help students understand **epithets,** invite them to think of examples for themselves. Model this by doing a few together—for instance, "teacher, giver of homework" or "Makiah, player of soccer." Discuss how the epithet influences opinion as well as conveys information about the person or thing that it describes.

Explain that **allusions** refer to something or someone outside of the work itself. (Make sure that students understand the difference between the similar-sounding words *allusion* and *illusion*.) Note that students use allusions as a kind of shorthand. When they say the name of a particular place or a person, their friends understand that they are referring to pertinent events, people, and more. Allusions in classic works of literature such as *The Odyssey* also provide historical context.

EXAMINING THE HOMERIC EPICS

Tell students that Heinrich Schliemann, a German businessman and archaeologist, excavated the site of ancient Troy in the 1870s and 1880s. His findings suggest that the story of the Trojan War may be based on fact. Troy was an ancient seaport on the Aegean Sea in present-day Turkey. Historians and archaeologists continue to excavate the site to learn more about this time in the Bronze Age.

Explain to students that Homer's epics are the earliest written record of ancient Greece. They incorporate Greek myths that explain natural phenomena; tell stories; and pass down values, beliefs, and customs. They also tell us of Greek **heroes** like Odysseus.

Greek myths are the origin of some expressions we use today. When a person's weakness is described as his or her "Achilles' heel," for example, the reference is to the story of the Greek hero Achilles. His mother dipped him in the River Styx to make him immortal; but she was holding him by the heel, which was the only place on his body that he could be injured. He died when an arrow hit him in that very spot.

Connect to the ESSENTIAL QUESTION

Homer's *The Odyssey* can be read from many different perspectives. One is as a study of what drives the hero Odysseus to take on challenges that would be insurmountable to an ordinary human. The challenges at the center of each story of this poem are all undertaken to achieve the ultimate challenge of finding the way home to Ithaca—where yet more challenges await.

from THE ODYSSEY

Epic Poem by **Homer**
translated by Robert Fitzgerald

ESSENTIAL QUESTION:

What drives us to take on a challenge?

498 Unit 6

LEARNING MINDSET

Plan Explain to students that completing work efficiently and well is one goal of a learning mindset. Planning well requires being able to estimate how long an assignment will take and then deciding how to allocate this time. People are not magically able to do this; it takes practice. Give students opportunities to practice planning their assignments. Coach them to break out the steps required and to look at how long each step will realistically take. Suggest that students follow the example of people who set the deadline a little before the actual one, to build in wiggle room in case the assignment takes longer than planned. Tell students that the practice they get now with planning will serve them well as adults, who have to meet deadlines all the time—both in their work and personal lives.

QUICK START

Think about someone you think is a hero. What qualities or characteristics do you admire in this person? Brainstorm a list of up to 20 heroic traits. Share your list with a partner, and note any overlapping traits. Ask your classmates or teacher to explain any terms you are not familiar with.

EPIC HEROES

Odysseus is an **epic hero**—a larger-than-life character who embodies the ideals of a nation or race. Epic heroes take part in long, dangerous adventures and accomplish great deeds. They are considered **archetypes** because they can be found in many works from different cultures throughout the ages. Often their character traits provide clues to the epic's **themes**. In addition, the form, style, and point of view of epics provides insight into the historical time in which they were written.

Although epic heroes may have superhuman abilities, they still have human flaws. These flaws make them more complex and also more believable. For example, Odysseus demonstrates extraordinary strength and courage, but his overconfidence results in a tendency to dismiss warnings. His imperfections help make him more likable than a perfect character would be, and the audience can relate to his mistakes.

As you read, take notes in the chart below to help you analyze how the complex character of Odysseus develops over the course of the epic.

GENRE ELEMENTS: EPIC POEM

- a long, narrative poem on a serious subject in an elevated or formal style
- tells adventures of a hero whose traits reflect the ideals of a nation or race
- addresses universal themes
- occurs across cultures and time periods

QUESTION ABOUT ODYSSEUS	NOTES FROM THE EPIC
What do you learn about Odysseus' character through how he faces various conflicts?	
What traits, or qualities, does Odysseus show through his interactions with other characters?	
What do Odysseus' character traits tell you about what the ancient Greeks found admirable? What themes do you predict Homer might develop?	

TEACH

QUICK START

In some ways, Odysseus is not a modern hero, nor would some modern heroes be recognized as such in Homer's time. Consider keeping students' lists. Revisit them after students have a deeper understanding of Odysseus's character, and how he is portrayed as an epic hero. How might they revise the lists to represent the heroic traits envisioned by Homer?

EPIC HEROES

Tell students that as they take notes on Odysseus, what they learn about his character as he confronts conflict will overlap with the traits he displays through interactions—since many of the interactions are also conflicts. How often and to what degree Odysseus is in conflict with other characters will also tell students something about him.

As Odysseus reveals his character traits through conflict, interactions, and problem-solving tactics, he will seem recognizably human through his failings and flaws, while other traits will make him seem superhuman. Point out that the ancient Greeks didn't necessarily admire Odysseus's negative traits; what, then, was Homer trying to say by portraying these particular weaknesses and vulnerabilities? Students will need to **make inferences** about what the Greeks admired when they come upon examples of Odysseus's human frailty.

ENGLISH LEARNER SUPPORT

Expand Vocabulary Ask pairs of students to read lines 105–106, 148–155, and 227–230 in Book 9 of the selection. First, tell students to underline words they don't know. As a class, define those words together. Next, instruct students to circle the words that describe how Odysseus is feeling or acting. Make a word wall that students can refer to as they read. Include high-frequency words and words that describe the character traits and feelings of Odysseus.
SUBSTANTIAL/MODERATE

TEACH

EPIC POETRY

Choose a short section of *The Odyssey* to model reading aloud while students follow along on the page. Review poetic devices such as **alliteration, meter,** and **rhyme.** Discuss a couple of lines that contain one or more of these poetic devices and instruct students to write down those examples in their charts. Tell them to continue finding examples as they read and see how many examples they can find for their charts.

To show students why the punctuation is so important, read a line aloud and pause at the end (where there is no punctuation) before reading the next line. Then read the lines again, pausing where the punctuation falls. Discuss how the meter and flow are affected accordingly.

LANGUAGE CONVENTIONS

Explain to students that **absolute phrases** are always set off by commas, which is one clue to finding them. They describe, or modify, the entire main clause of the sentence. Students can remember what this term means if they think of the word *absolute* as meaning "complete" or "total." In other words, absolute phrases modify the sentence as a whole.

ANNOTATION MODEL

Students can review the Reading Model introduction if they have questions about any of the signposts. Suggest that they underline important phrases or circle key words that help them identify signposts. They may want to color-code their annotations by using a different color highlighter for each signpost. Point out that they may follow this suggestion or use their own system for marking up the selections in their write-in texts.

GET READY

EPIC POETRY

An **epic** is a long narrative poem, usually an adventure story. An epic plot spans many years and involves a long journey. Often, the fate of an entire nation is at stake. An epic **setting** spans great distances and foreign lands. Epic **themes** reflect timeless concerns, such as courage, honor, life, and death. To appreciate *The Odyssey* as poetry, follow these steps:

- Read the epic aloud. Listen for sound devices, such as alliteration, meter, and rhyme, and notice how they reflect and enhance meaning.
- Pay attention to structure by following punctuation closely. Remember that the end of a line does not indicate the end of a thought.
- Consider how imagery and figurative language, including epic similes, develop characters and reveal plot events. Note allusions and epithets.

As you read, make notes in the chart about poetic elements you notice.

POETIC DEVICE	EXAMPLE
Sound devices	
Imagery and figurative language	
Allusions and epithets	
Other poetic elements	

LANGUAGE CONVENTIONS

Absolute Phrases In this lesson, you will learn about the usefulness of **absolute phrases** in adding information and imagery to writing. An absolute phrase consists of a noun and a participle, a verb form ending in *-ed* or *-ing* that acts as an adjective. An absolute phrase describes the main clause. As you read, note Homer's use of absolute phrases. Here is an example.

I drove them, all three wailing, to the ships . . .

ANNOTATION MODEL

NOTICE & NOTE

As you read, notice and note signposts, including **Tough Questions, Again and Again,** and **Contrasts and Contradictions.** Here is how one reader responded to the beginning of *The Odyssey*.

He saw the townlands
and learned the minds of many distant men,
and weathered many bitter nights and days
in his deep heart at sea, while he fought only
to save his life, to bring his shipmates home.

epic poem setting—a wanderer who sees many lands

"fought"—Odysseus will perform heroic deeds

NOTICE & NOTE

BACKGROUND

Homer *may have lived sometime between 900 and 800 BC—if he ever lived at all. Although the ancient Greeks credited him with composing* The Iliad *and* The Odyssey, *people have long argued about whether or not he really existed. Many theorists speculate on who Homer may have been and where he may have lived. Details in the stories suggest that he was born and lived in the eastern Aegean Sea, either on the island of Chios or in Smyrna, and that he was blind.*

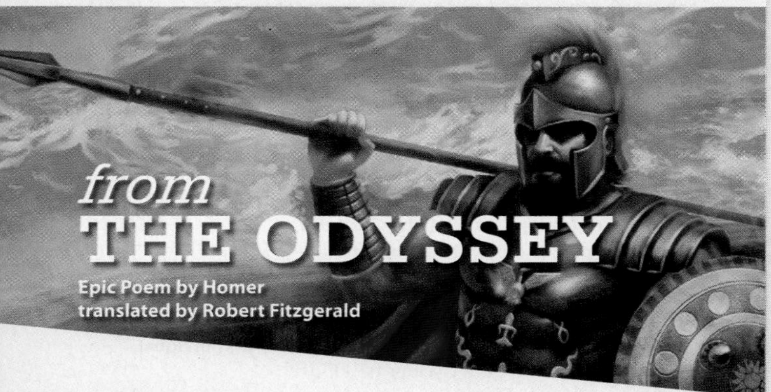

from THE ODYSSEY

Epic Poem by Homer
translated by Robert Fitzgerald

Whatever position modern scholars take on the debate, most believe that one or two exceptionally talented individuals created the Homeric epics. The Iliad *and* The Odyssey *each contain 24 books of verse, but they probably predate the development of writing in Greece. The verses, which were originally sung, gradually became part of an important oral tradition. Generations of professional reciters memorized and performed the poems at festivals throughout Greece. By 300 BC, several versions of the books existed, and scholars undertook the job of standardizing the texts.*

Homer's poems profoundly influenced Greek culture and, as a result, contributed to the subsequent development of Western literature, ideas, and values. The Roman poet Virgil wrote a related poem, the Aeneid, *in Latin, and Odysseus appears in Dante's* Inferno. *Poets throughout English literature, from Geoffrey Chaucer in the Middle Ages to William Shakespeare in the Renaissance to John Keats in the Romantic era, have found inspiration in Homer. James Joyce's 1922 novel* Ulysses *(the Latin form of Odysseus' name) transforms one ordinary Dublin day into an Odyssean journey. Dozens of movies have retold the saga of the Trojan War and the long journey home, both directly and symbolically. For thousands of years people have taken the tales of a wandering Greek bard and made them their own.*

BACKGROUND

Although Homer may have composed *The Odyssey* in the eighth or ninth century BC, scholars believe that the epic takes place during Greece's Bronze Age, an era that ended approximately 500 years earlier. It was a time when warrior chieftains lived in elaborate palaces and led colonizing expeditions to expand trade and territory.

Display a map of the Mediterranean region and point out Greece and the Aegean Sea. Indicate the area in the northwest of present-day Turkey believed to be the site of the Trojan War. Ask a volunteer to point out the island of Ithaca off the west coast of Greece. Explain that scholars have tried to correlate the route Odysseus took back to Ithaca with places around the Mediterranean Sea. Maps of this route show a circuitous path, full of backtracking and landings far away from the island of Ithaca.

TEACH

SETTING A PURPOSE

Direct students to use the Setting a Purpose prompt to focus their reading.

ENGLISH LEARNER SUPPORT

Practice Pronouncing Phonetically Direct students to the list of characters from *The Odyssey* on page 502 and point out the pronunciations shown in parentheses. Explain that learning the phonetic symbols—especially those for the vowel sounds of English—will make it a lot easier to pronounce unfamiliar words. Have students turn to the Pronunciation Key provided in the Student Resources section of their Student Edition. Review the phonetic symbol for each vowel sound. Pronounce the vowel sound and then the example word. Then model how to look up and use the phonetic symbols in the Pronunciation Key to pronounce *Helios*.

Guide students to repeat this process with *Thrinacia* and *Zeus*. Then have pairs of students use the Pronunciation Key to help them pronounce each of the remaining names in the list on page 502.

Tell students that knowing how to use these phonetic symbols will help them to pronounce English words that they look up in a dictionary. They can also remember how a word is pronounced by using the symbols to write the word phonetically when they hear it.
ALL LEVELS

NOTICE & NOTE

Notice & Note

You can use the side margins to notice and note signposts in the text.

SETTING A PURPOSE

As you read, monitor your comprehension by rereading and referring to the explanatory notes in the margins. Ask for help from a peer or teacher when you come across other unfamiliar words or phrases.

IMPORTANT CHARACTERS IN THE ODYSSEY (in order of mention)

Book 1

Helios (hē´lē-ŏs), the sun god, who raises his cattle on the island of Thrinacia (thrĭ-nā´shə)
Zeus (zo͞os), the ruler of the Greek gods and goddesses; father of Athena and Apollo
Telemachus (tə-lĕm´ə-kəs), Odysseus' son
Penelope (pə-nĕl´ə-pē), Odysseus' wife

Book 9

Alcinous (ăl-sĭn´ō-əs), the king of the Phaeacians (fē-ā´shənz)
Cyclopes (sī-klō´pēz), a race of one-eyed giants; an individual member of the race is a Cyclops (sī´klŏps)
Apollo (ə-pŏl´ō), the god of music, poetry, prophecy, and medicine
Poseidon (pō-sīd´n), the god of the seas, earthquakes, and horses; father of the Cyclops who battles Odysseus
Athena (ə-thē´nə), the goddess of war, wisdom, and cleverness; goddess of crafts

Book 12

Circe (sûr´sē), a goddess and enchantress who lives on the island of Aeaea (ē-ē´ə)
Sirens (sī´rənz), creatures, part woman and part bird, whose songs lure sailors to their death

WHEN STUDENTS STRUGGLE . . .

Pronounce Greek Names Instruct students to pronounce each Greek name after you. Organize the class into groups of four.

- Distribute flash cards. Tell students to write the names of characters on them. Have students practice pronouncing the names of the characters on their set of cards.
- Have each student quiz the group on pronouncing the characters' names.
- After one round, have students shuffle all the cards together, redistribute, and become experts on the new set before quizzing each other.

NOTICE & NOTE 

BOOK 1

A GODDESS INTERVENES

Sing in me, Muse, and through me tell the story
of that man skilled in all ways of contending,
the wanderer, harried for years on end,
after he plundered the stronghold
on the proud height of Troy.
He saw the townlands
and learned the minds of many distant men,
and weathered many bitter nights and days
in his deep heart at sea, while he fought only
to save his life, to bring his shipmates home.
But not by will nor valor could he save them,
for their own recklessness destroyed them all—
children and fools, they killed and feasted on
the cattle of Lord Helios, the Sun,
and he who moves all day through heaven
took from their eyes the dawn of their return.

Of these adventures, Muse, daughter of Zeus,
tell us in our time, lift the great song again. . . .

The story of Odysseus begins with the goddess Athena appealing to Zeus to help Odysseus, who has been wandering for ten years on the seas, to find his way home to his family on Ithaca. While Odysseus has been gone, his son, Telemachus, has grown to manhood and Odysseus' wife, Penelope, has been besieged by suitors wishing to marry her and gain Odysseus' wealth. The suitors have taken up residence in her home and are constantly feasting on the family's cattle, sheep, and goats. They dishonor Odysseus and his family. Taking Athena's advice, Telemachus travels to Pylos for word of his father. Meanwhile, on Ithaca, the evil suitors plot to kill Telemachus when he returns.

1 Muse: a daughter of Zeus, credited with divine inspiration.

3 harried: tormented; harassed.

11–13 their own recklessness . . . the Sun: a reference to an event occurring later in the poem—an event that causes the death of Odysseus' entire crew.

CLOSE READ SCREENCAST

Modeled Discussion In their eBook, have students view the Close Read Screencast, in which readers discuss and annotate the explanation of what happened to Odysseus's crew (Book 1, lines 5–15).

As a class, view and discuss the video. Then have students pair up to an independent close read of Book 9, lines 335–352. Students can record their responses on the Close Read Practice PDF.

Close Read Practice PDF

TEACH

ENGLISH LEARNER SUPPORT

Rephrase Unfamiliar Vocabulary To aid comprehension, replace terms that are new to students with more common ones. When a sentence is long and complex, help students to rephrase it in simpler, shorter, sentences. Together, reread Book 9, lines 8–12, aloud. Provide this list of substitutions:

- *have no muster* = don't get together
- *no consultation* = don't share information
- *dwells* = lives
- *rough justice* = punishment
- *indifferent to* = not caring about

Tell pairs of students to reread the passage with the substitutions. Discuss the meaning as a class.

Encourage students to add this strategy to their toolkit for understanding difficult passages. **MODERATE**

NOTICE & NOTE

BOOK 9

NEW COASTS AND POSEIDON'S SON

The Cyclops

Odysseus has spent ten years wandering the Mediterranean Sea. By Book 9, he has reached the island of Scheria, where King Alcinous has welcomed him with a banquet. Odysseus agrees to tell King Alcinous stories about his adventures, including the following story about a race of creatures called the Cyclopes.

In the next land we found were Cyclopes,
giants, louts, without a law to bless them.
In ignorance leaving the fruitage of the earth in mystery
to the immortal gods, they neither plow
nor sow by hand, nor till the ground, though grain—
wild wheat and barley—grows untended, and
wine-grapes, in clusters, ripen in heaven's rain.
Cyclopes have no muster and no meeting,
no consultation or old tribal ways,
but each one dwells in his own mountain cave
dealing out rough justice to wife and child,
indifferent to what the others do. . . ."

Across the bay from the land of the Cyclopes is a lush, deserted island. Odysseus and his crew land on the island in a dense fog and spend days feasting on wine and wild goats and observing the mainland, where the Cyclopes live. On the third day, Odysseus and his company of men set out to learn if the Cyclopes are friends or foes.

"When the young Dawn with finger tips of rose
came in the east, I called my men together
and made a speech to them:
'Old shipmates, friends,
the rest of you stand by; I'll make the crossing
in my own ship, with my own company,
and find out what the mainland natives are—
for they may be wild savages, and lawless,
or hospitable and god fearing men.'
At this I went aboard, and gave the word
to cast off by the stern. My oarsmen followed,
filing in to their benches by the rowlocks,
and all in line dipped oars in the gray sea.

1 Cyclopes (sī-klō´pēz): refers to the creatures in plural; Cyclops is singular.

22 stern: the rear end of a ship.

NOTICE & NOTE

TEACH

As we rowed on, and nearer to the mainland,
at one end of the bay, we saw a cavern
yawning above the water, screened with laurel,
and many rams and goats about the place
inside a sheepfold—made from slabs of stone
earthfast between tall trunks of pine and rugged
towering oak trees.

A prodigious man

slept in this cave alone, and took his flocks
to graze afield—remote from all companions,
knowing none but savage ways, a brute
so huge, he seemed no man at all of those
who eat good wheaten bread; but he seemed rather
a shaggy mountain reared in solitude.
We beached there, and I told the crew
to stand by and keep watch over the ship;
as for myself I took my twelve best fighters
and went ahead. I had a goatskin full
of that sweet liquor that Euanthes' son,
Maron, had given me. He kept Apollo's
holy grove at Ismarus; for kindness
we showed him there, and showed his wife and child,
he gave me seven shining golden talents
perfectly formed, a solid silver winebowl,
and then this liquor—twelve two-handled jars
of brandy, pure and fiery. Not a slave
in Maron's household knew this drink; only
he, his wife and the storeroom mistress knew;
and they would put one cupful—ruby-colored,
honey-smooth—in twenty more of water,
but still the sweet scent hovered like a fume
over the winebowl. No man turned away
when cups of this came round.

A wineskin full

I brought along, and victuals in a bag,
for in my bones I knew some towering brute
would be upon us soon—all outward power,
a wild man, ignorant of civility.

We climbed, then, briskly to the cave. But Cyclops
had gone afield, to pasture his fat sheep,
so we looked round at everything inside:
a drying rack that sagged with cheeses, pens
crowded with lambs and kids, each in its class:
firstlings apart from middlings, and the 'dewdrops,'

27 screened with laurel: partially hidden by laurel trees.

42–43 Euanthes (yo͞o-ăn´thēz); **Maron** (mâr´ŏn).

46 talents: bars of gold or silver of a specified weight, used as money in ancient Greece.

57 victuals (vĭt´lz)**:** food.

66–67 The Cyclops has separated his lambs into three age groups.

For **reading support** for students at varying proficiency levels, see the **Text X-Ray** on page 494D.

IMPROVE READING FLUENCY

Targeted Passage Tell students that when they read this poem aloud, they should imagine that they are reciting it to an audience that has no text to follow along in. The speaker must pause when the punctuation calls for it and must use expression and emphasis to help listeners understand and enjoy the language of the poem.

Model reading Book 9, lines 38–56, aloud while students follow along in their textbooks. Then have pairs of students read the passage aloud, changing speakers for each new sentence.

Go to the **Reading Studio** for additional support in developing fluency.

EPIC HEROES

Remind students that an **epic hero** such as Odysseus shows **character traits** that are both superhuman and believably human. Ask students to reread lines 75–77 and consider what human flaws Odysseus displays here. The statement "how sound that was" acknowledges that the men had made a good suggestion; *sound* means "showing good sense." But Odysseus admits that he did not follow this suggestion because he was curious to see the Cyclops. "No pretty sight" hints—or **foreshadows**—that the men will not benefit from the curiosity of their leader. (***Answer:*** *The passage suggests that Odysseus is recklessly curious and heedless of potential danger.*)

■ English Learner Support

Analyze the Language of Foreshadowing Explain **foreshadowing** as giving readers clues about something that hasn't happened yet. Choral read Book 9, lines 75–77. Model how to analyze the language in this example of foreshadowing by thinking aloud: "I know that the phrase *how sound that was* is a clue about something that Odysseus hasn't talked about yet. He knows that the advice was good—but he knows it now only because of what happened when he didn't take that advice. That's what he means when he uses the expression *it turned out*". Discuss this expression together, making sure students understand that it means "as it happened" or "I later realized."

Ask students to write and share sentences using the expression *it turned out* regarding an event that they know about or in which they participated. **MODERATE/LIGHT**

NOTICE & NOTE

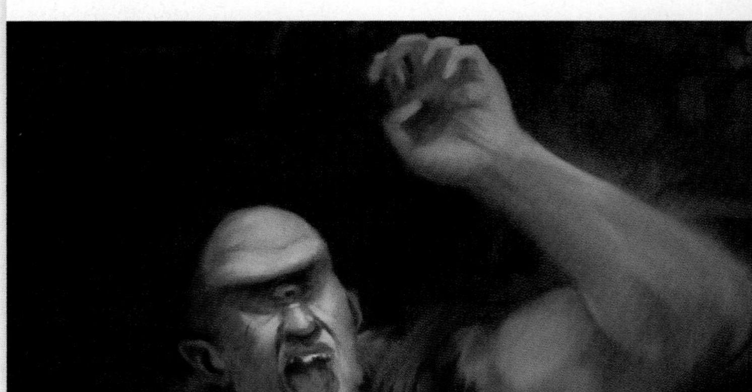

68 whey: the watery part of milk, which separates from the curds, or solid part, during the making of cheese.

74 good salt water: the open sea.

EPIC HEROES
Annotate: Mark foreshadowing in lines 75–77 suggesting that Odysseus has a weakness that may bring trouble to him and his men.

Evaluate: What flaws might be revealed in these lines?

78 burnt an offering: burned a portion of the food as an offering to secure the gods' goodwill. (Such offerings were frequently performed by Greek sailors during difficult journeys.)

or newborn lambkins, penned apart from both.
And vessels full of whey were brimming there—
bowls of earthenware and pails for milking.
My men came pressing round me, pleading:
'Why not
take these cheeses, get them stowed, come back,
throw open all the pens, and make a run for it?
We'll drive the kids and lambs aboard. We say
put out again on good salt water!'
how sound that was! Yet I refused. I wished
to see the caveman, what he had to offer—
no pretty sight, it turned out, for my friends.
We lit a fire, burnt an offering,
and took some cheese to eat; then sat in silence
around the embers, waiting. When he came
he had a load of dry boughs on his shoulder
to stoke his fire at suppertime. He dumped it
with a great crash into that hollow cave,
and we all scattered fast to the far wall.
Then over the broad cavern floor he ushered
the ewes he meant to milk. He left his rams
and he-goats in the yard outside, and swung
high overhead a slab of solid rock
to close the cave. Two dozen four-wheeled wagons,
with heaving wagon teams, could not have stirred

the tonnage of that rock from where he wedged it
over the doorsill. Next he took his seat
and milked his bleating ewes. A practiced job
he made of it, giving each ewe her suckling;
thickened his milk, then, into curds and whey,
sieved out the curds to drip in withy baskets,
and poured the whey to stand in bowls
cooling until he drank it for his supper.
When all these chores were done, he poked the fire,
heaping on brushwood. In the glare he saw us.

'Strangers,' he said, 'who are you? And where from?
What brings you here by sea ways—a fair traffic?
Or are you wandering rogues, who cast your lives
like dice, and ravage other folk by sea?'

We felt a pressure on our hearts, in dread
of that deep rumble and that mighty man.
But all the same I spoke up in reply:

'We are from Troy, Achaeans, blown off course
by shifting gales on the Great South Sea;
homeward bound, but taking routes and ways
uncommon; so the will of Zeus would have it.
We served under Agamemnon, son of Atreus—
the whole world knows what city
he laid waste, what armies he destroyed.
It was our luck to come here; here we stand,
beholden for your help, or any gifts
you give—as custom is to honor strangers.
We would entreat you, great Sir, have a care
for the gods' courtesy; Zeus will avenge
the unoffending guest.'

He answered this

from his brute chest, unmoved:

'You are a ninny,

or else you come from the other end of nowhere,
telling me, mind the gods! We Cyclopes
care not a whistle for your thundering Zeus
or all the gods in bliss; we have more force by far.
I would not let you go for fear of Zeus—
you or your friends—unless I had a whim to.
Tell me, where was it, now, you left your ship—
around the point, or down the shore, I wonder?'

96 withy baskets: baskets made from twigs.

102 fair traffic: honest trading.

117–120 It was a sacred Greek custom to honor strangers with food and gifts. Odysseus is reminding the Cyclops that Zeus will punish anyone who mistreats a guest.

TO CHALLENGE STUDENTS . . .

Write a Scene Have students work in small groups to interpret this meeting between the Cyclops, Odysseus, and his men into a scene from a play. Tell them that the audience they are writing for has no knowledge of *The Odyssey* or ancient Greek history. How would they make this scene come alive? What instructions would they give the actors? What would they have the actors say—would they keep the dialogue verbatim, or would they modernize it?

Tell students to research playwriting conventions and to write their scenes. Then have them perform their scenes for their classmates or for students who are not studying *The Odyssey*.

TEACH

TOUGH QUESTIONS

Remind students that characters are faced with **Tough Questions** when they are struggling with a decision and experiencing **internal conflict.** When they come upon a Tough Question, the question to ask themselves is, *What does this make me wonder about?*

In lines 151–168, the situation is dire for Odysseus and his men. They are in shock and horror from witnessing the gruesome spectacle of their companions being ripped apart and devoured. If Odysseus kills the Cyclops in the cave, he and his remaining men will not be able to move the stone away from the cave entrance to escape. Discuss the internal conflict Odysseus feels. Ask students to read carefully to discern the emotions he is experiencing. These factors add more weight to the urgent, vengeful question that Odysseus considers. (***Answer:*** Ponder *means "to think about something in a careful, thorough way." Odysseus thinks carefully and thoroughly about how to rescue his surviving men and avenge the deaths of the men whom the Cyclops has eaten. He wants to get everyone out, and he wants the Cyclops to suffer—and he may have only one chance to accomplish both.)*

ENGLISH LEARNER SUPPORT

Practice Sequencing Read Book 9, lines 136–155, aloud. Discuss common sequencing words: *first, then, so, finally*. Instruct students to practice using sequencing words by retelling this passage. Give pairs the following sentence frames to fill out together:

In the beginning of this passage, the Cyclops ______.

The men reacted by ______.

Then the Cyclops fell asleep. Odysseus wanted to ______.

However, Odysseus realized that he couldn't do that because ______.

So they had to wait until ______.

MODERATE

NOTICE & NOTE

He thought he'd find out, but I saw through this,
and answered with a ready lie:

'My ship?

Poseidon Lord, who sets the earth a-tremble,
broke it up on the rocks at your land's end.
A wind from seaward served him, drove us there.
We are survivors, these good men and I.'

Neither reply nor pity came from him,
but in one stride he clutched at my companions
and caught two in his hands like squirming puppies
to beat their brains out, spattering the floor.
Then he dismembered them and made his meal,
gaping and crunching like a mountain lion—
everything: innards, flesh, and marrow bones.
We cried aloud, lifting our hands to Zeus,
powerless, looking on at this, appalled;
but Cyclops went on filling up his belly
with manflesh and great gulps of whey,
then lay down like a mast among his sheep.
My heart beat high now at the chance of action,
and drawing the sharp sword from my hip I went
along his flank to stab him where the midriff
holds the liver. I had touched the spot
when sudden fear stayed me: if I killed him
we perished there as well, for we could never
move his ponderous doorway slab aside.
So we were left to groan and wait for morning.

When the young Dawn with fingertips of rose
lit up the world, the Cyclops built a fire
and milked his handsome ewes, all in due order,
putting the sucklings to the mothers. Then,
his chores being all dispatched, he caught
another brace of men to make his breakfast,
and whisked away his great door slab
to let his sheep go through—but he, behind,
reset the stone as one would cap a quiver.
There was a din of whistling as the Cyclops
rounded his flock to higher ground, then stillness.
And now I pondered how to hurt him worst,
if but Athena granted what I prayed for.
Here are the means I thought would serve my turn:

a club, or staff, lay there along the fold—
an olive tree, felled green and left to season
for Cyclops' hand. And it was like a mast

TOUGH QUESTIONS

Notice and Note: Mark the question Odysseus faces in lines 151–168.

Evaluate: What does it say about his approach to problems that Odysseus "pondered"?

154 ponderous: heavy in a clumsy way; bulky.

161 brace: pair.

163–164 The Cyclops reseals the cave with the massive rock as easily as an ordinary human places the cap on a container of arrows.

171 left to season: left to dry out and harden.

a lugger of twenty oars, broad in the beam—
a deep-sea-going craft—might carry:
so long, so big around, it seemed. Now I
chopped out a six foot section of this pole
and set it down before my men, who scraped it;
and when they had it smooth, I hewed again
to make a stake with pointed end. I held this
in the fire's heart and turned it, toughening it,
then hid it, well back in the cavern, under
one of the dung piles in profusion there.
Now came the time to toss for it: who ventured
along with me? whose hand could bear to thrust
and grind that spike in Cyclops' eye, when mild
sleep had mastered him? As luck would have it,
the men I would have chosen won the toss—
four strong men, and I made five as captain.

At evening came the shepherd with his flock,
his woolly flock. The rams as well, this time,
entered the cave: by some sheep-herding whim—
or a god's bidding—none were left outside.
He hefted his great boulder into place
and sat him down to milk the bleating ewes
in proper order, put the lambs to suck,
and swiftly ran through all his evening chores.
Then he caught two more men and feasted on them.
My moment was at hand, and I went forward
holding an ivy bowl of my dark drink,
looking up, saying:
'Cyclops, try some wine.
Here's liquor to wash down your scraps of men.
Taste it, and see the kind of drink we carried
under our planks. I meant it for an offering
if you would help us home. But you are mad,
unbearable, a bloody monster! After this,
will any other traveller come to see you?

He seized and drained the bowl, and it went down
so fiery and smooth he called for more:

'Give me another, thank you kindly. Tell me,
how are you called? I'll make a gift will please you.
Even Cyclopes know the wine-grapes grow
out of grassland and loam in heaven's rain,
but here's a bit of nectar and ambrosia!'

173 lugger: a small, wide sailing ship.

182 profusion: abundance.

EPIC POETRY

Annotate: In lines 198–208, mark a passage indicating one of Odysseus' character traits.

Analyze: How does Odysseus' behavior in this passage reflect Greek ideas and values and suggest a theme?

213 nectar (nĕk′tər) **and ambrosia** (ăm-brō′zhə)**:** the drink and food of the gods.

EPIC POETRY

Remind students that one of the features that distinguishes epic poetry from other forms is the portrayal of an **epic hero** who embodies traits and values that are admired in a particular culture. Epic poetry reveals the mores, or traditions and customs, of a historical period.

Lines 198–208 reveal important character traits of Odysseus as well as cultural values of the ancient Greeks. Tell students to look for both **explicit** lines of text and **implicit** clues as they analyze the passage.

(***Answer:*** *Odysseus demonstrates bravery by striding up to the Cyclops and offering him wine. He is also foolhardy to tell the Cyclops what he thinks of him. A second trait is his cleverness. Odysseus has devised a cunning plan and prepared carefully; now he is executing it. The reader can gather that the Greeks expected a hero to think on his feet, be smart, and take advantage of the enemy's weaknesses in order to win.*

These lines show that they also valued hospitality. The Cyclops violates the customs of welcoming and honoring guests. In the guise of honoring another hospitable custom, Odysseus offers the host a gift.

A possible theme is that it takes courage, cleverness, and the exploitation of weakness to defeat an enemy.)

WHEN STUDENTS STRUGGLE . . .

Chart the Sequence of Events Students can see how Odysseus outwits the Cyclops by making a sequence chart. Pick a starting point such as when the Cyclops traps them in the cave. As needed, fill in some boxes together. Encourage students to add boxes to their sequence chart as the story unfolds.

For additional support, go to the **Reading Studio** and assign the following **Level Up Tutorial: Plot: Sequence of Events.**

TEACH

LANGUAGE CONVENTIONS

An **absolute phrase** is different from other modifiers such as adjectives and adverbs. Rather than modifying one word in a sentence, it modifies the main clause of the sentence. Remind students that absolute phrases are always set off with commas and that they contain a noun and a **participle.** Participles are verbs often ending in *-ed* or *-ing* that can act as adjectives—in this case, modifying the noun of the absolute phrase. Review the following example and have a volunteer point out the noun and participle that make up the absolute phrase (three *and* wailing).

Main clause	absolute phrase	prepositional phrase
↓	↓	↓
I drove them,	all three wailing,	to the ships.

Point out that an absolute phrase can come before the main clause, after the main clause, or between parts of the main clause, as in the example sentence. Explain that often an absolute phrase will contain several modifiers such as prepositional phrases. Ask students to locate the absolute phrase in line 224, and have them identify the noun, the participle, and any modifiers in that phrase. *(noun: head; participle: lolling; modifiers: his great, to one side)* Then discuss the meaning that the phrase brings to the sentence.

*(**Answer:** The absolute phrase "his great head lolling to one side" modifies the main clause of the sentence—"he reeled and tumbled backward"—and it helps readers visualize the drunken state of the Cyclops.)*

ENGLISH LEARNER SUPPORT

Clarify Grammar Transfer Issues Speakers of Spanish, Haitian Creole, Hmong, Khmer, and Vietnamese usually place adjectives after nouns in their primary language. Explain that in English, adjectives usually appear before the nouns they modify.

Ask students to locate and say aloud the adjectives and the word that each one modifies in lines 250–254. *(bloody spike, wild hands, windy peaks)*
SUBSTANTIAL/MODERATE

NOTICE & NOTE

215 fuddle and flush: the state of confusion and redness of the face caused by drinking alcohol.

LANGUAGE CONVENTIONS
Annotate: Mark the absolute phrase in lines 221–226.

Analyze: How does the absolute phrase add to the meaning of the sentence?

231 the pike: the pointed stake.

244 smithy: blacksmith's shop.

245 adze (ădz)**:** an axlike tool with a curved blade.

Three bowls I brought him, and he poured them down.
I saw the fuddle and flush come over him,
then I sang out in cordial tones:
'Cyclops
you ask my honorable name? Remember
the gift you promised me, and I shall tell you.
My name is Nohbdy: mother, father, and friends,
everyone calls me Nohbdy.'
And he said:
'Nohbdy's my meat, then, after I eat his friends.
Others come first. There's a noble gift, now.'

Even as he spoke, he reeled and tumbled backward,
his great head lolling to one side: and sleep
took him like any creature. Drunk, hiccupping,
he dribbled streams of liquor and bits of men.

Now, by the gods, I drove my big hand spike
deep in the embers, charring it again,
and cheered my men along with battle talk
to keep their courage up: no quitting now.
The pike of olive, green though it had been,
reddened and glowed as if about to catch.
I drew it from the coals and my four fellows
gave me a hand, lugging it near the Cyclops
as more than natural force nerved them; straight
forward they sprinted, lifted it, and rammed it
deep in his crater eye, and I leaned on it
turning it as a shipwright turns a drill
in planking, having men below to swing
the two-handled strap that spins it in the groove.
So with our brand we bored that great eye socket
while blood ran out around the red hot bar.
Eyelid and lash were seared; the pierced ball
hissed broiling, and the roots popped.
In a smithy
one sees a white-hot axehead or an adze
plunged and wrung in a cold tub, screeching steam—
the way they make soft iron hale and hard—:
just so that eyeball hissed around the spike.
The Cyclops bellowed and the rock roared round him,
and we fell back in fear. Clawing his face
he tugged the bloody spike out of his eye,
threw it away, and his wild hands went groping;
then he set up a howl for Cyclopes
who lived in caves on windy peaks nearby.

Some heard him; and they came by divers ways
to clump around outside and call:
'What ails you,
Polyphemus? Why do you cry so sore
in the starry night? You will not let us sleep.
Sure no man's driving off your flock? No man
has tricked you, ruined you?'
Out of the cave
the mammoth Polyphemus roared in answer:
'Nohbdy, Nohbdy's tricked me, Nohbdy's ruined me!'
To this rough shout they made a sage reply:
'Ah well, if nobody has played you foul
there in your lonely bed, we are no use in pain

255 divers: various.

257 Polyphemus (pŏl-ə-fēʹməs)**:** the name of the Cyclops.

263 sage: wise.

264–267 Odysseus' lie about his name has paid off.

APPLYING ACADEMIC VOCABULARY

☑ **motivate** ☐ **objective** ☐ **pursuit** ☑ **subsequent** ☐ **undertake**

Write and Discuss Have students turn to a partner to discuss the following questions. Guide students to include the academic vocabulary words *motivate* and *subsequent* in their responses. Ask volunteers to share their responses with the class.

- Why did Polyphemus's reply fail to **motivate** the other Cyclopes to help him?
- When Odysseus lied about his name, were the **subsequent** effects what he had hoped for? Explain your answer.

TOUGH QUESTIONS

Explain to students that sometimes Tough Questions in a work of fiction will be abstract or rhetorical, in that there is no way to answer the questions effectively. The questions that can cause a character a great deal of **internal conflict** often have no answer. At other times, the Tough Question is directly addressing the situation at hand, as in this case. *(**Answer:** Odysseus uses the traits he has already shown: quick reasoning, cleverness, and resourcefulness. He is just as adept at using materials at hand in this situation—willow boughs from the Cyclops's bed to tie his men to the undersides of three sheep, who are also corded together, so that the men can escape without detection in the morning.)*

English Learner Support

Visualize Text Details Help students to draw upon text details to visualize the escape plan Odysseus devises. Slowly read aloud lines 280–302. Instruct students to underline the words and phrases that catch their attention as they listen. Then pair students at different levels of proficiency. Have them discuss the details and then collaborate on illustrating the escape plan in a series of several pictures. When they are finished, have them listen as you again read the passage aloud. This time, ask partners to point to the pictures they drew to depict the relevant part of the plan.
ALL LEVELS

272 breach: opening.

TOUGH QUESTIONS

Notice & Note: Mark the question Odysseus asks himself while he is trapped in the Cyclops's cave.

Analyze: How does Odysseus' strategy reflect traits he has shown previously?

298 pectoral fleece: the wool covering a sheep's chest.

given by great Zeus. Let it be your father,
Poseidon Lord, to whom you pray.'

So saying
they trailed away. And I was filled with laughter
to see how like a charm the name deceived them.
Now Cyclops, wheezing as the pain came on him,
fumbled to wrench away the great doorstone
and squatted in the breach with arms thrown wide
for any silly beast or man who bolted—
hoping somehow I might be such a fool.
But I kept thinking how to win the game:
death sat there huge; how could we slip away?
I drew on all my wits, and ran through tactics,
reasoning as a man will for dear life,
until a trick came—and it pleased me well.
The Cyclops' rams were handsome, fat, with heavy
fleeces, a dark violet.

Three abreast
I tied them silently together, twining
cords of willow from the ogre's bed;
then slung a man under each middle one
to ride there safely, shielded left and right.
So three sheep could convey each man. I took
the woolliest ram, the choicest of the flock,
and hung myself under his kinky belly,
pulled up tight, with fingers twisted deep
in sheepskin ringlets for an iron grip.
So, breathing hard, we waited until morning.
When Dawn spread out her finger tips of rose
the rams began to stir, moving for pasture,
and peals of bleating echoed round the pens
where dams with udders full called for a milking.
Blinded, and sick with pain from his head wound,
the master stroked each ram, then let it pass,
but my men riding on the pectoral fleece
the giant's blind hands blundering never found.
Last of them all my ram, the leader, came,
weighted by wool and me with my meditations.
The Cyclops patted him, and then he said:

'Sweet cousin ram, why lag behind the rest
in the night cave? You never linger so,
but graze before them all, and go afar
to crop sweet grass, and take your stately way
leading along the streams, until at evening

you run to be the first one in the fold.
Why, now, so far behind? Can you be grieving
over your Master's eye? That carrion rogue
and his accurst companions burnt it out
when he had conquered all my wits with wine.
Nohbdy will not get out alive, I swear.
Oh, had you brain and voice to tell
where he may be now, dodging all my fury!
Bashed by this hand and bashed on this rock wall
his brains would strew the floor, and I should have
rest from the outrage Nohbdy worked upon me.'

He sent us into the open, then. Close by,
I dropped and rolled clear of the ram's belly,
going this way and that to untie the men.
With many glances back, we rounded up
his fat, stiff-legged sheep to take aboard,
and drove them down to where the good ship lay.
We saw, as we came near, our fellows' faces
shining; then we saw them turn to grief
tallying those who had not fled from death.
I hushed them, jerking head and eyebrows up,
and in a low voice told them: 'Load this herd;
move fast, and put the ship's head toward the breakers.'
They all pitched in at loading, then embarked
and struck their oars into the sea. Far out,
as far off shore as shouted words would carry,
I sent a few back to the adversary:

'O Cyclops! Would you feast on my companions?
Puny, am I, in a Caveman's hands?
How do you like the beating that we gave you,
you damned cannibal? Eater of guests
under your roof! Zeus and the gods have paid you!'

The blind thing in his doubled fury broke
a hilltop in his hands and heaved it after us.
Ahead of our black prow it struck and sank
whelmed in a spuming geyser, a giant wave
that washed the ship stern foremost back to shore.
I got the longest boathook out and stood
fending us off, with furious nods to all
to put their backs into a racing stroke—
row, row, or perish. So the long oars bent
kicking the foam sternward, making head
until we drew away, and twice as far.
Now when I cupped my hands I heard the crew
in low voices protesting:

AGAIN AND AGAIN

Notice & Note: Mark the name the Cyclops repeats.

Analyze: What effect does the repeated pun have?

330 put . . . the breakers: turn the ship around so that it is heading toward the open sea.

334 adversary: opponent; enemy.

335–339 Odysseus assumes that the gods are on his side.

340–348 The hilltop thrown by Polyphemus lands in front of the ship, causing a huge wave that carries the ship back to the shore. Odysseus uses a long pole to push the boat away from the land.

351 cupped my hands: put his hands on either side of his mouth in order to magnify his voice.

AGAIN AND AGAIN

Cyclops repeats the name *Nohbdy*, which Odysseus craftily claimed to be his own name. Choosing this name is another example of how clever Odysseus is. For the ruse to work, he had to size up the intelligence of the Cyclops and take a calculated risk that the Cyclops would not be smart enough to recognize that he was being fooled.

The name *Nohbdy* is an example of a **pun,** or play on words. Although Odysseus is pretending that it is the name of a person, it is really the word *nobody*.

(***Answer:*** *This extended play on words creates a humorous tone. "Nohbdy will not get out alive" in line 313 is a double negative, so it really means that everybody will get out alive. While the Cyclops is talking to the ram about Odysseus and thinking that the ram is sympathetic to his plight, Odysseus is actually hanging on beneath the ram, listening. At no point does it dawn on the Cyclops that he has been duped.*)

The Odyssey 513

NOTICE & NOTE

'Godsake, Captain!
Why bait the beast again? Let him alone!'
'That tidal wave he made on the first throw
all but beached us.'

'All but stove us in!'
'Give him our bearing with your trumpeting,
he'll get the range and lob a boulder.'

'Aye
He'll smash our timbers and our heads together!'

I would not heed them in my glorying spirit,
but let my anger flare and yelled:

'Cyclops,
if ever mortal man inquire
how you were put to shame and blinded, tell him
Odysseus, raider of cities, took your eye:
Laertes' son, whose home's on Ithaca!'

At this he gave a mighty sob and rumbled:

'Now comes the weird upon me, spoken of old.
A wizard, grand and wondrous, lived here—Telemus,
a son of Eurymus; great length of days
he had in wizardry among the Cyclopes,
and these things he foretold for time to come:
my great eye lost, and at Odysseus' hands.
Always I had in mind some giant, armed
in giant force, would come against me here.
But this, but you—small, pitiful and twiggy—
you put me down with wine, you blinded me.
Come back, Odysseus, and I'll treat you well,
praying the god of earthquake to befriend you—
his son I am, for he by his avowal
fathered me, and, if he will, he may
heal me of this black wound—he and no other
of all the happy gods or mortal men.'

Few words I shouted in reply to him:
'If I could take your life I would and take
your time away, and hurl you down to hell!
The god of earthquake could not heal you there!'

At this he stretched his hands out in his darkness
toward the sky of stars, and prayed Poseidon:
'O hear me, lord, blue girdler of the islands,

366 Now comes . . . of old: Now I recall the destiny predicted long ago.

367–375 A wizard . . . you blinded me: Polyphemus tells of a prophecy made long ago by Telemus, a prophet who predicted that Polyphemus would lose his eye at the hands of Odysseus.

377 the god of earthquake: Poseidon.
378 avowal: honest admission.

ENGLISH LEARNER SUPPORT

Practice Phonology Speakers of Spanish, Vietnamese, Hmong, Cantonese, Haitian Creole, and Korean may have difficulty pronouncing the short *i* vowel sound. Cantonese speakers may also have difficulty pronouncing the long *i* vowel sound. Use the following supports with students at varying proficiency levels:

- Echo read Book 9, lines 372–375, with students. Model pronouncing the long and short *i* vowel sounds of the words in this passage, with students repeating after you. Ask pairs of students to circle the words with a long *i* vowel sound *(I, mind, giant, wine, blinded)* and underline the words with a short *i* vowel sound *(in, this, pitiful, twiggy)*. **SUBSTANTIAL**
- In pairs, ask students to take turns reading aloud Book 9, lines 372–375. Ask them to make two lists: words with long *i* vowel sounds and words with short *i* vowel sounds. **MODERATE**

if I am thine indeed, and thou art father:
grant that Odysseus, raider of cities, never
see his home: Laertes' son, I mean,
who kept his hall on Ithaca. Should destiny
intend that he shall see his roof again
among his family in his father land,
far be that day, and dark the years between.
Let him lose all companions, and return
under strange sail to bitter days at home.'

In these words he prayed, and the god heard him.
Now he laid hands upon a bigger stone
and wheeled around, titanic for the cast,
to let it fly in the black-prowed vessel's track.

But it fell short, just aft the steering oar,
and whelming seas rose giant above the stone
to bear us onward toward the island.

There
as we ran in we saw the squadron waiting,
the trim ships drawn up side by side, and all
our troubled friends who waited, looking seaward.
We beached her, grinding keel in the soft sand,
and waded in, ourselves, on the sandy beach.
Then we unloaded all the Cyclops' flock
to make division, share and share alike,
only my fighters voted that my ram,
the prize of all, should go to me. I slew him
by the sea side and burnt his long thighbones
to Zeus beyond the stormcloud, Cronus' son,
who rules the world. But Zeus disdained my offering;
destruction for my ships he had in store
and death for those who sailed them, my companions.

Now all day long until the sun went down
we made our feast on mutton and sweet wine,
till after sunset in the gathering dark
we went to sleep above the wash of ripples.

When the young Dawn with finger tips of rose
touched the world, I roused the men, gave orders
to man the ships, cast off the mooring lines;
and filing in to sit beside the rowlocks
oarsmen in line dipped oars in the gray sea.
So we moved out, sad in the vast offing,
having our precious lives, but not our friends."

NOTICE & NOTE 

CONTRASTS AND CONTRADICTIONS

Notice & Note: How does the Cyclops's behavior in lines 386–397 contrast with his previous behavior? Mark key details.

Infer: Based on what you know of epic poetry, what do you think will happen as a result of Cyclops's prayer?

400 titanic for the cast: drawing on all his enormous strength in preparing to throw.

402 aft: behind.

404 the island: the deserted island where most of Odysseus' men had stayed behind.

415 Cronus' son: Zeus' father, Cronus, was a Titan, one of an earlier race of gods.

428 offing: the part of the deep sea visible from the shore.

TEACH

CONTRASTS AND CONTRADICTIONS

The behavior of the Cyclops in lines 386–397 contrasts with his previous behavior in several ways, giving readers insights into this **character.** In lines 123–125, in his first conversation with Odysseus, he claims contempt for the gods and boasts that the Cyclopes are more powerful than the gods; here, he respectfully entreats Poseidon and acknowledges him as his father. His beseeching tone contrasts with the boorish tone he has been using. Both of these changes accompany the Cyclops's realization that a prophecy has come to pass. He suddenly changes his demeanor because Poseidon is capable of returning his sight. (***Answer:*** *The gods play a major role in epic poetry. Students can infer that Poseidon will respond to the Cyclops's prayer and that Odysseus will be in trouble again.)*

For **listening and speaking support** for students at varying proficiency levels, see the **Text X-Ray** on pages 494C–494D.

CONTRASTS AND CONTRADICTIONS

The Sirens' song is beautiful and enchanting (bewitching). But its effects on the men who listen to it are deadly: They will become piles of skin and bones if they are lured to the Sirens through their song. This type of contrast, in which what seems beautiful and sweet is actually sinister, occurs in other places in *The Odyssey;* students may infer a **theme** from this repetition. (***Answer:*** *Answers will vary. The author may want readers to understand that Odysseus and his men will continue to face challenges. The contrast, expressed by Circe, also is a reminder that appearances can be deceiving—that things are not always as they seem.)*

NOTICE & NOTE

BOOK 12

SEA PERILS AND DEFEAT

The Sirens

Odysseus and his men continue their journey home toward Ithaca. They spend a year with the goddess Circe on the island of Aeaea. Circe sends Odysseus and his crew to the Land of the Dead (the underworld), after which they return to Circe's island. While the men sleep, Circe takes Odysseus aside to hear about the underworld and to offer advice.

"Then said the Lady Circe:
'So: all those trials are over.
Listen with care
to this, now, and a god will arm your mind.
Square in your ship's path are Sirens, crying
beauty to bewitch men coasting by;
woe to the innocent who hears that sound!
He will not see his lady nor his children
in joy, crowding about him, home from sea;
the Sirens will sing his mind away
on their sweet meadow lolling. There are bones
of dead men rotting in a pile beside them
and flayed skins shrivel around the spot.
Steer wide;
keep well to seaward; plug your oarsmen's ears
with beeswax kneaded soft; none of the rest
should hear that song.
But if you wish to listen,
let the men tie you in the lugger, hand
and foot, back to the mast, lashed to the mast,
so you may hear those harpies' thrilling voices;
shout as you will, begging to be untied,

2–3 In Circe, Odysseus has found a valuable ally. In this section, she describes in detail the dangers that he and his men will meet on their way home.

CONTRASTS AND CONTRADICTIONS

Notice and Note: According to lines 4–12, how does the Sirens' song sharply contrast with the effect the song has on men who listen to it?

Analyze: Why do you think the author introduces such a contrast at this point in the poem?

18 those harpies' thrilling voices: the delightful voices of those horrible female creatures.

IMPROVE READING FLUENCY

Targeted Passage Ask students to review Book 12, lines 13–21. Then have them imagine Circe, who has come to know Odysseus over their year together. Her advice will save him and his crew from the deadly Sirens. Briefly discuss how to deliver Circe's lines to express her intention of saving the lives of Odysseus and his crew.

Place students in small groups and tell them to take turns reading these lines aloud. Their delivery shoud be serious and persuasive.

 Go to the **Reading Studio** for additional support in developing fluency.

your crew must only twist more line around you
and keep their stroke up, till the singers fade.

At dawn, Odysseus and his men continue their journey. Odysseus decides to tell the men of Circe's warnings about the Sirens, whom they will soon encounter. He is fairly sure that they can survive this peril if he keeps their spirits up. Suddenly, the wind stops.

"The crew were on their feet
briskly, to furl the sail, and stow it; then,
each in place, they poised the smooth oar blades
and sent the white foam scudding by. I carved

NOTICE & NOTE

30–31 plumb amidships: exactly in the center of the ship.

39 Perimedes (pĕr-ĭ-mē´dēz).

a massive cake of beeswax into bits
and rolled them in my hands until they softened—
no long task, for a burning heat came down
from Helios, lord of high noon. Going forward
I carried wax along the line, and laid it
thick on their ears. They tied me up, then, plumb
amidships, back to the mast, lashed to the mast,
and took themselves again to rowing. Soon,
as we came smartly within hailing distance,
the two Sirens, noting our fast ship
off their point, made ready, and they sang. . . .

The lovely voices in ardor appealing over the water
made me crave to ligten, and I tried to say
'Untie me!' to the crew, jerking my brows;
but they bent steady to the oars. Then Perimedes
got to his feet, he and Eurylochus,
and passed more line about, to hold me still.
So all rowed on, until the Sirens
dropped under the sea rim, and their singing
dwindled away.
My faithful company
rested on their oars now, peeling off
the wax that I had laid thick on their ears;
then set me free.

ENGLISH LEARNER SUPPORT

Practice Phonology Speakers of other languages often find the *r* sound difficult to pronounce. Discuss how to position the tongue and have students repeat the words *carved, rolled, burning, lord, forward,* and *carried* after you. Then use the following supports with students at varying proficiency levels:

- Have students review Book 12, lines 24–30, and circle words with *r*. Guide students to read each of those words. **SUBSTANTIAL**
- Ask pairs of students to take turns reading Book 12, lines 24–30, to each other, making a special effort to correctly pronounce the words they just practiced. **MODERATE**
- Have pairs of students review Book 12, lines 36–38, and mark the words containing the letter *r*. Then have partners take turns reading lines 36–38 aloud. Ask: Which two words sound similar and almost rhyme? *(ardor, water)* **LIGHT**

CHECK YOUR UNDERSTANDING

Answer these questions before moving on to the **Analyze the Text** section on the following page.

1 Which of the following sentences shows how Odysseus first uses his cleverness to outwit the Cyclops?

- **A** *Steer wide; keep well to seaward; plug your oarsmen's ears with beeswax kneaded soft.*
- **B** *If I could take your life I would and take your time away, and hurl you down to hell!*
- **C** *Why not take these cheeses, get them stowed, come back, throw open all the pens, and make a run for it?*
- **D** *Poseidon Lord, who sets the earth a-tremble, broke it up on the rocks at your land's end.*

2 Odysseus and his surviving men ultimately escape from the Cyclops by —

- **F** hiding underneath the Cyclops's sheep
- **G** removing the door to the Cyclops's cave
- **H** promising the Cyclops that they will return
- **J** giving the Cyclops the rest of their wine

3 Odysseus is tied to the mast because he —

- **A** ran out of beeswax and cannot cover his own ears
- **B** did not want to leave Circe's island
- **C** is offering himself as a sacrifice to Helios, lord of high noon
- **D** wants to hear the song of the Sirens without dying

CHECK YOUR UNDERSTANDING

Have students answer the questions independently.

Answers:

1. *D*
2. *F*
3. *D*

If they answer any questions incorrectly, have them reread the text to confirm their understanding. Then they may proceed to ANALYZE THE TEXT on page 520.

ENGLISH LEARNER SUPPORT

Oral Assessment Use the following questions to assess students' comprehension and speaking skills.

1. What does Odysseus say when the Cyclops asks where his ship is? *(He says the ship was wrecked.)*
2. How do Odysseus and his men escape from the Cyclops? *(They hide under sheep.)*
3. Why does Odysseus ask his men to tie him to the mast? *(He wants to hear the Sirens sing without dying.)* **MODERATE/LIGHT**

APPLY

ANALYZE THE TEXT

Possible answers:

1. **DOK 2:** *Invoking Muse shows that Homer is respectful of the gods and that he takes the telling of this epic seriously.*
2. **DOK 4:** *Odysseus sees the Cyclops and the entire race of Cyclopes as barbaric. Their ignorance, lawlessness, laziness, and lack of traditions or compassion for others are abhorrent to Odysseus. He shares the values of the ancient Greeks, who revere knowledge and cleverness, abide by laws, cherish traditions, work hard, and take care of their families.*
3. **DOK 4:** *Odysseus wants the Cyclops to know who outwitted him because the Cyclops killed his men and insulted him. He allows his rage to get the better of him. He also reveals his pride and tendency to dismiss potential danger. In consequence, his ship is nearly destroyed and the Cyclops asks his father, Poseidon, to take revenge on Odysseus.*
4. **DOK 4:** *Odysseus deceives the Cyclops and outwits him several times in order to escape. Other themes include the following: keep pride in check, beware of strangers' intentions, treat guests honorably, and respect the gods.*
5. **DOK 4:** *Repeating epithets such as these reminds readers that Odysseus is not only a powerful leader but also a cunning hero, unafraid to use trickery to accomplish his goals.*

RESEARCH

Tell students to choose audio recordings that don't require installing an application in their browser or that ask them to pay a fee. Note that students should narrow their search by including the term *audiobook;* it will also help if they type in the number of the book they want to hear.

Extend In addition to incorporating characteristics they find effective from the audio recordings, encourage students to bring something of their own to this activity. Ask them to practice their fluency before recording and to think about how to bring the text to life using just their voices.

RESPOND

ANALYZE THE TEXT

Support your responses with evidence from the text. NOTEBOOK

1. **Interpret** In the opening lines of Book 1, the poet calls upon Muse, a daughter of Zeus often credited with inspiration. Why would he open the epic in this way? What does this allusion tell you about him as a poet?
2. **Analyze** How does Odysseus regard the Cyclops, based on the description in lines 1–12 of Book 9? What does this description reveal about Odysseus' values as well as the values of the ancient Greeks?
3. **Analyze** Why does Odysseus continue to taunt the Cyclops as he pulls away from the shore? What traits does he demonstrate through this behavior, and what are the consequences?
4. **Evaluate** One theme in *The Odyssey* is that a hero must rely on clever deceit, or guile, to survive. Explain how this theme is conveyed. What other themes can you identify?
5. **Notice & Note** The author uses many epithets for Odysseus, such as "carrion rogue" and "raider of cities." What effect does the repetition of these epithets have on your understanding of the character of Odysseus?

RESEARCH

Like other classic epic poems, *The Odyssey* was spoken before it was written. This great adventure was passed down orally from generation to generation. Find two audio recordings of *The Odyssey* and listen to the parts you have read in this unit. Pay attention to elements of **prosody**—timing, phrasing, emphasis, and intonation—the readers use. Use the chart below to make notes about how the audio version makes the action and/or the characters more vivid; and how it helps you better understand the text.

	HOW IT INCREASES MY ENJOYMENT OF THE TEXT	HOW IT HELPS ME UNDERSTAND THE TEXT
Audio Recording 1	*The speaker is very dramatic and serious. It makes me interested in hearing the story.*	*Hearing the names of characters and places pronounced makes it easier to remember them.*
Audio Recording 2		

RESEARCH TIP
When researching audio recordings, keep in mind that some readings may be of higher quality than others. A classic such as *The Odyssey* has been recorded by several organizations and actors with varying success. Look for audio recordings with positive reviews or those that have received awards.

Extend With a small group, create your own audio recording of the selections from *The Odyssey* in this unit. When planning your own recording, integrate the qualities you appreciated most about the two recordings you researched. Play your recording for the class.

LEARNING MINDSET

Problem Solving Remind students that learning and solving problems often go together; it is the process of solving the problem that makes the learning happen. When students get stuck, asking for help is an excellent strategy because they can learn how other people solve problems and add these methods to their own toolbox. If they are having trouble answering Analyze the Text questions, tell them to try working with a partner. Talking the question through may be the right strategy for coming up with a good response.

CREATE AND PRESENT

Write a Narrative The point of view in *The Odyssey* rarely wavers from that of Odysseus. Nevertheless, other characters' words and actions hint at what they are thinking. Write a one-page narrative of an event from *The Odyssey* from the point of view of a character or object other than Odysseus. For example, you could narrate Odysseus's escape from the Cyclops from the point of view of the Cyclops, one of the rams, or one of the Sirens as Odysseus and his crew sailed by.

- ❑ Review the main events covered in the selections from *The Odyssey*. Choose an event and a point of view.
- ❑ Write your narrative. Speak in the voice of the character you chose.
- ❑ Use dialogue and description to engage and orient the reader, set up the situation, and create a smooth progression of events.
- ❑ Use precise words and phrases, telling details, and sensory language to convey a vivid picture of the events.

Deliver a Presentation With a group, create and deliver a 3- to 5-minute multimodal presentation of your narrative. A multimodal presentation includes two or more media, such as audio elements, written elements, visual aids, lighting effects, and presentation software.

- ❑ Research ways to integrate your the media you choose. Look for images online or create your own graphics to illustrate your presentation.
- ❑ Rehearse your presentation, including all multimedia elements. Share your presentation with the class. If time allows, offer to answer questions from the audience about your work.

Go to the **Writing Studio** for more on writing a narrative.

Go to the **Speaking and Listening Studio** for help with using media in a presentation.

RESPOND TO THE ESSENTIAL QUESTION

What drives us to take on a challenge?

Gather Information Review your annotations and notes on the selection from *The Odyssey*. Then, add relevant information to your Response Log. As you determine which information to include, think about:

- Odysseus' motivations as he takes on challenges
- flaws that hold Odysseus back on his quest to return home
- how cultures might influence what people take on as challenges

At the end of the unit, use your notes to help you write an explanatory essay.

ACADEMIC VOCABULARY

As you write and discuss what you learned from the narrative presentations, be sure to use the Academic Vocabulary words. Check off each of the words that you use.

- ❑ **motivate**
- ❑ **objective**
- ❑ **pursuit**
- ❑ **subsequent**
- ❑ **undertake**

APPLY

CREATE AND PRESENT

Write a Narrative Students who have been tracking the story through their sequence charts can also use them to help pick a character for this writing task. The sequence chart is a good way to review main events for all students.

Encourage students to practice using some of the elements of epic poetry in their narratives. Challenge them to include an **epic simile,** a lengthy and intricate method of comparison. They can incorporate **epithets,** which will help their readers understand their character; and they can try their hand at writing an **allusion,** a vivid shorthand for referring to a person, place, or event outside the story they are telling.

For **writing support** for students at varying proficiency levels, see the **Text X-Ray** on page 494D.

Deliver a Presentation Have students form groups and take turns presenting their narratives. Then have group members reach consensus on the narrative that they will use for their multimodal presentation. Instruct students to choose their media elements with care. Their goal is to have the media work together and not seem chosen at random. Students should ask themselves:

- What is the overall effect that we want to achieve?
- What would help most to create a particular mood or impression?
- Which elements would contribute the most to our narrative?

RESPOND TO THE ESSENTIAL QUESTION

Allow time for students to add details from *The Odyssey* to their Unit 6 Response Logs.

APPLY

VOCABULARY STRATEGY: Words from Latin

Possible answers:

1. *sol-, solitary; trem-, tremblor; plac-, placid; vers-, reversible*
2. *solitary — the state of being alone; tremblor — a shaking at the surface of the earth; placid — calm, peaceful; reversible — able to be turned around or undone*
3. *All meanings are confirmed by a dictionary.*
4. *All we could hear was the call of a* ***solitary*** *bird.*
   The ***tremblor*** *caused massive trees to shake and fall.*
   Not one ripple disturbed the ***placid*** *lake.*
   Her winter coat was ***reversible;*** *it was blue on one side, red on the other.*

RESPOND

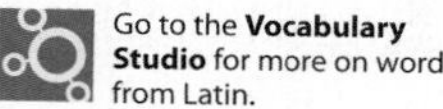

Go to the **Vocabulary Studio** for more on words from Latin.

VOCABULARY STRATEGY: Words from Latin

Recognizing **word roots** can help you determine the meanings of unfamiliar words. For example, the word *desolation*, meaning "a feeling of loneliness," contains the Latin root *sol*, which means "alone." This root is found in numerous other English words. Study the Latin roots and their meanings in the chart, along with example words that contain each root.

LATIN ROOT	MEANING	EXAMPLES
sol-	alone	soliloquy, solo
trem-	tremble	tremor, tremulous
plac-	calm	implacable, placate
vers	turn	adversity, versatile

Practice and Apply For each Latin root in the chart, follow these steps:

1. Look online or in print resources for one additional example of a word that uses the Latin root.
2. Use your knowledge of the root's meaning to write a definition for each example word.
3. Consult a dictionary to confirm each example word's meaning.
4. Use each example word in a sentence.

ENGLISH LEARNER SUPPORT

Spanish Cognates Tell students that many words in both Spanish and English come from Latin. For this reason, many English and Spanish words have similar roots. These Latin roots provide Spanish cognates: **ALL LEVELS**

Root	English word	Spanish cognate
sol-	solitary	*solitario*
trem-	trembling	*tembloroso*
plac-	placid	*plácido*

LANGUAGE CONVENTIONS: Absolute Phrases

An **absolute phrase** consists of a noun and a participle, a verb form ending in *-ed* or *-ing* that acts as an adjective. Absolute phrases must be set off with commas and may also contain objects of the participle and any modifiers. Rather than modifying a specific word in a sentence, absolute phrases describe the main clause of a sentence. Absolute phrases are a helpful way to add information to a sentence.

Look at this example of an absolute phrase from *The Odyssey*.

There
as we ran in we saw the squadron waiting,
the trim ships drawn up side by side, and all
our troubled friends who waited, looking seaward.

In this sentence, the absolute phrase *the trim ships drawn up side by side* is a description. The phrase adds information and helps explain how the waiting squadron looked. The noun *ships* is modified by the adjective *trim*, the participle *drawn*, and the additional modifiers *up side by side*. The absolute phrase modifies the first part of the sentence: *There as we ran in we saw the squadron waiting.*

Practice and Apply Look back at the narrative you wrote for Create and Present. Revise your narrative to include one or two absolute phrases. Share your revised narrative with a partner and discuss how your revisions add variety and interest.

Go to the **Grammar Studio** for more on participial phrases.

APPLY

LANGUAGE CONVENTIONS: Absolute Phrases

Discuss the meaning of the term **absolute phrase,** emphasizing that the function of an absolute phrase is to modify the thought expressed in a main clause.

Review the information on page 523. Clarify for students that a **participle** is a verb form that can function in different ways—within an absolute phrase, it acts as an adjective to modify the noun. Point out that while most participles end in *-ing* or *-ed*, some end in *-en* and a few have irregular spellings (such as *begun* or *drawn*). Display and discuss the following examples.

Absolute phrases can be just two words:

Eyes flashing, she stomped out of the room.

[Eyes is the noun and *flashing* is the participle.]

Absolute phrases can include objects:

Eyes flashing sparks, she stomped out of the room.

[*Sparks* is the object of *flashing*.]

Absolute phrases can include modifiers in addition to objects:

Eyes flashing menacing sparks of anger, she stomped out of the room.

[*Menacing* and *of anger* modify *sparks*.]

Practice and Apply As students practice incorporating absolute phrases into their narratives, encourage them to try phrases that vary in complexity. They can build lengthier, more complex phrases by starting with just a noun and a participle. They can also experiment with putting absolute phrases at the beginning of the sentence, as in these examples, or within the sentence, in which case they are set off with commas.

ENGLISH LEARNER SUPPORT

Distinguish Two Uses of Participles Review that participles are verb forms that usually end in *-ing*, *-ed*, or *-en*, and that one way they can be used is as part of a verb phrase. Ask students to name something they are learning now, something they have discussed, and something they have written. Use their responses to write example sentences; have volunteers underline the participles. *(For example: We are learning about participles. We have discussed an epic poem. We have written narratives.)*

Next, review that participles can also be used to form absolute phrases. Ask students to describe how Odysseus was able to escape the tempting song of the Sirens; then use their response to write an example. *(The ship sailed safely past the Sirens, Odysseus tied to the mast.)* Ask volunteers to underline the absolute phrase, and identify the noun and the participle in the absolute phrase. *(absolute phrase—"Odysseus tied to the mast"; noun—Odysseus; participle—tied)* **LIGHT**

MENTOR TEXT

ARCHAEOLOGY'S TECH REVOLUTION SINCE INDIANA JONES

Informational Text by Jeremy Hsu

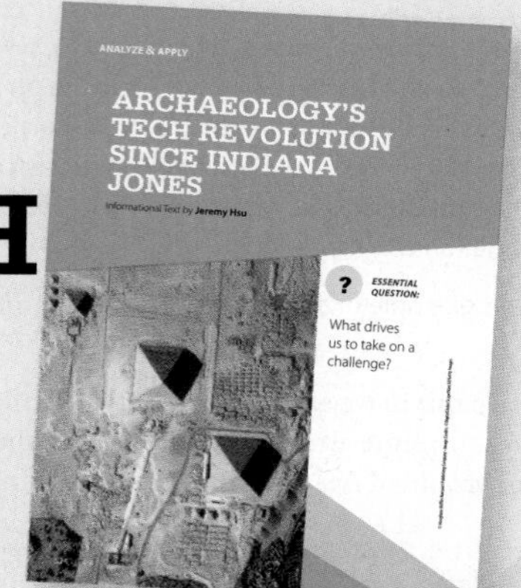

This article serves as a **mentor text,** a model for students to follow when they come to the Unit 6 Writing Task: Write an Explanatory Essay.

GENRE ELEMENTS

INFORMATIONAL TEXT

There are many forms of **informational text,** such as news articles, essays, and scientific writing. Informational text provides factual information and may contain text features to organize and clarify ideas. It also contains domain-specific vocabulary. **Technical informational text** includes supporting evidence, relevant examples, and a conclusion. In this lesson, students will analyze the technical text "Archaeology's Tech Revolution Since Indiana Jones."

LEARNING OBJECTIVES

- Make predictions while reading.
- Analyze the structure and characteristics of technical texts.
- Learn how to use appositives effectively.
- Use resource materials to understand text references.
- Research technologies available to archaeologists in the past.
- Present a slideshow about a technology used by archaeologists.
- Write summaries of student presentations.
- **Language** Discuss text features using the term *predict*.

TEXT COMPLEXITY

Quantitative Measures	**Archaeology's Tech Revolution Since Indiana Jones**	Lexile: 1330L
Qualitative Measures	**Ideas Presented** Mostly requires weighing of different perspectives.	
	Structures Used Text features such as headings and captioned images guide the reading.	
	Language Used Mostly complex sentence structure including expository and quoted content.	
	Knowledge Required Cultural, scientific, and historical references.	

Online Ed

RESOURCES

- Unit 6 Response Log
- Selection Audio
- Reading Studio: Notice & Note
- Level Up Tutorial: Main Idea and Supporting Details; Drawing Conclusions
- Writing Studio: Using Textual Evidence
- Speaking and Listening Studio: Using Media in a Presentation
- Vocabulary Studio: Using References
- Grammar Studio: Module 3: Lesson 8: Appositives and Appositive Phrases
- "Archaeology's Tech Revolution Since Indiana Jones" Selection Test

SUMMARIES

English

In the 1981 movie *Raiders of the Lost Ark*, the portrayal of archaeologist Indiana Jones inspired many students to learn about archaeology. Nonetheless, it gave a misleading picture of what archaeologists really do. Today's archaeologists employ many kinds of advanced technology to find and analyze ancient ruins and remains. These include 3-D mapping, infrared satellite imaging, ground-penetrating radar, and forensic analysis.

Spanish

A pesar de que la representación de un arqueólogo en la película "Cazadores del arca perdida" dio una imagen falsa de lo que los arqueólogos hacen, la película inspiró a muchos estudiantes a aprender de arqueología. Los arqueólogos de hoy en día utilizan muchas formas de tecnología avanzada para encontrar y analizar ruinas y restos antiguos. Entre ellas el mapeo tridimensional, las imágenes de satélite por infrarrojos, el radar de penetración de suelo y el análisis forense.

SMALL-GROUP OPTIONS

Have students work in small groups to read and discuss the selection.

Numbered Heads Together

- After students have read and analyzed "Archaeology's Tech Revolution Since Indiana Jones," have them form groups of four, and then number off 1-2-3-4 within the group.
- Ask students to discuss the following question: How might innovations in existing technology, such as robots, provide archaeologists with more information about the past?
- Have students discuss their responses in groups.
- Then call a number from 1 to 4. Students with that number respond for their group.

Think-Pair-Share

- After students have read and analyzed the excerpt from "Archaeology's Tech Revolution Since Indiana Jones," pose this question: Which innovation did you find most interesting? Explain.
- Have students think about the question individually and take notes.
- Then have pairs discuss their ideas about the question.
- Finally, ask pairs to share their responses with the class.

Text X-Ray: English Learner Support
for "Archaeology's Tech Revolution Since Indiana Jones"

Use the Text X-Ray and the supports and scaffolds in the Teacher's Edition to help guide students at different proficiency levels through the selection.

INTRODUCE THE SELECTION

DISCUSS ARCHAEOLOGY

In this text, Jeremy Hsu explains some of the technological innovations that have advanced the study of archaeology. Read the title of the selection to students. Write and display the word *archaeology*. Use images as needed to provide the following explanations:

- Archaeology is the study of past human life and culture.
- Archaeologists are people who study archaeology.
- Archaeologists find the places where humans lived in the past. They study objects made and used by humans.

Encourage students to share what they know about archaeology. Use these sentence frames:

- *I saw an archaeologist in a movie about* ______.
- *I read about an archaeologist who studied* ______.

CULTURAL REFERENCES

The following words or phrases may be unfamiliar to students:

- *Indiana Jones* (paragraph 1): the lead character, a professor of archaeology, in *Raiders of the Lost Ark* and other movies.
- *bullwhip* (paragraph 1): a long braided whip
- *pinpoint* (paragraph 4): to locate or identify exactly
- *Egyptologist* (paragraph 5): a person who studies ancient Egyptian culture
- *surveys* (paragraph 11): close examinations of something

LISTENING

Analyze Details

Point out to students that analyzing details in a technical text will help them identify and understand central ideas. Have students write down details as you read aloud passages from the essay.

Have students listen as you read aloud paragraph 7, followed by the section titled "Dusting off old bones," paragraphs 12–15. Use the following supports with students at varying proficiency levels.

- Reread paragraph 7 aloud. Ask: Can archaeologists see mud brick on Google Earth? *(yes)* **SUBSTANTIAL**
- As you read aloud paragraphs 12–15, pause after each paragraph and ask a comprehension question. For example, after paragraph 13, ask: What can we learn from the bones of ancient people? *(the foods they ate)* **MODERATE**
- After listening, ask partners to work in pairs to identify details that support the article's central idea. **LIGHT**

SPEAKING

Discuss Reading Predictions

Have partners or small groups discuss their reading predictions based on text features. Point out elements that will help students to analyze technical texts, including subheadings, scientific terms, and quotations from experts.

Use the following supports with students at varying proficiency levels.

- Point out the word *tech* in the selection title. Then display and read aloud these sentences: *The title tells me about the article. I predict the article is about technology*. Have partners practice saying the sentences. **SUBSTANTIAL**
- In the selection title, have students mark the words *archaeology's* and *tech*. Then have students use this frame to express their predictions about the article: *I predict the article is about* _____. **MODERATE**
- Have partners discuss how specific words in the selection title and subheadings help them make predictions about the text that follows. **LIGHT**

READING

Understand Central Ideas

Help students identify and understand central ideas in a technical text.

Work with students to reread paragraphs 1–4, followed by the article's conclusion, the section titled "Back to the future," paragraphs 16–19. Use the following supports with students at varying proficiency levels.

- Point out that the quotations in paragraph 3 represent the central idea of the essay. Have students echo read paragraph 3. Ask: Do archaeologists depend on technology? Can they work without it? **SUBSTANTIAL**
- Guide students to identify a central idea shared between the two passages. Supply sentence frames to express the idea. For example: *Each passage states that archaeologists need technology because* ______. **MODERATE**
- Have students identify a shared central idea in the passages using this frame: *The shared central idea in these passages is* _____. Then have students identify a supporting detail. **LIGHT**

WRITING

Write a Summary

Work with students to help them summarize from notes taken during their classmates' slideshows in the activity on Student Edition page 533. Encourage students use Critical Vocabulary in their summaries.

Use the following supports with students at varying proficiency levels.

- Provide students with sample notes from one of the slideshow presentations. Have students mark the words they recognize, then look them up in a dictionary to be sure the spelling is correct. **SUBSTANTIAL**
- Provide students with sample notes prior to the presentations. Provide a word bank for students to use in taking notes on the presentations. Work with students to write a summary. Have partners peer edit summaries for correct spelling of familiar English words. **MODERATE**
- Have partners compare notes before writing individual summaries. Review English spelling patterns and rules. Then, have partners peer edit summaries for correct spelling. **LIGHT**

Connect to the

ESSENTIAL QUESTION

Archaeologists are driven by curiosity to explore human history. Patient in the gathering of information, they locate and study artifacts and other evidence of ancient individuals and societies. Finding more evidence than is obvious to the naked eye is a challenge that new technology is helping them accomplish.

MENTOR TEXT

At the end of the unit, students will be asked to write an explanatory essay. The article, "Archaeology's Tech Revolution Since Indiana Jones," provides a model for how an author can write informational text effectively and support ideas with evidence.

ANALYZE & APPLY

ARCHAEOLOGY'S TECH REVOLUTION SINCE INDIANA JONES

Informational Text by **Jeremy Hsu**

?

ESSENTIAL QUESTION:

What drives us to take on a challenge?

524 Unit 6

LEARNING MINDSET

Persistence Discuss the value of persistence with your students. Explain that they are going to read a selection about archaeologists, who are persistent in trying out new tools and methods to discover more about human history. Remind students that making persistent effort is a key to growth, and encourage them not to give up when they encounter something challenging—challenges are an essential part of learning. Tell students to remember to use positive self-talk when they encounter challenges. Give them an example of positive self-talk, such as "I know I can do this if I keep at it." Ask them to suggest a few other examples.

QUICK START

Look at the title, headings, and images in this article. What do you predict it will be about? Discuss your prediction with the class.

MAKE PREDICTIONS

We make predictions every day—about our lives, about current events, and about texts we are reading. When we **predict** while reading, we make a reasonable guess about what is likely to happen next in a text. We usually base our predictions on several factors:

- prior knowledge—what we already know about a situation or subject
- information gleaned from scanning a text to read titles, headings, and photos or illustrations
- details from the text

As we gather more information, our predictions may change.

GENRE ELEMENTS: INFORMATIONAL TEXT

- provides factual information
- includes evidence to support ideas
- may contain text features to organize and clarify ideas
- includes domain-specific vocabulary

ANALYZE TECHNICAL TEXTS

Authors of informational or technical texts often present one central idea or make one central claim. They can't however, just make their claim or present their idea. They must provide relevant examples and evidence to support those claims.

As you read, note the central ideas the author presents and the evidence and relevant examples he provides to support those ideas. Also, think about the organizational design the author uses to present the thesis and supporting information. Use a chart like the one below to help you analyze the structure and characteristics of technical texts as they appear in Jeremy Hsu's article.

Introduction: What is this article mostly about? What is the central thesis?	
Central Ideas	**Supporting Evidence and Relevant Examples**
1.	
2.	
3.	
4.	
Conclusion: How does the author pull it all together?	

TEACH

QUICK START

Encourage students to examine the four headings and the illustrations in the article and consider how they relate to the title. Some students may need help understanding the cultural reference to fictional archaeologist Indiana Jones. Note that satellites, referred to in the first heading, are an example of the new technology being used by archaeologists.

MAKE PREDICTIONS

Note that prior knowledge about a situation or subject can have several origins. Students may have read about archaeologists and their work in different sources—for example, books, online newspapers and magazines, blogs, and interviews. On the other hand, their understanding of the topic might be limited to the actions of characters in movies, such as the archaeologist Indiana Jones. In either case, explain that predictions based on this prior knowledge can change as more information is acquired during reading.

ANALYZE TECHNICAL TEXTS

Note that an author's thesis, the main point he or she wants to make about a subject, is usually stated directly or implied within the first paragraph of a text. Ask students to read the first paragraph of the article and identify its thesis. *(The thesis, stated in the paragraph's last sentence, is that modern archaeologists are successful because they use advanced technology.)*

Next, explain that a well-written technical text will contain relevant examples— examples directly related to the thesis. Ask students which of the following would be relevant examples to support this thesis: the methods used by Indiana Jones; the use of airborne technology to find ancient ruins; handheld tools such as trowels and picks; or computer analysis of data acquired from the field. *(airborne technology, computer analysis)*

WHEN STUDENTS STRUGGLE . . .

Use Prereading Support Review the chart. With students, work to complete one numbered row of the chart. Tell them that they may want to wait to complete the Introduction row of the chart until they have read more of the article. By that time, the topic of the article will be clear and they can reread the first paragraph and identify the thesis. Have students work in pairs to complete the chart with information from the article. Remind them to use quotation marks if they are quoting directly from the article.

For additional support, go to the **Reading Studio** and assign the following **Level Up Tutorial: Main Idea and Supporting Details.**

CRITICAL VOCABULARY

As a clue to determining meaning, point out that an analysis is something a person does to determine facts and key ideas. Forensic analysis is conducted by a person studying evidence such as human remains.

Answers:

1. *infrared*
2. *GPS*
3. *artifact*
4. *forensic analysis*
5. *innovation*

■ English Learner Support

Use Cognates Tell students that some of the Critical Vocabulary words have Spanish cognates: *innovation/innovación, forensic/forense, infared/infrarrojo, analysis/análisis.* **ALL LEVELS**

LANGUAGE CONVENTIONS

Review the information about appositives. Point out that appositives and appositive phrases provide detail and clarity to writing. While many appositives are set off with commas, parentheses and dashes are sometimes used as well. Give students more examples of appositives and appositive phrases.

ANNOTATION MODEL

Suggest that students bracket central ideas as they read. They may also underline supporting details and evidence. Encourage them to develop their own system for marking up the selection in their write-in text. They may want to color-code their annotations using highlighters. Their notes in the margin may include questions about ideas that are unclear or topics they want to learn more about.

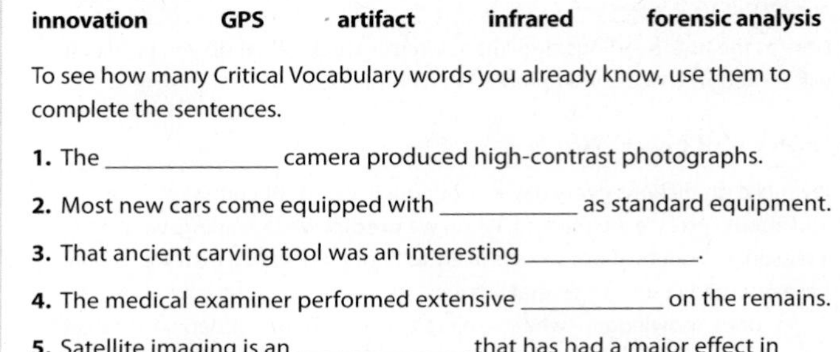

CRITICAL VOCABULARY

innovation **GPS** **artifact** **infrared** **forensic analysis**

To see how many Critical Vocabulary words you already know, use them to complete the sentences.

1. The _____________ camera produced high-contrast photographs.
2. Most new cars come equipped with ___________ as standard equipment.
3. That ancient carving tool was an interesting _____________.
4. The medical examiner performed extensive ___________ on the remains.
5. Satellite imaging is an _____________ that has had a major effect in many areas of life and work.

LANGUAGE CONVENTIONS

Appositives In this lesson, you will learn about the effective use of appositives. An **appositive** is a noun or pronoun that writers use to identify, rename, or provide extra information about a noun. An appositive phrase includes an appositive and modifiers of it.

The movie, **a documentary about inventors,** has won several awards.

Rachel, **the chef,** prepared a delicious dinner for her guests.

Most appositives are set off with commas. As you read "Archaeology's Tech Revolution Since Indiana Jones," note the author's use of appositives.

ANNOTATION MODEL

NOTICE & NOTE

As you read, develop your understanding of this technical text by noting examples and details of central ideas. In the model, you can see one reader's notes about the text's main ideas.

Let's face it, Indiana Jones was a pretty [lousy archaeologist. He destroyed his sites, used a bullwhip instead of a trowel and was more likely to kill his peers than co-author a paper with them.] Regardless, "Raiders of the Lost Ark," which celebrates its 30th anniversary on June 12, did make studying the past cool for an entire generation of scientists. Those modern archaeologists whom "Raiders" inspired luckily learned from the mistakes of Dr. Jones, and [use advanced technology such as satellite imaging, airborne laser mapping, robots and full-body medical scanners] instead of a scientifically useless whip.

things a good archaeologist shouldn't do

things a good archaeologist should do

NOTICE & NOTE

BACKGROUND

Jeremy Hsu *has been working as a science and technology journalist since 2008, and has written on subjects as diverse as supercomputing and wearable electronics. He contributes to a variety of publications, including* Scientific American, Discover, *and* Popular Science. *In this article, Hsu uses Indiana Jones, the iconic archaeologist of a series of popular movies, to introduce how the field of archaeology has changed with advancements in technology.*

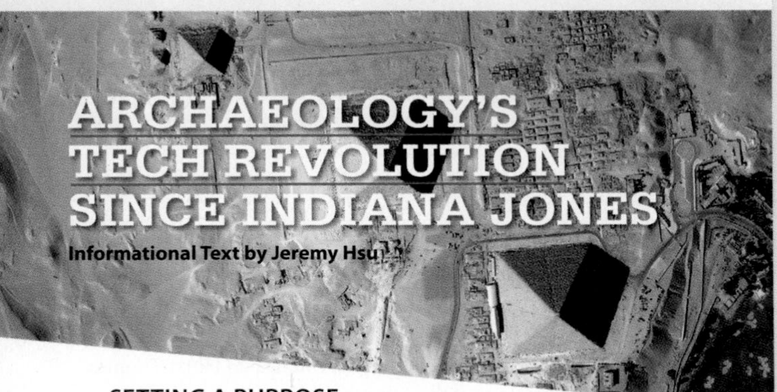

ARCHAEOLOGY'S TECH REVOLUTION SINCE INDIANA JONES

Informational Text by Jeremy Hsu

SETTING A PURPOSE

As you read, pay attention to examples the author gives to build the central idea. Many of those examples include technical terms. When you come across an unfamiliar term, ask your teacher or a peer for help or consult reference material.

1 Let's face it, Indiana Jones was a pretty lousy archaeologist. He destroyed his sites, used a bullwhip instead of a trowel[1] and was more likely to kill his peers than co-author a paper with them. Regardless, "Raiders of the Lost Ark," which celebrates its 30th anniversary on June 12, did make studying the past cool for an entire generation of scientists. Those modern archaeologists whom "Raiders" inspired luckily learned from the mistakes of Dr. Jones, and use advanced technology such as satellite imaging,[2] airborne laser mapping, robots and full-body medical scanners instead of a scientifically useless whip.

2 Such **innovations** have allowed archaeologists to spot buried pyramids from space, create 3-D maps of ancient Mayan ruins from the air, explore the sunken wrecks of Roman ships and find

[1] **trowel** (trou′əl): a small implement with a pointed, scoop-shaped blade used for digging.

[2] **satellite imaging**: the scanning of the earth by satellite or high-flying aircraft to obtain information about it.

Notice & Note

You can use the side margins to notice and note signposts in the text.

MAKE PREDICTIONS

Annotate: Mark words or phrases in the title and paragraph 1 that help you predict what this article is about.

Predict: What do you expect to learn from reading this article?

innovation
(ĭn-ə-vā′shən) *n.* something newly introduced.

ENGLISH LEARNER SUPPORT

Learning Strategies Use this strategy to help students learn how to take notes as they read.

- Provide students with a two-column chart with the following headings: Main Idea (column 1) and Details (column 2). Explain that the rows of the chart will be used to take notes on the main idea(s) and supporting details of each passage.
- Display and read aloud the first four paragraphs of the selection. Guide students to summarize and record the main idea. *(Archaeologists use technology to explore sites.)*
- Have pairs identify supporting details from paragraphs 1–4, and then share them with the class. **ALL LEVELS**

BACKGROUND

After students read the Background note, tell them that tools used in the early days of archaeology were for the most part limited to what archaeologists could hold in their hands, such as maps and digging tools. Several famous archaeological sites were discovered because of hints in written texts and information provided by local people. Some sites were found by accident or sheer luck.

SETTING A PURPOSE

Direct students to use the Setting a Purpose prompt to focus their reading.

MAKE PREDICTIONS

Ask students what they already know about archaeology, perhaps from movies or reading. Then point out the title of the article, and discuss the term "tech revolution." Invite their thoughts about how the term might relate to the field of archaeology. (***Answer:*** *Students may predict that they will learn about technological advancements in archaeology.)*

For **speaking** support at varying proficiency levels, see the **Text X-Ray** on page 524D.

ENGLISH LEARNER SUPPORT

Understand Complex Syntax Read aloud the last sentence in paragraph 1. Guide students to analyze the sentence:

- Set aside modifying words *(whom "Raiders" inspired, luckily, from the mistakes of Dr. Jones)* and look for the subject and verbs *(modern archaeologists, learned, use).*
- Review the technical vocabulary. Help students find words that might be familiar, such as *map, robot,* and *body*. Explain the meaning of *full-body medical scanners.* **MODERATE/LIGHT**

CRITICAL VOCABULARY

innovation: In the first paragraph, the author mentions several examples of newly developed technology, such as satellite imaging and airborne laser mapping.

ASK STUDENTS to explain how these innovations help archaeologists learn about the past. *(They help them find things that the human eye could not spot, especially things underground or under water.)*

TEACH

LANGUAGE CONVENTIONS

Remind students that an **appositive** gives more information about a noun or a pronoun. Details that name, identify, describe, or explain help readers to understand the point the writer is trying to make. Ask students to identify the **appositive phrase** in paragraph 5. Discuss the purpose of the appositive phrase in the sentence. (***Answer:*** *The appositive phrase is "an Egyptologist at the University of Alabama in Birmingham." It identifies Sarah Parcak as an Egyptologist, which explains her role in researching the Egyptian desert.)*

ENGLISH LEARNER SUPPORT

Language Conventions Read aloud the sentence from paragraph 5 that includes the appositive, "an Egyptologist from the University of Alabama in Birmingham." Ask: Why is the information in the appositive necessary for understanding the rest of the sentence?

- Have student pairs read the sentence with and without the appositive.
- Ask: Is the name "Sarah Parcak" a proper noun? Who is Sarah Parcak? **MODERATE/LIGHT**

CRITICAL VOCABULARY

GPS: Archaeologists use Global Positioning System (GPS) technology to identify the exact locations of sites.

ASK STUDENTS what other ways archaeologists might use GPS. *(GPS provides assistance with navigation and with measurement of distances within and between sites.)*

artifact: Archaeologists search for objects created by ancient humans, such as cooking utensils and weapons.

ASK STUDENTS what archaeologists can learn from studying ancient artifacts. *(They can learn about people's daily lives.)*

infrared: Infrared technology has helped archaeologists discover pyramids buried beneath the Egyptian desert.

ASK STUDENTS what other kinds of things infrared technology might help archaeologists discover. *(It may show sites covered by lava or hidden by overgrown vegetation.)*

NOTICE & NOTE

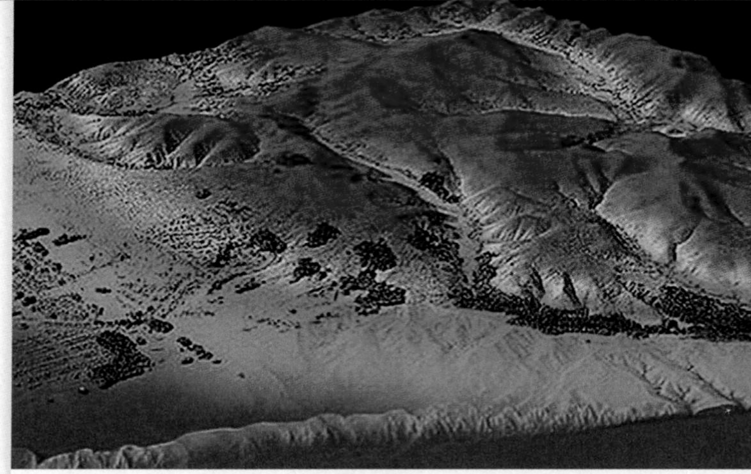

A LIDAR (Light Detection and Ranging) image created with data from NOAA's National Geodetic Survey.

evidence of heart disease in 3,000-year-old mummies. Most of the new toolkit comes from fields such as biology, chemistry, physics or engineering, as well as commercial gadgets that include **GPS**, laptops and smartphones.

GPS
n. Global Positioning System, a utility that provides positioning, navigation, and timing services.

3 "If we dig part of a site, we destroy it," said David Hurst Thomas, a curator in anthropology at the American Museum of Natural History in New York. "Technology lets us find out a lot more about it before we go in, like surgeons who use CT and MRI scans.[3]"

4 Archaeologists have harnessed such tools to find ancient sites of interest more easily than ever before. They can dig with greater confidence and less collateral damage[4], apply the latest lab techniques to ancient human **artifacts** or remains, and better pinpoint when people or objects existed in time.

artifact
(är′tə-făkt) *n.* an object produced or shaped by human workmanship.

Satellites mark the spot

5 One of the current revolutions in archaeology relies upon satellites floating in orbit above the Earth. Sarah Parcak, an Egyptologist at the University of Alabama in Birmingham, and an international team recently used **infrared** satellite imaging to peer as far down as 33 feet (10 meters) below the Egyptian desert. They found 17 undiscovered pyramids and more than 1,000 tombs.

infrared
(ĭn′ frə-rĕd) *adj.* pertaining to electromagnetic radiation having wavelengths greater than those of visible light and shorter than those of microwaves.

LANGUAGE CONVENTIONS
Annotate: Mark a sentence in paragraph 5 where the author has used an appositive.
Analyze: Which part of the sentence is the appositive? What noun does it describe?

6 The images also revealed buried city streets and houses at the ancient Egyptian city of Tanis, a well-known archaeological site that was featured in "Raiders of the Lost Ark" three decades ago.

7 Even ordinary satellite images used by Google Earth have helped. Many of the old Egyptian sites have buried mud brick architecture

[3] **CT and MRI scans:** special X-ray tests that produce cross-sectional images.
[4] **collateral damage** (kə-lăt′ər-əl dăm′-ĭj): unintended injury or damage.

IMPROVE READING FLUENCY

Targeted Passage Use echo reading to help students use appropriate phrasing and emphasis in reading both expository text and quoted speech. Begin by reading aloud paragraphs 3 and 4, emphasizing phrasing and pauses within sentences and between sentences and paragraphs. Point out the difference between the two paragraphs—the first contains quoted speech and the second is expository. Then have students echo your reading as you read the paragraphs a second and third time. You may choose to conclude by having students choral read the paragraphs.

Go to the **Reading Studio** for additional support in developing fluency.

Satellite imagery of the Giza pyramid complex on the outskirts of Cairo, Egypt.

that crumbles over time and mixes with the sand or silt above them. When it rains, soils with mud brick hold moisture longer and appear discolored in satellite photos.

8 "In the old days, I'd jump into the Land Rover and go look at a possible site," said Tony Pollard, director of the Centre for Battlefield Archaeology at the University of Glasgow in Scotland. "Now, before that, I go to Google Earth."

Digging with less damage

9 Tools such as ground-penetrating radar can also help archaeologists avoid destroying precious data when they excavate ancient sites, Thomas said.

10 "Many Native American tribes are very interested in remote sensing that is noninvasive and nondestructive, because many don't like the idea of disturbing the dead or buried remains," Thomas explained.

11 Magnetometers[5] can distinguish between buried metals, rocks and other materials based on differences in the Earth's magnetic field. Soil resistivity surveys detect objects based on changes in electrical current speed.

Dusting off old bones

12 Once objects or bones have surfaced, archaeologists can return them to the lab for **forensic analysis** that would impress any CSI[6] agent. Computed tomography (CT) scanners commonly used in

[5] **magnetometer** (măg-nĭ-tom´ ĭ-tər): an instrument for comparing the intensity and direction of magnetic fields.

[6] **CSI:** crime scene investigator.

NOTICE & NOTE

ANALYZE TECHNICAL TEXTS

Annotate: Mark words and phrases that explain magnetometers.

Analyze: How could the use of a magnetometer help preserve Native American sites?

forensic analysis (fə-rĕn´ sĭk ə-năl´ĭ-sĭs) *n.* the scientific collection and analysis of physical evidence in criminal cases.

TO CHALLENGE STUDENTS . . .

Research Archaeology of Native American Sites Read aloud paragraphs 9 and 10, and explain that archaeological evidence of ancient Native American societies has been found across North America. The information gathered has sometimes been useful to native tribes, and many have cooperated with students of their ancient cultures; on the other hand, the activity has not been without controversy. For example, many Native Americans are concerned about the disturbance and possible destruction of sacred sites by excavation. Invite students to do online research about this controversy and write a few paragraphs summarizing what they have found. Encourage them to include some contemporary examples in their summaries. Once they have completed their research and summaries, invite students to share their findings in small groups.

ANALYZE TECHNICAL TEXTS

Note that supporting **evidence** provided within a **technical text** may include unfamiliar vocabulary. Unfamiliar technical words can sometimes be understood by definition and examples. Point out that the technical term *magnetometer* is defined in a footnote and that more information is provided in the text. (***Answer:*** *A magnetometer could detect where bones are buried. Archaeologists could avoid digging there.)*

ENGLISH LEARNER SUPPORT

Identify Context Clues Explain that students can sometimes use context clues to identify the meaning of technical vocabulary. Have them find the clue that suggests the meaning of *soil resistivity surveys* in line 13. *("detect objects based on changes in electrical current speed")* **MODERATE/LIGHT**

ENGLISH LEARNER SUPPORT

Use Cognates Point out that identifying cognates is a useful strategy to find the meaning of scientific vocabulary. Tell students that several terms in the selection have Spanish cognates:

English	Spanish
distinguish	*distinguir*
magnetic	*magnético*
electrical current	*corriente eléctrica*

Discuss how using this strategy helps them determine the meaning of *magnetometer.*
LIGHT

CRITICAL VOCABULARY

forensic analysis: Archaeologists use forensic analysis to determine information about the health, diet, and other physical information about ancient people.

ASK STUDENTS to explain the similarities between the forensic science practiced by medical examiners, who examine dead bodies, and that practiced by forensic archaeologists. *(Forensic science helps both groups gather facts about the health and causes of death of human beings.)*

ANALYZE TECHNICAL TEXTS

Remind students that a technical text includes a clear thesis that is supported with evidence and relevant examples. By the same token, without a clear thesis, a list of evidence and examples has no real purpose or foundation. (***Answer:*** *These examples show how technology allows archaeologists to "see" into the past and learn about the daily lives of people, in many cases by examining preserved remains of those who lived hundreds, even thousands, of years ago.)*

For **listening and reading support** for students at varying proficiency levels, see the **Text X-Ray** on pages 524C–524D.

NOTICE & NOTE

A rover robot to be sent into an air shaft of the Pyramid of Khufu in Giza, Egypt.

medicine have revealed blocked arteries in an ancient Egyptian princess who ended up mummified 3,500 years ago.

13 Looking at the ratios of different forms of elements, called isotopes, in the bones of ancient people may reveal what they ate. The dietary details can include whether they favored foods such as corn or potatoes, or if they were strictly hunters.

ANALYZE TECHNICAL TEXTS

Annotate: Mark text that describes the kinds of information archaeologists can obtain from bones.

Analyze: What does this text reveal about the use of technology in archaeology?

14 A similar chemical signature[7] based on the isotope ratio of different geographical locations can reveal where humans originally grew up. Archaeologists used it to identify the origins of dozens of soldiers found in a 375-year-old mass grave in Germany.

15 "Once they excavated them, they did analysis on bones and identified in most cases where individual soldiers came from," Pollard said. "Some came from Finland, some came from Scotland."

Back to the future

16 Archaeologists have many other new tools in the toolkit. The laser mapping technique used on the Mayan ruins, called LIDAR (Light Detection And Ranging), has become a norm for archaeology in just a few years. Robots have begun exploring pyramids and caves as well as underwater shipwrecks.

[7] **chemical signature:** a unique pattern, produced by an analytical instrument, indicating the presence of a particular molecule.

WHEN STUDENTS STRUGGLE . . .

Draw Conclusions Encourage students to refer to their graphic organizer for analyzing technical texts on page 525. Have them draw a conclusion from the ideas and information they have recorded. Refer them to the thesis they identified at the beginning of the selection, and explain that a conclusion often restates a thesis. Encourage them to find a direct or indirect restatement of the thesis in the final section, paragraphs 16 and 17. *("Archaeologists have many other new tools in the toolkit. . . . 'We do all we can to keep up technologically.'")*

For additional support, go to the **Reading Studio** and assign the following  **Level Up Tutorial: Drawing Conclusions.**

NOTICE & NOTE 

17 "When I was a bad boy and went into archaeology instead of med school, my mother thought I'd spent all my time in the past," Thomas said. "It couldn't be further from the truth; we do all we can to keep up technologically."

18 Technology won't eliminate the need to dig anytime soon, archaeologists say. But if that day comes, "archaeology will get a lot more boring," Pollard said. He wasn't alone with that sentiment.

19 "It's all very well to use satellite imaging, but until you get out into the field, you're stuck in your lab," Parcak said. "It's a constant in archaeology; you've got to dig and explore."

CHECK YOUR UNDERSTANDING

Answer these questions before moving on to the **Analyze the Text** section on the next page.

1 Which of the following is true?

- **A** Archaeologists have little regard for preserving sites.
- **B** Archaeologists are technologically savvy scientists.
- **C** Archaeology is a science developed by Native Americans.
- **D** The tech revolution has made archaeology boring.

2 Which of the sentences from the selection most strongly supports the idea that some people miss the way archaeology used to be practiced?

- **F** *In the old days, I'd jump into the Land Rover and go look at a possible site*
- **G** *It's all very well to use satellite imaging, but until you get out into the field, you're stuck in your lab*
- **H** *When I was a bad boy and went into archaeology instead of med school, my mother thought I'd spend all my time in the past*
- **J** *Now, before that, I go to Google Earth.*

3 Which of these is not an important idea in the article?

- **A** Archaeologists do not like to damage precious sites.
- **B** Archaeologists do much of their work in a lab.
- **C** Indiana Jones used a bullwhip instead of a trowel.
- **D** Archaeologists use tools from a variety of fields.

ENGLISH LEARNER SUPPORT

Oral Assessment Use the following questions to assess students' comprehension and speaking skills. Ask students to respond in short, complete sentences.

1. Do archaeologists know a lot about technology? *(Yes, archaeologists know a lot about technology.)*
2. Do all archaeologists like using technology? *(No, some prefer to dig and explore in the field.)*
3. Are the details about Indiana Jones important? *(No, Indiana Jones is a fictional character and his tools are not representative of a real archaeologist.)* **ALL LEVELS**

CHECK YOUR UNDERSTANDING

Have students answer the questions independently.

Answers:

1. *B*
2. *G*
3. *C*

If they answer any questions incorrectly, have them reread the text to confirm their understanding. Then they may proceed to ANALYZE THE TEXT on page 532.

APPLY

ANALYZE THE TEXT

Possible answers:

1. **DOK 2:** *Answers will vary. Students should give reasons and examples to confirm or correct their predictions.*
2. **DOK 3:** *New tools and technology borrowed from other fields of study have enabled archaeologists to learn about the past while doing less damage to ancient sites and artifacts.*
3. **DOK 2:** *Sample answer: The ability of archaeologists to locate and identify sites with little or no damage during the "hunt" is the most significant result of the technology revolution. The use of radar and satellite imaging not only allows for less destruction but also allows scientists to locate sites they might not have known existed before.*
4. **DOK 3:** *The satellite image of the Giza Pyramid complex (page 529) shows variations in the soil colors around the pyramids. This supports the text (paragraph 7) that states, "buried mud brick architecture . . . mixes with the sand or silt above them. When it rains, soils with mud brick . . . appear discolored in satellite photos."*
5. **DOK 4:** *Students should cite an example and explain how it supports one of the ideas in the article. Sample answer: A CT scanner revealed blocked arteries in the mummified corpse of a 3,500-year-old Egyptian. The use of this noninvasive technology supports the author's idea that technology borrowed from other fields, in this case medicine, helps archaeologists learn more about the past.*

RESEARCH

Remind students to use sites that are trustworthy in order to locate credible and relevant sources. Before students begin their research, discuss tips for determining the reliability of sites. For this topic, for example, students might visit museum and university websites, which often end with *.org* or *.edu* in their URLs.

Connect Encourage students to describe the research they found most interesting or surprising.

RESPOND

ANALYZE THE TEXT

Support your responses with evidence from the text. NOTEBOOK

1. **Confirm Predictions** Recall the predictions you made before reading the article. Which ones can you confirm? Which do you need to correct?
2. **Draw Conclusions** What is the author's main idea about the technology revolution in archaeology?
3. **Summarize** What would you say is the most significant result of the technology revolution in archaeology?
4. **Cite Evidence** Describe one of the images in the article. How does it help support the author's claims?
5. **Notice & Note** The article contains several numbers and statistics. Find one instance, and explain how it supports the author's main idea.

RESEARCH TIP
As you find information and begin to write it in the chart, be sure to document every source you use so that you can give proper credit to it. The main elements of a source citation are the author name, publisher name, publisher location (for books), date created or published, title, URL (for websites), and page number(s).

RESEARCH

Jeremy Hsu mentions a variety of technologies that are available to archaeologists today. To understand the changes those technologies have brought to archaeology, you need to know how archaeologists worked in the past. Research some of the tools and technologies available to archaeologists 100 years ago, around the early 1900s. Record what you learn in the chart.

TASK	TOOL OR TECHNOLOGY USED 100 YEARS AGO
Locating a site	*visual survey by traveling on foot, pack animal, or vehicle; maps, written records, oral history; shovels, pickaxes, baskets*
Field work	*grid system; trowels, shovels, brushes, cameras*
Lab work	*microscopes, magnifying glasses, visual dating of soil layers (Varve method)*

Connect Share your findings with classmates. You will incorporate some of your findings into the slideshow presentation you will create.

LEARNING MINDSET

Problem Solving If students get stuck when trying to respond to the Analyze the Text questions, help them by asking them to apply problem-solving strategies as they work through the questions. Encourage students to look at the question from a different angle or to try a different learning strategy. For example, students might rephrase a question as a statement and then use what they know from the text to complete the idea.

CREATE AND DISCOVER

Present a Slideshow Work with a partner or a small group to research one of the technologies Jeremy Hsu mentions in his article. Then create a slideshow to accompany instructions for the technology or process.

- ❑ Work with your classmates to create a list of these technologies.
- ❑ In small groups or pairs choose one of the technologies to research.
- ❑ Consult at least three sources.
- ❑ Use the information to create a slideshow you will share with the class. In your show, give oral instructions on how the tool or technology is used.
- ❑ Remember to use appropriate technical vocabulary in your presentation.

Write a Summary Write a summary of what you learn from your classmates.

- ❑ Take notes as each pair or group of classmates gives its presentation.
- ❑ Review your notes and write a summary of what you learned.
- ❑ Share what you learned during a class discussion.

Go to **Using Media in a Presentation** in the **Speaking and Listening Studio** for more help.

Go to **Using Textual Evidence: Paraphrasing and Summarizing** in the **Writing Studio** for more on writing a summary.

RESPOND TO THE ESSENTIAL QUESTION

? What drives us to take on a challenge?

Gather Information Review your annotations and notes on "Archaeology's Tech Revolution Since Indiana Jones." Then add relevant information to your Response Log. As you determine which information to include, think about:

- the challenges that archaeologists face
- changes in archaeology
- what quests motivate archaeologists

At the end of the unit, use your notes to help you write an explanatory essay.

ACADEMIC VOCABULARY

As you write and discuss what you learned from the text, be sure to use the Academic Vocabulary words. Check off each of the words that you use.

- ❑ **motivate**
- ❑ **objective**
- ❑ **pursuit**
- ❑ **subsequent**
- ❑ **undertake**

APPLY

CREATE AND DISCOVER

Present a Slideshow Point out that the directions in this section can serve as a guide for students' work. Encourage students to find images that clearly illustrate the technology or process they find interesting. Remind students to provide clear source information for the images they present, as well as facts and details they convey. Challenge them to use appropriate technical vocabulary and be prepared to define that vocabulary during the presentation.

Write a Summary Remind students that a summary includes only the most important ideas and information. For their summaries, they likely will not use all the information in the notes they have taken.

For **writing support** for students at varying proficiency levels, see the **Text X-Ray** on page 524D.

RESPOND TO THE ESSENTIAL QUESTION

Allow time for students to add details from "Archaeology's Tech Revolution Since Indiana Jones" to their Unit 6 Response Logs.

ENGLISH LEARNER SUPPORT

Present a Slideshow Use the following supports with students at various proficiency levels.

- Provide the following sentence frame: *This slide shows* _____. Work with students to complete the sentence frame by identifying a key idea about how their tool or technology is used. Have them practice saying the sentence aloud. **MODERATE**
- Provide the following sentence frames to help students present their research: *This photograph shows* _____. *This technology is important because* _____. _____ *use(s)* _____ *to learn about* _____. **MODERATE**
- Have partners discuss key ideas from their presentations. Partners may practice using words from a bank of technical vocabulary relevant to their topic. **LIGHT**

APPLY

CRITICAL VOCABULARY

Answers:

1. *As engineers and designers continue to make cars that use and deliver new technologies, the automobile continues to be an innovation.*
2. *GPS is a popular utility because it is very useful and available. It is now standard equipment in most new cars. Anyone with a smartphone has GPS—and uses it. GPS has largely replaced paper maps and made navigation easier.*
3. *Answers will vary. Students should mention any object made by humans.*
4. *Infrared is a kind of radiation. Objects radiate infrared light that can be sensed using infrared satellite technology.*
5. *Archaeologists use forensic analysis to solve mysteries and gather evidence about how humans from the past lived and died. Forensic analysis can reveal health problems, dietary habits, and even where a person grew up.*

VOCABULARY STRATEGY:
Use References

Answers:

1. ***Raiders of the Lost Ark****—a movie released in 1981. In the film, archaeologist Indiana Jones is hired to find the Ark of the Covenant before the Nazis do.*
2. **curator***—a person in charge of a museum.*
3. **Google Earth***—a computer program that maps the Earth using images from satellite imagery, aerial photography, and GIS data onto a globe, allowing users to see cities and landscapes from various angles.*
4. **isotopes***—two or more forms of a chemical element that have the same number of protons or the same atomic number but different numbers of neutrons or atomic weights. Isotopes of a single element have almost identical properties.*
5. **Mayan ruins***—pyramids and other buildings, some as old as 3,000 years. Hundreds of Mayan ruins have been found throughout Mexico, Belize, Honduras, and Guatemala.*
6. **LIDAR (Light Detection and Ranging)***—a remote sensing method that uses a pulsed laser to measure variable distances to Earth. A LIDAR instrument principally consists of a laser, a scanner, and a specialized GPS receiver.*

RESPOND

WORD BANK
innovation
GPS
artifact
infrared
forensic analysis

CRITICAL VOCABULARY

Practice and Apply Answer each question to demonstrate your understanding of the Critical Vocabulary words. Then, explain your responses.

1. The automobile was once an **innovation**. Is it still?
2. Why is **GPS** a popular utility?
3. Imagine your class is gathering **artifacts** for a time capsule. What will you contribute?
4. How is **infrared** satellite imaging able to see underground?
5. **Forensic analysis** is used in criminal cases. Why do archaeologists use it?

VOCABULARY STRATEGY:
Use References

Go to the **Vocabulary Studio** for more on using references.

The author of the article you have just read incorporates popular, historical, and scientific references into the text. Though you may be able to understand the author's main idea without knowing what these references are, knowing them will enhance your comprehension and make the article more interesting to you.

Practice and Apply Use print or digital resource materials, including glossaries, dictionaries, and encyclopedias, to define or explain each reference from the article.

1. *Raiders of the Lost Ark*
2. curator
3. Google Earth
4. isotopes
5. Mayan ruins
6. LIDAR (Light Detection and Ranging)

ENGLISH LEARNER SUPPORT

Vocabulary Strategy Give students additional practice in explaining references from the selection. Suggest that they use a dictionary to define *noninvasive* (paragraph 10) and *blocked arteries* (paragraph 12). Have partners write and then share sentences using the words.

ALL LEVELS

LANGUAGE CONVENTIONS: Use Appositives Effectively

An **appositive** is a noun or pronoun that identifies or renames another noun or pronoun. An **appositive phrase** includes an appositive and modifiers of it.

An appositive can be either essential or nonessential. An essential appositive provides information that is needed to identify what is referred to by the preceding noun or pronoun.

> **The author Jeremy Hsu has written several articles about technology.**

A nonessential appositive adds extra information about a noun or pronoun whose meaning is already clear.

> **Indiana Jones, played by Harrison Ford, was a popular movie character.**

In "Archaeology's Tech Revolution Since Indiana Jones," the author uses appositives in the following ways.

- To name or identify

> **Looking at the ratios of different forms of elements, called isotopes, in the bones of ancient people may reveal what they ate.**

> **"If we dig part of a site, we destroy it," said David Hurst Thomas, a curator in anthropology at the American Museum of Natural History in New York.**

- To describe or explain

> **The images also revealed buried city streets and houses at the ancient Egyptian city of Tanis, a well-known archaeological site that was featured in "Raiders of the Lost Ark" three decades ago.**

Practice and Apply Write your own sentences with appositives, using the examples from "Archaeology's Tech Revolution Since Indiana Jones" as models. Your sentences can be about your own experiences with technology. When you have finished, share your sentences with a partner and compare your use of appositives.

! Go to the **Grammar Studio** for more on appositives.

LANGUAGE CONVENTIONS: Use Appositives Effectively

Review the distinction between appositives that are essential (needed to identify the preceding noun and pronoun) and nonessential (not needed to clarify the meaning of a noun or pronoun). Have volunteers provide examples of each kind.

Point out that an appositive can appear in the middle of a sentence, where it may be set off by two commas, or at the beginning or end of a sentence, where it may be set off from the rest of the sentence with one comma. A comma should not be used when an appositive is needed to understand the meaning of a sentence. Discuss the following examples:

- *My cousin Elena lives in Mexico City.* (*Elena* is an essential appositive. When used this way, the writer means, "I have more than one cousin and am using her name to identify which cousin I mean.")
- *My cousin, Elena, lives in Mexico City*. (The commas indicate that the writer is adding extra information. The writer means, "I have only one cousin and am using her name as extra information.")

Practice and Apply After students share their sentences with a partner, have them discuss whether the appositives have been used effectively and how they might be made more effective.

ENGLISH LEARNER SUPPORT

Language Conventions Provide instruction and practice in using appositives with the following example sentences:

1. Give groups of students strips of paper with the following sentence cut into its three parts: *Jorge, a student, is good at math.* Have students organize the strips into a sentence. Ask: Is this an appositive? *(yes)* **SUBSTANTIAL**
2. Provide students with a sentence without an appositive, such as *Jorge discovered a tomb*. Have student pairs rewrite the sentence with an appositive of their choice. **MODERATE**
3. Provide students with a sentence without an appositive, such as *Jorge studied the sites at Giza*. Have students rewrite the sentence to include two appositives. *(Jorge, an archaeologist, studied sites near Giza, a city in northern Egypt.)* **LIGHT**

from THE CRUELEST JOURNEY

Travel Writing by Kira Salak

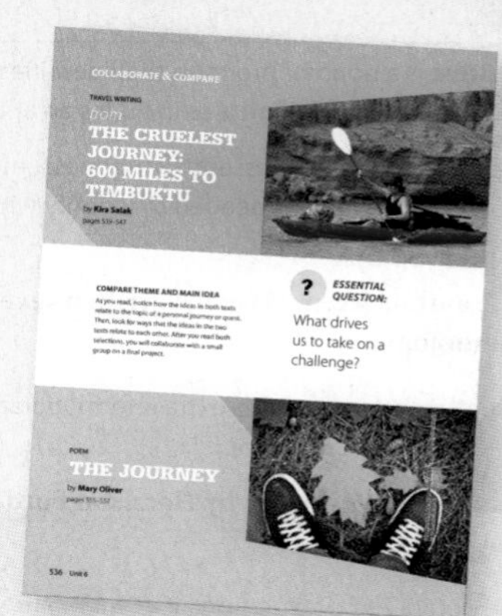

GENRE ELEMENTS

TRAVEL WRITING

Travel writing is a kind of **nonfiction narrative** that is also part informational text, true adventure story, and personal essay. It typically provides information about the history, geography, and culture of a particular place as well as maps and photographs. It is the true account of its author's unique journey in that place, making it engaging with conflicts, resolutions, characters, vivid sensory details, and a clear narrative voice. It is also often an author's exploration of personal challenges, thoughts, and feelings, and of human nature itself.

LEARNING OBJECTIVES

- Analyze key elements of travel writing, including imagery, mood, central idea, and purpose.
- Evaluate how graphic features achieve specific purposes.
- Analyze the effects of sentence variety on a narrative.
- Research transportation options within a community.
- Create oral and written directions with a small group.
- **Language** Discuss maps and photographs to evaluate how they help to achieve an author's purpose.

TEXT COMPLEXITY

Quantitative Measures	**The Cruelest Journey**	Lexile: 1030L
Qualitative Measures	**Ideas Presented** More than one purpose implied, but easily identified from context.	
	Structures Used Clearly stated sequential, chronological organization.	
	Language Used Some figurative, foreign, and less accessible language.	
	Knowledge Required Some difficult social studies concepts required.	

Online Ed

RESOURCES

- Unit 6 Response Log
- Selection Audio
- Reading Studio: Notice & Note
- Level Up Tutorial: Reading for Details
- Vocabulary Studio: Foreign Words Used in English
- Grammar Studio: Module 1: Lesson 10: Classifying Sentences by Purpose
- *from* The Cruelest Journey/"The Journey" Selection Test

SUMMARIES

English

This excerpt from Kira Salak's book, *The Cruelest Journey,* describes the beginning and end of a 600-mile trip along the Niger River in Africa. It is an exciting and dangerous journey in a kayak, something that had never been accomplished before. Along with descriptions of the natural world around her, Salak tries to make sense of her motivations to go on journeys that pose physical, emotional, and mental challenges.

Spanish

Este pasaje del libro de Kira Salak, *El viaje más cruel,* describe el comienzo y el fin de un viaje de 600 millas a lo largo de río Níger en África. Es un viaje emocionante y peligroso en cayac, algo nunca antes logrado. Con descripciones de la naturaleza a su alrededor, Salak intenta darle sentido a sus motivos de emprender un viaje que representa retos mentales, físicos y emocionales.

SMALL-GROUP OPTIONS

Have students work in small groups to read and discuss the selection.

Activate Academic Vocabulary

- Form groups of five students per group or five groups with about an equal number of students.
- Assign each member of a group (or each group if five groups) one of the Academic Vocabulary words for the unit: *motivate, objective, pursuit, subsequent, undertake*.
- Tell individuals (or groups) to provide a definition written in their own words, a question about the selection using the word, and a possible answer to the question using the word.
- Call on students or groups to share their work with the class.

Think-Write-Pair-Share

- After students have read and analyzed the excerpt from *The Cruelest Journey,* pose these questions: Is Salak's journey up the Niger River something she *wants* to do or something she *needs* to do? What is the difference?
- Have students think about the questions individually and write brief responses.
- Then have pairs share their responses and discuss their ideas.
- Finally, ask pairs to share their responses with another pair or the class and discuss their ideas.

Text X-Ray: English Learner Support
for The Cruelest Journey

Use the Text X-Ray and the supports and scaffolds in the Teacher's Edition to help guide students at different proficiency levels through the selection.

INTRODUCE THE SELECTION

DISCUSS CHALLENGES AND MOTIVATIONS

In this lesson, students will need to be able to discuss challenges and motivations, so provide the following explanations:

- *Challenges* are typically activities that are hard or goals that are not easy to reach. *Challenge* may also be used as a verb to call someone to a contest or competition *(I challenge you to a game of chess).*
- *Motivation* refers to a reason a person does something. In most cases, people have multiple motivations for doing what they do—some of which they don't consciously know or fully understand.

Invite volunteers to share some of their own motivations for attempting specific challenges. Supply the following sentence frames:

- *I attempted* ____________ *because* ____________.
- *My main motivation for challenging myself to* ____________ *was* ____________.

CULTURAL REFERENCES

The following words or phrases from the selection may be unfamiliar to students:

- *"Let's do it,"* (paragraph 2): "Let's get started."
- *the boons* (paragraph 4): great gifts
- *a whiff* (paragraph 5): literally, a slight smell; figuratively, a possibility
- *in synch* (paragraph 17): in the same rhythm
- *El Dorado* (paragraph 17): an imaginary city of gold in South America sought by Spanish adventurers
- *blasphemy* (paragraph 25): literally, speaking words that attack a god or religion; figuratively, questioning something that is well-established

LISTENING

Understand Key Ideas

Give students a framework for understanding what they will hear. Explain that in the first part of paragraph 3 Salak describes herself in Old Ségou.

Read sentences 1–4 of paragraph 3 aloud. Then use the following supports with students at varying proficiency levels:

- As you read, pause after each sentence and confirm students' understanding of its meaning. Then have students draw an image that shows what Salak describes in the first part of the paragraph. **SUBSTANTIAL**
- Encourage students to note questions they have as you read. When finished, have students ask their questions to clarify their understanding of the text. Remind them to use this strategy, asking you or other students questions, as they read to make sure they understand key ideas. **MODERATE**
- Have partners work together to provide an oral summary of what they heard. Give them the following to begin: *Challenges make the author feel* ____. *When she walks through Old Ségou she sees* _____. **LIGHT**

SPEAKING

Discuss Graphic Features

Guide students to realize that Salak has two main purposes: to describe her journey and to explain her motivations for taking it. Write these on the board. Explain that graphic features, such as maps and photographs, help authors achieve their purposes.

Use the following supports with students at varying proficiency levels:

- Guide students to review the map on page 545. Ask: What does the map help you to understand? How does the map help Salak? Supply these sentence frames: *The map helps me to see* ______________. *The map helps Salak* ______________ *her journey.* **SUBSTANTIAL**
- Have pairs discuss a graphic feature of their choice, using this sentence frame: *I think this [photograph/ map] helps the author to achieve her purpose of* ______________ *because it shows* ______________. **MODERATE**
- Have partners find and discuss two graphic features, one to support each purpose. Listen in to make sure they use the words *photographs, maps,* and *author's purpose.* **LIGHT**

READING

Recognize Elements of Travel Writing

Remind students that travel writing uses imagery, mood, graphic features, and central ideas to achieve its author's main purposes.

Use the following supports with students at varying proficiency levels:

- Echo read paragraph 11, pausing at details that create strong imagery. Guide students to circle these details. Clarify terms and expressions as necessary. Then guide them to use the details to draw an illustration of Salak paddling in her kayak. **SUBSTANTIAL**
- Choral read paragraphs 11 and 14. Direct students to identify the two different moods and to mark details that contribute to those moods. **MODERATE**
- Have students read paragraphs 11–13. Then have small groups determine the central idea of paragraph 13. Ask them to clarify what the "bargain" is and with whom Salak makes this bargain. Discuss how this setting connects to themes of challenges and motivations. **LIGHT**

WRITING

Write Directions

Work with students to read the writing assignment on Student Edition page 549.

Use the following supports with students at varying proficiency levels:

- Allow students to create maps to serve as directions. Then help them write map labels for buildings and locations for their directions, such as "Turn left" and "Go straight." **SUBSTANTIAL**
- Guide students in creating a word wall of prepositions to use to give directions. Prepositions might include *left, right, up, down, over, under, around, behind,* and *inside.* When possible, accompany prepositions with directional arrows or pictures to aid understanding. **MODERATE**
- Have students work in pairs to draft their directions. Allow them to refer to the word wall of prepositions you created. **LIGHT**

Connect to the ESSENTIAL QUESTION

The Cruelest Journey: 600 Miles to Timbuktu is written by a woman who takes on many challenges as a traveler and adventurer. As a part of her personal observations, she asks herself about her own drive to face challenges in general and this one in particular. The answers she finds are a unique expression of her personality, but at the same time, reflect some universal truths about overcoming fears and accepting challenges.

COMPARE THEME AND MAIN IDEA

Point out that *The Cruelest Journey* and "The Journey," are different genres, but the titles of both include the word *journey*, which can describe both physical and mental movement. Remind students that the main idea of a piece of literature and its theme are somewhat different. A **theme** is a larger message about life or human nature, while a **main idea** is the most important idea about a topic that the writer conveys — not necessarily about life or human nature. Students will analyze both selections so they can identify the main idea and theme and make comparisons between them.

COLLABORATE & COMPARE

TRAVEL WRITING

from THE CRUELEST JOURNEY: 600 MILES TO TIMBUKTU

by **Kira Salak**

pages 539–547

COMPARE THEME AND MAIN IDEA

As you read, notice how the ideas in both texts relate to the topic of a personal journey or quest. Then, look for ways that the ideas in the two texts relate to each other. After you read both selections, you will collaborate with a small group on a final project.

ESSENTIAL QUESTION:

What drives us to take on a challenge?

POEM

THE JOURNEY

by **Mary Oliver**

pages 555–557

LEARNING MINDSET

Plan Remind students that planning is a valuable skill for achieving any life goal. Mapping out the steps they need to take to arrive at a goal actually helps them get there more efficiently and without leaving out anything essential. If students are familiar with hiking or going on a long-distance trip, liken planning to marking a trail or setting out a route. Explain that even if they think they know what steps to follow, mapping the steps will allow them to take those steps with more confidence and ensure that they have allowed enough time for each one. Show them how to map steps backwards from a goal on a calendar or how to write them as a list and then order them with numbers.

from The Cruelest Journey: 600 Miles to Timbuktu

QUICK START

Traveling provides us with enduring memories, but it can also lead to some uncomfortable experiences and feelings. With a group, discuss your most memorable travel experiences.

ANALYZE TRAVEL WRITING

Travel writing is a type of nonfiction that records an author's experiences exploring new places. Travel writers don't just present a series of facts; they present a narrative that describes a setting, reflects a purpose, and communicates messages about life. In this excerpt, Kira Salak uses narrative techniques to reveal her reflections about her journey. She doesn't just tell you what she sees, she shows you how she feels. By including vivid details and **imagery** to describe people, places, and events, Salak builds tension and gets readers involved in her adventure. In addition to imagery, Salak's narrative reflects other literary elements:

- **Mood:** The mood of a work is the emotional response it creates in readers. What details does Salak include to create the mood of her narrative?
- **Central Idea:** The central idea of a work refers to a larger message about life. How is the setting of the narrative important to Salak's central idea?
- **Purpose:** When reading, think about why Salak wrote the narrative. Look for how she uses text structure and language to achieve her purpose.

GENRE ELEMENTS: TRAVEL WRITING

- type of narrative nonfiction
- usually illustrated with photographs, maps, or other visuals that help the reader visualize the places being described
- provides author's impressions about places visited
- includes vivid details and imagery to describe people, places, and events

EVALUATE GRAPHIC FEATURES

Graphic features help a reader better understand what a text is trying to communicate. They may include diagrams, charts, tables, time lines, illustrations, photographs, and maps. In particular, maps that accompany travel writing help the reader better understand where the narrative occurs geographically.

As you read the excerpt from *The Cruelest Journey: 600 Miles to Timbuktu*, note how the graphic features help the author achieve her purpose.

ENGLISH LEARNER SUPPORT

Build Academic Language Proficiency Review the meanings and pronunciations of the following literary terms: *mood, imagery,* and *author's message.* As you pronounce the words, emphasize that the first syllable of each word is stressed. For students whose primary language is Spanish, explain that here *mood* refers to *el ambiente* and not *el humor, el ánimo,* or *el modo*. Also share the following cognates: *image/imagen (imagery/la imaginería), author/autor,* and *message/mensaje.* **SUBSTANTIAL/MODERATE**

QUICK START

If some students do not have experience traveling over long distances, note that traveling a short distance to a different environment can create some of the same feelings. For example, traveling to a different school for sports or another event, or even to visit a relative in a different part of the city or area can expose them to new sights, sounds, and experiences. Students might extend the discussion by considering the relationship between "enduring memories" and "uncomfortable experiences and feelings." How often are they the same? Why is discomfort often memorable?

ANALYZE TRAVEL WRITING

Note that **imagery** consists of words and phrases that appeal to a reader's five senses. In travel writing, imagery is particularly important because it helps readers to imagine the look, feel, smell, sound, and taste of the unfamiliar things the author is encountering.

Mood is the reader's emotional response to descriptions. A narrative may inspire a wide variety of emotions, from sad and gloomy to happy and elated.

Clarify for students that a **central idea** is the author's main idea or message about a topic. One good way to determine the main idea in travel writing is to look for statements that reveal what the author thinks and feels about the journey and its impact on her.

Explain that while author's purpose may be stated explicitly, more often readers must infer it from what they read. Remind students that authors often have more than one purpose for writing.

Students may also be able to determine a central idea by creating a series of summaries for paragraphs or sections and then drawing a conclusion from them.

EVALUATE GRAPHIC FEATURES

Point out that maps and photos are common graphic features in modern travel writing. Explain that the photos that accompany this selection were taken by a professional photographer who was assigned the job of providing vivid images to accompany the writing but who did not travel continuously alongside her. Suggest that students note instances where the photos illustrate or expand on the text descriptions. For example, they can look for descriptions of Salak's kayak on the initial pages and compare these to the visual images of Salak with her kayak to evaluate the importance of these graphic features.

TEACH

CRITICAL VOCABULARY

Answers:

1. *c*
2. *d*
3. *a*
4. *e*
5. *b*

English Learner Support

Use Cognates Tell students that three of the Critical Vocabulary words have direct Spanish cognates: *circuit/circuito, integrity/integridad, embark/embarcar.*
ALL LEVELS

LANGUAGE CONVENTIONS

Remind students that noticing and analyzing language conventions often requires reading text very carefully or rereading a second or third time. To support the analysis of sentence lengths, encourage students to notice when their reading is slowed down by long sentences, sped up by short sentences, or involves significant pauses or breaks due to punctuation such as dashes. When they notice such changes in their pace, they should reread the section a second or third time to see whether the sentence length mirrors the action or the nature of the person, place, thing, or idea it is describing.

ANNOTATION MODEL

Remind students of the ideas in Analyze Travel Writing on page 537. The Model on this page shows that the student chose to underline phrases that establish a particular mood through imagery and reveal the author's purpose. Point out that they may follow this model or use their own system for marking up the selection in their write-in text. They may want to color-code their annotations using highlighters. Their notes in the margin may also include questions about ideas that are unclear or topics they want to learn more about.

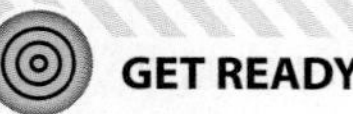

GET READY

CRITICAL VOCABULARY

To preview the Critical Vocabulary words, match the words to their definitions

1. circuitously	a. consistency and strength of purpose
2. disingenuous	b. not flowing or progressing
3. integrity	c. in an indirect and lengthy manner
4. embark	d. lacking in honesty
5. stagnant	e. to begin a journey or project

LANGUAGE CONVENTIONS

Authors often use **sentence variety** to keep their writing from becoming monotonous. In addition, sometimes they introduce varied sentences to mirror the ideas they describe.

- Long, winding sentences slow down a reader. They may also reflect a long journey or a detailed plot.
- Short, choppy sentences can be read more quickly. They can be used to add tension to a plot or reflect on quickly moving events.
- Breaks in sentences, such as the use of dashes, cause readers to pause and reflect on what they have just read.

As you read the excerpt from *The Cruelest Journey: 600 Miles to Timbuktu*, watch for how the author uses varying sentence length—and punctuation breaks within sentences—to effectively express her ideas.

ANNOTATION MODEL

NOTICE & NOTE

Here is an example of how one student annotated the beginning of "The Cruelest Journey: 600 Miles to Timbuktu."

In the beginning, my journeys feel at best ludicrous, at worst insane. This one is no exception. The idea is to paddle nearly 600 miles on the Niger River in a kayak, alone, from the Malian town of Old Ségou to Timbuktu. And now, at the very hour when I have decided to leave, a thunderstorm bursts open the skies, sending down apocalyptic rain, washing away the very ground beneath my feet.

When the author says her "journeys feel at best ludicrous, at worst insane" I think she is creating a mood of chaos. This is reinforced by the thunderstorm at the beginning of the journey.

The purpose of the text is to describe the author's kayaking trip from Old Ségou to Timbuktu.

NOTICE & NOTE

BACKGROUND

Kira Salak *(b. 1971) wrote her book,* The Cruelest Journey: 600 Miles to Timbuktu, *to document her 600-mile solo kayak trip on the Niger River. The first person to ever achieve this feat, she traveled through a remote and dangerous region in Africa. Salak is an adventurer, an explorer, and a journalist. She has covered the civil war in the Democratic Republic of Congo, traveled across Papua New Guinea, and biked across Alaska. In 2005, she received a National Geographic Emerging Explorer Award, which recognizes people who are helping build knowledge about the world through exploration. This selection is an excerpt from her book.*

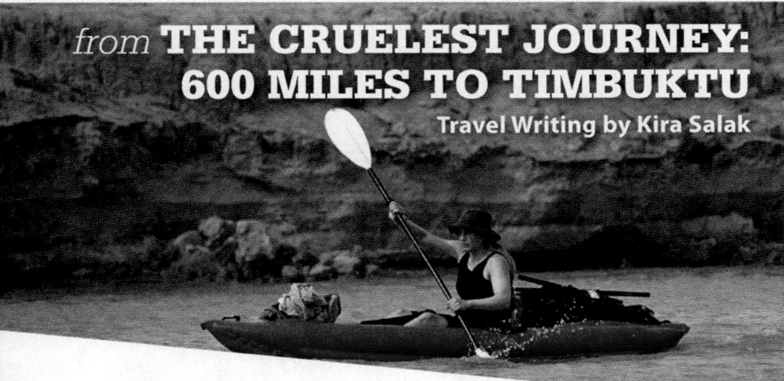

from THE CRUELEST JOURNEY: 600 MILES TO TIMBUKTU

Travel Writing by Kira Salak

PREPARE TO COMPARE

What does Salak think and feel about her journey? Make note of her thoughts, comments, and any telling details you notice. Write down any questions you generate during reading.

1 In the beginning, my journeys feel at best ludicrous, at worst insane. This one is no exception. The idea is to paddle nearly 600 miles on the Niger River in a kayak, alone, from the Malian town of Old Ségou to Timbuktu. And now, at the very hour when I have decided to leave, a thunderstorm bursts open the skies, sending down apocalyptic rain, washing away the very ground beneath my feet. It is the rainy season in Mali, for which there can be no comparison in the world. Lightning pierces trees, slices across houses. Thunder racks the skies and pounds the earth like mortar fire, and every living thing huddles in tenuous shelter, expecting the world to end. Which it doesn't. At least not this time. So that we all give a collective sigh to the salvation of the passing storm as it rumbles its way east, and I survey the river I'm to leave on this morning. Rain or no rain, today is the day for the journey to begin.

Notice & Note

You can use the side margins to notice and note signposts in the text.

ANALYZE TRAVEL WRITING

Annotate: Mark the author's description of the rainstorm.

Respond: How does she use details to create a mood?

BACKGROUND

After students read the Background paragraph, note that Salak began traveling on her own at the age of nineteen and went on a solo backpacking trip in Africa at twenty-one. Ask: Why might a person want to travel alone in remote or dangerous places? *(to test his or her survival skills, to be more deeply immersed in the experience, to have time and opportunity to reflect)* What are the possible dangers involved in traveling to remote or hostile places? *(Some may try to harm unsuspecting travelers; an injury or illness could be difficult to treat when far from medical help; and a lost or ruined food or water supply may be difficult to replace.)*

PREPARE TO COMPARE

Direct students to use the Prepare to Compare prompt to focus their reading.

ANALYZE TRAVEL WRITING

Note that **mood** within a selection may shift depending on the events and feelings in the narrative. However, introductory sentences and paragraphs often establish a continuing or recurring mood that can affect the reader throughout the selection. Discuss the possible effects of extreme weather on people who are settled as well as on travelers without permanent shelter. The danger associated with exposure to the elements is emphasized in the opening paragraph and the power of the natural world versus a lone traveler will be emphasized throughout the narrative. *(**Answer:** The description of the torrential rainstorm creates a mood of chaos and danger.)*

TEACH

LANGUAGE CONVENTIONS

Remind students that varying sentence lengths are often used to speed up or slow down one's reading pace so that it mirrors the action or setting that is being described. Contrast the long sentences in the description of walking through winding streets to the short sentences in the first lines of paragraph 2. Note that those short sentences describe several different actions that happened quickly (leaving the hut, pointing to the north, the promise to pray for her).

Also point out that long sentences often require punctuation to make them understandable and to guide the reader in phrasing. In this case, the author uses commas to break the long sentences into phrases that aid comprehension and create a rhythm. (***Possible answers:*** *The sentences are detailed and winding, just like the labyrinth of streets being described. The long yet rhythmic quality of the sentences mirrors a slow walking pace.)*

For **listening support** for students at varying proficiency levels, see the **Text X-Ray** on page 536C.

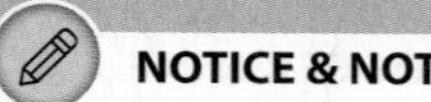

NOTICE & NOTE

LANGUAGE CONVENTIONS

Annotate: Mark the author's description of walking through Old Ségou.

Respond: How does the sentence structure mirror the topic?

And no one, not even the oldest in the village, can say for certain whether I'll get to the end.

2 "Let's do it," I say, leaving the shelter of an adobe hut. My guide from town, Modibo, points to the north, to further storms. He says he will pray for me. It's the best he can do. To his knowledge, no man has ever completed such a trip, though a few have tried. And certainly no woman has done such a thing. This morning he took me aside and told me he thinks I'm crazy, which I understood as concern and thanked him. He told me that the people of Old Ségou think I'm crazy too, and that only uncanny[1] good luck will keep me safe.

3 Still, when a person tells me I can't do something, I'll want to do it all the more. It may be a failing of mine. I carry my inflatable kayak through the narrow passageways of Old Ségou, past the small adobe huts melting in the rains, past the huddling goats and smoke of cooking fires, people peering out at me from the dark entranceways. It is a labyrinth[2] of ancient homes, built and rebuilt after each storm, plastered with the very earth people walk upon. Old Ségou must look much the same as it did in Scottish explorer Mungo Park's time

[1] **uncanny:** mysterious or impossible to explain.

[2] **labyrinth:** a complex collection of paths, such as a maze.

TO CHALLENGE STUDENTS . . .

Reflect on Personal Motivations Direct students to the first two sentences of paragraph 3. Salak uses provocative words to describe one of her general motivations and suggests that it is a possible "failing." Ask students whether they consider Salak's reaction a failing or a strength and why. Then have them reflect on their own motivations for accepting challenges. Are they the same as Salak's? If not, what other motivations push them ahead? Suggest they write a personal essay in which they share one of their biggest or most frequent motivators for accepting challenges and compare this to Salak's as expressed either in this paragraph or elsewhere in the selection, such as in paragraph 5. Tell them to include at least one example of an experience in which this motivation played a large role and the outcome of that experience, including whether they learned something in the process.

when, exactly 206 years ago to the day, he left on the first of his two river journeys down the Niger to Timbuktu, the first such attempt by a Westerner. It is no coincidence that I've planned to leave on the same day and from the same spot. Park is my benefactor of sorts, my guarantee. If he could travel down the Niger, then so can I. And it is all the guarantee I have for this trip—that an obsessed 19th-century adventurer did what I would like to do. Of course Park also died on this river, but I've so far managed to overlook that.

4 I gaze at the Niger through the adobe passageways, staring at waters that began in the mountainous rain forests of Guinea and traveled all this way to central Mali—waters that will journey northeast with me to Timbuktu before cutting a great circular swath through the Sahara and retreating south, through Niger, on to Nigeria, passing **circuitously** through mangrove swamps and jungle, resting at last in the Atlantic in the Bight of Benin.[3] But the Niger is more than a river; it is a kind of faith. Bent and plied by Saharan sands, it perseveres more than 2,600 miles from beginning to end through one of the hottest, most desolate regions of the world. And when the rains come each year, it finds new strength of purpose, surging through the sunbaked lands, giving people the boons of crops and livestock and fish, taking nothing, asking nothing. It humbles all who see it.

5 If I were to try to explain why I'm here, why I chose Mali and the Niger for this journey—now that is a different matter. I can already feel the resistance in my gut, the familiar clutch of fear. I used to avoid stripping myself down in search of motivation, scared of what I might uncover, scared of anything that might suggest a taint of the pathological.[4] And would it be enough to say that I admire Park's own trip on the river and want to try a similar challenge? That answer carries a whiff of the **disingenuous**; it sounds too easy to me. Human motivation, itself, is a complicated thing. If only it was simple enough to say, "Here is the Niger, and I want to paddle it." But I'm not that kind of traveler, and this isn't that kind of trip. If a journey doesn't have something to teach you about yourself, then what kind of journey is it? There is one thing I'm already certain of: Though we may think we choose our journeys, they choose us.

6 Hobbled donkeys cower under a new onslaught of rain, ears back, necks craned. Little children dare each other to touch me, and I make it easy for them, stopping and holding out my arm. They stroke my white skin as if it were velvet, using only the pads of their fingers, then stare at their hands to check for wet paint.

7 Thunder again. More rain falls. I stop on the shore, near a centuries-old kapok tree under which I imagine Park once took shade. I open my bag, spread out my little red kayak, and start to pump it up. I'm doing this trip under the sponsorship of *National*

[3] **Bight of Benin:** a gulf on Africa's west coast between Ghana and Nigeria.
[4] **taint of the pathological:** trace of mental illness.

NOTICE & NOTE

circuitously
(sər-kyo͞o´ĭ-təs-lē) *adv.*
in an indirect and lengthy manner.

ANALYZE TRAVEL WRITING
Annotate: In Paragraph 5, underline the author's strongest belief about travel.

Respond: Why do you think she chose to make this trip?

disingenuous
(dĭs-ĭn-jĕn´yo͞o-əs) *adj.*
insincere, deceitful.

TEACH

ANALYZE TRAVEL WRITING

Tell students that a rhetorical question is not always just a question with such an obvious answer that it does not require a reply. It may be a question used to make a point or create an effect, rather than to get an answer. Ask students to find the first rhetorical question in paragraph 5. *("And would it be enough to say that I admire Park's own trip on the river and want to try a similar challenge?")* Then guide students to recognize that Salak poses this question to move smoothly into a deeper exploration of her personal motives for undertaking this particular journey.

Explain that mountain climbers have often answered the question of why they made a tough and dangerous climb up a mountain with the statement, "Because it was there." Ask students to speculate on how Salak would classify this answer based on her thoughts in this paragraph. *(probably as too easy and somewhat disingenuous)* (***Answer:*** *The author most likely chose the trip to learn more about herself. However, her last sentence in paragraph 5 suggests that she felt compelled to take the journey—that "it chose her.")*

APPLYING ACADEMIC VOCABULARY

☑ **motivate** ☑ **objective** ☐ **pursuit** ☐ **subsequent** ☑ **undertake**

Write and Discuss Have students turn to a partner to discuss the following questions. Guide students to include the academic vocabulary words *motivate, objective,* and *undertake* in their responses. They should write out a response before beginning discussion. Ask volunteers to share their written responses orally with the class.

- What does Salak say **motivates** her to choose this journey down the Niger? Is she clear about her **objective**?
- Why did Salak **undertake** such a dangerous journey?

CRITICAL VOCABULARY

circuitously: The river flows and turns in many directions.

ASK STUDENTS to explain what details Salak provides to show that the river flows circuitously. *(The Niger does not flow directly to the Atlantic but indirectly through desert, swamps, and jungles. She also notes that the river runs northeast before retreating southward.)*

disingenuous: An insincere person often tries to deceive others.

ASK STUDENTS why Salak thinks it would be disingenuous to say that she took this trip just because she admired Park's trip and wanted to try a similar challenge. *(The truth is usually complicated—not as simple as her answer would make it seem.)*

ENGLISH LEARNER SUPPORT

Use Pronouns Native Vietnamese speakers may tend to use the same noun repeatedly rather than substituting pronouns in English. Explain that in English, appropriate pronouns are substituted for nouns to avoid repetition. Show how this is done by guiding students to use pronouns to refer to the underlined nouns in the sentences below from paragraphs 7–9.

- *The magazine presented the best compromise ____ could. (it)*
- *Paddles fitted together and ready. Modibo is standing on the shore, watching me.*
  "I'll pray for you," ____ reminds me. (he)

SUBSTANTIAL/MODERATE

For **reading support** for students at varying proficiency levels, see the **Test X-Ray** on page 536D.

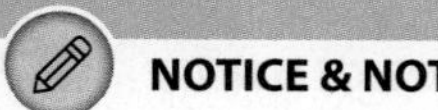

NOTICE & NOTE

integrity
(ĭn-tĕg´rĭ-tē) *n.*
consistency and strength of purpose.

Geographic Adventure, which hopes to run a magazine story about it. This means that they need photos, lots of photos, and so a French photographer named Rémi Bénali feverishly snaps pictures of me. I don't know what I hate more—river storms or photo shoots. I value the privacy and **integrity** of my trips, and I don't want my journey turning into a circus. The magazine presented the best compromise it could: Rémi, renting a motor-driven pirogue,[5] was given instructions to find me on the river every few days to do his thing.

8 My kayak is nearly inflated. A couple of women nearby, with colorful cloth wraps called *pagnes* tied tightly about their breasts, gaze at me cryptically, as if to ask: *Who are you and what do you think you're doing?* The Niger churns and slaps the shore, in a surly mood. I don't pretend to know what I'm doing. Just one thing at a time now, kayak inflated, kayak loaded with my gear. Paddles fitted together and ready. Modibo is standing on the shore, watching me.

9 "I'll pray for you," he reminds me.

10 I balance my gear, adjust the straps, get in. And, finally, irrevocably, I paddle away. . . .

11 The storm erupts into a new overture. Torrential rains. Waves higher than my kayak, trying to capsize me. But my boat is self-bailing[6] and I stay afloat. The wind drives the current in reverse, tearing and ripping at the shores, sending spray into my face. I paddle madly, crashing and driving forward. I travel inch by inch, or so it seems, arm muscles smarting and rebelling against this journey. I crawl past New Ségou, fighting the Niger for more distance. Large river steamers rest in jumbled rows before cement docks, the town itself looking dark and deserted in the downpour. No one is out in their boats. The people know something I don't: that the river dictates all travel.

12 A popping feeling now and a screech of pain. My right arm lurches from a ripped muscle. But this is no time and place for such an injury, and I won't tolerate it, stuck as I am in a storm. I try to get used to the pulses of pain as I fight the river. There is only one direction to go: forward. Stopping has become anathema.[7]

embark
(ĕm-bärk´) *v.*
to set out on a course or a journey (often aboard a boat).

13 I wonder what we look for when we **embark** on these kinds of trips. There is the pat answer that you tell the people you don't know: that you're interested in seeing a place, learning about its people. But then the trip begins and the hardship comes, and hardship is more honest: it tells us that we don't have enough patience yet, nor humility, nor gratitude. And we thought that we did. Hardship brings us closer to truth, and thus is more difficult to bear, but from it alone comes compassion. And so I've told the world that it can do what it wants with me during this trip if only, by the end, I have learned something more. A bargain, then. The journey, my teacher.

[5] **pirogue** (pĭ-rōg´): a canoe made from a hollowed tree trunk.
[6] **self-bailing:** the boat has holes, or scuppers, that allow water to drain from the cockpit.
[7] **anathema:** something hated or despised.

CRITICAL VOCABULARY

integrity: Someone whose words and actions are consistent is able to keep focused on what is important.

ASK STUDENTS to explain why Salak uses the word *integrity* to describe her trips. *(She takes the trips on her own terms, establishing the conditions that will assure her privacy and singleness of purpose.)*

embark: Setting out on a trip, a traveler has many expectations.

ASK STUDENTS what does Salak say we often tell people we don't know when we embark on a trip. *(When we set out on a journey, we often tell people we don't know that we are going to see a place and learn about its people and culture.)*

WHEN STUDENTS STRUGGLE . . .

Analyze Travel Writing Help students add examples to each row from paragraphs 1–13.

Technique	Example
Imagery	*vivid picture of Old Ségou, paragraph 3*
Mood	*rejecting physical pain, paragraph 12*
Central idea	*challenges posed by nature, paragraphs 8–11*
Purpose	*explaining motivation, paragraphs 3–5*

For additional support, go to the **Reading Studio** and assign the following **Level Up Tutorial: Reading for Details.**

NOTICE & NOTE 

14 And where is the river of just this morning, with its whitecaps that would have liked to drown me, with its current flowing backward against the wind? Gone to this: a river of smoothest glass, a placidity unbroken by wave or eddy, with islands of lush greenery awaiting me like distant Xanadus.[8] The Niger is like a mercurial god, meting out punishment and benediction on a whim. And perhaps the god of the river sleeps now, returning matters to the mortals who ply its waters? The Bozo and Somono[9] fishermen in their pointy canoes. The long passenger pirogues, overloaded with people and merchandise, rumbling past, leaving diesel fumes in their wake. And now, inexplicably, the white woman in a little red boat, paddling through waters that flawlessly mirror the cumulus clouds above. We all belong here, in our way. It is as if I've entered a very lucid dream, continually

[8] **Xanadus** (zăn´ə-do͞oz): Xanadu, the summer palace of Kublai Khan; connotes an elaborate, ideal paradise.
[9] **Bozo and Somono**: ethnic groups native to Mali and the Niger River delta.

ENGLISH LEARNER SUPPORT

Recognize Informal English Explain that formal English consists of complete sentences—those that have a subject and verb. However, authors often break this rule for effect by using fragments in their writing or by beginning their sentences with conjunctions such as *and*. Have students listen as you read sentences 4–7 of paragraph 14 aloud. Then use the following supports with students at varying proficiency levels.

- Read aloud only sentence 5. Ask: Is this a complete sentence? *(no)* **SUBSTANTIAL**
- Pause after you read each sentence, and ask a volunteer to explain why it is or is not complete. **MODERATE**
- Help students rewrite the sentences in standard, formal English, using new punctuation, subjects, and action verbs or forms of the linking verb to be. The following is a sample revision:

  Perhaps the god of the river sleeps now, returning matters to the mortals who ply its waters: the Bozo and Somono fishermen in their pointy canoes; the crowds of people with their merchandise stuffed onto the long passenger pirogues that rumble past, leaving diesel fumes in their wake; and, inexplicably, a lone white woman in a little red boat, paddling through waters that flawlessly mirror the cumulus clouds above.

Discuss with students how the revised version compares to the original. Ask: What is gained in the rewrite? *(grammatical correctness, proper parallelism in subject-verb order by repositioning "the crowds of people")* What is lost? *(the informal tone that suggests the thought processes of a first-person narrator)* **LIGHT**

TO CHALLENGE STUDENTS . . .

Investigate Details Salak's adventures and writing offer a unique perspective on the challenges of exploration. Encourage students to prepare an oral, written, or multimedia presentation that provides more information on this journey of hers and/or others she has taken. They may want to read more from *The Cruelest Journey* and/or excerpts from her other books or articles. Tell students that along with providing summaries of her adventures, they should share their answers to these questions: By describing their travels, can Salak and other explorers make the world a better place? Can they help us become better people? Why or why not?

LANGUAGE CONVENTIONS

Note that some types of punctuation (such as commas, colons, and dashes) allow authors to construct longer yet grammatically correct sentences. These sentences can provide fuller descriptions and prompt the reader to focus on a particular thought or description. Point out that the longer sentences in this selection serve a number of purposes, including creating a slower pace that not only mirrors the narrator's thought process but also allows readers more time to follow and absorb her thoughts and feelings. Note that no action is described in these sentences, but rather a static scene in the author's mind. (***Answer:*** *The dash provides a pause for the reader to think about why the author is surprised to find herself on the journey. The colon also causes the reader to pause, but since it is in such an early and surprising place in the sentence, the pause created by the colon suggests that the narrator is having a stunned moment of realization. The commas and periods help with the reader's pacing.)*

ENGLISH LEARNER SUPPORT

Derive Meaning from Signs Point out the sign on page 544. Explain that words, numbers, symbols, and images often appear on signs. Even if a person doesn't fully understand a sign, he or she can still get information from it. For example, draw students' attention to the directional arrow and numbers on the sign. Guide students to the conclusion that the sign is pointing to a destination and a distance one must travel to reach that destination. **ALL LEVELS**

NOTICE & NOTE

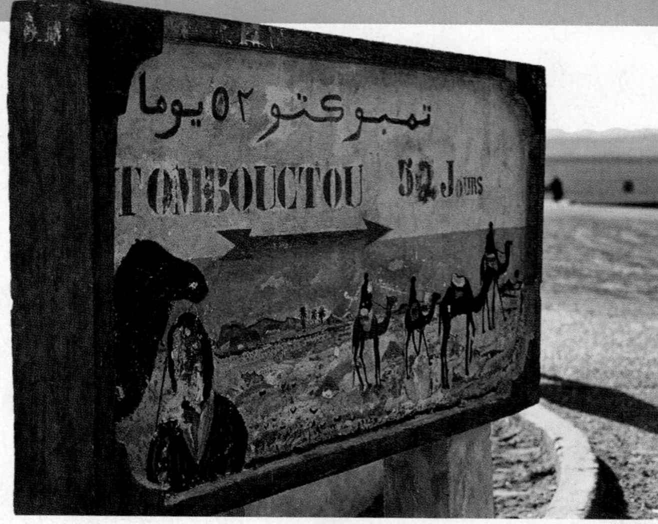

LANGUAGE CONVENTIONS

Annotate: Notice the punctuation within the last two sentences of Paragraph 14. Mark each one.

Respond: How does each one affect how you read these sentences?

surprised to find myself here on this river—I've become a hapless actor in a mysterious play, not yet knowing what my part is, left to gape at the wonder of what I have set in motion. Somehow: I'm in a kayak, on the Niger River, paddling very slowly but very surely to Timbuktu.

15 *As Salak continues on her journey—including a side trip on a tributary of the Niger—she encounters raging storms, dangerous hippos, and unrelenting heat. Because she is traveling in a small kayak and unable to carry many supplies, she comes ashore each night, seeking shelter and food from the locals, who live along the banks of the river. The locals are very curious about a woman undertaking such a dangerous journey alone. Some of them greet her warmly and generously; others with hostility. Finally, weak from dysentery, she approaches her final destination—Timbuktu.*

from Chapter Thirteen

16 "This river will never end," I say out loud, over and over again, like a mantra. My map shows an obvious change to the northeast, but that turn hasn't come for hours, may never come at all. To be so close to Timbuktu, and yet so immeasurably far away. All I know is that I must keep paddling. I *have* to be close. Determined still to get to Timbuktu's port of Korioumé by nightfall, I shed the protection of my long-sleeved shirt, pull the kayak's thigh straps in tight, and prepare for the hardest bout of paddling yet.

17 I paddle like a person possessed. I paddle the hours away, the sun falling aside to the west but still keeping its heat on me. I keep up a cadence in my head, keep my breaths regular and deep, in synch with my arm movements. The shore passes by slowly, but it passes. As the sun gets ominously low, burning a flaming orange, the river turns almost due north and I can see a distant, square-shaped building

IMPROVE READING FLUENCY

Targeted Passage Use echo reading to help students practice appropriate phrasing and emphasis in reading the summary text in paragraph 15. Explain that this paragraph is not written by Salak as part of her book, but created by editors who need to summarize intervening events. Begin by reading the paragraph aloud, emphasizing pauses and phrasing. Then have students echo your reading as you read it a second and third time, first by pausing after each phrase or clause and then reading it again with pauses after each sentence. Consider concluding with a choral reading so all can enjoy reading the paragraph aloud together.

 Go to the **Reading Studio** for additional support in developing fluency.

NOTICE & NOTE

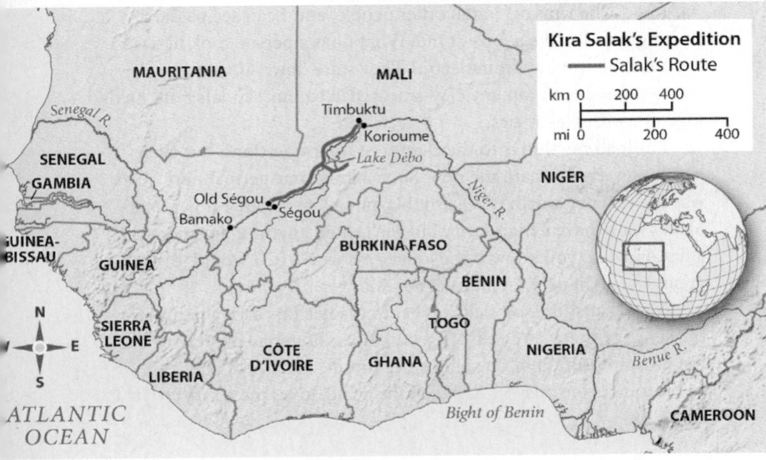

made of cement: the harbinger of what can only be Koriouмé. Hardly a tower of gold, hardly an El Dorado, but I'll take it. I paddle straight toward it, ignoring the pains in my body, my raging headache. *Timbuktu, Timbuktu!* Bozo fishermen ply the river out here, and they stare at me as I pass. They don't ask for money or cadeaux[10]—can they see the determination in my face, sense my fatigue? All they say is, *"Ça va, madame?"*[11] with obvious concern. One man actually stands and raises his hands in a cheer, urging me on. I take his kindness with me into the final stretch, rounding the river's sharp curve to the port of Koriouмé. . . .

18 Just as the last rays of the sun color the Niger, I pull up beside a great white river steamer, named, appropriately, the *Tombouctou*. Rémi's boat is directly behind me, the flash from his camera lighting up the throng of people gathering on shore. There is no more paddling to be done. I've made it. I can stop now. I stare up at the familiar crowd waiting in the darkness. West African pop music blares from a party on the *Tombouctou*.

19 Slowly, I undo my thigh straps and get out of my kayak, hauling it from the river and dropping it onshore for the last time. A huge crowd has gathered around me, children squeezing in to stroke my kayak. People ask where I have come from and I tell them, "Old Ségou." They can't seem to believe it.

20 "Ségou?" one man asks. He points down the Niger. His hand waves and curves as he follows the course of the river in his mind.

21 "Oui," I say.

22 "Ehh!" he exclaims.

23 "Ségou, Ségou, Ségou?" a woman asks.

[10] **cadeaux** (kə-dō´): French word meaning "gifts."

[11] **Ça va, madame?** (sä vä, mä-däm´): French for "How are you, madam?"

EVALUATE GRAPHIC FEATURES

Annotate: Trace the route of the Niger River on the map.

Respond: How does the map help you better understand the author's journey?

WORD GAPS

Notice & Note: Mark the footnote for "cadeaux."

Respond: Why do you think the author chooses to use the French word for "gifts" instead of the English one?

EVALUATE GRAPHIC FEATURES

Note that the map displays the entire route of the Niger River and that Salak's journey covered only a portion. Ask students to review the text and identify the names of the cities where Salak's journey begins and ends. *(Old Ségou, Timbuktu)*

To help students make best use of the map, ask them to review the title and identify the length of the journey. *(600 miles)* Ask them to estimate the entire length of the Niger River based on the distance of her journey. *(possibly about 2400–3000 miles if Ségou and Timbuktu are 600 miles apart)* Ask them to compare this estimate with the distance between the oceans in America: about 3000 miles. Discuss whether this comparison helps them to better comprehend the length of her journey. *(**Answer:** Seeing the route helps the reader better appreciate the length of the journey.)*

For **speaking support** for students at varying proficiency levels, see the **Text X-Ray** on page 536D.

WORD GAPS

Notice & Note Point out that French is spoken in the areas Salak travels through, along with people's native languages. Foreign words may be used by authors for particular reasons. In this case, the author uses a word that she hears often on her journey as she encounters fishermen on the river. Note the second use of French in this section in paragraph 21 as Salak answers in French rather than English. *(**Answer:** Using the French word reflects the setting of the text, since French is spoken in Mali.)*

ENGLISH LEARNER SUPPORT

Confirm Understanding Use the following supports for students at varying proficiency levels:

- Read aloud the last two sentences of paragraph 17 and the first two sentences of paragraph 18. Have students draw a graphic-novel style illustration of Salak engaged in this final push to reach her goal. **SUBSTANTIAL/MODERATE**
- Read aloud paragraphs 17–18. Then have students dramatize the scene, using movements and facial expressions to convey the mood. **MODERATE/LIGHT**

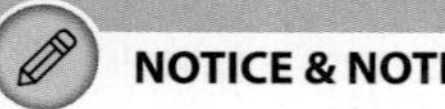

NOTICE & NOTE

24 I nod. She runs off to tell other people, and I can see passersby rushing over to take a look at me. What does a person look like who has come all the way from Ségou? They stare down at me in my sweat-stained tank top, my clay-smeared skirt, my sandals both held together with plastic ties.

25 I unload my things to the clamor of their questions, but even speaking seems to pain me now. Such a long time getting here. And was the journey worth it? Or is it blasphemy to ask that now? I can barely walk, have a high fever. I haven't eaten anything for more than a day. How do you know if the journey is worth it? I would give a great deal right now for silence. For stillness.

26 My exhaustion and sickness begin to alter this arrival, numbing the sense of finish and self-congratulation and replacing it with only the most important of questions. I've found that illness does this to me, quiets the busy thoughts of the mind, gives me a rare clarity

ENGLISH LEARNER SUPPORT

Use Learning Strategies Help students to recognize details that convey imagery, create mood, support a central idea, and/or reveal the author's purpose by using the following supports with students at varying proficiency levels:

- Tell students to mark words that prompt mental images. Then have them make a list of these words and draw images based on these details, checking them off their lists as they incorporate them. Then have students share their drawings with a partner and discuss the mood of each picture. **SUBSTANTIAL**
- Tell students to reread paragraphs 14–27 and focus on looking for just one type of detail at a time. Allow students to work in small groups or pairs for this purpose, with students taking turns reading paragraphs aloud while the listener(s) write down significant details. **MODERATE**
- After individuals have found examples that convey imagery, mood, central ideas, and author's purpose, have them meet in small groups to compare and discuss their findings. **LIGHT**

WHEN STUDENTS STRUGGLE . . .

Analyze Travel Writing Help students fill in more examples from paragraphs 14–27.

Technique	Example
Imagery	*description of hot sun, paragraph 17*
Mood	*changing aspect of river, paragraph 14*
Central idea	*avoiding a stagnant life, paragraph 27*
Purpose	*to explain feelings during the journey as well as the success of arrival, paragraphs 26–27*

that I don't usually have. I see the weeks on the river, the changing tribal groups, the lush shores down by Old Ségou metamorphosing[12] slowly into the treeless, sandy spread near Timbuktu. I'm wishing I could explain it to people—the subtle yet certain way the world has altered over these past few weeks. The inevitability of it. The grace of it. Grace, because in my life back home every day had appeared the same as the one before. Nothing seemed to change; nothing took on new variety. It had felt like a **stagnant** life.

27 I know now, with the utter conviction of my heart, that I want to avoid that stagnant life. I want the world to always be offering me the new, the grace of the unfamiliar. Which means—and I pause with the thought—a path that will only lead through my fears. Where there are certainty and guarantees, I will never be able to meet that unknown world.

[12] **metamorphosing:** completely changing into another form.

NOTICE & NOTE

stagnant
(stăg´nənt) *adj.* unchanging; without activity or development.

CHECK YOUR UNDERSTANDING

Answer these questions before moving on to the **Analyze the Text** section on the following page.

1 What mood is conveyed as the excerpt from Chapter 13 begins?
- **A** Enjoyment and excitement
- **B** Serenity and uncertainty
- **C** Calm and quiet
- **D** Tedium and exhaustion

2 How does the author mainly support her ideas?
- **F** With descriptions of her experiences
- **G** With facts about geography
- **H** With impressions of other writers
- **J** With information about the region

3 What is the purpose of the map in the text?
- **A** It shows the reader the geography of the continent.
- **B** It helps the reader visualize what the author saw.
- **C** It shows the reader where the author traveled.
- **D** It helps the reader plan a trip similar to the author.

TEACH

CHECK YOUR UNDERSTANDING

Have students answer the questions independently.

Answers:

1. *D*
2. *F*
3. *C*

If they answer any questions incorrectly, have them reread the text to confirm their understanding. Then they may proceed to ANALYZE THE TEXT on page 548.

ENGLISH LEARNER SUPPORT

Oral Assessment Use the following questions to assess students' comprehension and speaking skills. Ask students to respond in complete sentences.

1. Reread paragraph 16. What is the mood conveyed by this paragraph? *(The paragraph conveys a mood of tedium and exhaustion.)*
2. What kind of support does the author mainly use—descriptive details, facts, quotations, or statistics? *(She mostly uses descriptive details as support.)*
3. What is the purpose of the map on page 545? *(Its purpose is to show the route the author traveled and the surrounding area.)* **MODERATE/LIGHT**

CRITICAL VOCABULARY

stagnant: A life that consists of unchanging routines doesn't promote personal growth.

ASK STUDENTS why Salak believes her life was stagnant before she embarked on her journey. *(Her life was unchanging and lacking in new variety.)*

APPLY

ANALYZE THE TEXT

Possible answers:

1. **DOK 2:** *Salak says she might be doing it because she admired Park's voyage on this river and wanted the challenge, or that because the Niger is there, she wants to paddle it. But really she embarks on this trip to learn something about herself, and she believes that the trip has chosen her in order to teach her something.*
2. **DOK 4:** *The dialogue illustrates public reactions to the author's accomplishment: people cannot believe that she has paddled all the way from Old Ségou. While most of the narrative recounts solitary actions and private thoughts, the dialogue offers another perspective and provides some variation.*
3. **DOK 3:** *Facts: The Niger River flows 600 miles from Old Ségou to Timbuktu. Salak begins her river journey on the same day of the year and in the same spot as 19th century Scottish explorer Mungo Park. Opinions: Normal life is stagnant. People think the author is unstable.*
4. **DOK 3:** *Students might suggest more detailed maps; more photos; or videos of the journey.*
5. **DOK 4:** *Pointing out the statistics shows how rare the journey is, reinforces the danger the author faces, and expands upon how the author likes to push boundaries.*

RESEARCH

Remind students to list at least two community locations, each with one or more transportation options and observations in the Positives and Negatives column.

Extend Discussions should include contributions from all members of the small group and a respectful discussion related to selecting a location for the group. Students might prioritize locations by how commonly people go there, the subjective value they place on the location, and/or the challenges involved in traveling there and in giving directions.

RESPOND

ANALYZE THE TEXT

Support your responses with evidence from the text. NOTEBOOK

1. **Interpret** Reread paragraphs 5 and 6. What reasons does Salak give for making this trip? Why does she really undertake this journey? What does she expect to learn from the experience?
2. **Analyze** What does the dialogue in paragraphs 19–23 add to the narrative? How does it contribute to the central idea of the selection?
3. **Cite Evidence** The text includes both facts and opinions. Identify two facts and two opinions from the text.
4. **Critique** The selection includes a map showing Salak's journey. What other visual aids would you have found helpful in visualizing her journey?
5. **Notice & Note** In paragraph 2, why does the author point out the number of people who have completed the journey?

RESEARCH

Find out about the places in your community by learning how to travel around it.

- Think about two places in your community that students might like to visit.
- How could students travel to each place? Could they walk, use public transportation, or bike? Is a car necessary? Research online as needed.
- Think about how easy or confusing it would be to give directions to each location. Write positives and negatives about giving directions to each place.

LOCATIONS	TRANSPORTATION OPTIONS	POSITIVES AND NEGATIVES
SAMPLE ANSWERS *Library*	*Walking* *Bicycle* *Car*	*Close enough to need limited directions* *One-way streets make driving complicated*
Public park	*Car* *Bicycle* *Bus*	*Distance too long for walking Bus transfer needed from school* *Some streets do not have bike lanes so directions need to use other streets*

Extend As a group, discuss the locations and transportation options in the chart. Choose a place for which you will provide directions using a mode of transportation the group agrees on.

LEARNING MINDSET

Problem Solving Remind students that valuable learning often takes a circuitous path. To attain a final goal, they may need to solve unexpected problems, just as Salak did on her journey to Timbuktu. Encourage them to use a variety of strategies to solve problems like the challenge of giving or following directions, including asking for help from adults and peers. Note that understanding the world spatially is a skill that is easier for some than others. Suggest students discuss how they'd find their way around a city or country without smartphones or GPS systems. Discuss how collaborating with others and working to improve one's own skills and knowledge can result in facing challenges successfully.

CREATE AND GIVE INSTRUCTIONS

Create Directions With your group, create a set of directions that you will deliver orally to another group.

- ❑ Decide what the group will create to accompany your oral instructions. Consider a written version of the directions, a map or maps, clues, and pictures.
- ❑ Then, create clear, detailed directions for another team to travel from school to the location using your chosen mode of transportation.

Give Directions Present your directions to another group.

- ❑ Be sure to give the group all the information they need to follow the directions.
- ❑ Speak slowly and clearly, using appropriate vocabulary.
- ❑ Answer any clarifying questions the group may have.

Receive Directions Use another group's directions to find a place of interest in your community.

- ❑ Listen carefully and examine the directions thoroughly.
- ❑ Ask questions to clarify anything you do not understand.

Discuss the Directions As a class, discuss the processes of creating and following directions.

- ❑ What was the hardest part about giving and/or following directions?
- ❑ What surprised you the most about giving and/or following directions?

RESPOND TO THE ESSENTIAL QUESTION

What drives us to take on a challenge?

Gather Information Review your annotations and notes on the excerpt from *The Cruelest Journey: 600 Miles to Timbuktu* and highlight those that help answer the Essential Question. Then, add relevant details to your Response Log.

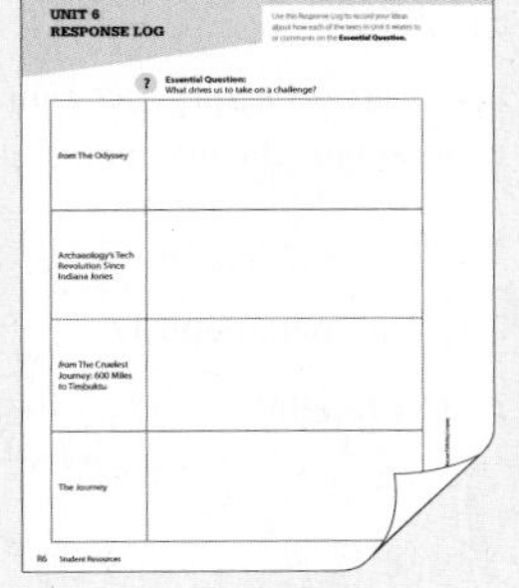

ACADEMIC VOCABULARY

As you write and discuss what you learned from travel writing, be sure to use the Academic Vocabulary words. Check off each of the words that you use.

- ❑ **motivate**
- ❑ **objective**
- ❑ **pursuit**
- ❑ **subsequent**
- ❑ **undertake**

CREATE AND GIVE INSTRUCTIONS

Create Directions First, students can discuss ways to give directions, considering the strengths of different students in the group. For example, some students may have skills in creating maps or other visual aids, while others might enjoy and feel more comfortable with providing oral instructions. Note that a group may select a combination of methods, such as a map with oral instructions, to best use the talents of group members.

Once a format is chosen, suggest that students break the journey down into steps that involve going straight until there is a need to turn. Also note that more than one set of directions may be necessary if there is more than one transportation option available (for example, public transportation and driving a car or walking).

For **writing support** for students at varying proficiency levels, see the **Text X-Ray** on page 536D.

Give Directions Students can follow the tips listed on the page. Individuals can seek help from members of their own group as necessary to clarify directions or answer questions.

Receive Directions Emphasize careful listening skills during the presentation. If directions are given orally, tell students to take notes to be sure they remember specifics.

Discuss the Directions Lead the class in discussion with the prompts listed. Encourage students to be honest in their assessments of challenges. You might extend the discussion with consideration of how GPS programs on smartphones and other handheld devices minimize or enhance the importance of being able to give and receive directions personally.

RESPOND TO THE ESSENTIAL QUESTION

Allow time for students to add details from *The Cruelest Journey: 600 Miles to Timbuktu* to their Unit 6 Response Logs.

ENGLISH LEARNER SUPPORT

Use Direction Words Use the following support with students of varying proficiency levels.

- Preview the meanings of the following direction words: *right, left, before, after, up, down, inside, outside*. **SUBSTANTIAL**
- Tell students to create maps on which they write numerals where each numbered direction begins. **MODERATE**
- Encourage students to include "You've gone too far if . . . " notes in their directions that state what students will see if they have gone past their turn-off or stopping point. Also emphasize the importance of spelling the names of streets and landmarks correctly. **LIGHT**

APPLY

CRITICAL VOCABULARY

Possible answers:

1. *Traveling in a meandering, roundabout fashion is not the quickest way to travel, but you might see something along the way that you otherwise would have missed.*
2. *Once, when I didn't want to admit something, I answered insincerely and withheld some information.*
3. *I regularly act with integrity when I take exams and write reports, because I never cheat or plagiarize.*
4. *Before setting off on a trip around the world, I'd probably pack, get somebody to take care of my pet, and say goodbye to family and friends.*
5. *If I were stuck in an unchanging, monotonous life, I would make an abrupt change in the way I live to make things more interesting.*

VOCABULARY STRATEGY: Foreign Words

Answers:

1. *gifts*
2. *How are you?*
3. *Literal translation: Good appetite! The phrase is used to tell someone to enjoy their meal.*

RESPOND

WORD BANK
circuitously
disingenuous
integrity
embark
stagnant

CRITICAL VOCABULARY

Practice and Apply Answer each question in a way that demonstrates your comprehension of the Critical Vocabulary word.

1. What might be the benefits of traveling *circuitously* to an unfamiliar destination?
2. Have you ever given a *disingenuous* answer? Explain.
3. When have you acted with *integrity*? Explain.
4. What would you do to get ready to *embark* on a trip around the world?
5. What would you do if you felt your life was *stagnant*?

VOCABULARY STRATEGY: Foreign Words

Did you notice how Kira Salak worked foreign words into the text? Take a look at how one student marked an example.

A couple of women nearby, with colorful cloth wraps called *pagnes* tied tightly around their breasts, gaze at me cryptically, as if to ask: *Who are you and what do you think you're doing?*	Pagnes is not an English word. By reading the context around the word, I can figure out that pagnes are a type of colorful cloth that women wrap around themselves to create a dress.

In addition to using context clues, footnotes also sometimes provide definitions of foreign words. If neither of those is included in the text, you can often use an online translation tool to figure out the meaning of a non-English word.

Practice and Apply Use context clues, footnotes, and a dictionary if needed, to determine the meaning of the following French words.

1. cadeaux (paragraph 17)
2. Ça va? (paragraph 17)
3. Bon appétit!

ENGLISH LEARNER SUPPORT

Use Text Features Be sure that students understand the system of footnotes that is standard in English texts. Direct their attention to paragraph 17 and ask them the reason that *cadeaux* and *"Ca va, madame?"* are followed by a small number that is elevated (superscript). Explain that footnotes are used in all types of selections to provide additional information that does not directly relate to the text. In some cases, footnotes are used to cite references used for evidence. Explain that most long selections (books, chapters of books, long articles) number footnotes consecutively beginning with "1." Direct them to the footnotes on pages 540–545. Ask: If there was a footnote on page 546, what number would it be? *(12)* Where would the word's definition appear? *(the bottom of the page)* **SUBSTANTIAL**

LANGUAGE CONVENTIONS: Sentence Variety

Authors vary **sentence length and style** to keep a piece from becoming monotonous. Authors also use sentence length to achieve a specific effect. For example, long sentences tend to slow readers down, while short sentences are read more quickly. A series of short, choppy sentences can also add tension.

Read this sentence from the selection:

> **I gaze at the Niger through the adobe passageways, staring at waters that began in the mountainous rain forests of Guinea and traveled all this way to central Mali—waters that will journey northeast with me to Timbuktu before cutting a great circular swath through the Sahara and retreating south, through Niger, on to Nigeria, passing circuitously through mangrove swamps and jungle, resting at last in the Atlantic in the Bight of Benin.**

Salak could have written the passage this way:

> **I gaze at the Niger through the adobe passageways. I stare at waters that began in the mountainous rain forests of Guinea and traveled all this way to central Mali. These waters will journey northeast with me to Timbuktu. Then they will cut a great circular swath through the Sahara and retreat south, through Niger, on to Nigeria. Along the way, they will pass circuitously through mangrove swamps and jungle. They will rest at last in the Atlantic in the Bight of Benin.**

By using a long, winding sentence, the author mirrors the flow of the river she is describing.

Later, Salak changes her sentence style as shown in this example:

> **Just one thing at a time now, kayak inflated, kayak loaded with my gear. Paddles fitted together and ready.**

Here, Salak uses shorter phrases and sentences to mirror the sequence of quick actions she is performing.

Authors also use breaks in sentences for effect. Consider this sentence:

> **Which means—and I pause with the thought—a path that will only lead through my fears.**

The use of dashes to offset Salak's side comment causes readers to pause with her and think carefully about the insight she is sharing.

Practice and Apply Write a short narrative about a trip you have taken or something meaningful you have experienced. In the narrative, use a variety of sentence lengths to mirror what you describe.

APPLY

LANGUAGE CONVENTIONS: Sentence Variety

Reinforce the idea that authors may make conscious and unconscious choices in sentence length to achieve their purpose. In some cases, their choices may flow naturally as a part of a first draft, or they may change sentence lengths as a part of the editing process.

Note that the content that is communicated may not change at all in changing sentence length, as indicated by the first and second example paragraphs. Varying sentence length as a writer is a part of the craft of writing rather than the process of creating content. This is true for both fiction and nonfiction.

Practice and Apply Suggest limits on the narrative to provide students with parameters. For example, you might suggest the draft for the narrative be limited to 1 page or 3 paragraphs or 10 minutes of writing time. This will help make the editing of sentences for length more manageable for students.

ENGLISH LEARNER SUPPORT

Language Conventions Provide instruction and practice in varying sentences using these two sentences from the text: "Just one thing at a time now, kayak inflated, kayak loaded with my gear. Paddles fitted together and ready."

- Read the first sentence aloud. Ask: Does this sentence have a subject? *(no)* Think aloud: *If I want to rewrite this as a complete sentence, I need to add a subject: Salak. I'll write: "I do just one thing at a time now, so first, I inflate my kayak, and then I load it with my gear."* **SUBSTANTIAL**
- Use the preceding support. After reading your revision aloud, work with students to add a second sentence. Ask: How could you rewrite the second sentence with *I* as the subject? *(Next, I fit my paddles together so they are ready.)* **MODERATE**
- Challenge pairs to rewrite the sentences as one long, complete sentence using the frame: *I do just one thing at a time now: ____. (I do just one thing at a time now: inflate the kayak, load the kayak, and fit the paddles together so they are ready.)* **LIGHT**

THE JOURNEY

Poem by Mary Oliver

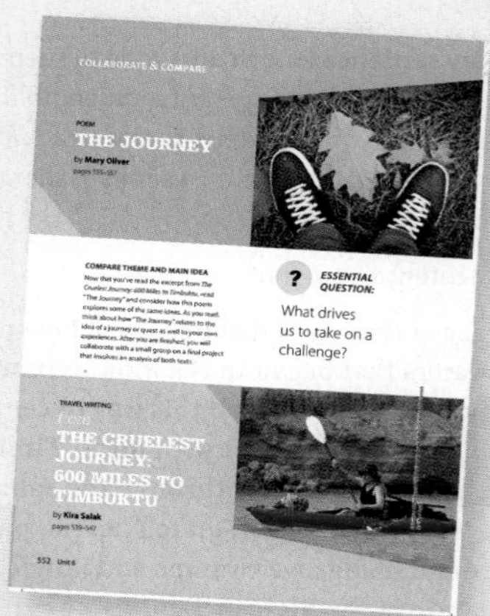

GENRE ELEMENTS

POEM

Remind students that **poetry** is one of the oldest forms of written expression. In many of its earliest forms, it followed strict rules for the number of syllables in each line and required that the final word in certain lines rhyme in a predictable pattern. Many modern poets write in **free verse,** which does not use rules for rhyme and meter. Most poetry employs **figurative language** (language used to communicate meanings beyond the literal meanings of words) to convey a **theme** (central idea or message).

LEARNING OBJECTIVES

- Analyze figurative language.
- Make connections with the selection.
- Create and discuss a theme statement and visual response to the selection.
- Compare and contrast two selections of different genres.
- **Language** Identify figurative language using the word *personification.*

TEXT COMPLEXITY

Quantitative Measures	**The Journey**	Lexile: N/A
Qualitative Measures	**Ideas Presented** Includes multiple levels of meaning and multiple themes.	
	Structures Used Free verse; no pattern for rhyme or meter.	
	Language Used Some figurative language requiring interpretation.	
	Knowledge Required Theme involves complex analysis.	

Online 

RESOURCES

- Unit 6 Response Log
- Selection Audio
- Reading Studio: Notice & Note
- Level Up Tutorial: Figurative Language
- Writing Studio: Task, Purpose, Audience
- Speaking and Listening Studio: Listening and Responding
- *from* The Cruelest Journey/"The Journey" Selection Test

SUMMARIES

English

Mary Oliver illustrates the challenges and importance of making tough, personal changes. She uses an extended metaphor that involves a person in a comfortable house during a windy night who accepts the challenge of going outside on a cluttered road. The first step is hard because the person knows that the journey towards personal change is worthwhile but challenging.

Spanish

Mary Oliver ilustra los retos y la importancia de realizar cambios difíciles y personales. Utiliza una metáfora extendida que involucra a una persona en una casa cómoda durante una noche ventosa que acepta el reto de salir a una calle abarrotada. El primer paso es duro porque la persona sabe que el camino que lleva al cambio personal es desafiante, pero vale la pena.

SMALL-GROUP OPTIONS

Have students work in small groups to read and discuss the selection.

The Poem as Theater

- Students work in small groups to present the poem as a short theatrical production.
- Explain that one half of each group should dramatize the literal meaning of the poem and the other half should dramatize the figurative meaning.
- Tell students that they can use simple actions and explanations. For example, while trembling, a student might say, *I am in the house, but I'm scared to go outside. I want to try ________, but I'm scared to begin.*
- Have groups present their dramatizations.

Reciprocal Teaching

- Form groups of two to three students.
- Have students write three or more discussion prompts related to the selection, using these sentence frames: *The poem reminds me of a time when I ________. The image in the poem of ________ affects me the most. I think making changes by facing challenges is important/not important because ________.*
- Tell students to complete each prompt.
- Have students share and discuss their completed prompts.

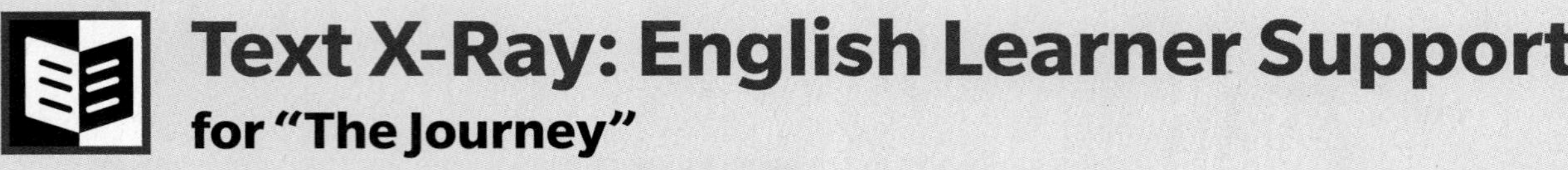

Text X-Ray: English Learner Support
for "The Journey"

Use the Text X-Ray and the supports and scaffolds in the Teacher's Edition to help guide students at different proficiency levels through the selection.

INTRODUCE THE SELECTION

DISCUSS SYMBOLS

In this lesson, students will need to be able to understand and discuss symbols in an extended metaphor.

Explain that a **symbol** is something that represents or stands for something else. Sometimes a tangible object—something you can see or touch—stands for something intangible, like an idea or concept. For example:

- *A crown is a symbol of the power and control of a king or queen.*
- *A country's flag is a symbol of the country and its ideals.*

Provide these frames for discussing interpretations of symbols:

- *I think the* ______ *is a symbol of* ______.
- ______ *is/is not a good symbol of* ______ *because* ______.

CULTURAL REFERENCES

The following words or phrases from the selection may be unfamiliar to students:

- *"Mend my life!"* (line 10): make my life better; fix a problem in my life
- *little by little* (line 23): slowly
- *kept you company* (line 30): stayed with you so you wouldn't be lonely

LISTENING

Understand Key Ideas

Explain that in a poem, a key idea—an important message—may be communicated by the speaker.

Tell students to listen for key ideas as you read lines 1–9 aloud. Use the following supports with students at varying proficiency levels:

- Paraphrase lines 1–9. After each paraphrase, have students indicate with a thumbs up (understood) or thumbs hidden (still don't understand) what the line is saying. Keep simplifying each paraphrase until everyone understands it. **SUBSTANTIAL**
- Tell students to think of a question they have about what you read. Have pairs discuss their questions and then share their questions and answers with the class. **MODERATE**
- Confirm students' understanding by asking them to explain what the speaker is conveying in these lines. **LIGHT**

SPEAKING

Speak with Expression

Have students practice reading a passage from the poem aloud with expressive intonations, emphasis, and proper pauses.

Read lines 10–18 aloud with expression. Then, use the following supports with students at varying proficiency levels:

- Ask students to echo your reading with appropriate emphasis and rhythm. **SUBSTANTIAL**
- Ask students why your voice changed for line 10 and why you paused after line 13. Then ask students to repeat your reading with appropriate emphasis and rhythm. **MODERATE**
- Discuss how the quotation in line 10 and the comma after line 13 should affect one's reading of these lines. Then prompt students to read the lines with the emphasis and rhythm they think is appropriate. **LIGHT**

READING

Recognize Figurative Language

Review **personification** as the giving of human qualities to an animal, object, or idea. Explain that identifying personification and other types of figurative language will help them appreciate the poet's craft and better understand the poem.

Work with students to reread lines 13–18. Use the following supports with students at varying proficiency levels:

- Explain that to identify instances of personification students should look for descriptions of human qualities that are given to things. Ask: What human qualities are mentioned in these lines? To whom or what are they given? Accept single words or phrases as answers. **SUBSTANTIAL**
- Ask: Does wind really have "stiff fingers"? *(no)* Suggest students think of personification as "making into a person." Next, direct them to lines 15–18. Explain the meaning of *melancholy* and *foundations,* and then ask: Whose melancholy was terrible? *(the foundations)* Ask: What is being personified here? *(the foundations)* **MODERATE**
- Have students mark instances of personification in lines 13–18. To prompt students to recognize the personification of the home's foundations in lines 17–18, ask: Whose melancholy was terrible? **LIGHT**

WRITING

Write Theme Statements

Work with students to address the writing assignment on Student Edition page 559.

Use the following supports with students at varying proficiency levels:

- Have students draw or collect images that reflect the poem's ideas. Work with students to discuss how their images suggest a message about life or human nature. **SUBSTANTIAL**
- Provide sentence frames such as the following for students to use to draft their theme statements: *Making a major life change can feel like ______. When you try to make a major life change, it is typical to ________.* **MODERATE**
- Remind students that a poem can suggest more than one theme. Then have them work with partners to discuss and write the messages the poem conveys. **LIGHT**

Connect to the ESSENTIAL QUESTION

"The Journey" explores the often difficult path that must be taken to live one's own life, rather than the lives of others. Mary Oliver's poem addresses the challenges of turning away from the voices of the past or present, so that the future may be fully realized. Like the excerpt from *The Cruelest Journey: 600 Miles to Timbuktu*, this poem explores the compelling forces that can drive a person toward discovery.

COMPARE THEME AND MAIN IDEA

Point out that comparing theme and main idea involves identifying both similarities and differences, which may be obvious or subtle. For example, the titles indicate one obvious similarity: both deal with a "journey." But finding more subtle similarities and differences may be a greater challenge. Remind students that in a poem they may be able to compare and contrast both literal and abstract messages with those in the prose selection.

POEM

THE JOURNEY

by **Mary Oliver**

pages 555–557

COMPARE THEME AND MAIN IDEA

Now that you've read the excerpt from *The Cruelest Journey: 600 Miles to Timbuktu*, read "The Journey" and consider how this poem explores some of the same ideas. As you read, think about how "The Journey" relates to the idea of a journey or quest as well to your own experiences. After you are finished, you will collaborate with a small group on a final project that involves an analysis of both texts.

ESSENTIAL QUESTION:

What drives us to take on a challenge?

TRAVEL WRITING

from

THE CRUELEST JOURNEY: 600 MILES TO TIMBUKTU

by **Kira Salak**

pages 539–547

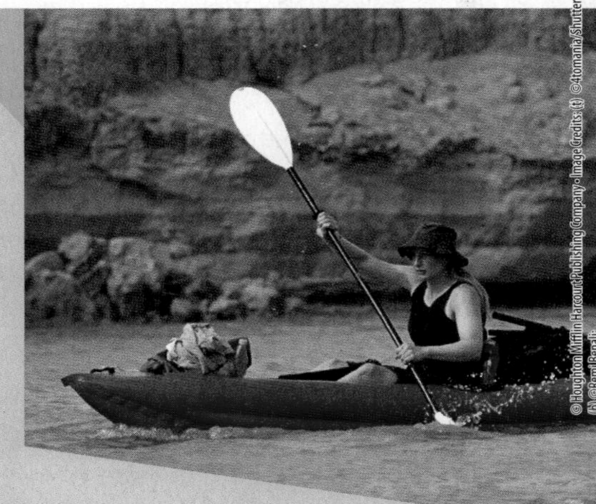

The Journey

QUICK START

Journeys can involve physical travel or they can be more metaphorical. During the course of their lives, many people pursue emotional journeys that lead to great change in their lives. Think about a period of time when you have changed. In a small group, describe your journey.

ANALYZE LANGUAGE

Figurative language is language that communicates meanings beyond the literal meanings of words. In figurative language, words are often used to represent ideas and concepts they would not otherwise be associated with. Poets use figurative language to make revealing comparisons and to help readers see subjects in a new light.

In "The Journey," Mary Oliver uses two types of figurative language: personification and metaphor.

PERSONIFICATION	METAPHOR
Authors use **personification** to give human qualities to an object, animal, or idea. For example, Oliver describes the wind as having stiff fingers, like a human.	Authors use **metaphors** to compare two things that are basically unlike but have something in common. Unlike similes, metaphors do not use the words *like* or *as*. In "The Journey," Oliver compares the subject's emotional state to a trembling house. An **extended metaphor** is a longer metaphor that continues the comparison at length, even throughout an entire poem or literary work.

GENRE ELEMENTS: POEM
- uses figurative language
- uses structure to communicate ideas
- expresses a theme, or a message about life
- uses imagery, rhythm, and word choice to elicit emotion from readers

ENGLISH LEARNER SUPPORT

Practice Personification Help students understand personification by providing a chart like the one below. Have them use various subject-verb-object combinations to form sentences that personify the subjects. **SUBSTANTIAL**

Subjects	Verbs	Objects
the ocean	grabbed	my toes
the wind	tickled	my cheek
the tree	kissed	her hair

TEACH

QUICK START

If students have trouble visualizing a part of their lives as a journey, suggest that they imagine events, viewpoints, or feelings on a timeline or a map. Select an end point and give it a title (e.g., Me After 3 Years of Dance). Then move backwards to an earlier time when their views or feelings differed and give it a name also (e.g., Me Before I Started Dance). Their journey would then consist of whatever happened to change their views or feelings between the two points. For example, did they strive for and meet a challenging goal? Did they experience something that had a profound impact on them? Did they practice hard and grow physically stronger and taller?

ANALYZE LANGUAGE

Elaborate upon the key terms described in the skill lesson. Explain that **figurative language** is used in various genres to communicate the author's thoughts, feelings, and ideas. It plays a major role in poetry, which often communicates abstract ideas about the emotional challenges of life. Poets often use figurative language to connect literal and actual events and situations with their psychological effects.

Personification is a way for the writer to make inanimate objects or forces of nature almost literally "come alive" by suggesting that they have some of the same qualities as humans.

Metaphors make comparisons—without using *like* or *as*—between two things that may not seem comparable. For example, "The teacher was a bear" creates an image of a large, strong, demanding presence even though the teacher herself might have been small and slight.

An **extended metaphor** is a comparison made and explored at length. However, as a writer seeks to find more similarities between two subjects, an extended metaphor may break down because finer details aren't comparable or simply don't fit. For example, comparing a large family to a tree is a common extended metaphor that can involve roots (an initial couple), branches (their children), and smaller twigs as grandchildren. However, if a writer were to attempt to extend that metaphor any further, it would likely break down because there are not appropriate parts of a tree to represent aunts and uncles, great-grandchildren, and others.

TEACH

MAKE CONNECTIONS

For students who struggle to understand or engage with poetry, making connections is a way to allow them to experience the genre in a personal way.

Connecting through **personal experiences** allows the reader to say "I know what the writer is feeling" or "The writer knows what I am feeling." Note that the events surrounding a feeling do not have to match for the feeling to make a connection. For example, a poem might describe a student's disappointment in not making a school team, while the student may have felt disappointment at not being invited to a party. The feeling of disappointment is similar even if the events leading to it are not.

Students may also make connections through **other texts** or through movies or TV shows. Something as small as a word or phrase may bring a connection to mind.

Note that students are often keen observers of the world around them and they may find similarities in a poem to a situation they have observed or heard about. **Society at large** may provide many examples of a feeling or event described in a poem.

ANNOTATION MODEL

Remind students of the ideas in Analyze Language on page 553 and Make Connections on this page. The Model shows that the student chose to write notes in the side column as a way to make connections with the text through personal experiences. Point out that they may follow this model or use their own system (such as circling, underlining, or highlighting) for marking up the selection in their write-in text. Their notes in the margin may also include questions about ideas that are unclear or topics they want to learn more about.

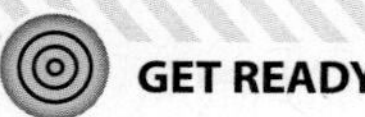

GET READY

MAKE CONNECTIONS

As a good reader, you make connections between the text and issues outside of the text. Doing so broadens your understanding of the text and helps you see how the text applies to the human experience.

- **Personal experiences:** Think about whether the text reminds of anything you have personally experienced in your life. Consider how your experiences influence your understanding or impressions of the text.
- **Other texts:** Notice if the text reminds you of something else you have read. Perhaps it is similar in genre, or maybe the theme reminds you of another text you have read.
- **Society at large:** Consider whether the text comments on or relates to issues in society at large. Remember that while the text may not seem to resonate with one particular group, people in another group may strongly identify with the text.

When reading "The Journey," think about any personal connections that you can make with the ideas in the poem.

ANNOTATION MODEL

NOTICE & NOTE

As you read, make notes about how ideas in the poem relate to your personal experiences. In the model, you can see one reader's notes about a portion of "The Journey."

One day you finally knew
what you had to do, and began,
though the voices around you
kept shouting
their bad advice—

This reminds me of the time I decided to try a new sport. I felt it was important to challenge myself to try something new, even though many people thought that I should just keep playing the same sports I always had.

ENGLISH LEARNER SUPPORT

Use Linguistic Support Provide students with the language and grammatical structures needed to express personal, textual, and societal connections by sharing the following sentence frames:

- *"[Quotation from poem]" reminds me of when I ____.*
- *The [image/symbol/idea] in line [line number] reminds me of the [image/symbol/idea] in ____ by ____.*
- *This poem speaks to the issue of ____ in society today.* **MODERATE**

NOTICE & NOTE

BACKGROUND

Mary Oliver *(b.1935) is known for observing the natural world in a way that is both romantic and unflinchingly honest. Oliver's poems often draw attention to small details—a bird calling, a still pond, a grasshopper. Her vivid imagery of the natural world opens a window for her to explore larger issues, such as love, loss, wonder, and grief. Oliver has published numerous other collections, and has won the Pulitzer Prize for Poetry and a National Book Award. She has also written many essays, as well as two books about the craft of writing poetry. Oliver has taught at colleges and universities including Bennington College in Vermont.*

THE JOURNEY

Poem by Mary Oliver

PREPARE TO COMPARE

Pay attention to details that describe barriers to the journey in the poem. Write down any questions you generate during reading.

One day you finally knew
what you had to do, and began,
though the voices around you
kept shouting
their bad advice—
though the whole house
began to tremble
and you felt the old tug
at your ankles.
"Mend my life!"
each voice cried.
But you didn't stop.

Notice & Note

You can use the side margins to notice and note signposts in the text.

TEACH

BACKGROUND

Have students read the Background information about the author. Note that Oliver has always been a private person and that when she won the Pulitzer Prize for Poetry in 1984, few people knew who she was. Her early poems focused on observations about the natural world and did not touch on her personal life. After her collection *American Primitive* won the Pulitzer, however, she broadened her subject matter to include the personal challenges people face throughout life. Consequently, her later works, including poetry and essays, reflect more of her life and personality, along with her lifelong attitude of amazement at the natural world.

PREPARE TO COMPARE

Direct students to use the Prepare to Compare prompt to focus their reading.

For **listening support** for students at varying proficiency levels, see the **Text X-Ray** on page 552C.

APPLYING ACADEMIC VOCABULARY

☑ **motivate** ☐ **objective** ☑ **pursuit** ☐ **subsequent** ☑ **undertake**

Write and Discuss Have students turn to a partner to discuss the following questions. Guide students to include the academic vocabulary words *motivate, pursuit,* and *undertake* in their responses. Have them write out a response before beginning the discussion. Ask volunteers to share their written and oral responses with the class.

- What **motivates** the person in the poem to **undertake** the journey, even in the face of so many obstacles?
- What does the poem say or imply about the **pursuit** of happiness?

TEACH

ANALYZE LANGUAGE

Review the extended metaphor that begins in lines 6–9 with references to a "house" that gives a "tug at your ankles." Note that a house is a common image that everyone can imagine. A common reference is also added with the reference to "wind" in line 14. Discuss the feelings typically associated with imagery of living in a house. *(feelings of safety or comfort)* Then, discuss the feeling related to a wind that pries at the house. *(a feeling of a threat)* Next, move on to the images and feelings related to a cluttered road in front of a house. *(The road is a way out but it is not clear or easy.)* *(**Answer:** The metaphor compares the challenges and obstacles in the speaker's life to fallen branches and stones.)*

English Learner Support

Use Linguistic Support Provide students with language and grammatical structures needed to discuss figurative language, using the following sentence frames:

- *In "The Journey," Oliver personifies ________ by describing [it/them] as "[quotation]."*
- *Oliver compares ________ to ________.*
- *She extends that metaphor in lines [00–00] by saying, "[quotation]," which I think means ________.*
- *In my opinion, Oliver's extended metaphor is ________ because ________.*

MODERATE

For **speaking and reading support** for students at varying proficiency levels, see the **Text X-Ray** on page 552D.

AHA MOMENT

Ask students to point out the clues in the language that indicate a moment of new understanding for the subject. *(a new voice, recognized as your own)* What words emphasize this important moment in the lines that follow? *(kept you company, determined to do the only thing you could do)* *(**Answer:** The speaker is beginning to recognize her own voice and authentic self.)*

NOTICE & NOTE

ANALYZE LANGUAGE

Annotate: Mark the metaphor in lines 19–22.

Infer: What is the speaker comparing in this metaphor?

AHA MOMENT

Annotate: Mark the moment when the speaker begins to come to a new realization.

Infer: What is the speaker beginning to recognize?

You knew what you had to do,
though the wind pried
with its stiff fingers
at the very foundations—
though their melancholy
was terrible.
It was already late
enough, and a wild night,
and the road full of fallen
branches and stones.
But little by little,
as you left their voices behind,
the stars began to burn
through the sheets of clouds,
and there was a new voice,
which was slowly
recognized as your own,
that kept you company
as you strode deeper and deeper
into the world,
determined to do
the only thing you could do—
determined to save
the only life you could save.

IMPROVE READING FLUENCY

Targeted Passage As you read aloud lines 19–31, tell students that whenever you pause, they should echo what you just read in the same the way to learn how to read the poem aloud with the poet's intended phrasing. Then, go back and point out the comma after *enough* in line 20, the period in line 22, the lack of a comma after line 25, and the dash in line 34. Explain that these standard punctuation marks—like notations in music—signal where to pause and for how long. Also note that they may need to read the poem several times to master the phrasing. Finally, explain that reading a poem as the poet intended it to be read can help them discover what the author wants to emphasize.

Go to the **Reading Studio** for additional support in developing fluency.

CHECK YOUR UNDERSTANDING

Answer these questions before moving on to the **Analyze the Text** section on the following page.

1 In lines 6–9, what is the speaker revealing?

A The speaker knows from experience that it is time to make a change.

B The speaker is afraid of an approaching tornado and is trying to escape.

C The speaker feels concerned and has decided to resist the upcoming changes.

D The speaker is worried about how the house will survive the coming storm.

2 Which of the following is an example of personification?

F *One day you finally knew / what you had to do*

G *the wind pried / with its stiff fingers / at the very foundations*

H *But little by little, / as you left their voices behind*

J *as you strode deeper and deeper / into the world*

3 An important message in "The Journey" is —

A people should take advice from those around them

B storms are frightening to experience

C it is always rewarding to make changes

D it can be difficult to do what is best for oneself

CHECK YOUR UNDERSTANDING

Have students answer the questions independently.

Answers:

1. *A*
2. *G*
3. *D*

If they answer any questions incorrectly, have them reread the text to confirm their understanding. Then they may proceed to ANALYZE THE TEXT on page 558.

ENGLISH LEARNER SUPPORT

Oral Assessment Use the following questions to assess students' comprehension and speaking skills. Ask students to respond in complete sentences.

1. Reread lines 6–9. What is the speaker saying? *(The current situation is too familiar, and the speaker wants to make a change.)*
2. Reread lines 13–18. What is being personified? *(the wind)*
3. What is one main idea in the poem? *(It isn't always easy to do what is best for yourself, but it is the right thing to do.)* **MODERATE/LIGHT**

APPLY

ANALYZE THE TEXT

Possible answers:

1. **DOK 4:** *The wind "pried / with its stiff fingers / at the very foundations—" in lines 14-16. It could mean a strong force is trying to rip away the foundation of the person's life.*
2. **DOK 2:** *The metaphor of the person summoning his or her strength to leave the house (make a major life change in the face of many obstacles) is carried throughout the stanza. By not breaking the poem into shorter stanzas, the poet creates the impression that the person does not pause to take a breath, because to hesitate would be to risk losing his or her resolution.*
3. **DOK 4:** *Images of the wind prying "with its stiff fingers," the "wild night," and "the road full of fallen branches and stones" all suggest obstacles for the person who wants to set out on a journey. The stars that "began to burn through the sheets of clouds" suggest hope and strength; they confirm that the person has made the right decision.*
4. **DOK 2:** *The theme is that a person must follow his or her own path in life and not be held back by the opinions of other people or any other factors that stand in the way. The title suggests that life itself is a journey, and the extended metaphor, which unfolds throughout the poem, implies that getting past one's fears and doubts and taking the first few steps may be the hardest part.*
5. **DOK 4:** *The poem's conclusion is a logical follow-up to the speaker's desire for change: The only life whose path we can determine is our own.*

RESEARCH

Suggest that students write two separate paraphrases: one that describes the literal content of the poem's words, and a second that interprets the extended metaphor. To prepare to create a visual response to the poem, have students begin by focusing on an important change they may have experienced, such as a physical move, entering a new school, or adding a sibling to the family. Then, encourage them to think about times they felt hesitant or fearful during this period and how they felt once they began to adjust to the change. Images collected in response to the poem may range from the concrete to the abstract.

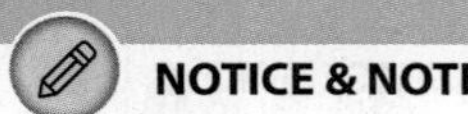

NOTICE & NOTE

ANALYZE THE TEXT

Support your responses with evidence from the text. NOTEBOOK

1. **Analyze** How does Oliver personify the wind? What is the figurative meaning of this strong wind outside the home of a person who is undertaking a journey?
2. **Interpret** Notice that the poem is written in one long stanza, not broken into smaller stanzas. How does Oliver use this structure to develop an extended metaphor?
3. **Synthesize** Trace the nature images that occur throughout the poem. How does Oliver use each image to develop the extended metaphor in the poem?
4. **Infer** What is the **theme**, or underlying message, of the poem? How do the title and structure of the poem help convey the theme?
5. **Notice & Note** In the last line the speaker expresses determination to "save / the only life you could save." How does this expand on the speaker's Aha Moment that a change had to be made?

RESEARCH

In the chart below, write a paraphrase for "The Journey." Remember that when you **paraphrase** a text, you put the text in your own words. The paraphrase should capture the essential points of the text without using the exact words from it. A paraphrase, even of a poem, should be written in prose.

Next, think about how the poem reminds you of experiences in your life. Select images to create a visual personal response to the poem. The images may be photographs you take, photos from magazines, drawings, or images in the public domain.

MY PARAPHRASE
Sample answer: *You make a long-awaited decision to change your life, and it scares everyone in your house—everyone close to you. They try to talk you out of changing or leaving—they want you to fix their lives, instead. But you don't listen to their sadness. Even though the future seems like a dark and treacherous path, you walk down it. As you get farther away from your old ways, the familiar voices grow quiet. Your spirits lift and you are free to hear your own voice and live your own, new life.*

WHEN STUDENTS STRUGGLE . . .

Reteaching: Analyze Language Review personification. *(giving human qualities to an object, animal, or idea)* Use lines 6–7 as an example. Then work with students to explain how these examples illustrate personification:

- In the wind, the tree shivered. *(Shivering is a human action.)*
- The angry sea crashed on the shore. *(Anger is a human emotion.)*
- At night, the town slept. *(Sleep is a human action.)*

For additional support, go to the **Reading Studio** and assign the following  **Level Up Tutorial: Figurative Language.**

CREATE AND DISCUSS

Create a Visual Response Use images to create a visual personal response to "The Journey."

- ❑ Arrange the images in a logical order in a visual display, whether the order mirrors the poem or the chronological order of the event about which they remind you.
- ❑ Using your paraphrase, develop a theme statement for "The Journey." Remember the **theme** of a text is the larger message it states about humanity. Add your theme statement to your visual display.

Discuss Visuals and Theme In small groups, share your theme statements and personal visual responses.

- ❑ Discuss each group member's theme statement. Notice how people may interpret the theme in different ways.
- ❑ Allow each member to share and discuss his or her visuals and how they connect to the poem.
- ❑ Reflect on similarities and differences in how group members reacted to the poem.

NOTICE & NOTE

Go to the **Speaking and Listening Studio** for help with having a group discussion.

RESPOND TO THE ESSENTIAL QUESTION

What drives us to take on a challenge?

Gather Information Review your annotations and notes on "The Journey" and highlight those that help answer the Essential Question. Then, add relevant details to your Response Log.

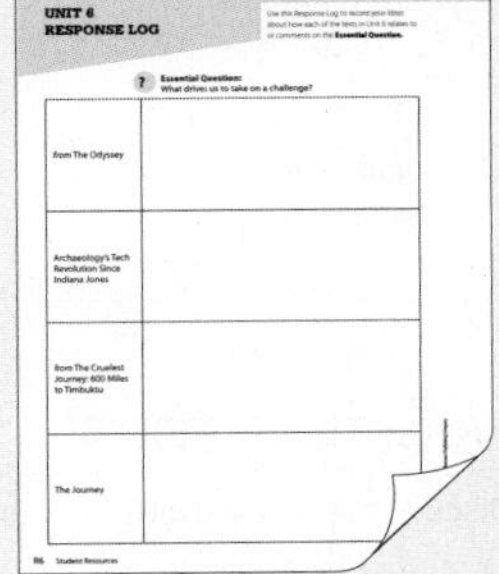

ACADEMIC VOCABULARY

As you write and discuss what you learned about "The Journey," be sure to use the Academic Vocabulary words. Check off each of the words that you use.

- ❑ **motivate**
- ❑ **objective**
- ❑ **pursuit**
- ❑ **subsequent**
- ❑ **undertake**

APPLY

CREATE AND DISCUSS

Create a Visual Response Students may create their visual response using the following suggestions.

- If their images represent the actions, feelings, ideas, and images described in the poem, suggest they present their images in the same order that those appear. Referring to their paraphrase of the poem may help. If they do not want to use a chronological approach or are planning only to represent their own personal experience visually, suggest that they accompany their visual story with one or two images representing those moments in the poem that reminded them of their own experience.
- Students may identify a theme using this question: What is the poem's overall message about life or the nature of our personal journeys?

Discuss Visuals and Theme Remind students to listen carefully without interruption and to respect the ideas of others. Point out that they should ask questions to clarify, and offer comments that further the discussion.

- When discussing theme statements, remind students that there is not one correct answer. However, students should be able to provide textual evidence that supports their interpretation.
- Depending on the available time, suggest a rough time limit for each presentation to keep the discussion moving (for example, 3 minutes for the presentation, 2 minutes for questions).
- One way to identify similarities is to find words, phrases, or ideas that are repeated in more than one statement. Differences may show up as contrasting reactions to the poem or in a range of personal experiences.

For **writing support** for students at varying proficiency levels, see the **Text X-Ray** on page 552D.

ENGLISH LEARNER SUPPORT

Provide Language Supports Assist students in preparing for the small-group discussion by offering the following sentence frames.

- *The message I took from lines _____ of the poem was that ___________.*
- *I chose to represent the message that ___________ with this image because the image ___________.*
- *The [idea/feeling] expressed in lines ______ reminded me of _________.*
- *I felt like the speaker does in lines _______ when I __________.* **MODERATE**

RESPOND TO THE ESSENTIAL QUESTION

Allow time for students to add details from the selection "The Journey" to their Unit 6 Response Logs.

APPLY

COMPARE THEME AND MAIN IDEA

Before small groups begin work to fill in the chart, note that students will need to look at the authors' conflicts, purposes, and messages to find similarities between the selections. To help students compare the selections, remind them that each work has a narrator revealing specific thoughts, feelings, and ideas about a journey. (***Answers:*** *Both selections describe a thought process and the mental challenges in taking on a new or difficult activity. The travelogue describes the actual physical effects of the journey on the writer's body, while the poem describes emotional effects that seem to feel physical. Some students may connect more strongly with the literal, physical journey described by Salak and others with the emotional challenges suggested by Oliver.)*

ANALYZE THE TEXTS

Possible answers:

1. **DOK 4:** *Both journeys challenge the person taking them. At times the journeys are emotionally hard and physically frightening, but they are both ultimately rewarding.*
2. **DOK 2:** *Both authors are writing to describe for their audience what they went through to complete their journey. However, Salak's journey was about a physical experience and challenging herself to do something specific. The exact nature of the speaker's journey in Oliver's poem is unknown. She never specifically stated whether the journey was a physical experience, emotional upheaval, or a lifestyle change.*
3. **DOK 2:** *Salak uses varied sentence lengths to mirror the experiences she discusses, in addition to using vivid vocabulary. Oliver uses personification and metaphor to convey the threats experienced on the journey.*
4. **DOK 4:** *When taking on a challenge, you have to keep moving toward your goal and do what you know you have to do despite the obstacles before you.*

RESPOND

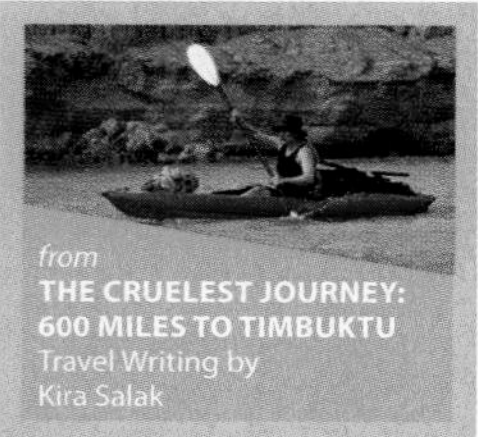
from THE CRUELEST JOURNEY: 600 MILES TO TIMBUKTU
Travel Writing by Kira Salak

THE JOURNEY
Poem by Mary Oliver

Collaborate & Compare

COMPARE THEME AND MAIN IDEA

Think about the journey portrayed in "The Journey" and the journey Kira Salak undertakes in the excerpt from *The Cruelest Journey: 600 Miles to Timbuktu*. What similarities and differences are there between the journeys? How have you connected with each journey?

Review both selections and consider how you might answer the questions. To develop your response, complete the graphic organizer below.

	THE CRUELEST JOURNEY	THE JOURNEY
Purpose	*Share her kayak journey along the Niger River*	*Let reader know that change is hard, but good.*
Message	*Always keep pushing to avoid a stagnant life.*	*Don't be afraid of change that is good for you.*
Text Structure	*Chronological prose*	*Poem*
Language	*Varied sentence structure with vivid descriptions*	*Metaphors, personification*
Personal Connection	*Answers will vary.*	*Answers will vary.*

ANALYZE THE TEXTS

Discuss these questions in your group.

1. **Connect** What similarities do you see between the journey described by Salak and the journey discussed in the poem?
2. **Compare and Contrast** How would you describe each writer's purpose? How are Salak's and Oliver's purposes similar and different?
3. **Infer** How does each author use language to effectively convey her point?
4. **Synthesize** What have you learned from these sources together about how to take on a challenge?

WHEN STUDENTS STRUGGLE . . .

Compare Texts Use the following questions to help students compare the selections.

1. What type of journey does Salak describe? What type of journey does Oliver describe?
2. What type of language does each author use to create vivid images?
3. What advice would each author likely give people about taking on challenges?
4. Have you had any similar feelings to those that Salak or Oliver describes? Explain.

RESPONDD 

COLLABORATE AND PRESENT

Now your group can continue exploring the ideas in these texts by collaborating on a response to the text. Follow these steps:

1. **Discuss** In your group, discuss which journey you more closely identify with. Think about how these and similar journeys can apply to the broader human experience.
2. **Use Text Evidence** Support your response with evidence from the texts. Refer to your notes in the graphic organizer on the previous page.
3. **Listen** Consider your group members' points of view. Think about how personal experiences have shaped each person's point of view. Adjust your own response as you reflect on your classmates' comments.
4. **Ask Questions** Ask questions for clarification or to gain information.
5. **Write** In the chart below, take notes on the discussion. Then compose a brief summary of your group's discussion. Include what you have learned and what insights you have gained.

NOTES FROM THE DISCUSSION

SUMMARY

Go to the **Speaking and Listening Studio** for help with having a group discussion.

APPLY

COLLABORATE AND PRESENT

Reinforce the idea that working together as a group can result in a product that includes a broader view and a more balanced approach than what might be created by an individual. Note that each numbered step is important and, when used conscientiously, adds value to the final product.

1. **Discuss** Note that identifying more strongly with one selection or the other does not mean one is better than the other. Encourage groups to listen respectfully to responses from all members.
2. **Use Text Evidence** The most appropriate responses are those supported by text evidence. Remind students to be as specific as possible in citing evidence (refer to specific lines, sentences, or paragraphs).
3. **Listen** Encourage students to modify or expand their opinions and responses based on others' comments. Learning from peers is a great way to add to or refine their knowledge and understanding.
4. **Ask Questions** Encourage students to ask the kinds of questions that seek clarification. Open-ended questions, such as those that begin with *how* or *why*, encourage discussion more than those requiring a *yes/no* response.
5. **Write** Remind the group that writing a summary of the discussion can be a group endeavor, with multiple writers and reviewers.

TO CHALLENGE STUDENTS . . .

Write or Create a Work with a Similar Theme After students have identified a common theme for the selections, challenge them to write or create another work that expresses a similar theme. They can choose any literary genre that is different from the selections. They can also choose a different type of creative expression that might include one or more of the following: music, theater, art or images, movies, graphic novels or cartoons, dance or movement. After their work has been completed, they should prepare to present it to the class and explain as necessary how they intended to communicate the theme.

INDEPENDENT READING

READER'S CHOICE

Setting a Purpose Have students review their Unit 6 Response Log and think about what they've already learned about what drives us to take on a challenge. As they choose their Independent Reading selections, encourage them to consider what more they want to know.

NOTICE  NOTE

Explain that some selections may contain multiple signposts; others may contain only one. And the same type of signpost can occur many times in the same text.

LEARNING MINDSET

Grit Remind students that our brains are muscles; the more we work them, the stronger they become. Encourage students to approach their Independent Reading with flexible thinking and determination. Reinforce students for making the effort to understand challenging parts of the text and for sticking with a selection until they complete it.

INDEPENDENT READING

ESSENTIAL QUESTION:

What drives us to take on a challenge?

Reader's Choice

Setting a Purpose Select one or more of these options from your eBook to continue your exploration of the Essential Question.

- Read the descriptions to see which text grabs your interest.
- Think about which genres you enjoy reading.

Notice & Note

In this unit, you practiced noticing and noting these signposts: **Tough Questions, Again and Again,** and **Contrasts and Contradictions.** As you read independently, these signposts and others will aid your understanding. Below are the anchor questions to ask when you read literature and nonfiction.

Reading Literature: Stories, Poems, and Plays		
Signpost	**Anchor Question**	**Lesson**
Contrasts and Contradictions	Why did the character act that way?	p. 419
Aha Moment	How might this change things?	p. 171
Tough Questions	What does this make me wonder about?	p. 494
Words of the Wiser	What's the lesson for the character?	p. 171
Again and Again	Why might the author keep bringing this up?	p. 170
Memory Moment	Why is this memory important?	p. 418

Reading Nonfiction: Essays, Articles, and Arguments		
Signpost	**Anchor Question(s)**	**Lesson**
Big Questions	What surprised me? What did the author think I already knew? What challenged, changed, or confirmed what I already knew?	p. 248 p. 2 p. 84
Contrasts and Contradictions	What is the difference, and why does it matter?	p. 3
Extreme or Absolute Language	Why did the author use this language?	p. 85
Numbers and Stats	Why did the author use these numbers or amounts?	p. 249
Quoted Words	Why was this person quoted or cited, and what did this add?	p. 85
Word Gaps	Do I know this word from someplace else? Does it seem like technical talk for this topic? Do clues in the sentence help me understand the word?	p. 3

ENGLISH LEARNER SUPPORT

Develop Fluency Select a passage from a text that matches students' abilities. Read the passage aloud while students follow along silently.

- Echo read the passage by reading aloud one sentence and then having students repeat the sentence back to you. Be sure to emphasize proper pauses for different forms of punctuation. Check comprehension by asking yes/no questions. **SUBSTANTIAL**
- Have students work in pairs. Ask each student to read the passage aloud focusing on expression, tone, and correct pauses for punctuation. Have partners talk about how hearing the intonation helps them understand the passage. **MODERATE**
- Allow more fluent readers to select their own texts. Set a specific time for students to read silently (for example, 30 minutes). Check their comprehension by having them write a summary of what they've read. **LIGHT**

Go to the **Reading Studio** for additional support in developing fluency.

You can preview these texts in Unit 6 of your eBook.

Then, check off the text or texts that you select to read on your own.

EPIC POEM

from **The Odyssey**
Homer

Odysseus faces daunting challenges as he tries to return home to Ithaca after the Trojan War.

POEM

Siren Song
Margaret Atwood

What is it really like to be a Siren stuck on an island? Not as glamorous as it might seem.

DRAMA

from **The Odyssey: A Dramatic Retelling of Homer's Epic**
Simon Armitage

What's the best path between two evils? Odysseus orders his ship to sail straight between an abyss and a monster!

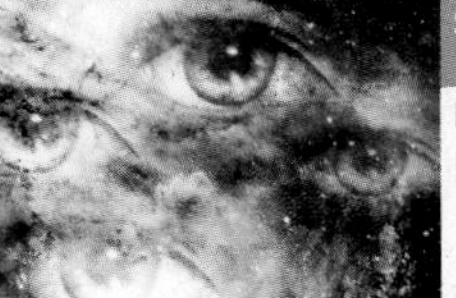

SHORT STORY

Ilse, Who Saw Clearly
E. Lily Yu

A traveling magician steals the eyes from everyone in Ilse's village, so Ilse goes on a quest to get them back.

ARGUMENT

The Real Reasons We Explore Space
Michael Griffen

What is it about space that challenges us to go there?

Collaborate and Share Get with a partner to discuss what you learned from at least one of your independent readings.

- Give a brief synopsis or summary of the text.
- Describe any signposts that you noticed in the text and explain what they revealed to you.
- Describe what you most enjoyed or found most challenging about the text. Give specific examples.
- Decide whether you would recommend the text to others. Why or why not?

Go to the **Reading Studio** for more resources on **Notice & Note.**

INDEPENDENT READING

MATCHING STUDENTS TO TEXTS

Use the following information to guide students in choosing their texts.

***from The* Odyssey**
Genre: epic poem
Overall Rating: Challenging

Siren Song
Genre: poem
Overall Rating: Accessible

***from* The Odyssey: A Dramatic Retelling of Homer's Epic**
Genre: drama
Overall Rating: Challenging

Ilse, Who Saw Clearly — **Lexile: 830L**
Genre: short story
Overall Rating: Accessible

The Real Reasons We Explore Space — **Lexile: 1170L**
Genre: argument
Overall Rating: Challenging

Collaborate and Share To assess how well students read the selections, walk around the room and listen to their conversations. Encourage students to be focused and specific in their comments.

for Assessment

- Independent Reading Selection Tests

Encourage students to visit the **Reading Studio** to download a handy bookmark of **NOTICE & NOTE** signposts.

WHEN STUDENTS STRUGGLE . . .

Keep a Reading Log As students read their selected texts, have them keep a reading log for each selection to note signposts and their thoughts about them. Use their logs to assess how well they are noticing and reflecting on elements of their texts.

Reading Log for (Title)		
Location	**Signpost I Noticed**	**My Notes About It**

UNIT 6 Tasks

- **WRITE AN EXPLANATORY ESSAY**
- **PARTICIPATE IN A COLLABORATIVE DISCUSSION**

MENTOR TEXT

ARCHAEOLOGY'S TECH REVOLUTION SINCE INDIANA JONES

Informational Text by JEREMY HSU

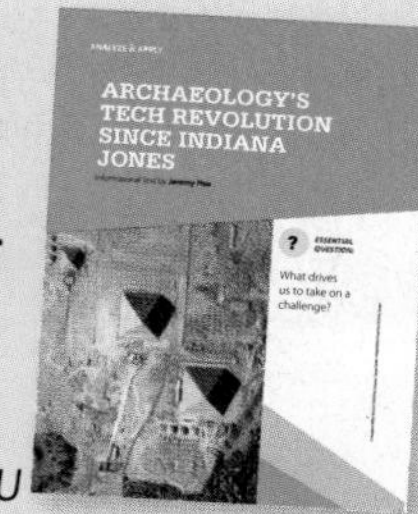

LEARNING OBJECTIVES

Writing Task

- Write an explanatory essay about how humans meet the need for challenges.
- Use strategies to plan and organize ideas for an explanatory essay.
- Develop a focused, structured draft of an explanatory essay.
- Use the Mentor Text as a model for an explanatory essay.
- Revise drafts to include narrative details, strengthen ideas, and incorporate peer feedback.
- Edit drafts to incorporate standard English conventions.
- Use a rubric to evaluate writing.
- Publish writing to share it with an audience.
- **Language** Practice spelling homophones correctly.

Speaking and Listening Task

- Use an explanatory essay as the basis for participating in a collaborative discussion.
- Listen actively and speak in a collaborative discussion.
- **Language** Discuss text structure using the academic vocabulary *main idea* and *supporting details*.

Assign the Writing Task in ***Ed.***

RESOURCES

- Unit 6 Response Log
- Reading Studio : Notice & Note
- Writing Studio: Writing Informative Texts; Writing as a Process
- Speaking and Listening Studio: Participating in Collaborative Discussions
- Grammar Studio: Module 13: Lesson 6: Commonly Misspelled Words

Language X-Ray: English Learner Support

Use the instruction below and the supports and scaffolds in the Teacher's Edition to help you guide students at different proficiency levels.

INTRODUCE THE WRITING TASK

Review the elements of a strong **explanatory essay:** The introduction presents a thesis statement that expresses the main point the writer wants to convey about the topic. Each subsequent paragraph in the body of the essay offers a key idea along with evidence to support it. Paragraphs are logically ordered, with smooth transitions from one to the next. The conclusion reinforces the main idea of the essay in a meaningful way. Note that the explanatory essay for this unit will be based on one or more unit selections.

Point out that the selections in this unit deal with the theme of the human need to meet challenges. Use sentence frames to help students explore ideas related to this theme. For example: *A person who likes challenges is able to ______. One challenge that people meet is ______. Another is ______.* Brainstorm words and phrases related to the theme and display them. Have pairs of students work together to write an original thesis sentence related to the theme, which they can use to begin their essays.

WRITING

Spell Homophones Correctly

Provide practice in which students identify, use, and correctly spell homophones.

Use the following supports with students at varying proficiency levels:

- Display sentences that include homophones. Example: *Those two boxes are too heavy to carry by yourself*. Have students copy the sentence and circle the homophones. Spell each word and have students repeat. Discuss its meaning as a class. **SUBSTANTIAL**
- Dictate a sentence that provides context for a homophone, such as *I accept your offer*, and have students write the word correctly. **MODERATE**
- Provide these homophone pairs: *male/mail, ate/eight, one/won, sore/soar,* and *write/right*. Then instruct students to write sentences with them and read them aloud to a partner. Have partners identify each homophone and write it correctly. **LIGHT**

SPEAKING AND LISTENING

Identify Main Ideas and Supporting Details

Using the model paragraphs from unit selections, provide oral practice in which students identify main ideas and supporting details.

Use the following supports with students at varying proficiency levels:

- Read aloud a paragraph from the mentor text as students follow along. Provide a sentence that states the main idea. Have students echo the sentence. **SUBSTANTIAL**
- Reread aloud a paragraph from the mentor text. Provide these sentence frames for students to complete: *The main idea of this paragraph is ______. One supporting detail is ______.* **MODERATE**
- Assign pairs a paragraph from the reading selection. Have one student read it aloud as the other listens for the main idea. Reverse roles and instruct the listener to note details. **LIGHT**

WRITE AN EXPLANATORY ESSAY

Read aloud the introductory paragraph and discuss the writing task with students. Encourage them to refer to the notes they recorded in the Unit 6 Response Log before they begin planning and writing their drafts.

USE THE MENTOR TEXT

Explain to students that their explanatory essays will be similar to "Archaeology's Tech Revolution Since Indiana Jones." Their essays also will express a central message with main ideas presented in a series of logically structured paragraphs. The ideas will be supported by evidence. In the conclusion, students will summarize the key points of their explanatory essays.

WRITING PROMPT

Discuss the way the writing prompt is expressed by identifying its key elements—the type of writing required and the topic on which it will focus. Encourage students to ask questions about any part of the assignment they find unclear. Emphasize that the purpose of their essay is to explain how an activity described in a unit selection relates to the human need for challenges.

Review the checklist of key points that students should consider as they write their essays.

WRITING TASK

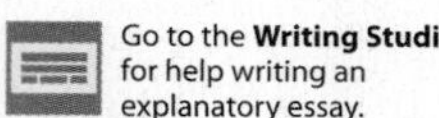

Go to the **Writing Studio** for help writing an explanatory essay.

Write an Explanatory Essay

This unit focuses on the very human need to pit ourselves against forces that may be stronger than we are. These challenges might be more than we can meet; or they might provide us with the most satisfying moments of our lives. For this writing task, you will write an explanatory essay focusing on one of the challenges you have read about in the unit. In your essay, you will give a clear explanation of how that particular activity might meet the human need for challenge. For an example of a well-written explanatory essay you can use as a mentor text, review the article "Archaeology's Tech Revolution Since Indiana Jones."

As you write your essay, you will want to look at the notes you made in your Response Log after reading the texts in this unit.

Writing Prompt

Read the information in the box below.

This is the topic or context for your essay.

> **The human need for challenge takes many forms, from traveling through forbidding places to exploring the mind.**

This is the Essential Question for the unit. How would you answer this question, based on the texts in this unit?

Think carefully about the following question.

> **What drives us to take on a challenge?**

Mark the words that describe exactly what you are supposed to write.

Write an explanatory essay about how an activity described in one of the unit selections meets the human need for challenge.

Review these points as you write and again when you finish. Make any needed changes.

Be sure to—

- ❑ include a clear thesis about the activity and the need for challenge
- ❑ engage readers with an interesting observation, quotation, or detail
- ❑ organize central ideas in a logically structured body that clearly develops the thesis
- ❑ use domain-specific vocabulary and logical transitions to clarify and connect ideas
- ❑ include evidence from the texts to illustrate central ideas
- ❑ have a concluding section that follows logically from the body of the essay and sums up the central ideas of the explanation

564 Unit 6

LEARNING MINDSET

Asking for Help Emphasize that an essential part of the learning process is dealing with new and challenging tasks. Explain that one strategy when confronted with a difficult problem or challenge is to ask someone for help. Discuss possible sources of help including teachers, other school staff, classmates, older siblings, and parents and guardians. Stress the fact that asking others for help is not a sign of failure or lack of responsibility, but a "smart" learning strategy. Consider offering an anecdote about a time when you sought help or advice, or setting up a role-playing opportunity for students to gain skills and experience in seeking help.

1 Plan

Begin the planning process by choosing your topic. Go over your notes from this unit to see what appeals to your personal interests or engages you emotionally and intellectually. It may help to discuss the selections in this unit with a partner to generate ideas. Then choose a topic, keeping in mind your purpose for writing and your audience. Write a thesis statement and consider how you can explore and support it. A hierarchy diagram like the one below can help you organize your ideas and develop evidence for the body of your essay.

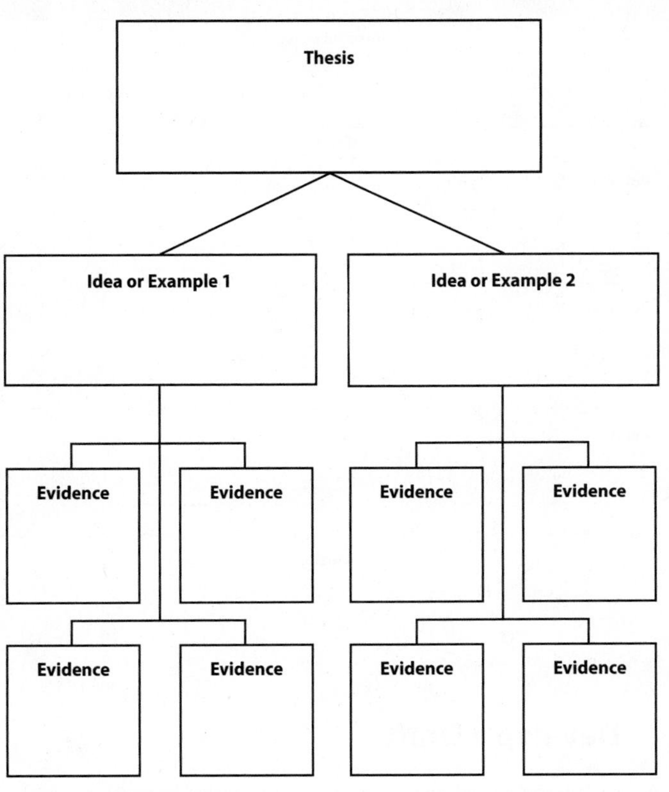

Background Reading Review the notes you have taken in your Response Log after reading the texts in this unit. These texts provide background reading that will help you think about what you want to say in your essay.

Go to **Writing Informative Texts: Developing a Topic** for help planning your essay.

Notice & Note

From Reading to Writing

As you plan your explanatory essay, apply what you've learned about signposts to your own writing. Remember that writers use common features, called signposts, to help convey their message to readers.

Think about how you can incorporate **Numbers and Stats** into your argument.

Go to the **Reading Studio** for more resources on **Notice & Note**.

Use the notes from your Response Log as you plan your essay.

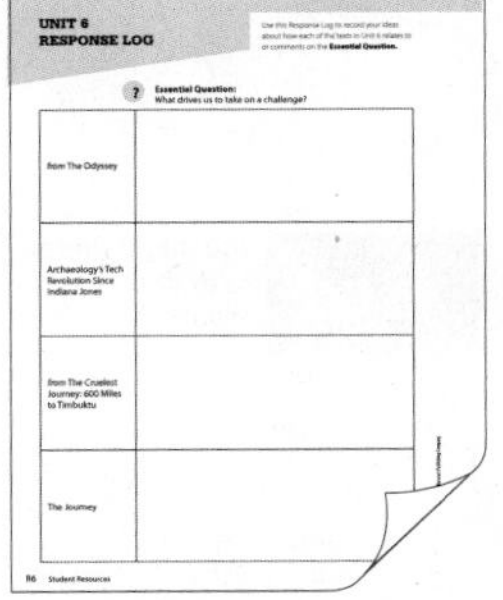

1 PLAN

Read the introductory text. Then, review some of the strategies students should consider as they explore possible topics for their explanatory essays. Ask: Which activities described in the selections do you think were most challenging? Do you think most people would agree with your choices? Why or why not? Suggest that students design a quick flash poll to get a sense of which activities their classmates consider most challenging.

Once they have chosen a topic, point out the hierarchy diagram and discuss how it can be used to organize central ideas, examples, and evidence that will support the thesis of their explanatory essays.

English Learner Support

Discuss Academic Language Review the meaning of the following words:

- **thesis:** the main point a writer wants to make
- **evidence:** facts and examples that support the thesis

Ask: What is a thesis statement? *(a sentence that includes the thesis)* What are different kinds of evidence? *(examples, statistics, and quotations)* With a partner, have students state their thesis and explain what evidence they will use to support it. **ALL LEVELS**

NOTICE & NOTE

From Reading to Writing Review the focus of the **Numbers and Stats** signpost. Explain that they can provide specific numbers or statistical information as evidence for the main ideas in their essays. When deciding whether to incorporate numbers or statistics, students should ask, "Can I use numbers to make an important comparison?" "How could these details help readers better grasp my topic?"

Background Reading As students plan their explanatory essays, encourage them to review the notes in their Response Log for Unit 6. Suggest that they look back at the unit's selections to identify content that may help them select topics.

WHEN STUDENTS STRUGGLE . . .

Narrow a Topic Explain that when writers first choose a topic for an explanatory essay, it often is too broad. A topic is too broad when:

- there are so many ways to develop it that it becomes unfocused
- you can write only general statements about it
- there is an overwhelming amount of research available

Discuss strategies that students can use to narrow their topic. These might include:

- subdividing the topic
- expressing the topic in one main question
- relating the topic to a specific event or example

WRITING

Organize Your Ideas Emphasize the importance of organizing ideas in an outline before students begin drafting their explanatory essay. Tell students that one way they can plan their essay is to organize it into an introduction, two or three body paragraphs with one main point and supporting evidence in each, and a conclusion. Explain that this organization helps a writer keep his or her focus and helps the reader follow the writer's ideas.

Provide the following sample outline based on the chart:

I. Introduction: Thesis Statement with Interesting Example, Observation, or Quotation

II. Body Paragraph 1: Main Idea with Examples/Evidence

III. Body Paragraph 2: Main Idea with Examples/Evidence

IV. Body Paragraph 3: Main Idea with Examples/Evidence

V. Conclusion: Restate Thesis and Key Points, and Offer New Observation

2 DEVELOP A DRAFT

Remind students that their outlines will provide a natural path to the development of their explanatory essays. Emphasize that an outline is only a preliminary step in the writing process and that it can and should be revised if better ideas occur to them.

English Learner Support

Use Transitions Students might need help connecting ideas. Use a few transitions in sentences *(next, before, after, then, for example, also, therefore, because, finally)*. Instruct students to ask questions for clarification. Next, put the transition words on a "transition word wall" and have students work in pairs to add at least three of these transitions to their drafts. **SUBSTANTIAL/MODERATE**

WRITING TASK

Go to **Writing Informative Texts: Organizing Ideas** for more help.

Organize Your Ideas Now it's time to take the ideas and information from your planning activities and organize them in a way that will help you draft your essay. First, decide what organizational pattern best serves your purpose—chronology, main idea and supporting details, cause and effect, or another organizing structure. You may use the chart below to organize your ideas, or create an outline of your own. Present your information in logically ordered paragraphs. Each paragraph should have a central idea related to your thesis with relevant evidence, details, quotations, and examples to support it. Write a conclusion that summarizes your thesis and presents a final synthesis of your central ideas.

EXPLANATORY ESSAY
Introduction
Body
Point 1:
Point 2:
Point 3:
Conclusion

2 Develop a Draft

You might prefer to draft your argument online.

Once you have completed your planning activities, you will be ready to begin drafting your explanatory essay. Be sure to use precise language, including domain-specific terms, to make your explanation clear for readers. Use transitions to connect the main sections of your essay and to clarify the relationships among your ideas. Refer to your Graphic Organizer and the outline you have created, as well as any notes you took as you studied the texts in this unit.

WHEN STUDENTS STRUGGLE . . .

Choose an Organizational Pattern Use the chart to review different ways students might organize their explanatory essays.

Organizational Pattern	How It Works
Chronology	Presents ideas and details in time order
Comparison and Contrast	Explains how things are similar and different
Cause and Effect	Describes why something happens, and what then results
Classification	Explains ways to group related ideas

Use the Mentor Text

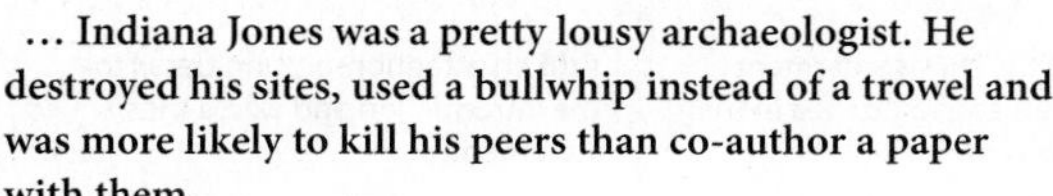

Author's Craft

You can use narrative text effectively when you write an explanatory essay. A longer piece of narrative can present important information. Just a tiny piece of a story can engage the reader, as it does in the mentor text "Archaeology's Tech Revolution Since Indiana Jones."

... Indiana Jones was a pretty lousy archaeologist. He destroyed his sites, used a bullwhip instead of a trowel and was more likely to kill his peers than co-author a paper with them.

I never thought about Indiana Jones that way!

Apply What You've Learned Use a narrative structure, when it's appropriate, to make your ideas clear and draw in your reader.

Genre Characteristics

An explanatory narrative is built on a thesis and ideas, but evidence is always necessary for support. Here is how the author of "Archaeology's Tech Revolution Since Indiana Jones" supports one idea with evidence.

Those modern archaeologists whom "Raiders" inspired luckily learned from the mistakes of Dr. Jones, and use advanced technology such as satellite imaging, airborne laser mapping, robots and full-body medical scanners ...

These examples show the kinds of technology that archaeologists use now. They support the idea that there has been a "tech revolution" in archaeology.

Apply What You've Learned Support your thesis and central ideas with evidence.

WHY THIS MENTOR TEXT?

"Archaeology's Tech Revolution Since Indiana Jones" provides a strong example of an explanatory essay. Use the instruction below to model how narrative text and a clear thesis supported by evidence can be highly effective ways to provide explanations and support ideas.

USE THE MENTOR TEXT

Author's Craft Have a volunteer read aloud the introduction to this section and the example from the mentor text. Ask: How does this narrative detail grab a reader's attention? *(The film character known as Indiana Jones is careless and destructive. This characterization contrasts with the image of a meticulous, cautious archaeologist.)*

Genre Characteristics Have a volunteer read this introduction and the excerpt from the text. Ask: What main idea from the text does the evidence In this passage support? *(New technologies have led to dramatic changes in the way archaeologists work.)* What specific details does the author provide as evidence to support this main idea? *(satellite imaging, airborne laser mapping, robots, and full-body medical scanners)*

ENGLISH LEARNER SUPPORT

Use the Mentor Text Use the following supports with students at varying proficiency levels:

- Point out the word *narrative* in the introduction to Author's Craft. Explain that a narrative is a kind of story, either true or made up. Provide the following sentence frame for students to complete: *My essay tells a story about* _____. **SUBSTANTIAL**
- Tell students that narratives are stories with a beginning, middle, and end. Provide the following sentence frames for students to complete: *My essay tells a story about*_____. *The first part describes/explains* ________. *The next part describes/explains* _______. **MODERATE**
- Have students discuss the narrative arc of their essay and explain how the story relates to their essay's thesis. **LIGHT**

WRITING

3 REVISE

Have students determine how they might improve their drafts by answering each question posed in the Revision Guide. Call on volunteers to model their revision techniques.

With a Partner Have students work with peer reviewers to evaluate their drafts. Use the following questions as a guide for peer review:

- Does the introduction to the essay grab the reader's attention with an engaging detail?
- Does the introduction include a thesis statement that clearly responds to the writing prompt?
- Does each body paragraph express a key idea and provide supporting details?
- Does the conclusion clearly restate the essay's thesis?
- Are the style and vocabulary appropriate to the writing task?

Encourage partners to offer specific comments about what they liked and how the explanatory essays might be improved.

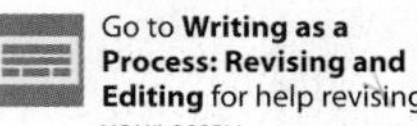

WRITING TASK

3 Revise

Go to **Writing as a Process: Revising and Editing** for help revising your essay.

On Your Own A draft is where you get your ideas down on paper. It is the process of revision that allows you to go back and find ways to improve your explanatory essay. The Revision Guide will help you focus on specific elements to make your writing stronger.

REVISION GUIDE

Ask Yourself	Tips	Revision Techniques
1. Does the introduction engage readers and state a clear thesis?	**Underline** the thesis statement and **mark** an engaging idea in the introduction.	**Add** an attention-getting detail to the introduction and **add** a thesis statement.
2. Are ideas organized logically and linked with transitions?	**Note** the idea explored in each paragraph. **Mark** transitional words and phrases.	**Reorder** evidence to center each paragraph on one idea. **Add** appropriate transitions to connect ideas and clarify the organization.
3. Does text evidence support the ideas in each paragraph?	**Underline** each supporting fact, definition, example, or quotation.	**Add** facts, details, examples, or quotations to support ideas.
4. Does the conclusion effectively summarize ideas?	**Underline** the restated thesis or summary of ideas in the conclusion.	**Add** a restatement of the thesis or summary of the essay's ideas.
5. Is the style appropriately formal, including domain-specific vocabulary?	**Note** slang or informal word choices. **Underline** domain-specific terms.	**Replace** informal language. **Add** scientific or academic language as appropriate.

ACADEMIC VOCABULARY

As you conduct your **peer review**, try to use these words.

- ❑ **motivate**
- ❑ **objective**
- ❑ **pursuit**
- ❑ **subsequent**
- ❑ **undertake**

With a Partner After you have worked through the Revision Guide on your own, exchange papers with a partner. Evaluate each other's drafts in a **peer review**. Pay particular attention to the organization of the ideas and the style. Think about ways your partner could better accomplish his or her purpose in writing.

In your discussion, describe your specific revisions suggestions and explain how they would improve the essay. As you give feedback, include praise for what he or she has done well.

ENGLISH LEARNER SUPPORT

Use Quotations Use the following supports with students at varying proficiency levels:

- Review the punctuation students should use to incorporate quotations into their essays. Then provide the following sentence frame that students can use to introduce a quotation: *The ____ says, "[quotation]."* **SUBSTANTIAL**
- Give students several wordings they can use to introduce quotations into their writing. These might include, *As the author says, "____"; In the author's words, "____"*; and *According to the author, "____."* Have them add a quotation to their essay using one of these structures. **MODERATE**
- Explain that quotations can appear at any point in a sentence and that correct punctuation is essential. Have students practice putting a quotation at the beginning of a sentence, in the middle of a sentence, and at the end of a sentence. **LIGHT**

4 Edit

Edit for the proper use of standard English conventions and make sure to correct any misspellings or grammatical errors. One of the most common causes of spelling errors is confusing one word for another. These types of errors will not show up in a computer spell check.

Go to **Commonly Misspelled Words** in the **Grammar Studio** to learn more.

Spelling Commonly Confused Words

There are many words in the English language that are pronounced the same way but are spelled differently and have different meanings. These types of words are called **homophones**. You are familiar with some of them, such as *your* and *you're*. There are also many words that are close in pronunciation, but different in spelling and meaning. When you're editing, make sure you have used the right word. This chart includes a few that you might use in an explanatory essay.

WORDS	DEFINITIONS	EXAMPLES
accept / except	***Accept*** is a verb meaning "to receive or believe," while ***except*** is a preposition meaning "excluding."	**Except** for some of the more extraordinary events, I can **accept** that *The Odyssey* recounts a real journey.
affect/ effect	As a verb, ***affect*** means "to influence," while ***effect*** as a verb means "to cause." If you want a noun, you will almost always want ***effect***.	Did Circe's wine **affect** Odysseus' mind? It did **effect** a change in Odysseus' men. In fact, it had an **effect** on everyone else who drank it.
loose / lose	***Loose*** is an adjective that means "free, not restrained," while ***lose*** is a verb meaning "to misplace or fail to find."	Who turned the horses **loose**? I hope we won't **lose** any of them.
than / then	Use ***than*** in making comparisons. On all other occasions, use ***then***.	I enjoyed this story more **than** that one. **Then** I read a third one and liked it best of all.

5 Publish

Finalize your essay and choose a way to share it with your audience. Consider these options:

- Post your essay as a blog.
- Participate in a Collaborative Discussion with your peers.

4 EDIT

Encourage students to read their drafts aloud multiple times. During their first reading, have students focus on the clarity of their key ideas and supporting details. During their second reading, suggest that students read for the use of effective transitions. During a third reading, students should focus on the correct use of English conventions including grammar and usage, spelling, capitalization, and punctuation.

LANGUAGE CONVENTIONS

Spelling Commonly Confused Words Explain that the word *homophone* means "same sound." Introduce the definition of *homophone;* then direct students' attention to the chart.

Read aloud the pairs of homophones in the left-hand column of the chart. Then have volunteers read the meanings of the words in the middle column and the model sentence(s) that use them correctly in the right-hand column. Test students' understanding by asking questions such as these: Which word—*accept* or *except*—describes what you do after winning an award? *(accept)* Which word would use to explain why one example doesn't fit with the other examples? *(except)* Call on other students to come up with similar model sentences for the other pairs of homophones in the chart.

For **writing support** for students at varying proficiency levels, use the **Language X-Ray** on page 564B.

5 PUBLISH

Discuss the suggested publishing options. If available, have students post their explanatory essays as blog posts on a school website. Encourage other students to read the essays before they engage in a collaborative discussion.

TO CHALLENGE STUDENTS . . .

Create a Homophone Handbook Organize small groups to prepare entries for a homophone handbook that can be used as a classroom writing resource. Have each group prepare a page that presents the meanings and model sentences for two or more easily confused words. Challenge them to write some model sentences that include both words. In addition to the homophones presented on page 569, possible entries might include:

plain/plane	flew/flu	site/cite/sight	your/you're	ceiling/sealing
lone/loan	past/passed	main/mane	band/banned	their/they're/there
higher/hire	it's/its	shown/shone	by/buy/bye	ate/eight

USE THE SCORING GUIDE

Allow students time to read the scoring guide. Encourage them to ask questions about any ideas, sentences, phrases, or words they find unclear. Tell partners to exchange their final explanatory essays and score them using the guidelines. Have each student reviewer write a paragraph explaining the reason for the score he or she awarded for each major category.

WRITING TASK

Use the scoring guide to evaluate your essay.

WRITING TASK SCORING GUIDE: EXPLANATORY ESSAY

	Organization/Progression	Development of Ideas	Use of Language and Conventions
4	• The organization is effective and appropriate to the purpose. • All ideas are focused on the topic specified in the prompt. • Varied transitions clearly show the relationship among ideas.	• The introduction catches the reader's attention and clearly states the thesis. • The topic is well developed with clear main ideas supported by specific and well-chosen facts, details, examples, etc. • The conclusion effectively summarizes the information.	• Language and word choice is purposeful and precise. • Care has been taken to avoid errors with commonly confused words. • Spelling, capitalization, and punctuation are correct. • Grammar, usage, and mechanics are correct.
3	• The organization is, for the most part, effective and appropriate to the purpose. • Most ideas are focused on the topic specified in the prompt. • Transitions generally clarify the relationships between ideas.	• The introduction could be more engaging. The thesis statement identifies the topic but may be cursory. • Most ideas are adequately developed and supported with facts, details, examples, and quotations. • The conclusion summarizes the information presented.	• Language is for the most part specific and clear. • Generally, care has been taken to avoid errors with commonly confused words. • There are some spelling, capitalization, and punctuation mistakes. • Some grammar and usage errors occur.
2	• The organization is evident but is not always appropriate to the purpose. • Only some ideas are focused on the topic specified in the prompt. • More transitions are needed to show the relationship among ideas.	• The introduction is not engaging. The topic is not clear and the thesis statement does not express a clear point. • The development of ideas is minimal. The writer uses facts, details, examples, etc. that are inappropriate or ineffectively presented. • The conclusion is only partially effective.	• Language is somewhat vague and unclear. • There are problems with commonly confused words. • Spelling, capitalization, and punctuation, as well as grammar and usage, are often incorrect but do not make reading difficult.
1	• The organization is not appropriate to the purpose. • Ideas are not focused on the topic specified in the prompt. • No transitions are used, making the essay difficult to understand.	• The introduction is missing or confusing and the thesis statement is missing. • The development of ideas is weak. Supporting facts, details, examples, or quotations are unreliable, vague, or missing. • The conclusion is missing.	• Language is inappropriate for the text. • There are many problems with commonly confused words. • Many spelling, capitalization, and punctuation errors are present. • Grammatical and usage errors confuse the writer's ideas.

SPEAKING AND LISTENING TASK

Participate in a Collaborative Discussion

This unit focuses on ways people seek out and often thrive during life's challenges. Look back at the Reading Model text, "Archaeology's Tech Revolution Since Indiana Jones," and at the other texts in the unit. How do different people meet the need for challenges in life? Synthesize your ideas by holding a collaborative discussion on how the different selections explore the answers to this crucial question. As you discuss, share findings from your essay.

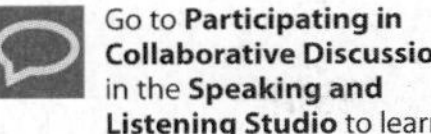

Go to **Participating in Collaborative Discussions** in the **Speaking and Listening Studio** to learn more.

1 Use Your Essay as the Basis for Your Participation

Review your essay, and use the chart below to guide you as you make notes to use in the collaborative discussion.

NOTES FOR COLLABORATIVE DISCUSSION	
Key Point	**Evidence**
Key Point	**Evidence**
Key Point	**Evidence**

SPEAKING AND LISTENING

PARTICIPATE IN A COLLABORATIVE DISCUSSION

Introduce students to the Speaking and Listening Task by describing the characteristics of an effective collaborative discussion. Emphasize the importance of referring to the text and the way it relates to the question of how different people meet the need for challenges in their life. Remind students to ask for clarification of issues that they find confusing and to stick to the main point under discussion. Encourage participants to talk to each other, not just to the moderators of the discussion. Stress that the main purpose of a collaborative discussion is for everyone to participate by offering ideas and supporting evidence such as examples, details, and quotations from the text.

1 USE YOUR ESSAY AS THE BASIS FOR YOUR PARTICIPATION

Introduce students to the Notes for Collaborative Discussion. Encourage them to review their essays before they begin to make their notes. Emphasize that students should keep their completed charts readily accessible during the collaborative discussion. Explain that they can and should modify the format of their notes to suit their needs and participation style. If needed, provide additional support for students in identifying main ideas and supporting details so that they are prepared to actively participate in the discussion.

For **speaking and listening support** for students at varying proficiency levels, see the **Language X-Ray** on page 564B.

WHEN STUDENTS STRUGGLE . . .

Take Notes Suggest that students review the outlines they created in the planning stage of their writing. Each paragraph in their essay will include a main idea and supporting evidence. As they review their essays, have students note the main idea (key point) and supporting evidence from each paragraph in a row of the chart.

2 GET ORGANIZED AND PRACTICE

Discuss each of the discussion rules presented in the margin and provide examples of how these rules will look, sound, and feel in action.

Review the meaning of key content and academic vocabulary that likely will be referenced during the collaborative discussion, including *thesis statement, topic, main idea, supporting details*, and *evidence*.

Have students refer to previous activities to decide which questions they will pose to group members for further discussion.

3 PARTICIPATE IN THE COLLABORATIVE DISCUSSION

Review the checklist of guidelines for effective participation in a collaborative discussion presented in the text. Provide adequate time for students to make notes about how well they think they participated in the discussion. Encourage them to use their notes as they write their self-evaluation summary paragraphs. If time permits, have students share and discuss some of their follow-up questions.

SPEAKING AND LISTENING TASK

As you work to improve your presentations, be sure to follow discussion rules:

- ❑ **listen closely to each other**
- ❑ **don't interrupt**
- ❑ **stay on topic**
- ❑ **ask helpful, relevant questions**
- ❑ **provide clear, thoughtful answers**

2 Get Organized and Practice

Join a group of four classmates. Try to include students who have chosen different selections to write about in their explanatory essays. Each student will be the expert on the text.

Present your ideas to your group, using content and academic vocabulary that is appropriate to your topic. Encourage classmates to ask questions about your ideas and examples, preparing you to "think on your feet" during the large-group discussion.

As a group, choose one or two questions you would like to pose to the class for further discussion.

Participate in the Collaborative Discussion

Present your group's discussion questions to the class. Help make the questions clear to other students and participate actively in the discussion that follows. Refer to your notes when needed.

An effective participant in a collaborative discussion

- ❑ makes a clear, logical, and well-defended generalization about the challenges people seek and meet
- ❑ uses relevant quotations and specific examples to illustrate ideas
- ❑ listens actively and responds thoughtfully and politely to the ideas of other speakers
- ❑ builds on the ideas of other speakers' contributions
- ❑ summarizes the discussion by synthesizing ideas

After the discussion, think about what you learned. Were there interesting new insights into the theme of the unit? Did you learn about ideas you had not thought of on your own by participating in the discussion? Write a paragraph about what you learned. Include any follow-up questions you would like to pursue further.

ENGLISH LEARNER SUPPORT

Ask Questions Use the following supports with students at varying proficiency levels:

- Provide a list of question words. Work with students to write three general questions that are effective in collaborative discussions, such as these: Why do you think that? What do you think about _____? Where did you find that example? **SUBSTANTIAL**
- Have students come up with a list of general questions they could use in collaborative discussions. **MODERATE**
- Tell students to add a third column labeled "Questions for Discussion" to their charts on page 571. Have them trade charts with a partner and write questions about their partner's key points. **LIGHT**

Reflect on the Unit

When you were writing your explanatory essay, you pulled together and expressed many of your thoughts about the reading you have done in this unit. Now is a good time to reflect on what you have learned.

Reflect on the Essential Question

- What drives us to take on a challenge? How has your answer to this question changed since you first considered it when you started this unit?
- What are some examples from the texts you've read that show the human need to seek and meet challenges?

Reflect on Your Reading

- Which selections were the most interesting or surprising to you?
- From which selection did you learn the most about why challenges are important to us?

Reflect on the Writing Task

- What difficulties did you encounter while working on your explanatory essay? How might you avoid them next time?
- What part of the essay was the easiest and what part was the hardest to write? Why?
- What improvements did you make to your essay as you were revising?

UNIT 6 SELECTIONS

- **The Epic**
- **from *The Odyssey***
- **"Archaeology's Tech Revolution Since Indiana Jones"**
- **from *The Cruelest Journey: 600 Miles to Timbuktu***
- **"The Journey"**

REFLECT

REFLECT ON THE UNIT

Have students reflect independently on the questions and write their responses. Next, have them discuss their responses in small groups. During these discussions, move about the classroom and note questions that seem to produce the liveliest conversations. Use these questions as the basis for a whole-class discussion that wraps up the unit.

LEARNING MINDSET

Self-Reflection Explain to students that developing a learning mindset that embraces growth means recognizing one's own strengths and weaknesses (skills and areas that could be strengthened). As students reflect on the unit, encourage them to ask themselves questions such as these: Did I ask for help when I got stuck or confused? Did I review my work for errors? Did I think about ways to improve my work or process? Am I proud of the effort I put into this task? Have I thought about how my experiences with writing and participating in a discussion can help me in the future?

Student Resources

HMH *Into Literature* Studios

For more instruction and practice, visit the HMH *Into Literature* Studios.

 Reading Studio

 Writing Studio

 Speaking & Listening Studio

 Grammar Studio

 Vocabulary Studio

UNIT 1 RESPONSE LOG

Use this Response Log to record your ideas about how each of the texts in Unit 1 relates to or comments on the **Essential Question.**

? **Essential Question:**
How can we come together despite our differences?

A Quilt of a Country	
Unusual Normality	
Once Upon a Time	
The Vietnam Wall	
The Gettysburg Address	
from Saving Lincoln	

UNIT 2 RESPONSE LOG

Use this Response Log to record your ideas about how each of the texts in Unit 2 relates to or comments on the **Essential Question.**

Essential Question:
How do people find freedom in the midst of oppression?

I Have a Dream	
Interview with John Lewis	
from Hidden Figures	
The Censors	
Booker T. and W.E.B.	
from Reading Lolita in Tehran	
from Persepolis 2: The Story of a Return	

UNIT 3 RESPONSE LOG

Use this Response Log to record your ideas about how each of the texts in Unit 3 relates to or comments on the **Essential Question.**

? **Essential Question:**
How do we form and maintain our connections with others?

The Grasshopper and the Bell Cricket	
Monkey See, Monkey Do, Monkey Connect	
With Friends Like These . . .	
AmeriCorps NCCC: Be the Greater Good	
Loser	
At Dusk	

UNIT 4 RESPONSE LOG

Use this Response Log to record your ideas about how each of the texts in Unit 4 relates to or comments on the **Essential Question.**

Essential Question:
How can love bring both joy and pain?

The Price of Freedom	
Love's Vocabulary	
My Shakespeare	
The Tragedy of Romeo and Juliet	
Having It Both Ways	
Superheart	

UNIT 5 RESPONSE LOG

Use this Response Log to record your ideas about how each of the texts in Unit 5 relates to or comments on the **Essential Question.**

Essential Question:
What does it take to survive in a crisis?

The Leap	
Is Survival Selfish?	
The End and the Beginning	
from Night	
from The Pianist	

UNIT 6 RESPONSE LOG

Use this Response Log to record your ideas about how each of the texts in Unit 6 relates to or comments on the **Essential Question.**

Essential Question:
What drives us to take on a challenge?

from The Odyssey	
Archaeology's Tech Revolution Since Indiana Jones	
from The Cruelest Journey: 600 Miles to Timbuktu	
The Journey	

R6 Student Resources

Using a Glossary

A glossary is an alphabetical list of vocabulary words. Use a glossary just as you would a dictionary—to determine the meanings, parts of speech, pronunciation, and syllabification of words. (Some technical, foreign, and more obscure words in this book are defined for you in the footnotes that accompany many of the selections.)

Many words in the English language have more than one meaning. This glossary gives the meanings that apply to the words as they are used in the selections in this book.

The following abbreviations are used to identify parts of speech of words:

adj. adjective *adv.* adverb *n.* noun *v.* verb

Each word's pronunciation is given in parentheses. A guide to the pronunciation symbols appears in the Pronunciation Key below. The stress marks in the Pronunciation Key are used to indicate the force given to each syllable in a word. They can also help you determine where words are divided into syllables.

For more information about the words in this glossary or for information about words not listed here, consult a dictionary.

Pronunciation Key

Symbol	Examples
ă	**pat**
ā	**pay**
ä	**father**
âr	**care**
b	**bib**
ch	**church**
d	**deed, milled**
ĕ	**pet**
ē	**bee**
f	**fife, phase, rough**
g	**gag**
h	**hat**
hw	**which**
ĭ	**pit**
ī	**pie, by**
îr	**pier**
j	**judge**
k	**kick, cat, pique**
l	**lid, needle*** (nēd´l)

Symbol	Examples
m	**mum**
n	**no, sudden*** (sud´n)
ng	**thing**
ŏ	**pot**
ō	**toe**
ô	**caught, paw**
oi	**noise**
o͝o	**took**
o͞o	**boot**
o͝or	**lure**
ôr	**core**
ou	**out**
p	**pop**
r	**roar**
s	**sauce**
sh	**ship, dish**
t	**tight, stopped**
th	**thin**
th	**this**
ŭ	**cut**

Symbol	Examples
ûr	**urge, term, firm, word, heard**
v	**valve**
w	**with**
y	**yes**
z	**zebra, xylem**
zh	**vision, pleasure, garage**
ə	**about, item, edible, gallop, circus**
ər	**butter**

Sounds in Foreign Words

Symbol	Examples
KH	*German* **ich, ach;** *Scottish* **loch**
N	*French*, **bon** (bôN)
œ	*French* **feu, œuf;** *German* **schön**
ü	*French* **tu;** *German* **über**

*In English the consonants *l* and *n* often constitute complete syllables by themselves.

Stress Marks

The relative emphasis with which the syllables of a word or phrase are spoken, called stress, is indicated in three different ways. The strongest, or primary, stress is marked with a bold mark (´). An intermediate, or secondary, level of stress is marked with a similar but lighter mark (´). The weakest stress is unmarked. Words of one syllable show no stress mark.

Pronunciation Key R7

GLOSSARY OF ACADEMIC VOCABULARY

attribute (ăt′rə-byo͞ot) *n.* a characteristic, quality, or trait.

capacity (kə-păs′ĭ-tē) *n.* the ability to contain, hold, produce, or understand.

commit (kə-mĭt′) *v.* to carry out, engage in, or perform.

confer (kən-fûr′) *v.* to grant or give to.

decline (dĭ-klīn′) *v.* to fall apart or deteriorate slowly.

dimension (dĭ-mĕn′shən) *n.* a feature, scale, or measurement of something.

emerge (ĭ-mûrj′) *v.* to come forth, out of, or away from.

enable (ĕ-nā′bəl) *v.* to give the means or opportunity.

enforce (ĕn-fôrs′) *v.* to compel observance of or obedience to.

entity (ĕn′tĭ-tē) *n.* a thing that exists as a unit.

expose (ĭk-spōz′) *v.* to make visible or reveal.

external (ĭk-stûr′nəl) *adj.* related to, part of, or from the outside.

generate (jĕn′ə-rāt) *v.* to produce or cause something to happen or exist.

impose (ĭm-pōz′) *v.* to bring about by force.

initiate (ĭ-nĭsh′ē-āt) *v.* to start or cause to begin.

integrate (ĭn′tĭ-grāt) *v.* to pull together into a whole; unify.

internal (ĭn-tûr′nəl) *adj.* inner; located within something or someone.

motivate (mō′tə-vāt) *v.* to provide a cause for doing something.

objective (əb-jĕk′tĭv) *n.* an intention, purpose, or goal.

presume (prĭ-zo͞om′) *v.* to take for granted as being true; to assume something is true.

pursuit (pər-so͞ot′) *n.* the action of chasing or following something.

resolve (rĭ-zŏlv′) *v.* to decide or become determined.

reveal (rĭ-vēl′) *v.* to show or make known.

statistic (stə-tĭs′tĭk) *n.* a piece of numerical data.

subsequent (sŭb′sĭ-kwĕnt) *adj.* coming after or following.

sustain (sə-stān′) *v.* to support or cause to continue.

trace (trās) *v.* to discover or determine the origins or developmental stages of something.

underlie (ŭn-dər-lī′) *v.* to be the cause or support of.

undertake (ŭn-dər-tāk′) *v.* to assume responsibility for or take on a job or course of action.

utilize (yo͞ot′l-īz) *v.* to make use of.

R8 Student Resources

GLOSSARY OF CRITICAL VOCABULARY

adulate (ăj´ə-lāt) *v.* to praise or admire excessively.

allocate (ăl´ə-kāt) *v.* to assign or designate for.

analytical (ăn-ə-lĭt´ĭ-kəl) *adj.* able to analyze, or understand something by breaking it down into parts.

annihilate (ə-nī´ə-lāt) *v.* to destroy completely.

artifact (är´tə-făkt) *n.* an object produced or shaped by human workmanship.

assess (ə-sĕss´) *v.* to determine the qualities or abilities of something.

audacious (ô-dā´shəs) *adj.* bold, rebellious.

berate (bĭ-rāt´) *v.* to criticize or scold.

circuitously (sər-kyōō´ĭ-təs-lē) *adv.* in an indirect and lengthy manner.

cognition (kŏg-nĭsh´ən) *n.* the process or pattern of gaining knowledge.

comply (kəm-plī´) *v.* to obey an instruction or command.

conceive (kən-sēv´) *v.* to form or develop in the mind: devise.

conscientiously (kŏn-shē-ĕn´shəs-ly) *adj.* doing something thoroughly.

constrict (kən-strĭkt´) *v.* to limit or impede growth.

consume (kən-sōōm´) *v.* to completely destroy or eradicate.

contagion (kən-tā´jən) *n.* the spreading from one to another.

convert (kən-vûrt´) *v.* to change one's system of beliefs.

counterparts (koun´tər-pärts) *n.* people or things that have the same characteristics and function as another.

decisive (dĭ-sīs´ĭv) *adj.* final or concluding.

decoy (dē´koi) *n.* a means to trick or attract.

default (dĭ-fôlt´) *v.* to fail to keep a promise to repay a loan.

degenerate (dĭ-jĕn´ər-āt) *v.* to decline morally.

demented (dĭ-mĕn´tĭd) *adj.* suffering from dementia, crazy, foolish.

deprecating (dĕp´rĭ-kāt-ing) *adj.* belittling or downplaying something.

derive (dĭ-rīv´) *v.* to obtain or extract from.

desolate (dĕs´ə-lĭt) *adj.* unhappy; lonely.

detract (dĭ-trăkt´) *v.* to take away from.

din (dĭn) *n.* loud noise.

discernable (dĭ-sûr´nə-bəl) *adj.* recognizable or noticeable.

discordant (dĭ-skôr´dnt) *adj.* conflicting or not harmonious.

Glossary of Critical Vocabulary R9

GLOSSARY OF CRITICAL VOCABULARY

disingenuous (dĭs-ĭn-jĕn´yo͞o-əs) *adj.* insincere, deceitful.

distend (dĭ-stĕnd´) *v.* to bulge or expand.

diversity (dĭ-vûr´sĭ-tē) *n.* having varied social and/or ethnic backgrounds.

edict (ē´dĭkt) *n.* an official rule or proclamation.

emaciated (ĭ-mā´shē-āt-id) *adj.* made extremely thin and weak.

emanate (ĕm´ə-nāt) *v.* to emit or radiate from.

embark (ĕm-bärk´) *v.* to set out on a course or a journey (often aboard a boat).

empathy (ĕm´pə-thē) *n.* the ability to understand and identify with another's feelings.

encroach (ĕn-krōch´) *v.* to gradually intrude upon or invade.

execute (ĕk´sĭ-kyo͞ot) *v.* to carry out, or accomplish.

extricate (ĕk´strĭ-kāt) *v.* to release or disentangle from.

forensic analysis (fə-rĕn´sĭk ə-năl´ĭ-sĭs) *n.* the scientific collection and analysis of physical evidence in criminal cases.

GPS *n.* Global Positioning System, a utility that provides positioning, navigation, and timing services.

gradation (grā-dā´shən) *n.* a slight, successive change in color, degree or tone.

horde (hôrd) *n.* a large group or crowd; a swarm.

implication (ĭm-plĭ-kā´shən) *n.* consequence or effect.

increment (ĭn´ krə-mənt) *n.* an addition or increase by a standard measure of growth.

inextricably (ĭn-ĕk´strĭ-kə-blē) *adv.* in a way impossible to untangle.

infiltration (ĭn-fĭl-trā´shən) *n.* the act or process of passing in secret through enemy lines.

infrared (ĭn´frə-rĕd) *adj.* pertaining to electromagnetic radiation having wavelengths greater than those of visible light and shorter than those of microwaves.

innovation (ĭn-ə-vā´shən) *n.* something newly introduced.

insistent (ĭn-sĭs´tənt) *adj.* demanding that something happen or refusing to accept that it will not happen.

intangible (ĭn-tăn´jə-bəl) *n.* something that is difficult to grasp or explain.

integrity (ĭn-tĕg´rĭ-tē) *n.* consistency and strength of purpose.

intention (ĭn-tĕn´shən) *n.* purpose or plan.

interwoven (ĭn-tər-wō´vən) *adj.* blended or laced together.

intrusion (ĭn-tro͞o´shən) *n.* act of trespass or invasion.

irrelevant (ĭr-rĕl´ə-vənt) *adj.* insignificant, unimportant.

irreproachable (ĭr-ĭ-prō´chə-bəl) *adj.* without fault or blame; perfect.

isolation (ī-sə-lā´shən) *n.* the condition of being alone or apart from others.

knack (năk) *n.* a special talent for doing something.

laud (lôd) *v.* to praise.

loiter (loi´tər) *v.* to stand or wait idly.

lozenge (lŏz´ĭnj) *n.* a diamond-shaped object.

maneuver (mə-nōō´vər) *v.* to make a series of controlled movements.

naïve (nī-ēv´) *adj.* lacking in worldly experience, everyday knowledge, or understanding.

perish (pĕr´ĭsh) *v.* to die or come to an end.

pluralistic (plŏŏr´ə-lĭs´tĭc) *adj.* consisting of many ethnic and cultural groups.

redemptive (rĭ-dĕmp´tĭv) *adj.* causing freedom or salvation.

rehabilitation (rē-hə-bĭl-ĭ-tā´shən) *n.* the act of being restored to good health or condition.

reprieve (rĭ-prēv´) *n.* the cancellation or postponement of punishment.

resolve (rĭ-zŏlv´) *v.* to decide or become determined.

sabotage (săb´ə-täzh) *n.* deliberate destruction of property; an act of damage to stop something.

scam (skăm) *n.* a plan to cheat others, often out of money.

seductive (sĭ-dŭk´tĭv) *adj.* tempting, alluring.

segregate (sĕg rĭ-gāt) *v.* to cause people to be separated based on gender, race, or other factors.

serrated (sĕr´ā-tĭd) *adj.* having a jagged, saw-toothed edge.

sheepish (shē´pĭsh) *adj.* showing embarrassment.

simulate (sĭm´yə-lāt) *v.* to create in a controlled setting conditions similar to those a person or machine might face in the real world.

skeptic (skĕp´tĭk) *n.* someone who doubts something.

stagnant (stăg´nənt) *adj.* unchanging; without activity or development.

stereotype (stĕr´ē-ə-tīp) *n.* one that is thought of as conforming to a set type or image.

subversive (səb-vûr´sĭv) *adj.* intending to undermine or overthrow those in power.

supple (sŭp´əl) *adj.* flexible or easily adaptable.

synchronization (sing-krə-nĭ-zā´shən) *n.* coordinated, simultaneous action.

tentative (tĕn´tə-tĭv) *adj.* with caution and without confidence.

transfix (trans-fĭks´) *v.* to captivate or make motionless with awe.

validate (văl´ĭ-dāt) *v.* to establish the value, truth, or legitimacy of.

Glossary of Critical Vocabulary R11

Index of Skills

Key

Teacher's Edition subject entries and page references are printed in **boldface** type. Subject entries and page references that apply to both the Student Edition and Teacher's Edition appear in lightface type.

D

N

O

P

Q

R

S

INDEX OF TITLES AND AUTHORS

R20 Student Resources

ACKNOWLEDGMENTS

Excerpts from *The American Heritage Dictionary of The English Language, Fifth Edition*. Text copyright © 2016 by Houghton Mifflin Harcourt Publishing Company. Reprinted by permission of Houghton Mifflin Harcourt Publishing Company.

Excerpt from "Archaeology's Tech Revolution Since Indiana Jones" from *Live Science* by Jeremy Hsu. Text copyright © 2011 by Purch. Reprinted by permission of Wright's Media on behalf of Purch.

"At Dusk" from *Native Guard* by Natasha Trethewey. Text copyright © 2006 by Natasha Trethewey. Reprinted by permission of Houghton Mifflin Harcourt Publishing Company.

"Booker T. and W.E.B" by Dudley Randall, from *Roses and Revolutions: The Selected Writings of Dudley Randall* edited by Dr. Melba Joyce Boyd. Text copyright © 1969 by Dudley Randall. Reprinted by permission of the Estate of Dudley Randall.

"The Censors" by Luisa Valenzuela, translated by David Unger from *Short Shorts: An Anthology of the Shortest Stories* edited by Irving Howe. English translation copyright © 1982 by David Unger. First published in *Short Shorts* edited by David Godine Howe. Text copyright © by Luisa Valenzuela. Reprinted by permission of Luisa Valenzuela and David Unger.

"Chapter 3: Bodies Talking to Bodies" from *The Age of Empathy: Nature's Lessons for a Kinder Society* by Frans de Waal. Text copyright © 2009 by Frans de Waal. Reprinted by permission of Harmony Books, an imprint of the Crown Publishing Group, a division of Penguin Random House LLC. All rights reserved. Any third party use of this material, outside of this publication, is prohibited. Interested parties must apply directly to Penguin Random House LLC for permission.

Excerpt from *The Cruelest Journey: 600 Miles to Timbuktu* by Kira Salak. Text copyright © 2005 by Kira Salak. Adapted and reprinted by permission of the National Geographic Society and Kira Salak.

Excerpt from *Deep Survival* by Laurence Gonzales. Text copyright © 2003 by Laurence Gonzalez. Reprinted by permission of W. W. Norton & Company, Inc.

"The End and the Beginning" from *Miracle Fair* by Wisława Szymborska, translated by Joanna Trzeciak. Text copyright © 2001 by Joanna Trzeciak. Used by permission of W. W. Norton & Company, Inc.

"The Grasshopper and the Bell Cricket" from *Palm in the Hand and Other Stories* by Yasunari Kawabata and translated by Lane Dunlop and J. Martin Holman. Translation copyright © 1988 by Lane Dunlop and J. Martin Holman. Reprinted by permission of North Point Press, a division of Farrar, Straus and Giroux, LLC.

"Having It Both Ways" from *New Collected Poems* by Elizabeth Jennings. Text copyright © 2002 by David Higham Associates. Reprinted by permission of David Higham Associates.

Excerpt from *Hidden Figures Young Readers' Edition* by Margot Lee Shetterly. Text copyright © 2016 by Margot Lee Shetterly. Reprinted by permission of HarperCollins Publishers, and Margot Lee Shetterly.

"I Have a Dream" speech by Martin Luther King, Jr. Text copyright © 1963 by Martin Luther King, Jr., renewed © 1991 by Coretta Scott King. Reprinted by permission of Writers House LLC on behalf of the Heirs of the Estate of Martin Luther King, Jr.

Excerpts from "Introduction: Love's Vocabulary" from *A Natural History of Love* by Diane Ackerman. Text copyright © 1994 by Diane Ackerman. Reprinted by permission of Penguin Random House LLC and the author. All Rights reserved. Any third party use of this material, outside of this publication, is prohibited. Interested parties must apply directly to Penguin Random House LLC for permission.

Adaptation of "Is Survival Selfish?" by Lane Wallace from *The Atlantic*, January 29, 2010. Text copyright © 2010 by Lane Wallace. Adapted and reprinted by permission of Lane Wallace.

"The Journey" from *Dream Work* by Mary Oliver. Text copyright © 1986. Reprinted by permission of Grove Atlantic, Inc., and Charlotte Sheedy Literary Agency.

"The Leap" by Louise Erdrich from *Harper's Magazine*, March 1990. Text copyright © 1990 by Harper's Magazine. Reprinted by permission of Harper's Magazine. All rights reserved.

"Loser" from *The Girl in the Flammable Skirt* by Aimee Bender. Text copyright © 1998 by Aimee Bender. Reprinted by permission of Penguin Random House LLC and Dunow, Carlson & Lerner Literary Agency. All rights reserved. Any third party use of this material, outside of this publication, is prohibited. Interested parties must apply directly to Penguin Random House LLC for permission.

Excerpt from "Monkey See, Monkey Do, Monkey Connect" from *The Age of Empathy: Nature's Lessons for a Kinder Society* by Frans de Waal. Text copyright © 2009 by Frans de Waal. Reprinted by permission of Souvenir Press, Ltd.

"My Shakespeare" by Kate Tempest. Text copyright © 2012 by Kate Tempest. Reprinted by permission of Johnson & Alcock on behalf of the author.

Excerpt from *Night* by Elie Wiesel, translated by Marion Wiesel. Text copyright © 2006 by Elie Wiesel. CAUTION: Users are warned that this work is protected under copyright laws and downloading is strictly prohibited. The right to reproduce or transfer the work via any medium must be secured with Farrar, Straus and Giroux. Reprinted by permission of Hill and Wang, a division of Farrar, Straus and Giroux, Georges Borchardt, Inc., and Recorded Books.

Excerpts from *The Odyssey* by Homer and translated by Robert Fitzgerald. Translation copyright © 1961, 1963 and copyright © renewed 1989 by Benedict R.C. Fitzgerald on behalf of the Fitzgerald children. This edition copyright © 1998 by Farrar, Straus and Giroux, LLC. Reprinted by permission of Farrar, Straus and Giroux, LLC.

"Once Upon a Time" from *Jump and Other Stories* by Nadine Gordimer. Text copyright © 1991 by Felix Licensing B.V. Reprinted by permission of Farrar, Straus and Giroux, LLC.

Acknowledgments R21

ACKNOWLEDGMENTS

Excerpt from *Persepolis 2: The Story of a Return* by Marjane Satrapi, translated by Anjali Singh. Text copyright © by Marjane Satrapi. Translation copyright © 2004 by Anjali Singh. Any third party use of this material, outside of this publication, is prohibited. Interested parties must apply directly to Penguin Random House LLC for permission. Reprinted by permission of Pantheon Books, an imprint of the Knopf Doubleday Publishing Group, a division of Penguin Random House LLC, The Random House Group, Limited, and Marjane Satrapi. All rights reserved.

Excerpt from *The Pianist* by Władysław Szpilman. Text Copyright © 1999 by Władysław Szpilman. Used by permission of St. Martin's Press.

"The Price of Freedom" by Noreen Riols, from *The Moth Presents All These Wonders: True Stories About Facing The Unknown,* edited by Catherine Burns. Text copyright © 2017 by Noreen Riols. Any third party use of this material, outside of this publication, is prohibited. Interested parties must apply directly to Penguin Random House LLC for permission. Reprinted by permission of Crown Archetype, an imprint of the Crown Publishing Group, a division of Penguin Random House LLC, Serpant's Tail Press, and The Moth. All rights reserved.

"A Quilt Of A Country" from *The Daily Beast* by Anna Quindlen. Text copyright © 2001 by Anna Quindlen. Reprinted by permission of ICM Partners.

Quote by Kofi Annan from "What Can I Do to Make Things Better?" by Kofi Annan from *Parade Magazine*. Text copyright © by Kofi Annan. Reprinted by permission of Kofi Annan.

Excerpt from *Reading Lolita in Tehran: A Memoir in Books* by Azar Nafisi. Text copyright © 2002 by Azar Nafisi. Any third party use of this material, outside of this publication, is prohibited. Interested parties must apply directly to Penguin Random House LLC for permission. Reprinted by permission of Random House, an imprint and division of Penguin Random House LLC and Penguin Books UK. All rights reserved.

"Superheart" by Marion Shore. Text copyright © by Marion Shore. Reprinted by permission of Marion Shore.

"Unusual Normality" by Ishmael Beah from *All These Wonders* edited by Catherine Burns. Text copyright © 2017 by Ishmael Beah. Reprinted by permission of SLL/Sterling Lord Literistic, Inc.

"The Vietnam Wall" from *The Lime Orchard Woman* by Alberto Ríos. Text copyright © 1988 by Alberto Ríos. Reprinted by permission of the author.

Excerpt from "With Friends Like These . . ." by Dorothy Rowe from the series "How to Understand People," from *The Observer*, March 8, 2009. Text copyright © 2009 by Guardian News and Media Ltd. Reprinted by permission of Guardian News and Media Limited.

R22 Student Resources